Manual of Accounting
New UK GAAP – 2013

UK Accounting Consulting Services
PricewaterhouseCoopers LLP

Published by

Bloomsbury Professional

Bloomsbury Professional, an imprint of Bloomsbury Publishing Plc, Maxwelton House, 41–43 Boltro Road, Haywards Heath, West Sussex, RH16 1BJ

ISBN 978 1 78043 416 2

British Library Cataloguing-in-Publication Data.
A catalogue record for this book is available from the British Library.

Printed in Great Britain.
Typeset by YHT Ltd, 4 Hercies Road, Hillingdon, Middlesex UB10 9NA

Authors

PricewaterhouseCoopers' Manual of Accounting – New UK GAAP is written by the PricewaterhouseCoopers LLP's UK Accounting Consulting Services team.

Writing team led by
Iain Selfridge
Helen McCann

Authors, contributors and reviewers

Satyajeet Beekarry	Peter Holgate	Armon Nakhai	Veenit Surana
Claire Burke	Claire Howells	Rebecca Nelson	Sandra Thompson
Howard Crossland	Barry Johnson	Harivadan Patel	Sarah Troughton
Sallie Deysel	Simon Johnson	Peter Piga	Mike Vickery
Fredré Ferreira	Yasir Khan	Olaf Pusch	Barbara Willis
Philip Garcia	Hannah King	Tom Quinn	Michelle Winarto
Michael Gaull	Luis De Leon Ortiz	Priya Rabheru	James Wong
Jyoti Ghosh	Avni Mashru	Alfredo Ramirez	Katie Woods
Susan Grun	Michelle Millar	Thomas Roberts	
Margaret Heneghan	Janet Milligan	Mike Simpson	
Peter Hogarth	Stephen Moseley	Peter Smith	

Foreword

By Roger Marshall
Chairman
UK FRC's Accounting Council

Over the last twelve months the FRC has issued completely revised financial reporting standards in the UK and Republic of Ireland. These revisions fundamentally reform UK financial reporting, replacing almost all extant standards with three Financial Reporting Standards: FRS 100 – Application of Financial Reporting Requirements; FRS 101 – Reduced Disclosure Framework: and FRS 102 – The Financial Reporting Standard applicable in the UK and Republic of Ireland. The accounting provisions of the Companies Act 2006 also continue to apply. The standards take as their base IFRS for SMEs but have been substantially tailored to take account of UK law and UK needs, which in some cases are more sophisticated than those for which IFRS for SMEs was designed.

The standards not only are much shorter than those they replace but address previously neglected areas in the UK such as accounting for derivatives.

These standards combined form the 'New UK GAAP' – the subject of this Manual – which in practice will be based on the application of judgement as well as the guidance in the standards. To assist in the promulgation and understanding of new UK GAAP, I commend this Manual of Accounting. The book, which will assist preparers and practitioners with the challenges they face in transitioning to new UK GAAP, benefits from the extensive experience and professional judgement of PricewaterhouseCoopers.

October 2013

Preface

PwC's Manual of Accounting – New UK GAAP 2013 is a practical guide to the new UK accounting regime (based on the IFRS SME standard but tailored to the UK environment), which can be applied in the UK now and becomes mandatory from 2015. The book encompasses: the requirements of the new accounting standards; FRS 100 – Application of financial reporting requirements, FRS 101 – Reduced disclosure framework – Disclosure exemptions from EU-adopted IFRS for qualifying entities and FRS 102 – The financial reporting standard applicable in the UK and Republic of Ireland; and the accounting requirements of the Companies Act 2006 that together make up the new UK GAAP.

The Manual offers a clear explanation of the new UK reporting requirements, which we hope will help you implement these new requirements and deal with day-to-day issues as well as the more complex areas under the new standards. In addition to providing reliable up-to-date guidance on the new UK GAAP, the Companies Act and relevant statutory instruments, it includes practical worked examples to help illustrate the explanations.

Written by PwC's Accounting Consulting Services team of specialists, the Manual will be of particular interest to finance directors, chief accountants and others concerned with preparing and using UK GAAP and reduced disclosure company financial statements.

The new UK GAAP is still in its infancy as it is only just starting to be applied by a relatively small number of companies, and will continue to evolve over time. Hence any manual on new UK GAAP should only be considered a snapshot of how the new requirements were understood at the time of writing – interpretations will move on constantly. As with this publication, most books contain wording that professional advice should be sought prior to entering into a transaction or making a major business decision. This will be similar with any book about new UK GAAP at the present time.

Even in a book of this size it is not possible to cover every aspect of company reporting. For example, the manual does not cover the specific accounting requirements that apply to banking companies, although much of the guidance given in the text will assist them.

We have also written a sister publication, Manual of Accounting – IFRS for the UK, which explains the rules that apply to UK listed companies and to other UK companies that choose to apply IFRS.

Iain Selfridge
PricewaterhouseCoopers LLP
London
October 2013

Contents

List of abbreviations

International standards

Accounts	financial statements
AESOP	all employee share ownership plan
the 2006 Act	the Companies Act 2006
ACT	advance corporation tax
AFS	available-for-sale
AG	Application Guidance
AGM	Annual General Meeting
AIM	Alternative Investment Market
AITC	Association of Investment Trust Companies
App	Application note of a Financial Reporting Standard
App	Appendix
ARC	Accounting Regulatory Committee
BC	Basis for Conclusions (to an accounting standard)
BIS	Department for Business, Innovation and Skills (formerly BERR before that DTI)
CA06	the Companies Act 2006
CCAB	Consultative Committee of Accountancy Bodies Limited
CGU	cash-generating unit
Chp	Chapter
chapter (1)	'PwC's Manual of accounting new UK GAAP' – chapter (1)
CIF	cost, insurance, freight
CODM	chief operating decision maker
CTD	cumulative translation difference
DCF	discounted cash flow
the 7th Directive	EC 7th Directive on Company Law
DRC	depreciated replacement cost
EBITDA	earnings before interest, tax, depreciation and amortisation
EC	European Community
ED	exposure draft
EPS	earnings per share
ESOP	employee share ownership plan
ESOT	employee share ownership trust
EU	European Union
EU 2005 Regulation	Regulation (EC) No 1606/2002 on the application of International Accounting Standards
FIFO	first-in, first-out
financial statements	Accounts
FOB	free on board
Framework	Framework for the preparation and presentation of financial statements
FRED	Financial Reporting Exposure Draft
FRC	Financial Reporting Council
FRRP	Financial Reporting Review Panel

List of abbreviations

FRS	Financial Reporting Standard
FRSSE	Financial Reporting Standard for Smaller Entities
FSA	Financial Services Authority
FVTPL	at fair value through profit or loss
GAAP	generally accepted accounting principles (and practices)
GAAS	generally accepted auditing standards
HMRC	HM Revenue & Customs
IAS	International Accounting Standard (see also IFRS)
IASB	International Accounting Standards Board
ICAEW	Institute of Chartered Accountants in England and Wales
IFRIC	International Financial Reporting Interpretations Committee
IFRS	International Financial Reporting Standard (see also IAS)
IG	Implementation Guidance (to an accounting standard)
IPO	initial public offering
ISA (UK & Ire)	International Standard on Auditing (UK and Ireland)
LIBOR	London inter-bank offered rate
LIFO	last-in, first-out
NPV	net present value
para(s)	paragraph(s) of Schedules to the Companies Acts, or IFRSs or IASs or FRSs, or SSAPs, or FREDs, or EDs, or DPs, or text
PFI	Private Finance Initiative
PPE	property, plant and equipment
QUEST	qualifying employee share ownership trust
R&D	research and development
Reg	regulation of a statutory
Sch	Schedule to the Companies Act 1985 (eg CA85 4A Sch 85 = Schedule 4A, paragraph 85)
Sec(s)	Section(s) of the 1985 Act/Sections(s) of the 2006 Act
SERPS	State earnings related pension scheme
SI	Statutory Instrument
SIC	Standing Interpretation Committee of the IASC (see IFRIC)
SIPs	share incentive plans
SMEs	small and medium-sized entities
SoP	Statement of principles
SORP	Statement of Recommended Practice
SPE	special purpose entity
SPV	special purpose vehicle
SSAP	Statement of Standard Accounting Practice
Stock Exchange (or LSE)	the London Stock Exchange
TR	Technical Release of the ICAEW
UITF	Urgent Issues Task Force
UK	United Kingdm
US	United States of America
VAT	value added tax
WACC	weighted average cost of capital

UK accounting standards

FRS 100	Application of financial reporting requirements
FRS 101	Reduced disclosure framework – Disclosure exemptions from EU-adopted IFRS for qualifying entities

FRS 102   The financial reporting standard applicable in the UK and Republic of Ireland

International accounting standards

IFRS 1	First-time adoption of International Financial Reporting Standards
IFRS 2	Share-based payment
IFRS 3	Business combinations
IFRS 4	Insurance contracts
IFRS 5	Non-current assets held for sale and discontinued operations
IFRS 6	Exploration for and evaluation of mineral resources
IFRS 7	Financial instruments: Disclosures
IFRS 8	Operating segments
IFRS 9	Financial instruments
IFRS 10	Consolidated financial statements
IFRS 11	Joint arrangements
IFRS 12	Disclosure of interests in other entities
IFRS 13	Fair value measurement
IAS 1	Presentation of financial statements
IAS 2	Inventories
IAS 7	Cash flow statements
IAS 8	Accounting policies, changes in accounting estimates and errors
IAS 10	Events after the balance sheet date
IAS 11	Construction contracts
IAS 12	Income taxes
IAS 16	Property, plant and equipment
IAS 17	Leases
IAS 18	Revenue
IAS 19	Employee benefits
IAS 20	Accounting for government grants and disclosure of government assistance
IAS 21	The effects of changes in foreign exchange rates
IAS 23	Borrowing costs
IAS 24	Related-party disclosures
IAS 26	Accounting and reporting by retirement benefit plans
IAS 27	Separate financial statements
IAS 28	Investment in associates and joint ventures
IAS 29	Financial reporting in hyper-inflationary economies
IAS 31	Interests in joint ventures
IAS 32	Financial instruments: presentation
IAS 33	Earnings per share
IAS 34	Interim financial reporting
IAS 36	Impairment of assets
IAS 37	Provisions, contingent liabilities and contingent assets
IAS 38	Intangible assets
IAS 39	Financial instruments: Recognition and measurement
IAS 40	Investment property
IAS 41	Agriculture

Interpretations

IFRIC 1	Changes in existing decommissioning, restoration and similar liabilities

List of abbreviations

IFRIC 2	Members' shares in co-operative entities and similar Instruments
IFRIC 4	Determining whether an arrangement contains a lease
IFRIC 5	Rights to interests arising from decommissioning, restoration and environmental rehabilitation funds
IFRIC 6	Liabilities arising from participating in a specific market – Waste electrical and electronic equipment
IFRIC 7	Applying the restatement approach under IAS 29 Financial reporting in hyper-inflationary economies
IFRIC 9	Re-assessment of embedded derivatives
IFRIC 10	Interim financial reporting and impairment
IFRIC 12	Service concession arrangements
IFRIC 13	Customer loyalty programmes
IFRIC 14	IAS 19 – The limit on a defined benefit asset, minimum funding requirements and their interaction
IFRIC 15	Agreements for the construction of real estate
IFRIC 16	Hedges of a net investment in a foreign operation
IFRIC 17	Distributions of non-cash assets to owners
IFRIC 18	Transfers of assets from customers
IFRIC 19	Extinguishing financial liabilities with equity instruments
IFRIC 20	Stripping costs in the production phase of a surface mine
IFRIC 21	Levies
SIC-7	Introduction of the euro
SIC-10	Government Assistance – No specific relation to operating activities
SIC-12	Consolidation - Special purpose entities
SIC-13	Jointly controlled entities – Non-Monetary contributions by venturers
SIC-15	Operating leases – Incentives
SIC-25	Income taxes – Changes in the tax status of an entity or its shareholders
SIC-27	Evaluating the substance of transactions in the legal form of a lease
SIC-29	Service Concession Arrangements: Disclosures
SIC-31	Revenue – Barter transactions involving advertising services
SIC-32	Intangible assets – Web site costs

Chapter 1

Scope

Chapter 1

Scope

Background

1.1 Despite the use of international financial reporting standards (IFRS) by listed entities and some others, UK GAAP continues to be important and is still used by most unlisted companies and groups and by many individual entities – parent entities and UK subsidiaries – in listed groups. Hence, by number at least, the majority of entities in the UK use UK GAAP. But UK GAAP is undergoing a fundamental change. The SSAPs and FRSs, and UITF Abstracts ('old UK GAAP'), that have been familiar for 40 years or more, are being swept away and replaced by a new system, involving new choices (see below), some changes to accounting principles and changes (mostly reductions) to disclosure. These new rules are found in FRS 100, FRS 101 and FRS 102, which are explained below. In summary: FRS 100 sets out the overall framework; FRS 101 sets out the reduced disclosure framework; and FRS 102, 'The financial reporting standard applicable in the UK and the Republic of Ireland', sets out in detail the requirements that entities adopting the new UK GAAP will need to follow.

1.2 The old regime of SSAPs and FRSs needed to be replaced for two main reasons. First, it was a very detailed and complex system, reflecting the fact that it used to apply, until 2005, to listed companies as well as others. But, since listed companies have had to follow IFRS in their group accounts from 2005, UK GAAP has applied to smaller and/or privately owned entities; and, for them, this degree of complexity is unnecessary. In short, the old regime is no longer fit for purpose. Secondly, UK GAAP had become an unholy mixture of old UK GAAP (all the SSAPs and FRS 1 to FRS 19) and standards based on importing IFRS into the UK (broadly, FRS 20 to FRS 29). It was neither one thing nor the other. At the same time, the general view was that a different, nationally based system of accounting was no longer realistic in a world increasingly dominated by IFRS.

1.3 In the world of IFRS, there was, in the period leading up to 2009, a realisation that IFRS was becoming overly complex for many unlisted and smaller entities in countries that use IFRS. As a result, the IASB developed the International Financial Reporting Standard for Small and Medium-sized Entities (IFRS for SMEs). This was published in 2009. It does not apply in the UK but has provided the basis for FRS 102. In developing FRS 102, however, the UK Accounting Council and the Financial Reporting Council adapted IFRS for SMEs, partly to make FRS 102 consistent with UK company law, partly to retain some accounting treatments that were considered useful in the UK, and partly to clarify the standard. Despite these changes, FRS 102 is quite similar to IFRS for SMEs and has the same overall philosophy, namely that it is based on IFRS but with simplifications and other changes aimed at making it more suitable for entities other than listed groups.

The new UK GAAP framework

Summary of framework

1.4 New UK GAAP is considerably simpler than its predecessor, but the question of who can, or should, apply which requirements is quite complex. Moreover, there are important choices for entities to make. The requirements and options can be summarised as follows:

New framework

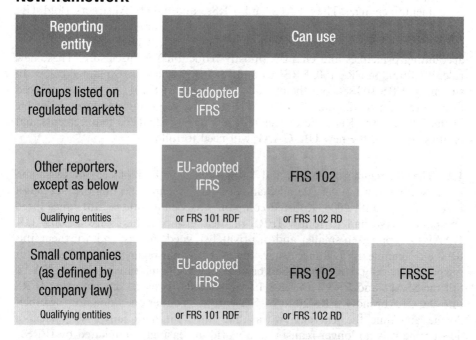

Reporting entity	Can use		
Groups listed on regulated markets	EU-adopted IFRS		
Other reporters, except as below	EU-adopted IFRS	FRS 102	
Qualifying entities	or FRS 101 RDF	or FRS 102 RD	
Small companies (as defined by company law)	EU-adopted IFRS	FRS 102	FRSSE
Qualifying entities	or FRS 101 RDF	or FRS 102 RD	

1.5 As has been the case since 2005, the consolidated accounts of groups that are listed on a regulated market (for example, the Main Market of the London Stock Exchange) must use EU-adopted IFRS. Also, other entities and groups can opt to use EU-adopted IFRS if they so wish; this, too, is the same as the old position. EU-adopted IFRS is the subject of PwC's 'Manual of Accounting – IFRS for the UK' and is not discussed in detail in this book.

1.6 The Companies Act 2006 ('the Act') sets out its accounting requirements in the following way. Under section 395, a company's individual accounts can be prepared *"(a) in accordance with section 396 ('Companies Act individual accounts'), or (b) in accordance with international accounting standards ('IAS individual accounts')"*. Section 403 of the Act sets out the equivalent for group accounts. The Act's reference to 'IAS' means the same as IFRS for all practical purposes. Importantly, only EU-adopted IFRS ('IFRS') is regarded as 'IAS' for this purpose. In particular, FRS 101's reduced disclosure framework does not count as IAS accounts: it is a type of 'Companies Act accounts' for legal purposes. Neither do accounts under FRS 102 count as IAS accounts, even though FRS 102 is based on IFRS for SMEs. This point is important because, for entities following 'IAS accounts' (that is, IFRS), some detailed accounting requirements of the Act are disapplied. The detailed accounting rules in question (that is, those that apply to companies preparing 'Companies Act accounts' but that are disapplied for those preparing 'IAS accounts') are set out in the Small Companies and Groups (Accounts and Directors' Report) Regulations 2008 (SI 2008/409) and the Large and Medium-sized Companies and Groups (Accounts and Reports) Regulations 2008 (SI 2008/410). These Regulations primarily set out the accounting principles, formats, valuation rules and disclosures.

1.7   Put another way, all of the following count as 'Companies Act accounts':

■   FRS 101 – IFRS as regards recognition and measurement but with reduced disclosures;

■   FRS 102 – the new UK GAAP;

■   FRS 102 – the new UK GAAP with reduced disclosures; and

■   the Financial Reporting Standard for Smaller Entities (FRSSE).

The relationship between the Act and FRS 102 is explored in Appendix IV to FRS 102.

Listed groups and other users of IFRS

1.8   As shown in the table above, it is open to any entity (except charities) to use IFRS. IFRS must be used in the consolidated accounts of groups listed on a regulated market of an EU member state; for other entities, it is optional. Some listed groups have also used IFRS in their UK subsidiaries and/or in the parent entity. This has had the advantage of easing the consolidation process, but at the cost of needing to prepare overly complex entity accounts. Such groups might wish to continue with this approach; but we believe that many will find it attractive to move the accounts of the entities onto FRS 101, or perhaps onto FRS 102. Other entities that have adopted IFRS on a voluntary basis might similarly continue with this approach, but they might find it attractive to move to FRS 102 (or FRS 101, or the FRSSE, if available).

Small companies

1.9   As shown in the bottom line of the table above, small companies (as defined in the Act) have a number of choices. The least onerous approach is to use the Financial Reporting Standard for Smaller Entities (FRSSE), a highly simplified system for small companies. This continues to be available to such companies and is unchanged – that is, it is not amended to be consistent with, or based on, IFRS or IFRS for SMEs. Eligibility to use the FRSSE is set out in full in paragraphs 8 and 9 of the FRSSE. The key points are that the following are eligible:

- a company or group that is small as defined in the Companies Act; or

- an entity that would also qualify under the Act if it had been incorporated under companies legislation, with the exception of building societies.

1.10 The definition of a small company in the Act is currently one that meets two out of three of the following:

- turnover – not more than £6.5m;

- balance sheet total – not more than £3.26m; and

- employees – not more than 50.

For this purpose, turnover and balance sheet total should be measured in accordance with the FRSSE. That is, the equivalent measures under FRS 101 or FRS 102 need not be considered. [CA06 Sec 382; FRS 100 para 4].

1.11 Small companies are also able to use FRS 102 or IFRS if they wish. Those that are 'qualifying entities' (see below) are able to use the reduced disclosure version of IFRS (that is, FRS 101) or the reduced disclosures in FRS 102.

Other entities

1.12 The middle line of the table above deals with those entities that do not have to follow IFRS and do not qualify to use the FRSSE. This is a large category; it will include many subsidiaries and parent entities of listed and other groups, the consolidated accounts of unlisted groups, and large and medium-sized private single entities.

1.13 Such entities can choose between:

- EU-adopted IFRS ('IFRS');

- the reduced disclosure framework of FRS 101, if they are qualifying entities;

- FRS 102; and

- FRS 102 with reduced disclosures, if they are qualifying entities.

Qualifying entities

1.14 A 'qualifying entity' is defined as *"A member of a group where the parent of that group prepares publicly available consolidated financial statements which are intended to give a true and fair view (of the assets, liabilities, financial position and profit or loss) and that member is included in the consolidation"*. [FRS 100, FRS 101, FRS 102 Glossary of terms]. Hence, an individual entity (that is, one that is not part of a group) cannot be a qualifying entity. Also, under FRS 101, a charity cannot be a qualifying entity.

1.15 The phrase 'publicly available' is used in the definition above of qualifying entity. No definition of this phrase is given in the FRSs, but it seems clear that it means available to the public in general and not, for instance, just to shareholders. Section 436 of the Companies Act 2006 refers to the publication of accounts and states:

> *"For the purposes of those sections a company is regarded as publishing a document if it publishes, issues or circulates it or otherwise makes it available for public inspection in a manner calculated to invite members of the public generally, or any class of members of the public, to read it."*

1.16 We consider that 'publicly available' can be interpreted in this way. However, the test should be judged, in practice, by reference to whether a copy of the consolidated financial statements can be acquired relatively easily. The financial statements might be on a public register, for example; but, if the financial statements themselves cannot be easily obtained, they would not be regarded as publicly available. Where there is no public register but the address from which they can be obtained is given, the financial statements would be regarded as publicly available.

1.17 Qualifying entities are able, in defined circumstances, to take advantage of the reduced disclosures in FRS 101 and FRS 102.

FRS 101 – the reduced disclosure framework

1.18 FRS 101 comprises the use of IFRS as regards recognition and measurement (with some amendments for the Companies Act, where necessary) but with extensive disclosure reductions. Indeed, the whole purpose of FRS 101 is to provide a reduced disclosure framework for individual entities that otherwise comply with the recognition and measurement rules of IFRS.

1.19 The disclosure reductions are only available in specified conditions, where: (a) shareholders have been notified in writing and do not object; (b) the entity otherwise applies the recognition, measurement and disclosure requirements of EU-adopted IFRS, but amended where necessary to comply with the Act (as the accounts are Companies Act accounts); and (c) various disclosures are made, including a brief narrative summary of the disclosure exemptions adopted. [FRS 101 para 5].

1.20 The disclosure exemptions are limited or not available in the following circumstances:

- The disclosure exemptions do not apply in consolidated financial statements. [FRS 101 para 3].

■ Some disclosures required by the Act continue to be required, despite the standard's exemptions. [FRS 101 para 6]. The description is complex and is discussed more fully in the paragraph below.

■ A qualifying entity that is a financial institution (as defined in the glossary of FRS 101; see also chapter 34) is not exempt from the disclosure requirements of:

    ■ IFRS 7 on financial instruments;

    ■ IFRS 13 on fair value measurement, to the extent that they apply to financial instruments; and

    ■ paragraphs 134-136 of IAS 1 on management of capital. [FRS 101 para 7].

1.21 As noted in the second bullet point above, the Act requires various disclosures, and this is described as follows:

> *"A qualifying entity which is not a financial institution may take advantage in its individual financial statements of the disclosure exemptions set out in paragraphs 8 to 9 of this FRS. In relation to paragraphs 8(d) and (e), for financial liabilities that are held at fair value that are part of a trading portfolio or are derivatives, the qualifying entity can take advantage of those exemptions. Where the qualifying entity has financial instruments held at fair value subject to the requirements of section 36(4) of Schedule 1 to the Regulations, it must apply the disclosure requirements of paragraphs 8(e), 9(c), 10, 11, 17, 20(a)(i), 25, 26, 28, 29, 30, 31 of IFRS 7 and paragraph 93 of IFRS 13 to those financial instruments held at fair value. For accounting periods beginning before 1 January 2013, paragraph 93 of IFRS 13 should be replaced with paragraphs 27, 27A and 27B of IFRS 7."* [FRS 101 para 6].

1.22 This can be explained as follows:

■ Financial institutions, even if they follow FRS 101, are not exempt from disclosures relating to financial instruments.

■ Non-financial institutions following FRS 101 are exempt from the disclosures in IFRS 7 and IFRS 13.

■ However, there are various disclosure requirements relating to the 'fair value accounting' provisions of the Act, that still have to be given (if applicable).

■ Paragraph 36(4) of Schedule 1 to each of the Regulations incorporates into law some requirements of the international standards on financial instruments.

■ Because those requirements are rules of law, the standard-setter cannot provide exemptions from them. Hence, the disclosures required by the paragraphs of IFRS 7 and 13 (as listed in the quoted paragraph above) need to be given, even though there are wider-ranging exemptions. See Appendix 1 to this chapter for further details

1.23 The disclosure exemptions, subject to the limitations described above, are set out in paragraphs 8 and 9 of FRS 101. Some of these require that 'equivalent' disclosures are included in the consolidated financial statements in which the entity is consolidated. See paragraph 1.41 below for a discussion of equivalence. In summary, the disclosure exemptions are:

- There are extensive exemptions from share-based payment disclosures in a subsidiary's financial statements, using equity instruments of another group entity; and in an ultimate parent's separate financial statements, using its own equity instruments. [FRS 101 para 8(a)].

- There are extensive exemptions from the business combination disclosures. [FRS 101 para 8(b)]. This exemption would apply to the disclosures regarding a business combination in which the reporting entity has acquired an unincorporated business.

- Cash flow information relating to discontinued operations need not be given. [FRS 101 para 8(c)]. But there is a broader exemption from cash flow statements as a whole (see below).

- There is an exemption from the disclosure requirements for financial instruments in IFRS 7. [FRS 101 para 8(d)]. But this exemption does not extend to financial institutions. Also, non-financial institutions that have specified financial instruments held at fair value are required to give some disclosures under company law (see para 1.22).

- There is an exemption from the disclosure requirements for fair value measurement in IFRS 13. [FRS 101 para 8(e)]. But, similar to the previous bullet point, this exemption does not extend to financial institutions for disclosures in respect of financial instruments.

- There are exemptions from the reconciliations from opening to closing amounts (sometimes called 'movements tables') for comparatives in respect of:

    - number of shares outstanding;

    - property, plant and equipment;

    - intangible assets;

    - investment property; and

    - biological assets.

  [FRS 101 para 8(f)].

- There are various exemptions from IAS 1 relating to the third (earliest) balance sheet and to the management of capital. [FRS 101 para 8(g)].

- No cash flow statement is required. [FRS 101 para 8(h)].

- No details are required about new IFRSs that have been published but are not yet effective. [FRS 101 para 8(i)].

- As regards related party disclosures:

  - no disclosures are required about compensation of key management personnel. [FRS 101 para 8(j)];

  - no disclosures are required about transactions between wholly owned subsidiaries or between the parent and wholly owned subsidiaries. [FRS 101 para 8(k)]; but

    - the other related party disclosures *are* required.

- There are exemptions from many of the impairment disclosures in IAS 36; these relate to estimates used to measure recoverable amounts of cash-generating units containing goodwill or intangible assets with indefinite useful lives. [FRS 101 para 8(l)].

Companies Act amendments in FRS 101

1.24 Although FRS 101 essentially comprises IFRS as regards recognition and measurement, but with reduced disclosures, it is not quite that simple. FRS 101 is a form of 'Companies Act accounts', not IFRS, for legal purposes. Hence, the accounting requirements of the Act continue to apply. Because of that, some amendments need to be made to IFRS; these are set out in the Application Guidance to FRS 101 and summarised below:

- Contingent consideration in a business combination is recognised at its estimated amounts if it is probable. Goodwill is adjusted for subsequent changes.

- Negative goodwill is not immediately recognised in profit or loss.

- The analysis of results of discontinued operations needs to be presented on the face of the income statement.

- Generally, only realised profits can be included in profit or loss (but there are exceptions under the Act's fair value accounting rules).

- Government grants cannot be netted against the related asset.

- Government grant income cannot be netted against expenses.

- Impairments of goodwill are reversed if the reasons for the impairment loss cease to apply.

- Assets and liabilities of a parent or subsidiaries on first-time adoption of IFRS need to be measured in line with the above amendments in FRS 101.

1.25 In addition to the above, the formats in IAS 1 cannot be used unless they comply with the formats in the Regulations. Differences in the primary statement formats might result from:

- The definition of 'fixed assets' (company law) and 'non-current assets' (IFRS).

- The definition of current assets.

- The definitions of creditors falling due within, or after, one year (company law) and current/non-current liabilities (IFRS).

- Presentation of debtors falling due after more than one year within current assets (company law). Under IFRS, those items would be presented in non-current assets.

If there are differences, the company law formats must be followed.

1.26 Also, the non-amortisation of goodwill under IFRS conflicts with Schedule 1 to the Regulations, which requires goodwill to be depreciated over its useful economic life. So, non-amortisation of material goodwill will require the use of a true and fair override.

FRS 102 – the new UK GAAP

General principles

1.27 Small companies can use the FRSSE, and many subsidiaries of listed and other groups are likely to use FRS 101. These are both part of UK GAAP and are regarded as 'Companies Act' accounts for legal purposes. Nevertheless, it is FRS 102 that, for large numbers of companies in the UK and the Republic of Ireland, will become the new accounting standard to which they migrate in or before 2015.

1.28 FRS 102 is based on IFRS for SMEs. But the Financial Reporting Council adapted IFRS for SMEs, partly to make FRS 102 consistent with UK company law, partly to retain some accounting treatments that were considered useful in the UK, and partly to clarify the standard. Despite these changes, FRS 102 is quite similar to IFRS for SMEs and has the same overall philosophy, namely that it is based on IFRS but with simplifications and other changes aimed at making it more suitable for entities other than listed groups. Hence FRS 102 is short and concise.

Scope

1.29 FRS 102 applies to financial statements that are intended to give a true and fair view. [FRS 102 para 1.1]. That is, a true and fair view is deemed to arise from a proper application of the standard, even though it is less demanding in terms of recognition, measurement and disclosure than either IFRS or, indeed, old UK GAAP. FRS 102 uses the term 'fair presentation', which is generally taken to be equivalent to the legal requirement for a true and fair view. Fair presentation is discussed in chapter 3. [FRS 102 para 3.2].

1.30 As discussed above, FRS 102 can be used by any UK company, except those that are required to use IFRS by Regulation (EC) 1606/2002 on the application of international accounting standards ('the IAS Regulation').

1.31 The standard is also applicable to public benefit entities and other entities, not just companies. Paragraph numbers prefixed with 'PBE' should only be applied by public benefit entities and should not be applied, either directly or by analogy, by entities that are not PBEs, other than (where specifically directed) by entities within a PBE group. [FRS 102 para 1.2]. Also, for example, the standard can be used by LLPs; indeed, it should be used by LLPs unless they opt for IFRS or are eligible to use the FRSSE.

1.32 A *single entity* that is listed on a regulated market is not bound by the IAS Regulation to use IFRS in the way that a listed *group* must do for its consolidated accounts. Such listed entities have been able to use UK GAAP in the past, although some have adopted IFRS voluntarily. Such entities can use FRS 102, but the standard adds two aspects of IFRS for listed entities:

- *"An entity whose ordinary shares or potential ordinary shares are publicly traded, or that files, or is in the process of filing, its financial statements with a securities commission or other regulatory organisation for the purposes of issuing ordinary shares in a public market, or an entity that chooses to disclose earnings per share"* should apply IAS 33. [FRS 102 para 1.4].

- *"An entity whose debt or equity instruments are publicly traded, or that files, or is in the process of filing, its financial statements with a securities commission or other regulatory organisation for the purpose of issuing any class of instruments in a public market, or an entity that chooses to provide information described as segment information"* should apply IFRS 8. If an entity discloses disaggregated information, but the information does not comply with IFRS 8, it should not describe the information as segment information. [FRS 102 para 1.5].

FRS 102 compared with old UK GAAP

1.33 FRS 102 differs considerably from the previous version of UK GAAP. Most noticeably, it is much shorter and more concise. As noted above, it is based on IFRS for SMEs, but with some adaptations for UK use. In terms of accounting treatments, the following are the principal differences.

Financial instruments:

- Initial measurement of financial instruments varies between transaction price (excluding transaction costs) for those held at fair value through profit or loss (FVTPL), present value of future payments for financing transactions, and transaction price (including transaction costs) for those that are not held at FVTPL or financing transactions.

- Derivatives will need to be fair valued and recognised on the balance sheet; this is a change for those not applying FRS 26.

- Many equity investments will need to be fair valued, with changes recognised through profit or loss.

- There are additional disclosures in FRS 102 for financial institutions.

Deferred tax:

- Deferred taxes will need to be recognised on asset revaluations, and on assets (except goodwill) and liabilities arising on a business combination.

- Deferred taxes cannot be discounted.

Employee benefits:

- Interest and return on assets is calculated as a net amount by applying the discount rate to the net pension deficit/surplus. 'Expected return on assets' will no longer apply.

- The deficit or surplus relating to a group defined benefit pension scheme can no longer be recognised only in the group accounts. Where group companies cannot individually account for their portion of the surplus/deficit, the total must be recognised in the sponsoring company's accounts.

- A liability is recognised for multi-employer pension plans where there is an agreement to fund a deficit relating to past service, even if the plan is otherwise accounted for as defined contribution. Under FRS 17, there was no clear guidance in this situation.

- An accrual for short-term employee benefits (such as holiday pay) will need to be made.

Goodwill and intangible assets:

- All intangible assets, including goodwill, are assumed to have finite lives, so they have to be amortised. Intangibles with indefinite lives were possible under old UK GAAP.

- The rebuttable presumption of useful life of goodwill has been reduced from 20 years to 5 years, to comply with EU legislation.

- The definition of 'intangible assets' has changed. There could be more intangible assets recognised as part of a business combination.

Investment property:

- Changes in the fair value of investment properties will need to be recognised in profit or loss, instead of through the statement of total recognised gains and losses.

Other significant changes:

- Groups are exempt from consolidating subsidiaries held as part of an investment portfolio; this is because these are considered to be held for resale. All portfolio investments are measured at fair value through profit or loss. These subsidiaries would be consolidated under old UK GAAP.

- Sales and purchases in a foreign currency can no longer be measured at the forward contract rate.

- The cash flow statement is similar to that under IFRS, showing movements on cash and cash equivalents (thus broader than the focus on *cash* in FRS 1), but with fewer standard headings than under FRS 1. Qualifying entities are exempt.

- Lease incentives are recognised over the lease term. Under old UK GAAP, lease incentives are spread over the shorter of the lease term and the period to the first market rent review.

FRS 102 compared with IFRS for SMEs

1.34 An important difference between the two is that FRS 102 applies to a wider range of entities than IFRS for SMEs envisages. That is, apart from groups that are required by the IAS Regulation to apply IFRS, the 'publicly accountable' test in IFRS for SMEs is not used. The scope and application of FRS 102 is described above.

1.35 In addition, a number of specific accounting treatments have been changed. Examples include:

- Development costs can be capitalised in some circumstances.

- Borrowing costs can be capitalised in some circumstances.

- Property, plant and equipment can be revalued.

- Merger accounting is permitted for group reconstructions.

A table in Appendix 2 to FRS 102 sets out the differences in detail.

FRS 102's disclosure reductions

1.36 FRS 102 contains a lower level of disclosure than IFRS and, depending on the topic, a lower level of disclosure than old UK GAAP. But FRS 102 goes further than this and provides for a still lower level of disclosures for 'qualifying entities'. Qualifying entities are defined in the same way as in FRS 100 and 101 (see above). But, unlike FRS 101, charities can take advantage of the FRS 102 exemptions if they are qualifying entities.

1.37 However, the exemptions are not the same as the exemptions in the FRS 101 reduced disclosure framework, as the starting points of the two sets of disclosure requirements differ.

1.38 In summary, exemptions from disclosure are available in FRS 102 for:

- Cash flow statements.

- Financial instrument disclosures (but the exemption does not apply to financial institutions). Also, non-financial institutions that have specified financial instruments held at fair value need to give some disclosures under company law.

- Share-based payment disclosures in a subsidiary's financial statements, using equity instruments of another group entity; and in an ultimate parent's separate financial statements, using its own equity instruments.

- Key management personnel compensation (but company law disclosures for directors' remuneration still apply).

- Related party transactions entered into between two or more members of a group (for wholly owned subsidiaries) – this exemption is not restricted to 'qualifying entities.

[FRS 102 paras 1.8, 1.9, 1.12, 33.1A].

1.39 The exemptions are not available in the preparation of consolidated accounts. [FRS 102 para 1.10]. Also, the following conditions must be satisfied: (a) shareholders have been notified in writing and do not object; (b) the entity otherwise applies the recognition, measurement and disclosure requirements of FRS 102; and (c) various disclosures are made, including a brief narrative summary of the disclosure exemptions adopted. [FRS 102 para 1.11].

1.40 As spelled out in paragraph 1.12 of FRS 102, some of these disclosure reductions are available only if 'equivalent' disclosures are given in the group's publicly available consolidated financial statements in which the entity in question is consolidated. The meaning of 'equivalent' is discussed below. The reduced disclosures are summarised in Appendix 2 to this chapter.

Disclosure reductions and 'equivalence'

1.41 There are disclosure reductions in FRS 101 and FRS 102 but these are different from each other (as described above). In each case, some of the disclosure reductions are available only if 'equivalent' disclosures are included in the consolidated financial statements of the group in which the entity is consolidated. The Application Guidance to FRS 100 explains what 'equivalent' means in this context.

1.42 Paragraph AG1 of FRS 100 starts by referring to section 401 of the Act, which deals with the exemption from preparing consolidated accounts where the group in question is part of a larger group. This is not directly relevant to FRS 101 or FRS 102 but is used as a starting point because it is an established use, albeit in a different context, of the notion of 'equivalence'. Paragraph AG2 notes that FRS 101 and FRS 102 give disclosure exemptions but only, in some cases, where equivalent disclosures are included in the consolidated accounts of the group in which the entity is consolidated. The remainder of the Application Guidance interprets equivalence and applies to both situations – that is, the exemption from consolidation under section 401 of the Act and the disclosure exemptions under FRS 101 and FRS 102. Only the second of these situations is discussed here.

1.43   The key aspects of the guidance can be summarised as follows:

- The guidance starts by noting that *"In the absence of this guidance, companies and auditors might feel obliged to take an overly cautious approach in response to uncertainty about whether the exemptions can be used"*. [FRS 100 AG4]. This seems to be a strong steer by the standard-setter that one should take a broad view in considering equivalence.

- Reference to equivalence does not mean compliance with every detail. [FRS 100 AG5].

- It is necessary to consider whether the consolidated financial statements of the parent provide disclosures that meet the basic disclosure requirements of the relevant standard, without requiring strict conformity with each and every disclosure. This assessment should be based on the particular facts, including the similarities to and differences from the requirements of the relevant standard from which relief is provided. [FRS 100 AG8].

- Disclosure exemptions for subsidiaries are permitted where the relevant disclosures are given in the consolidated accounts, even if these disclosures are given (as will generally be the case) in aggregate or abbreviated form. But, if no disclosure is made in the consolidated accounts on grounds of materiality, the relevant disclosure (if material) should be made by the subsidiary in its financial statements. [FRS 100 AG10]. Groups might therefore find that a summarised disclosure in the group accounts can take the place of comprehensive disclosure in the accounts of one or more subsidiaries.

- In the context of the section 401 exemption from consolidation, FRS 100 notes that, as well as IFRS being equivalent to the EU seventh directive on consolidated accounts, accounts drawn up under US, Japanese, Chinese, Canadian or Korean GAAP are regarded as equivalent to IFRS, as is Indian GAAP on a short-term basis. [FRS 100 AG7]. Of course, the most common example is likely to be where the consolidated accounts are drawn up under IFRS, and here the test of equivalence is most obviously met. A related question is whether disclosures could be considered equivalent if the consolidated accounts are drawn up under FRS 102 or, if abroad, IFRS for SMEs. There is no single answer to this question; it would have to be considered on the facts of each case. Voluntary additional disclosure by the group might be a solution where equivalence is not otherwise achieved. In any event, it is unlikely that the accounts of the subsidiary would be drawn up using the recognition and measurement rules of IFRS (which are the basis of FRS 101), with the accounts of the group drawn up on a simpler basis.

Effective date, transition and consistency

Effective date

1.44 The effective date of FRS 100, FRS 101 and FRS 102 is periods beginning on or after 1 January 2015. As with most changes of accounting policy, comparatives are re-stated. Hence, the date of transition is, in effect, 1 January 2014. A company can early adopt FRS 100 and 101; it can early adopt FRS 102 also, but only from periods ended on or after 31 December 2012. In each case, it must note that it has done so.

Transition

1.45 FRS 100 sets out detailed requirements relating to the various transitions that might arise [FRS 100 paras 10–13]. In summary:

- An entity transitioning to IFRS must apply IFRS 1's rules on first-time adoption.

- A qualifying entity transitioning to FRS 101 should (unless it applied IFRS before the date of transition - see next bullet) apply the requirements of paragraphs 6 to 33 of IFRS 1 including the relevant appendices; references to IFRSs in IFRS 1 are interpreted to mean EU-adopted IFRS as amended by paragraph 5(b) of FRS 101 (see para 1.24 above).

- A qualifying entity transitioning from IFRS to FRS 101 requires some thought; this is because, although (in simple terms) FRS 101 involves using the recognition and measurement rules of IFRS, FRS 101 accounts are 'Companies Act accounts' in law and so have to comply with the relevant parts of the Companies Act; this could lead to adjustments to the IFRS information and, where these are material, some additional disclosures and reconciliations are required. The rules are set out fully in paragraphs 11 and 12 of FRS 100.

- An entity transitioning to FRS 102 or to the FRSSE should follow the transitional arrangements in those standards. Transition to FRS 102 is conventional – that is, prior years' figures are re-stated onto FRS 102. There are some exceptions and exemptions from retrospective application for first-time adopters of FRS 102 (see chapter 35). A further complication arises in connection with SORPs. For entities that are within the scope of a SORP, early application is permitted for periods ended on or after 31 December 2012, provided it does not conflict with the requirements of a current SORP or legal requirements for the preparation of accounts. [FRS 102 para 1.14].

1.46 There is nothing in FRS 100, FRS 101 or FRS 102 that requires a number of entities (say, all UK subsidiaries of a group) to transition at the same time.

Transitioning from IFRS

1.47 Previous restrictions on changing GAAP have been relaxed. Until 2012, it was difficult, under the Companies Act, to revert to UK GAAP (strictly, to 'Companies Act accounts') once a company had adopted IFRS: section 395 of the Act permitted this only if there was a 'relevant change in circumstances'. However, the Act has been updated such that a company that has adopted IFRS is now permitted to revert to 'Companies Act accounts'. The Regulations provide that company directors who prepare a company's individual accounts in accordance with IFRS can switch to Companies Act accounts for a reason other than a relevant change of circumstances, provided they have not switched to Companies Act accounts in the period of five years preceding the first day of the financial year in which they wish to implement the change of accounting framework. The same applies in relation to group accounts, provided those accounts are not required by the IAS Regulation to be prepared in accordance with IFRS. [SI 2012/2031].

1.48 The most obvious application of this is in respect of groups that have moved their UK subsidiaries onto IFRS for reasons of consistency with the consolidated accounts, but which view the preparation of IFRS accounts for subsidiaries as onerous, and so would benefit from moving to FRS 101's reduced disclosure framework or, potentially, to FRS 102.

Consistency of GAAP within a group

1.49 The Companies Act requires that, where a parent company prepares group accounts, individual entities within the group should follow either IFRS or UK GAAP (in Companies Act terms, they should prepare either 'IAS accounts' or 'Companies Act accounts'), rather than have a mixture of the two within a group. There is an exception to this, in that the parent entity can use IFRS if the group uses IFRS in its consolidated accounts (for example, in a listed group), even if all the other UK subsidiaries use UK GAAP. [CA06 Sec 407]. See further chapter 10.

1.50 Any intermediate parent entity that prepares consolidated IFRS financial statements can also use IFRS for its parent entity accounts without breaching the GAAP consistency rule.

1.51 This rule remains in place, but will apply in a different way from before. This is because all of FRS 101, FRS 102 and the FRSSE, including the reduced disclosure variant of FRS 102, are a form of Companies Act accounts. Subject to the exception for the parent entity (see previous paragraph), a group can have all of its UK subsidiaries on (a) IFRS ('IAS accounts') or (b) one or more of FRS 101, FRS 102 and (less likely) the FRSSE, including the reduced disclosure variant of FRS 102 ('Companies Act accounts'). So, for example, some subsidiaries could follow FRS 101 and others could follow FRS 102 without breaching the Act.

Selecting an approach within the new regime

1.52 Entities following old UK GAAP (SSAPs, FRSs 1-30 etc) cannot continue to use it indefinitely. They must switch to their selected approach within the new regime for periods beginning on or after 1 January 2015 at the latest.

1.53 As already noted, entities in the second and third lines of the table in paragraph 1.4 have various choices open to them. It is worthwhile spending time making well-informed choices. The factors to take into account in selecting an approach include:

- *Reported results.* The accounting rules for recognition and measurement are different as between IFRS and FRS 102 in some areas. For example, goodwill is amortised under FRS 102 but retained at cost (subject to impairment review) under IFRS. Other differences are described above. Although private companies and subsidiaries will typically be less concerned about their reported results than listed groups, there might still be concerns about the reported results (for example, if a private company is planning a trade sale). So an analysis of the effect on reported results of FRS 102 compared with IFRS will be an important exercise in these circumstances.

- *Tax liabilities.* Differences in accounting treatment between IFRS and FRS 102 might lead to differences in the amount or timing of tax payments.

- *Distributable profits.* Similarly, differences in accounting treatment between IFRS and FRS 102 might lead to different amounts of distributable profits. Whether this is a concern will depend on the amount of accumulated distributable profits and the entity's plans for future distributions.

- *Amount of work in preparing financial statements.* Other things being equal, most preparers would prefer a regime under which financial statements can be prepared quickly and efficiently. So the reduced disclosure approach of FRS 101 is likely to be attractive for the subsidiaries of many groups. Financial statements drawn up under FRS 102 will also tend to be simpler and quicker than those under IFRS.

- *Regulatory capital.* This is an important matter for many financial services companies.

- *Bonus schemes.* These could be based on, for example, operating profit drawn from old UK GAAP.

- *Consistency with group policies.* A consolidation is eased where the financial statements of subsidiaries are drawn up under the same GAAP as the group accounts. And so listed groups, and other groups that report under IFRS, will find it helpful if the financial statements of subsidiaries are drawn up under IFRS, in particular as regards recognition and measurement. In this respect, therefore, FRS 101's reduced disclosure framework will be attractive.

1.54 As well as the choice of GAAP (that is, what change to make), there is a related question of when to change. For example, a group might wish to take advantage of the reduced disclosure framework as soon as possible. It is open to such a group to change its subsidiaries' and parent entity's accounting to FRS 101 immediately; there is no need to wait until 2015, as the standard can be early adopted. A second example is that a change – for example, from old UK GAAP to FRS 102 – might have different tax consequences if it occurs earlier as opposed to in 2015. Note that, within a group, whilst it might make sense to change all the entity accounts to the selected new regime at the same time, there is no requirement to do so; changing the regime for some subsidiaries one year and for others another year might have various advantages, including spreading the work-load over a period.

Other matters

Insurance and FRS 103

1.55 FRS 103, 'Insurance contracts', is being developed, as there would otherwise be nothing on that topic once FRS 27 is withdrawn. There is no material in IFRS for SMEs on insurance contracts. An entity should apply FRS 103 to: (a) insurance contracts (including reinsurance contracts) that it issues and reinsurance contracts that it holds; and (b) financial instruments with a discretionary participation feature that it issues. [FRS 102 para 1.6]. The current requirements for insurance companies are considered in chapter 34.8.

SORPs

1.56 Statements of Recommended Practice (SORPs) have been an important feature of UK GAAP. The question arose as to their role and status in the context of FRS 100 to FRS 102. FRS 100 indicates that *"if an entity's financial statements are prepared in accordance with the FRSSE or FRS 102, SORPs will apply in the circumstances set out in those standards"*. [FRS 100 paras 5–8]. This is slightly puzzling because the only significant reference to SORPs in FRS 102 is in section 10 on accounting policies, where the standard discusses what management should do when FRS 102 does not specifically deal with an issue: in developing an accounting policy that results in information that is relevant and reliable, management should consider the guidance in SORPs. [FRS 102 paras 10.4–10.5]. As to the future, although two SORPs will be withdrawn, most will be updated based on FRS 102 (according to paras 21–23 of the Accounting Council's advice to the FRC (set out as an appendix to FRS 100)).

Statement of compliance

1.57 All financial statements need to state clearly the basis on which they have been prepared. This has two aspects. The first is simple clarity. But also there is a need to avoid unwarranted claims or implications. For example, it is not appropriate to state or claim compliance with IFRS if the financial statements do not comply with the whole of IFRS. Reflecting this principle, *"Where a qualifying entity prepares its financial statements in accordance with FRS 101, it shall state in the notes to the financial statements: 'These financial statements were prepared in accordance with Financial Reporting Standard 101 Reduced Disclosure Framework'"*. [FRS 101 para 10]. FRS 102 requires an 'explicit and unreserved statement of compliance'; this is discussed in chapter 3.

The new regime in context

1.58 As discussed above, the new UK accounting regime, for those companies and groups that do not follow IFRS, comprises FRS 100 to FRS 102 (and once published, FRS 103 on insurance contracts). The FRC is also issuing Staff Guidance Papers and Examples, containing material to assist in understanding FRS 102. The FRSs are developed by the UK Accounting Council and approved and published by the Financial Reporting Council (FRC). The FRSs are not the whole picture, and the following are also part of UK GAAP:

■   UK company law contains various accounting requirements: the requirement to prepare accounts that give a true and fair view; the separate rules for 'IAS accounts' and 'Companies Act accounts', and the more detailed requirements that apply to Companies Act accounts. The Act contains much more, of course, but that is beyond the scope of this book.

■   There are various other pronouncements and sources of guidance that are part of UK GAAP. The UK Accounting Standards Board (the predecessor of the Accounting Council) published guidance statements on interim reporting, preliminary announcements and the operating and financial review. In practice, these are mainly relevant to UK listed companies.

■   A further source is guidance from the professional bodies, in particular the ICAEW Technical Releases, such as the very useful and highly regarded Tech 02/10, 'Guidance on the determination of realised profits and losses in the context of distributions under the Companies Act 2006', and ICAEW accounting recommendations, such as the members' handbook statements on materiality and 'Accounting for goods sold subject to reservation of title'.

■   Established practice. Quite literally, practices that are generally accepted, even though not codified in official literature, can be regarded as part of UK GAAP. Much of this practice is set out in the guidance from leading accounting firms, such as in this book.

1.59 The Accounting Council is one of many bodies within the FRC. The FRC and its operating bodies cover a wide range of accounting, auditing, actuarial and governance matters. Of particular relevance here, as well as the work of the Accounting Council, is the work of the Conduct Committee's Financial Reporting Review Panel (FRRP). The FRRP's role is to examine material departures from the Act's accounting requirements, including the accounting standards. The Companies Act 2006 provides for the Secretary of State to inquire into the accounts of companies and, where necessary, to apply for a court order requiring their revision. [CA06 Secs 455, 456]. Pursuant to its operating procedures, the FRRP handles cases involving public and large private companies (according to its website, 2012); all other cases fall to the Department for Business, Innovation and Skills (BIS). The following types of company fall within the FRRP's authority:

- public limited companies;

- companies within a group headed by a PLC;

- any private company that does not qualify as small or medium-sized and is not excluded from being treated as such under sections 382 to 384 and 465 to 467 of the Act; and

- any private company within a group that does not qualify as a small or medium-sized group.

[Conduct Committee operating procedures para 15].

1.60 So, although most of the FRRP's cases concern the group accounts of listed companies, there are some occasions on which it investigates the accounts of individual entities, including private entities, some of which follow UK GAAP. This is likely to be the case under the new UK GAAP too.

1.61 More details about the wider context of UK GAAP can be found in chapter 1 of PwC's *Manual of Accounting – IFRS for the UK*. The website of the FRC (frc.org.uk) is also a useful source of information.

Appendix 1: FRS 101 reduced disclosure framework

The disclosure exemptions that a qualifying entity can take advantage of in its individual financial statements under FRS 101 are summarised below. These are not available in consolidated financial statements.

Non-financial institution No financial instruments at fair value	Non-financial institution – With financial instruments held at fair value	Financial institutions
Disclosure exemptions available (*provided that equivalent disclosures for these exemptions are included in the group's consolidated financial statements):		
IFRS 2* *Share-based payment*		
Exemption from all disclosure requirements in IFRS 2 *except* for the following: ■ Paragraph 45(a) – A description of each type of share-based payment arrangement, including general terms and conditions, vesting requirements, term of options granted and method of settlement. ■ Paragraph 45(c) – For share options exercised during the period, the weighted average share price at the date of exercise. If options were exercised on a regular basis throughout the period, the weighted-average share price during the period can be disclosed. ■ Paragraph 45(d) – For outstanding share options, the range of exercise prices and weighted average remaining contractual life. Note: These disclosure exemptions are available if the equity instruments in the share-based payment arrangements are of another group entity. If the entity has share-based payment arrangements with its own equity instruments, these disclosure exemptions do not apply (except in the case of the ultimate parent s separate financial statements).		
IFRS 3* *Business combinations*		

■ Paragraph 62 – The information specified in paragraph B67 (see below).
■ Paragraph B64 –
   (d)   The primary reasons for the business combination and a description of how the acquirer obtained control of the acquiree.
   (e)   A description of the factors that make up the goodwill recognised.
   (g)   Information on contingent consideration arrangements and indemnification assets.
   (h)   Information on acquired receivables.
   (j)   Information on contingent liabilities.
   (k)   The total amount of goodwill expected to be deductible for tax purposes.
   (l)   Information on transactions that are recognised separately from the business combination.
   (m)   Information on acquisition-related costs.
   (n)(ii)   In a bargain purchase, a description of the reasons why the transaction resulted in a gain.
   (o)(ii)   For each non-controlling interest measured at fair value, the valuation techniques and key model inputs used for determining that value.
   (p)   Information on a business combination achieved in stages.
   (q)(ii)   The combined entity's revenue and profit or loss as though the acquisition date had been as of the beginning of the annual reporting period.
■ Paragraph B66 – Disclosure in respect of business combinations after the balance sheet date.
■ Paragraph B67 –
   (a) Information on provisional fair values.		

    1021

(b)	Information on contingent consideration.
(c)	Information on contingent liabilities recognised in a business combination.
(d)	A reconciliation of the carrying amount of goodwill at the beginning and end of the reporting period (but this is still required by company law).
(e)	Information on material gains or losses relating to previously recognised assets acquired or liabilities assumed in a business combination.

IFRS 5* *Non-current assets held for sale and discontinued operations*

Paragraph 33(c) – The net cash flows attributable to the operating, investing and financing activities of discontinued operations.

IFRS 7* *Financial instruments: Disclosures*

Exemption from all requirements of IFRS 7.	Exemption from IFRS 7 (and IFRS 13) depends on the types of financial instruments held at fair value.	No disclosure exemptions.
	Exemption from all disclosures applies for:	
	<ul><li>financial assets required to be held at fair value under IAS 39, such as held for trading assets and derivatives;</li><li>financial liabilities held as part of a trading portfolio; and</li><li>financial liabilities that are derivatives.</li></ul>	
	However, for financial instruments held at fair value under paragraph 36(4) of Schedule 1 to SI 2008/410, the exemption is restricted. These financial instruments include financial liabilities other than the above and financial assets that would not normally be carried at fair value but which are permitted to be if certain criteria are met under IAS 39. In these cases, there is exemption from all except the following paragraphs:	
	8(e) – Disclosures in respect of the carrying amount of financial liabilities at fair value through profit or loss.	
	9(c) – Where an entity has designated a loan or receivable (or group of loans or receivables) as at fair value through profit or loss, information of changes in fair value attributable to credit risk.	
	10 and 11 – Where an entity has designated a financial liability as at fair value through profit or loss, information on changes in fair value attributable to credit risk; and disclosure of the difference between the financial liability's carrying amount and the amount contractually required to be paid at maturity.	
	17 – Disclosure of existence of multiple embedded derivatives in compound financial instruments.	
	20(a)(i) – Disclosures in respect of the net gains or net losses on financial assets or financial liabilities at fair value through profit.	
	25, 26 – Disclosure of fair value for each class of financial assets and financial liabilities.	

| | 27 – Disclosure for each class of financial instruments the methods and, when a valuation technique is used, the assumptions applied in determining fair values of each class of financial assets or financial liabilities.

27A, 27B – Disclosures relating to the classification of financial instruments based on their fair value measurement hierarchy, significant transfers between level 1 and level 2 with reasons there for and a reconciliation and sensitivity analysis for level 3.

28 – Disclosure if there is a difference between the fair value at initial recognition and the amount that would be determined at that date using a valuation technique.

29 – Situations where disclosures of fair value are not required.

30 – Additional disclosures in situations where disclosures of fair value are not required.

31 – Information enabling users to evaluate the nature and extent of risks arising from financial instruments to which the entity is exposed at the end of the reporting period.

Note: For accounting periods beginning on or after 1 January 2013, replace paragraphs 27, 27A and 27B with paragraph 93 of IFRS 13. | |

IFRS 13* *Fair value measurement*

| Exemption from all disclosures. | Exemptions from all disclosures *except* paragraph 93.

Note: For accounting periods beginning before 1 January 2013, replace paragraph 93 with paragraphs 27, 27A and 27B of IFRS 7 listed above. | Exemptions from disclosure except those relating to financial instruments. |

IAS 1 *Presentation of financial statements*

- Paragraph 10(d) – A statement of cash flows for the period.
- Paragraph 10(f) – A balance sheet as at the beginning of the earliest comparative period when an entity makes a prior year adjustment.
- Paragraph 16 – A statement of compliance with IFRS.
- Paragraph 39 – Detail in respect of minimum comparative information, including prior year opening balance sheet.
- Paragraph 40 – Detail in respect of narrative information.
- Paragraph 79(a)(iv) – A reconciliation of the number of shares outstanding at the beginning and end of the period for each class of shares need not be presented for prior periods.
- Paragraph 111 – Cash flow information.

| - Paragraph 134 to 136 – Information on an entity's objectives, policies and processes for managing capital (qualitative and quantitative). | Not available to financial institutions |

May 2012 annual improvements (effective 1 January 2013)

The following exemptions in place of paragraphs 39 and 40 above (all other exemptions remain the same)

- Paragraph 38A-38B – Detail in respect of minimum comparative information.
- Paragraph 38C-38D – Additional comparative information.

Scope

● Paragraph 40A-40D – Detail in respect of third balance sheet presented on a change in accounting policy, retrospective restatement or reclassification.
IAS 16 *Property, plant and equipment*
Paragraph 73(e) – A reconciliation showing the carrying amounts of property, plant and equipment at the beginning and end of the period need not be presented for prior periods.
IAS 38 *Intangible assets*
Paragraph 118(e) – A reconciliation showing the carrying amounts of intangible assets at the beginning and end of the period need not be presented for prior periods.
IAS 40 *Investment property*
Paragraphs 76 and 79(d) – Comparatives are not required for the notes showing movements in investment properties (under both the fair value model and the cost model).
IAS 41 *Agriculture*
Paragraph 50 – Comparatives are not required for the note showing movements in biological assets.
IAS 7 *Statement of cash flows*
Full exemption from IAS 7.
IAS 8 *Accounting policies, changes in accounting estimates and errors*
Paragraph 30-31 – Disclosure in respect of new standards and interpretations that have been issued but which are not yet effective.
IAS 24 *Related party disclosures*
■ Paragraph 17 – Disclosure of key management personnel compensation in total and for each of the following categories: (a) short-term employee benefits;   (b) post-employment benefits;   (c) other long-term benefits;   (d) termination benefits; and   (e) share-based payment.   (but company law disclosures for directors' remuneration still apply)   ■ Related party transactions entered into between two or more members of a group, provided that any subsidiary which is a party to the transaction is wholly-owned by such a member.
IAS 36* *Impairment of assets*
■ Paragraph 134 – For each cash-generating unit (group of units) with significant amounts of goodwill or indefinite-lived intangibles assets: (d) if recoverable amount is based on value in use, information on key assumptions, cash flow projection periods, growth rates and discount rates.   (e) if recoverable amount is based on fair value less costs to sell, details of the methodology used, key assumptions, cash flow projection periods, growth rates and discount rates.   (f) sensitivity analysis for key assumptions.   ■ Paragraph 135(c)-(e) – Information where goodwill or indefinite-lived intangible assets are allocated across multiple cash-generating units (groups of units), including key assumptions in determining recoverable amount and sensitivity analysis for key assumptions.

Appendix 2: FRS 102 reduced disclosures

The disclosure exemptions that a qualifying entity can take advantage of in its individual financial statements under paragraph 1.12 of FRS 102 are summarised below. These are not available in consolidated financial statements.

Non-financial institution No financial instruments at fair value	Non-financial institution – With financial instruments held at fair value	Financial institutions
Disclosure exemptions available (*provided that equivalent disclosures for these exemptions are included in the group's consolidated financial statements):		
Section 3 *Financial statement presentation* **Section 7** *Statement of cash flows*		
■ Paragraph 3.17(d) and Section 7 – Exempt from the requirement to prepare a statement of cash flows.		
Section 4 *Statement of financial position*		
■ Paragraph 4.12(a)(iv) – A reconciliation of the number of shares outstanding at the beginning and at the end of the period.		
Section 11* *Basic financial instruments*		
Exemption from all disclosure requirements.	Exemption from section 11 disclosures depends on the types of financial instruments held at fair value. Exemption from all disclosures in section 11 applies for: ■ financial assets required to be held at fair value, such as held for trading assets and derivatives; ■ financial liabilities held as part of a trading portfolio; and ■ financial liabilities that are derivatives. However, for financial instruments held at fair value under paragraph 36(4) of Schedule 1 to SI 2008/410, the exemption is restricted. These financial instruments include financial liabilities other than the above and financial assets that would not normally be carried at fair value but which are permitted to be if certain criteria are met under the international standard (IAS 39). In these cases, the entity must apply the disclosure requirements of section 11 to those financial instruments held at fair value.	No disclosure exemptions.
Section 12* *Other financial instruments*		
Exempt from all disclosure requirements.	Exempt from all disclosure requirements.	No disclosure exemptions.
Section 26* *Share-based payment*		
Exemption from all disclosure requirements in section 26 except for the following:		

Scope

- Paragraph 26.18(a) – A description of each type of share-based payment arrangement, including general terms and conditions, vesting requirements, term of options granted, method of settlement.
- Paragraph 26.22 – An entity that is part of a group share-based payment plan, and which recognises and measures its share-based payment expense on the basis of a reasonable allocation of the expense recognised for the group, should disclose that fact and the basis for the allocation.

Note: These disclosure exemptions are available if the equity instruments in the share-based payment arrangements are of another group entity. If the entity has share-based payment arrangements with its own equity instruments, these disclosure exemptions do not apply (except in the case of the ultimate parent's separate financial statements).

Section 33 *Related party disclosures*

- Paragraph 33.7 – Disclosure of key management personnel compensation (but company law disclosures for directors' remuneration still apply).
- Paragraph 33.1A – Related party transactions entered into between two or more members of a group, provided that any subsidiary which is a party to the transaction is wholly-owned by such a member[1].

[1]This disclosure exemption is contained in paragraph 33.1A of FRS 102 (not in the reduced disclosures in paragraph 1.12) and is not restricted to 'qualifying entities'.

Chapter 2

Concepts and pervasive principles

Chapter 2

Concepts and pervasive principles

Introduction

2.1 Section 2 of FRS 102 is different from the remainder of the standard because it sets out the underlying concepts of accounting and the pervasive principles. It acknowledges that there might be inconsistencies between section 2 and the rest of the standard; and that, in these circumstances, the specific requirements of another section take precedence. [FRS 102 para 2.1A]. This is a pragmatic approach and is in line with the difference in status between old UK GAAP's Statement of principles for financial reporting (SoP) and the individual standards (and, in IFRS, between the Conceptual framework for financial reporting and the individual IFRSs).

2.2 FRS 102's concepts and pervasive principles are drawn from, and are similar to, the IFRS Framework, the UK SoP and the equivalent section in IFRS for SMEs. But some differences of wording exist, and these are discussed selectively below. The concepts and pervasive principles are also similar to the 'accounting principles' set out in the Companies Act 2006 (SI 2008/410 1 Sch).

2.3 Section 2 does not spell out clearly why the concepts and pervasive principles are included. But the IFRS Framework and the old UK GAAP SoP do explain their purpose. Briefly stated, the purpose is: to assist standard-setters in developing standards based on a coherent set of principles; to assist preparers in determining the accounting treatment of a transaction that is not covered by the specific standards (in this context, therefore, something that is not covered by the other sections of FRS 102); to assist auditors in forming an opinion on compliance with the standards; and to assist users in interpreting financial statements. It could well be that section 2 of FRS 102 is referred to more than the IFRS Framework and the old UK SoP; this is because FRS 102 is a much slimmer standard that necessarily is not as comprehensive as either IFRS or old UK GAAP. So it might become more common to refer, for example, to section 2's definitions of an asset and a liability.

2.4 Section 2 of FRS 102 includes commentary on the following matters:

- the objectives of financial statements;

- the qualitative characteristics of financial statements;

- definitions relating to financial position (that is, assets, liabilities and equity);

- definitions relating to performance (that is, income and expenses);

- recognition criteria;

- measurement considerations;

- accrual accounting; and

- offsetting.

Objectives of financial statements

2.5 Discussion among standard-setters and other constituents about the objectives of financial statements is surprisingly heated. There is a tension between those who consider that the objective is to provide information that is useful in making decisions (essentially a forward-looking purpose) and those who stress the stewardship role (essentially a backward-looking purpose). FRS 102 comes down on both sides of the fence:

> *"The objective of financial statements is to provide information about the financial position, performance and cash flows of an entity that is useful for economic decision-making by a broad range of users who are not in a position to demand reports tailored to meet their particular information needs."* [FRS 102 para 2.2].

But this is followed by: *"Financial statements also show the result of the stewardship of management – the accountability of management for the resources entrusted to it"*. [FRS 102 para 2.3].

2.6 In this respect, FRS 102 places more emphasis on stewardship than the Framework and SoP. This is realistic, because the financial statements of entities following FRS 102 (such as subsidiaries of listed groups) will tend to be historical documents of record; but the financial statements of entities following IFRS (such as listed groups) will tend to be used more for the purposes of investment analysis, including forecasting future cash flows.

Qualitative characteristics of financial statements

2.7 FRS 102 sets out the following qualitative characteristics:

- *Understandability.* Information should be presented in such a way as to be comprehensible by users. It is assumed that users have a reasonable knowledge of business and economic activities and a willingness to study the information with reasonable diligence. [FRS 102 para 2.4].

- *Relevance.* Relevance means relevant to the decision-making needs of users. Information is relevant when it is capable of influencing the economic decisions of users. [FRS 102 para 2.5].

- *Materiality.* This is closely related to relevance. Information is material *"... if its omission or misstatement, individually or collectively, could influence the economic decisions of users taken on the basis of the financial statements ..."*. [FRS 102 para 2.6]. FRS 102 adds: *"Materiality depends on the size and nature of the omission or misstatement judged in the surrounding circumstances. The size or nature of the item, or a combination of both, could be the determining factor".*

The ICAEW issued a statement in June 2008, Tech 03/08, containing guidance to help those preparing financial statements decide what information is material, in the context of the principle that an item is material if it could influence users' economic decisions. This guidance is relevant in applying FRS 102.

Similar to FRS 102, Tech 03/08 considers that there are three aspects to consider when deciding whether an item is material and then discusses each aspect in turn. These aspects are:

■ *Size*. While the monetary value of items needs to be taken into account, materiality can never be judged purely on the basis of absolute size, and no specific rule of thumb tests are recommended. In some cases, size might be irrelevant (for example, where the quality of management stewardship or corporate governance is at issue).

■ *Nature*. Consideration needs to be given to the events or transactions giving rise to the item, as well as their legality, sensitivity, normality and potential consequences. In addition, the identity of the parties involved in the events or transactions (and the accounts captions and disclosure affected) might also impact on users' decisions.

■ *Circumstances*. When preparers consider the potential impact of information on users, they should not take a narrow view of the financial statements for a single period. They will often need to modify their views on the materiality of an item in the light of comparative figures, expected future trends, the financial statements of comparable entities and other information relating to the economic and industry background.

The standard notes that it is inappropriate to make, or leave uncorrected, immaterial departures from the FRS to achieve a particular presentation of an entity's financial position, financial performance or cash flows.

■ *Reliability*. Information is reliable if it is *"free from material error and bias"* and *"represents faithfully"* that which it purports to represent. [FRS 102 para 2.7]. Excessive use of prudence, for example, would be a bias. Note also that the criteria for the recognition of assets and liabilities involve the characteristic of reliability; that is, assets and liabilities should not be recognised if they cannot be measured reliably (see below).

■ *Substance over form*. Substance over form has been a predominant concept in the application of UK GAAP for some years, chiefly as a result of FRS 5. FRS 102 continues this emphasis: *"Transactions and other events and conditions should be accounted for and presented in accordance with their substance and not merely their legal form".* [FRS 102 para 2.8]. Substance over form is also required by the

Companies Act 2006: *"The company's directors must, in determining how amounts are presented within items in the profit and loss account and balance sheet, have regard to the substance of the reported transaction or arrangement, in accordance with generally accepted accounting principles or practice"*. [SI 2008/410 1 Sch 9]. Substance over form enhances the reliability of financial statements. But the application of substance is subject to the specific rules in other sections of FRS 102. For example, the rules on classification of financial instruments as debt or equity have a specific way of identifying the substance of the contractual terms, and this can give a result that is at odds with a broader notion of substance. The more specific rules have to be followed in such a case. Nevertheless, substance over form is a powerful concept and applies where there are no specific rules or where the rules are not detailed.

- *Prudence.* Despite rumours to the contrary, prudence still has a role in financial reporting, but not as great a role as in earlier years. As noted above, prudence is not valid where it represents a bias. But it does have a role as a response to uncertainty: *". . . Prudence is the inclusion of a degree of caution in the exercise of the judgements needed in making the estimates required under conditions of uncertainty, such that assets or income are not overstated and liabilities or expenses are not understated . . ."*. [FRS 102 para 2.9]. This is also reflected in the requirements of the Act: *"The amount of any item must be determined on a prudent basis and in particular (a) only profits realised at the balance sheet date are to be included in the profit and loss account, and (b) all liabilities which have arisen in respect of the financial year to which the accounts relate or a previous financial year must be taken into account, including those which only become apparent between the balance sheet date and the date on which it is signed on behalf of the board of directors . . ."*. [SI 2008/410 1 Sch 13]. The wording of the Act could be taken to be very strict on prudence. But there is an exception to the realised profits rule as regards gains and losses on certain items that are carried at fair value (see SI 2008/410 1 Sch 36-41 and chapter 22). Also, the wording within sub-section (b) above is not taken to mean that companies should provide for all post-balance sheet liabilities; the guidance in section 32 of FRS 102 is regarded as consistent with the Act and should be followed in this regard.

- *Completeness.* Completeness is a matter of degree. FRS 102 says that, to be reliable, information in financial statements must be complete within the bounds of materiality and cost. [FRS 102 para 2.10]. But an important feature of FRS 102 (and, more so, FRS 101) is the reduction in disclosures that are permitted. This is not inconsistent with the idea of completeness because the idea of comparing benefits and costs (see below) also applies. Financial statements drawn up under FRS 102 (and FRS 101) are still regarded as giving a true and fair view.

- *Comparability.* This refers both to comparability of information of an entity over time and also to comparability of information from one entity to another. [FRS 102 para 2.11]. As with completeness, this is a matter of degree: financial statements drawn up under FRS 102 are not entirely comparable with financial statements drawn up under IFRS, but they would generally be regarded as similar. The equivalent requirement of the Act is: *"Accounting policies must be applied consistently within the same accounts and from one financial year to the next"*. [SI 2008/410 1 Sch 12].

■ *Timeliness.* Information that is made available too late for the relevant decisions to be taken would fall at this hurdle. [FRS 102 para 2.12]. Nonetheless, this qualitative characteristic does not override the UK statutory filing deadlines.

■ *Balance between benefit and cost.* Assessing the costs and the benefits is difficult, because the benefits are inherently judgemental; also, the costs are incurred by the reporting entity and the benefits largely gained by other parties. The general principle is that the benefits derived from the information should exceed the costs of providing it. [FRS 102 para 2.13]. In the context of companies using FRS 102 (that is, primarily unlisted companies and subsidiaries of listed groups), the benefits will tend to be lower than, say, the benefits from the financial statements of listed groups; so it is appropriate to reduce the costs of preparation, and this explains the simplified approach and the disclosure reductions.

Financial position

2.8 The financial position of an entity is defined as the *"relationship of"* its assets, liabilities and equity as presented in the statement of financial position. [FRS 102 para 2.15]. Although that wording is rather odd, the meaning is reasonably clear. The 'statement of financial position' is the new term, introduced in IFRS in recent years, for the balance sheet, but many people continue to refer to the balance sheet as a practical matter.

2.9 Developments in accounting standards in the last 20 years have placed increased emphasis on the balance sheet. The current model focuses on getting the balance sheet right and letting the income statement (that is, the profit and loss account) reflect the consequences; this is in contrast to the earlier focus of matching transactions in the profit and loss account, with assets and liabilities being what is left over as a result of the matching process. Paragraph 2.45 of FRS 102 notes that *"generally, this FRS does not allow the recognition of items in the statement of financial position that do not meet the definition of assets or liabilities regardless of whether they result from applying the notion commonly referred to as the 'matching concept' for measuring profit or loss"*.

2.10 So the definitions of assets and liabilities are particularly important. Section 2 defines these as follows:

■ *"An asset is a resource controlled by the entity as a result of past events and from which future economic benefits are expected to flow to the entity"*. [FRS 102 para 2.15].

This is the same as the definition in the Framework for IFRS. It differs from the UK SoP's definition, which is *"assets are rights or other access to future economic benefits controlled by an entity as a result of past transactions or events"*. As a practical matter, it is doubtful if the new definition will yield different results from the definition in the SoP.

Section 2 adds the following points. First, the *"future economic benefit"* of an asset is its potential to contribute, directly or indirectly, to the flow of cash and cash equivalents, through use or sale of the assets. Secondly, physical form is not essential, as many assets are intangibles. And, thirdly, ownership is not essential (for example, property held on a lease is an asset if the entity controls the expected benefits). [FRS 102 paras 2.17-2.19].

■ *"A liability is a present obligation of the entity arising from past events, the settlement of which is expected to result in an outflow from the entity of resources embodying economic benefits"*. [FRS 102 para 2.15].

This also is the same as the definition in the Framework for IFRS. It differs from the UK SoP's definition, which is *"liabilities are obligations of an entity to transfer economic benefits as a result of past transactions or events"*. The new definition emphasises that the obligation must be a '*present* obligation'. But this is unlikely, as a practical matter, to lead to a different result from the definition in the SoP.

Section 2 adds the following points. An obligation might be a legal obligation or it might be constructive. A constructive obligation derives from an entity's actions when:

■ *"By an established pattern of practice, published policies or a sufficiently specific current statement, the entity has indicated to other parties that it will accept certain responsibilities; and*

■ *As a result, the entity has created a valid expectation on the part of those other parties that it will discharge those responsibilities"*. [FRS 102 para 2.20].

■ *"Equity is the residual interest in the assets of the entity after deducting all its liabilities"*. [FRS 102 para 2.15].

This also is the same as the definition in the Framework for IFRS. The UK SoP uses the term *"ownership interest"*, which it defines as *"the residual amount found by deducting all of the entity's liabilities from all of the entity's assets"*. Again, the practical effect seems to be very similar.

Section 2 points out that equity might be sub-classified; in a UK context, this most obviously refers to the line items for share capital and reserves in the Companies Act formats.

2.11 Importantly, items that meet the definitions of assets and liabilities are recognised on the balance sheet, but only if they also meet the recognition criteria (see below).

Performance

2.12 An entity's performance is defined as the *'relationship of'* its income and expenses during a reporting period. The wording is curious but reasonably clear. As noted above, the measurement of performance is driven by the recognition and measurement of assets and liabilities.

2.13 FRS 102 permits two approaches to the presentation of performance: (1) a single 'statement of comprehensive income'; or (2) an income statement and a statement of comprehensive income. The 'income statement' is the new term, introduced in IFRS in recent years, for the profit and loss account, but many people continue to refer to the profit and loss account as a practical matter. In terms of the transition from old UK GAAP, the statement of comprehensive income (when presented as a separate, second statement) is similar to the statement of total recognised gains and losses. But the idea of a *single* statement of comprehensive income is new to UK GAAP.

2.14 Items that are presented in the statement of comprehensive income in the two-statement approach, or the second part of the single statement, are termed 'other comprehensive income' (OCI). Although there are various rules in other sections of FRS 102 about what is presented in OCI, there is no underlying principle or concept that determines this.

Income

2.15 Income is defined as *"increases in economic benefits during the reporting period in the form of inflows or enhancements of assets or decreases of liabilities that result in increases in equity, other than those relating to contributions from equity investors".* [FRS 102 para 2.23(a)]. This definition includes an important point: in effect, any item that increases net assets is income, except for those items that are transactions with shareholders in their capacity as such. So, for example, a sale of goods in the ordinary course of business (even a sale to a shareholder) is income; and so is the increase in value of an investment property carried at fair value. But an increase in net assets as a result of shareholders subscribing new equity is not income.

2.16 Income encompasses both revenue and gains:

- *"Revenue is income that arises in the course of the ordinary activities of an entity and is referred to by a variety of names include sales, fees, interest, dividends, royalties and rent".* [FRS 102 para 2.25(a)]. Put another way, whether these items are revenue depends on the entity's business model. If its main business is making and selling goods, sales of those goods will be revenue. If the main business is property investment, rent would be revenue. But rent that is the incidental income of a manufacturing entity would not be presented as revenue; it would be presented as other operating income or similar.

■ *"Gains are other items that meet the definition of income but are not revenue. When gains are recognised in the statement of comprehensive income, they are usually displayed separately because knowledge of them is useful for making economic decisions".* [FRS 102 para 2.25(b)]. Gains, in other words, are the residual category of income. Rent received by a manufacturing entity (see previous bullet) would be a gain, not revenue. Increases in value of investment property are also gains, as they are not presented as top-line revenue. It appears that 'gains' are not limited to items that form part of other comprehensive income.

Expenses

2.17 Expenses are defined as *"decreases in economic benefits during the reporting period in the form of outflows or depletions of assets or incurrences of liabilities that result in decreases in equity, other than those relating to distributions to equity investors".* [FRS 102 para 2.23(b)]. As with the definition of assets, this definition points out that transactions with shareholders in their capacity as such are different from expenses. So, for example, paying a salary to a shareholder for work done is an expense; but paying a dividend to that shareholder is a transaction with a shareholder in their capacity as such, and therefore not an expense.

2.18 Expenses encompass both expenses arising in the course of an entity's ordinary activities and losses:

■ *"Expenses that arise in the course of the ordinary activities of the entity include, for example, cost of sales, wages and depreciation. They usually take the form of an outflow or depletion of assets such as cash and cash equivalents, inventory, or property, plant and equipment."*

■ *"Losses are other items that meet the definition of expenses and may arise in the course of the ordinary activities of the entity. When losses are recognised in the statement of comprehensive income, they are usually presented separately because knowledge of them is useful in making economic decisions."* [FRS 102 para 2.26].

2.19 The distinction between expenses and losses is far from clear. Fortunately, not much seems to hang on the distinction. As noted above, there is no underlying principle or concept that determines what is presented in OCI as opposed to in the income statement. It might be thought that expenses are presented in the income statement and losses are presented in OCI, but there is no such general rule or principle.

Recognition

2.20 An item might meet the definition of an asset, liability, income or expense, but it is not automatically incorporated into financial statements. It also has to meet the recognition criteria, which are first stated by section 2 of FRS 102 in general terms as follows:

- It must be *probable* that any future economic benefit associated with the item will flow to or from the entity. Probability is assessed based on evidence at the balance sheet date. The assessments are made individually for significant items, and by group for a large population of individually insignificant items.

- The item has a cost or value that can be measured *reliably*. This is not a high hurdle. The need to estimate numbers is commonly encountered in accounting and this is not a reason to fail to recognise an item. But, if there is considerable uncertainty regarding the amount of an item (for example, an entity is likely to be fined by a regulator but it is difficult to make any sensible guess as to the range of the fine), it would not be recognised until the uncertainty is reduced. In the meantime, disclosure might be appropriate, depending on the materiality of the item. [FRS 102 paras 2.27-2.32].

2.21 These general principles are applied as follows:

- *Assets.* Assets are recognised when it is probable that the future economic benefit will flow to the entity and the asset has a cost or value that can be measured reliably. Conversely, if expenditure has been incurred for which it is not probable that economic benefits will flow to the entity beyond the current reporting period, the item is expensed. Contingent assets are not recognised. [FRS 102 paras 2.37-2.38].

- *Liabilities.* Liabilities are recognised when: (a) the entity has an obligation at the end of the reporting period as a result of a past event; (b) it is probable that the entity will be required to transfer resources embodying economic benefits in settlement; and (c) the settlement amount can be measured reliably. Contingent liabilities are not recognised, except in a business combination. [FRS 102 paras 2.39-2.40].

- *Income.* The recognition of income (that is, revenue and gains) results directly from the recognition of assets and liabilities. Income is recognised when an increase in future economic benefits related to an increase in an asset or a decrease of a liability has arisen that can be measured reliably. [FRS 102 para 2.41]. Under this approach, most obviously, sales activity will result in the recognition of revenue when a debtor is established. Equally, income arises when an asset (such as an investment property or a financial asset carried at fair value) is re-measured at an amount higher than its previous carrying value. Also, the re-measurement of a provision at an amount lower than its previous carrying value would appear to give rise to income.

- *Expenses.* As with the recognition of income, recognition of expense (that is, expenses and losses) results directly from the recognition of assets and liabilities. An expense arises when a decrease in future economic benefits related to a decrease in an asset or an increase of a liability has arisen that can be measured reliably. [FRS 102 para 2.42].

Measurement

2.22 Measurement means determining the monetary amounts at which an entity measures assets, liabilities, income and expense.

2.23 Historical cost and fair value (*"two common measurement bases"*) are defined in paragraph 2.34 of FRS 102.

2.24 The definition of historical cost is as follows:

■   For assets, historical cost is the amount of cash or cash equivalents paid or the fair value of the consideration given to acquire the asset at the time of its acquisition.

■   For liabilities, historical cost is the amount of proceeds of cash or cash equivalents received or the fair value of non-cash assets received in exchange for the obligation when the obligation is incurred, or in some circumstances (for example, income tax) the amounts of cash or cash equivalents expected to be paid to settle the liability in the normal course of business.

2.25 The definition of fair value is similar to that in IAS 39, 'Financial instruments: recognition and measurement' (FRS 26 in old UK GAAP), that is: *"fair value is the amount for which an asset could be exchanged, a liability settled, or an equity instrument granted could be exchanged, between knowledgeable, willing parties in an arm's length transaction …".* [FRS 102 para 2.34(b)]. In the absence of any specific guidance provided in the relevant section of FRS 102, where fair value measurement is permitted or required, the guidance in paragraphs 11.27-11.32 of FRS 102 should be applied (see chapter 11).

2.26 As described in paragraphs 2.46-2.51 of FRS 102, various sections of the standard specify the measurement bases for a selection of financial and non-financial assets and liabilities. But there is no single principle determining how items should be measured. In particular, the 'cost versus fair value' debate is not settled by FRS 102. The measurement bases described in those paragraphs are discussed in other chapters of this book.

Recognition and measurement – selection of accounting policies

2.27 Paragraph 2.35 of FRS 102 refers to the requirements of section 10 relating to the selection of accounting policies. Paragraphs 10.4 and 10.5 explain that, if FRS 102 does not specifically address a transaction, other event or condition, there is a role in applying the judgements and the hierarchy for section 2's definitions, recognition criteria and measurement concepts for assets, liabilities, income and expenses and the pervasive principles. See chapter 10 for further discussion.

Other matters

2.28 Section 2 of FRS 102 makes brief reference to the accruals basis and to offsetting.

Accruals basis

2.29 Section 2 confirms that, in preparing financial statements, except for cash flow information, the accruals basis should be used. This is, of course, the fundamental and well-established basis of accounting. What is different is the way in which the accruals basis is described. Historically, it has been thought of in terms of recognising transactions when they occur (and not when cash is received or paid); that is, they are accounted for in the periods to which they relate. In FRS 102, accrual accounting is described as follows: *"On the accruals basis, items are recognised as assets, liabilities, equity, income or expenses when they satisfy the definitions and recognition criteria for those items"*. [FRS 102 para 2.36]. Although the approach is different, this wording will, in most cases, give rise to accrual accounting in a similar way to previous practice, although it might change the accounting treatment in some situations because it is more fundamentally based on definitions of assets and liabilities. The Companies Act 2006 describes accrual accounting in the more traditional way: *"All income and charges relating to the financial year to which the accounts relate must be taken into account, without regard to the date of receipt or payment"*. [SI 2008/410 1 Sch 14].

Offsetting and separate determination

2.30 In relation to offsetting, *"an entity shall not offset assets and liabilities, or income and expenses, unless required or permitted by an FRS"*. [FRS 102 para 2.52]. The standard gives two examples. First, it points out that to carry an asset net of a valuation allowance (for example, for uncollectible receivables or slow-moving stock) is not offsetting; it is just part of the valuation of the asset. Second, it refers to the practice of reporting a gain or loss (that is, a net figure) on disposing of fixed assets. It does not make it clear whether this is not offsetting or is permissible offsetting. Nevertheless, it endorses the treatment. The Act sets out the requirement in an equivalent way: *"Amounts in respect of items representing assets or income may not be set off against amounts in respect of items representing liabilities or expenditure (as the case may be), or vice versa"*. [SI 2008/410 1 Sch 8].

2.31 Closely related to not offsetting is the idea of separate determination of each item. The Act says: *"In determining the aggregate amount of any item, the amount of each individual asset or liability that falls to be taken into account must be determined separately"*. [SI 2008/410 1 Sch 15]. This guards against offsetting profits on some items in a population against losses on other items.

Going concern

2.32 Curiously, there is no reference in section 2 of FRS 102 to 'going concern', despite its featuring in the IFRS Framework as an 'underlying assumption'.

Going concern is instead addressed in Chapter 3 and this is consistent with the Companies Act statement that *"The company is presumed to be carrying on business as a going concern"*. [SI 2008/410 1 Sch 11].

Chapter 3

Financial statement presentation

Chapter 3

Financial statement presentation

Introduction

3.1 FRS 102 does not prescribe which entities prepare financial statements. Whether an entity prepares financial statements is determined by applicable legislation, regulation or its own internal rules and customs. For those entities falling within its scope (see chapter 1), FRS 102 sets out the requirements for a complete set of financial statements that give a fair presentation of the entity's financial position, financial performance and cash flows, regardless of whether the financial statements are prepared to meet legal or other requirements. [FRS 102 para A4.14]. It does not address the presentation of interim financial reports. An entity preparing such a report should disclose the basis for preparing and presenting the information. [FRS 102 para 3.25].

Fair presentation

3.2 FRS 102 states:

> "Financial statements shall present fairly the financial position, financial performance and cash flows of an entity. Fair presentation requires the faithful representation of the effects of transactions, other events and conditions in accordance with the definitions and recognition criteria for assets, liabilities, income and expenses set out in Section 2 Concepts and Pervasive Principles.
>
> a.   The application of this FRS, with additional disclosure when necessary, is presumed to result in financial statements that achieve a fair presentation of the financial position, financial performance and cash flows within the scope of this FRS".

[FRS 102 para 3.2].

3.3 Disclosure additional to that set out in the standard is required where it is necessary to enable the users of the financial statements to understand particular transactions, other events and conditions of the entity. [FRS 102 para 3.2]. This requirement of the standard is consistent with the legal requirement for additional disclosure to be made when compliance with accounting and disclosure requirements would be insufficient to give a true and fair view. [CA06 Secs 396(4), 404(5)]. But, in either case, disclosure or explanation is not a substitute for proper accounting.

Compliance with FRS 102

3.4 FRS 102 requires an "*explicit and unreserved statement of compliance*" in the notes to the financial statements. Entities cannot state that their financial statements are FRS 102-compliant if they do not comply with all the requirements of the standard. [FRS 102 para 3.3]. Financial statements either comply with FRS 102 or they do not; there is no middle ground. In addition, a public benefit entity (PBE) that applies the standard's PBE-prefixed paragraphs is required to make an explicit and unreserved statement that it is a public benefit entity. [FRS 102 para PBE3.3A].

3.5 The standard envisages that, in extremely rare circumstances, management might conclude that compliance with the standard would conflict with the objective of financial statements (see chapter 2); if this is the case, the entity needs to depart from the relevant requirement. [FRS 102 para 3.4]. Similarly, in special circumstances, if compliance with the provisions of the Companies Act and its supporting regulations would be inconsistent with the requirement to give a true and fair view, the directors must depart from those provisions. [CA06 Secs 396(5), 404(5)]. In both cases, this is often referred to as a 'true and fair override'. FRS 102 requires that, when an entity departs from a requirement of the standard or applicable legislation, it should disclose the following:

■ that management has concluded that the financial statements present fairly the entity's financial position, financial performance and cash flows;

■ that it has complied with the standard or applicable legislation, except that it has departed from a particular requirement of the standard or applicable legislation, to achieve a fair presentation; and

■ the nature of the departure, including the treatment that the standard or company law would require, the reason why that treatment would be so misleading in the circumstances that it would conflict with the objective of financial statements set out in section 2, and the treatment adopted.

[FRS 102 para 3.5].

3.6 In departing from the standard or applicable legislation, an entity should consider the objective of the requirement in question and determine why the objective is not met or is not relevant in its particular circumstances. It should also consider how its own circumstances differ from other entities that comply with the relevant requirement. Where other entities in similar circumstances comply with the requirement, it is unlikely that the entity's non-compliance would be justified. Because 'true and fair overrides' of FRS 102 would be rarely justified, the standard requires extensive disclosures in the event of a departure from the requirements.

3.7 A departure from a requirement of the standard might affect more than a single financial year. For example, if an entity departs from a requirement in respect of the measurement of assets or liabilities, in the following period there will be a consequential effect on the measurement of changes in assets and liabilities. In the year of departure from the standard, the entity should give the disclosures set out in paragraph 3.5. In the following period, where the prior year departure affects amounts recognised in that period, the entity should give the disclosures shown in the final bullet of paragraph 3.5. [FRS 102 para 3.6].

Going concern

3.8 Financial statements are normally prepared on the assumption that the entity is a going concern. An entity is a going concern unless management either intends to liquidate the entity or to cease operations, or has no realistic alternative but to do so. [FRS 102 para 3.8]. Management is required to assess, at the time of preparing the financial statements, the entity's ability to continue as a going concern and this assessment should cover the entity's prospects for at least 12 months from the date when the financial statements are authorised for issue. [FRS 102 para 3.8]. The 12-month period for considering the entity's future is a minimum requirement; an entity cannot, for example, prepare its financial statements on a going concern basis if it intends to cease operations 18 months from the date when the financial statements are authorised for issue. Where an entity does not prepare its financial statements on a going concern basis, it discloses that fact, together with the basis on which it prepared the financial statements and the reason why the entity is not regarded as a going concern. [FRS 102 para 3.9].

3.9 In many cases, the assessment of the entity's status as a going concern will be a simple matter. A profitable entity with no financing problems will almost certainly be a going concern. In other cases, management may need to consider very carefully the entity's ability to meet its liabilities as they fall due. Detailed cash flow and profit forecasts may be required before management can be satisfied that the entity is a going concern. The existence of significant doubts about the entity's ability to continue as a going concern is not sufficient reason to depart from preparing financial statements on a going concern basis. Where there are significant doubts about the entity's ability to continue as a going concern, details of those material uncertainties should be disclosed, even if the financial statements continue to be prepared on a going concern basis. [FRS 102 para 3.9].

3.10 Further, events that occur after the reporting period might indicate that the entity is no longer a going concern. In a situation where management believed at the reporting date that the entity was a going concern, but its later assessment leads it to conclude that it is not, any financial statements that are prepared after that assessment (including the financial statements in respect of which management is making the assessment) should not be prepared on a going concern basis. See chapter 32.

3.11 An example of a situation where disclosure of an uncertainty is required is given below.

Example – Uncertainty about the entity being a going concern

An entity has incurred losses during the last four years and its current liabilities exceed its total assets. The entity was in breach of its loan covenants and has been negotiating with its bankers in order to keep them supporting its business. These factors raise significant doubt that the entity will be able to continue as a going concern. How should management disclose uncertainties that affect the entity's ability to continue as a going concern?

Management should state clearly that there is a material uncertainty related to events or conditions which might cast significant doubt on the entity's ability to continue as a going concern and, therefore, that it might be unable to realise its assets and discharge its liabilities in the normal course of business. Management should describe the events and conditions that give rise to the material uncertainty, as well as the actions proposed to address the situation. This disclosure should preferably be made in the same note where the basis for preparation of the financial statements is described. Management should also disclose the possible effects on the financial position, or that it is impracticable to measure them. Additionally, management should state whether or not the financial statements include any adjustments that result (or might result in the future) from the outcome of these uncertainties.

3.12   Under the going concern basis, both assets and liabilities are usually recorded on the basis that their carrying amounts will be recovered or discharged in the normal course of business. For example, the carrying values of property, plant and equipment (such as depreciated cost or recoverable amount) reflect costs or values that the business expects to recover from future cash flows relating to their continued use and ultimate disposal. But if the business is not a going concern, these bases might not be appropriate.

3.13   If an entity is not a going concern, but is preparing its financial statements under FRS 102, the measurement of assets and liabilities might be affected by changes in judgements that can arise when the going concern assumption ceases to be valid. For example, estimates of recoverable amounts of assets might require revision, and this could result in the recognition of impairments to the carrying value of some assets. But, in such circumstances, it would not be appropriate to recognise the expected profit on the intended disposal of assets, either as a reduction in the amounts recognised as impairments or provisions or as uplifts in the carrying value of the relevant assets (although some entities might revalue property, plant and equipment in accordance with previously established accounting policies in the normal way). Some contracts might be regarded as onerous, requiring a provision. However, provisions should not be made in respect of executory contracts (unless onerous) or restructuring costs that do not qualify as obligations under section 21 of the standard at the reporting date.

3.14   In some situations, the effect of ceasing to regard the business as a going concern might be negligible in terms of the amounts reported in the financial statements. Nevertheless, FRS 102 requires the financial statements to disclose that the entity is no longer regarded as a going concern. Unless there is a statement to the contrary, the standard allows a reader to *presume* that an entity is carrying on business as a going concern.

Frequency of reporting

3.15 The standard requires that a complete set of financial statements is presented at least annually. When an entity changes its reporting date (termed 'accounting reference date' in the Companies Act) and presents financial statements that are longer or shorter than one year, the entity should disclose the reason for using a period other than one year and state the fact that the comparative amounts are not entirely comparable. [FRS 102 para 3.10].

3.16 There are legal restrictions on a company's ability to extend its reporting period. These are discussed further in chapter 3 of the Manual of Accounting – Other statutory requirements.

Consistency of presentation

3.17 FRS 102 requires entities to present the financial statements in a consistent manner. The standard states that an entity should retain the presentation and classification of items in its financial statements from one period to the next unless:

■ it is apparent, following a significant change in the nature of the entity's operations or a review of its financial statements, that another presentation or classification would be more appropriate, having regard to the criteria for selection and application of accounting policies set out in chapter 10; or

■ the FRS, or another applicable FRS or FRC Abstract, requires a change in presentation.

[FRS 102 para 3.11].

3.18 Once management has selected a particular presentation, it should use it consistently. An entity will seldom have good reason to change its presentation and, therefore, management should consider carefully the presentation to be adopted when preparing the entity's first set of financial statements after incorporation or on transition to FRS 102. A change in presentation or classification is a change in accounting policy, and changes in accounting policy are discussed further in chapter 10.

3.19 Unless FRS 102 requires a change in presentation, an entity is only permitted to change its presentation if the revised presentation provides reliable and more relevant information; that is, the new presentation should be an improvement on the previous presentation. Just as entities should not change an accounting policy on recognition or measurement to another acceptable, but not more relevant, accounting policy, they should not change presentation to another acceptable, but not more relevant, presentation. [FRS 102 para 10.8(b)].

3.20 If the presentation or classification of items is changed, the comparative figures should be reclassified to conform to the new presentation, unless reclassification is impracticable. The entity should disclose the nature and amounts of each item or class of items that is reclassified and the reasons for the reclassification. [FRS 102 para 3.12]. In addition, where the formats for the primary statements are changed, the notes to the financial statements should disclose:

- particulars of the change (that is, the fact that the entity has adopted a different format); and

- the reasons for the change.

[SI 2008/410 1 Sch 2(2)].

3.21 In rare situations, reclassification is impracticable; in such a case, the entity should disclose why this is so. [FRS 102 para 3.13].

Comparative information

3.22 FRS 102 requires an entity to present comparative information in respect of the preceding period for all amounts reported in the current period's financial statements. A comparative amount is still reported if the current period amount is nil. [SI 2008/410 1 Sch 5(1), (2)]. So an entity should present, as a minimum, two of each of the required financial statements and notes. [FRS 102 para 3.20]. Comparative information for narrative and descriptive information is also disclosed if it is relevant to understanding the current period's financial statements. [FRS 102 para 3.14].

3.23 An exemption from the requirement to present comparative numerical information is given in some sections of the standard for reconciliations of opening and closing positions. For example, section 21 requires a reconciliation of the opening and closing provisions, but does not require the disclosure of a comparative reconciliation. [FRS 102 para 21.14]. Similarly, sections 16, 17 and 18 (on investment property, intangible assets, and property, plant and equipment respectively) do not require the disclosure of a comparative reconciliation. [FRS 102 paras 16.10, 17.31, 18.27]. On the other hand, no exemption exists for the statement of changes in equity; so entities will usually present a reconciliation of the opening and closing positions for the comparative period, immediately followed by a reconciliation of the opening and closing positions for the current period.

3.24 Comparative narrative information need not be given if the information is no longer relevant. Where a legal dispute was outstanding at the previous reporting date and has still not been resolved, the financial statements for the current period should disclose details of that dispute and of the steps that have been taken to resolve the dispute. If a legal dispute is settled during the year, the result of the dispute might need to be disclosed if the related income or expense is considered to be of such size or nature that its separate disclosure is necessary to explain the entity's financial performance for the period.

3.25 Where an amount for the previous year is not comparable with the amount to be shown in respect of the current year, the previous year's amount should be adjusted. Where this applies, particulars of the adjustment and the reasons for it should be disclosed. This requirement applies in respect of every item in a reporting entity's primary statements and in respect of each item shown in the notes to the financial statements. [SI 2008/410 1 Sch 7(2)].

Materiality and aggregation

3.26 Each material class of similar items should be presented separately in the financial statements. Items of a dissimilar nature or function should be presented separately, unless they are immaterial. [FRS 102 para 3.15]. Conversely, an immaterial line item should be aggregated with other items, either on the face of the primary statements or in the notes. An item that is not sufficiently material to warrant separate presentation on the face of the financial statements might nevertheless be sufficiently material that it should be presented separately in the notes.

3.27 FRS 102's disclosure requirements only apply to material items. [FRS 102 para 3.16, 3.16A]. Similarly, accounting policies in the standard need not be applied when the effect of applying them is immaterial. [FRS 102 para 10.3]. The Glossary of Terms gives the following definition of 'material':

> *"Omissions or misstatements of items are material if they could, individually or collectively, influence the economic decisions that users make on the basis of the financial statements. Materiality depends on the size and nature of the omission or misstatement judged in the surrounding circumstances. The size or nature of the item, or a combination of both, could be the determining factor."*

3.28 Section 2 of the standard makes clear that financial statements are prepared for users who have a reasonable knowledge of business and economic activities and accounting and who study the information diligently. [FRS 102 para 2.4]. So materiality is assessed against the decision-making of reasonably knowledgeable individuals. The concept of materiality is discussed further in chapter 2.

3.29 The FRC discussion paper, 'Cutting clutter', published in April 2011, drew attention to the need to focus on key messages in corporate reports and for these not to be obscured by unnecessary detail. In its 2011 report, the Financial Reporting Review Panel (FRRP) noted that, when preparing their financial statements, some boards do not appear to apply a materiality threshold, or consider whether an item is material by nature, because clearly immaterial or irrelevant detail is often disclosed. The FRRP noted that this can lead a user to conclude that the directors consider such amounts to be material and that all amounts greater than this have been disclosed. In its 2012 report, the FRRP noted that some companies have reduced unnecessary and obscuring detail from their reports, but other companies have not. The FRRP continues to encourage boards to use their judgement to determine and apply a quantitative threshold and qualitative assessment for materiality in relation to disclosures as part of their financial statements preparation process. It notes that a more rigorous approach might result in financial statements that are more meaningful, focused and relevant to users because inconsistencies and superfluous material will have been excluded.

3.30 As described in greater detail in chapters 4 and 5, SI 2008/410, 'The Large and Medium-sized Companies and Groups (Accounts and Reports) Regulations 2008', requires the presentation of some line items in the balance sheet (that is, the statement of financial position) and the profit and loss account in accordance with prescribed formats. (FRS 102 clarifies that these profit and loss account line items are included in the statement of comprehensive income.) Whichever format is used, the entity should show the items in the order and under the headings and the sub-headings set out in the particular formats that it has selected. [SI 2008/410 1 Sch 3]. But there are exceptions to this rule, as explained below.

3.31 An item is permitted to be shown in greater detail than the particular format requires. [SI 2008/410 1 Sch 3(1)]. An entity should present additional line items, headings and subtotals in its statement of financial position and in its statement of comprehensive income (and income statement, if presented) when such a presentation is relevant to an understanding of the relevant financial statement. [FRS 102 paras 4.3, 5.9]. For example, most entities include motor vehicles under the sub-heading 'Fixtures, fittings, tools and equipment'. But, where such motor vehicles are significant in value, they could be presented as a separate category of asset.

3.32 An item representing an asset or a liability, or an item of income or expenditure that is not covered in any of the prescribed formats, could be shown separately.[SI 2008/410 1 Sch 3(2)]. An example is where an entity holds inventory that does not fall easily within the sub-headings of raw materials and consumables, work in progress, finished goods and goods for resale, and payments on account.

3.33 The formats list items either as main headings or as sub-headings. In the balance sheet, main headings are designated either by letters or by Roman numerals, and sub-headings are designated by Arabic numerals. Items in the profit and loss account formats are all preceded by Arabic numerals. Items that are preceded by Arabic numerals could be combined in the entity's financial statements where either of the following circumstances apply:

- Their individual amounts are not material to assessing the entity's state of affairs or profit or loss for the financial year in question. [SI 2008/410 1 Sch 4(2)(a)].

- The combination facilitates the assessment of the entity's state of affairs or profit or loss (that is, it results in greater clarity). Where this applies, the detailed breakdown of the combined items must be given in the notes to the financial statements. [SI 2008/410 1 Sch 4(2)(b),(3)].

3.34 The arrangement, the headings and the sub-headings of items set out in the formats and preceded by Arabic numerals must be adapted if required by the special nature of the entity's business. [SI 2008/410 1 Sch 4(1)].

3.35 Although the law prescribes the headings and sub-headings of items, many entities in practice depart from this requirement (for example, describing 'land and buildings' as 'property', 'stocks' as 'inventories', or 'turnover' as 'sales'. This practice is considered permissible, provided that the revised wording is unlikely to mislead users of the financial statements.

Offsetting

3.36 Assets and liabilities are not permitted to be set off against one another. Similarly, income and expenditure cannot be offset. [SI 2008/410 1 Sch 8]. See chapter 2.

Contents of a complete set of financial statements

3.37 A complete set of financial statements comprises the following statements, all of which should be presented with equal prominence: [FRS 102 para 3.21].

- A statement of financial position as at the reporting date.
- Either:
  - a single statement of comprehensive income for the reporting period; or
  - a separate income statement and a separate statement of comprehensive income.
- A statement of changes in equity for the reporting period.
- A statement of cash flows for the reporting period.
- Notes comprising a summary of significant accounting policies and other explanatory information.

[FRS 102 para 3.17].

3.38 Entities can choose whether to present a single statement of comprehensive income, or a separate income statement and a separate statement of comprehensive income. If an entity elects to prepare a single statement, all items of income and expense are presented in that single statement, and profit or loss is presented as a sub-total followed by items of other comprehensive income (that is, the items of income and expense that are not recognised in profit or loss). If the entity elects to prepare two statements, it presents the profit or loss items as an income statement immediately followed by a statement of comprehensive income presenting the total profit or loss for the period and the items of other comprehensive income. [FRS 102 para 3.17]. All income and expenses should be included in a 'performance statement', rather than just being shown in the statement of changes in equity. See chapter 5.

3.39 The title of the primary statements reflects the function of those statements. Nevertheless, an entity is permitted to use titles for the statements other than those used in FRS 102. An entity can, for example, present a 'balance sheet' rather than a 'statement of financial position', should it wish to do so. However, it is important that the titles used are not misleading. [FRS 102 para 3.22].

3.40 Where, in both the current and comparative periods, an entity has only items of profit or loss, payment of dividends, corrections of prior errors or changes in accounting policy, and no other items that create a change in equity, it could present a single statement of income and retained earnings instead of the statement of comprehensive income and statement of changes in equity. [FRS 102 para 3.18]. See chapter 6.

3.41 If an entity has no items of other comprehensive income in either the current or comparative periods, it could present only an income statement or it could present a statement of comprehensive income in which the 'bottom line' is 'profit or loss'. [FRS 102 para 3.19].

3.42 A qualifying entity (that is, a member of a group whose parent prepares publicly available financial statements, which give a true and fair view, in which that member is consolidated) is exempt from the requirement to prepare a statement of cash flows. [FRS 102 para 1.12(a)]. See chapter 1. A parent entity must prepare a 'performance statement', but it might be exempt from publishing it with the consolidated financial statements. See chapter 5.

Identification of the financial statements

3.43 FRS 102 requires that entities should clearly identify the financial statements and distinguish them from other information in the same published document. [FRS 102 para 3.23]. Reports and statements presented outside financial statements are outside the scope of FRS 102, which deals only with the financial statements.

3.44 The Companies Act 2006 requires directors to prepare a directors' report, including a business review. Some entities also provide additional reports and statements (for example, environmental reports and value added statements), as well as other financial data, within documents containing their financial statements. FRS 102 does not encourage entities to prepare such additional reports and information, and it does not discourage them from doing so; but such reports and information do not form part of the financial statements. This fact should be made clear from the presentation and disclosures accompanying such information.

3.45 Where the financial statements are audited, it is particularly important that the audited FRS 102-compliant financial statements can be distinguished from unaudited information that might or might not comply with FRS 102. The use of alternative measures of performance, often referred to as 'non-GAAP measures', might give a different picture of the entity's performance from the profit determined in accordance with FRS 102. Entities should exercise care – when presenting alternative performance measures in their published documents – to ensure that they are distinguished from the financial statements themselves.

3.46 FRS 102 also requires disclosure of the following:

- The name of the reporting entity and any change in its name since the end of the preceding reporting period.

- Whether the financial statements are of an individual entity or a group of entities.

- The date of the end of the reporting period or the period covered by the set of financial statements.

- The presentation currency, as defined in chapter 30.

- The level of rounding used in presenting amounts in the financial statements.

[FRS 102 para 3.23].

3.47 Entities should determine the best way of presenting the information to meet the overall objective of clarity. The above requirements are usually met by presenting appropriate headings for items, such as pages, statements and columns; but, where financial statements are presented electronically, a different approach might be required. Also, entities could make their financial statements clearer by presenting the information in thousands or millions of the presentation currency. This is permitted as long as the level of rounding is stated and material information is not omitted.

3.48 The following information should be included in the notes to financial statements:

- The entity's domicile and legal form, its country of incorporation and address of the registered office (or principal place of business if different from the registered office).

- A description of the nature of the entity's operations and principal activities.

[FRS 102 para 3.24].

Transitional issues

3.49 No special exemptions on financial statement presentation are available to first-time adopters under section 35 of FRS 102. So a first-time adopter must prepare its first FRS 102 financial statements as though the requirements of section 3 of FRS 102 had always applied.

3.50 The requirements of section 3 of FRS 102 are broadly consistent with the existing company law requirements and with old UK GAAP (such as FRS 21), so transitioning entities should have little difficulty in applying the section.

3.51 As discussed in chapter 32, comparative amounts are presented on the basis of the information available when the previous financial statements were approved.

Chapter 4

Statement of financial position

Statement of financial position

Chapter 4

Statement of financial position

Introduction

4.1 The statement of financial position presents an entity's assets, liabilities and equity as at the end of the reporting period (the 'reporting date'). [FRS 102 para 4.1]. This chapter deals with the presentation of the statement of financial position (or 'balance sheet' as it is referred to in the Companies Act) and with related disclosure requirements set out in section 4 of FRS 102. Additional disclosure requirements related to specific balance sheet items are dealt with in the relevant chapters. Whether an entity is required to prepare consolidated and/or separate financial statements is considered in chapter 9.

4.2 The requirements specific to banking companies, insurance companies and limited liability partnerships are outside the scope of this chapter. The requirements for insurance companies are considered in chapter 34.8. This chapter deals only with matters related to the presentation of the statement of financial position; matters applying to the presentation of financial statements more generally are dealt with in chapter 3.

Scope

4.3 The standard requires the statement of financial position (and the profit and loss account items in the statement of comprehensive income – see chapter 5) to be presented in accordance with the general rules and formats in SI 2008/410, 'The Large and Medium-sized Companies and Groups (Accounts and Reports) Regulations 2008', or SI 2008/1913, 'The Large and Medium-sized Limited Liability Partnerships (Accounts) Regulations 2008'.

4.4 Under the law, only entities that report under the Companies Act are required to adopt the general rules and formats set out in these regulations. Those rules and formats should be applied by any entity that purports to comply with FRS 102, whether or not it reports under the 2006 Act. [FRS 102 paras 4.1, 5.1]. So, a general partnership that does not report under the Companies Act but reports under FRS 102 presents according to the rules and formats set out in the law, even though that law does not apply to it.

4.5 The formats contained in the law are suitable for use by most businesses. But, as discussed in chapter 3, the law recognises that these formats might need to be adapted to fit the entity's particular business. This is more likely to be the case when the entity does not report under the Companies Act, because it is constituted under other legislation or regulation. Where entities do not report under the Companies Act, it might be that the statutory framework under which they report does not permit full compliance with the requirements of sections 4 and 5 of FRS 102, or with the regulations referred to in those sections. In such cases, the entities are permitted to depart from those requirements to the extent required by the statute under which they operate. [FRS 102 para 4.1]. The appendix to the standard summarises the applicable legislation for certain types of entity and sets out how it interacts with the standard's requirements. [FRS 102 paras A4.41, A4.42].

Format of individual accounts

4.6 FRS 102 requires an entity to present its statement of financial position in accordance with one of the following:

- Part 1 General Rules and Formats of Schedule 1 to SI 2008/410. These apply to companies generally.

- Part 1 General Rules and Formats of Schedule 2 to SI 2008/410. These apply to 'banking companies' only.

- Part 1 General Rules and Formats of Schedule 3 to SI 2008/410. These apply to 'insurance companies' only.

- Part 1 General Rules and Formats of Schedule 1 to SI 2008/1913. These apply to limited liability partnerships.

[FRS 102 para 4.2].

4.7 For simplicity, this chapter refers only to SI 2008/410 but equivalent provisions exist in SI 2008/1913 for limited liability partnerships.

Formats

4.8 Schedule 1 to SI 2008/410 sets out two alternative balance sheet formats. Format items preceded by Arabic numerals can be combined on the face of the balance sheet provided the individual amounts are immaterial and the combination results in greater clarity. [SI 2008/410 1 Sch 4(2)]. The standard requires an entity to present additional line items, headings and sub-totals when such presentation is relevant to an understanding of the entity's financial position. [FRS 102 para 4.3]. This is permitted by SI 2008/410 which states that any balance sheet item can be presented in greater detail than required by the particular format. [SI 2008/410 1 Sch 3(1)].

Format 1

4.9 In the format 1 balance sheet, net assets can be shown as equal in total to the aggregate of share capital and reserves. This method of presentation is probably the most common in the UK. But SI 2008/410 does not prescribe where the totals should be struck. So, in this format an entity can equate total assets less current liabilities, on the one hand, with the aggregate of creditors falling due after more than one year, provisions for liabilities, and capital and reserves, on the other hand.

4.10   The format 1 balance sheet is set out below.

Balance sheet — Format 1

A   Called up share capital not paid

B   Fixed assets

    I   Intangible assets

        1   Development costs

        2   Concessions, patents, licences, trade marks and similar rights and assets

        3   Goodwill

        4   Payments on account

    II   Tangible assets

        1   Land and buildings

        2   Plant and machinery

        3   Fixtures, fittings, tools and equipment

        4   Payments on account and assets in course of construction

    III   Investments

        1   Shares in group undertakings

        2   Loans to group undertakings

        3   Participating interests

        4   Loans to undertakings in which the company has a participating interest

        5   Other investments other than loans

        6   Other loans

        7   Own shares

C   Current assets

    I   Stocks

        1   Raw materials and consumables

        2   Work in progress

        3   Finished goods and goods for resale

        4   Payments on account

Statement of financial position

  II Debtors

  1 Trade debtors

  2 Amounts owed by group undertakings

  3 Amounts owed by undertakings in which the company has a participating interest

  4 Other debtors

  5 Called-up share capital not paid

  6 Prepayments and accrued income

  III Investments

  1 Shares in group undertakings

  2 Own shares

  3 Other investments

  IV Cash at bank and in hand

D Prepayments and accrued income

E Creditors: amounts falling due within one year

  1 Debenture loans

  2 Bank loans and overdrafts

  3 Payments received on account

  4 Trade creditors

  5 Bills of exchange payable

  6 Amounts owed to group undertakings

  7 Amounts owed to undertakings in which the company has a participating interest

  8 Other creditors including taxation and social security

  9 Accruals and deferred income

F Net current assets (liabilities)

G Total assets less current liabilities

H Creditors: amounts falling due after more than one year

  1 Debenture loans

  2 Bank loans and overdrafts

  3 Payments received on account

  4 Trade creditors

     5   Bills of exchange payable

     6   Amounts owed to group undertakings

     7   Amounts owed to undertakings in which the company has a participating interest

     8   Other creditors including taxation and social security

     9   Accruals and deferred income

I   Provisions for liabilities

     1   Pensions and similar obligations

     2   Taxation, including deferred taxation

     3   Other provisions

J   Accruals and deferred income

K   Capital and reserves

    I   Called-up share capital

    II   Share premium account

    III   Revaluation reserve

    IV   Other reserves

     1   Capital redemption reserve

     2   Reserve for own shares

     3   Reserves provided for by the articles of association

     4   Other reserves

    V   Profit and loss account

Format 2

4.11 In the format 2 balance sheet, assets are shown as equal in total to liabilities (which include capital and reserves). Because the information disclosed in format 2 is identical in all respects (apart from one) to the information disclosed in format 1, format 2 has not been reproduced here. The only difference between format 1 and format 2 is that format 2 aggregates, on the face of the balance sheet, creditors due within one year and those due after more than one year. But, in respect of each item included in creditors, the split between the amount due within one year and the amount due after more than one year, together with the aggregate, must still be disclosed either on the face of the balance sheet or in the notes. [SI 2008/410 1 Sch Balance sheet formats note 13]. This method of presentation is more common in some other EU countries (for example, France and Germany) than in the UK.

Alternative positions in the balance sheet

4.12   The following items can be shown in alternative positions in the balance sheet (references given are for format 1):

- Called-up share capital not paid (A or C.II.5).

- Prepayments and accrued income (C.II.6 or D) – see paragraph 4.20.

- Accruals and deferred income (E.9, H.9 or J) – see paragraph 4.43.

Alternative positions in the balance sheet

4.12   The following items can be shown in alternative positions in the balance sheet (references given are for format 1):

- Called-up share capital not paid (A or C.II.5).

- Prepayments and accrued income (C.II.6 or D) – see paragraph 4.20.

- Accruals and deferred income (E.9, H.9 or J) – see paragraph 4.43.

Investments

4.13   An entity presents investments in its balance sheet as either fixed asset investments or current asset investments depending on how it intends to use them. A entity's investments that are *"…intended for use on a continuing basis in the company's activities"* are classified as fixed assets. Holding an investment for a long time does not necessarily make it a fixed asset. Generally, investments should be classified as fixed where the entity intends to hold them for the long-term and this intention can clearly be demonstrated. Other investments are classified as current assets.

4.14   Whether an entity intends to use an investment on a continuing basis (that is, hold it for the long-term) will often be obvious from the nature of the investment. Also, where there are practical restrictions on an investor's ability to dispose of the investment, classification as a fixed asset investment might be appropriate. Fixed asset investments will, therefore, comprise:

- Equity shareholdings in, or loans to, subsidiaries and associates.

- Investments arising from other trading relationships.

- Investments that either cannot be disposed of or cannot be disposed of without a significant effect on the operations of the investing entity.

- Investments that are intended to be held for use on a continuing basis by investing entities whose objective is to hold a portfolio of investments to provide income and/or capital growth for their members.

Participating interests

4.15 'Participating interest' (item B.III.3 in the format 1 balance sheet) means an interest held by an undertaking in the shares of another undertaking that it holds on a long-term basis for the purpose of securing a contribution to its activities by the exercise of control or influence arising from or related to that interest. [SI 2008/410 10 Sch 11(1)]. A holding of 20% or more of the shares of an undertaking is presumed to be a participating interest unless the contrary is shown. [SI 2008/410 10 Sch 11(2)]. In this context, a participating interest does not include an interest in a subsidiary undertaking. [SI 2008/410 10 Sch 11(5)]. But it will include associates (see further chapter 14).

Own shares

4.16 The formats include a line item within investments (fixed and current) for 'own shares'. But, under section 22 of FRS 102, 'treasury' shares (that is, own shares) are dealt with as a deduction from equity, and so the line item for 'own shares' within investments cannot be used.

Payments on account

4.17 'Payments on account' relate, as appropriate, to advance payments that an entity makes in respect of the acquisition of intangible assets, tangible assets or stocks (see further chapters 18, 17 and 13 respectively).

Presentation of debtors

4.18 The balance sheet formats include 'debtors' as a component of current assets. The amount of each item to be shown under the heading 'debtors' must be split between those receivable within one year of the balance sheet date and those receivable later than that. [SI 2008/410 1 Sch Balance sheet formats note 5]. For this purpose, a debtor is considered to be receivable on the earliest date on which payment is due, rather than on the earliest date on which payment is expected. But SI 2008/410 does not require this disclosure to be given on the face of the balance sheet. This means that there is an imbalance between the treatment of long-term debtors and long-term creditors, where the latter are disclosed as long-term on the face of the balance sheet and not included in net current assets. In some instances, the absence of disclosure of long-term debtors on the face of the balance sheet might mean that users misinterpret the financial statements.

4.19 As a result of this imbalance, the standard requires debtors due after more than one year to be disclosed on the face of the balance sheet if the amount is so material (in the context of total net current assets) that readers might otherwise misinterpret the balance sheet. [FRS 102 para 4.4A]. This might arise where, for example, the entity is a lessor with long-term trade debtors or the entity is to receive substantial deferred consideration on the sale of assets. The long-term debtor is still included in current assets, but is shown separately on the face of the balance sheet, normally as an additional line item, 'Debtors: amounts falling due after more than one year', in the current assets section. In most cases, however, disclosure of the long-term element of debtors in the notes will suffice. [FRS 102 para 4.4A].

Prepayments and accrued income

4.20   Prepayments and accrued income can be disclosed in one of two alternative positions. [SI 2008/410 1 Sch Balance sheet formats note 6]. They can be disclosed either as a category of debtors (within current assets), or as a separate category in their own right. Where prepayments and accrued income are disclosed within debtors, SI 2008/410 requires disclosure of the amount due in more than one year. But, if they are included as a separate category, no such analysis is strictly required under SI 2008/410. However, the standard requires separate disclosure of debtors due after more than one year where the amount is highly material in the context of the total net current assets. We consider that this applies to prepayments and accrued income regardless of whether the total is included in debtors or shown as a separate category.

Cash at bank and in hand

Definition of cash

4.21   Schedule 1 to SI 2008/410 requires cash at bank and in hand to be included as a separate line item within current assets. The statutory instrument does not define cash, but FRS 102 defines cash as 'cash on hand and demand deposits'. It does not include cash equivalents, which are defined as 'short-term, highly liquid investments that are readily convertible to known amounts of cash and that are subject to an insignificant risk of changes in value'. [FRS 102 Glossary of terms]. So cash equivalents are shown as a separate category in the statement of financial position. The cash flow statement deals with inflows and outflows of both cash and cash equivalents. Section 7 of the standard includes a requirement to provide a reconciliation between the components of cash and cash equivalents and the equivalent items in the statement of financial position. See chapter 7 for more details.

Right of set-off of bank balances

4.22   Assets and liabilities are only offset against each other in the balance sheet where there is a legally enforceable right of set-off between the balances. This stems from the requirement in paragraph 8 of Schedule 1 to SI 2008/410, which states that amounts in respect of items that represent assets or income are not permitted to be offset against amounts in respect of items that represent liabilities or expenditure, or *vice versa*.

4.23 Section 2 of the standard includes a general prohibition on offsetting assets and liabilities. (See chapter 2). Section 11 expands on this and sets out conditions that have to be met in order for offset to apply for financial assets and financial liabilities. The standard's rules require offset where, and only where, both the following conditions are met:

- The entity has a legally enforceable right to offset the recognised amounts.

- The entity intends either to settle on a net basis, or to realise the asset and settle the liability simultaneously.

[FRS 102 para 11.38A].

4.24 Extreme care needs to be taken in consolidated financial statements, where it might be difficult to arrange for an amount that one group entity owes to another party (such as a bank) to be offset against the amount of a deposit that another member of the group has lodged with that party. But, where a bank funds members of a group of entities, this situation would be different if all of the following conditions applied:

- Each individual depositing entity in the group has a joint and several liability to pay the same debts as the borrowing entities (that is, each is deemed to be a principal debtor for the same debts).

- The bank has a liability to each individual depositing entity in respect of its deposit.

- The group has a demonstrable intention to net settle these balances.

4.25 In these circumstances, such assets and liabilities are permitted to be offset against each other; but the restrictions imposed by section 11 of the standard make this relatively rare.

Restricted cash balances

4.26 Cash at bank and in hand will sometimes include balances that can only be used for a specific purpose or where access is restricted. If these amounts are material, they should be disclosed, normally in the notes to the financial statements.

Net current assets and liabilities

4.27 In determining the amount to be shown under 'net current assets (liabilities)' in format 1, an entity must take into account any amount that is shown separately under the heading 'prepayments and accrued income'. [SI 2008/ 410 1 Sch Balance sheet formats note 11]. This applies whether the amount in question is shown as a sub-heading of debtors (C.II.6) or as a main heading (D). But, because the alternative positions of this heading within Format 1 both automatically fall within net current assets (liabilities), this seems to be a self-evident requirement. In practice, it is fairly rare for prepayments to be disclosed as a main heading.

Liabilities

Disclosure

4.28 All items included under creditors must be analysed between amounts that will fall due within one year of the balance sheet date and amounts that will fall due after more than one year. [SI 2008/410 1 Sch balance sheet formats note 13]. SI 2008/410 requires that creditors are analysed into the following categories:

- Debenture loans.

- Bank loans and overdrafts.

- Payments received on account.

- Trade creditors.

- Bills of exchange payable.

- Amounts owed to group undertakings.

- Amounts owed to undertakings in which the company has a participating interest.

- Other creditors including taxation and social security.

- Accruals and deferred income.

[SI 2008/410 1 Sch formats].

4.29 An item representing a liability that is not covered by the prescribed format can be shown separately. [SI 2008/410 1 Sch 3(2)]. The following are examples of creditors that are sometimes shown as separate categories within total creditors: amounts due in respect of factored debts or bills of exchange discounted with recourse; finance lease payables; and deferred consideration in respect of acquisitions.

4.30 Where any item shown under the heading 'creditors' includes liabilities for which the company has given security, these liabilities must be disclosed in aggregate. Also, the notes must give an indication of the nature of the securities given. [SI 2008/410 1 Sch 61(4)]. For this requirement to be meaningful, the financial statements should show some disaggregation of the relevant liabilities. This is because it could be misleading merely to disclose the aggregate of securities compared with the aggregate of liabilities.

Classification as short-term or long-term

4.31　An entity classifies a liability as due within one year if it does not have the unconditional right at the end of the reporting period to defer its settlement for at least 12 months after the reporting date. [FRS 102 para 4.7].

4.32　Many loan agreements include a change of control clause under which a borrowing becomes repayable if there is a change of control event. This raises the question as to whether the borrowing is required to be classified as a current liability if an entity is unable to prevent a controlling shareholder selling its shares to a third party, even if there is no expectation that a change of control might happen within 12 months. Our view is that a change of control clause does not result in classification as a current liability if there has been no change of control event at the reporting date. In this respect, we consider that a change of control clause is similar in substance to a covenant (see para 4.34). So a borrowing is not classified as current if the counter-party does not have a right (as of the balance sheet date) to demand repayment within 12 months of that date.

4.33　A rescheduling or refinancing of debt that is at the lender's discretion and occurs after the reporting date does not alter the liability's condition at the reporting date. Such rescheduling or refinancing is regarded as a non-adjusting post balance sheet event and it is not taken into account in determining the current/long-term classification of the debt. But, if the entity has the right (at the reporting date) to defer payments for more than one year, a liability should be classified as falling due in more than one year. The entity must have full discretion to roll the obligation over; the potential for a refinancing alone is not sufficient to classify an obligation as non-current.

4.34　It is common practice for financial institutions to include borrowing covenants in the terms of loans. Under some borrowing covenants, a loan which would otherwise be long-term in nature becomes immediately repayable if certain items related to the borrower's financial condition or performance are breached. Typically, these items are measures of liquidity or solvency based on ratios derived from the entity's financial statements. Where these types of breach occur before the balance sheet date, the borrowings should be classified as a current liability (unless a sufficient waiver of the covenant is granted by the lender before the balance sheet date, such that the borrowing does not become immediately repayable). Where the borrower has breached a covenant of this nature by the balance sheet date, and the lender agrees (after the balance sheet date but before authorisation of the financial statements) not to require immediate repayment of the loan, the lender's agreement is regarded as a non-adjusting post balance sheet event. This is because the lender's agreement had not been obtained at the balance sheet date, and the borrower did not have the unconditional right to defer payment for at least 12 months after the balance sheet date.

4.35　Some borrowings might include 'cross default' clauses, such that the terms of the borrowing are assessed, at least in part, against compliance with covenants of another borrowing. Once the related borrowing covenant is breached, the borrowing with the 'cross default' clause (and any similarly linked borrowings) might become immediately repayable, and so they are classified as a current liability.

4.36 There might be a period between the measurement date of the covenants and the date at which the borrower needs to report any breach to the bank. If the covenant test date is at or before the balance sheet date, the fact that the borrower need not report the breach until after the period end does not indicate that the covenant has not been breached. Classification of the borrowing as a current liability would still be required.

> **Example – Covenant breach reported after period end**
>
> A company has a long-term loan with a bank. The terms of the loan require quarterly testing of certain covenant ratios. The bank requires the company to file covenant compliance certificates within 60 days of the measurement date of the covenants. The company's year end is 31 December 20X1. The company was within the acceptable parameters based on the calculation of the ratios for the third quarter (that is, 30 September 20X1). The covenant testing date in the fourth quarter is 31 December 20X1. The financial results were finalised in January 20X2. Based on these, the company was in breach of its covenants at 31 December 20X1. The company is due to file the covenant compliance certificates on 2 March 20X2, which will show the breach. The company believes that the breach in covenant does not occur until the filing date, because this is the date at which the bank would call the loan in the absence of any remedy. How should the loan balance be classified at the year end?
>
> Although reporting of the breach was not required until after the balance sheet date, the company was, in effect, in breach of its covenants at 31 December 20X1. This is the case, even though the reported financial figures were not finalised until January. The company did not have the unconditional right to defer settlement of the loan for at least 12 months after the balance sheet date: so the loan balance should be classified as current.

4.37 Following a breach of a borrowing covenant, lenders often agree to a period of grace during which the borrower could rectify the breach. The lender agrees not to demand repayment during this time; but, if the breach is not rectified, the debt becomes immediately repayable at the end of the period of grace. If, before the balance sheet date, the lender has agreed to such a period of grace and that period ends at least 12 months after the balance sheet date, the liability should be shown as long-term. If the breach of the borrowing covenant occurs after the balance sheet date, the liability is still shown as long-term. The presentation of the loan is dictated by the condition of the loan as at the balance sheet date. Events after the balance sheet date might give evidence of that condition, but they do not change it. This is consistent with section 32 of the standard ('Events after the end of the reporting period').

4.38 In contrast, some borrowing agreements include a period of grace, the effect of which is that the borrower does not lose the unconditional right to defer payment of the liability until the period of grace has expired. In this case, where the breach does not occur until this later date, the entity continues to present the borrowings as non-current.

> **Example – Borrowing agreement includes a period of grace**
>
> A term loan agreement includes a provision that the borrower must sell a foreign branch of its operations by 31 December 20X1. But the agreement states that the borrower is permitted an additional two months to complete the sale if it is not able to sell the branch by that date. The borrower has not been able to find a buyer by 31 December 20X1. In its financial statements for the period ended 31 December 20X1, how will the borrowings be classified?
>
> The entity should continue to classify the loan balance as non-current, as the agreement allows for a period of grace such that the actual breach of the loan conditions does not occur until two months after the end of the reporting period. The entity should consider the impact of the potential breach and the appropriateness of including disclosure on this item in the financial statements.

4.39 Where an entity experiences a downturn in trading results, in addition to the impact of these results on banking covenants, management should consider if there is an impact on the entity's borrowing powers. For example, a company's articles of association might contain a borrowing restriction that requires the directors to restrict borrowings to a multiple of capital and reserves (as defined in the articles). So a significant loss might affect the amount of any new borrowing that the company can take out, or it might affect the roll-over of existing borrowings. If management considers that the company might breach (or has breached) the borrowing powers in its articles, it should discuss remedies (for example, ratification by shareholders) with its legal advisers.

Debenture loans

4.40 There is no precise definition of a debenture loan, either in law or in practice. In legal terms, it is generally construed as formal acknowledgment of a debt. However, section 738 of the Companies Act 2006 refers to debentures as including *"debenture stock, bonds and any other securities of a company, whether or not constituting a charge on the assets of the company"*. This definition does not distinguish clearly between a debenture loan and any other loan. Whether a particular loan is a debenture or not will depend on the documentation. A formal loan agreement, whether containing security or not, will often constitute a debenture. Although a bank loan might be a debenture loan, the balance sheet formats distinguish between bank loans and other debenture loans. For accounting measurement and disclosure purposes, there is no difference between debentures, loans and other debt instruments.

Amounts received on account

4.41 Unless an entity shows the payments that it has received on account of orders as a deduction from 'stocks', it must show them under creditors. [SI 2008/410 1 Sch Balance sheet formats note 8]. 'Stocks' in SI 2008/410 comprises raw materials and consumables, work in progress, finished goods and goods for resale. Under FRS 102, these items are dealt with as inventory and work in progress under construction contracts. It is not permissible under FRS 102 to deduct payments on account from inventory, and section 2 of the standard prohibits offsetting. Inventory is measured at the lower of cost and estimated selling price less costs to complete and sell. [FRS 102 para 13.4]. Payments on account of inventory are included in creditors. In respect of work in progress on construction contracts dealt with under the percentage of completion method, payments on account are dealt with as a deduction from amounts receivable from customers, with any excess included as a creditor.

Other creditors including taxation and social security

4.42 The line 'other creditors including taxation and social security' must be analysed between other creditors, on the one hand, and taxation and social security on the other. [SI 2008/410 1 Sch Balance sheet formats note 9]. 'Other creditors including taxation and social security' contrasts with the line under provisions for 'taxation, including deferred taxation'. The latter item will comprise all income tax liabilities.

Accruals and deferred income

4.43 In the same way that 'prepayments and accrued income' can be shown in either of two positions in the formats (see para 4.20), the item 'accruals and deferred income' can be disclosed either as a category of creditors or as a separate category in its own right. [SI 2008/410 1 Sch Balance sheet formats note 10]. Where 'accruals and deferred income' is disclosed under creditors, it must be analysed between those amounts that will fall due within one year and those amounts that will fall due after more than one year. [SI 2008/410 1 Sch Balance sheet formats note 13]. No such analysis is required if 'accruals and deferred income' is included as a separate category.

4.44 'Accruals and deferred income' could include government grants that are accounted for as deferred credits. These are discussed in chapter 24.

Other liabilities

4.45 SI 2008/410 requires the amount of any convertible loans included in the caption of debenture loans to be shown separately. [SI 2008/410 1 Sch Balance sheet formats note 7]. Section 22 of the standard requires the debt component of convertible debt (which is treated as a compound financial instrument) to be reported within liabilities. We consider that, in order to comply with the company law requirements, the liability element of convertible loans should be separately disclosed as part of debentures. Section 22 of the standard is considered in detail in chapter 22.

Interests in and amounts due to and from group undertakings

4.46 The format 1 balance sheet specifies where amounts owed to and from, and any interests in, group undertakings should be presented. These items can be summarised as follows:

B   Fixed assets

    III   Investments

        1   Shares in group undertakings

        2   Loans to group undertakings

C   Current assets

    II   Debtors

        2   Amounts owed by group undertakings

    III   Investments

        1   Shares in group undertakings

E   Creditors: amounts falling due within one year

        6   Amounts owed to group undertakings

H   Creditors: amounts falling due after more than one year

        6   Amounts owed to group undertakings

4.47 The amounts owed and owing have to be ascertained on an undertaking-by-undertaking basis. [SI 2008/410 1 Sch 8]. So, for accounting disclosure purposes in the parent's financial statements, amounts that one subsidiary owes to the parent cannot be offset against amounts that the parent owes to another subsidiary. As explained in paragraph 4.23, set-off can be allowed only in circumstances where there is a legal right of set-off and the entity has an intention to settle net (see further chapter 11).

4.48 Undertakings are required to analyse 'amounts owed by (and to) group undertakings' between amounts that will fall due within one year and amounts that will fall due after more than one year. [SI 2008/410 1 Sch Balance sheet formats notes 5 and 13]. The results of this analysis will largely depend both on the way in which group undertakings are financed and on the terms of any formal or informal agreements between the undertakings.

Format of consolidated accounts

4.49 Where an entity presents a consolidated statement of financial position, it should be presented in accordance with the requirements for a consolidated balance sheet in Schedule 6 to SI 2008/410 or Schedule 3 to SI 2008/1913. [FRS 102 para 4.2]. SI 2008/410 requires consolidated financial statements to comply as far as practicable with the provisions of Schedule 1 to SI 2008/410 as if the undertakings included in the consolidation were a single company. [SI 2008/410 6 Sch 1(1)]. The consolidated financial statements should also comply with the provisions of the relevant regulations as to their form and content. [CA06 Sec 404(3)].

4.50 Schedule 6 to SI 2008/410 includes provisions that modify the formats detailed in Schedule 1 to SI 2008/410 to include additional items that require disclosure in the consolidated balance sheet. [SI 2008/410 6 Sch 17(2), 20(2)]. The format 1 balance sheet set out below includes the requirements of both Schedules 1 and 6 to SI 2008/410 (the additional requirements of Schedule 6 are shown in italics, and modifications to the numbering and lettering have been made for illustrative purposes). The format 2 balance sheet is not set out (for the same reasons given in para 4.11).

4.51 The format chosen by the group's parent for its individual balance sheet would normally also be used to present the consolidated balance sheet. There is nothing in the legislation to prevent the parent from adopting a different format for its consolidated balance sheet, but this is unlikely to happen in practice, unless the group has banking or insurance activities and the parent does not.

Consolidated balance sheet — Format 1

A   Called up share capital not paid

B   Fixed assets

    I   Intangible assets

        1   Development costs

        2   Concessions, patents, licences, trade marks and similar rights and assets

        3   Goodwill

        4   Payments on account

    II   Tangible assets

        1   Land and buildings

        2   Plant and machinery

        3   Fixtures, fittings, tools and equipment

        4   Payments on account and assets in course of construction

    III   Investments

        1   Shares in group undertakings

        2   Loans to group undertakings

        3   *Interests in associated undertakings*

        4   *Other participating interests*

5   Loans to undertakings in which the company has a participating interest

6   Other investments other than loans

7   Other loans

8   Own shares

C   Current assets

   I   Stocks

     1   Raw materials and consumables

     2   Work in progress

     3   Finished goods and goods for resale

     4   Payments on account

   II   Debtors

     1   Trade debtors

     2   Amounts owed by group undertakings

     3   Amounts owed by undertakings in which the company has a participating interest

     4   Other debtors

     5   Called-up share capital not paid

     6   Prepayments and accrued income

   III   Investments

     1   Shares in group undertakings

     2   Own shares

     3   Other investments

   IV   Cash at bank and in hand

D   Prepayments and accrued income

E   Creditors: amounts falling due within one year

     1   Debenture loans

     2   Bank loans and overdrafts

     3   Payments received on account

     4   Trade creditors

     5   Bills of exchange payable

     6   Amounts owed to group undertakings

    7   Amounts owed to undertakings in which the company has a participating interest

    8   Other creditors including taxation and social security

    9   Accruals and deferred income

F   Net current assets (liabilities)

G   Total assets less current liabilities

H   Creditors: amounts falling due after more than one year

    1   Debenture loans

    2   Bank loans and overdrafts

    3   Payments received on account

    4   Trade creditors

    5   Bills of exchange payable

    6   Amounts owed to group undertakings

    7   Amounts owed to undertakings in which the company has a participating interest

    8   Other creditors including taxation and social security

    9   Accruals and deferred income

I   Provisions for liabilities

    1   Pensions and similar obligations

    2   Taxation, including deferred taxation

    3   Other provisions

J   Accruals and deferred income

K   Capital and reserves

    I   Called-up share capital

    II   Share premium account

    III   Revaluation reserve

    IV   Other reserves

    1   Capital redemption reserve

    2   Reserve for own shares

    3   Reserves provided for by the articles of association

    4   Other reserves

    V   Profit and loss account

4.52 Schedule 6 to SI 2008/410 also requires that, in the balance sheet formats, there should be shown, as a separate item and under an appropriate heading, the amount of capital and reserves attributable to shares in subsidiary undertakings included in the consolidation held by minority interests. [SI 2008/410 6 Sch 17(2)]. The position of the line item for minority interests (or 'non-controlling interests' as they are referred to in the standard) is not specified in the statutory instrument. The presentation of minority interests is considered further in chapter 9.

Related undertakings

4.53 Schedule 4 to SI 2008/410 requires companies to disclose considerable detail about their investments in subsidiaries and other related undertakings. The schedule sets out disclosures applying to all companies, and then has separate sections for companies not required to prepare group accounts, companies required to prepare group accounts, and additional disclosures for banking companies and groups. The disclosures are grouped in the following categories:

- Subsidiaries included in consolidated financial statements (considered in chapter 9).

- Subsidiaries that are excluded from consolidation (considered in chapter 9).

- Disclosures about subsidiaries where the parent does not prepare consolidated financial statements (considered in chapter 9).

- Joint ventures, associated undertakings and other significant holdings (considered in chapters 14 and 15).

- Membership of certain undertakings, such as qualifying partnerships (considered in chapter 9).

Share capital, reserves and dividends

4.54 FRS 102 requires an entity with share capital to disclose the following for each class of share capital, either on the face of the statement of financial position or in the notes:

- The number of shares issued and fully paid, and issued but not fully paid.

- Par value per share, or that the shares have no par value.

- A reconciliation of the number of shares outstanding at the beginning and at the end of the period. (A qualifying entity (that is, a member of a group that prepares publicly available consolidated financial statements which give a true and fair view) could take advantage of the exemption from this disclosure set out in paragraph 1.12(a) of FRS 102 (see chapter 1)).

- The rights, preferences and restrictions attaching to that class, including restrictions on the distribution of dividends and the repayment of capital.

- Shares in the entity held by the entity or by its subsidiaries, associates or joint ventures.

- Shares reserved for issue under options and contracts for the sale of shares, including the terms and amounts.

[FRS 102 para 4.12(a)].

4.55 An entity without a share capital, such as a partnership or trust, discloses information equivalent to that above, showing changes during the period in each category of equity, and the rights, preferences and restrictions attaching to each category of equity. [FRS 102 para 4.13].

4.56 FRS 102 requires disclosure of a description of each reserve within equity. [FRS 102 para 4.12(b)]. The Companies Act also requires disclosure of the following:

- Any amount set aside or proposed to be set aside to, or withdrawn or proposed to be withdrawn from, reserves.

- The aggregate amount of dividends paid in the financial year (other than those for which a liability existed at the immediately preceding balance sheet date).

- The aggregate amount of dividends that the company is liable to pay at the balance sheet date.

- The aggregate amount of dividends that are proposed before the date of approval of the accounts, and not otherwise required to be disclosed.

[SI 2008/410 1 Sch 43].

Off-balance sheet arrangements

4.57 The Companies Act 2006 requires the disclosure of 'off-balance sheet arrangements'. The premise underlying the disclosure requirement is that certain arrangements undertaken by a company might have a material impact on the company, but might not be included in the company's balance sheet. So, if a company is or has been party to arrangements that are not reflected in its balance sheet, and the risks or benefits are material, the company should disclose:

- the nature and business purpose of the arrangements; and

- the financial impact of the arrangements on the company, to the extent necessary for enabling the company's financial position to be assessed.

[CA06 Sec 410A].

4.58 Where the company belongs to a group, the group's financial position as a whole might also be affected. So aggregated disclosures need to be made in the notes to the consolidated financial statements.

4.59 Application guidance from the BIS (formerly BERR) draws attention to Recital (9) to the EU Corporate Reporting Directive (2006/46/EC) which states:

> *"Such off-balance-sheet arrangements could be any transactions or agreements which companies may have with entities, even unincorporated ones, that are not included in the balance sheet. Such off-balance sheet arrangements may be associated with the creation or use of one or more Special Purpose Entities (SPEs) and offshore activities designed to address, inter alia, economic, legal, tax or accounting objectives. Examples of such off-balance-sheet arrangements include risk and benefit-sharing arrangements or obligations arising from a contract such as debt factoring, combined sale and repurchase agreements, consignment stock arrangements, take or pay arrangements, securitisation arranged through separate companies and unincorporated entities, pledged assets, operating leasing arrangements, outsourcing and the like. Appropriate disclosure of the material risks and benefits of such arrangements that are not included in the balance sheet should be set out in the notes to the accounts or the consolidated accounts."*

4.60 We consider that FRS 102 generally goes well beyond the minimum requirements of the law in ensuring that assets and liabilities are not inappropriately excluded from the balance sheet. It also imposes disclosure requirements on some types of arrangements which are not included in the balance sheet, such as operating leases and contingent liabilities. So, in most cases, compliance with FRS 102 should be sufficient to ensure compliance with the law. But FRS 102 does not necessarily provide for all circumstances, and entities should consider making disclosures where, for example, they have had discussions with their auditors about off-balance sheet implications of transactions that their companies undertake or whether entities should be consolidated. In this respect, compliance with the requirements in section 8 of the standard (that is, to disclose critical judgements and sources of estimation uncertainty) should assist in formulating an appropriate disclosure that meets the legal requirement.

4.61 Furthermore, the recent financial crisis and the ensuing problems with liquidity in the markets have highlighted concerns about latent risks and exposures that had not previously been considered an issue. Concerns have focused on, amongst others, unconsolidated special purpose entities, liquidity facilities, loan commitments, guarantees and derivatives. In meeting the disclosure requirement on off-balance sheet arrangements, entities might need to consider a broader concept of financial impact of their off-balance sheet arrangements, in terms of, for example, liquidity, capital resources and credit risk.

Disposal groups

4.62 A disposal group is defined as follows:

"A group of assets to be disposed of, by sale or otherwise, together as a group in a single transaction, and liabilities directly associated with those assets that will be transferred in the transaction. The group includes goodwill acquired in a business combination if the group is a cash-generating unit to which goodwill has been allocated in accordance with the requirements of Section 27 paragraphs 24 to 27 of this FRS."

[FRS 102 Glossary of terms].

4.63   The following disclosure in the notes is required if, at the reporting date, an entity has a binding sale agreement for a major disposal of assets or a disposal group:

- A description of the asset(s) or the disposal group.

- A description of the facts and circumstances of the sale or plan.

- The carrying amount of the assets or, for a disposal group, the carrying amounts of the underlying assets and liabilities.

[FRS 102 para 4.14].

4.64   As discussed in chapter 32, an entity might plan to sell an asset or disposal group but the sale is subject to conditions. For example, an entity might have a binding sale agreement to sell a site after the reporting date, provided that planning permission is obtained before the completion date. Although the sale is conditional (and so it is not recognised until completion occurs), there is a binding sale agreement and the disclosures above are required.

Transitional issues

4.65   No special exemptions on the presentation of the balance sheet are available to first-time adopters under section 35 of FRS 102. So a first-time adopter must prepare its first FRS 102 financial statements as though the requirements of section 4 of FRS 102 had always applied.

4.66   The requirements of section 4 of FRS 102 are mainly derived from the existing requirements in company law and in old UK GAAP (UITF 4), so transitioning entities should have little difficulty in applying the section.

Chapter 5

Statement of comprehensive income and income statement

Chapter 5

Statement of comprehensive income and income statement

Introduction

5.1 Total comprehensive income is the change in equity during a period resulting from transactions and other events, other than those resulting from transactions with owners in their capacity as owners; in other words, it reflects the entity's financial performance in the period. This chapter describes the requirements of section 5 of FRS 102 dealing with financial performance presentation in the financial statements. Like section 4 of the standard, section 5 applies to all entities, regardless of whether they report under the Companies Act (see chapter 4).

5.2 The requirements specific to banking companies, insurance companies and limited liability partnerships are outside the scope of this chapter. The requirements for insurance companies are considered in chapter 34.8. This chapter deals only with matters related to the presentation of the statement of comprehensive income and income statement; matters applying to the presentation of financial statements more generally are dealt with in chapter 3.

Presentation of total comprehensive income

5.3 An entity can present total comprehensive income under a single-statement or two-statement approach:

■ Single-statement approach: The entity presents a single statement of comprehensive income, presenting all items of income and expense recognised in the period.

■ Two-statement approach: The entity presents an income statement (called the 'profit and loss account' in the Companies Act) presenting all items of profit or loss, and a separate statement of comprehensive income that begins with the total profit or loss for the period and also presents all items of other comprehensive income (that is, all income and expense items not dealt with through profit or loss). Where an entity has no items of other comprehensive income to present, it might be eligible to present a combined statement of income and retained earnings. See chapter 6 for more details.

5.4 A change from one approach to the other is a change in accounting policy under section 10 of the standard. [FRS 102 para 5.3]. See chapter 10 for more details.

5001

Profit and loss account items

5.5 The standard requires the items of profit or loss to be presented in accordance with company law formats, regardless of whether a single-statement or two-statement approach is adopted. An entity presents items of profit or loss in accordance with the general rules and formats for the profit and loss account contained in the Large and Medium-sized Companies and Groups (Accounts and Reports) Regulations 2008 (SI 2008/410) or the Large and Medium-sized Limited Liability Partnerships (Accounts) Regulations 2008 (SI 2008/1913). [FRS 102 paras 5.5, 5.7]. Under the law, only entities that report under the Companies Act are required to adopt the general rules and formats set out in these regulations. Those rules and formats should be applied by any entity that purports to comply with FRS 102, whether or not it reports under the 2006 Act. [FRS 102 paras 4.1, 5.1]. So, a general partnership that does not report under the Companies Act but reports under FRS 102 presents according to the rules and formats set out in the law, even though that law does not apply to it.

5.6 Entities can combine format items preceded by Arabic numerals provided the individual amounts are immaterial and the combination results in greater clarity. [SI 2008/410 1 Sch 4(2)]. A breakdown of the amounts combined is disclosed in the notes to the financial statements. [SI 2008/410 1 Sch 4(3)]. All profit and loss account items are preceded by an Arabic numeral but SI 2008/410 requires entities to present, as a minimum, the profit or loss before taxation on the face of the profit and loss account. [SI 2008/410 1 Sch 6]. Also, the standard requires entities to present turnover on the face of the income statement (or statement of comprehensive income). [FRS 102 para 5.7C].

5.7 As discussed in chapter 4, formats are adapted when the special nature of the business requires it. Additional line items, headings and sub-totals are added to the statement of comprehensive income (and income statement, if presented) when such presentation is relevant to an understanding of the entity's financial performance. [FRS 102 para 5.9]. Where entities do not report under the Companies Act, it might be that the statutory framework under which they report does not permit full compliance with the requirements of sections 4 and 5 of FRS 102, or with the regulations referred to in those sections. In such cases, the entities are permitted to depart from those requirements to the extent required by the statute under which they operate. [FRS 102 para 4.1]. The appendix to the standard summarises the applicable legislation for certain types of entity and sets out how it interacts with the standard's requirements. [FRS 102 paras A4.41, A4.42].

Individual accounts – profit and loss account items

5.8 FRS 102 requires an entity to present its profit and loss account items in its separate financial statements (known as 'individual accounts' in the Companies Act) in accordance with one of the following:

- Part 1 General Rules and Formats of Schedule 1 to SI 2008/410. These apply to companies generally.

- Part 1 General Rules and Formats of Schedule 2 to SI 2008/410. These apply to 'banking companies' only.

- Part 1 General Rules and Formats of Schedule 3 to SI 2008/410. These apply to 'insurance companies' only.

- Part 1 General Rules and Formats of Schedule 1 to SI 2008/1913. These apply to limited liability partnerships.

[FRS 102 paras 5.5, 5.7].

5.9   Unlike the choice between the balance sheet formats, the choice between the profit and loss account formats is significant. A company can choose between not only a vertical presentation (formats 1 and 2) and a presentation in which charges are shown separately from income (formats 3 and 4), but also between classifying expenses by function or by nature. This latter choice is mirrored in section 5 of the standard, which also requires such an analysis. [FRS 102 para 5.11].

5.10   For simplicity, this chapter refers only to SI 2008/410; equivalent provisions exist in SI 2008/1913, except that limited liability partnerships cannot adopt a format in which charges are shown separately from income.

Classification of expenses by function

5.11   In formats 1 and 3, expenses are classified by function (such as cost of sales, distribution costs, and administrative expenses). Format 1, which is the vertical presentation, is set out below. Format 3 is not set out, because it is rarely used and replicates the information in format 1.

Profit and loss account — Format 1

1   Turnover

2   Cost of sales

3   Gross profit or loss

4   Distribution costs

5   Administrative expenses

6   Other operating income

7   Income from shares in group undertakings

8   Income from participating interests

9   Income from other fixed asset investments

10   Other interest receivable and similar income

11   Amounts written off investments

12   Interest payable and similar charges

13   Tax on profit or loss on ordinary activities

14   Profit or loss on ordinary activities after taxation

15   Extraordinary income

16   Extraordinary charges

17   Extraordinary profit or loss

18   Tax on extraordinary profit or loss

19   Other taxes not shown under the above items

20   Profit or loss for the financial year

Turnover, cost of sales, distribution costs and administrative expenses

5.12   As discussed in paragraph 5.6, the standard requires that, as a minimum, turnover is presented on the face of the income statement (or statement of comprehensive income). [FRS 102 para 5.7C]. Turnover (or revenue) is discussed in chapter 23.

5.13   Cost of sales will normally include:

■   Opening (less closing) inventory.

■   Direct materials.

■   Other external charges (such as the hire of plant and machinery or the cost of casual labour used in the productive process).

■   Direct labour.

■   All direct production overheads, including depreciation, and indirect overheads that can reasonably be allocated to the production function.

■   Product development expenditure.

■   Cash discounts received on 'cost of sales' expenditure (this is not an offsetting, but an effective reduction in the purchase price of an item).

■   Inventory write-downs.

5.14   Distribution costs are generally interpreted more widely than the name suggests and often include selling and marketing costs. Items normally included in this caption comprise:

■   Payroll costs of the sales, marketing and distribution functions.

■   Advertising.

■   Salesperson's travel and entertaining.

■   Warehouse costs for finished goods.

- Transport costs concerning the distribution of finished goods.

- All costs of maintaining sales outlets.

- Agents' commission payable.

5.15 Administrative expenses will normally include:

- The costs of general management.

- All costs of maintaining the administration buildings.

- Professional costs.

- Research and development expenditure that is not allocated to cost of sales (sometimes this is shown as a separate item).

5.16 In some specific instances, the allocation of costs between the headings proposed above might not be appropriate. For example, in the context of a mail-order company, agents' commission payable might be regarded as a cost of sale rather than as a distribution cost.

5.17 The way in which a company analyses its costs will depend very much on the nature of its business. Where a company incurs significant operating expenses that it considers do not fall under any one of the headings 'cost of sales', 'distribution costs' and 'administrative expenses', there is nothing to prevent the company from including an additional item for these expenses in format 1 or 3. The overriding consideration is that a company should analyse its operating expenses consistently from year to year.

Depreciation (including other amounts written off assets)

5.18 If format 1 or 3 is adopted, charges for depreciation (or the diminution in value of assets) have to be analysed under the headings set out in paragraph 5.11. [SI 2008/410 1 Sch Profit and loss account formats note 14]. The type of analysis will depend on the function of the related assets. Where an entity prepares its profit and loss account in accordance with either format 1 or 3, expenses are classified by function. So, any provisions for depreciation or the diminution in value of tangible and intangible fixed assets will not be disclosed in the profit and loss account format. Accordingly, this information must be disclosed separately in the notes to the financial statements. [SI 2008/410 1 Sch Profit and loss account formats note 17].

5.19 Company law also requires separate disclosure of the aggregate amount of:

- Any provision against a fixed asset investment for diminution in value.

- Any provision against a fixed asset for permanent diminution in value.

- Any write back of such provisions which are no longer necessary.

[SI 2008/410 1 Sch 19, 20].

5.20 Accounting for depreciation and diminutions in value of tangible and intangible fixed assets is considered in chapters 17 and 18.

Classification of expenses by type

5.21 In formats 2 and 4, expenses are classified by type (such as raw materials and consumables, staff costs, and depreciation). Format 2, which is the vertical presentation, is set out below. Format 4 is not set out, because it is rarely used and replicates the information in format 2.

Profit and loss account — Format 2

1   Turnover

2   Change in stocks of finished goods and in work in progress

3   Own work capitalised

4   Other operating income

5   (a)   Raw materials and consumables

    (b)   Other external charges

6   Staff costs:

    (a)   Wages and salaries

    (b)   Social security costs

    (c)   Other pension costs

7   (a)   Depreciation and other amounts written off tangible and intangible fixed assets

    (b)   Exceptional amounts written off current assets

8   Other operating charges

9   Income from shares in group undertakings

10   Income from participating interests

11   Income from other fixed asset investments

12   Other interest receivable and similar income

13   Amounts written off investments

14   Interest payable and similar charges

15   Tax on profit or loss on ordinary activities

16   Profit or loss on ordinary activities after taxation

17   Extraordinary income

18   Extraordinary charges

19   Extraordinary profit or loss

20   Tax on extraordinary profit or loss

21   Other taxes not shown under the above items

22   Profit or loss for the financial year

Own work capitalised

5.22   Where an entity has constructed some of its own property, plant and equipment or intangible assets, and it adopts either format 2 or 4 (which classify expenses by nature) for its profit and loss account, it should include the costs of direct materials, direct labour and overheads that it has capitalised as a credit under the heading 'own work capitalised'. The costs of direct materials, direct labour and overheads are charged in the profit and loss account (income statement) by including these amounts under the relevant expenditure headings. The amount capitalised is then credited in the profit and loss account as own work capitalised, and it is debited to property, plant and equipment or intangible assets, as appropriate (see chapters 17 and 18). So, items such as raw material costs in the profit and loss account will include the costs connected with such work.

Depreciation (including other amounts written off assets)

5.23   Paragraph 5.18 sets out disclosure requirements that apply regardless of the profit and loss account format adopted. Accounting for depreciation and diminutions in value of tangible and intangible fixed assets is considered in chapters 17 and 18.

Other operating charges (including other external charges)

5.24   The relevant formats (formats 2 and 4) place 'other external charges' next to 'raw materials and consumables' under a single item number. Therefore, such charges are likely to include any production costs from external sources that are not included under other headings (for example, equipment rentals and the costs of subcontractors).

5.25   'Other operating charges' is a separate line item which tends to be a residual class of all charges relating to a business's trading activities that do not fall into any other category. In practice, the distinction between 'other external charges' and 'other operating charges' is blurred. Some companies do not attempt to make a distinction, and include only one heading to cover all residual operating costs.

Operating profit

5.26   FRS 102 does not require entities to disclose results from operating activities. But entities will often present 'operating profit', an undefined term; the standard emphasises that, where an entity does so, it should ensure the amount disclosed *"... is representative of activities that would normally be regarded as* '*operating*'...". An item is not 'non-operating' just because it occurs irregularly or infrequently (for example, inventory write-downs, restructuring and relocation expenses) or because it does not involve cash flows (for example, depreciation and amortisation expenses). [FRS 102 para 5.9B]. So entities should ensure that all operating-type items are appropriately included when presenting a measure that is intended to represent operating activity. See paragraph 5.55 on presentation in consolidated financial statements of the share of profits from associates and 'jointly controlled entities'.

Material and exceptional items

5.27 Paragraph 5.9A of FRS 102 requires separate disclosure of the nature and amount of any material items of *profit or loss*. Materiality could be determined by reference to an item's size or nature, or a combination of both. For example, the Financial Reporting Review Panel (FRRP) concluded in one case that the payment of fines was an important matter that should be brought specifically to the attention of the users of the financial statements. The panel argued that the nature and circumstances of the fines concerned made them material, even though (as the preparer of the financial statements argued) the amounts involved were not material.

5.28 The following are other examples of items that might warrant separate disclosure, if material:

- Writing down inventories to net realisable value, or impairments of property, plant and equipment, as well as the reversal of such write downs or impairments.

- Restructuring provisions or their reversal.

- Profits or losses on disposals of items of property, plant and equipment.

- Profits or losses on disposals of investments.

- Litigation settlements.

- Other reversals of provisions.

5.29 Disclosure of such information should be made on the face of the statement of comprehensive income (or, if presented, the income statement) by means of additional line items or headings if such presentation is relevant to understanding the entity's financial performance. [FRS 102 para 5.9]. Otherwise, these items should be disclosed in the notes.

5.30 FRS 102 does not include a specific name for the types of item that should be separately disclosed. The term 'exceptional items' is commonly used, but should not be confused with the term 'extraordinary items' (see para 5.50). Those companies that choose to disclose a category 'exceptional items' in their financial statements should ensure that the notes to the financial statements include a definition of this term, because the term 'exceptional item' is not defined within FRS 102. Similarly, where an entity uses any other term not defined in FRS 102 (for example, 'significant items' or 'unusual items'), a definition should be given in the notes to the financial statements or as a footnote to the statement of comprehensive income. Typically, companies include the definition of such terms in their principal accounting policies. The presentation and definition of these items should be applied consistently from year to year. Also, some regulators might take a restrictive view of the suitability of presentation and definition of terms such as 'exceptional' or 'unusual', and regulated companies will need to consider these constraints.

5.31 Entities sometimes show 'operating profit before exceptional items', 'exceptional items' and 'operating profit'. This might be acceptable, provided that (i) it does not clutter the statement of comprehensive income (or, if presented, the income statement) such that it dilutes clarity, and (ii) it does not undermine the expense analysis required, by excluding amounts that would otherwise be included. Headings such as 'underlying business performance' (or similar) should not normally be used to describe 'operating profit before exceptional items'; this is because these types of heading tend to imply that the exceptional item has not arisen from the entity's ordinary activities. Also, 'operating profit before exceptional items' should not receive more prominence than 'operating profit' by, say, being shown in bold print.

5.32 In an analysis of expenses by nature, care should be taken to ensure that each class of expenses contains all items related to that class. An exceptional restructuring cost might, for example, include redundancy payments (an employee benefit cost), inventory write-downs (changes in inventory) and impairments in property, plant and equipment. It would not normally be acceptable to show restructuring costs as a separate line item in an analysis of expenses by nature where there is an overlap with other line items. But it might sometimes be possible to present line items that do not create such an 'overlap', although this will depend on the nature of each of the costs. For example, payments made in a litigation settlement might be included as exceptional costs, if this cost did not form a component of any of the other categories.

5.33 When using a 'function of expense' format, exceptional items should be included within the function to which they relate. It will still be possible to show exceptional items separately on the face of the statement of comprehensive income (or, if presented, the income statement) by using a 'boxed presentation', under which the operating profit is analysed into 'operating profit before exceptional items' and 'exceptional items'. This form of presentation could also be used when a 'nature of expense' presentation is adopted. The objective of analysing the entity's expenses will need to be balanced against the objectives of achieving clarity and avoiding clutter in reporting.

Discontinued operations

5.34 A discontinued operation is a component of an entity that has been disposed of and which:

- represents a separate major line of business or geographical area of operations;

- is part of a single co-ordinated plan to dispose of a separate major line of business or geographical area of operations; or

- is a subsidiary acquired exclusively with a view to resale.

[FRS 102 Glossary of terms].

5.35 The word 'component' from the definition above is further defined as *"operations and cash flows that can be clearly distinguished, operationally and for financial reporting purposes, from the rest of the entity"*. [FRS 102 Glossary of terms]. This means that a component will have been a single cash-generating unit (CGU), or a collection of CGUs, while held for use in the business.

5.36 A discontinued operation must have been disposed of (that is, sold or closed) by the balance sheet date. Merely having started the process of closure is not sufficient. It should be noted that not all disposal groups will meet the criteria to be classified as discontinued operations.

5.37 Paragraph 5.7D of FRS 102 requires an entity to disclose, either on the face of the statement of comprehensive income (or income statement, if presented) or in the notes, an amount comprising the total of:

- the post-tax profit or loss of discontinued operations; and

- the post-tax gain or loss attributable to the impairment or on the disposal of the net assets constituting discontinued operations.

5.38 The standard also requires an entity to provide an analysis between continuing operations and discontinued operations of each of the line items on the face of the income statement, up to and including post-tax profit or loss for the period. [FRS 102 para 5.7D]. Items of other comprehensive income in the statement of comprehensive income need not be analysed between continuing and discontinued operations.

5.39 When an entity presents an operation as discontinued in a current period, it also presents that operation as discontinued in the comparative information; in other words, if the operation was continuing in the prior period financial statements, the prior period results are re-presented as discontinued in the comparatives for the current period financial statements. [FRS 102 para 5.7E].

5.40 FRS 102 includes an example showing the presentation of discontinued operations. This is reproduced below.

Statement of comprehensive income for the year ended 31 December 20X1

	Continuing operations 20X1 £	Discontinued operations 20X1 £	Total 20X1 £	Continuing operations 20X0 £ (as restated)	Discontinued operations 20X0 £ (as restated)	Total 20X0 £
Turnover	**4,200**	**1,232**	**5,432**	3,201	1,500	4,701
Cost of Sales	**(2,591)**	**(1,104)**	**(3,695)**	(2,281)	(1,430)	(3,711)
Gross profit	**1,609**	**128**	**1,737**	920	70	990
Administrative expenses	**(452)**	**(110)**	**(562)**	(418)	(120)	(538)
Other operating income	**212**	-	**212**	198	-	198
Profit on disposal of operations	-	**301**	**301**	-	-	-
Operating profit	**1,369**	**319**	**1,688**	700	(50)	650
Interest receivable and similar income	**14**	-	**14**	16	-	16
Interest payable and similar charges	**(208)**	-	**(208)**	(208)	-	(208)
Profit on ordinary activities before tax	**1,175**	**319**	**1,494**	508	(50)	458
Taxation	**(390)**	**(4)**	**(394)**	(261)	3	(258)
Profit on ordinary activities after taxation and profit for the financial year	**785**	**315**	**1,100**	247	(47)	200
Other comprehensive income						

			Total 20X1			Total 20X0
Actuarial losses on defined benefit pension plans			(108)			(68)
Deferred tax movement relating to actuarial losses			28			18
Total comprehensive income for the year			1,020			150

[FRS 102 Appendix to section 5].

Income from investments

5.41 Each of the four profit and loss account formats for individual companies contains the same four investment income captions:

- Income from shares in group undertakings.

- Income from participating interests.

- Income from other fixed asset investments.

- Other interest receivable and similar income.

5.42 The last two items referred to above (that is, income from other fixed asset investments and other interest) are required to be split between that derived from group undertakings and that derived from other sources. [SI 2008/410 1 Sch Profit and loss account formats note 15].

5.43 Dividends received and receivable from both subsidiary and fellow subsidiary companies will be included in 'income from shares in group undertakings'. In a group's consolidated financial statements, this line will appear only if dividends are received or receivable from subsidiaries that have not been consolidated. The accounting for dividend income is dealt with in chapter 23.

5.44 In an investing company's individual profit and loss account, 'Income from participating interests' will include, for example, income from the following undertakings in which the investing company holds 20% or more of the shares:

- Income from bodies corporate (including dividends received from associated undertakings).

- Share of profits from partnerships.

- Share of profits from unincorporated associations carrying on a trade or business, with or without a profit.

5.45 Chapter 14 explains the meaning of participating interests and associated undertakings; it also describes the accounting treatment of income from interests in associated undertakings in consolidated financial statements.

Interest payable and similar charges

5.46 'Interest payable and similar charges' appears as a separate item in all the profit and loss account formats. Apart from interest, the caption could include other finance costs such as:

- Accrued discounts in respect of zero coupon and deep discount bonds.

- Accrual of the premium payable on the redemption of debt.

- Dividends on preference shares that are classified as liabilities under section 22 of FRS 102.

5.47 Company law requires certain additional disclosures in respect of interest. Note 16 to the profit and loss account formats requires that interest payable to group undertakings must be disclosed separately. In addition, disclosure is required of the amount of the interest on (or any similar charges in respect of):

- Bank loans and overdrafts.

- Loans of any other kind made to the company.

[SI 2008/410 1 Sch 66(1)].

5.48 The requirement to give the above analyses does not apply to either interest or charges on loans from group undertakings. But it does apply to interest or charges on all other loans, whether or not these are made on the security of a debenture. [SI 2008/410 1 Sch 66(2)].

Ordinary activities and extraordinary activities

5.49 Ordinary activities are *"any activities which are undertaken by a reporting entity as part of its business and such related activities in which the reporting entity engages in furtherance of, incidental to, or arising from, these activities. Ordinary activities include the effects on the reporting entity of any event in the various environments in which it operates, including the political, regulatory, economic and geographical environments, irrespective of the frequency or unusual nature of the events"*. [FRS 102 para 5.10].

5.50 Extraordinary items are *"material items possessing a high degree of abnormality which arise from events or transactions that fall outside the ordinary activities of the reporting entity and which are not expected to recur. The additional line items required to be presented by paragraph 5.9A are not extraordinary items when they arise from the ordinary activities of the entity Extraordinary items do not include prior period items merely because they relate to a prior period"*. [FRS 102 para 5.10A]. As to paragraph 5.9A of the standard, see paragraph 5.27 above.

5.51 Extraordinary items do not arise in practice. The last sentence of the definition of 'ordinary activities' is all embracing; and so even the effects of events such as a war (political environment), a natural disaster (geographical environment), a devaluation (economic environment) or a fundamental change in the basis of taxation (regulatory environment) would be material items arising from ordinary activities rather than extraordinary items.

Consolidated accounts – profit and loss account items

5.52 Where the entity presents consolidated financial statements, the profit or loss items in the consolidated statement of comprehensive income (or separate consolidated income statement, if presented) should be presented in accordance with Schedule 6 to SI 2008/410 or Schedule 3 to SI 2008/1913. [FRS 102 paras 5.5, 5.7]. These regulations detail the items that should be added to the formats prescribed in Schedule 1 to SI 2008/410. [SI 2008/410 6 Sch 17(3), 20(3)]. The formats set out below include the requirements of Schedules 1 and 6 to SI 2008/410 (the additional requirements of Schedule 6 are shown in italics, and modifications to the numbering have also been made for illustrative purposes). Formats 3 and 4 are not set out, because they are rarely used and they replicate the information in formats 1 and 2.

Consolidated profit and loss account — Format 1

1   Turnover

2   Cost of sales

3   Gross profit or loss

4   Distribution costs

5   Administrative expenses

6 Other operating income

7 Income from shares in group undertakings

8 *Income from interests in associated undertakings*

9 *Income from other participating interests*

10 Income from other fixed asset investments

11 Other interest receivable and similar income

12 Amounts written off investments

13 Interest payable and similar charges

14 Tax on profit or loss on ordinary activities

15 Profit or loss on ordinary activities after taxation

16 Extraordinary income

17 Extraordinary charges

18 Extraordinary profit or loss

19 Tax on extraordinary profit or loss

20 Other taxes not shown under the above items

21 Profit or loss for the financial year

Consolidated profit and loss account — Format 2

1 Turnover

2 Change in stocks of finished goods and in work in progress

3 Own work capitalised

4 Other operating income

5 (a) Raw materials and consumables

   (b) Other external charges

6 Staff costs:

   (a) Wages and salaries

   (b) Social security costs

   (c) Other pension costs

7 (a) Depreciation and other amounts written off tangible and intangible fixed assets

   (b) Exceptional amounts written off current assets

8 Other operating charges

9 Income from shares in group undertakings

10 *Income from interests in associated undertakings*

11 *Income from other participating interests*

12 Income from other fixed asset investments

13 Other interest receivable and similar income

14 Amounts written off investments

15 Interest payable and similar charges

16 Tax on profit or loss on ordinary activities

17 Profit or loss on ordinary activities after taxation

18 Extraordinary income

19 Extraordinary charges

20 Extraordinary profit or loss

21 Tax on extraordinary profit or loss

22 Other taxes not shown under the above items

23 Profit or loss for the financial year

5.53 In addition, the profit and loss account formats should show, as a separate item and under an appropriate heading, the amount of any profit or loss on ordinary activities and the amount of any profit or loss on extraordinary activities that are attributable to shares in subsidiary undertakings included in the consolidation held by minority interests (known as 'non-controlling interests' in the standard). [SI 2008/410 6 Sch 17(3)]. Similarly, FRS 102 requires an entity to present (as allocations of profit or loss and total comprehensive income for the period) the amounts attributable to:

■ Non-controlling interest.

■ Owners of the parent.

[FRS 102 paras 5.6, 5.7A, 5.7B]

5.54 In the vast majority of cases, this disclosure meets the legal disclosure requirement. This is because extraordinary items (see para 5.50) will rarely, if ever, arise under FRS 102; and it is highly unlikely that any amount would fall to be disclosed under the heading 'Other taxes not shown under the above items'.

5.55 Under SI 2008/410, joint ventures ('jointly controlled entities' under FRS 102) can be dealt with by proportional consolidation; but this is not permitted under the standard. 'Associated undertakings' must be included in the consolidated financial statements under the equity method (see chapter 14). Entities in which the investor has a long-term investment and over which it has significant influence, and which are not subsidiaries or joint ventures included by proportional consolidation, are 'associated undertakings' under SI 2008/410. In short, associates and 'jointly controlled entities', as defined in FRS 102, are 'associated undertakings' under the law, and the share of their profits is presented as 'income from associated undertakings'.

5.56 As discussed in paragraph 5.26, 'operating profit' is not a required line item. The share of profits from associates is generally shown after operating profit (if presented); this recognises that the share of profits from associates (and 'jointly controlled entities') arises from what is essentially an investing activity, rather than part of the group's operating activities. But, where associates (and 'jointly controlled entities') are an integral vehicle for the conduct of the group's operations and its strategy, it might be more appropriate to include the share of profits from associates and joint ventures in arriving at operating profit (if presented). It would not be appropriate to include the share of associates (and 'jointly controlled entities') within 'revenue' (and so within 'gross profit'). The share of associates (and 'jointly controlled entities') does not represent a 'gross inflow of economic benefits' that is part of the definition of 'revenue' in FRS 102; rather, it is in the nature of a net gain.

Parent's profit and loss account

5.57 When a parent company publishes consolidated financial statements in accordance with the Companies Act 2006, it is not required to include its own statement of comprehensive income (single-statement approach) or income statement (two-statement approach) and related notes. [FRS 102 para A4.15]. This exemption is conditional on the following requirements:

- The notes to the parent company's individual balance sheet show the company's profit or loss for the financial year determined in accordance with the provisions of the Act. [CA06 Sec 408(1)(b)].

- The parent company's board of directors must approve the company's individual profit and loss account in accordance with the rules concerning approval of the company's financial statements. [CA06 Sec 408(3)].

- The notes to the financial statements disclose the fact that the parent company has taken advantage of this exemption. [CA06 Sec 408(4)].

5.58 Where the published consolidated financial statements do not include the company's profit and loss account, they need not include certain supplementary information when presented to the board for their approval. [CA06 Sec 408(2); SI 2008/410 Reg 3(2)]. The information that can be excluded is specified in section 411 of the Companies Act 2006 and in paragraphs 65 to 69 of Schedule 1 to SI 2008/410 and includes the following:

- Employee numbers and employee costs. [CA06 Sec 411].

- Interest and similar charges. [SI 2008/410 1 Sch 66].

- Detailed particulars concerning tax. [SI 2008/410 1 Sch 67].

- Disaggregated information concerning turnover. [SI 2008/410 1 Sch 68].

- Certain miscellaneous matters including:

  - The effect of including any preceding year items in the current year's profit and loss account.

  - Particulars of extraordinary income or extraordinary charges.

  - The effect of any exceptional items.

[SI 2008/410 1 Sch 69].

5.59 Where the parent's profit and loss account is not reproduced, suitable wording for a note to be included in the consolidated financial statements would be:

> **Example**
>
> As permitted by section 408(3) of the Companies Act 2006, the parent company's individual statement of comprehensive income has not been included in these financial statements. The parent company's profit for the financial year was £x (20XX: £y).

Other comprehensive income

5.60 The standard requires an entity to present items of other comprehensive income (that is, income and expenses not dealt with through profit or loss) on the face of its statement of comprehensive income, whether this statement is presented under either the single-statement or two-statement approach. The following should be presented:

- The components of other comprehensive income, classified by nature, and presented either:

  - net of related tax effects; or

  - before the related tax effects, with one amount shown for the aggregate amount of income tax relating to those components.

- The entity's share of the other comprehensive income of associates and 'jointly controlled entities' accounted for by the equity method (note that this amount does not need to be analysed by nature).

- Total comprehensive income.

[FRS 102 paras 5.5A, 5.7B].

5.61 Where an entity adopts the two-statement approach, the statement of comprehensive income should have profit or loss as its first line item. [FRS 102 para 5.7B]. The standard does not require the statement of comprehensive income to follow immediately after the income statement, but this will usually be the most appropriate presentation.

Transitional issues

5.62 Except as described in paragraphs 5.63 and 5.64, no special exemptions on the presentation of the statement of comprehensive income and the income statement are available to first-time adopters under section 35 of FRS 102. So, except as described in paragraphs 5.63 and 5.64, a first-time adopter must prepare its first FRS 102 financial statements as though the requirements of section 5 of FRS 102 had always applied.

5.63 FRS 102 requires separate disclosure to be given in the statement of comprehensive income (or income statement, if presented) in respect of discontinued operations. The definition of a discontinued operation in FRS 102 is similar to that in IFRS, but differs from that in old UK GAAP (FRS 3). But, on first-time adoption of FRS 102, a company should not retrospectively change the accounting that it followed under its previous financial reporting framework for discontinued operations. [FRS 102 para 35.9(d)]. So, no reclassification or remeasurement is recognised for discontinued operations previously accounted for under the previous financial reporting framework.

5.64 Paragraph 5.6 of FRS 102 requires profit or loss and total comprehensive income to be allocated between non-controlling interests and owners of the parent. This requirement is applied prospectively from the date of transition to the standard (or, from such earlier date as the standard is applied to restate business combinations). [FRS 102 para 35.9(e)]. See chapter 9.

5.65 Transitioning companies should have no difficulty presenting items of profit or loss and items of other comprehensive income. The requirements of section 5 of FRS 102 in respect of profit or loss items are mainly derived from the existing requirements in company law. Although section 5 deals with the presentation of items of 'other comprehensive income', a term not used in old UK GAAP, many entities will have an FRS 102 presentation of financial performance that is similar to that which would have applied under FRS 3 (profit and loss account and statement of total recognised gains and losses). This will be the case particularly for those entities that adopt the two-statement approach to the statement of comprehensive income and present items of other comprehensive income before tax (with total related tax presented separately).

5.66 Under paragraph 20 of FRS 3, some exceptional items are presented after operating profit; these are often known as 'super-exceptional items' or 'non-operating exceptional items'. These are:

■ Profits and losses on the sale or termination of an operation.

■ Costs of a fundamental reorganisation or restructuring that have a material effect on the nature and focus of the company's operations.

■ Profits or losses on the disposal of fixed assets.

Under FRS 102, although separate disclosure or presentation of material items is required (see para 5.27 onwards), if 'operating profit' is presented, it must include all items that are operating in nature. This means that the items that were presented after operating profit under old UK GAAP are presented before operating profit under FRS 102. Comparative amounts are restated accordingly.

Chapter 6

Statement of changes in equity and statement of income and retained earnings

Chapter 6

Statement of changes in equity and statement of income and retained earnings

Introduction

6.1   Equity is the residual interest in the assets of an entity after deducting all of its liabilities. [FRS 102 Glossary of terms]. The amount of the change in an entity's net assets in a reporting period is equivalent to the amount of the change in its equity; this change occurs through transactions with equity-holders (that is, owners) and through the entity's financial performance and, sometimes, through changes in accounting policy or correction of errors. This chapter deals with section 6 of FRS 102, which sets out how the changes in equity are reported.

6.2   An entity is required to present a statement of changes in equity unless the only changes in equity in both the current and prior periods arise from profit or loss, payment of dividends, corrections of prior period errors and changes in accounting policy. If this is so, the entity could present a statement of income and retained earnings instead of a statement of comprehensive income and a statement of changes in equity. [FRS 102 para 6.4]. In other words, the single statement of income and retained earnings could be presented if the entity has no items of other comprehensive income and no transactions with equity-holders other than dividends.

Statement of changes in equity

6.3   The statement of changes in equity includes the following information:

■   Total comprehensive income for the period, showing separately the total amounts attributable to the parent's owners and to non-controlling interests.

■   For each component of equity, the effects of retrospective application or retrospective restatement recognised in accordance with section 10 of the standard (see chapter 10).

■   For each component of equity, a reconciliation between the carrying amount at the beginning and the end of the period, separately disclosing changes resulting from:

(i)   profit or loss;

(ii)   other comprehensive income; and

(iii)   the amounts of investments by, and dividends and other distributions to, owners, showing separately issues of shares, treasury share transactions, dividends and other distributions to owners, and changes in ownership interests in subsidiaries that do not result in a loss of control.

[FRS 102 para 6.3].

6.4 For each component of equity, an analysis of other comprehensive income by item is presented either in the statement of changes in equity or in the notes. [FRS 102 para 6.3A].

6.5 So, the statement of changes in equity includes the following:

■ Share issues and redemptions.

■ Purchase and sale of treasury shares.

■ Equity component of convertible bonds issued.

■ Dividends on instruments classified as equity.

■ Credit entries reflecting the issue of equity instruments in connection with an equity-settled share-based payment arrangement (see chapter 26).

■ Transactions with non-controlling interests that do not result in a change of control (see chapter 9).

6.6 The presentation of the group's share of associates and joint ventures' changes in equity is dealt with in chapters 14 and 15.

6.7 Comparative information is required for all amounts reported in the financial statements, unless a standard permits or requires otherwise. There is no exemption from the requirement to give comparative information for the statement of changes in equity.

Statement of income and retained earnings

6.8 Where the only changes in equity in both the current and prior periods arise from profit or loss, dividends or prior period adjustments, an entity could present a statement of income and retained earnings instead of a statement of comprehensive income and statement of changes in equity. This is a simplification of the usual requirements for those entities that have no items of other comprehensive income and no transactions with owners other than the payment of dividends.

6.9 The statement of income and retained earnings presents the line items required in a separate income statement (see chapter 5) plus the following items:

■ Retained earnings at the beginning of the reporting period.

■ Dividends declared and paid or payable during the period.

- Restatements of retained earnings for corrections of prior period material errors.

- Restatements of retained earnings for changes in accounting policy.

- Retained earnings at the end of the reporting period.

[FRS 102 para 6.5].

6.10 The standard is not specific about the positioning of the above line items in the statement of income and retained earnings. The profit and loss account formats in the Companies Act regulations (see chapter 5) set out the line items that are required and the order in which they appear. The final line item required is 'profit for the financial year'; this is a measure of performance, whereas the additional line items set out in paragraph 6.9 are not. So, it is important that, for example, dividends paid or payable are presented outside the profit and loss account items (and not as a deduction) in arriving at profit for the financial year. Such dividends are not an expense, and the presentation should make this clear. The term 'dividends' in this context means dividends on equity instruments; it does not include dividends on shares that are classified as debt.

Transitional issues

6.11 No special exemptions on the presentation of the statement of changes in equity and statement of income and retained earnings are available to first-time adopters under section 35 of FRS 102. So, a first-time adopter must prepare its first FRS 102 financial statements as though the requirements of section 6 of FRS 102 had always applied.

6.12 Transitioning enities should have little difficulty in applying section 6 of the standard, because its requirements are no more onerous than those applying under old UK GAAP.

Chapter 7

Statement of cash flows

Chapter 7

Statement of cash flows

Introduction

7.1 The success, growth and survival of every reporting entity depend on its ability to generate or otherwise obtain cash. Reported profit is important to users of financial statements, but is merely one indicator of financial performance; what enables an entity to survive is the tangible resource of cash. Thus, owners look for dividends, suppliers and lenders expect payments and repayments, employees receive wages for their services, and the tax authorities are legally entitled to collect tax receipts due. So, a cash flow statement is an important part of corporate reporting.

7.2 A cash flow statement presents the cash effects of transactions with parties that are external to the reporting entity and the impact of those transactions on the entity's cash position. Only those transactions that involve a cash flow should be reported in the cash flow statement. [FRS 102 para 7.18]. For this purpose, cash flows are defined as *"inflows and outflows of cash and cash equivalents"*. [FRS 102 Glossary of terms].

Scope

7.3 Section 7 of FRS 102 requires all entities to prepare a cash flow statement, except:

- Mutual life assurance companies.

- Retirement benefit plans.

- Investment funds that meet all the following conditions:

  - substantially all of the fund's investments are highly liquid;

  - substantially all of the fund's investments are carried at market value; and

  - the fund provides a statement of changes in net assets.

[FRS 102 para 7.1A].

7.4 Also, a qualifying entity (that is, a member of a group that prepares publicly available consolidated financial statements which give a true and fair view) could take advantage of the exemption from publishing a cash flow statement set out in paragraph 1.12(b) of FRS 102 (see chapter 1).

Definition of cash and cash equivalents

7.5 A cash flow statement prepared in accordance with section 7 of FRS 102 includes not just cash but also cash equivalents. This represents an important difference from previous UK GAAP, which required a cash flow statement in a literal sense (see para 7.81).

7.6 *Cash is* defined as *"cash on hand and demand deposits"*. [FRS 102 Glossary of terms]. No definition is provided for demand deposits, but these are generally accepted to be deposits with financial institutions that are repayable on demand and available within 24 hours (or one working day) without penalty. So, demand deposits will include accounts where additional funds can be deposited at any time and funds withdrawn at any time without prior notice (for example, a bank current account).

7.7 Bank overdrafts are normally considered financing activities similar to borrowings. But, where bank overdrafts are repayable on demand and form an integral part of an entity's cash management, they should be included as a component of cash and cash equivalents. [FRS 102 para 7.2].

7.8 *Cash equivalents* are defined as:

"Short-term, highly liquid investments that are readily convertible to known amounts of cash and that are subject to an insignificant risk of change in value."

[FRS 102 para 7.2].

7.9 In order to meet the definition of cash equivalents, an investment will normally have to have a *'short maturity'*. Paragraph 7.2 of FRS 102 states that a short maturity period would be a period of three months or less from the acquisition date of the investment. The use of a short maturity period, when considering investments as cash equivalents, incorporates the fact that the investments should be so near to cash that there must be an insignificant risk of changes in value. Investments classified as cash equivalents are not restricted to investments with financial institutions, such as banks. Other investments, such as short-term gilts, certificates of deposit, certain money market instruments and short-term corporate bonds, can also be classified as cash equivalents, provided they are highly liquid and subject to insignificant risk of change in value.

7.10 In limited circumstances, deposits with a term of more than three months might be classified as cash equivalents. Judgement will be necessary to determine the appropriate classification. For example, term deposits for longer than three months that can be redeemed (subject to the interest income being forfeited) might be classified as cash equivalents if the deposit has no significant risk of a change in value as a result of an early withdrawal.

7.11 The three-month maturity period commences from the time when the investment is acquired. Any investment, such as a government bond or a certificate of deposit, purchased with a maturity period of more than three months without an early redemption option will not be a cash equivalent; this is because the maturity of these instruments exposes them to fluctuations in capital value. They will not become a cash equivalent when their remaining maturity period (measured from a subsequent reporting date) becomes three months or less, because the maturity period is measured from the date of acquisition.

7.12 The term 'readily convertible' implies that the investment is convertible into cash without an undue period of notice and without incurring a significant penalty on withdrawal. Monies deposited in a bank account for an unspecified period, but which can only be withdrawn by advance notice, should be evaluated carefully to determine whether they meet the definition of cash and cash equivalents. Factors to be considered should include whether there are other restrictions on the withdrawal, the period of advance notice, and the risk of significant change in value during that period.

7.13 A deposit having a short maturity period with no early redemption option might still be considered 'readily convertible' and be included as cash and cash equivalents if the other conditions are met. The facts of each situation, and how management intends to use the deposits, should be taken into account to determine the classification of the deposits in the cash flow statement.

7.14 Where the counterparty to any short-term investment experiences financial problems, there could be doubt over its ability to fulfil the requirements of the agreement. In such circumstances, the investment should not be classified as a cash equivalent; this is because there is a risk that the instrument will not be a highly liquid investment and, also, it would have significant risk of changes in value.

7.15 Transfers between those deposits or investments that qualify as cash and cash equivalents do not result in cash inflows and outflows; they are movements within the overall cash and cash equivalents balance. But all charges and credits on accounts or investments qualifying as cash and cash equivalents (such as bank interest, bank fees, deposits or withdrawals other than movements wholly within them) represent inflows and outflows to be reported in the cash flow statement.

7.16 Section 7 of FRS 102 only provides guidance on how an entity might define cash equivalents (and not a rigid rule relating to the nature and maturity of items treated as cash equivalents), so it would be appropriate for an entity to disclose its policy for determining the composition of cash equivalents. Like any other accounting policies, it should be applied consistently, and any changes should be regarded as a change in accounting policy that should be accounted for in accordance with section 10 of the standard.

Format of a cash flow statement

7.17 A cash flow statement prepared in accordance with section 7 of FRS 102 presents cash flows under three standard headings

Statement of cash flows

- Operating activities.

- Investing activities.

- Financing activities.

[FRS 102 para 7.3].

7.18 Also, although it is not a cash flow itself, the effect of exchange movements on cash and cash equivalents held or due in a foreign currency should also be presented on the face of the cash flow statement (separately from cash flows from operating, investing and financing activities) in order to reconcile cash and cash equivalents at the beginning and end of the period. [FRS 102 para 7.13].

7.19 The standard provides guidance for classifying cash flows under the three standard headings, and gives examples of cash flows that would be *expected* to be classified under each heading; but, in practice, an entity is required to exercise judgement in determining which cash flows go where. For example, dividends received by a venture capital entity are likely to be operating activities (because its business is to receive a return on investments), but a manufacturing entity would be likely to classify such dividends received under investing activities.

Gross or net cash flows

7.20 Major classes of receipts and payments should be reported gross in the cash flow statement, except to the extent that net presentation is permitted. [FRS 102 para 7.10].

7.21 Cash flows from operating activities are often presented on a net basis under the 'indirect method' described in paragraph 7.32 onwards. The following cash flows can also be reported on a net basis:

- Cash receipts and payments on behalf of customers when the cash flows reflect the activities of the customer rather than those of the entity (see para 7.22).

- Cash receipts and payments for items in which the turnover is quick, the amounts are large, and the maturities are short (see para 7.23).

[FRS 102 para 7.10A].

7.22 Examples of cash receipts and payments on behalf of customers include the following:

- The acceptance and repayment of demand deposits of a bank.

- Funds held for customers by an investment entity.

- Rents collected on behalf of, and paid over to, the owners of properties.

[FRS 102 para 7.10B].

7.23 Examples of cash receipts and payments for items in which the turnover is quick, the amounts are large, and the maturities are short include advances made for, and repayment of, the following:

- Principal amounts relating to credit card customers.

- The purchase and sale of investments.

- Other short-term borrowings (for example, those which have a maturity period of three months or less).

[FRS 102 para 7.10C].

7.24 Financial institutions can also report the following cash flows on a net basis:

- Cash receipts and payments for the acceptance and repayment of deposits with a fixed maturity date.

- The placement of deposits with, and withdrawal of deposits from, other financial institutions.

- Cash advances and loans made to customers and the repayment of those advances and loans.

[FRS 102 paras 7.10D, 34.33].

7.25 A financial institution that undertakes the business of effecting or carrying out insurance contracts (other than a mutual life assurance company that is scoped out of section 7 of the standard – see para 7.3 above) should include the cash flows of their long-term business only to the extent of cash transferred and available to meet the obligations of the entity or group as a whole. [FRS 102 para 7.10E].

Classification of cash flows by standard headings

Cash flow from operating activities

7.26 Operating activities are defined as *"the principal revenue-producing activities of the entity"*. [FRS 102 para 7.4]. So, cash flows from operating activities generally (but not always) result from transactions and other events and conditions that are shown in the income statement in arriving at profit or loss. The separate disclosure of operating cash flows allows the user of the financial statements to assess the extent to which the operating activities generate cash flows to maintain the operating capability of the entity and support the cash flows for financing and investing activities.

7.27 Despite the general presumption that components of profit or loss give rise to operating cash flows, some transactions giving rise to amounts included in profit or loss are not classified as operating cash flows. For example, the cash flow relating to a gain on the sale of a fixed asset will normally be reported under investing activities.

7.28 The following are examples of cash flows that are expected to be classified as operating activities:

- Receipts from the sale of goods and the rendering of services.

- Receipts from royalties, fees, commissions and other revenue.

- Payments to suppliers for goods and services.

- Payments to and on behalf of employees.

- Payments and refunds of income taxes (unless they can be specifically identified as financing or investing).

- Receipts and payments from investments, loans and other contracts held for dealing or trading purposes, which are similar to inventory acquired specifically for resale.

- Cash advances and loans made to other parties by financial institutions.

[FRS 102 para 7.4].

7.29 Operating cash flows can be reported using either the direct method (see para 7.30) or the indirect method (see para 7.32). [FRS 102 para 7.7].

Direct method

7.30 The direct method reports the major classes of *gross* operating cash receipts (for example, cash collected from customers) and gross operating cash payments (for example, cash paid to suppliers and employees). These gross operating cash flows are aggregated to arrive at the net operating cash flow of the entity. This presentation is consistent with that of investing and financing activities.

7.31 There are two ways in which gross operating cash receipts and payments can be derived under the direct method: they could be captured directly from a separate cash-based accounting system that records amounts paid or received in any transaction; or they could be determined indirectly by adjusting operating profit and loss account items for non-cash items, changes in working capital and other items that relate to investing and financing cash flows. [FRS 102 para 7.9]. For example, cash collected from customers could be derived indirectly by adjusting sales for the changes in amounts receivable from customers during the period. Similarly, cash paid to suppliers for goods used in manufacture or resale could be determined indirectly by adjusting cost of sales for changes in inventory and amounts due to suppliers during the period.

Indirect method

7.32 The indirect method is described as a method *"... whereby profit or loss is adjusted for the effects of non-cash transactions, any deferrals or accruals of past or* *future operating cash receipts or payments, and items of income or expense associated with investing or financing cash flows".* [FRS 102 para 7.7(a)].

7.33 Under the indirect method, net cash flows from operating activities must be the same as under the direct method, except that the figure is produced by adjusting the profit or loss to remove the effects of non-cash items (such as depreciation and provisions), changes in working capital (such as inventory, receivables and payables) and items that relate to investing and financing activities. [FRS 102 para 7.8].

7.34 Paragraph 7.7(a) of FRS 102 specifies that 'profit or loss' is the starting point for the reconciliation to net cash flow from operating activities. 'Profit or loss' is defined as *"the total of income less expenses, excluding the components of other comprehensive income"* (that is, profit after tax). [FRS 102 Glossary of terms]. The FRC's Financial Reporting Lab reported in November 2012 that *"most investors prefer the [reconciliation] to start from a sub-total on the income statement that represents operating income or loss".* But this would not appear to be consistent with the definition of profit or loss provided in the standard. Nevertheless, if management believes that another measure of profit or loss (for example, operating profit or loss) might be considered a more helpful starting point to the users of the financial statements, it would be possible to include a sub-total in the reconciliation.

7.35 In general, the reconciliation of profit or loss to net cash flows from operating activities will disclose movements in inventory, debtors and creditors related to operating activities, other non-cash items (for example, depreciation, provisions, gain or loss on sale of assets, share of profits of associates, charges relating to share-based payment) and other items, such as interest (see para 7.43) and taxation (see para 7.46), which are required to be shown separately. It might be necessary to analyse the movements in opening and closing debtors and creditors to eliminate those movements that relate to items reported in financing or investing activities. For example, an entity might purchase a fixed asset before the year end on credit. In this situation, the closing creditors balance would need to be adjusted to eliminate the amount owing for the fixed asset purchase before working out the financial position movements for operating creditors.

7.36 Section 7 of the standard does not specify where the reconciliation of profit or loss to net cash flow from operating activities should be presented. In our view, it could be presented either on the face of the cash flow statement or in a note.

Cash flow from investing activities

7.37 Investing activities are defined as "*the acquisition and disposal of long-term assets and other investments not included in cash equivalents".* [FRS 102 para 7.5]. Investing cash flows also include cash flows relating to the acquisition or disposal of equity interests in other entities (including obtaining or losing control of subsidiaries, and investments in or disposals of associates and joint ventures) or business units. The disclosure of cash flows from investing activities provides users with information on the extent of expenditure that has been incurred in order to generate the future cash flows and profits of the business.

7.38 The following are examples of cash flows expected to be classified as investing activities:

- Payments to acquire property, plant and equipment (including self-constructed property, plant and equipment), intangible assets and other long-term assets. These payments include those relating to capitalised development costs and self-constructed property, plant and equipment.

- Receipts from sales of property, plant and equipment, intangibles and other long-term assets.

- Payments to acquire equity or debt instruments of other entities and interests in joint ventures (other than payments for those instruments classified as cash equivalents or held for dealing or trading). See further paragraph 7.56 onwards.

- Receipts from sales of equity or debt instruments of other entities and interests in joint ventures (other than receipts for those instruments classified as cash equivalents or held for dealing or trading). See further paragraph 7.56 onwards.

- Advances and loans made to other parties (except those made by a financial institution). See paragraph 7.28.

- Receipts from the repayment of advances and loans made to other parties (except those received by a financial institution). See paragraph 7.28.

- Payments for futures, forwards, options and swaps, except when the contracts are held for dealing or trading, or the payments are classified as financing activities.

- Receipts from futures, forwards, options and swaps, except when the contracts are held for dealing or trading, or the receipts are classified as financing activities.

[FRS 102 para 7.5].

7.39 Paragraph 7.5 of FRS 102 goes on to clarify that, when a contract is accounted for as a hedge in accordance with section 12 of the standard, the contract's cash flows should be classified in the same manner as the cash flows of the item being hedged.

7.40 The amount paid in respect of fixed assets during the year might not be the same as the amount of additions shown in the fixed asset note. The difference could arise for a number of reasons. For example, fixed assets might be purchased on credit (in which case, the amounts for additions shown in the fixed asset note would need to be adjusted for the outstanding payables, to arrive at the cash paid). Also, the change in fixed asset creditors should be eliminated from the total change in creditors, to arrive at the movement in operating creditors; this figure is needed for the reconciliation of profit to net cash flow where the indirect method is used to report cash flows from operating activities. A further example arises where assets have been acquired under finance leases. Most entities do not show assets acquired under finance leases separately, but include them in the total additions figure in their fixed assets movements note. Assets acquired under finance leases do not involve any cash outlay at the inception of the lease, so the amount in respect of leased assets that is included in the figure for fixed assets additions needs to be eliminated so that the true cash outflow for fixed assets purchased can be reflected in the cash flow statement.

Cash flow from financing activities

7.41 Financing activities are defined as *"activities that result in changes in the size and composition of the contributed equity and borrowings of an entity"*. [FRS 102 para 7.6]. So, cash flows from financing activities generally comprise receipts or payments in relation to obtaining, servicing and repaying or redeeming debt and equity finance.

7.42 The following are examples of the cash flows expected to be classified as arising from financing activities:

- Proceeds from issuing shares or other equity instruments.

- Payments to owners to acquire or redeem the entity's shares.

- Proceeds from issuing debentures, loans, notes, bonds, mortgages and other short- or long-term borrowings.

- Repayments of amounts borrowed.

- Capital element of finance lease repayments.

[FRS 102 para 7.6].

Interest and dividend cash flows

7.43 The cash flows arising from dividends and interest receipts and payments should be presented separately in the cash flow statement under the activity appropriate to their nature. Classification should be on a consistent basis from period to period. [FRS 102 para 7.14].

7.44 Section 7 of the standard does not dictate how dividends and interest cash flows should be classified, but rather allows an entity to determine the classification appropriate to its business. An entity could classify interest paid (and interest and dividends received) as operating cash flows, because they are included in profit or loss. Similarly, an entity could classify dividends paid as operating cash flows, because they are paid out of operating cash flows. Or the entity could classify interest and dividends paid as financing cash flows, and interest and dividends received as investing cash flows; this is because they represent costs of obtaining financial resources or returns on investments respectively. [FRS 102 paras 7.15, 7.16].

7.45 Section 25 of the standard permits an entity to capitalise borrowing costs that are directly attributable to the acquisition, construction or production of a qualifying asset. Where an entity adopts such a policy, section 7 is silent as to the appropriate classification of this interest in the cash flow statement. As noted above, the section suggests that interest paid is either an operating or a financing cash flow. It does not specify whether it permits interest payments capitalised as part of the cost of an asset to be classified as an investing cash flow. But paragraph 7.5(a) of FRS 102 requires that cash payments to self-constructed property, plant and equipment are classified as investing activities. So, in our view, cash flows arising from interest paid that are capitalised as assets in the statement of financial position would be eligible for classification as cash flows from investing activities. But the amount classified as such should be presented separately (as described in para 7.43 above).

Taxation cash flows

7.46 Cash flows relating to income tax should be presented separately as operating cash flows, unless they can be specifically attributed to financing or investing activities. [FRS 102 para 7.17]. But it could be inappropriate and misleading to allocate tax cash flows between the three economic activities. A payment of income or corporation tax usually involves only one cash flow, that is arrived at by applying the rate of tax to the entity's total income. The total income is the result of aggregating taxable income arising from all sources, including taxable gains arising on the disposal of assets. The taxation rules under which taxable total income is calculated often do not easily lend themselves to subdivision between operating, investing and financing activities. Nevertheless, where taxation cash flows are allocated over more than one class of activity, the total amount of income tax paid should be disclosed. [FRS 102 para 7.17].

7.47 Section 7 of the standard does not provide any guidance on the treatment of sales taxes in the cash flow statement. Sales taxes are not a tax on income, so they are not covered by the previous paragraph. Two issues arise in relation to the treatment of sales tax in the cash flow statement: whether the cash flows should be reported gross or net of sales tax; and how the net amounts paid to, or repaid by, the tax authorities should be reported in the cash flow statement.

7.48 In our view, where sales tax is recoverable, cash flows should be presented net of tax. Where sales tax is irrecoverable (for example, where the entity operates in a territory where local law does not provide for the recovery of sales tax incurred by the entity), the cash flows should be shown gross of the irrecoverable tax.

7.49 The second issue can be resolved by taking a simple and pragmatic approach. The net movement on the balance of sales tax payable to, or receivable from, the tax authorities would be presented as cash flows from operating activities, unless it is more appropriate to allocate it to another heading. Where the direct method is used, customer payments received inclusive of sales tax should be shown gross, and any sales tax payments made should be presented separately.

7.50 Taxation cash flows (excluding those in respect of income tax and sales taxes) should be included in the cash flow statement under the same standard headings as the cash flow that gave rise to them. This presentation is consistent with the manner in which transactions are presented in the statements of comprehensive income and financial position.

Consolidated cash flow statements

7.51 A parent entity of a group that is required to prepare consolidated financial statements should prepare a consolidated cash flow statement reflecting the cash flows of the group entity. In preparing consolidated cash flow statements, adjustments should be made to eliminate intra-group cash flows (that is, only those cash receipts and payments that flow to and from the group as a whole should be included). Many important issues arise in preparing consolidated cash flow statements, and these are considered below.

Non-controlling interests

7.52 The treatment of a non-controlling interest in the consolidated cash flow statement should be consistent with the overall approach to non-controlling interests followed in preparing the group financial statements. Dividends paid to non-controlling shareholders will generally be classified as financing cash flows (but see para 7.43 above regarding dividend payments generally).

7.53 Changes in ownership interests in a subsidiary that do not result in a loss of control, such as the purchase or sale by a parent of a subsidiary's equity instruments, are accounted for as equity transactions (that is, as transactions with owners). So the resulting cash flows are classified in the same way as other transactions with owners (that is, as cash flows from financing activities).

Investments accounted for under the equity method

7.54 Where a group has investments in associates or joint ventures that are accounted for using the equity method, the cash flow statement should include only the cash flows between the group and those investees, and not the cash flows of those entities. This means that the following cash flows should be included:

- Cash flows from sales or purchases between the group and the associates or joint ventures.

- Cash flows from investments in, and dividends from, the associates or joint ventures.

7.55 Specifically, cash flows related to equity accounted entities should be classified in the following manner:

■ Dividends received from these entities should be classified under operating or investing activities in line with the group's policy for dividends received (see para 7.43 above).

■ Cash flows relating to acquisitions and disposals should be shown under investing activities.

Acquisitions and disposals of subsidiaries and other businesses

7.56 When a subsidiary undertaking (or other business unit) is acquired (that is, control is obtained) or disposed of (that is, control is lost) during a financial year, the aggregate cash flows relating to the consideration should be reported separately under investing activities in the cash flow statement. Although there is no specific requirement to present the cash flows from a major acquisition or disposal separately on the face of the cash flow statement, we consider that this would be in line with the spirit of the standard, because section 7 requires major classes of gross cash receipts and gross cash payments to be reported separately.

7.57 Section 7 of the standard does not specify how cash and cash equivalent balances transferred on acquisition or disposal should be treated. But, in our view, it would be appropriate to present the consideration described in the previous paragraph net of any cash and cash equivalent balances transferred as part of the acquisition or disposal.

7.58 Where the consideration for the acquisition has been discharged partly in *cash* and partly by the issue of *shares*, the cash flow statement would show only the cash element of the consideration paid. The shares that are issued as part of the consideration do not give rise to any cash flows, and so they should not be shown in the cash flow statement. Instead, they should be disclosed as non-cash transactions (see para 7.77).

Foreign currency

7.59 An entity could engage in foreign currency activities in the following ways:

■ It might enter directly into business transactions that are denominated in foreign currencies.

■ It might conduct its foreign operations through a subsidiary, associate, joint venture or branch whose operations are based or conducted in a country other than that of the investing entity (a 'foreign operation').

Individual entities

7.60 Where an individual entity has cash receipts or makes cash payments in a foreign currency, those receipts and payments should be translated into the entity's functional currency (that is, the currency of the primary economic environment in which the entity operates – see chapter 30) at the rate ruling at the date on which the cash is received or paid. An exchange rate that approximates to the actual rate (such as a weighted average exchange rate for the period) could be used instead. [FRS 102 para 7.11].

7.61 Exchange differences might arise because of a rate change between the transaction date (that is, the date at which the transaction is recorded) and the settlement date. Exchange differences also arise where a transaction remains unsettled (that is, it is not realised in cash and cash equivalents) at the reporting date and is required to be translated at that date.

Settled transactions

7.62 Where a transaction is *settled* at a different exchange rate from that used when the transaction was initially recorded, the exchange difference will be recognised in profit or loss in the period in which the settlement takes place. Where the direct method (see para 7.30 above) is used to present the cash flows from operating activities, the cash payment itself is presented, and so any exchange differences between recognition and settlement do not cause any complications. Where the indirect method is used (see para 7.32 above), a reconciliation is required between profit and operating cash flows. Any exchange gain or loss on a settled transaction that relates to operating activities is already included in arriving at profit or loss, so the exchange gain or loss does not need to be adjusted in reconciling profit to operating cash flows when the transaction is settled.

7.63 But, where a settled transaction does not relate to operating activities and the exchange gain or loss is included in the income statement, the exchange gain or loss should be removed from the reconciliation required under the indirect method; this is because it will, in effect, be included as part of the cash flows arising from the settlement disclosed under investing or financing activities. An example would be dividend income from a foreign investment shown under investing activities as dividends received. In this situation, the functional currency equivalent of foreign cash actually received would be shown under investing activities, and it would reflect any exchange gain or loss that arises at the time of receipt and reported in the income statement.

Unsettled transactions

7.64 Where a transaction remains *outstanding* at the reporting date, an exchange difference arises as a consequence of recording the foreign currency transaction at the rate ruling when the transaction was recorded (or when it was translated at a previous reporting date) and the subsequent translation to the rate ruling at the reporting date. This exchange difference will generally be included in the income statement. Normally, such exchange differences arise on monetary items (for example, foreign currency loans, debtors and creditors). In the context of an individual entity's operations, these exchange gains or losses will ultimately be reflected in cash flows. But the way in which they affect the cash flow statement will depend on the nature of the monetary assets or liabilities (that is, whether they relate to operating, investing or financing activities).

7.65　Where the direct method is used to present operating cash flows, the cash payment itself is reflected, so no complications should arise in preparing the cash flow statement. Where the indirect method is used, exchange differences that arise on translation of monetary items that form part of operating activities (such as debtors and creditors) will require no adjustment in the reconciliation of profit to net cash flow from operating activities, even though they do not involve any cash flows. This is because increases or decreases in the debtor or creditor balances will include the exchange differences on their translation at the reporting date, which would be offset against their equivalent exchange gain or loss included in profit for the year. The effect is that the net cash flow from operating activities will not be distorted by such translation differences.

7.66　So, as a general rule, movements in foreign currency trade receivables and payables (except where they relate to foreign subsidiaries) will include the impact of exchange differences reported in the income statement, and no separate adjustments for such exchange differences are necessary in the reconciliation. It should be noted, however, that some entities prefer to split the movement on the receivables/payables into cash, foreign exchange, acquisitions and other movements, including only the movement in cash in the reconciliation. In this case, the exchange gain or loss included in arriving at profit will not be offset by the total movement in receivables or payables, and so it must be adjusted in order for the reconciliation to balance.

7.67　Exchange differences on monetary items that form part of investing or financing activities, such as long-term loans, will normally be reported as part of the profit or loss for the financial year. They need to be eliminated in arriving at the net cash flows from operating activities when performing the reconciliation for the indirect method. This is because they are not operating activity items, so the actual movement on long-term monetary items that includes the relevant exchange difference is not reported in the reconciliation of profit to operating cash flow.

7.68　Where exchange differences arise on the translation of foreign currency cash and cash equivalent balances themselves, these are not cash flows, but they should be reported in the cash flow statement in order to reconcile opening and closing balances of cash and cash equivalents. [FRS 102 para 7.13].

Consolidated financial statements

7.69 Section 30 of FRS 102 requires each individual entity included in a group to determine its functional currency (that is, the currency of the primary economic environment in which the entity operates) and measure its results and financial position in that currency (see further chapter 30). Where a group conducts part of its business through a foreign operation (that is, where the operation's functional currency differs from the group's presentation currency), different considerations arise from those for individual transactions discussed above. This is because the cash flows of the foreign operation are considered as a whole rather than as a series of single transactions.

7.70 The method of translation for foreign operations under section 30 of the standard requires monetary and non-monetary assets and liabilities to be translated at the closing rate; it also requires income and expense items to be translated at the rate ruling at the date of the transaction or an average rate that approximates to the actual exchange rates (for example, an average rate for the period). Exchange differences arising on translation of foreign operations are recognised in other comprehensive income. The foreign subsidiary's cash flow statement should be translated (for the purpose of inclusion in the consolidated cash flow statement) using the exchange rate at the date of the actual cash flows or an exchange rate that approximates to the actual rate (such as a weighted average exchange rate for the period). [FRS 102 para 7.12].

7.71 It is possible (although, we believe, unusual) to use different weighted average rates for the translation of a foreign operation's cash flow statement and for its income statement. This would give rise to a reconciling item in the cash flow statement. For example, consider a foreign operation with annual subscriptions running from January to December. Cash is mainly received during January of each year, and revenue is recognised over the whole year. If there are large exchange rate movements over the course of the year, such that the exchange rate for January is significantly different from the average rate for the year, it might be appropriate to use different exchange rates for the translation of the income statement and for the cash flow statement.

7.72 All exchange differences relating to the translation of a foreign operation's opening net assets to the closing rate will have been recognised in other comprehensive income. As such, exchange differences have no cash flow effect; and so they will not be included in the consolidated cash flow statement. But, where the opening net assets include foreign currency cash and cash equivalents, the exchange difference arising on their translation at the closing rate for the current period will have been reflected in the closing balances. Such translation differences should be reported in the cash flow statement to determine the total movement in cash and cash equivalents in the period (see para 7.68 above).

7.73 The group translates a foreign operation's income statement at an average (or actual) rate, so a further translation difference (between the result translated at the average rate and the result translated at the closing rate) will be recognised in other comprehensive income. This difference will include the exchange rate effect of the movement in foreign currency cash and cash equivalents from the average rate to the closing rate. This exchange difference will be included (with the exchange differences arising on the translation of the opening foreign currency cash and cash equivalents, as stated in the preceding paragraph) in the cash flow statement.

7.74 The treatment of foreign currency exchange differences in the consolidated cash flow statement can be complex. In practice, a reporting entity presenting its consolidated financial statements in, say, sterling will find it simpler to require each of its foreign subsidiaries to prepare a cash flow statement (with supporting notes) in its functional currency. This cash flow statement can then be translated into sterling. The sterling equivalent of each subsidiary's cash flow statement can be consolidated with the reporting entity's cash flow statement, after eliminating intra-group items such as dividends and inter-group loans.

Disclosure

Components of cash and cash equivalents

7.75 An entity is required to present a reconciliation of the amounts shown in the cash flow statement to the equivalent items shown in the statement of financial position. In most situations, the reconciliation between opening and closing cash and cash equivalents is relatively straightforward, because the opening balance of cash and cash equivalents (together with the increase or decrease in cash and cash equivalents, as shown in the cash flow statement) will equate to the closing balance. Where totals for cash and cash equivalents are not readily identifiable, because they relate to different balance sheet amounts, sufficient detail should be shown to enable the movements to be understood. This is because cash and cash equivalents according to the cash flow statement are not necessarily the same as the single figure on the balance sheet. An entity is not required to present this reconciliation if the amount of cash and cash equivalents presented in the statement of cash flows is identical to the amount similarly described in the statement of financial position. [FRS 102 para 7.20].

7.76 Entities applying Part 1 General Rules and Formats of Schedule 2 to the Regulations should include only the following items as cash: cash and balances at central banks and loans and advances to banks repayable on demand. [FRS 102 para 7.20A].

Non-cash transactions

7.77 Many significant transactions do not result in cash flows. Examples include:

- Acquisition of assets by finance lease.

- It might conduct its foreign operations through a subsidiary, associate, joint venture or branch whose operations are based or conducted in a country other than that of the investing entity (a 'foreign operation').

- Conversions of debt to equity.

- Acquisition of an entity by means of a share issue.

- Share-based payments.

7.78 Transactions that do not require the use of cash or cash equivalents should not be reported in the cash flow statement. Instead, such non-cash transactions should be disclosed elsewhere in the financial statements in a way that provides all the relevant information about those transactions. [FRS 102 para 7.18].

Restricted cash

7.79 Where a significant amount of cash and cash equivalent balances are not available for use by the group, disclosure is required of the relevant amounts, with a commentary on their restriction. [FRS 102 para 7.21]. A typical example of disclosure is where a foreign subsidiary is prevented from remitting funds to its overseas parent because of local exchange control regulations. Other examples where disclosure might be relevant, depending on the regulatory environment, relate to cash balances in escrow, deposited with a regulator or held within an employee share ownership trust.

Comparative figures

7.80 Section 3 requires comparative figures to be given for all amounts reported in the current period's financial statements, unless a section permits or requires otherwise. [FRS 102 para 3.14]. So, comparative figures are required for all items reported in the cash flow statement.

Transitional issues

7.81 There are two main presentational differences between section 7 of FRS 102 and FRS 1. The first is that the cash flows reported under section 7 relate to movements in cash and cash equivalents, whereas FRS 1 requires reporting of the movement in cash, being cash in hand and deposits repayable on demand less overdrafts.

7.82 FRS 1 has a category labelled 'management of liquid resources'. Liquid resources are defined as *"current asset investments held as readily disposable stores of value. A readily disposable investment is one that: (a) is disposable by the reporting entity without curtailing or disrupting its business; and is either: (b)(i) readily convertible into known amounts of cash at or close to its carrying amount, or (b)(ii) traded in an active market"*. [FRS 1 para 2]. The definition is substantially the same as that of cash equivalents in FRS 102 (see para 7.8 above), and the amounts that form part of cash equivalents for section 7 of FRS 102 will generally be included in the category of 'liquid resources' in an FRS 1 cash flow statement. Under both standards, the short-term characteristic is generally taken to mean a maturity of three months or less from the date of acquisition of the instrument.

7.83 The other main difference between FRS 102 and FRS 1 is that section 7 of FRS 102 has three categories (operating, investing and financing activities) in its format, whereas FRS 1 has nine. FRS 102 (with its various options of presenting cash flows) is more flexible than FRS 1, and so there is likely to be diversity of presentation in practice.

7.84 One final key difference between FRS 102 and FRS 1 is in their scope. FRS 1 exempts entities that are 90% owned from presenting a cash flow statement, as long as the consolidated financial statements in which the subsidiary is included are publicly available. FRS 102 provides a broader exemption for 'qualifying entities', which does not impose a 90% ownership requirement (see further para 7.4 above).

Chapter 8

Notes to the financial statements

Chapter 8

Notes to the financial statements

Introduction

8.1 This chapter describes the requirements of section 8 of FRS 102 dealing with notes to the financial statements. It also deals with disclosure requirements contained in the law that are not replicated in FRS 102. Other sections of the standard contain other disclosure requirements that are normally dealt with in the notes; and these are set out in the relevant chapters.

8.2 FRS 102 describes the purpose of the notes as being to provide narrative descriptions or disaggregations of items presented in the primary statements and information about items that do not qualify for recognition in those statements. [FRS 102 para 8.1].

Structure of the notes

8.3 The notes to the financial statements should disclose the following:

■ The basis of preparation and accounting policies adopted in the preparation of the financial statements.

■ Information required by the standard that is not presented elsewhere in the financial statements.

■ Additional information that is not presented elsewhere in the financial statements but is relevant to their understanding.

[FRS 102 para 8.2].

8.4 These requirements overlap with legal disclosure requirements. Schedule 1 to SI 2008/410 requires companies to disclose considerable detail in the notes to their financial statements. The objects of the requirements are:

■ To supplement the information given in the financial statements in respect of any particular items that are shown in either the balance sheet or the profit and loss account.

■ To give details of anything else that is relevant, in the light of the information so given, to the assessment of the state of the company's affairs.

■ To explain any particular circumstances that affect items shown in the profit and loss account.

[SI 2008/410 1 Sch 46, 65].

8.5 The notes should, as far as practicable, be presented in a systematic manner. Each item in the financial statements should be cross-referenced to any related information in the notes. [FRS 102 para 8.3]. Typically, the notes are presented in the following order:

- Statement of compliance with FRS 102 (see chapter 3).

- A summary of significant accounting policies (see para 8.8).

- Information relating to line items presented on the face of the financial statements in the order of the items in the financial statements.

- Any other disclosures.

[FRS 102 para 8.4].

8.6 Schedule 1 to SI 2008/410 requires companies to state whether the financial statements have been prepared in accordance with applicable accounting standards. Also, if there are any material departures from these standards, the particulars and the reasons for the departure must be given. [SI 2008/410 1 Sch 45]. These requirements are dealt with in chapter 3.

8.7 Although the standard recognises that the notes to the financial statements will usually be presented in the order of the financial statement line items to which they relate, this is not a requirement. In determining the order of the information presented in the notes, management should aim to maximise the transparency and accessibility of the information.

Accounting policies

8.8 Entities should disclose, in a summary of significant accounting policies, the measurement basis used in preparing the financial statements and each accounting policy that is relevant to understanding the financial statements. [FRS 102 para 8.5]. This will be particularly important where no policy is prescribed or where alternative policies are allowed, so that users can make proper comparisons of the financial statements of different entities.

8.9 The notes to the financial statements should set out the accounting policies adopted by a company in determining the amounts to be included in the financial statements. [SI 2008/410 1 Sch 44]. In particular, this disclosure must include:

- The method of determining the provision both for depreciation and for diminution in the value of assets. [SI 2008/410 1 Sch 44].

- The method of translating foreign currency amounts into sterling. [SI 2008/410 1 Sch 70].

8.10 Where a company's financial statements have been drawn up under the alternative accounting rules in Schedule 1 to SI 2008/410, the accounting convention used should be stated in those financial statements. The company should also refer to the specific policy for each item that it has accounted for under the alternative rules. [SI 2008/410 1 Sch 34(2)].

8.11 Entities might disclose accounting policies related to the following:

- Revenue recognition.

- Consolidation principles.

- Business combinations.

- Application of the equity method of accounting for investments in associates and 'jointly controlled entities'.

- Share-based payments.

- Depreciation and amortisation of tangible and intangible assets.

- Capitalisation of borrowing costs and other expenditure.

- Construction contracts.

- Investment properties.

- Derivative financial instruments and hedging.

- Other financial instruments and investments.

- Impairment of assets.

- Leases.

- Inventories.

- Taxes, including deferred taxes.

- Provisions.

- Employee benefit costs.

- Functional currency and presentation currency.

- Foreign currency translation and hedging.

- Government grants.

In order to avoid disclosing immaterial information, entities should restrict their disclosure to *significant* accounting policies. Accounting policies related to immaterial items, or items that the entity does not have, should not be disclosed.

Judgements

8.12 An entity should disclose the judgements, apart from those involving estimations (see para 8.16), that management has made in the process of applying the accounting policies and that have the most significant effect on the amounts recognised in those financial statements. [FRS 102 para 8.6].

8.13 This disclosure requirement has the effect of requiring management to justify the view they have taken on some items. This is already done, to a limited extent, by other sections of the standard. For example, section 9 requires a parent to disclose (in its consolidated financial statements) the basis for concluding that it controls an investee, even though it does not own (directly or indirectly through subsidiaries) more than half of the voting power. [FRS 102 para 9.23].

8.14 Similarly, disclosure might be relevant in respect of lease arrangements. A lease is either an operating lease (where the leased asset and lease liability are off-balance sheet) or a finance lease (where both the leased asset and lease liability are shown on the balance sheet). The judgement as to which category applies to a specific lease depends on management's assessment of whether the risks and rewards of ownership have been transferred to the lessee. In some cases, the required classification will be clear, and no additional disclosure will be required under section 8. But, in some cases, the classification will not be so obvious. Operating leases are not always fundamentally different from finance leases; the change in one term of a lease could transfer it from one classification to the other. Indeed, lease arrangements are sometimes constructed so that they marginally meet the definition of a particular type of lease. Paragraph 8.6 of FRS 102 requires disclosure of the judgements made in such cases, thereby making the accounting more transparent. In effect, section 8 of the standard fills a gap by placing a general obligation on management to disclose the judgements made where there are no specific requirements in other standards.

8.15 There is also a legal requirement to disclose off-balance sheet arrangements (see chapter 4 for more details).

Key sources of estimation uncertainty

8.16 Information about the key assumptions concerning the future, and other key sources of estimation uncertainty at the reporting date, that have a significant risk of resulting in a material adjustment to the carrying amounts of assets and liabilities within the next financial year should be disclosed. [FRS 102 para 8.7].

8.17 In respect of the assets and liabilities referred to in the previous paragraph, an entity should disclose:

■ their nature; and

■ their carrying amount as at the end of the reporting period.

[FRS 102 para 8.7].

8.18 The nature and extent of the information provided will vary according to the nature of the assumption and other circumstances; but the overriding consideration is that the information should be provided in a way that helps users of the financial statements to understand the judgements made by management where there is estimation uncertainty. The following are examples of the types of disclosure that might be made:

- Nature of the assumption or other estimation uncertainty.

- Sensitivity of carrying amounts to the methods, assumptions and estimates underlying their calculation, including the reasons for the sensitivity.

- Expected resolution of an uncertainty and the range of possible outcomes within the next financial year in respect of the carrying amounts of the assets and liabilities affected.

- Explanation of changes made to past assumptions concerning those assets and liabilities, if the uncertainty remains unresolved.

8.19   The estimation uncertainty disclosures deal with situations where the entity has incomplete or imperfect information, often relating to the future. On the other hand, an entity might have complete information but still have to exercise judgement in applying accounting policies. For example, an entity might have complete knowledge of its ownership and voting rights in another entity but, in complex situations, it will still have to exercise judgement to determine whether it has control of that entity.

8.20   Disclosure of estimation uncertainty is only required where there is a significant risk of material adjustment to the carrying amount of assets and liabilities within the next financial year. It might be that management makes estimates in respect of material amounts in the financial statements, but this does not necessarily mean that there is a significant risk of material adjustment. Material adjustments are most likely to arise in difficult, subjective or complex judgements. As the number of variables and assumptions increases, so the judgements become more complicated and the potential for future material adjustment increases accordingly.

8.21   The standard restricts the required disclosures to those that have a significant risk of material adjustment *within the next financial year*. A longer period than the next financial year might obscure the most relevant information with other disclosures. The longer the future period to which the disclosures relate, the greater the number of items that would qualify for disclosure and the less specific the disclosures that could be made about particular assets and liabilities. But the assessment of the carrying amount of assets and liabilities is not based solely on expectations for the following financial year, but on the full amount of time in which the asset will be recovered or the liability settled. So, a material adjustment to the carrying amount of an asset or liability could occur in the following financial year as a result of a reappraisal in that period of the recoverability of an asset or settlement of a liability over a much longer period. As a result, entities will need to take care that they do not narrow their disclosures excessively.

Staff costs and numbers

Employee costs

8.22 Disclosure is required in the financial statements of the costs that a company incurs in respect of the persons it employs under contracts of service. [CA06 Sec 411]. A contract *of service* (or 'employment contract') is an agreement under which the employer agrees to employ the employee for a wage or a salary in return for the employee's labour. This agreement must be made in writing. Self-employed persons are not employed by the company, but merely have contracts to perform specific services for that company. The costs of self-employed people should normally be excluded from staff costs, because their contracts will be contracts *for services*. Examples of such persons are consultants and contractors. Their costs should normally be included under 'other external charges' in Formats 2 and 4, and under an appropriate functional expense heading in Formats 1 and 3.

8.23 The item 'staff costs' does not appear in the profit and loss account Formats 1 and 3. This is because expenses are classified in these formats by function, rather than by type. But, where a company prepares its profit and loss account in either Format 1 or 3, it has to disclose (in the notes to the profit and loss account) the equivalent information to that given when Formats 2 and 4 are used.

8.24 In summary, the legal requirement in section 411 of the Companies Act 2006 is that either the profit and loss account or the notes should disclose, in aggregate, each of the following amounts:

- The wages and salaries that were paid to employees, or are payable to them, in respect of the financial year in question.

- Social security costs that the company has incurred on behalf of its employees. For this purpose, social security costs are any contributions that the company makes to any social security or pension scheme, or fund or arrangement that the State runs. These costs will include the employer's national insurance contributions.

- Other pension costs that the company has incurred on behalf of employees. For this purpose, pension costs include:

  - Any costs incurred by the company in respect of any non-State occupational pension scheme that is established to provide pensions for employees or past employees.

  - Any sums that the company has set aside for the future payment of pensions directly to current or former employees.

  - Any amounts that the company has paid in respect of pensions, without those amounts having first been so set aside.

So, pension costs will include the cost in respect of the company's participation in any pension scheme other than the State scheme. [CA06 Sec 411; SI 2008/410 10 Sch 14].

8.25 Wages and salaries should be determined by reference to the payments that the company makes, or the costs that it incurs, in respect of all persons whom it employs. [SI 2008/410 10 Sch 14(3)].

Average number of employees

8.26 In addition to requiring that the notes to the profit and loss account should disclose employee costs, the legislation requires that those notes should include information in respect of the number of employees.

8.27 The two disclosures that the notes must contain, in connection with the number of employees, are:

- The average number of employees in the financial year. The number should be calculated by:

    - ascertaining the number of persons employed under contract of service, whether full-time or part-time, for each month in the year;

    - adding together all the monthly numbers; and

    - dividing the resulting total by the number of months in the financial year.

    The average number of employees includes persons who work wholly or mainly overseas, as well as persons who work in the UK.

- The average number of employees by category. This number should be calculated by applying the same method of calculation as outlined above to each category of employees. For this purpose, the categories of persons employed should be such categories as the directors select, having regard to the way in which the company's activities are organised.

[CA06 Sec 411].

8.28 Because the guidance on how to select categories is rather vague, company directors have chosen a variety of different categories. Methods have included splitting: between part-time employees and full-time employees; between hourly paid, weekly paid and salaried staff; between production, sales and administration staff; and between staff employed in different geographical areas.

8.29 There is no exemption from disclosure where, for example, a company is a wholly owned subsidiary.

Notes to the financial statements

Directors

8.30   Directors who have a contract *of service* (that is, an employment contract) with the company are regarded as employees. So, their salaries, social security costs and other pension costs must be included in the required analysis under staff costs, even if a note is included stating that directors' emoluments are shown elsewhere. Directors' emoluments should also be disclosed separately under Schedule 5 to SI 2008/410. In that disclosure, their emoluments will exclude those social security costs that the company bears, because such amounts are neither paid to the director nor paid in respect of a pension scheme.

8.31   In contrast to payments under a contract *of service* (where the director is employed), amounts paid to directors under contracts *for services* (equivalent to the director being self-employed) should not be disclosed under staff costs. But, under Schedule 5 to SI 2008/410, they should be disclosed as directors' emoluments in the notes to the financial statements. Whether a director's contract with the company is a contract *of service* or a contract *for services* is a question of fact in each circumstance. Usually, executive directors will have contracts *of service*, but non-executive directors will have contracts *for services*. Contracts *for services* might include, for example, consultancy arrangements.

8.32   Directors' remuneration is dealt with further in chapter 5 of the Manual of Accounting – Narrative Reporting. Section 413 of the 2006 Act also sets out disclosure requirements for specified transactions and other arrangements involving directors; these are dealt with in the Manual of Accounting – Other Statutory Requirements.

Disclosures by groups

8.33   Where a parent company prepares group financial statements, the disclosure of staff costs and numbers is required to be presented for the consolidated group.

8.34   Where a parent company prepares group financial statements, it is not required to present particulars of employee numbers and costs for the company. This is the case whether or not the parent company takes the exemption from presenting its own profit and loss account. [CA06 Sec 408].

Practical problems relating to employee costs

8.35   In practice, deciding on the employees to include in staff costs and identifying the average number of employees might cause problems. One of the most common problems is where employees clearly work for one company, but their contracts of service are with another company (for example, the holding company). Further complications arise when that other company pays the wages and salaries of these employees. A strict interpretation of section 411 of the Companies Act 2006 could lead to the disclosure of misleading information in the financial statements. So, as well as giving the statutory disclosures, a company might need to include additional information so that its financial statements give a true and fair view.

8.36 Some of the more common problems that arise in this respect are considered in the examples that follow.

Example 1 – Contracts of service with another group company

Employees work full time for, and are paid by, a subsidiary company, but their contracts of service are with the parent company.

It would be misleading if no staff costs or numbers were disclosed in the subsidiary company's financial statements. So, the wages and salaries paid by the subsidiary company to those employees should be disclosed as 'staff costs' in its financial statements; and those employees should be included in the calculation of the average number of staff employed.

The notes to the subsidiary company's financial statements should explain that those staff have contracts of service with another group company; and they should also explain why their remuneration and average number are disclosed in the financial statements.

The parent company's consolidated financial statements will generally not be affected (unless the subsidiary is not included in the consolidated financial statements); this is because they will show the average number of employees and staff costs of the group as a whole, as well as those of the parent company separately. So, no explanatory note should be necessary in the parent company's financial statements.

(If the contracts of service are with a fellow subsidiary company, that fellow subsidiary company's financial statements should include those employees in the calculation of staff costs and average number of employees; and they should explain that some employees – who have service contracts with the company – work for and are paid for wholly by a fellow subsidiary company.)

Example 2 – Subsidiary company incurs management charge

Employees work full time for the subsidiary company, but they are not paid by the subsidiary company and they do not have service contracts with it. But the subsidiary company bears a management charge for their services from the company that pays the employees, and it can ascertain the proportion of the management charge that relates to staff costs.

Again, in this situation it could be misleading if the subsidiary company's financial statements disclosed no information about staff costs or numbers. So the proportion of the management charge that relates to staff costs should be disclosed in the subsidiary company's financial statements as 'staff costs'. The employees concerned should be included in the calculation of the average number of employees. The notes to the financial statements should explain that the employees do not have contracts of service with the company, and they should also explain why their costs and average number are disclosed in the financial statements.

(If the contracts of service are with, and the employees are paid by, a fellow subsidiary company, that fellow subsidiary's financial statements should disclose the staff costs and average number of employees in respect of all its employees, and they should give details regarding the staff costs that are recharged to the fellow subsidiary.)

Example 3 – Subsidiary company incurs non-specific management charge

The facts are the same as in example 2, except that the subsidiary company is unable to break down the management charge and ascertain the part of it that relates to staff costs.

The notes to the subsidiary company's financial statements should explain that the employees' contracts of service are with the parent company and that their remuneration is included in the parent company's financial statements. The notes should also explain that the management charge that the parent company makes includes the cost of these employees, but that it is impossible to ascertain separately the element of the management charge that relates to staff costs.

(If the employees' contracts of service are with a fellow subsidiary, rather than with the parent company, and that fellow subsidiary also pays the employees, the fellow subsidiary's financial statements should disclose the employees' remuneration in its staff costs and should also include the employees in the calculation of average number of employees. The notes should explain that these employees work for a fellow subsidiary company and that the company recharges the cost of their employment to that fellow subsidiary as part of a management charge.)

Example 4 – Subsidiary company does not incur management charge

The facts are the same as in example 2, except that no management charge is made for the employees' services. This will often apply where staff work, either full-time or part-time, for small companies.

In this situation, the notes to the subsidiary company's financial statements should explain that the company is not charged for the services provided by the employees who work for it. If appropriate, the notes should also indicate that the cost of these employees and their average number are included in the parent company's consolidated financial statements.

(Once again, if it is a fellow subsidiary that employs and pays the employees, its financial statements should include the cost of these employees in its staff costs and should include these employees in the average number of employees. If appropriate, the notes to the financial statements should explain that these employees work for a fellow subsidiary company, but that no management charge is made for their services to that company.)

Auditors' remuneration

8.37 The Companies Act 2006 requires separate disclosure of the amounts of remuneration receivable by a company's auditors, in their capacity as auditors and in respect of services other than audit. The legal requirements are set out in SI 2008/489, 'The Companies (Disclosure of Auditor Remuneration and Liability

Limitation Agreements) Regulations 2008'. These are dealt with in the Manual of Accounting – Other Statutory Requirements.

Transitional issues

8.38 No special exemptions in respect of the requirements of section 8 are available to first-time adopters under section 35 of FRS 102. So, a first-time adopter must prepare its first FRS 102 financial statements as though the requirements of section 8 of FRS 102 had always applied.

8.39 The requirement to disclose information about judgements in applying accounting policies and about key sources of estimation uncertainty will be a new disclosure for transitioning entities . Where relevant to an understanding of the current period financial statements, an entity should disclose comparative narrative information. [FRS 102 para 3.14]. This might be the case where the judgements and estimates have changed since the previous balance sheet date. As discussed in chapter 32, comparative amounts are presented on the basis of the information available when the previous financial statements were approved.

Chapter 9

Consolidated and separate financial statements

Chapter 9

Consolidated and separate financial statements

Introduction

9.1 This chapter refers to the requirements of section 9 of FRS 102. FRS 102 contains references to the Companies Act 2006.

Scope of provisions of the Act and section 9 of FRS 102

9.2 The Companies Act 2006 requires 'parent companies' (subject to specified exemptions) to prepare consolidated financial statements, and it sets out the form that those financial statements should take. [CA06 Secs 399, 403].

9.3 The provisions of section 9 of FRS 102 go further and apply to 'all parents', not just 'parent companies'. Subject to specified exemptions, 'all parents' that present financial statements are required to prepare and present consolidated financial statements (see further para 9.10 below). [FRS 102 para 9.1]. Section 9 of the standard directs a parent that qualifies for one of the exemptions from the requirement to prepare consolidated financial statements, but prepares individual financial statements, to include some additional disclosure (see para 9.11 below).

9.4 Section 9 of FRS 102 also deals with the individual financial statements of a parent (see para 9.172 below) and separate financial statements (see para 9.173 below).

9.5 Although section 9 of the standard does not conflict with the Act, there are circumstances where the standard is more restrictive than the Act; for example, section 9 requires some subsidiaries to be excluded from consolidation, whereas the Act permits rather than requires exclusion (see further para 9.11 below). Furthermore, the standard states that:

> "...Parents that do not report under the Act should comply with the requirements of this section, and of the Act where referred to in this section, except to the extent that these requirements are not permitted by any statutory framework under which such undertakings report..."

[FRS 102 para 9.1].

9.6 By referring to sections of the Act and applying them to parents that are not subject to the Act, section 9 of the standard achieves a single set of rules that apply to parents preparing consolidated financial statements, whether or not they are companies.

Concept of the 'group'

9.7 The 'group' is defined to mean "*a parent and all its subsidiaries*". [FRS 102 Glossary of terms]. The concept of a 'group' under FRS 102 is based on the economic entity model. The economic entity model considers the group as a single entity. So, any entities that are controlled by the parent would be consolidated. Where the parent holds less than 100% of the ownership interests, the non-controlling interests' share of assets and liabilities is recognised as part of shareholders' funds, thereby emphasising the control that the parent and its shareholders have over a subsidiary.

Accounting for investments

9.8 Under FRS 102, the way in which an entity accounts in its consolidated financial statements for an investment in another entity depends on the control or influence that the entity has over the investee. These different situations are summarised below:

- Where the investing entity does not exercise significant influence or control over the other entity (normally holdings of below 20%), its investment is accounted for under the guidance in sections 11 and 12 of the standard (see further chapters 11 and 12).

- Where the investing entity has significant influence over another entity (presumed for holdings of over 20% but less than 50%), or the investing entity has joint control over another entity, it is accounted for as an associate or joint venture respectively. If the investment in an associate or joint venture is held as part of an investment portfolio, the investment is measured at fair value, with changes in fair value recognised in profit or loss (see further chapters 14 and 15).

- Where the investing entity has the power to control the other entity (normally holdings of more than 50%), its investment is consolidated in full as a subsidiary, and any non-controlling interests are recognised. Determining whether the investing entity has control is discussed further at paragraph 9.38 below onwards.

Form of consolidated financial statements

9.9 A parent is required to prepare consolidated financial statements, unless it is exempt from preparing such financial statements; consolidated financial statements should present financial information about the group as a single economic entity; and the consolidation process is described as the parent and its subsidiaries being combined on a line-by-line basis by adding together like items of assets, liabilities, equity, income and expenses. [FRS 102 para 9.13].

9.10 Consolidated financial statements should include:

- A consolidated statement of financial position dealing with the parent and its subsidiaries.

- There is a choice between including:

  - a consolidated statement of comprehensive income. The statement of comprehensive income under this approach deals with both the profit or loss of the parent and its subsidiaries and changes in equity other than those arising from transactions with equity shareholders (including the non-controlling interest); and

  - a consolidated income statement and a separate consolidated statement of comprehensive income. The consolidated income statement deals with the profit or loss of the parent and its subsidiaries. The statement of comprehensive income deals with changes in equity other than those arising from transactions with equity shareholders (including the non-controlling interest).

- A consolidated statement of changes in equity, showing all changes in equity, identifying separately the amounts attributable to equity shareholders and to non-controlling interests.

- A consolidated statement of cash flows dealing with the parent and its subsidiaries.

- Notes to the consolidated financial statements dealing with accounting policies and additional disclosure requirements.

[FRS 102 para 3.17].

Exemption from preparing consolidated financial statements

9.11   There are four broad situations where a parent could be exempt from the general requirement to prepare consolidated financial statements:

- Parents of small groups (see para 9.12 below). [FRS 102 para 9.3(e)].

- Some parents that are also subsidiaries (that is, intermediate parents – see para 9.13 below). [FRS 102 para 9.3(a)–(d)].

- Parents, all of whose subsidiaries are permitted or required to be excluded from consolidation (see para 9.15 below). [FRS 102 para 9.3(f)].

- Parents not reporting under the Act, if the relevant statutory framework does not require the preparation of consolidated financial statements. [FRS 102 para 9.3(g)].

Small groups

9.12   Under the Companies Act 2006 a parent company under the small companies regime is not required to prepare consolidated financial statements. Companies that are subject to the small companies regime are those that qualify as small in size and are not excluded from the regime. [CA06 Secs 398, 382–384]. For further information please refer to the chapter on small and medium-sized companies on PwC's Inform.

Intermediate parent exemption

9.13 An intermediate holding entity is not required to prepare consolidated financial statements where either of two potential exemptions applies. These are found in sections 400 and 401 of the Companies Act 2006. The two exemptions differ because their requirements vary depending on the group structure. The exemption under section 400 of the Act is only available if the immediate parent is established under the law of an EEA state. The section 401 exemption is wider and is available to any entity which has a non-EEA parent (not necessarily immediate parent). So, the section 401 exemption is potentially available to any subsidiary included in the consolidated financial statements of a larger group, irrespective of the parent's jurisdiction.

9.14 Depending on the group structure, it might be that a particular intermediate parent entity can look to one or both of these sections for its potential exemption. The following flow chart summarises this principle and highlights which exemption might be available in the circumstances in question.

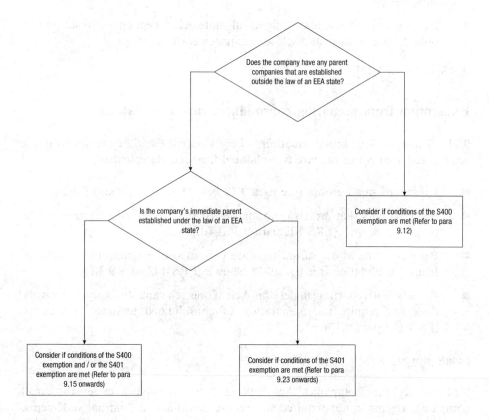

Immediate parent is an EEA entity exemption

9.15 An intermediate holding entity is not required to prepare consolidated financial statements where it is wholly owned by its immediate parent undertaking, and this immediate parent entity is established under the law of an EEA state. [CA06 Sec 400(1)(a)]. But a number of conditions apply before the exemption can be taken, and these are summarised in paragraph 9.21 below. The conditions stated in section 400 of the Act do not need to be satisfied at the intermediate holding entity's financial year end date; they can be satisfied during the period after the intermediate holding entity's year end date and before the filing date of its immediate parent's consolidated financial statements. The consolidated financial statements must include the intermediate holding entity and all of its subsidiaries, and all of the conditions must be met in order to obtain the exemption.

9.16 In addition to wholly owned subsidiaries, this exemption extends to the situation where the immediate parent holds more than 50% of the shares by number in the intermediate holding entity, and no notice has been served on the entity to prepare consolidated financial statements. Such notice must be made by either of the following:

■ Shareholders holding in aggregate more than half of the remaining shares in the entity.

■ Shareholders holding in aggregate 5% of the total shares in the entity.

The immediate parent entity must be established under the law of an EEA state (as with para 9.13 above).

[CA06 Sec 400(1)(b)].

9.17 The European Economic Area (EEA) encompasses the member states of the EC and the EFTA countries of Iceland, Liechtenstein and Norway. The member states of the EC are Austria, Belgium, Bulgaria, Cyprus, Czech Republic, Denmark, Estonia, Finland, France, Germany, Greece, Hungary, Republic of Ireland, Italy, Latvia, Lithuania, Luxembourg, Malta, Netherlands, Poland, Portugal, Romania, Slovakia, Slovenia, Spain, Sweden, and United Kingdom.

9.18 The notice must be served within six months of the end of the previous financial period (that is, normally within the first six months of the financial year for which the consolidated financial statements are being prepared). [CA06 Sec 400(1)]. So the onus is clearly on the minority shareholders to serve such notice if they require consolidated financial statements to be prepared for a sub-group.

9.19 The scope of the relevant sections of the Act outlined above is extended to apply to all parents, so reference to 'company' or 'entity' should be treated as applying to any undertaking, where appropriate. [FRS 102 para 9.3].

9.20 For the purposes of determining whether the entity is wholly owned or whether the parent holds more than 50% of the entity's shares, the rules below apply:

- Shares held by directors to comply with their share qualification requirements should be disregarded when determining whether an entity is wholly owned (see para 9.15 above). [CA06 Sec 400(5)].

- In determining whether the parent holds more than 50% of the shares of the entity (see para 9.16 above), shares held by a parent's wholly owned subsidiary should be attributed to the parent undertaking. Shares held on behalf of the parent, or by or on behalf of a wholly owned subsidiary, should also be attributed to the parent undertaking. [CA06 Sec 400(3)].

9.21 Both the exemptions outlined in paragraphs 9.15 and 9.16 above only apply, however, where the following conditions have been satisfied:

- The entity is 'included in' the consolidated financial statements of a larger group drawn up to the same date (or an earlier date in the same financial year – see para 9.30 below) by a parent undertaking established under the law of an EEA state. [CA06 Sec 400(2)(a)]. This parent does not have to be the EEA immediate parent referred to in paragraph 9.15 above; it could be an EEA parent further up the chain. This parent is referred to here as the 'reporting parent'. 'Included in', for this purpose, means by way of full consolidation; equity accounting or proportional consolidation is not sufficient.

- The reporting parent's consolidated financial statements and annual report must be drawn up and audited in accordance the law of the EEA state under which it is established, complying either:

  - with the provisions of the EC 7th Directive (as modified by the provisions of the Bank Accounts Directive or the Insurance Accounts Directive, where applicable); or

  - with IFRS.

[CA06 Sec 400(2)(b)].

- It must be noted in the entity's individual financial statements that it is exempt from preparing and delivering to the Registrar of Companies consolidated financial statements. [CA06 Sec 400(2)(c)].

- The reporting parent's name must be noted in the entity's individual financial statements, stating:

  - The reporting parent's country of incorporation, if it is incorporated outside Great Britain.

  - The address of the reporting parent's principal place of business, where it is unincorporated.

[CA06 Sec 400(2)(d)].

- The entity must deliver to the Registrar of Companies, within the period allowed for delivering its individual financial statements, a copy of the reporting parent's consolidated financial statements and annual report, together with the audit report on them. [CA06 Sec 400(2)(e)].

- Where any of the documents delivered to the Registrar of Companies in accordance with the previous requirement is not in English (or Welsh for an entity registered in Wales), a copy of a translation must be annexed to those documents. The translation must be certified in the prescribed manner to be a correct translation. [CA06 Sec 400(2)(f)].

- The entity cannot have any securities listed on a regulated market in an EEA member state. [CA06 Sec 400(4)]. For this purpose, 'securities' include shares and stocks, debentures (including debenture stock, loan stock, bonds, certificates of deposit and other similar instruments), warrants and similar instruments, and specified certificates and other instruments that confer rights in respect of securities. [CA06 Sec 400(6)].

9.22 As regards practical application of the requirement in the second bullet point of paragraph 9.21 above, the national GAAPs of the 27 countries that are members of the EC should have implemented the EC 7th Directive. In order for the exemption to be taken if the reporting parent is established in another country in the EEA, appropriate analysis will be needed to confirm that the GAAP under which the financial statements are prepared is either IFRS or a GAAP that is in accordance with the EC 7th Directive.

Parent entities included in non-EEA group accounts exemption

9.23 An intermediate holding entity is not required to prepare consolidated financial statements where it is wholly owned by a parent undertaking not established under the law of an EEA state. [CA06 Sec 401(1)(a)]. But a number of conditions must apply before the exemption can be taken, and these are summarised in paragraph 9.29 below. The conditions stated in section 401 of the Act do not need to be satisfied at the intermediate holding entity's financial year end date; they can be satisfied during the period after the intermediate holding entity's year end date and before the filing date of its parent's consolidated financial statements. The consolidated financial statements must include the intermediate holding entity and all of its subsidiaries, and all of the conditions must be met in order to obtain the exemption. There is a key difference here from the section 400 exemption requirement, because the parent undertaking identified need not be the 'immediate parent' of the entity, merely a 'parent'.

9.24 In addition to wholly owned subsidiaries, this exemption extends to the situation where the parent holds more than 50% of the shares by number in the entity looking to claim the exemption, and no notice has been served on the entity to prepare consolidated financial statements. Such notice must be made by either of the following:

- Shareholders holding in aggregate more than half of the remaining shares in the entity.

■ Shareholders holding in aggregate 5% of the total shares in the entity.

9.25 The parent undertaking identified must not be established under the law of an EEA state, but can be any parent of the entity, with no restriction to 'immediate parent' (as with para 9.23 above). [CA06 Sec 401(1)(b)].

9.26 The notice must be served within six months of the end of the previous financial period (that is, normally within the first six months of the financial year for which the consolidated financial statements are being prepared). [CA06 Sec 401(1)]. So the onus is clearly on the minority shareholders to serve such notice if they require consolidated financial statements to be prepared for a sub-group.

9.27 The scope of the relevant sections of the Act outlined above is extended to apply also to unincorporated parents, so reference to 'company' or 'entity' should be treated as applying to any undertaking, where appropriate. [FRS 102 para 9.3].

9.28 For the purposes of determining whether the entity is wholly owned or whether the parent holds more than 50% of the entity's shares, the rules below apply:

■ Shares held by directors to comply with their share qualification requirements should be disregarded when determining whether an entity is wholly owned (see para 9.15 above). [CA06 Sec 401(5)].

■ In determining whether the parent holds more than 50% of the shares of the entity (see para 9.16 above), shares held by a parent's wholly owned subsidiary should be attributed to the parent undertaking. Shares held on behalf of the parent, or by or on behalf of a wholly owned subsidiary, should also be attributed to the parent undertaking. [CA06 Sec 401(3)].

9.29 Both the exemptions outlined in paragraphs 9.23 and 9.24 above only apply, however, where the following conditions have been satisfied:

■ The entity and all of its subsidiary undertakings are 'included in' the consolidated financial statements of a larger group drawn up to the same date (or an earlier date in the same financial year – see para 9.30 below) by a parent undertaking. [CA06 Sec 401(2)(a)]. This group does not have to be the non-EEA parent referred to in paragraph 9.23 above; it could be an alternative parent in the group structure, referred to here as the 'reporting parent'.

Note that this is a stronger requirement than under section 400 of the Act, which does not include the requirement *"and all of its subsidiary undertakings"*.

'Included in', for this purpose, means by way of full consolidation; equity accounting or proportional consolidation is not sufficient.

■ The reporting parent's consolidated financial statements and annual report must be drawn up in accordance with the provisions of the EC 7th Directive (as modified by the provisions of the Bank Accounts Directive or the Insurance Accounts Directive, where applicable) or otherwise in a manner equivalent to consolidated accounts and annual reports so drawn up. [CA06 Sec 401(2)(b)].

- Consolidated financial statements of the higher parent will meet the test of equivalence in the Seventh Directive if they:

  - give a true and fair view and comply with FRS 102;

  - are prepared in accordance with EU-adopted IFRS;

  - are prepared in accordance with IFRS, subject to the consideration of the reasons for any failure by the European Commission to adopt a standard or interpretation; and

  - are prepared using other GAAPs which are closely related to IFRS, subject to consideration of the effect of any differences from EU-adopted IFRS.

  [FRS 100 para AG 6].

- A mechanism to determine the equivalence of the Generally Accepted Accounting Principles (GAAP) from third countries was established in 2007. Accordingly, the European Commission adopted a Decision and Regulation which identified as equivalent to IFRS the US GAAP, the Japanese GAAP, and accepted financial statements using the GAAP of China, Canada, India and South Korea within the EU on a temporary basis until 31 December 2011. In accordance with relevant EU legislation the European Commission has been updating the European Parliament at regular intervals on the progress made by these countries with their respective programmes to converge their GAAP with IFRS. This decision was amended on 11 April 2012 to state that from 1 January 2012, with regard to annual consolidated financial statements and half-yearly consolidated financial statements, the following standards shall be considered as equivalent to IFRS adopted pursuant to Regulation (EC) No 1606/2002:

  - GAAP of the People's Republic of China;

  - GAAP of Canada; and

  - GAAP of the Republic of Korea.

  Further, third country issuers shall be permitted to prepare their annual consolidated financial statements and half-yearly consolidated financial statements in accordance with the Generally Accepted Accounting Principles of the Republic of India for financial years starting before 1 January 2015.

  [FRS 100 para AG 7].

- The financial statements must also be audited by one or more persons authorised to audit accounts under the law under which the parent undertaking which draws them up is established. [CA06 Sec 401(2)(c)].

- It must be noted in the entity's individual financial statements that it is exempt from preparing and delivering to the Registrar of Companies consolidated financial statements. [CA06 Sec 401(2)(d)].

- The reporting parent's name must be noted in the entity's individual financial statements, stating:

  - The reporting parent's country of incorporation, if it is incorporated outside Great Britain.

  - The address of the reporting parent's principal place of business, where it is unincorporated.

  [CA06 Sec 401(2)(e)].

- The entity must deliver to the Registrar of Companies, within the period allowed for delivering its individual financial statements, a copy of the parent's consolidated financial statements and a copy of the parent's annual report, together with the audit report on them. [CA06 Sec 401(2)(f)].

- Where any of the documents delivered to the Registrar of Companies in accordance with the previous requirement is not in English (or Welsh for an entity registered in Wales), a copy of a translation must be annexed to those documents. The translation must be certified in the prescribed manner to be a correct translation [CA06 Sec 401(2)(g)].

- The entity cannot have any securities listed on a regulated market in an EEA member state. [CA06 Sec 401(4)]. For this purpose, 'securities' include shares and stocks, debentures (including debenture stock, loan stock, bonds, certificates of deposit and other similar instruments), warrants and similar instruments, and specified certificates and other instruments that confer rights in respect of securities. [CA06 Sec 401(6)].

Relevant dates

9.30   The relevant dates specified in the exemptions above can cause particular problems in practice, as explained in the example that follows.

Example – Relevant dates where year ends differ

A parent company acquires the whole of the company S sub-group in June 20X1 during its current financial year and, after the acquisition, the group has the following structure:

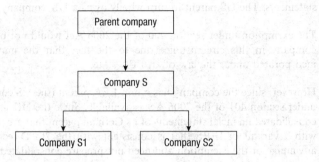

The parent company's year end is 31 December, but the year end of the company S sub-group is 30 September. The question arises whether company S can take advantage of the exemption to prepare consolidated financial statements for its sub-group (that is, including both company S1 and company S2). If it complies with the other conditions of the exemption, it will fail on the first condition in the year of acquisition (namely, 20X1). This is because at its year end, 30 September 20X1, it will not have been included in the parent's consolidated financial statements drawn up to the same date (that is, 30 September 20X1) or to an earlier date in company S's financial year. The company S sub-group will only be included in the parent's consolidated financial statement as at 31 December 20X1. In 20X2, company S does comply with this condition, because its results will be consolidated into its parent's financial statements to an earlier date in its financial year to 30 September 20X2 (that is, its parent's consolidated financial statements for the financial year to 31 December 20X1). So, in 20X1, company S will have to prepare consolidated financial statements; but, in 20X2, if it complies with the other conditions, it will not have to prepare them. The simple way round this problem is for company S to change its year end from 30 September to 31 December.

Applications of exemptions in practice

9.31 Care should be taken to ensure an understanding of which exemption is being taken and that the requirements of that exemption are fulfilled. The following examples assume that the conditions of the exemptions in question are met.

Example 1 – Company with a non-EEA immediate parent and an EEA ultimate parent

An ultimate parent company is incorporated in Germany and prepares its consolidated financial statements in accordance with EU-adopted IFRS. The German ultimate parent has a wholly-owned subsidiary in the US, which does not prepare consolidated financial statements. The US parent in turn wholly owns a UK company and its subsidiaries.

The exemption under section 400 of the 2006 Act would not be available to the UK company in this circumstance due to the fact that the immediate parent is not incorporated under the law of an EEA state.

However, since the company has a non-EEA parent (the US company) the exemption under section 401 of the 2006 Act is available. Since the UK group is included in the consolidated financial statements of its German parent that are prepared in accordance with a variant of IFRS that is consistent with the 7th Directive, it is able to take advantage of the exemption and need not prepare consolidated financial statements.

Example 2 – Company with an EEA immediate parent and an EEA ultimate parent

The facts are the same as in example 2, except that there is a Belgian company in the group structure instead of the US company.

In this example the immediate parent company and the reporting parent are both incorporated under the law of an EEA state. Hence the exemption under section 400 of the 2006 Act is available to the UK company. Since the UK company is included in the consolidated financial statements of its German parent that are prepared in accordance with the 7th Directive, it is able to take advantage of the exemption and need not prepare consolidated financial statements.

The exemption under section 401 of the 2006 Act would not be available to the UK company in this circumstance due to the fact that all of the UK company's parent undertakings are incorporated under the law of an EEA state.

Example 3 – Company with a non-EEA immediate parent preparing IFRS consolidated financial statements

The group's ultimate parent is incorporated in the US and prepares its consolidated financial statements in accordance with US GAAP. The US ultimate parent has a wholly-owned subsidiary incorporated in Bermuda that prepares and has audited consolidated financial statements in accordance with IFRS. The Bermuda subsidiary, in turn, owns a UK company and its subsidiaries.

The exemption under section 400 of the 2006 Act would not be available to the UK company in this circumstance due to the fact that the immediate parent is not incorporated under the law of an EEA state.

However, since the company has a non-EEA parent, the exemption under section 401 of the 2006 Act is potentially available. As the UK group is included in the consolidated financial statements of its Bermuda parent that are prepared in accordance with IFRS (which is consistent with the 7th Directive), it is able to take advantage of the exemption under section 401 of the 2006 Act and need not prepare consolidated financial statements.

Example 4 – Company with a non-EEA ultimate parent preparing US GAAP consolidated financial statements

The facts are the same as in example 3, except that the Bermuda parent does not prepare consolidated financial statements.

The exemption under section 400 of the 2006 Act would not be available to the UK company in this circumstance due to the fact that the immediate parent is not incorporated under the law of an EEA state.

However, since the company has a non-EEA parent the exemption under section 401 of the 2006 Act is potentially available. In this case, the UK parent company is included in the consolidated financial statements of its US parent prepared in accordance with US GAAP. It will be necessary to determine whether the US GAAP consolidated financial statements are prepared "*in a manner equivalent to the 7th Directive*". Such assessment should be made based on the principles in paragraph 9.29 above. If equivalence is agreed for the circumstances in question, then the UK group may take advantage of the exemption under section 401 of the 2006 Act and will not need to prepare consolidated financial statements. If equivalence cannot be agreed then the exemption will not be available.

Example 5 – Company with an EEA immediate parent and a non-EEA ultimate parent

An ultimate parent company is incorporated in the US and prepares its consolidated financial statements in accordance with US GAAP. The US ultimate parent has a wholly-owned subsidiary in France. The French parent in turn wholly owns a UK company and its subsidiaries.

In this example the immediate parent company is incorporated under the law of an EEA state. Hence, the exemption under section 400 of the 2006 Act is potentially available to the UK company. If the French company prepares consolidated financial statements in accordance with the 7th Directive, it is able to take advantage of the exemption and need not prepare consolidated financial statements.

Since the company has a non-EEA parent the exemption under section 401 under the 2006 Act is also potentially available. In this case, the UK parent company is included in the consolidated financial statements of its US parent prepared in accordance with US GAAP. It will be necessary to determine whether the US GAAP consolidated financial statements are prepared "*in a manner equivalent to the 7th Directive*". Such assessment should be made based on the principles in paragraph 9.29 above. If equivalence is agreed for the circumstances in question, then the UK group may take advantage of the exemption under section 401 of the 2006 Act and will not need to prepare consolidated financial statements. If equivalence cannot be agreed then the exemption under section 401 of the 2006 Act will not be available.

All subsidiaries excluded from consolidation

9.32   Where all of a parent's subsidiaries are permitted or required to be excluded from consolidation by sections 402 and 405 of the Companies Act 2006 and section 9 of FRS 102, that parent is exempt from the requirement to prepare consolidated financial statements. [FRS 102 para 9.3(f)]. The conditions for exclusion of subsidiaries from consolidation are considered in detail in paragraph 9.11 above.

Parent and subsidiaries

9.33 The term 'parent' is simply defined as an entity that has one or more subsidiaries. [FRS 102 Glossary of terms].

9.34 A subsidiary is defined as an entity (which includes both partnerships and unincorporated associations) that is controlled by another entity. [FRS 102 para 9.4]. Such entities are required to be consolidated by their parent entities.

9.35 Although the term 'entity' is used by FRS 102, it is not defined. 'Entity' generally means something that has real or distinct existence, such as an organisation or institution. An entity will often be an organisation that exists separately from its individual members; but this is not always the case, because the term 'entity' also applies to a partnership. So, entities include a corporation, partnership, trust, governmental body or agency, university, and any other organisation or body of persons. An entity is treated legally like a person; it can function legally, be sued and make decisions through its governing body.

Subsidiaries

9.36 Determining which entities are the parent's subsidiaries, and so should be consolidated, is fundamental in preparing consolidated financial statements. A subsidiary is an entity that is controlled by another entity (namely, its parent). [FRS 102 para 9.4]. A subsidiary can include any of the following entities:

- A company.
- A partnership.
- An unincorporated association carrying on a trade or business for profit.
- An unincorporated association not trading for profit.
- A trust.

9.37 The meaning of 'entity' is consider further in paragraphs 9.34 and 9.35 above.

Meaning of 'control'

9.38 The definition of 'control' is not based solely on legal ownership; it is the *"power to govern the financial and operating policies of an entity so as to obtain benefit from its activities"*. [FRS 102 para 9.3].

9.39 It should be noted that this definition of 'control' can be split into two parts:

- power over the financial and operating policies; and

- benefits must be obtained from that power in order for a subsidiary relationship to exist.

Financial and operating policies

9.40 The entity's particular financial and operating policies will need to be analysed in some detail to find out where control lies. There is little guidance in section 9 of the standard on the particular policies that an investor must govern. The two key financial and operating policies of an entity, that will often give the best indication of who has control, are the 'distribution and reinvestment' policy and approval of the annual business plan. Other important financial and operating policies that will have to be considered will include: the entity's strategic direction; ability to approve capital expenditure; and raising of finance and winding up the entity.

9.41 Typically rights of an investor are considered to be substantive (that is, giving power) or merely protective. Rights are considered substantive in nature if they enable an investor to initiate and approve or veto significant decisions made in the ordinary course of business. Decisions in the ordinary course of business are decisions about matters of a type consistent with those normally expected to be addressed in directing and carrying out an entity's current business activities. Protective rights are rights that allow a non-controlling interest shareholder or other party to block some decisions, but have limited impact on the majority shareholder's ability to control the entity's operations or assets.

9.42 In assessing whether an investor's rights are substantive or protective in nature, all relevant facts and circumstances should be assessed. If the holder of the right has a small economic interest, the right is more likely to be protective.

9.43 Examples of substantive rights include rights relating to:

- Selecting, terminating and setting the compensation of management responsible for implementing the investee's policies and procedures.

- Establishing operating and capital decisions of the investee, including budgets in the ordinary course of business (for example, approval of the annual business plan). Note that:

  - Rights over the approval of an operating budget are participative. However, consideration should be given as to whether the right is substantive. For example, in a mature business, if additional clauses in the shareholder agreement stipulate that, if the budget is not approved, it reverts back to last year's budget adjusted for inflation, the right is not substantive.

  - Rights that deal with operating and capital decisions that are not significant to the ordinary course of business are not substantive. For example, this might include decisions about the location of investee headquarters, name of investee, selection of auditors and selection of accounting policies.

- ■ Rights over decisions in the ordinary course of business that are remote are not substantive.

- Decisions covering acquisitions and disposals of assets.

- Decisions concerning financing requirements in the ordinary course of business.

- Blocking customary or expected dividends.

9.44 Examples of protective rights include rights relating to:

- Amendments to an entity's constitution or articles of incorporation.

- Pricing on transactions between the investor and investee.

- Liquidation of the investee or a decision to cause the investee to enter bankruptcy or other receivership.

- Restrictions on major acquisitions and disposals of assets that are not in the ordinary course of business.

- Issuance or repurchase of equity interests.

- Blocking extraordinary dividends.

Benefits

9.45 There is no requirement for the benefits obtained from the relationship to be those related to an ownership interest (that is, dividend flows or an interest in the entity's residual net assets). The potential benefits identifiable could include other benefits, such as cross-selling opportunities, brand-related goodwill generating more customers, access to a customer database of a subsidiary, and costs savings. The 'benefits test' is rarely failed in circumstances where the 'power to govern the financial and operating policies' test is passed, for two reasons:

- There is no requirement for the parent to receive the majority of benefits, so the 'hurdle' to be achieved is relatively low.

- It would be unusual that at least some benefit would fail to accrue to the entity with the 'power to govern'.

Passive control

9.46 Section 9 of FRS 102 does not refer to the demonstration or exercise of control, but only to the 'power to govern'.

9.47 There is no requirement to actually exercise control over an entity before it would be treated as a subsidiary; under the standard, the basic requirement is satisfied by having the power to govern. That power does not need to be actually exercised in practice; its mere existence will suffice.

Five situations of control

9.48   Section 9 of FRS 102 includes five situations where a parent has control over another entity (namely, its subsidiary). Control will arise where the parent:

- Owns more than half of the voting power of an entity, in which case control is presumed to exist; unless, in exceptional circumstances, it can be clearly demonstrated that such ownership does not constitute control (see further para 9.50 below).

- Owns half or less of the voting power of an entity where there is:

  - Power over more than one half of the voting rights by virtue of an agreement with other investors (see further para 9.63 below).

  - Power to govern the entity's financial and operating policies under a statute or an agreement (see further para 9.64 below).

  - Power to appoint or remove the majority of the members of the board of directors or equivalent governing body, and control of the entity is by that board or body (see further para 9.68 below).

  - Power to cast the majority of votes at meetings of the board of directors or equivalent governing body, and control of the entity is by that board or body (see further para 9.68 below).

- Has the power to exercise, or actually exercises, dominant influence or control over the undertaking.

- Is managed on a unified basis with the undertaking.

[FRS 102 paras 9.5, 9.6A].

9.49   In practice, control often arises through a combination of the factors noted above. For example, ownership of more than half the voting power would usually give an entity control, but the majority owner should also consider the existence of statutes, agreements and board control, because this might give control to another party. There could also be situations in practice where a party controls an entity by both majority ownership of the voting power and agreement of the board. The control situations explained in paragraph 9.48 above are similar to those included in section 1162 of the 2006 Act, and so there is not an issue of conflict between section 9 of FRS 102 and the legislative position. A parent has a subsidiary where the parent:

- Holds a majority of the voting rights in the undertaking.

- Is a member of the undertaking and has the right to appoint or remove directors holding a majority of the voting rights at meetings of the board on all, or substantially all, matters.

- Has a right to exercise dominant influence over the undertaking by virtue of provisions either in its memorandum or articles, or in a control contract.

- Is a member of the undertaking and controls alone, pursuant to an agreement with other shareholders or members, a majority of the voting rights in the undertaking.

- Has the power to exercise, or actually exercises, dominant influence or control over the undertaking.

- Is managed on a unified basis with the undertaking.

[CA06 Sec 1162(2)–(4)].

Majority of voting rights

9.50 A parent or its subsidiaries must have voting power over an entity before the control provisions apply. For entities, voting power is normally gained by having an ownership interest in the entity. However, it would be possible to gain voting power by other means.

9.51 An entity is a subsidiary where the parent owns (directly or indirectly through subsidiaries) more than one half of its voting power. [IAS 27 para 13]. This is the control provision that is applied most frequently in practice to identify subsidiaries. While ownership (equity shares) and voting rights (that is, voting power) are usually held in equal proportions, there are situations where an entity may own a majority of the equity shares in another entity and yet not hold more than one half of its voting power. In such a situation, the entity will not be a subsidiary (unless it is a subsidiary by virtue of one of the other control provisions set out in para 9.48 above).

9.52 'Voting power' can be taken to mean the ability to exercise the rights conferred on shareholders in respect of their shares to vote at the entity's general meetings on all, or substantially all, matters. This would apply also where an entity does not have share capital. If the entity does not have general meetings where matters are decided by exercising voting rights, 'voting power' can be taken to mean having the ability to exercise the right under the entity's constitution to direct its overall policy, or to alter the terms of its constitution.

9.53 Voting rights that relate to shares held as security would be treated as held by the entity providing the security where those rights (excluding any right to exercise them to preserve the value of the security, or to realise it) are only exercisable in accordance with that entity's instructions. This situation might arise for example, where entity A grants a loan to entity B, entity B gives entity A shares in entity C as security for the loan. However, entity A does not gain the voting rights on the shares in entity C, unless entity B defaults on the loan. Hence, entity B retains control of the voting rights in entity C (unless it defaults) even though they are held as security by entity A.

9.54   In determining whether an undertaking holds more than half of the voting power, options will generally only be taken into consideration, for the purposes of determining whether any party has a majority of voting rights or control of the board, when the option is currently exercisable (see para 9.80).

9.55   Note that intention with regard the voting rights is not relevant (unless *de facto* control can be demonstrated as per para 9.184 below).

Example – Control of the 'voting power' in an entity

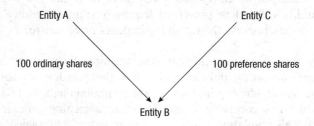

Entity A — 100 ordinary shares

Entity C — 100 preference shares

Entity B

The rights attached to entity B's shares are as follows:

- Ordinary shares (wholly owned by entity A).
- 100 C1 ordinary shares.
- All dividends after payment of preference dividends.
- Right to all surplus assets on a winding up of the entity after repayment of preference shares.
- Right to vote on all matters at any meetings of the entity.
- Preference shares (wholly owned by entity C).
- 100 C1 preference shares.
- Fixed preference dividend.
- Right on winding up to the repayment of par value and up to 25% of any sum standing to the credit of the share premium account.
- No rights to vote at entity meetings.

The distinction between ordinary share capital and other share capital is irrelevant in determining whether an entity is a subsidiary of another. The definition of a subsidiary looks at who controls the 'voting power' in the entity. The preference shares have no voting rights, while the ordinary shares do. Consequently, entity B is a subsidiary of entity A, but is not a subsidiary of entity C. This of course ignores who has the right to appoint the majority of the board of directors and the other control provisions (set out in para 9.48 above), which in practice would all have to be considered.

9.56   Control is presumed to exist when a parent owns more than 50% of the voting power of an entity unless in exceptional circumstances it can be clearly demonstrated that such ownership does not constitute control.

9.57   It is very unusual that an entity that holds more than one half of another entity's voting rights will be unable to exercise control. However, this might be the case where another party clearly does control the entity. These situations might include surrender of the right to control by contract (for example, in a joint venture), or legal restrictions on an acquirer's ability to exercise all of the voting rights acquired.

9.58   Virtually all entities are subject to some form of government regulation and the existence of regulation does not necessarily rebut the presumption that control exists. For example, an entity that owns more than half the voting rights of a regulated utility will not be prevented from governing the utility's financial and operating policies because the regulator imposes price controls.

9.59   Only regulation that prevents the acquirer from governing an entity's financial and operating policies will rebut the presumption of control. For example, the law might require that the state appoints half the board of directors of certain defence contractors and exercises a casting vote if the board is deadlocked. This regulation would prevent an entity that owned more than half the voting rights from governing the financial and operating policies.

9.60   An acquiree's charter might also restrict an acquirer's ability to exercise all of the voting rights acquired. It may restrict the rights to appoint the board of directors to the holders of a certain class of voting share or restrict the circumstances in which the acquirer can exercise its voting rights.

Example – Acquirer's voting rights restricted by acquiree's charter

Entity A entered into an agreement on 31 December 20X3, to sell 80% of a wholly-owned subsidiary B, to entity C. Entity A's representatives on the board of subsidiary B will immediately resign and will be replaced by the new owners.

Entity A has also provided subsidiary B with a short-term loan. Entity C has agreed to apply certain operating decisions defined by entity A, as stated in a memorandum of understanding, during the period when the loan is outstanding. Any operating decision proposed by entity C, which differs from the memorandum of understanding, is subject to entity A's veto, during that period.

Entity A has determined subsidiary B's operating decisions, stated in the memorandum of understanding as part of the purchase agreement. It is entitled to veto any different decision proposed by entity C, as long as the subordinated loan is outstanding.

Entity A, therefore, retains control over subsidiary B and should consolidate it, despite the fact that entity C owns 80% of subsidiary B.

9.61   A entity might appear to control over 50% of the entity's voting rights by having a holding of more than 50% of the share capital, but an agreement with the other shareholders might significantly restrict this control. It could, for example, require unanimous agreement between the shareholders before it could: pay a dividend; change direction of the entity's business; incur capital expenditure over a specified level; pay its directors and other employees; change other major operating and financial policies, etc. In this type of situation, the entity holding more than 50% of the share capital would not control the entity. However, it might still have joint control or significant influence. (See further chapters 14 and 15.)

9.62 Control can be contrasted with joint control, which is defined in FRS 102 section 15 to mean: *"the contractually agreed sharing of control over an economic activity, and exists only when the strategic financial and operating decisions relating to the activity require the unanimous consent of the parties sharing control (the venturers)"*. [FRS 102 para 15.2]. Where joint control exists over an entity, it falls within the requirements of FRS 102. (See further chapter 15).

Majority of voting rights by agreement with other shareholders

9.63 An entity will be a subsidiary where its parent can exercise power over more than one half of its voting rights by virtue of an agreement with other shareholders. [FRS 102 para 9.5].

> ### Example – Majority of voting rights by agreement with other shareholders
>
> Entity A owns 45% of the voting shares of entity B. Entity A also has an agreement with other shareholders that they will always vote a further 20% holding in the same way as entity A.
>
> The agreement between entity A and the other shareholders provides entity A with control over 65% of the voting rights of entity B. This is because the other shareholders will vote in accordance with the instructions of entity A. Entity A, therefore, controls entity B and entity B is its subsidiary and should be consolidated in entity A's consolidated financial statements.

Power to govern under a statute or an agreement

9.64 An entity will be a subsidiary where the parent has the power to govern the financial and operating policies of the entity under a statute or an agreement. [FRS 102 para 9.5].

9.65 In the UK it is possible for such a power to be embedded in a company's memorandum and articles of association or in a separate agreement.

9.66 It is likely that a parent will have such a power to govern where it has a right to give directions with respect to the operating and financial policies of another entity, which that entity's directors are obliged to follow whether or not they are for the benefit of that entity.

Example – Power to govern under a shareholder agreement

Entity D is an overseas entity applying FRS 102 in its individual financial statements. Three entities A, B and C invest in entity D to manufacture footballs. Entity A has considerable experience in manufacturing footballs and has developed new technology to improve their production. Entity B and entity C are both banks that have previously financed entity A's operations.

Entity A will contribute technology and know-how to entity D, whilst entity B and entity C will contribute finance. The share ownership will be entity A: 40%, entity B: 30%, and entity C: 30%. Each entity will appoint directors in proportion to their ownership percentage. An agreement between the shareholders states that all directors will be non-executive except for the managing director and the finance director, both of whom will be appointed by entity A in recognition of its expertise in the area of football manufacture.

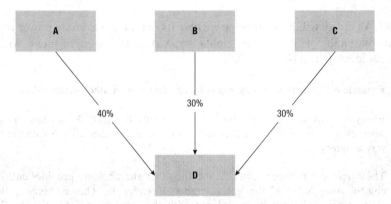

The shareholder agreement delegates to entity A's managing director and its finance director the power to set entity D's operating policies and operating budget. However, requests for additional financing must be considered by the full board.

The delegation of powers over the entity's operating policies and budget to the directors appointed by entity A, provides entity A with effective control of entity D. Although there are some powers retained by the full board, including decisions over changes to financing and share structure, these are limited and provide rights that are more protective, rather than participative in nature.

The decisions concerning financial and operating policies represent a substantial part of the total range of decisions to be taken in respect the operating entity. In particular, entity A has control over the distribution policy and can determine whether surplus funds are distributed or reinvested. Control over these financial and operating decisions, therefore, provides participative control over the entity.

Determining control in situations similar to this must be considered carefully since the identification of rights as participative or protective can be unclear and subject to interpretation (see para 9.43 above).

9.67 This position is unlikely to arise in a UK subsidiary, because in the UK, the entity's directors have a duty under UK law to act in the entity's best interest.

There is some doubt whether the directors of a UK subsidiary could be obliged to comply with the directions of the holder of control if to do so would not be for the benefit of the subsidiary as this might leave them in breach of their duties as directors.

Control of the board

9.68   There are two control situations relating to the board.

- Power to appoint or remove the majority of the members of the board of directors or equivalent governing body and control of the entity is by that board or body.

- Power to cast the majority of votes at meetings of the board of directors or equivalent governing body and control of the entity is by that board or body.

[FRS 102 para 9.5].

9.69   The first circumstance, "*the power to appoint or remove the majority of the members of the board of directors*" makes no reference to their voting power. Usually directors have equal voting rights at board meetings, so that power to appoint or remove the majority of the board will mean control of the board and the entity. However it is conceivable that sometimes some directors may have more votes than others at board meetings. If an entity controlled the appointment and removal of a majority of directors, but those directors did not have a majority of votes at board meetings, the entity might still appear to meet the definition under FRS 102 for it to have control. In this situation, it would be necessary to consider carefully whether an entity does indeed have control even though it appeared to meet the definition. If, for example another entity could appoint a minority of the directors, but those directors had a majority of votes at board meetings, that other entity might well have control. It appears that two unrelated entities could be identified as the parent, only one can have control in practice.

9.70   The second circumstance, "*the power to cast the majority of votes at board meetings*" can be taken to mean the power to cast the majority of the voting rights at board meetings on all, or substantially all, matters (without the need for any other person's consent or agreement).

9.71   The operation of these provisions is illustrated by the examples that follow.

Example – Control linked to whether preference dividends are in arrears

The rights attaching to the two different types of share are as follows:

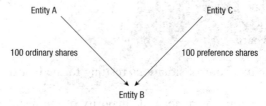

- ■ Ordinary shares:

  - ■ 100 C1 ordinary shares.

  - ■ All dividends after payment of preference dividends.

  - ■ Right to all surplus assets on a winding up of the entity after repayment of preference shares.

  - ■ Right to vote on all matters at any meetings of the entity.

  - ■ Power to appoint two directors of the entity with one vote each.

- ■ Preference shares:

  - ■ 100 C1 preference shares.

  - ■ Fixed preference dividend.

  - ■ Right on winding up to the repayment of par value and up to 25% of any sum standing to the credit of the share premium account.

  - ■ No rights to vote at entity meetings.

  - ■ No voting rights, but if a preference dividend is in arrears at any point, the shareholders have the power to appoint two directors with two votes each.

Where the preference dividend is not in arrears, entity A holds more than 50% of the voting power of entity B and entity B is a subsidiary of entity A. However, if the preference dividend is in arrears and, as a consequence, the preference shareholders appoint (or have the power to appoint) their two directors, entity B becomes a subsidiary of entity C, which then has the power to appoint or remove directors holding a majority of the voting power at entity B's board meetings.

9.72 The situation described in the example is unusual and it is possible that in this situation as soon as entity C is able to control the board of entity B, entity A might lose effective control and will have to exclude entity B from its consolidated financial statements. Where an entity owns more than half of the voting power (at shareholder meetings), as entity A does, control is presumed unless in exceptional circumstances it can be clearly demonstrated that control does not exist. Where more than one entity could be identified as a parent in such a situation, only one of those potential parents has control in practice. In the example, when the arrears of dividend are paid, the directors appointed to entity B by entity C might cease to hold office, in which case control would again reside with entity A. The circumstances and how a situation such as that described above is handled in practice, would need to be evaluated. The possible conclusions based on that evaluation might be any of:

- Entity A retains control but with certain restrictions, for example on spending levels, imposed by entity C to protect its investment.

- Entity C takes control and directs the operating and financial policies.

- There is joint control by agreement.

9.73 Where there are restrictions placed on the rights or the ability of the parent to exercise control, this would indicate that there is a loss of control and the entity is no longer a subsidiary (see para 9.155). Alternatively, in a situation where there is effectively deadlock in voting rights there might be joint control, in which case this might indicate the existence of a joint venture. See chapter 15 for further guidance on jointly controlled entities.

Example 1 – Control via right to appoint majority of the board

Entity A owns 45% of the shares in entity B but, based on the shareholders agreement, controls the composition of its board of directors by having the power to appoint or remove the majority of entity B's directors.

Amendments to entity B's articles of incorporation state that acquisitions and disposals of assets in an amount higher than 50% of the fair value of entity's B's total assets, and the decision to liquidate entity B, are reserved for shareholder vote.

The ability of entity A to control the composition of entity B's board, therefore, confers control of entity B to entity A. Although certain decisions are reserved for a shareholder vote, where entity A has control of only 45% of the votes, such decisions tend to be protective in nature. Provided the decisions reserved for shareholder vote do not interfere with the operations of entity B, entity A will be able to control entity B's operating and financial policies so as to obtain benefits from its activities. Hence, entity B would be regarded as entity A's subsidiary. (See para 9.38.)

Example 2 – Intervention by government (non-controlling interest holder) in operation and financial policy decisions

A government does not have a controlling shareholding in a company, but has a golden share that enables it to replace the board of directors with its nominees should the government disagree with the operating and financial policy decisions taken by the other shareholder.

Whilst the share exists to enable the government to protect its national interest, the power that this share gives the government extends beyond this as there are no restrictions on the circumstances in which it can intervene. The share gives the government power to control the board, which means the operating and financial policies are controlled by the government so as to obtain benefits from its activities. Conversely, if there were restrictions on when the government could intervene, for example only in preventing the issuance of additional shares or the sale of a material ownership interest to foreign shareholders, then as these rights are more protective in nature, this would indicate that the government does not control the company.

9.74   Where an entity has the right to appoint a director with a casting vote in the event of a board deadlock and because of this that entity controls more than half of the voting power on the board, it will effectively control the board and can, therefore, control any board decision.

> **Example – Control via the power to direct the board's votes**
>
> Entity A owns 50% of the voting shares of entity B. The board of directors consist of eight members. Entity A appoints four directors and two other investors appoint two directors each. One of entity A's nominated directors always serves as chairman of entity B's board and has the casting vote at board meetings.
>
> Entity A has the casting vote at board meetings in the event that the directors cannot reach a majority decision. This provides entity A with control of board decisions and, therefore, control of entity B. Hence entity B is a subsidiary of entity A and will be consolidated into entity A's consolidated financial statements.

9.75   In practice a further complication can arise. Many 50/50 jointly controlled entities are set up in the form of companies with each party owning 50% of the equity, holding 50% of the voting rights in general meeting and having the right to appoint directors with 50% of the votes on the board. In order to avoid total deadlock in the event of a disagreement a 'rotating' chairman is appointed with a casting vote. The chairman, who is chosen from the directors, is appointed in alternate years by each party to the joint venture. Therefore, in theory, by virtue of the casting vote, in years one, three and five the entity is the subsidiary of one of the venturers while in years two, four and six it is a subsidiary of the other.

9.76   The two parties appear to control the venture in alternate years. Such problems can be resolved in practice by considering the substance of the arrangement. There may be other arrangements in place that give one of the parties control or both parties joint control. It is likely that the arrangement outlined above would be treated as a joint venture with shared control. (See further chapter 15.)

Control via a number of factors

9.77   Although there is a presumption that the acquisition of more than one half of another entity's voting rights confers control, factors other than ownership can also hand control to a parent that does not own more than half the voting rights.

> **Example – Control via a of combination factors**
>
> Entity A owns 49% of entity B, an oil refiner. Access to entity B 's refining capacity is important to entity A. An agreement between entity A and the two other shareholders provides entity A with the right to obtain and unilaterally distribute entity B's output. The price paid for entity B's output is set by reference to a standard industry pricing formula. Additionally, entity A has guaranteed 75% of entity B's borrowings.
>
> Entity A should consolidate entity B because it has the power to control who has access to entity B 's operating capacity. Entity A has access to significant rewards and is significantly exposed to entity B's risks through the output agreement and the guarantee of entity B's borrowings.

Potential voting rights

9.78 All options and convertible instruments that are currently exercisable are required to be considered in determining whether control exists. [FRS 102 para 9.6].

9.79 An entity might own instruments that, if exercised or converted, give the entity voting power over the financial and operating policies of another entity; these are termed 'potential voting rights'. Potential voting rights might take the form of share warrants, share call options, debt or equity instruments that are convertible into ordinary shares.

9.80 The voting rights in shares under option do not vest with the holder until the option is actually exercised. However, where an option to acquire shares has not yet been exercised, but can be freely exercised by its holder (that is, the option is within its exercise period and would, if exercised, give the holder control), the holder in effect has a power of veto and has the power to control the entity's financial and operating policies.

9.81 An entity might hold currently exercisable potential voting rights in a company where the majority of ordinary shares are held by a third party. The third party might not be able to consolidate the company if the entity holding the potential voting rights could obtain control through exercise of the rights. The entity holding the rights would consolidate the company.

Control through an agent

9.82 Control can also be achieved by having an agent with the ability to direct the activities for the benefit of the controlling entity (that is, the principal). [FRS 102 para 9.6].

9.83 An agent is a party engaged to act on behalf of the principal. A principal might delegate some of its decision authority over the investee to the agent, but the agent does not control the investee when it exercises such powers on behalf of the principal. The decision-making rights of the agent should be treated as being held by the principal directly in assessing control. Power resides with the principal rather than with the agent.

9.84 The overall relationship between the decision-maker and other parties involved with the investee must be assessed to determine whether the decision-maker is acting as an agent. One feature indicating that an entity is acting as an agent is that the amount that the entity earns is predetermined, being either a fixed fee per transaction or a stated percentage of the amount billed to the customer. [FRS 102 Glossary of terms]. In practice, common examples of agents are investment and asset managers earning a market-based fixed or stated percentage fee based on a publicly traded, regulated fund.

Special purpose entities

9.85 Where it has been determined that an entity is not a subsidiary under the control guidance above, it might still be a subsidiary that is required to be consolidated if it is a special purpose entity (SPE), as described in section 9 of FRS 102. The guidance was written as an anti-abuse measure, to prevent the basic principles of control from being flouted by setting up an entity in such a way as to circumvent those rules. Groups have tried in the past to take items off balance sheet by using SPEs in this way. SPEs are also known as special purpose vehicles (SPVs) in the UK.

9.86 It should be noted that section 9 of the standard excludes post-employment or other long-term employee benefits plans, such as pension schemes. [FRS 102 para 9.12]. But section 9 of the standard must be considered when assessing SPEs used in employee share plans.

9.87 An SPE can be a company, trust, partnership, unincorporated entity or multi-user structure such as a protected cell company. An SPE is often created to accomplish a narrow and well-defined objective (for example, to effect a lease, undertake research and development activities, securitise financial assets, or facilitate employee shareholdings under remuneration schemes, such as employee share ownership plans (ESOPs)). [FRS 102 para 9.10].

9.88 An SPE is not defined, but a non-exhaustive list of circumstances indicates where an entity controls a SPE:

- the activities of the SPE are being conducted on behalf of the entity according to its specific business needs (see further guidance in para 9.92 below);

- the entity has the ultimate decision-making powers over the activities of the SPE, even if the day-to-day decisions have been delegated (see further guidance in para 9.93);

- the entity has rights to obtain the majority of the benefits of the SPE, and so might be exposed to risks incidental to the activities of the SPE (see further guidance in para 9.94); and

- the entity retains the majority of the residual or ownership risks related to the SPE or its assets (see further guidance in para 9.100 below).

[FRS 102 para 9.11].

9.89 In practice, common features that might identify an SPE are:

- 'Auto-pilot' arrangements that restrict the decision-making capacity of the governing board or management.

- Use of professional directors, trustees or partners.

- Thin capitalisation (that is, the proportion of 'real' equity is too small to support the SPE's overall activities).

- Absence of an apparent profit-making motive, such that the SPE is engineered to pay out all profits in the form of interest or fees.

- Domiciled in 'offshore' capital havens.

- Have a specified life.

- Exist for financial engineering purposes.

- The creator or sponsor can transfer assets to the SPE, often as part of a derecognition transaction involving financial assets.

9.90   The presence of any of the features identified above does not automatically make an entity an SPE, nor does the absence of one or more features mean that it is not an SPE.

9.91   The following examples illustrate how the control indicators are applied in practice.

Example 1 – Compliance with regulation

An insurance entity, H, would like to issue credit derivatives, but industry regulation prohibits insurance companies from issuing them. An unrelated bank B has a significant exposure to a number of its customers and would like to reduce that exposure through a credit derivative.

Bank B sets up an SPE, whose share capital is minimal and carries all of the voting rights. The share capital is wholly owned by a charitable trust. The SPE's articles of association restrict its activities to issuing credit derivatives and insuring the related risk with H.

The SPE issues a credit derivative to bank B in exchange for a premium. The credit derivative provides bank B with protection against the risks associated with bank B's concentration of credit risk. The SPE insures itself against any loss on the credit derivative by paying a premium for an insurance policy issued by entity H.

Entity H is permitted to insure against the risk of loss on a credit derivative. The arrangements, therefore, comply with insurance regulation.

Entity H should consolidate the SPE.

The SPE's activities are pre-determined. Entity H controls the SPE because its activities are pre-determined to meet H's business objectives.

The substance of the arrangements is that the SPE has allowed entity H to assume the risks of the credit derivative. Bank B's position is the same as it would have been if entity H itself had issued the credit derivative. The benefits of the SPE are that entity H has been able to take on the risk in the credit derivative. Entity H controls the SPE, as it receives all the benefits and is exposed to all risks.

Example 2 – Research and development

Entity A, which makes pharmaceutical products, sets up a charitable trust controlled by an independent trustee. The trust is funded initially by a donation of cash and research facilities from entity A. The trust's activities are the research and development of anti-ageing products. The trust is required to repay to entity A any amount of the donation that is not used for research and development purposes.

The trust is obliged to offer to sell entity A the intellectual property rights to any approved products before they are offered to other entities. Entity A will be able to purchase the intellectual property for an amount equal to the accumulated research and development cost.

The trust is an SPE. Entity A should consolidate it.

The SPE's activities are pre-determined. Entity A has control because the SPE's activities were pre-determined to meet entity A's specific business needs. Entity A is entitled to all of the benefits from the trust's activities, because it has the right of first refusal to acquire the rights to any successful development.

Example 3 – Non financial benefits

Entity Z manufactures and sells office equipment. Approximately half of its sales are made under leases that transfer substantially all the risks and rewards in the equipment to the customer. Entity Z accounts for its rights to receive lease payments as finance lease receivables.

Entity Z has examined ways to improve the efficiency of its leasing operations and has decided to set up an alliance with a bank to manage the lease portfolio. The bank has established an SPE, whose share capital is minimal and carries all the voting rights. The bank owns 50% of the share capital and entity Z owns 50%. The SPE acquires office equipment from entity Z at the selling price agreed with a customer and enters a finance lease agreement with the customer. The SPE's articles of association do not permit it to write leases in connection with products manufactured by any other parties. The SPE's investment in the finance lease is funded by a loan from the bank at a market rate of interest. The bank will manage the portfolio of receivables in exchange for a management fee calculated at market rates.

Entity Z has not guaranteed the lease receivables or the equipment's residual value. The price the SPE paid for the equipment, the interest on the bank borrowing and the management fee are all determined by market rates. Entity Z and the bank share the SPE's profits in proportion to their shareholdings. The financial advantage of the SPE arrangement is that the management services the bank provides will improve the efficiency and overall profitability of the leasing operation.

Entity Z has also agreed with the bank that entity Z will have the first right of refusal to acquire any office equipment that is repossessed or returned at the end of the lease period. Entity Z must acquire any office equipment at fair value. However, it is able to control the secondary market in office equipment and ensure that cheap second-hand products do not depress the price of new equipment.

Entity Z should consolidate the SPE.

The SPE's activities are pre-determined because it is only permitted to write finance leases in connection with equipment sold by entity Z. The bank and entity Z have participated equally in pre-determining the activities. Entity Z and the bank share the financial risks and rewards from the SPE equally.

There are non-financial benefits in these arrangements. Entity Z requires a finance lease alternative to selling equipment to its customers and the SPE provides that alternative. Entity Z originates all of the SPE's transactions. Entity Z also requires the ability to control the secondary market and the right of first refusal to purchase repossessed equipment provides that ability.

The financial benefits are shared equally, but entity Z receives the non-financial benefits and, therefore, receives most of the benefits and should consolidate the SPE.

Example 4 – Receivables factorisation

A bank has established an SPE, whose shares are owned by the bank. The SPE's constitutional documents state that its activities are restricted to the purchase and subsequent collection of receivables originated by entity D.

The SPE has a borrowing facility with the bank to finance the purchase of the receivables from entity D. The bank facility agreement states that the SPE cannot use the borrowing facility for any other purpose. The SPE will acquire the receivables from entity D for 95% of the face amount receivable. Entity D has agreed to manage the collection process in exchange for a fixed fee. The discount to the face amount receivable is expected to allow the SPE to meet its interest obligations to the bank and pay the management fee to D.

Entity D has provided a credit guarantee to the bank to cover any costs that arise from unexpected credit defaults and from late payment.

Entity D should consolidate the SPE.

The SPE operates on autopilot since all of its economic decisions are pre-determined (what receivables to purchase, how much to pay, etc). Entity D controls the SPE because it was set up in connection with entity D's business activities. Entity D is exposed to substantially all the receivables' risks through the guarantee to the bank.

The arrangements have been constructed so the bank obtains a lender's return on its loan to the SPE. The bank does not consolidate the SPE.

Example 5 – Investment portfolio and fiduciary

An SPE is used to conduct investment activities exclusively on behalf of entity B.

Entity B invests in the SPE by paying a premium to acquire a total return swap issued by the SPE. The total return swap transfers 90% of the profits and 100% of the losses in a specified portfolio of investments to entity B. Entity B is financing the SPE's investing activities. A specialist investment manager manages the SPE's investments and owns all of its share capital.

An operating agreement between the investment manager and entity B sets out investment guidelines and prohibits the investment manager from obtaining access to the investments for its own benefit. Payment on the swap occurs annually in relation to income and at the expiry of 5 years in relation to return of capital.

Entity B should consolidate the SPE.

The SPE operates on autopilot because the investment guidelines were established when the SPE was formed. Entity B controls the SPE because entity B established the investment guidelines. Entity B also receives 90% of the SPE's profits and is exposed to all of its losses.

The investment manager manages the SPE's investments, but does so within pre-determined guidelines. The investment manager incurs no risk and receives the premium and 10% of the profits as a fee for providing management services. The specialist investment manager can only benefit as a consequence of creating profits for the principal, entity B. The investment manager is a fiduciary and does not control the SPE.

Example 6 – Transfer of risks

Entity A has decided to realise the cash in its receivables. It sets up an SPE. Independent trustees hold the SPE's voting rights and share capital.

Entity A sells its receivables to the SPE for 95% of the amount receivable. The SPE has no recourse to entity A in the event of slow payment or default. The historical default rate by entity A's customers is 2%. The SPE finances the purchase of the receivables with a bank loan and uses the cash collected from the receivables to meet its obligations under the bank loan. Any surplus cash the SPE holds after the bank loan is repaid is payable to entity A (30%) and the bank (70%).

Entity A should not consolidate the SPE.

The SPE's activities are pre-determined, but entity A has transferred most of the risks in the receivables. Entity A is entitled to receive some, but not a majority, of the rest of the benefits from the receivables.

The risk in the receivables is the variability in the collection of the receivables transferred to the SPE. This risk has been transferred to the bank. Entity A and the bank will share in any surplus in the SPE, but the bank receives most of the rewards. Hence, the bank controls and should consolidate the SPE.

Example 7 – Lease arrangements

An SPE purchases an aircraft from entity A, a manufacturer. The purchase is financed by a loan from a bank on normal commercial terms. The SPE leases the aircraft to entity B, an airline, for an initial term of 15 years. When the initial lease term expires, entity B has the option to purchase the aircraft at market value or extend the lease on normal commercial terms, but not at less than the existing rental rates, for a further 5 years. The total lease term of 20 years covers the aircraft's expected economic life.

Entity A guarantees the aircraft's residual value at the end of year 15. The guaranteed residual ensures that the SPE will be able to repay the bank borrowing if entity B decides to purchase the aircraft.

Entity B should consolidate the SPE in its consolidated financial statements.

Entity B controls the SPE because it has the ability to obtain all the economic benefits from operating the aircraft. Entity B should record its interest in the aircraft and a bank borrowing in the consolidated financial statements.

Entity B has the power to control the day-to-day usage of the aircraft and obtain all the benefits from its operation even though entity B is protected against any decline in the value of the aircraft. Entity B also controls the principal economic decision that must be taken in connection with the SPE — whether the structure collapses at year 15 or continues to year 20. The SPE does not make any other economic decisions and operates on autopilot.

Entity A is exposed to any unexpected fall in the aircraft's value, but does not control the aircraft's use during the initial lease period or control whether the aircraft is sold at the end of the initial lease period. Entity A is exposed to the residual risk after 15 years, but does not consolidate the SPE. The guarantee might prevent entity A from recognising revenue on the sale of the new aircraft to the SPE.

The bank has no control over use of the aircraft. The bank obtains a commercial rate of return on its loan and it has no participation in the SPE's results. The bank does not consolidate the SPE.

Example 8 – Transfer of risks

Entity A is an airline operator that provides passenger services throughout Europe. It owns four aircraft, each of which has a carrying value of 50m and a remaining useful life of 15 years.

Entity A sets up an SPE: independent trustees own its share capital and voting rights. The corporate charter of the SPE restricts its activities to acquiring aircraft from entity A and leasing them to entity A. The SPE borrows money from a bank and pays entity A 200m to acquire the aircraft. Entity A and the SPE enter into a lease agreement under which entity A leases the aircraft back for an initial period of 10 years. When that period expires, the airline has the option to purchase the aircraft at market value or extend the lease for another five years.

Entity A separately guarantees the aircraft's residual value at year ten at 40m, which is the amount that will be outstanding on the SPE's borrowing at that date. The aircraft are expected to have a market value at year 10 approximately equal to the amount of the guarantee. There is a liquid secondary market for the aircraft.

Entity A should consolidate the SPE.

The SPE's activities are pre-determined. Entity A controls the SPE because it is exposed to all of its risks. The SPE has no independent activity and was set up only to be a party to the lease arrangement with entity A.

> The key risk is that the aircraft will not achieve the residual value. Entity A is exposed to that risk through the residual value guarantee, although it is not expected to be significant. The key benefit is the use of the aircraft and having the aircraft available to operate in the business. Entity A has a lease for the majority of the aircrafts' remaining useful life and thus will enjoy the majority of the benefits.

Activities

9.92   An SPE is likely to be a subsidiary where the activities of the SPE are being conducted on behalf of the entity according to its specific business needs. [FRS 102 para 9.11(a)]. For example, this might arise where:

■   The SPE is principally engaged in providing a source of long-term capital to an entity or funding to support an entity's ongoing major or central operations.

■   The SPE provides a supply of goods or services that is consistent with an entity's ongoing major or central operations which, without the existence of the SPE, would have to be provided by the entity itself.

Decision making

9.93   An SPE is likely to be a subsidiary where the entity has the ultimate decision-making powers over the activities of the SPE even if the day-to-day decisions have been delegated. [FRS 102 para 9.11(b)]. Such powers might be governed by an agreement in such a way that they unwind like clockwork without the need for significant further intervention. Examples of this type of control are the:

■   Power to unilaterally dissolve an SPE.

■   Power to change the SPE's charter or bylaws.

■   Power to veto proposed changes of the SPE's charter or bylaws.

Benefits

9.94   An SPE is likely to be a subsidiary where the entity has rights to obtain the majority of the benefits of the SPE and therefore may be exposed to risks incidental to the activities of the SPE. [FRS 102 para 9.11(c)]. Such rights to benefits in the SPE may be indicators of control when they are specified in favour of the originator, such that it stands to gain those benefits from the SPE's financial performance. The originator might also be exposed to the risks that are incidental to the SPE's activities. An originator might control such an SPE where it has:

■   Rights to a majority of any economic benefits distributed by the SPE in the form of future net cash flows, earnings, net assets, or other economic benefits. For example, the investing entity's ownership interest in an SPE might be only 40%, but it might have an economic interest in greater than 50% of the SPE's net assets and distributions.

- Rights to majority residual interests in scheduled residual distributions or in a liquidation of the SPE. For example, this is a typical device used in mortgage securitisation schemes.

9.95 The analysis of benefits and risk exposure covers not only financial, but also operational benefits and risks.

9.96 Some possible financial benefits are fees, reduced costs of borrowing or an ability to participate in the potential upside of the assets in a structure. Financial benefit encompasses both absolute income and reduction of costs.

9.97 The types of financial risk that need to be considered are currency, interest rates, equity prices, credit risk and residual value risk. Where risks can be easily hedged in the market (such as currency and interest rate risk), this is often an auto-pilot requirement of the SPE and these risks are seldom its principal risks. Financial risk is not measured in absolute terms, but rather by reference to the variability of the outcome.

9.98 In considering whether an entity has the majority of the benefits and bears the majority of the risks of an SPE, this is not measured in absolute terms, but rather it is measured by reference to whether an entity is exposed to the majority of the variability of the outcome.

9.99 Operational risks arise where assets that have been derecognised to the SPE are still used in the entity's business. It may be that the entity has an obligation to maintain or renew the assets.

Risks

9.100 An SPE is likely to be a subsidiary where the entity retains the majority of the residual or ownership risks related to the SPE or its assets. [FRS 102 para 9.11(d)]. An indication of control may be obtained by evaluating the risks of each party engaging in transactions with an SPE. Often, the originator guarantees a return or credit protection directly or indirectly through the SPE to outside investors who provide substantially all of the capital to the SPE. As a result of the guarantee, the originator retains residual or ownership risks and the investors are, in substance, only lenders because their exposure to gains and losses is limited. Examples of this type of control might arise where the providers of the capital:

- Do not have a significant interest in the SPE's underlying net assets.

- Do not have rights to the SPE's future economic benefits.

- Are not substantively exposed to the inherent risks of the SPE's underlying net assets or operations.

- In substance receive mainly consideration equivalent to a lender's return through their debt or equity interest.

Subsidiaries excluded from consolidation

9.101 The general rule, under both the Act and section 9 of the standard, requires that all subsidiary undertakings should be included in the consolidated financial statements. A parent entity need only prepare consolidated accounts under the Act if it is a parent at the year end. [CA06 Sec 405(1); FRS 102 para 9.2]. The Act *permits* exclusion of a subsidiary from consolidation where:

- Inclusion is not material for the purposes of giving a true and fair view (see further para 9.105 below). [CA06 Sec 405(2)].

- The information necessary for the preparation of consolidated financial statements cannot be obtained without disproportionate expense or undue delay. [CA06 Sec 405(3)(b)].

- There are severe long-term restrictions over a parent's rights in respect of a subsidiary (see further para 9.107 below). [CA06 Sec 405(3)(a)].

- The parent's interest is held exclusively with a view to resale (see further para 9.110 below). [CA06 Sec 405(3)(c)].

9.102 Within the constraints of the statutory framework set out in the Act, section 9 of FRS 102 refines the conditions for exclusion so that entities identify those undertakings that, even though they are defined by the Act as subsidiaries, are not controlled by the parent in a way that would, in principle, justify consolidation. Having identified such subsidiaries, section 9 of the standard *requires* their exclusion from consolidation.

9.103 Exclusion from consolidation is required in the situations outlined in the third and fourth bullet points above. [FRS 102 para 9.9]. For the fourth bullet point above, this is restricted to exclusion only when *"the subsidiary has not previously been consolidated in group accounts prepared by the parent undertaking"*. [FRS 102 para 9.9(b)]. Further, for the second bullet point above, exclusion on this basis is not permitted unless its inclusion of the subsidiary is not material for the purposes of giving a true and fair view. [FRS 102 para 9.8A].

9.104 Paragraph 9.8 of the standard specifically states that a subsidiary should not be excluded from consolidation where its activities are dissimilar to those of the rest of the group, unless its inclusion is not material (see para 9.105 below).

Immaterial subsidiaries

9.105 Careful consideration needs to be given to all aspects of the subsidiary when assessing materiality. Subsidiaries excluded from consolidation on the basis of materiality should be carefully reviewed each year to confirm that they continue to be immaterial. A change in financial circumstances of the group or of the subsidiary might mean that it becomes material. A parent should consolidate all subsidiaries in all periods rather than report changes in the group's composition from one period to the next.

9.106 If there were a number of immaterial subsidiaries, they should only be excluded where, taken together, they are still not material to the consolidation.

Severe long-term restrictions

Basis of exclusion

9.107 Consolidation of a subsidiary undertaking is not required by the Act where severe long-term restrictions substantially hinder the exercise of the parent entity's rights over the assets or over the management of the undertaking. The rights that must be restricted, in order for this exclusion to apply, are those that would result in the undertaking being a subsidiary of the parent and without which it would not be a subsidiary. [CA06 Sec 405(3); FRS 102 para 9.9(a)]. They include all such rights attributed to the parent undertaking under section 405(3) of the Act. The important difference is that the Act *permits* exclusion on these grounds, whereas section 9 of the standard *requires* exclusion.

9.108 There are a number of situations where a parent's control over its subsidiary might be subject to severe long-term restrictions. These include situations where the following exist:

■   A power of veto is held by a third party.

■   Severe restrictions exist over remittances.

■   Insolvency or administration procedures are in progress.

■   Two parent undertakings are identified under the definitions in the Act, but one does not control the subsidiary undertaking or they exercise joint control.

9.109 Where a parent's control over a subsidiary is subject to severe long-term restrictions, that subsidiary should be excluded from consolidation and treated as an investment in a subsidiary. The investment is measured using the accounting policy selected to account for investments in subsidiaries, associates and jointly controlled entities in the parent's separate financial statements. [FRS 102 para 9.9A]. See paragraph 9.175 below for further details.

Interest held exclusively with a view to subsequent resale

9.110 Consolidation of a subsidiary undertaking is not required where the interest of the parent entity is held exclusively with a view to subsequent resale. [CA06 Sec 405(3)(c)].

9.111 'Held exclusively with a view to subsequent resale' is defined as:

"An interest:

    (a)   for which a purchaser has been identified or is being sought, and which is reasonably expected to be disposed of within approximately one year of its date of acquisition; or

    (b)   that was acquired as a result of the enforcement of a security, unless the interest has become part of the continuing activities of the group or the holder acts as if it intends the interest to become so; or

    (c)   which is held as part of an investment portfolio."

[FRS 102 Glossary of terms].

9.112 In this situation, the 'interests' of the parent entity are the interests attributed to it under the definition of 'parent undertaking'. Again, this exemption is repeated in section 9 of the standard, but with the important difference that the Act *permits* exclusion on these grounds, whereas section 9 *requires* exclusion. [FRS 102 para 9.9(b)]. The circumstances in which a subsidiary held for resale is permitted (and required) to be excluded is also restricted to those where "*the undertaking has not previously been consolidated in group accounts prepared by the parent undertaking*". [FRS 102 para 9.9].

9.113 A subsidiary held exclusively with a view to resale and not previously consolidated, although controlled by its parent, does not form part of the group's continuing activities. The parent's control is temporary and is not used to deploy the underlying assets and liabilities of that subsidiary as part of the group's continuing activities and for the parent's benefit. So, the subsidiary should be excluded from consolidation on these grounds and be treated as a current asset.

9.114 Measurement of the current asset depends on whether or not the investment is held as part of an investment portfolio. If the investment is held as part of an investment portfolio, it is measured at fair value, with changes in fair value recognised in profit or loss. [FRS 102 para 9.9B]. The measurement at fair value through profit or loss prescribed by section 9 of the standard is a departure from the requirements of the Act for the purpose of the consolidated financial statements providing a true and fair view. [SI 2008/410 4 Sch 1(36); FRS 102 para A4.17]. The Act does not permit investments in subsidiaries, associates and joint ventures to be measured at fair value. In this circumstance, the notes to the financial statements must provide the "*particulars of the departure, the reasons for it and its effect*". [SI 2008/410 4 Sch 1(10(2))].

9.115 An investment that is not held as part of an investment portfolio is measured using the accounting policy selected to account for investments in subsidiaries, associates and jointly controlled entities in the parent's separate financial statements. [FRS 102 para 9.9B]. See paragraph 9.175 below for further guidance.

Consolidation procedures

9.116 In preparing its consolidated financial statements, a group should combine the financial statements of the parent and its subsidiaries and present that information as if the group were a single economic entity. [FRS 102 para 9.13]. Consolidated financial statements should generally incorporate all of the information contained in the individual financial statements of the entities included in the consolidation.

9.117 The accounting principles that are used in the consolidation process should be disclosed in the accounting policies note. The accounting principles that need to be considered when performing a consolidation, many of which should be covered in the accounting policy note, are as follows:

■ The effective dates and methods of accounting used to consolidate new subsidiaries; that is acquisition accounting (see further chapter 19) and how to account for disposals (see para 9.155 below).

■ The treatment of any goodwill arising on consolidation (see further chapter 19) and the treatment of other differences arising on consolidation.

■ The translation of foreign subsidiaries' financial statements (see chapter 30).

■ How to account for non-controlling interests (see para 9.138 below).

■ How associates and joint ventures are dealt with (see chapters 14 and 15).

■ How the non-coterminous year ends of the parent and subsidiaries are dealt with (see para 9.130 below).

■ The treatment of intra-group transactions (see para 9.132 below).

Procedure for consolidation

9.118 The income and expenses of a subsidiary are included in the consolidated financial statements from the acquisition date, except where a business combination is accounted for by using the merger accounting method under section 19 of FRS 102 (see chapter 19) or for some public benefit entity combinations falling under section 34 of the standard (see chapter 34). The income and expenses are no longer included from the date on which the parent ceases to control the subsidiary (see para 9.155 below). [FRS 102 para 9.18].

9.119 The consolidated statement of financial position and the consolidated statement of comprehensive income should incorporate the information contained in the individual financial statements of the entities included in the consolidation, subject to some consolidation adjustments. But section 9 of FRS 102 does not specify in detail how the aggregation of this information should be undertaken.

9.120 Section 9 of the standard makes little comment on the process of consolidation, apart from mentioning that, in preparing consolidated financial statements, an entity combines the financial statements of the parent and its subsidiaries line by line, adding together like items of assets, liabilities, equity, income and expenses. [FRS 102 para 9.13(a)]. Some of the steps in the consolidation process are then considered.

9.121 In practice, there are two methods of preparing consolidated financial statements. Under the first method, the individual financial statements of subsidiaries are aggregated centrally by adding together the income statement, statement of financial position and cash flow figures on a line-by-line basis. These aggregate figures taken from the subsidiaries' financial statements are then amended to deal with consolidation adjustments. Such adjustments would be necessary in order to:

- Adjust individual figures in the subsidiaries' financial statements to uniform accounting policies.

- Achieve the consolidation by, for example, dealing with goodwill and non-controlling interests and eliminating intra-group transactions.

9.122 The second method, more suitable for large groups, is for each subsidiary to prepare a consolidation return. The consolidation return is made up from the individual subsidiaries' financial statements which are:

- Adjusted to uniform accounting policies.

- Edited into a format and analysis that makes the consolidation process easier.

9.123 These returns are then aggregated to form the group's consolidated financial statements. Even using this method, consolidation adjustments might still need to be made. For example, entity A would not know how much intra-group profit to eliminate on goods sold to its subsidiary, entity B, because it would not know how much of that stock entity B had sold.

9.124 There are a number of reasons why a parent might have to make consolidation adjustments to its subsidiaries' financial statements in preparing the group's consolidated financial statements. Some of these reasons, and the rules relating to such adjustments, are considered in the paragraphs that follow.

Economic interest

9.125 The rules outlined above are concerned with determining whether an entity is a parent's subsidiary. But they do not determine the economic interest that needs to be taken into account in allocating a subsidiary entity's net assets between the parent and non-controlling interests in preparing consolidated financial statements.

9.126 The proportion allocated to the parent and non-controlling interests in preparing consolidated financial statements is determined solely on the basis of present ownership interests. Although currently exercisable potential voting rights are considered when assessing control, they are not taken into account when determining the economic interest, because this is based solely on present ownership interest. [FRS 102 para 9.14].

Consolidation adjustments

Uniform accounting policies

9.127 Uniform group accounting policies should be used to determine the amounts to be included in the consolidated financial statements. This might require adjustment, on consolidation, of the amounts that have been reported by subsidiaries in their individual financial statements. [SI 2008/410 6 Sch 3(1); FRS 102 para 9.17].

Other consolidation adjustments

9.128 Consolidation adjustments are required for a variety of reasons, and the group's accounting policies will often describe the areas where adjustments are made. The elimination of pre-acquisition reserves, although it would not generally be dealt with specifically in the accounting policies note, is another adjustment that is fundamental to the consolidation process (see further chapter 19).

9.129 A consolidation adjustment might also be necessary where a material 'subsequent event' occurs in a subsidiary between the date when the subsidiary's directors sign the subsidiary's own financial statements and the date when the holding entity's directors sign the consolidated financial statements. If the 'subsequent event' is material to the group and is an 'adjusting event' (which is a post balance sheet event that provides additional evidence of conditions that exist at the balance sheet date), a consolidation adjustment should be made for it in the consolidated financial statements.

Subsidiary year ends

9.130 The financial statements of all subsidiaries to be used in preparing the consolidated financial statements should, wherever practicable, be prepared to the same financial year end and for the same accounting period as those of the parent. [FRS 102 para 9.16]. The directors have an obligation under section 390(5) of the Companies Act 2006 to secure that the financial year of each of its subsidiary undertakings coincides with the parent entity's own financial year, unless in their opinion there are good reasons for this not to be so.

9.131 Where the reporting period and date of the subsidiary are not the same as those of the parent, the Act and section 9 of the standard provide two options. Consolidation of the subsidiary can be based on financial statements made up to its last reporting date before the parent's reporting date, provided the subsidiary's accounting period ends no more than three months before that of its parent. In such a case, the subsidiary's financial statements must be adjusted for the effects of any significant transactions or events that occur between the date of those financial statements and the date of the consolidated financial statements. [SI 2008/410 6 Sch 2(2)(a); FRS 102 para 9.16(a)]. Alternatively, the subsidiary must prepare interim financial statements to coincide with the end of the parent entity's financial year. [SI 2008/410 6 Sch 2(2)(b); FRS 102 para 9.16(b)].

Elimination of intra-group balances and transactions

9.132 Intra-group balances, transactions, income and expenses must be eliminated in full. [FRS 102 para 9.15].

9.133 The rules are as follows:

- Intra-group balances and transactions, including income and expenses and dividends, should be eliminated in full.

- Profits and losses resulting from intra-group transactions that are recognised in assets, such as inventory and fixed assets, should be eliminated in full.

- Intra-group losses might indicate an impairment that might need to be recognised in the consolidated financial statements.

- Section 29 of the standard should be applied to any temporary differences that arise from the elimination of profits and losses resulting from intra-group transactions. See chapter 29 for further guidance on deferred tax recognised on these eliminations.

[FRS 102 para 9.15].

9.134 The rationale for full elimination of unrealised profits or losses, even where the related transactions are between subsidiary entities with non-controlling interests, might not initially be obvious. However, transactions between subsidiaries included in the consolidation are wholly within the control of the parent entity, whether or not the subsidiaries are wholly owned. All the assets and liabilities of a subsidiary, and transactions between subsidiaries, are brought into the consolidation in full, again whether or not they are wholly owned. So, because the group includes 100% of all the subsidiaries' assets and liabilities, intra-group transactions that give rise to profits or losses that are unrealised at the balance sheet date are wholly unrealised to the group and do not represent any increase or decrease in the group's net assets. As a result, they should be eliminated in full, even where the transactions involve subsidiaries with non-controlling interests.

9.135 The following example deals with the elimination of intra-group profit on the sale of assets by a subsidiary to its parent and the elimination of intra-group profit on sale of assets by a parent to its subsidiary. For the purposes of the examples tax is ignored.

Example 1 – Elimination of intra-group profit on sale of assets by a subsidiary to its parent

A parent owns 60% of a subsidiary. The subsidiary sells some inventory to the parent for C70,000 and makes a profit of C30,000 on the sale. The inventory is in the parent's balance sheet at the year end.

The parent must eliminate 100% of the unrealised profit on consolidation. The inventory will, therefore, be carried in the group's balance sheet at C40,000 (C70,000 — C30,000). The consolidated income statement will show a corresponding reduction in profit of C30,000.

The double entry on consolidation is as follows:

		C'000	C'000
		Dr	**Cr**
Dr	Revenue	70	
	Cr Cost of sales		40
	Cr Inventory		30

The reduction of group profit of C30,000 is allocated between the parent company and non-controlling interest in the ratio of their interests – 60% and 40%.

Example 2 – Elimination of intra-group profit on sale of assets by a parent to its subsidiary

The situation is as above except that, on this occasion, it is the parent that makes the sale. The parent owns 60% of a subsidiary. The parent sells some inventory to the subsidiary for C70,000 and makes a profit of C30,000 on the sale. The inventory is in the subsidiary's balance sheet at the year end.

The parent must eliminate 100% of the unrealised profit on consolidation. The inventory will, therefore, be carried in the group's balance sheet at C40,000 (C70,000 — C30,000). The consolidated income statement will show a corresponding reduction in profit of C30,000.

		C'000	C'000
		Dr	**Cr**
Dr	Revenue	70	
	Cr Cost of sales		40
	Cr Inventory		30

9.136 Where an entity makes a loss selling assets (at fair value) to another group entity, careful consideration needs to be given to whether a consolidation adjustment is made. This is because the result of the transaction might indicate that there has been an impairment in the asset, and so it would be wrong to reinstate the asset at a value above its recoverable amount.

9.137 Profits or losses arising on transactions with undertakings excluded from consolidation, because they are held exclusively with a view to subsequent resale or because of severe long-term restrictions, need not be eliminated, except to the extent appropriate where significant influence is retained and the subsidiary is treated as an associate (that is, equity accounted).

Non-controlling interests

Definition and classification

9.138 'Non-controlling interest' is defined as *"the equity in a subsidiary not attributable, directly or indirectly, to a parent"*. [FRS 102 Glossary of terms]. The effect of the provision is, for example, that a parent owning 70% of a subsidiary must consolidate 100% of the subsidiary's results and net assets, and show non-controlling interests of 30%.

9.139 The non-controlling interest is reported as part of equity of the consolidated group, recorded separately from the parent's interests, and clearly identified and labelled (for example, 'non-controlling interest in subsidiaries') to distinguish it from other components of equity. [FRS 102 para 9.13(d)].

Measurement

9.140 Non-controlling interest is measured at each reporting date as:

(i)   the amount of the non-controlling interest at the date of the original combination (see chapter 19); and

(ii)   the non-controlling interest's share of changes in equity since the date of the combination (see para 9.143 below).

9.141 Profit or loss and comprehensive income or loss are attributed to the controlling and non-controlling interests. No particular method is specified for attributing earnings between the controlling interest and the non-controlling interest. [FRS 102 para 9.13(d)]. All earnings and losses of the subsidiary should be attributed to the parent and the non-controlling interest, even if the attribution of losses to the non-controlling interest results in a debit balance in shareholders' equity. [FRS 102 para 9.22].

9.142 If there are contractual arrangements that determine the attribution of earnings, such as a profit-sharing agreement, the attribution specified by the arrangement should be considered if it is determined to be substantive. If no such contractual arrangements exist, the relative ownership interests in the entity should be used if the parent's ownership and the non-controlling interest's ownership in the assets and liabilities are proportional. For example, if the controlling interest owns 60% and the non-controlling interest owns 40% of entity A, 60% of the earnings should be allocated to the controlling interest and 40% to the non-controlling interest. But, if the parties have a contractual arrangement specifying a 50/50 split of the earnings, 50% of the earnings should be allocated to the controlling interest and 50% to the non-controlling interest, provided the contractual arrangement is substantive.

Transactions with non-controlling interests

9.143 Where changes in a parent's ownership interest after control is obtained do not result in a change in control of the subsidiary, they are accounted for as equity transactions. So, the carrying amount of the non-controlling interest will be adjusted to reflect the change in the non-controlling interest's ownership interest in the subsidiary. Any difference between the amount by which the non-controlling interest is adjusted and the fair value of the consideration paid or received is recognised in equity and attributed to the equity holders of the parent. [FRS 102 para 22.19]. See paragraph 9.146 below for further guidance on increases in a controlling interest in a subsidiary.

9.144 Changes in a parent's ownership interest in a subsidiary can also arise as a result of a share-based payment, whereby the parent might grant some of its shares in its subsidiary to that subsidiary's employees, thereby reducing its interest. Such transactions fall within the scope of section 26 of the standard (see chapter 26 for further guidance).

9.145 Entities that owned a controlling interest in a subsidiary before adopting FRS 102 will also record subsequent changes in ownership interests that do not result in a change in control (after adoption of FRS 102) as equity transactions.

9.146 A subsidiary might also issue additional shares to a third party, thereby diluting the controlling interest's ownership percentage. If this dilution does not result in a change in control, it is accounted for as an equity transaction.

> **Example 1 – Sale of a 20% interest in a wholly-owned subsidiary**
>
> Entity A sells a 20% interest in a wholly-owned subsidiary to outside investors for C200 million in cash. Entity A still maintains an 80% controlling interest in the subsidiary. The carrying value of the subsidiary's net assets is C600 million, including goodwill of C130 million from the subsidiary's initial acquisition.
>
> The accounting entry recorded on the disposition date for the 20% interest sold is as follows:
>
> | | | | Cm Dr | Cm Cr |
> |---|---|---|---|---|
> | Dr | Cash | | 200 | |
> | | Cr | Non-controlling interest (20% × C600m) | | 120 |
> | | Cr | Equity | | 80 |

The carrying value of the 20% non-controlling interest which is recognised is calculated at its proportionate interest in the carrying value/net assets of the subsidiary.

Example 2 – Acquisition of a 20% interest in a subsidiary

Entity A acquired 60% of entity B some years ago for C3,000. At the time entity B's fair value was C5,000. It had net assets with a fair value of C3,000 (which for the purposes of this example was the same as book value). Goodwill of C1,200 was recorded (being C3,000 — (60% × C3,000)). On 1 July 20X5, entity A acquires a further 20% interest in entity B, taking its holding to 80%. At that time the fair value of entity B is C10,000 and entity A pays C2,000 for the 20% interest. At the time of the purchase the fair value of entity B's net assets is C6,000 and the carrying amount of the non-controlling interest is C2,000.

The accounting entry recorded for the purchase of the non-controlling interest is as follows:

		C Dr	C Cr
Dr	Non-controlling interest	1,000	
	Equity	1,000	
Cr	Cash		2,000

The carrying value of the 20% non-controlling interest which is eliminated is calculated at the proportionate interest in the carrying value of the non-controlling interest.

Options and forward contracts over shares relating to non-controlling interests

9.147 A parent might write a put option on shares in an existing subsidiary that are held by non-controlling interests. The put option provides the non-controlling shareholder with the right to force the parent to purchase the shares that are subject to the put in accordance with the terms and conditions of the put option. The option might be issued when the parent acquires the controlling interest in the subsidiary or at some later date. The option's exercise price might be a fixed price, fair value or a formula (for example, a multiple of EBITDA). A purchased call option might also accompany the put option, on exactly the same (or similar) terms as the put. The call option provides the parent with the right to force the non-controlling shareholder to sell its shares to the parent in accordance with the terms and conditions of the call option. Alternatively, a forward purchase contract might be entered into, which specifies that the parent will acquire the non-controlling shareholding on a future date at a particular price (which might be, for example, fixed, formula-based or fair value), with no ability for either party to avoid the transaction.

9.148 Section 19 of FRS 102 does not give guidance on how such contracts should be accounted for in a business combination. There is also a lack of guidance where such contracts are entered into by a parent following the business combination. In determining the appropriate accounting treatment, the guidance in both sections 9 and 12 of the standard needs to be considered.

9.149 The main accounting principles are as follows:

(a) The ownership risks and rewards of the shares relating to the forward or option should be analysed, to determine whether they remain with the non-controlling interest or have transferred to the parent. The non-controlling interest is recognised to the extent that the risks and rewards of ownership of those shares remain with them.

(b) Regardless of whether the non-controlling interest is recognised, a derivative financial liability is recorded to reflect the forward or put option. The derivative financial liability is measured at fair value; but, where the derivative is to purchase the stake at fair value, this value would be zero. All subsequent changes to the liability are recognised in profit or loss. For further guidance, refer to chapter 12, because the subsequent treatment is the same as that of other derivatives.

(c) Where the risks and rewards of ownership remain with the non-controlling interest, the derivative financial liability recognised in (b) above is a reduction of controlling interest equity. The non-controlling interest continues to be recognised and is allocated its share of profits and losses in the normal way.

(d) We consider that, where the significant risks and rewards of ownership reside with the controlling interest, the derivative financial liability recognised in (b) above is offset against the non-controlling interest balance:

- If the derivative liability is greater than the non-controlling interest (which is unlikely to be the case), the difference is debited to controlling interest equity. This is to avoid the non-controlling interest becoming negative.

- If the derivative liability is less than the non-controlling interest, it is likely that the non-controlling interest has retained some residual rights, which might be, for example, to future dividends. In this situation, the balance is shown as a non-controlling interest.

- Dividends paid to the non-controlling interest that do not reduce the contracted future purchase price are deducted from the carrying value of the non-controlling interest. Profits and losses are allocated to the non-controlling interest to the extent that it is necessary to cover the dividend payment so that the non-controlling interest does not become negative.

- If the forward or put option states that dividend payments reduce the contracted future purchase price, this will be taken into account when calculating the fair value of the derivative. Dividend amounts paid are treated as part settlement of the derivative liability.

Analysis of risks and rewards

9.150 The terms of the forward and option contracts should be analysed in detail to assess whether they provide the parent with access to the economic benefits and risks associated with the actual ownership of the shares during the contract period. The non-controlling shareholder might have substantially retained the risks and rewards associated with the continued ownership until the contract is settled. Factors to consider in making this assessment include the pricing of the forward contract or options and whether share price movements during the contract period result in benefits and losses being borne by the parent or by the non-controlling shareholder.

9.151 Typically, forwards or options that will be settled with a transfer of the non-controlling interest's shares for a fair value price do not result in a transfer of the risks and rewards of ownership to the parent until the contract is settled. But fixed-price forwards do result in a transfer of risks and rewards of share ownership to the parent from the date when the contract is written. Written put options with a fixed exercise price (where they are accompanied by a similarly priced call option, exercisable at the same future date) are similar, in substance, to a fixed-price forward. If symmetrical put and call options exist, it is often virtually certain that either the parent or the non-controlling shareholder will exercise the option. This is because it will be in the economic interests of one of them to do so. If the share price falls below the fixed strike price, the non-controlling shareholder will exercise the put option and sell the shares (that is, the parent has retained the risks of decline in value during the option period). If the share price increases above the fixed strike price, the parent will exercise the call option and buy the shares (that is, the parent has retained access to the benefits from increases in value during the option period).

9.152 A non-controlling interest is recognised in equity to the extent that the risks and rewards of ownership substantially remain with the non-controlling interest during the contract period. Where all the risks and rewards of ownership have transferred to the parent, a non-controlling interest is not recognised.

9.153 If the forward or symmetrical put and call options are entered into at the same time as the business combination, and an amount is recognised for non-controlling interest, it is recorded in accordance with section 9 of FRS 102. If the contracts are entered into after the date of the business combination, the non-controlling interest is derecognised to the extent that the risks and rewards of ownership have transferred to the parent.

9.154 Evaluating whether the risks and rewards of ownership transfer to the parent or remain with the non-controlling interest is a matter of judgement and requires consideration of all the contract's terms and conditions. There might also be circumstances where the exercise price of the forward or symmetrical put and call options to acquire the non-controlling interest is based on a formula that is not akin to a fair value price. These are complex situations, and determining where the risks and rewards of ownership lie depends on the specific facts and circumstances. So, these types of situation cannot be fully addressed in this guidance.

Loss of control

9.155   A parent will lose control of an entity (that is, its subsidiary) where it no longer has the power to govern the financial and operating policies of that entity, and so cannot gain the benefits from its activities. Such a loss in control might arise even where there has been no change in the absolute or relative ownership interest in the subsidiary. [FRS 102 para 9.18]. There are a number of situations where a parent's control over its subsidiary might be lost, and so it should no longer be treated as a subsidiary. These could include the following situations:

- A parent sells all or part of its ownership interest in its subsidiary, thereby losing its controlling interest in the subsidiary.

- A contractual agreement that gave control of the subsidiary to the parent expires.

- The subsidiary issues shares, thereby reducing the parent's ownership interest in the subsidiary, so that the parent no longer has a controlling financial interest in the subsidiary.

- A power of veto is granted to a third party.

- The parent enters into an agreement with a non-controlling interest holder that gives joint control to both parties.

- A subsidiary becomes subject to the control of a government.

- Insolvency or administration procedures are in progress.

9.156   A subsidiary's income and expenses must be included in the consolidated financial statements until the date on which the parent ceases to control the subsidiary. [FRS 102 para 9.18].

9.157   The gain or loss on disposal of a subsidiary (or disposal of a portion of the shareholding of a subsidiary, with control retained) is calculated as:

(a)   the proceeds from the disposal or the event that resulted in the loss of control; and

(b)   the carrying amount of the subsidiary's net assets, including any related goodwill (or proportion thereof if a portion is disposed of), at the date of disposal or the date when control is lost.

9.158   The gain or loss calculated above is recognised in the consolidated statement of comprehensive income. It should be noted that the cumulative amount of any exchange differences recognised in equity that relate to a foreign subsidiary is not recognised in profit or loss as part of the gain or loss on disposal of the subsidiary. [FRS 102 para 9.18A].

9.159 It is important to identify any gains or losses deferred in accumulated other comprehensive income attributable to the subsidiary. This is because those amounts are included in the gain or loss on the disposal and are required to be reclassified to profit or loss on disposal in accordance with other sections of FRS 102. Amounts that are not required to be reclassified to profit or loss on disposal should be transferred directly to retained earnings. [FRS 102 para 9.18B].

9.160 Where an entity ceases to be a subsidiary, its parent might retain an ownership interest. The retained interest might still be an associate or a joint venture or merely an investment (that is, financial asset). The gain or loss on disposal is calculated using the method described in paragraph 9.155 above. A loss of control is an economic event, similar to that of gaining control, and so it is not a remeasurement event. The carrying amount of the retained interest at the date when the entity ceases to be a subsidiary is regarded as the cost on initial measurement of the financial asset, investment in associate or jointly controlled entity, as appropriate. [FRS 102 para 9.19].

Increasing a controlling interest in a subsidiary

9.161 On the date when the controlling interest is increased, the subsidiary's identifiable assets and liabilities (including contingent liabilities) are not revalued to fair value, and no additional goodwill is recognised. [FRS 102 para 9.19C].

9.162 For details on the accounting for the non-controlling interest, see paragraph 9.138 above.

Exchanges of businesses or other non-monetary assets for an interest in a subsidiary, jointly controlled entity or associate

9.163 Disposals often arise where a parent sells a subsidiary for shares in another entity, which results in that other entity becoming an associate, jointly controlled entity or subsidiary of the vendor. In such a case, there is a disposal of part of the interest in the subsidiary together with an acquisition of the interest in the new associate, jointly controlled entity or subsidiary. The disposal is recognised at the date on which control of the subsidiary is lost; and the acquisition is recognised on the date when the investor gains significant influence, joint control or control over the entity.

9.164 Where entity A exchanges a business or other non-monetary asset for an interest in entity B, which thereby becomes entity A's subsidiary or which becomes entity A's jointly controlled entity or associate, the following accounting treatment is required in entity A's consolidated financial statements:

- To the extent that entity A retains an ownership interest in the original business or non-monetary asset, that retained interest (including any related goodwill) should be included at its pre-transaction carrying amount (that is, it should not be fair valued).

- Entity A's share of net assets acquired through its new interest in entity B should be accounted for at fair value, with the difference between these fair values and the fair value of the consideration given being accounted for as goodwill.

- To the extent that the fair value of the consideration received by entity A exceeds the book value of the part of the business or non-monetary assets no longer owned by entity A (and any related goodwill), together with any cash given up, entity A should recognise a gain. Any unrealised gain should be recognised in other comprehensive income.

- Where the fair value of the consideration received by entity A is less than the book value of the part of the business or non-monetary assets no longer owned by entity A (and any related goodwill), together with any cash given up, entity A should recognise a loss, either as an impairment in accordance with section 27 of the standard or, for any loss remaining after an impairment review of the relevant assets, in entity A's profit and loss account.

[FRS 102 para 9.31].

9.165 As regards the third bullet point above, any unrealised gain should be recognised in other comprehensive income in accordance with paragraph 13(a) of Schedule 1 to SI 2008/410. Under this guidance, the income statement can only include those profits that have been realised at the reporting date. Realisation is an accounting concept rather than a legal concept. Entities (and auditors) need guidance in determining realised profits, because:

- Directors need to know what profits recognised in the financial statements are realised, so that they can determine the amount of profits available for lawful distribution.

- Entities need to comply with paragraph 10(2) of Schedule 1 to SI 2008/410 if there is a departure from the accounting principle of including in the profit and loss account only those profits that are realised – this requires the effect of the departure to be quantified.

- The law assumes that accountants will be in a position to determine what is meant by realised.

9.166 The ICAEW and ICAS have developed detailed guidance (Tech 02/10) on determining realised profits in the context of distributions under the Act. This is *de facto* GAAP on what constitutes a realised profit. The concepts of 'realised' and 'distributable' profits are considered further in chapter 22.

9.167 In rare cases, the artificiality or lack of substance of the transaction might be such that a gain or loss on the exchange could not be justified. In this case, no gain or loss should be recognised. Where a gain or loss on the exchange is not taken into account because the transaction is artificial or has no substance, the circumstances should be explained in the notes to the financial statements. [FRS 102 para 9.32].

9.168 The method required for calculating the gain or loss and goodwill is as follows:

- The book value of assets and liabilities effectively disposed of, plus attributable goodwill, is compared to the fair value of the consideration received (that is, the fair value of the part of the business that is acquired). This is not necessarily the same as the fair value of the net assets acquired, because the fair value of the business includes the goodwill of that element of the business that is acquired. The result is either a gain or a loss arising on the exchange.

- The fair value of the consideration given, which is the fair value of the part of the business disposed of (which, again, might be different from the fair values of the assets and liabilities given up, because it will include a value for the unrecognised goodwill of the business) is compared with the fair values of the assets and liabilities acquired, and the result is recognised as goodwill (either positive or negative).

- The above calculations will be affected if cash settlements are made as part of the exchange.

9.169 To illustrate the first bullet point above, if the book value of the net assets disposed of is £50 and the fair value of the net assets acquired is £60, but the fair value of the business acquired (which contains the net assets acquired) is £70, the comparison is between £50 and £70, and not between £50 and £60.

9.170 Similarly, to illustrate the second bullet point, if the book value of the net assets disposed of is £50 and their fair value is £55, but the fair value of the business given up is £70, it is £70 that is compared with the fair value of the net assets acquired in order to determine the goodwill arising.

9.171 The method prescribed by section 9 of FRS 102 calculates the gain or loss only on the element that has been disposed of to a third party. So, no intra-group profit or loss arises, which would otherwise need to be eliminated on consolidation.

Individual and separate financial statements

Individual financial statements

9.172 The requirements for the preparation of individual financial statements are set out in the Act or other statutory framework.

Separate financial statements

9.173 Separate financial statements are defined as "*those presented by a parent in which the investments in subsidiaries, associates or jointly controlled entities are accounted for either at cost or fair value rather than on the basis of the reported* *results and net assets of the investees. Separate financial statements are included within the meaning of individual financial statements".* [FRS 102 para 9.24].

9.174 The parent entity's financial statements that are required in the UK by section 394 of the 2006 Act, and presented in addition to the consolidated financial statements, are 'separate' financial statements.

9.175 Section 9 of the standard requires the parent to select and adopt an accounting policy for its investments in subsidiaries, associates or jointly controlled entities either:

(a) at cost less impairment;

(b) at fair value, with changes in fair value recognised in other comprehensive income in accordance with section 17 of FRS 102 (see chapter 17); or

(c) at fair value, with changes in fair value recognised in profit or loss.

9.176 As regards accounting policy choice a) above, sections 611 to 615 of the Act set out the treatment where 'merger relief' or 'group reconstruction relief' are available. These reliefs reduce the amount required to be included in share premium; they also (in section 615) allow the initial carrying amount to be adjusted downwards, so it is equal to either the previous carrying amount of the investment in the transferor's books or the nominal value of the shares issued, depending on which relief applies. If the fair value model (accounting policy choices b) and c) above) is used, the relief in section 615 is not available, so the investment's carrying value cannot be reduced, although the provisions in sections 611 and 612 remain relevant in respect of amounts required to be recorded in share premium.

9.177 As regards accounting policy choice c) above, section 11 of FRS 102 provides guidance on fair value (see chapter 11).

9.178 The accounting policy chosen for a class of investment must be applied consistently to each class (that is, investments in subsidiaries, associates or jointly controlled entities). Different accounting policies can be chosen for different classes.

9.179 An investor that does not have investments in subsidiaries, but does have investments in jointly controlled entities or associates, must prepare 'economic interest' financial statements in which these investments are equity accounted; or, where these investments are held as part of an investment portfolio, they must be measured at fair value, with changes in fair value recognised in profit or loss. This is a requirement of sections 14 and 15 of the standard (see chapters 14 and 15).

9.180 The term 'economic interest' financial statements is used throughout this book to describe such financial statements. The term has been used to distinguish such financial statements from consolidated financial statements that are prepared by investors that have subsidiaries as well, and from separate financial statements.

9.181 The situations where 'separate' financial statements and 'economic interest' financial statements are required are summarised in the following diagram.

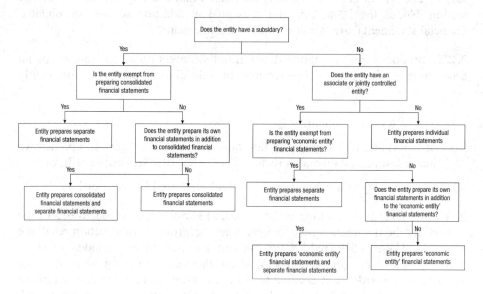

Intermediate payment arrangements

9.182 Section 9 of FRS 102 applies not only to trusts but also to other intermediaries with similar features, for example:

- Although such arrangements are most commonly used to pay employees, they are sometimes used to compensate suppliers of goods and services other than employees. The sponsoring entity's employees and other suppliers are not always the only beneficiaries of the arrangement. Other beneficiaries might include past employees and their dependants, and the intermediary might be entitled to make charitable donations.

- The precise identity of the persons or entities that will receive payments from the intermediary, and the amounts that they will receive, are not usually agreed at the outset.

- The relationship between the sponsoring entity and the intermediary might take different forms. For example, where the intermediary is constituted as a trust, the sponsoring entity will not have a right to direct the intermediary's activities. But, in these and other cases, the sponsoring entity might give advice to the intermediary or might be relied on by the intermediary to provide the information that it needs to carry out its activities. Sometimes, the way in which the intermediary has been set up gives it little discretion in the broad nature of its activities.

- The sponsoring entity often has the right to appoint, or veto the appointment of, the intermediary's trustees (or its directors or equivalent).

- The payments made to or by the intermediary are often cash payments, but might involve other transfers of value.

9.183 Common examples of intermediate payment arrangements are employee share ownership plans (ESOPs) and employee benefit trusts that are used to facilitate employee shareholdings under remuneration schemes. [FRS 102 para 9.33].

De facto control

9.184 The trustees of an intermediary must act at all times in accordance with the interests of the beneficiaries of the intermediary. Most intermediaries are specifically designed to serve the purposes of the sponsoring entity, and to ensure that there will be minimal risk of any conflict arising between the trustees' duties and the sponsoring entity's interest, such that, in practice, there is nothing to encumber implementation of the sponsoring entity's wishes. Where this is the case (most often for trusts established as a means of remunerating employees), the sponsoring entity has *de facto* control. [FRS 102 para 9.33].

Accounting for intermediate payment arrangements

9.185 There is a rebuttable presumption that, where a sponsoring entity makes payments (including asset transfers) to an intermediary, the entity has exchanged one asset for another, and the payment itself does not represent an immediate expense.

9.186 This presumption can be rebutted, at the time when the payment is made to the intermediary, if the entity can demonstrate that:

(a) it will not obtain future economic benefit from the amounts transferred; or

(b) it does not have control of the right or other access to the future economic benefit that it is expected to receive. [FRS 102 para 9.34].

9.187 Where the assets and liabilities of the intermediary are under de facto control of the sponsoring entity, they should be accounted for as an extension of the sponsoring entity's business and recognised in its own financial statements. An example of an asset ceasing to be recognised as an asset of the sponsoring entity is where the intermediary's asset vests unconditionally with the identified beneficiaries. [FRS 102 para 9.35].

9.188 Intermediaries (such as ESOPs and employee benefit trusts) under *de facto* control often hold the sponsoring entity's equity instruments. In this case, the sponsoring entity should account for the equity instruments as if it had purchased them directly. The accounting treatment in the sponsoring entity's individual financial statements is as follows:

Consolidated and separate financial statements

(a) Until the sponsoring entity's equity instruments vest unconditionally with employees, the consideration paid for the equity instruments is deducted from equity.

(b) Consideration paid or received for the purchase or sale of the sponsoring entity's own equity instruments is shown separately in the statement of changes in equity.

(c) The sponsoring entity's assets and liabilities include the other assets and liabilities of the intermediary.

(d) No gain or loss is recognised in profit or loss or other comprehensive income on the purchase, sale, issue or cancellation of the entity's own equity instruments.

(e) Finance costs and any administration expenses are accrued for, rather than recognised when funding payments are made to the intermediary.

(f) Dividend income from the sponsoring entity's own equity instruments is excluded from profit or loss and deducted from the aggregate of dividends paid.

[FRS 102 para 9.37].

Disclosure requirements

Consolidated financial statements

9.189 The following disclosures are required to be made in consolidated financial statements:

(a) the fact that the statements are consolidated financial statements;

(b) the basis for concluding that control exists where the parent does not own, directly or indirectly through subsidiaries, more than half of the voting power;

(c) any difference in the reporting date of the financial statements of the parent and its subsidiaries used in the preparation of the consolidated financial statements;

(d) the nature and extent of any significant restrictions (for example, resulting from borrowing arrangements or regulatory requirements) on the ability of subsidiaries to transfer funds to the parent in the form of cash dividends or to repay loans; and

(e) the name of any subsidiary excluded from consolidation and the reason for exclusion.

[FRS 102 para 9.23].

9.190 In addition to the requirement in (e) above, the Act prescribes the following disclosure concerning subsidiaries *excluded* from consolidation:

- The aggregate amount of the subsidiary's capital and reserves at the end of its relevant financial year and its profit or loss for the period. [SI 2008/410 4 Sch 2(1)]. However, this information does not need to be given where any of the following conditions is satisfied:

  - The group's total investment in its subsidiaries' shares is included in the consolidated financial statements by the equity method of valuation (see chapter 27). [SI 2008/410 4 Sch 2(3)].

  - The entity is exempt by virtue of section 400 (see para 9.15 above) or section 401 of the Companies Act 2006 from the requirement to prepare consolidated financial statements. [SI 2008/410 4 Sch 2(2)].

  - The undertaking is not required under the Act to file its balance sheet with the Registrar of Companies or publish it in Great Britain or elsewhere. Exemption is only allowed under this provision, however, if the group's holding in the undertaking is less than 50% of the nominal value of that undertaking's shares. [SI 2008/410 4 Sch 2(4)].

9.191 The Act requires disclosure of the following information concerning subsidiaries that are included in consolidation:

- Place of origin and reason for consolidation.

- Name of each subsidiary undertaking.

- The country of incorporation, if incorporated outside Great Britain.

- The address of the principal place of business, if the undertaking is unincorporated.

- Whether the subsidiary is included in the consolidation and, if not, the reasons for excluding it.

[SI 2008/410 4 Sch 1(1)–(3), 16(2)].

9.192 Also, it is necessary to disclose the particular definition of 'subsidiary undertaking' that makes an undertaking a subsidiary under the provisions of the Act. [SI 2008/410 4 Sch 16(2)]. But there is an exemption where the undertaking is a subsidiary because the parent holds a majority of its voting rights and it holds the same proportion of shares in the subsidiary as it holds voting rights. This will obviously be the reason for consolidating most subsidiaries, and so disclosure will only be required for other subsidiary undertakings, of which there will be relatively few.

Holdings in subsidiary undertakings

9.193 The following information needs to be given separately (where different) concerning the subsidiary's shares held by the parent and the group:

- The identity of each class of shares held.

■ The percentage held of the nominal value of each of those classes of shares. [SI 2008/410 4 Sch 17].

9.194 Shares that are held on the parent's or group's behalf by any other person should be treated for this purpose as if they are held by the parent. [SI 2008/410 4 Sch 22(1)(2)(a)(3)]. But shares held on behalf of a third party other than the parent or the group should be disregarded for this purpose. [SI 2008/410 4 Sch 22(3)].

9.195 A subsidiary company cannot generally own shares in its parent company. [CA06 Sec 136(1)]. This prohibition applies equally to subsidiaries incorporated overseas. This provision extends to sub-subsidiaries holding shares in their immediate parent companies and in their ultimate parent companies. It also includes any shares held on behalf of the subsidiary by another person as its nominee. [CA06 Sec 144]. But the prohibition does not apply where the subsidiary is acting as a personal representative for a third party, or as a trustee. This exemption only applies, however, where the subsidiary or a parent company is not beneficially interested under the trust. [CA06 Sec 138(1)(2)]. An exemption is also given to market makers. [CA06 Sec 141(1)(2)].

Parent company shares held by subsidiaries

9.196 For the purposes of sections 136 to 138 and 141 to 143 of the Companies Act 2006, the definitions of 'holding company' and 'subsidiary' in section 1159 of the Companies Act 2006 are relevant and not those in section 1162.

9.197 Where a corporate body became a subsidiary company because of the changes to the definition of subsidiaries included in section 1159 of the Companies Act 2006, it can retain any shares that it already held in its parent. But, where shares are held in this way, they will carry no right to vote at company meetings. [CA06 Sec 137(1)].

9.198 In some situations, a subsidiary might find that it does hold shares in its parent. This could arise, for example, where the parent has recently acquired a subsidiary which owned shares in the parent before it became a group member. Sections 136 to 138 and 141 to 143 of the Companies Act 2006 expressly provide that, where a company acquires shares in its parent, but before it becomes a subsidiary of the parent, it can retain those shares. In this circumstance also, those shares will carry no right to vote at company meetings. [CA06 Sec 137(2)].

9.199 The notes to a parent's consolidated financial statements must disclose the number, description and amount of any of its shares that subsidiaries or their nominees hold. [SI 2008/410 4 Sch 3(1)]. But this information is not required where the subsidiary holds the shares as personal representative or as a trustee. [SI 2008/410 4 Sch 3(2)]. However, the exemption for a subsidiary acting as a trustee will not be available if the entity or any of its subsidiaries is beneficially interested under the trust, unless the beneficial interest is by way of security for the purpose of a transaction entered into by it in the ordinary course of a business which includes the lending of money. [SI 2008/410 4 Sch 3(2)].

Significant investment holdings of the parent or group

9.200 Where the parent or any of its subsidiaries has significant holdings in undertakings, additional information is required to be disclosed in the consolidated financial statements. A 'significant holding' means one where the investment in the undertaking concerned amounts to 20% or more of the nominal value of any class of shares in the undertaking. [SI 2008/410 4 Sch 4(2)(a), 20(2)(a)]. (Joint ventures and associated undertakings are considered separately in chapters 14 and 15.)

9.201 The disclosure is also required where the holding by the parent or its subsidiaries exceeds 20% of the amount of the parent's (or the group's) assets. [SI 2008/410 4 Sch 4(2)(b), 20(2)(b)]. The information to be disclosed is as follows:

■   The name of the undertaking.

■   The country of incorporation of the undertaking, if it is incorporated outside Great Britain.

■   The address of its principal place of business, if it is unincorporated.

■   The identity of each class of shares held.

■   The percentage held of the nominal value of each of those classes of shares.

[SI 2008/410 4 Sch 5].

9.202 Additional information is required to be disclosed as follows:

■   The aggregate amount of the capital and reserves of the undertaking at the end of its 'relevant financial year'. 'Relevant financial year' means the financial year ending with, or the last one before, that of the entity.

■   Its profit or loss for the year.

[SI 2008/410 4 Sch 6(1)(4)].

9.203 This additional information need not be disclosed if the undertaking is not required by the Act to deliver to the Registrar of Companies a copy of its balance sheet and does not otherwise publish it (for example, if it is a partnership). But this exemption only applies where the entity's holding is less than 50% of the nominal value of the undertaking's shares. [SI 2008/410 4 Sch 6(2)]. As a result, this exemption is likely to apply to investments in partnerships where the interest in the partnership is less than 50%. The information is also not required if it is immaterial.

9.204 For investments in unincorporated undertakings with capital, 'shares' for the purposes of the paragraphs above means the rights to share in the capital of the undertaking, by virtue of section 1161(2)(b) of the Companies Act 2006. In respect of an undertaking that does not have capital, the term 'shares' refers to any right to share in the profits or liability to contribute to losses of the undertaking, or an obligation to contribute to its debts or expenses on winding up. [CA06 Sec 1161(2)(c)].

Interpretation of 'shares held by the group'

9.205 In the paragraphs above, references to 'shares held by the group' are to shares held by the parent entity or any of its subsidiaries, or to shares held on their behalf. But such references do not include shares held on behalf of third parties. [SI 2008/410 4 Sch 22(3)]. Also, shares held by way of security must be treated as held by the person providing the security where both of the following apply:

■　The rights attached to the shares are exercisable only in accordance with that person's instructions (apart from the right to exercise them for the purpose of preserving the value of the security, or of realising it).

■　The shares are held in connection with granting loans as part of normal business activities, and the rights attached to the shares are exercisable only in that person's interest (apart from the right to exercise them for the purpose of preserving the value of the security, or of realising it).

[SI 2008/410 4 Sch 22(4)].

Disclosure 'seriously prejudicial'

9.206 In some circumstances, the information required by Schedule 4 to SI 2008/410 concerning subsidiaries and other significant holdings in undertakings (summarised above) need not be given where the undertaking is established under the law of a country outside the UK, or it carries on business outside the UK. [CA06 Sec 409(3)(4)]. This exemption will apply where, in the directors' opinion, disclosing information would be seriously prejudicial to the business of that undertaking, or to the business of the parent company, or to any of the parent's subsidiaries. Permission to exclude the information also needs to be obtained from the Secretary of State before this exemption can be used. A group that takes advantage of this exemption is required to disclose this fact in its financial statements. [CA06 Sec 409(5)].

9.207 The section 409(5) statement that exemption has been taken is required to be given, whether or not the group has taken advantage of section 410(1)(2) (see para 9.209 below), which only requires information for subsidiaries that principally affect the group's reported figures to be given in its financial statements. Under section 410(1)(2), the full information for all subsidiaries must be annexed to the company's next annual return; but, where the Secretary of State has granted exemption under section 409(3)(4), this need not include the information regarding the subsidiary excluded on seriously prejudicial grounds.

9.208 The exemption does not apply, however, to the information required by paragraph 3 of Schedule 4 to the 2008/410, which is summarised in paragraph 9.101 above.

Disclosure of excessive information

9.209 There is a further relaxation of the disclosure requirements of Schedule 4 to SI 2008/410 that applies if, in the directors' opinion, the resulting disclosure would be excessively lengthy. This will often be the situation where the group has a significant number of subsidiaries. Where this is so, the directors need only give the required information concerning the undertakings whose results or financial position principally affect the figures shown in the company's annual accounts. [CA06 Sec 410(1)(2)]. However, the directors are required to give the necessary information that relates to undertakings excluded from consolidation, except where they are excluded on the ground of materiality (see para 9.105 above).

9.210 Where the directors take advantage of this exemption, they need to note in the financial statements that the information given is only in respect of principal subsidiaries and significant investments. [CA06 Sec 410(3)(a)]. In addition, the full information (including that disclosed in the financial statements) needs to be annexed to the parent's next annual return. [CA06 Sec 410(3)(b)].

Distributable reserves

9.211 The restrictions on distributions contained in the Act apply to individual entities and not to groups. This is because individual entities make distributions, whereas groups do not. However, users of consolidated financial statements might wish to know the amount that the holding entity could distribute if all the group's subsidiaries were to pay up their realised profits by way of dividends to the parent entity. In the past, some groups have voluntarily disclosed this amount or have stated in their reserves note any amounts that are not available for distribution.

9.212 Entities might also consider it necessary to give such disclosure when the size of a dividend paid or proposed is substantial, in the context of the total distributable reserves of the entity, and there is the risk that the shareholders might be under the mistaken impression that the same level of dividends can be maintained in the future.

Separate financial statements

9.213 Where a parent prepares separate financial statements, those separate financial statements are required to disclose:

(a)   that the statements are separate financial statements; and

(b)   a description of the methods used to account for the investments in subsidiaries, jointly controlled entities and associates.

[FRS 102 para 9.27].

9.214 Where a parent uses one of the exemptions from presenting consolidated financial statements, it needs to disclose the grounds on which it is exempt. [FRS 102 para 9.27A].

9.215 In addition to the requirements above, the Act requires a parent which uses one of the exemptions from presenting consolidated financial statements to disclose the following:

- Details about subsidiaries, including: name; country of incorporation or registration; proportion of shares held; profit/loss for the year; aggregate capital and reserves at the year end; details about non-coterminous year ends; and holdings in shares of the parent.

- Details about significant holdings of greater than 20% in undertakings other than subsidiary undertakings, including: name; country of incorporation; and proportion of shares held.

- Additional information about significant holdings of greater than 20% in undertakings other than subsidiary undertakings, including aggregate capital and reserves, and profit or loss for the year.

- Details about parents, including: name of ultimate parent; name of largest group of undertakings for which consolidated financial statements are drawn up of which the undertaking is a member; and name of the smallest such group.

9.216 The disclosure requirements are extensive and are set out in Parts 1 and 2 of Schedule 4 to SI 2008/410.

9.217 Where a parent adopts a policy of accounting for its investments in subsidiaries, associates or jointly controlled entities at fair value, with changes in fair value recognised in profit or loss, it must comply with the requirements of paragraph 36(4) of Schedule 1 to SI 2008/410 by applying the disclosure requirements of section 11 of FRS 102 to those investments. [FRS 102 para 9.27B].

Disclosure of parent company

9.218 The Companies Act 2006 deals with the disclosures concerning a company's parent (or parents) in Schedule 4 to SI 2008/410. Part 1 of Schedule 4 sets out the disclosures to be made by all companies; Part 2 sets out the disclosures to be made by companies not required to prepare consolidated financial statements; and Part 3 deals with the disclosure requirements for companies that are required to prepare consolidated financial statements. These requirements are identical. The paragraphs that follow summarise these disclosures and make reference to the paragraphs of Schedule 4 that are duplicated.

9.219 Where, at the end of a financial year, a company is a subsidiary, or where the company is a parent company and is itself a subsidiary, it should disclose the name of its ultimate parent company and, if incorporated outside Great Britain, the country of its incorporation (if known). 'Company' includes any corporate body in this context. [SI 2008/410 4 Sch 9].

9.220 Also, where the parent company is itself a subsidiary, similar information has to be disclosed for the parent undertaking (whether or not it prepares consolidated financial statements) that heads the following:

- the largest group of undertakings that prepares consolidated financial statements and of which the company is a member; and

- the smallest group of undertakings that prepares consolidated financial statements and of which the company is a member.

[SI 2008/410 4 Sch 8(1)].

9.221 The information to be disclosed in respect of both of these undertakings is similar to that required by paragraph 9.219 above:

- The name of the parent undertaking.

- The country of incorporation of the undertaking, if it is incorporated outside Great Britain.

- The address of its principal place of business, if it is unincorporated.

- If copies of the undertaking's consolidated financial statements are available to the public, the address from which copies of the financial statements can be obtained.

[SI 2008/410 4 Sch 8(2)(3)(4)].

9.222 Where the ultimate parent company prepares consolidated financial statements, the information in paragraph 9.221 disclosed in the sub-group parent's financial statements need be given only for the ultimate parent and for the smallest group of undertakings that prepare consolidated financial statements which include the sub-group (if such an undertaking exists).

Table 9.1 – Disclosure of ultimate parent company

The Fiction plc – Annual Report and accounts – 31 December 2014

Notes to the accounts (extract)

32. Ultimate parent company

Howarths Inc., incorporated in Canada and listed on the Toronto, Montreal and Vancouver stock exchanges, is regarded by the directors of the company as the company's ultimate parent company.

The largest group in which the results of the company are consolidated is that of which Howarths Inc. is the parent company. The consolidated accounts of Howarths Inc. may be obtained from 18 York Street, Suite 2600, Toronto, Ontario, M5J 0B2.

> The smallest such group is that of which Fiction Holdings Limited is the parent company, whose consolidated accounts may be obtained from 21 Wilson Street, London EC2M 2TQ. Fiction Holdings Limited is registered in England and Wales.

9.223   But, where the ultimate parent does not prepare consolidated financial statements, the information in paragraph 9.219 above needs to be disclosed in the sub-group parent's financial statements. The information set out in paragraph 9.221 above might also be required to be disclosed concerning the largest and smallest groups that prepare consolidated financial statements which include the sub-group. These provisions can be very confusing and are best illustrated by an example.

Example – Disclosure of parent company

Consider the group structure set out in the diagram below:

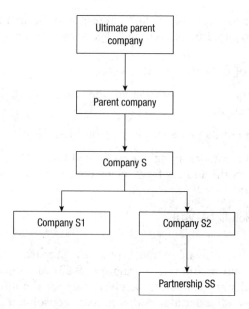

Where the ultimate parent company prepares consolidated financial statements, the following disclosure applies:

- Company A needs to disclose, in respect of the ultimate parent company (being the largest group parent), the information set out in paragraphs 9.219 and 9.221 above. [SI 2008/410 4 Sch 8, 9].

- If company A prepares consolidated financial statements (because it is the parent of the smallest group that prepares consolidated financial statements), company S needs to disclose, in respect of company A, the information set out in paragraph 9.221 above. [SI 2008/410 4 Sch 8]. Company S also needs to disclose, in respect of the ultimate parent company (being also the largest group parent), the information set out in paragraphs 9.219 and 9.221 above. [SI 2008/410 4 Sch 8, 9].

- Company S2 needs to disclose, in respect of the ultimate parent company (being also the largest group parent), the information set out in paragraphs 9.219 and 9.221 above. [SI 2008/410 4 Sch 8, 9]. If company S prepares consolidated financial statements, company S2 also needs to disclose, in respect of company S (being the parent of the smallest group that prepares consolidated financial statements), the information set out in paragraph 9.221 above. [SI 2008/410 4 Sch 8]. If company A prepares consolidated financial statements (because it is the parent of the smallest group that prepares consolidated financial statements), and company S does not prepare consolidated financial statements, company S2 needs to disclose the same information in respect of company A.

Where the ultimate parent company does not prepare consolidated financial statements, the following disclosure applies:

- Company A needs to disclose, in respect of the ultimate parent company, the information set out in paragraph 9.219 above. [SI 2008/410 4 Sch 9].

- If company A prepares consolidated financial statements (because it is the parent of the largest group that prepares consolidated financial statements), company S needs to disclose, in respect of company A, the information set out in paragraph 2.221 above. [SI 2008/410 4 Sch 8]. Company S also needs to disclose, in respect of the ultimate parent company, the information set out in paragraph 2.219 above. [SI 2008/410 4 Sch 9].

- Company S2 needs to disclose, in respect of the ultimate parent company, the information set out in paragraph 2.219 above. [SI 2008/410 4 Sch 9]. If company A prepares consolidated financial statements (because it is the parent of the largest group that prepares consolidated financial statements), company S2 needs to disclose, in respect of company A, the information set out in paragraph 2.221 above. [SI 2008/410 4 Sch 8]. The same information needs to be given in respect of company S (if company S prepares consolidated financial statements because it is the parent of the smallest group that prepares consolidated financial statements). This means that, in the situation described, company S2 is required to disclose information concerning three parent companies. Also, the situation might arise, for example, where another intermediate parent undertaking exists in the group structure between company S and company A. Even where such an undertaking prepares consolidated financial statements, company S2 is still only required to give information concerning company A, company S and its ultimate parent. This is because the legislation only requires the information concerned to be disclosed in respect of the largest and smallest groups preparing consolidated financial statements, and it is not concerned with any other intermediate parents that prepare consolidated financial statements.

9.224 In the majority of situations, these provisions mean that, in practice, the information required by paragraph 2.221 above needs to be given for the next parent undertaking in the group that prepares consolidated financial statements that include the sub-group, and also for the ultimate parent company that prepares consolidated financial statements.

Membership of a qualifying undertaking

9.225 Where a parent company or group is a member of a qualifying undertaking at the year end, it needs to give the following information in its financial statements:

- The name and legal form of the undertaking.

- The address of the undertaking's registered office or, if it does not have such an office, its head office.

[SI 2008/410 4 Sch 7(1)(2)].

9.226 Where the qualifying undertaking is a qualifying partnership, one of the following must also be stated:

- That a copy of the latest financial statements of the undertaking has been, or is to be, appended to the copy of the company's financial statements sent to the Registrar under section 444 of the Act.

- The name of at least one body corporate (which might be the company) in whose consolidated financial statements the undertaking has been, or is to be, dealt with by the method of full consolidation, proportional consolidation or the equity method of accounting.

[SI 2008/410 4 Sch 7(3)].

9.227 For the purpose of these rules, 'qualifying undertakings' can either be companies or partnerships. A qualifying company (or qualifying partnership) is an unlimited company (or partnership) incorporated in (or governed by the laws of any part of) Great Britain, if each of its members is:

- a limited company; or

- another unlimited company, or a Scottish partnership, each of whose members is a limited company.

The references to 'limited company', 'another unlimited company' and 'Scottish partnership' also encompass any comparable undertakings incorporated in, or formed under the law of, any country or territory outside Great Britain. [SI 2008/ 410 4 Sch 7(6); SI 2008/569 Reg 3].

9.228 The information required to be disclosed in the third bullet point of paragraph 9.221 need not be given if the partnership is dealt with either by consolidation, proportional consolidation or equity accounting in the consolidated financial statements prepared by:

- a member of the partnership that is established under the law of a member state; or

- a parent undertaking of such a member established in the same way.

[SI 2008/410 4 Sch 7(5); SI 2008/569 Reg 7(1)].

9.229 The exemption can only be used, however, where the following two conditions are complied with:

- The consolidated financial statements are prepared and audited under the law of the member state in accordance with the provisions of the EC 7th Directive.

- The notes to those consolidated financial statements disclose that the exemption has been used.

[SI 2008/410 4 Sch 7(5); SI 2008/569 Reg 7(2)].

Table 9.2 – Exemption from the requirement to deliver to the Registrar account of a qualifying partnership

ABC p.l.c. – Annual report – 31 December 2014

42 Subsidiary and associated undertakings and joint ventures (extract)

The more significant subsidiary and associated undertakings and joint ventures of the group at 31 December 2014 and the group percentage of equity capital or joint venture interest (to nearest whole number) are set out below. The principal country of operation is generally indicated by the company's country of incorporation or by its name. Those held directly by the parent company are marked with an asterisk (*), the percentage owned being that of the group unless otherwise indicated. A complete list of investments in subsidiary and associated undertakings and joint ventures will be attached to the parent company's annual return made to the Register of Companies. Advantage has been taken of the exemption conferred by schedule 7 of SI 2008/410 from the requirements to deliver to the Register of Companies and publish the annual accounts of ANC P.l.c.

Intermediate payment arrangements

9.230 Where a sponsoring entity recognises the assets and liabilities held by an intermediary, it should disclose sufficient information in the notes to its financial statements to enable users to understand the significance of the intermediary and the arrangement in the context of the sponsoring entity's financial statements. This should include:

(a) a description of the main features of the intermediary, including the arrangements for making payments and for distributing equity instruments;

(b) any restrictions relating to the assets and liabilities of the intermediary;

(c) the amount and nature of the assets and liabilities held by the intermediary, which have not yet vested unconditionally with the beneficiaries of the arrangement;

(d) the amount that has been deducted from equity and the number of equity instruments held by the intermediary, which have not yet vested unconditionally with the beneficiaries of the arrangement;

(e) for entities that have their equity instruments listed or publicly traded on a stock exchange or market, the market value of the equity instruments held by the intermediary, which have not yet vested unconditionally with employees;

(f) the extent to which the equity instruments are under option to employees, or have been conditionally gifted to them; and

(g) the amount that has been deducted from the aggregate dividends paid by the sponsoring entity.

[FRS 102 para 9.38].

Transferring a business around a group

9.231 Group reconstruction relief can be taken in certain situations where assets are transferred around the group where the acquiring company issues shares and where the subsidiaries concerned are wholly-owned. However, many transfers of business are transacted for cash or are left outstanding on the inter-company account and often transactions of this type within a group are not transacted at fair value.

Transfer of a business from a subsidiary to its parent

9.232 An issue arises where a parent acquires a subsidiary and transfers the business of that subsidiary to its parent. This is often referred to as a 'hive-up'. These transfers are carried out at fair value, at book value or at some other amount. This transaction can happen at the same time as the original acquisition of the subsidiary or at a later date.

9.233 These transactions are commonly undertaken at book value (perhaps to achieve a certain tax result). Often the consideration is payable *via* an inter-company account. The issue is how to account for the transaction and in particular whether it is necessary to impair the investment in the subsidiary after the hive-up has taken place. From a group perspective, such a transaction does not result in any loss of value.

9.234 A hive up where the parent acquires a business from its wholly-owned subsidiary can be accounted for in two ways. An entity can account for such a transaction using merger accounting principles (that is, predecessor values) or account for the transaction using acquisition accounting in accordance with FRS 6. If an entity has undertaken such transactions before, then it should generally account for the transaction using the same accounting policy it has previously used.

Example – Hive up immediately after acquisition

Company A acquires company B for fair value £100. Immediately after the acquisition, 100% of company B's business (net assets) is transferred to company A for £40, the carrying value of the business in company B's financial statements. The fair value of the net assets is £80 and the consideration is payable *via* the inter-company account.

This is the first transaction of this type company A has undertaken, hence it should select an appropriate accounting policy and apply this consistently to all future transactions of this type. The initial investment in company B would be recorded as follows:

Company A:

			£	£
Dr		Investment in company B	100	
	Cr	Cash		100

To recognise the initial purchase of the investment in company B.

If predecessor values are used, then generally it is necessary to look to the values in the highest level of the group.

If company A had prepared consolidated financial statements immediately after the acquisition but before the hive-up, it would have recorded net assets acquired of £80 and goodwill of £20 for company B.

Using predecessor values would give the following accounting entries:

			£	£
Dr		Net assets acquired	80	
		Goodwill	20	
	Cr	Investment in company B		60
		Inter-company payable		40

To record the acquisition of the business of company B at its predecessor values that would have arisen in the consolidated financial statements of company A had those been prepared immediately after the acquisition. The credit to the investment in company B is in substance part of the consideration for the acquisition (that is, part of the investment's value is given up as consideration). (Note: that the same principles would apply if company A were a NewCo.)

Company B:

			£	£
	Cr	Net assets transferred		40
Dr		Inter-company receivable	40	

To record the transfer of assets to company A.

If acquisition accounting is used in accordance with the acquisition accounting rules in chapter 19, a full fair value exercise would need to be carried out on acquisition. Where a hive-up takes place immediately after an acquisition, applying acquisition accounting to the hive-up results in the same accounting entries as if predecessor values had been used.

The use of predecessor values or acquisition accounting is a policy choice for the company. Normally this choice would result in different accounting, but in the circumstance where the transfer of the business is made immediately after the acquisition, both policies result in the same accounting.

9.235 Where the transaction takes place some time after the original acquisition it can be argued that there has not been another business combination, because company A and its group acquired company B some time ago. If this argument is followed it is necessary to develop an accounting policy for this transaction and following this approach using merger accounting principles (that is, predecessor values) is an appropriate method. However, there might be other situations where the facts and circumstances could justify a different accounting approach.

Example – Hive up some time after original acquisition

Using the same basic facts as in the example in paragraph 9.232, except that, the business is transferred to company A for £45, the net assets of company B in the consolidated financial statements are £90 and the goodwill recognised is £20 at the date of the transfer. Taking the values in the highest level of the group, using predecessor values this would give the following accounting entries.

Company A

			£	£
Dr	Net assets acquired		90	
Dr	Goodwill		22	
	Cr	Investment in company B		55
	Cr	Inter-company payable		45
	Cr	Unrealised reserve		10

To record the reorganisation of the business of company B at its predecessor values in the consolidated financial statements of company A and to recognise an increase in shareholders' funds.

The credit to the investment in company B is in substance part of the consideration for the reorganisation (that is, part of the investment's value is given up as consideration).

Transfer of a subsidiary from one group member to another

9.236 Groups may reorganise themselves by transferring subsidiaries or businesses around the group for less than the carrying amount of the investment, for example, for the carrying amount of the subsidiary's net assets or for no consideration. This can appear to cause an impairment of the parent's investment in the transferor. Consider this example:

Example – Impairment in a group reorganisation

Company A has direct 100% subsidiaries B and C. Company C has a 100% subsidiary D:

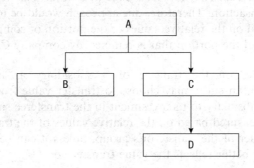

Company A:
Investment in company B	£100m
Investment in company C	£200m

Company C:
Investment in company D	C150m
Other assets	C50m

Company D:
Net assets	C120m

The recoverable amounts of company A's investments in company B and company C exceed their carrying amounts. Company A accounts for investments in subsidiaries at historical cost.

In this reorganisation company C transfers its investment in company D to company B for £120m cash, being the carrying amount of company D's net assets. Company C accounts for the transaction at transaction price and records a loss of £30m. Following the transaction, the recoverable amount of company A's investment in company C falls to £170m. Hence, company A's investment in company C appears to be impaired. However, company A has not suffered any loss of value and so it would not be appropriate to recognise an impairment.

Company A should account for a transfer of value from the investment in company C to the investment in company B. As this type of transaction is not covered by UK GAAP an accounting policy should be developed to support this treatment. This treatment is supported by paragraph 2.8 of FRS 102, as this requires transactions to be accounted for and presented in accordance with their substance and economic reality and not merely their legal form.

> This method recognises that the cost to company A of this transaction is a reduction in the value of its investment in company C, so recognition of this value as part of the investment in company B is a cost method.

9.237 In many cases it is inappropriate to transfer the full carrying amount of the investment in company C to the investment in company B, because company C may retain other assets, and company D may be one of many subsidiaries of company C. The transfer should be done at a value that reflects the economic effect of the transaction. Therefore, one approach would be to measure the value transferred based on the relative values of the portion of company C's group that is transferred and the portion that is retained by company C.

9.238 Therefore, on the transfer of a subsidiary as in the example in paragraph 9.236, an entity may choose to transfer value from its investment in the transferor subsidiary to its investment in the transferee subsidiary. The value transferred is measured based on the relative values of the transferred subsidiary and the remainder of the transferor's group, unless it can be demonstrated that another method better reflects the value transferred.

> **Example – Transfer of investment value based on relative values**
>
> This example uses the same facts as the example in paragraph 9.236. If the fair value of company D is £170m and the fair value of company C's group after the transaction is £170m, company A transfers half of its investment in company C to the investment in company B, that is, £100m, because company A's investment in company C before the transfer was £200m.

Transfer of a subsidiary by dividend

9.239 Where the transfer of the subsidiary is achieved by means of a dividend between companies under common control, the transferee recognises the dividend at the fair value of the investment received. The transferor has an accounting policy choice as to whether to recognise the dividend at the book value or fair value of the investment that is being distributed.

Transition issues

Non-controlling interests

9.240 Section 35 of FRS 102 requires that on first time adoption of the FRS, an entity should not retrospectively change the accounting that it followed under its previous financial reporting framework for measuring non controlling interests. So, an entity applies the following requirement prospectively from the date of transition:

"*The requirements:*

(i) *to allocate profit or loss and total comprehensive income between non-controlling interest and owners of the parent;*

9072

(ii) for accounting for changes in the parent's ownership interest in a subsidiary that do not result in a loss of control; and

(iii) for accounting for a loss of control over a subsidiary

shall be applied prospectively from the date of transition to this FRS (or from such earlier date as this FRS is applied to restate business combinations — see paragraph 35.10(a))."

[FRS 102 para 35.9(e)].

Individual and separate financial statements

9.241   Where an entity prepares individual or separate financial statements, Section 9 of FRS 102 requires the entity to account for its investments in subsidiaries, associates, and jointly controlled entities either:

"(i)   at cost less impairment; or

(ii)   at fair value."

[FRS 102 para 35.10(f)].

9.242   Where a first-time adopter elects to measure such an investment at cost, it determines this in accordance with section 9, 14 or 15 of the standard or at deemed cost. The deemed cost is the carrying amount at the date of transition as determined under the entity's previous GAAP. [FRS 102 para 35.10(f)].

9.243   Where an entity does not have a policy of revaluation going forward for its investments and did not have a policy of revaluation prior to the conversion to FRS 102, it would not be able to use fair value at the date of transition as deemed cost, as the exemption in paragraph 35.10(f) of FRS 102 does not allow for this.

Subsidiary, joint venture or associate adopts later than the group

9.244   There are two options where an entity adopts FRS 102 at a date later than the group headed by its parent (or entity that has significant influence or joint control over it). It may measure its assets and liabilities at either:

"(i)   the carrying amounts that would be included in the parent's consolidated financial statements, based on the parent's date of transition to this FRS, if no adjustments were made for consolidation procedures and for the effects of the business combination in which the parent acquired the subsidiary; or

(ii)   the carrying amounts required by the rest of this FRS, based on the subsidiary's date of transition to this FRS ..."

[FRS 102 para 35.10(r)].

9.245 It should be noted that, if the subsidiary was acquired after the parent's date of transition to FRS 102, the first option would not be available. This is because the *"carrying amounts that would be included in the parent's consolidated financial statements, based on the parent's date of transition to this FRS ..."* simply would not exist. Since the parent did not have control over the subsidiary at its date of transition, the subsidiary was not included in the parent's consolidated financial statements at that date.

9.246 Where a parent entity that prepares consolidated financial statements adopts FRS 102 for the first time, it will require information from its subsidiary for those consolidated financial statements as at the date of transition. From this date onwards, the subsidiary will have to produce the information as if it had adopted FRS 102 for the first time from the parent's date of transition. The subsidiary might not ever have produced full financial statements under FRS 102. It makes sense that, when the subsidiary moves to FRS 102 at a later date, it has the option to use the same assumptions, exemptions and figures as it produced when its parent moved to FRS 102.

9.247 Where the subsidiary uses the group's date of transition as the basis of its own financial statements, the subsidiary's assets and liabilities on its transition can be stated at *"the carrying amounts that would be included in the parent's consolidated financial statements, based on the parent's date of transition to this FRS, if no adjustments were made for consolidation procedures and for the effects of the business combination in which the parent acquired the subsidiary"*, for example, to eliminate inter-company profit in inventory, to align group accounting policies and any adjustments relating to the subsidiary's acquisition. [FRS para 35.10(r), emphasis added].

9.248 This is illustrated in the example below.

> **Example – Subsidiary adopts FRS 102 later than group: measurement of assets and liabilities**
>
> Group M has a date of transition to FRS 102 of 1 January 2013, producing its first FRS 102 financial statements for the year to 31 December 2014.
>
> On transition to FRS 102, group M decides to use the deemed cost exemption and measures its buildings at their fair value at 1 January 2013 of C1.2m, using these fair values as deemed cost. The buildings had previously been stated at a net book value of C400,000, being cost of C600,000 less depreciation of C200,000, at 31 December 2012. One of the buildings, with a fair value of C450,000, a cost of C200,000 and a net book value of C150,000, was held in subsidiary N. The asset is being depreciated over 20 years and had 15 years remaining. Group M assesses that all of its buildings have a remaining useful economic life at the date of transition of 15 years.
>
> Subsidiary N has a transition date of 1 January 2014 and produces its first FRS 102 financial statements for the year to 31 December 2015 with one year of comparatives. Subsidiary N did not revalue its property under old UK GAAP. The net book values at 31 December are as follows:

Year to	Subsidiary N (old UK GAAP) C'000	Consolidation adjustment C'000	N adjusted C'000	Rest of group C'000	Group M consolidated (FRS 102) C'000
31 December 2012	150[1]	300	450	750	1,200[2]
31 December 2013	140	280[3]	420	700[4]	1,120
31 December 2014	130	260	390	650	1,040

[1] 200 — 50
[2] Deemed cost on transition
[3] (450 — (450 ÷ 15)) — 140
[4] 750 — (750 ÷ 15)

In its old UK GAAP financial statements at 31 December 2014 subsidiary N has a net book value for the building of C130,000, represented by cost of C200,000 less 7 years of depreciation of C70,000.

When subsidiary N moves to FRS 102 in 2015 it may use the exemption for the assets and liabilities of subsidiaries and, at its date of transition of 1 January 2014, measure its building at the carrying amount that would be included in the consolidated financial statements based on the parent M's date of transition.

This means using the 'deemed cost' at the time of parent M's transition of C450,000 less depreciation of C30,000 to give a net book value of C420,000 in subsidiary N's own separate financial statements at 1 January 2014.

The value in entity N's financial statements is the C420,000 'based on' the C450,000 value used in group M's consolidated financial statements at its date of transition, rather than the actual C450,000 'fair value as deemed cost' used in group M's consolidated financial statements.

Entity N should state the assets at a net book value of C420,000 at its date of transition of 1 January 2014, being deemed cost of C450,000 less deprecation to date of C30,000. Our view is that the gross cost and depreciation (C450,000 and C30,000) should be reported in the subsidiary's own separate FRS 102 financial statements, and not a deemed cost of C420,000, as this provides more information to the users of the financial statements. At entity N's reporting date of 31 December 2015 the building will be stated at cost of C450,000 less depreciation of C90,000, giving a net book value of C360,000.

The other option open to entity N in its own separate first FRS 102 financial statements is to use the deemed cost exemption. It could then fair value its buildings at the date of transition, 1 January 2014 and either continue to value them going forward or treat this as deemed cost and adopt a cost less depreciation model.

Entity N could also choose to carry forward its previous cost and depreciation. The building will be stated at cost of C200,000 less depreciation of C80,000, giving a net book value of C120,000 at entity N's reporting date. This will result in a consolidation adjustment being required for the M group going forward.

The consolidation adjustment in this example reflects only the fair value adjustment to entity N's fixed assets on parent M's transition. This is not a consolidation adjustment that should be ignored for the purposes of the assets and liabilities of subsidiaries exemption, such as adjustments for the elimination of intra group profits.

9.249 The second option given by the 'assets and liabilities of subsidiaries' exemption is that a subsidiary may use carrying amounts based on the subsidiary's own date of transition. This allows the subsidiary to adopt FRS 102 independently of the group to which it belongs. The subsidiary can make its own choice from the exemptions available, at its own date of transition to FRS 102. The standard notes that the carrying amounts under the second option could differ from those under the first option when the exemptions in FRS 102 result in measurements that depend on the date of transition to the FRS, or when the accounting policies used in the subsidiary's financial statements differ from those in the consolidated financial statements. For example, for property plant and equipment, the subsidiary may use as its accounting policy the cost model in section 17, whereas the group many use the revaluation model.

9.250 The same exemption is available to associates or joint ventures that adopt FRS 102 at a date later than the entities that have significant influence or joint control over them. [FRS 102 para 35.10(r)]. This could give more options to associates or joint ventures where more than one party has significant influence or joint control, or the investors or joint venturers have different transition dates.

Group adopts later than subsidiary, joint venture or associate

9.251 There are no similar options when a group becomes a first-time adopter later than its subsidiary, associate or joint venture. The standard sets out the carrying amounts for assets and liabilities that must be used. The entity, in its consolidated financial statements, should measure the assets and liabilities of the subsidiary, associate or joint venture at the "*same carrying amounts as in the financial statements of the subsidiary (or associate or joint venture), after adjusting for consolidation (and equity accounting) adjustments and for the effects of the business combination in which the entity acquired the subsidiary (or transaction in which it acquired the associate or joint venture)*". [FRS 102 para 35.10(r)]. Once part of the group has moved to FRS 102, the group as a whole should use the carrying amounts adopted by that subsidiary, associate or joint venture.

9.252 It is necessary to establish which assets and liabilities existed at the date of acquisition, and which assets and liabilities have since been acquired or assumed, to determine the carrying amounts of assets or liabilities. The business combination exemption requirements are applied to the carrying amounts of assets and liabilities that existed at the date of acquisition. The carrying amounts of assets and liabilities acquired or assumed after the subsidiary, associate or joint venture was acquired are measured at the same carrying amounts as in the subsidiary, associate or joint venture's own financial statements after adjusting for the effect of consolidation (and equity accounting adjustments). These might include accounting policy alignment, profits and losses included in assets. [FRS 102 para 35.10(r)].

Example – Group adopts later than associate

An investor acquired a 25% stake in an associate in 20X1. The associate had net assets of 400 with a fair value of 600. Goodwill is ignored in this example.

Since acquisition, the associate has acquired a property that cost 200. The associate adopts FRS 102 before the investor, did not use the deemed cost exemption and continues to recognise all property at historical cost. The associate has net assets of 600 in its own FRS 102 financial statements at the date the investor transitions to FRS 102 (depreciation is ignored for the purpose of this example).

When the investor adopts FRS 102 it bases its 25% share on net assets of 800, being 600 in respect of the fair value assigned to the property that the associate owned at the time of acquisition in 20X1 and 200 in respect of the property subsequently purchased (the investor must base its share on the carrying amount in the associates own FRS 102 financial statements – as the associate did not take advantage of the fair value deemed cost exemption and chose to continue with historical cost, so must the investor).

Parent entities adopting earlier or later than the group

9.253 The rules are slightly different for parent entities. A parent entity that becomes a first-time adopter in its own separate financial statements at a different date from that used for its consolidated financial statements should use the same carrying amounts (except for consolidation adjustments) in both sets of financial statements. [FRS 102 para 35.10(r)]. The position in consolidated financial statements of a parent that moves to FRS 102 before the group does is the same as that for a subsidiary that moves before the group: the consolidated financial statements should use the measurements from the parent's individual financial statements. However, the parent does not have the same option as a subsidiary that moves to FRS 102 later than the group in its own separate financial statements. It cannot adopt FRS 102 at its 'own' transition date, but rather has to base its measurements on those that the group used.

Example – Parent adopts FRS 102 later than subsidiary: property, plant and equipment measurement

Entity C prepares its first FRS 102 financial statements for the year ending 31 December 2015. The date of transition to FRS 102 is 1 January 2014 and the opening FRS balance sheet is prepared as at that date.

Entity C applies UK GAAP in its consolidated financial statements. It has two subsidiaries in the UK which already apply FRS 102 in their local statutory financial statements.

The existence of subsidiaries that already apply FRS 102 restricts the exemptions available to entity C.

Entities A and B measured their property, plant and equipment at cost. Entity C is not permitted to apply the revaluation method and must use the amounts recorded by entities A and B in the consolidated opening FRS 102 balance sheet.

Entity C's management may elect to follow a different accounting policy from that applied by entities A and B, for example the revaluation model, but it must use the cost measurement that the subsidiaries recorded as a starting point.

Chapter 10

Accounting policies, estimates and errors

Chapter 10

Accounting policies, estimates and errors

Selecting and applying accounting policies

Definition

10.1 Accounting policies are the specific principles, bases, conventions, rules and practices applied by an entity in preparing and presenting financial statements. [FRS 102 para 10.2]. Accordingly, they are essential for a proper understanding of the information contained in the financial statements.

Accounting policies contained in an FRS or FRC Abstract

10.2 Where an FRS or FRC Abstract specifically addresses a transaction, other event or condition, the accounting policy or policies applied to that item must conform to that FRS or FRC Abstract. [FRS 102 para 10.3].

10.3 It is not necessary to apply those policies if the effect of applying them is immaterial. [FRS 102 para 10.3]. But this does not mean that immaterial departures from an FRS or FRC Abstract can be made, or left uncorrected, in order to achieve a particular presentation of an entity's financial position, financial performance or cash flows. The concept of materiality is discussed in chapter 2.

Policies not contained in an FRS or FRC Abstract

10.4 An entity might have a particular transaction, other event or condition that is not specifically addressed by an FRS or FRC Abstract. In this case, management should use its judgement in developing and applying an accounting policy that results in information that is:

- relevant to the economic decision-making needs of users; and
- reliable, in that the financial statements:
    - represent faithfully the financial position, financial performance and cash flows of the entity;
    - reflect the economic substance of transactions, other events and conditions, and not merely the legal form;
    - are neutral (that is, free from bias);
    - are prudent; and
    - are complete in all material respects.

[FRS 102 para 10.4].

10.5 The freedom from bias (or the requirement to be neutral) might have to be tempered by prudence because of uncertainties that inevitably surround many events and circumstances. Such uncertainties are acknowledged by the entity disclosing their nature and extent and by the entity exercising prudence. But the exercise of prudence does not allow an entity to deliberately understate its assets or income, or overstate its liabilities or expenses. In short, prudence does not permit bias. [FRS 102 para 2.9].

10.6 When management selects an accounting policy, it must refer to the following sources, and consider their applicability, in the order set out below:

- the requirements and guidance in an FRS or FRC Abstract dealing with similar and related issues;

- where an entity's financial statements are within the scope of a Statement of Recommended Practice (SORP), the requirements and guidance in that SORP dealing with similar and related issues; and

- the definitions, recognition criteria and measurement concepts for assets, liabilities, income and expenses and the pervasive principles in section 2 of FRS 102 (see chapter 2).

[FRS 102 para 10.5].

10.7 FRS 102 notes that management may also consider the requirements and guidance in EU-adopted IFRS dealing with similar and related issues, although this is not a requirement. [FRS 102 para 10.6]. But the standard requires specified entities to apply IAS 33, 'Earnings per share', IFRS 8, 'Operating segments' or IFRS 6, 'Exploration for and evaluation of mineral resources'. [FRS 102 paras 10.6, 1.4-1.7].

10.8 FRS 102 is silent on whether entities may refer to another national GAAP where a transaction, other event or condition is not addressed by an FRS or FRC Abstract. We believe that the absence of a specific reference to consider other national GAAPs is not in itself significant and should not cause difficulty, in practice, in developing a suitable accounting policy. For instance, if an accounting treatment is specified in another national GAAP, for which there is no equivalent guidance in the sources above, but the particular accounting treatment accords with the definitions, recognition criteria and measurement concepts discussed in section 2 of the standard, that accounting policy should be appropriate under the standard because it would provide information that is still relevant and reliable.

10.9 Also, an accounting treatment for a transaction or event that is not specifically addressed in the sources above (but which nevertheless applied previously under UK GAAP) might continue to be appropriate under an FRS or FRC Abstract. In practice, this situation is likely to be relevant to industry-specific issues for which there is no guidance in an FRS, FRC Abstract or in a SORP.

Consistency

10.10 An entity selects and applies its accounting policies consistently for similar transactions, other events and conditions, unless an FRS or FRC Abstract specifically requires or permits categorisation of items for which different policies might be appropriate. If an FRS or FRC Abstract requires or permits such categorisation, management should select an appropriate accounting policy and apply it consistently to each category. [FRS 102 para 10.7].

10.11 FRS 102 allows choice; for example, a property interest held under an operating lease that is subsequently sublet and meets the definition of an investment property might be treated as an investment property, while another property interest held under an operating lease (that also qualifies as an investment property) might be treated as an operating lease (see chapter 16). Property interests that are treated as investment properties and those that are treated as operating leases are regarded as different categories. The principle of consistency requires that, where an entity adopts different policies for different categories, the policy adopted for each category should be applied consistently for all property interests included in that category and from one accounting period to another.

Issues for groups

10.12 Where consolidated financial statements are prepared, FRS 102 requires that uniform accounting policies are applied in their preparation. Where individual group entities do not apply the group accounting policies, the standard requires the necessary adjustments to be made, as part of the consolidation process, to achieve uniformity. [FRS 102 para 9.17]. The Companies Act envisages that, in exceptional circumstances, non-uniform accounting policies might be applied in preparing group accounts [SI 2008/410 6 Sch 3(2)], but this is overridden by the requirement of the standard.

10.13 Where the individual financial statements of the parent and subsidiaries are being prepared, questions might arise as to whether consistent accounting policies need to be adopted in the different sets of financial statements. There are two aspects to this issue:

■ Do all group entities need to apply the same accounting framework?

■ Do all group entities need to apply the same accounting policies?

Consistent accounting framework

10.14 The directors of a parent company must ensure that the individual accounts of a parent company and each of its subsidiaries are prepared using the same financial reporting framework (except where, in the directors' opinion, there are good reasons for not doing so). [CA06 Sec 407].

10.15 The two financial reporting frameworks under the Act are EU-adopted IFRS and 'Companies Act accounts'. It is important to note that 'Companies Act accounts' encompasses both FRS 101 and FRS 102 (and also the Financial Reporting Standard for Smaller Entities). At first glance, this seems counter-intuitive because FRS 101 is based on EU-adopted IFRS, whereas FRS 102 is adapted from the IFRS for SME standard; but, in legal terms, they are both Companies Act accounts and so are treated as being the same financial reporting framework. It is thus possible for a group to comprise a parent and subsidiaries, some of which prepare their accounts using FRS 101 and some using FRS 102, whilst meeting the Act's requirement for a consistent reporting framework.

10.16 Under the Act, the requirement for the same financial reporting framework across the group does not apply:

■ where the directors do not prepare group accounts for the parent company;

■ to subsidiaries that are not required to prepare individual accounts under the Act;

■ to subsidiary charities (whose financial reporting framework can be different to the non-charity subsidiaries and/or the parent); or

■ where the directors of the parent company prepare both the group accounts and parent individual company accounts using EU-adopted IFRS (in which case there only has to be a consistency of framework across the subsidiaries).

Consistent accounting policies

10.17 FRS 102 does not include any requirement for each group entity to adopt the same accounting policies. The Companies Act similarly does not require the accounting policies of the parent, the subsidiaries and the group to be the same in their individual financial statements. Indeed, paragraph 4 of Schedule 6 to SI 2008/410 requires differences between the accounting policies used in the parent's own financial statements and the group financial statements to be disclosed and the reasons given.

10.18 Overseas subsidiaries that do not prepare individual financial statements under the Companies Act are beyond the jurisdiction of FRS 102, so the question is not relevant. For example, in the standard, LIFO inventory valuations are considered to be likely to be incompatible with the requirement to give a true and fair view. But such valuations are allowed by GAAP in some other countries (for example, the US). So, there might be good reasons for subsidiaries in different jurisdictions having different policies.

10.19 For each group entity that reports under FRS 102, the standard requires the directors to go through the same accounting policy selection process described in paragraphs 10.6 to 10.9 above. The factors that the parent entity's management would take into account in selecting accounting policies for the group's consolidated financial statements would generally also apply to the individual entities; so, in most cases, it would be reasonable to expect that the same accounting policies would be selected for the group, the parent and the subsidiaries reporting under FRS 102.

10.20 But there might be special reasons for adopting different policies. The particular circumstances of different reporting entities, or the cost-benefit equations between different reporting entities and their users, could differ significantly. As an example, comparability with other GAAPs might score highly in the selection of accounting policies for the consolidated financial statements, but might be less of an issue for the users of the individual entities' financial statements; and so other factors, such as the effect of different accounting policies on subsidiaries' distributable profits, might weigh more heavily in the selection of the most appropriate accounting policies for them.

10.21 Deciding to adopt consistent or different policies to some extent involves the judgements of different management teams. If different policies are adopted, an entity should be able to justify this with sound business or commercial reasons.

Disclosure of accounting policies

10.22 An entity is required to disclose a summary of its significant accounting policies. [FRS 102 para 3.17(e)]. This comprises the measurement basis (or bases) used in preparing the financial statements, together with any other accounting policies used that are relevant for an understanding of the financial statements. [FRS 102 para 8.5]. See also chapter 8.

10.23 Management needs to exercise its judgement as to which accounting policies it considers to be significant and relevant to an understanding of the financial statements. But FRS 102 specifically requires the following accounting policies, where material, to be disclosed:

- In individual financial statements, the policies for accounting for subsidiaries, jointly controlled entities and associates. [FRS 102 para 9.27(b)].

- Financial instruments. [FRS 102 para 11.40].

- Inventories. [FRS 102 para 13.22(a)].

- Investments in associates. [FRS 102 para 14.12(a)].

- Investments in jointly controlled entities. [FRS 102 para 15.19(a)].

- Measurement bases and depreciation methods for property, plant and equipment. [FRS 102 para 17.31(a) and (b)].

- Revenue recognition. [FRS 102 para 23.30(a)].

- Government grants. [FRS 102 para 24.6(a)].

- Termination benefits. [FRS 102 para 28.43].

- Heritage assets. [FRS 102 para 34.55(c)].

- Public benefit entity concessionary loans. [FRS 102 para PBE34.95].

10.24 The Companies Act 2006 also specifically requires disclosure of the accounting policies in respect of depreciation and diminution in the value of assets. [SI 2008/410 1 Sch 44].

10.25 In some cases, an FRS or FRC Abstract permits a choice of accounting policies. For example, borrowing costs might be included in the cost of the asset or recognised as an expense immediately (see chapter 25). In such situations, entities will need to make clear which of the available options they have chosen, if the FRS or FRC Abstract does not otherwise require the entity to disclose this.

Changes in accounting policies

10.26 An entity should only change an accounting policy if the new policy:

- is required by a change to an FRS or FRC Abstract; or

- results in the financial statements providing reliable and more relevant information about the effects of transactions, other events or conditions on the entity's financial position, financial performance or cash flows.

[FRS 102 para 10.8].

10.27 So, an entity applies the same accounting policy from one period to the next, unless a change in policy meets at least one of the two conditions specified above. This is because users of the financial statements need to be able to compare the financial statements of an entity over time in order to appreciate trends in its financial position, financial performance and cash flows.

10.28 A change in accounting policy encompasses changes in the recognition and measurement principles for assets, liabilities, income and expenses; it also includes changes in the way in which such items are classified and presented in the financial statements. For example, where an entity changes its classification of certain overheads from cost of sales to administrative expenses, this would represent a change in accounting policy. Similarly, if an entity that has previously presented a single statement of comprehensive income decides instead to present two statements (or vice versa), this constitutes a change in accounting policy. [FRS 102 para 5.3].

10.29 Where an FRS or FRC Abstract allows a choice of accounting treatment (including a choice in the selection of the measurement basis) for a specified transaction or other event or condition and an entity changes its choice, that is a change in accounting policy. [FRS 102 para 10.10].

10.30 Once an entity has selected an accounting policy for a particular transaction or event that is prescribed in an FRS or FRC Abstract, there is a presumption that the entity will continue to apply that policy in future periods.

This presumption is understandable, given that the consistent use of accounting policies enhances the usefulness of financial statements. But the technological, market, economic and legal environment in which the entity operates is constantly changing, and entities must adapt to such changing circumstances and events. This might cause an entity to revisit its previous policies and practices and, if necessary, change them. This voluntary change in policy is permissible (as noted in the second bullet point in para 10.26 above) only if management believes that the change will result in reliable and more relevant information being presented in the financial statements.

10.31   The following are not changes in accounting policy:

- The application of an accounting policy for transactions, other events or conditions that are different in substance from those previously occurring.

- The application of a new accounting policy for transactions, other events or conditions that did not occur previously or were not material.

- A change to measurement at cost when a reliable measure of fair value is no longer available (or vice versa) for an asset that an FRS or FRC Abstract would otherwise require or permit to be measured at fair value.

[FRS 102 para 10.9].

10.32   Where management voluntarily applies an accounting policy based on another acceptable GAAP, and there is a change in the requirements of the source GAAP, this does not automatically require management to change its accounting policy. Instead, management should only change its accounting policy to adopt the new requirements if the new policy results in the financial statements providing reliable and more relevant information about the effects of transactions, other events or conditions on the entity's financial position, financial performance or cash flows. (But where an entity has voluntarily adopted IAS 39/IFRS 9 or where FRS 102 requires the entity to apply an entire IFRS standard, management has no discretion about adopting changes to that underlying standard – see paras 10.35 and 10.36).

Applying changes in accounting policies

Change resulting from a change in an FRS or FRC Abstract

10.33   An entity should account for a change in accounting policy that results from a change in the requirements of an FRS or FRC Abstract in accordance with the transitional provisions (if any) specified in that amendment. [FRS 102 para 10.11(a)].

10.34   Specific transitional provisions might be included to allow alternative approaches to implementation. For example, prospective (rather than retrospective) application of the change might be permitted, or retrospective application might only be required for certain transactions. Typically, alternatives might be permitted if full retrospective application would be impracticable or unduly onerous because the information needed to restate comparative amounts is either unavailable or difficult to obtain without significant cost.

Change resulting from an amendment to the requirements of IAS 39 and/or IFRS 9

10.35   FRS 102 is a stand-alone standard that does not require an entity applying it to look to EU-adopted IFRS in addition to the standard. But it does include an option that allows an entity to use IAS 39, 'Financial instruments: recognition and measurement', and/or IFRS 9, 'Financial instruments', in accounting for financial instruments instead of sections 11 and 12 of FRS 102. Where an entity elects to take this option and the requirements of IAS 39 and/or IFRS 9 change, the entity should account for that change in accounting policy in accordance with the transitional provisions (if any) specified in the revised IAS 39 and/or IFRS 9. [FRS 102 para 10.11(b)].

Change resulting from an amendment to IAS 33, IFRS 8 or IFRS 6

10.36   In addition, FRS 102 requires some entities to apply IAS 33 'Earnings per share', IFRS 8 'Operating segments' or IFRS 6 'Exploration for and evaluation of mineral resources'. The standard also permits other entities to adopt any of these three standards voluntarily. Where the entity applies any of these standards, if the requirements in those standards subsequently change, the entity accounts for that change in accounting policy in accordance with the transitional provisions (if any) set out in the amended standard [FRS 102 para 10.11(c)].

Voluntary changes in accounting policies

10.37   All voluntary changes in accounting policies should be applied retrospectively. [FRS 102 para 10.11(d)]. But FRS 102 contains an exception to retrospective restatement where an entity decides to apply a policy of revaluing assets in accordance with section 17 or 18 of the standard. Such a change in accounting policy is dealt with instead as a revaluation in accordance with those sections. [FRS 102 para 10.10A].

10.38   Where management applies an accounting policy based on another acceptable GAAP and, following a change in the source GAAP, chooses to amend its policy, that voluntary change is applied retrospectively in accordance with FRS 102. In other words, if the source GAAP contains transitional provisions for the change, the entity cannot make use of them. (But this does not apply to changes in IAS 39, IFRS 9, IAS 33, IFRS 8 or IFRS 6 where an entity applies those standards, as described in paras 10.35 and 10.36 above.)

Retrospective application

10.39   Retrospective application means that the entity applies the new accounting policy to comparative information for prior periods to the earliest date for which it is practicable, as if the new accounting policy had always been applied. [FRS 102 para 10.12]. In other words, the entity adjusts prior years' comparative amounts on a basis consistent with the newly adopted accounting policy. In general, retrospective application involves:

- Adjusting the carrying amounts of assets and liabilities (as of the beginning of the earliest prior period presented), with a corresponding adjustment to the opening balance of each affected component of equity (for example, retained earnings).

- Adjusting all the comparative information disclosed for each prior period presented. For the avoidance of doubt, there is no requirement to present an additional balance sheet as of the beginning of the earliest comparative period.

10.40   The use of hindsight is not permitted when applying a new accounting policy (or when correcting prior period errors), either to second-guess management's intentions in the earlier period or in estimating amounts recognised, measured or disclosed in the prior period.

Impracticability of retrospective application

10.41   It might sometimes be impracticable to restate the financial statements of prior years for a change in accounting policy. Applying a requirement is impracticable when the entity cannot apply it after making every reasonable effort to do so. [FRS 102 Glossary of terms]. This could arise in the following circumstances: where the relevant information for prior years is not available; where the company is unable to recreate the information after expending every reasonable effort to do so; or where the restatement requires assumptions about management's intent in a prior period. Furthermore, retrospective application becomes potentially difficult if it requires significant estimates of amounts. Estimation becomes more difficult and subjective the longer the period of time that has passed since the relevant transaction, event or condition occurred. As a result, the company might not be able to objectively verify the necessary information to develop these estimates. An example would be an estimate of fair value that is not based on observable price or observable inputs.

10.42   Where it is impracticable to determine the individual-period effects of a change in accounting policy on comparative information for one or more prior periods presented, the entity should apply the new accounting policy to the carrying amounts of assets and liabilities as at the beginning of the earliest period for which retrospective application is practicable. This might be the current period. Corresponding adjustments are made to the opening balance of each affected component of equity for that period. [FRS 102 para 10.12]. This means that, for periods where restatement is impracticable, no restatements are made. The new policy is applied prospectively from the start of the earliest date practicable, which might be the current period.

Disclosure of changes in accounting policy

Changes arising from an amendment to an FRS or FRC Abstract

10.43 Where an amendment to an FRS or FRC Abstract has an effect on the current period or any prior period, or might have an effect on future periods, an entity should disclose the following:

- The nature of the change in accounting policy.

- For the current period and each prior period presented (so far as practicable), the amount of the adjustment for each financial statement line item affected.

- The amount of the adjustment relating to periods before those presented (so far as practicable).

- An explanation if it is impracticable to determine the amounts to be disclosed under the second or third bullet point above.

[FRS 102 para 10.13].

10.44 Financial statements of later periods need not repeat these disclosures.

Voluntary changes

10.45 Where a voluntary change in accounting policy has an effect on the current period or any prior period, an entity should disclose the following:

- The nature of the change in accounting policy.

- The reasons why applying the new accounting policy provides reliable and more relevant information.

- So far as practicable, the amount of the adjustment for each financial statement line item affected, shown separately:
  - for the current period;
  - for each prior period presented; and
  - in the aggregate for periods before those presented.

- An explanation if it is impracticable to determine the amounts of the adjustments above.

[FRS 102 para 10.14].

10.46 Financial statements of later periods need not repeat these disclosures.

Changes in accounting estimates

10.47 Inherent uncertainties in business activity mean that many items in the financial statements cannot be measured accurately, and so they have to be estimated. Estimates involve judgements based on the latest available, reliable information. Estimates are made, for example, in determining an impairment for doubtful debts, impairments for slow-moving or obsolete inventory, the useful lives of property, plant and equipment and intangible assets, fair values of financial assets and financial liabilities, recoverability of deferred tax assets, and warranty provisions. Chapter 3 provides guidance on the disclosure of information about key estimates and judgements made by management.

10.48 FRS 102 defines a change in accounting estimate as *"an adjustment of the carrying amount of an asset or a liability, or the amount of the periodic consumption of an asset, that results from the assessment of the present status of, and expected future benefits and obligations associated with, assets and liabilities"*. It might sometimes be difficult to distinguish a change in an accounting policy from a change in an accounting estimate; in that case, the change should be treated as a change in an accounting estimate. [FRS 102 para 10.15].

10.49 Accounting estimates might change as a result of changes in the circumstances on which the estimate was based, or because of new information, more experience or later developments. Such changes are to be expected in view of the uncertainty inherent in making accounting estimates, and they are not corrections of errors. [FRS 102 para 10.15].

10.50 A change in estimate can also occur because later information reveals that the original estimate was in error. For example, the estimate might have been based on wrong assumptions, it might have contained errors of calculation, or it might not have reflected the latest information available (or capable of being obtained) at the time. It is sometimes difficult in practice for an entity to determine whether it overlooked the information in earlier periods (an error), or whether it obtained new information (a change in estimate). Proper classification is important because of the difference in accounting treatment for correcting errors (retrospective application) versus changes in estimates (prospective application), and this requires the exercise of judgement. If the present change in the estimate corrects the previous error, it should be dealt with as the correction of an error (as described later in this chapter), rather than as a change of estimate.

Recognition of changes in accounting estimates

10.51 The standard notes that, by its nature, the revision of an estimate does not relate to prior periods and is not the correction of an error. Also, an entity should prospectively recognise the effect of a change in an accounting estimate (except as referred to in para 10.53 below) by including it in profit or loss:

■   in the period of the change, if the change affects that period only; or

■   in the period of the change and future periods, if the change affects both.
[FRS 102 para 10.16].

10.52   An example of a change in accounting estimate that would affect the current period profit and loss but not the profit and loss in future periods is a change in the allowance for doubtful debts. Conversely, a change in the estimate of the useful life of an item of property, plant and equipment would affect both the current and future periods; this is because the depreciation charge is affected for both current and future periods until the end of the asset's useful life.

10.53   In some circumstances, a change in estimate might affect the carrying amounts of assets or liabilities, or relate to an equity item, rather than affecting profit or loss. In those circumstances, the entity recognises the change by adjusting the carrying amount of the related asset, liability or equity in the period of the change. [FRS 102 para 10.17].

Disclosure

10.54   An entity should disclose the nature of any change in an accounting estimate and the effect of the change on assets, liabilities, income and expense for the current period. If it is practicable for the entity to estimate the effect of the change in one or more future periods, the entity should disclose those estimates. [FRS 102 para 10.18].

Corrections of prior period errors

Identifying prior period errors

10.55   From time to time, errors are discovered that relate to one or more prior periods for which financial statements have already been issued. Such errors include the effects of mathematical mistakes, mistakes in applying accounting policies, oversights or misinterpretations of facts, and fraud. [FRS 102 para 10.20]. Prior period errors are defined as *"…omissions from, and misstatements in, the entity's financial statements for one or more prior periods arising from a failure to use, or misuse of, reliable information that:*

■   *was available when financial statements for those periods were authorised for issue; and*

■   *could reasonably be expected to have been obtained and taken into account in the preparation and presentation of those financial statements."*

[FRS 102 para 10.19].

10.56   In straightforward situations, reliable information will have been available *"when financial statements for those periods were authorised for issue"*. For example, where an error involves the under-accrual of a significant item of expense, evidence in the form of an invoice or creditor's statement might have been available but overlooked.

10.57 In less straightforward situations (such as deliberate manipulation of results or fraud), it could be more difficult to establish whether reliable information existed at the time when the financial statements were issued, particularly where management was involved in carrying out the manipulation or fraud. The reason why such situations cause difficulty is that reliable information might have been deliberately suppressed or destroyed (or false and unreliable information might have been created) in order to conceal or justify the incorrect accounting. In the UK, when fraud is discovered, auditors sometimes add a statement in their report that a company has failed to keep proper accounting records. Such failure to keep proper accounting records, by definition, implies an absence of reliable information.

Correction of material prior period errors

10.58 Material prior period errors should be corrected by restating the comparative information presented in the current period's financial statements. Except where it is impracticable (see para 10.59 below), the error is corrected retrospectively in the first set of financial statements authorised for issue after the discovery of the error:

- restating the comparative amounts for the prior period(s) presented in which the error occurred; or

- if the error occurred before the earliest prior period presented, by restating the opening balances of assets, liabilities and equity for the earliest prior period presented.

[FRS 102 para 10.21].

10.59 Sometimes, it might not be possible to restate the comparative information to correct a material prior period error (for example, where the records needed to quantify the effect of the error have not been kept and cannot be recreated). In such situations, an entity should instead restate the opening balances of assets, liabilities and equity for the earliest period for which restatement is practicable (which might be the current period). [FRS 102 para 10.22].

Disclosure of prior period errors

10.60 An entity should disclose the following information about material prior period errors:

- The nature of the error.

- For each prior period presented (so far as practicable), the amount of the correction for each financial statement line item affected.

- So far as practicable, the amount of the correction at the beginning of the earliest prior period presented.

- An explanation if it is not practicable to determine the amounts to be disclosed in the second or third bullet point above.

[FRS 102 para 10.23].

10.61   Financial statements of later periods need not repeat these disclosures.

10.62   FRS 102 does not contain any exemption from disclosure of a prior period error that might be prejudicial to the entity's interests. So, An entity must disclose the correction of a prior period error, even where such disclosure might, for example, lead to a risk of legal action against the entity, or reveal that the entity violated its borrowing covenants.

10.63   Where the current period includes amounts for the correction of a prior period error (for example, where the error is immaterial, or retrospective restatement is impracticable), the Companies Act 2006 requires the company to disclose those amounts. [SI 2008/410 1 Sch 69(1)].

Re-issue of prior year financial statements

10.64   Restatement of the financial statements for prior years does not necessarily mean that an entity has to withdraw and amend the financial statements that it has already issued, approved and filed for those prior financial years. The Companies Act 2006 includes provisions for revising and re-issuing defective accounts; but, if a company corrects errors by way of a prior year adjustment in the latest financial statements, it would not normally take advantage of those provisions. Paradoxically, if the company did withdraw and amend such earlier years' financial statements, the revised financial statements would become the statutory financial statements for the year or years in question. In that case, the company would not need to show a prior year adjustment for a material prior period error in the current year's financial statements; this is because the comparatives would be presented to reflect the revised amounts for that year filed at Companies House. Chapter 32 provides additional guidance.

Transitional issues

10.65   The requirements of FRS 102 are similar in most respects to the requirements of FRS 18, which should minimise transition issues. But there is a significant difference between old UK GAAP and FRS 102 relating to correction of errors. Under old UK GAAP (FRS 3), a prior period adjustment was made only for a change in accounting policy or for the correction of a fundamental error. A fundamental error is an error of such significance as to destroy the true and fair view, and hence the validity, of financial statements. By contrast, FRS 102 requires correction of material errors, which need not be fundamental. On transition to FRS 102, any uncorrected material prior period errors in the financial statements will need to be restated at the date of transition, unless restatement is impracticable.

10.66 An entity adopting FRS 102 for the first time must (except as expressly permitted in section 35 of FRS 102) restate its financial statements in accordance with the accounting policies it applies under the standard and, where appropriate, another FRS or an FRC Abstract. Where an entity used an accounting estimate in a previous financial period under its previous financial reporting framework, and that estimate is also appropriate under an FRS or FRC Abstract, the entity should not retrospectively alter the amount recognised originally. [FRS 102 para 35.9(c)]. The accounting and disclosures on transition to FRS 102 are dealt with in chapter 35.

Chapter 11

Basic financial instruments

Chapter 11

Basic financial instruments

Introduction

11.1 Accounting for financial instruments is split into two sections of FRS 102: section 11 covers basic financial instruments, and section 12 covers other financial instrument issues. This chapter deals with the requirements of section 11, which sets out the rules for the recognition and measurement of basic financial instruments comprising financial assets and financial liabilities. It also deals with derecognition of financial instruments and impairment of financial assets. In addition, this chapter also mandates disclosures that apply to all financial instruments. Chapter 12 addresses the requirements of section 12 of the standard, which deals with more complex financial instruments and hedge accounting. Disclosures about hedges and hedge accounting are also considered in chapter 12.

11.2 All entities should review section 12 of FRS 102 to determine whether they have financial instruments that fall within its scope.

Accounting policy choice

11.3 An entity should account for all its financial instruments in accordance with either:

- the provisions of sections 11 and 12 (if applicable) in full, or
- the recognition and measurement provisions of IAS 39, 'Financial instruments: Recognition and measurement' (as adopted in the EU) and/ or IFRS 9, 'Financial instruments', and the disclosure requirements of sections 11 and 12. As the use of IFRS 9 is via FRS 102, the FRC has noted that EU endorsement is not relevant.

[FRS 102 para 11.2].

11.4 The option selected above is an accounting policy choice and should be applied consistently. Chapter 10 provides guidance on accounting policy changes and when they might be appropriate.

Scope

11.5 Where an entity elects to account for its financial instruments in accordance with section 11 of FRS 102, it must apply the section to its basic financial instruments, and it must apply section 12 of the standard to its other financial instruments (except those excluded from the scope of sections 11 and 12). The following are, or might be, basic financial instruments which are excluded from the scope of section 11:

- Investments in subsidiaries, associates and joint ventures. [FRS 102 para 11.7(a)]. See Chapters 9, 14 and 15.

- Rights and obligations under leases (see para 11.6 below). See Chapter 20.

- Reimbursement assets and financial guarantee contracts. These are accounted for in accordance with section 21 of FRS 102. See Chapter 21.

11.6   Finance lease contracts that give rise to financial assets for lessors and financial liabilities for lessees are financial instruments that are specially dealt with in section 20 of FRS 102. Therefore, they are outside the scope of section 11. But finance lease receivables recognised by lessors are included in section 11's scope for derecognition and impairment accounting requirements; and finance lease payables recognised by lessees are included in section 11's scope for derecognition purposes only. [FRS 102 para 11.7(c)].

Definitions relating to financial instruments

Financial instruments

11.7   Financial instruments embrace a broad range of assets and liabilities. They include both primary financial instruments – financial assets (such as cash, receivables and equity securities of another entity) and financial liabilities (such as debt) – and derivative financial instruments such as financial options, forwards, swaps and futures.

11.8   A financial instrument is any *"contract that gives rise to a financial asset of one entity and a financial liability or equity instrument of another entity"*. [FRS 102 Glossary of terms]. The basic definitions of 'financial assets' and 'financial liabilities' are set out below. For further discussion on financial assets and liabilities, see the IFRS Manual of Accounting.

Financial assets

11.9   *"A financial asset is any asset that is:*

a) Cash.

b)   An equity instrument of another entity.

c)   A contractual right:

> *i)   to receive cash or another financial asset from another entity; or*

> *ii)   to exchange financial assets or financial liabilities with another entity under conditions that are potentially favourable to the entity.*

d)   *A contract that will or may be settled in the entity's own equity instruments and:*

   i)   *under which the entity is or may be obliged to receive a variable number of the entity's own equity instruments; or*

   ii) *that will or may be settled other than by the exchange of a fixed amount of cash or another financial asset for a fixed number of the entity's own equity instruments. For this purpose the entity's own equity instruments do not include instruments that are contracts for the future receipt or delivery of the entity's own equity instruments."*

[FRS 102 Glossary of terms].

Financial liabilities

11.10   *"A financial liability is any liability that is:*

a)   *A contractual obligation:*

   i)   *to deliver cash or another financial asset from another entity; or*

   ii) *to exchange financial assets or financial liabilities with another entity under conditions that are potentially unfavourable to the entity.*

b)   *A contract that will or may be settled in the entity's own equity instruments and:*

   i)   *under which the entity is or may be obliged to deliver a variable number of the entity's own equity instruments; or*

   ii) *that will or may be settled other than by the exchange of a fixed amount of cash or another financial asset for a fixed number of the entity's own equity instruments. For this purpose the entity's own equity instruments do not include instruments that are contracts for the future receipt or delivery of the entity's own equity instruments."*

[FRS 102 Glossary of terms].

11.11   As an exception to the above, some financial instruments that meet the definition of a financial liability are classified as an equity instrument because they represent residual interests in the net assets of the entity. This is considered further in chapter 22.

Classification of financial instruments

11.12   The above paragraphs considered financial instruments generally. FRS 102 classifies all financial assets and liabilities into two categories:

■   Basic financial instruments that are accounted for under an amortised cost model in accordance with section 11 of the standard, provided they meet specified conditions. Investments in non-convertible, non-puttable preference shares and non-puttable ordinary shares which are also basic financial instruments are measured at fair value (or cost, if a reliable measure of fair value cannot be determined) in accordance with section 11. Basic debt instruments which meet specified requirements may be designated as at fair value through profit or loss as a policy choice under section 11.

■ All other financial instruments that do not satisfy the definition of basic financial instruments. They are accounted for at fair value through profit or loss in accordance with section 12 of the standard.

Basic financial instruments

Definition

11.13 An entity should account for the following as basic financial instruments:

■ Cash.

■ A debt instrument (such as an account, note or loan receivable or payable) that meets the conditions in paragraph 11.14 below.

■ A commitment to receive a loan that:

  ■ cannot be settled net in cash, and

  ■ when the commitment is executed, is expected to meet the conditions in paragraph 11.14 below.

■ An investment in non-convertible preference shares and non-puttable ordinary shares or preference shares.

[FRS 102 para 11.8].

Debt instruments as basic financial instruments

11.14 A debt instrument will qualify as a basic financial instrument if it meets all of the conditions noted below:

■ Returns to the holder are:

  ■ a fixed amount;

  ■ a fixed rate of return over the life of the instrument;

  ■ a variable return that, throughout the life of the instrument, is equal to a single referenced quoted or observable interest rate (such as LIBOR); or

  ■ some combination of such fixed rate and variable rates (such as LIBOR plus 200 basis points), provided that both the fixed and variable rates are positive (for example, an interest rate swap with a positive fixed rate and negative variable rate would not meet this criterion). For fixed and variable rate interest returns, interest is calculated by multiplying the rate for the applicable period by the principal amount outstanding during the period.

■ There is no contractual provision that could, by its terms, result in the holder losing the principal amount or any interest attributable to the current period or prior periods. The fact that a debt instrument is subordinated to other debt instruments is not an example of such a contractual provision.

■ Contractual provisions that permit the issuer (the debtor) to prepay a debt instrument or permit the holder (the creditor) to put it back to the issuer before maturity are not contingent on future events other than to protect:

   ■ the holder against the credit deterioration of the issuer (for example, defaults, credit downgrades or loan covenant violations), or a change in control of the issuer; or

   ■ the holder or issuer against changes in relevant taxation law.

■ There are no conditional returns or repayment provisions except for the variable rate return described in the first bullet point above and prepayment provisions described in the third bullet point above.

[FRS 102 para 11.9(a)–(d)].

11.15 A debt instrument referred to above might be a financial asset or a financial liability. It is a financial asset of the entity to which the debt is owed, because it has a contractual right to receive cash. It is a financial liability of the entity that is required to pay the debt, because it has a contractual obligation to pay cash. Examples are deposits held in banks, trade receivables and payables, bonds issued and loan liabilities. Investments in convertible debt and convertible preference shares are examples of instruments which are not basic financial instruments, because they do not meet the requirements of paragraph 11.14 above.

11.16 Debt instruments often have a fixed maturity, but they can also be repayable on demand. The contractual terms of the instrument will define the amounts and dates of payments, such as interest and principal payments. But the terms and the cash flows do not always need to be pre-determined. A debt instrument might contain terms under which the amount or timing of the contractual cash flows could vary. FRS 102 distinguishes between 'basic' debt instruments (that are accounted for at amortised cost) and 'complex' debt instruments by providing a set of criteria for making the distinction (as noted in para 11.14 above).

11.17 The first condition in paragraph 11.14 above refers to the returns to the holder of the debt instrument. However expressed, the return comprises the interest cash flows that compensate the holder for the time value of money and the credit risk associated with the instrument. Credit risk is the risk that one party to a financial instrument will cause a financial loss for the other party by failing to discharge an obligation (that is, failing to repay principal and interest when due).

11.18 An example of a debt instrument – where the return is a fixed amount – is a zero coupon bond issued at a discount to its face amount. For such a bond, the interest is the difference between the amount finally payable or receivable (the face amount of, say, £100) and the amount of the consideration received or paid when the instrument was issued (say, £80). The discount of £20 in this case is the interest which will be recognised over the term of the bond.

11.19 Where an interest rate is specified in the instrument, the interest rate must either be fixed (for example, 5%), providing a fixed rate of return over the life of the instrument, or it could be a variable rate equal to a single referenced quoted or observable interest rate (such as LIBOR). A combination of a fixed and a variable rate is also permitted, provided both the fixed and the variable rates are positive. Consider the following example:

> **Example – Fixed and variable interest payments**
>
> An entity takes out a loan from a bank. The terms of the loan contract specify that the interest rate on the principal is calculated as 12-month LIBOR + 5%.
>
> In this example, the loan consists of a fixed return (5%) and a variable return (12-month LIBOR). As 12-month LIBOR can never be negative, the return on the instrument is always positive and above 5%. So, this meets the first condition of a basic debt instrument.
>
> On the other hand, if the terms of the loan specifies that the interest rate on the principal is calculated as 12-month LIBOR minus 5%, this would not meet the definition of a basic financial instrument as both the fixed and variable rates are not positive.

11.20 A debt instrument that pays interest based on a rate that is not quoted or observable, or on an index that is not an interest rate (for example, a price index, a commodity index or a government-published inflation rate), would not satisfy the first condition in paragraph 11.14 above, because the returns are not fixed or variable based on a single referenced quoted or observable interest rate. Therefore, such instruments are not basic financial instruments accounted for at amortised cost. Rather, they would qualify as 'complex' financial instruments and would fall to be accounted for at fair value through profit or loss in accordance with section 12 of FRS 102. Similarly, a bond which pays a variable return based on the issuing entity's profits or sales revenues has a return which is not based on a quoted or observable interest rate, and as such, the bond is not a basic debt instrument.

11.21 The second condition in paragraph 11.14 above stipulates that there should be no terms in the debt instrument that would cause the holder to lose the principal amount or any interest that has been earned in the current or any prior periods.

Example – Acquisition of an interest-only strip

An entity buys a fixed-rate interest-only strip on a bond (that is, the stream of future interest payments on a fixed-rate bond, but not the principal cash flows from the bond). The strip was created in a securitisation and is subject to prepayment risk (in other words, some, or all, of the cash flows might be paid in advance of the scheduled maturity).

For a debt instrument to satisfy the condition in paragraph 11.9(b) of FRS 102, there must be no contractual provision that could, by its terms, result in the holder losing the principal amount. In this case, the principal amount is the original investment by the entity (namely, the amount that it paid to buy the interest-only strip). If the issuer of the bond (the creditor) chooses to settle the bond early, the entity might not recover its investment, because no interest payments will be incurred after settlement of the principal. Since the entity could lose some or all of its original investment (because it will not receive the interest payments that it paid for), the fixed-rate interest-only strip is not a basic financial instrument and so cannot be accounted for under the amortised cost model in accordance with section 11 of FRS 102. It must be accounted for at fair value through profit or loss in accordance with section 12 of the standard.

11.22 The standard makes it clear that, if the terms of the debt instrument in question specify that it is subordinated to other debt instruments (such that the principal amount is repaid only after all the other debt instruments have been paid off), this provision would not, in itself, cause a violation of the second condition. The fact that the issuer has issued other debt instruments that have priority over the claims of the debt instrument in question does not affect the contractual right of the holder of the debt instrument in question to unpaid principal. Similarly, the possibility that the holder of a debt instrument will not recover some or all of the amounts due, because of financial difficulties of the debtor, is not a contractual provision of the instrument and so would not violate this condition.

11.23 The third condition in paragraph 11.14 above refers to a contractual term under which the debt instrument could be repaid early, before its maturity date. Many debt instruments contain terms that allow the issuer to repay the debt early (an issuer call option), sometimes on payment of a penalty to compensate the holder for loss of interest arising from early repayment. Alternatively, the investor might have a put option to force early redemption of the outstanding principal. Such call and put options would not cause the instrument to violate this condition, provided they are not contingent on future events (a possible, but uncertain, future event), other than to protect the holder against the credit deterioration of the issuer (such as defaults, credit downgrades or loan covenant violations), or a change in control of the issuer, or to protect the holder or issuer against changes in relevant taxation law.

11.24 The prepayment amount must be substantially equal to the unpaid amounts of principal and interest; in our view, this could include reasonable additional compensation for the early termination of the contract, as noted above. This is consistent with the second condition.

Example 1 – Prepayments on credit downgrade of the issuer

Entity A holds an investment in a debt instrument issued by entity B. The instrument includes a prepayment clause whereby, if the credit rating of entity B falls by two or more notches, entity A can require the debt to be repaid.

The existence of the early repayment feature is to protect the holder against credit deterioration of the issuer and, as such, does not breach the requirements of paragraph 11.14 above. Provided the other terms of the instrument are not in breach of the requirements in paragraph 11.14 above, the instrument would be a basic financial instrument.

Example 2 – Change in tax legislation triggering a repayment

An entity issues a debt instrument which, based on tax legislation in force at the time of issuance, allows it to claim tax deductions for the purposes of its tax computation. This gives rise to a benefit that arises as a result of the structuring of the debt. This benefit is priced into the fixed interest rate payable on the debt and, as such, is attractive to an investor. As part of the terms of the instrument, an early repayment clause is added whereby a change in tax legislation – which removes the ability of the issuing entity to claim the deductions referred to – will give rise to an option of the issuer to redeem the instrument.

The tax-related clause referred to above protects the issuer against changes in relevant taxation law and, as such, is not in breach of the requirements set out in paragraph 11.14 above. Provided the other terms of the instrument do not breach the requirements of paragraph 11.14 above, the instrument would be a basic financial instrument.

11.25 The fourth condition in paragraph 11.14 above stipulates that there should be no conditional returns or prepayment provisions, other than the variable return described in the first condition and the prepayment provision described in the third condition above. If such terms are present, it would mean that returns to the holder are not certain to be fixed or variable on the basis of a single referenced quoted or observable interest rate. This would violate the first condition and, hence, the instrument would not qualify for amortised cost accounting.

Example – Principal repayment linked to a commodity price index

The following is an example of an instrument which does not meet the requirement in paragraph 11.14 above in relation to the returns to the holder.

An entity issues a £10m debt security at par in year 1. Quarterly interest payments, which are payable in pounds sterling, are set at LIBOR + 2%. The principal amount is due for repayment in full at the end of year 5 and is adjusted for the indexed movement in the price of Brent Crude compared to that index at the beginning of year 1.

In this example, although the quarterly interest payments are equal to a single referenced quoted or observable interest rate, the instrument fails the first condition in paragraph 11.14 above, because the returns to the holder in respect of the principal adjustment are not fixed or variable on the basis of a single referenced quoted or observable interest rate. So, the instrument would not be a basic financial instrument.

11.26 Another example of debt instruments that would meet the conditions in paragraph 11.14 above is given below.

Example – Perpetual debt instruments

An entity issues a perpetual bond at its par amount of £1m. The terms of the bond require the entity to make annual payments in perpetuity equal to a stated interest rate of 8% applied to the principal amount.

In this example, the instrument is perpetual and non-redeemable, because the holder has no right to receive a return of principal: rather the issuing entity is required to pay a fixed rate of 8% in perpetuity. The fact that the bond is non-redeemable does not result in the holder losing the principal amount of £1m (the second condition in paragraph 11.14 above). Assuming that 8% represents the market rate of interest when the bond was issued, the present value of annual interest payments of £80,000 in perpetuity is equal to the principal amount. Therefore, the instrument qualifies as a basic debt instrument for both the holder and the issuer.

Loan commitments

11.27 Loan commitments are firm commitments to provide credit under pre-specified terms and conditions. They are usually entered into by financial institutions (such as banks) for providing loans to third parties at a specified rate of interest during a fixed period of time. Such commitments might provide the borrower with the option to borrow money in the future, or they might require it to do so (non-optional).

11.28 From both the borrower's and lender's perspective, a commitment to receive or extend a loan is considered a basic financial instrument and not a derivative if the following two conditions are met:

- The commitment cannot be settled net in cash.
- The loan to be received, when the commitment is executed, is expected to be a basic financial instrument under section 11 (that is, it is expected to meet the conditions in paragraph 11.14 above).

[FRS 102 para 11.8(c)].

Example – Revolving facility

A bank enters into an agreement with an entity to provide a revolving loan facility of £10m for a period of three years. The bank charges the entity a fee of 0.5% of the total revolving facility which is paid as an upfront payment. The commitment cannot be settled net in cash, and the terms of the loan (if drawn) are such that the instrument would be considered a basic financial instrument in accordance with paragraph 11.14 above.

Both the lender and the borrower recognise the commitment at cost, which is the transaction price of £50,000.

Investments in non-puttable and non-convertible shares

11.29   To be within the scope of section 11 of the standard, investments in ordinary or preference shares must be non-puttable. [FRS 102 para 11.8(d)]. An entity has an investment in non-puttable shares if:

■   the entity does not have an option to sell the shares back to the issuer of the shares for cash or another financial asset; or

■   there is no arrangement that could result in the shares being automatically redeemed or repurchased by the issuer on the occurrence of an uncertain future event or the death or retirement of the instrument holder.

[FRS 102 para 22.4(a)].

11.30   Investments in equity instruments (other than investments in subsidiaries, associates and joint ventures) are basic financial instruments that fall within the scope of section 11 of FRS 102 if they are either non-convertible, non-puttable preference shares or non-puttable ordinary shares.

11.31   For investments in preference shares to be within the scope of section 11 of the standard, they must be both non-convertible (that is, they cannot be converted into equity shares) and non-puttable. A conversion feature would provide a return to the holder that can vary with the price of the issuer's equity shares, rather than just with market interest rates, and so would fall within the scope of section 12 of FRS 102. On the other hand, a non-convertible, non puttable preference share can be within the scope of section 11, whether or not the principal amount is redeemable at maturity or is non-redeemable (a perpetual instrument). From the holder's perspective, if the preference shares are both non-convertible and non-puttable, paragraphs 11.48 and 11.49 below apply and the investment is accounted for at fair value (or cost, if a reliable measure of fair value is not available). Paragraph 11.14 above is not applicable.

11.32 From the perspective of the issuer, if the preference share's terms meet the requirements of paragraph 11.14 above, the instrument is accounted for as a basic debt instrument.

Other financial instrument

11.33   The standard provides the following examples of financial instruments that do not satisfy the conditions in paragraph 11.14 above, and so are accounted for at fair value through profit or loss under section 12 of FRS 102:

■   An investment in another entity's equity instruments, other than non-convertible preference shares and non-puttable ordinary and preference shares (see para 11.31 above).

- An interest rate swap that returns a cash flow that is positive or negative, or a forward commitment to purchase a commodity or financial instrument that is capable of being cash-settled and that, on settlement, could have positive or negative cash flow, because such swaps and forwards do not meet the first condition in paragraph 11.14 above.

- Options and forward contracts, because returns to the holder are not fixed and the first condition in paragraph 11.14 above is not met.

- Investments in convertible debt, because the return to the holder can vary with the price of the issuer's equity shares, rather than just with market interest rates.

[FRS 102 para 11.11].

Identification of basic and other financial instruments

11.34 For ease of understanding and as a practical aid, the table below provides a list of common balance sheet items, and applies the concepts discussed above to determine whether each item meets the definition of a financial instrument and, if so, whether it falls within the scope of section 11 or 12 of FRS 102 (the list is by no means exhaustive):

Balance sheet items	Financial instruments Yes = ✓ No = X	Included within the scope of section 11 Yes = ✓ No = X	Included within the scope of section 12 Yes = ✓ No = X
Intangible assets	X	n/a	n/a
PPE	X	n/a	n/a
Investment property	X	n/a	n/a
Interests in subsidiaries, associates and JVs	✓	X (Sections 9, 14, 15)	X (Sections 9, 14, 15)
Inter-entity trading balances with subsidiaries, associates and JVs	✓	✓	X
Investments in shares of entities other than subsidiaries, associates and JVs	✓	Note 2	Note 2
Inventories	X	n/a	n/a
Construction contract work in progress	X	n/a	n/a
Construction contract receivables	✓	✓	X
Finance lease receivables (recognised by a lessor)	✓	Note 3	Note 3
Trade receivables	✓	✓	X
Pre-payments for goods and services	X	n/a	n/a
Cash and cash equivalents	✓	✓	X
Trade payables	✓	✓	X

Basic financial instruments

Balance sheet items	Financial instruments Yes = ✓ No = X	Included within the scope of section 11 Yes = ✓ No = X	Included within the scope of section 12 Yes = ✓ No = X
Contingent consideration in a business combination (acquirer)	✓	X (Section 19)	X (Section 19)
Accruals for goods and services (settlement in cash)	✓	✓	X
Deferred income	X	n/a	n/a
Debt instruments	✓	Note 4	Note 4
Derivative instruments	✓	X	✓
Net settled commodity-based contracts	✓	X	✓
Retirement benefit obligations	✓	X (Section 28)	X (Section 28)
Provisions for constructive obligations	X	n/a	n/a
Vacant leasehold property provision	✓	n/a	n/a
Warranty obligations (settled by delivery of goods or services)	X	n/a	n/a
Dividends payable	Note 1	Note 1	Note 1
Current and deferred tax	X	n/a	n/a
Redeemable preference shares	✓	Note 5	Note 5
Entity's own equity shares	✓	X	X
Employee share options	✓	X	X
Other equity options over own equity	✓	X	X
Non-controlling interest	✓	X (Section 9 and 22)	X (Section 9 and 22)

Notes:

1.   Dividends payable on the balance sheet are a financial liability when the dividend has been formally approved by the members in a general meeting and becomes a legal obligation of the entity to deliver cash to shareholders for the amount of the declared dividend. [FRS 102 section 23].

2.   The investment in shares of the other entity must be non-convertible preference shares and non-puttable ordinary shares or preference shares to be the scope of section 11; otherwise, they are in the scope of section 12.

3.   Although not in the scope of section 11 or 12 of the standard for the purposes of recognition and measurement, finance lease receivables are in the scope of section 11 for the purposes of derecognition and impairment (discussed in paras 11.95 and 11.62 respectively).

4.   Debt instruments which do not meet the requirements of paragraph 11.14 above are not basic financial instruments, and so they are in the scope of section 12 (see the example in para 11.21 above).

5.   Investments in convertible and puttable preference shares are not included in the scope of section 11 of FRS 102, and so are treated in accordance with section 12 of the standard.

Initial recognition

11.35   An entity should recognise a financial asset or a financial liability when, and only when, it becomes a party to the contractual provisions of the instrument. [FRS 102 para 11.12]. For instance, unconditional receivables or payables are recognised as assets or liabilities when the entity becomes a party to the contract and, as a consequence, has a legal right to receive (or a legal obligation to pay) cash.

11.36   A consequence of the above recognition rule is that a contract to buy or sell a financial instrument at a future date is itself a financial asset or liability that is recognised on the balance sheet at contract inception date.

11.37   Planned future transactions, no matter how likely, cannot give rise to assets and liabilities; this is because the entity has not become a party to a contract. Such future transactions are future events to be recognised in the future periods when contractual rights are acquired or obligations incurred.

Initial measurement

11.38   Where a basic financial asset or financial liability is recognised initially, an entity should measure it at the transaction price (including transaction costs, except in the initial recognition of financial assets or financial liabilities that are subsequently measured at fair value through profit or loss), unless the arrangement constitutes, in effect, a financing transaction. [FRS 102 para 11.13].

11.39   In most situations, the initial transaction price is also the fair value of the financial instrument. But there might be situations where the financial instrument is not recognised initially at its transaction price because it does not, in the economic sense, represent fair value. The standard recognises this and identifies arrangements that are, in effect, financing transactions. Most financing transactions in connection with the sale of goods or services are carried out on an arm's length basis and on normal commercial terms, especially between unrelated parties. However, sometimes a purchase or sale agreement might contain an implicit financing element (for example, where payment is deferred beyond normal business terms or is financed at a rate of interest that is not a market rate). In those situations, the standard requires the entity to measure the financial asset or financial liability at the current estimate of the present value of the future payments, discounted at the market rate of interest for a similar debt instrument. [FRS 102 para 11.13].

11.40   Discounting is unlikely to be material for short-term receivables or payables and, hence, the standard permits them to be measured at an undiscounted amount, which is normally the invoice price. The standard also provides a number of examples where discounting would be appropriate, but is silent on how the difference between the transaction price paid or received and the present value of the future cash flows should be accounted for. Consider the following examples:

Example 1 – Interest-free loan to an entity

Entity A lends £1,000 to entity B for five years. The loan carries no interest. The loan satisfies all the conditions for a basic debt instrument. The market rate of interest for a similar five-year loan with payment of interest at maturity is 10% per year.

By agreeing not to charge any interest on the loan, entity A is effectively providing entity B with implicit financing, in addition to the underlying loan. Therefore, as stated above, entity A recognises the loan at the present value of the future payments, discounted at a market rate of interest for a similar loan (similar as to currency, term, type of interest and other factors).

The present value of the future payment of £1,000, discounted using the market rate of interest for a similar loan of 10% for five years, is £621 ($1,000/(1.10)5$). Therefore, entity A recognises the loan at its initial fair value of £621 that will accrete to £1,000 over the term of the loan using the effective interest method (see further para 11.53 below).

However, the standard is silent on how the difference between the consideration given for the loan of £1,000 and its initial recognised amount of £621 (that is, £379) should be accounted for.

We believe that the additional amount lent is not a financial asset, since it is something other than a right to receive payment on the loan asset. Therefore, the amount should be written off as an expense, unless entity A expects to receive any future economic benefits from entity B, such as an implicit right to receive goods or services at favourable prices. If that is so, the additional amount lent could be capitalised as an intangible asset in accordance with section 18 of FRS 102.

In practice, it is unlikely that entity A would make a loan on such terms to an unrelated party. Providing interest-free loans or loans at significantly below market rates is, however, quite common between a parent entity and its subsidiaries. So, entity A would recognise the additional amount as part of the cost of investment in entity B, if entity B is its subsidiary. Similarly, subsidiary B would recognise the loan liability at £621 and record the difference of £379 in equity as a capital contribution from the parent.

Note; Public benefit entities have an accounting policy in respect of concessionary loans made and received which is dealt with in Section 34 and is discussed in Chapter 34.5

Example 2 – Interest-free loan to an employee

An entity grants an interest-free loan of £1,000 to an employee for a period of two years. The market rate of interest to this individual, for a two-year loan with payment of interest at maturity, is 10%.

The loan carries no interest, so the present value of the future cash flows is not equal to the transaction price of £1,000. Accordingly, the loan is recorded at the present value of the future payments discounted at a market rate of interest for a similar loan. The present value is £826 ($£1,000/(1.10)2$).

The difference of £174 is accounted for as employee compensation in accordance with section 28 of FRS 102.

Transaction costs

11.41 Transaction costs are defined in FRS 102 as incremental costs that are directly attributable to the acquisition, issue or disposal of a financial asset or financial liability. They include costs such as fees and commissions paid to agents, advisers, brokers and dealers, levies by regulatory agencies and securities exchanges, and transfer taxes and duties. They also include fees that are an integral part of generating an involvement with the resulting financial instrument (such as evaluating the borrower's financial condition, evaluating and recording guarantees, collateral and other security arrangements, negotiating the instrument's terms, and preparing and processing documents). These fees are often referred to as arrangement fees, commitment fees or facility fees. Transaction costs do not include debt premiums or discounts, financing costs or internal administrative costs.

11.42 Transaction costs are accounted for in a financial instrument's initial measurement as follows:

- Where a financial asset or financial liability is recognised initially and is subsequently measured at amortised cost or cost (see para 11.14(a), (b), (c)(ii) of FRS 102), transaction costs (net of fees received) are included in the initial amount recognised. For financial assets, such costs are added to the amount originally recognised. For financial liabilities, such costs are deducted from the amount originally recognised. Transaction costs will, therefore, be included in the calculation of amortised cost using the effective interest method, and consequently are recognised in profit or loss over the life of the instrument or a shorter period, if appropriate (see para 11.54 below for guidance on the period used). [FRS 102 para 11.18].

- For financial instruments that are subsequently measured at fair value through profit or loss, transaction costs (net of any fees received or paid) are not added to or deducted from the amount initially recognised. Instead, they are expensed immediately on initial recognition of the financial instrument, because the payments do not result in any future economic benefits. [FRS 102 para 12.12].

- Transaction costs expected to be incurred on a financial instrument's transfer or disposal are not included in the initial or subsequent financial instrument's measurement. [FRS 102 para 11.14].

[FRS 102 para 11.11].

Subsequent measurement

11.43 At the end of each reporting period, an entity should measure basic financial instruments as follows.

Debt instruments

11.44 Basic debt instruments that meet the conditions discussed in paragraph 11.14 above should be measured at amortised cost using the effective interest rate method. [FRS 102 para 11.14(a)]. The amortised cost method of accounting is discussed at paragraph 11.52 below.

11.45 Unless the arrangement constitutes, in effect, a financing transaction (see para 11.39 above), debt instruments that are payable or receivable within one year should be measured at the undiscounted amount of the cash or other consideration expected to be paid or received (net of any impairment). [FRS 102 para 11.14(a)].

Fair value option

11.46 Debt instruments which meet the conditions included in paragraph 11.14 above, can, at initial recognition, be designated by the entity as at fair value through profit or loss, provided doing so results in more relevant information, either because:

- it eliminates or significantly reduces a measurement or recognition inconsistency (sometimes referred to as 'an accounting mismatch') that would otherwise arise from measuring assets or debt instruments or recognising the gains and losses on them on different bases; or

- a group of debt instruments or financial assets and debt instruments is managed and its performance is evaluated on a fair value basis, in accordance with a documented risk management or investment strategy, and information about the group is provided internally on that basis to the entity's key management personnel (as defined in chapter 23), such as members of the entity's board of directors and its chief executive officer.

[FRS 102 para 11.14(b)].

> **Example – Investments in quoted bonds**
>
> A bond held by an entity which is traded in an active market has fixed coupons and a fixed maturity date on which the par value of the bond becomes repayable. Depending on the difference between the coupon rate and the market rate of interest, the bond might be trading at a premium or at a discount to its par value.
>
> The fact that the bond is quoted in an active market does not preclude it from being a basic financial instrument that can be measured at amortised cost. However, the entity might, on initial recognition, designate a debt instrument as at fair value through profit or loss, provided doing so results in more relevant information.

Loan commitments

11.47 Commitments to receive a loan, or to make a loan to another entity, that meet the conditions stated in paragraph 11.28 above should be measured at cost (which is sometimes nil) less impairments. [FRS 102 para 11.14(c)].

Investments in non-puttable and non-convertible shares

11.48 Investments in non-convertible preference shares and non-puttable ordinary or preference shares that are publicly traded, or shares whose fair values can be measured reliably, should be measured at fair value through profit or loss. For this purpose, publicly traded means *"traded, or in process of being issued for trading, in a public market (a domestic or foreign stock exchange or an over-the-counter market, including local and regional markets)"*. [FRS 102 Glossary of terms].

11.49 Other investments in non-convertible preference shares and non-puttable ordinary or preference shares should be measured at cost less impairment. [FRS 102 para 11.14(d)(ii)].

> **Example – Investments in equity shares**
>
> An entity acquires 100 non-puttable ordinary shares of a listed entity at the quoted price of £20 per share, for a total consideration of £2,000. The entity also pays purchase commission of £200 to acquire the shares. At the end of the entity's financial year, the share's quoted market price is £25. If the shares were to be sold, a commission of £250 would be payable.
>
> On initial recognition, the entity recognises its investment in the shares at its transaction price of £2,000. Because the shares are publicly traded, the entity should measure the investment at its fair value of £2,500 at the end of its reporting period. The change in fair value of £500 is recognised in profit or loss. The purchase commission of £200 is recognised immediately on acquisition as an expense. The commission of £250 that the entity would incur on the sale of the shares is disregarded.
>
> If, on the other hand, the shares are not publicly traded, and the fair value of the shares cannot otherwise be measured reliably, the entity recognises the shares at its transaction price, inclusive of the purchase commission (that is, at £2,200). The entity continues to measure the investment at its initial cost price at each subsequent reporting date for as long as the asset is held, unless the asset becomes impaired. As before, the commission of £250 that the entity would incur on the sale of the shares is disregarded.

Amortised cost and the effective interest method

General

11.50 The amortised cost of a financial asset or financial liability at each reporting date is the net of the following amounts:

- the amount at which the financial asset or financial liability is measured at initial recognition,

- minus any repayments of the principal,

- plus or minus the cumulative amortisation using the effective interest method of any difference between the amount at initial recognition and the maturity amount,

- minus, in the case of a financial asset, any reduction (directly or through the use of an allowance account) for impairment or uncollectability.

[FRS 102 para 11.15].

11.51 Financial assets and financial liabilities that have no stated interest rate, and are payable or receivable within one year, are initially measured at an undiscounted amount in accordance with paragraph 11.45 above. Therefore, the third bullet above does not apply to them. [FRS 102 para 11.15].

11.52 The effective interest method is a method of calculating the amortised cost of a financial asset or a financial liability (or group of financial assets or financial liabilities) and of allocating the interest income or interest expense over the relevant period. The amortised cost of a financial asset (liability) is the present value of future cash flows discounted at the effective interest rate. The interest income (expense) equals the carrying amount of the financial asset (liability) at the beginning of a period multiplied by the effective interest rate for the period. The effective interest method's principal features are as follows:

- The effective interest rate is the rate that exactly discounts estimated future cash payments or receipts through the financial instrument's expected life or, where appropriate, a shorter period, to the net carrying amount of the financial asset or financial liability (see para 11.54 below). The effective interest rate is determined on the basis of the carrying amount of the financial asset or liability at initial recognition. [FRS 102 para 11.16]. An examples to illustrate the application of the effective interest method is given in paragraph 11.54. below.

- When calculating the effective interest rate, an entity should estimate cash flows, taking into account all contractual terms of the financial instrument (for example, pre-payment, call and similar options) and known credit losses that have been incurred, but it should not consider future credit losses that have not yet been incurred. [FRS 102 para 11.17].

- The calculation should include all fees and 'points' paid or received between parties to the contract that are an integral part of the effective interest rate, transaction costs, and all other premiums or discounts. [FRS 102 para 11.18].

In some cases, financial assets are acquired at a deep discount that reflects incurred losses (for example, purchase of impaired debt). Such losses are already reflected in the price, so they should be included in the estimated cash flows when computing the effective interest rate. [FRS 102 para 11.17].

Expected life

11.53 As noted above, the effective interest rate is the rate that exactly discounts estimated future cash payments or receipts through the financial instrument's expected life or, when appropriate, a shorter period, to the net carrying amount of the financial asset or financial liability. The entity should be able to estimate reliably the expected life of an instrument from the terms of the instrument and the entity's future intentions in respect of that instrument. Call or put options in debt instruments that cause the instrument to be settled prior to its contractual maturity date, and that are not contingent on future events, are particularly relevant in determining the instrument's expected life. In determining the instrument's expected life at inception, an entity needs to assess whether it or the other party is likely to exercise the option, which, in turn, would influence the estimation of future cash flows. Furthermore, this assessment should continue in subsequent periods until the debt instrument is settled. This is because the likelihood of the option being exercised will affect the timing and amount of the expected future cash flows, and any change in these will have an immediate impact in profit or loss (see further para 11.56 below). Under no circumstances can the expected life of the instrument exceed its contractual term.

11.54 Transaction costs and fees should be amortised over the instrument's expected life. However, a shorter period should be used when the variable (for example, interest rates) to which the fee, transaction costs, discount or premium relates is re-priced to market rates before the instrument's expected maturity. In such a case, the appropriate amortisation period is the period to the next such re-pricing date. [FRS 102 para 11.18].

Example – Fixed interest loan asset repayable at maturity

On 1 January 20X0, entity A originates a 10-year 7% £1 million loan. The loan carries an annual interest rate of 7% payable at the end of each year and is repayable at par at the end of year 10. Entity A charges a 1.25% (£12,500) non-refundable loan origination fee to the borrower, and also incurs £25,000 in direct loan origination costs.

The contract specifies that the borrower has an option to pre-pay the instrument and that no penalty will be charged for pre-payment. At inception, the entity expects the borrower not to pre-pay.

The initial carrying amount of the loan asset is calculated as follows:

	£
Loan principal	1,000,000
Origination fees charged to borrower	(12,500)
Origination costs incurred by lender	25,000
Carrying amount of loan	1,012,500

Since the entity expects the borrower not to pre-pay, the amortisation period is equal to the instrument's full term. In calculating the effective interest rate that will apply over the term of the loan at a constant rate on the carrying amount, the discount rate necessary to equate 10 annual payments of £70,000 and a final payment at maturity of £1 million to the initial carrying amount of £1,012,500 is approximately 6.823%.

So, the carrying amount of the loan over the period to maturity will be as follows:

	Cash inflows (coupon)	Interest income @ 6.823%	Amortisation of net fees	Carrying amount
	£	£	£	£
1 Jan 20X0				1,012,500
31 Dec 20X0	70,000	69,083	917	1,011,588
31 Dec 20X1	70,000	69,025	975	1,010,613
31 Dec 20X2	70,000	68,959	1,041	1,009,572
31 Dec 20X3	70,000	68,888	1,112	1,008,460
31 Dec 20X4	70,000	68,812	1,188	1,007,272
31 Dec 20X5	70,000	68,731	1,269	1,006,003
31 Dec 20X6	70,000	68,644	1,356	1,004,647
31 Dec 20X7	70,000	68,552	1,448	1,003,199
31 Dec 20X8	70,000	68,453	1,547	1,001,652
31 Dec 20X9	70,000	68,348	1,652	1,000,000
	700,000	687,500	12,500	
31 Dec 20X9	Repayment of principal			(1,000,000)
;				
31 Dec 20X9	Carrying value of loan			Nil

As can be seen from the above, the effective interest income for the period is calculated by applying the effective interest rate of 6.823% to the loan's amortised cost at the end of the previous reporting period. The annual interest income decreases each year, to reflect the decrease in the asset's carrying value as the initial net fee is amortised. Thus, the difference between the calculated effective income for a given reporting period and the loan's coupon is the amortisation of the net fees during that reporting period. The loan's amortised cost at the end of the previous period, plus amortisation in the current reporting period, gives the loan's amortised cost at the end of the current period. By maturity date, the net fees received are fully amortised, and the loan's carrying amount is equal to the face amount, which is then repaid in full.

Changes in estimated cash flows

11.55   The cash flows that are discounted to arrive at the effective interest rate are the cash flows that are expected to occur over the instrument's expected life. However, in practice, circumstances change, and the entity might need to revise its estimation of future cash flows. Such revisions could affect the amount or timing of the cash flows, or both. Differences from the original estimates need to be adjusted for. If the variation is ignored, either the asset or liability will amortise before all of the cash flows occur, or a balance might remain after the last cash flow.

11.56   The standard, therefore, requires that, if an entity revises its cash flow estimates, it should adjust the carrying amount of the financial asset or financial liability (or group of financial instruments) to reflect actual and revised estimated cash flows. The entity recalculates the carrying amount by computing the present value of the revised estimated future cash flows at the financial instrument's original effective interest rate. The difference between this amount and the previous carrying amount is recognised in profit or loss as income or expense at the date of the revision. [FRS 102 para 11.20].

Floating rate instruments

11.57   For variable rate instruments that, for example, pay interest linked to a reference rate such as LIBOR, periodic re-estimation of cash flows to reflect movements in market rates of interest alters the instrument's effective interest rate. [FRS 102 para 11.19].

11.58   Where a floating rate instrument is recognised initially at an amount equal to the principal receivable or payable at maturity, re-estimating the future interest payments normally has no significant effect on the carrying amount of the asset or liability. [FRS 102 para 11.19]. The effective yield will always equal the rate under the interest rate formula (for example, LIBOR + 1%) in the instrument. The result is that changes in LIBOR are reflected in the period in which the change occurs.

11.59   However, if a floating rate instrument is issued or acquired at a discount or premium, or the entity receives or incurs transaction costs, the question arises as to whether the premium or discount and other transaction costs should be amortised over the period to the next re-pricing date, or over the instrument's expected life. The answer depends on the nature of the premium or discount and its relationship with market rates:

■   An amortisation period to the next re-pricing date should be used if the premium or discount on a floating rate instrument reflects interest that has accrued on the instrument since interest was last paid, or changes in the market interest rate since the floating interest rate was reset to market rates. This is because the premium or discount relates to the period to the next interest reset date as, at that date, the variable to which the premium or

11021

discount relates (that is, the interest rate) is reset to market rates. In this case, the loan's fair value at the next re-pricing date will be its par value.

- The instrument's expected life should be used as the amortisation period if the premium or discount results from changes in the credit spread over the floating rate specified in the instrument, or other variables that are not reset to market rates. In this situation, the date that the interest rate is next reset is not a market-based re-pricing date of the entire instrument, since the variable rate is not adjusted for changes in the credit spread for the specific issue.

[FRS 102 para 11.18].

11.60 There is no specific guidance in the standard as to how transaction costs incurred in originating or acquiring a floating rate instrument should be amortised. Since such costs are sunk costs and are not subject to re-pricing, they will be amortised over the instrument's expected life. Any methodology that provides a reasonable basis of amortisation could be used. For example, entities might find it appropriate to amortise the fees and costs using the effective interest rate method or to simply adopt a straight-line amortisation method.

Perpetual debt instruments

11.61 An entity might issue a perpetual debt instrument on which interest is paid at a fixed rate or a variable rate in perpetuity. At initial recognition, assuming there are no transaction costs, the debt instrument will be recorded at the amount received. Since there is no repayment of principal, there is no amortisation of the difference between the initial amount and the maturity amount (zero). This is because the amortised cost, which is the present value of the stream of future cash payments discounted at the effective interest rate, equals the principal amount in each period. If, on the other hand, the entity incurs transaction costs, the debt instrument will be recorded in each reporting period at its initial amount, which is the amount received less transaction costs. The result is that the transaction costs are never amortised, but they are reflected in the carrying amount indefinitely.

Impairment of financial assets

11.62 Impairment issues are only relevant to financial assets that are measured at cost or amortised cost. A financial asset that is carried at fair value through profit or loss does not give rise to any impairment issues, since any diminution in value due to impairment is already reflected in the fair value and, therefore, in profit or loss.

11.63 Section 11 of FRS 102 deals with impairment of financial assets through a two-step process. First, an entity must carry out an impairment review of its financial assets at the end of each reporting period. The aim of this review is to determine whether there is objective evidence that impairment exists for a financial asset. Secondly, if there is objective evidence of impairment, the entity should measure and record the impairment loss immediately. [FRS 102 para 11.21]. For further guidance regarding objective evidence of impairment, see the IFRS Manual of Accounting.

Objective evidence of impairment

11.64 Section 11 of the standard states that objective evidence of impairment includes observable data that comes to the attention of the holder of the asset about the following loss events:

■ Significant financial difficulty of the issuer or obligor.

■ A breach of contract, such as a default or delinquency in interest or principal payments.

■ The creditor, for economic or legal reasons relating to the debtor's financial difficulty, granting to the debtor a concession that the creditor would not otherwise consider.

■ It becomes probable (that is, more likely than not) that the debtor will enter bankruptcy or other financial reorganisation.

■ Observable data indicating that there has been a measurable decrease in the estimated future cash flows from a group of financial assets since the initial recognition of those assets, even though the decrease cannot yet be identified with the individual financial assets in the group, such as adverse national or local economic conditions or adverse changes in industry conditions.

[FRS 102 para 11.22].

11.65 Other factors might have an adverse effect on the issuer and affect its ability to pay the holder, and hence might also be objective evidence that an impairment loss has been incurred when considered either individually or taken together. These include information about significant changes with an adverse effect on:

■ The debtor's liquidity.

■ The solvency, business and financial risk exposures of the debtor.

■ National and local economic trends and conditions that affect the debtor, including the technological, market, economic or legal environment in which the debtor operates.

■ Levels of, and trends in, delinquencies for similar financial assets.

■ A downgrade of an entity's credit rating is not, of itself, evidence of impairment, although it could be evidence of impairment when considered with other available information.

Impairment assessment on an individual or group basis

11.66 Impairment assessments should be performed as follows:

- All equity investments should be assessed for impairment on an individual basis, regardless of significance. [FRS 102 para 11.24(a)]. This would apply to non-puttable ordinary shares and preference shares and non-convertible preference shares which are not publicly traded or whose fair value cannot otherwise be measured reliably.

- All other financial assets that are considered to be individually significant are assessed for impairment individually.

- All other assets that are not individually significant are assessed for impairment, either individually or collectively on a group basis, as indicated below.

[FRS 102 para 11.24].

11.67 For the purpose of a collective evaluation of impairment, financial assets should be grouped on the basis of similar credit risk characteristics. [FRS 102 para 11.24]. Credit risk characteristics are indicative of the debtor's ability to pay all amounts due, according to the contractual terms. Such a grouping might be done on the basis of a credit risk evaluation or grading process that considers asset type, industry, geographical location, collateral type, past-due status and other relevant factors. If an entity does not have a group of assets with similar risk characteristics, such assets should be individually assessed for impairment.

Measurement of impairment loss

Financial assets carried at amortised cost

11.68 For a debt instrument measured at amortised cost, the impairment loss should be measured as the difference between the asset's carrying amount and the present value of estimated cash flows discounted at the asset's original effective interest rate (that is, the effective interest rate computed at initial recognition). [FRS 102 para 11.25(a)].

11.69 However, if the financial asset is a variable rate instrument, the discount rate for measuring any impairment loss is the current effective interest rate determined under the contract. [FRS 102 para 11.25(a)]. For example, if the rate under the contract is LIBOR + 100 basis points, and the asset is found to be impaired when LIBOR is 5% compared with the rate at inception of 4%, the appropriate discount rate for measuring the impairment loss is 6% and not the original rate at inception of 5%; this is because the original credit risk spread of 100 basis points is held constant and not adjusted to reflect changes in credit risk spreads, as noted above.

11.70 The carrying amount of the asset is reduced, either directly or through the use of an allowance account, such as a provision for bad and doubtful debts. In the latter case, the asset's carrying amount in the entity's statement of financial position is stated net of any related allowance. Whichever presentation is used, the amount of the impairment loss should be recognised in profit or loss.

11.71   The expected future cash flows that are included in the calculation are the contractual cash flows of the instrument itself, reduced or delayed based on the current expectations of the amount and timing of these cash flows as a result of losses incurred at the balance sheet date. Where the amount outstanding is expected to be collected in full, but the collection period is delayed, an impairment loss must still be recognised, unless the creditor receives full compensation (for example, in the form of additional interest) for the period of the delinquency and expects to recover this additional interest.

Recognition of interest income on impaired assets

11.72   An entity should not stop accruing interest on loans that are non-performing. Once a financial asset or a group of similar financial assets has been written down as a result of an impairment loss, interest income is thereafter recognised using the rate of interest used to discount the future cash flows for the purpose of measuring the impairment loss (that is, the discount in the carrying amount is unwound). This would be the original effective rate for fixed rate instruments, and the current interest rate for floating rate instruments.

Financial assets carried at cost

11.73   Instruments measured at cost less impairment are those investments in non-convertible and non-puttable preference shares and non-puttable ordinary shares that are not publicly traded and whose fair value cannot be measured reliably, and some commitments to receive a loan (see para 11.27 above). For such instruments, if there is objective evidence that an impairment loss has been incurred, the amount of the impairment loss is measured as the difference between the asset's carrying amount and the best estimate (which will necessarily be an approximation) of the amount (which might be zero) that the entity would receive for the asset if it were to be sold at the reporting date. [FRS 102 para 11.25(b)].

Reversal of impairment losses

11.74   As stated in paragraph 11.63 above, an impairment review should be carried out at the end of each reporting period. If, in a subsequent period, the amount of the impairment loss decreases, and the decrease can be related objectively to an event occurring after the impairment was recognised (such as an improvement in the debtor's credit rating), the previously recognised impairment loss should be reversed, either directly or by adjusting an allowance account. The reversal should not result in a carrying amount of the financial asset that exceeds what the amortised cost would have been if the impairment had not been recognised at the date of reversal. The amount of the reversal should be recognised in profit or loss immediately. [FRS 102 para 11.26].

Fair values

11.75 The only instruments in the scope of section 11 of FRS 102 that are measured at fair value are investments in non-convertible preference shares and non-puttable ordinary or preference shares if the shares are publicly traded or their fair value can otherwise be measured reliably. Financial instruments within the scope of section 12 of the standard must also apply the guidance on measuring fair values from section 11, which is considered from paragraph 11.76 below. Section 12 of FRS 102 provides further fair value guidance for financial instruments in its scope.

11.76 Fair value is *"the amount for which an asset could be exchanged, a liability settled, or an equity instrument granted could be exchanged, between knowledgeable, willing parties in an arm's length transaction".* [FRS 102 Glossary of terms]. In looking for a reliable measure of fair value, the standard provides a hierarchy for estimating fair valued, as shown below:

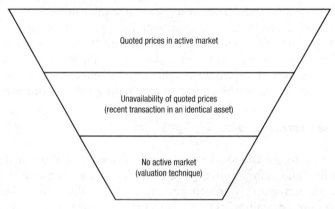

Quoted prices in active market

Unavailability of quoted prices
(recent transaction in an identical asset)

No active market
(valuation technique)

11.77 As can be seen from the above, the hierarchy gives the highest priority to quoted prices in active markets. Unfortunately, for some financial assets for which fair values are required, there might be no active market.

Quoted prices in an active market

11.78 The best evidence of fair value is a quoted price for an *identical* asset in an active market [FRS 102 para 11.27(a)]. Two assets are identical if they have identical terms and conditions. Therefore, if entity X holds A and B ordinary shares having slightly different rights in entity Y, the two shares are not identical. So, if only the A ordinary shares are quoted, their quoted price cannot be inferred as the fair value of the B ordinary shares.

11.79 The existence of published price quotations in an active market for identical assets, where available, must always be used. [FRS 102 para 11.27(a)]. An active market is defined as one in which all the following conditions exist: the items traded in the market are homogeneous; willing buyers and sellers can normally be found at any time; and prices are available to the public. The phrase 'quoted price in an active market' means that quoted prices are readily and regularly available from an exchange, dealer, broker, industry groups, pricing service or regulatory agency, and those prices represent actual and regularly occurring market transactions on an arm's length basis.

11.80　The objective of determining fair value for a financial instrument that is traded in an active market is to arrive at the price at which a transaction would occur at the end of the reporting period in that instrument (that is, without modifying or repackaging the instrument) in the most advantageous active market to which the entity has immediate access. This means that, if an entity has immediate access to different markets having different prices for essentially the same financial asset, the most advantageous market is the one with the price that maximises the net amount that would be received in a current transaction for the financial asset.

11.81　A market is considered to be active if transactions occur with sufficient frequency to provide reliable information on prices on a continuous basis. However, if the market is not well-established, and only a small volume of a particular instrument is traded relative to the amount of the instrument in issue (or trading is infrequent), quoted prices in those markets might not be suitable for determining fair value. See paragraph 11.85 below for further guidance on this point.

11.82　In an active dealer market, bid prices (that is, the price at which a dealer is willing to purchase) and ask prices (that is, the price at which a dealer is willing to sell) are readily available. Financial assets held at the reporting date are usually valued at current bid price. [FRS 102 para 11.27(a)]. This is consistent with the definition of fair value being *"the amount for which an asset could be exchanged, or a liability settled, between knowledgeable, willing parties in an arm's length transaction"*. [FRS 102 Glossary of terms]. Therefore, the price at which an asset could be exchanged is the price that an entity would have received if it had sold the asset.

Unavailability of quoted prices

11.83　Where current prices of financial instruments are unavailable at the reporting date, the price of the most recent transaction for an identical asset should be used, provided there has not been a significant change in economic circumstances or a significant lapse of time since the transaction took place. This is a fairly simple technique and provides a foundation for estimating fair value. [FRS 102 para 11.27(b)].

11.84　Similarly, if the entity can demonstrate that the last transaction price is not a good estimate of fair value (for example, because it reflects the amount that an entity would receive or pay in a forced transaction, involuntary liquidation or distress sale), that price should be adjusted. [FRS 102 para 11.27(b)].

Valuation techniques in the absence of an active market

11.85 If the market for the asset is not active, and recent transactions of an identical asset on their own are not a good estimate of fair value, an entity should estimate the fair value by using a valuation technique. The objective of using a valuation technique is to estimate what the transaction price would have been on the measurement date in an arm's length exchange motivated by normal business considerations. [FRS 102 para 11.27(c)].

11.86 The objective of the valuation process is to arrive at a reasonable estimate of a financial instrument's fair value, so the technique used should reasonably reflect how the market could be expected to price the instrument. That expectation is likely to be met if the valuation technique makes maximum use of market inputs, and relies as little as possible on entity-specific inputs. Also, the inputs should reasonably represent market expectations and measures of the risk-return factors inherent in the financial instrument. In other words, an acceptable valuation technique should incorporate all factors that market participants would consider in setting a price, and should be consistent with accepted economic methodologies for pricing financial instruments.

11.87 A valuation technique should, therefore, reflect how the market could be expected to price the instrument under the conditions that exist at the measurement date. Even where a market is considered to be inactive, the most recent transaction prices should be considered as an input to a valuation model, provided that these are not forced or non-arm's length transactions. Current market conditions cannot be ignored. In practice, an entity could begin the valuation process by using its own data, which is adjusted if reasonably available information indicates that other market participants would use different data. An entity does not need to undertake exhaustive efforts to obtain information about market participant assumptions; but it cannot ignore information about market participant assumptions that is reasonably available.

11.88 Valuation techniques that are well-established in financial markets include recent market transactions, reference to a transaction that is substantially the same, price/earnings models, discounted cash flows and option pricing models. If there is a valuation technique commonly used by market participants to price the asset, and that technique has been demonstrated to provide reliable estimates of prices obtained in actual market transactions, the entity should use that technique. [FRS 102 para 11.28]. Whatever technique is used to value a particular instrument, it should be used on a consistent basis. A change in the valuation techniques used is appropriate only if the change results in a more reliable estimate of fair value (for example, as new markets develop, or as new and improved valuation techniques become available).

Fair value – own credit risk

11.89 Where financial liabilities are measured at fair value, changes in their credit risk should be reflected in their fair value measurement. Because financial statements are prepared on a going concern basis, credit risk affects the value at which liabilities could be repurchased or settled. Accordingly, a financial liability's fair value reflects the credit risk relating to that liability.

11.90 Where an entity uses a valuation technique to estimate fair value, credit risk would generally be built into the valuation model. Therefore, fair value should incorporate the impact of credit risk to the extent that credit risk affects the price for which the liability could be exchanged between willing parties in an arm's length transaction. In the particular case of derivatives, the entity's own credit risk will need to be incorporated where the derivative is in a liability position at the reporting date. In many cases, the only way in which an entity can settle a derivative liability at the reporting date is through paying the counterparty a 'close-out amount' that does not incorporate changes in the entity's credit risk since the inception of the contract. In other words, an entity often has no practical ability to realise gains by settling liabilities at a lower amount, due to deterioration in its own credit risk.

11.91 In our view, either of the following approaches is acceptable for measuring the fair value of liabilities not traded in an active market:

- Fair value based on a presumption that an entity has the practical ability to settle the liability in a way that enables it to realise gains and losses from changes in its own credit risk ('the full own credit risk approach').

- Fair value based on a 'close-out amount' that would be paid to the counterparty. This reflects the amount that the entity would pay to settle the liability with the counterparty at the reporting date ('the counterparty close-out approach').

The chosen accounting policy should be applied consistently in both measuring and disclosing fair value. The policy selected should be disclosed where it has a significant effect on either measurement or disclosure.

No reliable measure

11.92 It is normally possible to estimate, with sufficient reliability, the fair value of equity instruments or preference shares that do not have a quoted market price in an active market by applying valuation techniques based on reasonable assumptions. The fair values of such instruments are deemed to be reliably measurable if:

- the variability in the range of reasonable fair value estimates is not significant for that instrument; or

- the probabilities of the various estimates within the range can be reasonably assessed and used in estimating fair value.

[FRS 102 para 11.30].

11.93 There are many situations in which the variability in the range of reasonable fair value estimates is likely not to be significant, and so the fair value is reasonably measurable. However, if the range of reasonable fair value estimates is significantly wide, and the probabilities of the various estimates cannot be reasonably assessed, an entity is precluded from measuring the instrument at fair value. [FRS 102 para 11.31]. It is not permissible for the entity to measure the instrument at fair value, for instance, by arbitrarily picking a fair value estimate within a wide range.

11.94 If a reliable measure of fair value is no longer available for an asset measured at fair value (for example, an equity instrument measured at fair value through profit or loss), its carrying amount at the last date when the asset was reliably measurable becomes its new cost. The entity should measure the asset at this cost amount less impairment until a reliable measure of fair value becomes available.

Derecognition of financial assets

11.95 Although section 11 of FRS 102 applies to basic financial instruments measured at amortised cost, and to those investments in ordinary shares or preference shares measured at fair values if their fair values can be measured reliably, the derecognition requirements also apply to other financial instruments that are accounted for in accordance with section 12 of the standard at fair value through profit or loss. [FRS 102 para 12.14].

11.96 Section 11 of the standard provides different requirements for derecognition of financial assets and liabilities. In the context of a financial asset, derecognition is not achieved simply by transferring the legal title. The substance of the arrangement needs to be assessed to determine whether the entity has transferred the economic rights and exposures inherent in the asset. That assessment is made by applying a combination of risks and rewards and control tests.

11.97 An entity should derecognise a financial asset if any one of the following conditions is met:

- The contractual rights to the cash flows from the financial asset expire or are settled.

- The entity transfers to another party substantially all of the risks and rewards of ownership of the financial asset.

- The entity, despite having retained some significant risks and rewards of ownership, has transferred control of the asset to another party, and the other party has the practical ability to sell the asset in its entirety to an unrelated third party and is able to exercise that ability unilaterally and without needing to impose additional restrictions on the transfer. In this case, the entity should:

- derecognise the asset, and

- recognise separately any rights and obligations retained or created in the transfer.

[FRS 102 para 11.33].

11.98 A financial asset is derecognised when the rights to the cash flows from the asset expire or are settled.

Transfer of substantially all the risks and rewards of ownership of the asset

11.99 If an entity transfers substantially all the risks and rewards of ownership of the financial asset, it derecognises the financial asset in its entirety. The entity might need to recognise any rights or obligations retained or created in the transfer.

11.100 The standard does not provide any specific guidance on how to determine whether the entity has transferred 'substantially all' the risks and rewards of ownership. In most types of transfer of financial assets expected to be undertaken by entities in the scope of FRS 102, it will often be readily apparent from the terms and conditions of the transfer arrangements whether this is so. The analysis should be based on all facts and circumstances, considering all the risks associated with the financial assets. The types of risk that would normally be considered include credit risk, late payment risk, interest rate risk, foreign exchange risk and equity price risk, depending on the particular asset that is being considered for derecognition. For example, in the case of short-term receivables, the main risks that would be considered are credit risk and late payment risk, and perhaps foreign currency risk if they are denominated in a foreign currency.

11.101 Examples of transactions that transfer substantially all the risks and rewards of ownership include:

- An unconditional sale of a financial asset for a fixed amount of non-returnable consideration. This is the most obvious example.

- A sale of a financial asset, together with an option to repurchase the financial asset at its fair value at the time of repurchase. In this situation, the entity is no longer exposed to any value risk (that is, potential for gain and exposure to loss) on the transferred asset, which is borne by the buyer. The option for the seller to buy the asset back at its fair value at the date of repurchase is economically no different from buying a new asset.

- A sale of a financial asset at its fair value, with an option for the purchaser to require the transferor (the seller) to repurchase the asset at the price it was sold for if the market price of the asset falls, within the next month, by a large amount that is so large it is very unlikely to happen. The purchaser's put option is so far 'out of the money' that it is highly unlikely to go 'into the money' before expiry. In this situation, the seller has no substantial risks and rewards, because there is no real possibility that the put option will be exercised. As the option has little or no value, such a sale is economically little different from an unconditional sale. A similar analysis would apply to a call option, held by the transferor, whose terms were such that it was highly unlikely to be exercised.

- A sale of a financial asset, with a right of first refusal to repurchase the transferred asset at fair value if the transferee subsequently sells it. On the other hand, if the right of first refusal is at a price other than the asset's fair value at that date, the analysis would be similar to the transferor having a call option.

11.102 If the above analysis indicates that the entity has retained substantially all the risks and rewards of ownership, the entity cannot derecognise the asset. Examples of such transactions would be:

- A sale of short-term receivables in which the entity guarantees to compensate the transferee for all credit losses and late payments which are likely to occur.

- A sale of a financial asset, together with a deep 'in the money' put or call option (that is, an option that is so far 'in the money' that it is highly likely to be exercised before expiry).

Transfer of control of the financial asset

11.103 If the entity (transferor) has neither transferred nor retained substantially all the risks and rewards of ownership of the transferred financial asset – in other words, it has retained some significant risks and rewards – it is in a middle ground in which the risks and rewards analysis does not provide a clear answer. In this situation, the transferor needs to determine whether it has retained control of the asset.

11.104 Whether the entity has retained control of the transferred asset depends on the transferee's ability to sell the asset. If the transferee has the 'practical ability' to sell the transferred asset, the transferor has lost control and derecognises the asset. In all other cases, the entity has retained control and continues to recognise the asset.

11.105 'Practical ability' to sell the transferred asset means that:

- the transferee can sell the asset in its entirety to an unrelated third party; and

- the transferee is able to exercise that ability 'unilaterally and without imposing additional restrictions'.

[FRS 102 para 11.33(c)].

11.106 The above conditions should be evaluated by considering what the transferee is able to do in practice, not what contractual rights it has with respect to the transferred asset (or, indeed, what contractual prohibition exists).

Accounting treatment

11.107   The accounting treatment that should be followed by the transferor following a transfer of financial assets is discussed below, with examples.

Transfers that qualify for derecognition

11.108   Where the entity determines that a transfer qualifies for derecognition (as noted in para 11.97 above), an entity should derecognise the asset in its entirety and recognise any new rights and obligations created at fair value at the transfer date. Any difference between the consideration received and the amounts derecognised should be recognised in profit or loss in the period of the transfer. [FRS 102 para 11.33].

> **Example – Factoring without recourse**
>
> Entity A (the transferor) holds a portfolio of accounts receivables with a carrying value of £1m. It enters into a factoring arrangement with entity B (the factor) under which it transfers the receivables portfolio to entity B in exchange for £900,000 of cash.
>
> Entity A continues to handle collections from the debtors on behalf of the bank, including sending monthly statements, and the bank pays the entity a market-rate fee for servicing the receivables. Entity A is obliged to remit promptly to the entity B any and all amounts collected, but it has no obligation to entity B for slow payment or non-payment by the debtors. In other words, entity B has no recourse to entity A whatsoever.
>
> In this example, entity B has no recourse to entity A for either late payment risk or credit risk arising on the transferred receivables. Accordingly, entity A has transferred substantially all the risks and rewards of ownership of the portfolio to entity B.
>
> Hence, entity A derecognises the entire portfolio. The difference between the carrying value of £1m and cash received of £900,000 (that is, the entire discount of £100,000) is recognised immediately as a financing cost in profit or loss.
>
> No new rights or obligations are created in the transfer, except that entity A recognises a liability for sums collected from the debtors, but not yet remitted to entity B.
>
> As entity A continues to provide accounting services to entity B for which it receives a market-rate fee, it recognises income and expense for providing the services in the normal way.

11.109   In circumstances where the entity has transferred control of the asset, but has retained some significant risks and rewards (as noted in the third bullet point in para 11.97 above), the carrying amount of the transferred asset should be allocated between the rights or obligations retained and those transferred, on the basis of the relative fair values at the transfer date. Any difference between the consideration received and the amounts recognised and derecognised should be recognised in profit or loss in the period of the transfer. [FRS 102 para 11.33].

Example – Transfer of asset measured at fair value subject to call option

Entity A has a 1% equity holding in a listed entity, B, that is measured at fair value thought profit or loss and whose fair value is £190,000. This holding is treated as a trade investment and classified as at fair value through profit or loss. On 31 December 20X0, the fair value of the asset is £190,000. On the same date, entity A sells its entire holding in entity B to a bank for a consideration of £180,000, but retains a call option to purchase the investment for £200,000 on 31 December 20X1.

It is judged that the entity has neither transferred nor retained substantially all the risks and rewards of ownership of the transferred asset through the operation of the option. This is because:

- entity A can exercise its call option so as to benefit from movements in the asset's fair value above the call option exercise price of £200,000; and

- entity A is not exposed to movements in the asset's fair value below the call option exercise price.

Furthermore, because the investment is actively traded, the bank has the practical ability to sell the asset to an unrelated third party and is able to do so unilaterally and without needing to impose any additional restrictions on the transfer. This is so because, if entity A decides to exercise its option, the bank can buy the asset in the market and fulfil its obligations under the contract. Therefore, entity A has transferred control of the investments to the bank.

As a result, entity A is able to derecognise its investments in entity B and recognise the option asset (a new right created in the transfer). At the date of transfer, the call option is 'out of the money' (that is, the option's exercise price of £200,000 is greater than the fair value of the shares at £190,000). The premium paid on the option (all time value) is £10,000 (fair value of the asset of £190,000 less consideration received of £180,000). Therefore, entity A recognises the following accounting entries:

	Dr £	Cr £
Cash received on sale	180,000	
Fair value of call option (premium paid)	10,000	
Investments in entity B		190,000
	190,000	190,000

The call option is a derivative financial instrument that would be measured at fair value through profit or loss in accordance with section 12 of FRS 102 until its expiry on 31 December 20X1.

Transfers that do not qualify for derecognition

11.110   Where a transfer does not result in derecognition because the entity has retained significant risks and rewards of ownership of the transferred asset, the entity continues to recognise the transferred asset in its entirety and recognises a financial liability for the consideration received. The asset and the associated liability cannot be offset. In subsequent periods, the entity recognises any income on the transferred asset and any expense incurred on the financial liability. [FRS 102 para 11.34]. Again, the entity cannot offset the income and the expense. This reflects the transaction's substance, which is accounted for as a collateralised borrowing.

Example – Factoring with limited recourse (late payment risk retained)

Entity A (the transferor) holds a portfolio of trade receivables with a carrying value of £1m. Entity A enters into a factoring arrangement with entity B (the transferee) under which it transfers the portfolio to entity B in exchange for £900,000 of cash. Entity A transfers the credit risk, but retains the late payment risk up to a maximum of 180 days. After 180 days, the receivable is deemed to be in default, and entity B suffers any resulting loss. A charge is levied on entity A for these late payments, using a current rate of 6%. Apart from late payment risk, entity A does not retain any credit or interest rate risk and does not carry out any servicing of the portfolio. There is no active market for the receivables, and both late payment risk (up to 180 days) and credit risk (including the risk of slow payment beyond 180 days) have been assessed to be significant.

Entity A has transferred some but not all the risks and rewards of ownership – it has retained late payment risks, but has transferred credit risks. Furthermore, as there is no active market for the receivables, entity B does not have the practical ability to sell the transferred asset. Since entity B is constrained from selling the asset, the 'practical ability' test fails, with the result that control of the transferred asset is retained by entity A.

As a result of the above, entity A recognises a financial liability for the consideration received of £900,000. The liability is measured at amortised cost, with interest expense recognised over the period to maturity of the receivables, in line with the interest rate charged by the factor.

In the unlikely event that entity B is able to transfer the receivables to a third party freely and without imposing additional restrictions on the transfer, entity A would be considered to have lost control of the receivables.

In that situation, entity A would derecognise the receivables and recognise separately the financial instrument (guarantee) created in the transfer that might cause entity A to repay 6% × £1m × 180/360 = £30,000. This is the maximum amount of the consideration received in the transfer that entity A would be required to repay if all the debtors in the portfolio fail to pay within the 180-day period. This guarantee is a financial instrument, because entity A has agreed to reimburse entity B in the event that all the debtors default. The guarantee does not meet the definition of a basic financial instrument, and so is outside the scope of section 11 of FRS 102. The financial instrument is accounted for in accordance with section 12 of the standard. If the fair value of the guarantee is assumed to be £1,000, entity A would record the following entries:

	Dr £	Cr £
Cash received	900,000	
Receivables		1,000,000
Fair value of guarantee		1,000
Loss on disposal in profit or loss	101,000	
	1,001,000	1,001,100

The fair value of the guarantee of £1,000 would be amortised to profit or loss over the guarantee period of 180 days, subject to the need to increase the guarantee liability to reflect any amounts expected to be paid, in accordance with section 21 of the standard.

Accounting for Collateral

11.111 A transfer of financial assets might require the transferor to provide non-cash collateral (such as a debt or equity instruments) to the transferee. If collateral is transferred to the transferee, the custodial arrangement is commonly referred to as a pledge. Transferees sometimes are permitted to sell or re-pledge (or otherwise transfer) collateral held under a pledge. The accounting for the collateral by the transferor and the transferee depends on whether the transferee has the right to sell or re-pledge the collateral and on whether the transferor has defaulted, as shown in the table below:

Circumstance	Accounting by transferor	Accounting by transferee
Transferee has the right, by contract or custom, to sell or re-pledge the collateral.	The transferor reclassifies that asset in its balance sheet (for example, as a loaned asset, pledged equity instruments or repurchase receivable) separately from other assets that are not so encumbered. [FRS 102 para 11.35(a)]. This is because the transferor retains all the risks and rewards of ownership of the asset pledged as collateral and, therefore, cannot derecognise it under the normal rules for derecognition.	The transferee will not recognise the collateral as an asset. If the transferee sells the collateral pledged to it, it recognises the proceeds from the sale and a liability measured at fair value for its obligation to return the collateral. [FRS 102 para 11.35(b)].

Transferor defaults under the terms of the contract and is no longer entitled to redeem the collateral.	Transferor derecognises the collateral. [FRS 102 para 11.35(c)].	Transferee recognises the collateral as its asset initially measured at fair value; or, if it has already sold the collateral, derecognises its obligation to return the collateral. [FRS 102 para 11.35(c)].

This is because the risks and rewards of ownership of the collateral have passed to the transferee. |
| All other situations, except as referred to above. | Transferor continues to recognise the collateral as its asset. [FRS 102 para 11.35(d)]. | Transferee does not recognise the collateral as an asset. [FRS 102 para 11.35(d)]. |

Derecognition of financial liabilities

11.112 The derecognition rules for financial liabilities are somewhat different from those relating to financial assets. Whereas the derecognition rules for financial assets tend to focus on risks and rewards (and might not lead to derecognition, even though legal transfer has occurred), the derecognition rules for financial liabilities focus solely on the legal release of the contractual obligations. Consequently, the provisions in section 11 of FRS 102 relating to derecognition of financial liabilities, in whole or in part, are relatively straightforward and less subjective than those for derecognition of financial assets. The rules in section 11 of the standard deal with extinguishment of financial liabilities, their modification by lenders, and the recognition and measurement of any gains or losses that arise from extinguishment and modification. These issues are considered in detail below.

Extinguishment of a financial liability

General principles

11.113 A financial liability (or part of it) is derecognised when it is extinguished – that is, when the obligation is discharged, is cancelled or expires. [FRS 102 para 11.36]. This condition is met when:

- the debtor discharges the liability (or part of it) by paying the creditor, normally with cash, other financial assets, goods or services; or

- the debtor is legally released from settling the liability (or part of it) by the creditor or by process of law.

Legal release by process of law

11.114   A financial liability will also be extinguished if the entity is released from settling the liability by process of law. For example, in England and Wales, under the Limitation Act 1980, creditors are given a fixed period of time to chase their debtors. The time scale mainly depends on the type of debt and can be extended at the court's discretion. For example, the limitation period for enforcing payment under a contract is six years. Thus, a supplier would no longer be able to legally enforce payment by a customer if the supplier did not claim payment within six years from the date that the goods were provided. Until six years have passed, the customer would be legally required to pay the supplier, if the supplier made a claim, and so it would not be appropriate for the customer to derecognise any debt due to the supplier.

Gain or loss arising on extinguishment

11.115   Where a financial liability (or a part of it) is extinguished or transferred to another party, the entity should recognise, in profit or loss, any difference arising between the carrying amount of the financial liability (or part of it) extinguished or transferred and the consideration paid, including any non-cash assets transferred or liabilities assumed. [FRS 102 para 11.38].

Exchange and modification of debt instruments

11.116   Section 11 of FRS 102 requires an exchange between an existing borrower and lender of debt instruments with substantially different terms to be accounted for as an extinguishment of the original financial liability and the recognition of a new financial liability. Similarly, a substantial modification of the terms of an existing financial liability (or part of it), whether or not attributable to the financial difficulty of the debtor, should be accounted for as an extinguishment of the original financial liability and the recognition of a new financial liability. [FRS 102 para 11.37].

11.117   The standard does not provide any specific guidance on how to determine whether the terms are 'substantially different' following an exchange of financial instruments, or whether a modification of the terms is 'substantial'. Therefore, an entity would need to exercise judgement. In exercising that judgement, factors that should be considered include, but are not limited to, the following:

- A change in interest rate basis from fixed to floating, or vice versa, between original debt and new/replacement debt, or as a result of modification of the terms of the original debt instrument.

- Material difference in maturity between the remaining maturity of the old debt and the new debt, or as a result of modification of the original terms.

- Material changes in covenants between the old and new debt, or as a result of modification of the original terms.

- Material change in conversion terms between the old and new debt, or as a result of modification of the original terms.

- A change in currency denomination between the old and new debt, or as a result of modification of the original terms.

11.118   The factors discussed above are qualitative in nature. Another way of establishing whether there are substantially different terms is to consider quantitative changes in cash flows. For example, if the discounted present value of the cash flows under the new terms, including any fees paid net of any fees received and discounted using the original effective interest rate, is at least 10% different from the discounted present value of the remaining cash flows of the original financial liability. A 10% differential is the criteria used in IFRS and therefore is not a requirement for FRS 102 but in our view, a 10% change in cash flows would normally represent a substantial modification of the terms. [IAS 39 para AG 62; IFRS 9 B3.3.6].

11.119   In the absence of any specific guidance, but following the hierarchy of sources set out in paragraph 10.5 of FRS 102, we believe that it is appropriate to account for an insubstantial modification of a debt instrument, that does not lead to extinguishment, in the same way as a change in estimated cash flows (discussed in para 11.56 above). This means that any difference in present value between the cash flows under the old terms and the new terms, discounted using the original effective interest rate, is recognised immediately in profit or loss.

Treatment of costs and fees incurred on debt restructuring

11.120   Section 11 of FRS 102 does not provide any specific guidance on to how account for costs and fees incurred when an entity restructures its own debt, unlike IAS 39. In our view, for a change in terms which is accounted for as an extinguishment, the transaction costs and fees incurred would be expensed as incurred. If the change in terms is not accounted for as an extinguishment, directly attributable costs and fees should be spread over the life of the instrument by adjusting the effective interest rate.

Presentation and disclosure

Disclosures

11.121   Disclosures required by a reporting entity include those in sections 11 and 12 of FRS 102, and the Companies Act. In all cases, the Companies Act disclosures are required, whether the entity is a qualifying entity or not.

11.122   A qualifying entity which is not a financial institution is exempt from making the disclosures required by sections 11 and 12 of FRS 102, provided equivalent disclosures required by FRS 102 are included in the consolidated financial statements of the group in which the entity is consolidated. The disclosure requirements of section 11 that are considered in paragraphs 11.124–

11.137 below are not relevant to such an entity. This exemption includes financial liabilities measured at fair value that are part of a trading portfolio or are derivatives. However, for financial liabilities designated as at fair value through profit or loss under the fair value option (see para 11.46 above), the effect of the Companies Act is that the exemption is not available, and so the disclosures required by section 11 of the standard must be given (see further para 11.146 below).

11.123 The disclosure requirements noted below apply to basic financial instruments, as well as to financial instruments measured at fair value through profit or loss (as discussed in chapter 12).

Balance sheet – Categories of financial assets and liabilities

11.124 An entity should disclose the carrying amounts of each of the following categories of financial assets and financial liabilities at the reporting date, in total, either in the statement of financial position or in the notes:

- Financial assets measured at fair value through profit or loss.

- Financial assets that are debt instruments measured at amortised cost. These would include debt instruments classified as current assets that are measured at an undiscounted amount (for example, trade and other receivables).

- Financial assets that are equity instruments measured at cost less impairment.

- Financial liabilities measured at fair value through profit or loss in accordance with section 12 of FRS 102. Financial liabilities that are not held as part of a trading portfolio and are not derivatives should be separately disclosed.

- Financial liabilities measured at amortised cost. These would include debt instruments classified as current assets that are measured at an undiscounted amount (for example, trade and other payables).

- Loan commitments measured at cost less impairment.

[FRS 102 para 11.41].

11.125 The above information for financial assets and financial liabilities is best presented in a tabular form where an entity has many different types of financial instrument. However, if an entity has only basic financial instruments that are already presented as separate line items on the balance sheet, there is no need to group them all in a table and show a cumulative total.

11.126 An entity should present financial assets and liabilities in accordance with the classification set out in section 4 of FRS 102 (discussed in chapter 4). In most cases, it will be satisfactory to disclose the size of debtors due after more than one year in the notes to the accounts. There will be some instances, however, where the amount is so material in the context of the total net current assets that, if the debtors due after more than one year are not disclosed on the face of the balance sheet, readers might misinterpret the accounts. In such circumstances, the amount should be disclosed on the face of the balance sheet within current assets.

Derecognition

11.127   An entity might have transferred financial assets to another party in a transaction that does not qualify for derecognition. In that situation, the entity should disclose, for each class of such financial assets:

■   The nature of the assets.

■   The nature of the risks and rewards of ownership to which the entity remains exposed.

■   The carrying amounts of the assets, and of any associated liabilities that the entity continues to recognise.

[FRS 102 para 11.45].

Collateral

11.128   Where an entity has pledged financial assets as collateral for liabilities or contingent liabilities, it should disclose the following:

■   The carrying amount of the financial assets pledged as collateral.

■   The terms and conditions relating to its pledge.

[FRS 102 para 11.46].

Defaults and breaches on loans payable

11.129   An entity is required to disclose the following information on defaults and breaches of loans payable at the reporting date for which there is a breach of terms (or default of principal, interest, sinking fund, or redemption terms) that has not been remedied by the reporting date:

■   Details of that breach or default.

■   The carrying amount of the related loans payable at the reporting date.

■   Whether the breach or default was remedied, or the terms of the loans payable were renegotiated, before the financial statements were authorised for issue.

[FRS 102 para 11.47].

Disclosures — Income statement

Items of income, expense, gains and losses

11.130 An entity should disclose the following items of income, expense, gains or losses:

- Income, expense, gains or losses, including changes in fair value, recognised on:

  - Financial assets measured at fair value through profit or loss.

  - Financial liabilities measured at fair value through profit or loss, with separate disclosure of movements on those which are not held as part of a trading portfolio and are not derivatives.

  - Financial assets measured at amortised cost.

  - Financial liabilities measured at amortised cost.

- Total interest income and total interest expense (calculated using the effective interest method) for financial assets or financial liabilities that are not measured at fair value through profit or loss.

- The amount of any impairment loss for each class of financial asset. A class of financial asset is a grouping that is appropriate to the nature of the information disclosed and that takes into account the characteristics of the financial assets.

[FRS 102 para 11.48].

Other disclosures

Accounting policies

11.131 In accordance with paragraph 8.5 of FRS 102, an entity should disclose, in the summary of significant accounting policies, the measurement basis (or bases) used for financial instruments, and the other accounting policies used for financial instruments that are relevant to an understanding of the financial statements. [FRS 102 para 11.40].

Information about financial instruments

11.132 An entity should disclose information that enables users of its financial statements to evaluate the significance of financial instruments for its financial position and performance. For example, such information for long-term debt would normally include the terms and conditions of the debt instrument (such as interest rate, maturity, repayment schedule, and restrictions that the debt instrument imposes on the entity). [FRS 102 para 11.42].

Fair values

11.133 For all financial assets and financial liabilities measured at fair value, the entity should disclose the basis for determining fair value (for example, quoted market price in an active market or a valuation technique). [FRS 102 para 11.43]. For instance, if investments in shares that are not actively traded are fair valued using a valuation technique, the valuation technique used (recent market transactions, reference to other observable transaction that is substantially the same, discounted cash flow or option pricing models) should be disclosed.

11.134 When a valuation technique is used, the entity should disclose the assumptions applied in determining fair value for each class of financial assets or financial liabilities. For example, an entity discloses information (if applicable) about the assumptions relating to prepayment rates, rates of estimated credit losses, and interest rates or discount rates. [FRS 102 para 11.43].

11.135 If a reliable measure of fair value is no longer available for ordinary or preference shares measured at fair value through profit or loss, the entity should disclose that fact. [FRS 102 para 11.44].

11.136 An entity is required to make the following disclosures for financial instruments at fair value which are neither derivatives nor held as part of a trading portfolio (see chapter 34 for a discussion relating to credit risk, market risk and liquidity risk within the similar disclosures for financial institutions):

- The amount of change, during the period and cumulatively, in the fair value of the financial instrument that is attributable to changes in the credit risk of that instrument, determined either:

  - as the amount of change in its fair value that is not attributable to changes in market conditions that give rise to market risk; or

  - using an alternative method that, in management's opinion, more faithfully represents the amount of change in its fair value that is attributable to changes in the credit risk of the instrument.

- The method used to establish the amount of change attributable to changes in own credit risk; or, if the change cannot be measured reliably or is not material, that fact.

- The difference between the financial liability's carrying amount and the amount that the entity would be contractually required to pay at maturity to the holder of the obligation.

- If an instrument contains both a liability and an equity feature, and the instrument has multiple features that substantially modify the cash flows, and the values of those features are interdependent (such as a callable convertible debt instrument), the existence of those features.

- Any difference between the fair value at initial recognition and the amount that would be determined at that date using a valuation technique, and the amount recognised in profit or loss.

- Information that enables users of the entity's financial statements to evaluate the nature and extent of relevant risks arising from financial instruments to which the entity is exposed at the end of the reporting period. These risks typically include (but are not limited to) credit risk, liquidity risk and market risk. The disclosure should include both the entity's exposure to each type of risk and how it manages those risks.

[FRS 102 para 11.48A].

Additional disclosure requirements for financial institutions

11.137 Additional disclosures are required to be made in the individual financial statements of a financial institution (other than a retirement benefit plan) and consolidated financial statements of a group containing a financial institution (other than a retirement benefit plan) where the financial instruments held by the financial institution are material to the group. In such a case, the disclosures apply, whether the principal activity of the group is being a financial institution or not, but are restricted to financial instruments held by entities within the group that are financial institutions. [FRS 102 para 34.17]. These disclosures are considered in chapter 34.

Additional disclosure requirements for retirement benefit plans

11.138 Retirement benefit plans are also required to apply the disclosure requirements of paragraph 34.39 to 34.48 in Section 34 of FRS 102. See Section 34 of the Standard for these disclosure requirements.

Companies Act disclosure requirements

11.139 The Companies Act has extensive disclosure requirements in respect of accounting for investments. Not all financial instruments are investments, and so not all investments are within the scope of sections 11 and 12 of FRS 102, but there is a significant overlap between financial instruments and investments.

11.140 The Act does not provide a formal definition of investments, although the model formats for the balance sheet include a heading for 'investments' under the general heading of both 'fixed assets' and 'current assets'. Moreover, there are separate sub-headings for investments under both the fixed and the current categories:

- The sub-headings identified for fixed asset investments are:

  - Shares in group undertakings.

  - Loans to group undertakings.

- ■ Participating interests.

- ■ Loans to undertakings in which the entity has a participating interest.

- ■ Other investments other than loans.

- ■ Other loans.

- ■ Own shares.

- ■ The sub-headings identified for current asset investments are:

  - ■ Shares in group undertakings.

  - ■ Own shares.

  - ■ Other investments.

11.141 Under the Act, a company can treat investments in its balance sheet as either fixed asset investments or current asset investments, depending on how it intends to use them. A company's investments that are "... *intended for use on a continuing basis in the company's activities*" should be classified as fixed assets in the company's financial statements. Generally, investments should be classified as fixed where the company intends to hold them for the long term and this intention can be clearly demonstrated. Furthermore, such a situation might arise where the company's ability to dispose of an investment is restricted for a particular reason. If a company's investments do not fall within the category described above, and so they are not considered to be fixed asset investments, they will fall to be classified as current asset investments.

11.142 Whether a company intends to use an investment on a continuing basis (that is, hold it for the long term) will often be obvious from the nature of the investment. Treatment as a fixed asset might also arise where there are practical restrictions on an investor's ability to dispose of the investment. Fixed asset investments will, therefore, comprise:

- ■ Equity shareholdings in, or loans to, subsidiaries and associates.

- ■ Investments arising from other trading relationships.

- ■ Investments that either cannot be disposed of, or cannot be disposed of without a significant effect on the operations of the investing company.

- ■ Investments that are intended to be held for use on a continuing basis by investing companies whose objective is to hold a portfolio of investments to provide income and/or capital growth for their members.

11.143 It should be remembered, however, that the mere fact that an investment has been held for a long time does not necessarily make it a long-term asset, unless it also falls within one of the categories indicated in the paragraph above.

11.144 The Companies Act allows some financial instruments to be measured at fair value. However, the following financial instruments cannot be fair valued (except in the circumstances noted in para 11.145 below):

- Financial liabilities, unless they are held as part of a trading portfolio or they are derivatives.

- Financial instruments (other than derivatives) held to maturity.

- Loans and receivables originated by the company and not held for trading purposes.

- Interests in subsidiary undertakings, associated undertakings and joint ventures.

- Equity instruments issued by the company.

- Contracts for contingent consideration in a business combination.

- Other financial instruments with such special characteristics that (according to generally accepted accounting principles or practice) they should be accounted for differently from other financial instruments.

[SI 2008/410 1 Sch 36].

11.145 If an entity fair values any of the financial instruments listed above under FRS 102 (or the optional use of IAS 39/IFRS 9), the disclosures in section 11 of FRS 102 discussed in this chapter must be given for those instruments, to comply with the Companies Act. This is the case, even if the entity is a qualifying entity that would otherwise be exempt from such disclosures. [SI 2008/410 1 Sch 36(4)].

11.146 Companies applying fair value accounting under FRS 102, IAS 39 or IFRS 9 are required by the Companies Act, whether they are a qualifying entity for the purposes of FRS 102 disclosures or not, to disclose:

- The significant assumptions underlying the valuation models and techniques used.

- For each category of financial instrument, the fair value of the instruments in that category and the amounts:

    - included in the profit and loss account; or

    - credited to or debited from the fair value reserve,

    in respect of instruments in that category.

- For each class of derivative financial instruments, the extent and nature of the instruments, including significant terms and conditions that might affect the amount, timing and certainty of future cash flows.

- Where any amount is transferred to or from the fair value reserve during the financial year, there should be stated in tabular form:

    - the amount of the reserve as at the beginning of the financial year and as at the balance sheet date;

    - the amount transferred to or from the reserve during that year; and

- the source and application respectively of the amounts so transferred.

[SI 2008/410 1 Sch 55(2)(3)].

11.147 In addition, where:

- a company has financial fixed assets that could be included at fair value;

- the amount at which those assets are included in the financial statements is in excess of their fair value; and

- the company has not made provision for diminution in value of those assets,

the following disclosures must be made:

- The amount at which either the individual assets or appropriate groupings of those individual assets are stated in the company's financial statements.

- The fair value of those assets or groupings.

- The reasons for not making a provision for diminution in value of those assets, including the nature of the evidence that provides the basis for the belief that the amount at which they are stated in the financial statements will be recovered.

[SI 2008/410 1 Sch 57].

11.148 A company must give the following information in the directors' report (unless such information is not material):

- The financial risk management objectives and policies of the company and its consolidated subsidiaries, including the policy for hedging each major type of forecasted transaction for which hedge accounting is used.

- The exposure of the company and its consolidated subsidiaries to price risk, credit risk, liquidity risk and cash flow risk.

[SI 2008/410 7 Sch 6].

11.149 Under the Act, capital instruments in the form of debentures, loans and debt instruments fall to be included under the general heading of 'Creditors'. All items included under creditors must be analysed between amounts that will fall due within one year of the balance sheet date and amounts that will fall due after more than one year. [SI 2008/410 1 Sch Balance sheet formats note 13].

11.150 In distinguishing between the above two categories, a loan is regarded as falling due for repayment (or an instalment is regarded as falling due for payment) on the earliest date on which the lender could require repayment (or payment) if he were to exercise all options and rights available to him. [SI 2008/410 10 Sch 9].

11.151   For each item shown under creditors (whichever balance sheet format is adopted), the aggregate amounts of debts falling into the two categories below must be disclosed separately:

- Debts that are payable or repayable otherwise than by instalments, and falling due for payment or repayment after the end of the five-year period beginning with the day after the end of the financial year.

- Debts that are payable or repayable by instalments, any of which will fall due for payment after the end of that five-year period.

[SI 2008/410 1 Sch 61(1)].

11.152   The requirement is to disclose one figure showing the aggregate of the above two items, but the aggregation of instalment and non-instalment debts results in a figure that is rather meaningless. The Act's intention seems to have been to require disclosure of the amount of debts and instalments which are payable in over five years, to bring the disclosure in line with that required by Article 43(1)(6) of the Fourth Directive. In practice, it seems sensible to give the intended disclosure, because this is more meaningful

11.153   The terms of payment or repayment and the applicable rate of interest for each debt covered by the disclosure under the preceding paragraph must also be given. [SI 2008/410 1 Sch 61(2)]. Where the number of debt instruments is such that, in the directors' opinion, this requirement would result in a statement of excessive length, this information need be given only in general terms. [SI 2008/ 410 1 Sch 61(3)].

11.154   Where any item that is shown under the heading 'Creditors' includes debts for which the company has given security, these debts must be disclosed in aggregate. Also, the notes must give an indication of the nature of the securities given. [SI 2008/410 1 Sch 61(4)]. For this requirement to be meaningful, the financial statements should show some disaggregation of the relevant liabilities. This is because it could be misleading merely to disclose the aggregate of a basket of securities compared with the aggregate of a basket of liabilities. However, in practice, companies often describe the charge in general terms, referring, for example, to 'mortgages on freehold land and buildings' rather than specifying the particular properties involved.

11.155   If a company has issued any debentures during the financial year, the notes to the financial statements must disclose:

- The classes of debentures issued.

- The amount issued and the consideration received by the company in respect of each class of debentures issued.

[SI 2008/410 1 Sch 50(1)].

Significant holdings greater than 20 per cent

11.156 Where a company, at the end of its financial year, has a 'significant holding' of shares of any class in another undertaking (other than a subsidiary undertaking, a joint venture or an associated undertaking), the Act requires the company to disclose specified information. [SI 2008/410 4 Sch 4].

11.157 For this purpose, a significant holding is a holding of 20% or more of the nominal value of any class of shares in an undertaking, or a holding for which the carrying amount exceeds one-fifth of the company's assets, as stated in its balance sheet. [SI 2008/410 4 Sch 4(2)].

11.158 Where a company has significant holdings, the notes to the financial statements must disclose, in respect of each undertaking in which the company has a significant holding:

- Its name.

- Its country of incorporation, where it is incorporated outside Great Britain.

- If it is unincorporated, the address of its principal place of business.

- The identity of each class of shares that the investing company holds.

- The proportion of the nominal value of the shares of each class that the investing company holds.

[SI 2008/410 4 Sch 5].

11.159 In addition, the following information should be given:

- The aggregate amount of the capital and reserves of the undertaking at the end of its relevant financial year (see below).

- The profit or the loss of that undertaking, as disclosed by those financial statements.

[SI 2008/410 4 Sch 6].

11.160 The 'relevant financial year' is the financial year ending on or before the investing company's balance sheet date. [SI 2008/410 4 Sch 6(4)].

11.161 Except as described below, where any of the information required by Schedule 5 to SI 2008/410 relates to either an undertaking that is established under the law of a country outside the UK or an undertaking that carries on its business outside the UK, and the directors believe that disclosure would be seriously prejudicial to the business of that undertaking or to the business of the company or any of its subsidiary undertakings, and the company has obtained the Secretary of State's agreement, that information does not need to be disclosed. [CA06 Sec 409(3)(4)]. Where advantage is taken of this exemption, this must be stated in the notes to the financial statements. [CA06 Sec 409(5)]. Exemption is not available in respect of disclosures regarding shares in a company held by its subsidiary undertakings or membership of a qualifying undertaking.

11.162 Where a company has a significant number of investments such that, in the directors' opinion, compliance with the requirements of Schedule 5 to SI 2008/410 would result in disclosure of excessive length, information need only be given in respect of those undertakings whose results or financial position principally affect the figures shown in the company's financial statements. [CA06 Sec 410(1)(2)]. Where advantage is taken of this exemption, this must be stated in the notes to the financial statements. [CA06 Sec 410(3)]. In addition, the full information (including both the information that is disclosed in the notes to the financial statements and the information that is not) must be annexed to the company's next annual return. [CA06 Sec 410(3)]. Failure to do so will result in the company, and any officer of it who is in default, being liable to a fine. [CA06 Sec 410(4)(5)].

11.163 The statement in section 409(5) of the Companies Act 2006 (that is, that the 'seriously prejudicial' exemption has been taken) is required to be given, whether or not the group has taken advantage of the exemption in section 410(1) described above. Under section 410(1), the full information for all subsidiaries must be annexed to the company's next annual return; but, where the Secretary of State has granted exemption under section 409(3), this need not include the information regarding the subsidiary excluded on seriously prejudicial grounds.

11.164 The information described in paragraph 11.159 above need not be given if it is immaterial. Furthermore, it need not be given in either of the following two situations:

- Where the company is exempt, by virtue of section 400 or 401 of the 2006 Act, from the requirement to prepare consolidated financial statements (see chapter 24). But, for this exemption to apply, the company's investment in all such undertakings must be shown, in aggregate, in the notes to the company's financial statements by way of the equity method of valuation (that is, by stating the company's share of the undertaking's net assets). [SI 2008/410 4 Sch 13(1)].

- Where the company's investment is in an undertaking that is not required by any of the Act's provisions to deliver a copy of its balance sheet to the Registrar of Companies, and it does not otherwise publish that balance sheet in Great Britain or elsewhere. Where this situation exists, the information need not be given, provided the company's holding is less than 50% of the nominal value of the shares in the undertaking. [SI 2008/410 4 Sch 6(2)].

Transitional issues

11.165   In the area of financial instrument accounting, old UK GAAP had a two-tier regime for unlisted UK entities, depending on whether they fair valued their financial instruments. The transitional issues will differ for entities falling in one or the other tier, as discussed below.

11.166   The first-tier entities are those that fair valued their financial instruments in accordance with the Companies Act fair value accounting rules and apply FRS 25, 'Financial instruments: Presentation', FRS 26, 'Financial instruments: Recognition and measurement' and FRS 29, 'Financial Instruments: Disclosure'. As these three standards are replicas of IAS 32, IAS 39 and IFRS 7 respectively, entities applying them are unlikely to face any problems on transition to FRS 102. This is because the accounting for financial instruments under FRS 102 is the only section of the standard for which there is an optional fallback to the recognition and measurement principles of full IFRS. Consequently, those UK entities that currently apply FRS 26 could choose to move to IAS 39, whose requirements are the same, and they will be unaffected.

11.167   The second-tier entities are those that did not fair value their financial instruments in accordance with the Companies Act fair value accounting rules and applied FRS 4, 'Capital Instruments', and the presentation requirements of FRS 25. Although not mandatory, such entities were encouraged to comply with some disclosure requirements of FRS 29, adapting them in line with the entity's accounting policies.

11.168   An entity that applied pre-FRS 26 standards (or those from the first tier that choose not to apply IAS 39 after transition to FRS 102) would need to consider, at the date of transition to FRS 102, whether its financial instruments meet the definition of a basic financial instrument. If not, the entity would need to measure such instruments at fair value in its opening balance sheet at its date of transition (that is, at the beginning of the earliest period presented). Any adjustments to previous carrying amounts should be made against retained earnings. However, if it is impractical to measure the instruments at fair value at the date of transition, the entity should measure them in the earliest period presented. that it is practical to do so [FRS 102 para 35.11].

11.169   There is, however, an exception from the application of retrospective application. This relates to derecognition of financial assets and financial liabilities. Financial assets and liabilities derecognised under old UK GAAP are not recognised on adoption of FRS 102. Conversely, for financial assets and liabilities that would have been derecognised under FRS 102 in a transaction that took place before the date of transition, but that were not derecognised under old GAAP, an entity can choose either to derecognise them on adoption of FRS 102 or to continue to recognise them until disposed of or settled. [FRS 102 para 35.9(a)].

11051

11.170 Under FRS 5 of old UK GAAP, an entity might have adopted linked presentation in respect of transferred assets (that is, some specialised transactions such as securitisations, where non-recourse finance is involved). The only recourse allowed to the provider of the finance in such a transaction is to the specific assets being financed and not to the entity's other assets (where the associated FRS 5 requirements had been met), such that derecognition was not appropriate. There is no concept of linked presentation in FRS 102 and, as such, the entity will, in this situation, need to recognise the assets in their entirety and the associated liability on a gross basis.

11.171 A debt instrument which meets the conditions of paragraph 11.9 of FRS 102 (discussed in para 11.14 above) can, on transition, be voluntarily designated as at fair value through profit or loss, provided it meets the requirements of paragraph 11.14(b)(i) or (ii) of the standard (discussed in para 11.46 above). [FRS 102 para 35.10(s)].

Chapter 12

Other financial instruments issues

Other financial instruments issues

Chapter 12

Other financial instruments issues

Introduction

12.1 The previous chapter dealt with basic financial instruments. This chapter deals with the provisions of section 12 of FRS 102 which relate to the recognition and measurement of financial instruments that do not meet the definition of basic financial instruments as well as hedge accounting.

12.2 Entities that only have basic financial instruments within the scope of section 11 of the standard do not need to apply section 12. However, such entities should consider the scope of section 12 to ensure that they are exempt.

Accounting policy choice

12.3 As noted in chapter 11, entities that apply the disclosure requirements of sections 11 and 12 of FRS 102 nevertheless have an option to apply the recognition, measurement and hedge accounting requirements of IAS 39 or IFRS 9 to all financial instruments. Alternatively, entities can opt to follow the provisions for financial instruments set out in sections 11 and 12 of FRS 102.

12.4 The option described above is an accounting policy choice. Once an option is selected, a change to the other option would be a change in accounting policy. Chapter 10 provides guidance on accounting policy changes and when they might be appropriate.

Scope

12.5 Where an entity elects to account for its financial instruments in accordance with section 12 of FRS 102, it must apply the section to all its financial instruments, except for those specifically covered by section 11 of the standard and those that are outside the scope of section 12. The latter are discussed in the following paragraphs.

Own equity instruments

12.6 Financial instruments issued by an entity, including options and warrants that meet the definition of an equity instrument in section 22 of the standard, or instruments that are required to be classified as equity in accordance with that section, are outside the scope of section 12. [FRS 102 para 12.3(e)].

12.7 Similarly, share-based payment transactions (to which section 26 of the standard applies) are outside the scope of section 12. [FRS 102 para 12.3(i)].

Employee rights and obligations

12.8 Employee rights and obligations under employee benefit plans are accounted for under section 28 of the standard, and so they are outside the scope of section 12. [FRS 102 para 12.3(c)].

Reimbursement assets and financial guarantee contracts

12.9 Reimbursement assets and financial guarantee contracts are accounted for in accordance with section 21 of the standard, and so they are also outside the scope of section 12. [FRS 102 para 12.3(k),(l)].

Rights under insurance contracts

12.10 An insurance contract is defined as *"a contract under which one party (the insurer) accepts significant insurance risk from another party (the policyholder) by agreeing to compensate the policyholder if a specified uncertain future event (the insured event) adversely affects the policyholder"*. [FRS 102 Glossary of terms]. Rights under insurance contracts (including reinsurance contracts) are outside the scope of section 12 of the standard, because the policyholder transfers to the insurer significant insurance risk rather than financial risk (see chapter 34.8). [FRS 102 para 12.3(d)].

Rights and obligations under leases

12.11 Finance lease contracts that give rise to financial assets for lessors, and financial liabilities for lessees, are financial instruments that are specially dealt with in section 20 of the standard. Therefore, they are outside the scope of section 12 unless the lease could, as a result of non-typical contractual terms, result in a loss to the lessor or lessee. Examples of typical contractual terms include (but are not limited to) terms related to changes in the price of the leased asset, changes in interest rates or foreign exchange rates, or the consequences of a default by one of the counterparties. The derecognition requirements included in section 11 of the standard (see chapter 11) do, however, apply to lease receivables and payables. [FRS 102 para 12.3(f)].

12.12 It is unlikely that lessors will price leases or set rentals based on variables that might cause the lessor to lose its investment in the lease (see further chapter 20). However, if the lease payments are wholly contingent or are highly leveraged, the lessor might not be able to recover its net investment in the lease. In other words, such rental payments are unlikely to be payments relating solely to the use of the asset. In those situations, the lease contract would fall to be treated as a financial instrument and accounted for in accordance with section 12 of FRS 102.

Contingent consideration and forward contracts in a business combination

12.13 Contracts for contingent consideration in a business combination are addressed in section 19 of the standard. Such contracts are outside the scope of section 12. This exemption only applies to the acquirer. [FRS 102 para 12.3(g)]. From the perspective of the seller, contingent consideration will be a financial asset that would fall within the scope of this section.

12.14 A forward contract between an acquirer and a selling shareholder to buy or sell an entity, which will result in a business combination at a future acquisition date, is outside the scope of section 12. [FRS 102 para 12.3(h)]. The term of the contract should not exceed a reasonable period that is normally necessary to obtain any required approvals and to complete the transaction.

Contracts to buy or sell non-financial items

12.15 Contracts to buy or sell non-financial items (such as commodities, inventories, plant and machinery, that is, firm commitments) are, in general, not financial instruments.

12.16 A contract to buy or sell a non-financial item would fall within the scope of section 12 of FRS 102 if it can be settled net in cash or by exchanging financial instruments, as if the contract were a financial instrument. This is so, unless the contract was entered into and continues to be held for the purpose of receipt or delivery of non-financial items to meet the entity's expected purchase, sale or usage requirements (often referred to as 'own use' purchase or sale exception). In other words, if the 'own use' exception is met, the contract is not a financial instrument for the purpose of this section (that is, the application of the 'own use' exception is not a choice). [FRS 102 para 12.5].

12.17 Net settlement means that the entity will pay or receive cash (or an equivalent value in other financial assets) to and from the counterparty, equal to the net gain or loss on the contract on exercise or settlement.

12.18 In addition, contracts that impose risks on the buyer or seller that are not typical of contracts to buy or sell non-financial items (such as contractual terms that could result in a loss to the buyer or seller that are unrelated to changes in the price of the non-financial item, changes in foreign exchange rates, or default by one of the counterparties) are also in the scope of section 12. [FRS 102 para 12.4].

12.19 Contracts that might result in a loss to the buyer or seller that is unrelated to the above factors are likely to contain terms that include a financial risk component that alters the settlement amount of the contract. Because there is no concept in FRS 102 of embedded derivatives, the whole instrument is measured at fair value through profit or loss.

Initial recognition

12.20 An entity should recognise a financial asset or a financial liability falling within the scope of section 12 of the standard only when it becomes a party to the contractual provisions of the instrument. [FRS 102 para 12.6]. At this point, the entity recognises all its contractual rights and obligations that give rise to the financial assets or liabilities on its balance sheet. This is the same recognition rule that applies to basic financial instruments, discussed in chapter 11.

Initial measurement

12.21 Where a financial asset or financial liability falling within the scope of section 12 is recognised initially, an entity should measure it at its fair value, which is normally the transaction price. [FRS 102 para 12.7].

12.22 Like basic financial instruments, if payment for a financial asset falling within the scope of section 12 is deferred (or is financed at a rate of interest that is not a market rate), the entity should measure the financial asset at the present value of the future payments discounted at a market rate of interest. [FRS 102 para 12.7].

12.23 For financial instruments that are subsequently measured at fair value through profit or loss, transaction costs (net of any fees received or paid) are not added to or deducted from the amount initially recognised. Instead, they are expensed immediately on initial recognition of the financial instrument, because the payments do not result in any future economic benefits. [FRS 102 para 12.12]. However, for those equity instruments that are measured at cost less impairment (see para 11.14(d)(ii) of FRS 102), transaction costs are included in the amount initially recognised (see further chapter 11).

Subsequent measurement

12.24 At the end of each reporting period, an entity should measure all financial instruments within the scope of section 12 at fair value and recognise changes in fair value in profit or loss, except:

(a) > investments in equity instruments that are not publicly traded and whose fair value cannot otherwise be measured reliably and contracts linked to such instruments, which are measured at cost less impairment; and

(b) hedging instruments in a designated hedging relationship, which are accounted for as discussed below.

[FRS 102 para 12.8].

12.25 A financial asset that is carried at fair value through profit or loss does not give rise to any impairment issues; this is because diminution in value due to impairment is already reflected in the fair value and, hence, in profit or loss.

12.26 If an equity instrument is measured at fair value through profit or loss, and a reliable measure of fair value is no longer available, its fair value at the last date when the instrument was reliably measured is treated as the cost of the instrument until a reliable measure of fair value becomes available. [FRS 102 para 12.9].

Fair value

12.27 Guidance for measuring fair value of financial instruments is provided in chapter 11. That guidance applies to all instruments falling within the scope of section 12 that are measured at fair value. [FRS 102 para 12.10].

12.28 The fair value of a financial liability that is due on demand is not less than the amount payable on demand, discounted from the first date that the amount could be required to be paid. [FRS 102 para 12.11].

Derecognition of financial asset or financial liability

12.29 An entity is required to apply the derecognition requirements discussed in chapter 11 to financial assets and financial liabilities that fall within the scope of section 12 of the standard. [FRS 102 para 12.14].

Hedge accounting

Introduction

Scope of hedge accounting under FRS 102

12.30 The hedge accounting model in FRS 102 contains only a limited number of allowable hedges which are specified in paragraphs 12.17 and 12.18 of the standard. To allow greater flexibility under FRS 102, and to accommodate entities which might apply more sophisticated hedging strategies, the standard contains the option to apply the recognition, measurement and hedging provisions of IAS 39 (or IFRS 9) plus the disclosures required by section 12. However, an entity that chooses this option must apply all of the recognition and measurement provisions of IAS 39 (or IFRS 9) and not only those relating to hedge accounting.

12.31 The Accounting Council has stated it may amend section 12 of FRS 102 for any consequential changes following publication of the hedge accounting chapter of IFRS 9.

What is hedging?

12.32 Entities face many types of business risk, including financial risks (such as interest rate, currency, equity price and commodity price risk). Successful entities manage risk by deciding the risk to which they should be exposed, and to what extent, by monitoring the actual exposure and taking steps to reduce risks to within agreed limits, often through the use of derivatives.

12.33 Entering into a derivative or other transaction, to eliminate or reduce an entity's exposure to a particular risk, is referred to as 'hedging'. Hedging mitigates risk because the derivative's value or cash flows move inversely to, and offset changes in, the value or cash flows of the 'hedged position' or item. An entity might arrange its affairs so as to be naturally hedged. For example, if an entity's portfolio of fixed-interest securities is financed by fixed-rate borrowings of the same amount and duration, a rise in interest rates will decrease the value of both asset and liability positions by approximately the same amount, so the entity has no net exposure to interest rate risk. Hedging in an economic sense, therefore, reduces or eliminates financial risks associated with the hedged position. It is a common risk management activity.

What is hedge accounting?

12.34 For financial statements to show how hedges mitigate risk, it might be necessary to apply special 'hedge accounting' to them. The aim is that the accounting for the hedging transaction should be consistent with the objective of entering into it. This consistency can be achieved if both the hedging instrument and the hedged position are recognised and measured on symmetrical bases, and offsetting gains and losses are reported in profit or loss in the same periods. Unfortunately, without hedge accounting, this might not be the case. For instance, all derivatives must be carried at fair value, with gains and losses recognised in the income statement under FRS 102. But derivatives commonly hedge financial risks associated with a hedged position that is measured at cost or amortised cost, or hedge items such as highly probable forecast transactions or firm commitments that are not yet recognised in the financial statements. This creates a mismatch in the timing of gain and loss recognition. Hedge accounting has developed to mitigate these mismatches.

In simple terms, 'hedge accounting' modifies the normal basis for recognising gains and losses (or revenues and expenses) on associated hedging instruments and hedged items, so that both are recognised in profit or loss in the same accounting period. It seeks to eliminate or reduce the income statement volatility that would arise if the hedged items and hedging instruments were accounted for separately, without regard to the hedge's business purpose.

Criteria for obtaining hedge accounting

12.35 Hedge accounting is an exception to the normal accounting principles for financial instruments (and, sometimes, non-financial instruments). So, section 12 of FRS 102 requires hedge relationships to meet specified criteria to qualify for hedge accounting. A hedging relationship will qualify for hedge accounting only if all of the following conditions are met:

■ The entity designates and documents the hedging relationship, so that the risk being hedged, the hedged item and the hedging instrument are clearly identified, and the risk in the hedged item is the risk being hedged with the hedging instrument (see para 12.36 below).

■ The hedged risk is one of the risks specified in paragraph 12.17 of the standard (see para 12.38 below).

- The hedging instrument is as specified in paragraph 12.18 of the standard (see para 12.42 below).

- The entity expects the hedging instrument to be highly effective in offsetting the designated hedged risk. The effectiveness of a hedge is the degree to which changes in the fair value or cash flows of the hedged item that are attributable to the hedged risk are offset by changes in the fair value or cash flows of the hedging instrument (see para 12.49 below).

[FRS 102 para 12.16].

Documentation and designation

12.36 As noted in the first bullet point above, an entity is required to designate and document the hedge relationship. Unlike IAS 39 or the previous FRS 26, the guidance does not state that this documentation should be 'formal' or that it must be prepared at inception of the hedge. However, management should prepare the documentation at the inception of the hedge, because hedge accounting will only apply from the date when all the conditions are met. The documentation should specify the nature of the risk being hedged (for example, whether the hedged risk is interest rate risk, currency risk or commodity price risk), and clearly identify both the hedged item (for example, whether it is a recognised asset/liability, a firm commitment or a highly probable forecast transaction) and the hedging instrument (for example, whether the instrument is a forward or a swap).

12.37 There is no specific requirement to state in the documentation how the entity plans to assess whether the hedge is expected to be highly effective, although the entity does need to have such an expectation in order to qualify for hedge accounting. However, for most hedges under FRS 102, it is likely that the key terms of the hedging instrument (such as notional amounts, maturity dates and underlying risk) will match those of the hedged item, in which case this might be sufficient to demonstrate that the hedge is expected to be highly effective (see further para 12.49 below).

Eligible hedged risks

12.38 Section 12 of FRS 102 permits only the following hedged items and hedged risks:

- Interest rate and foreign exchange risk of a debt instrument measured at amortised cost.

- Foreign exchange and interest rate risk in a firm commitment or a highly probable forecast transaction.

- Price risk of a commodity that the entity holds or price risk in a firm commitment or highly probable forecast transaction to purchase or sell a commodity.

- Foreign exchange risk in a net investment in a foreign operation.

[FRS 102 para 12.17, Glossary of terms].

12.39 A commodity hedge will qualify for hedge accounting only if the hedged risk is the price risk of a commodity itself. Commodities are generally basic resources extracted through mining (such as gold, copper, aluminium, coal, crude oil and iron ore) and agricultural products (such as coffee beans and soybeans) that are traded in the spot and derivative markets. Where an entity holds such commodities in inventory (for example, as raw materials), or enters into transactions to buy or sell a commodity, it can hedge its exposure to changes in the price risk of those commodities.

12.40 FRS 102 does not permit hedging risks identified in other non-financial items held. However, the foreign currency risk in a debt instrument measured at amortised cost, a firm commitment, a highly probable purchase or sale of a non-financial asset, or a net investment in a foreign operation, can be designated as a hedged item; this is because changes in cash flows attributable to currency risk are separately measurable.

Eligible hedging strategies under section 12 of FRS 102

12.41 The standard does not use the terms 'cash flow hedge', 'fair value hedge' or 'net investment hedge'. However, as such terms are now commonly used and understood in the UK and can be mapped to the descriptions in section 12, we will use them throughout this chapter as a convenient shorthand. The following table sets out the hedges that are permitted under FRS 102:

	Interest rate risk	Foreign exchange risk	Commodity price risk
Fixed-rate debt instruments	FV	FV or CF	–
Floating-rate debt instruments	CF	FV or CF	–
Commodities held	–	–	FV
Highly probable forecast transactions	CF	CF	CF
Firm commitments	CF	CF	FV
Net investment in a foreign operation	–	CF	–

Key:
FV = 'fair value' hedge (FRS 102 para 12.19)
CF = 'cash flow' hedge (FRS 102 para 12.23)

Hedging instruments and hedged items

12.42 A financial instrument can be used as a hedging instrument only if it meets all of following conditions:

■ It is an interest rate swap, a foreign currency swap, a cross-currency interest rate swap, a forward or future foreign currency exchange contract, a forward or future commodity exchange contract, or any financial instrument used to hedge foreign exchange risk in a net investment in a foreign operation, provided that it is expected to be highly effective in offsetting the designated hedged risk(s) identified in paragraph 12.17 of FRS 102.

- It involves a party external to the reporting entity (that is, external to the group, segment or individual entity being reported on).

- Its notional amount is equal to the designated amount of the principal or notional amount of the hedged item.

- It has a specified maturity date not later than:

  - the maturity of the financial instrument being hedged:

  - the expected settlement of the commodity purchase or sale commitment: or

  - the later of the occurrence and settlement of the highly probable forecast foreign currency or commodity transaction being hedged.

- It has no prepayment, early termination or extension features other than at fair value.

[FRS 102 para 12.18].

12.43 For hedge accounting purposes, only instruments external to the group, segment or individual entity that is being reported on can be designated as hedging instruments. It follows that internal derivative contracts between members of a group (for example, an operating subsidiary entering into a derivative contract with group treasury) cannot be designated as a hedging instrument in the group's consolidated financial statements or in a hedge of transactions between divisions of the same legal entity in that entity's individual or separate financial statements.

12.44 The notional amount of the derivative instrument should be equal to the designated amount of the principal or notional amount of the hedged item. [FRS 102 para 12.18(c)]. 'Notional amount' is defined as the quantity of the currency units, shares, bushels, pounds or other units specified in a financial instrument contract [FRS 102 Glossary of terms]. It is not clear whether the notional amount of the derivative should be the entire amount or could be a proportion of the nominal amount – we believe it could be interpreted either way.

12.45 Paragraph 12.18(c) of the standard similarly refers to the designated amount of the hedged item, but does not clarify whether the designated amount could be only some (rather than all) of the exposure to interest rate risk, currency risk or commodity price risk of the hedged item. In the absence of any specific prohibition, our view is that an entity could designate a proportion of the principal or notional amount of the hedged item, or a portion of one or more selected cash flows of a debt instrument, as illustrated below.

Example – Hedging only a portion of the hedged item

Entity A, whose functional currency is the pound sterling, enters into a US$10m forward contract on 1 June 20X1 to hedge highly probable forecast US$-denominated sales of US$12.5m occurring in March 20X2.

In this situation, entity A could designate only US$10m of US$12.5m highly probable US$ sales as the hedged item, because paragraph 12.18(c) of FRS 102 allows a hedging instrument to hedge the 'designated amount' of the principal or notional, which could be less than the full notional. The hedge documentation should clearly identify the hedged risk as being the foreign exchange risk attributable to only US$10m of the highly probable sales of US$12.5m. This could be specified either as the first US$10m of sales (commonly referred to as a bottom layer) or as 80% of forecast sales. Note that, if sales fell below US$12.5m, the 80% designation would result in some ineffectiveness being recorded through the profit and loss account, whereas there would be no ineffectiveness in respect of volume in the former designation unless total sales fell below US$10m.

12.46 Similarly, an entity could hedge only some of the life of a financial instrument, such as a borrowing or debt investment. This is because paragraph 12.18(d) of the standard only requires that the hedging instrument has a *"specified maturity date not later than the maturity of the financial instrument being hedged"* and not that it must have the same maturity. For example, management could swap some but not all interest payments on a debt instrument from fixed to floating, or vice versa, as the following example illustrates.

Example – Partial term hedging

Entity A acquires a 10% fixed rate government bond with a remaining term to maturity of 10 years. On the same date, to hedge against fair value exposure on the bond associated with the first five years, the entity acquires a five-year pay-fixed, receive-floating swap. The swap has a fair value of zero at the inception of the hedge relationship.

The swap could be designated as hedging the fair value exposure of the interest rate payments on the government bond until year 5 and the change in value of the principal payment due at maturity to the extent affected by changes in the yield curve relating to the five years of the swap.

The same principle applies if the hedged item had been a financial liability instead of a financial asset with the same terms. In that situation, the entity could designate the fair value exposure of the first five years due to changes in interest rate only and hedge that exposure using a five-year receive-fixed, pay-floating interest rate swap.

The entity is also able to achieve effective partial term cash flow hedges. For instance, assume that an entity issues a 10-year floating rate debt and wishes to hedge the variability in the first three years of interest payments. This could be easily done by using a three-year receive-floating, pay-fixed interest rate swap.

This is, of course, also subject to the proviso that the hedge is expected to be highly effective and the other hedge accounting criteria are met.

12.47 The maturity date of the hedging derivative cannot be later than the maturity date of the financial instrument being hedged or the expected settlement date or occurrence of a highly probable forecast transaction or firm commitment. [FRS 102 para 12.18(d)]. This condition ensures that a hedging relationship cannot be designated for only a portion of the time period during which a hedging instrument remains outstanding, as illustrated below.

> **Example – Portion of the outstanding life of a derivative as a hedging instrument**
>
> An entity enters into a pay-fixed, receive-variable interest rate swap to hedge the cash flow exposure of a floating rate debt instrument. Both the swap and the debt instrument are entered into on the same date and have the same notional amounts. The floating rate debt instrument has a term of five years and the swap has a term of seven years.
>
> Because the swap has a maturity date that extends beyond the maturity date of the debt instrument, it cannot be designated as a hedging instrument. Designating the cash flows arising in the first five years of the seven-year swap as a hedging instrument is not possible. This is because the swap's fair value derives from the present value of the net settlements over the entire seven-year period, and not just the first five years. In addition, the fair value of the swap cannot be time apportioned using linear interpolation, because the change in the swap's fair value per unit of time is non-linear.
>
> On the other hand, if the maturities of the swap and the debt are reversed, so that they are five and seven years respectively, the five-year swap could be designated as a hedge of the first five years of the debt instrument. This is referred to as 'partial term' hedging (see the example in para 12.46 above).

12.48 The hedging derivative should not have any prepayment, early termination or extension features other than at fair value. [FRS 102 para 12.18(e)]. Contracts for potential hedging instruments would need to be reviewed carefully to identify any optionality at other than fair value which might prevent hedge accounting. This means that forward contracts or swaps used as hedging instruments should be simple or plain vanilla types, with no optional features.

Effectiveness

12.49 As noted in paragraph 12.35 above, one of the conditions for hedge accounting is that the hedging instrument is expected to be highly effective in offsetting the designated hedged risk. To the extent that the changes do not fully offset, such differences reflect ineffectiveness that is recognised in profit or loss.

12.50 Hedge accounting is discontinued where the hedge no longer meets the conditions for hedge accounting. This means that hedge effectiveness should be assessed at the inception of the hedge and then at least annually, to demonstrate that the expectation that the hedge will be highly effective continues to be met. Unlike full IFRS, there is no requirement under FRS 102 to assess whether the hedge has actually been effective throughout the reporting period for which the hedge was designated.

12.51 The standard does not specifically address how an entity should demonstrate that the hedge relationship is expected to be highly effective. Qualitative methods should be sufficient for most simple hedging transactions where the principal terms of the hedging instrument match those of the hedged item, as explained further below. But, where a transaction is more complex, quantitative testing might be necessary.

12.52 If the principal terms of the hedging instrument and of the hedged item are the same, the changes in fair value and cash flows attributable to the risk being hedged could be expected to offset each other fully, both when the hedge is entered into and afterwards. An entity can expect that the hedge will be highly effective on a prospective basis if the following conditions are met:

- The notional amount of the derivative is equal to the designated amount of the principal or notional amount of the hedged item (as required by para 12.18(c) of FRS 102 – see para 12.44 above for more details).

- The maturity of the derivative equals the maturity of the hedged position (see para 12.46 above for discussion of partial term hedges).

- The underlying of the derivative matches the underlying hedged risk.

- The fair value of the derivative is zero at inception.

- There are no prepayment, early termination or extension features other than at fair value (as required by para 12.18(e) of FRS 102).

- There is insignificant risk of non-payment for the hedging instrument due to the credit risk of the counterparty being low.

12.53 For instance, a hedge of a debt instrument with an interest rate swap is expected to be highly effective if the notional and principal amounts, term, re-pricing dates, interest payment dates and basis for measuring interest rates are the same for the hedging instrument and the hedged item, and the other points above are met. Similarly, a hedge of a highly probable forecast purchase of a commodity with a forward contract is likely to be highly effective if the forward contract is for the purchase of the same quantity of the same commodity at the same time and location as the hedged forecast purchase, and the fair value of the forward contract at inception is zero. The fair value would be zero where the entity enters into the forward contract at (or very close to) the same time that it establishes the hedging relationship. A forward contract with a value other than zero at inception includes a 'financing element' that is a source of ineffectiveness.

12.54 A quantitative calculation would be needed where the critical terms do not match, or where the entity uses partial term hedging or hedges a proportion of an item (for example, so that the entity can measure and recognise any resulting ineffectiveness). The accounting treatment of ineffectiveness is dealt with in paragraphs 12.69 and 12.79 below.

Accounting for specific hedges

12.55 The standard permits hedge accounting only for a number of specific hedging relationships. These are considered to form the bulk of the hedging activities likely to be undertaken by entities applying FRS 102.

12.56 Some of the hedges permitted in FRS 102 relate to a hedge of the exposure to changes in the fair value of a recognised debt instrument (due to interest rate risk or foreign exchange risk) or changes in the fair value of a commodity due to price risk (either in a currently held commodity or in a firm commitment). Because the risks being hedged affect the fair value of the recognised asset or liability, such hedges are referred to in this chapter as 'fair value hedges', although the standard does not use the term (see further para 12.58 below).

12.57 The remaining hedges permitted in FRS 102 relate to a hedge of the exposure to variability in cash flows. Such changes can be attributable to any of the following: interest rate risk or foreign exchange risk in a recognised debt instrument; foreign exchange risk or interest rate risk in a firm commitment or highly probable forecast transaction; foreign exchange risk in a net investment in a foreign operation; or commodity price risk in a highly probable forecast transaction. [FRS 102 para 12.23]. Because the risks being hedged affect the variability of the cash flows relating to the hedged position, such hedges are referred to in this chapter as 'cash flow hedges', to distinguish them from fair value hedges (see further para 12.70 below), although once again the standard does not use the term.

Fair value hedge accounting

12.58 If a fair value hedge (referred to in para 12.56 above) meets the hedge accounting conditions discussed in paragraph 12.35 above during the period, it should be accounted for as follows:

- the hedging instrument should be recognised as an asset or liability, and the change in fair value of the hedging instrument should be recognised in profit or loss; and

- the change in the fair value of the hedged item related to the hedged risk should be recognised in profit or loss and as an adjustment to the carrying amount of the hedged item.

[FRS 102 para 12.19].

12.59 In a fully effective hedge, the gain and loss recognised in profit or loss exactly offset each other. If the hedge is not fully effective, the derivative and the hedged item will change in value by unequal amounts. In any event, the entire change in fair value of the hedged item due to the hedged risk must be reported in profit or loss.

Fair value hedge of fixed interest rate risk of a recognised debt instrument

12.60 An entity that has issued a fixed rate debt instrument measured at amortised cost might be concerned about the change in the debt's fair value due to changes in the market rate of interest. The instrument's fair value moves inversely in line with changes in market interest rate, so an entity might decide to manage the interest rate exposure by entering into a receive-fixed, pay-variable interest rate swap. This has the effect of converting the fixed rate debt into a variable rate debt whose fair value moves in line with market rates. Similarly, if the entity acquired a fixed rate bond, it could enter into a pay-fixed, receive-variable interest rate swap to hedge the change in the fair value of the bond due to interest rate movements.

12.61 Where the hedged risk is the fixed interest rate risk of a debt instrument measured at amortised cost, the entity should recognise the periodic net cash settlements on the interest rate swap (that is, the hedging instrument) in profit or loss in the period in which the net settlements accrue. [FRS 102 para 12.20].

Fair value hedge of fixed interest rate risk and foreign exchange risk of a recognised debt instrument

12.62 The standard permits the hedging of interest rate risk and foreign exchange risk of a recognised debt instrument, but it is not explicit on whether both these risks can be hedged simultaneously. However, paragraph 12.18(a) of FRS 102 explicitly permits the use of cross-currency interest rate swaps as hedging instruments, so we believe that both the interest rate and foreign exchange risk can be hedged in a recognised debt instrument simultaneously.

Fair value hedge of price risk of a recognised commodity

12.63 An entity might hold a commodity (such as gold, silver or copper) as inventory for use in the manufacture of its products. The entity might be concerned about the change in the fair value of its commodity inventory, due to changes in the market price of the commodity. As a result, the entity might decide to hedge the price risk of a commodity that it holds by entering into a futures contract or forward contract. When an entity enters into a futures or forward contract, it agrees to buy or sell the commodity at a predetermined price at a future date. Futures contracts are very similar to forward contracts except that, unlike a forward contract that is traded over the counter, a futures contract is a standardised contract that is regulated and traded on a commodity exchange.

Fair value hedge of commodity price risk in a firm commitment

12.64 Exposure to commodity price risk can also occur through a firm commitment to buy or sell a commodity. By fixing a price in advance, the entity might be required to buy or sell for a price which is different from the spot rate at the date of settlement. Although the cash flows are fixed, the fair value of the contract will vary according to the price of the commodity. This fair value exposure can be hedged by taking out a commodity futures or forward contract, to offset the movement in fair value of the firm commitment.

Adjustments to hedged items

12.65 The adjustment to the carrying amount of a hedged asset or liability for the fair value changes attributable to the hedged risk (as required by para 12.19(b) of FRS 102), would be dealt with according to the normal accounting treatment for that item. The adjustment is often referred to as a 'basis adjustment', because the hedging gain or loss adjusts the carrying value of the hedged item, resulting in an amount that is neither cost nor fair value. Thus, in a fair value hedge of silver inventory, changes in the fair value of silver are adjusted against the carrying value of silver inventory, and the adjusted carrying amount becomes the cost basis for the purposes of applying the lower of cost and selling price less cost to complete and sell under section 13 of the standard. In other words, the basis adjustment remains part of the carrying value of inventory and enters into the determination of earnings when the inventory is sold.

12.66 Where hedge accounting is discontinued, the hedged item will cease to be basis adjusted. If the hedged item is an asset or liability carried at amortised cost (such as a debt instrument), any gains or losses recognised as adjustments to the hedged item should be amortised using the effective interest method over the remaining life of the hedged instrument. [FRS 102 para 12.22].

> **Example – Amortisation of adjustments to carrying amount of hedged item carried at amortised cost**
>
> Entity A enters into an interest rate swap contract to hedge changes in the fair value of a fixed rate borrowing of £100m due for settlement in five years. The terms of the borrowing and the swap exactly match. Interest rates rise, so that the carrying amount of the borrowing (adjusted for changes in fair value attributable to interest rate risk) falls to £90m, and the swap's fair value changes from zero to minus £10m.
>
> Under fair value hedge accounting, the swap is carried as a liability of £10m (less any settlement paid). The carrying amount of the borrowing is reduced to £90m. Both the loss and the gain are recognised in profit or loss. Under the amortised cost method, the carrying amount of the liability at £90m would be amortised back up to £100m, giving rise to additional finance cost of £10m over the remaining period to maturity.
>
> Amortisation could be deferred until hedge accounting is discontinued. If the swap is in place until the borrowing's maturity date, the debt's carrying amount will be adjusted back to £100m through further hedge accounting adjustments. In other words, any fair value adjustments to the debt's carrying value would be reversed by maturity, because the fair value of the liability immediately before settlement must be £100m. Therefore, no amortisation will be necessary.
>
> If hedge accounting is discontinued (say, at the end of year 2), a significant income statement impact could result in later periods, as a result of amortising the cumulative basis adjustments made to the hedged item during the two-year period when the hedge

was in place. This is because the entity would need to 'catch up' the basis of the hedged item to its settlement amount of £100m over the remaining three years.

Discontinuing fair value hedge accounting

12.67   Fair value hedge accounting should be discontinued prospectively if any of the following occurs:

- The hedging instrument expires or is sold or terminated.

- The hedge no longer meets the conditions for hedge accounting specified in paragraph 12.16 of the standard.

- The entity revokes the designation.

[FRS 102 para 12.21].

12.68   Where an entity ceases to apply hedge accounting because the hedge no longer meets the conditions for hedge accounting during the accounting period, hedge accounting is discontinued prospectively from that point. For instance, if the hedging instrument no longer exists, hedge accounting is discontinued from the date when the instrument ceases to exist.

12.69   The table below sets out an appropriate accounting treatment to apply when fair value hedge accounting is discontinued, although the standard itself is silent on this issue:

Discontinuance of fair value hedges (including firm commitments)				
	Hedging instrument			**Hedged item**
Hedge termination events	**Continue mark-to-market accounting Note 1**	**Derecognise from the balance sheet**	**Derecognise from the balance sheet Note 2**	**Freeze basis adjustments Note 3**
Hedging instrument no longer exists (that is, it is sold, terminated, extinguished, exercised or expired)		✓		✓
The hedge no longer meets the criteria for hedge accounting (effectiveness)	✓			✓
The entity revokes the hedge designation	✓			✓
The hedged item is sold or extinguished	✓		✓	

Note 1 – The hedging instrument will continue to be marked to market, unless it is re-designated as a hedging instrument in a new hedge that qualifies as a cash flow hedge.
Note 2 – The derecognition of the hedged item occurs through profit or loss – for example, the gain or loss on sale or extinguishment of the hedged item (inclusive of fair value basis adjustments) is recognised in profit or loss.
Note 3 – The hedged item ceases to be adjusted for changes in its fair value attributable to the risk being hedged and continues to be accounted for as it was before being hedged. Once the basis adjustment on the hedged item is frozen, it either:

- continues as part of the carrying amount of the asset, up to the date when the carrying value is recovered through use or sale or the asset becomes impaired. This will apply for commodities, and firm commitments to buy or sell commodities, that have been hedged for price risk; or

- is amortised through profit or loss (for interest-bearing financial assets and liabilities measured at amortised cost) using the effective interest method over the remaining life of the hedged item. [FRS 102 para 12.22]. See also example in para 12.66 above.

Cash flow hedges

12.70 Cash flow hedges were referred to in paragraph 12.57 above. Hedging for variability in cash flows is permitted only for the following risks:

- The variable interest rate risk or foreign exchange risk in a debt instrument measured at amortised cost.

- The foreign exchange risk or interest rate risk in a firm commitment or a highly probable forecast transaction.

- The commodity price risk in a highly probable forecast transaction.

- The foreign exchange risk in a net investment in a foreign operation.

[FRS 102 para 12.23].

12.71 If an entity hedges one of the hedged risks noted in paragraph 12.70 above, and the hedge meets the hedge accounting conditions discussed in paragraph 12.35 above during the period, it should be accounted for as follows:

- The portion of the gain or loss on the hedging instrument that is determined to be an effective hedge, in offsetting the change in the fair value of the expected cash flows of the hedged item, should be recognised in other comprehensive income (OCI).

- The ineffective portion of the gain or loss on the hedging instrument – that is, the excess (in absolute terms) of the cumulative change in fair value of the hedging instrument since the inception of the hedge over the cumulative change in fair value of the expected cash flows since the inception of the hedge – should be recognised in profit or loss.

■   The hedging gain or loss recognised in OCI should be reclassified to profit or loss when the hedged item is recognised in profit or loss or when the hedging relationship ends (see para 12.79 below). However, unlike IFRS, the cumulative amount of any exchange differences that relate to a hedge of a net investment in a foreign operation recognised in other comprehensive income shall not be reclassified to profit or loss on disposal or partial disposal of the foreign operation.

[FRS 102 para 12.23].

12.72   We believe that paragraph 12.25 of the standard implies that the hedging relationship ends only when the entity no longer has the hedged item (for example, a hedged debt instrument is derecognised or a hedged forecast transaction is no longer expected to take place). That would defer release of the amount in OCI if the hedged item still exists.

Variable interest rate risk in a recognised debt instrument

12.73   An entity that has issued a floating rate debt instrument measured at amortised cost might be concerned about the change in the debt's future cash flows due to changes in the benchmark interest rate. An entity might decide to manage the interest rate exposure by entering into a receive-floating, pay-fixed interest rate swap. This has the effect of converting the variable rate debt into a fixed rate debt whose interest payments are fixed. Similarly, if the entity acquired a floating rate bond, it could enter into a pay-floating, receive-fixed interest rate swap to hedge the variability of future cash flows due to interest rate movements. For an example of this type of hedge, see para 12.96 below).

12.74   If the hedged risk is the variable interest rate risk in a debt instrument measured at amortised cost, the entity should subsequently recognise in profit or loss the periodic net cash settlements on the interest rate swap (that is, the hedging instrument) in the period in which the net settlements accrue. [FRS 102 para 12.24].

Hedges of foreign exchange and interest rate risk in a firm commitment

12.75   A firm commitment is a binding agreement for the exchange of a specified quantity of resources at a specified price on a specified future date or dates. The firm commitment is a binding agreement, so it is usually legally enforceable.

12.76   Hedges of firm commitments are treated as cash flow hedges under section 12 of FRS 102 (with the exception of commodity price risk, covered in para 12.64 above). The firm commitment itself might well be outside of the scope of section 12 of the standard. This is because (as noted in para 12.16 above), contracts to buy or sell non-financial assets that are entered into and continue to be held to meet the entity's normal purchase, sale or usage requirements – whether or not they can be settled net in cash or by exchanging financial instruments – are not financial instruments. The net fair value of the firm commitment cannot be recognised as an asset or liability, so it cannot qualify as a fair value hedge for changes in foreign exchange rates. However, the foreign exchange risk in a firm commitment can be the hedged item in a cash flow hedge (as noted in para 12.70 above).

Hedges of highly probable forecast transactions

12.77 To qualify for cash flow hedge accounting, it is not necessary for the hedged cash flows to be committed. The hedged cash flows could be those that arise in a forecast transaction (for example, sales or purchases that are forecast to occur in a future period but for which the entity has not yet entered into a contract). A forecast transaction is an uncommitted but anticipated future transaction. [FRS 102 Glossary of terms]. However, such a forecast transaction can only be hedged if it is highly probable to occur [FRS 102 paras 12.17(b),(c), 12.23(b),(c)]. The term 'highly probable' is defined as significantly more likely than probable. [FRS 102 Glossary of terms]. This means that there must be a high probability that the forecast transaction will occur; in other words, there must be a small probability that the forecast transaction will not occur. Also, the forecast transaction must present an exposure to variations in cash flows for the hedged risk (foreign currency risk or price risk) that would affect profit or loss. This follows from the requirement (in the last bullet point in para 12.71 above) for the hedging gain or loss that is recognised in other comprehensive income to be reclassified to profit or loss as the hedged item is recognised in profit or loss.

> **Example – Forecast purchase of a non-monetary asset in foreign currency**
>
> Entity A is planning to buy, from a foreign supplier, a large piece of machinery to be used in its production process. The forecast purchase will be denominated in a foreign currency, so the entity enters into a forward contract to hedge the risk of movements in the relevant foreign exchange rate.
>
> The forecast purchase can be designated as a hedged item in a cash flow hedge of foreign currency risk, provided that the forecast purchase is highly probable and the other conditions for hedge accounting are met. The hedged risk (movements in exchange rates) will affect the amount paid for the machine and will affect profit or loss as the machine is depreciated.

Discontinuing cash flow hedge accounting

12.78 Cash flow hedge accounting (described in para 12.71 above) should be discontinued prospectively if any of the following occurs:

- The hedging instrument expires or is sold or terminated.

- The hedge no longer meets the conditions for hedge accounting specified in paragraph 12.35 above.

- In a hedge of a forecast transaction, the forecast transaction is no longer highly probable.

- The entity revokes the designation.

[FRS 102 para 12.25].

12.79 However, for a hedge of a forecast transaction that is no longer highly probable, any hedging gain or loss that has been recognised in OCI should be reclassified to profit or loss only if the hedged item is no longer expected to occur. The table below sets out an appropriate accounting treatment to be applied when cash flow hedge accounting is discontinued:

Discontinuance of cash flow hedges				
	Hedging instrument		**Amount accumulated in OCI**	
Hedge termination events	**Begin mark-to-market accounting** **Note 1**	**Derecognise from the balance sheet**	**Reclassify immediately to profit or loss**	**Retain amounts in OCI** **Note 2**
Hedging instrument no longer exists (that is, sold, terminated, extinguished, exercised, or expired) but hedged item does still exist		✓		✓
The hedge no longer meets the effectiveness criteria for hedge accounting	✓			✓
A hedged forecast transaction is no longer highly probable, but is still expected to occur	✓			✓
The entity revokes the hedge designation	✓			✓
A hedged forecast transaction is no longer expected to occur	✓		✓	
A hedged debt instrument measured at amortised cost is derecognised	✓		✓	

Note 1 – The hedging instrument will be marked to market through profit or loss, unless it is re-designated as a hedging instrument in a new cash flow hedge.

Note 2 – The cumulative gain or loss on the hedging instrument (previously recognised directly in other comprehensive income) is reclassified to profit or loss when the hedged item is recognised in profit or loss or when the hedging relationship ends. The latter includes the case where a hedged forecast transaction is not expected to occur. [FRS 102 para 12.23].

12.80   Where an entity ceases to apply cash flow hedge accounting because the hedge no longer meets the condition for hedge accounting during the accounting period, hedge accounting is discontinued prospectively from that point, and the entity applies the guidance in paragraph 12.79 above.

> **Example – Discontinuance of cash flow hedge**
>
> On 1 January 20X1, entity A has a highly probable sale that is expected to occur on 31 May 20X1. Entity A expects to collect the cash on 30 June 20X1. Entity A's functional currency is pound sterling and the sale is denominated in US dollars. At the same time on 1 January 20X1, entity A takes out a £/US$ forward contract to hedge the future sale. This forward contract matures on 30 June 20X1. Entity A has put in place all the documentation required to achieve cash flow hedge accounting.
>
> On 1 March 20X1, the forecast sale is no longer considered to be highly probable, but is still expected to occur. On 1 April 20X1, the transaction is no longer expected to occur. The entity does not close out the forward contract before maturity.
>
> The fair value of the forward contract at each date is as follows:
>
> | | Fair value of forward (maturity 30 June 20X1) £'000 |
> | --- | --- |
> | 31 January 20X1 | 35,000 |
> | 28 February 20X1 | 30,000 |
> | 31 March 20X1 | 25,000 |
> | 30 April 20X1 | 27,000 |
> | 31 May 20X1 | 28,000 |
> | 30 June 20X1 | 32,000 |

The accounting entries from the inception of the hedge to settlement of the forward contract, assuming perfect effectiveness (that is, the hedged risk is the forward rate and no other mismatches occur), are as follows:

Date	Transaction	Cash £000	Forward contract £000	OCI £000	Debit (Credit) Profit or loss £000
31 Jan 20X1	Change in fair value of forward		35	(35)	
28 Feb 20X1	Change in fair value of forward		(5)	5	
	Hedge accounting ceases prospectively from 1 March 20X1. Gain deferred in OCI remains there, but the forward is now marked to market through profit or loss				
31 Mar 20X1	Change in fair value of forward		(5)		5
30 Apr 20X1	Change in fair value of forward		2		(2)
30 Apr 20X1	Recycling of gain from OCI because hedged transaction is no longer expected to occur			30	(30)
31 May 20X1	Change in fair value of forward		1		(1)
30 Jun 20X1	Change in fair value of forward		4		(4)
30 Jun 20X1	Settlement of forward	32	(32)	-	-
		32	-	-	(32)

If the transaction had continued to be highly probable, the movements on the forward contract (to the extent that the hedge was effective) would continue to be taken to OCI until the sale occurred in May, at which date the gain would be recycled from OCI to profit or loss. Management could then re-designate the forward contract as a hedge of the receivable, in which case the fair value movements would be recorded through the income statement between May and June, and this should offset the gain or loss on the receivable (settlement due on 30 June 20X6) caused by currency fluctuations. There would be some ineffectiveness, because the interest element (forward points) included in the forward contract's fair value is not present in the undiscounted trade receivable. This is very similar to the accounting that would result if hedge accounting was not applied, so, in practice, entities might choose not to re-designate the forward contract as a hedge once a receivable has been recognised.

Hedges of a net investment hedge in a foreign operation

12.81 A net investment in a foreign operation is the amount of the reporting entity's interest in the net assets of that operation. Such foreign operations might be subsidiaries, associates, joint ventures or branches. Section 30 of FRS 102 requires the net assets of the foreign operation that are included in the financial statements of the reporting entity to be translated from the functional currency of the foreign operation into the functional currency of the reporting entity, with the resulting exchange gains or loss recognised in other comprehensive income. It is the translation of those net assets into the reporting entity's functional currency that is designated as the hedged risk in a hedge of a net investment. Because the net assets of the foreign operation are reported only in the reporting entity's consolidated financial statements, the foreign exchange risk, for which hedge accounting can be applied under section 12 of the standard, only exists on consolidation. Therefore stand-alone entities cannot hedge the foreign exchange risk of the net assets of a foreign operation. An exception is that for branches that are foreign operations, hedge accounting can be applied to the foreign exchange risk in the net assets of the branch.

12.82 Goodwill and any fair value adjustments arising on the acquisition of a foreign operation are treated as assets and liabilities of the foreign operation. They are expressed in the functional currency of the foreign operation and translated at the closing rate, so they are considered part of the net investment in the foreign operation. [FRS 102 para 30.23]. Similarly, a monetary item that is receivable from or payable to a foreign operation – for which settlement is neither planned nor likely to occur in the foreseeable future – is, in substance, part of the entity's net investment in the foreign operation. Exchange differences arising on such items are hedgeable currency risks.

12.83 Foreign currency borrowings can be used as a hedging instrument to hedge the foreign exchange risk in the net investment in the foreign operation. Alternatively, other financial instruments – such as forward contracts and fixed to fixed cross-currency swaps (which are effectively a series of forwards) – can be used to hedge a net investment in a foreign operation. However, fixed to floating cross-currency interest rate swaps are unlikely to be effective hedging instruments, because the interest element of the swap does not reduce foreign exchange risk of the net investment in the foreign operation.

12.84 A hedge of a net investment in a foreign operation (assuming that it meets all the criteria for hedge accounting in para 12.35 above) is accounted for in the same way as a cash flow hedge, as set out in paragraph 12.71 above. This means that the portion of the gain or loss on the hedging instrument that is determined to be an effective hedge (offsetting the loss or gain on the net investment) is recognised in other comprehensive income. However, the cumulative exchange difference recognised is not reclassified to profit or loss on disposal or partial disposal of the foreign operation, unlike under IFRS. [FRS 102 para 12.23]. This is because the hedged item (foreign exchange differences on the foreign operation) are not themselves recognised in profit or loss on disposal of the foreign operation in accordance with paragraph 30.13 of FRS 102, so the hedged item will never affect profit or loss.

Presentation and disclosure

Presentation

12.85 The presentation and disclosure requirements in section 11 of FRS 102 (see chapter 11) for basic financial instruments also apply to other financial instruments that fall within the scope of section 12 of the standard.

Disclosures about hedge accounting

12.86 If an entity uses hedge accounting, it should make the following disclosures separately for each of the risks described in paragraph 12.38 above.

■ A description of the hedge.

■ A description of the financial instruments designated as hedging instruments and their fair values at the reporting date.

■ The nature of the risks being hedged, including a description of the hedged item.

[FRS 102 para 12.27].

12.87 In addition, the entity should disclose the following for fair value hedges:

■ The amount of the change in fair value of the hedging instrument recognised in profit or loss for the period.

■ The amount of the change in fair value of the hedged item recognised in profit or loss for the period.

[FRS 102 para 12.28].

12.88 Similarly, the entity should disclose the following additional information for cash flow hedges:

■ The periods when the cash flows are expected to occur and when they are expected to affect profit or loss.

■ A description of any forecast transaction for which hedge accounting had previously been used, but which is no longer expected to occur.

■ The amount of the change in fair value of the hedging instrument that was recognised in other comprehensive income during the period.

■ The amount that was reclassified from other comprehensive income to profit or loss for the period.

■ The amount of any excess of the fair value of the hedging instrument over the change in the fair value of the expected cash flows that was recognised in profit or loss for the period.

[FRS 102 para 12.29].

Transitional requirements

12.89 The transitional issues for UK companies – that were discussed in chapter 11 for basic financial instruments – also apply to other financial instruments falling within the scope of section 12 of FRS 102.

12.90 In the context of hedge accounting, UK entities that fair value their financial instruments according to the Companies Act fair value accounting rules, and that apply the suite of financial instruments standards (that is, FRS 25, FRS 26 and FRS 29), are unlikely to face any significant transitional issues. However, the requirements for hedge accounting under FRS 102 are fundamentally different from those that applied historically under old UK GAAP. Those UK entities that do not fair value their financial instruments in accordance with the Companies Act fair value accounting rules, and that apply FRS 4 and the presentation requirements of FRS 25, will be impacted by the following hedging accounting requirements when transitioning from old UK GAAP to new UK GAAP.

12.91 An entity should not change its hedge accounting before the date of transition to FRS 102 for hedging relationships that no longer exist at the date of transition. [FRS 102 para 35.9(b)]. For hedge relationships that exist at the date of transition, entities should first consider whether the relationship that has been designated as a hedge under previous UK GAAP would qualify as a hedge under FRS 102.

12.92 Where an entity has a hedging relationship under previous UK GAAP that does not meet the conditions to qualify as a hedge under new UK GAAP, the entity should apply the requirements for discontinuing hedge accounting, as specified in new UK GAAP. [FRS 102 para 35.9(b)]. This means that the hedging relationship must not be reflected in the opening statement of financial position as of the entity's date of transition to new UK GAAP. The only entries recognised on the opening balance should be the derivative at fair value and the hedged item measured in accordance with the normal measurement rules for that type of asset or liability set out under new UK GAAP.

12.93 Where the hedging relationship does meet the conditions in new UK GAAP, the entity should follow the hedge accounting requirements in section 12 of the standard. [FRS 102 para 35.9(b)]. This could require an entity to make adjustments in its opening statement of financial position as of its date of transition to FRS 102 (that is, the beginning of the first period presented). In essence, the adjustments put entities in the position as if they had hedge accounted under section 12 of FRS 102 up to the date of transition to new GAAP. For fair value hedges, entities should adjust the carrying value of the hedged item, as illustrated in the example below.

Example – Fair value hedge of fixed rate debt with an interest rate swap

Entity A prepares its first FRS 102 financial statements at 31 December 20X3 and its transition date is 1 January 20X2.

Entity A has a £100,000 5% fixed-rate loan asset that is hedged in a fair value hedge relationship under previous GAAP using a pay-fixed, receive-floating interest rate swap. The loan was accounted for at cost and the derivative was not recognised under previous GAAP.

The former hedge relationship meets the conditions for hedge accounting under new GAAP (see para 12.35 above). At 1 January 20X2 the loan has an amortised cost of £100,000, the interest rate swap has a positive fair value of £5,100, and the negative fair value change of the loan attributable to the hedged interest rate risk is £4,900. Management has also prepared all the necessary designation and documentation that meets the hedge accounting requirements by 1 January 20X2. The hedge is expected to be highly effective.

Management should recognise the derivative at its fair value of £5,100 at 1 January 20X2, with the corresponding entry to retained earnings. The loan's carrying amount is also adjusted by £4,900, with the corresponding entry to retained earnings.

The changes in fair value of the derivative and the changes in fair value attributable to the hedged risk of the loan are recognised in the income statement in the subsequent periods.

Although the hedging relationship might qualify for hedge accounting under section 12 of FRS 102, there was no requirement under old UK GAAP to formally designate and document the hedging relationship or assess whether the hedge is expected to be highly effective (that is, requirements which are essential if hedge accounting is to continue under new GAAP for hedging relationships that exist at the date of transition). This might be read to imply that entities transitioning to new GAAP will be unable to use hedge accounting for qualifying hedges; but we believe that, if an entity complies with the requirements for hedge accounting set out in paragraph 12.35 above before or at the date of transition, hedge accounting could be continued.

12.94 For qualifying cash flow hedges existing at the date of transition to FRS 102, the entity should record the cumulative change in fair value of the hedging instrument as a separate component of other comprehensive income (for example, cash flow hedging reserve). [FRS 102 para 12.23]. The amounts recorded in the cash flow hedging reserve should be reclassified to the income statement in the period(s) that the transaction affects profit or loss or when the hedging relationship ends. This means that the amount that is recorded in the cash flow hedging reserve at the transition date should reflect the extent to which the transaction has not yet affected profit or loss. If some or all of the transaction had affected profit or loss before the transition date, the reserve should be adjusted at transition to reflect this, with the amount that would have been recorded in the income statement being transferred to the profit and loss reserve.

> **Example – Cash flow hedge of a variable rate debt with an interest rate swap**
>
> Entity B prepares its first FRS 102 financial statements to 31 December 20X3 and its transition date is 1 January 20X2.
>
> Entity B has a floating rate loan asset that is hedged in a cash flow hedge relationship under previous GAAP, using a pay-floating, receive-fixed interest rate swap. The loan was accounted for at amortised cost and the derivative was not recognised under previous GAAP.
>
> The former hedge relationship is of a type that qualifies for hedge accounting under FRS 102 (see para 12.35 above).
>
> Management should measure the derivative at fair value (with the corresponding entry to the cash flow hedging reserve). The loan balance is not adjusted for the hedge relationship. The impact in equity is the fair value of the derivative.
>
> The effective portion of future changes in fair value of the derivative is recognised in other comprehensive income and in the cash flow hedging reserve in the subsequent periods, and the ineffective portion of the changes in fair value of the derivative is recognised in profit or loss. The amounts accumulated in other comprehensive income are reclassified to profit or loss where the hedged risk (that is, the variable interest payments) affects profit or loss.

12.95 Where a hedging instrument was terminated but the hedged item still exists at the date of transition for a hedging relationship that is permitted under FRS 102, the gain or loss arising on termination of the hedging instrument is generally deferred on the balance sheet and spread over what would have been the remaining period of the original hedge under previous GAAP. Depending on the type of the hedge (that is, fair value or cash flow), the entity should follow the guidance for discontinuing hedge accounting and make the appropriate adjustments described in paragraphs 12.69 and 12.79 above.

Illustrative example

12.96 An illustration of how hedge accounting can be applied in practice is given below. The objective is to present the mechanics of applying the requirements of FRS 102.

12.97 The accounting treatment that an entity would follow, if it hedged the variable interest rate risk in debt that it has issued, is illustrated below.

> **Example – Cash flow hedge of a variable rate debt with an interest rate swap**
>
> On 1 January 20X1, entity A, a UK company, enters into a three-year £10 million variable interest rate borrowing at six-month LIBOR + 1%, with semi-annual interest payments and semi-annual interest reset dates. No transaction costs were incurred in issuing the debt. Entity A does not expect to repurchase the debt before maturity.

On the same date, in order to hedge the risk of changes in the variability of the cash flows due to changes in market interest rates (that is, six-month LIBOR), the entity enters into a three-year interest rate swap with a bank to convert the debt's variable rate to a fixed rate. Under the terms of the swap, entity A pays interest at a fixed rate of 7.5% and receives interest at a variable rate equal to the six-month LIBOR, based on a notional amount of £10 million. Both the debt and the swap require payments to be made or received on 30 June and 31 December each year. The six-month LIBOR rate on each reset date determines the variable portion of the interest rate swap for the following six-month period. Entity A designates the swap as a cash flow hedge, which hedges the exposure to variability in the cash flows of the variable rate debt, and changes in cash flows that are due to changes in the six-month LIBOR are the specific risk that is hedged.

Diagrammatically:

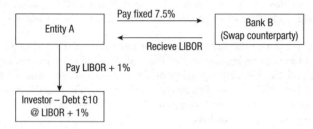

Entity A expects the hedge to be highly effective, both at inception of the hedge and on an ongoing basis. It has documented the assessment and has assumed that there is no ineffectiveness in the hedging relationship involving the interest-bearing debt and the interest rate swap, because all of the following conditions are met:

- The risk being hedged is a variable six-month LIBOR interest rate risk only. The credit spread of 1% is not hedged. Hence, the hedged risk matches the risk in the interest rate swap, whose variable leg also reflects six-month LIBOR.

- The notional amount of the swap matches the principal amount of the borrowing.

- The expiration of the swap matches the maturity date of the borrowing.

- The swap is a plain vanilla type, with no prepayment or early termination features and no floor or ceiling on the variable interest rate of the swap.

- The reset and payment dates on the borrowing match those in the swap.

- The fair value of the swap is zero at inception.

- The swap counterparty is highly rated, so there is no significant risk of non-payment on the hedging instrument due to counterparty credit risk.

The interest payments on the borrowing are variable, which will cause the future interest payments to change if the market interest rate changes. Changes in the fair value of the swap are designated as a hedge of the variable future cash interest payments on the borrowing. Over the life of the swap, its cash flows (represented by changes in its fair value) will exactly offset the impact of interest rate changes on interest payments. So, the swap is assumed to be 100% effective in offsetting the hedged risk.

The six-month LIBOR rates, the swap's fair value and the carrying amount of borrowing (following adjustment for changes in fair value attributable to the hedged interest rate risk) are as follows for the first year of the swap and the debt agreements:

Date	Six-month LIBOR rate[1]	Settlement paid/ (received)	Swap fair value asset/ (liability)[2]
	£	£	£
1 Jan 20X1	6.0%	Nil	Nil
30 June 20X1	7.0%	75,000	323,000
31 Dec 20X1	5.5%	25,000	(55,000)

1 All rates changes are assumed to take place on the date indicated.

2 The fair value of the swap represents the present value of the cash flows that entity A expects to pay under the swap and is after net swap settlements. These rates were obtained from dealer quotes.

The interest payments on the variable rate borrowing and the net payments/(receipts) on the interest rate swap are as follows for the first two semi-annual periods:

	30 June 20X1	31 Dec 20X1
	£	£
Variable rate borrowing (£10m @ LIBOR + 1%) × 6 months)	350,000[1]	400,000[2]
Swap payment	75,000[3]	25,000[4]
	425,000	425,000

1 £10m × (6% + 1%) × 6 months = £350,000
2 £10m × (7% + 1%) × 6 months = £400,000
3 (Pay fixed £10m @ 7.5% – receive LIBOR £10m @ 6%) × 6 months = £375,000 – £300,000 = £75,000
4 (Pay fixed £10m @ 7.5% – receive LIBOR £10m @ 7%) × 6 months = £375,000 – £350,000 = £25,000

The swap is separately recognised and measured at its fair value. Initially this is zero, so no entry is made for the swap at inception. At the next interest reset date, when the swap's fair value changes, the swap is recorded on the balance sheet as an asset or a liability, and changes in fair values are recorded in other comprehensive income (to the extent that the hedge relationship is effective). Any ineffectiveness is immediately recognised in net profit or loss. Amounts accumulated in other comprehensive income are reclassified to profit or loss where the hedged risk (that is, the variable interest payments) affects profit or loss. Periodic net settlements on the swap are recognised in profit or loss in the period when they accrue.

The accounting entries for the period 1 Jan 20X1 to 31 Dec 20X1 are shown below:

Other financial instruments issues

Period 1 Jan 20X1 to 30 June 20X1	Debit (Credit)				
	Debit	**Swap**	**Cash**	**OCI**	**Profit or loss**
	£	£	£		£
Recognise issue of borrowing	(10,000,000)		10,000,000		
Recognise interest payments on borrowing			(350,000)		350,000
Recognise net swap settlement			(75,000)		75,000
Recognise change in fair value of swap		323,000		(323,000)	
	(10,000,000)	323,000	9,700,000	(323,000)	425,000
Period 1 Jul 20X1 to 31 Dec 20X1					
Recognise interest payments on borrowing			(400,000)		400,000
Recognise net swap settlement			(25,000)		25,000
Recognise change in fair value of swap		(378,000)		378,000	
	(10,000,000)	(55,000)	9,275,000	55,000	850,000

The profit or loss shows a charge of £425,000, which is half of 8.5% on debt of £10 million, in both six-month periods. This gives an effective interest yield of 8.5% for the year. The net effect of the swap and the borrowing is that the entity has fixed its cost of borrowings at 8.5% and has eliminated the variability in interest cash flows on its variable rate debt.

Under old UK GAAP, entity A would have recorded the same profit or loss charge for the first six-month period of £425,000, consisting of a half-yearly interest payment of £375,000 plus net swap payments of £75,000. Similarly, it would have recorded an interest charge of £400,000 in the next six-month period plus a net swap payment of £25,000, giving a total charge of £425,000. Entity A would not have recorded the swap as an asset or liability on the balance sheet at fair value, with the change in fair value in OCI. Amounts accumulated in OCI are indirectly recognised in profit or loss, as periodic settlements of the swap occur and the fair value of the swap declines to zero.

Chapter 13

Inventories

Chapter 13

Inventories

Introduction and scope

13.1 Section 13 of FRS 102 considers the accounting treatment for inventories. The principal issues that it considers are the types of costs that should be included in the carrying value of inventories and their measurement, the subsequent recognition of expense (including any write-downs as a result of impairment), and the cost formulas that are used to assign cost to inventories.

13.2 Inventories comprise assets that are:

■ held for sale in the ordinary course of business;

■ in the process of production for such sale; or

■ in the form of materials or supplies to be consumed in the production process or in the rendering of services.

[FRS 102 para 13.1].

13.3 The first category above refers to goods purchased and held for resale (such as merchandise purchased by a retailer, or land and other property held for resale). Financial assets, such as investments held for sale, are not inventories. The second category includes work-in-progress of a manufacturing company and labour costs incurred by a service provider for producing intangible assets (such as software) for sale. The third category generally refers to raw materials, spare parts, tools and consumables. These are not used for more than one period, but are consumed in the production process. Another example is given below.

> **Example – Reusable containers**
>
> A company produces and sells bottled drinks. Customers are required to pay a deposit for each bottle when drinks are sold. The company is required to buy back empty bottles, which are then reused in the production of drinks.
>
> The bottles are not inventory. They are used for more than one period and are not repurchased for the purpose of resale. They are items of equipment to which section 17 of FRS 102 applies.

13.4 Section 13 of FRS 102 applies to all inventories except:

■ work in progress arising under construction contracts, including directly related service contracts (see section 23 of FRS 102);

■ financial instruments (see sections 11 and 12 of FRS 102); and

- biological assets related to agricultural activity and agricultural produce at the point of harvest (see section 34 of FRS 102).

[FRS 102 para 13.2].

13.5 In addition, section 13 of FRS 102 does not apply to the measurement of the following types of inventories (but does apply in all other respects, such as disclosure) measured at fair value less costs to sell through profit or loss at each reporting date. [FRS 102 para 13.3].

Recognition of inventories

13.6 Section 13 of FRS 102 does not specifically address when inventory should be recognised, although it deals with derecognition of inventory (see para 13.46 below). Perhaps this is rather obvious but, for the sake of clarity, the matter is discussed below.

13.7 A company should initially recognise inventory when it has control of the inventory, it expects the inventory to provide future economic benefits, and the cost of the inventory can be measured reliably (see section 2 of FRS 102).

13.8 A company has control of the inventory at the date when it obtains the risks and rewards of ownership of the inventory. In some situations, ownership transfers when the company takes physical delivery of the goods; in other situations, ownership is determined when legal title passes. For example, when goods are shipped f.o.b (free on board), legal title to these goods passes to the buyer on shipment of the goods. So, goods shipped to the company f.o.b (but in transit at the reporting date) are included in inventory.

13.9 Goods out on consignment are another example. Under this arrangement, a company (the consignor) ships goods to the consignee, who acts as the company's agent in selling the consigned goods. Such goods remain the property of the consignor, and so are held in inventory of the consignor. The consignee never includes goods held on consignment as its inventory.

Measurement of inventories

13.10 A company should measure its inventory at the lower of cost and estimated selling price less costs to complete and sell. 'Estimated selling price less costs to complete and sell' is synonymous with 'net realisable value' although this term is not used in FRS 102.

13.11 It should be noted that 'estimated selling price less costs to complete and sell' is not necessarily the same as 'fair value less cost to sell'. Assuming that the cost to sell an inventory is constant, the estimated selling price is the amount that a company actually expects to make from selling the inventory in the ordinary course of business, and is therefore a company-specific measure. Fair value is the amount that could be obtained for the same inventory from a knowledgeable willing party in the marketplace, and so it is not company-specific. An example where the two will differ is where the sale of inventory is assured under a binding forward contract that is not affected by more recent fluctuations in market prices.

13.11.1 Inventories held for distribution at no or nominal consideration should be measured at cost, adjusted (where applicable) for any loss of service potential. [FRS 102 para 13.4A].

Inventories held for distribution at no or nominal consideration are assets that are:

(a) held for distribution at no or nominal consideration in the ordinary course of operations;

(b) in the process of production for distribution at no or nominal consideration in the ordinary course of operations; or

(c) in the form of material or supplies to be consumed in the production process or in the rendering of services at no or nominal consideration.

Items such as promotional material can meet the definition of inventories held for distribution at no or nominal cost.

Cost of inventories

13.12 Cost of inventories comprises:

■ All costs of purchase.

■ Costs of conversion.

■ Other costs incurred in bringing the inventories to their present condition and location.

[FRS 102 para 13.5].

13.12.1 Inventories could also be acquired through non-exchange transactions. A non-exchange transaction is defined as a *"transaction whereby an entity receives value from another entity without directly giving approximately equal value in exchange, or gives value to another entity without directly receiving approximately equal value in exchange"*. [FRS 102 Glossary of terms]. The cost of inventories for this type of transaction should be measured at its fair value as at the date of acquisition. For public benefit entities (PBEs) and entities within a public benefit entity group, this requirement only applies to inventory that is recognised as a result of the incoming resources from non-exchange transactions, as prescribed in section 34 of FRS 102. [FRS 102 para 13.5A]. This requirement should not be applied directly (or by analogy) by companies that are not PBEs.

Costs of purchase

13.13 The costs of purchase of inventories include:

- Purchase price.

- Import duties and other taxes (other than those subsequently recoverable by the company from the taxing authorities).

- Transportation and handling costs.

- Other costs directly attributable to the acquisition of finished goods, materials and services.

- Any trade discounts or rebates received are deducted in determining the costs of purchase.

[FRS 102 para 13.6].

13.14 There is no guidance in section 13 of FRS 102 as to when rebates and volume discounts that reduce the cost of inventories should be recognised. Rebates are often given when a company has purchased a specified volume of goods over a given period. Like any contingent asset, rebates and discounts should be recognised when it is virtually certain that they will be received (that is, the conditions for receiving them have been largely met). In that situation, it would be appropriate to recognise the discount as a receivable, with a corresponding reduction in the purchase price of inventory. Otherwise, they should be recognised on receipt. Examples 2 and 3 illustrate.

Example 1 – Point at which import duties are included in inventory valuation

A car dealer imports cars, bringing them initially into a customs-free zone. The cars remain there until they are sold and delivered to customers; at this point, import duties will become payable by the importer.

Should the estimated import duties on inventory held in a customs-free zone be included in the cost of inventories?

No, import duties are not included in the inventory valuation for inventory held in a customs-free zone. Import duties do not arise from shipping the cars to the customs-free zone, so they are not included in the inventory valuation at that point. Import duties payable are included in the cost of inventory when the cars leave that zone.

Example 2 – Bonus related to sale of inventory

A car dealer receives bonuses from car manufacturers when it reaches certain sales targets of motor vehicles. The sales-related bonuses are received only after the cars have been sold (that is, when they are no longer in inventory).

When can the car dealer recognise the bonus?

The bonus from the manufacturers is a contingent asset and should be recognised only when it becomes virtually certain. As it is a sales-related bonus in respect of inventory that has been sold, it is appropriate to take the credit to income as a reduction in cost of sales.

Example 3 – Treatment of rebates

A car distributor values its items of inventory at the year end. Rebates are only received from the car manufacturers once a year and are only known after the year end, but they relate to purchases in the current period. Should the rebates be taken through the income statement as a deduction in the cost of sales without allocation to the items in inventory at the balance sheet date, or should a proportion of the rebates be allocated to the inventory items at the year end?

A proportion of the rebates should be allocated to inventory items at the year end. For example, if purchases during the year are 100, and there is inventory with a cost of 10 at the year end, 10% of the rebate should be applied to the inventory items at the year end, and 90% should be taken through the income statement as a deduction in the cost of sales. The reasoning is that the rebates cannot be allocated to particular items in the year, so they should be spread over all the items purchased during the year, whether sold or unsold.

13.15 When payment for inventory is deferred beyond normal credit terms, the arrangement effectively contains an unstated financing element that results in the imputation of interest. Where interest is imputed, the interest cost is not added to the cost of inventory unless the inventory is a qualifying asset (per section 25 of FRS 102) and the entity adopts a policy of capitalisation of borrowing costs. Rather, the inventory is recorded at the price that the company would pay under normal credit terms (which assumes that there is no financing element). The difference between the purchase price for normal credit terms and the deferred settlement amount is recognised as interest expense over the period of the financing. [FRS 102 para 13.7]. Where a price is not available under normal credit terms, the cost is arrived at by discounting the deferred settlement amount (the future cash flows) at a market rate of interest.

Costs of conversion

13.16 Costs of conversion comprise:

- Costs that are specifically attributable to units of production (for example, direct labour, direct expenses and sub-contracted work).

- A systematic allocation of fixed and variable production overheads incurred in converting raw materials into finished goods. Fixed production overheads are indirect costs of production that remain relatively constant, regardless of the level of production (such as rent, local taxes including business rates, depreciation and maintenance of factory buildings and equipment, and the cost of factory management and administration). Variable production overheads are those that vary according to the volume of production (such as indirect materials and indirect labour).

[FRS 102 para 13.8].

Allocation of production overheads

13.17 The allocation of fixed production overheads should be based on the company's normal level of productive capacity. This level of capacity is the average production expected to be achieved over a number of periods in normal circumstances, taking account of production loss due to planned maintenance. Actual production levels can be used where they approximate to normal capacity. Allocation of fixed production overheads is not increased where production is abnormally low or plant is idle. But, in periods of abnormally high production, the allocation is decreased so that inventory is not measured above cost. Unallocated overheads are recognised as an expense in the period in which they are incurred. Variable production overheads are allocated to each unit of production on the basis of the actual use of the production facilities. [FRS 102 para 13.9]. Examples 1 and 2 illustrate.

> **Example 1 – Allocation of overheads (production less than normal)**
>
> The following is relevant information for company A:
>
> - Full capacity is 10,000 labour hours in a year.
> - Normal capacity is 7,500 labour hours in a year.
> - Actual labour hours for current period are 6,500 hours.
> - Total fixed production overhead is £1,500.
> - Total variable production overhead is £2,600.
> - Total opening inventory is 2,500 units.
> - Total units produced in a year are 6,500 units.
> - Total units sold in a year are 6,700 units.
> - Total ending inventory is 2,300 units.
> - The cost of inventories is assigned by using FIFO cost formula.
>
> Management should allocate fixed and variable overhead costs to units produced at a rate of £0.20 per hour and £0.40 per hour respectively.
>
> Fixed production overhead absorption rate:
>
> = fixed production overhead / labour hours for normal capacity
> = £1,500/7,500
> = £0.20 per hour
>
> So, fixed production overheads allocated to 6,500 units produced during the year (one unit per hr) = 6,500 × £0.20 = £1,300. The remaining £200 of overheads incurred that remains unallocated is recognised as an expense.
>
> The amount of fixed overhead allocated to inventory is not increased as a result of low production by using normal capacity to allocate fixed overhead.

Variable production overhead absorption rate:

= variable production overhead / actual hours for current period
= £2,600/6,500
= £0.40 per hour

The above rate results in the allocation of all variable overheads to units produced during the year.

As each unit has taken one hour to produce (6,500 hours/6,500 units produced), total fixed and variable production overhead recognised as part of cost of inventory is:

= number of units of closing inventory × number of hours to produce each unit × (fixed production overhead absorption rate + variable production overhead absorption rate)
= 2,300 × 1 × (£0.20 + £0.40) = £1,380

The remaining £2,720 (that is, (£1,500 + £2,600) – £1,380) is recognised as an expense in the income statement as follows:

	£
Absorbed in cost of goods sold (FIFO basis) (6,500 – 2,300) = 4,200 × £0.60	2,520
Unabsorbed fixed overheads — also included in cost of goods sold	200
Total	2,720

Example 2 – Allocation of overheads (production greater than normal)

The following is relevant information for company A:

- Full capacity is 10,000 labour hours in a year.
- Normal capacity is 7,500 labour hours in a year.
- Actual labour hours for current period are 9,000 hours.
- Total fixed production overhead is £4,000.
- Total opening inventory is 2,000 units.
- Total units produced in a year are 9,000 units.
- Total units sold in a year are 8,700 units.
- Total ending inventory is 2,300 units.
- The cost of inventories is assigned by using FIFO cost formula.

In this situation, each unit produced has taken one hour (9,000 hours/9,000 units produced).

Production overhead absorption rate:

= production overhead/labour hours for normal capacity
= 4,000/7,500
= £0.53 per hour

Generally, management should allocate overhead costs to goods produced at the normal overhead absorption rate of £0.53 per unit, as calculated above. But, if this absorption rate is used, the amount allocated to all units produced = 9,000 × 0.53 = £4,770, where the overhead actually incurred during the year is £4,000. So this absorption rate would result in closing inventory being recorded above cost.

Consequently, in periods of high production, as is the situation in this example (labour hours used are 9,000; normal capacity is 7,500), the absorption rate should be adjusted to reflect actual production; that is, the absorption rate should be £0.44 per hour (£4,000/9,000); otherwise, inventory would be recorded at an amount in excess of cost. At this rate, production overhead recognised as part of inventory = 2,300 × 0.44 = £1,012 and not £1,219 (2,300 × 0.53).

13.18 There is no guidance in section 13 of FRS 102 for determining what constitutes 'normal capacity'. The following factors should be considered:

- The volume of production that the production facilities are intended (by their designers and by management) to produce under the working conditions (for example, single or double shift) prevailing during the year.

- The budgeted level of activity for the year under review and for the following year.

- The level of activity achieved both in the year under review and in previous years.

Although temporary changes in the level of activity can be ignored, consideration should be given to revising the normal capacity if actual production is substantially different from normal capacity over a period of time.

Allocation of costs to joint products and by-products

13.19 The production process might result in more than one product being produced at the same time. Allocation of costs to each of the 'joint products' could present problems. Allocation of costs should be made on a rational and consistent basis. For example, such allocation might be based on the relative sales value of each product. This allocation can be made at the point in the production process where the joint products become separately identifiable or at the completion of production. [FRS 102 para 13.10].

13.20 In other cases, the production process might not result in joint products that are each important, but rather in a main product and a relatively unimportant by-product. Where this is the case, such by-products should be measured at selling price less costs to complete and sell. This amount is then deducted from the total costs to give a net cost for the main product. The value of the by-product is immaterial, so this deduction does not result in the cost of the main product being materially different from cost. [FRS 102 para 13.10].

Borrowing costs

13.20.1 The Companies Act 2006 allows interest to be included in cost of inventory if it relates to capital borrowed to finance the production of the asset, insofar as it arises in the period of production. [SI 2008/410 1 Sch 27(3)(b)]. Further, FRS 102 allows a company to adopt a policy of capitalising borrowing costs that are directly attributable to the construction or production of a qualifying asset. This includes inventories that take a substantial period of time to produce. But the financing cost of inventories purchased on deferred settlement terms is recognised as an expense. [FRS 102 para 13.7; section 25].

Other costs included in inventories

13.21 Other costs are included in the cost of inventories only if they are incurred in bringing the inventories to their present location and condition. [FRS 102 para 13.11]. For example, the cost of designing products for a particular customer can be included in inventory. The example below shows that, in specific circumstances, storage costs would qualify for inclusion in the cost of inventories.

13.22 The following costs should be excluded from the cost of inventories and recognised as expenses in the period in which they are incurred:

- Abnormal amounts of wasted materials, labour or other production costs.

- Storage costs, unless those costs are necessary during the production process before a further production stage.

- Administrative overheads that do not contribute to bringing inventories to their present location and condition.

- Selling costs.

[FRS 102 para 13.13].

> **Example – Storage costs included in cost of inventory**
>
> The production of whisky involves storing whisky in a cask to age it before bottling.
>
> Storage costs can only be capitalised if the storage is necessary in the production process before a further production stage. So, in this situation, the storage cost that the company incurs during the distilling process should be capitalised, as ageing is integral to making the finished product saleable.

13.23 No matter how overheads are allocated, it is necessary to ensure that only 'normal' costs are included. So, 'abnormal' costs (such as wasted materials, labour and costs of excess facilities) are expensed in the period in which they are incurred. This would automatically happen in a standard costing system (see para 13.29

below). In the absence of such a system, the company should carry out an exercise to identify abnormal costs.

13.24   Storage costs are not costs which would normally be incurred in bringing inventory to its present location and condition. But, where it is necessary to store raw materials and work in progress before a further stage in the production process, the cost of storage should be included in production overheads (see para 13.22 above). This means that warehousing costs and overheads of a retail outlet cannot be included in inventory, because neither of these costs is incurred in a further production process.

13.25   Classifying overheads for the purpose of the allocation takes the function of the overhead as its distinguishing characteristic (for example, whether it is a function of production, marketing, selling or administration), rather than whether the overhead varies with time or with volume. The costs of general management (as distinct from functional management) are not directly related to current production, and so they are excluded from cost of conversion. But, in smaller organisations, there might not be a clear distinction between the various management functions. In such organisations, it would be appropriate to allocate fairly the cost of management on a suitable basis to the functions of production, marketing, selling and administration. Overheads relating to service departments (such as accounts and personnel departments) should be allocated to main functions, depending on the amount of support they provide to the main functions. Only those costs of the service department that can reasonably be allocated to the production function should be included in the cost of conversion.

13.26   Selling and advertising costs should not be included in the cost of inventory. Similarly, costs of distribution to the customer cannot be included in inventory, because they are selling costs. Note that this is also in line with SI 2008/ 410, which states that distribution costs cannot be included in production cost. [SI 2008/410 1 Sch 27(4)]. But a company can include a proportion of the costs incurred in distributing goods from its factory to its sales depot, because these are costs incurred in bringing the product to its present location.

Example – Costs that can be included in inventories

The following table highlights examples of the types of costs that can be included in the cost of inventories.

Description of costs	Include in inventory		Expense Selling and admin
	Direct	Indirect	
Production materials	✓		
Production labour	✓		
Employment costs of direct labour (for example, pension costs)	✓		
Normal amounts of materials wastage	✓		
Supervisor salaries and employment costs		✓	
Other indirect labour		✓	
Indirect materials		✓	
Rent, maintenance, heat, light, some taxes (excluding income taxes) and other indirect costs of running factory		✓	
Depreciation of production equipment and related facilities and property		✓	
Amortisation of related acquired intangibles		✓	
Product research			✓
Abnormal amounts of wastage, labour and other costs			✓
Selling costs			✓
Storage costs (but see example in para 13.22)			✓
General management costs			✓

Costs of inventories of a service provider

13.27   Inventories (work in progress) of service providers are costs incurred in providing the services for which the company has not recognised revenues. In relation to a service provider, to the extent that it has inventories, the cost of these is mainly the labour and other costs of the personnel who are directly engaged in providing the service, including supervisory personnel and attributable overheads. Labour and other costs attributable to sales and general administration are not included and are recognised as expenses as incurred. The cost of inventories of a service provider does not include profit margins or non-attributable overheads that are sometimes included in the price charged to customers by service providers. [FRS 102 para 13.14].

Cost of agricultural produce harvested from biological assets

13.28   As discussed in section 34 of FRS 102, inventories comprising agricultural produce that a company has harvested from its biological assets are measured on initial recognition at their fair value less estimated costs to sell. This becomes the cost of the inventories at that date for application of section 13 of FRS 102. [FRS 102 para 13.15]. However, if the fair value of a biological asset cannot be measured reliably, the entity shall apply the cost model until such time that the fair value can be reliably measured. In applying the cost model, agricultural produce harvested from an entity's biological assets should be measured at the point of harvest at either:

(a) the lower of cost and estimated selling price less costs to complete and sell; or

(b) its fair value less costs to sell. [Section 34 of FRS 102].

Techniques for the measurement of cost

13.29 Various techniques for measuring cost instead of using actual costs are permitted, where those techniques give a result that approximates to cost [FRS 102 para 13.16]. Such techniques are often used where there are a large number of similar items. Section 13 of FRS 102 specifically allows the use of standard costing method or the retail method. Rather surprisingly, it also permits the use of the most recent purchase price to measure cost (see further para 13.32 below).

13.30 The standard costing method is mostly used in the manufacturing industry for allocating both fixed and variable overheads to units of production. The standard cost of a unit of production is based on the budgeted levels of materials, supplies, labour and efficiency and normal capacity use of the production facilities. Standard costs are revised to take account of variances between standard cost that are based on budgets and actual costs. Where standard costs are used for year end inventory valuation purposes, they should be revised or adjusted for the recorded variances to arrive at actual costs incurred during the period.

13.31 The retail method is often used in the retail industry for measuring the cost of large numbers of rapidly changing items that have similar margins and for which there is no other practicable costing method. The cost of inventory is arrived at by reducing the selling price by the percentage gross margin. The reduction takes account of any reductions already made from the original selling price (for example, where the items have been marked down in a sale). Sometimes, an average gross margin for each retail department is used. [FRS 102 para 13.16].

13.32 The use of the most recent purchase price for measuring the cost of inventories is allowed, provided it results in a valuation that approximates to cost. This might be appropriate in periods of low inflation where market prices remain relatively stable. But, in times of rising prices, it will have the effect of overstating the value of closing inventory and result in the recognition of profit that has not yet been earned.

Cost formulas

13.33 A company should measure the cost of inventories of items that are not ordinarily interchangeable, and goods or services produced and segregated for specific projects, by using specific identification of their individual costs. [FRS 102 para 13.17]. Specific identification means that specific costs are attributed to each item sold or held in inventory that is easily distinguishable and not ordinarily interchangeable. Car dealers, jewellers and sellers of antiques and works of art would use this method. Manufacturers would use this method where they produce bespoke items for specific customers.

13.34 Where the use of this specific identification method is inappropriate (for example, because there are large number of interchangeable items such as nuts and bolts), cost should be allocated by the use of a cost formula. A company is permitted to choose between two cost formulas: first-in first-out (FIFO) and weighted average cost formula.

13.35 The FIFO method assumes that a company uses goods in the order in which it purchases them. So, in a retail concern, the first goods purchased are the ones sold first. Similarly, in a manufacturing concern, the first goods purchased are the ones used first. This cost flow assumption results in the remaining inventory representing the most recent purchases. But the weighted average cost method, as the name implies, prices items in the inventory on the basis of the average cost of all similar goods available during the period, using the number of units as the weights. This method is simple to apply, and it is objective.

13.36 A company should use the same cost formula for all inventories having a similar nature and use to the company. For inventories with a different nature or use, different cost formulas might be justified. For example, a manufacturer using a particular type of microprocessor in different industrial and domestic appliances might be justified in measuring the cost of the microprocessor differently for the different end products. But it might not be appropriate to use different cost formulae for similar items located in different geographical locations.

13.37 FRS 102 does not permit the use of the last-in, first-out (LIFO) method. [FRS 102 para 13.18]. The LIFO method results in inventory being stated in the balance sheet at amounts that bear little relation to recent cost levels.

13.37.1 From the perspective of the Companies Act 2006, SI 2008/410 allows companies to use various methods for arriving at the purchase price or the production cost of stocks and other 'fungible items'. For this purpose, 'fungible items' are those items that are indistinguishable one from another (for example, identical nuts and bolts). [SI 2008/410 10 Sch 5]. The Act permits the use of FIFO, LIFO, weighted average price or any other similar method. [SI 2008/410 1 Sch 18(1)(2)]. Note that, although the Act permits LIFO, it is not an acceptable valuation method in the UK (for the reasons set out in para 13.37 above).

Impairment of inventories

13.38 At each reporting date, a company must assess whether any inventories are impaired (that is, the carrying amount is not fully recoverable from future revenue). Impairment could occur because of damage, obsolescence or a decline in selling prices. If an item of inventory (or group of similar items) is impaired, the company should measure the inventory (or the group) at its selling price less costs to complete and sell, and it should recognise the irrecoverable carrying amount as an impairment loss immediately in profit or loss. [FRS 102 para 13.19; section 27].

> **Example 1 – Recognising an impairment loss**
>
> Company A sells potatoes. Management has a policy of holding high inventory levels. Due to unexpected high levels of imported potatoes coming onto the market, it was not possible to sell the expected volumes to food producers and wholesalers. As a result, the condition and quality of the potatoes deteriorated and they could only be sold at low prices for animal feed.
>
> Management should write the inventories of the affected potatoes down to the net value at which they can be realised (that is, the price net of selling costs at which the potatoes can be sold to the animal feed producers).
>
> Any quantities of potatoes in excess of those likely to be sold to the animal feed producers and unlikely to be sold to any other party should be written down to nil.

13.39 The write-down of inventory to selling price less cost to complete and sell is normally made on an item-by-item basis. But, if it is impracticable to determine the selling price less costs to complete and sell for each individual item, the company can group items of inventory. A group basis is appropriate where the items in a group are similar or related. This would be where items relate to the same product line, have a similar purpose and end use, and are produced and marketed in the same geographical area (see section 27 of FRS 102). However, it would not be appropriate to group items for this purpose by reference to general categories or classifications of inventory, such as finished goods.

13.40 Service providers generally collect costs in respect of each service for which a separate selling price is charged. So, each such service is considered separately when applying the lower of cost and selling price less cost to complete and sell.

13.41 Estimates of selling price less cost to sell should take into account the reason or purpose for which the inventory is held. For example, inventories might be held to satisfy a particular sales or service contract. The specified contract price is used as the basis for determining impairment. So, where the carrying value of the inventory in such a firm sales contract is above the contract sales price, it should be written down to the selling price less cost to sell. In such situations, it would also be necessary to consider whether any existing purchase commitments to buy parts or raw materials that are to be used in the firm sales contract are at a price above the contract sales price. Where this is so, the purchase commitments are onerous contracts and provisions should be made in accordance with section 21 of FRS 102.

13.42 Where a write-down is required to reduce the value of finished goods below cost, any inventory of the parts and sub-assemblies held for the purpose of the manufacture of such products, together with inventories on order, needs to be reviewed to determine if a write-down is also required against such items.

13.43 A write-down is not necessary when the carrying value of raw material inventories is above selling price, provided that the finished goods into which the materials are to be incorporated can still be sold at a profit after incorporating the materials at cost price. This is illustrated in the example below.

> **Example – Fall in market value of materials used in production**
>
> A manufacturing company uses copper in the manufacture of its products. The market value of copper fluctuates significantly and, at the end of the accounting period, its market price has fallen below historical cost. The finished goods are expected to be sold at prices well above production cost.
>
> The copper inventory does not need to be written down to its market price, because it is not held for resale. The copper is held for use in the production of finished goods, and it will be incorporated into the goods expected to be sold at or above cost.

13.44 Events occurring between the company's financial reporting date and the date of authorisation of the financial statements need to be considered in determining whether inventory held at the reporting date should be impaired. For example, the sale of inventories after the end of the reporting period might give evidence about their selling prices at the end of the reporting period for the purposes of assessing impairment at that date.

> **Example — Impact of post balance sheet events in assessing impairment**
>
> A company supplies car parts to a major manufacturer. At the year end, it had inventories of parts with a carrying value of £1m. But, after the year end, the manufacturer changed its car models, and so the inventories became obsolete (the part is not interchangeable between models). Should the company recognise an impairment loss against the inventories at the year end?
>
> In this situation, judgement needs to be exercised. It might be argued that the change of model by the manufacturer is a condition that did not exist at the year end, and so any loss recognition should be deferred to the next accounting period.
>
> But it is likely that the manufacturer would have been considering the change over a long period (including the period before the year end), even if it did not announce the change until after the year end. In addition, the high inventory levels could have indicated slow demand from the manufacturer. This is confirmed by the post balance sheet announcement confirming the over-supply at the year end. The condition (that is, the likelihood that the models would change and the resultant potential loss) is likely to have existed at the year end, and so the post balance sheet confirmation of the change and the resultant loss should be reflected in the carrying value of the inventories at the year end.

Reversal of impairment

13.45 After a write-down has been made, a company should make a new assessment of selling price less costs to complete and sell at each subsequent reporting date. Where the circumstances that previously caused inventories to be impaired no longer exist (or there is clear evide nce of an increase in selling price less costs to complete and sell because of changed economic circumstances), the company should reverse the amount of the impairment. The reversal is limited to the amount of the original impairment loss, so that the new carrying amount is the lower of the cost and the revised selling price less costs to complete and sell (see section 27 of FRS 102). The reversal should be recognised in the income statement in the period in which the reversal occurs, and the carrying amount of inventories is increased accordingly. The reversal is included in cost of sales, as this is the line in the income statement against which the original impairment would have been charged (with disclosure of the amount of the reversal – see para 13.50 below).

Derecognition

13.46 When inventories are sold, the company should recognise the carrying amount of those inventories as an expense in the period in which the related revenue is recognised. [FRS 102 para 13.20]. Section 23 of FRS 102 sets out the condition for when the sale of goods should be recognised. So, these conditions need to be met before inventory is derecognised (unless it is being written off as obsolete). The carrying amount of inventories held for distribution at no or nominal consideration should be recognised as an expense when those inventories are distributed. [FRS 102 para 13.20A].

13.47 Inventory might be used for the production of other assets (for example, parts used in constructing property, plant or equipment for own use). The cost of such inventory is added to the cost of the item produced and subsequently accounted for in accordance with the guidance that applies to the produced item. [FRS 102 para 13.21].

13.48 Certain types of more complex transaction (such as consignment sales or sale and repurchase transactions) require careful consideration as to whether inventory should be derecognised. As stated in paragraph 13.46 above, the application of the revenue recognition criteria to such transactions will determine whether inventory should be recognised.

Presentation and disclosure

Presentation

13.49 Section 4 of FRS 102 outlines information to be presented in the statement of financial position. In that section, a company should present a statement of financial position in accordance with one of the formats allowed by the Companies Act. Different choices exist for individual company accounts and for consolidated financial statements (see section 4 of FRS 102). The different formats under the Companies Act require inventory (stocks) to be analysed into different categories (as described in para 13.51 below). Inventories are current assets by nature. But, if there are inventories that are expected to be realised more than 12 months after the reporting date, it would be appropriate to classify them separately as non-current assets.

Disclosure

13.50   A company should disclose the following in respect of inventories:

- The accounting policies adopted in measuring inventories, including the cost formula used.

- The total carrying amount of inventories and the carrying amount in classifications appropriate to the company.

- The amount of inventories recognised as an expense during the period.

- Impairment losses recognised or reversed in profit or loss in accordance with section 27 of FRS 102.

- The total carrying amount of inventories pledged as security for liabilities.

[FRS 102 para 13.22].

13.51   In respect of the second bullet point above, the Companies Act includes further guidance and requires inventories (referred to as 'stocks' within the Act) to be analysed between the following four categories:

- Raw materials and consumables.

- Work in progress.

- Finished goods and goods for resale.

- Payments on account – this represents the payments that a company makes on account of stocks and not the payments it receives from customers.

[SI 2008/410 1 Sch formats].

13.51.1   The Companies Act requires a company to follow this categorisation so long as it produces true and fair financial statements. But, in certain circumstances, the special nature of a company's business might mean that the company needs to adapt the formats. For example, a property development company might include additional categories for show homes and part-exchange properties within stocks.

13.51.2   A further disclosure requirement of the Act relates to the replacement value of stocks. Where the historical cost of stocks or fungible assets is calculated using a method permitted by the Act (for example, FIFO, weighted average or any similar method), and if that valuation differs materially from the 'relevant alternative amount' of those items, the difference should be disclosed in a note to the financial statements. [SI 2008/410 1 Sch 28].

13.51.3 The 'relevant alternative amount' will normally be the amount at which the assets would have been disclosed if their value had been determined according to their replacement cost as at the balance sheet date. [SI 2008/410 1 Sch 28(4)]. The replacement cost of these types of asset will normally be their current cost. However, a company could instead determine the relevant alternative amount according to the most recent actual purchase price or the most recent actual production cost of assets of that class before that date. But it can do this only where this method gives a more appropriate standard of comparison for assets of the class in question. [SI 2008/410 1 Sch 28(5)]. The Act leaves it to the company's directors to form an opinion as to whether the method does this. The example below considers the disclosure of the replacement cost of stocks.

> **Example – Disclosure of replacement cost of stocks**
>
> Companies A and B have identical opening and closing stocks and purchases in a particular year, but company A chooses to determine the value of its closing stocks by the FIFO method, and company B does so by the 'weighted average price' method. In these circumstances, the amount to be included in the balance sheets would be calculated as follows:
>
> Company A: £3,175
> Company B: £2,825
> The value of the stocks at replacement cost is £3,300.
>
> If the difference between the balance sheet value of stocks and their replacement cost is material in the context of their balance sheet value, it must be disclosed under the requirement outlined above in paragraph 13.51.2. The difference for company A is £125 (£3,300 − £3,175), which is unlikely to be considered material. The difference for company B is £475 (£3,300 − £2,825), which is likely to be considered material. If it is, it must be disclosed.

13.51.4 Counsel has advised that a 'method' is not used when stocks are valued at either their actual purchase price or their production cost. So, it would appear that, where companies value their stocks at actual purchase price or production cost, they do not need to disclose in their financial statements the difference between this value and the replacement value of those stocks.

13.51.5 In many situations, it is likely that some items of stocks will be valued by one of the methods mentioned above, and that other items will be valued at actual purchase price or production cost. Where a company does this, the company will need to disclose not only the difference between the figure of stocks valued by a method and their replacement cost, but also the actual purchase price or production cost of the stocks that it has valued by that method. Otherwise, it could be misleading for the company to disclose the figure that represents the difference, without also giving an indication of the proportion of the total stock value to which this difference relates.

13.52 The way in which a company would disclose the amount of inventories recognised as an expense during the period would depend on whether the company presents an analysis of expenses according to their nature or their function. Either method of presentation is permitted by FRS 102 (see section 5 of FRS 102). For example, a company that adopts the 'function of expense' approach would disclose the amount of inventories recognised as an expense in cost of sales. That category would also include unallocated production overheads, abnormal costs, impairments and their reversals. But a company that adopts the 'nature of expense' approach would disclose the cost of raw materials and consumables, labour costs and other costs, together with the amount of the net change in inventories for the period.

13.53 Sometimes, impairment losses might be of such significance that they should be separately disclosed. Inventories that are written down in previous periods but sold in the current period will inevitably result in higher gross margins and profits. So, disclosure of the reversals of impairment losses that boost profits in the current period improves financial transparency.

Reduced disclosures for subsidiaries

13.53.1 In respect of inventories, there are no disclosure exemptions for qualifying companies. [FRS 102 para 1.12].

Transitional issues

13.54 UK companies transitioning from old UK GAAP to FRS 102 are unlikely to face any significant issues on transition in accounting for inventory. This is because the requirements of old UK GAAP (SSAP 9) are for the most part similar to those in FRS 102. Accounting for construction contracts, which is also covered by SSAP 9, is addressed by section 23 of FRS 102. The main issues arising on transition are as follows:

13.55 Company law permits companies to carry inventory at current value, although this was not commonly used, as it involved a departure from SSAP 9. Section 13 of FRS 102 requires inventory to be carried at the lower of cost and estimated selling price less cost to complete. Where a UK company carries inventory at current value at the transition date that does not approximate to cost, the carrying value of the inventory might need to be adjusted. Any adjustment should be made against opening retained profits.

13.56 One area where new information will be required on transition to FRS 102 is to meet the disclosure requirements of section 13 of FRS 102. This section requires disclosure of the amount of any reversal of a write-down of inventories (see para 13.50 above). There was no such disclosure requirement in old UK GAAP, and UK companies will have to find ways of obtaining this information if it was not recorded under old UK GAAP.

Chapter 14

Investments in associates

Chapter 14

Investments in associates

Scope

14.1 This chapter applies to accounting for investments in associates in consolidated financial statements or the individual financial statements of an investor that is not a parent. [FRS 102 para 14.1]. A 'parent' is defined by the standard as *"an entity that has one or more subsidiaries"*. The accounting for investments in associates in the parent's separate financial statements is described in chapter 9.

Definition

14.2 The term associate is defined by both the Companies Act 2006 and FRS 102. An associate is defined by the standard as *"an entity, including an unincorporated entity such as a partnership, over which the investor has significant influence and that is neither a subsidiary nor an interest in a joint venture"*. [FRS 102 para 14.2].

14.3 As mentioned above, the key criteria for determining whether an investment should be accounted for as an associate is whether the investor has significant influence over it. [FRS 102 para 14.2]. Significant influence is defined as *"the power to participate in the financial and operating policy decisions of the associate but is not control or joint control over those policies"*. [FRS 102 para 14.3]. In this context, power refers to the ability to do or affect something. It is not necessary for an investor to actually exercise this power. It is just sufficient to have the ability to do so. So significant influence can be exercised passively, for example through potential voting rights (see para 14.18 onwards below).

Participating interest versus significant influence

14.4 An *'associated undertaking'* is defined in the Companies Act in the following terms:

> *"... an undertaking in which an undertaking included in the consolidation has a participating interest and over whose operating and financial policy it exercises a significant influence, and which is not—*
>
> *(a)   a subsidiary undertaking of the parent company, or*
>
> *(b)   a joint venture dealt with in accordance with paragraph 18."*

[SI 2008/410 6 Sch 19(1)].

14.5 Whilst there is similarity between the definitions, there are two key differences. The Act requires the relationship to be based on a *'participating interest'* which is not mentioned by FRS 102. The other difference concerns how significant influence is exercised.

14.6 Participating interest is defined in paragraph 11 of Schedule 10 to SI 2008/ 410, 'The Large and Medium-sized Companies and Groups (Accounts and Reports) Regulations 2008', to mean *"... an interest held by an undertaking in the shares of another undertaking which it holds on a long-term basis for the purpose of securing a contribution to its activities by the exercise of control or influence arising from or related to that interest"*.

14.7 The meaning of 'shares' in the definition is explained in section 1161(2) of the Act. For this purpose, references to shares also include rights to share in the capital of an undertaking that has no share capital, rights to share in the profits or liability to contribute to the losses of an undertaking without capital or interest giving rise to an obligation to contribute to the debts or expenses of an undertaking without capital in the event of a winding up.

14.8 It is also quite clear under the Act that a participating interest includes an option to acquire shares or any interest that is convertible into shares. [SI 2008/ 410 10 Sch 11(3)]. For this purpose, it does not matter whether the options can be exercised now or in the future, their mere existence is taken into account whether or not they are currently exercisable. An interest or option in shares falls within this definition even if the share to which it relates, until conversion or the exercise of the option, is unissued. [SI 2008/410 10 Sch 11(3)]. In addition, interests held on behalf of an undertaking should be treated as held by it. [SI 2008/410 10 Sch 11(4)].

Voting power

14.9 Significant influence is presumed to exist when an investor holds directly or indirectly 20% or more of the voting power of the investee. Conversely, it is presumed that significant influence does not exist if the investor holds directly or indirectly less than 20% of the voting power of the investee. Indirect holdings that are taken into account in assessing significant influence are those held through subsidiaries but not through associates or joint ventures. [FRS 102 para 14.3(a)(b)].

14.10 The presumptions mentioned in the previous paragraphs can be overturned where the ability or lack of ability, to have significant influence can be clearly demonstrated. [FRS 102 para 14.3(a)(b)].

14.11 More than one entity can have significant influence over another entity at the same time and a substantial or majority ownership by another investor does not preclude an investor from having significant influence. [FRS 102 para 14.3]. For example, entity A might hold 25% of the voting power in entity B, which is presumed to be its associate, even though another entity C might control entity B through its holding of the remaining 75% of the voting power. In practice, however, the substance of the investor's 25% interest should be examined carefully to determine whether it gives that investor significant influence.

14.12 The standard gives no further definition or guidance as to the meaning of 'voting power'. We consider voting power to mean the rights that shareholders have to vote at general meetings of the entity on all, or substantially all, matters.

14.13 UK entities should follow the definitions given in UK law. For the purposes of the definition of an associated undertaking, *'voting rights in the undertaking'* means the rights conferred on the shareholders in respect of their shares to vote at general meetings of the undertaking on all, or substantially all, matters. Where the undertaking has no share capital, it can also mean any other rights conferred on members to vote at the undertaking's general meetings on all, or substantially all, matters. [SI 2008/410 6 Sch 19(3)].

14.14 Voting rights should not be treated as held by a person (which includes an undertaking) if they are held in a fiduciary capacity. Similarly, voting rights held by a person as nominee should not be treated as held by him. Such voting rights will be considered held 'as nominee' if they can only be exercised on the instructions or with the consent of another person. It is not possible to treat voting rights held by a parent undertaking as held by a subsidiary by using nominee holdings. [SI 2008/410 6 Sch 19(4); CA06 7 Sch 6, 7 Sch 7(2), 7 Sch 9(2)].

14.15 Voting rights that are attached to shares held as security should be treated as held by the person providing the security where those voting rights (excluding any right to exercise them to preserve the value of the security, or to realise it) are only exercisable in accordance with his instructions. This rule applies where the shares are held in connection with granting loans in the normal course of business and the rights are exercised only in the interest of the person providing the security. This provision cannot be used to require voting rights held by a parent to be treated as held by any of its subsidiaries. Furthermore, voting rights should be treated as being exercisable in accordance with the instructions of, or in the interests of, an undertaking if they are exercisable in accordance with the instructions of, or in the interests of, any group undertaking. [SI 2008/410 6 Sch 19(4); CA06 7 Sch 8, 7 Sch 9(2), 7 Sch 9(3)].

14.16 The voting rights in an undertaking should also be reduced by any voting rights held by the undertaking itself. [SI 2008/410 6 Sch 19(4); CA06 7 Sch 10].

Potential voting rights

14.17 Potential voting rights held by an investor are considered when assessing whether an entity has significant influence. [FRS 102 para 14.8(b)]. Potential voting rights exist where an entity owns share warrants, share call options, debt or equity instruments that are convertible into ordinary shares or other similar instruments that have the potential if exercised, or converted, to give the entity additional voting power or reduce another party's relative voting power over the financial and operating policies of another entity.

14.18 In assessing significant influence, the impact of potential voting rights that are currently exercisable or convertible, including potential voting rights held by another entity, are considered. Potential voting rights are not currently exercisable or convertible when, for example, they cannot be exercised or converted until a future date or until the occurrence of a future event. All facts and circumstances (including the terms of exercise of the potential voting rights and any other contractual arrangements whether considered individually or in combination) that affect potential rights, should be considered.

14.19 An entity might initially conclude that it has significant influence over another entity after considering the potential voting rights that it can currently exercise or convert. However, the entity might not have significant influence over the other entity when potential voting rights held by other parties are also currently exercisable or convertible. As a result, an entity considers all potential voting rights held by it and by other parties that are currently exercisable or convertible when determining whether it has significant influence over another entity.

Demonstrating significant influence in practice

14.20 There is no practical guidance in the standard on how significant influence can be demonstrated in practice. So it is necessary to exercise judgement to ascertain the substance of the relationship between the investor and the investee. Typically, significant influence is demonstrated via one or more of the following:

■ representation on the board of directors or equivalent governing body;

■ participation in policy-making processes, including decisions about dividends or other distributions;

■ material transactions between the entity and its investee;

■ interchange of managerial personnel; or

■ provision of essential technical information.

14.21 The presence or absence of one or more of the above qualitative factors might indicate whether significant influence exists. The list, however, is not exhaustive. There might be other factors (such as the existence of a right of veto over significant policy decisions, absence of concentration of other shareholdings, special agreements between the investor and the investee to extend credit, guarantee of indebtedness etc) which are equally important in understanding the substance of the relationship between the two parties.

14.22 Significant influence might be called into question if the investor has failed in an attempt to gain board representation or to obtain timely financial information from the investee, or if the investee is actively opposing the investor's attempts to exercise influence over it.

14.23 There is a potential conflict between FRS 102 andthe Act which requires the investor to have a participating interest and to actually exercise significant influence through active participation in the operating and financial policy decisions, whereas FRS 102 only requires the power to participate. We do not expect that this conflict will arise often in practice as generally demonstrating significant influence will be very closely linked to exercising significant influence.

14.24 Chapter 27 of the IFRS Manual of Accounting includes further discussions and examples concerning assessing whether an investor has significant influence.

Loss of significant influence

14.25 Significant influence could be lost, for example, when an associate becomes subject to the control of a government, court, administrator or regulator. An entity might also lose significant influence if the associate issues shares to third parties, or options and warrants held by other parties (that are not currently exercisable or converted) are exercised or converted, thus diluting the investor's interest, or as a result of a contractual agreement. The facts of each case need to be examined carefully. In these circumstances, there could be a change in the absolute or relative ownership levels (see further paras 14.56 – 14.61 below)

Measurement

14.26 An investor is required to account for an associate by using the equity method of accounting in its consolidated financial statements. If the associate is held as part of an investment portfolio it is measured at fair value with changes recognised in profit or loss. [FRS 102 paras 14.4A, 14.4B].

14.27 An investor that is not a parent (and therefore does not prepare consolidated financial statements) can choose to account for its investment in the associate by using either the cost model or the fair value model. [FRS 102 para 14.4 (a)(c)(d)].

Equity method of accounting

14.28 An investment in an associate is accounted for under the equity method from the date on which it becomes an associate. Under the equity method, an investment is initially recorded at the transaction price which includes any related transaction costs. The carrying amount of the investment is subsequently adjusted for:

- The investor's share of the post-acquisition profit or losses of the associate, which are recognised in the investor's profit or loss.

■   The investor's share of the other comprehensive income of the associate, (for example, foreign exchange translation differences, actuarial gains and losses and changes in fair values of hedging instruments). These are recognised directly in other comprehensive income of the investor.

■   The investor's share of equity.

[FRS 102 para 14.8].

Share accounted for

14.29   Before it is possible to equity account for associates, it is necessary to establish what share the group owns. The meaning of a group's share or holding is not defined in the standard. In a simple situation, where the investor only has an interest in the associate's equity share capital, it is easy to ascertain the share to be equity accounted: it will normally be the number of shares held as a percentage of the total number of equity shares in issue. There are a number of matters that need to be considered in determining what is the appropriate share because, in many situations, the percentage will not be apparent.

14.30   Where investments in associates are held by group members, all of the interests held by group members are aggregated to determine the share of the associate that falls to be equity accounted. However, indirect interests held through associates or joint ventures are excluded in computing the group's share, because these entities are not controlled by the group.

14.31   In many situations, the share to be taken into account will be derived from the percentage holding in shares; in some situations the economic interest might differ from the shareholding, but it will be the appropriate interest to take into account. For example, although the shareholding in an associate might be 40:60, the investors might share profits in the ratio 30:70. So it would be appropriate to equity account for the economic share rather than the equity participation. As a result, considerable care needs to be taken in establishing the appropriate share to be equity accounted.

14.32   Associates might have outstanding cumulative preference shares in issue that are not owned by the investor. In that situation, the investor's share of the associate's profits should be calculated after deducting the dividends on such shares, whether paid or not.

Distributions and other adjustments to carrying amount

14.33   Any distribution from the associate should be treated as a reduction in the carrying amount of the investment. The investor might also need to adjust the carrying amount as a result of changes in the associate's equity arising from items of other comprehensive income. [FRS 102 para 14.8(a)].

Potential voting rights

14.34 Although potential voting rights are taken into account in determining whether the investor has significant influence, such interests are not taken into account in determining the share to be equity accounted. Only the investor's present ownership interest is used to measure its share of profits or losses and other comprehensive income and its share of changes in the associate's equity under the equity method. Those measurements do not reflect the possible exercise or conversion of potential voting rights. [FRS 102 para 14.8(b)].

14.35 Having an option interest or a convertible interest is very different from holding the shares to which such an option relates.

> **Example – Significant influence with presently exercisable options**
>
> An investor has significant influence over its associate by virtue of its present ownership interest of 15% and presently exercisable options to acquire a further 10% for a fixed price. The investor equity accounts for its investment in the associate using its present ownership interest of 15%. The option to acquire a further 10% share is ignored for this purpose. However, the option is a derivative that is accounted for as at fair value through profit or loss in accordance with FRS 102 section 12, 'Other financial instruments issues'.

Implicit goodwill and fair value adjustments

14.36 On the associate's acquisition, management should measure any implicit goodwill as the difference between the cost of the acquisition and the share of fair values of the net identifiable asset acquired. [FRS 102 para 14.8(c)]. Although measurement of implicit goodwill is as described in section 19 of FRS 102 the implicit goodwill is not treated as a separate asset in the same way as goodwill arising on the acquisition of a subsidiary, but is included as part of the carrying amount of the investment in the associate. [FRS 102 para 14.8(c)].

14.37 Where the goodwill is negative, the entity needs to reassess the identifiable fair value of the net assets acquired to ensure that fair values of the identifiable assets and liabilities have been appropriately determined. Any excess of the revised net fair value over cost is recognised in profit or loss over the time frame in which the non-monetary assets are recovered. [FRS 102 para 19.24(a)(b)].

14.38 Subsequent to acquisition, the goodwill should be amortised over its useful life on a systematic basis as set out in section 19 of FRS 102. The amortisation should be charged against the investor's share of the associate's profits or losses after acquisition. [FRS 102 paras 14.8(c), 19.23(a)].

14.39 In addition, the investor should also adjust its share of the associate's profits or losses to account for any additional depreciation or amortisation of the associate's depreciable or amortisable assets on the basis of the excess of their fair values over their carrying amounts at the time of acquisition. [FRS 102 para 14.8(c)]. The additional depreciation or amortisation is calculated over the remaining useful life of the relevant assets. Any gain or loss arising on the disposal of those assets by the associate subsequent to acquisition would also need to be adjusted by the investor to reflect the fair value recognised on acquisition.

Example – Equity method accounting

Entity A acquired a 30% interest in entity B and achieved significant influence. The cost of the investment was £250,000. The associate has net assets of £500,000 at date of acquisition. The fair value of those net assets is £600,000, as the fair value of property, plant and equipment is £100,000 higher than its book value. This property, plant and equipment has a remaining useful life of 10 years. The entity determines the useful life of the goodwill to be five years.

After acquisition, entity B recognised profit after tax of £100,000 and paid a dividend out of these profits of £10,000. Entity B also recognised exchange losses of £20,000 directly in other comprehensive income. Its net assets at the end of the year is £570,000.

	£
Calculation of goodwill	
Consideration paid	250,000
Share of the fair value of the net assets acquired (30% of £600,000)	180,000
Goodwill	70,000
Amortisation of goodwill over five years	14,000
Entity A's share of entity B's profit for the year:	
Share of entity B's profit after tax (30% of £100,000)	30,000
Amortisation of goodwill	(14,000)
Additional depreciation of property (30% of 10% of £100,000)	(3,000)
	13,000
Entity A's share of entity B's other comprehensive income for the year:	
Share of entity B's exchange loss (30% of £20,000)	(6,000)
Entity A's interest in entity B at the end of the year:	
Cost including goodwill	250,000
Share of entity B's profit for the year	13,000
Share of entity B's other comprehensive income for the year	(6,000)
Share of dividend's received in the year (30% of £10,000)	(3,000)
Entity A's interest in entity B under the equity method	254,000
Reconciliation of the carrying amount under the equity method:	
Entity A's share of net assets at end of the year (30% of £570,000)	171,000
Unamortised goodwill on acquisition (£70,000 – £14,000)	56,000
Unamortised fair value adjustment on property (30% of £90,000)	27,000
	254,000

Impairment

14.40 Various indicators might suggest that an investment in an associate is impaired(for example, where the investee is incurring losses or experiencing significant liquidity crisis that affects the level of dividend payments and therefore the investor might not be able to recover the carrying value of its investment. Another impairment indicator could be a significant or a prolonged decline in associate's the fair value below cost. If any such indication exists, the investor is required to perform an impairment test on the associate in accordance with section 27 of FRS 102. [FRS 102 para 14.8(d)].

14.41 As discussed in paragraph 14.36 above, the goodwill forms part of the investment's carrying value and, as such, the impairment test is performed for the associate as a single asset. [FRS 102 para 14.8(d)].

14.42 An estimate of recoverable amount is only required if there is an indication of impairment. [FRS 102 para 27.7]. The recoverable amount can be estimated by aggregating the present value of the dividends that the investor expects to receive in future and the proceeds from ultimate disposal. An impairment loss should be recognised to the extent that the recoverable amount of the investment is below the cost. This applies even if the investee has accounted for any impairment in the underlying assets.

14.43 In addition to having an equity interest in the associate, the investor might have made loans to the associate that do not form part of the net investment. Such loans are financial assets, so they should be assessed in accordance with section 11, 'Basic financial instruments' of FRS 102.

Transaction with associates

14.44 The investor should eliminate unrealised profits and losses resulting from both upstream and downstream transactions, to the extent of its interest in the associate. [FRS 102 para 14.8(e)].

14.45 The standard requires the investor's share of unrealised profits or losses to be eliminated from transactions between the investor and the associate only where such profits or losses are included in the carrying amount of assets in either the investor or the associate. Amounts due to or from the associate arising from normal trading transactions (such as payable and receivables, or loans to or from associates) are not eliminated under the equity method of accounting.

> **Example 1 – Upstream: elimination is made against the carrying amount of the associate**
>
> An investor has a 20% interest in an associate. The associate sells inventory costing £300 to the investor for cash of £500. The inventory has not been sold to third parties at the balance sheet date. The profit attributable to the investor is required to be eliminated from the consolidated financial statements. The associate recorded a profit of £200 on this transaction. The investor's share of this profit is £40 (£200 × 20%).

The investor eliminates its share of the profit against the carrying amount of the associate. The investor's interest in its associate is not increased by the profits that it generates from selling upstream until the transaction has been crystallised by an onward sale to a third party. The accounting entries are to debit the share of profit of associates £40 and to credit the investment in associate £40.

Assuming the investor sells the inventory to a third party in the following year for £500, it is necessary to reverse the profit elimination entry made on consolidation in the prior year; this is because the unrealised profit has now been crystallised by an onward sale. Overall, there is a profit on the transaction of £200, and the group's share of this profit is taken up in the share of its associate's result. Any additional profit made by the investor by selling the inventory would be recorded as part of operating profit in the normal way.

Example 2 – Downstream: elimination is made against the carrying amount of the associate

An investor has a 20% interest in an associate. The investor sells inventory to the associate of £500. The original cost of the inventory was £300. The inventory has not been sold to a third party at the balance sheet date.

T he investor records a profit of £200. However, as the sale was to an associate an element of this profit is unrealised and should be eliminated. The unrealised profit is £40 (20% × £200).

The adjustments required to be made in the investor's books are to debit revenue £100 (£500 × 20%), credit cost of sales £60 (£300 × 20%) (alternatively, the investor could debit the share of profit of associates by £40) and credit the investment in associate £40.

The adjustments will be reversed by the investor when the associate sells the inventory onto a third party.

14.46 It is not uncommon for an investor to contribute its own business in exchange for an investment in an associate. The accounting for such contributions can be complex and is explained in chapter 9.

14.47 Unrealised losses on both upstream and downstream transactions could provide evidence of an impairment of the asset transferred (see para 14.41 onwards above). [FRS 102 para 14.8(e)].

Date of associate's financial statements

14.48 Where the investor incorporates its investment into its consolidated financial statements by using the equity method of accounting, it should use the associate's financial information for the same date as its own financial information. This means that, where the financial year ends are different, the investor would require the associate to prepare financial statements for its (that is, the investor's) year end. [FRS 102 para 14.8(f)].

14.49   The standard acknowledges that preparation of an 'extra' set of financial statements by the associate is sometimes impracticable. If it is impracticable, the investor should use the most recent available financial statements of the associate. However it should make adjustments for any significant transactions and events that occur between the associate's and the investor's year end. [FRS 102 para 14.8(f)]. There is no requirement, unlike in IAS 28, 'Investments in associates', that the difference between the associate's and the investor's reporting date should not be more than three months.

Associate's accounting policies

14.50   In arriving at the amounts to be included by the equity method of accounting, the associate needs to use the same accounting policies as those of the investor. Where the accounting policies used by the associate and the investor for similar transactions and events are different, the investor should adjust the associate's financial statements to harmonise accounting policies, unless it is impracticable to do so (for example, where the information necessary to make the adjustments is not available). [FRS 102 para 14.8(g)].

Losses in excess of investment

14.51   A problem might arise where an associate starts to make losses, particularly where those losses are such that the associate has net liabilities. Where an investor's share of losses of an associate equals or exceeds its interest in the associate, the investing group should discontinue recognising its share of further losses. [FRS 102 para 14.8(h)].

14.52   After the carrying amount of the investor's interest is reduced to nil, no further losses should be recorded, unless the investor has incurred legal or constructive obligations or made payments on behalf of the associate (that is, amounts that the investor has guaranteed or otherwise committed, whether funded or not). [FRS 102 para 14.8(h)]. The standard does not deal with the situation where an investor has lent funds to, or invested in preference shares of, the associate. As this is not specifically mentioned in FRS 102, it will be necessary to consider whether such interests are recoverable and provide against them where necessary in accordance with the requirements in section 27, 'Impairment of Assets' of the standard (see above and chapter 27).

14.53   In practice, an investor might have a constructive obligation to its associate if, for example, it is unwilling to abandon its investment, and it would continue to record its share of the associate's losses. If the investor does have a constructive obligation to its associate and continues to account for its share of losses, such losses should be recognised as a provision in accordance with section 21, 'Provisions and contingencies' of the standard. [FRS 102 para 14.8(h)].

14.54   If the associate subsequently reports profits, the investor resumes including its share of those profits only after its share of the profits equals the share of net losses not recognised (that is, in most cases when its share of net assets becomes positive again).

Discontinuing the equity method

14.55 When significant influence is lost, equity accounting should cease. [FRS 102 para 14.8(i)]. The words *"from the date that significant influence cease"* indicate clearly that neither the results for the period before the change in status nor the comparatives should be restated to reflect the changed status. Associate status could be lost for example, when the associate becomes a subsidiary or a joint venture by virtue of the investor acquiring control or joint control of the investee, or as a result of a full or partial disposal of the investor's equity interest in the associate. Loss of significant influence can also occur with or without a change in the absolute or relative ownership interest.

14.56 If significant influence is lost due to a full or partial disposal, the gain or loss is calculated as the difference between the proceeds from the disposal and the carrying amount of the investment in the associate relating to the proportion disposed of, or lost, at the date when significant influence is lost. [FRS 102 para 14.8(i)(i)].

14.57 When an investor loses significant influence due to partial disposal, the investor should account for the retained interest using section 11, 'Basic financial instruments' or section 12, 'Other financial instruments issues' of the standard, as appropriate. [FRS 102 para 14.8(i)(i)]. The carrying amount of the investment is treated as its cost on initial measurement as a financial asset.

14.58 An investor might lose significant influence for reasons other than by partial disposal, as noted in paragraph 14.24 above. Where this is the case, the investor should regard the carrying amount of the investment under the equity method at the date it when ceases to exercise significant influence as the cost of the interest which would then be recognised as an investment. Subsequently, the investment should be accounted for in accordance with section 11 or section 12 of the standard. [FRS 102 para 14.8(i)(ii)].

14.59 If the associate becomes a subsidiary due to a step up acquisition (in accordance with section 19, 'Business Combinations and Goodwill') or a joint venture in accordance with section 15, 'Investments in Joint Ventures', the investor should account for these transactions in accordance with those specific sections of the standard. [FRS 102 para 14.8(i)].

14.60 Illustrative examples on step acquisitions and disposals are included in the IFRS Manual of Accounting 27.169 onwards

Exemption from equity accounting – Investment portfolio

14.61 The standard explains that:

"an *associate that is held as part of an investment portfolio shall be measured at fair value with changes in fair value recognised in profit or loss in the consolidated financial statements*". [FRS 102 para 14.4B].

Consequently, investments of this nature are specifically exempted from the requirements to be equity accounted as associates. However, it does appear that such investments might still fall to be treated as associates under the Act, that is, the investor exercises significant influence. In situations where an entity adopts FRS 102's relaxation in respect of its associates included in its investment portfolio, if the investor still exercises significant influence over those undertakings, it should recognise a departure from the Act by giving the particulars, reasons and effect as required by the Act. The reason should include the fact that FRS 102 specifies the accounting treatment to be adopted.

14.62 Investment companies might also have investments that should be treated as associates that are held outside their investment portfolio. Such associates often carry on businesses which are similar or complementary to those of the investor. In these circumstances, the provisions of section 14 of FRS 102 should be applied and such associates should be equity accounted in accordance with the normal rules.

Cost model

14.63 An entity that does not prepare consolidated financial statements can choose to account for its investment in the associate by using either the cost model or the fair value model (as noted in para 14.26 above).

14.64 Under the cost model the investor should measure its investments in associates at cost less any accumulated impairment losses recognised. Cost is the transaction price including transaction cost. [FRS 102 para 14.5].

14.65 The guidance relating to impairment for an investment in an associate measured using the equity method of accounting (discussed in para 14.41 onwards above) is also applicable for investments in associates measured under the cost model. [FRS 102 para 14.5].

14.66 Where the cost model is applied, any distributions (including dividends) from the associate should be recognised in the profit or loss account as income. Such receipts should not reduce the carrying amount of the investment. [FRS 102 para 14.6]. The standard does not differentiate between distributions received from pre- and post-acquisition accumulated reserves; however, in our view, receipt of a dividend paid out of pre-acquisition reserves shortly after the acquisition of an associate could be an impairment indicator.

Fair value model

14.67 Where an investor that is not a parent elects to measure its investment in an associate at fair value, it initially recognises the investment at transaction price, which is the investment's fair value. Transaction price, therefore excludes transaction costs which are immediately recognised in profit or loss on initial recognition. [FRS 102 para 14.9].

14.68 At each reporting date, an investor that is not a parent should where it chooses to do so measure its investments in associates at fair value, with changes in fair value recognised in:

- other comprehensive income if the fair value movement is positive. Such increase should be accumulated in the revaluation reserve in equity.

- profit or loss, if the fair value movement is negative unless the entity has a positive revaluation reserve (as described above) for the same asset. In such cases the investor should reverse the accumulated reserve first.

[FRS 102 paras 14.10, 17.15E, 17.15F].

14.69 However, if the investor had previously recognised losses in relation to the fair value movement in the profit or loss account, it should reverse such movements first before recognising any subsequent revaluation gain in equity. [FRS 102 para 17.15E].

14.70 The fair value of the investment should be determined in accordance with the guidance provided in chapter 11. Where it is impracticable to measure fair value reliably without undue cost or effort, the investment should be measured at cost (see para 14.68 above). [FRS 102 paras 14.10, 14.10A].

Presentation and disclosure

Presentation

14.71 Sections 4 and 5 of FRS 102 govern the presentation of balance sheets (statement of financial positions) and income statements, they and require investors to follow the formats prescribed by Section B of the SI 2008/410, 'The Large and Medium-sized Companies and Groups (Accounts and Reports) Regulations 2008'.

14.72 An investor should classify its investments in associates as investments under the heading 'fixed assets' in the balance sheet. [FRS 102 para 14.11, SI 2008/410 Section 1].

14.73 Loans to associates that are due on demand are basic financial instruments. [FRS 102 para 11.10(c)]. They are disclosed as financial assets on the face of the balance sheet. [FRS 102 para 4.2(c)(m)].

Disclosures

General requirements

14.74 An investment in an associate should be classified by the investor as a fixed asset. [FRS 102 para 14.11]. The investor should also disclose the following:

- *the accounting policy for investments in associates;*
- *the carrying amount of investments in associates; and*
- *the fair value of investments in associates accounted for using the equity method for which there are published price quotations. "*

[FRS 102 para 14.12].

Consolidated financial statements of parent entities

14.75 Where the investor uses the equity method of accounting for its associates, it should separately disclose its share of profit or loss from the associate together with its share of discontinued operations of the associate. [FRS 102 para 14.14].

14.76 Where the associate is accounted for under the equity method, the investor should disclose the share of its associates other comprehensive income in the investor's consolidated statement of comprehensive income. This might relate to a number of items. There is no requirement however to analyse this share into its component parts. [FRS 102 para 5.5A].

14.77 If the investor recognised an impairment during the period, the following should also be disclosed:

"(a) the amount of impairment losses recognised in profit or loss during the period and the line item(s) in the statement of comprehensive income (or in the income statement, if presented) in which those impairment losses are included; and

(b) the amount of reversals of impairment losses recognised in profit or loss during the period and the line item(s) in the statement of comprehensive income (or in the income statement, if presented) in which those impairment losses are reversed. "

[FRS 102 para 27.34].

14.78 Schedule 4 to SI 2008/410 requires investors to disclose the following additional information in the consolidated financial statements about an undertaking's investments in associates:

- The name of the principal associates.
- If the associate is incorporated outside Great Britain, the country of its incorporation.

- Where the associate is unincorporated, the address of its principal place of business.

- In respect of shares held by the parent entity or by other members of the group:

  - The identity of each class of shares.

  - The proportion held of the nominal value of each class.

The disclosures above need to be split between those held by the parent and those held by the group.

[SI 2008/410 4 Sch 19].

14.79 The information required by Schedule 4 to SI 2008/410 outlined above need not be disclosed where the joint venture or associate is established under the law of a country (or carries on a business) outside the UK if, in the directors' opinion, the disclosure would be seriously prejudicial to the business of the joint venture or associate, or to the investor's business or any of its subsidiaries. But this information can only be withheld in this type of situation where the Secretary of State agrees that it need not be disclosed, and this fact must be stated in the notes to the financial statements. [CA06 Sec 409(3)(4)].

14.80 Where the entity's directors consider that the number of undertakings in respect of which the entity is required to disclose the above information (required by Schedule 4 to SI 2008/410) would result in excessive disclosure being given, the information need only be given in respect of associates whose results or financial position, in the opinion of the directors, principally affected the figures shown in the financial statements. Where this provision is used, the notes to the financial statements should state that the information is given only with respect to principal joint ventures and associates, and they should state that the full information (both that disclosed in the notes and that which is not) will be annexed to the entity's next annual return. [CA06 Sec 410(1)(2)(3)].

Investors that are not parents

14.81 For investments in associates accounted for using the cost model, an investor should disclose the amount of dividends and other distributions recognised as income. [FRS 102 para 14.13].

14.82 For investments in associates accounted for by the fair value model, an investor should make the following disclosures:

- The carrying amount of the investment measured at fair value. [FRS 102 para 14.12].

- The basis for determining fair value, for example, quoted market price in an active market or a valuation technique. [FRS 102 paras 14.15, 11.43].

■ Where a valuation technique is used, assumptions made in determining fair value for the associate. [FRS 102 paras 14.15, 11.43].

■ If a reliable measure of fair value is no longer available for an equity instrument measured at fair value through profit or loss, that fact. [FRS 102 paras 14.15, 11.44].

■ The changes in fair values of associates in the other comprehensive income (as described in paras 14.69 and 14.70 above). [FRS 102 para 5.4(iv)].

Transitional issues for UK entities

14.83 There are some important issues for UK entities to consider on transition from old UK GAAP based on FRS 9, 'Associates and joint ventures,' to new UK GAAP based on IFRS for SMEs. These issues are considered below.

Investment not accounted for as an associate under previous GAAP

14.84 Some entities that were not previously classified as associates under FRS 9 might be classified as an associate under FRS 102. This is because, eventhough the definitions of associates are similar, there is a subtle difference in the definition of significant influence and the way it is exercised. As noted in paragraph 14.7 above, FRS 102 defines significant influence as *"the power to participate in the financial and operating policy decisions of the associate"*. So, if an investor elects to be passive, significant influence will still exist, so long as the investor has the power to participate in policy decisions when it so wishes. FRS 9, on the other hand, required the investor to have a participating interest (meaning that the investor actually had an equity interest and/or options to acquire further shares in the associate) and to exercise significant influence through active participation in the operating and financial policy decisions. In other words, a passive role was clearly not sufficient. So, UK entities transitioning from FRS 9 to FRS 102 should look closely at their relationships with entities that are not classified as associates, because there is no significant influence (but there is a participating interest). However, this type of situation is unlikely to be a problem in practice (see para 14.8 above).

14.85 Nevertheless, for any such entities that are classified as associates under FRS 102 but were treated as passive investments under FRS 9, the investing entity would need to adjust the carrying amounts of the associate's assets and liabilities to the amounts that FRS 102 would require in the associate's separate balance sheet at the investor's date of transition. The deemed goodwill is the difference between the investing entity's share of those adjusted carrying amounts and the cost of the investment under FRS 9.

14.86 Although the above issue is also relevant to the individual financial statements of the entity that is not a parent but has investments in associates, it will not have any impact. This is because under FRS 9 the UK entity that was not a parent but had investments in associates would have carried its investment at cost and, therefore, would be expected to continue with that policy under new UK GAAP.

Associates in net liability position at date of transition

14.87 It is possible that at the date of transition the associate is in a net liability position. There is a difference in accounting treatment under FRS 9 and FRS 102 for an associate with net liabilities. When applying equity accounting under FRS 9, an investor continued to recognise losses, even if this resulted in an interest in net liabilities, as long as significant influence existed. This contrasts with the position under FRS 102, where losses of associates are recognised only until the point at which the carrying amount of the investment is reduced to zero. A liability in respect of the investment in the associate is recognised only to the extent that the investor has incurred legal or constructive obligations or has made payments on behalf of the associate. Consequently, in the absence of a constructive or legal obligation, the liability should be adjusted against retained earnings at the date of transition, and no further losses should be recognised. Subsequent accounting is discussed in paragraph 14.54.

Chapter 15

Investments in joint ventures

Chapter 15

Investments in joint ventures

Introduction and scope

15.1 This chapter deals with accounting for investments in joint ventures in consolidated financial statements and in a parent's separate financial statements for investments in jointly controlled operations and jointly controlled assets. A venturer that is a parent should account for interests in jointly controlled entities in its separate financial statements in accordance with paragraphs 9.26 and 9.26A of FRS 102 as appropriate. [FRS 102 para 15.1]. This chapter also deals with how to account for investments in joint ventures in the individual financial statements of a venturer that is not a parent.

Joint ventures

Definition

15.2 A joint venture *"is a contractual arrangement whereby two or more parties undertake an economic activity that is subject to joint control"*. [FRS 102 para 15.3]. The standard uses the term economic activity rather than entity. This is because joint ventures take many different forms and structures, and the standard does not limit itself to only those joint arrangements housed in a legal entity.

15.3 In organising an economic activity, venturers form structures to represent their best interests. The following are examples of joint ventures:

- Property development.
- Property management.
- Property investment.
- Consortia to jointly produce products.
- Shared distribution network.
- Shared use of an asset (such as a pipeline or football teams sharing a ground).
- Pharmaceutical companies sharing research.

15.4 Although joint ventures can take different forms and structures, the two key characteristics that must be present in all joint ventures (as evident from the definition in para 15.2 above) are *contractual arrangement* and *joint control*. These terms are explained below.

Contractual arrangement

15.5　The contractual arrangement is important because this is how joint control is created between the parties; without which such an agreement a joint venture cannot exist. The existence of a contractual agreement between the parties to the venture distinguishes a joint venture from a subsidiary or an associate.

15.6　Although not specifically discussed in the standard, the contractual arrangement might take the form of a contract, or minutes of discussions between venturers, or it might appear in the articles of association or by-laws of the entity subject to the joint control. Whatever the form, the contractual agreement is usually in writing and deals with such matters as noted below:

- The nature and duration of the joint venture activity.

- The rules for appointment of the board of directors or equivalent governing body and the voting rights of the venturers.

- Capital contributions by the venturers.

- The sharing of the output, income, expenses or results of the joint venture between the venturers.

- The delegation of the entity's day-to-day management, which could be to one of the venturers or to a third party.

- The joint venture's financial and operating policies.

> **Example – Clause in articles of association that meets definition of joint venture**
>
> Entities A and B form a new joint venture, entity J. By a clause in the articles of association of entity J, only entities A and B together can determine the strategic financial and operating decisions relating to entity J's activities. Entities A and B do not enter into any other agreement related to the management of entity J's activities.
>
> Even though there is no separate joint venture agreement, the clause included in entity J's articles of association is sufficient for the definition of a joint venture to be met, provided entity J's articles of association are legally binding.

15.7　The contractual agreement might identify one of the venturers as the manager of the day-to-day operations. The venturer acting in the capacity of a manager does not control the joint venture. As long as it acts within the financial and operating policies that have been collectively agreed between it and the other venturers and documented in the contractual agreement, it is not precluded from managing the joint venture. However, if the venturer managing the day-to-day operations has the power to govern the venture's financial and operating policies, it controls the venture, and so the venture is a subsidiary of that venturer and not a joint venture.

Joint control

15.8   The standard defines joint control as *"the contractually agreed sharing of control over an economic activity, and exists only when the strategic financial and operating decisions relating to the activity require the unanimous consent of the parties sharing control (the venturers)"*. [FRS 102 para 15.2]. Each of the parties sharing control must consent to all essential decisions relating to the entity's strategic operating, investing and financing activities. Joint control ensures that no single venturer is in a position to control unilaterally the activities of the joint venture. This means, for example, that each party will have a power of veto over strategic financial and operating decisions that would prevent the other party from exercising unilateral control.

15.9   The standard does not give examples of the type of strategic decisions that require unanimous consent, but the decisions would include matters such as:

- Issuing shares.

- Capital expenditure.

- Significant asset disposals.

- Approving a business plan.

- Changing the strategic direction of the business such as changes in products, markets and activities.

- Remuneration policy.

- Major financing.

- Distributions and investment.

- Nomination or revocation of the governing bodies' members.

15.10   The joint venture agreement must require unanimity for these important decisions of strategy, but not for lesser issues that arise in the day-to-day management of the business. It is impractical for the venturers to unanimously agree to every decision required in carrying out an economic activity. Consideration should be given to the nature of the decisions that are subject to unanimous consent. To qualify as strategic financial and operating decisions, rights should be over substantive operating and financial decisions that would be taken in the ordinary course of business.

15.11   Therefore, the venturers must identify at the outset the types of strategic financial and operating decisions that require unanimous agreement and set this out in the joint venture agreement. The venturers would normally also agree arbitration procedures in the event that the parties to the venture cannot agree. Other decisions might be made by a small group of venturers acting like a management committee, while those employees designated as management make day-to-day decisions.

15.12 For the parties to exercise joint control there is no requirement for every venturer to have an equal financial interest in the venture. Venturers could have different interests in the net assets and profit and loss of a venture, but still be equal in terms of exercising joint control. For example, it would be possible to have an arrangement whereby the venturers' interests were 30:35:35 or 25:35:40. But, in order for the arrangement to meet the definition of a joint venture, there must be joint control, including the ability for one party to veto the wishes of the other parties. However, a very uneven split, such as 90:10, might call into question whether the venture is a joint venture and, in this situation, it would be necessary to look at the specific facts and circumstances.

> **Example 1 – Investors in joint venture share joint control**
>
> Entities A, B and C (venturers) hold 25%, 35% and 40% in entity J. Strategic decisions in entity J need to be approved by venturers holding only 60% of the voting power. Each entity has equal representation on the management board.
>
> Provided that the three entities have entered into a contractual arrangement that establishes joint control, from the perspective of the three venturers, entity J is jointly controlled. This is because for joint control to exist the contractual arrangements would require unanimous consent between those investors holding 60% of the voting power. This is the case here, because only two of the three venturers must be in agreement to achieve joint control. Accordingly, each of the investor entities, A, B and C, individually has joint control and accounts for its investment in entity J as a joint venture.

> **Example 2 – Investors in joint venture do not share joint control**
>
> Entities A, B, C and D (venturers) each hold 25% in entity J. Strategic decisions in entity J need to be approved by a 75% vote of the venturers. Each entity has equal representation on the management board.
>
> From the perspective of the four venturers, entity J is not jointly controlled. For this to be the case, the voting arrangements would have to require unanimous agreement between those investors sharing joint control of entity J. However, the contractual voting arrangements of entity J allow agreement of any combination of three of the four partners to make decisions. Accordingly, no fixed combination of investors has joint control over entity J.
>
> Each investor must, therefore, account for its interest in entity J as an associate; this is because they each have significant influence, but they do not have joint control.
>
> If any investor does not have significant influence over entity J, then it would account for its investment in entity J in accordance with FRS 102 section 11, 'Basic financial instruments', or FRS 102 section 12, 'Other financial instruments'.

15.13 Joint control might not exist if the joint venture is operating under restrictions that effectively impair the venturer's ability to implement essential decisions, including the ability to transfer funds. This might happen where the venture is in legal reorganisation or in bankruptcy, or it operates in a jurisdiction where government restrictions apply.

Forms of joint venture

15.14 Although joint ventures can take many different forms, both legal and in substance, the standard identifies three forms of joint ventures. These are:

- Jointly controlled operations.
- Jointly controlled assets.
- Jointly controlled entities.

[FRS 102 para 15.3].

Jointly controlled operations

15.15 A jointly controlled operation is one that involves the use of the assets and other resources of the venturers without establishing a corporation, partnership or other entity, or a financial structure that is separate from the venturers themselves to carry out those activities. The venturers will use their own property, plant and equipment and carry their own inventories. Each venturer will generally incur its own expenses and liabilities and need to raise its own finance. Often activities of the joint venture will be carried out by the venturer's employees alongside those of its main business activities. The joint venture agreement will typically determine how revenue from the sale of the joint product and any expenses incurred in common should be shared among the venturers. [FRS 102 para 15.4].

15.16 An example of a jointly controlled operation is where two or more venturers combine their operations, resources and expertise in order to manufacture, market and distribute jointly a particular product, such as an aircraft or a drug. Different parts of the manufacturing process are carried out by each of the venturers. Each venturer bears its own costs and takes a share of the revenue from the sale of the product, such share being determined in accordance with the contractual arrangement. The accounting for jointly controlled operations is considered in paragraph 15.21 below.

15.17 Some joint ventures involve the joint control, and possibly joint ownership, of an asset (or assets) contributed to, or acquired by, the joint venture. [FRS 102 para 15.6]. The assets are used to obtain benefits for the venturers. Each venturer can take a share of the output from the assets and each bears an agreed share of the expenses incurred. This type of joint venture involves the joint ownership of a single asset that is not a separate entity. In such arrangements, it is important to distinguish between shared costs and revenues and those that each venturer incurs separately.

Jointly controlled assets

15.18 A common example of a jointly controlled asset is a property that is jointly owned by two entities, each taking a share of the rents and bearing a share of the expenses. The separate costs that the venturers might incur are loan interest to finance their share of the property. Another example is where two oil companies with adjoining wells build and operate a pipeline to transport oil to an on-shore refinery. The jointly controlled asset is the pipeline that each venturer uses to transport its own product. The shared costs are the building costs, maintenance costs and any future decommissioning costs. The separate costs that the venturers incur might include the cost of the stocks of oil that pass through the pipeline and any liability incurred to finance their share of the pipeline. The accounting for jointly controlled assets is considered in paragraph 15.24 below.

Jointly controlled entities

15.19   Jointly controlled entities differ from the other two forms of joint venture in that they involves the creation of a separate entity, such as a corporation or a partnership in which each venturer has an interest. The jointly controlled entity will operate in the same way as other entities, except that there will be a contractual arrangement between the venturers that establishes joint control over the entity's economic activities. [FRS 102 para 15.8].

15.20   A common example found in practice is where two venturers set up an entity and transfer assets and liabilities to it in order to combine their activities in a particular business. The activity of the joint venture is undertaken and managed by the jointly controlled entity and not the venturers themselves. It is a separate legal entity. The entity will enter into contracts in its own name and can raise finance in its own name for the purposes of the joint venture activity. The jointly controlled entity controls its assets, incurs liabilities and expenses and earns income. The results of the jointly controlled entity are shared amongst the ventures depending on their entitlement as set out in the joint venture agreement. The accounting for jointly controlled entities is considered in paragraph 15.27 below.

Accounting for jointly controlled operations

15.21 The accounting method specified in the standard for jointly controlled operations effectively treats the operations as if the venturer conducted them independently. Consequently, in respect of its interests in jointly controlled operations, a venturer recognises in its financial statements:

- assets that it controls and liabilities that it incurs; and

- expenses that it incurs and its share of the joint venture's income that it earns from the sale of goods or services.

[FRS 102 para 15.5].

15.22   The accounting entries are booked in the venturer's own financial statements and, therefore, they flow through into the consolidated financial statements (if the venturer prepares them). No further adjustments or consolidation procedures are required.

15.23 Where the ventures provide funds for the operations of a jointly controlled operation, the question arises as to how such funding should be recognised, given that a jointly controlled operation is not a separate legal entity that can recognise its own assets and liabilities. Consider the following example:

Example 1 – Loans to jointly controlled operations

Entities A and B each own 50% of a jointly controlled operation. The initial funding of the operation was provided by both venturers – entity A lending £500 and entity B lending £300.

In this example, each venturer shares 50% of the total loan of £800 payable by the jointly controlled operation.

Entity A cannot recognise a receivable of £250 (50% of £500) and a payable of £150 (50% of £300) due from/to the jointly controlled operation. This is because the jointly controlled operation is not a separate entity that controls its own assets and incurs its own liabilities. Instead, entity A will recognise a net receivable of £100 (£500 – £400) due from its business partner, entity B. Similarly, entity B will recognise a net payable of £100 (£400 – £300) due to entity A.

Example 2 – Jointly controlled operation

Entities A and B have entered into a joint operation to develop products for sale. Entity A builds the product and provides the day-to-day management of the production. Entity A makes a 10% margin on the products that it sells to the joint operation. Entity B identified the opportunity and contributed £40,000. Entity A contributed £10,000. Profits are shared 55/45.

During the joint operation's first year, entity A incurred costs of £70,000 in respect of work in progress, of which £50,000 was charged to the joint operation at £55,000. The joint operation made product sales to third parties of £40,000 and the cost of those sales in the joint operation was £30,000. There are no third party receivables or payables at the year end, because all transactions have been settled.

	Entity A £'000	JO £'000	55% JO £'000	Adjustments £'000	Entity A adjusted £'000
Income statement					
Sales	55.00	40.00	22.00	(30.25)[a]	46.75
Cost of sales	(50.00)	(30.00)	(16.50)	27.50[b]	(39.00)
Net profit	5.0	10.0	5.5	(2.75)	7.75

Balance sheet					
Contribution	10.00	–	–	(10.00)[(c)]	–
Inventory and work in progress					
Costs	70.00	55.00	30.25	(30.25)[(a)]	70.00
Transfer to cost of sales	(50.00)	(30.00)	(16.50)	27.50[(b)]	(39.00)
	30.00	25.00	13.75	(12.75)	31.00
Cash/loan	(25.00)	35.00	19.25	–	(5.75)
	5.00	60.00	33.00	(12.75)	25.25
Liability to entity B	–	50.00	27.50	(10.0)[(c)]	17.50
Retained earnings	5.00	10.00	5.50	(2.75)	7.75
	5.00	60.00	33.00	(12.75)	25.25

(a) 45% of entity A's sales have in effect been made to entity B and these can continue to be recognised by entity A. But £30,250 (that is, 55% of £55,000) of entity A's sales need to be eliminated and replaced by its share of the sales made by the joint operation (that is, £22,000).

(b) Similarly, 45% of entity A's cost of sales relates to sales made in effect to entity B; the other £27,500 (that is, 55% of £50,000) relate to the goods sold to the joint operation at a profit margin of 10% and these need to be eliminated. The balance of inventory of £31,000 is made up of entity A's inventory and work in progress of £20,000 together with the share outstanding in the joint operation of £13,750 (55% of £25,000), less the profit element included in this inventory of £2,750, which has been eliminated.

(c) The jointly controlled operation has total borrowings of £50,000 of which entity A's share is £27,500. However as entity A contributed to £10,000, it has a net obligation of £17,500 (£27,500 – £10,000), because entity B contributed 80% of the funds.

Accounting for jointly controlled assets

15.24   The accounting method specified for jointly controlled assets apportions to each venturer its share of revenues, expenses, assets and liabilities. The venturer recognises its share in its own financial statements. Consequently, as for jointly controlled operations, the accounting entries flow through into the consolidated financial statements (if the venturer prepare them), and no further adjustments or consolidation procedures are necessary.

15.25   With regard to a venturer's interest in a jointly controlled asset, it recognises in its financial statements:

■   The venturer's share of the jointly controlled assets, classified by their nature. For example, a share in a jointly controlled pipeline is shown within property, plant and equipment and not as an investment in the joint venture.

■ Any liabilities that the venturer has incurred, for example, those incurred to finance its share of the asset.

■ The venturer's share of any liabilities incurred jointly with other venturers (for example, the decommissioning liability of a jointly controlled asset).

■ Any income from the sale or use of the venture's share of the output of the joint venture, together with its share of any expenses incurred by the joint venture.

■ Any expenses that the venturer has incurred in respect of its interest in the venture (for example, those related to financing the venturer's interest in the assets and selling its share of the output).

[FRS 102 para 15.7].

15.26 Funds provided to finance jointly controlled assets are treated in the same way as those provided to finance jointly controlled operations (as discussed in para 15.23 above). An example is given below.

Example – Jointly controlled asset

Entities A, B and C are oil companies that together own and operate an offshore loading platform. The platform is close to producing fields that they own and operate independently from each other. The entities own 45%, 40% and 15% respectively of the platform and have agreed to share services and costs accordingly. Decisions regarding the platform require the unanimous agreement of the three parties. The platform is a jointly controlled asset under FRS 102.

The platform cost £10m to construct and the entities each contributed to this cost based upon their percentage ownership. Construction was completed on 31 December 20X0. Local legislation requires the dismantlement of the platform at the end of its 10 year useful economic life, resulting in a decommissioning liability of £800,000 upon construction. The platform costs £500,000 a year to run and 100,000 barrels of oil are loaded each year from the independent oil fields of entities A, B and C.

In the year to 31 December 20X1, entity A sold 40,000 barrels of oil for £250 each and its cost of inventory was £200 per barrel.

Entity A should recognise the following in its financial statements as at 31 December 20X0 in the year to 31 December 20X1:

| | 31 Dec 20X0 | | | | | | 31 Dec 20X1 |
	Note 1 £'000	Note 2 £'000	Note 3 £'000	Note 4 £'000	Note 5 £'000	Note 6 £'000	£'000
Income statement							
Revenue	-					10,000	10,000
Operating expenses	-	(486)		(225)		(8,000)	(8,711)
Finance expense	-		(25)				(25)
Net profit	-	(486)	(25)	(225)		2,000	1,264

Investments in joint ventures

Balance sheet							
PPE	4,860	(486)					4,374
Cash	(4,500)			(225)	(9,000)	10,000	(3,725)
Inventory	-				9,000	(8,000)	1,000
Provisions	(360)		(25)				(385)
Net assets	-	(486)	(25)	(225)		2,000	1,264
Retained earnings	-						1,264

Note 1 – Entity A's share of the property, plant and equipment £4,500,000 (45% of £10m) plus its share of the decommissioning provision £360,000 (45% of £800,000).

Note 2 – Depreciation of property, plant and equipment over the 10 year useful economic life = £486,000 (10% of £4,860,000).

Note 3 – Unwinding of the discount on the decommissioning provision of, say, £25.

Note 4 – Entity A's share of annual operating costs for the platform = £225,000 (45% of £500,000).

Note 5 – Cost of entity A's share of the 100,000 barrels loaded at the platform in the year at £200 each. = £9,000,000 (45% of 100,000 x £200).

Note 6 – Entity A's sale of 40,000 barrels @ £250 each = £10,000,000; and associated costs of sale = £8,000,000 (40,000 x £200).

Accounting for jointly controlled entities

Measurement

15.27 A venturer that is not a parent in its individual financial statements is required to choose one of the following three methods of accounting for its interests in jointly controlled entities:

■ Cost model (see para 15.28 below).

■ Fair value model (see para 15.34 below).

■ Fair value model with changes in fair value recognised in profit or loss (see chapter 11).

Cost model

15.28 A venturer that is not a parent measures its investments in jointly controlled entities at cost less any accumulated impairment losses recognised in accordance with FRS 102 section 27, 'Impairment of assets'. [FRS 102 para 15.10]. The impairment issues that apply to associates accounted for under the cost model also apply to jointly controlled entities measured at cost (see para 40 of chapter 14, 'Investments in associates').

15.29   The investor recognises dividends and other distributions received from the investment as income without needing to consider whether the distributions are from accumulated profits of the jointly controlled entity before or after acquisition. [FRS 102 para 15.11]. However, a receipt of a dividend paid out of pre-acquisition profits shortly after acquisition might be an impairment indicator.

Example 1 – Investment in a jointly controlled entity measured at cost without impairment

On 1 January 20X1 entities A and B each acquired 30% of the ordinary shares that carry voting rights at a general meeting of shareholders of entity Z for £300,000. Entities A and B immediately agreed to share control over entity Z. For the year ended 31 December 20X1 entity Z recognised a profit of £400,000.

On 30 December 20X1, entity Z declared and paid a dividend of £150,000 for the year 20X1. At 31 December 20X1 the fair value of each venturer's investment in entity Z is £425,000. However, there is no published price quotation for entity Z.

Entities A and B (the venturers) must each recognise dividend income of £45,000 (that is, 30% × £150,000 dividend declared by entity Z) in profit or loss for the year ended 31 December 20X1.

At 31 December 20X1 the venturers must report their investments in entity Z (a jointly controlled entity) at £300,000 (that is, cost). Each venturer must also consider whether there are any indicators that might indicate that its investment is impaired and, if so, conduct an impairment test in accordance with the provisions explained in chapter 27, 'Impairment of assets'. In this case there would not be an impairment, because the fair value (£425,000) less costs to sell of the investment exceeds its carrying amount (£300,000).

Example 2 – Investment in a jointly controlled entity measured at cost with impairment

On 1 March 20X1 entities A and B each acquired 30% of the ordinary shares that carry voting rights at a general meeting of shareholders of entity Z for £300,000. Entities A and B immediately agreed to share control over entity Z.

On 31 December 20X1 entity Z declared a dividend of £100,000 for the year 20X1.

Entity Z reported a profit of £80,000 for the year ended 31 December 20X1.

At 31 December 20X1 the recoverable amount of each venturer's investment in entity Z is £290,000 (that is, fair value of £293,000 less costs to sell of £3,000). There is no published price quotation for entity Z. Entities A and B must each recognise dividend income of £30,000 in profit or loss (that is, 30% × £100,000 dividend declared by entity Z).

The payment of the dividend partly out of pre-acquisition profits on 1 March 20X1 is an impairment indicator that could trigger an impairment at 31 December 20X1. At 31 December 20X1 the recoverable amount of the investment is £290,000 (because fair value less cost to sell is higher than its value in use), which exceeds it carrying amount of £300,000. Hence, in accordance with FRS 102 section 27, 'Impairment of assets', entities A and B must each report their investment in entity Z at its recoverable amount of £290,000 (that is, at cost of £300,000 less accumulated impairment of £10,000). Each venturer recognises the impairment loss of £10,000 in profit or loss for the year ended 31 December 20X1.

Equity method

15.30 A venturer that is a parent measures its investments in jointly controlled entities in its consolidated financial statements using the equity method of accounting as explained in chapter 14. [FRS 102 para 15.13]. In fact, all issues that are dealt with in paragraph 14.27 in chapter 14 relating to the equity method of accounting for associates are equally applicable to jointly controlled entities. Consequently, those issues are not discussed again in this chapter.

> **Example 1 – Investment in a jointly controlled entity measured using the equity method**
>
> On 1 January 20X1 entities A and B each acquired 30% of the ordinary shares that carry voting rights at a general meeting of shareholders of entity Z for £300,000. Entities A and B immediately agreed to share control over entity Z.
>
> For the year ended 31 December 20X1 entity Z recognised a profit of £400,000. On 30 December 20X1 entity Z declared and paid a dividend of £150,000 for the year 20X1. At 31 December 20X1 the fair value of each venturer's investment in entity Z is £425,000. However, there is no published price quotation for entity Z.
>
> Entities A and B must recognise £120,000 as their share of entity Z's income (that is, 30% × £400,000 entity Z's profit for the year) in profit or loss for the year ended 31 December 20X1.
>
> At 31 December 20X1 entities A and B must each report their investment in entity Z (a jointly controlled entity) at £375,000 (that is, £300,000 cost + £120,000 share of earnings less £45,000 dividend). The venturers must also consider whether there are any indicators that their investment is impaired and, if so, conduct an impairment test in accordance with FRS 102 section 27, 'Impairment of assets' (see chapter 27). In this case there would not be an impairment because the fair value (£425,000) less costs to sell of the investment (its recoverable amount in this case) exceeds its carrying amount (£375,000).

> **Example 2 — Investment in a jointly controlled entity measured using the equity method**
>
> The facts are the same as in example 1 above. However, in this example, on 1 January 20X1 each venturer's share of the fair values of the net identifiable assets of entity Z is £280,000 and the fair value of one of entity Z's assets (a machine) exceeded its carrying amount (in entity Z's statement of financial position) by £50,000. That machine is depreciated on the straight-line method to nil residual value over its remaining five-year useful life.
>
> Entities A and B estimated the useful life of the implicit goodwill as five years.
>
> The tax effects of the fair value adjustments and implicit goodwill have been ignored.

Entities A and B must recognise income from their jointly controlled entity of £113,000 in profit or loss for the year ended 31 December 20X1, as follows:

Entity Z's profit for the year £400,000 × 30%	120,000
Amortisation of goodwill (note 1)	(4,000)
Additional depreciation on machine £10,000 × 30% (note 2)	(3,000)
	113,000

Note 1 – £300,000 cost of acquisition less £280,000 share of the fair values of the net identifiable assets = £20,000 goodwill; £20,000 goodwill ÷ 5-year useful life = £4,000 amortisation.

Note 2 – £50,000 additional cost of machine ÷ 5-year useful life = £10,000 depreciation.

At 31 December 20X1 the venturers must each report their investment in entity Z (a jointly controlled entity) at £368,000 (that is, £300,000 cost + £113,000 share of earnings less £45,000 dividend). Entities A and B must also consider whether there are any indicators that the investment is impaired and, if so, conduct an impairment test in accordance with the provisions outlined in chapter 27.

Fair value model

15.31 Where an interest in a jointly controlled entity is measured at fair value, the venturer initially recognises the interest at transaction price, which is generally its fair value. Transaction price excludes transaction costs because these are immediately recognised in profit or loss on initial recognition. [FRS 102 para 15.14].

15.32 At each reporting date, the venturer measures its interest in jointly controlled entities at fair value, with changes in fair value recognised in profit or loss. The fair value of the investment should be determined in accordance with the guidance provided in chapter 11, 'Financial assets and liabilities'. Where it is impracticable to measure fair value reliably without undue cost or effort, the investment is measured at cost. [FRS 102 para 15.15].

15.33 The venturer recognises dividends and other distributions received from its investment in a joint venture as income. It does not need to consider whether the distributions are from accumulated profits of the jointly controlled entity arising before or after acquisition, because the accounting is the same. [FRS 102 para 15.15A].

> **Example — Investment in a jointly controlled entity measured at fair value**
>
> On 1 January 20X1 entities A and B each acquired 30% of the ordinary shares that carry voting rights at a general meeting of shareholders of entity Z for £300,000. Entities A and B immediately agreed to share control over entity Z.
>
> For the year ended 31 December 20X1 entity Z recognised a profit of £400,000. On 30 December 20X1 entity Z declared and paid a dividend of £150,000 for the year 20X1. At 31 December 20X1 the fair value of each venturer's investment in entity Z is £425,000. However, there is no published price quotation for entity Z. In determining their profit or loss for the year ended 31 December 20X1 entities A and B must each:
>
> - Recognise dividend income of £45,000 (that is, 30% × £150,000 dividend declared by entity Z). The venturer recognises a dividend from its jointly controlled entity in profit or loss when its right to receive the dividend is established.
>
> - Recognise the increase in the fair value of its investment in entity Z of £125,000 (that is, £425,000 fair value at 31 December 20X1 less £300,000 carrying amount on 1 January 20X1).
>
> At 31 December 20X1 entities A and B must each report their investment in entity Z (a jointly controlled entity) at its fair value of £425,000.

Transactions between a venturer and a joint venture

15.34 It is common for a venturer to enter into transactions with its joint venture. Such transactions might include the contribution or sale of assets by a venturer to its joint venture (downstream transactions). In particular non-monetary assets such as properties or businesses are often contributed by venturers for equity interests in the jointly controlled entity at the time of formation of the joint venture. Similarly, a venturer might purchase assets from the joint venture (upstream transactions) after the joint venture has been formed. Such transactions can give rise to gains and losses. The question arises as to how such gains and losses should be recognised.

15.35 When a venturer contributes or sells assets to a joint venture, any portion of a gain or loss recognised should reflect the transaction's substance. While the assets are retained by the joint venture the venturer recognises only that portion of the gain or loss that is attributable to the interests of the other venturers. This is allowed provided the venturer has transferred the significant risks and rewards of ownership. [FRS 102 para 15.16]. In other words, the venturer recognises only that part of the gain or loss that arises from the sale of the asset to the other venturers. The balance of the gain or loss that is attributable to the venturer is not recognised until the assets have been disposed of by the joint venture. If the asset contributed is a depreciable asset, the unrealised gain or loss would be realised as the asset is depreciated.

15.36 Where the transaction gives rise to a loss, the venturer should recognise the full amount of the loss when the contribution or sale provides evidence that the asset is impaired. [FRS 102 para 15.16]

15.37 An example illustrating the treatment of gain or loss arising on contribution of an asset to a jointly controlled entity is given below.

Example – Contribution of asset in exchange for shares in a jointly controlled entity

On 1 January 20X1 entities A and B (the venturers) establish a joint controlled entity Z. Entities A and B each take up 50% of the share capital of entity Z. In return for their interests in entity Z entities A and B each contribute £100,000 to entity Z. Entity A contributes a machine with a fair value of £100,000 and a carrying amount of £80,000. Entity B's contributes cash amounting to £100,000.

The machine contributed by entity A has an estimated useful life of 10 years with nil residual value. During the year ended 31 December 20X1, entity Z made a profit of £30,000 (after deducting depreciation expense of £10,000 on the machine contributed by entity A).

Entity A accounts for jointly controlled entities using the equity method.

Gain recognised by entity A on contribution of machine to entity Z

	£
Fair value of asset transferred to entity Z	100,000
Carrying amount of asset prior to transfer	80,000
Gain	20,000
Amount unrealised (gain attributable to entity A – note 1)	(10,000)
Amount realised (gain attributable to entity B)	10,000

Note 1 – The unrealised gain of £10,000 will be realised over the life of the machine as it is depreciated at 10% each year by entity Z.

Carrying amount of entity A's equity interest in entity Z

		£
Carrying amount of machine contributed to entity Z		80,000
Gain attributable to interest of entity B		10,000
Carrying amount at 1 January 20X1		90,000
Share of jointly controlled entity's profit (50% of £30,000)	15,000	
Portion of unrealised gain of C10,000 realised in the year	1,000	
Share of profit of jointly controlled entity	16,000	
Carrying amount at 31 December 20X1		106,000

On the other hand, if the carrying amount of the machine in entity A's financial statement amounted to £120,000 prior to transfer, a loss of £20,000 arises on the transfer. Entity A would recognise the entire loss in profit or loss and there is no unrecognised element to carry forward. In effect, this is the same treatment that would result if entity A had recognised an impairment loss of £20,000 prior to sale and then recognised no gain or loss when the asset is transferred at its fair value of £100,000.

Carrying amount of entity A's equity interest in entity Z

	£
Fair value of machine contributed to entity Z	100,000
Share of entity Z's profit (50% of £30,000)	15,000
Carrying amount at 31 December 20X1	115,000

15.38 In the situation where a venturer purchases assets from the joint venture, it should not recognise its share of any profits arising on the transaction in the joint venture until it resells the assets to an independent third party. However, where there is a loss on such a transaction, the venturer recognises its share of the losses in the same way as profits except that losses are recognised immediately when they represent an impairment loss. [FRS 102 para 15.17].

15.39 The standard does not give specific guidance as to whether the portion of any unrealised gain or loss on upstream transactions should be eliminated against the carrying amount of the joint venture, or against the asset transferred.

Example – Venturer buys an asset from its jointly controlled entity

On 1 January 20X1 entities A and B each acquired 30% of the ordinary shares that carry voting rights at a general meeting of shareholders of entity Z for £300,000. Entities A and B immediately agreed to share control over entity Z.

For the year ended 31 December 20X1 entity Z recognised a profit of £400,000. On 30 December 20X1 entity Z declared and paid a dividend of £150,000 for the year 20X1. At 31 December 20X1 the fair value of each venturer's investment in entity Z is £425,000. However, there is no published price quotation for entity Z.

In 20X1 entity A purchased goods for £100,000 from entity Z. At 31 December 20X1 £60,000 of the goods purchased from entity Z were in entity A's inventories (that is, they had not been sold by entity A). Entity Z sells goods at a 50% mark-up on cost.

Entities A and B account for jointly controlled entities using the equity method.

Entity A

Entity A would recognise income from its jointly controlled entity in profit or loss for the year ended 31 December 20X1 of £114,000 (that is, 30% × £400,000 of entity Z's profit for the year = £120,000 less 30% × £20,000 = £6,000, the unrealised profit on the inventory still held by entity Z).

In this example it is assumed that entity A follows an accounting policy of eliminating the unrealised profits from upstream transactions with its jointly controlled entity against the carrying amount of its investment in the jointly controlled entity. At 31 December 20X1 entity A would report its investment in entity Z (a joint venture) at £369,000 (that is, £300,000 cost + £114,000 share of earnings (after adjusting for the elimination of the unrealised profit) less £45,000 dividend). Entity A must also consider whether there are any indicators that its investment is impaired and, if so, conduct an impairment test in accordance with FRS 102 section 27, 'Impairment of assets'.

Entity B

Entity B would recognise £120,000 as its share of entity Z's income (that is, 30% × £400,000 entity Z's profit for the year) in profit or loss for the year ended 31 December 20X1.

At 31 December 20X1 entity B would report its investment in entity Z (a jointly controlled entity) at £375,000 (that is, £300,000 cost + £120,000 share of earnings less £45,000 dividend). Entity B would also consider whether there are any indicators that its investment is impaired and, if so, conduct an impairment test in accordance with FRS 102 section 27, 'Impairment of assets'.

Investor does not have joint control

15.40 To be a joint venture partner the investor must have joint control with its other investors. In some situations, an investor could be party to a joint venture but not be one of the venturers sharing joint control. Such an investor would account for its investment in accordance with FRS 102 section 11, 'Basic financial instrument' (see chapter 11) or, if it has significant influence over the investment in the joint venture, as an associate in accordance with FRS 102 section 14, 'Investments in associates' (see chapter 14). [FRS 102 para 15.18].

> **Example – Investor in joint venture does not share joint control**
>
> Entities A, B and C have 60%, 30% and 10% equity interests in entity D. Entity D has ten board members, six from entity A, three from entity B and one from entity C. Each board member has one vote. Operational decisions require a 51% majority, however, per the contractual agreement that governs entities A, B and C's investment in entity D specifies that strategic financing and operating decisions require all of entity A's and entity B's board members to unanimously agree.
>
> Entities A and B jointly control entity D in this scenario, because the directors representing entities A and B on entity D's board must unanimously agree on key strategic business decisions. This prevents entity A from controlling entity D, because it does not have complete power to govern the financial and operating policies.
>
> Although entity C is a party to the contractual agreement, it does not have joint control because it cannot veto the key decisions. With a seat on the board, entity C could however have significant influence over entity D. This would mean that entity C would account for its investment in entity D in accordance with FRS 102 section 14. If this is not the case, entity C would account for its investment in accordance with FRS 102 section 11.

Presentation and disclosure

Presentation

15.41 An investor should classify investments in joint controlled entities accounted for using the equity method as non-current assets and disclose them as a separate line item in the statement of financial position. Other interests such as loans to associates should not be included within this line item. Loans to associates that are due on demand are basic financial instruments. [FRS 102 para 11.10(c)]. They would be disclosed as financial assets on the face of the statement of financial position.

Disclosure

15.42 An investor in a joint venture should disclose the following:

- Its accounting policy for recognising its interests in jointly controlled entities.

- The carrying amount of its investments in jointly controlled entities.

- The fair value of its investments in jointly controlled entities accounted for using the equity method of accounting where there are published price quotations.

- The aggregate amount of its commitments to joint ventures, including its share in the capital commitments that have been incurred jointly with other venturers, as well as its share of the capital commitments of the joint ventures themselves.

[FRS 102 para 15.19].

15.43 For jointly controlled entities that are accounted for in accordance with the equity method of accounting, the venturer should also disclose:

- its share of the profit or loss of jointly controlled entities; and

- its share of any discontinued operations of such jointly controlled entities.

[FRS 102 para 15.14].

This is consistent with the disclosures required for associates that are accounted for using the equity method of accounting; the share of profits or losses is included net of tax (see chapter 14).

15.44 Where the jointly controlled entity is accounted for under the equity method, the investor should also disclose in its statement of comprehensive income, its share of the jointly controlled entity's other comprehensive income net of tax that is recognised directly in the statement of comprehensive income of the jointly controlled entity. This might relate to a number of items as mentioned in paragraph 5.5A(b) of FRS 102. There is no requirement to analyse this share into its component parts.

15.45 The disclosures required for jointly controlled entities that are accounted for in accordance with the fair value model are those required by paragraphs 11.42 and 11.43 in section 11 of FRS 102 . [FRS 102 para 15.21].This would include the basis of determining fair value; that is a quoted market price in an active market or a valuation technique. Where a valuation technique is used, the entity should disclose the assumptions made to assess fair value. [FRS 102 para 11.43].

Transitional issues

15.46 There are some important issues for UK entities to consider on transition from old UK GAAP based on FRS 9 to FRS 102. Given that for jointly controlled entities FRS 9 required the gross equity method of accounting (which differs from the equity method in presentation only) in the consolidated financial statements, the issues for jointly controlled entities on transition are similar to those for associates. These issues are discussed in chapter 14.

15.47 In addition to jointly controlled entities as defined in FRS 102, FRS 9 also deals with joint arrangements that are not entities (known as JANEs). A JANE is a contractual arrangement under which the ventures engage in joint activities that do not create an entity because it does not carry on a trade or business of its own. Often these arrangements are similar to jointly controlled operations (see para 15.21 above) and jointly controlled assets (see para 15.24 above) and, therefore, are accounted for by incorporating in the consolidated (and individual) financial statements the assets and liabilities, or share thereof, that the venturer controls. Consequently, these types of arrangement should not generally give rise to any adjustments to assets and liabilities recognised under previous GAAP at the date of transition.

15.48 However, in some circumstances, UK entities might find that an interest previously accounted for as a JANE would be accounted for as a jointly controlled entity under FRS 102. That is because, under FRS 102, a jointly controlled entity is a legal entity such as a corporation or a partnership. This contrast with FRS 9 where a corporation or a partnership could have been a JANE; because it was the nature of the trading relationship between the venturers (that is, the substance of the arrangement), not how it was legally constituted, that determined whether an arrangement was a JANE. As a result, the previously recognised share of assets and liabilities of the joint arrangement would need to be reclassified as a single carrying amount under the equity method in accordance with paragraph 35.7(c) of FRS 102. Any consequential adjustments should be made against opening retained earnings in the venturer's opening statement of financial position as of its date of transition, unless it is impracticable to make the adjustments. The impracticability exemption that applies to first time adopters is discussed further in chapter 35.

Chapter 16

Investment property

Chapter 16

Investment property

Introduction and scope

16.1   The classification of certain properties as 'investment properties' for financial reporting purposes arises because it is argued that properties held as investments differ sufficiently from properties held for consumption in the business (owner-occupied properties) that there is a need for separate guidance on investment property. In such a case, the current value of such properties and changes in that current value are of prime importance rather than a calculation of systematic annual depreciation.

16.2   The scope of section 16 of FRS 102 is fairly wide. It applies to investments in land and buildings held by property investment entities, and it also applies to investment properties held by entities whose main activity is other than investment holding and management.

16.3   The measurement requirements of section 16 of the standard apply not only to investment property owned outright by the entity, but also to investment property held by the entity under a lease. Where the property is held under a finance lease, an entity must apply the measurement requirements of section 16 rather than those in section 20 of the standard. Furthermore, where the entity holds a property interest under an operating lease and specified conditions are met, it can elect to apply the measurement requirements of this section (see further para 16.19 below).

16.4   Entities do not have an accounting policy choice to measure an investment property at cost or fair value. Rather, the application of cost or fair value measurement is driven by circumstances.

16.5   For the fair value measurement basis to apply, the entity must be able to determine the fair value of investment property without undue cost or effort on an ongoing basis. Where this is so, the investment property is accounted for in accordance with section 16 at fair value through profit or loss. All other investment property is accounted for as property, plant and equipment (using the guidance in section 17 of FRS 102). In practice, it might be unlikely that the term 'undue cost or effort' could be applied consistently, because circumstances might change (see further para 16.34 below).

16.6   In addition, where property is held to provide social benefits (for example, social housing), the property is not in the scope of investment property and is accounted for as property, plant and equipment in accordance with section 17 of the standard. [FRS 102 para 16.3A].

Definition and initial recognition of investment property

16.7 Investment property is property (that is, land or a building, or part of a building, or both) held by the owner or by the lessee under a finance lease to earn rentals or for capital appreciation or both, rather than for:

- use in the production or supply of goods or services or for administrative purposes; or

- sale in the ordinary course of business.

[FRS 102 para 16.2].

16.8 A key feature that distinguishes an investment property from an owner-occupied property is that it generates cash flows (from rentals or sale) independently of other assets of the entity. By contrast, an owner-occupied property used by an entity for the production or supply of goods or services does not generate cash flows by itself, but it does so in conjunction with other assets such as plant and machinery and inventory used in the production or supply process. Section 17 of FRS 102 applies to such owner-occupied property.

16.9 Although the definition in paragraph 16.7 above appears relatively straightforward, it is not always easy to distinguish investment property from owner-occupied property. Some difficult issues arise in practice, and judgement is often needed to determine whether a property qualifies as an investment property. Some of these issues are discussed below.

Land and building

16.10 An investment property can comprise land, a building or part of a building, or both. A structure that is not a building in its own right, such as car park, is often regarded as an integral part of the land, and might qualify as an investment property.

16.11 Land that is held for sale in the short term will not qualify as an investment property. Similarly, if the entity intends to build residential homes for sale in the future, classification of the land as an investment property would not be appropriate. So, the entity's intention regarding the property is key to the classification. But, if an entity is undecided whether to occupy the land for own use or for short-term sale in the ordinary course of business, the land should be regarded as held for capital appreciation and classified as an investment property. Consider the following examples.

> **Example 1 – Land held for undetermined future use**
>
> Entity A is a supplier of industrial products. In 20X9, the entity purchased a plot of land on the outskirts of a major city. The area has mainly low-cost public housing and very limited public transport facilities. The government has plans to develop the area as an industrial park in five years' time, and the land is expected to greatly appreciate

in value if the government proceeds with the plan. Entity A's management has not decided what to do with the property. How should management classify such a property that is held for undetermined future use?

Management should classify the property as an investment property. Although management has not determined a use for the property after the park's development takes place, in the medium term the land is held for capital appreciation. So it satisfies the definition of an 'investment property' in paragraph 16.7 above.

Assuming that the area is developed as an industrial park as intended, management will need to decide in year 5 what it intends to do with the land. Based on that decision, the land might continue to meet (or it might cease to meet) the definition of an investment property.

Example 2 – Land held for currently undetermined future use

Entity A is involved in real estate development. Entity A has purchased land in London through the exercise of a purchase option that had been acquired some years ago. The purchase price was C10m and the land's fair value (as determined by an independent valuer) is C23.7m. The entity is undecided about whether to develop the land for sale, but will determine a use within the next accounting period. How should management recognise land held for a currently undetermined future use?

In this scenario, the land should be classified as inventory. Although the entity has not determined a use, the property is being held either for sale or for further development and eventual sale in the ordinary course of business. If the entity had decided to hold the land for long-term capital appreciation rather than short-term sale in the ordinary course of business, the land would be classified as an investment property.

16.12 The purchase of a property that is to be redeveloped for resale is not treated as an investment property, because it was not acquired for its rental potential or for capital appreciation.

Other assets

16.13 The definition of 'investment property' in paragraph 16.7 above refers to land or building or both. The question arises whether 'other assets' (such as fixtures and fittings and equipment) could be included as part of the investment property. For example, lifts, air-conditioning units, escalators and fitted furniture are often an integral part of a building. A literal reading of the definition could suggest that these 'other assets' are not investment properties, and so they should be recognised separately as property, plant and equipment under section 17 of the standard.

16.14 But, in practice, a lessor normally views such assets as an integral part of the building and includes them in the fair value of the investment property to set the amount of the lease rental. So, in our view, where such assets form an integral part of the building and the income stream in the lease contract relates to the entire group of assets, it is appropriate to include such assets as part of the investment property, rather than recognising them separately so as to avoid double counting. Similarly, where investment property is leased out on a furnished basis, the fair value of the property will generally include the fair value of the furniture; this is because the rental income relates to a furnished property as opposed to an unfurnished property. As a result, such assets form part of the investment property and are not accounted for as separate assets.

Ancillary services provided to occupants of property

16.15   The owner of an office building might provide ancillary services, such as cleaning, maintenance and security for the tenants. Provided such services are 'insignificant' to the arrangement as a whole (which is likely to be so in most instances), the building is treated as an investment property. But, in other situations, services provided might be significant. Consider the following examples.

Example 1 – Provision of services

An entity provides a bed and breakfast service from a building that it owns. The entity also provides its guests with other services, including housekeeping, satellite television and broadband internet access. The daily room rental includes these services. Furthermore, on request, the entity conducts tours of the surrounding area for its guests. Tour services are charged for separately.

It is apparent from the arrangement that the building is not simply a passive investment, held to earn rental income. Rather, it is used for the provision of a significant level of ancillary services to the guests. As a result, the building would be classified as owner-occupied and accounted for under section 17 of FRS 102.

Example 2 – Provision of services

The owner of an office building provides security and maintenance services to the lessees who occupy the building. There are no other ancillary services that the owner provides to the lessees. The security and maintenance services are considered to be insignificant to the arrangement as a whole. As a result, the building would be classified as an investment property by the owner.

16.16   In many instances, it might be difficult to determine whether ancillary services provided are significant or not, and judgement must be used. In making that judgement, it is important to bear in mind the principal operation of the entity's business, its business model and the spirit of the provisions discussed above. Information about such judgements made by management might need to be disclosed. [FRS 102 para 8.6].

Property occupied by group members, associates and joint ventures

16.17   Within a group, one group entity might lease property to another group entity for its occupation and use. In the consolidated financial statements, such property is not treated as investment property because, from the group's point of view as a single entity, the property is owner-occupied. In the separate financial statements of the entity that owns the property or holds it under a lease accounted for as a finance lease, the property will be treated as an investment property if it meets the conditions set out in the definition in paragraph 16.7 above.

16.18   In contrast, property owned or held under a finance lease by a group entity and occupied by an associate or joint venture should be accounted for as investment property in the consolidated financial statements if it meets the conditions set out in the definition in paragraph 16.7 above. Associates and joint ventures are not considered part of the group for consolidation purposes, and so the property is not owner-occupied from the group's perspective.

Property interest held under an operating lease

16.19   Where a lessee leases an asset under an operating lease (rather than a finance lease), the asset and the related obligation are not recognised in the balance sheet. But, if the lessee then leases the asset under a sub-lease to earn rental income, the lessee *could* treat the asset as an investment property if (and only if) the property would otherwise meet the definition of an investment property, and the lessee can measure the fair value of the property interest without undue cost or effort on an ongoing basis. [FRS 102 para 16.3]. In other words, the sub-lease is treated as if it were a finance lease by the sub-lessor, even though the interest might well be accounted for as an operating lease by the sub-lessee (see further para 16.30 below).

16.20   If, as a result of undue cost or effort, the entity is unable to measure the fair value of the property interest held under an operating lease reliably on an ongoing basis, it is prohibited from treating the property interest as an investment property. Where this is the case, the treatment for operating leases in section 20 of FRS 102 applies.

16.21   The option to treat an operating leasehold property interest as investment property, if fair value is measurable, is available on a property-by-property basis. This means that, where an entity is able to measure the fair values of all its property interests held under operating leases without undue cost or effort, there is no requirement to treat all of them as investment properties, which would be the case if those property interests were all held under finance leases. In other words, the entity can choose the ones that it intends to treat as investment properties.

Mixed-use property

16.22   There might be instances where a property is partially owner-occupied, and the remainder is held for rental income or capital appreciation. In such circumstances, as stated above, the portion that is owner-occupied is accounted for under section 17 of FRS 102 as property, plant and equipment, and the portion that is held for rental income or capital appreciation, or both, is treated as investment property.

16.23 For example, an entity might own a four-storey block and use the bottom two storeys for its administrative function, whilst renting out the upper two floors. If the entity is able to measure the fair value of the upper two floors without undue cost or effort, it treats them as investment properties at fair value through profit or loss. If the entity is unable to determine a reliable fair value, the entire property is treated as property, plant and equipment.

16.24 In some situations, the portion that is owner-occupied might be insignificant compared to the portion that is held for its investment potential. Provided the fair value is reliably measurable without undue cost or effort, it would be appropriate to treat the entire property as an investment property and ignore the insignificant owner-occupied portion. Similarly, if the portion held as an investment property is insignificant in relation to the portion that is owner-occupied, the entire property will be treated as owner-occupied. In practice, 'insignificant' might be assessed, for example, by reference to value and/or usable floor space. But judgement is required in determining what is 'insignificant' on a property-by-property basis.

Measurement at initial recognition

16.25 Investment property should be measured initially at cost. Cost is the purchase price, including any directly attributable expenditure (such as legal and brokerage fees, property transfer taxes and other transaction costs). [FRS 102 para 16.5].

16.26 Costs incurred in undertaking market studies before the purchase of a property cannot be capitalised, but instead they are expensed as incurred. This is because these costs are not directly related to the property.

16.27 Similarly, internal indirect employee costs cannot be included in the initial cost of an investment property. For example, a proportion of the staff cost relating to the time spent by an entity's in-house lawyer in drafting the purchase agreement and negotiating legal terms with the vendor's lawyers cannot be included in the cost of an investment property. Such internal costs relate to the 'general and administrative costs' and are not directly attributable costs; this is because these costs would have been incurred even if the property in question was not acquired.

16.28 Borrowing costs incurred in funding the acquisition or construction of an investment property can be capitalised as part of the initial cost of an investment where the entity has adopted a policy of capitalising borrowing cost (see para 25.2 of FRS 102).

Deferred payment terms

16.29 The cost of an investment property for which payment is deferred beyond normal credit terms is the present value of all future payments. There is no guidance in paragraph 16.5 of FRS 102 on how the discount rate should be determined. We believe that it would be appropriate to discount all future payments using the market rate of interest for a similar debt instrument (similar as to currency, term, type of interest rate and other factors – see also para 11.13 of the standard). The difference between the present value and the amount payable is recognised as an interest expense over the period of credit.

Property interest held under a lease

16.30   A property interest held by a lessee under an operating lease and classified as an investment property can be accounted for as if it were a finance lease (as explained in para 16.19 above). So, a lessee holding investment properties under both finance and operating leases applies the same accounting treatment. At the lease commencement date, the entity records the property asset and the related liability in its balance sheet at amounts equal to the fair value of the property at the lease inception date or, if lower, at the present value of the minimum lease payments in accordance with paragraph 20.9 of FRS 102. If the lease is an operating lease, the asset and the related liability will be recorded at the present value of the minimum lease payments, because this will be significantly lower than the fair value of the underlying property. Any initial direct costs that are directly attributable to negotiating and arranging a lease are added to the amount recognised as an asset.

Measurement after initial recognition

16.31   The measurement of an investment property subsequent to initial recognition is driven by circumstances (as stated in para 16.4 above). If an entity knows, or can measure, the fair value of an investment property without undue cost or effort, it must use the fair value through profit or loss model for that investment property. Otherwise, it must account for the investment property as property, plant and equipment (as set out in section 17 of the standard).

Determining fair value

16.32   Fair value is defined as *"the amount for which an asset could be exchanged, a liability settled, or an equity instrument granted could be exchanged, between knowledgeable, willing parties in an arm's length transaction"*. [FRS 102 Glossary of terms]. The guidance for measuring fair values is provided in paragraphs 11.27 to 11.32 of the standard.

16.33   In most circumstances, an investment property's fair value can be reliably determined on a continuing basis. But there could be rare situations where this is not so. For instance, an investment property might be located in a remote area where comparable market transactions are infrequent and/or market yields are not available to arrive at fair values using alternative valuation methods.

16.34   Even where the fair value of the investment property is readily measurable on a continuing basis, many entities might find that the cost of obtaining external valuation every year (or employing own staff with appropriate qualifications to carry out annual valuations) is a drain on their resources and does not provide a commensurate level of benefit to shareholders, often because the shareholders are also the directors. Furthermore, there could be circumstances where independent valuers with appropriate expertise are not available in some regions, and the effort required to obtain a valuation cannot be justified on cost-benefit grounds. In practice, no two entities are likely to find themselves in the same position. What comprises 'undue cost and effort' for one entity might not be so for another entity. So, entities should consider all factors, external (nature and location of properties) as well as internal (availability of resources), to determine whether there are genuine difficulties in terms of cost or effort in obtaining reliable estimates of fair values on an ongoing basis. In the absence of such difficulties, the investment property must be measured at fair value.

16.35 Paragraphs 11.27 to 11.32 of FRS 102 provide guidance on the methodology of valuations for determining fair values. That guidance is discussed in chapter 11. Although chapter 11 deals with financial instruments, the fair value measurement methodology discussed therein applies to investment properties for which fair value is required to be determined under section 16 of the standard (see para 16.7 of FRS 102).

16.36 Investment property whose fair value cannot be measured reliably without undue cost or effort is treated as property, plant and equipment and measured at cost using the cost model in section 17 of the standard. A consequence of adopting the cost model is that the property is likely to be depreciated systematically over its useful life to zero. This is because, if the fair value of the property cannot be determined reliably on a continuing basis, its residual value (which is a function of current fair value adjusted for age and condition expected at the end of its useful life) is unlikely to be reliable for measurement purposes.

Self-constructed property

16.37 An entity that constructs or develops a property for future use as an investment property must recognise the property initially at cost (as stated in para 16.25 above). This means that classification as an investment property should be made on acquisition of the property, rather than when development or construction is completed. Cost will include the purchase price of land, including legal fees and property taxes, borrowing costs (where an entity has elected to capitalise such costs), site preparation, construction costs and all other directly attributable costs necessary to bring the property to the condition for its use as an investment property. Further details of the type of costs that can or cannot be included are set out in paragraphs 17.10 to 17.14 of FRS 102.

> **Example – Directly attributable costs**
>
> An investment property entity develops office buildings for rental, and incurs expenses (such as security and utilities). The building was physically completed on 31 March 20X9, but the local health and safety regulator did not clear the property until 30 June

20X9. The delay of three months in receiving health and safety approval is standard for the type and location of the building. The entity incurred C400,000 for utilities and security in the period between 31 March and 30 June 2009.

Although the entity's management was not able to determine the fair value of the property during construction without incurring undue cost or effort, it would like to capitalise these costs as related to bringing the property into a condition in which it is ready to use.

The security and utility expenses should be capitalised for the expected period of delay. The legal requirement to receive the regulatory clearance meant that the building could not be put to its intended use as an investment property, although it was physically ready for its intended use on 31 March 20X9.

16.38 After initial recognition, the entity must measure the property at fair value through profit or loss if it is able to determine the fair value of the property during construction without undue cost or effort. Estimating the fair value of property in the course of construction is likely to be more challenging than valuing a completed property. In order to do so, management needs to consider a number of factors including, amongst others, the terms of the construction contract, nature of the property (typical for the market or non-standard), construction risks specific to the property and who bears it, the stage of completion, and the level of reliable cash flows after completion. In practice, many entities will need to engage the help of property valuation experts.

16.39 Once the decision is taken to measure the property at fair value on a continuing basis, the entity must use that valuation basis during the construction period at each reporting date. The change in the fair value must be recognised periodically in profit or loss from the date of acquisition over the construction or development phase. It is not possible to record the property at cost until construction or development is completed and the property available for letting. Consider the following example.

Example – Self-constructed property measured at fair value

An entity has recently acquired a plot of land to construct an office building. The land and building will be leased to a third party under an operating lease agreement when the development is completed. The entity started construction of the investment property on 1 January 20X1. Construction is expected to be completed on 30 June 20X3, and the property is expected to be let from 1 September 20X3. The entity prepares its accounts to 31 December each year. Management is able to obtain reliable fair values on a continuing basis without undue cost or effort. The following information is relevant:

	C'000
Cost of land	2
Construction cost incurred since commencement until 31 Dec 20X1	10
Additional construction costs incurred during 20X2	6
Additional construction costs incurred until 30 Jun 20X3	2
Fair value of property at 31 Dec 20X1	13
Fair value of property at 31 Dec 20X2	22

Fair value of property at 31 Dec 20X3	24

The entity will record the investment property at each reporting date as follows:

At 31 Dec 20X1: Initial recognition at cost (land plus construction)	12
Fair value gain recognised during 20X1 in profit or loss	1
At 31 Dec 20X1: Fair value	13
Additional cost incurred during 20X2	6
Fair value gain recognised during 20X2 in profit or loss	3
At 31 Dec 20X2: Fair value	22
Additional cost incurred during 20X3	2
At 31 Dec 20X3: Fair value	24

It is not possible to record the property at cost of C20 at date of completion on 30 June 20X3 and recognise the fair value gain of C4 (C24 – C20) in profit or loss during 20X3. The gain of C4 arose during 20X1 and 20X2 and is properly recognised in those periods.

Property interest held under a lease

16.40 Where an entity holds a property interest under an operating lease that is classified as an investment property, the entity records an asset and a liability at the present value of the minimum lease payments. Any up-front payment made on the lease (for example, a premium) is included in the cost of the asset and not in the finance lease obligation; this is because it has been paid. In an operating lease, the present value of the minimum lease payments is significantly less than the fair value of the property (as stated in para 16.30 above). So, if this interest is classified as investment property, it is the interest in the lease rather than the underlying property that is fair valued and recognised as an investment property.

16.41 In the UK, it is quite common to pay an up-front premium for very long property leases, together with ground rents at a nominal amount over the term of the lease. Contingent rents might also be payable (for example, based on turnover of the trade carried out from the property). The entity will record the investment property initially at the amount paid for the up-front premium, plus the present value of any ground rents payable, but excluding any contingent rentals. The entity will also recognise a liability for the present value of the ground rents payable.

16.42 After initial recognition, the leasehold investment property will be fair valued. Valuers often value long leasehold interests by reference to the fair value of the property (the freehold value) and any contingent rentals, but deduct the present value of any future lease payments and the present value of any residual (which is likely to be small for very long leases). The fair value of the investment property that should be recorded for accounting purposes is the gross value before deductions for any recognised lease liability. In other words, the liability is added back to the assessed value to ensure that the liability is not double counted.

Example – Valuation of leasehold investment property

On 1 January 20X9 an entity rents a building held under a lease for 50 years. On the same date, it sub-lets the building to various third parties under operating leases. At inception of the head lease, the entity pays a premium of C2.35m. Ground rent of C10,000 per annum is also payable. The present value of the ground rents payable amounts to C150,000 at a discount rate of 6.4%.

At the reporting date on 31 December 20X9, a valuer estimates that the fair value of the property (based on estimated future income net of all payments) amounts to C2.40m.

The entity will record the leasehold interest at initial recognition and at the next reporting date as follows:

	C'000
Initial recognition at 1 Jan 20X9	
Premium paid	2,350
Present value of ground rent of C10,000 pa @ 6.4% for 50 yrs	150
Cost at 1 Jan 20X9	2,500
Lease liability for ground rents payable	
At 1 Jan 20X9	150.0
Finance cost @ 6.4%	9.6
Less amount paid	(10.0)
At 31 Dec 20X9	149.6
Reporting date at 31 Dec 20X9	
Assessed fair value, net of all payments	2,400.0
Add: outstanding lease liability	149.6
Fair value at 31 Dec 20X9	2,549.6

If the entity also expects to receive any contingent rents, the valuer's estimate of the fair value of the contingent rents receivable would be included in the fair value for financial reporting purposes.

16.43 A similar issue arises in circumstances where a lessor provides operating lease incentives (such as rent-free periods) to a lessee. The incentive is required to be allocated over the lease term as a reduction in the rental income, so there might be accrued rent receivable in rent-free periods. To avoid double counting, the value of the investment property (which is arrived at by discounting the actual rents receivable) should be adjusted so that it excludes any amount that is reported as a separate asset on the balance sheet. The result is that an investment property will be stated on the balance sheet at fair value less the accrued rent receivable debtor.

16.44 It should be noted that the above requirement to recognise changes in fair value of investment property in profit or loss is markedly different from the requirements of old UK GAAP. This issue is discussed further at paragraph 16.55 below.

Transfers

16.45 In exceptional circumstances, an entity might not be able to determine the fair value of an investment property in the future without undue cost or effort. This could happen, for instance, where a significant employer in a particular area has relocated overseas, with the result that the area has become run down, and there is little or no prospect of a future recovery. In such circumstances, estimating the fair value of the property on an ongoing basis might be difficult, and the property should be treated as property, plant and equipment using the cost model in section 17 of FRS 102. The previously recorded fair value of the investment property becomes its cost at that date. The entity should also estimate the property's recoverable amount and, if necessary, recognise an impairment loss. The carrying amount of the property is depreciated over its remaining useful life, assuming a residual value of nil (see para 16.36 above). The reclassification should be disclosed as a change in circumstances, and not a change in accounting policy. [FRS 102 para 16.8].

16.46 The reverse situation can also happen. Where an investment property was previously carried at cost, a change in circumstances might make it possible to determine its fair value on an ongoing basis without undue cost or effort. In that situation, the entity continues to provide depreciation on the property until the date of transfer from cost to fair value. At the transfer date, the entity recognises the difference between fair value and carrying amount in profit and loss. Again, the reclassification from cost to fair value should be disclosed as a change in circumstances.

16.47 Transfers to and from investment property should also be made when the property first meets (or ceases to meet) the definition of an investment property. This would normally happen when there is a change in use of the property. The date when the property first meets (or ceases to meet) the definition of an investment property is critical.

16.48 The following table summarises how management should recognise and derecognise investment property, depending on the nature of the change in use. The treatment of gains and losses is applicable only to entities that are able to measure the fair value of the property without undue cost or effort on an ongoing basis. No gain or loss is recognised on transfers of investment property carried at historical cost.

Change in use	Transfer	FV gain/loss
(a) Start of owner occupation	From IP to PPE	N/A
(b) Start of development to sell	IP — Inventories	N/A
(c) End of owner occupation	PPE — IP	N/A or P&L
(d) Start of operating lease to third party	Inventory — IP	N/A or P&L

(a)   An investment property (IP) is transferred to property, plant and equipment (PPE) only when management starts to occupy the property. The fair value of the property at that date becomes deemed cost for subsequent accounting under section 17 of the standard, so no gain or loss arises.

(b) An investment property that will be developed prior to sale is transferred to inventory when the building is vacated by the tenants and redevelopment commences. The property remains in that category until development is complete. The fair value of the property at the transfer date becomes deemed cost for subsequent accounting under section 13 of the standard as inventory, so no gain or loss arises.

(c) An investment property is only transferred from PPE to investment property at the end of owner occupation. At that date, the property is classified as an investment property. If the entity is able to measure the fair value of the property without undue cost or effort on an ongoing basis, the difference between the fair value and the carrying value of the property at the date of transfer is recognised in profit or loss. Otherwise, there is no accounting effect for the change in use.

(d) A property previously held in inventory can be classified as an investment property when an entity enters into an operating lease with a third party, provided the entity is able to measure the fair value of the property without undue cost or effort on an ongoing basis. In that case, the difference between the fair value and the carrying value of the property at the date of transfer is recognised in profit or loss. This treatment is consistent with sales of inventories.

Disposals

16.49 Although not specifically dealt with in section 16 of FRS 102, an investment property should be derecognised on retirement (that is, withdrawn from permanent use or demolished) or disposal through sale or through entering into a finance lease. Any gain or loss between disposal proceeds and carrying value is recognised in profit or loss. The criteria that should be met for recognising revenue from sale is considered in paragraph 23.10 of FRS 102. Section 20 of the standard deals with accounting for finance leases, and sale and leaseback transactions.

Presentation and disclosures

16.50 A further issue that arises with investment properties is whether they should be treated as tangible fixed assets or fixed-asset investments. The description of such properties as 'investment' (and their non-depreciation for that reason) might suggest that they should be included within the 'investments' category. But Schedule 1 to SI 2008/410, 'The Large and Medium-sized Companies and Groups (Accounts and Reports) Regulations 2008', does not give any clear guidance on this question. So both methods are adopted in practice.

16.51 In addition, section 16 of FRS 102 and the Companies Act both require an entity to disclose the following for all investment property accounted for at fair value through profit or loss:

- The methods and significant assumptions applied in determining the fair value of investment property. [FRS 102 para 16.10(a)].

- The bases of valuation used. [SI 2008/410 1 Sch 58(2)].

- Comparable amounts determined under the historical cost accounting rules. or the differences between these amounts and the corresponding amounts shown on the balance sheet. [SI 2008/410 Sch 58(3)(a),(b)].

- The extent to which the fair value of investment property (as measured or disclosed in the financial statements) is based on a valuation by an independent valuer who holds a recognised and relevant professional qualification and has recent experience in the location and class of the investment property being valued. If there has been no such valuation, that fact should be disclosed. [FRS 102 para 16.10(b)].

- The existence and amounts of restrictions on the realisability of investment property or the remittance of income and proceeds of disposal. [FRS 102 para 16.10(c)].

- Contractual obligations to purchase, construct or develop investment property or for repairs, maintenance or enhancements. [FRS 102 para 16.10(d)]

- A reconciliation between the carrying amounts of investment property at the beginning and end of the period, showing separately:

  - additions, disclosing separately those additions resulting from acquisitions through business combinations;

  - net gains or losses from fair value adjustments;

  - transfers to property, plant and equipment where a reliable measure of fair value is no longer available without undue cost or effort (see paras 16.42 and 16.43 above);

  - transfers to and from inventories and owner-occupied property; and

  - other changes.

  This reconciliation need not be presented for prior periods. [FRS 102 para 16.10(e)].

16.52 It should be noted that the above disclosures apply to investment properties carried at fair value through profit or loss. The disclosure requirements for investment properties carried at cost are set out in section 17 of FRS 102. This should also include the Act's disclosure requirements as set out in paragraph 51 of Schedule 1 to SI 2008/410.

16.53 In accordance with section 20 of the standard, the owner of an investment property provides lessors' disclosures about leases into which it has entered. An entity that holds an investment property under a finance lease or operating lease provides lessees' disclosures for finance leases and lessors' disclosures for any operating leases into which it has entered.

16.54 The Companies Act also requires disclosure of an analysis of freehold, long leasehold and short leasehold. [SI 2008/410 1 Sch 53(a)(b)]. For this purpose, a lease includes an agreement for a lease of land and building. A lease will be a long lease if, at the end of the financial year in question, the remaining lease term is 50 years or more. Otherwise, it will be a short lease. [SI 2008/410 10 Sch 7(1)].

Realised profits

16.55 The fair value movements on investment properties are recognised in the profit and loss account (SI 2008/410 1 Sch 40).

16.56 Although these fair value movements on investment properties are shown in the profit and loss, this does not mean that they are realised profits available for distribution.

16.57 Fair value accounting profits that are 'readily convertible into cash' are realised. 'Readily convertible to cash' means that the entity has an unrestricted ability to convert the asset (or the change in the fair value of an asset or liability) to cash almost instantaneously at the balance sheet date (that is, without protracted negotiations). The changes in the fair value of many, but not all, financial instruments fulfil this definition. Some, such as unquoted equity instruments and investments held for strategic purposes, do not. [Tech 02/10 paras 4.10 — 4.11]. Changes in the fair value of non-financial assets (such as investment property) rarely, if ever, fulfil the definition.

16.58 As fair value gains on investment properties are not realised profits, entities can choose to transfer such fair value movements on investment properties to a revaluation reserve, instead of a transfer to retained earnings. The option of transferring the fair value movements to a revaluation reserve will assist with the identification of distributable reserve.

Transitional issues for UK entities

16.59 UK entities transitioning from old UK GAAP (SSAP 19) to FRS 102 must prepare their first financial statements as though the requirements of FRS 102 had always applied. But there are two 'valuation as deemed cost' exemptions relating to investment property that are available to first-time adopters under section 35 of FRS 102. A first-time adopter can elect:

- to measure an investment property on the date of transition to FRS 102 at its fair value and use that fair value as its deemed cost at that date; and

■ to use a previous GAAP revaluation of an investment property at, or before, the date of transition to FRS 102 as its deemed cost at the revaluation date.

[FRS 102 para 35.10(c),(d)].

16.60 But these exemptions are likely to be of limited use in the UK, given that entities with investment properties will have been carrying these at open market value under SSAP 19. Although section 16 of FRS 102 requires investment properties to be measured at 'fair value', in practice, 'fair value' and 'open market value' are unlikely to be different. So no adjustments to carrying values of investment properties are likely to be necessary at the transition date.

16.61 There are a number of other matters that UK entities need to note when they transition from old UK GAAP to FRS 102. These matters are discussed below.

16.62 Under old UK GAAP, investment properties had to be measured at open market value. On transition to FRS 102, the issue arises whether UK entities that measured their investment properties at open market value under old GAAP can move to the cost model. Some entities might argue that the measurement of open market value required by old GAAP entailed a significant amount of cost and effort which they found truly burdensome. Because this situation is unlikely to change after transition to new GAAP, they might argue that they are entitled to change to the cost model on the grounds of undue cost and effort. Others might argue that the concept of 'undue cost and effort' in the measurement process was never applicable under UK accounting standards nor permitted by the Companies Act. Furthermore, the move from a fair value measurement basis to cost is unlikely to provide reliable and relevant information. So, UK entities that were required to measure their investment properties at open market value should continue to do so. We support this latter argument.

16.63 Although the valuations might be similar under old GAAP and FRS 102, the reporting of gains and losses are fundamentally different (as noted in para 16.44 above). FRS 102 requires changes in fair value of investment properties to be recognised in profit or loss; whereas, under old UK GAAP, equivalent gains and losses were not reported in the profit and loss account, but were taken to the statement of total recognised gains and losses ('STRGL'), unless a deficit was expected to be permanent. So, reported profits are likely to be more volatile for UK entities under FRS 102. UK entities are unlikely to be able to avoid this volatility by moving to a cost model, as explained above.

16.64 Another matter that is going to affect UK property investment entities is deferred tax. Under old UK GAAP (that is, FRS 19), a deferred tax liability was not generally recognised on an increase in the fair value of an investment property. Under FRS 102, entities will generally have to provide significant deferred tax liabilities on fair value uplifts in their investment properties (see chapter 29).

Chapter 17

Property, plant and equipment

Property, plant and equipment

Chapter 17

Property, plant and equipment

Introduction and scope

17.1 Section 17 of FRS 102 considers the accounting treatment for property, plant and equipment (PPE) and investment property whose fair value cannot be measured reliably without undue cost or effort. The principal issues that it considers are the timing of recognition of assets (recognition), the determination of their carrying amounts (measurement), and the concepts and methods of depreciation. It does not deal with their impairments, which are dealt with in section 27 of the standard.

17.2 In terms of definition, the Companies Act gives only limited assistance, because its guidance is of a general nature. The formats in Schedule 1 to SI 2008/410 indicate that all assets are either fixed or current. The Act says that assets are fixed assets where they *"are intended for use on a continuing basis in the company's activities"*. So, current assets are *"assets not intended for such use"*. [CA06 Sec 835(6)].

17.3 FRS 102 defines property, plant and equipment as tangible assets that:

■ are held for use in the production or supply of goods or services, for rentals to others, or for administrative purposes; and

■ are expected to be used during more than one period.

[FRS 102 para 17.2].

17.4 Property, plant and equipment are tangible assets characterised by physical existence or substance. Examples include land, buildings, machinery, industrial and office equipment, computer hardware, fixtures and fittings, vehicles, etc. This differentiates them from intangible assets, such as patents or goodwill.

17.5 The definition excludes assets held for sale in the ordinary course of business, assets in the process of production for such sale, and assets in the form of materials or supplies to be consumed in the production process or in the rendering of supplies. Such assets are inventories, which are dealt with in section 13 of the standard.

17.6 Property, plant and equipment also exclude:

■ biological assets related to agricultural activity or heritage assets (see section 34 of the standard), or

17001

- mineral rights and mineral reserves, such as oil, natural gas and similar non-regenerative resources (see section 34 of the standard).

[FRS 102 para 17.3].

17.7 Property, plant and equipment are expected to be used over a number of years, so entities allocate the cost of the investment in these assets to future periods through periodic depreciation charges.

Recognition

General recognition criteria

17.8 An item of property, plant and equipment is recognised as an asset if (and only if):

- it is probable that future economic benefits associated with the item will flow to the entity; and

- the cost of the item can be measured reliably.

[FRS 102 para 17.4].

17.9 In general, costs incurred to achieve greater future benefits should be capitalised, whereas expenditures that simply maintain a given level of services should be expensed. Often, improvements and replacements result from a general policy to modernise or rehabilitate a piece of equipment or an old building. The issue is how to differentiate these types of expenditure from normal repairs. Good judgement is required to classify these expenditures correctly. (See further paragraphs 17.13 — 17.18 below).

17.10 Where it is apparent that an asset might be acquired as a whole (such as an integrated process plant or an aircraft), but that components of it have significantly different patterns of consumption of economic benefits, an entity should allocate the initial cost of the asset to its major components and depreciate each such component separately over its useful life. [FRS 102 paras 17.6, 17.16]. For example, an aircraft and its engines might need to be treated as separate depreciable assets, and this will be required if they have different useful lives. Another example of a component might be the lining of a blast furnace, where the lining has to be replaced periodically, and thus has a different useful life from the rest of the furnace (see further paras 17.11 and 17.12 below).

17.11 There is no guidance in the standard as to how the cost of the asset should be allocated amongst its major components where these have been identified as separately depreciable assets. In most cases, an invoice will specify a single amount for the whole asset, without further breakdown of the cost of the physical components. In that situation, the cost of the identifiable components should be estimated by reference to their current market prices or in consultation with the vendor. This information can then be used as a basis for allocating the cost of the asset to the remaining parts. In other words, the remaining parts of the asset that are not individually significant are grouped together, and the cost of the whole asset (less the sum of the costs of the individual identifiable parts) is attributed to it. Each component of cost is then depreciated over its estimated useful life (see further paras 17.89 — 17.96 below).

17.12   But there could be situations where the cost of a component is not available at inception (even though it is replaced subsequently), or the components are not physically identifiable (as happens when an item of property, plant and equipment is required to undergo major inspections or overhauls at regular intervals). The cost allocation issues that arise in these situations are considered below.

Spare parts and servicing equipment

17.13   Spare parts and servicing equipment are usually carried as inventories and expensed when they are consumed. However, these items are property, plant and equipment where an entity expects to use them during more than one period. Similarly, if the spare parts and servicing equipment can be used only in connection with an item of property, plant and equipment, they are considered property, plant and equipment. [FRS 102 para 17.5]. Where this is the case, the spare parts or servicing equipment would be depreciated over a period that does not exceed the useful life of the related asset. An example of the classification of spare parts and servicing equipment is shown below.

> **Example – Spare parts and servicing equipment**
>
> A private hospital has installed two identical back-up generators. The first back-up generator provides electricity when the supply from the national grid is interrupted. The second back-up generator will be used in the unlikely event that the first back-up generator fails.
>
> Both back-up generators are items of property, plant and equipment. This is because both items of stand-by equipment are expected to be used in more than one accounting period. The standard does not require such use to be regular. So they should be depreciated from the date when they become available for use.

Replacement parts

17.14   Costs incurred on a replacement part for property, plant and equipment are recognised as an asset if they meet the recognition criteria described in paragraph 17.8 above. If such costs meet those criteria, and are recognised in the carrying amount of the affected item of PPE, the carrying amount of the replaced part or parts is derecognised (that is, the accumulated cost and depreciation of the replaced parts is eliminated). [FRS 102 para 17.6]. This applies whether or not the replaced part or component had been separately depreciated. Examples of replacement parts are the lining of a blast furnace that might require replacement after a specified number of hours of use, or aircraft interiors (such as seats and galleys) that might require replacement several times during the airframe's life.

Property, plant and equipment

17.15 In some instances, it might not be possible to determine the carrying amount of the replaced component. In that situation, it might be acceptable to use the cost of the replacement as a proxy for the cost of the replaced part when it was acquired or constructed. This is consistent with the treatment discussed for major inspection (see para 17.18 below).

> **Example 1 – Replacement of machine part**
>
> An entity buys a machine for £100,000 and performs no separate identification of the component parts. The machine's useful life is estimated to be ten years. At the end of year 4, the machine breaks down and a significant component has to be replaced for £35,000. The rest of the machine is in good working order, and the entity expects to use the machine (subject to normal repair and maintenance) for its remaining useful life of six years.
>
> The cost of the new component meets the recognition criteria for an asset, because it will provide economic benefits to the entity. The original purchase price did not specify the cost of the component. But, as stated above, the new component's cost of £35,000 can be used as an indication of the likely cost of the component at the date of acquisition of the machine. This can be estimated by discounting, as indicated below.
>
> Assuming an appropriate discount rate of 6%, the discounted value of the cost of the new component of £35,000 amounts to £27,725 (that is, $£35,000/(1.06)^4$). After four years of depreciation, the current carrying value of the new component would be £16,635 (that is, £27,725 * 6/10) which is then derecognised from the unamortised carrying value of the asset of £60,000 at the end of year 4, and the cost of the new component of £35,000 would be added to the asset. The new carrying value of £78,365 (that is, £60,000 + £35,000 – £16,635) would be depreciated over its remaining useful life of six years.
>
> **Example 2 – Asset requiring periodic replacement**
>
> A small manufacturing entity has recently acquired a new factory, which cost £1m for the freehold and has a residual value of £100,000. This factory has a flat roof, which needs replacing every ten years at a cost of £100,000.
>
> The entity is considering two alternative approaches:
>
> ■ To regard the factory as one asset, and so depreciate the whole factory over its useful economic life of 30 years, charging £30,000 per annum.
>
> ■ To regard the roof as a significant part of the factory and depreciate the cost of the roof of £100,000 over ten years (giving a depreciation charge of £10,000 per annum), and to depreciate the remainder of the factory of £900,000 down to its residual value of £100,000 over 30 years (giving a depreciation charge of £26,667 per annum).
>
> Whichever approach is adopted, in year 10 (when the roof is replaced) the carrying amount attributable to the replaced roof will be written off.
>
> In the first accounting treatment above, the cost and accumulated depreciation of the old roof will be £100,000 and £33,333 respectively. So there will be a loss on disposal to

be recognised in the income statement of £66,667 (the £100,000 replacement cost is used as a proxy for the original cost of the old roof as the actual cost is not determinable; no residual value is assumed for the old roof in calculating the accumulated depreciation).

If the second accounting treatment is adopted, the carrying amount of the old roof in year 10 will be nil, and the cost and accumulated depreciation of £100,000 are written off, and no profit or loss arises on disposal.

The above alternative treatments have only been used to illustrate the principle. The second approach given is the correct method to use. Clearly, it more accurately reflects the entity's consumption of economic benefits of the factory, resulting in an even charge to the income statement of £36,667 per annum over the 30 years of the useful economic life of the factory. The component in this case is significant, so this second approach is the one required by the standard (see para 17.10 above).

Major inspections or overhauls

17.16 The standard notes that: *"A condition of continuing to operate an item of property, plant and equipment (eg a bus) may be performing regular major inspections for faults regardless of whether parts of the item are replaced".* [FRS 102 para 17.7]. This distinguishes pure inspection costs from costs of replacing parts.

17.17 Overhaul costs typically include replacement of parts and major repairs and maintenance. Replacement of parts is dealt with separately by the standard (see para 17.14 above), so the question remains whether major repairs and maintenance costs are included under the term 'inspection'. The answer will depend on whether or not these costs meet the standard's criteria for recognition as an asset. The costs of 'day-to-day servicing' of an item of property, plant and equipment are recognised in profit or loss in the period in which they are incurred. [FRS 102 para 17.15]. In other words, they do not meet the asset recognition criteria. But major repair and maintenance programmes that are carried out as part of a periodic inspection and overhaul, and that result in future economic benefits, might qualify for recognition. The dry-docking of a ship would be an example of such an event.

17.18 The standard requires that, when each major inspection is carried out, the cost is recognised as part of the carrying amount of the item of property, plant and equipment as a replacement if it meets the asset recognition criteria in the standard. Any remaining carrying amount relating to the previous inspection is derecognised. This treatment applies whether or not the cost of the previous inspection was separately identified and depreciated when the item was acquired or constructed. Where the cost of the previous inspection was not separately identified, the estimated cost of a future similar inspection could be used as a proxy for the cost of the previous inspection when calculating the carrying value of the previous inspection that needs to be derecognised. [FRS 102 para 17.7].

> **Example – Major inspection/overhaul**
>
> An airline purchases a new aircraft for £35m. The useful life of the aircraft is 15 years. The aircraft is expected to be inspected/overhauled every four years. The entity ascertains that, at acquisition date, the expected overhaul cost for similar aircraft that are four years old is £5m (at current prices, not the expected future price at year 4).
>
> Given that the overhaul/inspection cost represents a significant part of the total cost of the aircraft, a proportion of the cost of the asset equivalent to the expected cost of overhaul (that is, £5m) is depreciated over the period to the next inspection/overhaul. The remaining cost, which might need to be split into further components (such as seats and galleys that could require replacement several times during the airframe's life) is £30m. Any additional components would be depreciated over their own estimated useful lives.
>
> If, say, the aircraft is overhauled a year earlier than expected at an actual cost of £6m, the carrying amount relating to the original overhaul cost at the end of year 3 is £1.25m (£5m/4). This cost is removed from the asset's carrying amount, and the actual cost of the overhaul amounting to £6m is capitalised to avoid double counting.
>
> As explained above, component accounting for inspection or overhaul costs is intended to be used for major expenditure that occurs at regular intervals over the life of an asset. Costs associated with routine maintenance and repairs are expensed when incurred.

Measurement at initial recognition

Measurement at cost

17.19   An item of property, plant and equipment that qualifies for recognition should be initially measured at cost. [FRS 102 para 17.9].

17.20   Measurement of cost is normally straightforward, because it is generally the price paid. But land and buildings are separable assets, even though an entity might pay a single price when they are acquired together. Where an asset is self-constructed, the production cost will be ascertained by aggregating the price paid for material, labour and other inputs used in the construction.

17.21   Historical accounting rules require fixed assets to be shown at either their purchase price or their production cost, less any provision for depreciation or diminution in value. [SI 2008/410 1 Sch 17].

17.22   The Companies Act also defines purchase price, in relation to an asset of an entity or any raw materials or consumables used in the production of such an asset, as including *"any consideration (whether in cash or otherwise) given by the company in respect of that asset or those materials or consumables, as the case may be"*. [SI 2008/410 10 Sch 12]. It is ascertained by adding to the actual price that the entity paid for the asset any expenses that were incidental to its acquisition. [SI 2008/410 1 Sch 27(1)]. These incidental expenses include, for example, the expenses that the entity had to incur in order to bring the asset to its present location and into its present condition.

17.23   The amount to be shown as the production cost of an asset is ascertained by adding the following amounts:

- The purchase price of the raw materials and consumables that the entity used in producing the asset.

- The direct costs of production that the entity incurred (excluding distribution costs, in the case of current assets).

[SI 2008/410 1 Sch 27(2)].

17.24   The Act also permits the following costs to be included in the cost of tangible fixed assets, although FRS 102 provides further guidance on the circumstances in which these permitted costs should be included:

- A reasonable proportion of indirect overheads, to the extent that they relate to the period of production.

- Interest on any capital that the entity borrowed in order to finance the production of that asset, to the extent that it relates to the period of production. Where such interest has been included in the production cost, the fact that it has been included and its amount must be stated in the notes to the financial statements.

[SI 2008/410 1 Sch 27(3)].

17.25   The Act deals with circumstances where the purchase price and production cost are unknown. In certain circumstances, an asset's purchase price or production cost is to be taken as the value that the entity ascribed to the asset in the earliest available record of its value that the entity made on or after it acquired or produced the asset. These circumstances are where there is no record of either of the following:

- The actual purchase price or the actual production cost.

- Any price, any expenses or any costs that are relevant for determining the purchase price or the production cost.

17.26   This exemption applies also where the relevant record is available, but it could be obtained only with unreasonable expense or delay. [SI 2008/410 1 Sch 29].

17.27   Where an entity has determined, for the first time, an asset's purchase price or production cost according to its earliest known value, it must disclose this fact in the notes to its financial statements. [SI 2008/410 1 Sch 64(1)].

Property, plant and equipment

Elements of cost

17.28   The cost of an item of property, plant and equipment comprises all of the following:

- Its purchase price, including legal and brokerage fees, import duties and non-refundable purchase taxes, after deducting trade discounts and rebates.

- Any costs directly attributable to bringing the asset to the location and condition necessary for it to be capable of operating in the manner intended by management. These can include the costs of site preparation, initial delivery and handling, installation and assembly, and testing of functionality.

- The initial estimate of the costs (recognised and measured in accordance with section 21 of the standard) of dismantling and removing the item and restoring the site on which it is located, the obligation for which an entity incurs either when the item is acquired or as a consequence of having used the item during a particular period for purposes other than to produce inventories during that period.

- Any borrowing costs capitalised (refer to chapter 25).

[FRS 102 para 17.10].

17.29   Only costs that are directly attributable can be capitalised. Although it is tempting for management, particularly in start-up situations such as opening a new mine or a new manufacturing or retailing operation, to regard all the initial costs as capital to be carried forward and recovered when the operation is up and running successfully, this is forbidden by the standard. Only the costs that are directly attributable to the item of property, plant and equipment, and not general operating costs, can be capitalised. The standard lists types of costs that are not property, plant and equipment, and an entity should recognise these as an expense when they are incurred:

- costs of opening a new facility;

- costs of introducing a new product or service (including costs of advertising and promotional activities);

- costs of conducting business in a new location or with a new class of customer (including costs of staff training); and

- administration and other general overhead costs.

- Any borrowing costs capitalised (refer to chapter 25).

[FRS 102 para 17.11].

17.30   In addition to the guidance on asset recognition referred to in paragraphs 17.2 above and 17.127 below, the following three items cannot be treated as assets (either fixed or current) in any entity's balance sheet:

- Preliminary expenses.

- Expenses of, and commission on, any issue of shares or debentures.

- Costs of research.

[SI 2008/410 1 Sch 3(2)].

17.31 In view of the Act's prohibition, the above items should not be capitalised. Historically, they have been written off to the income statement, except where an entity had a share premium account, in which case the first two items could be written off to that account. [CA06 Sec 610(2)(3)]. Share issue costs connected with share premium accounts are considered further in chapter 22.

17.32 An example that illustrates the guidance for identifying the type of costs that should be included in the cost of an asset (as discussed above) is considered below.

> **Example – Capitalisation of directly attributable costs**
>
> Entity A, which operates a major chain of supermarkets, has acquired a new store location. The new location requires significant renovation expenditure. Management expects that the renovations will last for three months, during which time the supermarket will be closed. Management has prepared the budget for this period, including expenditure related to construction and remodelling costs, salaries of staff who will be preparing the store before its opening, and related utilities costs.
>
> Management should capitalise the costs of construction and remodelling the supermarket, because they are necessary to bring the store to the condition necessary for it to be capable of operating in the manner intended by management. The supermarket cannot be opened without incurring the remodelling expenditure, and thus the expenditure should be considered part of the asset.
>
> But the cost of salaries, utilities and storage of goods are operating expenditures that would be incurred if the supermarket was open. These costs are not necessary to bring the store to the condition necessary for it to be capable of operating in the manner intended by management, and so they should be expensed.

17.33 An example of where costs should not be capitalised relates to a new hotel or bookshop, which could operate at normal levels almost as soon as it has been constructed or opened, but where demand usually builds up slowly, and full use or sales levels will be reached only after several months. In such a case, initial operating losses in the start-up period should not be capitalised. Similarly, marketing and similar costs associated with generating demand for the services of the item of property, plant and equipment should not be capitalised as part of the asset. The following examples illustrate this.

> **Example 1 – Operating costs incurred in the start-up period**
>
> An amusement park has a 'soft' opening to the public, to trial run its attractions. Tickets are sold at a 50% discount during this period and the park is expected to operate at 80% capacity. The official opening day of the amusement park is three months later.
>
> Management claims that the soft opening is a trial run necessary for the amusement park to be in the condition capable of operating in the intended manner, so the net operating costs incurred should be capitalised.
>
> The net operating costs should not be capitalised, but should be recognised in the income statement. Running at 80% operating capacity is sufficient evidence that the amusement park is capable of operating in the manner intended by management.

> **Example 2 – Pre-opening rentals**
>
> A new store is being developed on a rented site. Can the rentals incurred before the store is opened be capitalised and then amortised over the period of the lease?
>
> No. The rentals would not qualify for capitalisation as part of the cost of the store fixed assets, because they are not costs directly attributable to bringing the assets to the location and condition necessary for them to be capable of operating in the manner intended by management. [FRS 102 para 17.10(b)]. The rentals are, in effect, part of the start-up costs, which should be expensed. [FRS 102 para 17.11].

Decommissioning costs

17.34   As mentioned in the third bullet point of paragraph 17.28 above, the cost of an item of PPE includes the estimated costs of dismantling and removing the asset and restoring the site on which it is located ('decommissioning costs'). But this is only allowed where there is a corresponding obligation recognised as a provision under section 21 of FRS 102. At first glance, it seems odd to capitalise decommissioning costs that are not going to emerge until later in the asset's life. But, where the entity has an obligation as a direct consequence of acquiring or constructing property, plant and equipment to incur further costs in the future that it cannot avoid, a provision is recognised in accordance with section 21 of the standard. So, the decommissioning costs at the end of the asset's life are just as much a cost of acquiring or constructing the asset as the costs incurred at the start of the asset's life.

> **Example – Restoration of property**
>
> An entity rents a property under an operating lease. The tenant has modified the property by building an internal wall, which is allowed under the terms of the lease, but on condition that the tenant returns the property at the end of the lease in its original state. This will entail dismantling the internal wall.
>
> On building the internal wall, the tenant creates an obligation to remove the wall, which it cannot avoid. At the end of the lease term, the entity is required to return the premises to the landlord in its original state.

In this situation, the entity should capitalise the cost of modifying the premises so that it is capable of operation in a manner intended by management. In addition, the entity has an obligation under the lease to return the premises in its original condition, so it should estimate the cost of restoring the wall and capitalise the cost at initial recognition, even though the cost is not expected to be incurred until the end of the lease term. This obligation should be calculated in accordance with paragraph 21.5 of the standard. As such, both costs are capitalised when the internal wall is built and will be recognised in the income statement over the useful economic life of the asset (generally the lease term) as part of the depreciation charge.

Incidental operations

17.35 Sometimes, an entity might undertake operations during the course of construction or development of an item of property, plant and equipment that are incidental to the construction or development activity. For example, it might earn income by using a building site as a car park until construction begins. These incidental operations are not necessary to bring the asset to the location and condition necessary for it to be capable of operating in a manner intended by management. For this reason, any revenue and costs attributable to such incidental operations are recognised in profit or loss. [FRS 102 para 17.12].

Measurement of cost

17.36 The cost of an item of property, plant and equipment is the cash price equivalent at the recognition date. [FRS 102 para 17.13]. This is the amount that the entity would need to pay if it paid cash for the asset immediately on purchase. This would be the case even if the asset was acquired at a bargain, and so the purchase price did not reflect the full value of the asset. However, as stated earlier, the purchase price includes legal and brokerage fees, import duties and non-refundable purchases taxes, after deducting trade discounts and rebates.

17.37 Where payment for an asset is deferred beyond normal credit terms, the cost is the present value of all future payments. [FRS 102 para 17.13]. The difference between the present value and the total payments is recognised as an interest expense over the period of credit.

Example – Deferred payment terms

Entity A manufactures computer chips, and entity B constructs the machinery used to manufacture the chips. Each machine that entity B manufactures is built to the customer's specifications. Due to the downturn in the chip market, entity A's management negotiates extended payment terms for a new machine to be constructed by entity B. Entity A will pay £2.5m to entity B 18 months after delivery of the new equipment. There is no list price to determine the equivalent price under normal credit terms because of the individual nature of the equipment.

Entity A should not record the asset at £2.5m. Instead, it should record the asset when it receives it at the present value of the financial liability of £2.5m, which establishes the purchase price of the asset.

The present value of the financial liability that carries no interest can be estimated by discounting all the future cash payments using the prevailing market rate of interest for a similar instrument with a similar credit rating.

Assuming the relevant discount rate for entity A is 7%, the asset and the price payable to entity B should be recorded at £2,258,730 (that is, £2,500,000/(1.07)$^{1.5}$). The entity also recognises interest expense of £158,111 in year 1 and £83,159 in year 2 over the 18-month period of credit, a total of £241,270; this is the difference between the amount payable and its present value.

Exchanges of assets

17.38 Where an item of property, plant or equipment is acquired in exchange for a non-monetary asset or assets (or a combination of monetary and non-monetary assets), the entity should measure the cost of the acquired asset at fair value unless:

- the exchange transaction lacks commercial substance, or

- the fair value of neither the asset received nor the asset given up is reliably measurable. In that case, the asset's cost is measured at the carrying amount of the asset given up.

[FRS 102 para 17.14].

17.39 Generally, entities account for the exchange of non-monetary assets on the basis of the fair value of the asset given up or the fair value of the asset received, whichever is clearly evident. Thus, entities should recognise immediately any gains or losses on the exchange. The rationale for immediate recognition of gains or losses is that most transactions have commercial substance, and so such gains or losses should be recognised.

17.40 But, if neither the fair value of the asset received nor the fair value of the asset given up is reliably measurable (which is rare in practice), the acquired item is measured at the carrying amount of the asset given up. This measurement basis also applies if the exchange transaction lacks commercial substance. The standard does not contain any guidance on how an entity should determine whether an exchange transaction involving non-monetary assets has 'commercial substance'.

17.41 Common sense would suggest that an exchange transaction has commercial substance if the economic positions of the two parties to the exchange transaction change (that is, the parties are in a different economic position before and after the exchange transaction). This will generally be evident if the future cash flows change as a result of the transaction. Consider the following examples.

Example 1 – Consideration received comprising a combination of non-monetary and monetary assets

Entity A exchanges surplus land (book value £100,000) for cash of £200,000 and plant and machinery (fair value £250,000) held by entity B.

In this example, it is likely that the timing and amount of the cash flows arising from the land will differ significantly from the cash flows arising from the equipment. As a result, both entities are in different economic positions. So the exchange has commercial substance, and the entities should recognise a gain or loss on the exchange.

Thus, entity A would record the plant and machinery at £250,000, which is equivalent to the fair value of the land of £450,000 less the cash received of £200,000. Entity A will also recognise a gain of £350,000 (fair value of assets received of £450,000 less book value of asset given up of £100,000).

Under current UK law, only £200,000 of the gain (limited to the amount of cash received by entity A) would be treated as a realised profit, and the remaining £150,000 would be unrealised. The realised profit is recognised in the income statement, whilst the unrealised profit is recognised in other comprehensive income.

Similarly, entity B would recognise the land at £450,000 and a gain or loss on the difference between the fair value of the plant and machinery and its carrying value prior to exchange.

Example 2 – Exchange of assets that lack commercial substance

An entity exchanges car X (with a book value of £13,000 and a fair value of £13,250) for car Y (which has a fair value of £13,100) and cash of £150.

The transaction lacks commercial substance, because, other than the cash of £150, the entity's future cash flows are not expected to change as a result of the exchange; it is in the same position overall as it was before the transaction.

The entity recognises the assets received at the book value of car X. So, it recognises cash of £150 and car Y as property, plant and equipment with a carrying value of £12,850. No gain or loss arises on the transaction.

17.42 In example 1 above, the unrealised profit is recognised in other comprehensive income in accordance with paragraph 13(a) of Schedule 1 to SI 2008/410. Following this guidance, the income statement can only include those profits that have been realised at the reporting date. The concepts of 'realised' and 'distributable' profits are considered further in chapter 22.

Measurement after initial recognition

17.43 After initial recognition, an entity should measure all items of property, plant and equipment using the cost model (in accordance with paragraph 17.15A of FRS 102) or the revaluation model (in accordance with paragraphs 17.15B - 17.15F of the standard). Where the revaluation model is selected, this is applied to all items of property, plant and equipment in the same class (that is, having a similar nature, function or use in the business). [FRS 102 para 17.15]. This ability to apply a revaluation model is also in line with the alternative accounting rules in Schedule 1 to SI 2008/410, which permits replacing the historical cost of a tangible fixed asset with a market value (as at the date of its last valuation) or its current cost. [SI 2008/410 1 Sch 32(2)].

Cost model

17.44   Under the cost model, an entity measures an item of property, plant and equipment at cost less accumulated depreciation and accumulated impairment losses. [FRS 102 para 17.15A]. Depreciation is discussed further at paragraph 17.69 onwards below; for impairment, see paragraph 17.106 onwards below.

Revaluation model

17.45   Under the revaluation model, an item of property, plant and equipment is carried at its revalued amount, being its fair value at the date of revaluation less any subsequent accumulated depreciation and subsequent accumulated impairment losses. The carrying amount of the item should not differ materially from its fair value at the reporting date. Revaluations should be carried out with sufficient regularity to ensure that this is the case. [FRS 102 para 17.15B].

17.46   Where an entity values its assets in accordance with the alternative accounting rules in SI 2008/410, it must value each asset separately, in order to comply with the separate valuation principle contained in paragraph 15 of Schedule 1. As above, the requirements of section 17 of the standard are stricter and require that, if a single tangible fixed asset is revalued, all fixed assets of the same class must also be revalued. [FRS 102 para 17.15]. This reduces the scope for picking out individual assets for revaluation, just because they happen to have significantly increased in value.

17.47   SI 2008/410 already defines quite broad categories or classes of assets, as follows:

■   Land and buildings.

■   Plant and machinery.

■   Fixtures, fittings, tools and equipment.

■   Payments on account and assets in the course of construction.

[SI 2008/410 1 Sch Part 1 Sec B].

17.48   But, for valuation purposes, an entity can adopt other, narrower, classes of assets, as the definition of a class of assets in paragraph 17.15 of FRS 102 is those that have a similar nature, function or use in the business. Other than ruling out classes of assets determined on a geographical basis, this definition is reasonably flexible, so that an entity can adopt meaningful classes that are appropriate to the type of business and assets held by an entity. When determining which classes of assets to adopt, it is worth bearing in mind that separate disclosures must be made for each class of assets. For example, as noted at paragraph 17.125 onwards below, each class of assets must be presented as a separate category in the reconciliation of movements in tangible fixed assets in the notes to the financial statements. [FRS 102 para 17.31]. In practice, this could prevent the adoption of many narrowly defined classes of assets.

17.49 Property is often revalued, although a class of assets for revaluation need not be confined to property. This is illustrated in the following example.

> **Example – Revaluation on a class-by-class basis**
>
> Entity A is a manufacturing entity. It owns a number of industrial buildings, such as factories and warehouses, and office buildings in several cities. The industrial buildings are located in industrial zones, whereas the office buildings are in central business districts of the cities. Entity A's management wants to apply the section 17 revaluation model to the subsequent measurement of the office buildings but continue to apply the historical cost model to the industrial buildings. Is this acceptable under section 17 of FRS 102?
>
> Entity A's management can apply the revaluation model to just the office buildings. The office buildings can be clearly distinguished from the industrial buildings in terms of their function, their nature and their general location. Assets can be revalued on a class-by-class basis. [FRS 102 para 17.15]. The different characteristics of the buildings enable them to be classified as different PPE classes. So, the different measurement models can be applied to these classes for subsequent measurement. As a result, all properties within the class of office buildings must be carried at revalued amounts.

Frequency of revaluation

17.50 One of the requirements of section 17 of the standard is that valuations should remain up to date. But there is no specific requirement for valuations to be performed every year or every reporting period. The standard sets out the general principle that revaluations should be made with sufficient regularity that the carrying amount does not differ materially from that which would be determined using fair value at the end of the reporting period. [FRS 102 para 17.15B]. This imposes no specific time interval for valuations, but rather the interval is determined by the movements in fair value.

17.51 So, the frequency of revaluations depends on movements in the fair value of property, plant and equipment. Where the fair value of a revalued item of property, plant and equipment at the balance sheet date differs materially from its carrying amount, a further revaluation is necessary. Where fair values are volatile (as might be the case with land and buildings), frequent revaluations could be necessary. Where fair values are stable over a long period (as might be the case with plant and machinery), valuations would be required less frequently.

17.52   A material change in value could be considered a change that would reasonably influence the decisions of a user of the accounts. It is a matter of judgement, which is ultimately the responsibility of management. But, in making that judgement, management would probably consult its valuers and consider, amongst other things, factors such as changes in the general market, the condition of the asset, changes to the asset and its location. Management should consider the combined effect of all the relevant factors.

17.53   Management should have a process by which it can monitor the movements in fair value each year, even if this does not amount to a full annual revaluation. This process could take the form of obtaining information on general fair value movements and periodic consultation with valuers.

17.54   Property, plant and equipment within a single class should all be valued at the same time, to avoid selective revaluation of assets and to avoid 'cherry picking' (that is, reporting a mixture of costs and values made at different dates in the financial statements). However, a class of assets could be revalued on a rolling basis, provided that the revaluation is completed within a short period of time and that the revaluations are kept up to date.

Valuers

17.55   Valuation of land and buildings is normally undertaken by professionally qualified valuers. [FRS 102 para 17.15C].

17.56 A qualified valuer would normally be a person who:

■   Holds a recognised and relevant professional qualification.

■   Has recent relevant post-qualification experience.

■   Has sufficient knowledge of the state of the market in the location and category of the asset being valued.

17.57   In the UK a qualified valuer will often be a member of the Royal Institution of Chartered Surveyors (RICS). As well as valuing properties, some members specialise in valuing plant and machinery and fine art and antiques. But the above definition of a qualified valuer does not preclude non-RICS members from carrying out valuations where appropriate.

17.58   In some cases, internal valuers might be used. An entity might have a policy of commissioning external valuations every three years, with a review by internal valuers each year to determine that the fair value has not changed significantly from the most recent valuation. An entity should disclose the basis on which it carried out valuations in the notes to the financial statements.

Fair value and bases of valuation

17.59 The Companies Act specifies that tangible fixed assets can be included in the balance sheet at a market value determined as at the date of their last valuation or at current cost. Section 17 of the standard gives more definitive guidance and requires the carrying amount of a revalued asset to be its fair value (less subsequent accumulated depreciation and impairment). [FRS 102 para 17.15B].

17.60 Fair value is defined as *"The amount for which an asset could be exchanged, a liability settled, or an equity instrument granted could be exchanged, between knowledgeable, willing parties in an arm's length transaction. In the absence of any specific guidance provided in the relevant section of this FRS, the guidance in paragraphs 11.27 to 11.32 shall be used in determining fair value"*. [FRS 102 Glossary of terms]. The fair value of land and buildings is usually determined from market-based evidence by an appraisal that is normally undertaken by a professionally qualified valuer. The fair value of plant and equipment is usually the market value of the item determined by appraisal. [FRS 102 para 17.15C].

17.61 Fair value is usually determined by reference to market-based evidence (for example, recent selling prices of comparable assets in a comparable condition in market transactions). Further guidance on determining fair value when market-based evidence is available, as well as where there is no market-based evidence, is contained in chapter 11.

17.62 Items of property, plant and equity are frequently valued using an income or depreciated replacement cost approach. There might be no market-based evidence of fair value, because the items are specialised in nature or are rarely sold except as part of a continuing business. [FRS 102 para 17.15D]. Secondhand plant and equipment is rarely sold, other than as part of a continuing business. Sales often result from a business closure or insolvency, and the price achieved for the plant and equipment is often far below what its value would be in a continuing operation. So, plant and equipment will often be valued on a depreciated replacement cost basis.

17.63 Specialised properties are defined in the RICS Appraisal and Valuation Standards as those properties that, because of their specialised nature, are rarely, if ever, sold in the market, except by way of a sale of the business or entity of which it is part, due to uniqueness arising from its specialised nature and design, its configuration, size, location or otherwise. Refer to chapter 16 of the Manual of Accounting for further discussion. All other properties (that is, the majority of properties) are non-specialised properties.

17.64 Depreciated replacement cost (DRC) is typically used to determine the fair value of specialised items of property, plant and equipment (for example, oil refineries, power stations, buildings for which there is no market, including isolated or remote buildings) that are rarely, if ever, sold on the open market except as part of a continuing business. This method involves estimating the value of land in its existing use and the gross replacement cost of buildings and other site works. Deductions ('depreciation') are made to allow for age, condition and economic or functional obsolescence, environmental and other factors. Often, indices are applied to both cost and depreciation.

Revaluation gains and losses

17.65 Any difference between the amount of an item that an entity has determined according to one of the alternative accounting rules, and the amount that the entity would have disclosed if it had adhered to the historical cost convention, must be credited or debited (as applicable) to a 'revaluation reserve'. [SI 2008/410 1 Sch 35(1)].

Revaluation gains

17.66 A revaluation gain is credited to other comprehensive income and accumulated in equity. An exception to this rule is where a gain on revaluation reverses a revaluation decrease on the same asset previously recognised as an expense. Gains are first credited to profit or loss to the extent that the gain reverses a loss previously recognised in profit or loss. [FRS 102 para 17.15E].

17.67 While not explicitly addressed in section 17 of FRS 102, the entire gain relating to a revalued asset is generally transferred from the revaluation reserve to retained earnings either when the asset is retired from use or disposed of or gradually as the asset is used by the entity. The amount transferred is the difference between depreciation based on the asset's revalued carrying amount and depreciation based on the asset's original cost.

Revaluation losses

17.68 A revaluation loss should be recognised in other comprehensive income to the extent of any previously recognised revaluation increase accumulated in equity, in respect of that same asset. Any balance of the decrease should then be recognised as an expense in profit or loss. [FRS 102 para 17.15F]. A negative revaluation amount recognised in equity cannot be created.

Example – Treatment of revaluation gains and losses

An entity has a policy of revaluing its tangible fixed assets. An asset cost £1,000 at the start of year 1. The asset has a useful economic life of ten years and is being depreciated on a straight line basis to nil residual value. It was revalued downwards at the end of year 1 to £850, which was assumed to be the asset's recoverable amount. The loss on revaluation in year 1 is recognised in the profit and loss account, because it is a fall in value below depreciated historical cost.

At the end of year 2, market values had risen to £1,050. The revaluation gain and loss are recognised as follows:

	Year 1	Year 2
Cost/valuation brought forward	1,000	850
Depreciation charge (*)	(100)	(94)
	900	756
(Loss)/gain on revaluation – profit and loss	(50)	44
Gain on revaluation – OCI	–	250
Carrying amount carried forward	**850**	**1,050**

* opening balance divided by remaining useful economic life

Of the £294 gain on revaluation in year 2, £44 is recognised in the profit and loss account. This reverses the £50 loss previously recognised in the profit and loss account, adjusted for depreciation of £6 (that is, £50 divided by 9), which is the additional depreciation charge that would have been recognised in year 2 had the opening balance been £900 (that is, if the £50 loss had not been recognised in year 1).

Note that the adjustment to depreciation of £6 is also the difference between depreciation that would have been charged of £100 (that is, 1,000 divided by 10) on the original cost of £1,000, and the depreciation actually charged for the year of £94.

Depreciation

17.69   After initial recognition, property, plant and equipment should be depreciated on a systematic basis over its useful life. Depreciation allocates the cost of property, plant and equipment in a systematic and rational manner to those periods expected to benefit from the use of the asset. Depreciation is defined as *"the systematic allocation of the depreciable amount of an asset over its useful life"*; and the depreciable amount is defined as *"the cost of an asset, or other amount substituted for cost (in the financial statements), less its residual value"*. [FRS 102 Glossary of terms]. This allocation process reduces an asset's depreciable amount to its residual value at the end of its useful life.

17.70   The depreciation charged for each period should be recognised in profit or loss, unless another section of FRS 102 requires the cost to be recognised as part of the cost of an asset. For example, the depreciation of manufacturing property, plant and equipment is included in the costs of inventories. [FRS 102 para 17.17].

17.71   Land and buildings are treated as separate assets and are accounted for separately, even though they could be acquired together. Land normally has an unlimited useful life, and so it is not depreciated. The passage of time and usage do not affect its future ability to provide economic benefits. [FRS 102 paras 17.8, 17.16]. But buildings have a limited useful life, and so they are depreciable assets. An increase in the value of land does not affect the determination of the depreciable amount of a building; nor does it remove the need for depreciation to be charged on the building.

17.72   It is apparent from the definitions in paragraph 17.18 of FRS 102 that there are three factors involved in the depreciation process. These are:

■   Determining the depreciable amount for the asset, or each major component (where applicable). This involves estimating the residual value.

■   Estimating the useful lives of each separately depreciable component.

■   Selecting an appropriate allocation method (depreciation).

These issues are discussed below.

Component depreciation

17.73   When an item of property, plant and equipment is first recognised, the entity should allocate the initial cost of the asset to its major components that are considered to have significantly different patterns of consumption of economic benefits (as noted in para 17.10 above). The standard goes on to state that each such component should be separately depreciated over its useful life. Other assets should be depreciated over their useful lives as a single asset. [FRS 102 para 17.16].

17.74   The major components are likely to be those that have costs that are significant to the total cost of the item. These components should be treated separately where they have significantly different useful lives. But, where the significant components have the same useful lives, they can be grouped together as a single asset and depreciated over their useful lives. As explained above, the separate components could be physical components that were identified at initial recognition, or they could be non-physical components that represent a major inspection or overhaul.

> **Example – Separately depreciable components**
>
> An entity buys a machine for £100 that is expected to be used for 10 years. The entity has identified two components, X (cost £35) and Y (cost £50), that have significant different patterns of consumption of economic benefits, and it estimates the useful lives of X and Y to be three and five years respectively.
>
> In this situation, cost attributable to the remainder of the asset that is not individually significant is £15. The entity will depreciate components X and Y over their useful lives of three and five years respectively. The remainder of the machine, which is treated as a single asset, should be depreciated over 10 years.

17.75 The above component approach should be used where it would be relevant. It is not necessary for an entity to attempt to allocate the cost of the assets amongst all its various components if the effect would be immaterial. For example, the tyres, motor and body of a truck could have different economic lives, but most entities would set a single depreciation rate for the entire truck. Entities can set separate depreciation rates, but it is often impractical. Hence, the standard focuses on major components that have significantly different useful lives.

Depreciable amount and residual values

17.76 As noted above, the depreciable amount of an asset is its cost less residual value. Residual value is defined as *"the estimated amount that an entity would currently obtain from disposal of an asset, after deducting the estimated costs of disposal, if the asset were already of the age and in the condition expected at the end of its useful life"*. [FRS 102 Glossary of terms].

17.77 Entities should assess whether indicators exist suggesting that the residual value or useful life of an asset has changed since the most recent financial reporting date. If such indicators exist, the entity should review its estimates for residual value, depreciation method and useful life of all items of PPE (and, therefore, all parts of them). Indicators include a change in how an asset is used, significant unexpected wear and tear, technological advancement and changes in market prices.

17.78 As the definition in paragraph 17.76 above implies, the residual value is the price that the asset will fetch today, but assuming that it is already of the age and condition it will be at the end of its useful life. The effect of this definition is that price changes (including changes due to inflation) should be taken into account when calculating an asset's residual value, but only up to the reporting date. Expected future changes (including inflation) after the reporting date should not be taken into account. So, strictly speaking, the value of the asset in question should be considered at the end of its useful life, but expressed in prices current at the reporting date.

> **Example – Revising the residual value of an asset**
>
> An asset is bought for £1,000. Its estimated useful life is six years. Its estimated residual value at the date of acquisition was £70, and this estimate has not changed up to year 3, because there have been no significant inflationary or other price changes. But the rate of inflation is now expected to increase and, at the end of year 4, the estimated residual value (based on prices at the end of year 4) is £130. If future inflation is taken into account, the estimated residual value at the end of the asset's useful life is estimated at £400. At the end of year 3, the asset has a carrying amount of £535, calculated as follows:

Property, plant and equipment

	£	
Cost	100	
Residual value	70	
Depreciable amount	930	
Depreciation	(465)	(3 years at £155 per year)
Carrying amount	535	(Cost of £1,000 less depreciation of £465)

In year 4 the residual value is revised to £130. The depreciable amount of the asset becomes £870. Deducting the depreciation charged to date of £465 leaves £405 to be depreciated over the remaining useful life of three years. So, depreciation of £135 is charged in year 4.

If future inflation had been taken into account in year 4, the depreciable amount would have been £600; and, after deducting depreciation to date of £465, the charge would have only been £45. But this treatment is not permitted by the standard.

The standard's treatment will ensure that, by the end of the asset's useful life, the total depreciation charged will normally be the same as that which would have been charged if future inflation had been taken into account. This is because, in years 5 and 6, the residual value will be revised so that, at the end of year 6, if expectations hold true, the revised residual value will be £400. Assuming that all the future inflation effect occurs in year 5, for example, the calculation of depreciation in year 5 will be:

Cost	1000
Residual value	400
Depreciable amount	600
Depreciation to year 5	600
Depreciation in years 5 and 6	Nil

(The example has been deliberately exaggerated, because it is unlikely that inflation between years 4 and 5 would be so high as to increase the residual value to £400, but the same effect could well occur over an extended period of time.)

As can be seen from this example, the depreciation charged in years 1 to 4 has been adequate to write the asset down to its residual value, as expressed in terms of prices at the end of years 5 and 6. But the charge for depreciation has not been evenly spread because, in each year, residual values (and, therefore, the depreciation charge) is based on residual values determined as at the balance sheet date.

The charge for depreciation over the six years is, therefore, as follows (for comparison purposes, the charge as it would have been if future inflation had been taken into account is also shown):

	Effect of future inflation	
	Not assumed	Assumed
	£	£
Year 1	155	100
Year 2	155	100
Year 3	155	100
Year 4	135	100
Year 5	Nil	100
Year 6	Nil	100
Total	600	600

Estimates of useful lives

17.79 Useful life is defined as either:

- the period over which an asset is expected to be available for use by an entity; or

- the number of production or similar units expected to be obtained from the asset by an entity.

[FRS 102 Glossary of terms].

17.80 Generally, the former of these two will apply; this is because, in most cases, it is more straightforward to assess useful lives by reference to time periods. But, for some types of asset, usage might be a more reliable measurement. For example, a machine might have the capacity to produce 100,000 units before it wears out. In that case, the useful life could be set at 100,000 units. However, if the same machine can produce 20,000 units per year and is expected to operate at its full capacity, a useful life of five years might be used instead.

17.81 The definition of useful life includes the phrase 'expected to be available for use'. So, it is clear that the useful life includes any period after acquisition when the asset is capable of operating in the manner intended by management, but has not yet been brought into use. This is consistent with the time at which depreciation commences (see para 17.86 below).

17.82 It is also clear from the definition that an asset's useful life is the period over which the entity expects to consume economic benefits from the asset. A piece of machinery might be capable of producing a given product for many years, but the entity might not use the equipment for all that time because the cost of producing the product in later years is too high. So, the useful life will often be less than its physical life. If an entity intends to hold an asset for the asset's whole physical life, the asset would only be good for scrap (that is, it will have nil or a negligible residual value).

17023

17.83 Many entities have a policy of disposing of assets after a period of use, in which case the value of the asset at the end of that life will reflect the asset's remaining economic life, and might be of benefit to another user. This is often the case with company cars which are disposed of well before the end of their economic lives. In this situation, the useful life of the asset will be shorter than its economic life. The economic life is the total period over which the asset is capable of providing economic benefits, whether to the entity or to a subsequent owner.

17.84 Judgement is required in order to estimate the useful life of an asset. The standard provides the following guidance about the factors that an entity should consider in determining the useful life of an asset:

■ The expected usage of the asset (for example, usage is assessed by reference to the asset's expected capacity or physical output).

■ Expected physical wear and tear, which depends on operational factors such as the number of shifts for which the asset is to be used and the repair and maintenance programme, and the care and maintenance of the asset while idle.

■ Technical or commercial obsolescence arising from changes or improvements in production, or from a change in the market demand for the product or service output of the asset.

■ Legal or similar limits on the use of the asset, such as the expiry dates of related leases.

[FRS 102 para 17.21].

17.85 As described in paragraph 17.76 above, entities should assess whether indicators exist suggesting that the residual value or useful life of an asset has changed since the most recent financial reporting date. If such indicators exist, the entity should review its estimates for residual value, depreciation method and useful life of all items of PPE (and, therefore, all parts of them). Indicators include a change in how an asset is used, significant unexpected wear and tear, technological advancement and changes in market prices.

Commencement of depreciation

17.86 Depreciation of an asset begins when it is available for use (that is, when it is in the location and condition necessary for it to be capable of operating in the manner intended by management). This is the same point in time when the asset's useful life begins (as noted in para 17.81 above).

Example 2 – Depreciation charged from date when asset is ready for use

Entity B constructs a machine for its own use. Construction is completed on 1 November 20X6, but the entity does not begin using the machine until 1 March 20X7.

The entity should begin charging depreciation from the date when the machine is ready for use (that is, 1 November 20X6). This is also the date when the machine's useful life commences. The fact that the machine was not used for a period after it was available for use is not relevant in considering when to begin charging depreciation.

Cessation of depreciation

17.87 Depreciation of an asset ceases when the asset is derecognised. So, depreciation does not stop when an asset is idle or has been removed from active use unless the asset is fully depreciated. But, where the entity is using the usage method of depreciation (see para 17.93 below), the depreciation charge might be nil when there is no production. In any event, when an asset becomes idle, or is retired from use, this could raise questions as to whether the asset is impaired.

Methods of depreciation

17.88 An entity should select a depreciation method that reflects the pattern in which it expects to consume the asset's future economic benefits. There is a variety of acceptable depreciation methods. The standard does not prescribe any particular methods, but mentions straight-line, diminishing balance and units of production as possibilities. Whatever method is used, it should result in a fair depreciation charge that reflects the consumption of economic benefits provided by the asset over its useful life.

Example – Selection of a depreciation method

An entity uses an item of machinery in the production of hazardous chemicals. Industry regulations limit the output of the machine to one million litres, after which the machine must be decommissioned, decontaminated and recycled.

The entity projects that the output of the machine will reach one million litres within four years of its acquisition, at which time the machine will be decommissioned. The unit of production method is probably the most appropriate depreciation method for the entity to apply in depreciating the machine. This method reflects the pattern in which the entity expects to consume the asset's future economic benefits. Using this method, one millionth of the cost of the machine would be included in the cost of each litre of chemical produced by the machine. If usage varied from one period to the next, the straight-line method of depreciation would not reflect the pattern in which it expects to consume the machine's future economic benefits.

Straight-line method

17.89 This is the most common method used in practice, because of its simplicity. The straight-line method considers depreciation a function of time rather than a function of usage. It is the most appropriate method when the level of consumption of an asset's economic benefits is either constant over the years or cannot be readily ascertained. Straight-line depreciation results in a constant charge over the useful life of the asset. For example, a machine costing £1,000 has a residual value of £100 and a useful life of 10 years. The annual depreciation charge is £90 each year, that will reduce the cost to its residual value of £100 at the end of year 10.

Diminishing balance method

17.90 Under the diminishing balance method (or reducing balance method), depreciation is measured as a fixed percentage of the opening carrying amount of the asset at the start of each period, resulting in higher depreciation charges in the earlier years and lower charges in later periods. This method is appropriate where the economic benefits of an asset decline as they become older (for example, because the asset becomes less reliable and more likely to breakdown, less capable of producing a high-quality product, or less technologically advanced).

17.91 Using the above example, the machine would be depreciated at a fixed rate of 20.5% per annum, in order to reduce the carrying amount to the residual value of £100 at the end of 10 years, as shown below.

Example – Depreciation charged using the diminishing balance method

	Yr 1	Yr 2	Yr 3	Yr 4	Yr 5	Yr 6	Yr 7	Yr 8	Yr 9	Yr 10
	£	£	£	£	£	£	£	£	£	£
Cost	1,000	795	632	502	399	317	252	200	159	126
Depn @ 20.5%	205	163	130	103	82	65	52	41	33	26
NBV	795	632	502	399	317	252	200	159	126	100

Sum of the digits method

17.92 This method is not mentioned in the standard, but is similar in its effect to the diminishing balance method, although the mechanics are different. The method results in a depreciation charge for each year that is based on a fraction of depreciable cost (that is, original cost less residual value) of an asset. The denominator of the fraction is equal to the sum of the years of the asset's estimated useful life, and it is a constant. So, if an asset has a life of four years, the denominator is the sum $(4+3+2+1 = 10)$. The numerator is the number of years of estimated life remaining at the beginning of the year, and it decreases year by year. So, the method results in a decreasing depreciation charge based on a decreasing fraction (4/10, 3/10, 2/10 and 1/10). At the end of the asset's useful life, the balance remaining should equal the residual value. Using the same example as before, the depreciation calculation is shown below.

Example – Depreciation charged using the sum of the digits diminishing balance method

	Yr 1	Yr 2	Yr 3	Yr 4	Yr 5	Yr 6	Yr 7	Yr 8	Yr 9	Yr 10
	£	£	£	£	£	£	£	£	£	£
Cost	1,000	836	689	558	433	345	263	198	149	116
Deprn (£900 x F)	164	147	131	115	98	82	65	49	33	16
NBV	836	689	558	433	345	263	198	149	116	100
F = Fraction	10/55	9/55	8/55	7/55	6/55	5/55	4/55	3/55	2/55	1/55

Sum of the units (units of production) method

17.93 This method assumes that depreciation is a function of use or productivity, instead of the passage of time. The entity considers the useful life of the asset in terms of either the output (such as estimated total number of units produced) or an input measure based on usage (for example, estimated total number of hours worked). The rate of depreciation per hour of usage or unit of production is given by dividing the depreciable amount by the asset's estimated total service capability, measured in terms of hours or units. This method is sometimes employed where the asset's usage varies considerably from period to period because, in these circumstances, it matches cost against revenue more satisfactorily. Examples of the types of asset that are often depreciated in this way are (for hourly rates) airline engines, and (for unit of production) landfill sites, and oil and gas facilities.

Example 1 – Depreciation charged based on unit of production method

A machine cost £100,000 and its expected residual value is £10,000. The total usage of the machine is expected to be 500,000 hours. So, the depreciation rate per hour's usage is £0.18 (£100,000 – £10,000 divided by 500,000). If the entity uses the machine for 80,000 hours in the first year, the depreciation charge is £14,400 (£0.18 x 80,000).

> **Example 2 – Depreciation charged based on estimated usage**
>
> Costs amounting to £5m are incurred in acquiring a landfill site. The landfill site comprises 2 million cubic metres of space. The rate of depreciation to be applied to the cost of the site is worked out as £2.50 per cubic metre of space used. In the first year, 200,000 cubic metres are used up, and depreciation charged at £2.50 per cubic metre amounts to £500,000.

Change in depreciation method

17.94 The depreciation method at each annual reporting date should be reviewed, to determine if there has been a significant change in the pattern by which an entity expects to consume an asset's future economic benefits. A significant change would be unusual, because it would mean that the entity's previous method of providing depreciation (for example, units of production) no longer reflects the pattern of consumption of an asset's benefits, and a new method that does so should be selected. Still, if there has been such a change, the change in the depreciation charge resulting from the new method should be accounted for as a change in accounting estimate in accordance with section 10 of the standard. [FRS 102 para 17.23]. This means that the resulting depreciation adjustment should be made prospectively (that is, the asset's depreciable amount at the date of change should be written off over current and future periods).

17.95 An example that illustrates this treatment is as follows.

> **Example – Change in estimate of useful life**
>
> Entity A purchased an asset on 1 January 20X0 for £100,000 and the asset had an estimated useful life of 10 years and a residual value of nil. The entity has charged depreciation using the straight-line method at £10,000 per annum. On 1 January 20X4, when the asset's net book value is £60,000, the directors review the estimated life and decide that the asset will probably be useful for a further four years, and so the total life is revised to eight years. The entity should amend the annual provision for depreciation to charge the unamortised cost (namely, £60,000) over the revised remaining life of four years. As a result, it should charge depreciation for the next four years at £15,000 per annum.

17.96 Consequently, in the example above (but assuming that the life remains as ten years) the entity might decide that, from the beginning of year 4, the 'sum of the digits' method of calculation would give a fairer presentation than the straight-line method. If so, the depreciation charge for year 4 would be £171 (that is, £600 × 6/6 + 5 + 4 + 3 + 2 + 1), because the asset still has a remaining useful life of six years.

Depreciation of revalued assets

17.97 Depreciation is charged on revalued property, plant and equipment, with the exception of investment properties accounted for a fair value under section 16 of FRS 102.

17.98 The revalued amount of an item of property, plant and equipment is the basis for the carrying amount and depreciable amount of an asset. This is also in line with the requirements of the Companies Act. So, any references to cost in SI 2008/410's depreciation rules must be substituted by a reference to the value determined by the alternative accounting rules that the entity applied. [SI 2008/410 1 Sch 33(1)]. The asset's value determined according to the latest valuation is the basis for determining depreciation rather than the historical cost of the asset.

17.99 The standard does not specify what asset value should be used as the basis for calculating the year's depreciation charge. The average value for the year might be the best measure; but, in practice, either the opening or closing balance could be used, provided that it is used consistently in each period. The opening balance is most commonly used, together with the cost of subsequent additions, for determining the current year's depreciation charge. This avoids the need to recalculate depreciation charged in the earlier part of the year, used, for example, in interim reports, should the entity report on interim periods. But an issue could arise where there is a material change arising from the revaluation at the end of the year.

17.100 Even where an entity chooses the revaluation method, the depreciation charge should be recognised as an expense. [FRS 102 para 17.17]. No depreciation previously charged should be written back to profit or loss on revaluation of an asset. A depreciation charge is made, even if the value of an asset exceeds its carrying amount.

17.101 It should be noted that section 841(5) of the Companies Act 2006 has a bearing on the way in which entities should treat depreciation on revalued assets. This section says that, if the revaluation of an asset produces an unrealised profit, an amount equal to any excess depreciation charged as a result of the revaluation can be treated as a realised profit. This section is concerned only with determining the amount of distributable profits (and not with the accounting treatment of excess depreciation).

17.102 Depreciation based on the revalued amount of an asset must be charged to the income statement. But an entity could also transfer an amount equal to the excess depreciation from the revaluation reserve to retained earnings (as noted in para 17.67 above). Because the amount transferred from the revaluation reserve to retained earnings represents a realised profit, this treatment does not contravene paragraph 35(3) of Schedule 1 to SI 2008/410.

Treatment of accumulated depreciation when tangible assets are revalued

17.103 While not explicitly addressed in section 17 of FRS 102, accumulated depreciation is generally treated in one of two ways when an item of property, plant and equipment is revalued:

- Eliminated against the gross carrying amount of the asset, with the net amount restated to equal the revalued amount. This method is normally used for buildings.

- Restated proportionate to the change in the gross carrying amount of the asset, such that the net book value of the asset after revaluation equals its revalued amount.

17.104 The amount of the adjustment to accumulated depreciation forms part of the revaluation increase or decrease. The first method described above simply compares the revalued amount with the net book amount immediately before revaluation, and accounts for the difference as further described in paragraph 17.65 above.

17.105 The gain or loss on revaluation is calculated in the same way as the difference between the net carrying value immediately before revaluation and the revalued amount, if both the gross carrying amount and accumulated depreciation are restated. But the cost and accumulated depreciation carried forward after the revaluation could instead reflect the gross cost and accumulated depreciation used to determine depreciated replacement cost.

Example – Treatment of depreciation when asset is revalued using DRC method

Details of an item of property, plant and equipment before revaluation are as follows:

	£
Property, plant and equipment at cost	1,000
Accumulated depreciation	(400)
Net book amount	600

The property, plant and equipment is revalued to £1,500 on a DRC basis, consisting of £2,500 gross cost and £1,000 depreciation.

Details of the property, plant and equipment after revaluation on a DRC basis are as follows:

	£
Property, plant and equipment at cost	1,000
Increase on revaluation	1,500
Property, plant and equipment at revalued gross replacement cost	2,500
Accumulated depreciation	(400)
Decrease (that is, additional depreciation) on revaluation	(600)
Accumulated depreciation after revaluation	(1,000)

The increase on revaluation is £900 (namely, £1,500 — £600).

Impairment

17.106   An entity should refer to section 27 of FRS 102 to determine whether an item or group of items of property, plant and equipment is impaired. Section 27 of the standard explains when and how an entity reviews the carrying amount of its assets, how it determines the recoverable amount of an asset, and when it recognises and reverses an impairment loss. [FRS 102 para 17.24].

Compensation for impairment

17.107   Where an asset is impaired, lost or given up, any compensation from third parties is included in the income statement when the compensation is virtually certain. [FRS 102 para 17.25]. Examples include reimbursement from an insurance company for impairment or loss due to fire or theft etc, compensation from government for expropriation of assets or for compulsory purchase of property, and physical replacement in whole or in part of an impaired or lost asset. Compensation should be recognised in the income statement separately from impairment.

> **Example – Gain on replacement of insured assets**
>
> Entity A carried plant and machinery in its books at £200,000. These were destroyed in a fire. The assets were insured 'new for old' and were replaced by the insurance company with new machines that cost £2m. The machines were acquired by the insurance company, and the entity did not receive the £2m for their purchase.
>
> Entity A should account for a loss in the income statement on derecognition of the carrying value of plant and machinery. Entity A should separately recognise a receivable and a gain in the income statement resulting from the insurance proceeds once the proceeds are virtually certain. The receivable should be measured at the fair value of assets that will be provided by the insurer.

Property, plant and equipment held for sale

17.108   Where an entity intends to dispose of an asset prior to its expected date, this is an indicator of impairment. If there is impairment, the carrying amount of the asset would be written down to its recoverable amount. Depreciation should continue until the date of disposal, at which time the asset will be derecognised. Also, the fact that the entity intends to dispose of the asset might indicate that the asset's residual value or its remaining life needs adjustment, even if there is no impairment.

17.109   Unlike full IFRS, FRS 102 does not require entities to stop depreciating, and measure assets or groups of assets held for sale at the lower of carrying amount and the fair value less costs to sell, and present them as a separate category on the face of the balance sheet. However, an entity applying FRS 102 might consider presenting such assets under a new sub-heading 'assets held for resale' within property, plant and equipment, either in the balance sheet or in the notes if such sub-classification is considered relevant to an understanding of the entity's financial position. Moreover, in many situations, assets that are disposed of quickly, rather than held for disposal for some time, are simply retired from the line item in which they have been held during their life.

17.110 If, at the reporting date, an entity has a binding sale agreement for a major disposal of assets, a description of the facts and circumstances of the planned sale, and the carrying amount of the assets, is required to be disclosed. [FRS 102 para 4.14]. See chapter 4.

Derecognition

17.111 An entity should derecognise an item of property, plant and equipment:

■ on disposal; or

■ when no future economic benefits are expected from its use or disposal.

[FRS 102 para 17.27].

17.112 An entity should recognise the gain or loss on derecognition of an item of property, plant and equipment in the income statement when the item is derecognised (unless the transaction is a sale and leaseback, and deferral is required). The gain or loss is determined as the difference between the net disposal proceeds, if any, and the carrying amount of the item. Any gain arising on derecognition should not be classified as revenue. [FRS 102 paras 17.28, 17.30].

17.113 The date of disposal of an asset is determined by applying the revenue recognition criteria in section 23 of FRS 102. This will normally be the date when the risks and rewards of ownership of the asset are transferred to the buyer. But, if the disposal is by sale and leaseback, section 20 of the standard applies. [FRS 102 para 17.29].

17.114 Where assets are transferred from fixed to current assets, it is not appropriate to include the asset in the balance sheet at an amount that exceeds cost, unless it is disclosed as a current asset investment. This is because the alternative accounting rules can only be adopted for stocks and current asset investments, and not for other current asset items. [SI 2008/410 1 Sch 32(4)(5)].

Presentation and disclosure

Presentation

17.115 Section 4 of FRS 102 requires an entity, other than a banking entity or an insurance entity, to present a statement of financial position (also known as the balance sheet) in accordance with Schedule 1 to SI 2008/410. Additional line items can be presented if they are relevant to understanding the reporting entity's financial position. [FRS 102 paras 4.2, 4.3].

17.116 Schedule 1 to SI 2008/410 sets out standard presentation formats. The balance sheet formats identify the following sub-classifications of tangible assets and their constituent parts:

- Land and buildings.

- Plant and machinery.

- Fixtures, fittings, tools and equipment.

- Payments on account and assets in course of construction.

17.117 SI 2008/410 requires entities to use the headings and sub-headings prescribed in the formats, except in specified instances where the special nature of the entity's business requires their adaptation.

17.118 However, many entities face practical problems when categorising their tangible fixed assets into these four fairly restrictive headings. In particular, some entities find it difficult to decide whether particular assets should be described as 'plant and machinery' or 'fixtures, fittings, tools and equipment'. Some entities also have difficulty in deciding the category in which to include motor vehicles.

17.119 In practice, entities categorise their assets according to the nature of their particular business. As a general rule, entities treat major manufacturing assets (including motor vehicles involved in the manufacturing process, such as fork-lift trucks and cranes) as plant and machinery. They include other assets not involved in the manufacturing process in 'fixtures, fittings, tools and equipment'.

17.120 Because the Companies Act allows an entity to show any item in greater detail than the formats require, an entity could, for example, disclose the amount for motor vehicles as a sub-division of either 'plant and machinery' or 'fixtures, fittings, tools and equipment'. [SI 2008/410 1 Sch 3(1)]. But, where an asset does not fall under any of the headings given in the formats, paragraph 3(2) of Schedule 4 allows an entity to include the amount of it under a separate heading. So, for example, motor vehicles could be included in the balance sheet as a separate item.

17.121 FRS 102 requires disclosures to be given for each class of assets (see para 17.125 below), which might be narrower than the Act's categories of assets.

17.122 All impairments of tangible assets that are charged to the income statement represent permanent diminutions in value under the Act, and they should be charged in arriving at operating profit (generally under the same statutory format headings as depreciation).

Disclosure

17.123 An entity should disclose, either in the statement of financial position or in the notes, the sub-categories or class of property, plant and equipment that is appropriate to the entity. For each such class of property, plant and equipment, the following should be disclosed:

- the measurement bases used for determining the gross carrying amount;

- the depreciation methods used;

- the useful lives or depreciation rates used;

- the gross carrying amount and the accumulated depreciation (aggregated with accumulated impairment losses) at the beginning and end of the reporting period; and

- a reconciliation of the carrying amount at the beginning and end of the reporting period, showing separately:

    - additions;

    - disposals;

    - acquisitions through business combinations;

    - revaluations;

    - transfers to or from investment property, if a reliable measure of fair value becomes available or unavailable (see chapter 16);

    - impairment losses recognised or reversed in profit or loss in accordance with section 27 of FRS 102;

    - depreciation; and

    - other changes.

This reconciliation does not need to be presented for prior periods.

[FRS 102 para 17.31; SI 2008/410 1 Sch 51].

17.124 The entity should also disclose the following

- the existence and carrying amounts of property, plant and equipment to which the entity has restricted title or that is pledged as security for liabilities; and

- the amount of contractual commitments for the acquisition of property, plant and equipment.

17.125 If items of property, plant and equipment are stated at revalued amounts, the following should be disclosed:

- the effective date of the revaluation;

- whether an independent valuer was involved;

- the methods and significant assumptions applied in estimating the items' fair values; and

- for each revalued class of property, plant and equipment, the carrying amount that would have been recognised if the assets had been carried under the cost model.

[FRS 102 para 17.32A].

17.126 Disclosures in respect of land and buildings required by the Act should include an analysis of freehold, long leasehold and short leasehold. [SI 2008/410 1 Sch 53]. For this purpose, a lease includes an agreement for a lease. It will be a long lease if it still has 50 years or more to run at the end of the financial year in question. Otherwise, it will be a short lease. [SI 2008/410 10 Sch 7].

Disclosure requirements relating to the revaluation of assets under the Act

17.127 In Practice Statement 5 (PS 5), the RICS Appraisal and Valuation Standards set out minimum disclosures that should be made in a published document, such as an entity's financial statements, that make reference to a valuer's report. The disclosure requirements of section 17 of FRS 102 broadly encompass and expand on those laid down by the RICS and those of SI 2008/410, but should be given for each class of revalued assets. The disclosure requirements in respect of valuations are:

- The name and qualification of the valuer or the valuer's organisation and a description of its nature. [SI 2008/410 1 Sch 52; PS 5.11].

- Whether the valuer is internal or external. [PS 5.11].

- The date of the valuation. [SI 2008/410 1 Sch 52; PS 5.11].

- The amounts of the valuation. [SI 2008/410 1 Sch 52].

- The basis or bases of valuation (including whether notional acquisition costs have been included or expected selling costs deducted). [SI 2008/410 1 Sch 34, 52]. The RICS Appraisal and Valuation Standards require disclosure of the valuation basis, together with any special assumptions made. [PS 5.11].

- Comment on the extent to which the values were determined directly by reference to market evidence or were estimated using other valuation techniques. [PS 5.11].

- Where appropriate, confirmation that the valuation has been made in accordance with the RICS Appraisal and Valuation Standards, or the extent of and reasons for departure from those standards. [PS 5.11].

- Where historical cost records are available, the net carrying amount that would have been shown under the historical cost method less depreciation (see also para 16.206 onwards in chapter 16). [SI 2008/410 1 Sch 34(3)].

17.128 Either the balance sheet or the notes should disclose, in respect of every item affected by the alternative accounting rules (except inventories), one or other of the following amounts:

- The comparable amounts determined according to the historical cost convention.

- The differences between those comparable amounts and the actual amounts shown in the balance sheet.

[SI 2008/410 1 Sch 34(3)].

17.129   For this purpose, 'comparable amounts' means the aggregate amount that the entity would have shown if it had applied the historical cost convention and the aggregate amount of the cumulative provisions for depreciation or diminution in value that would have been permitted or required in determining those amounts according to that convention. [SI 2008/410 1 Sch 34(4)].

17.130   To illustrate the requirement in paragraph 17.128 above, consider the following example.

Example

Details of an entity's fixed assets are as follows:

	Cost £	Valuation £
Fixed assets	10,000	15,000
Accumulated depreciation	6,000	4,000
	4,000	11,000

If the entity records the fixed assets in the balance sheet at valuation, the effect of the Act's provisions is to require the balance sheet or the notes to the financial statements to state either the comparable amounts (namely, cost £10,000 and depreciation £6,000) or the difference between the comparable amounts and the amounts at which they are actually stated (namely, £5,000 and £2,000 respectively).

The historical cost net book amount (namely, £4,000) or the difference between the comparable net book amounts (namely, £7,000) is another interpretation of the amounts that are required to be disclosed. This latter disclosure is arguable, because the Act refers to the amounts stated in the balance sheet, and the amounts so stated will be the net book amounts of the assets.

17.131   SI 2008/410 also requires disclosure in the directors' report of any substantial differences between the market value of properties and their carrying value, if the directors think the difference is of such significance that readers of the financial statements should be made aware of it. This difference is likely to be significant where, for example:

- Land and buildings are held at historical cost (or frozen at their previous GAAP valuations), and market values have significantly increased or decreased since the date of acquisition (or last valuation).

- For many companies, property, plant and equipment will be being used for its highest and best use. However, if the alternative use value is higher this value shall be disclosed. In such circumstances, additional disclosure noting that the higher fair value would not take into account issues such as business closure or disruption and the associated costs that would be incurred in achieving the alternative use may be useful information for the reader to consider.

[SI 2008/410 1 Sch 34(3)].

17.132   The revaluation reserve must be shown on the face of the balance sheet as a separate amount, although it need not be shown under that name. [SI 2008/410 1 Sch 35(2)]. This concession is necessary for several reasons. For example, where current cost financial statements are being prepared, the revaluation reserve might be described as the 'unrealised current cost reserve'.

17.133   The taxation implications of a revaluation are required by the Act to be noted in the financial statements. [SI 2008/410 1 Sch 35(4)].

17.134   The Act says that, where the value of any fixed asset has been determined according to the alternative accounting rules, the amount of any provision for depreciation to be charged in the income statement could be either the amount based on the valuation of the asset, or the amount based on its historical cost. But, where the amount so charged is based on historical cost, the difference between that charge and the charge based on the asset's valuation must be disclosed separately. It must be so disclosed either on the face of the income statement or in the notes. [SI 2008/410 1 Sch 33(2)(3)].

Transitional issues

17.135   There are a number of matters that entities need to note when they transition to FRS 102. These matters affect the measurement of property, plant and equipment that the entity recognises in its opening balance sheet at the date of transition.

17.136   Where an entity applies the cost model it would recognise items of property, plant and equipment at their original cost (less accumulated depreciation and, if relevant, impairment) at the date of transition. But it might be difficult and costly to determine the original cost of long-lived items of property, plant and equipment, and so the standard provides a number of exemptions, which are explained below. Any adjustment between the previous carrying amounts and the FRS 102 carrying amounts should be recognised directly in retained earnings (or, if appropriate, another category of equity) at the date of transition.

Property, plant and equipment

Valuations as deemed cost

17.137 Section 35 of the standard permits an entity to elect to measure an item of property, plant and equipment at the date of transition at its fair value, and to use that fair value at its deemed cost at that date. [FRS 102 para 35.10(c)]. Fair value is defined as *"the amount at which an asset could be exchanged, a liability settled, or an equity instrument granted could be exchanged, between knowledgeable, willing parties in an arm's length transaction"*. [FRS 102 Glossary of terms].

17.138 Section 35 of the standard also permits an entity to elect to use a previous GAAP revaluation of an item of property, plant and equipment at, or before, the date of transition to be frozen and treated as deemed cost at the revaluation date. [FRS 102 para 35.10(d)]. But, where the date of valuation is before the date of transition, the deemed cost should be depreciated from the valuation date. Estimates made to calculate the depreciation rate (such as residual values and useful lives) under old UK GAAP need not be revised. So entities will be able to use old UK GAAP revaluations or carry out fair value assessments at the transition date to create deemed cost on transition.

17.139 Whichever option the entity chooses, the question arises as to how any revaluation reserve under old UK GAAP that relates to the asset when deemed cost is determined should be treated. Section 35 of the standard does not specifically deal with this issue.

17.140 Where an entity will apply the cost model under FRS 102, in order to comply with the Act, an entity would retain the revaluation reserve arising under old UK GAAP that has been discussed in paragraph 17.67. Even though the entity applies the cost model under FRS 102, in terms of the Act, the entity still has revalued assets and so the disclosure requirements for the alternative accounting rules under the Act must be complied with on an ongoing basis. The Act's disclosure requirements are:

- The amounts of fixed assets held at valuation, the years of valuation, and the basis adopted.

- The historical cost equivalents for revalued assets.

- The amount of a revaluation reserve and any transfers from that reserve to realised reserves.

[SI 2008/410 1 Sch 34, 35, 52].

17.141 Where an entity will apply the revaluation model under FRS 102, it is our view that, where an asset has been revalued under FRS 15 and will continue to be revalued under FRS 102, it has a cost rather than a deemed cost, and the amount of the revaluation surplus disclosed should be based on the asset's original cost. UK entities are required by law to disclose the cost of revalued assets, and so they are able to carry forward any pre-existing revaluation reserve when moving to FRS 102 for those categories of asset that are to be revalued.

Component depreciation

17.142   Component depreciation is discussed in paragraph 17.73 above. FRS 102 takes a more prescriptive approach than old UK GAAP, so it seems likely that some entities will need to apply component accounting more extensively than they had done previously.

Residual values

17.143   In practice, the residual value of an asset is often not significant enough to affect materially the calculation of the depreciable amount. Residual value was based on prices at the date of acquisition or later revaluation. As noted in paragraph 17.78 above, the residual value under FRS 102 is calculated by reference to prices current at the reporting date. This means that, over time, residual value will change with prices under FRS 102 (but this was not the case under old UK GAAP as the effect is most pronounced for appreciating assets, such as buildings. In such a situation, first-time adopters should adjust the residual values of their assets at the date of transition to FRS 102, and then apply the procedure described in paragraph 17.78 above to determine the amended depreciation that this implies from the date of transition.

Renewals accounting

17.144   Renewals accounting is unlikely to be relevant to most UK entities transitioning to this standard. It is generally relevant to large infrastructure systems or networks, as typically found in the water industry, but it is discussed here for completeness. Briefly, under renewals accounting, the level of annual expenditure required to maintain the operating capacity of the infrastructure assets (regarded as one asset rather than definable major components with determinable finite lives) is treated as the depreciation charged for the period, and it is deducted from the carrying amount of the asset (as part of accumulated depreciation). Actual expenditure is capitalised as part of the cost of the asset as incurred. And the carrying amount of the part of the infrastructure that is replaced or restored by subsequent expenditure is removed by applying estimates based on the percentage of the system that is replaced each year.

17.145   Renewals accounting is not acceptable under FRS 102, which requires the cost or fair value of fixed assets to be depreciated over the expected useful life, but was permitted under old UK GAAP. In many cases, the actual cost of infrastructure assets is not known, through a combination of the assets being very old and the entities having been in the public sector, where fixed assets were not recorded. The 'fair value as deemed cost' exemption (discussed in para 17.138 above) grants some relief to first-time adopters. Entities will be allowed to record fixed assets at fair value at the date of transition, with the fair value becoming deemed cost, but there could be some practical difficulties in valuing the entire infrastructure network and then establishing an appropriate residual value and depreciable life.

Chapter 18

Intangible assets other than goodwill

Intangible assets other than goodwill

Chapter 18

Intangible assets other than goodwill

Introduction and scope

18.1 This chapter considers the accounting treatment for intangible assets. The principal issues considered are the nature, identification and recognition of intangible assets, initial measurement and measurement subsequent to initial recognition, determination of useful lives and amortisation methods. It does not deal with impairment of intangible assets, which is dealt with in chapter 27.

18.2 Section 18 of FRS 102 covers all intangible assets that are not addressed by other sections of the standard, but specifically excludes the following:

- Goodwill (dealt with in chapter 19).

- Deferred acquisition costs and intangible assets arising from contracts in the scope of FRS 103, 'Insurance contracts' (except for the disclosure requirements in this section which apply to intangible assets arising from contracts in the scope of FRS 103). This standard does apply to deferred acquisition costs that are not in scope of FRS 103.

- Intangible assets held for sale in the ordinary course of business (dealt with in chapters 13 and 23).

- Financial assets (dealt with in chapters 11 and 12).

- Mineral rights and mineral reserves, such as oil, natural gas and similar non-regenerative resources (see section 34 of FRS 102).

- Heritage assets (see section 34 of FRS 102).

[FRS 102 paras 18.1, 18.3].

18.3 An entity might be engaged in the sale of licences to third parties. Although each licence meets the definition of an intangible asset (as discussed below), they are classified as inventories and not intangible assets, because they are held for sale in the ordinary course of business.

18.4 The distinction between an intangible asset and a financial asset might be difficult to determine in practice. Generally, an intangible asset derives its value from the rights and privileges granted to the entities using it, whereas a financial asset derives its value from the right (claim) to receive cash or cash equivalents in the future.

> **Example 1 – Purchase of the rights to a proportion of a football club's revenue as opposed to the rights to sell the underlying tickets**
>
> An entity that purchases the rights to a proportion of the revenue that a football club generates from ticket sales will generally have acquired a financial asset as opposed to an intangible asset. Where the entity has no discretion over the pricing or selling of the tickets, and is only entitled to the cash generated from the sale of tickets, this would represent a financial asset, being a contractual right to receive cash. If, on the other hand, an entity has purchased the rights to sell tickets for a football club and is responsible for selling the tickets itself to generate revenue, this would represent an intangible asset.

> **Example 2 – Royalty income on intellectual property**
>
> An entity that creates and capitalises intellectual property such as patents grants the rights to use that intellectual property to a third party for a fee. That fee may be a proportion of the third parties revenue or may be a fixed periodic fee. Despite the fact that the entity is only entitled to a contractual right to receive cash as in the above example, the royalty income stream would not be a financial asset. This is because the royalty income represents economic benefits generated by the intellectual property which is already recognised as an intangible asset.

18.5   An entity might enter into a lease in respect of an intangible asset. If such a lease is determined to be a finance lease in accordance with section 20 of FRS 102, the underlying intangible asset after initial recognition is accounted for in accordance with section 18 of the standard. However, some rights are specifically excluded from the scope of section 20, including rights under licensing agreements for such items as motion picture films, video recordings, plays, manuscripts, patents and copyrights. Such licensing agreements are accounted for as intangible assets in accordance with section 18. [FRS 102 para 20.1(b)].

18.6   As noted in paragraph 18.2 above, section 18 of FRS 102 does not apply to expenditure incurred in the development and extraction of minerals, oil, natural gas and similar non-regenerative resources; this is because these activities are so specialised that they give rise to their own accounting issues. However, section 18 does apply to any other non-specialised intangible assets (for example, computer software) used in such activities. [FRS 102 para 34.11].

Characteristics of intangible assets

Definition

18.7   Intangible asset is defined as *"an identifiable non-monetary asset without physical substance"*. [FRS 102 para 18.2].

18.8 There are many different types of intangible asset, often classified into categories such as:

- Contract-related intangible assets (for example, licensing agreements, franchises, broadcast rights, and service or supply contracts).

- Market-related intangible assets (for example, trademarks or trade names, newspaper mastheads, quotas, market share, marketing rights and non-competition agreements).

- Customer-related intangible assets (for example, customer lists, order or production backlogs, and both contractual and non-contractual customer relationships).

- Technology-related intangible assets (for example, computer software, patented technology over innovations or technological advances).

- Artistic-related intangible assets (for example, ownership rights to plays, literary works, musical works, motion pictures, video and audio-visual material that are protected by copyrights).

- Goodwill (see chapter 19).

18.9 All the categories of intangible asset identified above (note that the list is by no means exhaustive) have the following key characteristics:

- identifiability;

- non-monetary asset (the definition of which encompasses 'control'); and

- lack of physical substance.

Identifiability

18.10 For physical assets, identifiability is straightforward, because it can be seen. For intangible assets, identifiability is more difficult and requires clear and practicable principles. An intangible asset is identifiable when:

- it is separable (that is, it is capable of being separated or divided from the entity and sold, transferred, licensed, rented or exchanged, either individually or together with a related contract, asset or liability), or

- it arises from contractual or other legal rights, regardless of whether those rights are transferable or separable from the entity or from other rights and obligations.

[FRS 102 para 18.2].

18.11 All assets that are separable, as defined above, are identifiable. This property of identifiability results in the recognition of intangible assets acquired in a business combination separately from goodwill.

18.12 However, separability is not the only indication of identifiability. Assets that arise from contractual or legal rights are also identifiable, even if they cannot be separated from the business. For example, a taxi licence that is needed to operate a vehicle as a taxi is identifiable because it arises from legal rights, even though the licence is not usually separable from the underlying taxi business, since it can only be transferred to other taxi operators.

18.13 The identifiability criterion is often the key factor in deciding whether an intangible asset should be recognised; this is because, if the asset is not separable or does not arise from legal rights, it is unlikely to meet the definition of an intangible asset. The same rights that demonstrate separability might also demonstrate control (see para 18.15 below).

Non-monetary asset (control)

18.14 Intangible assets are defined as being non-monetary. A non-monetary asset is an asset that is neither currency held nor an asset to be received in a fixed or determinable amount of money.

18.15 The definition of an asset encompasses control of a resource as a result of past events and from which future economic benefits are expected to flow to the entity. [FRS 102 para 2.15]. Control exists when the entity has the power to obtain the economic benefits that the asset will generate and to restrict the access of others to those benefits. In the context of an intangible asset, control is usually achieved through legal rights, such as those arising from a copyright, trademark or licence.

18.16 In the absence of legal rights, it is more difficult to demonstrate control. However, legal enforceability of a right is not a necessary condition for control, because an entity might be able to control the future economic benefits merely through custody. For example, control over the benefits of an intellectual property or know-how might be attained through secrecy.

18.17 Some intangible assets might be valuable to the entity, but the entity is unable to control the future economic benefits. For instance, an entity benefits from having a team of skilled workers or staff with specific management or technical talents, but is usually unable to exercise sufficient control over the workforce (that is, they can leave their employment) for it to be recognised as an intangible asset.

18.18 Customer relationships are another type of intangible asset where the issue of control presents challenges. For example, where an entity establishes relationships with its customers through fixed-term contracts, and those contracts contain legally enforceable contractual rights to future revenue (over which the entity has control), the definition of an intangible asset will be met. However, in the absence of legal rights to protect or control the relationship of customers, the entity usually has insufficient control over these items to meet the definition of intangible assets.

18.19 Nevertheless, even if an asset on its own is not separable or does not arise from contractual or legal rights, as in the case of non-contractual customer relationships (outside business combinations), it could meet the definition of an intangible asset if there are exchange transactions (for example, sale of the asset to third parties) for the same or similar non-contractual customer relationships. Such exchange transactions provide evidence that the asset is separable (a criterion for identifiability), because the entity is able to control the future economic benefits flowing from the customer relationships. However, the incidence of exchange transactions for non-contractual customer relationships is rare in practice.

18.20 It is worthwhile noting here that intangible assets should only be recognised where they meet the definition of an intangible asset and the applicable recognition criteria. For instance, expenditure incurred during the research phase of internally generated intangible assets is not recognised as an asset.

Lack of physical substance

18.21 Another essential characteristic of an intangible asset is that it lacks physical substance that is typical for a tangible asset. However, an intangible asset is often contained in or on a physical substance. Where this is the case, it might be difficult to categorise the asset as tangible or intangible. Examples are a DVD that contains computer software, legal documentation that evidences a patent or a licence, a building to which a trading licence attaches, a memory stick containing a film recording, or a computer system containing a database. The physical and non-physical elements might be incapable of separation in these instances, and judgement is required to determine which element is the more significant. For example, if a computer-controlled machine cannot operate without a particular piece of software, the specific software is regarded an integral part of the related hardware, and it is treated as property, plant and equipment (in accordance with section 17 of FRS 102). The same applies to the operating system of a computer. However, where the software is not an integral part of the related hardware, computer software is treated as an intangible asset.

18.22 There might also be situations where, although the tangible and intangible elements cannot operate independently of each other, their costs are each significant. It might be appropriate to account for each element separately in this case. For example, a database might be contained on expensive computer hardware, and the costs of the hardware are separately identifiable from those of the database. Each element might have a different useful life (for example, the hardware might become obsolete and the database could be transferred to another computer system). It is appropriate in this situation to account separately for the two components of the computer database, classifying the hardware as tangible and the database itself as intangible, because they are both significant components.

Recognition and initial measurement

18.23 Section 18 of FRS 102 sets out general principles for the recognition and measurement of intangible assets. It then considers in detail the following situations in which an entity obtains an intangible asset:

- By separate acquisition.

- As part of a business combination

- By exchange for other non-monetary assets.

- By way of a government grant.

- By developing or generating the assets internally.

18.24   The criteria for recognition are applied somewhat differently in each of the above situations. This is because the extent and reliability of the evidence available to the entity, in determining whether or not the criteria are met, vary depending on which situation is involved. For example, in each of the first three situations, there is an exchange transaction, which gives evidence that economic benefits are likely to flow to the entity.

General recognition principles

18.25   The recognition criteria for intangible assets are derived from the general principles for asset recognition established in section 2 of FRS 102. An intangible asset should be recognised as an asset if, and only if:

- it is probable that future economic benefits that are attributable to the asset will flow to the entity; and

- the cost or value of the asset can be measured reliably.

[FRS 102 para 18.4].

18.26   'Probable' is defined as 'more likely than not'. [FRS 102 Glossary of terms]. Therefore, if management considers it more likely than not that expected future economic benefits will flow to the entity, and this can be substantiated, this criterion will be met.

18.27   Future economic benefits include not only future revenues from the sale of products or services but also cost savings. For example, intellectual property used in a production process might reduce future production costs rather than increasing future revenues.

18.28   An entity should assess the probability of expected future economic benefits using reasonable and supportable assumptions. These assumptions should represent management's best estimate of the set of economic conditions that will prevail over the asset's useful life. [FRS 102 para 18.5]. Judgement is required in assessing the degree of certainty to attach to the flow of economic benefits expected from the asset's use, based on evidence available at the date of initial recognition. Management should place greater reliance on external evidence. [FRS 102 para 18.6].

18.29   The reference to the need to give greater weight to external evidence is important. Exchange transactions (referred to in para 18.19 above) provide external evidence of the expected future economic benefits, but other external evidence might include industry forecasts, market and competitor analysis provided by external experts, as well as general information on expected inflation and country growth rates.

18.30   Furthermore, the nature of many intangible assets is that there are often no additions to the asset or replacements of parts of it. Therefore, most subsequent expenditure is likely to be incurred in maintaining the expected future economic benefits embodied in an existing intangible asset, rather than in a way that meets the criteria for recognition as an asset. In addition, it is often difficult to attribute subsequent expenditure to a particular intangible asset rather than to the business as a whole. Most subsequent expenditure will, therefore, not qualify as an asset and will be expensed as incurred.

18.31   Consistent with the requirements in respect of initial recognition, subsequent expenditure on brands, mastheads, publishing titles, customer lists, and items that are similar in substance, is always expensed as incurred, because such subsequent expenditure cannot be distinguished from developing the business as a whole. This applies whether these intangible assets are acquired separately or in a business combination.

Initial measurement

18.32   Intangible assets should be measured on initial recognition at cost. [FRS 102 para 18.9]. Cost is defined as the amount of cash or cash equivalents paid, or the fair value of other consideration given, to acquire an asset at the time of its acquisition or construction.[FRS 102 para 2.24].

18.33   If payment for an intangible asset is deferred beyond normal credit terms, the asset's cost is its cash price equivalent, which is the discounted amount. The difference between this amount and the total payment is treated as interest payable over the period of credit.

Specific recognition and measurement requirements

Separate acquisition

Recognition criteria

18.34   The probability recognition criterion (referred to in the first bullet point of para 18.25 above) is always considered satisfied for intangible assets that are separately acquired. [FRS 102 para 18.7]. This is because the price that an entity pays to acquire an intangible asset separately will normally reflect expectations about the probability that the expected future economic benefits of the asset will flow to the entity. In other words, the entity expects there to be an inflow of economic benefits, even if there is uncertainty about the timing or the amount of the inflow. The greater the price paid, the higher the expectations of future economic benefits to be derived from the asset.

Measurement at cost

18.35 An intangible asset should be measured at cost. [FRS 102 para 18.9]. Measurement of cost is normally straightforward, because it is generally the price paid.

18.36 The cost of a separately acquired intangible asset comprises:

- the purchase price, including import duties and non-refundable purchase taxes (trade discounts and rebates are deducted in arriving at the purchase price); plus

- any directly attributable costs of preparing the asset for its intended use.

[FRS 102 para 18.10].

18.37 Examples of directly attributable costs of preparing the asset for its intended use are:

- costs of employee benefits (as defined in section 28 of FRS 102) arising directly from bringing the asset to its working condition;

- professional fees arising directly from bringing the asset to its working condition; and

- costs of testing whether the asset is functioning properly.

18.38 Examples of expenditures that does not form part of the cost of an intangible asset are:

- costs of introducing a new product or service (including costs of advertising and promotional activities);

- costs of conducting business in a new location or with a new class of customer (including costs of staff training); and

- administration and other general overhead costs.

18.39 Recognition of costs in the carrying amount of an intangible asset ceases when the asset is in the condition necessary for it to be capable of operating in the manner intended by management. Consequently, costs incurred in using or redeploying an intangible asset are not included in the carrying amount of that asset. This includes any incidental costs that are incurred while an asset is capable of operating in the manner intended by management and any initial operating losses, such as those that might be incurred while demand builds up for the asset's output.

Example – Measurement of intangible assets acquired separately

On 1 January 20X1, an entity purchased a new software package to operate its production equipment for £600,000, including £50,000 refundable purchase taxes. The purchase price was funded by incurring a loan of £605,000 (including £5,000 loan origination fees). The loan is secured against the software licences.

In January 20X1, the entity incurred the following costs in customising the software, so that it is more suited to the systems used by the entity:

- Labour – £120,000
- Depreciation of plant and equipment used to perform the modifications – £15,000.

In January 20X1, the entity's production staff were trained in how to operate the new software. Training costs included:

- Cost of an expert external instructor – £7,000
- Labour – £3,000.

In February 20X1, the entity's production team tested the software, and the information technology team made further modifications necessary to get the new software to function as intended by management.

The following costs were incurred in the testing phase:

- Material, net of £3,000 recovered from the sale of the scrapped output – £21,000
- Labour – £11,000
- Depreciation of plant and equipment while it was used to perform the modifications – £5,000.

The new software was ready for use on 1 March 20X1. However, because of low initial order levels, the entity incurred a loss of £23,000 on operating the software during March.

Expenditure that should be included in the cost of the intangible asset at initial recognition is as follows:

	£
Purchase price of £600,000 less refundable tax of £50,000:	550,000
The asset was not purchased on deferred credit terms, but funded by a loan. Hence, loan origination fees are included in the initial recognition of the liability.	
Directly attributable costs of preparing the asset for its intended use include: Customisation costs (labour £120,000, depreciation £15,000)	135,000
Cost of testing (material net £21,000, labour £11,000, depreciation £5,000)	37,000
Costs included in intangible asset at initial recognition	722,000
Training costs and initial operating losses are written off as incurred.	

18.40 In some situations, the determination of cost might cause problems in practice, where the consideration paid for an intangible asset is wholly or partly variable. Consider the following example.

> **Example – Acquisition of a licence for variable consideration**
>
> Entity A acquires a five-year licence to use patented technology owned by another entity. The technology is used in the production of specialised equipment. The consideration consists of an upfront payment of £10,000, and £40,000 due in one year's time. In addition, entity A is also required to pay 10% of its annual sales of specialised equipment in each year of the five-year term of the licence. Entity A estimates that annual sales are expected to be £500,000, increasing by 5% each year, for the following five years.
>
> The cost of entity A's licence should be based on the fixed upfront payment of £10,000 plus the present value of £40,000 payable in one year's time. The variable payment based on sales is akin to a royalty payable and is not a present obligation of entity A. Hence, these costs should be expensed as incurred, rather than included in the cost of the intangible asset to be amortised over the five-year term of the licence.

Assets acquired in a business combination

Recognition criteria

18.41 Section 19 of FRS 102 stipulates that, if an intangible asset is acquired in a business combination, the cost of that intangible asset is its fair value at the acquisition date. The fair value of an intangible asset, like an arm's length price, reflects expectations about the probability that the future economic benefits of the asset will flow to the entity. So, the probability criterion for recognition is always assumed to have been satisfied for intangible assets acquired in a business combination.

18.42 Therefore, an intangible asset acquired in a business combination is normally recognised as an asset separately from goodwill, because its fair value can be measured with sufficient reliability. [FRS 102 para 18.8]. This applies irrespective of whether the asset was previously recognised by the acquiree. This will include any in-process research and development project of the acquiree, if the project meets the definition of an intangible asset and its fair value can be measured reliably.

18.43 The only circumstances in which it might not be possible to measure reliably the fair value of an intangible asset acquired in a business combination are where the intangible asset arises from legal or contractual rights and there is no history or evidence of exchange transactions for the same or similar assets, and otherwise estimating fair value would be dependent on immeasurable variables. [FRS 102 para 18.8].

18.44 Many different types of intangibles (such as those noted in para 18.8 above) might be acquired in a business combination. Sometimes, it could be extremely difficult not only to identify particular types of intangibles but also to assign a value to them in a business combination. As a result, entities only record identifiable intangible assets that they can reliably measure (as noted above).

18.45 An example dealing with customer loyalty programmes is given below.

> **Example – Customer-related intangible assets acquired in a business combination**
>
> Entity A acquired another entity that operates a successful customer loyalty programme. Under the programme, customers receive a registration number and a membership card which accumulates points based on purchase values. These points can be exchanged for discounts on future purchases.
>
> The relationship established by the acquiree with its customers who have subscribed to the loyalty programme arises from contractual rights, because the parties have agreed to a number of terms and conditions, or have had a previous contractual relationship, or both. As the customer loyalty programme arises from a contractual or legal right, it can only be recognised as an intangible asset if there is history or evidence of exchange for the same or similar assets. So, the relationship meets the contractual-legal criterion for recognition of an intangible asset and, if its fair value can be determined reliably, entity A recognises an intangible asset separately from goodwill.

Measurement at fair value

18.46 The cost of an intangible asset acquired in a business combination is its fair value at the acquisition date. Fair value is defined as *"the amount for which an asset could be exchanged, a liability settled, or an equity instrument granted could be exchanged, between knowledgeable, willing parties in an arm's length transaction"*. [FRS 102 Glossary of terms]. The guidance for measuring fair values is provided in paragraphs 11.27 to 11.32 of the standard. Although chapter 11 of the standard deals with financial instruments, the fair value measurement methodology discussed therein could be applied to any asset for which fair value is required to be determined under FRS 102.

18.47 Where intangibles are traded on an active market, the quoted market prices provide the best evidence of fair value. Examples of intangible assets that might be quoted in an active market include emission rights, taxi licences, fishing licences or production quotas, such as milk quotas. However, many intangible assets acquired in a business combination are unlikely to have a quoted market price. For instance, an active market cannot exist for brands, newspaper mastheads, music and film publishing rights, patents or trademarks, because each such asset is unique.

18.48 Similarly, in the majority of cases, there are unlikely to be identical assets with observable prices that can be relied on to estimate the fair value of the acquired intangible assets in a business combination. Identifying similar assets (that is, similar in terms of intended use, useful economic life, pattern of cash flows, risk and opportunities, and so on) for which observable prices exist can also be difficult, since the majority of asset acquisitions are 'private' transactions, and information is not publicly available. In addition, making adjustments to observable prices, so that they can be used to assess the value of the acquired intangible asset, can be highly subjective.

18.49 So, it is expected that, in the majority of cases, the fair value of an intangible asset will need to be measured using valuation techniques. Some entities that buy and sell unique intangible assets might have developed techniques for estimating the fair value of such assets indirectly. These techniques could be used to value intangible assets acquired in a business combination if they are consistent with current transactions and practices in the industry to which the intangible asset relates. These techniques include:

■ Estimating the hypothetical costs that the entity avoids by owning the intangible asset and not needing to:

■ license it from another party in an arm's length transaction (as in the 'relief from royalty' approach); or

■ recreate or replace it (as in the 'cost' approach).

■ Discounting estimated future net cash flows from the asset.

Measuring fair value is complex, and entities might need to use external valuation specialists.

Acquisition by way of a government grant

Recognition criteria

18.50 An intangible might be acquired free of charge, or for nominal consideration, by way of a government grant. Where an intangible asset is acquired by way of a government grant, there is no exchange transaction. Assets that might be acquired through government grant include airport landing rights, emission rights, radio or television station operating licences, import licences and quotas.

18.51 No reference is made in section 18 of FRS 102 to the application of the recognition criteria for intangible assets acquired by way of a government grant. However, a non-monetary grant at fair value is recognised in income only when any performance conditions attaching to the grant are met or immediately if there are no performance conditions; and grants received before the revenue recognition criteria are met are recognised as a liability. [FRS 102 para 24.5B].

Measurement at fair value

18.52 The cost of an intangible asset acquired by way of a government grant is its fair value at the date the grant is received or receivable in accordance with section 24 of the standard. [FRS 102 para 18.12]. This applies even though government grants are sometimes received for nil or nominal consideration. Fair value is determined using an appropriate method.

Exchanges of assets

Recognition criteria

18.53 An intangible asset might be acquired in exchange for a non-monetary asset or assets, or a combination of monetary and non-monetary assets. The probability recognition criteria for intangible assets acquired separately in exchange for a non-monetary asset are deemed to be satisfied, as in the acquisition for monetary consideration. The asset acquired in a non-monetary exchange is measured at fair value, and the fair value reflects expectations about the probability of future economic benefits flowing to the entity. However, this assumes that the exchange transaction has commercial substance.

Measurement at fair value

18.54 An intangible asset acquired in an exchange for a non-monetary asset, or a combination of non-monetary and monetary assets, should be recognised initially at its fair value, unless:

- the exchange transaction lacks commercial substance, or

- the fair value of neither the asset received nor the asset given up is reliably measurable.

[FRS 102 para 18.13].

18.55 Generally, if the fair value of either the asset received or the asset given up is reliably measurable, entities account for the exchange transaction on the basis of the fair value of the asset given up, unless the fair value of the asset received is more clearly evident. Thus, entities should recognise immediately any gains or losses on the exchange. The rationale for immediate recognition of gains or losses is that most transactions have commercial substance, and so such gains or losses should be recognised.

> **Example – Exchange of patents**
>
> Entity A is the holder of a patent with a carrying amount of £3,000. Entity A agreed to exchange its patent for that of entity B. The fair value of entity A's patent has been assessed by both parties at £5,000. Entity B's patent cannot be measured reliably. No additional monetary or non-monetary consideration has been included in the exchange.
>
> Entity A will record its acquired patent at a cost of £5,000, because the asset's fair value that can be measured reliably is used by both parties as the value of the consideration if the fair value of the other asset cannot be measured reliably. A gain arises on the transaction of £2,000, being the difference between the carrying amount of entity A's original patent (£3,000) and the fair value of the patent given up (£5,000), and is recognised by entity A in the income statement. Patents are inherently unique, and so the exchange has commercial substance.

18.56 Where the consideration received or given comprises a combination of non-monetary and monetary assets, the fair value is adjusted by the amount of the monetary assets (for example, cash) given or received.

> **Example – Exchange of distribution rights in a region for cash and distribution rights in another region**
>
> An entity exchanges the rights to distribute a product in Japan that have a carrying amount of £1m (fair value of £1.2m) for £0.5m cash and the rights to distribute the same product in Europe, which are fair valued at £0.7m. The cash of £0.5m is effectively the difference between the fair value of the exchanged assets (£1.2m – £0.7m). The European distribution rights are, therefore, recorded at £0.7m, which is equivalent to the fair value of the Japanese rights of £1.2m less the cash received of £0.5m. A gain of £0.2m arises on the transaction and is recognised in the income statement.

18.57 However, if neither the fair value of the asset received nor the fair value of the asset given up is reliably measurable, which should be rare in practice, the acquired item is measured at the carrying amount of the asset given up. This measurement basis also applies if the exchange transaction lacks commercial substance.

18.58 An exchange transaction lacks commercial substance if the economic positions of the two parties to the exchange transaction do not change (that is, the parties are in the same economic position before and after the exchange transaction). This will be generally evident if the configuration of the cash flows of the asset received does not differ from the configuration of the cash flows of the asset given up. 'Configuration of the cash flows' in this sense means the risk, amount and timing of the cash flows. Consider the following example.

> **Example – Exchange of licences to provide telephone services**
>
> An entity acquired a licence from the government to provide fixed telecommunication services four years ago. The government has now offered to exchange the original licence for another that will allow the entity to operate both fixed and mobile services. The entity's management has accepted the offer of exchange. Management does not believe that there is sufficient demand for mobile phone services by the country's residents at the present time to make the venture profitable and does not intend to provide this facility in the near future. Management believes that the exchange lacks commercial substance and proposes to record the acquired licence using the carrying value of the licence given up.
>
> The transaction has commercial substance. The new licence provides management with the ability to obtain additional cash flows from the provision of mobile phone services. The decision not to capitalise on this opportunity is not relevant. The potential cash flows from the provision of mobile phone services will significantly increase the fair value of the new licence over that of the old fixed line licence. The new licence should be recorded at its fair value. The old licence should be derecognised, with any difference between the carrying amount of the old licence and the fair value of the new licence recognised in the income statement.

18014

Internally generated intangible assets

18.59 Intangible assets that are developed or generated internally must satisfy the recognition criteria if they are to be regarded as intangible assets. It is sometimes difficult to determine whether the cost incurred can be recognised as an intangible asset; this is because of problems in identifying and reliably measuring the costs associated with the particular intangible asset, and in determining the magnitude of the future benefits and length of time over which such benefits might be realised.

18.60 Generally, the difficulties associated with identifying internally generated intangible assets, and with satisfying the recognition and measurement criteria, mean that such assets either are indistinguishable from the rest of the business or cannot be reliably measured. So, there are specific procedures that must be followed to determine whether specified internally generated intangible assets can be recognised. There is an outright prohibition on recognising specific types of intangible asset where the recognition criteria can never be satisfied.

18.61 There are detail rules for determining whether an internally generated intangible asset should be recognised. These rules preclude recognition of internally generated intangible assets except development expenditures. For development expenditures, in addition to complying with the general requirements for the recognition and initial measurement of an intangible asset, the stringent conditions set out in paragraph 18.8H of FRS 102 must also be met before internally generated development expenditure can be capitalised.

Research and development

18.62 The process of generating an intangible asset is divided into a research phase and a development phase. If the two phases are indistinguishable, all of the expenditure on the asset should be attributed to the research phase. [FRS 102 para 18.8B].

18.63 'Research' is defined as *"original and planned investigation undertaken with the prospect of gaining new scientific or technical knowledge and understanding"*; and 'development' is defined as *"the application of research findings or other knowledge to a plan or design for the production of new or substantially improved materials, devices, products, processes, systems or services before the start of commercial production or use"*. [FRS 102 Glossary of terms]. The terms 'research phase' and 'development phase' have a broader meaning and are applied to a single project to distinguish the period of time and the quantum of the total project cost that is attributable to each type of activity.

18.64 Examples of research activities include:

■ Activities aimed at obtaining new knowledge, such as biotechnology research aimed at discovering how the presence of particular genes might affect the incidence of particular illnesses in humans.

- Searching for suitable applications of research findings or other knowledge, evaluating the applications and making a final selection of suitable applications (for example, determining whether the discovery of the effect of a particular interaction of chemicals might be used in developing a treatment for a particular disease, using criteria that include the treatment's likely effectiveness, cost, and the alternative existing treatments available).

- Searching for alternatives for materials, devices, products, processes, systems or services (for example, searching for alternatives that are more ecologically friendly as part of an entity's efforts to improve its corporate social responsibility).

[FRS 102 para 18.8G].

18.65   Examples of development activities include:

- Designing, constructing and testing pre-production or pre-use prototypes and models.

- Designing tools, jigs, moulds and dies involving new technology.

- Designing, constructing and operating a pilot plant that is not of a scale that is economically capable of commercial production.

- Designing, constructing and testing a selected alternative for new or improved materials, devices, products, processes, systems or services.

[FRS 102 para 18.8J].

Research phase

18.66   Expenditure on the research phase of an internal project should be expensed as incurred. No intangible asset arising from research or from the research phase of an internal project can be recognised. [FRS 102 para 18.8E]. During the research phase, an entity is unable to demonstrate that there will be future economic benefits. The absence of probability of future economic benefits means that the expenditure does not meet the definition of an intangible asset, nor does it meet the criteria for recognition.

18.67   An entity might purchase patents and other rights over processes that are used in a research and development project. These rights would qualify for recognition as separately acquired intangible assets, even though they are used in the research activity. This is because the 'future economic benefits' criterion is assumed to be automatically satisfied in the separate acquisition of an intangible asset. However, using the patent in a research project might not give rise to future economic benefits, but the fact that it has been bought for value means that it is probable that it could also be sold again for value.

18.68   The Glossary of terms in FRS 102 defines research as related to scientific or technical knowledge. The same accounting treatment of expensing the costs as incurred would apply to other forms of enquiry, such as market or customer research.

Development phase

18.69   There is an accounting policy choice for entities, either to recognise an internally generated intangible asset arising from the development phase of a project (if the recognition criteria are satisfied) or to write it off to profit or loss. The policy should be applied consistently to all expenditure that meets the requirement of paragraph 18.8H of FRS 102. Expenditure that does not meet the conditions of that paragraph is expensed as incurred. [FRS 102 para 18.8K].

18.70   The future economic benefits might become more apparent as a project progresses into the development stage. The measurement of development costs might become more reliable as this occurs. [FRS 102 para 18.8I]. Therefore, the recognition criteria might be satisfied. Section 18 of the standard sets out criteria to assist in determining the point at which an entity moves from the research phase (when costs are expensed) to the development phase (when subsequent costs might be recognised as an asset). If the criteria are met, expenditure might be recognised as an asset if the entity adopts a policy of capitalising expenditure in the development phase that meets the conditions of paragraph 18.8H of the standard. An entity must be able to demonstrate all of the following criteria before an intangible asset is recognised:

(a)   The technical feasibility of completing the intangible asset so that it will be available for use or sale.

(b)   Its intention to complete the intangible asset and use or sell it.

(c)   Its ability to use the intangible asset or to sell it.

(d)   How the intangible asset will generate probable future economic benefits. Among other things, the entity must be able to demonstrate the existence of a market for the intangible asset's output or for the intangible asset itself; or, if the asset is to be used internally, the entity must be able to demonstrate the usefulness of the intangible asset.

(e)   The availability of adequate technical, financial and other resources to complete the development and to use or sell the intangible asset.

(f)   Its ability to measure reliably the expenditure attributable to the intangible asset during its development.

[FRS 102 para 18.8H].

18.71   Management should consider the product life cycle, and then apply the above criteria at each stage of that cycle, as illustrated below.

Example – Application of recognition criteria to each stage of the product life cycle

Consider the development of a new technology to be used in a manufacturing plant. The process could be split into the following stages:

1. Identify a need for/benefit of new technology.

2. Commission a project to investigate the new technology.

3. Investigate other technologies available in the market.

4. Investigate competitors' use of other technology.

5. Commission the design of alternative types of new technology, and get input from the manufacturing floor for feasibility.

6. Prepare a shortlist of alternatives from commissioning stage and prepare costing.

7. Prepare a budget for the new technology and agree to the shortlist and the replacement of technology.

8. Send the shortlist to line managers for input, and list three based on feedback.

9. Present the final three to the board for final selection.

10. Finalise a development plan for the final selection.

11. Develop new technology.

12. Test new technology.

13. Train staff on new technology.

14. Roll out new technology to the production line.

Management needs to determine at what stage it should start to capitalise the costs of the project. The recognition criteria should be considered at each stage to determine when the criteria have been met in full. From that point on, the entity can capitalise all directly attributable costs.

At stage 5, criteria (a) and (c) have been met, because the feasibility of completing the intangible asset for use, and the entity's ability to use it, have been confirmed.

At the end of stage 7, criteria (a), (c), (d) and (e) have been met, because a budget has been produced, it has been agreed to proceed with replacing the technology, and adequate resources exist to complete the development.

At stage 10, all the criteria have been met because, in addition to the above, the board has approved the project (evidence of intention to complete the asset – criterion (b)), and the development plan, based on the budgets, evidences the ability to measure the expenditure reliably (criterion (f)).

18.72 Many entities incur significant expenditure on development, but the amount that is recognised as an intangible asset varies considerably, depending on the nature of the business and the nature of the products that are being developed. Consider, for example:

- An entity might make products for sale generally, such as cars. That entity might also incur significant expenditure on development of new models. Provided the recognition criteria were met, the entity could capitalise the development costs incurred after the criteria were met, and thus might carry significant amounts of development costs as an intangible asset.

- An entity that is involved in developing new drugs or vaccines might incur significant research and development costs and might reach a stage at which it is very confident that the product will be successful. However, because the release of a new drug is strictly controlled by legislation, and has to pass a number of clinical trials before it can be marketed, the entity might have to expense most of the costs. There is no definitive starting point for capitalising such internal development costs. Management must use its judgement, based on the facts and circumstances of each project. However, a strong indication that an entity might have met the recognition criteria in section 18 of FRS 102 arises when it files its submission to the regulatory authority for final approval. It is strong evidence that the technical feasibility of completing the project is proven, this being the most difficult criterion to demonstrate. Filing the submission with the regulatory authority for final approval will usually represent the starting point for capitalisation.

Expenditure which cannot be capitalised as internally generated intangible assets

18.73 The criteria for recognising internally generated intangible assets cannot be satisfied for some types of intangible asset. These include internally generated brands, mastheads, publishing titles, customer lists and items that are similar in substance. This is because it is extremely difficult to distinguish the costs of such items from the cost of developing the business as a whole. So, section 18 of the standard includes a specific prohibition on recognising those items as intangible assets. [FRS 102 para 18.8C].

18.74 Expenditure on intangible assets that cannot be capitalised should be expensed. However, such expenditure could be recognised as a pre-payment within current assets, where payment has been made in advance of delivery of goods or services. [FRS 102 para 18.8D]. Expenditure on an intangible item must be recognised as an expense when it is incurred, unless it forms part of the cost of an intangible asset that meets the criteria for recognition as an internally generated or a separately acquired intangible asset. Pre-payment for such expenditure can only be recognised as an asset until the entity obtains right of access to the related goods or receipt of services.

Measurement at cost

18.75 Cost for internally generated intangible assets that meet the recognition criteria is determined using similar principles to those used for separately acquired intangible assets. The cost of an internally generated intangible asset is the sum of expenditure incurred from the date when the intangible asset meets the recognition criteria in paragraphs 18.4 and 18.8H of the standard. [FRS 102 para 18.10A].

18.76 The cost of an internally generated intangible asset that meets the recognition criteria is the sum of directly attributable expenditure incurred to create, produce and prepare the asset, so that it is capable of operating in the manner intended by management. [FRS 102 para 18.10B].

18.77 Examples of directly attributable costs given in paragraph 18.10B of FRS 102 are:

- Costs of materials and services used or consumed in generating the intangible asset.

- The cost of employee benefits, as defined in section 28 of the standard that arise directly from the generation of the intangible asset.

- Fees paid to register a legal right, such as patent registration fees.

- Amortisation of patents and licences that are used to generate the intangible asset.

- Borrowing costs, to the extent that they are eligible for capitalisation as part of the cost (see chapter 25 for further guidance).

18.78 Only the costs that are directly attributable to generating the intangible asset, and not the general costs of the operation, can be capitalised. The following types of costs are not 'directly attributable' and, therefore, are not components of the cost of an internally generated intangible asset:

- Selling, administration and other general overhead costs, unless they can be directly attributed to preparing the asset for use.

- Inefficiencies and initial operating losses incurred before the asset achieves planned performance.

- Training costs for staff who will operate the asset.

18.79 The capitalisation of costs stops when the asset 'is capable of operating in the manner intended by management'. This means that, if an asset is internally generated (constructed) and can operate in that manner immediately, but is not brought into use immediately, costs incurred whilst the asset is standing idle cannot be capitalised. For example, staff costs in the development phase of a project might meet the capitalisation criteria; but, once the development project is completed, if the staff start work on another research project, their costs can no longer be capitalised. Costs incurred in using or redeploying an item are not included in its carrying amount.

> **Example – Promotion costs and operating losses related to entity's database**
>
> An entity has developed a database of names and addresses of professional people who reach their twenty-fifth birthdays between 2004 and 2010. Management intends to exploit this by selling the information to suppliers of life enhancement products and solutions for junior executives. The entity is incurring costs of promoting the databases to vendors of such solutions, such as adventure holiday companies. It is also incurring losses, because there are substantial administrative costs and no income as yet. Can it capitalise the promotion costs and the operating losses, because the database cannot work as intended by management unless a customer base is first established?
>
> The promotional costs are not eligible for capitalisation as part of the cost of the intangible asset. The database is already capable of operating in the manner intended by management (that is, it can provide the information that management wishes to exploit). Building up a customer base is not essential to the working of the database, although it is essential to ensuring that the future economic benefits expected from the asset are achieved. The start-up losses are also not eligible for capitalisation, because they are not directly attributable costs of the generation of the database.

18.80 An entity should recognise expenditure on the following items as an expense (such costs are generally indistinguishable from the costs of developing the business as a whole, and so they should not be recognised as intangible assets):

- Internally generated brands, logos, publishing titles, customer lists and items similar in substance.

- Start-up activities (that is, start-up costs), which include establishment costs such as legal and secretarial costs incurred in establishing a legal entity, expenditure to open a new facility or business (that is, pre-opening costs) and expenditure for starting new operations or launching new products or processes (that is, pre-operating costs).

- Training activities.

- Advertising and promotional activities.

- Relocating or reorganising part or all of an entity.

- Internally generated goodwill.

[FRS 102 para 18.8C].

18.81 Expenditure that does not meet the recognition criteria is recognised as an expense as incurred. This includes the general day-to-day expenditure on maintaining the business, such as wages and salaries, maintenance, and so on. Some of the types of expenditure that might seem to be at the margin between intangible assets and such routine expenditure is specifically put into the latter category by section 18 of FRS 102 and listed in the paragraph above.

18.82 Internally generated goodwill cannot be recognised as an asset. [FRS 102 para 18.8C]. The section of the standard explains that internally generated goodwill is not recognised as an asset because it is not an identifiable resource – that is, it is not separable and it does not arise from contractual or other legal rights that are controlled by the entity and that are reliably measurable.

> **Example – internally generated customer list**
>
> A supplier has been in the market for many years and has built a list of customers with which it currently transacts. This list is large and complete in terms of information about the customers. Management considers that the list has a significant value.
>
> The standard prohibits an entity from recognising an intangible asset for the internally-generated customer list despite the fact that the customer list is controlled by the entity and from which future economic benefits are expected to flow to the entity. This is because the cost of the list cannot be distinguished from the cost of developing the business as a whole.

Past expenses not to be recognised as an asset

18.83   Expenditure on an intangible item that was initially recognised as an expense should not be recognised at a later date as part of the cost of an asset. [FRS 102 para 18.17]. This is rather obvious, because expenditure (once it has been written off) is rarely restated.

Measurement after initial recognition

18.84   After initial recognition, an entity can adopt either the cost model or the revaluation model as its accounting policy. The revaluation model can only be adopted if the intangible assets are traded in an active market; so it is not frequently used. The policy should be applied to the whole of a class of intangible assets and not merely to individual assets within a class, unless there is no active market for an individual asset. A policy of revaluation might be more onerous, and involve more complex record keeping, than using the cost model. [FRS 102 para 18.18].

18.85   The cost model requires that, after initial recognition, intangible assets should be carried at cost less accumulated amortisation and impairment losses. [FRS 102 para 18.18A]. The revaluation model requires that, after initial recognition, intangible assets should be carried at fair value, determined by reference to an active market. [FRS 102 para 18.18B]. Revaluations should be carried out with sufficient regularity that the carrying amount of the asset does not differ materially from that which would be determined using fair value at the end of the reporting period. [FRS 102 para 18.18D].

Classes of intangible assets

18.86   If a single intangible asset is revalued, the entire class of intangible assets to which that item belongs should be revalued, although the policy need not be applied to all classes of intangible asset. [FRS 102 para 18.18].

18.87 An entity can adopt classes of asset that meet the following definition: *"A grouping of assets of a similar nature and use in an entity's operations"*. [FRS 102 Glossary of terms]. Other than ruling out classes of asset determined on a geographical basis, this definition is reasonably flexible. An entity can adopt meaningful classes that are appropriate to its business. Separate disclosures must be made for each class of assets. For example, each class of assets must be presented as a separate category in the table of movements in intangible assets in the notes to the financial statements. [FRS 102 para 18.27]. Most entities have a few broadly drawn classes of intangible asset.

18.88 Examples of classes of intangible asset are:

- Brand names.

- Mastheads and publishing titles.

- Licences and franchises.

- Copyrights, patents and other industrial property rights, service and operating rights.

- Recipes, formulae, models, designs and prototypes.

- Intangible assets under development.

- Emission rights.

[FRS 102 para 18.8C].

18.89 Items in the above list might be further analysed or combined, if that would give more relevant information to users of the financial statements. For example, further categories resulting from aggregation or disaggregation of items in the above list (that might sometimes be treated as separate classes of intangible asset) include:

- Website development costs.

- Computer software.

- Databases.

- Aircraft landing rights.

- Picture or music libraries.

- Mobile phone licences.

Application of the revaluation model

18.90 The revaluation model cannot be applied to intangible assets that have not previously been recognised as intangible assets. [FRS 102 para 18.18C]. The revaluation model can be applied to measure an intangible asset only after the asset's initial recognition and measurement at cost. The method cannot be used at initial recognition to record an intangible asset at a value other than cost. [FRS 102 para 18.18C].

18.91 However, if only part of the cost of an intangible asset is recognised as an asset, because the asset did not meet the criteria for recognition until part way through the process, the revaluation model could be applied to the whole of the asset. [FRS 102 para 18.18F].

18.92 Recording assets acquired in a business combination at fair value is not the application of the revaluation model. It is a method of determining the 'cost to the group' of individual assets acquired in a business combination.

18.93 Where a revalued asset's fair value can no longer be determined by reference to an active market, the carrying amount should be frozen at the revalued amount at the date of the last valuation. That carrying amount is then amortised and impaired, as necessary, in the normal way. [FRS 102 para 18.18E].

18.94 The only valuation basis permitted is fair value determined by reference to an active market. The definition of active market is a market in which all of the following conditions exist:

- The items traded in the market are homogeneous (similar in kind or nature).
- Willing buyers and sellers are always available.
- Prices are publicly quoted.

[FRS 102 Glossary of terms].

18.95 An active market exists for only a few types of intangible asset, and the revaluation model can only be used where such a market exists. Valuations should remain up to date, because old valuations that do not reflect current values are less meaningful. There is no requirement for valuations to be performed every reporting period. However, revaluations should be made with sufficient regularity that the carrying amount does not differ materially from fair value at the end of the reporting period. [FRS 102 para 18.18D].

Reporting gains and losses on revaluations

18.96 A revaluation increase should be recognised in other comprehensive income and accumulated in equity, unless it reverses a revaluation decrease on the same asset previously recognised as an expense. Reversals of previous revaluation decreases are credited to profit or loss to the extent that the decrease was recognised as an expense. [FRS 102 para 18.18G].

18.97 Any revaluation decrease should be recognised in profit or loss when it represents a permanent diminution in value of an asset. [FRS 102 para 18.18H]. Where the revaluation decrease does not represent a permanent diminution in value of an asset, the revaluation losses should be recognised as follows:

(i) In other comprehensive income, to the extent of any previously recognised revaluation increase accumulated in equity, in respect of that asset.

(ii) In the profit and loss, where the decrease exceeds the accumulated revaluation gains recognised in equity in respect of that asset.

[FRS 102 para 18.18H]

Amortisation

18.98 After initial recognition, an intangible asset should be amortised on a systematic basis over its useful life. Amortisation allocates the cost of property, plant and equipment in a systematic and rational manner to those periods expected to benefit from the use of the asset. 'Amortisation' is defined as *"the systematic allocation of the depreciable amount of an asset over its useful life"*, and the 'depreciable amount' is defined as *"the cost of an asset, or other amount substituted for cost, less its residual value"*. [FRS 102 Glossary of terms]. This allocation process reduces an asset's depreciable amount to its residual value at the end of its useful life.

18.99 The amortisation charged for each period should be recognised in profit or loss, unless another section of the standard requires the cost to be recognised as part of the cost of an asset, such as inventories or property, plant and equipment. [FRS 102 para 18.21].

18.100 Amortisation of an intangible asset ceases when the asset is derecognised. So, amortisation does not stop when the intangible asset is retained but no longer used, unless the asset has been fully amortised or has been derecognised. But, if the asset were no longer used because no future economic benefits were expected from it, it would be derecognised and a loss recorded. If an asset is temporarily unused, this would be an indication of impairment for the relevant cash-generating unit, and an impairment review should be carried out.

18.101 Amortisation of an intangible asset ceases when the asset is derecognised. So, amortisation does not stop when the intangible asset is retained but no longer used, unless the asset has been fully amortised or has been derecognised. But, if the asset were no longer used because no future economic benefits were expected from it, it would be derecognised and a loss recorded. If an asset is temporarily unused, this would be an indication of impairment for the relevant cash-generating unit, and an impairment review should be carried out.

18.102 It is apparent (from the definitions in para 18.98 above) that there are three factors involved in the amortisation process. These are:

■ Estimating the useful lives.

■ Determining the depreciable amount for the asset (where applicable); this involves estimating the residual value.

■ Choosing an amortisation method.

These issues are discussed below.

Estimates of useful lives

18.103 'Useful life' is defined as:

- the period over which an asset is expected to be available for use by an entity; or

- the number of production or similar units expected to be obtained from the asset by an entity.

[FRS 102 Glossary of terms].

18.104 Generally, the former of these two will apply; this is because, in most cases, it is more straightforward to assess useful lives by reference to time periods. However, for some types of asset, usage might be a more reliable measurement.

18.105 The definition includes the phrase 'expected to be available for use'. Thus, it is clear that the useful life includes any period after acquisition when the asset is *capable* of operating in the manner intended by management, but has not yet been brought into use. This is consistent with the time when amortisation commences.

18.106 It is also clear from the definition that an asset's useful life is the period over which the entity expects to consume economic benefits from the asset. However, the end of the asset's useful life is not necessarily the end of its economic life. The economic life is the period during which the asset produces economic benefits, no matter who is using it at the time. The useful life is the period when the asset is used by the entity. If the entity buys an intangible asset that has an economic life of ten years, but the entity intends to use the asset for only six years, the useful life that the entity assigns to the asset will be six years and not ten years. It would then be necessary to estimate the residual value at the end of six years.

18.107 For the purpose of section 18 of the standard, all intangible assets should be considered to have a finite useful life. [FRS 102 para 18.19]. Many intangible assets arise from contractual or legal rights. For these types of intangible asset, the useful life should not exceed the period of the contractual or other legal rights. However, the useful life could be shorter, depending on the period over which the entity expects to use the asset. [FRS 102 para 18.19]. If management is unable to make a reliable estimate of the useful life, the life should be presumed to be five years. [FRS 102 para 18.20].

> **Example — Legal life of copyright in excess of the economic life**
>
> An entity acquires a copyright that has a remaining legal life of 50 years. The entity determines that the copyright has an economic life of only 30 years (that is, it will only generate economic benefits for 30 years).
>
> The entity must amortise the copyright over 30 years. Useful economic life is defined as the period over which the entity is expected to use the asset, and this is limited to 30 years. The entity will not use the asset after 30 years, and must derecognise it when no future economic benefits are expected from its use.

18.108 If the contractual or other legal rights are conveyed for a limited term that can be renewed, the useful life of the intangible asset should include the renewal period(s) only if there is evidence to support renewal by the entity without significant costs. The existence of the following factors might indicate that management is able to renew the contractual or legal rights without significant costs:

■ There is evidence, possibly based on experience, that the contractual or legal rights will be renewed. This includes evidence that, where the consent of a third party is required, such consent will be forthcoming.

■ There is evidence that any conditions necessary to obtain renewal will be satisfied.

■ The cost to the entity is not significant when compared with the future economic benefits expected to flow to the entity from renewal.

18.109 Where the cost of renewal is significant, the original asset's useful life ends at the contractual renewal date, and the renewal cost is treated as the cost to acquire a new intangible asset. Management needs to exercise judgement in assessing what it regards as a significant cost.

18.110 Where an intangible asset does not arise from contractual or legal rights, such as non-contractual customer relationships, its useful life should be estimated. Many factors are considered in determining the useful life of an intangible asset, including:

■ Expected usage of the asset by the entity, and whether it could be managed efficiently by the management team.

■ The typical product life cycles for the asset, and public information about estimates of useful lives of similar assets that are used in a similar way.

■ Technical, technological, commercial or other types of obsolescence.

■ The stability of the industry in which the asset operates, and changes in the market demand for the products or services from or related to the asset.

■ Expected actions by competitors or potential competitors.

■ The level of maintenance expenditure required to maintain the asset's operating capability, and whether management intends to perform that level of maintenance. For example, management might have to spend on advertising to maintain the value of a trademark.

■ Whether the asset's useful life is dependent on the useful life of other assets of the entity. For example, use of a trademark or brand might cease if production of the goods represented by the trademark or brand is discontinued.

18.111 Although the useful life of an intangible asset is stated always to be finite, it might, in rare cases, be very long. Although the useful life cannot be infinite, it might still be indefinite, which means that there is no foreseeable limit on the period of time over which the intangible asset is expected to provide cash flows. Nevertheless, management must make an estimate of the useful life, even though cash flows are expected to continue indefinitely. However, both unjustifiably long and unrealistically short lives are not appropriate.

18.112   An indefinite life for an intangible asset will generally require a business, industry and products with a track record of stability and high barriers to market entry. Added to this, of course, is the commitment of management to continue to invest for the long term, to extend the period over which the intangible asset is expected to continue to provide economic benefits. Indefinite lives might be justified for some long-established brands and publishing titles that have demonstrated their ability to survive changes in the economic environment. Definite lives might be appropriate for other brands and publishing titles that are relatively new, dependent on an individual's reputation (such as a movie star), or which operate in more volatile sectors, where they are more likely to be affected by changes in fashions or technology.

> **Example – Useful life of customer relationships**
>
> Entity A acquired entity B, which operates a TV channel. Entity B negotiates the sale of air time directly with advertisers, who are mostly big companies. Advertisement contracts are negotiated annually, and management considers it likely that the relationships will continue indefinitely.
>
> Entity A's management has concluded that the criteria have been met in order to recognise such customer relationships as intangible assets separately from goodwill.
>
> It is unlikely that customer relationships have indefinite useful lives, because ownership of the customers might change, strategies might change, and further competitors might enter entity B's market.
>
> Entity A's management should consider all the relevant factors, such as historical experience, contracts periods, competitors and life cycle, to determine the useful lives of the customer relationships. This should be based on reliable assumptions about the period over which economic benefits are expected to be obtained from the relationships.
>
> Management should be able to estimate the useful lives of the customer relationships, considering all relevant factors as described above.

18.113   The useful life of an intangible asset must be reviewed at each financial reporting date. If there are indications that the useful life has changed since the most recent annual reporting date (as a result of the factors considered above), the entity should revise the useful life. The revision should be accounted for as a change in accounting estimate, in accordance with the requirements of section 10 of the standard. [FRS 102 para 18.24]. Where the original estimate of the useful life is revised, the unamortised cost should normally be written off over the revised remaining useful life.

Example – Revision of useful life

The facts are the same as in the example above. However, the licensing authority subsequently decides that it will no longer renew broadcasting licences, but instead will auction the licences. At the time that the licensing authority's decision is made, the entity's broadcasting licence has three years until it expires. The entity expects that the licence will continue to contribute to net cash inflows until the licence expires.

Because the broadcasting licence can no longer be renewed, its useful life is no longer presumed to be five years. The useful life of the acquired licence would be re-estimated, and the entity would conclude that it is the remaining three years until expiration.

Note: the change in the legal environment is an impairment indicator, and so the licence must be tested for impairment in accordance with section 27 of FRS 102.

Depreciable amount and residual values

18.114 As noted above, the depreciable amount of an asset is its cost less residual value. Residual value is defined as *"the estimated amount that an entity would currently obtain from disposal of an asset, after deducting the estimated costs of disposal, if the asset were already of the age and in the condition expected at the end of its useful life"*. [FRS 102 Glossary of terms]. The words 'currently obtain' make clear that the amount is based on current prices. The value takes account of inflationary increases since acquisition, but does not take account of expected future inflation after the reporting date.

18.115 An entity should assume that the residual value of an intangible asset is zero, unless:

- there is a commitment by a third party to purchase the asset at the end of its useful life; or

- there is an active market for the asset and:

  - residual value can be determined by reference to that market, and

  - it is probable that such a market will exist at the end of the asset's useful life.

[FRS 102 para 18.23].

18.116 If a third party has committed to buy the asset at the end of its useful life, its residual value would be the amount payable by the third party, adjusted to exclude future inflation. A residual value of greater than zero assumes that the entity expects to dispose of the intangible asset before the end of its economic life.

18.117 Like useful life, the residual value of an intangible asset must be reviewed at each financial reporting date. The revised estimate must be based on conditions and prices at the financial reporting date. If there are indications that the residual value has changed as a result of changing factors, or that the revised estimate differs significantly from previous estimates of residual value, the revision should be accounted for as a change in accounting estimate, in accordance with the requirements of section 10 of the standard. [FRS 102 para 18.24].

Methods of amortisation

18.118 Management should select an amortisation method that reflects the pattern in which it expects to consume the asset's future economic benefits. If management cannot determine that pattern reliably, it should use the straight line method. [FRS 102 para 18.22]. There is a variety of acceptable amortisation methods, including the straight-line method, the diminishing balance method, and the units of production method. These methods are illustrated in chapter 17. Whatever method is used, it should result in a fair amortisation charge that reflects the consumption of economic benefits provided by the asset over its useful life.

18.119 If the consumption of future economic benefit is through the passage of time (for example, patents and licences that operate for a fixed number of years), the straight-line method will often be the most appropriate method to use. However, if the consumption of future economic benefit is through usage or production, the entity should use that pattern of consumption if the entity can reliably determine that pattern. For example, assume that an entity purchases a licence to provide a limited quantity of a gene product, called Alpha. The entity should amortise the cost of the licence following the pattern of use of Alpha. If it cannot determine the pattern of production or consumption, the entity should use the straight-line method of amortisation. Where significant judgements are made when determining the amortisation method used, this should be disclosed in the notes to the financial statements. [FRS 102 para 8.6].

Change in amortisation method

18.120 There is a requirement to review the amortisation method at each annual reporting date, to determine if there has been a significant change in the pattern by which an entity expects to consume an asset's future economic benefits. It is unlikely that the pattern of consumption of an intangible asset would vary significantly over its useful life, and so changes in method should be rare. Nevertheless, if there has been such a change, the change in the amortisation charge resulting from the new method should be accounted for as a change in an accounting estimate, in accordance with the requirements of section 10 of the standard. [FRS 102 para 18.24]. This means that the resulting amortisation adjustment should be made prospectively (that is, the asset's depreciable amount at the date of change should be written off over current and future periods).

Impairment

18.121 An entity should refer to the requirements of section 27 of FRS 102 to determine whether an intangible asset is impaired. An entity should assess at each reporting date whether there is any indication that an intangible asset is impaired.

If such an indication exists, this could indicate that the entity should review its remaining useful life, amortisation method or residual value, even if no impairment loss is recognised for the asset. [FRS 102 para 27.10]. A recognised impairment loss reduces the asset's carrying amount to its recoverable amount (see chapter 27).

Derecognition

18.122 An entity should derecognise an intangible asset:

■ on disposal, or

■ when no future economic benefits are expected from its use or disposal.

[FRS 102 para 18.26].

18.123 An entity should recognise the gain or loss on derecognition of an intangible asset in profit or loss when the item is derecognised. The gain or loss is determined as the difference between the net disposal proceeds, if any, and the carrying amount of the item. Any gain arising on derecognition should not be classified as revenue, but in other income as gains and losses.

18.124 Intangible assets that are scrapped or abandoned should be derecognised, because there are no future economic benefits expected from the asset's continuing use or from its disposal.

> **Example – Impairment and derecognition of a patent**
>
> An entity sells cardboard boxes made out of a special type of cardboard, which it has protected by purchasing a patent. In late 20X4, the entity experienced several complaints from customers that they had received batches of defective cardboard boxes. This led to several important customers cancelling their future orders.
>
> In May 20X5, because of a significant drop in the level of sales, the entity temporary halted production of its patented cardboard boxes. Expecting that the customers would return and that demand for cardboard boxes would increase in the foreseeable future, the entity did not dispose of its cardboard manufacturing operations.
>
> On 30 June 20X6, management discovered that a competitor had developed a new type of cardboard that customers believed was superior to the entity's patented product. As a result, management gave up hope that sales would improve to the extent that it could recommence manufacturing cardboard boxes. Management therefore decided that the associated tangible and intangible assets (including the patent) should be scrapped.
>
> The entity has a year-end of 31 December.
>
> The entity must derecognise the patent on 30 June 20X6. From this date, no future economic benefits are expected from its use or disposal. The reduction in expected future economic benefits (that is, reduction in sales) due to customers cancelling their orders in late 20X4 is an impairment indicator, and hence the cardboard manufacturing operations should be tested for impairment under section 27 of

FRS 102 on 31 December 20X4. The subsequent significant drop in the level of sales is also an impairment indicator, and the cardboard manufacturing operations should therefore be tested again for impairment on 31 December 20X5.

Note: if expected future benefits are reduced, this is an impairment indicator. However, if no future benefits are expected, this results in derecognition of the asset.

Presentation and disclosure

Presentation

18.125 The presentation requirements under Part 1 of Schedule 1 to SI 2008/410 include a heading for 'Intangible assets'. Under that heading, there are separate sub-headings for:

- Concessions, patents, licences, trademarks, and similar rights and assets.
- Development costs.
- Goodwill.
- Payments on account

[FRS 102 para 18.26].

Disclosure

18.126 An entity should disclose the following for each class of intangible assets:

- The useful lives or the amortisation rates used.
- The amortisation methods used.
- The gross carrying amount and any accumulated amortisation (aggregated with accumulated impairment losses) at the beginning and end of the reporting period.
- The line item(s) in the statement of comprehensive income (and in the income statement, if presented) in which any amortisation of intangible assets is included.
- A reconciliation of the carrying amount at the beginning and end of the reporting period, showing separately:
  - additions;
  - disposals;
  - acquisitions through business combinations;
  - amortisation;
  - impairment losses; and
  - other changes.

This reconciliation does not need to be presented for prior periods. [FRS 102 para 18.27].

18.127 In addition, the entity should disclose the following:

- A description, the carrying amount and remaining amortisation period of any individual intangible asset that is material to the entity's financial statements.

- For intangible assets acquired by way of a government grant and initially recognised at fair value (see paragraph 18.52):

    - the fair value initially recognised for these assets, and

    - their carrying amounts.

- The existence and carrying amounts of intangible assets to which the entity has restricted title or that are pledged as security for liabilities.

- The amount of contractual commitments for the acquisition of intangible assets.

[FRS 102 para 18.28].

18.128 An entity should disclose the aggregate amount of research and development expenditure recognised as an expense during the period (that is, the amount of expenditure incurred internally on research and development that has not been capitalised as part of the cost of another asset that meets the recognition criteria).

18.129 If intangible assets are accounted for at revalued amounts, an entity should disclose the following:

- the effective date of the revaluation;

- whether an independent valuer was involved; and

- the methods applied in estimating the asset's fair values.

[FRS 102 para 18.29A].

18.130 The disclosure requirements for intangible fixed assets are governed by paragraph 51 of Schedule 1 to SI 2008/410. These requirements are identical to those for tangible fixed assets. The information should be given in respect of each of the sub-headings that are preceded in the formats by Arabic numerals.

18.131 Where an entity has applied the alternative accounting rules (that is, revaluation) to any intangible fixed asset, the notes must disclose the years in which the assets were separately valued (so far as the directors know these) and also the separate values. If any assets are valued during the financial year in question, the notes must also disclose the valuers' names or particulars of their qualifications and the basis of valuation used by them. [SI 2008/410 1 Sch 52].

18.132 Where an entity has elected to capitalise development costs, further disclosure should be made of the period over which the amount of those costs that were originally capitalised is being (or is to be) written off, together with the reasons for capitalising the development costs in question. [SI 2008/410 1 Sch 21(2)].

18.133 Where development expenditure is deferred by capitalising it, and the unamortised development expenditure is not treated as a realised loss, the notes to the financial statements must also state:

■   The fact that the amount of unamortised development expenditure is not to be treated as a realised loss for the purposes of calculating distributable profits.

■   The circumstances that the directors relied upon to justify their decision not to treat the unamortised development expenditure as a realised loss.

[CA06 Sec 844(2)(3)].

Transitional issues for UK entities

18.134 Entities transitioning from old UK GAAP (FRS 10) to FRS 102 must prepare their first financial statements as though the requirements of section 18 of FRS 102 for intangible assets had always applied. However, there are some exemptions relating to intangible assets that are available for first-time adopters under section 35 of the standard. The exemptions and the main issues that arise on transition are noted below.

Exemptions for first-time adopters

18.135 There are two 'valuation as deemed cost' exemptions relating to intangible assets that are available to first-time adopters under section 35 of FRS 102. A first-time adopter can:

■   Elect to measure an intangible asset, which meets the recognition criteria and the criteria for revaluation in section 18, on the date of transition to FRS 102 at its fair value, and use that fair value as its deemed cost at that date.

■   Elect to use a previous GAAP revaluation of an intangible asset which meets the recognition criteria and the criteria for revaluation in section 18 at, or before, the date of transition to FRS 102 as its deemed cost at the revaluation date.

[FRS 102 para 35.10(c),(d)].

18.136 However, these exemptions are likely to be of limited use in the UK, given that many intangible assets under old UK GAAP were subsumed in goodwill and, if groups use the exemption for business combinations in section 35 of FRS 102, these intangible assets are not recognised on transition to FRS 102. [FRS 102 para 35.10(a)]. Also, separately purchased intangible assets are not normally carried at a valuation.

18.137 In addition, a first-time adopter may elect to measure the carrying amount at the date of transition to FRS 102 for development costs deferred in accordance with SSAP 13 as its deemed cost. [FRS 102 para 35.10(n)]

18.138 Application of this election would prevent a first-time adopter from recognising an asset for expenditure that had previously been written off. This is an accounting policy choice. Should a first time adopter not make this election it is possible that costs incurred that did not meet capitalisation requirements under old UK GAAP and that do meet these requirements under section 18 of FRS 102 would be capitalised retrospectively on transition.

Recognition of intangible assets

18.139 Under the old UK GAAP, separability was a necessary condition for identifying an intangible asset, but this is not the case under section 18 of FRS 102. Under section 18 of the standard, an intangible asset is identifiable when it is separable or when it arises from contractual or other legal rights, regardless of whether those rights are transferable or separable from the entity or from the rights and obligations. We would expect more intangibles to be recognised when applying FRS 102 than under old UK GAAP.

Indefinite life intangible assets

18.140 Under old UK GAAP (FRS 10), the useful economic life of an intangible asset could be indefinite if the asset's durability could be demonstrated and the asset was capable of continued measurement so that annual impairment reviews were feasible. However, as stated in paragraph 18.107 above, under FRS 102 all intangible assets are considered to have a finite life. This means that a UK entity that did not amortise an intangible asset (because its life was considered to be indefinite under old UK GAAP) will have to determine its useful life under FRS 102. If a reliable estimate of useful life cannot be made, the intangible asset's life is presumed to be five years from date of acquisition under new GAAP. The intangible asset should be recognised at the relevant depreciated amount on transition taking into account the finite life determined during the transition process.

18.141 It was common practice for many entities to use the rebuttable presumption of a useful life of 20 years under old UK GAAP for goodwill and intangibles on acquisition. This implied that the entity was able to justify a 20-year life in the accounts under old GAAP. We therefore believe that it would be difficult to change this view on transition to FRS 102 and argue that the useful life for these assets defaults to five years. We would expect a change in circumstance to justify why the useful life should be changed from 20 years and, even then, five years might not be the answer, given that it is so widely different. Entities would need to consider whether there has been a change in circumstances that has occurred, and it might be that the starting point on transition is a 20 year life (as justified by management under old UK GAAP) and then a prospective adjustment to useful life when the change happens.

Chapter 19

Business combinations and goodwill

Business combinations and goodwill

Scope

19.1 This chapter considers the accounting treatment for business combinations. It provides guidance on identifying the acquirer, measuring a business combination's cost, and allocating that cost to the assets acquired and liabilities (including contingent liabilities) assumed. It also deals with the accounting for goodwill, both at the time of the business combination and after.

19.2 Section 19 of FRS 102 deals with the accounting for all business combinations except:

■ Forming a joint venture.

■ Acquiring a group of assets that do not constitute a business.

[FRS 102 para 19.2].

19.3 The first scope exclusion applies only where the venturers get together in setting up a joint venture. It does not apply where a business combination is entered into by a joint venture after its formation.

19.4 The second scope exclusion applies to the acquisition of a group of assets that do not constitute a business. In some transactions, it might be difficult to determine whether the acquiree is engaged in a business or simply holds a collection of assets and liabilities. This does not depend on whether or not the acquiree is a legal entity. The definition of a business is considered in paragraph 19.8 onwards below. If the transaction relates to a collection of assets, rather than a business, it does not give rise to goodwill in the acquirer's financial statements, but any identified assets are recorded at their cost, as evidenced by the purchase price (see chapters 17 and 18).

19.5 Section 19 of FRS 102 includes specific guidance on the accounting for group reconstructions (see para 19.165 onwards below).

19.6 In addition, public benefit entities need to consider the requirements of section 34 of FRS 102 in accounting for public benefit entity combinations (see chapter 34).

Identifying a business combination

19.7 A business combination is defined as *"the bringing together of separate entities or businesses into one reporting entity"*. [FRS 102 para 19.3, Glossary of terms]. The result of nearly all business combinations is that one entity (that is, the acquirer) obtains control of one or more other businesses (that is, the acquiree). [FRS 102 para 19.3]. For this purpose, a business is defined as indicated below.

Definition of a business

19.8   A 'business' is defined as:

> *"An integrated set of activities and assets conducted and managed for the purpose of providing:*
>
> *(a)   a return to investors; or*
>
> *(b)   lower costs or other economic benefits directly and proportionately to policyholders or participants.*
>
> *A business generally consists of inputs, processes applied to those inputs, and resulting outputs that are, or will be, used to generate revenues. If goodwill is present in a transferred set of activities and assets, the transferred set shall be presumed to be a business."*

[FRS 102 Glossary of terms].

19.9   So it is necessary to consider whether a transaction's substance is really the acquisition of a business or simply the purchase of assets. The above definition indicates that a significant characteristic of a business is that the underlying set of assets (inputs) and activities (processes) is integrated in some way to produce goods and services (output) that will generate revenue. A collection of assets without connecting activities is unlikely to represent a business. The three parts – inputs, processes and output – are explained below.

19.10   An input is an economic resource that creates, or has the ability to create, an output when one or more processes are applied to it. Examples include non-current assets (including intangible assets or rights to use assets), intellectual property, and the ability to obtain access to necessary materials or rights and employees.

19.11   A process is a system, standard, protocol, convention or rule that, when applied to an input or inputs, creates or has the ability to create outputs. Examples include strategic management processes, operational processes and resource management processes.

19.12   Administrative, billing, payroll and accounting processes are not required in order for a set of activities and assets to be a business, because those processes do not create outputs when applied to inputs. Processes are usually documented, but an organised workforce that has the skill and experience to follow rules can constitute the processes that, when applied to inputs, can create outputs.

19.13   Outputs are the results of the inputs and processes. The outputs can generally be sold or exchanged and provide, or are capable of providing, a return

19002

to investors, owners or participants. That return might be dividends, lower costs or other economic benefits. But outputs are not required to qualify as a business, provided the inputs (and the processes applied to the inputs) have the ability to create outputs.

Presence of goodwill

19.14   There is a presumption that, if goodwill is present in a transferred set of activities and assets, the transferred set is a business (see para 19.8 above). In this context, goodwill represents the acquiree's ability to earn a higher rate of return on an assembled collection of net assets than would be expected from those net assets operating separately, and the expected synergies and other benefits that arise from combining the acquiree's net assets with those of the acquirer.

19.15   But the lack of goodwill in an acquired entity does not create a presumption that the acquired entity is not a business. In other words, an acquired entity could constitute a business without any goodwill being present.

Distinguishing a business from an asset or group of assets

19.16   It will often be straightforward to determine whether a business has been acquired; the business will normally be carrying out a continuing trade with identifiable revenue. But, sometimes, determining whether a business has been acquired might not be easy. All relevant facts and circumstances must be analysed in assessing whether the definition of a business is met. Consider the following examples.

Example 1 – Development stage entity

Entity A has been formed to design computer games for the next generation of computer game systems. Entity A's current activities include researching and developing its first product, obtaining contracts to manufacture and package its product, and developing a market for the product.

Since its inception, entity A has produced no revenues and has received funding from third parties. With a workforce comprised primarily of engineers, entity A has the intellectual property needed to design the computer games, as well as the software and fixed assets required to develop them. Entity A does not have any commitments from customers to buy the computer games. The entity is being purchased by another entity.

Entity A is a business because it contains both inputs and processes. These include the intellectual property to design the software, fixed assets, employees, and strategic and operational processes to develop the software. The integrated set of assets and activities are being managed in a way to give the entity the ability to produce and sell goods and services to generate revenue in the future. The fact that there is no output at present is not in itself sufficient to disqualify entity A from being considered a business.

Example 2 – Outsourcing arrangement

Entity B provides information technology outsourcing services. Entity C generates and supplies electricity. Entity C's billing and other systems use significant computer and staff resources. Entity C uses these systems to provide billing and accounting services to a number of smaller utilities. Entity B and entity C have entered into an agreement under which entity B will provide all of entity C's information technology services for 15 years. Entity B will acquire all of entity C's back-office computer equipment, related buildings and third-party service contracts.

All staff currently employed by entity C in its information technology function will transfer to entity B. Entity B will, in addition to providing information technology services, restructure the information technology operations to improve efficiency.

The integrated set of assets and activities acquired by entity B is a business. This is because the elements in the acquisition include inputs (buildings, employees and computer equipment), processes (computer systems and operating processes) and outputs (the existing contracts with other utilities and the new service contract with entity B). The underlying set of assets and activities are all integrated in generating revenue.

Example 3 – Warehouses

A shipping and warehousing business, entity D, provides shipping and storage services to various third parties. A consumer retail business, entity E, plans to purchase several warehouses from entity D and intends to use the warehouses to enhance its inventory distribution system. The acquired group includes only the land and warehouses; it does not include warehousing contracts with third parties, employees or warehouse equipment, or information technology systems such as inventory-tracking systems.

The assets acquired by entity E are not a business. Entity E has purchased only inputs (the physical assets) and not the accompanying processes that can be applied to those inputs to produce outputs. A collection of assets without connecting activities does not represent a business.

Structuring a business combination

19.17 A business combination can be structured in a variety of ways for legal, taxation or other reasons. Possible structures include:

■ The purchase by an entity (the 'acquirer') of the equity of another entity, which becomes the acquirer's subsidiary.

■ The purchase of the net assets, comprising an unincorporated business, of another entity.

■ Acquiring an entity's business by assuming the liabilities of that entity.

■ The purchase of some of the net assets of another entity that together form one or more businesses.

[FRS 102 para 19.4].

19.18 A business combination might be effected by the issue of equity instruments, the transfer of cash, cash equivalents or other assets, or a mixture of these. The transaction could be between the shareholders of the combining entities, or between one entity and the shareholders of another entity. It could involve establishing a new entity to control the combining entities (see para 19.30 below) or net assets transferred, or restructuring one or more of the combining entities. [FRS 102 para 19.5].

19.19 The most common way for an entity to become a subsidiary of another is by the purchase of a controlling interest in its shares. As noted above, this purchase could be by cash, issuing equity interests, incurring liabilities, or a combination of these, or it might not involve any transfer of consideration. But it is also possible for a parent to gain a subsidiary by other means. This is illustrated in the following examples.

Example 1 – Share repurchase by investee

Entity A owns an equity investment in an investee that gives it significant influence but not control. Due to the investee's repurchase of its own shares from other parties, entity A's proportional interest increases, which causes entity A to obtain control of the investee.

This transaction qualifies as a business combination, and the purchase method (that is, business combination accounting) discussed in paragraph 19.20 onwards below is applied by the investor in its consolidated financial statements as a result of the investee's share repurchase transaction.

Example 2 – Change in the rights of other shareholders

Entity B owns a majority share of its investee's voting equity interests, but is precluded from exercising control over the investee due to contractual rights held by the other investors in the investee (for example, veto rights, board membership rights, or other substantive participation rights). The elimination or expiration of these rights causes entity B to obtain control of the investee.

This event qualifies as a business combination, and the purchase method would be applied by entity B in its consolidated financial statements.

Example 3 – Contracts or other arrangements

Entities C and D enter into a contractual arrangement to combine their businesses. Under the contract's terms, entity C will control the operations of both entities C and D. This transaction qualifies as a business combination, and the purchase method would be applied to the arrangement in entity C's consolidated financial statements.

Purchase method of accounting for business combinations

19.20 All business combinations are accounted for using the purchase method, except for:

- Group reconstructions, which can be accounted for using merger accounting (see para 19.165 onwards below).

- Public benefit entity combinations that are, in substance, a gift or that are a merger, which are accounted for under section 34 of FRS 102 (see chapter 34).

[FRS 102 para 19.6].

19.21 FRS 102 is consistent with the company law requirements in paragraph 8 of Schedule 6 to SI 2008/410, although FRS 102 restricts the use of merger accounting to group reconstructions.

19.22 The purchase method views a business combination from the perspective of the combining entity identified as the acquirer. The acquirer recognises the assets acquired and liabilities and contingent liabilities assumed, including those not previously recognised by the acquiree. Measurement of the acquirer's assets and liabilities is not affected by the transaction, and no additional assets or liabilities of the acquirer are recognised as part of the accounting for the transaction. For example, if, as a result of the business combination, the acquirer is able to recognise a previously unrecognised deferred tax asset of its own, this is not included in the accounting under the purchase method, and so it does not affect the calculation of goodwill. The accounting for the acquirer's deferred tax asset follows the guidance in chapter 29.

19.23 Under the purchase method, the acquirer allocates the business combination's cost by recognising the acquiree's identifiable assets, liabilities and contingent liabilities assumed at their fair values at the acquisition date. This is key to the reporting of post-acquisition performance relating to the business combination. As the standard indicates, the acquirer's statement of comprehensive income incorporates the acquiree's profits and losses after the acquisition date by including the acquiree's income and expenses based on the combination's cost to the acquirer. For example, post-acquisition depreciation expense relating to the acquiree's depreciable assets is based on those assets' fair values at the acquisition date (that is, their cost to the acquirer). [FRS 102 para 19.16; SI 2008/410 6 Sch 9].

19.24 Where a parent entity acquires a controlling interest in another entity, the purchase method applies in the parent's consolidated financial statements. In its separate financial statements, the parent will include its interest in the acquiree as an investment in a subsidiary (see chapter 9). Where the acquirer purchases an unincorporated business, the purchase method applies in the acquirer's individual (or separate) financial statements.

19.25 In summary, applying the purchase method involves the following steps:

- Identifying an acquirer (see para 19.26 onwards below).

- Determining the acquisition date (see para 19.33 onwards below).

■　　Measuring the business combination's cost (see para 19.37 onwards below).

■　　Allocating, at the acquisition date, the business combination's cost to the assets acquired and liabilities and provisions for contingent liabilities assumed.

[FRS 102 para 19.7].

Identifying the acquirer

19.26　An acquirer needs to be identified for all business combinations accounted for by applying the purchase method, and is the combining entity that obtains control of the other combining entities or businesses. [FRS 102 para 19.8].

19.27　'Control' is defined as *"the power to govern the financial and operating policies of an entity or business so as to obtain benefits from its activities"*. [FRS 102 para 19.9]. Control of one entity by another is dealt with in section 9 of the standard. There is a presumption that a combining entity has obtained control when it acquires more than half of another entity's voting rights, unless it can be clearly demonstrated that such ownership does not constitute control. Section 9 of FRS 102 also specifies circumstances in which the combining entity gains control where it obtains less than half the voting rights in the acquiree (see chapter 9).

19.28　Although it might sometimes be difficult to identify an acquirer, there are usually indications that one exists, as the following scenarios show:

■　　If the fair value of one of the combining entities is significantly greater than that of the other combining entity, the entity with the greater fair value is likely to be the acquirer. This is because the larger entity is likely to have the larger share of votes in the combined entity, or to be able to control it in some other way.

■　　If the business combination is effected through an exchange of voting ordinary equity instruments for cash or other assets, the entity giving up cash or other assets is likely to be the acquirer. The reason for this is that, when the equity of one of the entities is purchased for cash or other assets, its owners normally cease their involvement, and it is likely that the entity making the payment will control the purchased entity.

■　　If the business combination results in one of the management teams being able to dominate the selection of the combined entity's management team, the entity whose management is able to dominate is likely to be the acquirer.

[FRS 102 para 19.10].

19.29　The definition of control refers to 'obtaining benefits'. We consider that this should not be interpreted restrictively and covers a wide range of situations in practice, including obtaining benefits:

■　　In the form of current or future profits.

- By preventing another competitor from buying the business.

- By preventing a key supplier or distributor from going out of business.

- By reducing losses of the acquiring group.

New entity formed to effect a business combination

19.30   There can only be one acquirer in a business combination. Where a business combination involves the creation of a new entity to control the combining entities (as noted in para 19.18 above), determining who is the acquirer includes considering which entity initiated the combination and the relative sizes of the entities.

> **Example 1 – Business combination using a new entity**
>
>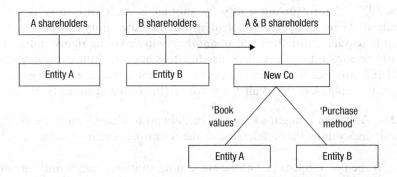
>
> The shareholders of entities A and B agree to join forces, to benefit from lower delivery and distribution costs. The business combination is carried out by setting up a new entity (New Co) that issues 100 shares to entity A's shareholders and 50 shares to entity B's shareholders in exchange for the transfer of the shares in those entities. The number of shares reflects the relative fair values of the entities before the combination.
>
> The transaction has brought together entities A and B. Legally, it has been effected by New Co acquiring entities A and B, rather than one of these entities acquiring the other. But New Co is a new entity that has been formed simply to issue equity shares to effect a business combination. It has little or no substance, and has probably been formed for legal, tax or other business considerations. In other words, the formation of New Co to issue equity shares to the owners of the combining entities A and B is, in substance, no different from a transaction in which one of the combining entities directly acquires the other. So it is necessary to look at all relevant facts and circumstances, to determine which of the combining entities is the acquirer.
>
> Based on the evidence available, and in the absence of any other information, it would appear that entity A is the acquirer. It is the larger of the two combining entities, and its previous owners control the combined group owning 67% of the total net assets (that is, 100/150).

New entity formed to acquire an existing group

19.31   The above example illustrates that, where a new entity is formed to issue equity shares to effect a business combination, it is not the acquirer. A question arises whether a new entity formed to effect a business combination, in which it pays cash as consideration for the business acquired, could be identified as the acquirer. Consider the following example.

Example – New entity formed to effect a business combination

Entity A intends to acquire all of the voting shares of entity B. For business reasons, entity A sets up New Co to effect the business combination. It provides New Co with the necessary funding at market interest rates to acquire 100% of the voting shares of entity B.

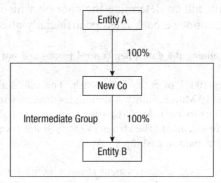

As noted in paragraph 19.26 above, the acquirer is the combining entity that obtains control of the other combining entities or businesses. Where such control is obtained through an exchange of voting ordinary equity instruments for cash or other assets, the entity giving up cash or other assets is likely to be the acquirer.

In this example, New Co is created to effect a business combination other than through the issue of equity shares. It pays cash to acquire all of the voting shares of entity B. In effect, New Co is considered to be an extension of entity A that has obtained control of entity B in an arm's length transaction. Although New Co, acting at the direction of entity A, has secured control of entity B for entity A, it would be identified as the acquirer at the intermediate group level (that is, Newco's group).

Even though New Co is the acquirer, in many situations (especially in the UK) New Co will not be required to account for the acquisition of entity B using the purchase method, because it will be exempt from preparing consolidated financial statements. Entity A, as the ultimate parent, will account for the acquisition of entity B using the purchase method, in its consolidated financial statements.

19.32   In contrast, the definition of a group reconstruction is met where a parent entity is added to an existing group by setting up a new entity that issues equity shares to the existing shareholders in exchange for the transfer of shares in the existing group (for instance, as part of a capital reconstruction), such that there is no change in the substance of the reporting entity. The accounting for group reconstructions is dealt with in paragraph 19.165 onwards below.

Determining the acquisition date

19.33   The acquisition date is the date on which the acquirer obtains control of the acquiree. [FRS 102 para 19.3, Glossary of terms]. Determining this date is important because the purchase method applies from this date. It will often be the date on which the acquirer legally transfers the consideration and acquires the assets and liabilities of the acquiree – that is, the transaction's closing date.

19.34   But control is the power to govern the financial and operating policies of an entity or business so as to obtain benefits from its activities, so it is not necessary for a transaction to be closed or finalised at law before the acquirer obtains control. All relevant facts and circumstances should be considered in assessing when the acquirer has obtained control. [FRS 102 para 19.17]. Although it might often be difficult to determine the date on which control passes, it is a matter of fact and cannot be backdated or artificially altered.

> **Example – Determining the date when control passes and not the date of agreement**
>
> Entity A acquires 100% of entity B for cash. The sale agreement specifies that the acquisition date is 10 March. Entity A nominates directors and appoints them in place of the existing directors on 1 April (that is, the date when all of the conditions in the sale agreement are satisfied). The shares in entity B are transferred to entity A when the consideration is paid in cash on 15 April.
>
> The date specified in the sale agreement is not binding for accounting purposes; the date when control passes to the acquirer can differ from the date set in the agreement.
>
> The acquisition date is 1 April, when entity A appoints the directors and, as a result, is able to govern entity B's financial and operating policies from that date. The consideration in this case is an obligation to make payment at a later date. The consideration is exchanged on 1 April, when control of entity B transferred to entity A. The payment of cash on 15 April does not affect the acquisition's recognition.

19.35   In determining the acquisition date, it should be remembered that control has two elements: the power to govern the financial and operating policies; and benefits must be obtained from that power. Both of these conditions must be met at the acquisition date. If a potential acquirer is given a right to profits from a date that is conditional on the completion of the purchase at some later date (or is given rights to past profits), this would impact the fair value of the combination's consideration, but not the acquisition date.

19.36   It can be seen that the key to control passing is dependent on *unconditional* terms. The negotiations to purchase a subsidiary might take place over a considerable period, and conditions (such as third party or shareholder approval) could take time to be satisfied. Until such time as agreement is reached and all conditions are satisfied, the transaction cannot be regarded as unconditional, and it is unlikely that control will have passed.

Measuring the business combination's cost

19.37　Having identified the acquirer, the next step is to measure the business combination's cost at the acquisition date. The cost is the aggregate of:

- the fair values, at the acquisition date, of assets given, liabilities incurred or assumed, and equity instruments issued by the acquirer, in exchange for control of the acquiree; and

- any costs directly attributable to the business combination.

[FRS 102 para 19.11].

19.38　The fair value of the consideration given is the basis for determining the amount that is allocated to the acquiree's identifiable assets, liabilities and contingent liabilities for the purpose of calculating the goodwill arising on the business combination.

19.39　The fair value of the consideration for a business combination is measured at the acquisition date. It is clear what this means where the business combination is achieved through a single transaction. But a business combination can also be achieved in stages (for example, where the acquirer purchases the shares of another entity in tranches at various dates until it achieves the majority of the voting shares and, hence, control). Where control is achieved following a series of transactions, the business combination's cost is the aggregate of the fair values of the assets given, liabilities assumed and equity instruments issued by the acquirer at the date of each transaction in the series. [FRS 102 para 19.11A]. Business combinations achieved in stages (sometimes referred to as 'step acquisitions') are considered in more detail in paragraph 19.127 onwards below.

Assets given and liabilities incurred or assumed by the acquirer

19.40　Where the purchase consideration is in the form of cash, its fair value will be the amount paid or payable. Where settlement of cash consideration is deferred, the fair value of the deferred cash consideration is normally determined by discounting the amounts expected to be payable to their present value. Guidance on determining fair values is given in chapter 11.

19.41　The business combination's cost includes liabilities incurred or assumed by the acquirer in exchange for control of the acquiree. The assumption of liabilities by the acquirer might take the form of the repayment of borrowings in an acquired entity owed to its former investors, including (in the case of the purchase of a subsidiary from its former parent) the repayment of an acquired entity's intra-group debt. The fair value of such consideration is the amount paid or payable (discounted to present value, if necessary, where settlement of the liabilities is due at a future date).

19.42　Future losses, or other costs that are expected to be incurred as a result of the business combination, are not deemed to be liabilities incurred by the acquirer, and so they are not included as part of the business combination's cost (see para 19.106 below). [FRS 102 para 19.18(b)].

Equity instruments issued by the acquirer

19.43 Where equity instruments issued by the acquirer are given as consideration for the business combination, the standard requires them to be fair valued at the acquisition date. Where fair value measurement is permitted or required, the guidance in paragraphs 11.27 to 11.32 of the standard should be applied. [FRS 102 para 2.34(b)].

19.44 Section 11 of the standard provides general guidance for measuring the fair value of equity instruments that are held as investments. We believe that it is appropriate to use the guidance in section 11 for determining the fair value of equity instruments given as consideration for a business combination.

19.45 Section 11 of FRS 102 provides that the fair value of unquoted equity instruments could be estimated by using valuation techniques such as discounted cash flows and option pricing models. The value can sometimes be estimated by reference to quoted securities issued by entities with similar characteristics. If the variability in the range of fair values arrived at using the various valuation techniques is not significant, or the probabilities of the various estimates within the range can be reasonably assessed and used in estimating fair value, the valuation of the equity instrument is likely to be reliable. Further guidance is given in chapter 11.

19.46 In the rare situation where valuation techniques are unable to provide a reliable estimate of fair value of the equity instrument issued by the acquirer, we consider that it might be appropriate to estimate the fair value of the equity instrument issued by reference to either the proportional interest in the fair value of the acquirer's operations obtained by the acquiree's shareholders, or the proportional interest in the fair value of the acquiree's operations acquired, whichever is the more clearly evident.

19.47 In the UK, where a company issues equity shares as part of the consideration to acquire a subsidiary, the difference between the consideration's fair value and the nominal value of the shares issued is credited to the share premium account, unless the company is eligible for 'merger relief' or 'group reconstruction relief' under the Companies Act 2006 (see chapter 22). If the company can obtain relief on the share issue, the difference between the fair value of the shares issued and their nominal value (and any minimum share premium) is credited to a merger reserve (as opposed to a share premium account) in the consolidated financial statements. The availability of the relief does not impact on the measurement of the shares' fair value for the purpose of determining the acquisition's consideration.

Payments to employees

19.48 It is not uncommon for selling shareholders to be key employees of the acquiree, particularly where smaller or unlisted entities are acquired. The selling shareholders might remain as employees of the acquired business following the business combination. Where payments are made to vendors who continue to be employees of the acquired entity after the acquisition, it will be necessary to look at the economic substance of the relevant transactions to determine the accounting treatment.

19.49 Payments for employee services are post-combination remuneration expenses that are included in the income statement in accordance with section 26 or 28 of the standard. Where consideration payable is automatically forfeited if the vendor ceases to provide employee services, the amount payable is normally treated as remuneration for post-combination employee services. Payments that are, in substance, consideration for the business acquired are part of the business combination's cost. There is some guidance on factors to be considered in making this assessment in chapter 25 of the IFRS Manual of Accounting.

Other consideration

19.50 If the consideration includes payment made for an agreement by the vendor not to compete with the acquirer for a number of years, the non-compete agreement might meet the criteria for separate recognition as an intangible asset by satisfying the 'contractual or other legal rights' criterion. [FRS 102 para 18.2]. In that situation, it would be accounted separately from the business combination.

19.51 Purchase consideration can take the form of a special dividend paid by the acquirer, after the acquisition date, to those vendors who became shareholders as a result of accepting the acquirer's shares in exchange for the acquiree. In principle, such dividends could be treated as part of the purchase consideration, where it can be demonstrated that the dividend payments were, in substance, part of the acquisition cost. The acquirer would need to ensure that the special dividend's cost is not double-counted in arriving at the fair value of the consideration shares. In other words, the consideration shares should be valued on an 'ex-div' basis (that is, excluding the special dividend).

Costs directly attributable to the business combination

19.52 Costs that are directly attributable to a business combination are included in the combination's cost (see para 19.37 above). This means that they are included in the goodwill calculation. These expenses might include fees payable to lawyers, accountants and other advisers for:

- Investigating and valuing the acquiree.
- Undertaking due diligence work.

- Negotiating the purchase price and drawing up the legal documentation.

- Finalising the purchase consideration, such as auditing the completion accounts.

19.53 Costs that are not directly attributable are excluded from the purchase consideration. Excluded costs might include:

- General administration costs, such as staff costs of the acquirer's finance and legal departments.

- The costs of senior management, even if they spend a considerable amount of time working on specific transactions.

- Overhead costs.

- Professional fees paid to investigate potential acquisition targets.

- Retainers paid to professional advisers.

19.54 The treatment of fees in respect of searching for and identifying the business that was later acquired is a matter of judgement. A finder's fee, resulting from work commissioned to identify a suitable target, might qualify to be included as part of the cost of the acquisition where it relates to the business being acquired; but, in general, other search and investigation fees incurred before a specific target has been identified would need to be written off.

19.55 Where services are provided by external advisers, they have to be directly attributable to the acquisition in order to be included in the business combination's cost, as illustrated in the following example.

> **Example – Directly attributable costs**
>
> Entity A acquired entity B during the year. After the acquisition, entity A has incurred external costs in determining the fair value of the assets (particularly intangible assets) acquired.
>
> Entity A's management argues that the costs would not have been incurred if the business combination had not occurred, and so they are directly attributable to the business combination.
>
> In our view, 'directly attributable' means that the costs have to have been incurred to 'effect the business combination'. Valuation costs of the acquired business prior to the acquisition date might qualify to be capitalised as part of the combination's cost. But costs incurred post-acquisition, to determine the fair value of the assets acquired or to perform the purchase accounting in accordance with the standard, should be expensed. This would also apply to other types of valuation costs (for example, tangible fixed assets and pension liabilities).

19.56 Costs of arranging and issuing debt instruments to finance the business combination are an integral part of the debt issue transaction, rather than costs directly attributable to the business combination. So they are not included in the business combination's cost, but are included in the financial liability's initial measurement. [FRS 102 para 11.13]. Similarly, costs of issuing equity instruments are not included in the business combination's cost, but are deducted from equity. [FRS 102 para 22.9].

Adjustments to the business combination's cost contingent on future events

19.57 Business combination agreements might allow for an adjustment to the combination's cost where the amount payable is uncertain because it is contingent on the outcome of future events. If the payment is linked to employee service, see paragraph 19.49 above. But contingent consideration is often used if the buyer and seller cannot agree on the value of the acquired business, or if the buyer and seller wish to share the risk of changes in the value of the business (for example, where the acquirer agrees to pay an additional amount based on a multiple of the acquired entity's profits, often referred to as 'earn-outs') or of particular projects (for example, where an additional amount is payable if an acquiree's product under development is successfully marketed).

19.58 The acquirer includes the estimated amount of an adjustment to the combination's cost contingent on future events in the combination's cost at the acquisition date, if the adjustment is probable (that is, more likely than not) and can be measured reliably. [FRS 102 para 19.12].

19.59 It is usually possible to estimate the amount of the contingent consideration at the time of initial accounting for the combination without impairing the reliability of the information, even though some uncertainty exists.

19.60 But it might sometimes be difficult to make a reliable estimate of the future consideration payable. For example, it might depend on the average of the acquired entity's profits for three years into the future and might not be payable at all, unless the average exceeds a specified amount. The acquired entity might be in a development phase, where any forecasts are very subjective and unreliable. When the acquirer's first post-acquisition financial statements are prepared, it could be difficult to assess the probable amount or, indeed, whether any amount will be payable. In these circumstances, the contingent consideration is not included in the combination's cost.

19.61 However, if the contingent consideration later becomes probable and can be measured reliably, the additional consideration should be treated as an adjustment to the combination's cost. [FRS 102 para 19.13].

19.62 Although not specifically stated in the standard, it follows from the above paragraph that an adjustment should continue to be made to the combination's cost (and so to goodwill) until the consideration is finally determined and payable in accordance with the terms of the agreement. In contrast, the adjustments to provisional fair values of assets and liabilities acquired to reflect new information obtained are finalised within 12 months of the acquisition date, and such adjustments are made retrospectively, as if they had occurred at the date of acquisition (see para 19.121 below).

19.63 This raises the question of how adjustments to the consideration contingent on future events should be accounted for – that is, retrospectively in line with the rule in section 19 of FRS 102 for finalising the initial accounting for a business combination; or prospectively in line with the normal rules for changes in accounting estimates in accordance with section 10 of the standard. The rule for finalising provisional fair values is a concession, permitting an acquirer to finalise fair values that it was not initially possible to finalise due to lack of time. This differs from the situation with contingent consideration where an initial estimate is made which is later adjusted, based on future events (for example, achieved profit levels). So, in our view, where this is the case, it appears reasonable to regard adjustments to contingent consideration as changes to estimates, and these should be accounted for prospectively by reflecting the effect of the change in the period that it is made.

19.64 Sometimes, under the terms of the purchase agreement, the vendor is required to give various representations and warranties that are not connected to the acquiree's future performance. For example, escrow adjustments and working capital adjustments (that are fairly common in business combinations) might require the vendor to refund part of the consideration paid by the acquirer. The question arises whether such refunds should be adjusted against the combination's initial cost. Consider the following example.

> **Example – Escrow arrangement**
>
> Entity E acquires entity F for £10m. Entity E seeks protection for false representations and warranties asserted by entity F's sellers. Entity E will pay £9m at the acquisition date and place £1m in an escrow account. Within one year after the acquisition date, the sellers will receive the £1m if there were no violations of the representations and warranties. Should any adjustments be made to the combination's cost by the acquirer at acquisition date?
>
> No. At the acquisition date, the acquirer has no way of knowing whether the representations and warranties made by the vendor will be violated. So the acquirer makes no adjustments to the combination's initial cost of £10m, because it is not probable that any amounts would be received back.
>
> On the other hand, if at the end of year 1, new facts and circumstances indicate that there would be an adjustment to the amount held in escrow, this is accounted for under the rules for contingent consideration in paragraphs 19.12 and 19.13 of FRS 102 (see paras 19.58 to 19.62 above). For example, if only £250,000 held in escrow would be released to the vendor, the refund of £750,000 received by entity E would be recognised as an adjustment to the consideration, resulting in a reduction of goodwill by that amount.

19.65 Adjustments to the combination's cost after the acquisition will rarely affect amounts attributed to assets and liabilities other than goodwill or negative goodwill. But an additional payment could bring the combination's cost above the fair value of the net assets acquired, thus converting negative goodwill into positive goodwill; and a later downward adjustment to the combination's cost could turn what was originally positive goodwill into negative goodwill.

Indemnities in a business combination

19.66 A purchase agreement might also provide that the seller indemnifies the buyer against specific contingencies (for example, tax risks, environmental problems or legal issues) existing at the acquisition date for which no liabilities have been recognised by the acquiree. As discussed in paragraph 19.109 below, the acquirer will be required to recognise a liability for the contingency at its fair value if it is able to measure the fair value reliably, even though the acquiree might not have recognised any liability for that contingency. The question arises of how the acquirer should account for the indemnity where the acquiree is required to refund part of the consideration paid by the acquirer if the contingency occurs or the uncertainty is resolved.

19.67 Under section 21 of FRS 102, where some or all of the amount required to settle a provision might be reimbursed by another party, the entity recognises the reimbursement as a separate asset if it is virtually certain that the entity will receive the reimbursement on settlement of the obligation. The amount recognised for the reimbursement should not exceed the amount of the provision. [FRS 102 para 21.9]. Applying this to a business combination, an indemnification asset is recognised by the acquirer at the acquisition date only if it relates to an indemnified asset or liability that is recognised at the acquisition date. The first stage of measuring the indemnification asset is to measure it on the same basis as the indemnified asset or liability. But, because the indemnification asset represents, in substance, a receivable from the perspective of the acquirer, it is subject to recoverability considerations. To the extent that some or all of the indemnification asset is considered uncollectable, a provision for recoverability of the receivable is included in the indemnification asset's carrying value. Similarly, the indemnification asset's value is adjusted to reflect any contractual limitations on the indemnified amount.

19.68 For example, the above accounting might be appropriate in the following circumstances for an indemnified liability or contingent liability:

■ The vendor agrees to specifically indemnify the acquirer for all or a specified proportion of the costs to be incurred and, subject to delivery of any required evidence, there is no doubt that the amount will be reimbursed.

■ There are no further negotiations to take place between the acquirer and vendor in relation to the subject matter of the claim or attached conditions. There are no clauses that allow for arbitration

■ The acquirer has not, in substance, economically assumed the liability as part of the business combination transaction. The liability has been 'set aside' in undertaking the purchase price negotiations.

In these circumstances, it could be argued that the receipt of the indemnification asset is virtually certain if the obligation is incurred, in which case the asset is recognised at the same time as the indemnified item.

19.69 In later periods, adjustments for changes in the value of the indemnification asset and the indemnified item (for items other than tax) can be offset in the statement of comprehensive income. [FRS 102 para 21.9].

Allocating the business combination's cost

19.70 Having determined the business combination's cost, it is necessary to allocate that cost to the assets acquired and liabilities and contingent liabilities assumed. For this purpose, the standard requires that, at the acquisition date, the acquirer allocates the business combination's cost by carrying out a fair value exercise. This involves recognising the acquiree's identifiable assets and liabilities and provision for contingent liabilities that satisfy the recognition criteria (see para 19.73 below) at their fair values at the acquisition date, except for the items specified in paragraph 19.74 below. [FRS 102 para 19.14; SI 2008/410 6 Sch 9].

19.71 Any difference between the business combination's cost and the acquirer's interest in the net amount of the identifiable assets, liabilities and provisions for contingent liabilities is goodwill (or negative goodwill). [FRS 102 para 19.14; SI 2008/410 6 Sch 9]. Accounting for goodwill is considered in paragraph 19.134 onwards below.

19.72 The standard is silent on how a non-controlling interest in the acquired entity should be determined. But goodwill is based on the acquirer's interest in the net amount recognised for the identifiable assets, liabilities and contingent liabilities, so any non-controlling interest in the acquired entity should be stated similarly at the non-controlling interest's proportion of the net amount of those items (see also para 19.136 below).

> **Example – Allocating the business combination's cost**
>
> Entity A acquired 80% of entity B for £250 in cash. Entity B's net assets were made up of property, plant and equipment, together with inventory, receivables and payables, and their carrying amount at the acquisition date was £100. The fair value of entity B's net assets at the date of acquisition was £200.
>
> In entity A's consolidated financial statements:
>
> - The carrying amount of entity B's net assets is £200.
>
> - Goodwill recognised is £90, being consideration given of £250, less entity A's 80% interest in the net fair value of £200 (that is, £160).
>
> - Non-controlling interest recognised is £40, being the 20% non-controlling interest in the net fair value of £200.

Identifiable assets and liabilities

19.73 Except for the items specified in paragraph 19.74 below, the acquirer recognises separately the acquiree's identifiable assets, liabilities and contingent liabilities at the acquisition date only if they satisfy the following criteria at that date:

■ For an asset other than an intangible asset, it is probable that any associated future economic benefits will flow to the acquirer, and the asset's fair value can be measured reliably.

■ For a liability other than a contingent liability, it is probable that an outflow of economic benefits will be required to settle the obligation, and its fair value can be measured reliably.

■ For an intangible asset or a contingent liability, its fair value can be measured reliably.

[FRS 102 para 19.15].

19.74 There are some exceptions to the general rule for recognising assets and liabilities at their fair value at the acquisition date, because to do so would conflict with other sections of the standard. These are as follows:

■ Deferred tax assets or liabilities arising from the assets acquired and liabilities assumed are recognised and measured in accordance with section 29 of FRS 102 (see chapter 29).

■ Liabilities (or assets, if any) related to the acquired entity's employee benefit arrangements are recognised and measured in accordance with section 28 of FRS 102 (see chapter 28).

■ Share-based payments are recognised and measured in accordance with section 26 of FRS 102 (see chapter 26). This follows on from the general rules in paragraph 19.14 of FRS 102 and so relates to the recognition of the acquired entity's assets and liabilities.

[FRS 102 paras 19.15A, 19.15B, 19.15C].

19.75 The standard does not define 'identifiable assets and liabilities', but the term is generally taken to mean assets or liabilities that are capable of being disposed of separately, without disposing of the business. In this context, goodwill is clearly not separable from a business as a whole (see para 19.134 below).

19.76 The identifiable assets and liabilities that are recognised under the purchase method include all of the acquiree's assets and liabilities that the acquirer purchases or assumes, including all of the financial assets and liabilities. They might also include assets and liabilities not previously recognised in the acquiree's financial statements, because they did not qualify for recognition prior to the business combination or because this was not permitted under local GAAP. For example, a tax benefit arising from the acquiree's past tax losses might not have been recognised by the acquiree before the business combination; but it will qualify for recognition as an identifiable asset in the fair value exercise if it is probable that the acquirer will have future taxable profits against which the unrecognised tax benefit can be applied.

19.77 The recognition rule for intangible assets and contingent liabilities is inconsistent with the general recognition rules for assets and liabilities set out in section 2 of FRS 102. The general recognition rule is that an asset is recognised if it is probable that the future economic benefit will flow to the entity, and the asset has a cost or value that can be measured reliably. Similarly, a liability is recognised if it is probable that an outflow of economic benefits will be required to settle the obligation, and the settlement amount can be measured reliably. [FRS 102 paras 2.37, 2.39]. But, for intangible assets and contingent liabilities acquired in a business combination, the probability recognition criterion is omitted, and the only criterion is that fair value can be measured reliably. The effect of probability is reflected in the fair value measurement. So, identifiable intangible assets and contingent liabilities might need to be recognised by the acquirer, even though they have not been recognised by the acquiree before the business combination.

19.78 Section 19 of the standard does not itself provide any guidance on how different categories of the acquiree's assets, liabilities and contingent liabilities should be valued at the date of the business combination. Where applicable, entities should refer to the guidance in the standard for specific assets and liabilities (for example, employee benefits and tax). For fair values, section 2 of FRS 102 states that, in the absence of any specific guidance provided in the relevant section of the standard, where fair value measurement is permitted or required, the guidance in paragraphs 11.27 to 11.32 of the standard should be applied. In applying the fair value guidance to assets and liabilities, the reference to shares in those paragraphs should be read to include the types of assets and liabilities being addressed. [FRS 102 paras 2.34(b), 11.27].

19.79 Section 11 of FRS 102 provides guidance on measuring fair values and includes a hierarchy for determining these. According to the hierarchy, the best evidence of fair value is a quoted price for an identical asset in an active market (that is, market value). In the absence of market values, fair values are estimated using valuation techniques. Management should follow this guidance in determining the fair values of assets and liabilities acquired in a business combination. In the absence of any specific guidance, management should use its judgement and might (but is not required to) look to the requirements and guidance in full IFRS. [FRS 102 para 10.6]. Based on this approach, see paragraph 19.82 onwards below for guidance on measuring fair values of specific assets and liabilities acquired in a business combination.

19.80 'Fair value' is defined as *"the amount for which an asset could be exchanged, a liability settled, or an equity instrument granted could be exchanged, between knowledgeable, willing parties in an arm's length transaction. The guidance in paragraphs 11.27 to 11.32 shall be used in determining fair value"*. [FRS 102

Glossary of terms]. It is apparent from this definition that fair value is based on assumptions made by market participants; it is not an entity-specific concept. This implies that the measurement of fair value should not take account of the acquirer's intentions or any acquirer-specific facts and circumstances, or any synergies created as a result of the combination.

Example 1 – Fair values not affected by the acquirer's intentions

Entity A acquires entity B in a business combination. Entity B's assets include a factory, carried at depreciated cost, which entity A plans to phase out over the next three to five years. Entity A also plans to align entity B's customer warranties with its own more favourable terms.

Entity A wishes to record the factory at a nominal amount in the business combination and to recognise a warranty provision based on its intended settlement terms. Can it do this?

No. The fair value attributed to assets and liabilities is not affected by the acquirer's intentions. The factory should be recorded initially at its fair value at the acquisition date. The factory's fair value will usually be its market value, which could differ from its carrying amount before the acquisition and give rise to a fair value adjustment. The fact that entity A might not use the factory after a period of time does not affect its fair value at that date.

The acquirer's decision to phase out the factory is unlikely to cause an impairment, due to the recoverable amount being the higher of fair value less costs to sell and value in use, but it will affect the useful life over which the factory will be depreciated post-acquisition.

The acquirer's intention to provide more generous warranty settlements is not recognised as part of the purchase accounting. The acquiree's warranty provision is valued based on contractual terms at the acquisition date. It is increased when a constructive obligation exists, with a corresponding charge to the post-acquisition income statement.

Example 2 – Fair values not affected by the acquirer's intentions

Entity C has acquired its principal competitor, entity D. Entity C's management has explained that its motivation for the acquisition was to acquire market share by taking its rival brand out of the market. Management has proposed to measure the brand at a minimal value, because it will be removed from the market shortly after the acquisition.

Management's proposal is not appropriate; the fair value attributed to assets and liabilities is not affected by the acquirer's intentions. The fair value is what a third party would pay for the assets.

The brand's value should be based on the assumption of cash flows from continuing use or sale to a third party. Buying a brand to 'take it out of the market' has a cost associated with it. It is not appropriate to mask this cost by assigning a low fair value to the brand in the purchase accounting.

Entity C's intentions and use of the brand will affect its useful life after the acquisition date. An entity could continue to receive indirect benefits from an asset if it prevents the asset from being used by others. The amount assigned to the brand is amortised over the period in which the brand is expected to contribute directly or indirectly to entity C's future cash flows, and it is tested for impairment. We would not expect such assets to be expensed immediately at the acquisition date, because there would presumably be a period of time over which entity D's business will be rebranded by entity C or in which indirect benefits are obtained, nor would we expect such assets to have an indefinite useful life.

19.81 Although an acquirer needs to carry out a fair value exercise as at the acquisition date, there is no general requirement to record these values in the acquired entity's books (unless, for example, they relate to asset impairments). So, a write down of inventory to its recoverable amount (where this is lower than cost) is recognised in the acquired entity's books. But it would not normally be possible for the acquired entity to record a fair value adjustment to inventory above cost.

Property, plant and equipment and related obligations

19.82 The acquirer should measure the fair value of land and buildings using the guidance in paragraphs 17.15C and 17.15D of FRS 102. The fair value of land and buildings is usually determined by professionally qualified valuers using market-based evidence (that is, 'market value'). [FRS 102 para 17.15C]. Accumulated depreciation in the acquiree is not carried forward in a business combination.

19.83 Plant and equipment should be measured using market values, normally determined by appraisal. If there is no market-based evidence of fair value, because of the specialised nature of the item of plant and equipment and the item is rarely sold, except as part of a continuing business, an acquirer might need to estimate fair value using an income or a depreciated replacement cost approach. [FRS 102 paras 17.15C, 17.15D].

19.84 If the acquiree received a government grant to fund an asset's acquisition, the asset is recognised at its fair value without regard to the government grant. The terms of the government grant are separately evaluated to determine whether there are on-going conditions or requirements that would indicate that a separate liability exists.

19.85 An acquirer might obtain a long-lived asset that, on its retirement, requires the acquirer to dismantle or remove it and restore the site on which it is located. If such a decommissioning obligation exists, it is recognised at fair value (using market participant assumptions), which could differ from the amount recognised by the acquiree.

> **Example – Effect of decommissioning on fair value**
>
> A power plant is acquired in a business combination. Entity A, the acquirer, determines that there is a decommissioning obligation of £5m associated with the plant. The valuer has included the expected cash outflows of £5m in the cash flow model, establishing the plant's value at £15m. Is this correct?
>
> No. For accounting purposes, the acquirer records the plant at its fair value of £20m and a separate liability of £5m for the decommissioning obligation.

Intangible assets

19.86   An intangible asset is recognised separately from goodwill if it meets the definition of an intangible asset and its fair value can be measured reliably (see para 19.73 above). An intangible asset acquired in a business combination is normally recognised as an asset, because its fair value can be measured with sufficient reliability. An exception to this is where it arises from legal or other contractual rights and there is no history or evidence of exchange transactions for the same or similar assets, and estimating fair value in some other way would depend on immeasurable variables. [FRS 102 para 18.8]. Otherwise, an intangible asset acquired in a business combination is measured at its fair value at the acquisition date. [FRS 102 para 18.11]. The recognition and measurement rules for intangible assets acquired in a business combination are covered in more detail in chapter 18.

Inventories

19.87   Inventories acquired in a business combination can be in the form of raw materials, work in progress and finished goods. There is no specific guidance in the standard for determining the fair value of inventories, other than the cross-reference to section 11 of FRS 102.

19.88   For inventories acquired in a business combination, fair values could be determined as follows:

- Raw materials at current replacement cost.

- Work in progress at selling prices of finished goods less the sum of (a) costs to complete, (b) costs of disposal, and (c) a reasonable profit allowance for the completing and selling effort, based on profit for similar finished goods.

- Finished goods at selling prices less the sum of (a) the costs of disposal and (b) a reasonable profit allowance for the selling effort of the acquirer, based on profit for similar finished goods.

19.89   Judgement is needed in determining a reasonable profit margin for the completion and selling efforts of the acquirer post-acquisition. That determination should be based on the finished goods' condition at the acquisition date, and not when it was manufactured; and it should be made on a market, and not an entity-specific, basis. Further guidance, including a worked example, is available in chapter 25 of the IFRS Manual of Accounting.

Financial instruments

19.90   Financial instruments are measured at fair value using the guidance in paragraphs 11.27 to 11.32 of FRS 102. See further chapter 11.

19.91   The fair value of most short-term receivables and payables is not usually significantly different from the book value, because the value reflects the amount expected to be received or paid in the short term. Fair value adjustments are usually limited to those arising from the acquirer's different estimates of amounts recoverable or payable.

> **Example – New evidence of fair value at acquisition date**
>
> A significant customer of an acquired entity has gone into liquidation between the acquisition date and the finalising of the initial accounting for the business combination. No provision was made against the receivables due from the customer in the acquired entity's books. Should a provision be included in the receivables' fair value at the acquisition date?
>
> Any new evidence that comes to light before the fair value exercise is completed in the permitted measurement period (see para 19.121 below), and that concerns the condition *as at the acquisition date* of the acquired entity's assets, is taken into account in arriving at fair value. The fair value of receivables is one area where further investigation might be necessary. The customer was not in liquidation at the acquisition date, but it is likely that it was in financial difficulties at that date. So, in the absence of a specific post-combination event causing the financial difficulties, we consider that the receivables' fair value should be measured including the effect of the liquidation.

19.92   For long-term monetary items, the time value of money also needs to be taken into account. The fair value of long-term receivables and payables is represented by their face values where they carry interest rates that are not significantly different from prevailing market rates at the acquisition date. But fair values of long-term receivables and payables might be materially different from their book or face values where they either carry no interest or carry interest at rates that are significantly different from market rates. Long-term monetary items include finance lease receivables and payables.

Unfavourable and beneficial contracts

19.93   Identifiable liabilities include unfavourable contracts, whether or not these are recognised as liabilities in the acquired entity's financial statements. First, a contract must be unfavourable to the acquired entity at the acquisition date and not have become unfavourable as a result of the acquirer's action. Secondly, whether or not a contract is unfavourable can often reasonably be interpreted as meaning whether or not the obligation exceeds the current (that is, at acquisition date) market value for that contract.

19.94   For the acquired entity's onerous contracts and other identifiable liabilities, the acquirer should use the present values of the amounts to be paid in settling the obligations, determined at current market rates. This is in accordance with the measurement principles for provisions discussed in chapter 21.

19.95   Similarly, identifiable assets include beneficial contracts, whether or not the assets were recognised in the acquired entity's financial statements. Again, the acquirer should use the present values of the amounts to be received for the acquired entity's beneficial contracts and other identifiable assets at appropriate current interest rates.

19.96   Unfavourable or beneficial contracts might be present in operating leases where the acquired entity is a lessee and the lease rentals payable are above or below market rates at the acquisition date.

> **Example – Property lease at above or below market rent**
>
> An acquired entity leases its head office on an operating lease. The rent for the next 15 years is fixed at a level that is in excess of the rents payable on leases of comparable buildings that are on the market at the time of the acquisition. This is not an onerous lease under section 21 of FRS 102, because the acquired entity continues to occupy the property, and its business makes adequate profits to absorb the lease costs.
>
> Although the acquirer does not generally recognise an asset for the acquiree's interest in an asset leased under an operating lease and a liability for the lease payments, it should recognise a net asset or liability to the extent that the lease is favourable or unfavourable compared to market rates at the acquisition date. This is consistent with the principle of identifying and measuring the acquiree's assets and liabilities at fair value, even though they might not be recognised by the acquiree.
>
> So, where lease rentals are higher than market rates at the acquisition date, the acquirer recognises a liability in the fair value exercise for the commitment to pay unfavourable rentals. The liability is not re-measured in later years if market rentals change, but it is amortised to reduce the rental expense during the lease term.
>
> Similarly, where the acquiree is obliged to pay rentals that are lower than market rates at the acquisition date, the acquirer should recognise an asset in the fair value exercise. The asset is amortised over the lease term, and it is not re-measured if market rentals change in later years.

19.97   A significant area of judgement in measuring favourable and unfavourable contracts is whether contract renewal or extension terms should be considered. The following factors are considered when determining whether to include renewals or extensions:

■   Whether renewals or extensions are at the acquiree's discretion without the need to renegotiate key terms. Renewals or extensions that are within the acquiree's control are likely to be considered if the terms are favourable to the acquirer.

■   Whether the renewals or extensions provide economic benefit to the holder of the renewal right. The holder of a renewal right, either the acquiree or the counterparty, is likely to act in their best interest. For example, if the acquiree is the lessee of an operating lease that is favourable to the lessee, the renewals would probably be considered, because the acquirer would plan to exercise the renewal right and realise the benefit of the favourable terms. On the other hand, if the acquiree is the lessee of an operating lease that is favourable to the lessor, the acquirer would usually not presume that the lessee would renew its unfavourable lease.

■   Whether there are any other factors that would indicate that a contract might or might not be renewed.

19.98   A contract that becomes onerous or beneficial as a result of actions taken by the acquirer is not included as an identifiable liability (or asset) in the fair value exercise.

> **Example – Rental property vacated after acquisition**
>
> An acquired entity had occupied a rented warehouse. After the acquisition, the acquiring group rationalised its distribution facilities and the warehouse was vacated. The group is making provision for the rentals payable under the unexpired lease. Is this provision included in assessing the fair values of the acquired entity's assets and liabilities?
>
> No, a liability is not recognised in the fair value exercise. The acquirer recognises liabilities for terminating or reducing the acquiree's activities as part of the business combination accounting only where the acquiree has, at the acquisition date, recognised an existing restructuring liability. The acquirer also does not recognise liabilities for future losses or other costs expected to be incurred as a result of the business combination.
>
> The cost of vacating the warehouse is accounted for as a post-combination event, because it was not a liability of the acquiree at the acquisition date.

Deferred income and charges

19.99   An acquirer recognises a liability related to deferred revenue only to the extent that the acquired entity has an obligation to perform (that is, an obligation to provide goods, services, or the right to use an asset or some other concession or consideration given to a customer) after the acquisition. The obligation assumed by the acquirer relating to deferred revenue should be based on the obligation's fair value on the acquisition date, which might differ from the amount previously recognised by the acquired entity. Also, the fair value will include an element of profit margin, but this might not equate to the profit that the selling entity will recognise over the period.

Example – Deferred income

An IT supplier has entered into a contract to provide support services to one of its larger customers for a period of five years, for which it received an up-front payment of £100,000. The advance payment is recognised in income over the five-year contract period. Entity X acquires the IT supplier. At the acquisition date, the contract still has three years to run (that is, there is deferred income of £60,000 in the IT supplier's books).

The IT supplier has a legal obligation to fulfil the contract. So, entity X recognises the fair value of the obligation to fulfil the contract. The obligation's fair value is the amount at which the liability could be settled between knowledgeable, willing parties in an arm's length transaction. Entity X identifies a sub-contractor that is prepared to assume the obligation for the same product support for the remaining three-year period for a price of £48,000 (or £80,000 for a similar five-year contract). The fair value of the deferred income in the acquiree's balance sheet is £48,000 for the remaining three-year period of service to be completed.

Restructuring provisions and future losses

19.100 As noted in paragraph 19.73 above, in allocating the business combination's cost, the acquirer recognises only the acquiree's identifiable assets, liabilities and contingent liabilities that existed at the acquisition date and that satisfy the recognition criteria.

19.101 This means that the acquirer recognises liabilities for terminating or reducing the acquiree's activities as part of allocating the combination's cost only to the extent that the acquiree has, at the acquisition date, an existing liability for restructuring recognised in accordance with section 21 of FRS 102. [FRS 102 para 19.18(a)]. For example, this will be the case where, before the acquisition date:

■ contracts for the restructuring have been entered into; or

■ a detailed formal plan for the restructuring has been developed, and a valid expectation has been raised in those affected that the restructuring will be carried out (either by publicly announcing the plan's main features, or by starting its implementation).

Example – Recognising restructuring or exit activities

On the acquisition date, entity B, the acquiree, has an existing liability related to a restructuring that was initiated one year before the business combination was contemplated. Also, in connection with the acquisition, entity A (that is, the acquirer) identified several operating locations to close and selected employees of entity B to make redundant to realise synergies from combining operations in the post-combination period.

The acquirer accounts for the two restructurings as follows:

- Restructuring initiated by entity B: entity A recognises the previously recorded restructuring liability at fair value as part of the business combination, because it is an obligation of the acquiree at the acquisition date.

- Restructuring initiated by entity A: entity A recognises the effect of the restructuring in profit or loss in the post-combination period when the recognition criteria in section 21 of FRS 102 are met, rather than as part of the business combination. The restructuring is not an obligation at the acquisition date, so the restructuring does not meet the definition of a liability and is not a liability assumed in the business combination.

19.102 Business combinations are normally agreed between willing buyers and willing sellers, so there is a possibility for restructuring provisions planned by the acquirer to be booked by the acquiree during the negotiations with the acquirer and before the acquisition date. An example is where reductions in excessive manpower in the acquiree are 'negotiated' during the course of the acquisition. In practice, it might be unlikely that management of an entity being acquired could commit the entity irrevocably to a particular course of action at the acquirer's request, unless the acquisition's completion was a foregone conclusion. If it did bind the acquired entity, this might suggest that the acquirer had *de facto* already obtained control.

19.103 If the acquirer had gained control, the acquisition date should be brought forward, and the new subsidiary should be consolidated from the earlier date. Hence, the profits and losses (including the restructuring provision) would be brought into the acquirer's post-acquisition income statement from that earlier date. It should be stressed that all aspects of the relationship between the acquirer and the acquiree would need to be considered before the acquisition date is brought forward.

19.104 But, if the acquirer suggests that negotiations cannot proceed until the acquiree arranges, for example, to restructure its workforce, and the acquiree takes the steps necessary to satisfy the recognition criteria for restructuring provisions in section 21 of FRS 102, it is appropriate to treat the restructuring obligations as the acquiree's pre-combination obligations and to recognise them as part of allocating the combination's cost. This is because the restructuring is not conditional on the entity being acquired and will proceed whether or not the business combination takes place.

19.105 For any restructuring that is conditional on acquisition, the acquiree has no present obligation immediately before the business combination; nor is it a contingent liability arising from a past event. So an acquirer does not recognise a liability for such restructuring plans as part of allocating the combination's cost (see further para 19.101 above).

19.106 In addition to specifying the treatment of restructuring provisions, the standard also makes it clear that liabilities for future losses (or other costs expected to be incurred as a result of the business combination) are not recognised as part of allocating the combination's cost. [FRS 102 para 19.18(b)].

Example – Vendor makes payments for future losses to acquirer

An entity is acquiring a business that will incur future operating losses. The vendor has agreed to make payments to the entity to cover the future losses for two years. Can the entity recognise a receivable in the fair value exercise for the payments that will be due from the vendor?

The payments that the vendor might make are effectively a refund of the consideration paid by the entity. Paragraphs 19.12 and 19.13 of FRS 102 address adjustments to the combination's cost that are contingent on future events (see para 19.57 above). The amount of the adjustment should be included in the combination's cost at the acquisition date if it is probable and can be measured reliably. If it is not, it is not included at the acquisition date; but, if it later becomes probable and can be reliably measured, the additional consideration (or reduction in consideration, in this situation) is treated as an adjustment to the combination's cost at that time, resulting in an adjustment to goodwill and recognising a debtor.

The acquirer, when allocating the combination's cost, should not recognise liabilities for future losses, or other costs expected to be incurred as a result of the business combination. So, the future losses are charged as incurred in the post-acquisition income statement.

Contractual payments

19.107   A payment that an entity is contractually required to make (for example, to its employees or suppliers if it is acquired in a business combination) is an entity's present obligation that is regarded as a contingent liability until it becomes probable that a business combination will take place. The contractual obligation is recognised as a liability by that entity in accordance with section 21 of FRS 102 when a business combination becomes probable and the liability can be measured reliably. So, when the business combination takes place, the acquirer recognises the acquiree's liability as part of the fair value exercise. This is in contrast to most restructuring provisions, which are not liabilities of the acquiree at the acquisition date (see paras 19.101 and 19.105 above).

Example – Contractual payments crystallising as a result of a business combination

The directors of entity A have clauses in their contracts entitling them to receive twice their basic annual salary, together with an amount for loss of pension benefits, if they decide to terminate their contracts within 28 days of entity A being acquired in a business combination. Entity A has been taken over, and the directors have exercised their rights to terminate their contracts and claim compensation.

In this example (which describes a so-called 'golden parachute'), the acquirer has no control over the decision to terminate the service contracts of entity A's directors and incur the costs. Because the change of ownership clauses were already in existence before the business combination took place, those directors had the right to claim compensation, regardless of the acquirer's intention towards the acquired entity. So, the compensation costs are identifiable liabilities resulting from the crystallisation of a pre-acquisition contingency for the purpose of allocating the business combination's cost.

> In contrast, if the acquirer decided to remove entity A's directors (where those directors had no such rights to terminate their contracts as a result of the business combination), or if the directors' rights to terminate their contracts depended on actions taken by the acquirer, the compensation costs are not recognised under the purchase method. This is because changes resulting from the acquirer's intentions or actions after the business combination are not part of the acquiree's identifiable assets and liabilities. So they should be treated as post-acquisition costs. Similarly, the costs would be post-acquisition if artificial arrangements were made between the acquirer and the vendors to put in place such clauses during the negotiations for the business combination.

19.108 The fair value measurement of acquired financial liabilities only takes into account any early payment of a financial liability, as a result of the business combination, if the payment is triggered by a 'change of control' clause included in the liability's contractual terms. If the payment of a financial liability is the acquirer's decision, it is a post-acquisition event and is not taken into account in measuring the financial liability's fair value at the acquisition date.

Contingent liabilities

19.109 An acquirer recognises an acquiree's contingent liabilities at the acquisition date only if their fair value can be measured reliably. [FRS 102 para 19.20]. Contingent liability has the same meaning as in section 21 of FRS 102 (see chapter 21 for the definition). As explained in paragraph 19.77 above, the recognition rules for a contingent liability acquired in a business combination differ from a liability's general recognition rules; this is because the effect of the probability of the transfer of economic benefits is reflected in a contingent liability's fair value, rather than being a criterion for recognition.

19.110 A contingent liability's fair value is based on the amount that a third party would charge to assume the contingent liability. This should reflect expectations about possible cash flows and not the single most likely, or the expected maximum or minimum, cash flow. This is relevant because, even if the expected minimum cash flow is zero, a third party will still charge a sum to assume the contingent liability.

19.111 If a contingent liability's fair value cannot be measured reliably, there is a resulting effect on the amount recognised as goodwill or negative goodwill. The acquirer needs to disclose the information about that contingent liability required by section 21 of FRS 102 (see chapter 21). [FRS 102 para 19.20].

19.112 After initial recognition, a contingent liability recognised in a business combination is measured at the higher of:

- the amount that would be recognised under section 21 of FRS 102; and

- the amount initially recognised less amounts previously recognised as revenue in accordance with section 23 of FRS 102.

[FRS 102 para 19.21].

19.113 The above guidance means that if, after initial recognition, the provision turns out to be higher than the amount initially recognised, the provision is increased, with a corresponding charge in the post-acquisition income statement. But, if the provision turns out to be lower than the amount initially recognised, the liability is not reduced but continues to be recognised at the fair value at the date of acquisition. It is only reduced if the contingency no longer exists or, if appropriate, for the amortisation of the liability under the revenue recognition guidance. The latter is only relevant if the contingent liability relates to a revenue-earning activity (for instance, a guarantee issued in connection with the sale of goods).

Deferred tax

19.114 Deferred tax assets or liabilities arising from the assets acquired and liabilities assumed are recognised and measured in accordance with section 29 of FRS 102. [FRS 102 para 19.15A]. In summary, for assets (other than goodwill) and liabilities recognised in a business combination:

- Where the amount that can be deducted for tax is less than the amount at which the asset is recognised, a deferred tax liability is recognised; and, where it is more, a deferred tax asset is recognised.

- Where the amount that will be assessed for tax is less than the amount at which the liability is recognised, a deferred tax asset is recognised; and, where it is more, a deferred tax liability is recognised.

[FRS 102 para 29.11].

19.115 A deferred tax asset for an acquired entity's past tax losses might not have been recognised by the acquired entity before the business combination. But the acquirer might determine that other entities within the group will have sufficient taxable profits in the future to realise the tax benefits through transfer of those losses, as permitted by the tax laws. So, if it is probable that the benefit from the tax losses will be recovered, a deferred tax asset is recognised in the purchase accounting.

19.116 The amount attributed to goodwill is adjusted by the amount of deferred tax recognised in the purchase accounting. [FRS 102 para 29.11]. The determination of deferred tax in a business combination is dealt with in chapter 29.

Initial accounting for the business combination

19.117 Under the purchase method of accounting, a business combination's cost is measured at its fair value plus any directly attributable costs (see para 19.37 above) and, subject to the exceptions for employee benefits and taxes, the acquiree's identifiable assets, liabilities and contingent liabilities are recognised at their fair values at the acquisition date (see para 19.70 above). So, the *initial* *accounting* for the business combination involves identifying and determining the fair values to be assigned to the combination's cost and to the acquiree's identifiable assets, liabilities and contingent liabilities.

19.118 The fair values should not generally be affected by matters arising after the acquisition date. But, in practice, it is often not possible for the acquirer to immediately identify and measure all the assets, liabilities and contingent liabilities existing at the date of acquisition date, especially those that have not been recognised by the acquiree.

Period for completing the initial accounting

19.119 The standard recognises that it is necessary to allow an acquirer a reasonable period of time in which to investigate the assets and liabilities that have been acquired, so that a reasonable allocation of the combination's cost can be made to them. The standard effectively requires the acquirer to complete the initial accounting of a business combination within 12 months of the acquisition date (as explained in para 19.121 onwards below).

19.120 If the initial accounting for the business combination is incomplete by the end of the reporting period in which the combination occurs, the acquirer recognises in its financial statements provisional amounts of the acquiree's assets and liabilities for which the accounting is incomplete. [FRS 102 para 19.19].

Adjustments completing the initial accounting

19.121 Where, as a result of completing the initial accounting within 12 months of the acquisition date, adjustment to the provisional amounts has been found to be necessary in the light of new information obtained, the acquirer retrospectively adjusts those provisional amounts (that is, accounts for them as if they had been made at the acquisition date). [FRS 102 para 19.19]. Any increases or decreases to provisional amounts of identifiable assets or liabilities, as a result of completing the initial accounting, results in a consequential adjustment to goodwill or negative goodwill.

19.122 New information that gives rise to adjustments to provisional fair values should provide further evidence of facts and circumstances existing at the acquisition date that, if known, would have impacted the item's recognition and/or measurement in the purchase accounting. It follows that new information reflecting events after the acquisition date does not cause any changes to the initial accounting. Factors to consider, in determining whether new information gives rise to such adjustment, include the timing of the receipt of new information and whether the acquirer can identify a reason for the adjustment. Information obtained shortly after the acquisition date, as opposed to information received several months later, is more likely to reflect facts and circumstances existing at the acquisition date.

19.123 The following example illustrates how new information gives rise to adjustments to provisional values in completing the initial accounting.

> **Example — Adjustments to provisional amounts in completing the initial accounting**
>
> Entity A acquired entity B on 30 September 20X4 and initially accounted for it in its consolidated financial statements for the year ended 31 December 20X4. Entity A commissioned an independent valuation for some equipment acquired in the combination, but this was not finalised by the time that entity A completed its 20X4 financial statements. Entity A recognised in its 20X4 financial statements a provisional fair value for the asset of £30,000 and a provisional value for goodwill of £100,000. The equipment had a remaining useful life at the acquisition date of five years. The useful life of goodwill is considered to be 10 years.
>
> Six months after the acquisition date, entity A received the independent valuation, which estimated the equipment's fair value at the acquisition date at £40,000. How should this information be reflected in the financial statements?
>
> The acquirer needs to recognise any adjustments to provisional values as a result of completing the initial accounting from the acquisition date. (The tax effects of the fair value adjustments are ignored in this example.)
>
> In the 20X5 financial statements, an adjustment is made to the equipment's opening amount at 1 January 20X5. That adjustment is measured as the fair value adjustment at the acquisition date of £10,000 (being £40,000 − £30,000), less the additional depreciation for the three-month period to 31 December 20X4 of £500 (being (£40,000 − £30,000)/5 × ¼) that would have been recognised if the equipment's fair value at the acquisition date had been recognised from that date; so, there is an overall increase of £9,500.
>
> The increase in the value of the equipment at the acquisition date of £10,000 reduces the carrying amount of the goodwill at that date by £10,000. Goodwill is amortised over a period of 10 years, so the adjustment will also result in a reduced amortisation charge for the three-month period to 31 December 20X4 of £250 (being £10,000/10 × ¼); so, there is an overall decrease of £9,750.
>
> The 20X4 comparatives are restated to reflect these adjustments as if the accounting for the business combination had been completed at the acquisition date. So, the 20X4 balance sheet is restated by increasing the carrying amount of equipment by £9,500, reducing goodwill by £9,750 and increasing retained earnings by £250. The 20X4 income statement is restated to include additional depreciation of £500 less goodwill amortisation of £250, giving a net increase of £250.

Adjustments after the initial accounting is complete

19.124 After the initial accounting for a business combination is complete within the permitted 12-month period, no further adjustments are allowed to the purchase accounting for acquired assets and liabilities, except to correct a material error in accordance with section 10 of FRS 102. [FRS 102 para 19.19]. Examples of errors might relate to those where the original cost allocation was based on misrepresentations of facts or on later discovery of issues relating to the acquired entity's activities before the acquisition date. A material error would be accounted for as a prior period adjustment (that is, by adjusting the goodwill arising on the combination). Accounting for errors is covered in chapter 10.

19.125   Amendments might still be necessary to fair values of the acquired assets and liabilities after the permitted investigation period has expired. Because the standard does not allow any further goodwill adjustments to be made, the effect of such amendments is dealt with (where applicable) in profit or loss for the current period. If material, the amendments might require separate disclosure.

19.126   In contrast, where there is contingent consideration in a business combination, adjustments continue to be made to the combination's cost (and so to goodwill) until the consideration is finally determined and payable in accordance with the terms of the agreement (see para 19.62 above).

Business combinations achieved in stages

19.127   The above guidance for applying the purchase method of accounting is based on a business combination that resulted from a single transaction. In practice, some investments that end up as subsidiaries might have started out by the investor acquiring smaller stakes that have increased gradually over time. Where an entity acquires another entity by successive share purchases over time, the business combination involves more than one transaction. This raises a number of questions, including how to determine the business combination's cost, the fair values of the net assets acquired and the resulting goodwill where a business combination is achieved in stages (sometimes referred to as 'step acquisitions').

19.128   The fair value of consideration for a business combination is measured at the acquisition date (see para 19.39 above). Where a business combination is achieved in a series of transactions (for example, where the acquirer purchases the shares of another entity in tranches at various dates until it acquires control), the business combination's cost is the aggregate of the fair values of the assets given, liabilities assumed and equity instruments issued by the acquirer at the date of each transaction in the series. [FRS 102 para 19.11A].

19.129   Where a group acquires a subsidiary in stages, it accounts for the allocation of the combination's total cost in line with the normal rules in paragraph 19.14 of FRS 102 (see para 19.70 onwards above). [FRS 102 para 9.19B]. This means that goodwill is determined on the basis of the fair values at the date of acquisition of the net amount of the identifiable assets, liabilities and contingent liabilities recognised.

19.130   This is consistent with the company law requirements in paragraph 9 of Schedule 6 to SI 2008/410, under which goodwill (or negative goodwill) is calculated as the difference between:

- the fair value of the group's share of the subsidiary's identifiable assets and liabilities at the date that control is achieved; and

- the total acquisition cost of the interests held by the group in that subsidiary.

This applies even where part of the acquisition cost arises from purchases at earlier dates. [FRS 102 para A4.18].

19.131 The FRC notes that, in most cases, this method provides a practical means of applying acquisition accounting, because it does not require retrospective assessments of the fair value of the subsidiary's identifiable assets and liabilities. But, in some circumstances, not using fair values at the dates of earlier purchases (while using acquisition costs that, in part, relate to earlier purchases) might result in accounting that is inconsistent with the way in which the investment has been treated previously, and so it might fail to give a true and fair view. For example, an investment that has been treated as an associate might be acquired by the group as a subsidiary. Using the method required by company law and paragraph 9.19B of FRS 102 to calculate goodwill means that the group's share of profits or losses and reserve movements of its associate becomes reclassified as goodwill (usually negative goodwill). A similar issue might arise where the group has substantially restated the carrying amount of an investment that subsequently becomes its subsidiary. For example, where an investment has been written down for impairment, the effect of applying the company law method of acquisition accounting would be to increase reserves and create an asset (goodwill). [FRS 102 paras A4.19–A4.20].

19.132 In the rare cases where the method for calculating goodwill set out in paragraph 9.19B of FRS 102 and SI 2008/410 would be misleading, the goodwill should be calculated as the sum of goodwill arising from each separate purchase (adjusted, as necessary, for any subsequent impairment). Goodwill arising on each purchase should be calculated as the difference between the cost of that purchase and the fair value at the date of that purchase of the identifiable assets and liabilities attributable to the interest purchased. The difference between the goodwill calculated using this method and that calculated using the method provided by FRS 102 and SI 2008/410 is shown in reserves. [FRS 102 para A4.21]. The particulars, reasons and effect of the departure need to be given (see chapter 3). [FRS 102 para 3.5; CA06 Sec 404(5)].

Exchange of businesses

19.133 Acquisitions of subsidiaries can also arise where a parent sells a subsidiary for shares in another undertaking, which results in that other undertaking becoming a subsidiary of the group. So, at the same time as the acquisition, there is a disposal. The accounting for these 'exchange of business' transactions, including those where the new interest is an associate or a joint venture, is dealt with in chapter 9.

Goodwill

19.134 'Goodwill' is defined as *"future economic benefits arising from assets that are not capable of being individually identified and separately recognised"*. [FRS 102 Glossary of terms]. So, goodwill acquired in a business combination represents a payment made by the acquirer in anticipation of future economic benefits from assets that cannot be individually identified and separately recognised. Purchased goodwill is, in effect, treated as an element of the investment in an acquired business (that is, the premium over its net asset value).

Recognising and measuring goodwill

19.135   At the acquisition date, the acquirer recognises goodwill acquired in a business combination as an asset. But, because goodwill is not an identifiable asset, no fair value is directly attributed to it under the purchase method. Instead, goodwill is initially measured at its cost, being the excess of the business combination's cost over the acquirer's interest in the net amount of the identifiable assets, liabilities and contingent liabilities recognised and measured in accordance with the standard (see para 19.70 above). [FRS 102 para 19.22].

19.136   Goodwill is measured as the business combination's residual cost after recognising the acquiree's identifiable assets, liabilities and contingent liabilities. Where a group acquires less than 100% of a subsidiary, the goodwill represents the group's share of the subsidiary's total goodwill and does not include the non-controlling interest's share.

> **Example – Goodwill recognised is the parent's share**
>
> Entity B is valued at £20m. Entity A acquires 60% of entity B for a cost of £12m. The fair value of entity B's identifiable net assets is £15m.
>
> The goodwill recognised in entity A's consolidated financial statements is determined as follows:
>
> | | £m |
> |---|---:|
> | Consideration paid | 12 |
> | Group's share of the fair value of net assets (£15m × 60%) | 9 |
> | Goodwill | 3 |

So, the goodwill recognised represents the group's share of the total goodwill of £5m (£20m – £15m) attributable to the group. It does not include the amount of the goodwill (in this case, £2m) attributable to the 40% non-controlling interest.

19.137   After initial recognition, goodwill acquired in a business combination is measured at cost less accumulated amortisation and accumulated impairment losses. The standard requires that the acquirer's management should follow the principles in paragraphs 18.19 to 18.24 of FRS 102 for amortising goodwill (see chapter 18) and section 27 of FRS 102 for recognising and measuring the impairment of goodwill (see chapter 27). [FRS 102 para 19.23].

Amortising over useful life

19.138 Goodwill is considered to have a finite useful life and, in line with section 18 of FRS 102 on intangible assets, it is amortised on a systematic basis over that life (see chapter 18). [FRS 102 para 19.23(a)]. It is seldom possible to justify a basis of amortising other than straight line. To do so requires identifying the goodwill's source and the pattern of future benefits arising from that source. If both these requirements are met, it is highly likely that the source of goodwill should be recognised as an identifiable intangible asset in its own right.

19.139 Under company law, goodwill is reduced by provisions for depreciation calculated to write it off in full (that is, to nil) systematically over a period chosen by the company's directors, which must not exceed its useful economic life. [SI 2008/410 1 Sch 22(2)(3)]. So, goodwill should be amortised down to nil over its useful life. No residual value falls to be attributed to goodwill, because it is not an asset that can be sold separately from the underlying business. The amortisation charge for each period is recognised in profit or loss.

19.140 Non-amortisation of goodwill is not permitted in FRS 102 (see para 19.142 below) and would be a departure from both the standard and company law. It would only be possible by using a 'true and fair override' of the Act's and standard's requirement for amortisation. Such a departure is only invoked in extremely rare circumstances, where compliance with the standard would be misleading and would not give a true and fair view. [FRS 102 para 3.4; CA06 Sec 404(5)].

Estimating useful life

19.141 There is no guidance in section 19 of FRS 102 on how to estimate the useful life of goodwill. But the factors discussed in chapter 18 for estimating the useful life of intangible assets are also relevant to goodwill. In particular, the acquirer's management should consider the following factors:

- Expected changes in products, markets or technology. A high-technology company that only has one main product might have considerable goodwill while that product is leading the market; but, if a competitor can produce a better product, the life of the company's goodwill might be short.

- Expected future demand, competition or other economic factors that might affect current advantages.

- The extent to which the acquisition overcomes market entry barriers that will continue to exist.

- The extent to which goodwill is linked to the economic lives of intangible assets.

19.142   Section 19 of FRS 102 states that goodwill is considered to have a finite useful life. Management needs to make an estimate of the useful life of goodwill and, while this cannot be infinite, it might still be long. This will depend on the circumstances, but both unjustifiably long and unrealistically short lives are not appropriate. Under the standard, if management is unable to make a reliable estimate of the useful life of goodwill, the life should not exceed five years. [FRS 102 para 19.23(a)]. What this means in practice is that entities will amortise goodwill over a 'default' period of five years, unless a different period can be justified.

19.143   A long life will generally require a business, industry and products to have a long track record of stability and achievement, and there should be high barriers to market entry. Added to this is the new management's commitment to continue to invest in the acquired business for the long term to maintain and enhance its value. Other businesses, industries and products might be relatively new, potentially much more volatile, and possibly requiring a payback for the acquirer over a much shorter period – in which case, a shorter amortisation period is appropriate. This might be so for products with expected short life cycles, or where there are few barriers to prevent new competitors from entering the market.

19.144   Where an acquired entity has different businesses, we consider that it makes sense to apportion the goodwill to those businesses for the purpose of determining useful lives and amortisation. It would be consistent with the rules for impairment, in section 27 of FRS 102, for goodwill attributable to dissimilar businesses to be amortised separately if the goodwill in those businesses clearly have different useful lives. The resulting amortisation charge would better reflect the depletion of the goodwill than using, say, an average of the useful lives of different components.

Revising useful life

19.145   Estimating the useful life of goodwill requires the exercise of judgement. Factors such as a change in the business, technological advancement and changes in market prices might indicate that the useful life has changed since the most recent annual reporting date. If there are such indications, management should revise the useful life. The revision is accounted for as a change in accounting estimate, in accordance with section 10 of FRS 102 (see chapter 10). [FRS 102 para 18.24]. Where the original estimate of the useful life is revised, the unamortised cost is written off over the revised remaining useful life.

Impact of contingent consideration payable on goodwill amortisation

19.146   A practical effect of the goodwill amortisation requirements arises where a business combination agreement provides for an adjustment to the combination's cost that is contingent on future events. As discussed in paragraph 19.58 above, the estimated amount of the adjustment is included in the combination's cost at the acquisition date if the adjustment is probable and can be measured reliably. Any such amounts recognised increase the goodwill that is recognised at the acquisition date. If the adjustment is not recognised at the acquisition date, but later becomes payable and can be measured reliably, the combination's cost is adjusted and a consequential adjustment is made to goodwill.

19.147 Where a material adjustment is made to the initial estimate of contingent consideration, reducing it because the acquired entity did not perform as well as expected, a question arises of the effect that this has on the amortisation of goodwill. There are two possible methods of dealing with this:

- Amortise the revised carrying amount of goodwill prospectively.

- Restore the excess amortisation previously charged (crediting profit or loss with the excess amount).

19.148 The first method overstates the goodwill's cumulative depletion, because an amount has previously been charged in profit or loss that, with hindsight, will not be paid for. It also arguably understates the cost of goodwill consumed over the remaining estimated useful life. The second method better reflects the goodwill's cumulative depletion, but the current year's amortisation charge would not reflect the goodwill consumed in that year, because it is credited with the excess charge of earlier years. Our view is that either method is acceptable. While we would normally expect the prospective treatment (first method) to be adopted where estimates are revised, the retrospective method could be used where the adjustment's effect is material to the pattern of goodwill amortisation. Whichever method is chosen, material debits should be treated consistently with material credits for different acquisitions.

Impairment

19.149 Management should assess at each reporting date whether there is any indication that goodwill is impaired. If such an indication exists, this might indicate that management should review the remaining useful life or amortisation method, even if no impairment loss is recognised for the asset. [FRS 102 para 27.10]. If there is an impairment loss, this reduces the asset's carrying amount to its recoverable amount (see chapter 27).

19.150 Measuring the recoverable amount of goodwill is complicated, because goodwill is, by definition, not a separable asset (that is, it attaches to a business as a whole). The details of impairment testing of goodwill are included in section 27 of FRS 102 (see chapter 27).

Negative goodwill

19.151 In some business combinations, the acquirer's interest in the net amount of the identifiable assets, liabilities and contingent liabilities recognised under the standard might exceed the business combination's cost. This 'excess' is sometimes referred to as 'negative goodwill' and might be due to one or more of the following reasons:

- Errors in measuring the fair value of either the combination's cost or the acquiree's identifiable assets, liabilities or contingent liabilities. For example, possible future costs and restructuring expenses expected to be incurred as a result of the business combination are not recognised as liabilities (see para 19.106 above) but, where the business (or part of it) is loss-making or under-performing and in need of restructuring, this will depress the fair value of the acquiree's identifiable assets, liabilities or contingent liabilities and might not have been reflected correctly in the fair value of those items.

- A requirement in the accounting standard to measure identifiable net assets acquired at an amount that is not fair value, but is treated as though it is fair value for the purpose of allocating the combination's cost. For example, the acquiree's tax assets and liabilities are not discounted (that is, fair valued).

- A bargain purchase. This might occur as a result of a distress sale (for example, where the seller is forced to dispose of the business quickly and cheaply to relieve cash flow problems).

19.152 Where an excess (or negative goodwill) arises, the acquirer should:

- Reassess the identification and measurement of the acquiree's assets, liabilities and contingent liabilities and the measurement of the combination's cost.

- At the acquisition date, recognise and separately disclose the negative goodwill on the face of the balance sheet, immediately below goodwill, followed by a subtotal of the net amount of goodwill and negative goodwill.

- Subsequently recognise negative goodwill up to the fair value of non-monetary assets acquired in profit or loss in the periods in which the non-monetary assets are recovered.

- Recognise any negative goodwill exceeding the fair value of non-monetary assets acquired in profit or loss in the periods expected to be benefited.

[FRS 102 para 19.24].

19.153 The standard seeks to restrict situations where negative goodwill is recognised. The requirement to reassess the fair values of the identifiable assets, liabilities and contingent liabilities could mean checking the fair values of identifiable assets for impairment, and checking the fair values of the identifiable liabilities to ensure that none has been omitted or understated. In particular, the acquirer ensures that it has recognised all contingent liabilities and measured them at fair value. Any reductions to the acquired net assets that need to be made as a result of this re-assessment exercise will reduce or eliminate the negative goodwill.

19.154 By matching the release of negative goodwill into profit or loss with the depreciation or cost of sales of the non-monetary assets acquired, different amortisation patterns are possible. If the release of negative goodwill is matched first with the depreciation of property, plant and equipment, it will be credited, say, over the average useful life of those assets acquired. This would seem to be a sensible treatment in most circumstances, considering that fair valuing those assets can sometimes be subjective. If the release of negative goodwill is matched first with the cost of sales relating to the sale of the inventory acquired, it will be credited more quickly. But, relative to property, plant and equipment, inventory is less likely to be subject to measurement uncertainty.

19.155 Situations where negative goodwill exceeds the fair values of the non-monetary assets acquired should be rare. If, for example, the only non-monetary asset was inventory, it would be logical to credit the excess negative goodwill in profit or loss over the period when the inventory was sold (or written down).

Disclosures for business combinations

Business combinations occurring during the reporting period

19.156 For each business combination (excluding group reconstructions, which are dealt with in para 19.185 onwards below) that was effected during the period, the following disclosures are required:

- The names and descriptions of the combining entities or businesses. Company law adds that, where a group was acquired, only the name of the acquired group's parent has to be disclosed.

- Whether the acquisition has been accounted for by the acquisition or the merger method of accounting (company law requirement).

- The acquisition date.

- The percentage of voting equity instruments acquired.

- The combination's cost and a description of the components of that cost (such as cash, equity instruments and debt instruments).

- The amounts recognised at the acquisition date for each class of the acquiree's assets, liabilities and contingent liabilities, including goodwill.

- The useful life of goodwill and, if this exceeds five years, supporting reasons for this.

- The periods in which the negative goodwill will be recognised in profit or loss.

[FRS 102 para 19.25; SI 2008/410 1 Sch 22(4), 6 Sch 13].

19.157 Although not specifically mentioned above, a description of the components of the combination's cost will also include the amount recognised as contingent consideration and costs directly attributable to the combination.

19.158 Company law requires the book values and fair values of each class of the acquired entity's assets and liabilities to be given in tabular form. The book values are those immediately before the acquisition, and so they are before any fair value adjustments. The book values of assets and liabilities of an acquired group include any necessary consolidation adjustments within that group. The disclosure should also include the amount of any goodwill or negative goodwill, together with an explanation of any significant adjustments made. [SI 2008/410 6 Sch 13(4)].

19.159 The standard does not specify where, in the income statement, the amortisation of negative goodwill should be shown. Section 5 of FRS 102 sets out the minimum line items to be presented on the face of the income statement. And it requires additional line items to be included when such presentation is relevant to an understanding of the entity's financial performance. [FRS 102 para 5.9]. So, if necessary, the negative goodwill should be shown on the face of the income statement in arriving at profit before tax and presented before financing items (as part of operating profit, where this is presented). Otherwise, it would be consistent with the treatment of goodwill to include negative goodwill as a negative component of goodwill amortisation charges that are treated as operating costs.

19.160 Management should disclose, separately for each material business combination that occurred during the reporting period, the amounts of the acquiree's revenue and profit or loss since the acquisition date included in the consolidated income statement for the reporting period. The disclosure can be provided in aggregate for business combinations that occurred during the reporting period which, individually, are not material. [FRS 102 para 19.25A].

19.161 If, in the directors' opinion, the disclosure of any of the information above that is required by paragraphs 13 to 15 of Schedule 6 (relating to an undertaking established under the law of a country, or one that carries on a business, outside the UK) would be seriously prejudicial to the business of the undertaking, its parent or its fellow subsidiaries, it need not be given if the Secretary of State's permission is obtained. [SI 2008/410 6 Sch 16].

Goodwill

19.162 In addition to the requirement, in the year of acquisition, to disclose the useful life of goodwill if it exceeds five years, with supporting reasons (see para 19.156 above), management should disclose a reconciliation of the carrying amount of goodwill at the beginning and end of the reporting period, showing separately:

- Changes arising from new business combinations.

- Amortisation.

- Impairment losses.

- Disposals of previously acquired businesses.

■   Other changes.

This reconciliation need not be presented for prior periods.

[FRS 102 para 19.26; SI 2008/410 1 Sch 51].

19.163   Disclosure is also required of the cumulative amount of goodwill that has been written off, other than in the consolidated profit and loss account for the current or any earlier financial year. This figure should be shown net of any goodwill attributable to subsidiaries or businesses disposed of prior to the balance sheet date. [SI 2008/410 6 Sch 14(1),(2)]. This relates to the aggregate of amounts of goodwill written off directly to reserves under old UK GAAP (pre-FRS 10) if groups still have this.

Negative goodwill

19.164   In addition to the requirement, in the year of acquisition, to disclose the periods in which negative goodwill will be recognised in profit or loss (see para 19.156 above), management should disclose a reconciliation of the carrying amount of negative goodwill at the beginning and end of the reporting period, showing separately:

■   Changes arising from new business combinations.

■   Amounts recognised in profit or loss (see para 19.152 above).

■   Disposals of previously acquired businesses.

■   Other changes.

This reconciliation need not be presented for prior periods.

[FRS 102 para 19.26A].

Group reconstructions

Applicability to group reconstructions

19.165   Group reconstructions can be accounted for by using the merger accounting method, provided that:

■   the use of the merger accounting method is not prohibited by company law or other relevant legislation;

■   the ultimate equity holders remain the same, and the rights of each equity holder, relative to the others, are unchanged; and

■   no non-controlling interest in the group's net assets is altered by the transfer.

[FRS 102 para 19.27].

19.166 A 'group reconstruction' is defined as any one of the following arrangements:

"(a) the transfer of an equity holding in a subsidiary from one group entity to another;

(b)   the addition of a new parent entity to a group;

(c)   the transfer of equity holdings in one or more subsidiaries of a group to a new entity that is not a group entity but whose equity holders are the same as those of the group's parent; or

(d)   the combination into a group of two or more entities that before the combination had the same equity holders."

[FRS 102 Glossary of terms].

19.167 The term 'group reconstruction' in FRS 102 is wider than that in the Companies Act 2006 for the purpose of group reconstruction relief. It includes several types of combination that are eligible for merger relief, rather than group reconstruction relief under the Act. Where any of the above forms of combination is planned, it will be necessary to determine whether relief from recognising share premium is applicable. These reliefs are explained in chapter 22.

19.168 It is noticeable that FRS 102 does not make merger accounting compulsory in the case of group reconstructions. However, it is likely that, in most cases where there is a group reconstruction and the conditions set out above for merger accounting are satisfied, groups will wish to use merger accounting, because this avoids the need to fair value assets and liabilities.

19.169 One of the conditions for using merger accounting is that it is not prohibited by company law. The conditions in company law, which are in Schedule 6 to SI 2008/410 and apply to consolidated financial statements, are as follows:

- At least 90% of the nominal value of the relevant shares in the acquired entity (excluding any shares held as treasury shares) is held by or on behalf of the parent and its subsidiaries. The reference to 'relevant shares' is to those carrying unrestricted rights to participate both in distributions and in the assets on liquidation.

- The proportion referred to above was attained under an arrangement providing for the issue of equity shares by the parent to one or more of its subsidiaries. Equity shares are defined in the Act as the issued share capital of a company excluding any part which, neither as respects dividends nor as respects capital, carries any right to participate beyond a specified amount in a distribution. [CA06 Sec 548].

- The fair value of any consideration, other than the issue of equity shares given under the arrangement by the parent and its subsidiaries, did not exceed 10% of the nominal value of the equity shares issued.

- Adoption of the merger method of accounting accords with generally accepted accounting principles or practice.

[SI 2008/410 6 Sch 10].

19.170 Under company law, 90% of the nominal value of the relevant shares must be attained under an arrangement providing for the issue of equity shares. This does not mean that, in order to merger account, the parent and its subsidiaries cannot hold more than 10% of the nominal value of the relevant shares before the acquisition; it merely means that, as a result of the offer, the company must have reached at least a 90% holding in the relevant shares (taking into account any prior holdings). Furthermore, any pre-existing holdings that are not part of the arrangement through which the 90% holding is acquired do not have to be taken into account in determining whether the cash or non-equity element of the consideration exceeds 10% of the nominal value of the equity shares issued.

19.171 Another of the conditions for merger accounting for a group reconstruction is that no non-controlling interest in the group's net assets is altered by the transfer. A non-controlling interest might be unaffected, for instance, where a subsidiary is transferred *within* a sub-group that has a non-controlling interest. But it is likely to be affected if a subsidiary is transferred *into* or *out of* such a group. This will be the case if the non-controlling interest has effectively acquired, or disposed of, rights to part of the net assets of the group.

Applicability to various structures of business combinations

19.172 The provisions of paragraphs 19.29 to 19.33 of FRS 102 on the merger accounting method, which are framed in terms of an acquirer or issuing entity issuing shares as consideration for the transfer to it of shares in the other parties to a combination, should also be read as applying to other arrangements that achieve similar results. [FRS 102 para 19.28]. This means that the principles of the merger accounting method also apply where an individual company acquires the trade and assets of an unincorporated business (including a division of a company) in a group reconstruction. However, in applying the merger accounting principles, consideration needs to be given to realised profit implications – for instance, it might be necessary to account for the transfer prospectively by bringing in the net asset book values at the date of the transfer of the trade and assets, and only recognising the profits of the acquired business from the date of transfer.

Merger accounting method

19.173 Where the merger accounting method is used, the carrying amounts of the acquired entity's assets and liabilities are not adjusted to fair value, although appropriate adjustments are made to achieve uniformity of accounting policies in the combining entities. [FRS 102 para 19.29]. So, no new goodwill arises under merger accounting, and the acquired entity's assets and liabilities are brought in at the amounts at which the entity recorded them in its books before the combination (subject to adjustment for uniform accounting policies). [SI 2008/ 410 6 Sch 11(2)].

19.174 The results and cash flows of all the combining entities are brought into the combined entity's consolidated financial statements from the beginning of the financial year in which the combination occurred, adjusted to achieve uniformity of accounting policies. That is to say, they should include the subsidiary's results for the part of the period before the business combination, as well as the subsidiary's results for the part of the period after the business combination, as if the subsidiary had always been part of this sub-group. In addition, the comparative information is restated by including the results for all the combining entities for the previous reporting period and their balance sheet for the previous reporting date (as if the entities had been combined throughout the prior period), adjusted as necessary to achieve uniformity of accounting policies. [FRS 102 para 19.30; SI 2008/410 6 Sch 11(3),(4)]. However, the restatement to show the acquired subsidiary as if it had always been part of the new sub-group is only made as far back as the date when the subsidiary joined the wider group.

19.175 The difference, if any, between the nominal value of the shares issued (and any minimum share premium) plus the fair value of any other consideration given, on the one hand, and the nominal value of the shares received in exchange, on the other, is shown as a movement on other reserves in the consolidated financial statements. Any existing balances on the share premium account or capital redemption reserve of the new subsidiary are brought in by being shown as a movement on other reserves. These movements are shown in the statement of changes in equity. [FRS 102 para 19.31; SI 2008/410 6 Sch 11(5)–(7)].

19.176 The inclusion of the subsidiary's share premium account and capital redemption reserve in the adjustment in other reserves reflects the fact that these are part of the subsidiary's capital. This contrasts with the subsidiary's distributable reserves that flow through into consolidated retained earnings. The share capital, share premium and capital redemption reserve (if any) in the consolidated balance sheet comprise only the amounts from the parent's balance sheet.

19.177 Where the nominal value of the shares issued (and any minimum share premium) plus the fair value of any other consideration given is less than the nominal value of the shares (plus any share premium and capital redemption reserve of the subsidiary) that the parent entity has acquired, the group treats the difference as an 'other reserve' that arises on consolidation. Where the nominal value of the shares issued (and any minimum share premium) plus the fair value of any other consideration given is greater than the nominal value of the shares (again, plus any share premium and capital redemption reserve) acquired, the difference represents the extent to which the group has effectively capitalised its reserves. So, the group should reduce its 'other reserves' by the amount of the difference.

19.178   The two examples below show how these consolidation differences arise and how they should be treated.

Example 1 – Investment's carrying amount is less than nominal value of shares acquired

Entity A acquires all of entity B's £200,000 share capital in a group reconstruction. The purchase consideration consists of new shares that entity A issues and these have a nominal value of £190,000 (assume that there is no minimum premium under section 611 of the Act). In its consolidated financial statements, entity A uses merger accounting for the group reconstruction. The respective balance sheets, after the combination, of the individual entities and the group are as follows:

	Entity A £'000	Entity B £'000	Group £'000
Net tangible assets	1,500	1,400	2,900
Investment in subsidiary	190	–	–
	1,690	1,400	2,900
Share capital	400	200	400
Profit and loss account	1,290	1,200	2,490
Other reserves	–	–	10
	1,690	1,400	2,900

The other reserve of £10,000 is calculated as follows:

	£'000
Nominal value of shares acquired	200
Nominal value of shares issued	190
Other reserves	10

The group treats the difference on consolidation as a reserve arising on consolidation, because the nominal value of shares issued (and, hence, the investment's carrying amount) is less than the nominal value of the shares acquired.

If entity B had existing balances on share premium account or capital redemption reserve, these would also be shown as a movement on other reserves.

Example 2 – Investment's carrying amount is greater than nominal value of shares acquired

The facts in this example are the same as those in example 1 above, except that the purchase consideration consists of new shares with a nominal value of £250,000 (again assume there is no minimum share premium under section 611 of the Act). In this example, the respective balance sheets, after the combination, of the individual entities and the group are as follows:

	Entity A £'000	Entity B £'000	Group £'000
Net tangible assets	1,500	1,400	2,900
Investment in subsidiary	250	–	–
	1,750	1,400	2,900
Share capital	460	200	460
Profit and loss account	1,290	1,200	2,490
Other reserve	–	–	(50)
	1,750	1,400	2,900

The other reserve of £50,000 is calculated as follows:

	£'000
Nominal value of shares acquired	200
Nominal value of shares issued	250
Other reserve	(50)

The nominal value of shares issued (and, hence, the investment's carrying amount) is greater than the nominal value of the shares acquired, and so the group reduces its reserves by the amount of the difference.

If entity B had existing balances on share premium account or capital redemption reserve, these would also be shown as a movement on other reserves.

19.179 Merger expenses are not included as part of the adjustment to 'other reserves', but are charged to the combined entity's profit or loss at the effective date of the group reconstruction. [FRS 102 para 19.32]. This includes share issue expenses, on the basis that there is a difference between the costs of issue of an equity instrument that raises new capital (from which the costs can be deducted) and the costs of a merger that is not considered to raise new capital, but which requires an expenditure of resources that should therefore be charged to the profit and loss account.

19.180 The standard does not prohibit such expenses from being charged to the share premium account, by means of a reserve transfer from the profit and loss account reserve, provided the expenses are eligible to be charged to the share premium account under section 610 of the Act. The relevant expenses that could be charged to the share premium account include the acquiring company's share issue expenses, or the preliminary expenses of any new parent company formed to effect the group reconstruction.

19.181 The aim of merger accounting is to show the combined entities' results and financial positions in the consolidated financial statements as if they had always been combined. So, any share capital issued for the purposes of the group reconstruction is shown as if it had always been issued.

> **Example – Treatment of shares issued in merger accounting**
>
> Entity B was transferred to entity A in 20X1 in consideration for the issue of shares by entity A to its parent. Entity A is accounting for the group reconstruction using merger accounting in its consolidated financial statements.
>
> Entity A's share capital (which is unchanged since the beginning of 20X0) is 100,000 £1 equity shares prior to the reconstruction and that of entity B is 200,000 50p shares. Entity A issues 100,000 equity shares to its parent in consideration for the transfer of entity B.
>
> Entity A's profits were £150,000 for 20X0 and £200,000 for 20X1. Entity B's profits were £190,000 for 20X0, and for 20X1 they were £100,000 to the date of transfer and £75,000 for the post-merger period. There were no adjustments required to achieve uniformity of accounting policies.
>
> The combined group's profits are presented as if entities A and B had always been combined. So, the group income statement shows profits for 20X0 of £340,000 (£150,000 + £190,000) and for 20X1 of £375,000 (£200,000 + £100,000 + £75,000).
>
> Entity A's share capital is adjusted so as to show the shares issued in respect of the group reconstruction as if they had been in existence at the start of 20X0. So, entity A's share capital at the beginning of 20X0 is shown at £200,000.
>
> There is no adjustment to other reserves; this is because the nominal value of shares issued as consideration is equal to the nominal value of shares acquired.

Accounting periods

19.182 Where a new parent company is formed to effect a group reconstruction, accounting issues can arise if the length of the new parent's accounting period differs from that of the other combining entities.

> **Example 1 – Different accounting periods (parent has a short period)**
>
> A new parent entity is formed on 1 July 20X1 and issues equity shares in exchange for the equity shares of entity A as part of a group reconstruction. Entity A's accounting period is the 12 months to 31 December 20X1. The accounting period of the new parent entity is the six months to 31 December 20X1. Entity A is preparing consolidated financial statements and accounting for the group reconstruction using merger accounting.

The question arises as to what figures for entity A should be included in the consolidated financial statements, which themselves must cover the period from 1 July to 31 December 20X1.

The consolidated financial statements could include entity A's results for the period from 1 July to 31 December 20X1, with comparatives for the period from 1 July to 31 December 20X0. But this means omitting the six months of entity A's trading from 1 January 20X1 to 30 June 20X1.

An alternative is for the consolidated financial statements to include the new parent's results for the six months to 31 December 20X1 and entity A's results for the 12 months to December 20X1. This is consistent with paragraph 2 of Schedule 6 to SI 2008/410, which requires the consolidated balance sheet and profit and loss account to incorporate the information contained in the individual financial statements of the undertakings included in the consolidation.

So, the consolidated financial statements for the six months to 31 December 20X1 would include the new parent's results for six months and entity A's results for 12 months. The comparative figures under merger accounting would comprise entity A's profit and loss account, cash flow statement and balance sheet for the year to 31 December 20X0.

Example 2 – Different accounting periods (parent has a long period)

A similar approach might be adopted if the new parent entity was formed on 1 October 20X0 and had its first year end on 31 December 20X1, giving a 15-month accounting period.

In this case, the consolidated financial statements to 31 December 20X1 would include the new parent's results for 15 months, from 1 October 20X0, and entity A's results for its accounting period of 12 months, from 1 January 20X1 to 31 December 20X1. Comparative figures would most sensibly be for the 12 months to December 20X0, because this would give a continuous record for the combined group.

Normally, the duplicated period (in this case, three months) is not an issue, because there is no trading in the new parent in the period to 31 December 20X0.

If the new parent does have significant results in the first three months to 31 December 20X0, this could mean that the December 20X1 consolidated financial statements would have to include both the parent and entity A for the 15-month period to 31 December 20X1, with the comparative period drawn up to 30 September 20X0, to avoid duplication of results.

19.183 As the above two examples show, the issues that arise, where the accounting periods of the new parent and the other combining entity differ, can be overcome. But it is simpler if it can be arranged that, where a new parent is to be formed and merger accounting used, it has the same accounting period as the entity that it combines with.

Comparison of acquisition accounting with merger accounting

19.184 The main differences between acquisition accounting and merger accounting are as follows:

- In acquisition accounting, the consolidated financial statements include the acquired entity's results from the date of acquisition only. In merger accounting, the consolidated financial statements incorporate the combined entities' results and cash flows for the current year as if they had always been combined, even though the business combination might have occurred part way through the year. Also, in merger accounting, the comparative figures in the consolidated financial statements reflect the combined entities' results, even though the business combination did not occur until the current year.

- In acquisition accounting, the acquiring group accounts for the assets and liabilities that it acquires at the combination's cost. It allocates that cost by attributing fair values to the assets and liabilities. But, in merger accounting, the group does not restate assets and liabilities at their fair values. Instead, it incorporates them at the amounts recorded in the acquired entity's books. Merger accounting shows the combining entities as if they had always been combined.

- Acquisition accounting normally gives rise to goodwill on consolidation. However, new goodwill does not arise in merger accounting. Merger accounting might lead to an adjustment to other reserves on consolidation (see para 19.175 above).

Disclosures for group reconstructions

19.185 For each group reconstruction that was effected during the period, the combined entity discloses the following:

- The names of the combining entities (other than the reporting entity). Company law adds that, where a group was acquired, only the name of the acquired group's parent needs to be disclosed.

- Whether the combination has been accounted for as an acquisition or a merger.

- The combination's date.

[FRS 102 para 19.33; SI 2008/410 6 Sch 13(2)].

19.186 In addition, further information is required to be disclosed as follows:

- The composition and the fair value of the consideration given by the parent and its subsidiaries. [SI 2008/410 6 Sch 13(3)].

- Any adjustment to other reserves arising on consolidation (see para 19.175 above). [FRS 102 para 19.31; SI 2008/410 6 Sch 11(6)].

19.187 If, in the directors' opinion, the disclosure of any of the information above that is required by paragraphs 13 to 15 of Schedule 6 (relating to an undertaking established under the law of a country, or one that carries on a business, outside the UK) would be seriously prejudicial to the business of the undertaking, its parent or its fellow subsidiaries, it need not be given if the Secretary of State's permission is obtained. [SI 2008/410 6 Sch 16].

Reverse acquisitions

19.188 Reverse acquisition accounting is a method of acquisition accounting that might be required, in some circumstances, to give a true and fair view of a business combination. Normally, where one company acquires another, the acquiring company's shareholders retain the majority holding in the combined group. But the positions might sometimes be reversed, and it is the acquired company's shareholders who effectively control the combined group, even though the other party is the legal acquirer. If so, the acquired company's management will normally dominate the combined group's management (unless there is a change in the acquired company's management at the same time).

19.189 Another example of a reverse acquisition is where a listed company with little or no business (sometimes called a 'cash shell') acquires a well-established unlisted trading company, which is much larger in size. The rationale for such acquisitions is often that, by combining with the cash shell, the unlisted trading company obtains a listing. It might not give a true and fair view to account for the combination as the acquisition of the trading company by the cash shell. A true and fair view might require the combination to be accounted for as the acquisition of the cash shell by the trading company (in other words, reverse acquisition accounting).

19.190 Company law and FRS 102 do not envisage reverse acquisition accounting, and to adopt that approach is a departure from the law and the standard. However, such a departure is required by both the Companies Act and the standard where it is necessary to give a true and fair view. In such cases, the particulars, reasons and effect of the departure need to be given.

19.191 The reasons given will normally be that the acquisition results in control passing from the legal parent to the legal subsidiary, and so the substance is an acquisition by the legal subsidiary (referred to as the 'acquirer'). Particulars will include the fact that the Act and accounting standards would normally require that the business combination is accounted for using the purchase method as an acquisition by the legal parent of the acquirer, but that (to reflect the transaction's substance) it has been accounted for as the acquisition of the legal parent by the acquirer, and reverse acquisition accounting has been adopted.

19.192 The effect will include disclosure of the fair value of assets and liabilities and of the goodwill that would have arisen if normal acquisition accounting in accordance with the Act and accounting standards had been adopted, together with the effect on reserves of adopting reverse acquisition accounting.

19.193 The accounting in the consolidated financial statements for reverse acquisitions will normally follow the principles outlined below:

- The assets and liabilities of the legal subsidiary (that is, the 'acquirer' for accounting purposes) are recognised and measured at their pre-combination carrying amounts.

- The assets and liabilities of the legal parent (that is, the 'issuer' – the acquiree for accounting purposes) are fair valued.

- The consideration for the reverse acquisition of the issuer is taken to be the number of the issuer's shares in issue immediately before the reverse acquisition multiplied by the market price of those shares when the offer becomes unconditional. The premium on these shares is taken to a reverse acquisition reserve.

- Where merger relief is available under section 612 of the Companies Act 2006, no share premium is recorded on the shares issued by the issuer for the combination with the acquirer.

- The acquirer's profit and loss reserve, revaluation reserve and 'other' reserves are shown in place of those of the issuer.

- The issuer's share capital, share premium and capital redemption reserves (being of a capital nature) are shown, because these are legal capital reserves and cannot be altered.

19.194 Detailed guidance on reverse acquisition accounting, including a worked example, is available in the IFRS Manual of Accounting (although this would need to take into account any GAAP differences in accounting for business combinations).

Transitional issues

19.195 Entities transitioning from old UK GAAP to FRS 102 will need to apply the requirements of section 19 of FRS 102 to all business combinations *after* the date of transition. So, any business combinations during the comparative periods presented by an entity are required to be restated in accordance with the standard. This also applies to accounting for goodwill that might not have been amortised, or has been amortised over a presumed life of 20 years, under old GAAP. The transitional issues applying to intangible assets (discussed in chapter 18) also apply to goodwill.

19.196 An entity can elect not to apply section 19 of FRS 102 to business combinations effected before the date of transition. But, if an entity chooses to restate any business combinations before this date to comply with section 19 of FRS 102, it is required to restate all later business combinations. [FRS 102 para 35.10(a)]. In any case, although the earlier business combinations are not restated to comply with section 19 of the standard, there might still be some restatement in recognising and measuring assets and liabilities (see para 19.200 below).

19.197 Applying these rules means that an entity using FRS 102 for the first time is allowed to choose any date before the date of transition, and account for business combinations going forward under new GAAP, without having to restate earlier business combinations. This is shown in the time line below:

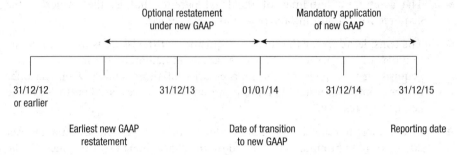

19.198 If a first-time adopter of FRS 102 uses the exemption for business combinations and does not apply section 19 of FRS 102 retrospectively, it recognises and measures all of its assets and liabilities acquired or assumed in a past business combination at the date of transition in accordance with section 35 of FRS 102, except that:

■   intangible assets subsumed within goodwill are not separately recognised; and

■   no adjustment is made to the carrying value of goodwill.

[FRS 102 para 35.10(a)].

19.199 The practical effect is that business combinations that occurred before the date of transition to FRS 102 are unlikely to be restated, because it would be impractical (for instance, in identifying intangible assets that were previously subsumed in goodwill).

19.200 The effect of the exemption is that, although business combinations before the transition date do not have to be restated in full, the assets and liabilities relating to those combinations have to be recognised and measured in accordance with FRS 102, subject to the exceptions and exemptions in section 35. The business combinations exemption is summarised in the table below:

	On transition	Adjustments
Classification (for instance, as an acquisition or a merger)	■ Classification is the same as it was under old UK GAAP.	■ None.
Recognition ■ Assets and liabilities previously recognised in the business combination.	■ Recognise all assets and liabilities in accordance with FRS 102, except some financial assets and liabilities derecognised under previous GAAP, where the derecognition exception is applied. ■ Do not recognise assets and liabilities whose recognition is not permitted by FRS 102.	■ To retained earnings.
■ Assets and liabilities not previously recognised in the business combination in acquirer's consolidated balance sheet.	■ Recognise assets and liabilities under FRS 102, but intangible assets subsumed within goodwill are not separately recognised. Contingent liabilities are recognised under FRS 102 if their fair value can be reliably measured; these might not have been recognised under previous GAAP.	■ To retained earnings.
Measurement	■ Measure all assets and liabilities in accordance with FRS 102. ■ Where FRS 102 requires measurement at fair value, measure on this basis. ■ For assets and liabilities measured at cost, the amount recorded on original combination is deemed cost for cost-based measurement. ■ Assets and liabilities not previously recognised are measured on the basis required by FRS 102 in the acquired entity's financial statements.	■ To retained earnings.

19.201 Where the exemption for past business combinations is used, the standard does not permit goodwill on previous business combinations to be adjusted, so any adjustments made in recognising and measuring the assets and liabilities relating to previous business combinations are made against opening retained earnings on transition to FRS 102.

19.202 Where an entity uses the exemption for past business combinations, deferred tax consequences might still arise in respect of those combinations. FRS 102's requirements apply in the same way to all the assets and liabilities of a group. Deferred tax is recognised when the amount attributable to an asset (other than goodwill) or liability for tax purposes differs from the amount at which it is recognised in a business combination. [FRS 102 para 29.11]. Even if an entity uses the exemption and does not have to restate past business combinations, it might still need to restate the deferred tax arising on those combinations. For example, if assets had been revalued to fair value on acquisition and no deferred tax had been provided under old UK GAAP, provision is required by FRS 102, because there is no specific exemption for this.

19.203 The adjustment for deferred tax and any other adjustments on transition relating to the business combination are made on transition against retained earnings, because goodwill cannot be adjusted where the exemption for past business combinations is used (see para 19.201 above). This means that, where a company has acquired an unincorporated business in a trade and asset deal, adjustments (for example, for deferred tax liabilities) will impact distributable profits.

19.204 If an entity previously determined that goodwill had an indefinite useful life, it will need to reassess this on transition. FRS 102 does not permit goodwill to have an indefinite useful life. So, on transition to FRS 102, entities that previously did not amortise goodwill (as permitted by FRS 10, using a 'true and fair override' of the Act) will need to determine its remaining useful life, and then amortise the goodwill over that period. [FRS 102 Advice to FRC para 161].

19.205 It was common practice for many entities to use a life of 20 years for goodwill under old UK GAAP, which implies that the entity was able to justify this life. We believe that it would be difficult to change this view on transition to FRS 102 and argue that the useful life for these assets defaults to five years. If the life is changed from 20 years, we would expect a change in circumstances in order to justify this; and, even then, five years might not be the answer, given that it is so widely different. Entities would need to consider whether there has been a change in circumstances that has occurred, and it might be that the starting point on restatement is 20 years (as justified by management under old UK GAAP), and then a prospective adjustment to useful life when the change happens.

Chapter 20

Leases

Chapter 20

Leases

Introduction

20.1 Section 20 of FRS 102 sets out the accounting treatment of leases in the financial statements of lessees and lessors in accordance with their commercial substance. A lease is *"an agreement whereby the lessor conveys to the lessee in return for a payment or series of payments the right to use an asset for an agreed period of time"*. [FRS 102 Glossary of terms]. In the UK, such agreements would include contracts for the hire of an asset (usually termed 'hire purchase contracts') or conditional sale agreements where title automatically passes to the hirer (lessee) on making the final lease payment.

Scope

20.2 The provisions of this chapter apply to all leases other than:

- Leases to explore for or use minerals, oil, natural gas and similar non-regenerative resources (see section 34 of the standard). [FRS 102 para 20.1(a)].

- Licensing agreements for such items as motion picture films, video recordings, plays, manuscripts, patents and copyrights (see section 18 of the standard). [FRS 102 para 20.1(b)].

- Leases that could lead to a loss to the lessor or the lessee as a result of non-typical contractual terms (see section 12 of the standard). [FRS 102 para 20.1(e)].

20.3 Licensing arrangements (for items such as those mentioned in the second bullet point above) are not accounted for as leases; they are intangible assets that are accounted for in accordance with section 18 of FRS 102. However, arrangements involving intangible assets could be accounted for as leases if they give exclusive rights to the lessee for the use of an intangible asset for a finite period (for example, a trademark that is licensed exclusively to the lessee).

20.4 Leases that could lead to a loss to the lessor or the lessee as a result of contractual terms that are unrelated to changes in the price of the leased assets (for example, changes in residual values), changes in foreign exchange rates (for example, where lease payments are denominated in foreign currencies), or a default by one of the counterparties are accounted for as financial instruments.

20.5 In practice, however, it is unlikely that lessors will price leases or set rentals based on variables that could cause them to lose their investment in the lease. If any such factors are present, they are likely to be contingent rentals over and above a minimum level of rentals. Such contingent rentals are included in profit or loss in the period in which they occur. But, if the entire stream of rentals is contingent, the lessor might not recover its investment, in which case the rentals are other than payment for use of the asset. Such agreements would be accounted for as financial instruments in accordance with section 12 of FRS 102.

20.6 In addition, the measurement rules of the standard do not apply to:

- Measurement of property held by lessees that is accounted for as investment property, and measurement of investment property provided by lessors under operating leases (see section 16 of the standard).

- Measurement of biological assets held by lessees under finance leases and biological assets provided by lessors under operating leases (see section 34 of the standard).

[FRS 102 para 20.1(c)(d)].

20.7 An entity might have an interest in a property that is leased to another party under an operating lease. If this property meets the definition of an investment property in section 16 of the standard, it should be measured in accordance with the rules of section 16 rather than section 20. The property interest held by the entity could be a freehold interest or a leasehold interest. If the interest is freehold or the lease is a finance lease, the entity is required to measure the investment property at fair value. But, if fair value cannot be measured reliably without undue cost or effort, the property interest is measured at cost. The same rule applies to a property interest held under an operating lease, but only if the entity wishes to treat the interest held as an investment property (see further chapter 16).

20.8 A property that is leased to a third party under a finance lease cannot be treated as an investment property; this is because leasing an asset under a finance lease is, in substance, no different from selling the property to the lessee. So the measurement rules of section 20 of the standard will apply.

20.9 Section 20 applies to agreements that transfer the right to use assets, even though substantial services by the lessor might be called for in connection with the operation or maintenance of such assets. [FRS 102 para 20.2]. For instance, entities often rent properties and equipment (such as motor vehicles, computers and photocopiers) from third parties. Such rental contracts often include an operation or a service contract, under which the third party is also required to maintain, repair, service and generally keep the rented asset in good working order. Such contracts fall within the scope of section 20 of the standard, because they convey the right to use assets from one contracting party to the other. The inclusion of other services in the contract does not change the characterisation of the contract as a lease. In these circumstances, the contract should be broken down into its lease and service components, and each component should be accounted for separately.

20.10 Conversely, section 20 of the standard does not apply to agreements that are contracts for services that do not transfer the right to use assets from one contracting party to the other. [FRS 102 para 20.2]. This means that separable service components in contracts that include both assets and services (for example, the maintenance and repair of motor vehicles, computers or photocopiers) are not leases.

Determining whether an arrangement contains a lease

20.11 Some arrangements do not take the legal form of a lease but convey rights to use assets in return for payments. Examples of arrangements in which one entity (the supplier) might convey a right to use an asset to another entity (the purchaser), often together with related services, include outsourcing arrangements, telecommunication contracts that provide rights to capacity, and take-or-pay contracts. [FRS 102 para 20.3].

20.12 The standard provides as follows:

> *"Determining whether an arrangement is, or contains, a lease shall be based on the substance of the arrangement and requires an assessment of whether:*
>
> *(a)* *fulfilment of the arrangement is dependent on the use of a specific asset or assets. Although a specific asset may be explicitly identified in an arrangement, it is not the subject of a lease if fulfilment of the arrangement is not dependent on the use of the specified asset. An asset is implicitly specified if, for example, the supplier owns or leases only one asset with which to fulfil the obligation and it is not economically feasible or practicable for the supplier to perform its obligation through the use of alternative assets; and*
>
> *(b)* *the arrangement conveys a right to use the asset. This will be the case where the arrangement conveys to the purchaser the right to control the use of the underlying asset."*

[FRS 102 para 20.3A].

Classification of leases

20.13 All leases should be classified as either finance leases or operating leases. The classification of leases under section 20 of FRS 102 is based on the extent to which risks and rewards incidental to ownership of the leased asset lie with the lessor or the lessee. The risks associated with assets include the possibilities of losses from idle capacity or technological obsolescence and of variations in return because of changing economic conditions. Rewards could include the expectation of profitable operation over the asset's life, the gain from increase in the capital value of the asset, or the right to sell the asset and realise the residual value.

20.14 A lease is classified as a finance lease if it transfers substantially all of the risks and rewards incidental to ownership. [FRS 102 para 20.4]. It follows that a finance lease is an arrangement that has the substance of a financing transaction for the lessee to acquire effective economic ownership of an asset. So, a finance lease usually involves payment by a lessee to a lessor of substantially all of the cost of the asset, together with a return on the finance provided by the lessor. Title to the asset might or might not transfer under such a lease.

20.15 A lease is classified as an operating lease if it does not transfer substantially all of the risks and rewards incidental to ownership. [FRS 102 para 20.4]. In practice, this means that a significant element of risk and rewards must remain with the lessor or some party other than the lessee. As a result, an operating lease is usually for a period that is substantially shorter than the asset's useful economic life, and the lessor will be relying on recovering a significant proportion of his investment from either the proceeds from the asset's sale or the asset's further hire after the end of the lease term.

Primary lease classification indicators

20.16   The standard provides as follows:

> *"Whether a lease is a finance lease or an operating lease depends on the substance of the transaction rather than the form of the contract. Examples of situations that individually or in combination would normally lead to a lease being classified as a finance lease are:*
>
> *(a)   the lease transfers ownership of the asset to the lessee by the end of the lease term;*
>
> *(b)   the lessee has the option to purchase the asset at a price that is expected to be sufficiently lower than the fair value at the date the option becomes exercisable for it to be reasonably certain, at the inception of the lease, that the option will be exercised;*
>
> *(c)   the lease term is for the major part of the economic life of the asset even if title is not transferred;*
>
> *(d)   at the inception of the lease the present value of the minimum lease payments amounts to at least substantially all of the fair value of the leased asset; and*
>
> *(e)   the leased assets are of such a specialised nature that only the lessee can use them without major modifications."*

[FRS 102 para 20.5].

20.17   When classifying a lease, it is important to recognise the substance of the agreement rather than its legal form. In analysing substance, more weight should be given to those terms of the agreement that are likely to have commercial effect in practice. Terms that are not likely to have commercial effect should be ignored. Paragraph 20.16 above sets out situations that 'would normally lead' to a lease being classified as a finance lease.

Lease term

20.18 The lease term is key to classifying a lease and is defined as *"the non-cancellable period for which the lessee has contracted to lease the asset together with any further terms for which the lessee has the option to continue to lease the asset, with or without further payment, when at the inception of the lease it is reasonably certain that the lessee will exercise the option"*. [FRS 102 Glossary of terms]. So, it is important to consider carefully those parts of the lease that deal with: the lease's non-cancellable period (sometimes referred to as the 'primary period'); cancellation (or 'break') clauses; exchange and upgrade conditions; and options to extend the lease. Further guidance on the lease term can be found in chapter 19 of the IFRS Manual of Accounting.

Transfer of ownership

20.19 A contractual clause that automatically transfers ownership of the leased asset at the end of the lease term is normally a strong indication of a finance lease. This is particularly the case if transfer of title is for no consideration or for a fixed consideration.

20.20 Transfer of ownership can also occur where the lessor has a put option to sell the asset at an amount that is more than the expected fair value at that date. In this situation, the option is priced in such a way that it is very likely to be exercised by the lessor, with the result that the lessee has no choice but to take ownership of the asset. But, where the put option is at market price, as determined at the end of the lease term, the residual value risk remains with the lessor, and such an option would not, in isolation, indicate finance lease treatment. In addition, it is important to consider whether there is any other commercial or economic compulsion for the lessee to exercise such options, even when the option appears to be priced at or above fair value.

20.21 The criterion in the second point in paragraph 20.16 above is an extension of the transfer of ownership situation. An option held by the lessee to purchase the leased asset below its fair value at the date of exercise is a bargain that is very likely to be exercised by the lessee. Such bargain purchase options are quite common in lease agreements, and they are designed to ensure that the lessor earns its expected return on its investment in the leased asset, but no more, over the term of the lease. So, a lease with such an option is classified as a finance lease. On the other hand, if ownership of the asset is transferred to the lessee at the end of the lease for a variable payment equal to the asset's then fair value, or if there are contingent rents, the lessee does not have substantially all of the risks and rewards incidental to ownership.

Economic life of asset

20.22 The criterion in the third point in paragraph 20.16 above refers to the asset's economic life. The standard does not define 'economic life' of an asset, but the term is understood to have the same meaning as defined in full IFRS. It is the period over which the asset is expected to be economically usable by one or more users; or, if the asset is a productive asset, the number of production or similar units expected to be obtained from the asset by one or more users.

20.23 Where the lease term is for a major part of the asset's economic life, the lease contract is indicative of a finance lease. This is because the residual value risk associated with the asset is likely to be small, and the lessor will look solely to the contracted rental stream to recover its investment in the lease. The lessor retains substantially no risks relating to the physical asset, so the contract will be a finance lease.

20.24 However, the standard does not explain what is meant to be a 'major part' of the asset's economic life. So, judgement must be used in determining its effect on the lease classification. A major part of the economic life must also be consistent with the transfer of 'substantially all' of the risks and rewards of ownership of an asset.

20.25 The period over which an asset is expected to be economically usable is not necessarily the same as the asset's useful life, which is the period over which the asset is expected to be available for use by the entity. For example, entity A might use a certain asset for two years before it replaces the asset due to its high performance requirements. However, another entity B might be able to use the same asset for a further period with no impact on performance. In this case, the economic life would encompass both periods, but the useful life to entity A is two years. So, the useful life of an asset might be shorter than its economic life.

20.26 Some assets, such as IT assets, can be subject to a higher risk of technical obsolescence than other assets. For example, an entity might lease computer hardware, that is capable of operating for seven years, for a period of only three years. Such a lease will probably qualify as a finance lease. This is because some factors, such as advances in technology, result in an economic life that is shorter than the physical life of the hardware. As a result, the economic value that can be obtained from the computer hardware will be concentrated in the first few years of the asset's physical life.

20.27 Where an asset that was previously leased is leased out again by the lessor, the term of the new lease should be compared with the remaining economic life of the asset measured from the commencement date of the new lease for the purposes of lease classification. For instance, if a lessor leases an asset having an economic life of 15 years to lessee A for four years and then to lessee B for eight years, lessee A will use the original economic life of 15 years and lessee B will use the remaining economic life of 11 years for comparison with the respective lease terms.

Present value of minimum lease payments

20.28 If, at inception of the lease, the present value of the minimum lease payments (MLP) amounts to at least substantially all of the fair value of the leased asset, the agreement can be viewed as a financing transaction. The 'present value' test of MLP is a quantitative test, and it can provide significant insight into the amount of residual risk retained by the lessor (or the risks and rewards obtained by the lessee).

20.29 'Fair value' is defined as the amount for which an asset could be exchanged between knowledgeable, willing parties in an arm's length transaction. [FRS 102 Glossary of terms]. But the standard provides no guidance as to what constitutes 'substantially all of the fair value of the asset'. Some national standards, such as old UK and US GAAP, have a bright-line threshold whereby, if the present value of the MLP amounts to 90% or more of the fair value of the asset, the lease must be classified as a finance lease. However, neither FRS 102 nor full IFRS includes such a quantitative threshold, and the final assessment of the lease classification should consider all the other criteria discussed above and should not be based solely on the 'present value' test.

20.30 In order to perform the above test, it is necessary to understand what is meant by 'minimum lease payments' and what 'discount rate' to use. These issues are considered at paragraph 20.44 onwards below.

Specialised nature of leased asset

20.31 Finally, where a leased asset is so highly specialised that only the lessee can use it without major modification, the lessor is unlikely to be able to sell the asset to a third party at the end of the lease. So, the lessor will look to recover its investment in the asset over the lease term, and the arrangement will be, in substance, a financing arrangement. An asset that has been tailor-made for, and leased to, entity A is unlikely to be a specialised asset if entity B, operating in the same industry as entity A, is able to use it without any major modification.

20.32 The assessment of the lease classification is usually not driven solely by the specialised nature of an asset. If, however, a leased asset is of a specialised nature, but the economic life and present value criteria do not indicate a finance lease, the underlying assumptions of these tests should be challenged.

> **Example – Analysis of lease terms**
>
> An entity operates a popular Alpine cable car route. It also owns and operates a restaurant and a shop at the top of the cable car route. The entity leases two new cable cars from a manufacturer. The terms of the lease are for an initial lease term of three years, renewable at the lessee's option. The renewal period is for a further 12 years. The cable cars' economic life is estimated at 15 to 20 years.
>
> The terms and conditions of this short three-year lease might suggest that the entity has only limited exposure to the risks and benefits of a lease asset; but this is not so.
>
> Although the primary lease term is only three years, the lessee has the option to renew the lease for a further period of 12 years. It is reasonably certain that the lessee will exercise the option, because the cable cars are essential for the operation of the cable

car business and for transporting tourists to the restaurant and shops at the top of the route.

In that case, the original period plus the renewal period will provide the entity with access to the rewards of ownership of the cable cars for substantially all of each cable car's economic life. Hence, the lease would qualify as a finance lease. Finance lease classification is also supported by the fact that the cable cars are specialised assets which are unlikely to be of any use to third parties without major modification.

Other lease classification indicators

20.33 In addition to the above primary indicators, the standard provides as follows:

"Indicators of situations that individually or in combination could also lead to a lease being classified as a finance lease are:

(a) *if the lessee can cancel the lease, the lessor's losses associated with the cancellation are borne by the lessee;*

(b) *gains or losses from the fluctuation in the residual value of the leased asset accrue to the lessee (eg in the form of a rent rebate equalling most of the sales proceeds at the end of the lease); and*

(c) *the lessee has the ability to continue the lease for a secondary period at a rent that is substantially lower than market rent."*

[FRS 102 para 20.6].

20.34 Although the above additional indicators do not provide conclusive evidence that a lease is a finance lease, they clearly impact on both the lease term and the minimum lease payments in a way that is likely to lead to a lease being classified as a finance lease. For instance, where the lessee makes a payment to terminate the lessee early, the lease term (for the purpose of the 'economic life' test or 'present value' test) will be based on the full length of the period, and so this is more likely to lead to a finance lease classification.

20.35 Similarly, where gains and losses from fluctuations in the fair value of the residual fall to the lessee, they are 'residual value guarantees' that might impact on the way in which leases are classified by both lessors and lessees. Obviously, if the lessee guarantees the whole of the asset's expected residual value at the end of the lease term, the lessor would not be taking any of the risks relating to the asset's performance or market value, and so the transaction would be clearly a finance lease. It would also mean that, by definition, the present value of the minimum lease payments would be equal to 100% of the asset's fair value. In practice, however, the residual value guarantee often takes the form of a first loss guarantee up to a stipulated amount, and the lessor (or other third party) only takes losses beyond that sum. The lessee is typically obliged to either purchase the asset at a pre-determined fixed amount at the end of the lease term, or sell the asset on the market and reimburse the lessor for any difference between the sales price and the pre-determined fixed amount.

20.36 Whether or not a lease passes substantially all of the risks and rewards of ownership to the lessee will normally be self-evident from the terms of the lease contract and an understanding of the commercial risks taken by each party. Where the lessor takes little or no asset-related risk, other than a credit risk on the lessee, the agreement will clearly be a finance lease. Similarly, where the lessor is exposed to significant levels of risks relating to movements in the asset's market value, utilisation, or performance (such as on a short-term hire agreement), the agreement will be easily classified as an operating lease. The difficulty tends to emerge on classifying leases where the lessor recovers most of his investment through the terms of the lease, but retains some element of risk relating to the asset's residual value at the end of the lease term.

Example 1 — Residual value guarantee

An entity (lessor) leases a truck to a customer for three years. The value of the truck at the end of the lease is estimated at 40% of its original cost. Market data suggest that the likely range of residual values after three years is 40% to 50% of original cost. The lessee will guarantee any fall in the truck's residual value below 40% down to 25% of original cost. The lessor will bear the cost of any fall in residual value below 25% of original cost.

From the given facts, the downside of the residual value risk appears to be shared between the lessee and the lessor. However, the lessor's exposure to residual value risk is remote and should be ignored, because it is unlikely that the truck's residual value will fall below 25% of original cost, even under the most pessimistic circumstances, unless the estimate of residual value of 40% to 50% of original cost is grossly overestimated. The residual value risk is, in substance, borne by the lessee, and the lease is likely to be classified as a finance lease (subject to the other terms). The minimum lease payment would include the guaranteed residual value of the truck that is 15% (40% − 25%) of original cost (see para 20.48 below).

Example 2 — Residual value guarantee

Entity A leases computers to its customers. The lessor's standard lease terms give the customer a right of exchange at any time. The customer can terminate the lease in return for entering into a new lease on new equipment.

The classification of the lease would depend on the economics of the exchange (in particular, the treatment of residual value risk). This is illustrated in the following two scenarios:

- The loss on exchange, calculated as the difference between the lessor's carrying value and the market value, is rolled into the replacement lease. This is achieved through higher lease payments than would otherwise be charged. Because the lessee bears the residual value risk, the lease is likely to qualify as a finance lease.

- The loss on exchange is borne by the lessor and not included in the rentals charged in the replacement lease. So the lease is likely to qualify as an operating lease.

Lease classification is carried at the inception of the lease, so the entity should consider the lessor's standard practice in setting the price of the replacement lease.

20.37 The ability to lease the asset for a secondary period at a nominal rent (or substantially below market rent) indicates that the lessor has received its required return from its initial investment during the primary period, and that the lessee is likely to choose to enter into such a secondary period. The secondary period, in these circumstances, would normally be included in the lease term, and so the economic life test or present value test will be based on the correct length of period.

20.38 It is evident from the above discussions that proper classification of a lease requires a large amount of judgement. Many of the situations described above are unlikely to be present in every lease, but (of the ones that are present) some are likely to be more persuasive than others. Emphasis will generally be placed on the risks that the lessor retains, rather than the benefits of ownership of the asset (for example, retention of legal title). Ultimately, the lease classification should be based on an overall assessment of whether substantially all of the risks and rewards of ownership of the leased asset have been transferred from the lessor to the lessee.

20.39 If other features in the contract make it clear that the lease does not transfer substantially all of the risks and rewards incidental to ownership, the lease is classified as an operating lease. For example, this might be the case if ownership of the asset is transferred to the lessee at the end of the lease for a variable payment equal to the asset's then fair value, or if there are contingent rents which mean that the lessee does not have substantially all of the risks and rewards incidental to ownership.

20.40 Although the definitions of 'operating lease' and 'finance lease' are the same for both the lessee and the lessor (and so the above classification criteria should lead to the same classification for both the lessee and the lessor), this is not always the case. In some situations, differing circumstances of the lessee and the lessor can result in the same lease being classified differently. For example, a lease might be an operating lease for the lessee and a finance lease for the lessor. This issue is discussed further in paragraph 20.65 below.

Inception and commencement of the lease

20.41 Lease classification is made at the inception of the lease. [FRS 102 para 20.8]. Although not defined in the standard, the inception date of the lease is the date on which the lease agreement is signed, which is consistent with the definition provided in full IFRS. Normally, this would also be the date from which the lease commences and the lessee begins to exercise its rights to use the leased asset. But this might not always be the case. For example, an entity might sign an agreement to lease a warehouse on 31 March, but is not able to take possession until 30 June. The inception date of the lease is 31 March and lease classification takes place at this date, but the lease is accounted for in the financial statements from the lease commencement date of 30 June. This later date is the date of initial recognition of the lease (that is, the recognition of the assets, liabilities, income or expenses resulting from the lease, as appropriate) (see para 20.43 below).

Changes in lease classification

20.42   Once a lease is classified as an operating or finance lease at the inception date, it continues to be accounted for as such during the lease term. Changes in estimates (for example, changes in economic life or residual value of the asset) or changes in circumstances (for example, default by the lessee) do not result in reclassification. But, if the lessee and the lessor agree to change the provisions of the lease (other than simply by renewing the lease) during the term of the lease, the lease classification is re-evaluated. [FRS 102 para 20.8].

> **Example 1 – Option to renew a lease**
>
> An entity enters into a five-year, non-cancellable lease on equipment that has an economic life of 11 years. The entity has the option to renew the lease at the end of the lease term for another five years at market rate.
>
> At the inception of the lease, it is not reasonably certain that the option will be exercised, and so, based on the indicators discussed above, the entity classifies the lease as an operating lease at inception.
>
> If the lessee decides later that it is likely to renew the lease, this would not give rise to a re-evaluation.
>
> **Example 2 – Option to purchase a leased asset**
>
> An entity enters into a five-year, non-cancellable lease on equipment that has an economic life of 11 years. At the end of year 5, the entity has the option to purchase the leased asset at a fixed amount that is also the equipment's expected market value at that date.
>
> At inception, the entity classified the lease as an operating lease, because there was no reasonable certainty that the purchase option would be exercised. But, two years into the lease, it became reasonably certain that the lessee would exercise the option at the end of year 5, because the option exercise price was expected to be significantly below the expected market price at that date.
>
> In this situation, the lessee's intention to exercise the purchase option is due to changed economic circumstances and not due to any change in the provisions of the lease. So, the lease will continue as an operating lease until the lessee exercises the option to repurchase. The equipment will be recorded at the option exercise price at that date.
>
> **Example 3 – Change in lease classification**
>
> Entity A leases a building. The original term of the lease was for 30 years, and the estimated useful and economic life of the building at the start of the lease was 45 years. At inception, the lease was classified as an operating lease. Now, nearing the end of the

30 years, the lease has been renegotiated. The new lease term is 20 years, which is equal to the revised expected remaining economic life of the building.

Should the classification of the lease be re-assessed?

The provisions of the lease have changed significantly. The lease is now for a major part of the economic life of the asset. Leases of this type would normally be classified as a finance lease. So the classification of the lease should be re-assessed.

This contrasts with the treatment of a change in estimate, where the lease classification would not be revisited. For example, if it had emerged during the first lease that the economic life of the building was not 45 years, but only 35 years, the original classification as an operating lease should still be kept until the end of the lease term.

Accounting by lessees

Finance leases

Initial recognition

20.43   At the commencement of the lease term, a lessee should recognise its rights of use and obligations under a finance lease as assets and liabilities in its statement of financial position. The leased assets and leased liabilities should be recorded at the lower of:

■   the fair value of the lease asset, determined at inception of the lease; and

■   the present value of the minimum lease payments, determined at inception of the lease.

[FRS 102 para 20.9].

20.44   If the lessee incurs any direct costs (for example, legal fees) in negotiating and arranging the lease, such costs are incremental costs that are added to the amount recognised for the leased asset. [FRS 102 para 20.9].

20.45   The present value of the minimum lease payments should be calculated using the interest rate implicit in the lease. If this cannot be determined, the lessee's incremental borrowing rate should be used. [FRS 102 para 20.10].

20.46   The interest rate implicit in the lease is defined as "... *the discount rate that, at the inception of the lease, causes the aggregate present value of (a) the minimum lease payments and (b) the unguaranteed residual value to be equal to the sum of (i) the fair value of the leased asset and (ii) any initial direct costs of the lessor*". [FRS 102 Glossary of terms]. In other words, the interest rate implicit in the lease is the lessor's internal rate of return from the lease, taking into account the normal cash price of the leased asset, rentals and the amount that the lessor expects to recover from the residual value. In practice, the interest rate implicit in the lease is unlikely to be stipulated in the agreement and, unless the lessor volunteers the information to the lessee, the lessee will need to derive an estimate of the rate from the information available.

20.47 A lessee can normally derive a reasonable estimate of the interest rate implicit in a lease where he either knows (or can make a reasonable estimate of) the cost of the asset and the anticipated residual value of the asset at the end of the lease term. But, where this is not possible (for example, where the lessee is unable to estimate the asset's residual value at the end of the lease term), the standard requires the lessee to use its incremental borrowing rate to determine the present value of the minimum lease payments. The lessee's incremental borrowing rate is the *"rate of interest the lessee would have to pay on a similar lease or, if that is not determinable, the rate that, at the inception of the lease, the lessee would incur to borrow over a similar term, and with a similar security, the funds necessary to purchase the asset"*. [FRS 102 Glossary of terms].

20.48 The minimum lease payments for a lessee are defined by the standard as the payments over the lease term that the lessee is, or can be, required to make, excluding contingent rent, costs for services and taxes to be paid by and reimbursed to the lessor, together with any amounts guaranteed by the lessee or any party related to the lessee (for example, another group entity). In addition, if a lessee has an option to purchase the asset at a price that makes it reasonably certain (at the inception of the lease) that the option will be exercised, the lessee should include the payment to exercise the option in its calculation of the minimum lease payments. If it is not reasonably certain that the option will be exercised, any penalty for non-exercise should be included in the minimum lease payments. It will be reasonably certain that an option will be exercised if (at the inception of the lease) it is expected that the option price will be sufficiently lower than the expected fair value of the asset at the date when the option is exercised.

20.49 The definition of minimum lease payments for a lessor is different from the definition for a lessee and is discussed in paragraph 20.65 below. The difference between the definitions could result in a different classification of the lease by the lessor and the lessee (see para 20.65 below).

Subsequent measurement

20.50 A lessee should apportion minimum lease payments between the finance charge and the reduction of the outstanding liability using the effective interest method (see chapter 11). The finance charge should be allocated to each period during the lease term so as to produce a constant periodic rate of interest on the remaining balance of the liability. [FRS 102 para 20.11].

20.51 A lessee should depreciate an asset leased under a finance lease over the shorter of the leased term and its useful life. But, if there is a reasonable certainty that the lessee will obtain ownership of the asset by the end of the lease term, the asset should be depreciated over its useful life. The depreciation policy used should be consistent with that for other depreciable assets of the same type that are owned by the entity. A lessee should also assess at each reporting date whether an asset leased under a finance lease is impaired in the same way as for assets that are owned by the entity (see section 27 of the standard). [FRS 102 para 20.12].

Example – Accounting for finance leases by lessee

Cost of leased asset	£100,000
Lease term	5 years
Rental six-monthly in advance	£12,000
Expected residual on disposal at the end of the lease term	£10,000
Lessee's interest in residual proceeds	97%
Economic life	8 years
Inception and commencement date	1 January 20X1
Lessee's financial year end	31 December

Initial direct costs are ignored for the purpose of this example.

In this example, the lease must obviously be a finance lease, because the lessor has only an insignificant interest in the residual value (3%).

The amounts that the lessor expects to receive and retain comprise the rentals, plus 3% of the residual at the end of the lease term. These amounts can be used to determine the interest rate implicit in the lease and the present value of the lessee's minimum lease payments as follows:

		Present value factor	Present value at 4.3535% C
Lessee's minimum lease payments:			
January 20X1 (1 period)	£12,000	1.0000	12,000
June 20X1 – January 20X5 (9 periods)	£12,000	7.3170[1]	87,804
			99,804
Lessor's residual			
December 20X5 (£10,000 – £9,700)	£300	0.6530[2]	196
Fair value			100,000

[1] $1/0.043535 \times (1 - 1/(1.043535)^9) = 7.3170$
[2] $1/(1.043535)^{10} = 0.6530$

The effective interest rate amounts to 4.3535%, compounded on a six-monthly basis. This is the rate that exactly discounts the ten six-monthly rentals of £12,000 plus the unguaranteed residual of £300 at the end of the lease term to the fair value of the asset of £100,000 (as shown above).

The amount that is capitalised as both an asset and an obligation at the commencement of the lease is £99,804, which is less than the fair value of the asset of £100,000.

The finance charge can be allocated to each accounting period using the effective interest method, as discussed in chapter 11:

Period commencing	Obligation at start of period £	Rental paid £	Obligation during period £	Finance charge at 4.3535% £	Obligation at end of period £
January 20X1	99,804	(12,000)	87,804	3,823	91,627
June 20X1	91,627	(12,000)	79,627	3,467	83,094
January 20X2	83,094	(12,000)	71,094	3,095	74,189
June 20X2	74,189	(12,000)	62,189	2,707	64,896
January 20X3	64,896	(12,000)	52,896	2,303	55,199
June 20X3	55,199	(12,000)	43,199	1,881	45,080
January 20X4	45,080	(12,000)	33,080	1,440	34,520
June 20X4	34,520	(12,000)	22,520	980	23,500
January 20X5	23,500	(12,000)	11,500	500	12,000
June 20X5	12,000	(12,000)	–	–	–
		(120,000)		20,196	

The finance charges for each year and, by deduction, the capital repayment element of the rental can be summarised as follows:

	Rental £	Finance charges £	Capital repayment £
20X1	24,000	7,290	16,710
20X2	24,000	5,802	18,198
20X3	24,000	4,184	19,816
20X4	24,000	2,420	21,580
20X5	24,000	500	23,500
	120,000	20,196	99,804

In this example, the lessee's financial year end coincides with the end of a rental period, and so no interest accrual is necessary.

Depreciation can be calculated as follows:

Lease term = 5 years
Economic life = 8 years
Lessee's interest in the proceeds of the residual = £9,700

So, the depreciation charge on a straight-line basis is: (£99,804 – £9,700)/5 = £18,021 per annum

The effects on the lessee's balance sheet and profit and loss account for each year can be summarised as follows:

	Obligations under finance leases £	Net book value of leased assets £	Depreciation £	Finance charges £	Total charges £
Start	99,804	99,804	18,021	7,290	25,311
20X1	83,094	81,783	18,021	5,802	23,823
20X2	64,896	63,762	18,021	4,184	22,205
20X3	45,080	45,741	18,021	2,420	20,441
20X4	23,500	27,720	18,020	500	18,520
20X5	–	9,700	90,104	20,196	110,300

The above example illustrates that, in addition to its impact on the lessee's balance sheet, lease capitalisation might also have a significant impact on the lessee's profit and loss account. For example, the lease rentals are £24,000 per annum, but the combined charge for depreciation and interest varies from £25,311 to £18,520 per annum. However, over the lease term, the total rentals of £120,000 differ from the sum of the finance charge (£20,196) and depreciation (£90,104) by £9,700, which is the residual value of the asset. Thus, differences between rental payments and profit and loss charges will be more pronounced on assets subject to long economic lives and leases with short primary lease periods, but which might have secondary periods at peppercorn rents.

20.52　It should be noted that finance lease payables are outside the scope of section 11 of FRS 102; this is because section 20 (the more specific section) provides the rules for recognition and measurement of these liabilities. The only exception to this is where an entity wishes to derecognise a finance lease liability. In this situation, the derecognition rules of section 11 apply.

20.53　A lease contract might sometimes contain a clause that requires the lessee to pay contingent rent. Contingent rent is that portion of the lease payments that is not fixed in amount, but is based on the future amount of a factor that changes other than with the passage of time (such as percentage of future sales, amount of future use, or future market rates of interest). For example, it is common in the retail sector for some of the rental paid by the lessee to be contingent on the lessee's sales. These contingent rentals are excluded from the calculation of minimum lease payments and are charged as expenses in the periods in which they are incurred. [FRS 102 para 20.11]. However, contingent rents must be carefully assessed to see whether they lack economic substance and whether they are, in fact, disguised minimum lease payments. For example, a lessor could charge fixed rents that are significantly below market rents, plus an element that is contingent on the happening of a specific event. If it is assessed that the contingent event is likely to occur, one would be sceptical and question why the fixed rents are set at a level below market rents.

Example – Contingent rentals

A car is leased under a three-year contract. The lease rentals during the three years are fixed, provided the mileage does not exceed a maximum amount during that period. Any mileage incurred above the maximum is subject to an additional charge. How should the minimum lease rentals be calculated?

The minimum lease payments should include only the fixed rent. The charges for excess mileage are contingent and should not be included in the minimum lease payments.

Disclosures

20.54 The standard provides as follows:

"A lessee shall make the following disclosures for finance leases:

(a) for each class of asset, the net carrying amount at the end of the reporting period;

(b) the total of future minimum lease payments at the end of the reporting period, for each of the following periods:
(i) not later than one year;
(ii) later than one year and not later than five years; and
(iii) later than five years; and

(c) a general description of the lessee's significant leasing arrangements including, for example, information about contingent rent, renewal or purchase options and escalation clauses, subleases, and restrictions imposed by lease arrangements."

[FRS 102 para 20.13].

20.55 In addition, lessees of assets held under a finance lease should give the disclosures required by sections 17 and 27 of the standard. [FRS 102 para 20.14].

Operating leases

Recognition and measurement

20.56 Operating leases should not be capitalised:

"A lessee shall recognise lease payments under operating leases (excluding costs for services such as insurance and maintenance) as an expense over the lease term on a straight-line basis unless either:

(a) another systematic basis is representative of the time pattern of the user's benefit, even if the payments are not on that basis, or

(b) the payments to the lessor are structured to increase in line with expected general inflation (based on published indexes or statistics) to compensate for the lessor's expected inflationary cost increases. If

> *payments to the lessor vary because of factors other than general inflation, then this condition (b) is not met."*

[FRS 102 para 20.15].

20.57 The user begins to enjoy the benefit of the leased asset from the date when the lease commences rather than the inception date, so rental expense will be recognised on a straight-line basis between commencement date and the lease termination date. A prepayment or an accrual will arise if the rental payments do not reflect the time pattern of the user's benefit.

20.58 The requirement to spread the lease rentals on a straight-line basis over the lease term, even if the payments are not made on such a basis, applies where the lessee is not using the leased asset. For example, it is common for entities in the retail sector to spend a period of time fitting out a shop before it is open to the public. Some entities have sought to argue that lease rentals on such properties should be spread over the period from the opening of the shop to the end of the lease term (that is, when the shop is generating revenues). But the lessee clearly has benefit from the leased asset during the fitting out of the shop (that is, the access to the property to perform the work). So, the lease rentals should be expensed over the whole of the lease term.

20.59 Prospective lessees are sometimes given incentives to sign operating leases for office or retail property. Such incentives can take many different forms. Examples include: contributions to relocation or start-up costs; the assumption of liabilities (such as the rentals under an old lease which would otherwise be a vacant property); or the gift of an asset (such as the lessor bearing directly all the costs of fitting out the property to the lessee's specifications or giving rent-free or reduced rental periods for an initial period of the lease). A lessee should recognise the aggregate benefit of lease incentives as a reduction to the expenses recognised over the lease term on a straight-line basis, unless another systematic basis is representative of the time pattern of the lessee's benefit from the use of the leased asset. [FRS 102 para 20.15A]. This requirement ensures that the income statement reflects the true effective rental charge for the property, irrespective of the particular cash flow arrangements agreed between the two parties.

> **Example 1 – Lease incentives – reimbursement of relocation costs**
>
> On 1 January 20X1, an entity entered into a new lease arrangement with a new lessor. The lessor agrees to pay the lessee's relocation costs as an incentive to the lessee for entering into the new lease. The lessee's moving costs are £10,000. The new lease has a term of 10 years, at a fixed rate of £20,000 per year.
>
> The lessee should recognise operating lease expenses of £19,000 per year, being rental expense of £20,000 less annual benefit of £1,000. The lessee will recognise moving costs of £10,000 in profit or loss in the year.

Example 2 – Lease incentives – rent-free periods

On 1 January 20X1, an entity entered into a non-cancellable lease on a retail premise for a period of 10 years. No rentals are payable for the first two years. Thereafter, the lessee pays rents of £10,000 each year until year 5. At the end of year 5, the rents are reviewed and adjusted to the prevailing market rates of £15,000 per annum for the remainder of the lease term.

In this situation, the lessee benefits from the first two years' rent-free period. The question is whether the benefit should be spread over the entire lease term or the shorter period until the next market rent review date at the end of year 5. There is no guidance in the standard, and we believe that arguments can be made in support of spreading the benefit either over the shorter period of five years (until the rent review date) or over the entire 10-year term of the lease. Whichever treatment is adopted, it should be applied on a consistent basis for all similar lease arrangements.

On the basis that the lessee decides to recognise the benefit over the entire lease term, and assuming that the benefit is the same for each year, the lessee will recognise rental expense of £10,500 in each of the 10 years of the lease (total cash payments of £105,000 (£10,000 × 3 + £15,000 × 5) divided by 10 years). By the end of year 2, the accrued rent will amount to £21,000, but that will diminish over the remaining lease term as payments are made.

20.60 Costs incurred by a lessee on its own behalf (for example, for the termination of a pre-existing lease, relocation or leasehold improvements) should be accounted for in accordance with the applicable section of the standard. [FRS 102 para 20.15A]. For example, an entity might decide to move out of an existing leasehold property and incur a termination penalty in order to move into a new property at lower rentals. The termination penalty should be expensed, because it does not meet the definition of an asset. Where costs would meet the definition of initial direct costs (that is, 'incremental costs directly attributable to negotiating and arranging a lease'), they should be capitalised and expensed over the lease term on a straight-line basis. This accounting treatment mirrors the accounting of the lessor in an operating lease (see para 20.84 below).

20.61 Where operating lease rental payments to the lessor are structured to increase in line with expected general inflation (based on published index), as noted in paragraph 20.56 above, the inflation adjustments should be recognised in the period in which they occur. In other words, inflation adjustments are treated in the same way as contingent rents. But, if the payments to the lessor vary because of factors other than general inflation, they are not recognised in the period in which they occur but spread on a straight-line basis, as illustrated in the following example given in the standard (with some modifications).

Example 1 – Operating lease rentals adjusted for inflation

X operates in a jurisdiction in which the consensus forecast by local banks is that the general price level index, as published by the government, will increase by an average of 10% annually over the next five years. X leases some office space from Y for five years under an operating lease. The lease payments are structured to reflect the expected 10% annual general inflation over the five-year term of the lease as follows:

Year 1	£100,000	£100,000
Year 2	£100,000 × 1.10	£110,000
Year 3	£100,000 × 1.10²	£121,000
Year 4	£100,000 × 1.10³	£133,000
Year 5	£100,000 × 1.10⁴	£146,000
		£610,000

X recognises annual rent expense equal to the amounts owed to the lessor as shown above. In other words, the inflationary adjustment of 10% is recognised in each year.

But, if the escalating payments are not clearly structured to compensate the lessor for expected inflationary cost increases based on published indexes or statistics, X recognises annual rent expense on a straight-line basis of £122,000 each year (that is, sum of the amounts payable under the lease £610,000 divided by five years).

Example 2 — Operating lease rentals adjusted for inflation

Entity A leases a property at an initial rent of £100,000 per annum. The lease term is 10 years. Under the provisions of the lease, rents will increase in line with the retail prices index at a minimum of 2.5% per year but capped at 4%.

In this situation, although the minimum lease payments will grow in line with expected inflation, there is a minimum floor of 2.5% and a cap of 4% per year. The minimum floor of 2.5% means that, even if inflation is below that level in any particular year, the lessee is committed to pay a 2.5% increase in rentals. Similarly, if the inflation rate in any particular year exceeds 4%, the lessee is committed to pay an increase up to 4%. This means that, when the inflation rate is outside the range of 2.5% to 4%, the rents paid in those periods either over-compensate or under-compensate the lessor for inflationary increases. As a result, the second condition in paragraph 20.56 above is not met.

So, the sum of the annual rents of £100,000 growing at a minimum rate of 2.5% (amounting to £1,120,338) would need to be spread over the lease term of 10 years, resulting in an annual charge of £112,034. Any rents payable in periods where inflation is higher than 2.5%, but less than 4%, will be charged to profit or loss as contingent rents.

Disclosures

20.62 The standard provides as follows:

> "*A lessee shall make the following disclosures for operating leases:*
>
> *(a) the total of future minimum lease payments under non-cancellable operating leases for each of the following periods:*
>
> *(i) not later than one year;*

> *(ii)   later than one year and not later than five years; and*
>
> *(iii)   later than five years; and*
>
> *(b)   lease payments recognised as an expense."*

[FRS 102 para 20.16].

Accounting by lessors

Finance leases

Initial recognition and measurement

20.63   A lessor should recognise assets held under a finance lease in its statement of financial position and present them as a receivable at an amount equal to the net investment in the lease. [FRS 102 para 20.17].

20.64   The net investment in a lease is the lessor's gross investment in the lease discounted at the interest rate implicit in the lease. The gross investment in the lease is the aggregate of:

■   the minimum lease payments receivable by the lessor under a finance lease; and

■   any unguaranteed residual value accruing to the lessor.

[FRS 102 para 20.17].

20.65   The definition of minimum lease payments for a lessor is slightly different from the definition used by a lessee. A lessor will include, in its calculation of minimum lease payments, any residual value that has been guaranteed (whether by the lessee, a party related to the lessee, or an independent third party) in addition to the payments required to be made by the lessee (see para 20.48 above). Third-party guarantors are, in essence, insurers who, for a fee, assume the risk of any deficiencies in leased asset residual value. A residual value guarantee given by a third party unconnected with the lessee, in addition to any given by the lessee, might indicate that substantially all of the risks and rewards were passed on by the lessor, not just to the lessee but to other parties as well. This might result in a different lease classification for the lessor and the lessee (for example, a finance lease for the lessor but an operating lease for the lessee).

20.66   For finance leases other than those involving manufacturer or dealer lessors, initial direct costs (that is, costs that are incremental and directly attributable to negotiating and arranging a lease) are included in the initial measurement of the finance lease receivable, and they reduce the amount of income recognised over the lease term. [FRS 102 para 20.18].

Subsequent measurement

20.67   At any time during the lease term, the net investment in the lease will be represented by the remaining minimum lease payments (that is, the amounts that the lessor is guaranteed to receive under the lease from either the lessee or third parties) less that part of the minimum lease payments that is attributable to future gross earnings (namely, interest). The lessor's net investment in the lease will also include any unguaranteed residual value. The unguaranteed residual value, which will be small in a finance lease, represents the amount that the lessor expects to recover from the value of the leased asset at the end of the lease term that is not guaranteed in any way, by either the lessee or third parties.

20.68   The recognition of finance income should be based on a pattern reflecting a constant periodic rate of return on the lessor's net investment in the finance lease; lease payments relating to the period (excluding costs for services) are applied against the gross investment in the lease to reduce both the principal and the unearned finance income. [FRS 102 para 20.19].

20.69   The method for allocating gross earnings to accounting periods is often referred to as the 'actuarial method'. The actuarial method allocates rentals between finance income and repayment of capital in each accounting period in such a way that finance income will emerge as a constant rate of return on the lessor's net investment in the lease. This is illustrated below.

Example – Accounting for finance leases by lessors

Lease term	7 years from 31 March 20X0
Rental payments	£1,787 payable annually in advance
Asset cost	£10,000
Expected residual value	£nil
Lessor's year end date	30 September

The lessor's gross investment in the lease is the total rent receivable of £12,509 (£1,787 × 7) plus the unguaranteed residual value which is nil. The gross earnings are therefore £2,509 (£12,509 – £10,000).

Finance income in each period must be recognised at a constant rate on the lessor's net investment in the lease at the beginning of the period, so it is necessary to determine the net investment. The net investment in the lease at inception is the present value of the gross investment discounted at the interest rate implicit in the lease. This must be equal to the initial carrying value of the asset of £10,000. The interest rate implicit in the lease, that discounts the advance rentals of £1,787 in each of the seven years to equal £10,000, is 8.1928%, as shown below.

Date	Cash flows	Interest 8.1928%	Balance
	£	£	£
31 Mar 20X0	10,000	–	10,000
31 Mar 20X0	(1,787)	–	8,213
31 Mar 20X1	(1,787)	673	7,099
31 Mar 20X2	(1,787)	582	5,894
31 Mar 20X3	(1,787)	483	4,590
31 Mar 20X4	(1,787)	376	3,179
31 Mar 20X5	(1,787)	260	1,652
31 Mar 20X6	(1,787)	135	–
	(2,509)	2,509	

This equates to a six-monthly interest rate of 4.0158% $[(1.081928)^{\frac{1}{2}} = 1.040158]$.

Once the interest rate implicit in the lease is known, finance income can be allocated to the appropriate accounting periods:

Date	Net investment = Receivable at start of period	Rents received	Interest income at 4.0158%	Gross investment	Gross earnings allocated to future periods	Net investment = Receivable at end of period	Annual finance income
	£	£	£	£	£	£	£
31 Mar 20X0	10,000	1,787	–	10,722	2,509	8,213	
30 Sep 20X0	8,213	–	330	10,722	2,179	8,543	330
31 Mar 20X1	8,543	1,787	343	8,935	1,836	7,099	–
30 Sep 20X1	7,099	–	285	8,935	1,551	7,384	628
31 Mar 20X2	7,384	1,787	297	7,148	1,254	5,894	–
30 Sep 20X2	5,894	–	237	7,148	1,017	6,131	534
31 Mar 20X3	6,131	1,787	246	5,361	771	4,590	–
30 Sep 20X3	4,590	–	184	5,361	587	4,774	430
31 Mar 20X4	4,774	1,787	192	3,574	395	3,179	–
30 Sep 20X4	3,179	–	128	3,574	267	3,307	320
31 Mar 20X5	3,307	1,787	133	1,787	134	1,653	–
30 Sep 20X5	1,653	–	66	1,787	68	1,719	199
31 Mar 20X6	1,719	1,787	68	–	–	–	–
30 Sep 20X6	–	–	–	–	–	–	68
		12,509	2,509				2,509

The gross investment in the lease at any time is the total rentals receivable in future periods and unguaranteed residual (if any). Thus, at 30 Sep 20X2, the gross investment is £7,148, which comprises four future rentals of £1,787. The net investment at 30 Sep 20X2 of £5,894, which is the amount of the receivable recorded in the balance sheet, is the present value of £7,148. The difference between the gross investment of £7,148 and the net investment of £5,894 (that is, £1,254) is the earnings to be allocated to future periods.

20.70 If there is an indication that the estimated unguaranteed residual value used in computing the lessor's gross investment in the lease has changed significantly, the income allocation over the lease term is revised, and any reduction in respect of amounts accrued is recognised immediately in profit or loss. [FRS 102 para 20.19].

Example – Revision of unguaranteed residual value

The facts are the same as in the example above, except that, at 30 September 20X3, the lessor estimates that the asset could realise £500 in the open market at the end of the lease term. The gross investment in the lease at that date is now £5,861, comprising three years' future rents receivable of £5,361 plus estimated unguaranteed residual value of £500. The present value of the gross investment, discounted at the original implicit rate of 8.1928%, amounts to £5,185. The income allocation is revised over the lease term, as shown below:

Date	Net investment = Receivable at start of period £	Rents received £	Interest income at 4.0158% £	Gross investment at end of period £	Gross earnings allocated to future periods £	Net investment = Receivable at end of period £	Annual finance income £
30 Sep 20X3	4,590	–	184	5,861	676	5,185	430
31 Mar 20X4	5,185	1787	208	4,074	468	3,606	
30 Sep 20X4	3,606	–	145	4,074	323	3,751	353
31 Mar 20X5	3,751	1787	151	2,287	172	2,115	
30 Sep 20X5	2,115	–	85	2,287	87	2,200	236
31 Mar 20X6	2,200	1787	87	500	0	500	
30 Sep 20X6	–	–					87
		5,361	860				

Because of the upward revision of the residual value, the lessor will need to recognise additional income of £411, being the difference between the revised net investment of £5,185 and the original net investment of £4,774. This is simply the present value of the residual value uplift of £500, being $500/(1.0458)^5 = 411$.

Manufacturer or dealer lessors

20.71 A manufacturer/dealer lessor is a lessor that either manufactures the leased asset or acquires the leased asset as part of its dealing activities. Because the manufacturer/dealer obtains the asset at its cost of manufacture or at a wholesale price, its cost will be below a normal arm's length selling price that would be the fair value of the asset in a normal financing lease transaction. The accounting issue is whether the manufacturer/dealer lessor should recognise a normal sale profit, and this will depend on the accounting classification of the lease.

20.72 Where the manufacturer/dealer enters into an operating lease, no selling profit is recognised. [FRS 102 para 20.29]. This is because the risks and rewards associated with the asset's ownership have not passed to the customer. So, the manufacturer/dealer will account for the lease in the same way as any other operating lessor.

20.73 Where a manufacturer/dealer enters into a finance lease with a customer, the manufacturer/dealer should recognise profit or loss equivalent to the profit or loss resulting from an outright sale of the asset being leased, at normal selling prices, reflecting any applicable volume or trade discounts. This is because the asset's risks and rewards of ownership have passed to the customer. Therefore, a finance lease of an asset by a manufacturer/dealer gives rise to two types of income: finance income; and a profit or loss equivalent to that arising on an outright sale. [FRS 102 para 20.20].

20.74 The sales revenue recognised at the commencement of the lease term by a manufacturer or dealer lessor is the fair value of the asset or, if lower, the present value of the minimum lease payments accruing to the lessor, computed at a market rate of interest. The cost of sale recognised at the commencement of the lease term is the cost (or carrying amount, if different) of the leased asset less the present value of the unguaranteed residual value. The difference between the sales revenue and the cost of sale is the selling profit, which is recognised in accordance with the entity's policy for outright sales. [FRS 102 para 20.21].

20.75 In determining the sales revenue, the standard requires a market rate of interest to be used; this is because manufacturer or dealer lessors sometimes quote artificially low rates of interest in order to attract customers. If such a low rate were used to determine the selling price, an excessive amount of income would be recognised at the time of the sale. So, if artificially low rates of interest are quoted, selling profit should be restricted to that which would apply if a market rate of interest were charged. [FRS 102 para 20.22].

20.76 Costs incurred by manufacturer or dealer lessors in connection with negotiating and arranging a lease should be recognised as an expense when the selling profit is recognised. [FRS 102 para 20.22]. This is because direct costs incurred by manufacturer or dealer lessors are assumed to relate mainly to earning the selling profit and not a reduction of the amount of income recognised over the lease term, as is the case with a normal finance lease by a lessor (see para 20.66 above).

20.77 For examples of the sale of assets by manufacturer/dealer lessors, refer to the IFRS Manual of Accounting.

Disclosures

20.78 The standard provides as follows:

> "*A lessor shall make the following disclosures for finance leases:*
>
> *(a)* *a reconciliation between the gross investment in the lease at the end of the reporting period, and the present value of minimum lease payments receivable at the end of the reporting period. In addition, a lessor shall disclose the gross investment in the lease and the present value of minimum lease payments receivable at the end of the reporting period, for each of the following periods:*

> (i) not later than one year;
>
> (ii) later than one year and not later than five years; and
>
> (iii) later than five years;
>
> (b) unearned finance income;
>
> (c) the unguaranteed residual values accruing to the benefit of the lessor;
>
> (d) the accumulated allowance for uncollectible minimum lease payments receivable;
>
> (e) contingent rents recognised as income in the period; and
>
> (f) a general description of the lessor's significant leasing arrangements, including, for example, information about contingent rent, renewal or purchase options and escalation clauses, subleases, and restrictions imposed by lease arrangements."

[FRS 102 para 20.23].

Operating leases

Recognition and measurement

20.79   A lessor should present assets subject to operating leases in its statement of financial position according to the nature of the asset. [FRS 102 para 20.24]. Leasing assets under operating leases means that the lessor has retained the risk and rewards of ownership of the asset, and so continues to present the asset on its balance sheet according to its nature (that is, property, plant and equipment, motor vehicles etc).

20.80   The standard provides as follows:

> "A lessor shall recognise lease income from operating leases (excluding amounts for services such as insurance and maintenance) in profit or loss on a straight-line basis over the lease term, unless either:
>
> (a) another systematic basis is representative of the time pattern of the lessee's benefit from the leased asset, even if the receipt of payments is not on that basis, or
>
> (b) the payments to the lessor are structured to increase in line with expected general inflation (based on published indexes or statistics) to compensate for the lessor's expected inflationary cost increases. If payments to the lessor vary according to factors other than inflation, then condition (b) is not met."

[FRS 102 para 20.25].

20.81   A lessor should recognise the aggregate cost of lease incentives as a reduction to the income recognised over the lease term on a straight-line basis, unless another systematic basis is representative of the time pattern over which the lessor's benefit from the leased asset is diminished. [FRS 102 para 20.25A].

20.82 A lessor should recognise as an expense any costs, including depreciation, incurred in earning the lease income. The depreciation policy for depreciable leased assets should be consistent with the lessor's normal depreciation policy for similar assets. [FRS 102 para 20.26]. So, if the asset falls to be treated as property plant and equipment, the rules of section 17 of FRS 102 for depreciation must be applied. That is, the method of depreciation adopted should reflect the pattern in which the asset's economic benefits are consumed. In general, this will result in straight-line depreciation.

20.83 A lessor might incur initial direct costs in negotiating and arranging an operating lease. They normally include:

■ External costs, such as commission and legal, arrangement and brokers' fees.

■ Other commissions and bonuses paid to procure business that are based on reaching sales volumes.

Such costs are added to the carrying amount of the leased asset and are recognised as an expense over the lease term on the same basis as the lease income. [FRS 102 para 20.27]. Recognition of initial direct costs as an immediate expense is not acceptable. If the initial direct costs are material, it is important that they are amortised separately from the asset; this is because they will be recognised as an expense over the lease term rather than over the life of the asset. The lease term is likely to be a significantly shorter period than the life of the asset.

20.84 To determine whether a leased asset has become impaired, a lessor should apply section 27 of the standard. [FRS 102 para 20.28]. This should be applied in the same way as for assets that are owned by the entity.

Disclosures

20.85 The standard provides as follows:

"*A lessor shall disclose the following for operating leases:*

(a) *the future minimum lease payments under non-cancellable operating leases for each of the following periods:*
   (i)   *not later than one year;*
   (ii) *later than one year and not later than five years; and*
   (iii) *later than five years;*

(b) *total contingent rents recognised as income; and*

(c) *a general description of the lessor's significant leasing arrangements, including, for example, information about contingent rent, renewal or*

> *purchase options and escalation clauses, and restrictions imposed by lease arrangements."*

[FRS 102 para 20.30].

20.86 In addition, lessors should give the disclosures required by sections 17 and 27 of the standard for assets provided under operating leases. [FRS 102 para 20.31].

Sale and leaseback transactions

20.87 A sale and leaseback transaction arises when a vendor sells an asset and immediately re-acquires the use of the asset by entering into a lease with the buyer. Such transactions are a popular method of releasing cash funds for new investment as an alternative to borrowing. The accounting treatment depends on the type of lease entered into. It also depends on whether the sale and the subsequent leaseback are on a strictly arm's length basis. In most cases, the lease rentals and the sales proceeds are interdependent, because they are negotiated as a package. Sale and leaseback transactions require careful consideration of all factors in order to arrive at the correct accounting.

Sale and finance leaseback

20.88 If a sale and leaseback transaction results in a finance lease, the seller-lessee does not recognise immediately, as income, any excess of sales proceeds over the carrying amount. Instead, the seller-lessee defers such excess and amortises it over the lease term. [FRS 102 para 20.33]. This treatment will have the effect of adjusting the overall charge to the profit and loss account for the depreciation of the asset to an amount consistent with the asset's carrying value before the leaseback.

> **Example — sale and finance leaseback**
>
> An entity owns a freehold building which is recorded in its books at £700,000. It sells the building to a bank for its fair value of £1,000,000 and leases it back on a finance lease for a period of 20 years, which also represents the major part of the building's economic life. Annual lease rentals amount to £88,218, giving an effective interest rate of 6.15%.
>
> The entity will record the transaction as follows:

On sale of asset	Dr £	Cr £
Cash	1,000,000	
Building		700,000
Deferred income (apparent profit)		300,000
To recognise the sale of the building		
Assets held under finance lease	1,000,000	
Finance lease obligation		1,000,000
To set up the finance lease asset and finance lease obligation		
Years 1–20		
Deferred income	15,000	
Profit or loss		15,000
To release the deferred income over the lease term (£300,000/20)		
Depreciation	50,000	
Assets held under finance lease		50,000

To recognise depreciation on the leased assets (£1,000,000/20)

The depreciation net of deferred income amounts to £35,000, which is consistent with amortising the previous carrying value of the building of £700,000 prior to the sale and leaseback over the remaining 20 years.

In addition, the entity would recognise interest expense calculated at 6.15% on the outstanding balance of the finance lease creditor, which will be amortised down to nil through annual lease payments of £88,218.

Sale and operating leaseback

20.89 Where the seller enters into a sale and operating leaseback, it effectively disposes of substantially all of the risks and rewards of owning the asset in the sale transaction; the seller might re-acquire some of the risks and rewards of ownership in the leaseback, but it does not re-acquire substantially all of them. So, the transaction should be treated as a disposal, and any profit or loss on the transaction should be recognised.

20.90 Where the sale transaction is established at fair value, any profit or loss on sale should be recognised immediately, because this is, in effect, a normal sale transaction. [FRS 102 para 20.34].

20.91 Where the sale price is below the fair value, any profit or loss should be recognised immediately. This recognises the fact that the entity, perhaps motivated by the need to raise cash quickly, might simply have negotiated a poor bargain. An exception is made, however, where a loss is compensated by future lease payments that are below market levels. In such a circumstance, the loss (to the extent that it is compensated by future rentals below market levels) should be deferred and amortised over the period for which the asset is expected to be used. [FRS 102 para 20.34]. The effect of this deferral is to reverse the effect of an artificial loss created by establishing, in an artificial way, the sale price and the subsequent rental.

20.92 Where the sale price is above the fair value, the excess of the sale price over the fair value does not represent a genuine profit. This is because the rentals payable in future years will almost certainly be inflated above the market value. So, the excess of the sale proceeds over the fair value should be deferred and amortised over the period for which the asset is expected to be used. [FRS 102 para 20.34]. This treatment will have the effect of reducing the annual expense for rentals to a basis consistent with the fair value of the asset.

Disclosures

20.93 Disclosure requirements for lessees and lessors apply equally to sale and leaseback transactions. The required description of significant leasing arrangements includes description of unique or unusual provisions of the agreement or terms of the sale and leaseback transactions. [FRS 102 para 20.35].

Transitional issues

20.94 UK entities transitioning from old UK GAAP (SSAP 21) to new UK GAAP must prepare their first financial statements as though the requirements of section 20 of FRS 102 had always applied. However, some exemptions relating to leases are available to first-time adopters under section 35 of FRS 102. The exemptions and the main issues that arise on transition are noted below.

20.95 In many respects, SSAP 21 was similar to section 20 of FRS 102 and had the same finance/operating classification basis for leases. But there was a rebuttable presumption in SSAP 21 that, where the present value of the lease payments amounted to substantially all of the fair value of the leased asset (normally 90% or more), the lease was a finance lease. [SSAP 21 para 15]. There is no such presumption in FRS 102. However, FRS 102 does provide the user with additional guidance on lease classification. Given the similarities in definitions, UK entities transitioning to FRS 102 should not encounter significant differences in lease classification.

20.96 Despite the similarities, entities should examine those leases whose classification was considered borderline under old UK GAAP. These would include outsourcing and other arrangements that are, in substance, leases. Normally, lease classifications are carried out at inception of the lease. But first-time adopters can elect to determine whether an arrangement existing at the date of transition contains a lease based on the facts and circumstances existing at that date, rather than when the arrangement was entered into. [FRS 102 para 35.10(k)]. Entities would normally take the exemption where the arrangement was entered into many years ago and there are difficulties in obtaining all the relevant information. In cases where a lease is reclassified or where an arrangement under old UK GAAP that might not have been classified as a lease is so classified at transition, this would result in an adjustment to retained earnings on transition.

20.97 Provided the term of the lease commenced before the date of transition to the new standard, a first-time adopter is not required to apply the standard's requirements to spread benefits received or receivable from lease incentives over the lease term on a straight-line basis or another systematic basis. The first-time adopter should continue to recognise any residual benefit or cost associated with these lease incentives on the same basis as that applied at the date of transition to the new standard. [FRS 102 para 35.10(p)].

20.98 Adjustments on transition to FRS 102 will be required where a lessor accounted for a finance lease under the net cash investment method allowed under SSAP 21 rather than the net investment method. As noted above, only the net investment method is permitted under FRS 102.

20.99 There are some differences in disclosure requirements between SSAP 21 and FRS 102 which are less detailed.

Chapter 21

Provisions and contingencies

Provisions and contingencies

Chapter 21

Provisions and contingencies

Scope

21.1 This chapter sets out the rules for recognising and measuring provisions, contingent liabilities and contingent assets. It also describes disclosures that are required to enable users to understand their nature and the uncertainties affecting their amount and timing.

21.2 This chapter deals with all provisions, contingent liabilities and contingent assets not covered by other sections of FRS 102. When those other sections contain no specific requirements to deal with contracts that have become onerous, section 21 applies to those contracts. [FRS 102 para 21.1].

21.3 Section 21 of FRS 102 applies to financial guarantee contracts unless the entity is either applying IAS 39 (and/or IFRS 9) to its financial instruments or has elected under FRS 103 to continue the application of insurance contract accounting. [FRS 102 para 21.1A]. It does not apply to financial instruments (including loan commitments) that are within the scope of sections 11 and 12 (see chapters 11 and 12). It also does not apply to insurance contracts (including reinsurance contracts) that an entity issues and reinsurance contracts that the entity holds, or financial instruments issued by an entity with a discretionary participation feature that are within the scope of FRS 103. [FRS 102 para 21.1B].

21.4 The requirements set out in this chapter do not apply to executory contracts unless they are onerous contracts. Executory contracts are contracts under which neither party has performed any of its obligations or both parties have partially performed their obligations to an equal extent. [FRS 102 para 21.2]. Executory contracts include commitments to purchase goods or to deliver services where performance has not yet happened. In some situations, these types of contract might be onerous; and, where they are, provisions should be made. Onerous contracts are dealt with in paragraph 21.67 onwards.

21.5 The word 'provision' is often used to describe amounts that are deducted from assets. For example, provisions are made for depreciation or amortisation or impairment of assets and for bad and doubtful debts. These types of provision are adjustments made to arrive at the asset's carrying amount; they are not liabilities, and so are not dealt with in this chapter.

Definition of provision

21.6 A provision is simply defined as *"a liability of uncertain timing or amount"*. [FRS 102 Glossary of terms]. A liability is defined in section 2 of FRS 102 as *"a* *present obligation of the entity arising from past events, the settlement of which is expected to result in an outflow from the entity of resources embodying economic benefits"*. [FRS 102 para 2.15(b)].

Provisions versus other liabilities

21.7 Provisions form a separate line item in the balance sheet under Schedule 1 to SI 2008/410. They differ from other categories of liabilities in the degree of certainty about the amount or the timing of payment. So, there is a clear distinction between provisions and other liabilities such as trade creditors (also a separate line item in the balance sheet) and accruals (included in the line item 'accruals and deferred income' in the balance sheet).

21.8 For example, trade creditors are liabilities to pay for goods or services that have been received or supplied and have been invoiced or formally agreed with the supplier. On the other hand, accruals are liabilities to pay for goods or services received where no invoice has been received or formally agreed with the supplier. Although there is little, if any, uncertainty relating to the amount of a trade creditor or the timing of when it becomes due, there is some uncertainty with regard to an accrual. But a very good estimate can generally be made of the amount due at the reporting date, and the timing of the payment is often certain (to within a short period of time). As a result, the degree of uncertainty as to the amount or timing is much less than that associated with a provision.

21.9 The following table identifies the types of liability that are usually presented as provisions and those that are presented as other liabilities:

Nature of the obligation	Provision	Other liabilities	Comments
Warranties given for goods or services sold (see para 21.77 below)	✓		
Refunds given for goods sold (see para 21.81)	✓		
Payments for damages connected with legal cases that are probable	✓		
Dilapidations payable at the end of an operating lease (see para 21.89)	✓		
Interest payments		✓	Accrual – the service has been received and the timing and amount of payment is known.
Holiday pay earned by employees		✓	Accrual – short-term compensated absences are recognised in accordance with section 28.
Utility payments for which invoices yet to be received		✓	Accrual – the service has been received, and the estimated amount and timing of payment are not significant.

Recognition criteria for provisions

21.10   Following from the definition of a provision above, the standard requires that a provision should only be recognised where the following conditions are met:

■   the entity has an obligation at the reporting date (that is, balance sheet date) as a result of a past event;

■   it is probable (that is, it is more likely than not) that the entity will be required to transfer economic benefits in settlement; and

■   the amount of the obligation can be estimated reliably.

[FRS 102 para 21.4].

21.11   A provision is recognised as a liability in the balance sheet, and the amount of the provision is charged as an expense, unless another section of FRS 102 requires the cost to be recognised as part of the cost of an asset such as inventories or property, plant and equipment (see para 21.26). [FRS 102 para 21.5].

Obligation and past event

21.12   Not all obligations require an entity to recognise a provision. Only obligations at the reporting date that arise as a result of a past event (that is, the first condition noted in para 21.10 above) give rise to a provision. This condition means that the entity has no realistic alternative to settling the obligation. [FRS 102 para 21.6]. An entity has no realistic alternative to settling the obligation when the obligation stems from a legal agreement (a 'legal obligation') or when, even without a legal agreement, the entity has created valid expectations in other parties that it will discharge the obligation (a 'constructive obligation' – see para 21.16).

21.13   A provision is made only where the obligation is created by a event occurring on or before the reporting date (a 'past event'), whether it arises through the entity's actions or due to external factors. Obligations that arise from an entity's future actions do not meet this condition, even if they are contractual or are virtually certain to occur. Where an entity can avoid future expenditure through its own actions, no provision is made, even if making the expenditure is commercially essential. [FRS 102 para 21.6].

Legal obligation

21.14   It will usually be relatively easy to establish in practice whether or not a legal obligation exists, because it derives either from a contract (through its explicit or implicit terms), or from legislation, or from the operation of the law. Only legislation that has been enacted or substantively enacted at the reporting date should be reflected in provisioning. Such legislation will only lead to a provision when it is retrospective (that is, applying to events that occurred before the reporting date).

21.15 A legal obligation can arise, for example, where a manufacturer gives warranties at the time of sale to purchasers of its products, even where the defect arises a number of years later (if the warranty is still effective); this is because the obligation arises from the contract entered into with the customer at the time when the original sale was made. The accounting for warranties is dealt with in more detail in paragraph 21.77 onwards. Obligations arising from onerous contracts are also examples of legal obligations, because they arise from a contractual burden (see para 21.67 below).

Constructive obligation

21.16 A constructive obligation might be more difficult to discern in practice than a legal obligation; this is because it derives from an entity's actions:

> "(a) by an established pattern of past practice, published policies or a sufficiently specific current statement, the entity has indicated to other parties that it will accept certain responsibilities; and
>
> (b) as a result, the entity has created a valid expectation on the part of those other parties that it will discharge those responsibilities."

[FRS 102 Glossary of terms].

21.17 Some constructive obligations will be obvious; for example, many retailers have a policy of giving cash refunds to dissatisfied customers, whether or not the goods that they bought are faulty. Such a policy might be over and above any legal obligation, but a constructive obligation arises from the retailer's established or published practice. [FRS 102 para 21A.5]. Ad hoc refunds would not be covered. In some circumstances, such as where an entity has published its environmental policies, a constructive obligation might arise where no legal obligation exists; this is because there is no law compelling the entity to carry out the environmental rectification. Clearly, the essence of a constructive obligation is the entity's commitment to a third party. That commitment arises through the entity's actions (that is, by establishing a pattern of practice or by publishing its policies or by making a statement setting out in detail its intended future actions).

Management decisions

21.18 In practice, entities might have difficulty in determining exactly when a constructive obligation arises from which they cannot realistically withdraw; the expectation of other parties is the key. A management decision alone does not give rise to a constructive obligation; this is because it does not create a valid expectation in others until that decision is communicated to them. For example, an entity's board might have taken a decision to undertake a major restructuring programme; but, until its plans are actually being carried out or they have been communicated to others so that it cannot realistically withdraw from its course of action (that is, when it has no realistic alternative but to carry it through), no obligation exists and no provision for restructuring should be made.

Past event

21.19 For there to be an obligation requiring a provision, something must have happened in the past (a 'past event') to trigger that obligation at the reporting date. The past event is often referred to as the 'obligating event'. Many obligating events are obvious; for example, when goods are sold under a warranty, the obligating event that triggers the warranty provision is the original sale. Some past events giving rise to an obligation can occur over a period of time. An example is open cast mining in a jurisdiction where environmental laws require the area to be restored to its pre-agreed condition. Here, the environmental damage is done as the top soil is removed and material is extracted. The obligation (whether legal or constructive) arises when the damage is caused, and provision should be made progressively for the necessary rectification work that will need to be undertaken in the future to restore the site to its pre-agreed condition.

Future actions

21.20 It is only those obligations arising from past events that exist independently of the entity's future actions that are recognised as provisions. Obligations that will arise from the entity's future actions (that is, the future conduct of its business) do not satisfy the first condition in paragraph 21.10 above, *no matter how likely they are to occur and even if they are contractual.* The standard gives an example of an entity that intends or needs to fit smoke filters in a particular type of factory for commercial or legal reasons. Because the entity can avoid the cost of fitting smoke filters by its future actions (for example, by changing its method of operation or selling the factory), it has no present obligation for that future expenditure, and so no provision is recognised. [FRS 102 para 21.6]. Similarly, an airline is legally required to carry out maintenance of its aircraft if it continues to operate them. Because it can stop operating the planes (even though this would make no commercial sense), no obligation to provide for the maintenance expenditure exists (see further para 21.86 below).

> **Example – Staff retraining as a result of changes in the income tax system**
>
> The government introduces changes to the income tax system. As a result of those changes, an entity in the financial services sector will need to retrain a large proportion of its administrative and sales workforce in order to ensure continued compliance with tax regulations. At the end of the reporting period, no retraining of staff has taken place.
>
> Does the entity provide for the cost of retraining at the end of the reporting period?

No, the entity does not recognise a provision. The tax law change does not impose an obligation on an entity to do any retraining. An obligating event for recognising a provision (that is, the retraining itself) has not taken place.

[FRS 102 para 21A.8]

21.21 Note that an event that does not give rise to an obligation initially might give rise to one at a future date. Changes in the law or an entity's actions might create an obligation after the event. For example, where environmental damage has occurred before the reporting date, but there is no current law to require clean-up, no legal obligation exists; this is because no obligation exists that can be enforced by law, even though the potentially obligating event has taken place (that is, the contamination of the land has occurred). But, if, in the following period, the law changed or, say, the entity made a public statement accepting responsibility for rectification of damage done historically, this would create an obligation for which provision is required in that period.

Example – Event giving rise to an obligation at a future date

An entity has been operating a plant where waste from its production process contaminated the groundwater for some years. The entity is not required by law to restore the contaminated environment. But, before the end of the current reporting period, the entity made a public announcement (consistent with its internal policies) that it would restore the contaminated environment within the next 12 months.

The entity has indicated to the public that it will accept responsibility for restoring the contaminated environment in line with its established internal policies and, as a result, it has created a valid expectation on the part of the public that it will discharge this responsibility. So, at the end of the reporting period, the entity has a constructive obligation to restore the damage caused to the environment. There is uncertainty about the amount of the cash flows to restore the environment. The entity has a liability of uncertain timing or amount (that is, it has a provision).

Uncertainty as to whether an obligation exists

21.22 In some cases, it might not be clear whether an obligation exists, even though a past event has occurred. The principal area of difficulty in this respect concerns litigation. Often in a legal case the events might be disputed by the parties. Because of the uncertainty concerning the past event, it might be unclear whether a present obligation exists. In this situation, it might be necessary for an entity to obtain a legal opinion to determine (after taking into account all the available evidence) whether a present obligation exists for which provision is required. This situation is illustrated in the following example, reproduced from paragraph 21A.9 of section 21 of the standard.

Example – A court case

A customer has sued Entity X, seeking damages for injury the customer allegedly sustained from using a product sold by Entity X. Entity X disputes liability on grounds that the customer did not follow directions in using the product. Up to the date the board authorised the financial statements for the year to 31 December 20X1 for issue, the entity's lawyers advise that it is probable that the entity will not be found liable. However, when the entity prepares the financial statements for the year to 31 December 20X2, its lawyers advise that, owing to developments in the case, it is now probable that the entity will be found liable.

(a) At 31 December 20X1

Present obligation as a result of a past obligating event — On the basis of the evidence available when the financial statements were approved, there is no present obligation as a result of past events.

Conclusion — No provision is recognised. The matter is disclosed as a contingent liability unless the probability of any outflow is regarded as remote.

(b) At 31 December 20X2

Present obligation as a result of a past obligating event — On the basis of the evidence available, there is a present obligation. The obligating event is the sale of the product to the customer.

An outflow of benefits in settlement — Probable.

Conclusion — A provision is recognised at the best estimate of the amount to settle the obligation at 31 December 20X2, and the expense is recognised in profit or loss. It is not a correction of an error in 20X1 because, on the basis of the evidence available when the 20X1 financial statements were approved, a provision should not have been recognised at that time.

21.23 Another example, where there is uncertainty over whether a past event gives rise to a present obligation, is set out below:

Example – Obligating events – regulatory notification

Entity A has received notice from the governmental environment agency that official investigations will be made into claims of pollution caused by the entity. Neighbours living near entity A's factory claim that its operations have caused groundwater contamination. The investigation will only consider whether entity A has caused contamination and, if so, what penalties and fines should be levied on it.

Manufacturing operations have been conducted at the site for 150 years; but entity A acquired the factory only 50 years ago. Entity A has used toxins at the plant, but not to an extent that is likely to cause pollution (according to available records). However, management is not sure whether it has all the information about the entire 50 years. So, neither management nor external experts are able to assess entity A's responsibility until the investigation is completed.

How should management account for a liability where it is not possible to assess reliably whether a present obligation exists?

The obligating event is the contamination caused in the past by entity A, and not the future investigation. But management cannot determine whether the obligating event has occurred until the investigation is complete. Under section 32 of FRS 102, any new evidence as to the existence of the obligating event that becomes available after the end of the reporting period up to the date of approval of the financial statements is an adjusting event in assessing whether a present obligation existed at the end of the reporting period.

If the entity is obligated at the end of the reporting period to meet any costs of the investigation, irrespective of the outcome of the investigation, the entity recognises a liability for such costs at the reporting date. If the investigation is not complete by the date of approval of the financial statements, the possible obligation to pay penalties and fines should be disclosed as a contingent liability (see para 21.30 onwards).

Transfer of economic benefits

21.24 Once it has been established that a present obligation exists, it is necessary to determine whether it is *probable* that the entity will be required to transfer economic benefits to settle the obligation (see para 21.10 above). Probable is defined as 'more likely than not'. [FRS 102 Glossary of terms]. 'More likely than not' means a probability of more than 50% that the transfer will occur. Where the probability of the outflow of economic benefits is below 50%, no provision is made, but a contingent liability will exist; this will need to be disclosed in the financial statements unless the contingency is remote.

Reliable estimate

21.25 The use of estimates is an essential part of preparing financial statements and does not undermine their reliability. [FRS 102 para 2.30]. This is especially true in the case of provisions, which by their nature are more uncertain than most other balance sheet items. An entity should normally be able to determine a range of possible outcomes, and so it can make an estimate of the obligation that is sufficiently reliable to use in recognising a provision. Where the amount (rather than the timing) is uncertain, it will be necessary to make a judgement about the appropriate amount to be provided. In many situations, this judgement will be relatively easy to make by using a variety of estimation techniques (see para 21.44 below). In the extremely rare case where no reliable estimate can be made, a liability exists that cannot be recognised. So that liability is disclosed as a contingent liability.

Where does the debit go?

21.26 The amount of the provision should be recognised as an expense, unless another section of the standard requires the cost to be recognised as part of the cost of an asset such as inventories or property, plant and equipment. [FRS 102 para 21.5]. So, the treatment of the debit will follow the requirements for recognising assets and expenses set out in section 2 of the standard. Where a provision (or a change in a provision) is recognised, an asset should also be recognised when the obligation incurred gives access to future economic benefits. [FRS 102 para 2.15(a)]. Where this is not so, the provision should be charged as an expense.

21.27 For example, the commissioning of an oil rig gives access to oil reserves over the years of the oil rig's operation; but it also creates an obligation to decommission the oil rig. The decommissioning cost represents a further element of the cost of the oil rig asset that is supported by future access to oil reserves, and is recognised as an asset concurrent with the provision for decommissioning.

Contingencies

21.28 In a general sense, all provisions are contingent; this is because they are uncertain in timing or amount. But the standard uses the term 'contingent' for assets and liabilities that are not recognised because their existence will be confirmed only by the occurrence or non-occurrence of one or more uncertain future events not wholly within the entity's control. In addition, the term 'contingent liability' is used for a liability that does not meet the recognition criteria in the standard.

21.29 Section 32 of FRS 102 gives further guidance about contingent assets and liabilities where further information is received after the reporting date but before the financial statements are authorised for issue. See chapter 32 for more details.

Contingent liabilities

21.30 A contingent liability is defined as:

> *"(a) a possible obligation that arises from past events and whose existence will be confirmed only by the occurrence or non-occurrence of one or more uncertain future events not wholly within the control of the entity; or*
>
> *(b) a present obligation that arises from past events but is not recognised because:*
> > *(i) it is not probable that an outflow of resources embodying economic benefits will be required to settle the obligation; or*
> > *(ii) the amount of the obligation cannot be measured with sufficient reliability."*

[FRS 102 Glossary of terms].

21.31 Except for those present obligations of an acquiree that are recognised as contingent liabilities in a business combination covered by the requirements of section 19 of FRS 102, contingent liabilities are not recognised. [FRS 102 para 21.12]. Possible obligations are not liabilities. Those present obligations that fall within (b) quoted in the paragraph above are not recognised; this is because they fail to meet the recognition criteria for a provision set out in the standard (see para 21.10).

21.32 The distinction between a provision and a contingent liability can be summarised as follows:

Where, as a result of past events, an entity might be required to settle ...

... a present obligation that will probably require an outflow of resources:	... a possible obligation or a present obligation that could, but probably will not, require an outflow of resources:	... a possible obligation or a present obligation for which the likelihood of an outflow of resources is remote:
A provision is recognised (see para 21.10 above).	No provision is recognised (see para 21.31 above).	No provision is recognised (see para 21.31 above).
Disclosures are required for the provision (see para 21.90).	Disclosures are required for the contingent liability (see para 21.95 below).	No disclosure is required.

A contingent liability also arises in the extremely rare case where a liability exists that cannot be recognised because it cannot be measured reliably. Disclosures are required for the contingent liability (see para 21.95 below).

21.33 The criteria for provision recognition (as discussed above) are illustrated by the use of a flow chart.

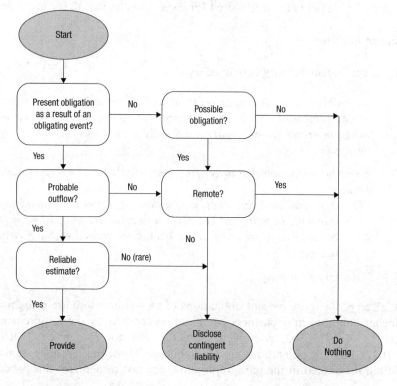

21.34 In some situations, entities are jointly and severally liable for an obligation. For example, in joint venture arrangements where two or more parties co-operate to build, develop or exploit a particular product, joint and several obligations often arise. The part of the obligation that is expected to be met by other parties is treated as a contingent liability. [FRS 102 para 21.12]. The accounting for the part of the obligation for which the entity is obligated in its own right will depend on the normal rules (as outlined above). The entity recognises a provision for any part of the obligation for which an outflow of economic benefits is probable. If an outflow of economic benefits is not probable, a contingent liability is disclosed, unless the outflow is a remote possibility.

21.35 Contingent liabilities might develop in a way that is not initially expected. So, they are continually assessed to determine whether a transfer of economic benefits has become probable. If it becomes probable that a transfer of future economic benefits will be required for an item previously dealt with as a contingent liability, a provision is recognised in the financial statements of the period in which the change in probability occurs (except in the extremely rare circumstances where no reliable estimate can be made).

Contingent assets

21.36 Contingent assets generally only arise from unplanned or other unexpected events that give rise to the possibility of an inflow of economic benefits to the entity. A contingent asset is defined as *"a possible asset that arises from a past event and whose existence will be confirmed by the occurrence or non-occurrence of one or more uncertain future events not wholly within the control of the entity"*. [FRS 102 Glossary of terms]. So, like contingent liabilities, contingent assets are not recognised. [FRS 102 para 21.13].

21.37 The reason for not recognising a contingent asset is that this could result in recognising income that might never be realised. So, it would be wrong to recognise a contingent asset where it is only probable that it would exist on the occurrence of an uncertain future event. But, where the inflow of economic benefits is virtually certain, the related asset is not contingent, and its recognition is appropriate. [FRS 102 para 21.13]. This means that the asset and the related income are recognised in the financial statements in the period in which the change occurs (that is, when the future event occurs and confirms the asset's existence or, if earlier, when it becomes virtually certain that the future event will confirm the asset's existence and it is virtually certain the asset will be realised).

21.38 Therefore, the spectrum that exists around contingent asset can be summarised as follows:

Where, as a result of past events, there is a possible asset whose existence and the inflow of economic benefits is...

... virtually certain:	... probable but not virtually certain:	... not probable:
The asset is not contingent.	No asset is recognised.	No asset is recognised.
	Disclosure is required (see para 21.96 below).	No disclosure is required.

21.39   As with contingent liabilities, any contingent assets should be assessed continually. If it has become virtually certain that there will be an inflow of economic benefits, the asset and the related profit are recognised in the financial statements of the period in which the change occurs. If an inflow of economic benefits has become probable, the contingent asset should be disclosed (see para 21.96 below).

Measuring provisions

21.40   By definition, provisions are uncertain as to either their amount or their timing. This uncertainty can cause a number of problems with their initial measurement. Even for those provisions where only the timing is uncertain, problems with measurement can arise due to the passage of time before the obligation is settled. The problems surround how to estimate a provision, whether it will be settled in the near future, and whether (and, if so, how) it should be discounted. These matters are considered in the paragraphs that follow.

Best estimate

21.41   An entity measures a provision at the best estimate of the amount required to settle the obligation at the balance sheet date. The best estimate of a provision represents the amount that an entity would rationally pay to settle the obligation at the reporting date or to transfer it to a third party. [FRS 102 para 21.7]. In practice, it will seldom be possible to settle the obligation or transfer it in this way, but this remains the best way in which to estimate the obligation.

21.42   Any estimation of the cost to settle or transfer will be a matter of judgement. It will generally be based on management's experience in similar situations. For example, with a warranty obligation, management will often have historical experience of the type and number of claims that have been made. From this past experience, it will be able to estimate (to a reasonable degree of certainty) the number and magnitude of claims for which provision is necessary. In other situations, management might need to seek the advice of an expert. For example, in a litigation case, it might be necessary to seek expert legal advice, not only on the likelihood of a liability arising (see para 21.22 onwards) but also on the quantum of any claim.

21.43   A provision is recognised only if an obligating event has taken place before the balance sheet date. In deciding the amount to be provided, it is appropriate for the entity to take into account any additional evidence arising from events that take place after the end of the reporting period. For example, a court case outstanding at the balance sheet date that is settled before the authorisation of the financial statements confirms that the entity had a present obligation at the balance sheet date. The settlement provides additional information that should be reflected in the measurement of the provision. See further chapter 32.

Estimation techniques

21.44 There are a number of different techniques that can be used to arrive at the best estimate of the amount of a provision, where the creditor does not wish to settle and where there is no market in obligations of the kind for which provision is being made. Generally, entities will use one of the following approaches:

- The most likely outcome (that is, the outcome with the highest probability). This approach is usually appropriate for estimating the amount of the provision that arises from a single obligation (see para 21.45).

- The expected value method (that is, the method that takes account of all possible outcomes, using probabilities to weight the outcomes). This approach is appropriate for estimating the amount of the provision that involves a large population of items (see para 21.47).

Most likely outcome for a single obligation

21.45 Where the provision arises from a single obligation, the individual most likely outcome (that is, the outcome with the highest probability) might be the best estimate of the amount required to settle the obligation. [FRS 102 para 21.7(b)]. Consider the following example.

> **Example – Most likely outcome**
>
> An entity is involved in a single legal case. It is expected that there is a 60% probability that the entity will have to pay damages of £1million and a 40% probability that the claim will be dismissed.
>
> The most likely outcome (that is, the one with the highest probability) is a 60% chance that the entity will lose the case. The entity will either win the case and pay nothing or lose the case and pay £1million. So the entity should recognise a provision of £1 million. For a single obligation, it is not appropriate to measure the provision at its expected value of £360,000 (£1,000,000 x 60% + £0 x 40%).

21.46 But, even in such a case, the entity considers other possible outcomes. Where other possible outcomes are either mostly higher or mostly lower than the most likely outcome, the best estimate will be a higher or lower amount. [FRS 102 para 21.7(b)]. For example, if an entity has to rectify a serious fault in a major plant that it has constructed for a customer, the individual most likely outcome might be for the repair to succeed at the first attempt at a cost of £1 million; but a provision for a larger amount is made if there is a significant chance that further attempts will be necessary.

Expected value method for large number of obligations

21.47 Where the provision involves a large population of items, an 'expected value' is used to arrive at the best estimate of the obligation. [FRS 102 para 21.7(a)]. This method is a statistical method that provides an estimate that reflects the entire probability distribution (that is, all the possible outcomes weighted by their probabilities). The example in paragraph 21.80 is based on the example in paragraph 21A.4 of the standard, which uses a warranty claim to apply the expected value method.

Discounting

21.48 Once the cash flows associated with an obligation have been estimated, it is necessary to consider whether or not the time value of money has a material effect on the sums to be paid. The standard requires that, where the effect of the time value of money is material, the amount of a provision should be the present value of the amount expected to be required to settle the obligation. [FRS 102 para 21.7]. Clearly, provisions for cash outflows that arise soon after the reporting date are more onerous than those where cash outflows of the same amount arise some time later. The main types of provision where the impact of discounting will be significant are those relating to lengthy periods of time, such as decommissioning and other environmental restoration liabilities.

21.49 The standard requires that the present value of a provision should be determined based on a pre-tax discount rate (or rates) that reflect(s) current market assessments of the time value of money. [FRS 102 para 21.7]. This is consistent with the notion that provisions are measured before tax. The tax consequences of the provision, and the tax consequences of a change in the measurement of a provision after it is initially recognised, are dealt with under section 29 of FRS 102.

21.50 As well as reflecting the time value of money, the standard requires that the discount rate should reflect the risks specific to the liability. The risks specific to the liability should be reflected either in the discount rate or in the estimation of the amounts required, but not both (because that would result in double counting for the risk). [FRS 102 para 21.7]. Generally, it is easier to adjust the cash flows for risk and to discount the risk-adjusted cash flows using a pre-tax risk-free discount rate. Adjusting the discount rate for risk can be quite complex and involve a high degree of subjectivity.

21.51 Typically, a government bond 'yield' rate (not the coupon rate on the bond) should be used, as this is a nominal, risk-free pre-tax rate; in other words, the income received is taxed in the hands of the recipient and is paid gross. The yield to redemption rates vary within a small range that depends upon the period of time to redemption. Government bond rates are typically quoted in bands of: up to five years; five to 15 years; and over 15 years. Within these bands, the rates remain fairly constant. So, in practice, it is logical to select a rate that matches the maturity of the liability being discounted. This is relatively straightforward where the amount being discounted is a single payment to be settled in the future; this is because a government bond will have a single capital repayment at the end of its term. But, where the provision is made up of a string of cash flows arising in different periods, it might be necessary to use different discount rates (yield on government bonds with different maturities) to reflect the different timing of the cash flows, as illustrated in the example on warranties in paragraph 21A.4 of the standard (see para 21.80).

Inflation adjustments

21.52 The standard provides no guidance as to whether the discount rate should include the effects of inflation. For the purposes of measuring provisions, cash flows are usually expressed in expected future prices (that is, including inflation), and so they should be discounted using a 'nominal' rate (that is, a rate that includes inflation). Alternatively, cash flows expressed in current prices should be discounted using a 'real' rate (that is, a rate that excludes the effects of inflation). Nominal discount rates are higher than real discount rates (unless there is deflation). Theoretically, discounting cash flows adjusted for price changes using a nominal rate should arrive at the same present value as using a real rate to discount cash flows that have been adjusted for inflation.

Expected disposal of assets

21.53 The measurement of a provision should not take account of any gains from the expected disposal of assets. [FRS 102 para 21.8]. This applies even if the expected disposal is closely linked to the event giving rise to the provision. For example, a restructuring provision cannot be reduced by an expected gain on disposal of a factory that is being sold as part of the restructuring. Instead, the gain will be recognised when the factory is sold.

Reimbursements

21.54 Sometimes, an entity is able to look to another party to pay part or all of the expenditure required to settle a provision (for example, through insurance contracts, indemnity clauses or suppliers' warranties). The other party might either reimburse amounts paid by the entity or pay the amounts directly. In most cases, the entity will remain liable for the whole of the amount in question, so a provision is recognised for the full amount of the liability.

21.55 But, where some or all of the amount required to settle a provision might be reimbursed by another party, the entity should recognise the reimbursement as a separate asset only when it is virtually certain that the entity will receive the reimbursement on settlement of the obligation.

21.56 To recognise the reimbursement as an asset, virtual certainty as to the amount of the reimbursement is not always necessary. Provided that it is virtually certain at the balance sheet date that the reimbursement will be received if the entity settles the obligation, the reimbursement asset is recognised; in other words, the asset is recognised provided that any post balance sheet negotiation in respect of the asset relates to agreement of final amount to be paid and not to whether the reimbursement will be paid if there is a related liability. In such a case, the virtual certainty of reimbursement (in the event of a liability arising) means that the reimbursement asset is not regarded as contingent (see para 21.37 above). The amount recognised for the reimbursement should not exceed the amount of the provision. [FRS 102 para 21.9].

21.57 The reimbursement receivable should be presented in the balance sheet as an asset and should not be offset against the provision. But, in the statement of comprehensive income (or in the income statement, where presented), the entity could offset any reimbursement from another party against the expense relating to the provision.[FRS 102 para 21.9]. This presentation in the income statement better reflects the substance of the transaction. The standard notes that this netting does not contradict the legal prohibition on the netting of expenditure against income. [FRS 102 Appendix IV para A4.22]. In practice, this concession has little impact; this is because both the provision and the recovery will often form part of operating profit, and so might only affect the allocation between, say, administrative expenses and other income.

21.58 In some situations, a provision made by a subsidiary could be settled by the parent without requiring any reimbursement from the subsidiary. The fact that the parent has undertaken to settle the obligation does not relieve the subsidiary from making a provision. When the parent settles the obligation on behalf of the subsidiary, the subsidiary should not write back the provision to profit or loss, but take it to equity as a capital contribution from the parent (that is, a transaction with an owner).

Subsequent measurement

Use of provision

21.59 After a provision's initial recognition, an entity should charge against the provision only those expenditures for which the provision was originally recognised. [FRS 102 para 21.10].

> **Example – Expenditure charged against a provision**
>
> An entity recognised a provision for £100,000 for a lawsuit at 31 December 20X1. In March 20X2 the case was dismissed without the right to appeal. In April 20X2, the entity undertook an advertising campaign costing £100,000 to repair the damage to its reputation caused by the adverse publicity from the case.
>
> In this situation, the entity cannot offset the cost of the advertising campaign against the provision because it is not an expenditure for which the provision was originally set up. Instead, the entity should write back the provision to profit or loss and recognise the cost of the campaign in profit or loss.

Changes in provisions

21.60 An entity should review its provisions at each reporting date and adjust each provision to reflect the current best estimate of the amount that would be required to settle the obligation at that reporting date. Adjustments to provisions might result from changes in the amount or timing of cash outflows or changes in the discount rate. Any adjustments to the amounts previously recognised are recognised in profit or loss, unless the provision was originally recognised as part of the asset's cost (see para 21.26). [FRS 102 para 21.11].

Unwinding of the discount

21.61 Where discounting is used to estimate the present value of the provision expected to be required to settle the obligation, the carrying amount will need to be adjusted each reporting date, even if the expected cash flows are unchanged. This adjustment increases the carrying amount of the provision as the discount unwinds due to the passage of time. This unwinding of the discount is recognised as finance cost in the profit or loss in the period in which it arises. [FRS 102 para 21.11]. The effect of revising the estimates of cash flows is not part of this unwinding and should be dealt with as an adjustment to the carrying amount of the provision.

> **Example – Change in cash outflow**
>
> An entity has a £1,000 obligation which is due at the end of year 5. It provides now for the net present value of the obligation of £802, which has been arrived at by using a nominal risk-free pre-tax rate of 4.5%. The amount of the provision is charged as an operating expense. At the end of year 3, based on new information, the entity estimates that it would need to pay £1,200 to settle the obligation at the end of year 5. The discount rate remains unchanged during the five-year period.
>
> The amount of the provision at the end of each year, based on the original estimate and the revised estimate at the end of year 3 (discounted at the 4.5%), is shown below:
>
> | | | NPV | Year 1 | Year 2 | Year 3 | Year 4 | Year 5 |
> |---|---|---|---|---|---|---|---|
> | | | £ | £ | £ | £ | £ | £ |
> | Original estimate | 4.5% | 802 | 839 | 876 | 916 | 957 | 1,000 |
> | Revised estimate | 4.5% | | | | 1,099 | 1,148 | 1,200 |

As noted above, the obligation at the beginning of year 3 is £876, and at the end of year 3 it would be stated at £1,099, based on the new estimate. The difference of £223 (£1,099 – £876) is made up of a finance cost (for the unwinding of the discount, that is £40 (£916 – £876)) and a change in estimate of the provision (due to the change in amount of the cash flows, that is £183 (£1,099 – £916)). The additional amount of £183 (to bring the provision to £1,099) would be charged as an operating expense.

Changes in discount rate

21.62 Changes in the value of the provision can also arise as a result of changes in the discount rate. The risk-free discount rate, represented by yield on government bonds, might change over time; and the effect could be significant, particularly where provision is for costs expected to be incurred a long time into the future, as is the case with decommissioning obligations. Furthermore, as mentioned in paragraph 21.51 above, it might sometimes be necessary to use different discount rates (yield on government bonds with different maturities) to reflect the different timing of the cash flows.

21.63 The standard provides no guidance on how to address changes in the discount rates used to measure the provision. Arguably, they could be treated in the same way as the unwinding of the discount and be included in finance cost. But we believe it is more appropriate to treat the change in discount rate as a change in accounting estimate (as discussed in chapter 10). Neither is there guidance on to how to calculate the adjustment where discount rate changes during the year. But, because the standard requires the amount of the provision to be reviewed at each year end, it makes sense to the use the rate prevailing at the year end to discount the future cash flows. Any change in the provision's carrying amount should be reported in the appropriate expense category in income statement, unless the provision was originally recognised as part of an asset's cost. This adjustment to the provision's carrying amount is treated in a similar way to changes in future cash outflows. Consider the following example:

Example – Change in discount rate

An entity has a £1,000 obligation which is due at the end of year 5. It provides now for the net present value of the obligation of £802, which has been arrived at by using a nominal risk-free pre-tax rate of 4.5%. At the end of year 3, the discount rate has changed to 4%.

The amount of the provision at the end of each year, based on the old discount rate of 4.5% and the new discount rate of 4%, is shown below:

		NPV	Year 1	Year 2	Year 3	Year 4	Year 5
		£	£	£	£	£	£
Original estimate	4.5%	802	839	876	916	957	1,000
Revised estimate	4.0%				925	962	1,000

As noted above, the obligation at the beginning of year 3 (measured at a discount rate of 4.5%) is £876 and, at the end of year 3, it would be stated at £916 if the rate were still 4.5%.

But, based on a current rate of 4%, the estimated net present value needs to be £925 (£1,000 discounted for two years at 4%). The difference of £49 (£925 – £876) is made

---

up of a finance cost (for the unwinding of the discount, that is £40 (£916 – £876)) and a change in estimate of the provision (due to the change in discount rate, that is £9 (£925 –£916)).

If the rate changed at the beginning of the year, it would be appropriate to charge £35 (that is, £876 × 4%) as a finance charge, representing the unwinding of the discount for the year. This would increase the provision to £911. The additional amount of £14 (to bring the provision to £925) would be charged as an operating item.

Applying the recognition and measurement rules

21.64 The following paragraphs examine a number of practical issues in applying the recognition and measurement rules for provisions. Many of these issues appear as examples in the Appendix to section 21, which does not form part of the standard. These examples provide useful application guidance and are reproduced below with modifications and additions of explanatory text where considered appropriate. Unless stated otherwise, the examples generally assume that a reliable estimate can be made of any outflows expected. References to 'best estimate' are to the present value amount, when the effect of the time value of money is material.

Future operating losses

21.65 Provisions should not be made for future operating losses; this is because there is no past event that obliges the entity to pay out resources, so they do not meet the definition of a liability. Also, future operating losses relate to an activity that will continue and are presumed to be avoidable (for example, by closure of the segment or operations). Hence, no present obligation exists. [FRS 102 paras, 21.11B, 21A.1].

21.66 But, where an entity is expected to incur future operating losses, this is an indication that an impairment review should be carried out on the appropriate cash generating unit (CGU) in accordance with section 27 of FRS 102. Such a review would determine whether those assets have suffered an impairment and need to be written down. [FRS 102 para 27.5]. Also, anticipated future operating losses might indicate that entity has one or more onerous contracts.

Onerous contracts

21.67 An onerous contract is one in which the unavoidable costs of meeting the obligations under the contract exceed the economic benefits expected to be received under it. [FRS 102 Glossary of terms]. Although future operating losses are not provided for, if an entity has a contract that is onerous, the entity recognises and measures the present obligation under the contract as a provision. [FRS 102 para 21.11A]. Many contracts can be cancelled without any compensation being paid to the other contracting party; and, clearly, because no obligation can arise in this type of situation, such contracts cannot be onerous. But other contracts establish both rights and obligations on each of the contracting parties. Where such contracts become onerous, provision should be made for the onerous obligations that arise. It is worth remembering that section 21 of FRS 102 excludes from its scope (and hence its rules concerning onerous contracts) contracts that are covered by more specific sections (for example, provision for construction contracts that fall within section 23).

21.68 A typical example of an onerous contract is an operating property lease which has been abandoned by an entity and cannot be sub-let. The contract is onerous because the entity expects to receive no further benefit under the contract but it is still committed to make rental payments to the landlord.

21.69 The 'unavoidable costs' under a contract reflect the least net cost of exiting from the contract, which is the lower of the cost of fulfilling it and any compensation or penalties arising from failure to fulfil it. [FRS 102 para 21A.2].

21.70 The interpretation of 'economic benefits expected to be received under the contract' is important because, if this is taken to mean only the direct benefits expected from the contract itself, this is likely to give rise to much larger provisions than if both the direct and indirect benefits are taken into account. We consider that this term should be interpreted in its widest sense to include all benefits arising either directly or indirectly under the contract.

21.71 The meaning of the above terms is best illustrated by using examples of two types of contract (long-term purchase contracts and property operating leases) that often arise in practice.

> **Example 1 – Purchase contract at above market price**
>
> An entity has a contract to purchase one million ball bearings at 23p per unit giving a contract price of £230,000. The current market price for a similar contract is 16p per unit giving a price of £160,000. The ball bearings are used in the production of components used in the manufacture of commercial vehicles. The entity sells all components manufactured (using the ball bearings purchased for 23p per unit) at a profit. The entity would have to pay £55,000 to exit the purchase contract.
>
> The economic benefits from the contract include the benefits to the entity of using the ball bearings in its business; and, because the component that is produced can be sold at a profit, the contract is not onerous.
>
> In practice, the entity could decide to terminate the existing contract and pay the penalty of £55,000, in order to enter into a more profitable purchase contract. But, as the existing contract is not onerous, no provision is made in advance of the order's cancellation. Instead, the termination costs are charged as incurred in the period in which the contract is terminated. It is not appropriate to defer the penalty over the new contract's term; this is because the cost to terminate the old contract is not a cost of obtaining the new contract, even though the decisions to terminate the old contract and to obtain a new, more lucrative one are commercially linked.

Example 2 – Sale to third party at below purchase price

The facts are the same as in example 1 with regard to the price of ball bearings subject to the contract and the market price. But, in this example, the entity sells the ball bearings under a sales contract to a component manufacturer at a price of 20p per unit (3p below purchase price). The entity would have to pay £55,000 to exit the purchase contract.

The only economic benefits to be derived from the purchase contract costing £230,000 are the proceeds from the sales contract, which are £200,000. So, a provision is made for the onerous element of £30,000, being the lower of the cost of fulfilling the contract and the penalty cost of cancellation (£55,000).

Example 3 – Sub-lease to third party at below head lease cost

An entity has a 10-year operating lease on a property at a rental of £50,000 per annum. The market rent is £30,000 per annum. It no longer occupies the property which is not used in the business. A sub-lease on the property has been arranged at a rent of £30,000 a year for 10 years. The entity has established that the present value of the net cost of continuing with the lease is less than the penalty for exiting the lease.

The maximum benefits to be derived from the contract are £30,000 for 10 years. The cash inflow of £30,000 should be deducted from the cash outflows of £50,000 and the balance of £20,000 each year should be discounted to give the amount that should be provided on the onerous element of the lease.

Example 4 – Sub-lease negotiation not complete

The facts are the same as in example 3 with regard to the lease. The entity no longer uses the property. It is going to make a provision for an onerous contract. It has not yet found a sub-lessee, but expects to do so soon. The question is whether or not it is acceptable for the entity to anticipate the future sub-lease in determining the provision to be made.

The definition of an onerous contract clearly states that the expected benefits to be received under the lease should be taken into account (see para 21.67). So, the entity should take account of the expected rent to be received under a sub-lease in determining the cost of continuing with the lease, provided that: the entity is actively seeking to sublet the property; there is evidence (from estate agents or similar) that the property can be let; and there is reasonable evidence as to the rent that could be obtained in an open market rental. The provision is calculated as the lower of the present value of the net cost of continuing with the lease and the cost of negotiating out of the lease with the landlord.

Restructurings

21.72 A restructuring is a programme that is planned and controlled by management and materially changes either the scope of a business undertaken by an entity or the manner in which that business is conducted. [FRS 102 Glossary of terms]. Examples of situations that would fall within the restructuring definition include:

- sale or termination of a line of business;

- the closure of business locations in a country or region or the relocation of business activities from one country or region to another;

- changes in management structure (for example, eliminating a layer of management); and

- reorganisations that have a material effect on the nature and focus of the entity's operations.

21.73   An entity recognises a provision for restructuring costs only when it has a legal or constructive obligation at the balance sheet date to carry out the restructuring. A restructuring gives rise to a constructive obligation only when an entity:

- has a detailed formal plan for the restructuring, identifying at least:

  - the business or part of a business concerned;

  - the principal locations affected;

  - the location, function and approximate number of employees who will be compensated for terminating their services;

  - the expenditures that will be undertaken; and

  - when the plan will be implemented; and

- has raised a valid expectation in those affected that it will carry out the restructuring by either:

  - starting to implement that plan; or

  - announcing its main features to those affected by it.

[FRS 102 para 21.11C]

21.74   An entity recognises a provision for restructuring costs only when it has a legal or constaructive obligation at the balance sheet date to carry out the restructuring. [FRS 102 para 21.11D]. It is not permissible to make a provision where only a management or board decision to restructure has been taken before the balance sheet date, because this does not, in itself, give rise to a constructive obligation; management could change its plans completely in the new year. So, the 'obligating event' does not take place until after the year end; it is a 'non-adjusting event' that would generally be disclosed. [FRS 102 para 32.11(e)]. See chapter 32 for more details.

21.75   In order to provide for a restructuring at the balance sheet date, the entity must have started to implement its restructuring plan; or it must at least have announced the main features of the restructuring plan to those affected by it in a sufficiently specific manner to raise a valid expectation in them that the entity will carry out the restructuring. Events that could provide evidence that the entity has 'started to implement' the restructuring plan might include dismantling plant, selling assets and making a public announcement of the plan's main features. This is illustrated in the following examples.

> **Example 1 – Announcing intentions**
>
> Entity A's management has prepared a plan for a reorganisation of its operations. The board has approved the plan, which involves the closure of 10 out of entity A's 50 retail outlets. Management will conduct further analysis before deciding which outlets to close. Management has announced its intentions publicly and believes that this has given rise to an obligation that should be recognised as a liability. Should a provision for restructuring costs be recognised? No, a provision for restructuring should not be recognised. A constructive obligation arises only when an entity both has a detailed formal plan for restructuring and also announces the plan to those affected by it. The current plan does not provide sufficient detail that would permit recognition of a constructive obligation. But disclosure should be made about the restructuring plan to reflect information after the end of the reporting period but before the financial statements are authorised for issue.

> **Example 2 – Announcing plans**
>
> An entity is planning a head office restructuring. The year end is 31 March 20X1. The entity will have made announcements about the plan's detail before the year end (say, in January 20X1). But there is a consultation period, and individual employees will not have been notified by the year end. Can the entity provide for the restructuring costs at 31 March 20X1?
>
> At the balance sheet date, there is a detailed plan in place which has been made public in sufficient detail to give rise to valid expectations in other parties such as customers, suppliers and employees (or their representatives) that the entity will carry out the restructuring.
>
> Our view is that it is not necessary for individual employees to have been notified at the year end, provided that employee representatives have been notified. It will be necessary to consider what is involved in the specific consultation; but, if it is negotiation of terms rather than something that could change the entity's plans (which have already been announced in detail), provision would be made.

21.76 A restructuring provision should only include the direct costs associated with the restructuring, such as employee termination costs, contract termination costs and onerous lease provisions. It should not include expenditures that relate to the future conduct of the business, such as retraining or relocating continuing staff, cost of moving assets or operations, or investing in new systems. These are not liabilities for restructuring at the end of the reporting period. Such expenditures are recognised on the same basis as if they arose independently of a restructuring. Identifiable future operating losses up to the date of a restructuring are not included in a provision, unless they relate to an onerous contract (as discussed in para 21.67 above onwards). Similarly (as discussed in para 21.53 above), gains on the expected disposal of assets are not taken into account in measuring a restructuring provision, even if the sale of assets is envisaged as part of the restructuring.

Warranties

21.77 A warranty is often provided in conjunction with the sale of goods. Warranty costs represent additional costs that the seller might have to incur to rectify defects in, or to replace, the product that it has sold. Whether provision is made for these costs depends on whether the warranty is a separate component of the sale transaction. The warranty obligation can arise either through the operation of the law (contract or statute) or through an entity's stated policies or practices (as explained in para 21.16 onwards).

21.78 Warranties that are recognised as provisions under this section are usually 'standard warranties' given at the time of sale. These offer the purchaser an assurance that, if an item purchased is not fit for purpose, the seller will be obliged to rectify or replace it. If the item is defective at the time of sale, it could be that the defect does not become apparent until, say, a year after the sale; in effect, a 'standard warranty' (say, for two years from sale) allows for a period in which such a defect can be identified. Such a warranty relates to the condition of the item sold at the date of sale. It is not usually considered separable from the sale of the item. Generally, the full consideration received is recognised as revenue on the sale, and a provision is recognised for the expected future cost to be incurred relating to the warranty. The obligating event is the sale of goods that turn out to be defective or faulty.

21.79 By contrast, where a warranty goes further than a standard warranty (for example, a warranty that extends the period of coverage provided by the manufacturer's warranty), such warranties are usually sold separately from the original product. In that situation, revenue from the sale of the warranty is usually deferred and recognised over the period of the warranty. In the case of an extended warranty, the defect is assumed to have arisen in the extension period. No provision should be made for costs at the start of the extended warranty; this is because the obligation to repair or replace arises when the defect arises, rather than at the time of selling the goods.

21.80 An entity recognises a provision for a standard warranty based on the probability of the goods requiring repair or replacement and the best estimate of the costs to be incurred in respect of the defective goods sold on or before the reporting date. The example below is based on the example in paragraph 21A.4 of FRS 102.

> **Example – Estimation based on expected values**
>
> A manufacturer gives warranties at the time of sale to purchasers of its product. Under the terms of the contract for sale, the manufacturer undertakes to make good, by repair or replacement, manufacturing defects that become apparent within three years from the date of sale. On the basis of experience, it is probable (that is, more likely than not) that there will be some claims under the warranties.
>
> In 20X0, goods are sold for £1,000,000. Experience indicates that 90% of products sold require no warranty repairs; 6% of products sold require minor repairs costing

30% of the sale price; and 4% of products sold require major repairs or replacement costing 70% of sale price.

Therefore, estimated warranty costs are:

	Expected value £
£1,000,000 x 90% x 0	0
£1,000,000 x 6% x 30%	18,000
£1,000,000 x 4% x 70%	28,000
Total	46,000

The expenditures for warranty repairs and replacements for products sold in 20X0 are expected to be made 60% in 20X1, 30% in 20X2, and 10% in 20X3 (in each case, at the end of the period). Because the estimated cash flows already reflect the probabilities of the cash outflows, and assuming there are no other risks or uncertainties that must be reflected, the entity determines the present value of those cash flows using a 'risk-free' discount rate based on government bonds with the same term as the expected cash outflows (6% for one-year bonds and 7% for two-year and three-year bonds). Calculation of the present value, at the end of 20X0, of the estimated cash flows, related to the warranties for products sold in 20X0, is as follows:

Year	Expected cash payments	Discount rate	Discount factor	Present value
1	£46,000 x 60% = £27,600	6%	1/(1.06) = 0.9434	26,038
2	£46,000 x 30% = £13,800	7%	1/(1.07)2 = 0.8734	12,053
3	£46,000 x 10% = £4,600	7%	1/(1.07)3 = 0.8163	3,755
Total				41,846

The entity recognises a warranty obligation of £41,846 at the end of 20X0 for products sold in 20X0.

Refunds

21.81 Many entities have refund policies which exceed the customers' rights under consumer law. A number of retailers, for example, give cash refunds for products returned, whether or not they are defective; whereas others make cash refunds even where the customer does not have the receipt showing when the goods were purchased. Yet these policies have been operated in such a way, and for so long, that the customer expects that they will be honoured. The example in paragraph 21A.5 of FRS 102 (on which the example below is based) illustrates the principles.

> **Example – Refunds policy**
>
> A retail entity has a policy of refunding purchases by dissatisfied customers, even though it is under no legal obligation to do so. Its policy of making refunds is generally known.
>
> The entity should make a provision for the best estimate of its refund obligation for the following reasons:
>
> ■ It has a present obligation that is constructive in nature, which is more likely than not to arise.
>
> ■ The obligating event is the sale of the goods, which has raised a valid expectation on the part of its customers from which the entity cannot realistically withdraw.
>
> ■ Past experience shows that it is more likely than not that the obligation will result in an outflow of economic benefits.
>
> ■ A reliable estimate of the obligation can be made from past refunds.

21.82   A situation where a refund might have to be made is where faulty goods have to be recalled. The example below considers the implications where goods sold before the period end are recalled after the period end.

> **Example – Product recalls**
>
> A retailer has to make a product recall on goods sold before its year end, because they have subsequently been found to be faulty. The recall notice was issued after the year end. Costs of the recall can be recovered from the supplier under the retailer's supply contract.
>
> The entity should make a provision for the best estimate of its refund obligation for the following reasons:
>
> (a)   Does the retailer need to make a provision at the year end for the recall costs?
>
> Provision for the costs of the recall should be made at the year end. The obligating event was the sale of the faulty goods, and not the recall notice. At the balance sheet date the entity has an obligation to recall the faulty goods.
>
> (b)   How should the retailer account for the recovery from the supplier?
>
> Recovery of the costs from the supplier can only be recorded if it is deemed to be virtually certain that the costs will be recovered in the event that recall expenditure is incurred. If it is not virtually certain (for example, if there was some doubt as to the legal enforceability of the recovery or the ability of the supplier to pay) but is probable, it is disclosed as a contingent asset in accordance with paragraph 21.16 of FRS 102 (see para 21.54).

Financial guarantee contracts

21.83 A financial guarantee contract is *"a contract that requires the issuer to make specified payments to reimburse the holder for a loss it incurs because a specified debtor fails to make payments when due in accordance with the original or modified terms of a debt instrument"*. [FRS 102 Glossary of terms]. Section 21 of FRS 102 applies to financial guarantee contracts unless the entity is either applying IAS 39 (and/or IFRS 9) to its financial instruments or has elected under FRS 103 to continue the application of insurance contract accounting. [FRS 102 para 21.1A]. Contracts that are within the scope of section 21 of the standard will either require provision to be made or require disclosure as a contingent liability; this is illustrated in the following example.

Example – Financial guarantee contract

On 31 December 20X0, entity A gives a guarantee of specified borrowings of entity B, whose financial condition at that time is sound. Under the guarantee's terms, entity A will make specified payments to reimburse the holder for any loss it incurs if entity B fails to make payment when due. During 20X1, entity B's financial condition deteriorates and, at 30 June 20X1, entity B files for protection from its creditors.

At 31 December 20X0

- The obligating event is the giving of the guarantee, which gives rise to a legal obligation.

- At 31 December 20X0, the financial position of entity B is sound. So an outflow of economic benefits is not probable at 31 December 20X0.

No provision is recognised. [FRS 102 para 21.4]. The guarantee is disclosed as a contingent liability, unless the probability of any transfer is regarded as remote. [FRS 102 para 21.15].

At 31 December 20X1

- The obligating event is the giving of the guarantee, which gives rise to a legal obligation.

- At 31 December 20X1, the financial position of entity B has deteriorated, so it is probable that an outflow of economic benefits will be required to settle the obligation.

A provision is recognised for the best estimate of the obligation. [FRS 102 para 21.4].

Parent company guarantees

21.84 The Companies Act 2006 exempts some subsidiary companies from the requirement to be audited. It also exempts some dormant subsidiaries from the requirement to prepare financial statements. These exemptions are subject to a number of conditions, principally that the parent gives a statutory guarantee of all the outstanding liabilities of the subsidiary at the end of the financial year for which the subsidiary is seeking the exemption. [CA06 Secs 394A, 479A]. The guarantee is enforceable against the parent by any person to whom the subsidiary company is obligated in respect of those liabilities until such time as those liabilities are settled in full. [CA06 Sec 394C(3), 479C(3)].

21.85 Because a guarantee given under Sec 479C is not a contract between the parent and the subsidiary, it is not a financial guarantee contract (see para 21.83). So, it is dealt with under section 21 of the standard. Where it is probable that the guarantee will be called upon by the subsidiary's creditors, the parent provides for the expected outflow of economic benefits. If it is possible (but not probable) that the guarantee will be called upon, the parent has a contingent liability which is not recognised but is disclosed in its separate financial statements. If it is only a remote possibility that the guarantee will be called upon, section 21 of the standard does not require recognition of a provision or disclosure in the parent's separate financial statements. Disclosure requirements are discussed from paragraph 21.97.

Major repairs and maintenance

Owned assets

21.86 Repairs and maintenance of owned assets cannot be provided for; this is because these are costs associated with the future use of the assets. The entity can choose not to repair the assets, and so there is no obligation to carry out the expenditure. But some assets require, in addition to routine maintenance, substantial expenditure every few years for major refits or refurbishment and the replacement of major components. Under section 17 of FRS 102, a component approach to depreciation is applied (see chapter 17), recognising that different components might have different useful lives. Under the components approach, each major component is depreciated over its useful life and derecognised when it is replaced. Replacement components are then capitalised.

21.87 Maintenance expenditure in respect of owned assets cannot be provided for in advance of being incurred, even if there is an external requirement for maintenance of those assets. For instance, aircraft are required to be overhauled after a fixed number of flying hours in accordance with aviation regulations. The entity can avoid the obligation by withdrawing the aircraft from service before it has flown the specified number of hours, so the cost of overhaul is not provided. Costs are recognised when the work is carried out. Another situation is illustrated in the following example.

> **Example – Covenants requiring maintenance**
>
> An entity has purchased some assets outright and borrowed from a bank to do so. The bank covenants include conditions that the entity should maintain the assets in good condition. Should the entity provide for maintenance on the owned assets that are financed by borrowings that contain the maintenance covenant?

Where an owned fixed asset is used as security for a loan, and the covenants require that the asset is maintained, there is no penalty as such in respect of non-maintenance. Of course, should the covenant be broken in any way, the bank could call in its loan. If the entity is unable to pay back the loan in cash, the bank could repossess the asset and consider this as settlement of the outstanding balance. In extreme cases, the bank might sue the entity for returning the asset in a state of disrepair.

But we do not consider that this would justify providing for maintenance on an ongoing basis. A failure to maintain an asset used for secured lending does no more than trigger a repayment of the lending which, in any case, has already been recognised as a liability. It does not trigger a claim for compensation for the maintenance work that the owner has to carry out. Costs should be recognised in the period when the work is carried out. The response would differ for assets held under operating leases, where the lease agreement can impose penalties for non-maintenance on the lessee. This is considered in paragraph 21.89 below onwards.

Assets held under finance leases

21.88 Major maintenance programmes can also arise under a finance lease and could be specified as part of the lease terms. The asset under a finance lease is accounted for as if it is owned by the lessee, so the lessee would generally account for major renewal and maintenance programmes in the same way as if it owned the asset outright. Accordingly, the lessee should apply the components approach and capitalise the costs and depreciate them over the life of the component. Normal repair and maintenance costs should be expensed as incurred.

Assets held under operating leases

21.89 Where an asset is held under an operating lease, a component approach to depreciation cannot be applied; this is because the asset is not on the entity's balance sheet. But obligations that arise under an operating lease might give rise to the need to make provision at an earlier stage. Some operating leases require the lessee to incur periodic charges for maintenance of the leased asset or to make good dilapidations or other damage occurring during the rental period. The general principle for fixed assets does not preclude the recognition of such liabilities arising under operating leases once the event giving rise to the obligation under the lease has occurred.

Example 1 – Refit and maintenance required under lease

An entity leases an aircraft on an operating lease on a 12-year lease, which includes options to cancel the lease at the end of years 4 and 8. The lease can only be terminated at these times. Every four years, the aircraft equipment has to undergo a major refit and maintenance programme in order to be able to continue to operate. The operating lease specifies that this work must be undertaken every four years and before the aircraft is returned to the lessor. In addition, the aircraft has to have its engines serviced about once a year after a specified number of flying hours has been reached, but this obligation is not mentioned in the operating lease.

As the lease is an operating lease, the aircraft does not appear on the lessee's balance sheet. The lessee charges its lease rentals to its income statement as they arise. Furthermore, because it has no asset on its balance sheet, it cannot recognise the wearing out of the asset to be replaced in the major refit over the period before the refit takes place. The operating lease creates an obligation on the entity to carry out the major refit. So, it is appropriate to provide for the costs of the major refit and maintenance over the four years to the refit (based on the value of the liability at each balance sheet date) for the following reasons:

- The lease imposes a legal obligation on the lessee to pay rent and to incur major refit and maintenance costs. While the aircraft is in use, the entity provides for these costs over the four years to refit. On the other hand, if the entity decided to mothball the aircraft (that is, put it beyond use), the entity's action would result in the operating lease becoming onerous. Provision for future rental payments and future refit costs to be incurred up to the end of the current four-year term would need to be made. (Onerous contracts are considered further in para 21.67 above onwards.)

- The past event is the action of using and flying the aircraft.

- The costs to be incurred do not relate to the entity's future operations, because it is clear from considering the final period (between years 9 and 12) that the aircraft has to be returned in a maintained state. So, the obligation in the last period clearly arises over the four-year term. Some might argue that the costs incurred at the end of years 4 and 8 relate to the following four-year terms, but this ignores the underlying obligation created by the lease, which is in effect to put right the damage that is caused through the asset's usage.

- An obligation arises under the lease that will result in an outflow of economic benefits.

- It will be possible to make a reliable estimate of the obligation to be provided each year based on the extent of wear and tear over the period.

The engine service each year is not covered by the lease, although it is an integral part of operating the aircraft. But, because the obligation does not arise from the lease agreement, the normal rules apply and provision cannot be made. These costs would be charged to the entity's income statement as they are incurred.

Example 2 – Repairs specified under property lease terms

The entity is currently a tenant of a property and is due to vacate it in five years' time. There is a clause in the tenancy agreement relating to dilapidation work which must be undertaken before the property is vacated. There is also a clause that enables the landlord to recharge the tenant for costs related to repairing the fabric of the building. In this regard, the landlord is intending to replace the cladding on the building and is obtaining quotes for this work.

Provision should be made for the estimated costs of the dilapidation repairs, spread over the period of the tenancy, for the following reasons:

- The tenant has a present legal obligation, arising from the lease agreement.

- The obligating event is the wear and tear to the property, which arises over the period of the tenancy, and its repair can be legally enforced.

- Because the obligation arises from the wear and tear to the property, it is not related to future operating costs.

- It is probable that the obligation will result in an outflow of economic benefits.

- It is possible to make a reliable estimate of the yearly obligation arising from the extent of the wear and tear taking place each year. This will not necessarily equate to one fifth of the estimated total.

With regard to repairing the fabric of the building, it should be clear from the lease whether or not an obligation arises. If the damage has already been done to the property, a provision should be made for the whole of the rectification work when the damage is identified.

Example 3 – Returning property to its condition at lease inception

An entity has entered into an operating lease for a warehouse. The entity wishes to use the warehouse for office accommodation. It has planning permission to build a mezzanine floor and partition the building for offices at a cost of £1.5 million. The operating lease is for a period of 15 years, and it is clearly specified in the lease that the property must be returned to the lessor in its original condition. The entity estimates that it will cost £500,000 to remove the improvements.

The entity should capitalise leasehold improvements of £1.5 million and amortise those over the term of the lease under section 17 of FRS 102. The entity has an obligation under the lease to remove the improvements at the end of the lease term. The obligation arises when the entity completes the improvements, and this represents a past event. So, if the improvements have been made by the entity's year end, a provision for the present value of £500,000 in 15 years' time should be made for their eventual removal. An asset of the same amount should also be recognised for what is, in effect, decommissioning; and this will be recovered from the benefits generated by the business over the lease's term. The asset should be amortised over the remaining lease term.

Presentation and disclosure

Presentation of provisions

21.90 SI 2008/410 sets out the required balance sheet formats. 'Provisions for liabilities' must be shown separately on the face of the balance sheet. No distinction is made on the face of the balance sheet between 'current' and 'non-current' provisions; but FRS 102 requires information to be disclosed about the timing of the expected payments (see para 21.91). SI 2008/410 requires 'Provisions for liabilities' to be analysed, either on the face of the balance sheet or in the notes, into the following categories:

- Pensions and similar obligations (see chapter 28).

- Taxation, including deferred taxation (see chapter 29).

Provisions and contingencies

- Other provisions.

[SI 2008/410 1 Sch formats].

Disclosures about provisions

21.91 Combining the requirements in FRS 102 and Schedule 1 to SI 2008/410, for each class of provision, an entity discloses all of the following:

- A reconciliation showing:

  - the carrying amount at the beginning and end of the period;

  - additions during the period, including adjustments that result from changes in measuring the discounted amount;

  - amounts charged against the provision during the period; and

  - unused amounts reversed during the period.

- A brief description of the nature of the obligation, and the expected amount and timing of any resulting payments.

- An indication of the uncertainties about the amount or timing of those outflows.

- The amount of any expected reimbursement, stating the amount of any asset that has been recognised for that expected reimbursement.

[FRS 102 para 21.14; SI 2008/410 1 Sch 59(2)].

21.92 In determining which provisions could be aggregated to form a class, it is necessary to consider the significance and nature of the individual provisions. For instance, warranties relating to different products can be shown as a single class amount, but would not be combined with litigation costs to form a single class. Generally, categories of provisions that would require separate disclosure include warranties, litigation, decommissioning liabilities, onerous contracts and restructuring costs.

21.93 All information about movements shown in the reconciliation should be disclosed gross, as required by the first bullet point in paragraph 21.91 above. For instance, if provision for legal costs has increased for a particular matter, but has decreased for another matter, the gross amount of the increases and decreases is disclosed and not offset.

21.94 Comparative information for prior periods in respective of the disclosures set out in paragraph 21.91 above is not required. [FRS 102 para 21.14]. For example, if a provision is made in the previous reporting period, there is no requirement to provide comparative narrative information, although it might be useful to do so to put the provision in its proper context.

Disclosures about contingent liabilities

21.95 Unless the possibility of any outflow of resources in settlement is remote, an entity should disclose, for each class of contingent liability at the balance sheet date, a brief description of the nature of the contingent liability:

■ An estimate of its financial effect, measured in accordance with paragraphs 21.7 — 21.11 of section 21 of FRS 102.

■ An indication of the uncertainties relating to the amount or timing of any outflow.

■ The possibility of any reimbursement.

[FRS 102 para 21.15]

If it is impracticable to make any of the above disclosures, that fact should be stated. [FRS 102 para 21.15].

In addition, SI 2008/410 requires the following disclosures:

■ The amount or estimated amount of the liability.

■ Its legal nature.

■ Whether any valuable security has been provided by the company in connection with the liability and a description of that security.

[SI 2008/410 1 Sch 63(2)].

Disclosures about contingent assets

21.96 Contingent assets are not recognised in the balance sheet unless their realisation is virtually certain. Contingent assets are disclosed when an inflow of economic benefits is probable (that is, more likely than not). The disclosure includes a description of the nature of the contingent assets at the end of the reporting period and (when practicable without undue cost or effort) an estimate of their financial effect, measured using the principles set out in paragraphs 21.7 — 21.11 of FRS 102. If it is impracticable to make this disclosure, that fact should be stated. [FRS 102 para 21.16].

Parent company guarantees

21.97 As discussed in paragraph 21.84, a parent may, subject to conditions, give a statutory guarantee so that one or more of its subsidiaries can use exemptions relating to audit or preparation of financial statements. Where the guarantee is given in connection with a subsidiary's exemption from the audit requirement, the law requires the parent to disclose in its consolidated financial statements that the subsidiary is exempt from the requirements of the Companies Act relating to the audit of individual accounts by virtue of section 479A. In the case of a dormant subsidiary taking an exemption from the requirement to prepare financial statements, the parent must disclose in its consolidated financial statements that the subsidiary is exempt from the requirement to prepare individual financial statements by virtue of section 394A

21.98   The law requires that the above disclosure is given in the parent's consolidated financial statements even though the subsidiary's liabilities are included in the group's balance sheet. From the group's point of view, the parent's guarantee is inter-company and is not disclosable under FRS 102 in the consolidated financial statements.

21.99   If management consider that it is only a remote possibility that the guarantee will be called upon, then the parent is not required to make any disclosure in its separate financial statements. But if it is probable that the guarantee will be called upon, then a provision is recognised in the parent's separate financial statements and disclosed in accordance with section 21 of the standard (see from para 21.91 above). If an outflow of economic benefits in respect of the guarantee is possible but not probable, the parent discloses a contingent liability in its separate financial statements (see para 21.95).

Other guarantees (including financial guarantee contracts)

21.100   Provision might be required where obligations under guarantees (including financial guarantee contracts) arise. Guarantees (including financial guarantee contracts) might be disclosed as contingent liabilities. Disclosure requirements in respect of provisions and contingent liabilities are dealt with in paragraphs 21.91 and 21.95 onwards respectively. Entities are also required to disclose the nature and purpose of any financial guarantee contracts that they have issued. [FRS 102 para 21.17A].

21.101   In addition, SI 2008/410 requires the notes to the financial statements to give details of:

- any charge on the company's assets that has been given in order to secure the liabilities of any other person; and

- the amounts so secured (where practicable).

[SI 2008/410 1 Sch 63(1)].

21.102   In addition to the requirement to disclose details of any charge on the company's assets, paragraph 63(2) of Schedule 1 to SI 2008/410 requires the notes to disclose whether any valuable security has been provided in respect of contingent liabilities and a description of that security.

Commitments

21.103   SI 2008/410 requires the notes to the financial statements to disclose details of:

- Where practicable, the aggregate amount or estimated amount of capital expenditure contracted for, but not provided for, at the balance sheet date.

  Pension commitments (see chapter 28).

- Other financial commitments that have not been provided for and are relevant to assessing the company's state of affairs.

[SI 2008/410 1 Sch 63(3)-(5)].

Prejudicial disclosures

21.104 Some information concerning provisions and contingent liabilities and assets – such as litigation and litigation recoveries (particularly through insurance) – might be very sensitive, and full disclosure could prejudice the outcome of a particular case. So, in extremely rare cases, disclosure of some or all of the information required in paragraph 21.91 above, where it might seriously prejudice the position of the entity in a dispute with other parties on the subject matter of the provision, contingent liability or contingent asset, need not be given. [FRS 102 para 21.17].

21.105 Where this exemption is used, the general nature of the dispute should be disclosed, together with the fact that, and reason why, the information has not been disclosed. [FRS 102 para 21.17]. An example is given below.

> **Example – Omission of disclosures**
>
> Entity A is in dispute with a competitor, which is alleging that entity A has infringed patents. The competitor is seeking damages of £100 million. Management recognises a provision for its best estimate of the obligation, but does not disclose the information required by paragraph 21.14 of section 21 of FRS 102 on the grounds that this would be prejudicial to the outcome of the case.
>
> Management should disclose that the litigation is in process against the entity relating to a dispute with a competitor, which alleges that the entity has infringed patents and is seeking damages. The information usually required by section 21 of FRS 102 is not disclosed, because the directors believe that to do so would seriously prejudice the outcome of the litigation.

21.106 As to what might fall into the category of 'extremely rare' is a matter of judgement. But it is clear that, if, for example, disclosure of specified information is likely to change the course of a particular legal action, this would justify non-disclosure. Whether this would extend to all of the required disclosures would depend on the particular circumstances. It should be noted, however, that the exemption only applies to the disclosure requirements of section 21 of the standard; it does not extend to the disclosures required by law, which are contained in paragraphs 59 and 63 of Schedule 1 to SI 2008/410 (see paras 21.91, 21.95, 21.101-21.103).

Transitional issues

21.107 No special exemptions on provisions, contingent liabilities and contingent assets are available to first-time adopters under section 35 of FRS 102. So, a first-time adopter must prepare its first financial statements as though the requirements of section 21 of FRS 102 had always applied.

21.108 Companies transitioning from old UK GAAP (FRS 12) to FRS 102 are unlikely to face any significant issues on transition. This is because there are no differences in substance between the requirements of old UK GAAP and those in section 21 of FRS 102.

21.109 Amounts reported under old UK GAAP will be carried forward without any modifications in the opening balance sheet as of the date of transition.

Chapter 22

Liabilities and equity

Chapter 22

Liabilities and equity

Introduction

22.1   Section 22 of FRS 102 contains the principles for distinguishing between liabilities and equity instruments in the financial statements of the issuing entity. The substance of the contractual arrangement of a financial instrument, rather than its legal form, governs its classification. The overriding criterion is that, if an entity does not have an unconditional right to avoid delivering cash or another financial asset to settle a contractual obligation, the contract is a liability.

22.2   Classifying instruments as liability and/or equity can be complex, and requires each component of an instrument's contractual terms to be assessed. The impact of an incorrect classification on gearing ratios, debt covenants and reported earnings can be highly significant to investors and other users of financial statements.

22.3   This chapter also deals with the impact of the Companies Act on debt and equity and related areas (including presentation of share capital, share premium and reserves). The chapter concludes with a discussion of the general principles around realised profits and some of the specific application issues. This chapter does not deal in depth with the provisions of the Companies Act; for further information, please consult chapter 23 of the Manual of Accounting.

Scope

22.4   Section 22 of FRS 102 should be applied by all entities when classifying financial instruments as either liabilities or equity, or as instruments with both liability and equity components (compound instruments).

22.5   The section applies to 'financial instruments', defined as *"[a] contract that gives rise to a financial asset of one entity and a financial liability or equity instrument of another entity"*. [FRS 102 Glossary of terms]. As can be seen from the definition, this section is contract-based. 'Contract' or 'contractual' refers to an agreement between two or more parties that has clear economic consequences that the parties have little, if any, discretion to avoid, usually because the agreement is enforceable by law. Contracts, and thus financial instruments, can take a variety of forms and need not be in writing. Liabilities or assets that are not contractual (for example, obligations established from local law or statute, such as income taxes) are not financial liabilities or financial assets. Similarly, constructive obligations, as defined in section 21 of the standard, do not arise from contracts and are not financial liabilities.

22.6 Section 22 of the standard should be applied to all types of financial instrument except:

(a) Investments in subsidiaries, associates and joint ventures that are accounted for in accordance with section 9, 14 or 15 of FRS 102.

(b) Employers' rights and obligations under employee benefit plans to which section 28 of the standard applies.

(c) Contracts for contingent consideration in a business combination (see section 19 of the standard). This exemption applies only to the acquirer.

(d) Financial instruments, contracts and obligations under share-based payment transactions to which section 26 applies, except that paragraphs 22.3 to 22.6 are applied to own equity instruments issued, purchased, sold, transferred or cancelled in connection with employee share option plans, employee share purchase plans, and all other share-based payment arrangements.

(e) Insurance contracts (including reinsurance contracts) that an entity issues and reinsurance contracts that it holds.

(f) Financial instruments issued by an entity with a discretionary participation feature.

(g) A reporting entity that issues or holds financial instruments set out in (e) and (f) is required by paragraph 1.5 to apply FRS 103, 'Insurance Contracts'.

[FRS 102 para 22.2].

Classification of an instrument as liability or equity

22.7 Before considering the general principles in section 22 of the standard for classifying a financial instrument as a financial liability or equity, it is appropriate to set out the section's basic definitions of a financial liability and an equity instrument.

22.8 A 'financial liability' is defined as any liability that is:

"*(a) a contractual obligation:*

- *to deliver cash or another financial asset to another entity; or*

- *to exchange financial assets or financial liabilities with another entity under conditions that are potentially unfavourable to the entity; or*

(b) a contract that will or may be settled in the entity's own equity instruments and:

- *under which the entity is or may be obliged to deliver a variable number of the entity's own equity instruments; or*

- *will or may be settled other than by the exchange of a fixed amount of cash or another financial asset for a fixed number of the entity's own equity instruments. For this purpose the entity's own equity instruments do not include instruments that are themselves contracts for the future receipt or delivery of the entity's own equity instruments."*

[FRS 102 para 22.3].

22.9   An equity instrument is defined as any contract that evidences a residual interest in an entity's assets after deducting all of its liabilities; and equity includes investments by an entity's owners, plus retained earnings less losses and distributions to owners. [FRS 102 para 22.3].

Contractual obligation to settle in cash or another financial asset

22.10   It is apparent from the above definitions of liability and equity instrument that the critical feature that distinguishes a liability from an equity instrument is the existence of a contractual obligation to deliver cash or another financial asset to the holder, or to exchange a financial asset or financial liability with the holder under conditions that are potentially unfavourable to the issuer. In other words, (ignoring share settlement) if the issuer does not have an unconditional right to avoid delivering cash or another financial asset to settle a contractual obligation, the obligation meets the definition of a liability, with the limited exception of puttable instruments and obligations arising on liquidation that meet the strict criteria set out in paragraph 22.32 onwards below.

22.11   Some examples of instruments that contain an obligation to transfer cash are considered below.

> **Example 1 – 6% mandatorily redeemable preference shares with mandatory fixed dividends**
>
> A preference share is the name given to any share that has some preferential rights in relation to other classes of shares, particularly in relation to ordinary shares. These preferential rights are of great variety, but refer normally to the right to a *fixed dividend*, although they could also refer to the right on winding up to receive a fixed part of the *capital* or otherwise to participate in the distribution of the company's assets (shares with such rights are often known as participating preference shares).
>
> In determining whether a preference share is a financial liability or an equity instrument, it is necessary to examine the particular contractual rights attaching to the instrument's principal and return components.
>
> The 6% mandatorily redeemable preference share with mandatory fixed dividends, in this example, provides for mandatory periodic fixed dividend payments and mandatory redemption by the issuer for a fixed amount at a fixed future date. Because there is a contractual obligation to deliver cash (for both dividends and repayment of principal) to the shareholder that cannot be avoided, the instrument is a financial liability in its entirety.

Example 2 – Non-redeemable preference shares with mandatory fixed dividends

It is necessary to examine the particular contractual rights attaching to the instrument's principal and return components. The shares are non-redeemable and thus the amount of the principal has equity characteristics, but the entity has a contractual obligation to pay dividends, and this provides the shareholders with a lender's return. This obligation is not negated if the entity is unable to pay the dividends because of lack of funds or insufficient distributable profits. Therefore, the obligation to pay the dividends meets the definition of a financial liability. The overall classification is that the shares may be a compound instrument, which might require each component to be accounted for separately (see further para 22.91 below). It would be a compound instrument if the coupon was initially set at a rate other than the prevailing market rate (an 'off-market' rate) or the terms specified payment of discretionary dividends in addition to the fixed coupon. If the coupon on the preference shares was set at market rates at the date of issue, and there were no provisions for the payment of discretionary dividends, the entire instrument would be classified as a financial liability; this is because the mandatory stream of cash flows is in perpetuity.

Contractual obligations: the entity versus the holder of the instrument

22.12 A contractual obligation does not give rise to a financial liability if the entity has an unconditional right to avoid delivering cash or another financial asset in settlement of that obligation. Shareholders as a collective body make key decisions affecting an entity's financial position and performance over its life (for example, regarding the distribution of dividends). Hence, their decisions have to be analysed from an accounting perspective. Shareholders can make decisions as part of the entity (that is, as members of the entity's corporate governance structure) or they can be separate and distinct from the entity itself when making these decisions (that is, as holders of a particular instrument). In light of the accounting principles under section 22 of FRS 102, the role of shareholders – that is, whether they are viewed as 'part of the entity' or as 'separate and distinct from the entity' – is critical in determining the classification of financial instruments where the entity's shareholders decide whether the entity delivers cash or another financial asset under those instruments.

22.13 Shares usually have voting rights leading to a two-fold role for a shareholder: (1) a holder of a financial instrument issued by the entity; and (2) a member of the corporate governance structure of the entity. In other words, in addition to the contractual rights to cash flows (for example, dividends), the shareholder has a contractual right to participate in the decision-making process of the entity's governing body. Shareholder rights in relation to the entity's decision-making process are generally exercised collectively in a general shareholder meeting (GSM). In many jurisdictions, including the UK, corporate law stipulates that the GSM is one of the governing bodies of the entity and prescribes a specific process regarding how a GSM is to be held, who is entitled to propose an agenda item, and how decisions are to be taken. In order to determine whether collective decisions of shareholders are decisions of the entity, it is necessary to determine whether these decisions are made as part of the entity's normal decision-making process for similar transactions.

22.14 If the decisions are made as part of the entity's normal decision-making process for similar transactions, the shareholders are considered to be part of the entity. For example, if an entity's equity instruments embody a contractual obligation to pay cash, but the shareholders can (as part of their normal decision-making process for this type of transaction) refuse to make such a cash payment, the shares would be classified as equity. The entity in this case has an unconditional right to avoid the payment of cash.

22.15 If the decisions are not made as part of the entity's normal decision-making process for similar transactions (for example, one shareholder or a class of shareholders can make the decision, and this is not the process that the entity generally follows to make financial decisions), the shareholders are viewed as separate and distinct from the entity. For example, if a single shareholder can make a decision that creates a contractual obligation for the issuer to pay cash for the entity's shares, and such decisions normally require a majority of the shareholder votes, these shares would be classified as a liability. The entity in this case does not have an unconditional right to avoid payment of cash. See further the examples to paragraph 22.26 below.

Payments that are discretionary or at the option of the issuer

22.16 If an instrument does not contain a contractual (including contingent – see para 22.25 onwards below) obligation to deliver cash or another financial asset, it is classified as an equity instrument. Therefore, where payments of interest/dividends or the principal amount, or both, are discretionary in nature, equity treatment is appropriate for some or all of the instrument. For example, dividends payable on non-puttable ordinary shares depend on the entity's profitability. However, the directors are not required to declare a dividend even though a past pattern of dividend payments might have created an expectation on the shareholders that a dividend will be declared and payable. Such discretionary payments do not create contractual obligations, because the directors cannot be required to deliver cash or another financial asset to the shareholders. Nevertheless, a liability must be recognised in respect of such non-puttable ordinary shares where the directors formally act to make a distribution and become legally obliged to the shareholders to do so. This might be the case following the declaration of a dividend, or where the entity is being wound up and any assets remaining after the satisfaction of liabilities become distributable to shareholders.

Contracts that will or might be settled in an entity's own equity instruments

22.17 The classification of contracts that will or might be settled in the entity's own equity instruments is dependent on whether there is variability in either the number of own equity instruments delivered and/or the amount of cash or other financial assets received, or whether both are fixed. [FRS 102 para 22.3(b)].

22.18   A contract that will be settled by the entity receiving (or delivering) a fixed number of its own equity instruments in exchange for a fixed amount of cash or another financial asset is an equity instrument. [FRS 102 para 22.3(b)]. This is commonly referred to as the 'fixed for fixed' requirement. For example, an entity will receive £100 from the holder in three years' time to issue 100 of the entity's own equity shares. This would meet the 'fixed for fixed' requirement, because both the number of own equity shares to be delivered and the cash to be received are fixed when the financial instrument is initially recognised. The instrument meets the definition of an equity instrument because the holder receives a residual interest in the entity. By fixing upfront the amount paid and the number of shares received, the holder benefits from any upside and suffers the loss from any fall in the residual value of the entity.

22.19   However, an entity might have a contractual obligation to receive or deliver a variable number of its own shares or other equity instruments. This might be, for example, so that the fair value of the entity's own equity instruments to be received or delivered equals the amount of the contractual right or obligation (that is, shares to a particular value). Such a contract might be for a fixed amount of currency or an amount that fluctuates (in part or in full) in response to changes in a variable. It would be inappropriate to account for such a contract as an equity instrument where an entity's own equity instruments are used 'as currency', because such a contract represents a right or obligation for a specified amount rather than a specified residual equity interest. Therefore, such a contract is classified as a financial liability. The underlying variable can include the entity's own share price.

> **Example 1 – Own shares to the value of £1 million**
>
> An entity receives £1m in exchange for its promise that it will deliver its own equity shares in an amount sufficient to equal a value of £1m at a future date. If the share price at the date on delivery of the contract is £5, the entity would be required to issue 200,000 shares (that is, a total value of £1m).
>
> On the day that the issuer delivers its own equity, the holder would be indifferent whether it received cash of £1m, on the one hand, or shares to the value of £1m which it could sell and receive £1m in cash, on the other. Therefore, the entity is using its own equity as currency and, as such, the holder does not receive a full residual interest. The entity has an obligation to deliver a variable number of shares, and so the financial instrument is a liability under paragraph 22.3(b)(i) of FRS 102.
>
> **Example 2 – Bermudan option with fixed but different strike prices**
>
> An entity issues an option to sell a fixed number of its own equity shares at a specified exercise price. The terms of the option state that the specified exercise price varies with the share price of the entity, such that:
>
> | Share price | Conversion ratio |
> | --- | --- |
> | £0–10 | 10 shares at £1 per share |
> | £11–20 | 10 shares at £1.50 per share |

The variability in the exercise price, as a function of share price of the entity, results in a variable amount of cash for a fixed number of shares. The 'fixed for fixed' requirement is, therefore, violated. So, the option is classified as a (derivative) financial liability under paragraph 22.3(b)(ii) of FRS 102 and not as an equity instrument.

Derivatives over own equity instruments

22.20 An entity might enter into a derivative contract for the purchase or sale of its own equity instruments. Depending on the nature of the contract (such as forward based or option based) and the settlement terms (for example, gross or net in cash) in particular, such contracts might be accounted for as equity instruments or derivatives.

Contracts accounted for as equity instruments

22.21 A derivative contract that will or might be settled by the entity receiving or delivering a fixed number of its own equity instruments, in exchange for a fixed amount of cash or another financial asset, is an equity instrument. This is because such an instrument is not a financial liability. [FRS 102 para 22.3(b)(ii)]. An example is a written share option that gives the counterparty a right to buy a fixed number of the entity's shares for a fixed price. The contract's fair value might change due to variation in the share price and market interest rates. However, provided that such changes in the contract's fair value do not affect the amount of cash or other financial assets to be paid or received, or the number of equity instruments to be received or delivered, on the contract's settlement, the contract is treated as an equity instrument.

22.22 Any consideration received (such as the premium received for a written option or warrant on the entity's own shares) on a derivative contract that is an equity instrument is added directly to equity. Any consideration paid (such as the premium paid for a purchased option) is deducted directly from equity. Changes in an equity instrument's fair value are not recognised in the financial statements.

Contracts accounted for as financial liabilities

22.23 Where a contract resulting in the issue of shares does not meet the requirements for it to be treated as equity, it is treated as a financial liability or asset under section 11 or 12 of FRS 102 (see further chapters 11 and 12). Net settlement of a derivative contract in cash or shares (either mandatory or at the option of the holder or issuer) means that the 'fixed for fixed' requirement is breached.

22.24 There are two types of contract that will or may be settled in shares that are accounted for as a financial liability rather than as equity instruments. The first is a contract that might require the entity to deliver a variable number of its own equity instruments. [FRS 102 para 22.3(b)(i)]. Such a contract is a (non-derivative) financial liability that is accounted for in accordance with section 11 or 12 of FRS 102, depending on its terms. The second is a contract that will or might be settled other than by the delivery of a fixed number of an entity's own equity instruments for a fixed amount of cash or another financial asset. [FRS 102 para 22.2(b)(ii)]. Such an instrument is a derivative financial liability (or asset) and is accounted for under section 12 of FRS 102. For example, an entity with a sterling functional currency might have a forward contract to deliver 100 of its ordinary shares in return for $1,000. The instrument is a derivative because the amount of cash is not fixed in the entity's functional currency.

Contingent settlement provisions

22.25 There is no requirement for an obligation to deliver cash or financial assets to be certain of occurring; the obligation could be contingent on the occurrence or non-occurrence of uncertain future events (or on the outcome of uncertain circumstances) that are beyond the control of the issuer or the holder of the instrument. Examples of such uncertain future events might include (but are not limited to):

- Changes in a stock market index or consumer price index.

- Changes in interest rates or exchange rates.

- Changes in tax laws or other regulatory requirements.

- Changes in the issuer's key performance indicators (such as revenue, net income or debt-to-equity ratios).

22.26 The instrument is a financial liability if cash or another financial asset must be transferred in the circumstances specified above, or if the instrument must otherwise be settled in such a way that it would be a financial liability. [FRS 102 para 22.3A]. The reason for this is that, at the time of the initial recognition, the issuer does not have an unconditional right to avoid delivering cash or another financial asset (or otherwise to settle it in such a way that it would be a financial liability), because it does not control the final outcome. A transfer of economic benefits as a result of a past event (that is, the issue of the instrument) cannot be avoided depending on the outcome of the future event. Such an event is known as a 'contingent settlement event', and financial instruments requiring payment on such an event should be classified as financial liabilities.

> ### Example 1 – Change of control events
>
> A contract between entity A and a third party contains a requirement for entity A to make payments to the third party in the event of a change of control of entity A (for example, where entity A is taken over by entity B, and entity B is not connected to entity A).
>
> The change of control event is outside the control of both entity A and the third party, provided that it does not need to be agreed by entity A at a general meeting (as discussed in para 22.12 onwards above). This will be the case if a purchaser could approach the individual shareholders of entity A and buy their shares. The payments to a third party that are contingent on a change of control event are, therefore, financial liabilities where no agreement by a general meeting of entity A is required.

Example 2 – Shares with an obligation to pay out a percentage of profits

A share includes an obligation to pay out a fixed 10% of profits each year and is mandatorily redeemable at par after 20 years.

The instrument has two liability components: a contractual obligation to redeem the instrument at par after 20 years; and a contractual obligation to pay 10% of profits until redemption. The latter is a financial liability because, although the payment depends on the issuing entity making profits (that is, an uncertain future event), the generation of future profits is outside the control of both the issuer and holder. If profits are made, the issuer cannot avoid making the payment, and so the definition of a contingent settlement event is met. The instrument does not meet the requirements of a basic financial instrument in section 11 of FRS 102, and so it is measured at fair value through profit and loss under section 12 of the standard (see further chapter 12).

Example 3 – Mandatory redemption where an IPO does not occur

An undated cumulative bond, whose interest payments are at the discretion of the entity in the absence of an IPO, contains a clause that states that the instrument (including all unpaid cumulative interest) will become mandatorily payable if there is not an IPO of the issuing entity by the end of three years from the instrument's date of issue. Although it might be within the entity's control to determine whether the IPO is attempted, market and regulatory forces determine whether any attempt is successful (that is, whether the market will accept an IPO and whether all regulatory approvals will be obtained). These forces are beyond the control of the issuing entity (and of the holder of the bond), and so redemption on an IPO event not occurring meets the definition of a contingent settlement event. This results in the bond being classified as a financial liability from inception.

22.27 Where the event that could trigger payment is within the control of the issuer but not the holder, it is possible for the issuer to avoid the event occurring and hence avoid settling the instrument. In such a case, the event does not meet the definition of a contingent settlement event. For example, an undated cumulative bond whose interest payments are at the discretion of the entity contains a clause stating that the instrument (including all unpaid cumulative interest) will become mandatorily payable if a successful IPO of the issuer occurs. It is within the issuing entity's control to determine whether an IPO is attempted and, as a result, the entity can avoid a successful IPO taking place. So, the clause does not meet the definition of a contingent settlement provision and results in the bond being classified as an equity instrument from inception. The issuing entity does not have an obligation to pay cash or transfer a financial asset.

22.28 There are three exceptions where uncertain events outside the control of the issuer are not contingent settlement events, as follows:

- Where the part of the contingent settlement provision that could require settlement in cash or another financial asset (or otherwise in such a way that it would be a financial liability) is not *genuine* (see para 22.29 below). [FRS 102 para 22.3A(a)].

- Where the issuer can be required to settle the obligation in cash or another financial asset (or otherwise to settle it in such a way that it would be a financial liability) only in the event of liquidation of the issuer (see para 22.31 below). [FRS 102 para 22.3A(b)].

- Where the instrument is puttable under particular circumstances or contains obligations arising on liquidation (as discussed in para 22.32 onwards below). [FRS 102 para 22.3A(c)].

Settlement terms that are not genuine

22.29 A non-genuine contingent settlement provision does not cause classification as a liability. A contingent settlement provision in a contract would be regarded as not genuine if, for example, it requires settlement in cash only on the occurrence of an event that is extremely rare, highly abnormal and very unlikely to occur.

22.30 In practice, terms are included in a contract for a purpose that is likely to have commercial effect. Therefore, it would be unusual to include settlement terms in a contract that are contingent on an event that is not genuine (that is, extremely rare, highly abnormal and very unlikely to occur). 'Not genuine' should not be equated to 'remote': it is not appropriate to disregard events that are merely 'remote'. The specific facts and circumstances would need to be considered.

> **Example 1 – Settlement terms based on increase in an index**
>
> An entity issues an instrument that is redeemable in cash if the FTSE 100 triples within a two-week period.
>
> In general, it is not for the entity to speculate whether an index will behave in a particular manner that might or might not trigger redemption of the instrument. Where an entity will be unable to avoid a settlement in cash if an index reaches a particular, the instrument should be treated as a financial liability.
>
> However, in this situation, the tripling of the FTSE 100 within such a short period of time is not genuine: it is extremely rare, highly abnormal and unlikely to occur. Furthermore, in practice, an investor is highly unlikely to advance funds on such redemption terms. Clearly, the terms are artificial and not genuine and should be ignored for classification purposes.

Settlements that arise only on liquidation

22.31 Obligations to deliver cash or other financial assets that are contingent only on the issuer's liquidation, and where liquidation is not certain to occur (see para 22.32 onwards below), should be ignored. This is because different rights and obligations associated with the instruments come into effect at liquidation that would not otherwise be triggered during the ordinary course of business and, hence, would be inconsistent with the going concern assumption. A contingent settlement provision that provides for payment in cash or another financial asset only on the entity's liquidation is similar to an equity instrument that has priority in liquidation. Such a provision does not, therefore, cause classification as a liability. However, if the instrument is redeemable on the occurrence of an event that could ultimately lead to eventual liquidation (for example, the entity becomes insolvent, goes into receivership or administration, all of which are beyond the control of the entity), the instrument component related to the redemption should still be classified as a financial liability.

Puttable instruments or instruments imposing an obligation only on liquidation

22.32 Financial instruments that give the holder the right to put them back to the issuer for cash or another financial asset (a 'puttable instrument'), other than those instruments that meet the criteria set out in paragraph 22.36 onwards below, are financial liabilities. For example, a preference share gives the holder the right to require the issuer to redeem the instrument for cash or another financial asset at some future date. The existence of an option for the holder to put the instrument back to the issuer for cash or another financial asset means that the issuer does not have an unconditional right to avoid delivering cash or cash equivalent, so the puttable instrument meets the definition of a financial liability.

22.33 Instruments resulting in an obligation only on liquidation are not liabilities (see para 22.31 above). Notwithstanding this, paragraph 22.4(b) of FRS 102 contains an exception stating that an instrument that contains an obligation to deliver a *pro rata* share of net assets on liquidation can be classified as equity, subject to specified conditions (see para 22.36 below). This seems to contradict the requirements in paragraph 22.3A(b) of the standard around obligations only arising on liquidation. The description (in para 22.4(b) of the standard) of a subordinate class of instruments that share in the net assets in liquidation seems to meet the definition of an equity interest and therefore do not require such an exemption in order to be classified as equity. In our view (based on the related guidance in IAS 32), paragraph 22.4(b) of FRS 102 refers to situations in which the obligation arises because liquidation is either certain to occur (such as in limited life entities) or is uncertain to occur but is at the option of the instrument holder in its capacity as holder of that instrument (and not in its capacity as a member of the entity – see further para 22.12 onwards above).

22.34 FRS 102 sets out an exception for specified puttable instruments and those where payment is required on liquidation. Financial instruments that would otherwise meet the definition of a financial liability are classified as equity where strict criteria are met. This is because such instruments represent the residual interest in the net assets of the issuing entity. [FRS 102 para 22.4].

22.35 The instruments addressed are:

- Puttable financial instruments, defined as *"a financial instrument that gives the holder the right to sell that instrument back to the issuer for cash or another financial asset or is automatically redeemed or repurchased by the issuer on the occurrence of an uncertain future event or the death or retirement of the instrument holder".* [FRS 102 para 22.4(a)].

■   Instruments, or components of instruments, that impose on the entity an obligation to deliver to another party a *pro rata* share of the entity's net assets only on liquidation. [FRS 102 para 22.4(b)]. We consider this to relate to situations where liquidation is certain or at the option of the instrument holder (as explained in para 22.33 above).

Criteria to be classified as equity

22.36   A non-derivative puttable instrument or obligation arising on liquidation (for example, arising in a limited life entity) is classified as equity only if all of the following criteria are met:

Criteria	Comment
1 The financial instrument is in the most subordinated class of instruments. [FRS 102 para 22.4(a)(ii), (b)].	If an open-ended investment fund has a small class of non-redeemable voting management shares that are the most subordinated, and a large class of non-voting investor shares that are puttable at fair value at the option of the holder, the investor shares are not the most subordinated class of instrument. So, the non-voting investor shares cannot be classified as equity, regardless of the value or number of the management shares.
2 For puttable instruments, all instruments in its class should have identical features. [FRS 102 para 22.4(a)(iii)].	To be considered identical, all puttable instruments in a class should, for example: ■ have the same formula or other method to calculate the redemption price; ■ rank equally on liquidation; ■ have identical voting rights; and ■ have all other features identical (for example, calls, management fees and currency of denomination). For example, an open-ended fund has two sub-funds (sub-fund A and sub-fund B) and two classes of puttable shares (A shares and B shares) whose returns are based on the performance of sub-funds A and B respectively. Both the A and B shares are the most subordinated class of shares in the fund's consolidated financial statements. But neither is classified as equity: they do

3   The instrument should entitle the holder to a *pro rata* share of the entity's net assets on liquidation. [FRS 102 para 22.4(a)(i), (b)].

An instrument with a preferential right on liquidation is not an instrument with an entitlement to a *pro rata* share of the entity's net assets. So, if a puttable instrument has a right to a fixed dividend on liquidation in addition to a share of the entity's net assets, but the other puttable instruments in the class do not have the same right on liquidation, none of the shares in that class are equity.

4   The total expected cash flows attributable to the instrument over the instrument's life should be based substantially on the profit or loss, the change in recognised net assets, or the change in the fair value of recognised and unrecognised net assets of the entity over the instrument's life (excluding any effects of the instrument). [FRS 102 para 22.4(a)(v), (b)].

Cash flows attributable to the instrument over its life should be based on the profit or loss or change in the entity's net assets as a whole, and not just part of the entity's business.

This condition would be met where the put is for cash equivalent to:

- fair value of the entity;
- FRS 102 book value of the entity's assets; or
- an approximation to fair value using a formula based on net profit, such as multiples of EBITDA, provided that the formula (for example, the multiple used) is reviewed regularly to ensure that it results in an approximation to fair value. For obligations arising on liquidation, the reference is only to 'share of net assets'. In a liquidation, this is equivalent to the value of the recognised and unrecognised net assets and to the profit or loss of the entity over its life.

5   For puttable instruments, the instrument should not contain any liability features, other than the put itself, and it should not be a contract that will or might be settled in the entity's own equity instruments, as set out in the liability definition (see para 22.8 above). [FRS 102 para 22.4(a)(iv)].

A puttable instrument cannot have another contractual obligation apart from the put itself, and so a compound instrument can never be classified as equity when it is puttable.

For example, a puttable financial instrument that contains an obligation:

- either to distribute current period profits on the demand of each holder based on a *pro rata* share of the entity's profits; or

Also at the top of the right column, before paragraph 3's commentary:

not have identical features, because they carry rights to different sub-funds.

      ■ to distribute all taxable income as a requirement of the entity's constitution, cannot be classed as an equity instrument.

Impact on consolidation

22.37 Instruments issued by a subsidiary that meet the criteria outlined above (and are therefore classified as equity at a separate or individual financial statements level) are treated as a liability in the consolidated financial statements of the group containing the subsidiary. [FRS 102 para 22.5(d)].

The following examples illustrate some aspects of the requirements.

> **Example 1 – Impact of distribution ceiling on liquidation**
>
> An instrument provides that, on liquidation, the holders of the instrument receive a *pro rata* share of the net assets, limited to a ceiling, and any excess net assets are distributed to a charity organisation or the government. The entity is a limited life entity, because it will be liquidated 10 years after start-up. The instrument is classified as a liability, because the holders are not entitled to a *pro rata* share of the net assets of the entity on liquidation. [FRS 102 para 22.5(a)].

> **Example 2 – Puttable instrument sharing in net assets**
>
> The terms of a puttable instrument determine that, when the put option is exercised, the holder receives a *pro rata* share of the net assets of the entity. The *pro rata* share is determined by:
>
> (i)   dividing the entity's net assets into units of equal amounts (as if the entity is in liquidation); and
>
> (ii)   multiplying that amount by the number of the units held by the financial instrument holder.
>
> This puttable instrument would be classified as equity. However, if the put entitled the holder to an amount measured on a different basis, the instrument is classified as a liability. [FRS 102 para 22.5(b)].

Members' shares in co-operative entities and similar instruments

22.38 Members' shares in co-operative entities and similar instruments are equity if:

■ the entity has an unconditional right to refuse redemption of the members' shares; or

■ redemption is unconditionally prohibited by local law, regulation or the entity's governing charter.

[FRS 102 para 22.6].

Examples of liability and equity classification – preference shares with various rights

22.39   Preference shares come with various rights: they could be redeemable at the option of the holder or the issuer, mandatorily redeemable or non-redeemable. Dividends on such shares might be either fixed or payable at the issuer's discretion, or their payment might be linked to payments on another instrument. Section 22 of FRS 102 requires the classification of preference shares, in common with other financial instruments, to be based on an assessment of the contractual arrangement's substance and the definitions of a financial liability and an equity instrument (as discussed above).

22.40   Preference shares are relatively common, so we summarise below, for ease of understanding and as a practical aid, the appropriate classification of preference shares for various combinations of redemption and dividend rights; it is assumed that the criteria for equity classification for puttable financial instruments and obligations arising on liquidation (summarised in para 22.36 above) have not been met:

Classification of preference shares			
Terms		**Classification**	
Redemption of principal	**Payment of dividends (assume all at market rates)**	**Type of Instrument**	**Reasons**
Non-redeemable	Discretionary	Equity	There is no contractual obligation to pay cash. Any dividends paid are recognised in equity (see para 22.98 below).
	Non-discretionary	Liability	Liability component is equal to the present value of the dividend payments in perpetuity. Assuming the dividends are set at market rates, the proceeds will be equivalent to the fair value (at the date of issue) of the dividends payable in perpetuity. So, the entire proceeds are classified as a liability.
Redeemable at the issuer's option at some future date	Discretionary	Equity	There is no contractual obligation to pay cash. An option to redeem the shares for cash does not satisfy the definition of a financial liability. Any dividends paid are recognised in equity (see para 22.98 below).

	Non-discretionary	Liability with an embedded call option feature	Liability component equal to the present value of the dividend payments in perpetuity. Assuming the dividends are set at market rates, the proceeds will be equivalent to the fair value (at the date of issue) of the dividends payable in perpetuity. So, the entire proceeds are classified as a liability. Whether the instrument will subsequently be measured at amortised cost or at fair value will depend on the features of the call option. It is most likely to be classified as 'basic' under section 11 of FRS 102 rather than as an 'other financial instrument' under section 12 of the standard (see further chapters 11 and 12).
Mandatorily redeemable at a fixed or determinable amount at a fixed or future date	Discretionary	Compound	Liability component is equal to the present value of the redemption amount. Equity component is equal to proceeds less liability component. Any dividends paid are related to the equity component and are recognised in equity (see para 22.98 below). However, if any unpaid dividends are added to the redemption amount, the whole instrument is a financial liability.
	Non-discretionary	Liability	The entity has an obligation to pay cash in respect of both principal and dividends.
Redeemable at the holder's option at some future date	Discretionary	Compound	Liability component equal to the present value of the redemption amount (on the basis that the criteria relating to puttables have not been met (see para 22.36 above)). Equity component is equal to proceeds less liability component (see para 22.93 below). Any dividends paid are related to the equity component and are recognised in equity (see para 22.98 below). Where any unpaid dividends are added to the redemption amount, the whole instrument is a financial liability.

	Non-discretionary	Liability	There is a contractual obligation to pay cash in respect of both the principal and dividend. Whether the instrument will subsequently be measured at amortised cost or at fair value will depend on the features of the put option. Often it will be classified as 'basic' under section 11 of FRS 102 rather than as an 'other financial instrument' under section 12 of the standard (see further chapter 11).

Original issue of shares or other equity instruments

Recognition

22.41 An entity recognises the issue of shares or other instruments that are classified as equity for accounting purposes when it issues those shares and another party is obliged to provide cash or other resources to the entity in exchange for those instruments. [FRS 102 para 22.7].

22.42 Where the entity receives cash or other resources before the equity instruments are issued, it recognises the corresponding increase in equity to the extent of consideration received if the shares are considered to be substantively issued in law. If the company believes that a shareholder is legally entitled to the shares (for example, is entitled to dividends), the consideration received is credited to paid-in capital (share capital/share premium) regardless of whether the certificate has been issued. If the shares have not been legally issued, the consideration received is credited to 'shares to be issued'. This is because the cash received is, in substance, equity: the entity cannot be forced to repay it and simply needs to issue the related instrument. [FRS 102 para 22.7(b)].

22.43 On the other hand, where the equity shares have not been issued (or called up), but they have been subscribed for and no consideration has been received, no increase in equity is recognised. [FRS 102 para 22.7(c)].

Partly paid shares

22.44 Under UK law, shares do not have to be fully paid at issue. For a private company, there are no rules to determine the minimum amount of consideration that must be paid, or how the consideration paid should be divided between the nominal value of the share and the share premium. A public company must have at least a quarter of the nominal value plus the whole of any premium paid up at issue. [CA06 Sec 586].

22.45 The accounting treatment for partly paid shares depends on the terms and conditions of the share issue and possibly the company's constitution. The issuer of equity shares records at least the amount received in cash on the partly paid shares as an asset and as a credit to equity (and the credit to equity is reduced by any transaction costs). The issuer then needs to consider whether to recognise the balance not yet paid on the shares as a receivable, with a corresponding credit to equity depending on the contractual terms – for indicators of whether an equity instrument should be recognised, see paragraph 22.42 above. If the shareholder is contractually obliged to pay any outstanding amounts, the related receivable is a financial asset and is accounted for in accordance with section 11 or 12 of FRS 102.

Measurement

22.46 Equity instruments are measured at fair value of cash or other consideration received, net of transaction costs. If payment of consideration is deferred and the time value of money is material, the initial measurement is on a present value basis. [FRS 102 para 22.8]. Transaction costs of an equity transaction are deducted from equity, net of any related income tax benefit. [FRS 102 para 22.9]. Transaction costs are defined as *"[i]ncremental costs that are directly attributable to the acquisition, issue or disposal of a financial asset, financial liability or equity instrument. An incremental cost is one that would not have been incurred if the entity had not acquired, issued or disposed of the financial instrument"*. [FRS 102 Glossary of terms]. Deducting transaction costs from equity is based on the view that the transaction costs incurred are a necessary part of completing the equity transaction and form an integral part of it. Linking the equity transaction and costs of the transaction reflects the net proceeds received from the transaction in equity.

22.47 An entity typically incurs various costs in issuing or acquiring its own equity instruments. Those costs might include registration and other regulatory fees, underwriting costs and brokerage fees, amounts paid to lawyers, accountants, investment bankers and other professional advisers, fees and commissions paid to agents, brokers and dealers, printing costs and stamp duties. Most such costs are transaction costs (that is, incremental costs that are directly attributable to the equity transaction that otherwise would have been avoided if the equity instruments had not been issued). Transaction costs arising on the issue of equity instruments, however, do not include indirect costs, such as the costs of management time and administrative overheads, or allocations of internal costs that would have been incurred if the equity instruments had not been issued. Nor do they include costs of researching different types of equity instruments or of ascertaining the suitability or feasibility of particular equity instruments.

Presentation

22.48 Presentation of increases in equity arising from the issue of shares or other equity instruments in the balance sheet is determined by the applicable laws. For example, the par value (or other nominal value) of shares and the amount paid in excess of par value (such as share premium) could be presented separately.

[FRS 102 para 22.10]. For UK entities, this is covered in the following paragraphs.

Legal aspects

22.49 The Companies Act 2006 and common law rules apply to all shares irrespective of their accounting classification.

22.50 Legal classification depends on the rights given to the shares in the company's memorandum and articles of association. The 2006 Act defines 'equity share capital' as a company's issued share capital except for any shares that, neither in regard to dividends nor in regard to capital, carry any right to participate beyond a specified amount in a distribution. [CA06 Sec 548]. Generally, ordinary shares are, in legal terms, equity shares. Some preference shares might also be, in legal terms, equity share capital. The distinction between equity share capital and non-equity share capital is important when considering the application of merger relief (see para 22.56 below). Clearly, FRS 102's definition of equity differs from this legal definition. There is another definition of equity shares for tax purposes.

22.51 Some financial instruments might be accounted for as equity (and the coupons as equity dividends) but they are, in legal terms, debt. They impact on distributable profits and capital maintenance as debt, and not as shares with dividends. Legally, compound instruments are either wholly debt or wholly shares, because the law does not contemplate that instruments will be broken into components. Determining the legal consequences can be complex, particularly for distributions and capital maintenance purposes. Section 6 of Tech 02/10, 'Guidance on the determination of realised profits and losses in the context of distributions under the Companies Act 2006', provides illustrative examples of the interaction between the accounting and legal rules. See also from paragraph 22.148 below.

22.52 Other instruments are classified as debt for accounting purposes but are legally shares, such as mandatorily redeemable preference shares. The nominal value and share premium of such instruments should be shown as a liability. Shares and share premium presented as liabilities are subject to the capital maintenance requirements of the 2006 Act. Companies should maintain sufficient records to ensure that, if legal shares presented as liabilities are repurchased, the company's capital base is preserved and appropriate amounts are transferred to the share premium account and capital redemption reserve in equity shareholders' funds.

22.53 The 2006 Act strictly governs the purchase of own shares by a company, and the rules governing the redemption of redeemable shares are very similar. If authorised by its articles, a company can issue shares that are redeemable at the option of the company or the shareholder, provided that there are also non-redeemable shares in issue. [CA06 Sec 684].

Equity arising from transactions with owners – legal implications

Equity share capital

22.54 If the equity shares have a par (nominal) value, paid-in capital is split between par value (reflected as share capital) and any premium at the date of issue (unless relief is available – see further para 22.56 onwards below). [CA06 Sec 610]. The 2006 Act restricts the use of the share premium account. For further information, refer to chapter 23 of the Manual of Accounting.

Non-equity share capital

22.55 Non-equity share capital's rights as regards dividends and capital are limited to a specified amount. [CA06 Secs 548, 616]. The 2006 Act does not specify whether those limited amounts contain obligations. Thus, a non-equity share might, for accounting purposes, be equity, a liability or a compound instrument. For example, a preference share redeemable at the option of the holder after 10 years that contains a fixed 10% non-cumulative, non-mandatory dividend is a compound instrument for accounting purposes: a liability for the present value of the principal amount, and an equity component for the non-mandatory dividends. Legal requirements in respect of share capital and share premium apply regardless of accounting classification.

Merger relief

22.56 Share premium is the excess of the proceeds received over the par value of shares issued, less any directly attributable transaction costs. [CA06 Sec 610]. Merger relief is a statutory relief from recognising share premium when issuing legal equity shares in order to acquire the legal equity shares of another company where specified conditions are met. It affects accounting for capital and reserves in the issuing company's financial statements. It does not affect the accounting treatment of acquisitions in consolidated financial statements (see further chapter 19). Applying merger relief means that shares issued are recorded at their nominal value; no share premium is recorded.

22.57 Where the conditions for merger relief are satisfied, applying the relief is compulsory. This is based on the wording of section 612(2) of the 2006 Act, which states that *"if the equity shares in the issuing company allotted in pursuance of an arrangement in consideration for the acquisition or cancellation of equity shares in the other company are issued at a premium, section 610 does not apply to the premium on these shares"*.

22.58 For merger relief to apply, a transaction must satisfy all of these conditions:

- A company (known either as the 'issuing company' or the 'acquiring company') secures at least 90% of the nominal value of each class of the equity share capital of another company (the 'acquired company') as a result of an arrangement.

- The arrangement provides for the allotment of equity shares in the issuing company. Such allotment will normally be made to the acquired company's shareholders.

- The consideration for the shares so allotted is either the issue or the transfer to the issuing company of equity shares in the acquired company, or the cancellation of those equity shares in the acquired company that the issuing company does not already hold.

[CA06 Sec 612(1)].

22.59 For further information on detailed conditions for merger relief, refer to chapter 23 of the Manual of Accounting.

22.60 The examples below illustrate how the provisions of the 2006 Act apply. Equity in these examples refers only to the legal nature of shares.

Example 1 – Equity share-for-share exchange

Company A issues equity shares and acquires 90% of company B's equity shares in a share-for-share exchange. This is the most obvious application of the provisions. Company A is entitled to merger relief. It records the shares issued at their nominal value. For discussion on the measurement of the related investment in company B, see below.

Example 2 – Cancellation of equity shares not held by acquirer

Company C owns 60% of company D's equity shares. The members of company D agree to cancel those equity shares that company C does not hold, in return for equity shares in company C.

Company C should apply merger relief. There are two factors in this:

- Cancelling the remaining shares increases company C's 60% holding to 100% (over the 90% threshold).

- The consideration for the allotment of company C's equity shares is the cancellation of those shares in company D that it does not already hold.

It is irrelevant that company C did not acquire the original 60% holding as part of the arrangement. Prior holdings are taken into account in determining whether company C has secured 90% of company D's equity share capital. Company C is only entitled to relief on the shares that it issues in consideration for the cancellation of those shares in company D that it does not hold. It cannot, however, write back any share premium that it set up on any shares that it issued when it acquired the 60% holding.

Example 3 – Differing classes of equity shares

Company E acquires all of company F's 'A' equity shares. Company F also has 'B' equity shares in issue, but company E holds none of these. Company E is not entitled to merger relief, because it has not secured a 90% holding of each class of equity shares in company F. [CA06 Sec 613(4)]. This applies even if the total 'B' shares represent 10% or less of the nominal value of company F's equity share capital.

Example 4 – Equity shares as consideration

Company G acquires 95% of company H's equity shares. The consideration for these shares is, in equal proportions, equity shares in company G and cash. Company G applies merger relief. There is no 'cash limit' criterion in the conditions for obtaining the relief, and there is no minimum proportion of the consideration that should consist of shares for merger relief to apply.

Application of merger relief – issue of non-equity shares

22.61 As part of the same arrangement when it issues equity shares for the equity shares of the target, the issuing company might also allot any shares for the acquisition or cancellation of the target's non-equity shares that are not held by the issuing company. In this case, the issuing company also takes merger relief on the shares that it issues. [CA06 Sec 612(3)].

Group reconstruction relief

22.62 Under the basic rule in section 610 of the 2006 Act (see para 22.54 above), the issuing company should transfer any premium on the issue of its shares to a share premium account, not only where a 'third party' acquisition of shares occurs but also where a group reconstruction occurs. The Act provides some relief from (but does not altogether dispense with) the requirement to recognise share premium when a group reconstruction occurs. [CA06 Sec 611]. Group reconstruction relief requires recognition of share premium of a 'minimum premium value'.

22.63 Merger relief provisions are not available for group reconstructions. [CA06 Sec 612(4)]. Group reconstruction relief does not affect the accounting for group reconstructions in consolidated financial statements. See further chapter 19.

22.64 Group reconstruction relief applies under the following conditions:

- A wholly owned subsidiary (the 'issuing company') allots some of its shares either to its holding company or to another wholly owned subsidiary of its holding company. [CA06 Sec 611(1)].

- The allotment is in consideration for the transfer to it of any assets (other than cash) of its holding company or of another wholly owned subsidiary of its holding company. [CA06 Sec 611(1)].

- 'Company' includes any body corporate, except where reference is made to the issuing company (that is, the acquiring company). [CA06 Sec 616(1)].

22.65 Use of the relief is not compulsory where the conditions are met, unlike merger relief.

22.66 Group reconstruction relief only applies to the transfer of 'non-cash' assets to the issuing company. [CA06 Sec 611(1)]. If the assets being transferred include cash, it must be determined how many of the shares in the issuing company have been allotted for that cash. Share premium must be recognised for those shares.

22.67 An example of a transaction to which group reconstruction relief might be applied is where an issuer allots shares in consideration for shares in a fellow subsidiary of the issuer's 100% parent. The fellow subsidiary does not need to be wholly owned by the issuer's parent, even though the issuer needs to be a 100% subsidiary of the parent. Applying group reconstruction relief, the issuing company need only transfer the 'minimum premium value' to the share premium account where the shares relating to the transfer are issued at a premium. [CA06 Sec 611(2)].

22.68 For this purpose, the following definitions apply:

- The 'minimum premium value' is the amount by which the base value of the consideration that the issuing company receives exceeds the aggregate nominal value of the shares that it allots in consideration for the transfer. [CA06 Sec 611(3)].

- The 'base value' of the consideration that the issuing company receives is the amount by which the base value of the assets transferred to it exceeds the base value of any liabilities that the issuing company assumes as part of that consideration. [CA06 Sec 611(4)].

- The 'base value of the assets transferred' is the lower of:

  - the cost to the transferor company of those assets; and

  - the amount at which the assets are stated, immediately before the transfer, in the transferor company's accounting records.

  [CA06 Sec 611(5)].

- The 'base value of the liabilities' assumed is the amount at which those liabilities are stated, immediately before the transfer, in the transferor company's accounting records. [CA06 Sec 611(5)].

Differences between merger and group reconstruction reliefs

22.69 The 'minimum premium' must be recognised in the share premium account when group reconstruction relief is applied. Merger relief is an absolute relief from recognising share premium. Furthermore, merger relief (where it applies) is compulsory, but group reconstruction relief is not.

22.70 In our view, crediting more to the share premium account in the financial statements than the 'minimum premium value' is unusual and potentially confusing to users of the financial statements. Users might infer that the excess over the 'minimum premium' is subject to the normal restrictions on the share premium account. [CA06 Sec 610]. We recommend that the excess premium over the 'minimum amount' in group reconstructions is credited to an 'other reserve', often called a 'merger reserve' or 'capital reserve', rather than to the statutory share premium account.

Carrying value of the investment

22.71 In legal terms, where a company acquires a subsidiary and qualifies for merger relief or group reconstruction relief, the cost of investment in the subsidiary can be recorded at either the nominal value plus any minimum premium or the fair value of the shares issued. [CA06 Sec 615].

22.72 Any difference between the initial carrying amount of an investment in a subsidiary and the legal share capital and share premium is credited to another reserve, generally called a 'merger reserve'.

22.73 Investments in subsidiaries can be carried at cost, at fair value through other comprehensive income, or at fair value through profit and loss. [FRS 102 para 9.26]. In our view, using 'cost' allows the investment in subsidiary to be carried at the nominal value, plus any minimum premium where relevant. See further chapter 9.

Multi-currency share capital

22.74 Companies might issue share capital denominated in a currency that is not their functional currency. Additionally, individual shares must be denominated in one particular currency, but different shares can be denominated in different currencies (see *Re Scandinavian Bank Group plc [1987] BCLC 220*).

22.75 Where foreign currency share capital is presented as a financial liability in the balance sheet, the liability is initially stated at the spot rate prevailing at the date of issue. Subsequently, the financial liability will be retranslated, as a monetary item, at each balance sheet date in accordance with section 30 of FRS 102. Foreign currency share capital that is presented as equity is initially stated at the spot rate prevailing at the date of issue, and is generally not retranslated. However, some companies do retranslate their foreign currency share capital and take the translation differences to reserves. This might seem contrary to section 30; however, the overall effect on equity (taking the retranslated foreign share capital and the cumulative translation differences together) is as if the foreign currency share capital is carried at the original historical spot rate.

22.76 The effect of exchange rate movements should be considered, even if no retranslation is recorded for accounting purposes. The common law has the effect of restricting distributions where to do otherwise would result in the net assets falling below the functional currency worth of the share capital. There is a rule of law that, where the share capital is denominated in another currency (other than the functional currency), the share capital is in fact fixed as that other currency amount. Thus, the current worth of the share capital in functional currency terms must be compared with the net assets in functional currency. To the extent that a distribution would result in the net assets falling below the current functional currency value of the share capital, the ability to make such a distribution is restricted. [Tech 02/10 paras 11.21–11.24].

22.77 Foreign currency share capital is generally redeemed or repurchased in the currency in which the shares are denominated. There will be a difference between the functional currency amount at redemption and the amount recorded at the issue of the shares (whether that amount is accounted for as a liability or as equity and, if equity, whether or not it has been retranslated). Based on the example in Appendix 7 of Tech 02/10, this seems to affect distributable profits (see further para 22.105 onwards below). A debit difference will absorb distributable profits. A credit difference should also be taken to distributable profits, provided that the shares were originally issued for qualifying consideration.

22.78 There are two legal views on the application of the 2006 Act's capital maintenance rules to the redemption or repurchase of foreign currency share capital (assuming that the shares are not redeemed or repurchased out of the proceeds of a fresh issue of shares made for this purpose). One view is that the nominal value of the shares concerned, translated at the original exchange rate, should be transferred from distributable profits to the capital redemption reserve. The alternative view is that the nominal value transferred is translated at the exchange rate ruling on the date of the redemption or repurchase. Companies redeeming or repurchasing foreign currency share capital should take legal advice.

22.79 The Act allows limited companies to redenominate their share capital easily. [CA06 Sec 622(1)]. A redenomination reserve is created, based on the rules for calculating the new nominal value for the redenominated shares in sections 622 and 623 of the Act. Such redenomination reserve can be used to allot fully paid bonus shares. [CA06 Sec 628(2)]. It is treated as paid up share capital of the entity for the purposes of a reduction in capital. [CA06 Sec 628(3)]. For further information about redenomination of share capital, refer to chapter 23 of the Manual of Accounting.

Reduction of share capital

22.80 A company might wish to reduce its share capital for a variety of reasons, the most common ones being:

■ Where the company has surplus capital in excess of its needs which it proposes to return to shareholders; this could be as part of reducing the scale of its trading operations.

■ Where the company has a dividend block (that is, it is unable to pay a dividend or make other distributions, because it has negative or insufficient distributable reserves).

■ Where the company wishes to release a liability to pay up capital. For example, it might have issued partly paid shares, and now wishes to cancel the unpaid amount.

■ Where the company is undertaking a major reconstruction, such as a scheme of arrangement of which a court-approved reduction forms part.

22.81 Private companies have the option of reducing their share capital either by applying to the court for approval or by issuing a solvency statement. [CA06 Sec 642]. It is no longer necessary for a company to have express authority in its articles of association to reduce its share capital (unless there is a specific prohibition or restriction in the articles). Public companies, however, still require court approval for a reduction of capital.

22.82 A company can reduce its share capital under the Companies Act 2006 as follows:

■ by extinguishing or reducing the liability on any unpaid share capital;

■ by cancelling any paid-up share capital which is lost or not represented by available assets; or

■ by repaying any surplus paid-up share capital.

[CA06 Sec 641(4)].

22.83 A company can reduce its issued share capital, share premium account and capital redemption and redenomination reserves, because share premium and these reserves constitute share capital for the purpose of a reduction. Other types of reserve (such as a revaluation reserve) cannot be reduced by way of a capital reduction, but could be capitalised into share capital by a bonus issue of shares prior to the reduction.

22.84 FRS 102 does not specify any accounting in respect of a reduction in capital. The accounting treatment, where the capital reduced has been presented as equity, should reflect the change in legal composition of capital and reserves. In the UK, private companies can acquire their own shares out of capital. Otherwise, under the Act, companies must maintain their capital after redeeming or acquiring their own shares or cancelling treasury shares. [CA06 Sec 733(1)]. Where a redemption or repurchase is wholly or partly funded specifically by a new or 'fresh' issue of shares, and the proceeds of the fresh issue are less than the nominal value of the shares redeemed or purchased, the difference is transferred to the capital redemption reserve. [CA06 Sec 733(3)]. Some of the capital might then be represented by share premium and some by the capital redemption reserve. For further information, including more on solvency statements, refer to chapter 23 of the Manual of Accounting.

Exercise of options, rights and warrants

22.85 The recognition, measurement and presentation principles (described in paras 22.41–22.47 above) are also applied to equity issued as a result of the exercise of options, rights, warrants and similar equity instruments. [FRS 102 para 22.11]. For accounting purposes, the options, rights or warrants might be recorded as financial assets or liabilities or they might be equity instruments (see further para 22.20 onwards above). If the option, right or warrant is recorded as a financial asset or liability (for example, the fair value of an option issued to a holder to buy the entity's shares), the carrying amount will be derecognised when exercised and affects the overall amount recorded in equity. Under company law, however, legal share capital is based on the exercise price of the option. The split between share capital and premium is based on the par value of the shares issued (as discussed in para 22.54 above). Any premium received on the issue of an option is a realised profit in law and forms part of distributable reserves. [Tech 02/10 para 6.17].

Capitalisation or bonus issues of shares, share splits or consolidation of shares

22.86 Some transactions do not change total equity. The issue of new shares to shareholders in proportion to their existing holding is a capitalisation or bonus issue (also sometimes referred to as a stock dividend). For example, an entity might give its shareholders one dividend or bonus share for every 10 shares held. Companies might issue bonus shares using share premium account, capital redemption reserve, retained earnings or the revaluation reserve, where this is permitted by their articles of association. The relevant reserve is debited with the nominal value of the shares issued. Paid-up share capital in equity is credited with an equivalent amount, if the bonus shares are accounted for as equity under section 22 of FRS 102 (as described above). If the bonus shares are not equity, they are recognised as financial liabilities in accordance with section 11 or 12 of the standard, as appropriate. An entity reclassifies amounts within equity as required by applicable laws, but it does not change the total amount of equity in its financial statements. [FRS 102 para 22.12].

22.87 The division of an entity's existing shares into multiple shares is called a share split. For example, in a share split, each shareholder might receive three additional shares for each share held. In some cases, the previously outstanding shares are cancelled and replaced by new shares. A share split or consolidation of shares impacts the number of shares in issue rather than the components of equity.

22.88 The Companies Act allows these types of transaction unless the company has prohibitions or restrictions in its articles. [CA06 Sec 618]. The resolution might give the company the power to sub-divide or consolidate the shares at any time in the future, or at particular times by reference to specified dates or circumstances. [CA06 Sec 618(4)].

Treasury shares

22.89 Where an entity purchases its own shares or other own equity instruments and holds them in treasury ('treasury shares'):

- The fair value of the consideration given is deducted from equity. This is because an entity's own equity instruments are not recognised as a financial asset, regardless of the reason for which they are acquired.

- No gain or loss is recognised on the purchase of an entity's own equity instruments. This is because the acquisition of treasury shares is a transaction with an entity's owners rather than a gain or loss to the entity. Similarly, no gain or loss is recognised when treasury shares are cancelled or reissued or resold by the entity.

[FRS 102 para 22.16].

22.90 The Companies Act permits only 'qualifying shares' to be purchased and held in treasury. [CA06 Sec 724(2)]. In essence, such shares need to be quoted ordinary shares, and so private companies without listed shares cannot hold shares in treasury. Any shares that are purchased that are not 'qualifying shares' need to be cancelled. Accounting and legal aspects related to the cancellation of shares are dealt with in paragraph 22.80 onwards above.

Convertible debt or similar compound financial instruments

Introduction

22.91 Not all financial instruments are either liability or equity in their entirety. Some, known as 'compound instruments', contain elements of both in a single contract. [FRS 102 para 22.13]. Typical examples of such instruments are:

- A mandatorily redeemable preference share that provides that dividend payments can be made at the issuer's discretion before the redemption date, and any dividends that are not made do not accumulate and become due on redemption. Such an instrument contains a liability component (that is, the issuer's contractual obligation to deliver cash or another financial asset for payment of the redemption amount) and an equity component (that is, the issuer's discretionary right to pay dividends if declared).

- A bond issued in the functional currency of the issuer that is convertible into a fixed number of equity shares at the holder's option. From the issuer's perspective, such an instrument comprises two components: a financial liability (that is, the issuer's contractual obligation to deliver cash or another financial asset for payment of interest and principal, if not converted) and an equity instrument (that is, a written call option granting the holder the right, for a specified period of time, to convert it into a fixed number of the entity's ordinary shares). The economic effect of issuing such an instrument is substantially the same as issuing simultaneously a debt instrument with an early settlement provision and warrants to purchase ordinary shares, or issuing a debt instrument with detachable share purchase warrants. In either case, the separate warrants would not meet the definition of a liability under paragraph 22.3(b)(ii) of FRS 102, and would instead be classified as equity.

Separation of a compound financial instrument on initial recognition

22.92   The issuer of a non-derivative financial instrument should first evaluate the financial instrument's terms, to determine whether it contains both a liability and an equity component. This evaluation should be done in accordance with the contractual arrangement's substance and the definitions of financial liability, financial asset and equity. If such components are identified, the issuer should account for the components separately as financial liabilities, financial assets or equity instruments. For example, for the conversion option of a convertible bond to be classified as an equity component, it must meet the definition of equity; in particular, it must be settled by delivery of a fixed amount of cash or other financial assets in return for the issue of a fixed number of equity instruments. [FRS 102 para 22.13].

22.93   Each component is accounted for separately. The initial allocation, illustrated by reference to a convertible bond but equally applicable to other compound instruments, allocates the fair value of the consideration for the compound instrument into its liability and equity components, as follows:

■   The fair value of the consideration in respect of the liability component is measured first, at the fair value of a similar liability (including any embedded non-equity derivative features, such as an issuer's call option to redeem the bond early) that does not have any associated equity conversion option. This becomes the liability component's carrying amount at initial recognition. [FRS 102 para 22.13].

■   In practice, the liability component's initial carrying value is determined by discounting the contractual stream of future cash flows (interest and principal) to the present value at the current rate of interest applicable to instruments of comparable credit status and providing substantially the same cash flows on the same terms, but without the equity component (the equity conversion option).

■   The liability is classified as 'basic' or 'other', in accordance with sections 11 and 12 of FRS 102, and it is subsequently accounted at either amortised cost or fair value through profit or loss. Where the liability is 'basic', any difference between the carrying amount of the liability component and the principal amount repayable at maturity is systematically recognised as an additional interest expense, using the effective interest method (see chapter 11). [FRS 102 para 22.15].

■ The equity component (the equity conversion option) is assigned the residual amount after deducting, from the fair value of the instrument as a whole, the amount separately determined for the liability component.

■ The equity component is excluded from the scope of sections 11 and 12 of the standard, and is never remeasured after initial recognition.

22.94 Transaction costs (see para 22.46 above) are allocated between the components, based on their relative fair values. [FRS 102 para 22.13].

22.95 Once a compound financial instrument has been separated into its liability and equity components on initial recognition, the classification of the liability and equity components is not revised. [FRS 102 para 22.14]. This is the case, whether or not the option's exercise might appear to have become economically advantageous to some or all holders.

> **Example – Separation of a convertible bond (based on the Appendix to section 22 of FRS 102)**
>
> On 1 January 20X5, an entity issues 500 convertible bonds. The bonds are issued at par with a face value of £100 per bond and are for a five-year term, with no transaction costs. The total proceeds from the issue are £50,000. Interest is payable annually in arrears at an annual interest rate of 4%. Each bond is convertible, at the holder's discretion, into 25 ordinary shares at any time up to maturity. At the time the bonds are issued, the market interest rate for similar debt that does not have the conversion option is 6%.
>
> The instrument contains two components: a liability for the interest and principal on the bonds, and an equity component for the holder's option to convert the bonds into a fixed number of equity shares.
>
> The liability component is valued first, and the difference between the total proceeds on issue (which is the fair value of the instrument in its entirety) and the fair value of the liability component is assigned to the equity component. The fair value of the liability component is calculated by determining its present value, using the discount rate of 6%. The calculations and journal entries are illustrated below:
>
> | | £ |
> |---|---|
> | Proceeds from the bond issue (A) | 50,000 |
> | Present value of principal at the end of five years (see calculations below) | 37,363 |
> | Present value of interest payable annually in arrears for five years | 8,425 |
> | Present value of liability, which is the fair value of liability component (B) | 45,788 |
> | Residual, which is the fair value of the equity component (A) – (B) | 4,212 |

The issuer of the bonds makes the following journal entry at issue on 1 January 20X5:

Dr	Cash	£50,000	
Cr	Financial Liability – Convertible bond		£45,788[1]
Cr	Equity		£4,212

1 Calculated as:

Present value of principal of £50,000 at 6%: £50,000/(1.06)^5 = £37,363

Present value of the interest annuity of £2,000 (= £50,000 × 4%) payable at the end of each of five years, using the formula PV = C/i × [1 – 1/(1 + i)^n]: (2,000/.06) × [1 – [(1/1.06)^5] = £ 8,425

Total value of liability component: £45,788

After issue, the carrying amount of the liability will be as follows:

	(a) Interest payment (£)	(b) Total interest expense (£) = 6% x (c)	(c) Net liability (£) = Opening balance – (a) + (b)
1/1/20X5			45,788
31/12/20X5	2,000	2,747	46,535
31/12/20X6	2,000	2,792	47,327
31/12/20X7	2,000	2,840	48,167
31/12/20X8	2,000	2,890	49,057
31/12/20X9	2,000	2,943	50,000
Totals	10,000	14,212	

At the end of 20X5, the issuer would make the following journal entry:

Dr	Interest expense	£2,747	
Cr	Financial liability – convertible bond		£747
Cr	Cash		£2,000

Conversion at or before maturity

22.96 Section 22 of FRS 102 contains no guidance on accounting for a convertible instrument when the conversion option is exercised. In our view, the accounting treatment that is applied under IAS 32 should be applied. The entity derecognises the liability component and recognises it as equity. The original equity component remains in equity. There is no gain or loss on conversion at maturity. The legal aspects of conversion are dealt with in paragraph 22.85 above.

Reserves and their purposes

22.97 Some reserves are disclosed in formats of accounts required by the Act, such as:

- Called up share capital.

- Share premium.

- Revaluation reserve.

- Other:

    - Capital Redemption Reserve.

    - Reserves for own shares.

    - Reserves provided for by articles of association.

    - Other reserves.

- Profit and loss account.

The following reserves are often presented as separate components of equity, even if they are not specifically required by FRS 102:

- Currency translation adjustment.

- Hedging reserve.

Distributions to owners

22.98 For companies in the UK, directors can propose final dividends to be approved by members. A dividend becomes a legally binding liability when approved by members of a public company in general meeting, or when a members' written resolution is passed in a private company, regardless of the date when it is to be paid. Owners of a company are holders of an entity's equity instruments. Distributions to owners are recognised in equity. [FRS 102 para 22.17]. The corresponding (credit) entry is made to cash if paid immediately, or it is recognised as a liability where settlement is to be made at a future date. Where there is no obligation at the balance sheet date, a liability is not recorded. [FRS 102 para 21.4]. A proposed unapproved final dividend is not a legal obligation to shareholders at the balance sheet date, and no liability is recorded. Where non-cash assets are distributed, their fair value needs to be disclosed, except where the assets are ultimately controlled by the same parties both before and after the distribution. [FRS 102 para 22.18].

22.99 A company's articles might provide that directors can declare interim dividends. Such dividends are never a liability until they are actually paid, because the directors can revoke their resolution any time before paying it; no contractual obligation is created by the declaration.

22.100 Dividends on shares accounted for as financial liabilities are accounted for as part of the effective interest method in profit and loss. Accounting for dividends on compound financial instruments that are divided into their liability and equity components, depends on whether the dividend relates to the equity component or the liability component. For example, the net present value of the redemption amount of a mandatorily redeemable non-cumulative preference share, whose dividends are payable at the discretion of the entity, is recognised as a financial liability. The balance of the proceeds of issue of the shares is allocated to the equity component. The unwinding of the discount is recognised as an interest expense. The discretionary dividends on the shares relating to the equity component are recognised as distributions in equity.

Distributable reserves – legal implications

22.101 Profits available for distribution are addressed in Part 23 of the 2006 Act. Companies are only permitted to make a distribution out of *"profits available for the purpose"*. The Act's requirements in respect of distributions apply to all UK companies.

22.102 Distributions might also be subject to any enactment, rule of common law or provision in the memorandum or articles of association that restricts either the amounts available for distribution or the circumstances in which a distribution can be made. [CA06 Sec 852]. Distributions must be paid in accordance with the company's memorandum and articles, which contain special provisions regarding dividends and other distributions.

22.103 Under common law, dividends cannot be paid out of capital. The directors should also consider their fiduciary duties in the exercise of the powers conferred on them and act in their company's best interests. Examples of fiduciary duties include the obligation on directors to safeguard the company's assets and to ensure that the company is in a position to settle its debts as they fall due. Consequently, even if the company has profits available for distribution under Part 23 of the 2006 Act, its directors should consider the future cash needs of their company before making a distribution. It would probably be unlawful to pay a dividend if, as a result, the company became insolvent or had insufficient working capital to carry on its business.

22.104 Tech 02/10, 'Guidance on the determination of realised profits and losses in the context of distributions under the Companies Act 2006', published in November 2010 by ICAEW and ICAS, is the relevant guidance for UK companies interpreting the requirements of the Companies Act on realised profits and distributions, and it is *de facto* GAAP for distributable profits.

General principles

Defining distributable profits

22.105 Any company (whether public or private) is permitted to make a distribution only out of *"profits available for the purpose"*. [CA06 Sec 830(1)]. In this context, 'make' means 'pay'. A company must have sufficient profits when the dividend is paid and not just when it is declared.

22.106 A company's available profits for distribution are *"... its accumulated, realised profits ... less its accumulated, realised losses"*. [CA06 Sec 831(2)]. The origin of these profits and losses might be either revenue or capital. [CA06 Sec 830(2),(3)]. 'Realised' is not exactly defined in the Act. Section 853(4) of the 2006 Act says that *"... references to realised profits and realised losses, in relation to a company's accounts, are to such profits or losses of the company as fall to be treated as realised in accordance with principles generally accepted, at the time when the accounts are prepared, with respect to the determination for accounting purposes of realised profits or losses"*.

22.107 Not only is this definition somewhat circular, but also there is little indication in case law of what is meant by 'realised'. All that can really be derived from previous court cases is that judges have interpreted 'realised' more widely than 'realised in cash', and that they, like the legislature, see realisation as an accounting concept rather than as a strictly legal concept.

22.108 Tech 02/10 identifies, interprets and applies the principles for determining realised profits and losses for the purposes of making distributions under the 2006 Act. It does not provide guidance on how transactions and arrangements should be accounted for in a company's financial statements.

22.109 Tech 02/10's guidance is based on the principle that realised profits are primarily those that are realised in the form of *"cash or of other assets the ultimate cash realisation of which can be assessed with reasonable certainty"*. [Tech 02/10 para 3.3].

22.110 In assessing whether a company has a realised profit, transactions and arrangements should not be looked at in isolation. A realised profit will arise only where the overall commercial effect on the company satisfies the definition of realised profit set out in the guidance. A group or series of transactions or arrangements should be viewed as a whole, particularly if they are artificial, linked (whether legally or otherwise) or circular, or any combination of these. This principle is likely to be of particular relevance for, but not limited to, intra-group transactions. [Tech 02/10 paras 3.5, 3.5A]. See further from paragraph 22.119 below.

Additional conditions applying to public companies — the 'net asset test'

22.111   A public company must not make a distribution that reduces the amount of its net assets below the aggregate of its called-up share capital and its undistributable reserves – the 'net asset test'. [CA06 Sec 831(1),(6)].

Principles of realisation

Realised profits — 'qualifying consideration'

22.112   Paragraph 3.9 of Tech 02/10 sets out when a profit is realised. First, a profit is realised where it arises from a transaction in which the consideration received by the company is 'qualifying consideration'. This is defined in paragraph 3.11 of Tech 02/10 as any of the following:

■   Cash.

■   An asset that is readily convertible to cash.

■   The release, or the settlement or assumption by another party, of all or part of a liability of the company.

■   An amount receivable in any of the above forms of consideration, where:

   (i)   the debtor is capable of settling the receivable within a reasonable period of time;

   (ii)   there is a reasonable certainty that the debtor will be capable of settling when called upon to do so; and

   (iii) there is an expectation that the receivable will be settled.

■   An amount receivable from a shareholder, where and to the extent that:

   (i)   the company intends to make a distribution to the shareholder of an amount equal to or less than its receivable from that shareholder;

   (ii)   the company intends to settle such distribution by off-setting against the amount receivable (in whole or in part); and

   (iii) within the meaning of paragraphs 3.5 and 3.5A of Tech 02/10 (that is, in assessing whether a company has a realised profit, transactions and arrangements should not be looked at in isolation; and a realised profit will arise only where the overall commercial effect on the company is such that the definition of realised profit set out is met), (i) and (ii) are linked.

[Tech 02/10 para 3.11].

22.113   For the purpose of applying paragraph 3.11 of Tech 02/10, references to 'settlement' include settlement by way of set-off with a liability to the same party. [Tech 02/10 para 3.11A].

Examples of realised gains

22.114 Examples of realised gains are:

■ The recognition in the financial statements of a change in fair value, where fair value has been determined in accordance with accounting standards, to the extent that the change recognised is readily convertible to cash. [Tech 02/10 para 3.9(c)].

■ The translation of a monetary asset that comprises qualifying consideration or a liability denominated in a foreign currency (see chapter 30). [Tech 02/10 para 3.9(d)].

■ The reversal of a loss previously regarded as realised. [Tech 02/10 para 3.9(e)]. This includes writing back a charge for impairment or releasing a provision for a specific loss.

■ A profit previously regarded as unrealised that has not been capitalised (for example, a revaluation reserve, merger reserve or other similar reserve) becoming realised as a result of:

  ■ Consideration previously received by the company becoming qualifying consideration. [Tech 02/10 para 3.9(f)(i)].

  ■ The related asset being disposed of in a transaction where the company receives qualifying consideration. [Tech 02/10 para 3.9(f)(ii)].

  ■ A realised loss being recognised on the scrapping or disposal of the related asset. [Tech 02/10 para 3.9(f)(iii)].

  ■ A realised loss being recognised on the write-down for depreciation, amortisation, diminution in value or impairment of the related asset. [Tech 02/10 para 3.9(f)(iv)].

  ■ The distribution *in kind* of the asset to which the unrealised profit relates. [Tech 02/10 para 3.9(f)(v)].

■ The remeasurement of a liability, to the extent that the change recognised is readily convertible to cash. [Tech 02/10 para 3.9(g)].

22.115 Regulation 3 of the Companies (Reduction of Share Capital) Order 2008 (SI 2008/1915) specifies the cases from 1 October 2008 in which a reserve arising from a reduction in a company's share capital is to be treated as a realised profit as a matter of law. Regulation 7(2) of the Companies Act 2006 (Commencement No.7, Transitional Provisions and Savings) Order 2008 (SI 2008/1886), in effect, provides that reserves arising prior to 1 October 2008 from specified reduction of capital transactions are treated, as a matter of law, as realised profits irrespective of when the reduction occurred or the reserves arose. For further information on these issues, refer to chapter 23 of the Manual of Accounting.

Readily convertible to cash

22.116   For the purposes of 'qualifying consideration', an *"asset or change in the fair value of an asset or liability that is readily convertible to cash"* means that:

- A value can be determined at which a transaction in the asset or liability could occur, at the date of determination, in its state at that date, without negotiation and/or marketing, to either convert the asset, liability or change in fair value into cash, or to close-out the asset, liability or change in fair value.

   In determining the value, information such as prices, rates or other factors that market participants would consider in setting a price is observable.

- The company's circumstances should not prevent immediate conversion to cash or close-out of the asset, liability or change in fair value; for example, the company should be able to dispose of, or close-out, the asset, liability or the change in fair value, without any intention or need to liquidate, to curtail materially the scale of its operations, or to undertake a transaction on adverse terms.

[Tech 02/10 para 3.12].

See further section 4 of Tech 02/10.

Other realised profits

22.117   In addition, the following are realised profits:

- The receipt or accrual of investment or other income receivable in the form of qualifying consideration.

- A gain arising on a return of capital on an investment where the return is in the form of qualifying consideration.

- A gift (such as a 'capital contribution') received in the form of qualifying consideration.

- The release of a provision for a liability or loss that was treated as a realised loss.

- The reversal of a write-down or provision for diminution in value or impairment of an asset that was treated as a realised loss.

[Tech 02/10 para 3.14].

Profits and losses made before 22 December 1980

22.118   The Companies Act 1980 introduced statutory distribution rules and the concept of realised and unrealised profits. Its commencement date was 22 December 1980. Where, after making all reasonable enquiries, the directors are unable to determine whether a profit or a loss that was made before 22 December

1980 is realised or unrealised, they can treat a profit as realised and a loss as unrealised. [CA06 Sec 850(1)–(3)]. This prevents problems from occurring if no record exists of the original cost of an asset or the amount of a liability.

Linked, circular and intragroup transactions

22.119   The term 'realised profits' is generally accepted as meaning profits that are realised in the form of cash or other assets readily convertible into cash. In assessing whether profit is realised, transactions and arrangements must not be looked at in isolation. The overall commercial effect on the company of a group or series of transactions should be looked at, particularly if they are linked (legally or otherwise), artificial or circular. [Tech 02/10 para 3.5A]. Issues typically occur in the case of intra-group transactions, where profits might arise from the transfer of cash and assets around a group, although linkage might also need to be considered when analysing some transactions with third parties.

22.120   A profit is not realised if it arises from a circular transaction. In other words, if a profit arises within a group from a transaction with a group entity that has directly or indirectly provided the funding for that transaction, that profit is not realised and is not distributable. If an intra-group transaction is funded by a company that then receives a dividend from the proceeds, there is a circular flow of cash. There is no incremental cash coming into the recipient group company or its sub-group. The company has effectively funded the dividend that it receives.

22.121   Section 9 of Tech 02/10 considers a number of intra-group transactions, including dividends received out of pre-acquisition profits and the sale of an asset by a parent to its subsidiary.

> **Example 1 – Intra-group sale of assets**
>
> A company creates a scheme to generate realised profits. It has 10 subsidiaries with a carrying value of £1 million. The subsidiaries have a fair value of £10 million. The company borrows £10 million from a bank, which it then injects as share capital into a newly formed subsidiary, Newco. Newco buys the subsidiaries for £10 million. Has the company realised a profit of £9 million?
>
> No realised profit has been created, because the parent has directly funded the purchase of the subsidiaries by injecting share capital of £10 million into Newco. [Tech 02/10 para 9.28(b)].
>
> **Example 2 – Transaction with a third party**
>
> A subsidiary is sold for cash to a third party on condition that the cash is applied in subscribing for shares in the purchaser. The transaction's substance or overall commercial effect is a sale with consideration in the form of shares of the purchaser. The profit will be unrealised unless the shares of the purchaser are readily convertible to cash (for example, because they are quoted on an active market).

22.122 The above example illustrates a clear instance of linkage. In practice, it could be far less clear (for example, if there is a period of time between the two transactions and perhaps no legal obligation to complete the second one). Judgement will often be required. Tech 02/10 aims to achieve greater consistency in those judgements by setting out a series of principles that should be followed. [Tech 02/10 paras 3.43–3.75].

Realised losses

22.123 Losses should be regarded as realised losses except to the extent that the law, accounting standards or guidance in Tech 02/10 provide otherwise. [Tech 02/10 para 3.10].

22.124 Realised losses include:

- A cost or expense (other than one charged to the share premium account) that results in a reduction in recorded net assets. [Tech 02/10 para 3.15(a)].

- A loss arising on the sale or other disposal or scrapping of an asset. [Tech 02/10 para 3.15(b)].

- The writing down or providing for the depreciation, amortisation, diminution in value or impairment of an asset. If the asset has previously been revalued, the appropriate proportion of the unrealised profit on revaluation becomes a realised profit, mitigating the effect of the realised loss. [Tech 02/10 para 3.15(c)].

- The creation of, or increase in, a provision for a liability or loss that results in an overall reduction in recorded net assets. However, where assets are revalued to their fair value, and any unrealised gain is included in the profit and loss account, the deferred tax on that gain should be treated as a reduction in that unrealised gain rather than as a realised loss. [Tech 02/10 para 3.15(d)].

- A gift made by the company (or the release of all or part of a debt due to the company or the assumption of a liability by the company) to the extent that it results in an overall reduction in recorded net assets. [Tech 02/10 para 3.15(e)].

- A loss arising from fair value accounting where profits on remeasurement of the same asset or liability would be treated as realised profits. [Tech 02/10 para 3.15(f)].

- Cumulative net losses arising on fair value accounting, unless:

  - profits on remeasurement of the same asset or liability would be unrealised; and

  - the losses would not have been recorded otherwise than pursuant to fair value accounting. [Tech 02/10 para 4.31].

Fair value accounting

22.125 Profits arising from the use of fair value accounting (where the change is readily convertible to cash) are realised or unrealised, irrespective of whether the profit is recognised in profit and loss (for financial instruments at fair value through profit or loss) or through other comprehensive income. [Tech 02/10 para 4.24]. Similarly, losses arising from fair value accounting are realised unless a cumulative net loss arises where both the profits on remeasurement of the same asset or liability would be unrealised, and the losses would not have been recorded otherwise than pursuant to fair value accounting. [Tech 02/10 para 4.31].

22.126 Fair value accounting profits that are 'readily convertible to cash' are realised. 'Readily convertible to cash' means that the entity has an unrestricted ability to convert the asset or the change in the fair value of an asset or liability to cash almost instantaneously at the balance sheet date — that is, without protracted negotiations. The changes in the fair value of many (but not all) financial instruments fulfil this definition. Some, such as unquoted equity instruments and investments held for strategic purposes, do not. [Tech 02/10 paras 4.10–4.11]. Changes in the fair value of non-financial assets (such as investment property and agricultural and biological assets) rarely, if ever, fulfil the definition. Although agricultural and biological assets (which are also held at fair value) are not specifically addressed in the guidance, the treatment of their fair value gains and losses should follow the same principles.

22.127 Paragraphs 4.14 to 4.22 of Tech 02/10 address profits and losses on remeasurement of financial instruments that might be affected by the company's own creditworthiness and block discounts for securities traded in an active market.

22.138 The fair value of financial instruments determined in accordance with section 12 of FRS 102 might be volatile. Directors will need to consider, given their fiduciary duties, whether it is prudent to distribute fair value gains. [Tech 02/ 10 para 2.4].

'Relevant accounts'

22.129 To determine whether a company has profits available, and (if it is a public company) whether the 'net assets test' has been met, reference is made to specified items in the company's 'relevant accounts':

- Profits, losses, assets and liabilities.
- Provisions of any kind.
- Share capital and reserves (including undistributable reserves).

[CA06 Sec 836(1)].

22.130 The 'relevant accounts' are normally the company's last audited individual financial statements that have been circulated to members in accordance with section 423 of the 2006 Act. Distributions are made by individual companies, and not by groups. A parent company's consolidated financial statements are not relevant for determining the parent's distributable profits.

22.131 If a proposed distribution exceeds the amount distributable according to the company's latest audited individual financial statements, *'interim accounts'* should be prepared and used in addition, to justify the payment. These additional financial statements are necessary to enable a proper judgement to be made of the profits, losses, assets and liabilities (including provisions), as well as share capital and reserves (including undistributable reserves). [CA06 Secs 836(2), 838(1), 839(1)].

22.132 *'Initial accounts'* are prepared and used where a company proposes to make a distribution during its first accounting reference period or before it circulates its first audited financial statements. [CA06 Secs 836(2), 838(1), 839(1)].

22.132.1 The legislation regarding 'relevant accounts' is particularly important for investment trusts, because they must distribute the majority of their reserves each year. Consequently, an interim dividend is unlikely to be covered by the remaining profits available for distribution derived from their last audited annual financial statements. Therefore, such companies generally prepare interim accounts so that they can legally pay an interim dividend.

22.133 The 2006 Act lays down strict requirements for relevant accounts. Failure to comply with these requirements means that the distribution is unlawful. [CA06 Sec 836(3),(4)]. The shareholders cannot agree to waive the requirements. [*Re Precision Dippings Ltd v Precision Dippings Marketing Ltd [1985] Ch 447*]. The requirements of sections 838 and 839 of the 2006 Act, regarding the form and content of interim and initial accounts of public companies, do not apply to private companies. Instead, private companies can use management accounts as interim or initial accounts to support a distribution, provided that the accounts enable the directors to make a reasonable judgement of distributable profits. [CA06 Sec 836]. However, management accounts might need to be adjusted, because they will often not deal with all relevant matters, and for the sort of closing adjustments made when preparing annual financial statements.

22.134 The requirements that apply to the published annual financial statements of all companies, and the interim and initial accounts of public companies, are discussed in detail in chapter 23 of the Manual of Accounting.

Specific issues

Effect of revaluations of PPE on distributable profits

22.135 The revaluation of property, plant and equipment (PPE) can affect the amounts recorded in profit or loss and distributable profits in the following ways:

■   Depreciation on revalued assets passes through profit or loss.

Liabilities and equity

- The profit on revalued assets that are subsequently sold cannot pass through the profit and loss account.

- The revaluation itself might involve reversing depreciation that has previously been charged to the profit and loss account.

- Diminutions in the value of assets might need to be taken to the profit and loss account.

Depreciation of revalued assets

22.136 When PPE is revalued, depreciation is charged to the income statement or statement of comprehensive income based on the asset's carrying value, and not its original cost. If depreciation on the revalued amount of the asset exceeds the depreciation that would have been charged on the asset's original cost then, for distributable profits purposes, a company treats an amount equal to the excess depreciation on the revaluation surplus as a realised profit. [CA06 Sec 841(5)].

> **Example 1 – Impact of revaluation of plant on distributable reserves**
>
> Company A carries its plant at £2,000, under the revaluation model permitted by FRS 102. This amount is depreciated over the asset's useful life of 10 years. The plant's cost was £1,700. During the year, depreciation of £200 was charged. Depreciation would have been £170 if the plant had been carried at cost. Therefore, following the charge of £200 for depreciation, £30 of the revaluation reserve is regarded as a realised profit, ensuring that the company is not in a worse position with respect to realised profits merely due to its revaluation policy.

Subsequent sale of revalued assets

22.137 Some items recorded in other comprehensive income need to be included in determining profits available for distribution. For example, an unrealised profit on a revaluation of an item of PPE is credited to a revaluation reserve. If that piece of PPE is disposed of, the gain or loss on the disposal reported in the income statement is calculated by reference to its carrying value, rather than its original cost. Not all of the profit on sale (based on original cost) necessarily passes through the income statement. However, if the asset is sold for qualifying consideration, the whole profit compared to original cost is clearly realised. When an item of PPE carried at valuation is sold, the balance on the revaluation reserve relating to the asset is transferred *via* reserves to retained profits.

Treatment of revalued assets in relevant accounts

22.138 A provision for depreciation or impairment in value of an item of PPE is normally a realised loss if it does not offset a previous revaluation surplus on that asset. Section 841(1) of the 2006 Act permits an exception to this rule that allows a fall in value to be treated as an unrealised loss, for distribution purposes, where a company revalues all of its 'fixed assets', even if the revaluation shows an overall deficit. These provisions are complex. A company seeking to rely on them, in order to have sufficient distributable profits to pay a dividend, is likely to have other difficulties and would be well advised to first seek legal advice.

Foreign currency translation

22.139 Section 30 of FRS 102 requires a company to translate monetary assets and liabilities (for example, foreign currency loans and creditors for PPE purchased from overseas) into its functional currency, using the rate of exchange at the balance sheet date (that is, the closing rate).

22.140 Exchange gains and losses arise both on completed foreign currency transactions during the year and on the retranslation of balance sheet foreign currency monetary items. Profits arising from the translation of a monetary asset that comprises qualifying consideration, or a liability denominated in a foreign currency, are realised. [Tech 02/10 para 3.9(d)].

22.141 Where a company has a foreign branch with a functional currency that is different from that of its parent, the exchange differences arising on the translation of the branch's assets and liabilities into the functional currency of the parent are taken directly to reserves *via* other comprehensive income. The issue is the extent to which these exchange differences are realised or unrealised. Gross profits and losses should be analysed separately, according to the nature of the assets and liabilities on which they arise. A profit that arises on the retranslation of an asset that comprises qualifying consideration, or a liability, is a realised profit. A profit arising on the retranslation of assets such as property, plant and equipment that do not constitute qualifying consideration is an unrealised profit. Losses on retranslation are realised losses, unless they reverse an unrealised profit. There could be a realised loss to be taken into account when determining profits available for distribution, even where the net amount on the reserve is a profit. [Tech 02/10 para 11.14].

22.142 This analysis applies only in straightforward situations, where the composition of the foreign branch's assets has not changed significantly during a period. Tech 02/10 addresses more complex situations, noting that reasonable approximations can be made in analysing whether profits arising on exchange differences are realised. [Tech 02/10 paras 11.15, 11.17].

Use of presentation currency

22.143 Realised profits and losses are measured by reference to the company's functional currency. The accounting gain or loss arising on the retranslation of the whole of the accounts from the company's functional currency to a presentation currency is not, as a matter of law, a profit or loss. Such an amount cannot, therefore, be a realised profit or loss. So, the position is similar to exchange differences arising on foreign currency share capital, as described above. [Tech 02/10 para 11.8].

22.144 Paragraphs 11.7 to 11.34 of Tech 02/10 set out seven principles to be applied in relation to foreign currency share capital and the use of presentation currencies. Examples of the application of the principles are set out in Appendix 5 to Tech 02/10.

Capitalisation of development costs

22.145 Where development costs are shown as an asset in the financial statements, any amount in respect of those costs should be treated as a realised loss, unless there are special circumstances justifying the directors' decision not to treat the costs as a realised loss, and the appropriate statements are made in the notes to the financial statements. [CA06 Sec 844]. Where development costs are capitalised in accordance with section 18 of FRS 102 (see chapter 18), these special circumstances generally exist. The note to the financial statements that states the special circumstances that permit the company to capitalise development costs must state also that the development costs have not been treated as a realised loss and the justification that the directors used for adopting this treatment. [CA06 Sec 844(2),(3)].

Goodwill

22.146 Goodwill arising on consolidation does not affect realised and distributable profits, because individual companies (and not groups) make distributions. Goodwill can arise in a company — for example, where a company purchases an unincorporated business. Where goodwill arises in a company's individual financial statements, it becomes a realised loss, because it is amortised or written down for impairment in accordance with relevant accounting standards.

Hedge accounting

22.147 Where hedge accounting is obtained, management should consider the combined effect of both sides of the hedging relationship, to determine whether there is a realised profit or loss. [Tech 02/10 para 3.19]. This applies both to changes in fair value of open contracts and to settled transactions.

Shares classified as financial liabilities and debt instruments classified as equity

22.148 The treatment of shares as financial liabilities, or debt instruments as equity, or either as compound instruments for accounting purposes, has a complex interaction with the legal rules on distributions and capital repayments. Section 6 of Tech 02/10 provides 10 key principles, underpinning statute and common law in respect of distributions and capital maintenance, for determining distributable profits when dealing with such contracts; and it illustrates the application of the principles to eight common scenarios involving shares and compound instruments.

22.149 Principles 1, 2 and 3 are particularly relevant for distributions presented as interest expense. Essentially, a dividend accounted for as interest expense is not a loss, as a matter of law; the accounting is an advanced recognition of a future distribution; and distributable profits are only consumed by a dividend when it is paid or when it is approved by members and becomes a legal liability. [Tech 02/10 paras 6.7–6.15]. Conversely, an interest amount presented in equity is a loss and not a distribution (for example, non-mandatory coupons on a bond). Consequently, when directors assess whether their companies have sufficient distributable profits to make a distribution, they will have to reverse the accounting for dividends that have been charged as interest expense, and *vice versa* for interest amounts treated as a distribution.

Transactions within a group

Capital contributions

22.150 'Capital contributions' or gifts are realised profits for the recipient company if they are received in cash or as an asset that is readily convertible to cash. If they are not received in qualifying consideration, the amount is unrealised, although it might become realised if the consideration is converted into qualifying consideration, or the asset is depreciated or sold. [Tech 02/10 para 3.9(f)].

Proposed dividends

22.151 Proposed dividends and intra-group dividends from UK companies are addressed in paragraphs 9.6 to 9.18 of Tech 02/10. Following legal advice, the Institutes have determined that companies that rely on dividends from UK subsidiaries to support their own distributions must require those subsidiaries to pay or approve those dividends before the balance sheet date of the recipient's relevant accounts.

22.152 Under FRS 102, dividends are recognised when a liability to pay the dividend is created. A receiving company recognises dividends at the same time as the paying company recognises the liability to pay a dividend. In the UK, this means that:

■ Interim dividends are booked when paid. As a matter of law, interim dividends do not become a legal liability until they are paid. This is because they are at the discretion of directors, who can reverse a decision to pay a dividend at any time up to the date of payment.

■ Final dividends are booked when they legally become a liability. This is when they are approved, either by the members in general meeting or, for private companies, by the members passing a written resolution. Companies can 'convert' an interim dividend into a final approved dividend (by approval by members in general meeting or, for private companies, by written resolution).

[Tech 02/10 para 2.10].

22.153 In some jurisdictions, the declaration of a dividend by the board of directors creates a liability for the company, because it would require a members' resolution to cancel the payment of that dividend. In such cases, the receiving company recognises the dividend receivable when it is declared by the directors.

22.154 Directors need to take into account the effect of the accounting standards in force when the dividend is proposed and when it is paid. In determining a dividend proposed in respect of one financial year but paid in the following financial year, directors should consider the known impact of new accounting standards on the latter year. Similarly, in paying an interim dividend in the current financial year, directors should consider the effect on opening distributable reserves of new accounting standards adopted in the current year, even if the 'relevant accounts' used to justify the distribution were prepared before implementation of the new standard. [Tech 02/10 paras 3.30–3.32].

Other matters covered by Technical Release 02/10

22.155 Tech 02/10 also considers the implications for distributable profits of the following:

- Cash box transactions. For further information, refer to chapter 23 of the Manual of Accounting.

- Business combinations, involving businesses under common control, carried out at fair value (see further chapter 19).

- Changes in circumstances, including changes in accounting policies.

Investment companies

22.156 An investment company can make a distribution at any time out of its accumulated realised *revenue* profits that have not previously been distributed or capitalised, less its accumulated revenue losses (realised and unrealised, and only insofar as they have not been previously written off in a reduction or reorganisation of capital). Capital profits and losses are ignored if the conditions in section 832(5) of the 2006 Act are met, including that the company's shares must be listed on a recognised UK investment exchange (other than an overseas investment exchange).

22.157 Section 832 of the 2006 Act is an alternative, rather than an additional, test for investment companies. An investment company might be able to make a distribution in accordance with section 831 of the 2006 Act, even if cannot comply with section 832 of that Act.

Long-term insurance business

22.158 The normal rules of section 830 of the 2006 Act (requirement for realised profits and the section 831 'net asset test') apply to insurance companies. However, for the purposes of determining whether there is a realised profit, the definition of 'realised profits' in section 853(4) of the 2006 Act, that refers to being determined by reference to generally accepted accounting principles, is displaced in favour of special rules in section 843 of the 2006 Act.

22.159 These special rules apply to an 'authorised insurance company' (as defined in section 1165 of the 2006 Act), other than an 'insurance special purpose vehicle' (as defined in section 843(8) of that Act), carrying on long-term insurance business. An amount included in the relevant part of the company's balance sheet is treated as a realised profit if it:

- represents a surplus in the fund or funds maintained by it in respect of its long-term business (as defined in section 843(7), and which includes both with-profits life business and other life business); and

- has not been allocated to policyholders or, as the case might be, carried forward unappropriated in accordance with asset identification rules made under section 142(2) of the Financial Services and Markets Act 2000.

22.160 For this purpose, the relevant part of the balance sheet is that part of the balance sheet that represents accumulated profit or loss. A surplus in the fund or funds maintained by the company in respect of its long-term business means an excess of the assets representing that fund or those funds over the liabilities of the company attributable to its long-term business, as shown by an actuarial investigation.

22.161 A deficit in the fund or funds maintained by the company in respect of its long-term business is treated as a realised loss. For this purpose, a deficit in any such fund or funds means an excess of the liabilities of the company attributable to its long-term business over the assets representing that fund or those funds, as shown by an actuarial investigation.

22.162 Subject to this, any profit or loss arising in the company's long-term business is left out of account when determining realised profits and losses.

22.163 For the purpose of these requirements, an actuarial investigation means an investigation made into the financial condition of an authorised insurance company, in respect of its long-term business, by an actuary appointed as actuary to the company:

- carried out once every period of 12 months in accordance with rules made under Part 10 of the Financial Services and Markets Act 2000; or

- carried out in accordance with a requirement imposed by section 166 of that Act.

22.164 Much of the guidance (such as in Tech 02/10) on identifying generally accepted principles used in determining realised profits and losses is in relation to section 853(4) of the 2006 Act. To that extent, it is not applicable to authorised insurance companies (other than special purpose vehicles), to which the above-mentioned special rule applies instead. That guidance, however, should not be overlooked, because, where such a company is a public company, it must also have regard to the section 831 'net asset test'.

Unlimited companies

22.165 An unlimited company can repay its share capital by passing a special resolution of members to reduce its share capital or share premium in any manner. The 2006 Act does not require a company to have the power to do so in its articles of association, as was the case under the 1985 Act. If the amount of the reduction is not repaid immediately or in an agreed schedule of staged repayments, it is credited to a reserve. Such a reserve in an unlimited company is still subject to the same rules on distribution of profit as a limited company (that is, that the profit must be realised and available for distribution).

22.166 Any reserve created by a reduction of capital prior to 1 October 2008 is treated as a realised profit available for distribution in accordance with Part 23 of the 2006 Act. [SI 2008/1886 Reg 7(2)]. Similarly, for capital reductions on or after 1 October 2008, the reserve is also realised and available for distribution in accordance with Part 23 of the 2006 Act. [SI 2008/1915]. As such, if the company has a deficit on distributable profits, the amount of any distribution from the reserve arising on the capital reduction must take this deficit into account. An unlimited company might have unrealised profits that it is not able to distribute. It can capitalise these profits as share capital, and it can then reduce its capital with immediate or staged repayment to shareholders.

Non-controlling interest and transactions in shares of a consolidated subsidiary

22.167 Further information is set out in chapter 19.

Transition requirements

22.168 On transition to FRS 102, an entity adopts the requirements of the standard retrospectively. That is, with some specified exceptions, the opening statement of financial position should be presented in accordance with the standard. [FRS 102 para 35.7]. Therefore, any changes from the previously applied accounting policies are accounted for retrospectively in accordance with the new standard. To ease the transition process, the standard allows a first-time adopter to take a number of exemptions. One of these is that it can elect not to separate the two components of a compound financial instrument, such as convertible debt, if the liability component is not outstanding at the date of transition to the new standard. [FRS 102 para 35.10(g)]. However, the principles of section 22 of FRS 102 are very similar to FRS 25, so it is unlikely that there would be classification differences when adopting FRS 102.

Chapter 23

Revenue

Revenue

Introduction and scope

23.1 Revenue is the top line in the statement of comprehensive income (or income statement where the two-statement approach is adopted) and is often used as a measure of the size (and so growth) of an entity. It is the key variable in a number of calculations and ratios that management and others might consider to be important indicators of the entity's financial performance. Not surprisingly, it is often viewed as the single most important item in the financial statements.

23.2 This chapter sets out criteria to be used in accounting for revenue arising from the following transactions and events:

■   The sale of goods (whether produced by the entity for the purpose of sale or purchased for resale).

■   The rendering of services.

■   Construction contracts in which the entity is the contractor.

■   The use by others of entity assets yielding interest, royalties or dividends.

[FRS 102 para 23.1].

23.3 This chapter does not deal with revenue or other income arising from transactions and events covered by other chapters of the book as noted below:

■   Lease agreements (see chapter 20).

■   Dividends and other income arising from investments that are accounted for using the equity method (see chapters 14 and 15).

■   Changes in the fair value of financial assets and financial liabilities or their disposal (see chapters 11 and 12).

■   Changes in the fair value of investment property (see chapter 16).

■   Initial recognition and changes in the fair value of biological assets related to agricultural activity (see chapter 34).

■   Initial recognition of agricultural produce.

■   Revenue or other income arising from transactions and events dealt with in FRS 103 'Insurance contracts'.

Definition of revenue

23.4 Income is defined as *"... increases in economic benefits during the accounting period in the form of inflows or enhancements of assets or decreases of liabilities that result in increases in equity, other than those relating to contributions from equity investors"*. [FRS 102 para 2.23(a)].

23.5 Revenue is a subset of income and is defined as *"...the gross inflow of economic benefits in the period arising in the course of the ordinary activities of an entity when those inflows result in increases in equity, other than increases relating to contributions from equity participants"*. [FRS 102 Glossary of terms].

23.6 Company law also uses the term 'turnover' and the Companies Act defines it as: *"The amounts derived from the provision of goods and services falling within the company's ordinary activities, after deduction of: (a) trade discounts; (b) value added tax; and (c) any other taxes based on the amounts so derived"*. [CA06 Sec 474]. The definition of turnover is repeated in the glossary to FRS 102. Turnover in both the standard and the Companies Act is a sub-set of revenue as it is specific to the revenue generated from the sale of goods and services and does not include, for example, revenue generated by a financial institution earning interest income.

23.7 The standard explains that income encompasses both revenue and gains. Revenue is income that arises in the course of the ordinary activities of an entity and is referred to by various names including sales, fees, interest, dividends, royalties and rent. Gains are other items that meet the definition of income, but are not revenue. They include items such as those arising on the disposal of non-current assets, for example, property, plant and equipment or long-term investments. [FRS 102 para 2.25].

23.8 The distinction between revenue and income is not always clear. The determination of whether a transaction should result in the recording of revenue will depend on the facts surrounding the business and the transaction itself. Consider the following example.

> **Example – Distinction between revenue and income**
>
> A chain of bicycle shops holds bicycles for short-term hire and for sale. The bicycles available for hire are used for two or three years and then sold by the shops as second-hand models. All shops sell both new and second-hand bicycles.
>
> The shops have three sources of revenue: (i) the sale of new bicycles, (ii) the sale of second-hand bicycles and (iii) the rental of bicycles.
>
> The sale of a second-hand bicycle is not a disposal of property, plant and equipment, even though the bicycle is held for use by the shops for a number of years in their hire business. The bicycle shops are in the business of selling both new and second-hand bicycles. So selling second-hand bicycles is part of the shops' ordinary, recurring activities and such sales represent revenue.

23.9   As is evident from the above definitions, both revenue and income exclude contributions from equity participants, which could include subscriptions for share capital and capital contributions.

General recognition principles

23.10   Revenue from the sale of goods, rendering of services, construction contracts and the use by others of entity assets yielding interest, royalties and dividends is recognised in the financial statements if it satisfies the following two general recognition criteria for incorporating an item in the financial statements as set out in section 2 of FRS 102:

■   It is probable that any future economic benefit associated with the transaction will flow to the entity.

■   The amount of revenue can be measured with reliability.

[FRS 102 paras 23.10(c)(d), 23.14(a)(b), 23.28(a)(b)].

23.11   In addition to the criteria above, there are further conditions that apply to the sale of goods (see para 23.57 below) and the rendering of services (see para 23.104 below).

Probability of future economic benefits

23.12   The probability that the economic benefits associated with the transaction will flow to the entity relates to the degree of uncertainty associated with the receipt of consideration. This is assessed on the basis of the evidence available when the financial statements are prepared, based on the conditions at the balance sheet date. Revenue is not recognised until the inflow of economic benefits is assessed as probable. Probable is defined in FRS 102 as meaning "*more likely than not*". [FRS 102 Glossary of terms]. In some situations, it might not be probable that the economic benefits will flow to the entity until the consideration is received by the entity or until an uncertainty is removed. An example might be where the receipt of consideration depends on whether or not the buyer could obtain funding (in which case recognition of the sale would be delayed until that uncertainty was removed).

23.13   Where uncertainty arises about the collectability of an amount that has already been included in revenue, any provision required as a result of that uncertainty is recognised as an expense and not as a reduction of revenue. Impairment of financial assets is addressed in chapter 11. The following example demonstrates the distinction between uncertainty at the time of sale and uncertainty arising after the sale.

Example – Timing of an uncertainty arising

Entity A has an existing manufacturing customer, entity B, which has recently announced that it expects to have to restructure its debts with current creditors, including entity A, in order to ensure sufficient operating liquidity to avoid bankruptcy. After the announcement, entity A ships an order of replacement parts to entity B based on a purchase order received from entity B before the announcement.

Entity A should not recognise revenue for the latest shipment to entity B, because it is not probable that the economic benefit related to the products shipped will flow to the entity. Entity A records revenue when entity B pays for the shipment of replacement parts, which is when it becomes probable that the economic benefit will flow to entity A and when the amount of revenue can be measured reliably.

In contrast, any allowance recorded against any existing receivable balance as a result of entity B's announcement of its need to restructure debts should be recorded as an expense, and not as a reversal of revenue.

Reliable measurement of revenue

23.14   It must be possible to reliably measure the amount of revenue in order to recognise it. In many revenue transactions, the value of consideration received or receivable is known. In other cases, the consideration receivable must be estimated. Reliable estimation could be problematic where the consideration receivable depends on the results of future events. In practice, concerns about reliability of measurement are more likely to arise from the rendering of services and construction activities than from the sale of goods. Where a reliable estimate cannot be made, no revenue should be recognised.

Measurement of revenue

23.15   Revenue is measured at the fair value of the consideration received or receivable. [FRS 102 para 23.3]. Fair value is defined as *"the amount for which an asset could be exchanged, a liability settled, or an equity instrument granted could be exchanged, between knowledgeable, willing parties in an arm's length transaction"*. [FRS 102 Glossary of terms]. Further detailed discussion of this definition can be found in chapter 11.

23.16   The fair value is generally the amount receivable where goods are sold or services provided in return for consideration in the form of cash or cash equivalents receivable at the time of the transaction. However, the following factors, and perhaps others, would require consideration in determining the amount of revenue to be recognised.

Trade discounts and similar items

23.17   The fair value of the consideration received or receivable should take into account the amount of any trade discounts, prompt settlement discounts and volume rebates allowed by the entity. [FRS 102 para 23.3].

23.18 In order to calculate the fair value of the revenue to be recognised, management needs to estimate the volume of sales or the expected settlement discounts to be given. The revenue recognised is reduced by this estimate. A common interpretation is that, if no reliable estimate can be made, the revenue recognised on the transaction should not exceed the amount of consideration that would be received if the maximum discounts were taken

Example 1 – Estimating cash volume discounts

A paint manufacturer with a 31 December year end offers several large customers stepped rebates on sales, based on the following volumes:

Up to 100,000 litres – no discount
Between 100,000 litres and 250,000 litres – 5% discount on all sales
Over 250,000 litres – 10% discount on all sales
Rebates are paid to customers after the end of their contract year.

At 31 December 20X0, a particular customer has purchased 140,000 litres of paint. That customer has a past history of purchasing over 250,000 litres of paint each contract year (which runs from 1 July to 30 June), spread evenly during the year.

The manufacturer has a contractual liability to pay the customer a rebate of 5% on all sales to date, because the volume threshold of 100,000 litres has been exceeded. But, based on all the available evidence, it is probable that the customer will also exceed the 250,000 litre threshold and that the manufacturer will pay a rebate of 10% on all sales. So, at 31 December 20X0 management reduces revenue by recognising a provision for the rebate based on 10% of the sales to date.

Example 2 – Estimating settlement discounts

A food manufacturer sells canned food and has 100 customers. The delivery of the goods is made on the last day of each month. Standard payment terms require settlement within 45 days of delivery. The entity's policy is to grant a settlement discount of 2% to customers who pay within 15 days of delivery. Experience shows that 45% of customers normally pay within 15 days. How much should the food manufacturer recognise as revenue on a month end delivery with an invoice value of £1,000?

The food manufacturer should deduct, from the total invoiced value of £1,000, the expected amount of discounts to be given of £9 (£1,000 × 45% × 2%) and recognise revenue of £991.

Gross or net

23.19 Following on from the definition of revenue (stated in para 23.5 above), the standard explains that an entity should include in revenue only the gross inflows of economic benefits received and receivable by the entity on its own account. Amounts collected on behalf of third parties (such as sales taxes, goods and services taxes and value added taxes) are not economic benefits that flow to the entity, so they are excluded from revenue. [FRS 102 para 23.4].

23.20 When determining whether revenue should be recognised gross or net of taxes, it is necessary to consider both the nature of the tax and whether the entity is acting as agent or a principal for the tax authority. For instance, in some jurisdictions excise duty payable by manufacturers of tobacco and alcoholic products might be treated as sales taxes and hence deducted from revenue; but in another jurisdiction, excise duty might be treated as a production tax and hence included in cost of sales. In the UK, value added tax is treated as a sales tax, which is collected on behalf of the government and so the entity simply acts as agent.

Principal or agent?

23.21 In an agency relationship, the entity collects consideration from its customers on behalf of the principal. The agent's revenue should include only the amount of its commission. Amounts collected on behalf of, and passed on to, the principal are not revenue of the entity. [FRS 102 para 23.4].

23.22 The glossary to FRS 102 includes definitions of '*principal*' and '*agent*'. The determination of whether an entity is acting as agent or principal will depend on the facts and circumstances of the relationship. If an entity is a principal, it has exposure to the significant risks and rewards associated with selling the goods or services. Indicators that an entity is a principal include:

- The entity has the primary responsibility for providing the goods or services to the customer or for fulfilling the order (for example, by being responsible for the acceptability of the products or services ordered or purchased by the customer).

- The entity has inventory risk before or after the customer order, during shipping or on return

- The entity has latitude in establishing prices, either directly or indirectly (for example by providing additional goods or services).

- The entity bears the customer's credit risk for the amount receivable from the customer.

[FRS 102 Glossary of terms].

23.23 Conversely, an entity is acting as an agent when it does not have exposure to the significant risks and rewards associated with the sale of goods or the rendering of services. One feature indicating that an entity is acting as an agent is that the amount the entity earns is predetermined, being either a fixed fee per transaction or a stated percentage of the amount billed to the customer. [FRS 102 Glossary of terms].

23.24 One of the indicators that management should consider in determining whether an entity is acting as principal or agent, is which entity retains the credit risk associated with the product. This factor is often presumed to carry a significant amount of weight because it relates to payment. But credit risk is determined to be a less significant factor in many cases, because risk could fall with either party. Where an entity is acting as agent, but retains the credit risk associated with the transaction, consideration, needs to be given as to whether this represents a financial guarantee. Accounting for financial guarantees is covered in chapter 21

Example – Goods sold under a distribution agreement

Entity A distributes entity B's products under a distribution agreement. The terms and conditions of the contract are such that entity A:

- Stores, transports and invoices the goods sold to the customer.

- Earns a fixed margin on the products sold, but has no flexibility in establishing the sales price.

- Has the right to return the goods to entity B without penalty.

- Is responsible for the goods while the goods are stored in entity A's warehouse, but entity B bears the risk of obsolete goods.

The credit risk rests with entity B.

Entity B is the principal in the distribution agreement. Entity B does not transfer the risks and rewards of ownership of the goods to entity A. Entity A has the option to return the goods and entity B bears the inventory risk. Entity B retains continuing managerial involvement over the goods by being able to set the sales price.

Entity A is acting as agent for entity B. It does not bear the significant risks and rewards of ownership of the goods. It earns a fixed margin on the goods sold and recognises this as revenue.

Deferred payment

23.25 If consideration to be received from the sale of goods or services is deferred beyond normal credit terms, and the arrangement is considered to include a financing transaction, this should be reflected in the accounting for the transaction. A financing transaction arises where, for example, an entity provides interest-free credit to the buyer or accepts a note receivable bearing a below-market interest rate from the buyer as consideration for the sale of goods. To calculate the fair value of the consideration receivable, all future receipts are discounted using an imputed rate of interest that is the more clearly determinable of either:

- the prevailing rate for a similar instrument of an issuer with a similar credit rating; or

- a rate of interest that discounts the nominal amount of the instrument to the current cash sales price of the goods or services.

[FRS 102 para 23.5].

23.26 The difference between the present value of all future receipts and the nominal value of the consideration is recognised as interest income over the credit period in accordance with the treatment specified for interest income from paragraphs 23.166 onwards below and in chapter 11. In other words, the consideration is split between the fair value of the consideration for the goods or services and the consideration for the financing element, and it is recognised accordingly. This is illustrated by example 11 in the appendix to section 23 [FRS 102 para 23A.13]. If the entity is in the business of both selling goods or services and providing finance to its customers, the interest income is presented as revenue in the income statement; this is because providing finance is part of the entity's ordinary activities. If not (for example if this is a one-off arrangement for a particular client) the interest income is disclosed separately from revenue as finance income.

> **Example – Sale with interest-free credit**
>
> Entity A is a retailer and offers interest-free credit to a customer as part of its marketing strategy. It sells the goods to the customer for £1,000, to be repaid by the customer over two years. The customer can borrow at 5% a year.
>
> Management should determine the fair value of revenue by calculating the present value of the cash flows receivable.
>
> On the transaction date, revenue of £907 is recognised, being £1,000 discounted for two years. The discounted receivable should be updated at each balance sheet date to reflect the passage of time. The resulting increase in the receivable represents interest income that should be recognised over the period from the date of sale to the expected receipt of cash.

Exchange of goods or services

23.27 Entities usually trade for cash or the right to receive cash. Sometimes, however, transactions are undertaken that involve the exchanging or swapping of goods or services. These are commonly known as barter transactions.

23.28 Where goods or services are exchanged for goods or services that are of a similar nature and value, the exchange is not considered to be a transaction that generates revenue. [FRS 102 para 23.6(a)]. There is no guidance on how to determine whether goods or services are similar in nature. In general, similar nature can be taken to mean that the items are used in the same line of business. Transactions of this nature are not often seen in practice, except perhaps in commodity trading such as oil or wheat where suppliers exchange or swap inventories in various locations to fulfil demand on a timely basis in a particular location. Other examples could include exchange of network capacity on the same route in the telecommunication industry and exchange of similar advertising services. For example, an exchange of banner advertising between two travel agent web-sites is an exchange of similar services which does not generate revenue.

23.29   Where goods or services are exchanged for dissimilar goods or services, the exchange is regarded as a transaction that gives rise to revenue, unless the transaction lacks commercial substance (in which case, no revenue is recognised). [FRS 102 para 23.6(b)]. The meaning of 'commercial substance' is discussed further in chapter 17 which also deals with exchange of non-monetary assets.

23.30   Where the transaction has commercial substance, the revenue is measured using the following measurement hierarchy:

- The fair value of the goods or services received, adjusted by the amount of any cash or cash equivalents transferred.

- If the amount under the first bullet point cannot be measured reliably, the fair value of the goods or services given up, adjusted by the amount of any cash or cash equivalents transferred.

- If the fair value of neither the goods or services received nor the goods or services given up can be measured reliably, the carrying amount of the goods or services given up, adjusted by the amount of any cash or cash equivalents transferred.

[FRS 102 para 23.7].

Contracts with both contingent and non-contingent consideration

23.31   Entities in a broad range of industries can enter into a single contract with both contingent and non-contingent revenue streams. For example, an entity could receive part of a contract's total consideration on delivery of a good, with the remainder being received over a future period, based on the outcome of a future event. If, on receipt of the initial consideration, the entity has further goods to supply or services to deliver in relation to the remaining consideration, this could indicate that there is a multiple element arrangement for which the consideration should be allocated to each of the elements (see para 23.44 onwards).

23.32   In some cases, on receipt of the initial consideration, the seller has supplied all the goods or delivered all the services, but some part of the consideration remains contingent on the outcome of future events.

23.33   FRS 102 is not explicit as to whether all elements of consideration must meet the revenue recognition criteria simultaneously in order for any portion of the revenue to be recorded, or if each element of consideration can be assessed separately and meet the revenue recognition criteria at different times. As a result, we believe that a policy choice can be made: either the contingent and non-contingent elements of consideration are considered separately, when determining when revenue is recognised; or the contract is assessed as a whole. Whichever policy choice is taken, the policy should be applied consistently and, where material, be disclosed as a key accounting policy. The two approaches are considered in turn below.

Approach 1: Separate assessment of each element of consideration

23.34 For contracts with both contingent and non-contingent elements of consideration, a separate assessment of each element of consideration is supportable based on FRS 102.

23.35 For example, an entity might determine that it has met the revenue recognition criteria for the non-contingent portion of the consideration when the goods and services are delivered, but has failed one of the revenue recognition criteria (such as the probable inflow of economic benefit or reliable estimation of revenue to be recognised) for the contingent portion. In such a situation, the entity records revenue for the non-contingent consideration when the goods or services are delivered. Revenue is recorded for the contingent portion of consideration when the revenue recognition criteria are met for that portion. In determining when the revenue recognition criteria are met for the contingent portion, an entity should consider, amongst other factors, historical trends and any specific features of the contract.

23.36 The revenue recognition criteria might be met for the contingent portion before the cash is received. If all of the revenue recognition criteria are met for the contingent consideration before the cash is received, an asset is recorded. Any such receivable should be measured initially at the fair value of the amount to be received, taking into account the time value of money and any related uncertainties.

> **Example – Sales transactions with contingent and non-contingent consideration**
>
> Entity A sells land to a developer for £100,000. Control and the risks and rewards of ownership of the land, transfer on completion of the sale. Entity A has no continuing involvement or obligation under the contract after the sale is complete. Entity A is also entitled to receive 5% of any future onward sales price in excess of £200,000.
>
> Entity A records revenue for the amount of initial cash received (£100,000) when control and the risks and rewards associated with the land are transferred to the developer (in this case on completion of the sale).
>
> Entity A records revenue for the contingent consideration when all the revenue recognition criteria for that element are met. When assessing whether all the criteria are met, entity A needs to consider the reliable measurement of the contingent revenue and the probability of inflow of economic benefits.
>
> Where entity A cannot predict or reliably measure any future sales price on completion of the sale to the developer, the recognition of revenue for the contingent portion of consideration will occur later than the recognition of revenue for the non-contingent portion

23.37 It is likely that the key judgements in determining when to recognise contingent revenue are the probability of inflow of economic benefit and the reliable measurement of contingent consideration. These two criteria might be difficult to assess, given the contingent nature of the revenue. Depending on the facts and circumstances, these criteria might be met either at the contract's inception or later. Nevertheless, in cases where contingent revenue arrangements are routinely part of the seller's business model and there is appropriate available evidence as to expected future contingent revenue amounts, it is likely that the revenue recognition criteria will be met before the contingent consideration is received.

Example – Timing of recognition for contingent revenue

Entity A develops cartoon characters. Entity B develops and sells cartoons and runs theme parks based on the cartoon characters. Entity B contracts with entity A to purchase the intellectual property rights over certain characters. The intellectual property agreement contains the following key terms:

1. The agreement grants entity B full ownership of the cartoon characters and related intellectual property. No further work will be required on the part of entity A, as entity B's in-house animation department will complete the development of all stories and required drawings.

2. On signing the agreement and providing all sketches and story ideas, entity A will be paid £1m up-front. This amount is non-refundable.

3. Entity A will also be paid an amount equal to 1% of all revenues generated from the use of the characters over the following five years.

Based on prior experience in numerous similar situations, entity B shares its projections with entity A. Entity B has estimated that the contingent revenues will be as follows:

Year	Revenues (£)	A's Share (£)
2010	10,000,000	100,000
2011	25,000,000	250,000
2012	50,000,000	500,000
2013	50,000,000	500,000
2014	25,000,000	250,000
Total	160,000,000	1,600,000

Entity B has entered into hundreds of similar agreements and the creative artist achieved these payment levels in the majority of cases.

On signing the agreement, how much revenue should entity A recognise? Would the accounting change if this were the first time that entity B had entered into such an agreement with a creative artist?

Where entity B has entered into hundreds of similar agreements with other artists, entity A might be satisfied that all of the revenue recognition criteria have been met in relation to the contingent revenue. Specifically with respect to probability of inflow of economic benefit and reliable measurement of revenue, entity A might consider that it has sufficient evidence to meet these criteria, given entity B's past experience with similar transactions. In that case, both the up-front payment of £1m and the fair value of the total expected future payments of £1.6m are recorded as revenue when the cartoons and related intellectual property are delivered. A corresponding receivable for the fair value of £1.6m is recorded, and adjusted each reporting period to the extent that relevant evidence indicates a change in the expected cash flows and to unwind any discount applied. (Note that the contingent revenue is discounted only to the extent that the impact is material.)

Where entity B has no experience of similar transactions, entity A might not be satisfied that all the revenue recognition criteria have been met in relation to the contingent revenue. Specifically, future payments might not be deemed probable or reliably measurable. For the up-front payment of £1m, revenue is recognised on delivery of the cartoons, because all the recognition criteria have been met for that non-contingent component of consideration. The expected future payments, being the contingent portion, are only recorded as revenue once all the recognition criteria have been met (that is, once it is deemed probable that economic benefits will flow and revenue can be reliably measured).

23.38   In some cases (but not in the example above), the contingent portion of consideration might make up a substantial proportion of the total expected consideration under the contract. Where the contingent portion of revenue is significant, and its recognition is delayed due to certain recognition criteria not being met, the entity should consider whether the significant risks and rewards of ownership have been transferred on delivery of the underlying good or service and payment of the non-contingent consideration. If this is not the case, it might not be appropriate to recognise revenue for the non-contingent portion of consideration until those criteria are met.

Approach 2: Contract considered as a whole

23.39   Where the contract is considered as a whole, revenue is recognised in the income statement when the revenue recognition criteria are met for the overall transaction. Following this approach, assuming that all other revenue recognition criteria are met and that the existence of non-contingent consideration means that the inflow of economic benefit from the contract is probable, the key judgement to be made (in determining when to recognise revenue) will be determining the date on which the total consideration for the contract can be reliably measured.

23.40   The total consideration on the contract includes the contingent portion of consideration. When assessing the date on which the total contract consideration can be reliably measured, an entity considers historic trends, factors specific to the contract and the uncertainties relating to the contingent consideration. The assessment of these factors is illustrated in the example in para 23.35 above. If all other criteria have been met on the contract's inception, revenue will be recognised when the total contract consideration can be reliably measured. This could occur at the contract's inception or later.

23.41   As noted above, in cases where contingent revenue arrangements are routinely part of the seller's business model and there is appropriate available evidence as to expected future contingent revenue amounts, it is likely that the contingent consideration will be reliably measurable before it is received. In such cases, the overall consideration on the contract will also be reliably measurable before the contingent element is received, and the revenue on the contract will be recognised in the income statement accordingly.

23.42 Where revenue is recognised in the income statement and consideration (contingent or non-contingent) has not been received, an asset is recognised. Any such receivable is measured initially at fair value, taking into account the time value of money and any related uncertainties.

23.43 Under both approaches, any asset recognised for contingent consideration is adjusted each reporting period where relevant evidence indicates a change in expected cash flows. Depending on the nature of the adjustment, it might be appropriate to recognise the adjustment as revenue, as an impairment of a financial asset, or (if the adjustment relates to the time value of money) as finance income or expense. The appropriate treatment depends on the factors driving the change in estimate and this should be assessed on a case-by-case basis.

Identification of the revenue transaction

Multiple elements

23.44 A single transaction or a contractual arrangement might require a seller to provide a number of different goods or services (components) to its customers. Where this is the case, an entity should apply the revenue recognition criteria to the separately identifiable components in order to reflect the substance of the transaction [FRS 102 para 23.8]. This means that the transaction has to be analysed in accordance with the economic substance to determine whether the various components should be considered together (a single unit of account) or individually for revenue recognition purposes (multiple units of account).

23.45 The transaction's substance should be assessed from the perspective of the customer and not of the seller. In other words what does the customer believe they are purchasing? If the customer views the purchase as one product, it is likely that the recognition criteria should be applied to the transaction as a whole. But, if the customer perceives there to be a number of elements to the transaction, then the revenue recognition criteria should be applied to each element separately. Consider the following example:

> **Example – Separation of components within a contract**
>
> A car dealership sells new cars to customers. As a limited period offer at no extra charge, the dealer undertakes to maintain the car for three years from the date of purchase. Normally the dealership charges extra for the maintenance services and it is possible for a customer to purchase both the car and the maintenance services separately.
>
> ■   sells a good (that is, the new car); and

- undertakes to provide maintenance services for three years.

Management allocates the fair value of the consideration received (that is, the amount received from the customer) to the separately identified components of the transaction. The two elements are generally sold separately, so it is possible to allocate the consideration based on the relative fair values of the individual elements when they are sold separately.

Furthermore, management must apply the recognition criteria to the separately identified components of the transaction (for the sale of the car, see para 23.57 onwards below; and, for the maintenance services, see para 23.104 onwards below).

23.46 When considering the separation of identifiable components in a single transaction or contract, if the seller sells the different components separately (or has done so in the past), this is a strong indicator that separation is necessary for the purposes of revenue recognition; but it is not a requirement. For example, even if the entity in question does not sell them separately, it could be that the transaction's components are sold separately by other sellers in the market. In such a situation, separation of the components might still be appropriate.

Allocation of consideration

23.47 The principles in FRS 102 require that the revenue in respect of each separable component of a transaction is measured at its fair value. The price that is regularly charged for an item when sold separately is often the best evidence of its fair value.

23.48 However, the total revenue arising from a transaction might sometimes be different from the aggregate fair value of the transaction's separate components. If it appears that the contract value exceeds the sum of the fair value of the separable elements, it is likely that the values being used are inappropriate, or additional goods or services provided have not been identified. Entities that find themselves in this situation should re-evaluate the components previously identified and the associated fair values.

23.49 In other situations, the contract value might be less than the fair value of the transaction's separable elements. Where this occurs, the difference should be allocated between the separable components based on the most appropriate method of allocating the separable components. Examples of revenue allocation methods include relative fair values, cost plus a reasonable margin, and the residual method (see examples below). Any loss on the overall contract should be recognised at the outset, in accordance with the guidance on onerous contracts in section 21. However, in general, if the contract is profitable as a whole, the entity should ensure that the revenue allocation policy adopted results in the most appropriate allocation of revenue to the elements of the contract.

Example 1 – Contract value is lower than the fair value of the separable elements

An entity sells boats for £30,000 each. The entity also provides mooring facilities for £2,000 per annum. The entity sells these goods and services separately. A purchaser of a boat who contracts to buy mooring facilities for a year receives a 5% discount on the whole package. Thus the 'package' costs £32,000 less 5% (that is £30,400). How should revenue be recognised?

The discount in this case is £1,600 (the difference between £32,000 and £30,400). Using the relative fair value approach, the element of the discount attributable to the boat is £1,500 (£1,600 × £30,000/£32,000) and the element of the discount attributable to the mooring facilities is £100 (£1,600 × £2,000/£32,000). So the revenue recognised on the sale of the boat should be £28,500 (£30,000 — £1,500), which will be recognised on delivery of the boat. The revenue recognised for the mooring facilities is £1,900 (£2,000 — £100), which will be recognised evenly over the year for which the mooring facility is provided.

Example 2 – Contract value is lower than the fair value of the separable elements

Entity A sells a copying machine in December 20X7 and will provide maintenance services for one year. The total consideration received for both the sale and the maintenance activity is £1,200. Costs expected to be incurred to fulfil the contract are £700 for the machine (being the cost of inventory) and £200 for the maintenance activity. The relative fair values are £1,050 and £150, respectively.

If the entity applied a relative fair value approach, this would result in a loss on the maintenance component of the contract. So the entity needs to consider whether this reflects the economics of the transaction. Where the economic substance of the transaction is that maintenance services are loss making, the entity should record an accrual to the extent that the remaining expected costs exceed the remaining expected revenue. After accruing for the loss, the remaining undelivered items will be at break-even once recognised.

But if this does not match the economics of the transaction, in these limited circumstances, an entity that uses relative fair values might apply cost plus a reasonable margin as an exception to the normal accounting policy. This is illustrated below.

Relative fair value policy

The cost of the maintenance activity of £200 exceeds the relative fair value of £150, resulting in a loss of £50. Costs of £750 are calculated as the total cost of the sale of the machine plus the loss of £50 relating to the maintenance contract. Following this allocation, the entries on the transaction would be as follows:

	Dr £	Cr £
December 20X7		
Cash	1,200	
Deferred revenue		150
Revenue		1,050
Cost of sales	700	
Cost for loss on maintenance element accrual	50	
Inventory		700
Accrual for loss on maintenance element		50

Revenue

Cost plus a reasonable margin policy

The overall profit is £300 (being the difference between the revenue of £1,200 and costs of £900). This profit might be allocated based on a reasonable margin (for example, £250 on the machine and £50 on the maintenance service). Following this allocation, the entries on the transaction date would be as follows:

	Dr £	Cr £
December 20X7		
Cash	1,200	
Deferred revenue (£200 + £50 margin on service)		250
Revenue (£700 + £250 margin on copier machine)		950
Cost of sales	700	
Inventory		700

Linked transaction

23.50 Sometimes, transactions are linked in such a way that the commercial effect cannot be understood without reference to the series of transactions as a whole. For example, if an entity sells goods and, at the same time, enters into a separate agreement to repurchase the goods at a later date, this could negate the original sale [FRS 102 para 23.8]. See paragraph 23.94 below.

23.51 Another example is so-called 'two-way trading transactions'. Entity A sells a product to entity B and entity B sells a different product to entity A. Provided the two transactions are not connected, no problem arises. But problems might arise where the transactions are connected. Consider the following examples:

Example 1 – Two-way trading transactions that are not linked

Entity A sells materials for making door profiles to a manufacturer who assembles the frames and puts glass in the door. Entity A then repurchases the doors and sells them to a house builder for installation in homes. It is argued that the sale of the profile material and the purchase of the doors are not linked because:

- The manufacturer buys profile material regardless of whether the doors which are assembled can be sold to entity A, as the manufacturer has other markets to which it can and does sell assembled doors.

- Entity A is not committed to buy doors from this manufacturer, as it could and does use other suppliers.

- The price of the door is not fixed when the profile material is sold, and so the manufacturer bears the risks of price fluctuations and obsolescence.

The question arises as to whether the sale of the materials for the door profiles to the manufacturer should be accounted for separately from the purchase of doors from the same manufacturer, or whether the transactions should be regarded as linked and conditional on each other for accounting purposes.

But if the facts had been different, the accounting might have been different too. For example, if entity A sold the materials (which cost it £5) for £10 per profile, and at that time agreed to buy back the materials made up into a finished door with glass fitted for £100, the two transactions would be linked. This is because the sale carries a corresponding commitment to repurchase the materials in the future at a fixed price. For that reason, entity A should not record a sale of the £10 materials (or a profit on that sale). Instead, the cost of the materials should be retained in inventory, and the £10 received from the manufacturer should be recorded as a liability. When the door is purchased, the additional net £90 paid by entity A will be recorded as inventory, giving an inventory value for the completed door of £95

Example 2 – Two-way trading transactions that are linked

A retailer enters into an arrangement with a supplier to purchase goods. The supplier proposes that, if the retailer purchases a minimum of £100,000 of goods and undertakes to display advertising for the goods on advertising boards in the retailer's stores for a period of six months, the supplier will pay the retailer C10,000. The retailer only provides the advertising on goods it purchases from suppliers.

The two transactions are clearly linked. The supplier has, in substance, offered the retailer a discount of £10,000. The provision of advertising is one of the conditions that the retailer must satisfy in order to obtain that discount, along with the purchase volume hurdle. As such, the supplier should make a best estimate of the future rebate to be given and recognise revenue net of the discount.

Equally, the retailer should not recognise revenue for the 'sale' of advertising to the supplier. The cash paid to the retailer by the supplier is a discount on purchase (cost of stock), which will be recognised within cost of sales once the stock is sold. The reduction in the cost of stock in respect of the agreement is earned over the period and is subject to significant performance conditions being satisfied (for example, the company must display advertising for the supplier's products). It could be argued that, until all of these conditions have been satisfied, none of the payment has been earned, and so it should be deferred in total until the conditions have been satisfied. But the satisfaction of the conditions is within the company's control and so it is reasonable that it should spread the credit over the period so provided it intends to abide by the conditions for the full period. It would not be acceptable, however, to recognise the full reduction in the cost of stock on day one; this is because the transaction extends over the period and, on day one, no part of the transaction has been completed.

Customer loyalty programmes

23.52 Sometimes, as part of a sales transaction, an entity grants vouchers, coupons or loyalty points to its customer that the customer can redeem in the future in exchange for free or discounted goods or services. Examples are airlines that offer air miles and supermarkets that offer money-off vouchers and loyalty cards that accumulate points that can be used to reduce the cost of future purchases. These are multiple element arrangements, as the customer is purchasing both goods or services and the award credits.

23.53 In accordance with the principle discussed above, the entity should account for the award credits as a separately identifiable component of the initial sales transaction. The entity allocates the fair value of the consideration received or receivable in respect of the initial sale between the award credits and the goods or services supplied to the customer. The consideration allocated to the award credits is measured by reference to their fair value (that is, the amount for which the award credits could be sold separately). [FRS 102 para 23.9]. The Appendix to section 23 of the standard includes an example (reproduced below) of how fair value should be calculated. It is clear from this example that the expected redemption rate of the credits can be taken into account. The entity should recognise the consideration allocated to the award credits as revenue when award credits are redeemed.

Example – Sale with customer loyalty award

An entity sells product A for £100. Purchasers of product A get an award credit enabling them to buy product B for £10. The normal selling price of product B is £18. The entity estimates that 40% of the purchasers of product A will use their award to buy product B at £10. The normal selling price of product A, after taking into account discounts that are usually offered but that are not available during this promotion, is £95. [FRS 102 para 23A.16].

The fair value of the award credit is $40\% \times [£18 - £10] = £3.20$. The entity allocates the total revenue of £100 between product A and the award credit by reference to their relative fair values of £95 and £3.20 respectively. Therefore:

(a) Revenue for product A is $£100 \times [£95 / (£95 + £3.20)] = £96.74$

(b) Revenue for product B is $£100 \times [£3.20 / (£95 + £3.20)] = £3.26$

23.54   If a redemption rate is taken into account when calculating the fair value of awards, the entity should have sufficient historical experience as a basis for making this estimate. If the scheme is new, it might be more appropriate not to adjust for redemption and only to release the liability when the awards are redeemed or when they expire.

23.55   Some more complex loyalty schemes allow customers to earn awards at one establishment and redeem them at a number of other establishments. In such schemes the entity is often acting as agent by issuing points, rather than as principal. In many cases such schemes are administered by a third party. FRS 102 does not address the accounting for these more complex schemes. But they are addressed by IFRIC 13, and we believe that the application of IFRIC 13 would be consistent with the overall principles of FRS 102. Guidance on the accounting more complex loyalty schemes can be found in the PwC International Manual of Accounting, chapter 9.

23.56   Vouchers are sometimes issued for cash or without consideration directly to customers (that is, the issue of vouchers is not part of a sales transaction). The accounting for these is considered at paragraph 23.91 onwards below.

Sale of goods

23.57 Revenue from the sale of goods is recognised when, in addition to the general recognition principles set out in paragraph 23.10 above, all of the following conditions are satisfied:

- The seller has transferred to the buyer the significant risks and rewards of ownership of the goods (see para 23.58 below).

- The seller retains neither continuing managerial involvement to the degree usually associated with ownership nor effective control over the goods sold (see para 23.72 below).

- The costs incurred or to be incurred in respect of the transaction can be measured reliably (see para 23.75).

[FRS 102 para 23.10].

Risks and rewards of ownership

23.58 In most cases, the transfer of the risks and rewards of ownership coincides with the transfer of legal title or the delivery of goods to the buyer, as in the case of most retail sales. As such, the laws relating to sales of goods in different countries where the entity is transacting may determine the point in time at which the entity transfer the significant risks and rewards of ownership. [FRS 102 para 23A.2]. Sometimes, transfer of risks and rewards of ownership occurs at a different time to the transfer of legal title or the passing of possession. [FRS 102 para 23.11]. The timing of the transfer will depend on the contract's specific terms and conditions.

23.59 If the entity retains the significant risks and rewards of ownership, the transfer is not a sale, and so no revenue should be recognised. Examples of situations where the transfer of significant risks and rewards has not taken place include:

- Where the entity retains an obligation for unsatisfactory performance not covered by normal warranty (for instance, where an entity supplies a new type of machine and guarantees that it will achieve a certain level of output or else a refund will be given and it is uncertain whether the required level of output will be achieved).

- Where the receipt of revenue from a particular sale is contingent on the buyer selling the goods (for instance, a sale to a distributor where payment is due only if the distributor sells the goods on to a third party).

- Where the goods are shipped subject to installation and the installation is a significant part of the contract that has yet to be completed (for instance, on the supply of a turnkey project where the seller is responsible for installing and making sure that the equipment is working to the customer's satisfaction).

■ Where the buyer has the right to rescind the purchase for a reason specified in the sales contract, or at the buyer's discretion without any reason, and the entity is uncertain about the probability of return (for instance, where goods are supplied on a sale or return basis).

[FRS 102 para 23.12].

23.60 If an entity retains only an insignificant risk of ownership, the transaction is a sale and the entity recognises the revenue. For example, a seller recognises revenue when it retains the legal title to the goods solely to protect the collectability of the amount due. Similarly an entity recognises revenue when it offers a refund if the customer finds the goods faulty or is not satisfied for other reasons, and the entity can estimate the returns reliably. In such cases, the entity recognises a provision for returns in accordance with section 21 of FRS 102. [FRS 102 para 23.13].

23.61 Some common situations illustrating whether the risk and rewards of ownership have or have not transferred are considered below.

Shipment terms

23.62 One of the considerations, in determining the point at which the significant risks and rewards of ownership have transferred to the buyer, is the shipment terms. Where goods are shipped FOB (free on board) or CIF (carriage, insurance and freight), this could impact the timing of revenue recognition. If the seller is responsible for carriage, insurance and freight until the goods are delivered, these form part of the entity's performance and so the risks and rewards of the item sold are retained until delivery to the client site has occurred. As a result, the timing of revenue recognition will be different depending upon the terms of delivery. Where goods are sold on a FOB basis, such that the seller has no further obligation and the buyer is responsible for all loss in transit, the significant risks and rewards of ownership pass to the buyer when the goods are loaded onto the ship, at which time title also passes. But it should not be assumed that use of the term 'FOB' leads to the treatments detailed above. Whether the insurance and freight risk is taken on by the customer will depend on the arrangement's exact terms, and these should be examined to ensure that the timing of revenue recognition appropriately reflects the time of transfer of risks and rewards for the transaction.

Example – Sale of goods on a CIF basis

Entity A sells steel from its factory on a CIF basis to entity B. The contractual terms state that insurance is taken out by entity A for the period when the steel is in transit. But the terms go on to say that:

"The seller must pay the costs and freight necessary to bring the goods to the named port of destination, but the risk of loss or of damage to the goods, as well as any additional costs due to events occurring after the goods cross the ship's rail, are transferred from the seller to the buyer when the goods pass the ship's rail."

In order to comply with these terms entity A takes out a bearer insurance document, which means that entity A would claim for any loss or damage to the steel until the steel passes the ship's rail (that is, the steel is officially documented as being loaded as part of the ship's cargo). From this point on, the insurance policy is transferred to entity B (now being the bearer of the insurance document). Entity B will need to make a claim directly to the insurers (that is, not via entity A) for any steel damaged in transit once the steel crosses the ship's rail.

The risk of loss is transferred when the steel cross the ship's rail, so revenue should be recognised by entity A at that point and should not be deferred until delivery. This conclusion is based on the assumption that all other conditions for revenue recognition have been satisfied.

If the terms of the contract state that the risk of loss remains with entity A until the goods are delivered, revenue recognition would be delayed until the steel is delivered to entity B.

Retention of legal title

23.63 Sometimes, a contract for the sale of goods includes a 'reservation of title' clause. This enables the seller to retain title to the goods until the purchaser has paid for them. In the UK, such clauses are often known as 'Romalpa clauses' following the Romalpa case [Aluminium Industrie Vaassen B.V. v Romalpa Aluminium Limited [1976] 1 WLR 676] in 1976. The main effect of trading with reservation of title is that the position of the unpaid seller might be improved if the purchaser becomes insolvent.

23.64 Retention of title could indicate that the risks and rewards of ownership have not passed to the buyer, although passing of title is not a required condition for recognition of revenue. So, provided the other revenue recognition conditions are satisfied, it is appropriate to recognise revenue at the time of sale.

Example – Retention of legal title

Entity A operates in a country where it is commonplace to retain title to goods sold as protection against non-payment by a buyer. The retention of title will enable entity A to recover the goods if the buyer defaults on payment.

After delivery of the goods to the buyer (entity B), entity A does not have any control over the goods. Entity B makes payments in accordance with the normal credit terms provided by entity A. Product liability is assumed by entity B. Settlement is due 14 days after delivery.

Entity A has sold the goods to entity B. The buyer controls the goods following the delivery and is free to use or dispose of them as it wishes. The most significant risk of ownership (that is, the product risk) has been transferred to entity B. Entity A's retention of legal title does not affect the substance of the transaction, which is the sale of goods from entity A to entity B. So entity A should, therefore, derecognise the inventory and recognise the revenue from the sale.

Rights of return

23.65   Some contracts give customers the right to return goods that they have purchased and obtain a refund or release from the obligation to pay. Rights of return can be explicit in the contractual terms or, they can be implicit as a matter of practice; they can also arise through statutory requirements.

23.66   In relation to rights of return, a contrast can be drawn between retailers that have a policy of giving refunds on returned goods, whether or not the goods are defective, and the situation where goods are sold on a consignment or a sale or return basis (as discussed below).

Goods sold with a right to be returned

23.67   Where goods are sold with a right of return, and management can reliably estimate the level of expected returns based on established historical record or other relevant evidence, revenue is recognised in full, and a provision is made against revenue for the expected level of returns. [FRS 102 para 23.13].

23.68   Where the entity can estimate the level of returns reliably, the liability recognised for expected returns will be measured in accordance with section 21 of FRS 102. The liability is not a financial liability, because the contract for return is executory and no cash will be paid unless the goods are returned. The liability should be measured at the best estimate of the amount necessary to settle the obligation. [FRS 102 para 21.7]. The entity has an accounting policy choice as to whether it adjusts revenue for the value of expected returns or whether it adjusts both revenue for the expected value of returns and cost of sales for the value of corresponding goods expected to be returned. The result of this second approach is that the provision for returns is measured as the margin on the sale. Where an adjustment is made to cost of sales, the value of the returned goods might be their original cost. But, if a reliable measurement of net realisable value is available, and this is lower than the original cost of the goods, net realisable value should be used when determining the liability to be recognised. In assessing the value of the returned goods, management will need to consider whether the returned goods will be impaired for damage or obsolescence.

23.69   Where goods are returned, an adjustment for the value of the goods is made to the provision, inventory and cash. The entity will need to assess whether the goods are impaired on return. Any remaining provision can be released to revenue when the period for returning goods has passed or the entity has assessed that it is probable that there will not be any further returns. If the original estimate of the provision is too low, returns might continue to be received once the provision has been written back in full. In such a situation, the returned goods would be accounted for as a debit to revenue and credit cash (or deferred income if the refund takes the form of store credit). The inventory received would be recognised at the lower of the original cost or its current net realisable value, and the related credit would be taken to cost of sales.

23.70 Where there is uncertainty about the possibility of return (or if the volume of expected returns cannot be reliably measured), the significant risk and rewards of ownership have not passed to the customer. Revenue is recognised when the shipment has been formally accepted by the buyer, or the goods have been delivered, and the time period for rejection has expired. [FRS 102 para 23A.5].

Goods shipped subject to conditions (sale or return/consignment)

23.71 Consignment sales, where the recipient (buyer) sells goods on behalf of the shipper (seller), that is as an agent, or items shipped on a sale or return basis, are situations where the risks and rewards of ownership do not pass until the goods are sold by the recipient to a third party. [FRS 102 para 23A.6].

> **Example – Goods delivered on the basis of sale or return**
>
> An entity imports sports clothing and has a number of distributors. It gives its distributors an extended credit deal whereby it supplies new fashion items worth £10,000 to each distributor for sale to third parties in order to encourage a market in these items. The distributor does not have to pay for the goods until payment has been received from the third party to which they are sold. If the goods are not sold within six months of receipt, the distributor can either return them to the entity or pay for them and keep them.
>
> The entity does not recognise revenue until the earlier of the distributor receiving payment for the sale of the goods to a third party or six months after the distributor receives them, provided that they are not returned. Only at this point can the entity determine that performance under the sales contract has occurred and that the risks and rewards of ownership have passed to the distributor. The goods should continue to be treated as the entity's inventory until they are sold.

Continuing managerial involvement and effective control

23.72 As noted above, one of the conditions for revenue recognition is that "*the entity retains neither continuing managerial involvement to the degree usually associated with ownership nor effective control over the goods sold*". The concept of control is relatively straightforward, since an asset is defined as: "*...a resource controlled by the entity as a result of past events and from which future economic benefits are expected to flow to the entity*". [FRS 102 para 2.15(a)]. It follows that, if the entity retains effective control over the goods sold, the transaction is not a sale, and so revenue is not recognised.

23.73 The phrase "*continuing managerial involvement to the degree usually associated with ownership*" is less straightforward, although it is highly unlikely that an entity would retain such involvement if it has transferred the risks and rewards of ownership of the goods to the buyer. Nor is it likely that a buyer would accept continuing managerial involvement from the seller to the degree envisaged where it had acquired the asset for fair consideration. Commercially, continuing managerial involvement to the degree associated with ownership would not normally occur where a genuine sale has taken place. But each situation should be judged on its own merits, because there might be features in the agreement that indicate that the seller has retained such continuing involvement.

23.74 Indicators of continuing managerial involvement, or retention of effective control, might include:

■ The seller can control the future onward sale price of the item.

■ The seller is responsible for the management of the goods after the sale (outside any other separable contract for management services).

■ The economics of the transaction make it likely that the buyer will return the goods to the seller.

■ The seller guarantees the return of the buyer's investment, or a return on that investment, for a significant period.

■ The seller has control over the re-sale of the item to third parties (for example, the seller can control the selling price, timing or counterparty of any re-sale transaction, or re-sale is entirely prohibited).

> **Example 1 – Ongoing involvement**
>
> Entity A sells a racehorse to entity B. As part of the arrangement entity A continues to house and train the horse, determine which races the horse will enter, and set stud fees for the horse. Should entity A recognise revenue on the sale of the horse to entity B?
>
> If a proper training agreement is in place that provides a market fee for the services that entity A provides, and that any winnings or fees achieved by the horse go to the buyer, it might be appropriate to recognise revenue on the sale. But it would also be necessary to consider whether entity A had given any guarantees, or incurred other obligations, that might indicate that it had not disposed of the significant risks and rewards of ownership of the horse.

Measurement of costs incurred related to the transaction

23.75 As noted above, management must be able to reliably measure the costs incurred, or to be incurred, in respect of the transaction in order to recognise revenue. Where such costs cannot be measured reliably, revenue is not recognised.

23.76 Costs incurred for the sale of goods produced by the entity are generally the manufacturing costs, which are calculated in accordance with section 13 of FRS 102 (see chapter 13). Where goods are purchased for resale, the costs generally comprise all costs of purchase. Measurement of each of these types of cost is usually relatively straightforward for an established business that is offering an existing product.

23.77 But this might not be so straightforward if an entity starts selling a new product and cannot reliably estimate warranty costs from the outset.

23.78 A warranty is often provided in conjunction with the sale of goods. Warranties represent guarantees made by the seller that a product will perform as specified for a period of time. Warranties should not be confused with general rights of return. A warranty permits a customer to return or exchange a product only if the product does not meet the specified performance criteria. Warranty costs represent additional costs that the seller might have to incur in relation to the product it has sold..

23.79 Where an entity sells a product subject to warranty, it must first determine whether the warranty represents a separable component of the transaction (for example, on the sale of a product and an extended warranty agreement).

23.80 When a warranty is not a separate element, the seller has completed substantially all the required performance and can recognise the full consideration received as revenue on the sale. The expected future cost to be incurred relating to the warranty should not be recorded as a reduction of revenue, but as a cost of sale; this is because the warranty does not represent a return of a portion of the purchaser's sale price. The costs of warranties should be determined at the time of the sale, and a corresponding provision for warranty costs recognised. Warranties and similar costs can normally be measured reliably, because entities have historical evidence of the costs associated with various products. But, if such costs cannot be measured reliably, revenue should not be recognised until the warranty period has expired and the related warranty costs are identified.

Practical issues

23.81 The following paragraphs examine a number of practical issues that illustrate the application of the revenue recognition criteria for the sale of goods. Many of these issues appear as examples in the Appendix to section 23 of FRS 102, which does not form part of the standard but provides useful guidance on its application. The examples are reproduced below with explanatory text where considered appropriate. Unless stated otherwise, the examples assume that the amount of revenue can be measured reliably, it is probable that the economic benefits will flow to the entity, and the costs incurred or to be incurred can be measured reliably.

'Bill and hold' sales

23.82 Bill and hold' sales occur where delivery is delayed at the buyer's request, but the buyer takes title and accepts billing. Normally, revenue on sale of goods is only recognised when all performance conditions have been satisfied, including delivery of the goods to the customer. So the issue arises as to whether, in the absence of delivery, revenue can be recognised in a bill and hold sale or whether inventory should continue to be recognised.

23.83 Under the guidance provided in the Appendix to section 23 of FRS 102, revenue is recognised when the buyer takes title, provided:

- it is probable that delivery will be made;

- the item is on hand, identified and ready for delivery to the buyer at the time the sale is recognised;

- the buyer specifically acknowledges the deferred delivery instructions; and

- the usual payment terms apply.

Revenue is not recognised where there is simply an intention to acquire or manufacture the goods in time for delivery. [FRS 102 para 23A.3].

Goods shipped subject to installation and inspection

23.84 Revenue relating to goods that are sold subject to installation and inspection is normally recognised when the buyer accepts delivery and the installation and inspection are complete. However, revenue is recognised on delivery where:

- the installation process is simple (for example, the installation of a factory-tested television receiver that requires only unpacking and connection of power and antennae); or

- the inspection is performed only for the purposes of final determination of contract prices (for example, shipments of iron ore, sugar or soya beans).

[FRS 102 para 23A.4].

23.85 Determining whether installation is incidental to the sale of a product is often difficult. In the case of the television receiver, for example, it is argued that the installation is straightforward. Where installation is more complicated, it might be identified as a separate component of the transaction. This approach is only possible where a reliable fair value can be ascertained for the installation. If installation is considered part of the single deliverable (that is, the entity is selling an 'installed machine' and not a machine with a separate installation service) revenue is not recognised until installation is complete.

> **Example – Sale of equipment is conditional on successful installation**
>
> Entity A manufacturers and sells complex bottling machines. Installation is a standard process, consisting principally of uncrating, calibrating and testing the equipment. However, a purchaser of the equipment could not complete the process itself since specialist testing equipment is needed. Installation is included in the equipment's overall sales price. The sale of each bottling machine is conditional on the equipment working as designed when the installation is complete.
>
> The sale of each machine is conditional on installation and installation is not an insignificant part of entity A's performance. As a result, entity A cannot record revenue relating to the machine's sale until installation is complete and customer acceptance has occurred or until the customer has declined the installation service.

Layaway sales

23.86 'Layaway sales' are those where goods are delivered only when the buyer makes the final payment in a series of instalments. Revenue from such sales is recognised when the goods are delivered. But, where experience indicates that most sales of this nature are consummated, revenue could be recognised when a significant deposit is received, provided the goods are on hand, identified and ready for delivery to the buyer. [FRS 102 para 23A.8].

Payments in advance

23.87 Sellers often require a deposit (that is, full or partial payments for goods when a customer places an order. Such a deposit might be received well in advance of delivery of the goods, which are not currently held in inventory, or are yet to be manufactured, or will be delivered direct to the buyer from a third party. In such situations, revenue is recognised only when the goods are delivered. This is because payments in advance of performance do not represent revenue because they have not been earned. Until the selling entity completes its contractual performance (that is, it delivers the goods to the buyer), the advance receipt is recognised as a liability. [FRS 102 para 23A.9].

Vouchers granted for consideration

23.88 FRS 102 does not deal specifically with vouchers issued for consideration, except where they meet the definition of a 'loyalty award' and are issued alongside the sale of a good or service; but, payment received in advance of future performance should be recognised as revenue only when the future performance to which it relates occurs.

23.89 The sale of a voucher is a contract with a customer in its own right; it should be considered together with the contract that arises if and when the voucher is exercised. The revenue from the sale of the voucher is generally accounted for when the seller performs under the latter contract (that is, when the seller supplies the goods or services on exercise of the voucher).

23.90 A common type of voucher issued for consideration is a gift voucher issued by retailers. The following example explains the accounting for gift vouchers.

> **Example – Accounting for gift vouchers**
>
> A retailer has a 31 December year end. While in store, customers can purchase a gift voucher that entitles the holder to purchase goods from the store up to the amount spent on the voucher. In December, the retailer sold gift vouchers with a face value of £1,000 ahead of the holiday season. None of the gift vouchers were redeemed in December, but all of the gift vouchers were redeemed in the following year. The gift vouchers expire one year from the date of purchase.

Where the retailer has only limited historical evidence of voucher redemption rates, it should not recognise revenue from the sale of the gift vouchers until the vouchers have been redeemed for merchandise, until the vouchers expire or until it can be reliably demonstrated that the vouchers are unlikely ever to be presented. Until this point, consideration received for the voucher should be deferred and recognised as a liability. This determination should be made for each individual voucher (or group of vouchers in an ageing profile) and not to the whole portfolio of vouchers.

If, however, the retailer maintains records on redemption rates that have historically been shown to be reliable, then the accounting might differ. With the additional fact that the retailer has a reliable, established pattern of 20% of vouchers not being redeemed before expiry, the retailer could choose to adopt a policy of allocating the consideration for the 20% (that is, the 'breakage') to the remaining 80% of the vouchers that are expected to be redeemed. The breakage revenue would then be recognised as the other vouchers are redeemed. If the retailer follows this approach, it must apply the policy consistently in future years, and it should adjust the non-redemption rate if estimates change.

Vouchers granted without consideration

23.91 Retailers, manufacturers and service providers often issue money-off vouchers for no consideration that can be redeemed in the future for goods or services. These are often included as part of marketing circulars or newspaper advertisements.

23.92 Where vouchers are distributed free of charge and independently of another transaction, they do not give rise to a liability, except where redemption of the vouchers will result in products (or services) being sold at a loss. This is because the voucher is an executory contract and neither side has performed, therefore, no provision is recognised unless the contract is onerous (see chapter 21). When the vouchers are redeemed, the seller should recognise revenue at the amount received for the product, that is, after deducting the discount granted on exercise of the vouchers from the normal selling price. This type of voucher is no different from a reduction in the sales price made during an annual or seasonal sale.

Free products

23.93 Some sales promotions are described as 'buy one, get one free' or 'two for the price of one', or a seller might price products below cost to attract volume. The revenue on such transactions is the actual sales proceeds and the purchase or production cost of the 'free' product or 'loss leader' is a cost of sale.

Example 1 – Buy one, get one half price

A retailer is offering a special 'buy one, get one half price' deal whereby customers who purchase one box of chocolates are entitled to purchase another box at the same time and obtain the second box for half the price. How should the retailer record the transaction?

The revenue recognised is the cash consideration received for the two boxes of chocolates. The additional cost from offering the second box at a discount to the normal price is recorded as a cost of sales, and not as a marketing expense.

Example 2 – First product is sold for free

A start-up entity retails an electronic product. It is attracting a customer base by allowing the customer to have the first product free. The customer is under no obligation to take further products.

There has been no inflow of economic benefit to the entity because this transaction was undertaken for nil consideration. The customer can just take the free product and walk away, so the transaction is not linked to any other transaction. Neither the customer nor the seller has any rights or obligations relating to future transactions as a result of giving (or taking) the free product. As a result, the cost of the goods given away is charged as a marketing cost. It is not a cost of sale, because no sale has been made.

In both examples, the entity should consider whether its inventory is being carried at an appropriate value , that is, these offers may indicate that net realisable value is less than cost (see chapter 13).

Sale and repurchase agreements

23.94 Sale and repurchase agreements (other than swap transactions) are transactions where the seller concurrently agrees to repurchase the same goods at a later date. In the absence of a formal buy-back agreement, the repurchase could also be effected through the exercise of an option. For instance, the seller might have a call option to repurchase, or the buyer might have a put option to require the seller to repurchase the goods.

23.95 Where such a sale and repurchase agreement on a non-financial asset is entered into, the agreement's terms need to be analysed to ascertain whether, in substance, the seller has transferred the significant risks and rewards of ownership to the buyer. If they have been transferred, the seller recognises revenue. Where the seller has retained the risks and rewards of ownership, even though legal title has been transferred, the transaction is a financing arrangement and does not give rise to revenue. For a sale and repurchase agreement on a financial asset, the derecognition provisions of section 11 of FRS 102 apply. [FRS 102 para 23A.10].

23.96 Where repurchase options are present, it is important to ascertain whether the seller or the buyer can significantly benefit from the exercise of the option. For instance, in a call option held by a seller, the seller might retain an important benefit of ownership by being able to profit from the difference between the fair value of the goods at the repurchase date and the option exercise price. This difference could be so significant that it precludes recognition of revenue. Similar considerations apply to put options held by a buyer. On the other hand, if the option exercise price is set at a price equal to the market value of the goods at the repurchase date and the goods are generally available in the market, revenue should be recognised at the time of delivery.

Example – Legal sale linked to a financing arrangement

The management of entity A is considering the following two alternative transactions:

(a) sale of inventory to a bank for £500,000, with an obligation to repurchase the inventory at a later stage; or

(b) sale of inventory to a bank for £500,000, with an option to repurchase the inventory at any time up to 12 months from the date of sale.

The repurchase price in both alternatives is £500,000 plus an imputed financing cost. The bank is required to provide substantially the same quality and quantity of inventory as was sold to it (that is, the bank is not required to return precisely the same physical inventory as was originally sold). The fair value of the inventory sold to the bank is £1,000,000.

Management should recognise the transactions as follows:

(a) Sale with repurchase obligation: management should not recognise revenue on the transfer of the inventory to the bank. The inventory should remain on entity A's balance sheet and the proceeds from the bank should be recognised as a collateralised borrowing.

Even though the inventory repurchased from the bank might not be the inventory sold, it is in substance the same asset. The substance of the transaction is that the sale and repurchase are linked transactions, and entity A does not transfer the risks and rewards associated with the inventory to the bank.

(b) Sale with repurchase option: management should not recognise revenue unless and until the repurchase option is allowed to lapse. The inventory should remain on entity A's balance sheet, and the proceeds should be recognised as a collateralised borrowing until entity A's right to repurchase the inventory lapses. (Entity A is unlikely to let the repurchase option lapse because the 'sale' was at significantly below fair value.)

Sales to intermediate parties

23.97 Where an entity makes a sale to an intermediate party (such as distributors, or dealers) for resale, revenue is recognised when the risks and rewards of ownership have transferred. But, where the buyer is acting as agent, the sale is treated as a consignment sale (see para 23.71 above).

Subscriptions to publications and similar items

23.98 In respect of subscriptions and similar items, revenue should be recognised on a straight-line basis over the period when the items are despatched, if they are of a similar nature in each time period, such as a typical magazine subscription. Where the items vary in value from one period to another, such as a 'wine of the month' club, revenue is recognised on the basis of the sales value of the item despatched as a proportion of the total estimated sales value of the items covered by the subscription. [FRS 102 para 23A.12].

Cash on delivery

23.99   Where goods are shipped subject to the condition that cash is received on delivery, revenue is recognised when the cash is received, either by the seller or its agent. [FRS 102 para 23A.7].

Agreements for the construction of real estate

23.100   Construction companies enter into transactions of different types. In some cases, they build developments where the properties could be 'pre-sold', so that the contract has been entered into before construction begins and all the terms and conditions of the sale are known. In other cases, they build houses or developments speculatively. In the real estate industry, entities that undertake the construction of real estate, directly or through subcontractors, could enter into agreements with one or more buyers before construction is complete. Such agreements can take diverse forms, so the issue arises as to whether the agreement should be accounted for as a sale of construction services or as the sale of goods.

23.101   The agreement should be accounted for using the percentage of completion method, only if:

- the buyer is able to specify the major structural elements of the design of the real estate before construction begins and/or specify major structural changes once construction is in progress (whether or not it exercises that right); or

- the buyer acquires and supplies construction materials and the entity provides only construction services.

[FRS 102 para 23A.14].

23.102   The agreement should be accounted for as a sale of goods where the entity provides construction services together with construction materials in order to perform its contractual obligation to deliver real estate. In this case, the buyer does not obtain control or the significant risks and rewards of ownership of the work in progress in its current state as construction progresses. Instead, the transfer occurs only on delivery of the completed real estate to the buyer.

> **Example – Property development business selling houses 'off plan'**
>
> Entity A operates a property development business. This involves entity A purchasing plots of undeveloped land in residential areas with the intention of building housing complexes on the land.
>
> In order to obtain financing at an early stage of the process, entity A advertises the developments at a discount well in advance of building the housing. Customers who wish to own a property could purchase them 'off plan' before any building has commenced. The customer pays a 15% deposit initially, and the remainder when the property is completed and transferred into the customer's name (that is, when the customer takes possession of the property).

When customers purchase the housing 'off plan', they must choose one of three designs specified by entity A. The customer could decide the type of tiling, flooring and wall colour of their property.

The contracts should be accounted for as a sale of goods. This is because the customers can only choose one of the three designs and do not have any opportunity to specifically negotiate the significant elements of the structural design. The agreement is a forward contract that gives the customer an asset in the form of a right to acquire, use and sell the completed real estate at a later date and an obligation to pay the purchase price in accordance with its terms. Although the customer might be able to transfer its interest in the forward contract to another party, the entity retains control and the significant risks and rewards of ownership of the work in progress in its current state until the completed real estate is transferred. So, revenue should be recognised only when all the criteria in paragraph 23.36 above are met (at completion in this example).

23.103 If the entity is required to provide services together with construction materials in order to perform its contractual obligation to deliver real estate to the buyer, the agreement shall be accounted for as a sale of goods. This is because the buyer does not obtain control or the significant risks and rewards of ownership of the work in progress as construction progresses. Instead the transfer occurs only on the delivery of the completed real estate to the buyer. [FRS 102 para 23A.15].

Sales of services

23.104 The key issue that arises in recognising revenue from rendering services is determining when services are transferred. The standard states that, when the outcome of a transaction involving the rendering of services can be estimated reliably, an entity shall recognise revenue associated with the transaction by reference to the stage of completion of the transaction at the end of the reporting period. This is often referred to as the 'percentage of completion method' (see further para 23.111 below).

23.105 The outcome of the transaction can be estimated reliably when, in addition to the general recognition principles set out in paragraph 23.10 above, both of the following conditions are satisfied:

■   the stage of completion of the transaction at the end of the reporting period can be measured reliably; and

■   the costs incurred for the transaction and the costs to complete the transaction can be measured reliably.

[FRS 102 para 23.14].

Contracts for services involving an indeterminate number of acts

23.106 Where a contract for services involves an indeterminate number of acts over a specified time, revenue is recognised on a straight-line basis, unless there is evidence that some other method gives a better reflection of the stage of completion at each year end. [FRS 102 para 23.15]. For example, revenue from a contract to provide maintenance services for a six month period would normally be reflected on a straight-line basis over the six months. This is because the frequency and timing of the provision of maintenance services cannot be determined and so the straight-line method of spreading revenue is the best practical method to use. In such situations, costs should be recognised as incurred and neither accrued nor deferred, unless they qualify for recognition as a liability or an asset.

Contracts for services containing significant acts

23.107 When a contract contains a specific act that is much more significant than any other acts to be performed under the contract, the recognition of revenue is postponed until the significant act is executed. [FRS 102 para 23.15]. The existence of a specific act that is much more significant than any other act might indicate that the other acts do not substantively advance the transaction's stage of completion.

23.108 In some cases, it might not be immediately obvious whether a contract contains a significant act or contingent consideration. A significant act is something that the entity must do itself. Where the contract contains a significant act, the entity has not earned revenue until the specific act is performed. In comparison, where a contract includes contingent consideration an entity will have performed all of its obligations under the contract, but the receipt of the consideration could be determined by events outside its control. Where a contract contains a significant act, no revenue is recognised until this act has occurred; this is because the entity has not yet performed under the contract. Where the entity has performed but consideration is contingent, revenue will be recognised to the extent that the entity can determine that there is a probable inflow of economic benefits that can be reliably measured. This approach can be used even if a further event outside the entity's control must occur so that the amount of revenue to be received can be determined. See from paragraph 23.31 onwards above for further discussion of contingent consideration.

23.109 The timing of cash payments should not, by itself, determine whether a single act is much more significant than any other in an arrangement. But, the terms of an arrangement that involve payment only on completion of a single act should be assessed to determine whether the timing of the payment suggests that one act is more significant than the others. Judgement will be required, in many circumstances, to determine whether a specific act is much more significant than any others.

23.110 When considering how to account for a service contract, it is essential that the contractual terms are understood. By agreeing to the terms in the contract, the buyer specifies the point at which the contract has value to them; and this will indicate when the criteria for revenue recognition are met. If the seller is seen to perform under the contract over the period of time the services are rendered, the revenue recognition profile should reflect this. If the seller has only performed under the contract after the fulfilment of a significant act, no revenue should be recognised until that act has occurred. This is illustrated below.

> **Example – Professional services**
>
> Mr A is an accountant who is half way through completing his client's tax return at the end of June (Mr A's year end). The client has agreed to pay £500 to Mr A for completion of the return. The contract specifies that Mr A has the right to receive payment for any work performed and will be paid for services rendered, even if the contract is broken off before completion. On this basis, Mr A has accounted for £250 of the revenue.
>
> In this case, the criteria for revenue recognition will be met over the period in which Mr A works on his client's tax return. Although it might seem that a half-completed tax return is of little practical use to the client, by agreeing to the terms of the contract, the client has agreed that Mr A is performing under the contract as he is performing his work. On this basis, the revenue would be recognised by reference to the contract's stage of completion and, as such, it would be appropriate to recognise £250 of the revenue at the end of June.
>
> If the contract specified that Mr A had no right to receive payment until the tax return was completed , revenue recognition would be postponed until that had occurred. This is because, under the agreed contractual terms, Mr A has not performed under the contract until this significant act is fulfilled. As such, the criteria for revenue recognition are not met until this point.

Percentage of completion method

23.111 Recognising revenue by reference to the stage of completion of a transaction is often referred to as the 'percentage of completion method'. Under this method, revenue is recognised in the accounting periods in which the work is performed. Recognising revenue on this basis provides useful information on the extent of service activity and performance during a period. This method is also used for recognising revenue under construction contracts [FRS 102 para 23.22].

23.112 The standard suggests the following possible methods for determining the stage of completion of the transaction, and, so the extent of progress toward completion at the reporting date:

- The proportion that costs incurred for work performed to date bear to the estimated total costs. Costs incurred for work performed to date do not include costs relating to future activity, such as for materials or prepayments.

- Surveys of work performed.

- Completion of a physical proportion of the contract work or the completion of a proportion of the service contract.

Progress payments and advances received from customers often do not reflect the work performed.

[FRS 102 para 23.22].

23.113 The first method set out above is an input measure; this is because it relates to inputs or efforts put into the contract that are measured in terms of costs. For instance, if the estimated total contract cost is £1,000, and £600 has been incurred by the reporting date, the contract is 60% complete. The other two methods are output measures, because they relate to the degree of output or work done by the reporting date. For instance, if the contract is for constructing a ten-storey building, and two floors have been completed by the reporting date, the contract is 20% complete.

23.114 The standard does not mandate the use of any particular method for revenue recognition on rendering services or construction contracts. The use of a particular method requires the exercise of judgement and careful tailoring to the nature of the contract. The entity should use the method that measures most reliably the work performed. In other words, the selected method must ensure that revenue relates only to work that has been performed, and it must exclude any element that relates to work that has yet to be carried out.

Reliable measurement of costs

23.115 As noted in paragraph 23.105 above, reliable measurement of costs incurred is one of the criteria to be satisfied before revenue can be recognised for the rendering of services. Estimating the cost of providing services might not be straightforward, especially where the contract for services spans several accounting periods. Determining the costs incurred to date should be relatively straightforward, but determining the future costs to be incurred in the transaction can present a greater challenge. Given the difficulty inherent in such judgement, entities should consider the need to disclose the judgements made as a key source of estimation uncertainty in the financial statements under paragraph 8.7 of FRS 102.

23.116 In some situations, the timing of costs can vary significantly from the profile of revenue recognition. This can happen, for example, in outsourcing contracts where the service provider might incur a number of expenses before revenue is received. Where this occurs, the question often arises as to whether these costs can be deferred. FRS 102 is clear that it "*does not allow the recognition of items in the statement of financial position that do not meet the definition of assets or of liabilities regardless of whether they result from applying the notion commonly referred to as the 'matching concept' for measuring profit or loss*". [FRS 102 para 2.45]. But, where expenses are incurred in advance (for example, where materials are purchased to be used in construction in a future period, or where the entity prepays for goods or services), these costs are deferred and recognised as an asset only if it is probable that the costs will be recovered. [FRS 102 para 23.23]. Where it is not probable that costs are recoverable, they should be expensed immediately. [FRS 102 para 23.24].

23.117   The treatment of costs will depend on the nature of the costs and the relevant facts and circumstances. It is appropriate to capitalise costs if the entity can recognise an asset under section 13 (inventories), section 17 (property, plant and equipment) or section 18 (intangible assets) of FRS 102. Some costs, although they do not meet the recognition criteria in these sections of standard, might be carried forward in accordance with section 23, provided the costs meet the definition of an asset:

"A resource controlled by the entity as a result of past events and from which future economic benefits are expected to flow to the entity." [FRS 102 Glossary of terms].

23.118   This could include costs that relate to future activity on the contract (provision of the service). But, such costs must meet the definition of an asset, and there are limited situations where this is the case. For example, staff training costs are costs that relate to the future activity of the business, but they do not meet the definition of an asset. This is because the trained member of staff can leave at any time, so the entity does not control any benefit associated with the training.

> **Example – Contract for the performance of services to numerous customers**
>
> A shipping entity provides specialised transportation services to numerous customers. A ship travels (empty) to the load port where it picks up cargo. It then loads the cargo and transports it to the discharge port. Costs are incurred on the voyage to the load port. The question arises as to whether these costs can be deferred until the vessel reaches the load port, so that they are recognised in the income statement in the same period as the revenue?
>
> Management should consider the nature of the costs incurred on a case-by-case basis. Only costs meeting the definition of inventory, property, plant and equipment or intangible assets (under sections 13, 17 and 18 respectively) or otherwise meeting the definition of an asset would be capitalised (in line with the relevant section). In all other cases, costs should be expensed as incurred. To illustrate, the cost of fuel used to travel to the load port would be expensed, but fuel purchased but not yet used would be capitalised as inventory. Other costs, such as staff training costs, would be expensed as incurred.

Reliable estimation of transaction outcome not possible

23.119   As discussed above, the stage of completion of the transaction determines the proportion of services delivered (under the contractual terms) and hence the revenue that should be recognised. But, where the outcome of the transaction involving the rendering of services cannot be estimated reliably, the entity should recognise revenue only to the extent of the expenses recognised that are recoverable. [FRS 102 para 23.16].

23.120   During the early stages of a transaction, it is often the case that the outcome of the transaction cannot be estimated reliably. Nevertheless, it might be probable that the entity will recover the transaction costs incurred. So, revenue is recognised only to the extent of costs incurred that are expected to be recoverable. As the outcome of the transaction cannot be estimated reliably, no profit is recognised

23.121 If costs have been expensed because it was not considered probable that they could be recovered, and that assessment changes in a future period, the amounts previously expensed are not reinstated, even if the costs are now considered recoverable and additional revenue might be recognisable in respect of such costs.

Practical issues

23.122 The following paragraphs examine a number of practical issues that illustrate the application of the revenue recognition criteria for the rendering of services. Many of these issues appear as examples in the Appendix to section 23 of FRS 102, which does not form part of the standard, but provide useful guidance on its application. These examples are reproduced below, with explanatory text where considered appropriate. Unless stated otherwise, the examples assume that the amount of revenue can be measured reliably, it is probable that the economic benefits will flow to the entity, and the costs incurred or to be incurred can be measured reliably.

Installation fees

23.123 Installation fees are recognised as revenue by reference to the stage of the installation's completion, unless they are incidental to the product's sale (in which case, they are recognised when the goods are sold). [FRS 102 para 23A.18].

Servicing fees included in the price of product

23.124 Where the selling price of a product includes an identifiable amount for subsequent servicing (for example, after-sales support and product enhancement on the sale of software), the seller defers that amount and recognises it as revenue over the period during which the service is performed. The amount deferred is that which will cover the expected costs of the services under the agreement, together with a reasonable profit on those services. [FRS 102 para 23A.19].

Advertising commissions

23.125 Advertising agency income might consist of media commissions for displaying advertising, and production commissions for the production of the advertisement. Revenue is recognised for media commissions when the advertisement appears before the public, and for production commissions according to the stage of completion of the project. [FRS 102 para 23A.20].

Insurance agency commissions

23.126 Insurance agency commissions received or receivable, that do not require the agent to render further services, are recognised as revenue by the agent on the effective commencement or renewal dates of the related policies. But, where it is probable that the agent will be required to render further services during the life of the policy, the agent defers the commission (or part of it), and recognises it as revenue over the period during which the policy is in force. [FRS 102 para 23A.21].

Financial services fees

23.127 There are three types of financial services fees contemplated in the appendix to Section 23:

■ Fees that are an integral part of the effective interest rate, which might include origination fees and commitment fees, are treated as an adjustment to the effective interest rate [FRS102 para 23.29(a)]. Calculation of the effective interest rate is discussed in chapter 11.

■ Fees that are earned as a service is provided, which might include, for example, loan servicing and investment management fees. Revenue should be recognised as the service is performed using the percentage of completion method.

■ Fees that are earned upon the execution of a significant act, which might include fees received on the allotment of shares or the arrangement of a loan. Revenue is recognised when the significant act is performed.

23.128 The example in the standard notes that the description of the fees might not be indicative of the nature and substance of the services performed. [FRS 102 para 23A.21A].

Admission fees

23.129 Admission fees (for example, from artistic performances, banquets and other special events) are recognised when the event takes place. Where a subscription to a number of events is sold, the fee is allocated to each event on a basis that reflects the extent to which services are performed at each event. [FRS 102 para 23A.22].

23.130 Where an event is held at a particular time, income and costs might be received and incurred in advance. For example, exhibitions, conferences and courses might involve delegates paying in advance of attending, and a number of costs (such as advertising), might also be incurred in advance. Performance does not occur and revenue is not earned until the exhibition is held or the course is given, so the payments received in advance represent a liability, which should be released in profit or loss when the event takes place. If income is deferred, costs incurred in advance of the event could be deferred if they meet the definition of an asset (see para 23.116 above). However, costs such as advertising of the event would not be held as an asset.

Tuition fees

23.131 Tuition fees should be recognised as revenue over the period of instruction. [FRS 102 para 23A.23].

23.132 This deals with the straightforward situation where a single session of tuition is given over a fixed time period, but some instruction courses are structured differently. For example, a course might be structured as a number of modules. Students might be able to choose to attend and complete a fixed number of modules at any time within, say, a two-year period. It would be more appropriate to recognise revenue as the modules are attended and completed by the student (that is, as the service is provided to the student) rather than recognising revenue on a straight-line basis as indicated above.

Initiation, entrance and membership fees

23.133 Recognition of revenue in respect of initiation, entrance and membership fees depends on the nature of the services provided. If the fee covers membership, or joining only, and other services or products are paid for separately, or if there is a separate annual subscription, the joining or membership fee is recognised as revenue where there is no significant uncertainty as to its collectability. If the joining or membership fee entitles the member to services or products during the membership period, or to purchase goods or services at prices lower than those charged to non-members, revenue is recognised on a basis that reflects the timing, nature and value of the benefits provided. [FRS 102 para 23A.24].

23.134 The issue is whether it is possible to separate clearly the membership or joining fee from other goods or services that are provided during the membership period. FRS 102 requires an analysis of the arrangement to see whether any part of the joining fee is, in fact, an advance payment for future goods or services. In practice, the annual subscription might well be discounted if the joining fee covers other services and, thus, the joining fee might not be solely for membership.

23.135 But where it can be demonstrated that the seller has no further obligations in respect of the fee once it has been received, the seller should recognise the fee on the date that it becomes entitled to receive it. The seller might have no further obligations in respect of the fee if the customer has to pay the full commercial price for all future goods or services, including any access to the organisation.

Franchise fees

23.136 Under a franchise agreement, the franchisor that grants business rights under the franchise normally provides a range of services to the franchisee. They include initial services, such as training and assistance to help the franchisee set up and operate the franchise operation, continuing services for the operation of the franchise, and the supply of equipment, inventory and other tangible assets and know-how. Therefore, these agreements could generate different types of revenue, such as initial franchise fees, profits and losses from the sale of fixed assets, and royalties.

23.137 In general, franchise fees should be recognised on a basis that reflects the purpose for which they were charged. That is, the franchisor recognises the fair value of the assets sold as revenue when the items are delivered or title passes. [FRS 102 para 23A.26]. Also, fees charged for the use of continuing rights granted by the agreement (or for other services provided during the period of the agreement) are recognised as revenue as the rights are used or the services are provided. [FRS 102 para 23A.31].

23.138 But, where the franchise agreement provides for the franchisor to supply equipment, inventory or other tangible assets at a price lower than that charged to others, or at a price that does not allow the franchisor to make a reasonable profit on the supplies, part of the initial franchise fee should be deferred. The amount of the initial franchise fee deferred should be sufficient to cover the estimated costs in excess of the price charged to the franchisee for any assets and to allow the franchisor to make a reasonable profit on these sales. This deferred income can then be recognised over the period when the goods are likely to be sold to the franchisee (as an adjustment to the selling price of the goods sold). The balance of the initial fee should be recognised as revenue when performance of all the initial services and other obligations (such as assistance with site selection, staff training, financing and advertising) has been substantially accomplished. [FRS 102 para 23A.28].

23.139 Similarly, if there is no separate fee for the supply of continuing services after the initial fee or services, or if the separate fee does not cover the cost of continuing services together with a reasonable profit then part of the initial fee sufficient to cover the cost of continuing services and provide a reasonable profit on those services is deferred and recognised as revenue as the services are rendered. [FRS 102 para 23A.27].

23.140 The initial services and other obligations under an area franchise agreement might depend on the number of individual outlets established in the area. In this case, the fees attributable to the initial services are recognised as revenue in proportion to the number of outlets for which the initial services have been substantially completed. [FRS 102 para 23A.29].

23.141 If the initial fee is collectable over an extended period, and there is a significant uncertainty that it will be collected in full, the fee is recognised as cash instalments are received. [FRS 102 para 23A.30].

23.142 Transactions might take place between the franchisor and the franchisee that, in substance, involve the franchisor acting as agent for the franchisee. For example, the franchisor might order supplies and arrange for their delivery to the franchisee at no profit. Such transactions do not give rise to revenue. [FRS 102 para 23A.32]. Agency agreements are considered in paragraph 23.21 above.

Construction contracts

Nature of construction contracts

23.143 A construction contract is "*a contract specifically negotiated for the construction of an asset or a combination of assets that are closely interrelated or interdependent in terms of their design, technology and function or their ultimate purpose or use*". [FRS 102 Glossary of terms]. Examples of the construction of a single asset might be a building, bridge or a pipeline; examples of the construction of a combination of assets might be the construction of refineries and other complex pieces of plant and machinery.

23.144 But, the production of a series of assets would not necessarily meet the definition of a construction contract. For example, a contract between a furniture manufacturer and a retailer for the supply of 2,000 sofas over a two-year term according to the retailer's specification would not be a construction contract. It is simply a contract for the production of goods. The contract is for the construction of a series of assets that are not interrelated, because one sofa is not connected to or dependent on another sofa in any way. Nor is the manufacture and sale of a single sofa a construction contract in its own right, as the contract is for the supply of 2,000 sofas.

23.145 There is no fixed contractual period stated in the above definition of a construction contract. Such contracts will in general last for more than a year, although some shorter contracts could also fall within the definition.

Segmentation and combination of contracts

23.146 The accounting for construction contracts set out below is usually applied separately to each construction contract. But it is sometimes necessary to break a single contract down into separable elements and apply the requirements to each of those elements separately. Conversely, there might be situations where a group of separate contracts should be treated as one contract because, in substance, they represent a single contract. [FRS 102 para 23.18]. Although the manner in which the contract has been negotiated will often determine whether, in substance, the contract is a series of separate individual contracts or one single contract for the construction of assets, the standard sets out a number of other factors that should be considered in this determination. This determination is important, because combining or segmenting will have a significant effect on the allocation of revenue and profit between accounting periods.

Segregating contracts

23.147   Where a contract covers the construction of a number of assets, the construction for each asset should be treated as a separate construction contract where:

- separate proposals have been submitted for each asset;
- each asset has been subject to separate negotiation, and the contractor and customer are able to accept or reject that part of the contract relating to each asset; and
- the costs and revenues of each asset can be identified.

[FRS 102 para 23.19].

23.148   These requirements are more onerous than the general disaggregation criteria set out in paragraph 23.8 of FRS 102; those criteria are discussed at paragraph 23.44 onwards above.

Combining contracts

23.149   Conversely, a group of contracts (whether with a single customer or with several customers), is treated as a single construction contract where:

- the group of contracts is negotiated as a single package;
- the contracts are so closely interrelated that they are, in effect, part of a single project with an overall profit margin; and
- the contracts are performed concurrently or in a continuous sequence.

[FRS 102 para 23.20].

Recognition of contract revenue and costs

23.150   Because of the nature of the activity undertaken in construction contracts the date at which the contract activity is entered into and the date when the activity is completed usually fall into different accounting periods. So, the primary issue in accounting for construction contracts is the allocation of contract revenue and contract costs to the accounting periods in which construction work is performed.

23.151   When the outcome of a construction contract can be estimated reliably, an entity should recognise contract revenue and contract costs by reference to the stage of completion of the contract activity at the end of the reporting period. The stage of completion method (referred to as the 'percentage of completion method') is discussed at paragraph 23.111 above. Under this method, contract costs, revenue and profits are recognised in the period in which the work is performed. Reliable estimation of the outcome requires reliable estimates of the stage of completion, future costs and collectability of billings. [FRS 102 para 23.17].

23.152 The measurement of revenue and costs is affected by a variety of uncertainties that depend on the outcome of future events. In particular, under a construction contract, the estimates of contract revenue and contract costs often need to be revised as events occur and uncertainties are resolved. So, at the end of each reporting period, an entity must review its estimates of contract revenue and contract costs and revise them if they have changed. The percentage of completion method is applied on a cumulative basis, and so revisions are treated as changes in estimates; this means that prior periods are not adjusted (see chapter 10). For example, in a four-year project, if contract revenue and contract costs are revised in year 2 of the project, no adjustment is made to the revenue or costs recognised in year 1. The change will be reflected in years 2, 3 and 4.

Contract revenue

23.153 No definition of contract revenue is given in FRS 102. The total amount of contract revenue will initially be specified in the contract: It could be a fixed price contract or costs incurred plus a margin. Revenue is measured at the fair value of the amount receivable. As noted above, the amount of revenue recognised in the reporting period is determined by applying the percentage of completion method. The percentage of completion method requires management to estimate the stage of completion of the contract at each reporting date, and this estimate will be revised as events change and uncertainties are resolved. As a result, the amount of revenue recognised in the period might increase or decrease.

23.154 Revision to original estimates might be due to variations in contract work, claims and incentive payments. For instance, variations in contract work could arise as from the customer requiring changes in the specification or design of the item to be constructed. Claims might arise when the contractor seeks to recover costs not specified in the contract (for example, due to customer-caused delays, errors in specifications or design, or disputed variations in contract work). Incentive payments could arise if specified performance standards are met or exceeded.

23.155 Following the general principles set out in the standard, changes in original revenue estimates (due to variations, claims and incentive payments) will be included in contract revenue where it is probable that such benefits will flow to the contractor and the amounts can be measured reliably. In practice, because of the frequency and large number of disputes that arise on construction contracts and the length of time over which negotiations might stretch, it is often more appropriate to take variations and claims into account only when they have actually been approved by the customer.

Contract cost

23.156 No definition of contract costs is given in FRS 102. But, contract costs would include costs that relate directly to the specific contract, costs that are attributable to contract activity in general and can be allocated to the contract and such other costs as are specifically chargeable to the customer under the terms of the contract.

23.157 Some costs could be attributable to contract activity in general (for example, construction overheads, insurance etc) and can be allocated to specific contracts. It would be acceptable to allocate such costs to specific contracts on a systematic and rational basis that is applied in a consistent manner to all costs that have similar characteristics. The allocation should be based on the entity's normal level of construction activity. But, borrowing costs should not be included in contract costs. Accounting for borrowing costs is discussed in chapter 25.

23.158 Other costs that are specifically chargeable to the contract could include general administration costs and development costs for which reimbursement is specified in the contract.

23.159 A contractor might incur various costs before securing the contract. Such costs would normally include design costs, external consultancy fees and the costs of preparing and presenting the bid documentation. There is no guidance in FRS 102 as to how such costs should be treated. But, in accordance with section 2 of FRS 102, such costs can be deferred and reported as an asset provided that they meet the definition of an asset (see para 23.116 above). It is only appropriate to defer pre-contract costs if it is probable that the contract will be obtained. If pre-contracts costs are expensed in the period in which they are incurred, they should not be reinstated if obtaining the contract becomes probable in a later period. If pre-contract costs are deferred, they will form part of the total contract costs once the contract begins.

23.160 When the percentage of completion method (which compares costs to date to total expected costs) is used, only those costs that reflect work performed to date are included in the contract costs to date. For example, the following are excluded:

- Contract costs that relate to future activity on the contract (such as costs of materials that have been delivered to a contract site or set aside for use in a contract but not yet installed, used or applied during contract performance). But, if materials have been made specifically for the contract, they are included in contract costs, even if they have not been used in the period, because it is unlikely that they will be used on other contracts.

- Payments made to sub-contractors in advance of work performed under the sub-contract.

23.161 Such costs are recognised as an asset, provided it is probable that they can be recovered. [FRS 102 para 23.23]. These costs are capitalised as assets (as described above) and are often described as work in progress. They are not taken into account for the purpose of determining the costs incurred to date for comparison with total expected contract costs; but they are included in the estimate of total contract costs. However, where recovery of costs is not probable, they should be recognised as an expense immediately. [FRS 102 para 23.24].

> **Example – Recognition of costs by reference to contract costs incurred to date**
>
> Entity A entered into a contract with entity B to construct a power station. The cost of the station is estimated at £150,000. The total revenue from the contract is estimated at £200,000. Entity A will take three years to construct the power station.
>
> At the end of year 1, entity A incurred costs of £70,000, including £10,000 of building materials held off site. The customer was invoiced for £50,000 at the end of year 1. Payment of this progress billing is due, early in year 2, in accordance with the normal credit terms that entity A offers.
>
> When the stage of completion is determined by reference to the contract cost incurred to date, entity A should compare the proportion of costs incurred to date to the total estimated costs.
>
> Based on the relationship between the costs incurred to date – that is, £60,000 (£70,000 – £10,000 relating to future activity) — and total estimated costs of £150,000, the contract is 40% (60,000/150,000) completed at the end of year 1.
>
> Entity A recognises revenue of £80,000 (40% of 200,000) and profit of £20,000 (£80,000 – £60,000) in year 1.
>
> The £10,000 of building materials that is held off site would be included in the statement of financial position as an asset (work-in-progress in inventories).
>
> The entity has invoiced the customer for C50,000 at the end of the year, so an amount of £30,000 (£80,000 – £50,000) would be included in accrued income (often also called 'Gross amount due from customers for contract work'). See further paragraph 23.185 below.

Reliable estimation of contract outcome not possible

23.162 Where the outcome of a construction contract cannot be estimated reliably:

■ revenue should be recognised only to the extent of contract costs incurred that it is probable will be recoverable, and

■ the entity shall recognise contract costs as an expense in the period in which they are incurred.

[FRS 102 para 23.25].

That is, revenue recognised is the amount required to show zero profit in the income statement for the period. Costs continue to be recognised in the period to which they relate, with future costs being deferred, unless they do not meet the definition of an asset.

> **Example – Outcome of contract cannot be estimated reliably**
>
> A construction contractor has a fixed price contract for £100,000 to construct a building of a design that has never before been constructed and using materials that have never before been used in the construction of a building (the project).The contractor began construction of the building in 20X1 and expects that construction will take at least five years. In 20X1 the contractor incurred £5,000 contract costs on the project.
>
> At the end of 20X1 the contractor cannot estimate the outcome of the contract with sufficient reliability to estimate the project's percentage of completion; in other words, the uncertainties arising from the new design and new materials mean that the entity cannot estimate total expected contract costs with sufficient reliability. However, the contractor has estimated that its total costs will be in the range £55,000 – £85,000 and as such it does not believe that the contract is onerous. It is highly likely that the contract price will be received from the customer.
>
> At the end of 20X1 the contractor must recognise revenue only to the extent of recoverable contract costs incurred (that is, £5,000 contract revenue and £5,000 expenses).

Recognition of losses

23.163 Where it is probable that total contract costs will exceed total contract revenue on a construction contract, the expected loss is recognised as an expense immediately, with a corresponding provision for an onerous contract (see chapter 21). [FRS 102 para 23.26]. A construction contract might become onerous even before any work has commenced on the contract.

> **Example 1 – Expected loss on a construction contract**
>
> A construction contractor has a fixed-price contract for £100,000 to construct a building. The contractor's initial estimate of total contract costs was £60,000.
>
> At the end of the first year of the project (20X1) the contractor has incurred £90,000 contract costs and it expects to incur a further £30,000 to complete the project. The contractor determines the stage of completion of the construction contract by reference to the proportion of costs incurred for work performed to date compared to the estimated total costs.
>
> At the end of year 1, the contractor will recognise the following revenue and costs:
>
> | | £ |
> | --- | --- |
> | Costs incurred to end of 20X1 | 90,000 |
> | Estimated cost to complete | 30,000 |
> | Total estimated costs | 120,000 |
> | Percentage of completion at end of year 1 (£90,000/£120,000) | 75% |

Contract revenue (75% of £100,000)	75,000
Contract costs incurred to date	(90,000)
Provision for further expected loss on contract (expected cost to complete of £30,000 is not covered by expected future revenue of £25,000)	(5,000)
Total loss on contract	(20,000)

Provisions for losses are set against the amount due from the customer (if an asset) or added to the amount of deferred income due to customers (if a liability).

23.164 Where revenue has been validly recognised on a contract, but an uncertainty arises later about the recoverability of the related amount due from the customer (it is no longer probable), any provision against the amount due is recognised as an expense, rather than as a reduction of contract revenue. [FRS 102 para 23.27].

Example 2 – Expected loss on a construction contract

Entity A is constructing a building for its customer. The construction is in its second year of the three-year project.

Management had originally assessed the contract to be profitable and recognised a profit in year 1 of £20,000, based on the percentage of the contract that had been completed at that time. Management now believes the contract will incur a loss of £30,000.

Management has proposed that a loss of £30,000 on the contract is recognised in year 2, but has questioned how the profit of £20,000 recognised in year 1 should be treated.

Management should recognise a loss in respect of the contract of £50,000 in year 2. This represents a reversal of the £20,000 profit recognised in year 1 and the £30,000 loss expected on the contract as a whole.

The loss has been assessed through a revision of the estimated costs to completion. So, the appropriate accounting treatment is, to recognise the adjustment in the current year's results rather than record a prior-period adjustment.

Revenue generated from assets

23.165 The general revenue recognition criteria discussed in paragraph 23.10 above apply to revenue arising from the use by others of entity assets yielding interest, royalties and dividends. [FRS 102 para 23.28]. The standard also sets out the bases for recognising revenue arising from interest, royalties and dividends (as noted below).

Interest income

23.166 Interest income is recognised using the effective interest method, as described and illustrated in chapter 11. When calculating the effective interest rate, an entity includes any related fees, finance charges paid or received (such as points), transaction costs and other premiums or discounts [FRS 102 para 23.29a]. Financial services fees are discussed further in paragraph 23.127 above.

23.167 In some circumstances, the cost of an interest-bearing investment might include accrued interest. In this case, the subsequent receipt of the interest will need to be allocated between the amount accrued and revenue as illustrated in the following example.

> **Example – Accrued interest included in cost of investment**
>
> On 31 January 20X1, an entity acquires £200,000 nominal, 9.5% treasury stock at £101.62 per £100 nominal of the stock. Interest is payable on 1 June and 1 December each year. The entity prepares its financial statements to 31 December each year.
>
> The acquisition price of £101.62 includes accrued interest for 62 days from 1 December 20X0 to 31 January 20X1. The accrued interest amounts to £1.62 (62/182 × £4.75) per £100 of stock. So the interest that the entity receives on 1 June 20X1 should be allocated between the accrued interest and interest revenue for the period from 1 February to 1 June 20X1.
>
> On 31 Jan 20X1, the entity will record the following entries:
>
> | | Dr £ | Cr £ |
> |---|---|---|
> | Investments | 200,000 | |
> | Interest receivable | 3,240 | |
> | Cash (C2000 × 101.62) | | 203,240 |
>
> The company will recognise the following interest revenue during the year ended 31 December 20X1:
>
> | | £ |
> |---|---|
> | Interest received on 1 June 20X1 (£200,000 × 4.75%) | 9,500 |
> | Less accrued interest adjusted against interest receivable | 3,240 |
> | Interest revenue for the period 1 Feb to 31 May 20X1 | 6,260 |
> | Interest received on 1 Dec 20X1 (£200,000 × 4.75%) | 9,500 |
> | Interest accrued to 31 Dec 20X1 (£200,000 × 31/183 × 4.75%) | 1,610 |
> | Interest revenue for the period to 31 Dec 20X1 | 17,370 |

Licence fees and royalties

23.168 Licence fees and royalties include fees for the use by others of entity assets such as trademarks, patents, software, copyright, record masters, films and television programmes. Royalties should be recognised on an accruals basis in accordance with the relevant agreement's substance. [FRS 102 para 23.29(b)]. As a practical matter, this may be on a straight-line basis over the life of the agreement, for example, when a licensee has the right to use specified technology for a specified period of time [FRS 102 para 23A.34].

Royalties

23.169 The terms of an agreement normally indicate when the revenue has been earned, that is, when the seller has performed all or substantially of its obligations under the terms of the contract. In a royalty agreement, cash flows can take place over a significant period of time. Management will need to consider when there is a probable inflow of economic benefits that is reliably measurable. Where royalties are based on future sales by the licensee, it may be that even where the seller has no further obligations, it is not probable that the revenue will be received and/or it is not possible to reliably measure the revenue. In these circumstances it is likely that royalty income should not be recognised until the licensee has made its sales.

23.170 So, if an agreement provides for a 5% royalty to be received on each sale by a third party, it would be normal to recognise royalty income on the basis of 5% of total sales made by the third party as those sales are made.

23.171 On the other hand, in a similar situation, an up-front non-refundable payment is made to the entity by the other party and then a royalty of 1% of sales is receivable thereafter. In that situation, it is important to consider the agreement's substance. Where the seller has no further performance obligations once the licence has been granted and in substance there has been a sale of a term licence (see paras 23.175-176) then the sale will be one with both contingent and non-contingent consideration. Guidance on accounting for such sales is provided in paragraphs 23.31-23.43. If, in contrast, management identifies that the entity has further obligations over the term of the agreement then the up-front receipt is in substance an advance royalty. As such it would be appropriate to defer the up-front receipt and recognise it as income on an appropriate basis over the period that the services are provided..

Licensing

23.172 In general, revenue should not be recognised under licensing agreements until performance under the contract has occurred and the revenue has been earned.

> **Example 1 – Licence fee with continuing obligation**
>
> Entity A grants a licence to a customer to use its web-site, which contains proprietary databases. The licence allows the customer to use the web-site for a two year period (1 January 20X1 to 31 December 20X2). The licence fee of £60,000 is payable on 1 January 20X1.
>
> How should entity A account for the licence fee received?

The substance of the agreement is that the customer is paying for a service that is delivered over time. Although entity A will not incur incremental costs in serving the customer, it will incur costs to maintain the web site.

The revenue from the licence fee should be accrued over the period that reflects the provision of the service. The entity has an obligation to provide services for the next two years, and so the fee of £60,000 received on 1 January 20X1 should be recognised as deferred income. Each month for the period January 20X1 to December 20X2, an amount of £2,500 should be released from the liability and recognised as income to reflect the service that is delivered.

Example 2 – Licence fee with a trigger event

A film distributor grants a licence to a cinema operator. The licence entitles the cinema to show the film once on a certain date for consideration of the higher of a non-refundable guarantee or a percentage of the box office receipts.

Based on the facts provided, the film distributor should recognise the revenue on the date the film is shown. It is only when the film is shown that the revenue has been earned.

23.173 An assignment of rights for a non-refundable amount – under a non-cancellable contract that permits the licensee to use those rights freely and where the licensor has no remaining obligations to perform – is, in substance, a sale. [FRS 102 para 23A.35].

23.174 Another example where a licensing agreement might be recognised as an outright sale is if a non-refundable, one-off fee has been received for the foreign exhibition rights to a film that allow the licensee to use the rights at any time in specified countries without restriction. In such a situation, it might be appropriate to recognise the income when the fee is due. The licensor has no control over the product's further use or distribution and has no further action to perform under the contract, so the licensor has effectively sold the rights detailed in the licensing agreement [FRS 102 para 23A.35].

23.175 If a licence is granted for a limited period of time, the question arises as to whether revenue should be recognised at one point in time (for the sale of the licence) or spread over the licence term. The appropriate treatment will depend on the facts and circumstances. A fixed licence term is an indicator that the revenue should be recognised over the period; but, this is not definitive. The fixed period suggests that all of the licence's risks and rewards have not been transferred to the customer. In some situations, there might be no clear performance obligation for the seller after the transaction, and the asset's risks and rewards might have been transferred for the asset's entire useful life. In such a case, it might be appropriate to recognise the revenue up-front, even if the licence rights are sold for a fixed period only.

23.176 Whether it is appropriate to recognise revenue over the period of the licence or as a sale of goods will be a matter of judgement. The following additional indicators should be considered when making that judgement (the presence of the indicator implying that treatment as a sale might be appropriate):

- Fixed fee or non-refundable guarantee. The fee is pre-determined in amount. It is non-refundable and is not contingent on the occurrence of a future event.

- The contract is non-cancellable. This will ensure that risks and rewards have been transferred and the inflow of economic benefit to the seller is probable.

- The customer is able to exploit the rights freely. For this to be possible, the licence rights must be a separable component that can meet the sale of goods criteria on their own. The seller should not have any significant involvement during the contractual period and should not have the right to control or influence how the customer uses the rights (provided the customer acts within the specified contractual terms). The ability to sub-sell the rights, or even to stop using the licence at any time, might indicate that the customer is able to exploit the rights freely.

- The seller has no remaining obligations to perform after delivery. Such obligations might include significant updating of the product (for example, software upgrades), marketing efforts and fulfilling specified substantive obligations to maintain the reputation of the seller's business and promote the brand in question.

Dividends

23.177 Dividend income should be recognised when the shareholder's right to receive payment is established. [FRS 102 para 23.29(c)]. Determining when a right to receive payment has been established will vary from one jurisdiction to another. But, the accounting for the receipt of dividends should mirror the accounting in the paying company under section 32 of FRS 102.

23.178 Dividends payable to holders of equity instruments that are declared (that is, the dividends are appropriately authorised and no longer at the company's discretion) after the end of the reporting period should not be recognised as a liability at the end of the reporting period. [FRS 102 para 32.8]. Similarly, dividends should not be recognised as receivable if they have not been declared by the end of the reporting period.

23.179 In the UK, directors are normally permitted by the company's articles of association to pay interim dividends without shareholder approval, but the dividend is not a liability for the company until it is paid (see chapter 32). Final dividends are usually recommended by the directors and then declared by the shareholders by ordinary resolution. The shareholders cannot declare a dividend that exceeds the amount recommended by the directors. Therefore, the shareholders' right to an interim dividend is normally established when it is paid, and the right to a final dividend is established when it is declared by the

© 2013 PricewaterhouseCoopers LLP. All rights reserved.   23051

shareholders in general meeting. If the right to the dividend cannot be established until the income is received, recognition should be delayed until then.

23.180 The situation for parent entities' investments in subsidiaries is no different from that where the shareholding is held as a trade investment.

23.181 Similar to the situation described in paragraph 23.146 above , shares may be acquired 'cum div' or with dividends. In that case, the subsequent receipt of the dividend will need to be allocated against the cost of the investment rather than recognised as revenue.

Presentation and disclosure

Disclosure

General disclosures about revenue

23.182 An entity should disclose.

- The accounting policies adopted for the recognition of revenue, including the methods adopted to determine the stage of completion of transactions involving the rendering of services.

- The amount of each category of revenue recognised during the period, showing separately, at a minimum, revenue arising from:

- The sale of goods.

- The rendering of services.

- Interest.

- Royalties.

- Dividends.

- Commissions.

- Grants.

- Any other significant types of revenue.

[FRS 102 para 23.30].

23.183 If an entity has different policies for different types of revenue transactions, the policy for each material type of transaction should be disclosed.

Disclosures relating to revenue from construction contracts

23.184 For revenue arising from construction contracts, an entity should disclose the following:

- the amount of contract revenue recognised as revenue in the period;

- the methods used to determine the contract revenue recognised in the period; and

- the methods used to determine the stage of completion of contracts in progress.

[FRS 102 para 23.31].

23.185 The entity should present:

- the gross amount due from customers for contract work, as an asset; and

- the gross amount due to customers for contract work, as a liability.

[FRS 102 para 23.31].

23.186 The gross amount due from customers for contract work is the net amount of costs incurred plus recognised profits less the sum of recognised losses and progress billings. The net amount is an asset where costs incurred plus recognised profits (less recognised losses) exceed progress billings.

23.187 Where progress billings exceed costs incurred plus recognised profits (less recognised losses), the balance will be a net credit balance and represents deferred revenue. This is included in liabilities as amounts due to customers for contract work. The negative balance is not offset against positive work in progress balances on other contracts.

23.188 Progress billings are amounts billed for work performed on a contract, whether or not they have been paid by the customer. The work in progress billings used in the calculation of the gross amounts due from and to customers are the amounts actually invoiced. It follows that, where the net amount is an asset, it represents unbilled contract revenue. Amounts invoiced to customers, for which payment has not been received by the end of the reporting period, should be included in trade receivables. An example is shown below.

Example – Disclosure about construction costs

An entity commenced two construction contracts in the year. Details of the two contracts in progress at the end of the first reporting period are as follows:

	Contract 1	Contract 2	Total
	£	£	£
Costs incurred	60	40	100
Profit	40	–	40
Losses	–	(20)	(20)
Progress billings – amount invoiced	(70)	(10)	(80)
Amount received from customers	(50)	–	(50)

Contract revenue	100	40	140
Less progress payments	(70)	(10)	(80)
Less provision for losses	–	(20)	(20)
Gross amount due from customers	30	10	40
Trade receivable	20	–	20

Transitional issues

23.189 No special exemptions on revenue are available to first-time adopters under section 35 of FRS 102. So a first-time adopter must prepare its first financial statements as though the requirements of FRS 102 for revenue had always applied.

23.190 Entities transitioning from old UK GAAP to new UK GAAP are unlikely to face any significant issues on transition. This is because the requirements of UK GAAP (Application note G to FRS 5 and UITF 40) are, for the most part, very similar to those in FRS 102 dealing with revenue recognition, excluding construction contracts. In respect of construction contracts, the requirements in FRS 102 are also fairly similar to the requirements in SSAP 9.

23.191 Amounts in respect of these topics reported under old UK GAAP are likely to be carried forward without any modifications in the opening balance sheet as of the date of transition

23.192 However, UITF 40 contains specific guidance on the accounting for contingent consideration, but section 23 of FRS 102 is silent on the matter, so general principles should be used to assess the most appropriate accounting treatment. Possible approaches are discussed in paragraph 23.33 above. Under old UK GAAP guidance, *"Where the substance of a contract is that a right to consideration does not arise until the occurrence of a critical event, revenue is not recognised until that event occurs. This only applies where the right to consideration is conditional or contingent on a specified future event or outcome, the occurrence of which is outside the control of the seller."* [UITF 40 para 19]. As such, an entity which earns revenue that is contingent on events outside its control might be able to recognise revenue earlier under FRS 102, since it might assess that there is a probable inflow that it can reliably measured, even where the event that makes the inflow certain has not yet occurred.

23.193 There are also some differences in disclosures for balances reported for long-term contracts. SSAP 9 required long-term contract balances to be analysed between amounts recoverable on contracts (a debtor), work-in-progress (inventory) and payments on accounts (deducted from the above items or shown as a creditor). Section 23 of FRS 102 does not distinguish between amounts recoverable on contracts and work in progress, but presents contract balances to which the section applies separately from inventory to which section 13 of FRS 102 applies.

Chapter 24

Government grants

Chapter 24

Government grants

Introduction and scope

24.1 This chapter applies to accounting and disclosure requirements for all government grants and to disclosure of other forms of government assistance.

24.2 Section 24 of FRS 102 establishes accounting requirements only for government grants and not for other government assistance. So, the standard does not cover:

- Forms of government assistance that cannot reasonably have a value placed on them (for example, export credit guarantees where no other party will provide such a guarantee).

- Transactions with government that cannot be distinguished from the normal trading transactions of the entity (for example, purchase by the government of goods and services normally provided by the entity to third parties).

- Government assistance that is provided to an entity in the form of benefits that are available in determining taxable profit or tax loss, or are determined or limited on the basis of income tax liability (such as income tax holidays, investment tax credits, accelerated depreciation allowances and reduced income tax rates).

[FRS 102 paras 24.2, 24.3].

Definitions

24.3 The term 'government' is not defined in this standard, but the glossary confirms that *"Government refers to government, government agencies and similar bodies whether local, national or international"*. [FRS 102 Glossary of terms]. government could include, for example, local authorities and the European Union

24.4 A government grant is *"assistance by government in the form of a transfer of resources to an entity in return for past or future compliance with specified conditions relating to the operating activities of the entity"*. [FRS 102 para 24.1]. The resources transferred to the entity could be either monetary or non-monetary.

24.5 Operating activies are *"the principal revenue-producing activities of the entity and other activities that are not investing or financing activities"*. [FRS 102 Glossary of terms]

24.6 A 'performance-related condition' is defined as *"A condition that requires the performance of a particular level of service or units of output to be delivered, with*

payment of, or entitlement to, the resources conditional on that performance". [FRS 102 Glossary of terms].

24.7   Set out below is one example of government assistance that would qualify as a government grant, and another that would not.

> **Example 1 – Receipt of a non-transferable licence**
>
> In 20X0 an entity received from the government, free of charge, a non-transferable licence to catch 10 tonnes of fish per year for each of the next five years, in that jurisdiction's waters. The licence is issued to the entity to prevent overfishing in the jurisdiction's waters. Under the licence the entity is not allowed to catch more than 10 tonnes of fish in a particular year or it will be fined severely.
>
> The transfer of the fishing licence from the government to the entity is a government grant. The resource transferred is the non-transferable right to remove 10 tonnes of fish per year from that jurisdiction's waters for each of the next five years. It is received in return for future compliance with specified conditions relating to the operating activities of the entity (that is, the entity must not catch more than 10 tonnes of fish in a particular year during that five-year period).

> **Example 2 – Privatisation of a public service**
>
> A local government decided to privatise its ambulance service and published its criteria in a public bidding document. The entity that won the bid has an exclusive licence to provide ambulance services in the jurisdiction for a five-year period and will earn revenue from the fees that it charges.
>
> The transfer of the licence is not a government grant. Although the winning bidder must comply with the conditions in the public bidding document, this is a business licence which has been acquired under an arm's length transaction and not a government grant. Indeed, it is possible that the contract should be accounted for as a service concession arrangement for the provision of a public service (see chapter 34).

Recognition

General principles

24.8   As described above, when an entity receives a grant, its resources (whether monetary or not) are increased. The entity receives an inflow of economic benefits through receiving either a financial or non-financial asset, so it has received income as defined in FRS 102. As a result, the receipt of a grant will lead to additional income recognised in profit or loss. The definition of income is considered in more detail in chapter 23.

24.9   Grants are not recognised until there is reasonable assurance that:

- the entity will comply with the conditions attaching to them; and

- the grants will be received.

[FRS 102 para 24.3A].

24.10 FRS 102 provides two models for recognising government grant income. Entities can use either:

- the performance model, which requires an entity to recognise grant income in line with the entity's performance of the grant conditions, or

- the accruals model, which requires the grant income to be matched against the related costs for which the grant is intended to compensate.

[FRS 102 para 24.4].

The model chosen is an accounting policy choice, which must be applied consistently on a class-by-class basis. [FRS 102 para 24.4]. Each model is considered in more detail below.

24.11 Under either model, the asset received or receivable by the entity must be recognised at its fair value. [FRS 102 para 24.5].

24.12 Under either model, if a grant becomes repayable, it is recognised as a liability, provided the requirement to make the repayment meets the definition of a liability. [FRS 102 para 24.5A].

Performance model

24.13 When considering the performance model, the entity must recognise grant income when the grant's performance-related conditions are met. In specified circumstances, government grants can be awarded unconditionally, without regard to the entity's future actions or any requirement to incur further costs. Such grants might be given for immediate financial support, to compensate an entity that has incurred losses due to natural disasters such as flood or earthquake, or to reimburse costs previously incurred. They might also be given to finance an entity's general activities over a specified period, or to compensate for a loss of income.

24.14 Where grants are awarded on such a basis (that is, they do not impose specified future performance-related conditions on the recipient), they should be recognised in income when the grant proceeds are receivable. [FRS 102 para 24.5B(a)].

> **Example – Grant received in return for past performance**
>
> Entity A incurred expenses of C5,000 that related to training employees during the period May 20X0 to September 20X0. The employee training was a government requirement. Entity A entered into negotiations with the government for compensation for the training expenses incurred during the period. In February 20X1 the government agreed that it would compensate the entity for the expenses incurred for the year ended 31 December 20X0.
>
> The transfer of C5,000 is a government grant given to the entity in return for complying with specific conditions relating to the training of its employees. Although

entity A incurred the expenses for the year ended 31 December 20X0 and submitted a claim to the government, the claim was not approved by the government by 31 December 20X0 Until the claim is approved, it is not clear whether all the conditions relating to the receipt of the training grant have been met. So, the entity should not recognise the income in 20X0. The grant of C5,000 will only become receivable for the year ended 31 December 20X1 (that is, the year in which the government agreed to compensate A for the training expenses).

24.15 Income relating to a grant that imposes specified future performance-related conditions on the recipient is recognised only when the performance-related conditions are met. [FRS 102 para 24.5B(b)]. So, it is the relationship between the grant and the performance-related conditions that is crucial to the accounting treatment.

24.16 Also, if the performance-related conditions are not met when the grant is received, the entity should recognise the grant as a liability. [FRS 102 para 24.5B(c)]. It will be credited to income when the performance-related conditions are met. In practice, performance-related conditions can be many and varied, as considered in the following examples.

Example – Construction of manufacturing plant in a development zone

On 1 January 20X0 an entity received C500,000 from a national government as an incentive to establish a manufacturing plant in a particular location (that is, a designated development zone). The incentive is conditional on the plant being erected in the development zone, meeting various specifications (including environment and safety criteria) and starting commercial production on or before 31 December 20X1. If these conditions are not met, the entity will be liable to refund the entire C500,000 to the government.

All the performance conditions were satisfied on 30 March 20X1 when the entity began commercial production at the plant.

On 1 January 20X0, the entity records C500,000 on receipt of the grant as a liability, as the conditions specified in the grant have not been met.

On 30 March 20X1, the conditions are met, and so the liability is derecognised and the grant is credited to income.

It should be noted that maintaining a level of employment is not an uncommon grant condition. If there were an additional condition that employment be kept at a certain level for a period of three years from 30 March 20X1, and the full amount of the grant must be repaid at any time during the three-year period if the employment condition is breached, this condition would also have to be met in order to recognise the grant income.

In that case, the grant could not be recognised in profit or loss until the condition was satisfied (that is, at the end of the three-year period, provided the employment criteria was not breached at any time during that three-year period).

However, if the amount repayable in the event of breaching the employment condition reduced with the passage of time (for example, evenly over the three-year period), the entity would recognise the grant in profit or loss as the grant became non-repayable (for example, evenly over the three-year period).

If the entity had adopted the accruals model, the accounting would have been very different. See paragraph 24.24 below.

Accruals model

24.17 Under the accruals method, a government grant is matched with the expenditure that it is intended to compensate, and so it is recognised in profit or loss over the relevant period. [FRS 102 para 24.5D]. So the relationship between the grant and the related expenditure is of paramount importance in establishing the accounting treatment.

24.18 Where the grant is receivable as compensation for expenses or losses already incurred, or for the purpose of giving immediate financial support, it can be recognised in income when it is received or receivable. [FRS 102 para 24.5E].

24.19 If the grant does not relate to expenses already incurred, management must determine whether the grant relates to revenue or to assets. [FRS 102 para 24.5C].

24.20 Grants relating to revenue are intended to compensate the entity for the ongoing expenses of the business and are recognised in income on a systematic basis over the periods in which the entity recognises the related costs for which the grant is intended to compensate. [FRS 102 para 24.5D].

24.21 Grants relating to assets are recognised in income on a systematic basis over the expected useful life of the asset. [FRS 102 para 24.5F].

24.22 It might not always be clear whether the grant relates to assets or to revenue. For example, project grants could relate to the project's capital expenditure costs and the number of jobs created or safeguarded. In such circumstances, the entity will need to classify the grant as either relating to the assets or revenue, according to what it believes best reflects the substance of the grant.

Example — Capital or revenue grant?

An entity obtains a grant from an industrial development agency for an investment project. The project is a building to house a manufacturing plant. The principal terms are that the grant payments relate to the level of capital expenditure, and the grant's intention is to help ensure that imports of the product can be replaced with products produced in the country and to safeguard 500 jobs. The grant will have to be repaid if there is an underspend on capital or if the jobs are not safeguarded until 18 months after the date of the last fixed asset purchase.

This grant is related to capital expenditure. The employment condition should be seen as an additional condition to prevent replacement of labour by capital, rather than as the reason for the grant. If the grant were revenue, it would be related to revenue expenditure (such as a percentage of the payroll cost or a fixed amount per job safeguarded).

24.23 Government grants related to assets should be presented in the balance sheet as deferred income and not deducted from the asset's carrying value. [FRS 102 para 24.5G].

24.24 The deferred grant income is recognised in the income statement on a systematic basis over the asset's expected useful life.

Example — Treatment of a capital grant

The facts are the same as in Example 1 in paragraph 24.16 above. The factory is expected to have a useful life of 10 years and was available for use on 31 March 20X1. In this instance, the entity has adopted the accruals model. Following the example in paragraph 24.22 above, although there are certain employment conditions, Entity A has identified this as a capital grant.

The C500,000 grant relates to the construction of an asset and should be initially recognised as deferred income.

The deferred income should be recognised as income on a systematic basis over the asset's useful life.

The entity should recognise a liability on the balance sheet for the year ending 31 December 20X0. Once the plant is available for use, C50,000 should be recognised in the income statement in each year of the asset's 10-year useful life to match depreciation.

24.25 Grants are sometimes receivable on a different basis (for example, on the achievement of a non-financial objective). In such situations, the grant should be matched with the identifiable costs of achieving that objective. Such costs must be identified or estimated on a reasonable basis. For example, if a grant to support the manufacture of a new product is given on condition that jobs are created and maintained for a minimum period, the grant should be matched with the cost of providing the jobs for that period. As a result, a greater proportion of the grant might be recognised in the project's early stages because of higher non-productive and set-up costs.

Example — Grant payable on achievement of a non-financial goal

Entity A is awarded a government grant of C60,000 receivable over three years (C40,000 in year 1 and C10,000 in each of years 2 and 3), contingent on creating 10 new jobs and maintaining them for three years. The employees are recruited at a cost of C30,000, and the wage bill for the first year is C100,000, rising by C10,000 in each of the subsequent years.

The income of C60,000 should clearly be recognised over the three-year period to match the related costs.

In year 1, C21,667 of the C40,000 received from government will match the related costs of C130,000 incurred during the year, and should be recognised as income. The amount of the grant that has not yet been credited to income (that is, C18,333, being C40,000 of cash received less C21,667 credited to income) is reflected in the balance sheet.

Year	Labour cost	Grant income	Grant calculations	Deferred income	Deferred income calculations
1			60,000		40,000
	130,000	21,667	× (130/360)	18,333	- 21,667
2			60,000		50,000
	110,000	18,333	× (110/360)	10,000	- 40,000
3			60,000		
	120,000	20,000	× (120/360)	-	
	360,000	60,000			

Measurement of non-monetary assets

24.26 Government grants are not always made in cash. Sometimes, a government grant might take the form of a non-monetary asset, such as land or other resources. An entity should measure such grants at the fair value of the asset received or receivable. [FRS 102 para 24.5]. This is consistent with the revenue recognition principle of measuring consideration received or receivable at its fair value. Fair value is defined in the Glossary of terms in FRS 102 and discussed in detail in chapter 11.

Example – Receipt of a non-transferable licence

The facts are the same as in example 1 in paragraph 24.7 above. The fair value of the licence received is C350,000.

The grant of a non-transferable fishing licence from the government is an intangible asset that should be recognised in the financial statements (in accordance with section 18 of FRS 102) at its fair value of C350,000. The intangible asset should be amortised over the five-year licence period.

Under the performance model, the government grant (that is, the grant of the non-transferable fishing licence) is recognised as income in profit or loss in the period in which it becomes receivable. The licence will not be revoked (because there are no future performance conditions), so recognition is likely to be on the date in 20X1 on which the fishing licence was granted to the entity by the national government.

Under the accruals model, the grant income should be matched against the amortisation of the intangible asset over the five-year licence period.

If, and only if, the entity catches more than 100 tonnes of fish it must recognise a provision to pay the fine in accordance with section 21 of FRS 102 (see para 24.27 below).

Repayment of government grants

24.27 Government grants sometimes become repayable because specified conditions are not fulfilled. It is important to consider whether the condition is a 'performance-related condition' (as defined in para 24.6 above) or another condition of the grant. Where the entity has adopted the performance model as its accounting policy for grants, no income is recognised until the performance-related condition is fulfilled. But there could be a further condition of the grant (not related to the entity's performance) which, if breached, could result in a fine or repayment of some or all of the grant received. Where the accruals model is adopted, income could be recognised in advance of all performance conditions being met; and so it is more likely that a breach of conditions, either performance-related or another condition, could result in an adjustment to the income statement.

24.28 So, management should consider regularly whether there is the likelihood of a breach of conditions on which the grant was made. If such a breach has occurred, the liability to repay the grant should be provided in accordance with section 21 of FRS 102.

24.29 A government grant that becomes repayable gives rise to a revision to an accounting estimate and not to a prior year adjustment. The provision for repayment should be accounted for by first offsetting the provision against any unamortised deferred income relating to the grant. Where the provision exceeds any such deferred income, or where no deferred income exists, the provision should be charged immediately to profit or loss.

24.30 Where a grant related to an asset becomes repayable, the entity might need to assess whether the asset to which the grant relates is impaired. For instance, the entity might have received funds from the government to build a manufacturing plant. During the period of construction, the entity might have breached specified conditions relating to the grant which results in the grant being repayable. It is possible that the entity is unable to raise external sources of finance (or is able to do so only at very high interest rates) to complete the construction. This provides objective evidence that the asset might be impaired, in which case an impairment loss would need to be recognised under section 27 of FRS 102.

Presentation and disclosure

Presentation

24.31 Any grant received should be presented separately from the assets to which it relates. The deferred income amount in the balance sheet might need to be split between current and non-current liabilities where the grant is recognised in income over a period longer than a year. Presentation in the statement of financial position is discussed further in chapter 4.

24.32 Section 24 of the standard does not specify where grant income is presented in the income statement. In our view, it would be acceptable to present grant income as a credit in the income statement, either separately or under a general heading such as 'other income'. Alternatively, if the accruals method is adopted, the grant income could be deducted from the related expense. Whichever presentation is chosen, it should be applied consistently to all grants and from year to year.

Disclosure

24.33 An entity should disclose the following about government grants:

- The accounting policy adopted for grants (that is, whether the performance or accruals model has been adopted).

- The nature and amounts of government grants recognised in the financial statements.

- Unfulfilled conditions and other contingencies attaching to government grants that have not been recognised in income.

- An indication of other forms of government assistance from which the entity has directly benefited.

[FRS 102 para 24.8].

24.34 In respect of the last bullet point above, examples of other forms of government assistance from which the entity has directly benefited include free technical or marketing advice, the provision of guarantees, and loans at nil or low interest rates. Although some of these forms of government assistance are not recognised directly in the financial statement because of the difficulty in placing a value on them, the disclosure of the nature, extent and duration of such assistance is still considered to be relevant to users.

Transitional issues for UK companies

24.35 The requirements of UK accounting standard SSAP 4, 'Accounting for government grants', are very similar to the accruals model in section 24 of FRS 102, and so entities choosing the accruals model should not face any significant issues on transition.

24.36 The performance model is fundamentally different from the accruals model, and could result in a significantly different pattern of income recognition.

Chapter 25

Borrowing costs

Chapter 25

Borrowing costs

Introduction and scope

25.1 This chapter specifies the accounting treatment for borrowing costs. Entities can adopt a policy to either expense or capitalise borrowing costs that are directly attributable to constructing, producing or acquiring qualifying assets. [FRS 102 para 25.2].

Definition

25.2 Borrowing costs are interest and other costs that an entity incurs in connection with the borrowing of funds. Borrowing costs include:

- interest expense calculated using the effective interest method as described in section 11 of FRS 102;

- finance charges in respect of finance leases recognised in accordance with section 20 of FRS 102; and

- exchange differences arising from foreign currency borrowings to the extent that they are regarded as an adjustment to interest costs.

[FRS 102 para 25.1].

25.3 Although the standard simply refers to borrowing of funds, and the list in paragraph 25.2 above refers to interest costs, an entity can borrow funds using capital instruments other than straightforward loans from banks and financial institutions. Such capital instruments are likely to include preference shares that are classified as liabilities. In that situation, the cost of servicing those shares (namely, the dividends) would be included in borrowing costs.

25.4 Note that, to comply with paragraph 27 of Schedule 1 to SI 2008/410, only items that would otherwise be charged to the income statement (and are not appropriations of profit) are eligible for capitalisation as part of the cost of a tangible fixed asset. So, the actual or implied costs (including issue costs) of equity instruments are not eligible for capitalisation. Dividends on equity instruments are not finance costs because they are paid at the discretion of the issuer.

25.5 In addition to interest costs, borrowing costs would include premiums or discounts on borrowings, such as the discount on a zero coupon bond. The discount would be amortised over the life of the bond, using the effective interest rate method. Entities also incur various transaction costs, in connection with the raising of finance, which are regarded as an integral part of the effective yield on the instruments. These transaction costs are also amortised using the effective interest method. The borrowings themselves are likely to be basic financial instruments that will be accounted for at amortised cost in accordance with section 11 of FRS 102, and the finance costs will be calculated using the effective interest method. The effective interest method is explained further in chapter 11. But, where the borrowings are not basic financial instruments, they would be accounted for at fair value through profit or loss (as discussed in chapter 12). In that situation, any transaction costs incurred in connection with such borrowings would be recognised immediately in profit or loss.

Exchange differences as borrowing costs

25.6 Entities may sometimes raise funds in a foreign currency, because the interest cost in the foreign currency over the term of the borrowing is less than an equivalent loan in the entity's functional currency over the same term. Where this is so, the last bullet point in paragraph 25.2 above makes it clear that exchange differences arising on the borrowing should be regarded as a borrowing cost 'to the extent that they are regarded as an adjustment to interest cost'. The standard is silent on how to estimate the extent to which foreign exchange differences should be included in borrowing costs.

25.7 We believe that, as a minimum, the interest cost in foreign currency, translated at the actual exchange rate on the date on which the interest expense is incurred, should be included in borrowing costs. What is not so clear is how much of the exchange difference arising on the retranslation of the principal should be treated as borrowing costs. We believe that, in most circumstances, it is appropriate to include all of the exchange differences on the borrowing as interest cost, on the grounds that the exchange rate movements are largely a function of the differential interest rate between the two currencies.

Recognition

25.8 An entity can either:

- capitalise borrowing costs that are directly attributable to the acquisition, construction or production of a qualifying asset as part of the cost of that asset, or

- recognise all borrowing costs as an expense in profit or loss in the period in which they are incurred.

[FRS 102 para 25.2].

For entities that adopt the policy of capitalising borrowing costs, this should be applied consistently to a class of qualifying assets.

Capitalisation of borrowing costs

25.9 A qualifying asset is defined as:

> *"An asset that necessarily takes a substantial period of time to get ready for its intended use or sale. Depending on the circumstances any of the following may be qualifying assets:*
>
> *a) inventories;*
>
> *b) manufacturing plants;*
>
> *c) power generation facilities;*
>
> *d) intangible assets; and*
>
> *e) investment properties.*
>
> *Financial assets, and inventories that are produced over a short period of time, are not qualifying assets. Assets that are ready for their intended use or sale when acquired are not qualifying assets."*

[FRS 102 Glossary of terms].

25.10 Qualifying assets require a 'substantial period of time' to bring them to a saleable condition. Section 25 of FRS 102 does not define 'substantial period of time'. Management exercises judgement when determining which assets are qualifying assets, taking into account the nature of the asset. An asset that normally takes more than a year to be ready for use will usually be a qualifying asset. Once management chooses the criteria and types of asset, it applies this consistently to those types of asset. The notes to the financial statements should disclose, where relevant, how the assessment was performed, which criteria were considered, and the types of asset that are subject to capitalisation of borrowing costs. Property, plant and equipment that fall within the definition might include a manufacturing plant, power generation facilities and the construction of investment properties. Assets that are ready for their intended use or sale when acquired are not qualifying assets.

25.11 Management should assess whether an asset, at the date of acquisition, is 'ready for its intended use or sale'. The asset may be a qualifying asset, depending on how management intends to use it. For example, where an acquired asset can only be used in combination with a larger group of fixed assets (or was acquired specifically for the construction of one specific qualifying asset), the assessment of whether the acquired asset is a qualifying asset is made on a combined basis.

Example 1 – Qualifying asset based on management intention

A telecom entity has acquired a 4G licence. The licence could be sold or licensed to a third party. However, management intends to use it to operate a wireless network. Development of the network starts on acquisition of the licence.

Should borrowing costs related to the 4G licence be capitalised until the network is ready for its intended use?

Yes. The licence has been exclusively acquired to operate the wireless network. The fact that the licence can be used or licensed to a third party is irrelevant. The acquisition of the licence is the first step in a wider investment project (namely, developing the network). The network investment meets the definition of a qualifying asset under section 25 of FRS 102.

Example 2 – Qualifying asset

An entity has incurred expenses in acquiring a permit for the construction of an office building to use as its local headquarters.

Can borrowing costs on the acquisition of the permit be capitalised until the construction of the building is complete?

Yes, in relation to a permit which is specific to the building being constructed. It is the first step in a wider investment project for which development activity has commenced, and is part of the construction cost of the office building, which meets the definition of a qualifying asset.

Costs eligible for capitalisation

25.12 Directly attributable borrowing costs should be capitalised. 'Directly attributable' means those borrowing costs that would have been avoided (for example, by avoiding additional borrowings or by using the funds paid out for the asset to repay existing borrowings) if there had been no expenditure on the asset. [FRS 102 para 25.2A].

25.13 Directly attributable borrowing costs that should be capitalised include specific borrowing costs. If an entity borrows specifically for the purpose of obtaining a qualifying asset, the borrowing costs attributable to obtaining that asset are readily identifiable and should be capitalised. The amount of borrowing costs capitalised is limited to the actual borrowing costs incurred on that borrowing during the period, less any investment income on the temporary investment of those borrowings.

25.14 Directly attributable borrowing costs that should be capitalised also include general borrowing costs. Where funds are borrowed generally, the amount of borrowing costs eligible for capitalisation should be determined by applying a capitalisation rate to the expenditure on qualifying assets. The capitalisation rate is determined as the weighted average of the borrowing rates applicable to the entity's borrowings that are outstanding during the period, other than specific borrowings. The amount of borrowing costs capitalised during a period should not exceed the amount of borrowing costs incurred during the period. A reasonable method of calculating expenditure would be to calculate the weighted average carrying amount of the asset during the period (including borrowing costs previously capitalised) and apply the capitalisation rate to that figure.

Judgement is required when looking at a group of entities to determine which general borrowings to include in the weighted average capitalisation rate and for consolidated financial statements capitalisation is limited by the total consolidated amount of borrowing costs.

25.15 You must incur borrowing costs so entities that finance the construction of qualifying assets from equity cannot capitalise the cost of equity or use a notional borrowing rate.

Period of capitalisation of directly attributable costs and borrowing costs

25.16 Borrowing costs, both general and specific, are not capitalised in the period before the commencement of the activities necessary to prepare the asset for use. These activities will often coincide with the commencement of the asset's physical construction. But they also encompass more than the asset's physical construction. Activities could include technical and administrative work prior to the commencement of physical construction (for example, drawing up site plans and obtaining planning permission). Activities exclude holding the asset when no production or development that changes the asset's condition is being undertaken. We do not consider that capitalisation is appropriate for borrowing costs incurred while land acquired for building purposes is held without any development activity taking place.

25.17 The capitalisation of borrowing costs should be suspended when active development of the qualifying asset has paused. [FRS 102 para 25.2D(b)]. Borrowing costs might be incurred during an extended period in which activities necessary to prepare an asset for its intended use are interrupted. These costs do not qualify for capitalisation. However, capitalisation continues during periods when substantial technical and administrative work is being carried out. Capitalisation also continues when a temporary delay is a necessary part of the process of preparing an asset for its intended use.

25.18 Directly attributable costs, where they are incurred during the period in which the activities necessary to bring the asset to the location and condition for it to be capable of operating in the manner intended by management are being undertaken, are capitalised. The capitalisation of costs should cease when substantially all the activities necessary to prepare the asset for use are complete, even if the asset has not yet been brought into use. [FRS 102 para 25.2D(c)]. We consider that similar criteria are used to determine when to cease the capitalisation of borrowing costs under section 25 of the standard, where 'ready for use' means when the asset's physical construction is complete, even though routine administrative work might still continue. For example, if minor decoration of a property to a purchaser's specification is all that is outstanding, this indicates that the asset is substantially complete.

25.19 The capitalisation of borrowing costs associated with each part should cease when each part is capable of being used, even if it has not yet been put into use.

25.20 Borrowing costs should be capitalised gross of tax. A deferred tax liability is recorded where the conditions in section 29 of FRS 102 are met.

Presentation and disclosure

25.21 Where finance costs are capitalised, the fact that interest is included in determining the production cost of particular assets, and the amount of interest so included, should be disclosed in the notes. [SI 2008/410 1 Sch 27(3)].

25.22 A separate line item for finance cost should be included in the income statement or the statement of comprehensive income, if presented. [FRS 102 paras 5.5(b), 5.7].

25.23 Paragraph 5.5 of FRS 102 sets out the presentation requirements for the statement of comprehensive income. Paragraph 11.48(b) of the standard requires disclosure of total interest expense (using the effective interest method) for financial liabilities that are not measured at fair value through profit or loss. Where a policy of expensing borrowing costs is adopted, no additional disclosure is necessary.

25.24 Where a policy of capitalisation is adopted, an entity is required to disclose:

■ the amount of borrowing costs capitalised in the period; and

■ the capitalisation rate used.

Transitional issues

25.25 There are a number of matters that UK entities need to note when they transition from old UK GAAP (FRS 15) to FRS 102. These matters affect the measurement of property, plant and equipment that the entity recognises in its opening balance sheet at the date of transition to FRS 102 and is dependent on the entity's accounting policy under old UK GAAP and under FRS 102, as explained in the paragraphs below. These transitional issues can also be applied by analogy when transitioning to FRS 102 from another GAAP.

Entities that capitalised borrowing costs under old UK GAAP that will continue to capitalise borrowing costs under FRS 102

25.26   The borrowing cost component under old UK GAAP will need to be assessed for FRS 102 compliance. Old UK GAAP required capitalisation of interest incurred on specific borrowings based on the actual expenditures incurred to date on the asset; in other words, gross interest payable was capitalised, but interest on 'excess' (or unspent) borrowings was ignored. [FRS 15 para 22]. Because old UK GAAP only allowed interest on specific borrowings to be capitalised to the extent of the expenditure on the asset, there was no need to offset investment income on any unspent borrowings, because the interest on unspent borrowings had not been capitalised. Entities should assess all borrowing costs capitalised under old UK GAAP to ensure that the correct amount of interest had been included in the cost of the asset. It might be that the 'net' amount of interest was not significantly different from the 'gross' amount, but this must be ascertained.

Entities that capitalised borrowing costs under old UK GAAP that will expense borrowing costs as incurred under FRS 102

25.27   As there is no transitional relief for an entity electing to adopt an accounting policy of expensing borrowing costs as incurred under FRS 102 it must recalculate the carrying value of qualifying assets to remove borrowing costs capitalised from the cost of the qualifying asset in the opening balance sheet as of the date of transition and adjust retained earnings.

Entities that expensed borrowing costs as incurred under old UK GAAP that will capitalise borrowing costs under FRS 102

25.28   An entity electing to adopt an accounting policy of capitalising borrowing costs as part of the cost of the qualifying asset may elect to treat the date of transition to FRS 102 as the date on which capitalisation commences. [FRS 102 para 35.10(o)].

25.29   This can be effected by either:

■   Capitalising borrowing costs prospectively from the date of transition to FRS 102 to the carrying value of qualifying assets. This occurs where a deemed cost (that is, a previous revaluation or transition date fair value) has been established for an asset and used at the date of transition (see chapter 17). Any borrowing costs incurred prior to measurement of the asset are effectively ignored on transition to FRS 102, or

■   Capitalising borrowing costs retrospectively by adjusting the carrying value of qualifying assets to include cumulative borrowing costs in the carrying value of qualifying assets at the date of transition to FRS 102.

Entities that expensed borrowing costs as incurred under old UK GAAP that will continue to expense borrowing costs as incurred under FRS 102

25.30   Entities that expensed borrowing costs as incurred under old UK GAAP that elect to continue expensing borrowing costs as incurred under FRS 102 will experience no change and will have no transition issues to consider.

Chapter 26

Share-based payment

Chapter 26

Share-based payment

Introduction

26.1 Entities often use their own equity instruments (including shares or share options) to remunerate directors and employees or as consideration to third parties to acquire goods and services. This chapter addresses the accounting for share-based payment transactions in which the entity acquires goods or services in return for issuing its own equity instruments (referred to as 'equity-settled share-based payment transactions'), or in return for payments based on the price (or value) of its equity instruments (referred to as 'cash-settled share-based payment transactions').

26.2 The principal issues addressed in this chapter are the classification, recognition and measurement of share-based payment transactions, including those which give the entity or the counterparty a choice of settling the transaction in cash (or other assets) or in equity instruments of the entity or of another group entity. This chapter also addresses the accounting for modifications to the terms and conditions on which equity instruments were granted and specifies the disclosures required for share-based payment transactions.

26.3 For the most part, section 26 of FRS 102 refers to 'share-based payment transactions' which are defined in the glossary to the standard. But, in a number of places in the standard, there are references to 'share-based payment arrangements' which are not defined in the glossary to the standard. For consistency, this publication uses the same references as are used in the corresponding sections of the standard, assuming that both terms have the same meaning.

Scope

26.4 A share-based payment transaction is defined as *"a transaction in which the entity: (a) receives goods or services (including employee services) as consideration for its own equity instruments (including shares or share options); or (b) receives goods or services but has no obligation to settle the transaction with supplier; or (c) acquires goods or services by incurring liabilities to the supplier of those goods or services for amounts that are based on the price (or value) of the entity's shares or other equity instruments of the entity or another group entity"*. [FRS 102 Glossary of terms].

26.5 Section 26 of the standard applies to all share-based payment transactions (as defined above) and also specifically includes government-mandated plans under which equity instruments are acquired by investors (such as employees), either without providing any goods or services, or where the goods or services provided are clearly of less value than the fair value of the equity instruments granted (see para 26.95 below for further guidance).

26.6   Additionally, transactions which are settled in equity instruments (or cash based on the value of equity instruments) of another group entity are within the scope of section 26. [FRS 102 para 26.1A and 26.16]. The group is defined as including a *"parent and all its subsidiaries"*. [FRS 102 Glossary of terms]. So, transactions where an investor entity grants equity instruments to the employees of its associates or joint ventures would not be within the scope of section 26. But, under the principles of paragraphs 10.4 to 10.6 of FRS 102, the most appropriate treatment in such an arrangement maybe to apply section 26. Further guidance on the accounting treatment for each of the entities involved in a group share-based payment transaction is provided from paragraph 26.98 below.

26.7   There are no scope exclusions in section 26 of FRS 102; but section 26 deals with transactions in which the entity acquires goods and services as consideration for equity instruments of the entity or a group entity (or incurs a liability based on the value of equity instruments of the entity or a group entity). It follows that only when a transfer of equity instruments is clearly for a purpose other than payment for goods or services would it be outside section 26's scope. So, equity instruments issued as consideration for the acquisition of businesses or for the purposes of forming joint ventures would fall outside section 26's scope. But equity instruments granted to employees of the acquiree (in return for services or equity instruments issued by a joint venture entity to investors in exchange for goods or services) would be within section 26's scope. Conversely, transactions between the entity and employees acting in their capacity as shareholders would also be outside the scope of section 26, because these transactions are not consideration for employee services. Guidance on determining whether or not a transaction with an employee is in section 26's scope is provided from paragraph 26.104 below.

Transactions within the scope of section 26

26.8   The following are examples of transactions that are within the scope of section 26 of FRS 102.

> **Example 1 – Shares issued as consideration for a patent acquisition**
>
> Entity A is developing a new product and purchased a patent from entity B. The parties agreed a purchase price of 1,000 of entity A's shares. These will be issued to entity B within 60 days of finalising the legal documentation that transfers the patent from entity B to entity A.
>
> This is a share-based payment transaction, because entity A is acquiring goods in exchange for its shares. Although not specifically stated in section 26 of the standard, goods includes inventories, consumables, property, plant and equipment, intangible assets and other non-financial assets.

Example 2 – Shares issued as consideration for services rendered

Entity A hired an external consultant to carry out a strategic review of its business. The service was provided over a three-month period and will be settled by entity A issuing 1,000 of its shares.

This is a share-based payment transaction. Entity A has received consultancy services that will be paid for in entity A's own shares.

Example 3 – Business combination and continued employee service

Entity D acquires 90% of the share capital of entity E. As part of the acquisition, entity D grants entity E's employees share options that vest after two years if the employees remain in service.

In this transaction, equity instruments are granted to employees of the acquiree in their capacity as employees, and so the transaction falls within section 26's scope.

Transactions outside the scope of section 26

26.9 The following are examples of transactions that are outside the scope of section 26 of FRS 102.

Example 1 – Commodity contracts

Entity H enters into a contract to purchase 100 tonnes of cocoa beans. The purchase price will be settled in cash at an amount equal to the value of 1,000 of entity H's shares. However, the entity could settle the contract at any time by paying an amount equal to the current market value of 1,000 of its shares less the market value of 100 tonnes of cocoa beans. The entity has entered into the contract as part of its hedging strategy and has no intention of taking physical delivery of the cocoa beans.

The transaction meets the definition of a share-based payment transaction (that is, entity H has acquired goods in exchange for a payment of which the amount will be based on the value of its shares). But the contract could be settled net and has not been entered into in order to satisfy entity H's expected purchase, sale or usage requirements. So, the transaction is outside section 26's scope and is instead dealt with under the requirements of sections 11 and 12 of the standard.

Example 2 – Cash payments dependent on earnings multiple

Entity J issued share appreciation rights (SARs) to its employees. The SARs entitle the employees to a payment equal to any increase in the entity's share price between the grant date and the vesting date. The arrangement's terms and conditions define the share price used to calculate payments to employees as five times EBITDA divided by the number of shares in issue.

Section 26 of the standard is unlikely to be applicable to this transaction; this is because a fixed multiple of EBITDA is not likely to reflect the fair value of the entity's share price. If it does not, management should apply section 28 to this transaction, because it is a deferred compensation arrangement.

Classification of share-based payment transactions

26.10 Share-based payment transactions are classified in the following three categories:

- Equity-settled share-based payment transactions.

- Cash-settled share-based payment transactions.

- Transactions with settlement alternatives.

[FRS 102 para 26.1].

The distinctions between these categories are explained below.

Equity-settled share-based payment transaction

26.11 An equity-settled share-based payment transaction is defined as a *"share-based payment transaction in which the entity: (a) receives goods or services as consideration for its own equity instruments (including shares or share options); or (b) receives goods or services but has no obligation to settle the transaction with the supplier"*. [FRS 102 Glossary of terms].

26.12 An example of an equity-settled share-based payment transaction is given below.

> **Example – Grant of equity instruments to employees**
>
> Entity F awards 100 share options to each of its 15 employees. The only condition associated with the award is that recipients must remain in entity A's employment until the entity is either sold or listed on a stock exchange. At the point of sale or listing, the employees can realise the value of their shares by exchanging them for either listed shares or for cash equal to the fair value of the shares. This is an equity-settled share-based payment transaction, because entity F is issuing its own equity instruments in exchange for employee services and because there is an external market for the shares, entity F is not required to pay cash to settle these shares.

Cash-settled share-based payment transaction

26.13 A cash-settled share-based payment transaction is defined as a *"share-based payment transaction in which the entity acquires goods or services by incurring a liability to transfer cash or other assets to the supplier of those goods or services for amounts that are based on the price (or value) of the entity's shares or other equity instruments of the entity or another group entity"*. [FRS 102 Glossary of terms].

26.14 The reference to equity or other equity instruments in the above definition might cause some confusion in practice. The definition of an equity instrument is the same under both sections 22 and 26 of FRS 102, but these sections establish different principles for classifying financial instruments as either equity or liabilities. As a result, the classification of an equity instrument as either equity or a liability might be different depending on which section of the standard is applied. Some share-based payment transactions might be based on the change in price of an instrument that takes the legal form of a share, but which falls to be classified as a liability under section 26, as a cash-settled share-based payment. Such payments that are within the scope of section 26 should be treated as cash-settled share-based payments, even though the instrument is not classified as an equity instrument under section 22. This is because there are differences between the sections of the standard dealing with financial instruments and share-based payments, particularly in the area of classification of financial instruments as equity or liabilities.

26.15 Typical examples of cash-settled share-based payment transactions include mandatorily redeemable shares, share appreciation rights (giving employees the right to receive future cash payments based on the increase in the entity's share price), 'phantom' share plans (where employees receive future cash payments equal to the value of the entity's shares) and other long-term incentive awards.

26.16 Sometimes, transactions that are actually settled in shares should be treated as cash-settled because this is reflective of their substance. For example, an entity might grant to its employees a right to shares that are redeemable mandatorily (such as on cessation of employment). The entity has an obligation to make cash payment, so the transaction would be treated as cash-settled.

26.17 In practice, it is unlikely that third parties providing goods and services to an unlisted entity would be willing to accept shares of the entity as consideration, because of the illiquid nature of the unlisted shares. This is despite the fact that the entity is able to measure the fair value of the equity instrument granted. For this reason, share-based payments settled with unlisted shares are more commonly encountered in transactions between an entity and its employees. In this situation, where the entity repurchases shares from employees to settle the award and provide the employees with value in the awards, the transaction should be classified as cash-settled. An example of an equity-settled share-based payment with employees is provided above.

> **Example – Repurchase of shares**
>
> Entity A is a private entity. Its shareholders have no plans to list or sell the business. Entity A grants shares to employees in exchange for services. These shares are non-transferable, and each employee has the obligation to sell the shares back to entity A on termination of employment, at the initial subscription price. But, after two years, if the individuals are still employed by entity A, they have the right to sell the shares to entity A at any time, for the market price of the shares on that date.
>
> This award is settled in cash, based on entity A's share price, and so the transaction should be accounted for as a cash-settled share-based payment award.

26.18 The accounting for cash-settled share-based payment transactions is considered at paragraph 26.80 onwards below.

Transactions with settlement alternatives

26.19 The terms of some share-based payment transactions, in which the entity receives or acquires goods or services, might offer a choice of settlement. The terms of the arrangement might give either the entity or the supplier of those goods or services a choice of whether the entity settles the transaction in cash (or other assets) or in equity instruments. The accounting for share-based payment transactions with cash alternatives is considered at paragraph 26.87 onwards below.

Recognition

General

26.20 The goods or services received or acquired in a share-based payment transaction should be recognised by the entity when the goods are obtained or as the services are received. A corresponding increase in equity is recognised if the goods or services were received in an equity-settled share-based payment transaction (see para 26.11 above). A liability is recognised if the goods or services were acquired in a cash-settled share-based payment transaction. [FRS 102 para 26.3].

26.21 Goods or services obtained in a share-based payment transaction are recognised as an expense, unless they qualify for recognition as assets (in which case, the expense will be charged to the income statement when the asset is sold, depreciated or impaired). For example, where the purchase cost of inventory is to be settled in equity shares or right to equity shares, the expense would only be recognised when the inventory is sold or written down.

26.22 For equity-settled transactions, section 26 of FRS 102 does not stipulate where in equity an entity should present the credit entry. It is often presented in the profit and loss reserve, or in a separate share-based payment reserve. But company law does not permit the credit to be presented in either share capital or share premium.

26.23 An entity should not present the credit entry in a statement of comprehensive income; this is because the credit reflects the issue of an equity instrument and does not represent a gain. So the credit entry should be presented in the statement of changes in equity.

Timing of recognition and vesting period

26.24 As noted above, the goods or services acquired in a share-based payment transaction should be recognised when they are received. Typically, it will be a question of fact as to when this occurs. In the case of goods, it will be obvious when this occurs. But, sometimes, as in the case of employee services, this will be less obvious. For example, an entity might grant share options to its employees whereby performance conditions need to be satisfied over three years, and even then they might only be exercised after a further year has elapsed, and the employee forfeits the options if they leave prior to exercise. Should an expense be recognised when the award is granted, over the three-year performance period, or over the longer period until the options vest (that is, the employees become unconditionally entitled to exercise the options)?

26.25 The period over which services are recognised should be determined by applying the standard's concept of 'vesting'. Vesting is defined as:

> "*Become an entitlement. Under a share-based payment arrangement, a counterparty's right to receive cash, other assets or equity instruments of the entity vests when the counterparty's entitlement is no longer conditional on the satisfaction of any vesting conditions.*" [FRS 102 Glossary of terms].

26.26 Section 26 concludes that, where share-based payment transactions granted to employees vest immediately (that is, the employee is not required to complete a service period before becoming unconditionally entitled to the award), in the absence of evidence to the contrary, the entity should presume that they represent consideration for services already rendered. So, the entity should recognise the services received in full, with a corresponding increase in equity or liabilities, on the date the share-based payments have been granted. [FRS 102 para 26.5].

26.27 On the other hand, if the share-based payments do not vest until the employees have completed a specified period of service, the entity should presume that services are to be rendered over that period. This is referred to as the 'vesting period', which is the period over which all the specified vesting conditions for a share-based payment transaction are to be satisfied. So, the entity should recognise the services over the vesting period, with a corresponding increase in equity or liabilities. [FRS 102 para 26.6]. As noted above, whether the corresponding entry is recognised in equity or liabilities will depend on the classification of the award.

26.28 The standard does not distinguish between vesting periods during which employees have to satisfy specific performance conditions and vesting periods during which there are no particular requirements other than to remain in the entity's employment (service conditions). The period over which employee services would be recognised is the period until the options vest and employees become unconditionally entitled to them, rather than any shorter period during which the employees must satisfy the performance conditions. Vesting conditions are considered further at paragraph 26.39 onwards.

26.29 The following examples illustrate the period over which all specified vesting conditions are to be satisfied, which could be different for different employees in the same award plan.

Example 1 – Options awarded instead of annual bonus

An entity normally awards options annually instead of an annual bonus. The entity grants options representing an annual bonus in 20X4, in respect of the year to December 20X3. The award is not exercisable for three years, and the employee must remain with the entity throughout this period.

In this situation, there is an expectation on the part of the employees that they will receive a bonus each year. So, employees are providing services in 20X3 to earn the right to equity instruments. But there is an additional period of service that the employee is required to complete until the equity instrument vests unconditionally with them. Therefore, the expense should be over the performance period (20X3) and the service period (20X4 to 20X6). The vesting period is a total of four years.

It should be noted that, if the employee was not required to remain with the entity for the three-year period, the vesting period would not include the three-year delay until the award is exercisable.

Example 2 – Award exercisable on chosen retirement date

An employee is currently 58 years old and is granted some options that vest over five years if he continues in employment. But this employee has the option to retire anytime between 60 and 65 (inclusive) without requiring the employer's consent. If the employee chooses to retire at the age of 60, the employee is able to keep the options, which become exercisable at that date. The vesting period for these options is two years, because the employee becomes entitled to (and can walk away with) the options at the age of 60, whether he chooses to continue working beyond that date or not.

Example 3 – Staged vesting (also known as tranched or graded vesting)

In some share-based payment plans, awards vest in stages or instalments over the vesting period. Section 26 of FRS 102 does not contain any accounting requirements on such vesting. Entities are therefore permitted to apply straight line vesting or alternatively to account for each instalment as a separate award (as explained in the example below). For the whole award, the second approach results in a front loaded share-based payment charge but has the advantage of being aligned with IFRS accounting requirements, so may be of more relevance to entities looking to have consistent reporting with IFRS. Further information on the application of staged vesting can be found in our Manual of Accounting – IFRS for the UK.

Measurement of equity-settled transactions

General

26.30 In an equity-settled share-based payment transaction, an entity should measure the goods or services received, and the corresponding increase in equity, at the fair value of those goods or services. Ideally, the entity should be able to measure the fair value of the goods or services received directly. But, if the entity cannot estimate reliably the fair value of the goods or services received, it should measure their value, and the corresponding increase in equity, by reference to the fair value of the equity instruments granted as consideration. [FRS 102 para 26.7].

This is sometimes referred to as the 'indirect method'. In these circumstances, the grant date fair value of the equity instrument represents the best surrogate for the price of the goods or services.

26.31 The principle described in the previous paragraph is best illustrated in the context of employee services. Shares and share options are often granted to employees as part of their remuneration package, in addition to a cash salary and other employment benefits. It is not generally possible to measure directly the services received for particular components of an employee's remuneration package. Further, options or shares might be granted as part of a bonus arrangement, rather than as an element of basic remuneration. By granting options, in addition to other remuneration, the entity is paying additional remuneration to obtain additional benefits. Estimating the fair value of those additional benefits is likely to be difficult. So, section 26 requires an entity to measure the fair value of the employee services (including similar services provided by others, discussed in para 26.32 below) received by reference to the fair value of the equity instruments. [FRS 102 para 26.7].

Transactions with employees (including others providing similar services)

26.32 For transactions with employees (including others providing similar services), the fair value of the equity instruments should be measured at grant date. [FRS 102 para 26.8]. Section 26 does not define 'others providing similar services'; but, in our view, 'others providing similar services' could include individuals who:

- Render personal services to the entity and are regarded as employees for legal or tax purposes.

- Work for the entity under its direction in the same way as individuals considered employees for legal or tax purposes.

- Render services that are similar to those rendered by employees.

Further reference to 'employees' in this chapter will include others providing similar services.

Transactions with parties other than employees

26.33 For transactions with parties other than employees (and others providing similar services), the measurement date is the date when the entity obtains the goods or when the services are rendered. [FRS 102 para 26.8]. This measurement date applies whether the fair value of the goods or services obtained can be measured directly or indirectly by reference to the fair value of the equity instrument granted. Contrast this with services provided by employees, where the measurement date is the date when equity instruments are granted. The overall position can be summarised as follows:

Counterparty	Measurement basis	Measurement date	Recognition date
Employees	Fair value of equity instrument granted	Grant date	Service date – when services are received
Non-employees	Fair value of goods or services received (or fair value of equity instrument granted, if fair value of goods or services received cannot be estimated reliably)	Service date – when goods or services are received	Date of receipt – when goods or services are received

26.34 Measurement of fair value when the goods or services are received is illustrated in the following examples.

Example 1 – Measurement of fair value by the direct method

Entity A is a small start-up company. To assist it in developing its business, it receives consultancy services from entity B. The entities have agreed that, because entity A has scarce cash resources, the consideration for the consultancy services will be in the form of entity A's ordinary shares. This is treated as an equity-settled share-based payment, because entity A has no obligation to pay cash to settle the shares. The agreed rate is one share for each hour of consultancy services. Entity B has a publicised schedule of scale rates, and the amount charged for a project of this nature is normally £100 per hour. So, an expense and an increase in equity of £100 should be recognised by entity A for each hour of consultancy services received.

Note that the counterparty providing services is an entity rather than an individual, and so does not fall within the category of employees or others providing similar services.

Example 2 – Measurement of fair value by the indirect method

The facts are similar to example 1, except that further shares are issued to entity B as it assists entity A in respect of a particular project, with 100 shares being awarded if the project is successful.

In this case, it might not be possible to measure reliably the fair value of the consultancy services themselves. The value of the transaction and shares received might have little to do with the value derived from the time spent by the consultants. Instead, the fair value should be measured as the services are rendered by reference to the fair value of the shares offered as consideration.

Grant date

26.35 Grant date is defined as *"the date at which the entity and another party (including an employee) agree to a share-based payment arrangement, being when the entity and the counterparty have a shared understanding of the terms and conditions of the arrangement. At grant date the entity confers on the counterparty the right to cash, other assets, or equity instruments of the entity, provided the* *specified vesting conditions, if any, are met. If that agreement is subject to an approval process (for example, by shareholders), grant date is the date when that approval is obtained".* [FRS 102 Glossary of terms].

26.36 As noted above, grant date is when both parties agree to a share-based payment transaction. The word 'agree' is used in its usual sense, which means that there must be both an offer and acceptance of that offer. Hence, the date at which one party makes an offer to another party is not the grant date. The date of grant is when that other party accepts the offer. For many share-based payment transactions with employees, the employees' agreement is often implicit (that is, the agreement is evidenced by their commencing to render services and not by signing an explicit contract).

26.37 It will often be clear when the parties in a share-based payment transaction have a shared understanding of the terms and conditions of the arrangement. But it might be that some terms need to be agreed on a later date; in that case, the grant date is on that later date, when all of the terms and conditions have been agreed. Similar questions are raised when equity instruments are granted subject to an approval process that takes place after the employees have begun rendering services in respect of that grant.

26.38 Section 26 of FRS 102 does not address situations where employees have already begun rendering services to the entity before the grant date is established. But section 26 does require the entity to recognise employee services as they are received over the vesting period. Our view is that the entity should start recognising the expense in the period in which the employees begin rendering services to the entity (in expectation of satisfying the award service condition), even if this is in advance of the grant date. The grant date fair value of the equity instruments should be estimated, for example, by reference to the fair value of the equity instruments at the balance sheet date. The expense should be based on an estimated amount until the date of grant has been established. Once the grant date is established, the entity should revise the earlier estimates, so that the amounts recognised for services received in respect of the grant are ultimately based on the grant date fair value of the equity instruments. This is considered in the following examples.

> **Example 1 – Individual notification of award**
>
> An award is approved by the board/shareholders on 1 December 20X1. The general terms and conditions of the award set out the relevant employee population that will participate in the award, but provide insufficient information to determine each employee's share. The general terms and conditions are posted to the entity's website on 31 December 20X1. The employees are individually informed of their shares on 1 February 20X2.
>
> Although the general terms and conditions are available on the website on 31 December 20X1, the employees only know about their individual entitlement on 1 February 20X2. So, the grant date is 1 February 20X2, because this is the date when all the terms and conditions of the award are finalised and accepted by the employees. But

the vesting period begins on 31 December 20X1 because this is when employees become aware of the award's general terms and conditions and begin providing services.

Example 2 – Award subject to shareholder approval

An award is communicated to individual employees on 1 December 20X1, subject to shareholder approval. The award is approved by shareholders on 1 February 20X2, with the same terms as had initially been communicated to employees. A letter to formalise the award is sent to individual employees on 1 March 20X2.

The award is subject to an approval process (in this example, by shareholders), so the grant date is the date when that approval is obtained. The letter to formalise the award is mainly administrative, both the employees and the employer have a shared understanding on 1 February 20X2, and so this is the grant date. The vesting period starts on 1 December 20X1 because this is when employees begin providing services in working towards the award.

If the entity's year end is 31 December 20X1, the entity should recognise the employee services as they are received. So, the entity should recognise the expense for services received during the period from service commencement date (1 December 20X1) to grant date (1 February 20X2). For this purpose, the entity should estimate the grant date fair value of the equity instruments by estimating the fair value of the equity instruments at the end of the reporting period (that is, 31 December 20X1). On the grant date of 1 February 20X2, management should revise the earlier estimate so that the amounts recognised for services received in respect of the grant are ultimately based on the 1 February 20X2 grant date fair value of the equity instruments.

Vesting conditions

26.39 A grant of equity instruments might be conditional on the counterparty (usually employees) satisfying specified vesting conditions. Vesting conditions are conditions that must be satisfied before the counterparty becomes unconditionally entitled to receive cash, other assets or equity instruments of the entity in a share-based payment transaction. Vesting conditions can be related to service or to performance. [FRS 102 para 26.9].

Service conditions

26.40 A service condition is one that requires the employees to complete a specified period of service. For example where an entity grants a share-based payment award conditional upon continued employment by the employee. Service conditions are treated in the same way as non-market performance conditions. The accounting for service conditions is discussed in paragraph 26.47 below.

Performance conditions

26.41 There might also be performance conditions that must be satisfied. Performance conditions can be either:

- Market vesting conditions where the vesting of equity instruments is related to the market price of the entity's shares.

- Non-market vesting conditions where the vesting of equity instruments is related to specific performance targets, other than targets related to the market price of the entity's shares, such as a specified growth in profit.

[FRS 102 para 26.9].

26.42 The following table illustrates some of the more common market and non-market conditions.

Market conditions	Non-market conditions
Achieve a minimum share price by a specified date.	Remain in employment for a specified period of time.
Achieve a total shareholder return target (for an entity in the group with listed shares).	Achieve earnings per share or profit targets.
Outperform a share price index.	Complete a particular project. Successful IPO (see para 26.109 below).

Non-vesting conditions

26.43 Section 26 of FRS 102 refers to 'non-vesting conditions' but does not define this term. In our view, a non-vesting condition is any other condition in a share-based payment transaction which is not a service condition or a performance condition. Examples of non-vesting conditions might include a requirement to make monthly savings during the vesting period (such as save as you earn ('SAYE') plans) or a restriction on the transfer of vested equity instruments. Although such requirements occur during the vesting period, they are often wholly within the control of the employee and the conditions are not related to duties specified in an employee's employment contract. So, they do not determine whether or not the entity receives the services linked to the shares.

Accounting for vesting conditions

26.44 All market vesting conditions (see para 26.42 above) and non-vesting conditions (see para 26.43 above) are taken into account when determining the fair value of shares or share options at the measurement date. Market conditions and non-vesting conditions are ignored for the purposes of estimating the number of awards that will vest; and there is no subsequent adjustment to the charge, whatever the outcome. [FRS 102 para 26.9]. In other words, equity instruments granted subject to such conditions are considered to vest, whether or not that market condition is fulfilled, on the grounds that the effect of the condition has already been taken into account in determining the grant date fair value of the award. This means that an expense is recognised even if the market performance condition is not met, provided that all other service and non-market vesting conditions (if any) are satisfied. An example of a share-based payment, where vesting is conditional on a market condition, is included in paragraph 26.48 below.

26.45 All vesting conditions other than market vesting conditions and non-vesting conditions (that is, those that relate solely to employee services (see para 26.40 above) or to non-market performance conditions (see para 26.42 above)) are not taken into account when estimating the fair value of the shares or share options at the measurement date. Instead, those vesting conditions are included in the measurement of the transaction amount by adjusting the number of equity instruments expected to vest. At each subsequent reporting date, the entity should revise that estimate if new information indicates that the number of equity instruments expected to vest differs from previous estimates. On vesting date, the entity should revise the estimate to equal the number of equity instruments that ultimately vested, based on the grant date fair value of the equity instrument. So, on a cumulative basis, no amount is recognised for goods or services received if the awards do not vest because of failure to satisfy a service condition or a non-market performance condition. [FRS 102 para 26.9].

26.46 The following diagram illustrates the principles discussed above.

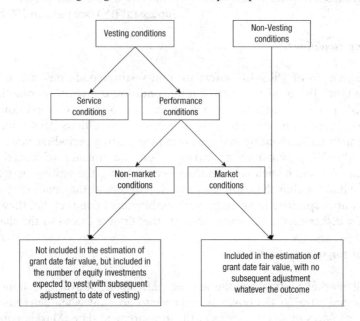

Non-market and service vesting conditions

26.47 The measurement of equity-settled share-based payment transactions that are subject to non-market or service vesting conditions has the overall objective that, at the end of the vesting period, the cumulative charge recognised in the income statement should be based on the number of equity instruments that have actually vested multiplied by their grant date fair value. The measurement of grant date fair value excludes the effect of non-market and service vesting conditions. The number of equity instruments expected to vest is re-estimated at each reporting period and at the vesting date. The amount of expense recognised in a reporting period is the difference between the cumulative expense so determined and the amount already charged in previous periods. A number of examples, categorised according to the type of non-market vesting condition, are given below to illustrate these points.

Example 1 – Grant of equity instruments with a time-based vesting condition

On 1 January 20X1, entity A made an award of 1,000 options to each of its 60 employees. The only condition associated with the award is that recipients must remain in entity A's employment for three years. The grant date fair value of each option is £5.

At the date of the award, management estimated that 10% of employees (that is, six employees) would leave the entity before the end of three years and so forfeit their rights to the share options.

During 20X2 it became apparent that fewer employees than expected were leaving, so management revised its estimate of the number of leavers to only 5% (that is, three employees). At the end of 20X3, awards to 55 employees actually vested.

Year	Calculation of cumulative expense	Cumulative expense £	Expense for period £
31/12/X1	(1,000 options x 90% x 60 x £5 x $^1/_3$ years)	90,000	90,000
31/12/X2	(1,000 options x 95% x 60 x £5 x $^2/_3$ years)	190,000	100,000
31/12/X3	(1,000 options x 55 x £5)	275,000	85,000

Example 2 – Grant of equity instruments in which the length of the vesting period varies

On 1 January 20X5, entity C granted 1,000 shares to each of its 500 employees, on condition that the employees remained in the employment of entity C throughout the vesting period. The shares will vest as follows: at the end of 20X5 if the entity's earnings increase by more than 20%; at the end of 20X6 if the entity's earnings increase by more than an average of 15% over the two-year period; and at the end of 20X7 if the entity's earnings increase by more than an average of 10% over the three-year period. If the entity's earnings increase by less than an average of 10% over the three-year period, no shares will vest. The grant date fair value of each share at 1 January 20X5 is £6 (which is assumed to be independent of the length of the vesting period, as no dividends are expected to be paid before 20X8).

During 20X5, earnings increased by 16% and 25 employees left the entity. Management forecast that earnings would grow at a similar rate in 20X6, so the share awards would vest at the end of 20X6. Management also estimated that a further 25 employees would leave the entity, so 450 awards would vest.

During 20X6, earnings increased by only 10%, resulting in an average for the two-year period of 13%; so the awards did not vest. But management forecast that earnings growth for 20X7 would be at least 4%, thereby achieving the average of 10% per year.

Thirty employees left the entity during 20X6, and management estimated a similar level of departures for 20X7, so 415 awards would vest.

During 20X7, earnings increased by 10% (resulting in an average over the three-year period of 12%) so the awards vested, and 27 employees left the entity.

The amount recognised as an expense in each year will be as follows:

Year	Calculation of cumulative expense	Cumulative expense	Expense for period
		£	£
31 December 20X5	1,350,000	1,350,000	$450 \times 1,000 \times 6 \times \frac{1}{2}$*
31 December 20X6	310,000	1,660,000	$415 \times 1,000 \times 6 \times \frac{2}{3}$
31 December 20X7	848,000	2,508,000	$418 \times 1,000 \times 6$

* $\frac{1}{2}$ not $\frac{1}{3}$ because, at the end of 20X5, management expected the award to vest at the end of 20X6

Example 3 – Grant with a performance condition in which the number of equity instruments varies

On 1 January 20X1, entity A made an award of shares to each of its 50 employees. The number of shares to which each employee will become entitled depends on growth in profit before tax (PBT) during the next three years, as noted below:

- If PBT increases by an average of 10% over the next three years, each employee will receive 100 shares.

- If PBT increases by an average of 15%, each employee will receive 200 shares.

- If PBT increases by an average of 20%, each employee will receive 300 shares.

No shares will be awarded if PBT increases by less than 10%.

The awards will vest at the end of 31 December 20X3, provided that the employees remain in the entity's employment for three years.

On the grant date of 1 January 20X1, the fair value of each share award is £12.

PBT is a non-market performance condition because it is not dependent on the market price of the entity's shares. So the PBT growth condition is relevant in determining the number of awards that will vest.

On the grant date of 1 January 20X1, management estimates that the PBT will increase by an average of 10% per year, and therefore expects that, for each employee who remains in service until the end of 31 December 20X3, 100 shares will vest. Management also estimates that 40% of employees (a total of 20) will leave before the end of year 3, so 30 awards will vest.

26016

By the end of 31 December 20X1 (the first accounting period end date), seven employees have left, and management expects that a total of 15 employees will leave by the end of 31 December 20X3, so that 35 awards would vest. Entity A's PBT increased by 16% and management forecast similar growth for the next two years. So, management predicts that each employee would receive 200 shares.

But 20X2 was a comparatively poor year and PBT increased by just 12%, resulting in an average increase for the two-year period of 14%. So management cut back its forecast, predicting growth of 14% for 20X3. On this basis, each employee would receive 100 shares. Six employees left during 20X2, bringing the total to 13 to date. Management now expects that only three additional employees will leave before 31 December 20X3, so 34 (= 50 – 7 – 6 – 3) awards would vest.

20X3 was actually a much better year and PBT increased by 17%, resulting in an average increase for the three-year period of 15%, so each employee did, in fact, receive 200 shares. But only one employee left during 20X3, so 36 (= 50 – 7 – 6 – 1) awards vested.

The amount recognised as an expense in each year will be as follows:

Year	Calculation of cumulative expense	Cumulative expense £	Expense for period £
31/12/X1*	35 x 200 x £12 x 1/3	28,000	28,000
31/12/X2	34 x 100 x £12 x 2/3	27,200	(800)
31/12/X3	36 x 200 x £12	86,400	59,200

This example illustrates how the impact of 'truing up' the cumulative expense in each period could result in the reversal of amounts previously charged.

*Note that management's expectations at grant date, 1 January 20X1 are superseded by their updated expectations at 31 December 20X1.

Market and non-vesting vesting conditions

26.48 The accounting treatment for both market vesting conditions and non-vesting conditions is included in paragraph 26.44 above. An illustrative example is provided below.

Example – Grant of equity instruments with a market condition

On 1 January 20X5, entity F made an award of 10,000 options to each of its 50 senior management employees, on condition that the employees remained in the entity's employment until the end of 20X7. But the share options cannot be exercised unless the market share price has increased from £10 at the beginning of 20X5 to at least £17.50 at the vesting date of 31 December 20X7; they can be exercised any time during the next two years.

At grant date, the fair value of each option (which takes into account the possibility that the share price will be at least £17.50 at 31 December 20X7) is £4.

Share-based payment

At the date of the award, management estimated that 10% of employees would leave the entity before the end of three years, so 45 awards would vest. During 20X6, it became apparent that more employees than expected were leaving, so management revised its estimate of the number of awards that would vest to 42. At the end of 20X7, awards to 40 employees actually vested.

Where awards are granted with market conditions, an entity should recognise the services received from a counterparty who satisfies all other vesting conditions, irrespective of whether the market conditions are satisfied. [FRS 102 para 26.9]. In other words, it makes no difference whether share price targets are achieved – the possibility that a share price target might not be achieved has already been taken into account when estimating the fair value of the options at grant date. So, the amounts recognised as an expense in each year will be the same, regardless of whether the share price has reached £17.50 by the end of 20X7.

Year	Expense for the year £	Cumulative expense £	Calculation of cumulative expense
31 December 20X5	C600,000	C600,000	45 × 10,000 × 4 × $^1/_3$
31 December 20X6	C520,000	C1,120,000	42 × 10,000 × 4 × $^2/_3$
31 December 20X7	C480,000	C1,600,000	40 × 10,000 × 4

26.49   An example with a non-vesting condition (the requirement for employees to save under a 'Save as You Earn'(SAYE) scheme) is provided in paragraph 26.115 below.

Measuring the fair value of equity instruments granted

26.50   In a share-based payment transaction, where the fair value of goods or services is measured by the indirect method, the fair value of the equity instrument granted (whether shares or share options) should be estimated at the relevant measurement date (see para 26.33 above). [FRS 102 para 26.7]. For example, an entity grants share options to its employees with a grant date fair value of £300,000. These options vest in three years' time with the only condition being that the employees remain in the entity's service for that period. Assuming that all of the options do vest (that is, none of the employees leave the entity), the amount charged as an expense each year will be £100,000. This will be the case regardless of any movements in the price of the entity's shares. So, even if the options have an intrinsic value of, say, £500,000 when they are exercised, the amount charged as an expense will be unchanged. Having determined the 'price' of employee services when the options were granted, this remains fixed.

26.51   In a government-mandated plan under which equity instruments are acquired by investors (such as employees), either without providing any goods or services, or where the goods or services provided are clearly of less value than the fair value of the equity instruments granted, the difference between the fair value of the equity instruments granted and the fair value of goods or services to be received (measured directly) should be calculated at the grant date. If the fair value of equity instruments granted is higher, the difference must be recognised as a share-based payment. [FRS 102 para 26.17]. Further information is included in paragraph 26.95 below.

26.52 There is a general presumption that fair value can be reliably measured for equity instruments. Nonetheless, the measurement process can be quite complex. Section 26 of FRS 102 contains a hierarchy approach for determining the fair value of shares, share options and share appreciation rights.

Shares

26.53 The following three-tier hierarchy should be applied to determine the fair values of shares (and the related goods or services):

- If an observable market price is available for the equity instrument granted, an estimate of fair value should be based on that price.

- If an observable market price is not available for the equity instrument granted, an estimate of fair value should be based on entity-specific observable market data, such as:

    - a recent transaction in the entity's shares, or

    - a recent independent fair valuation of the entity or its principal assets.

- If an observable market price is not available and obtaining a reliable measurement of fair value under the second point above is impracticable, then the fair value of equity instruments granted should be estimated using a valuation method to determine the price that would be paid for the equity instruments in an arm's length transaction between knowledgeable and willing parties, as at the grant date. The entity's directors should use their judgement in applying a generally accepted valuation methodology that is appropriate to the entity's circumstances.

Impracticable' is defined as *"Applying a requirement is impracticable when the entity cannot apply it after making every reasonable effort to do so"*. [FRS 102 Glossary of terms].

[FRS 102 para 26.10].

26.54 As can be seen from the above, the hierarchy gives the highest priority to observable market prices. But it is highly unlikely that an observable market price will exist for equity shares of unlisted entities, because their shares will not be traded in an active market.

26.55 In the absence of an observable market price, fair value could be estimated by using the price of the most recent transaction in the entity's shares, such as raising capital. Alternatively, a valuation of the entity might be available because management have commissioned an independent valuation for a special purpose (such as for resolving a dispute, repurchase of shares, entering into a joint venture agreement or for assessing the value of an offer for the entity made by a third-party bidder). A valuation of the entity might also be available if management generally uses value-based methods to review and target the performance of the entity's business operations. Such valuations could be used for estimating the fair value of the shares granted in a share-based payment transaction, but the valuation should be adjusted for any changes in conditions between the transaction/valuation date and the grant date for the equity shares. In limited circumstances, counterparties might have the right to shares which are not readily marketable. Only in this situation is it appropriate to apply a discount to the fair value for lack of marketability.

26.56 As a last resort, management should estimate the fair value of the shares indirectly by using a valuation method. The objective of using a valuation method is to establish what the price of the equity instruments would be on the grant date in an arm's length transaction between knowledgeable willing parties. So, to arrive at a reasonable estimate of fair value of the equity instrument, the method used should reasonably reflect how the market could be expected to price the instrument. That expectation is likely to be met if the valuation model used makes maximum use of market inputs and relies as little as possible on entity-specific inputs. So, any valuation method applied should use market data to the greatest extent that it is practicable to do so. [FRS 102 para 26.10(c)].

26.57 There are a number of generally accepted techniques for valuing equity instruments. The most common valuation methods are: asset-based valuation methods for valuing stable, asset-rich businesses; P/E ratios for valuing businesses with an established profitable history; and discounted cash flows, which is the most technical and depends heavily on assumptions about long-term business conditions and measurement of risk (used for estimating discount rates). Management should use its judgement to apply the most appropriate valuation method to determine the fair value of the shares. The valuation method selected should take into account all the terms and conditions on which the shares were granted, other than service and non-market vesting conditions that are excluded from the measurement of fair value (as explained in para 26.47 above).

26.58 For example, if the employee is not entitled to receive dividends during the vesting period, this factor should be taken into account when estimating the fair value of the shares granted. Similarly, if the shares are subject to restrictions on transfer after the vesting date, that factor is taken into account to the extent that the restrictions affect the price that a knowledgeable, willing market participant would pay for that share. For example, if the shares to employees vest after three years of service, but the employees are not allowed to sell the shares for a further two-year period, the two-year restriction is a post-vesting restriction (treated as a non-vesting condition) that should be taken into account in the grant date fair value measurement.

Share options and equity-settled share appreciation rights

26.59 A similar three-tier hierarchy to that for shares (see para 26.53 above) should be used to ascertain the fair value of share options and equity-settled share appreciation rights:

- If an observable market price is available for the share options or equity-settled share appreciation rights granted, the entity should use that price.

- If an observable market price is not available for the share options or equity-settled share appreciation rights granted, fair value should be measured using entity-specific observable market data, such as a recent transaction in the entity's share options.

- If an observable market price is not available and obtaining a reliable measurement of fair value under the second point above is impracticable, the fair value of equity instruments granted should be estimated using an alternative valuation method, such as an option pricing model. The inputs to the option pricing model (see para 26.61 below) should use external market data to the greatest extent possible. The standard also requires the entity to derive an estimate of expected volatility that is consistent with the valuation methodology applied.

[FRS 102 para 26.11].

Impracticable' is defined as *"Applying a requirement is impracticable when the entity cannot apply it after making every reasonable effort to do so"*. [FRS 102 Glossary of terms].

26.60 But the trading of private entity share options is not commonly encountered; so, for the majority of private entities, there will not be an observable market price for share options or equity-settled share appreciation rights granted. For that reason, private entities would normally apply an option pricing valuation methodology.

26.61 There are a number of option pricing models in use, such as Black Scholes, Binomial and Monte Carlo. The inputs for an option pricing model should use market data to the greatest extent possible. All option pricing models take into account, as a minimum, the following factors:

- The weighted average share price. Guidance for determining the fair value of shares used in determining the weighted average share price is set out at paragraph 26.53 onwards above.

- Exercise price of the option.

- Expected volatility of the share price. Management should derive an estimate of expected volatility consistent with the valuation methodology used to determine the fair value of the shares.

- Life of the option.

- Dividends expected on the underlying shares.

- Risk-free interest rate over the life of the option.

[FRS 102 para 26.11].

26.62 The first two items define the 'intrinsic value' of the option. The remaining four are relevant to its 'time value'. The time value of an option reflects the right of the holder to participate in future gains, if any. The valuation does not attempt to predict what the future gain will be, only the amount that a buyer would pay at the valuation date to obtain the right to participate in any future gains. In other words, option pricing models estimate the value of the share option at the measurement date, and not the value of the underlying share at some future date.

26.63 All other things being equal, a change in the expected volatility of the share price will have the greatest impact of the input assumptions listed above on the option's fair value (that is, an increase in volatility increases the fair value). A change to either the option's exercise price or its life has the next greatest impact on the option's fair value (in this case, an increase in the option's exercise price decreases its fair value, and an increase in the option's expected life increases its fair value). This will be the case, regardless of the option pricing model used.

26.64 The model selected should take into account all the terms and conditions on which the share options were granted, other than service and non-market vesting conditions that are excluded from the measurement of fair values (as explained in para 26.47 above). For example, a share option granted to an employee typically cannot be exercised during the vesting period.

26.65 Similarly, another factor common to employee share options is the possibility of early exercise of the option (for example, the option is not freely transferable, or the employee must exercise all vested options on cessation of employment). The effects of expected early exercise should be taken into account in the valuation.

26.66 Determining the fair value of shares and share options for entities is quite complex, particularly for those entities that are not listed. Preparers of financial statements might find it useful to refer to Chapter 12 of the 'Manual of Accounting, IFRS for the UK' for further guidance on estimating the fair value of equity instruments granted.

Modifications including cancellations and settlements

26.67 It is not uncommon for management to modify the terms and conditions of equity instruments awarded in a share-based payment transaction. This might happen, for example, where a share option's exercise price is significantly above the fair value of the shares, rendering the option worthless ('underwater' options). Similarly, a performance condition might have become so onerous that it is no longer achievable. The challenge for management is how to modify the terms of the award in order to continue to motivate and reward employees.

26.68 There are a number of ways in which management could revive share awards that have become valueless. For example, management could cancel awards, which would require the immediate recognition of any remaining expense. Or management might reduce the exercise price of options granted to employees (that is, re-price the options), reduce the vesting period, or modify or eliminate a performance condition. Alternatively, management could settle the award (that is, cancel it) in exchange for cash or other consideration. The approach taken would depend on a number of factors, such as meeting employee expectations, complying with legal and contractual obligations (for example, obtaining employees' approval to modify the terms and conditions) and managing the financial reporting consequences arising from the modification, cancellation or settlement.

Modifications

26.69 The manner in which modifications are accounted for depends on whether they are beneficial to the employee (for example, where the modified terms increase the fair value or the number of the equity instruments granted) or not (for example, where the modified terms reduce the total fair value or number of the equity instruments granted).

Modifications that are beneficial to employees

26.70 A modification is likely to be beneficial to the employee if it results in an increase in the fair value or number of equity instruments granted. Where a modification is beneficial to the employee, the entity should continue to recognise the amount based on the grant date fair value of the original equity instrument over the original vesting period, as if the award had not been modified. The entity should also recognise the incremental fair value of the award (that is, the difference between the fair value of the modified equity instrument and that of the original equity instrument, both estimated as at the modification date). This incremental fair value should be recognised for the services received over the period from the modification date until the date when the modified equity instrument vests. [FRS 102 para 26.12(a)].

26.71 Examples of modifications that increase the fair value of an equity instrument include:

- A reduction in the exercise price of the option.

- An increase in the number of equity instruments granted.

- A reduction in the vesting period.

- The modification or elimination of a performance condition.

- A combination of the above.

26.72 Accounting for share-based payment modifications is considered in the following examples.

Share-based payment

Example 1 – Reduction in option exercise price

On 1 January 20X1, entity A grants an award of 1,000 options to each of its 60 employees. The only condition associated with the award is that recipients must remain in the employment of entity A for three years. The grant date fair value of each option is £5.

Towards the end of 20X1, the fair value of entity A's shares dropped significantly; so, on 1 January 20X2, management chose to reduce the exercise price of the options. At the date of the re-pricing, the fair value of each of the original share options granted was £1, and the fair value of each re-priced option was £3. So, the incremental fair value of each modified option was £2.

At the date of the award, management estimated that 10% of employees would leave the entity before the end of three years (that is, 90% x 60 = 54 awards would vest).

During 20X2, it became apparent that fewer employees than expected were leaving, so management revised its estimate of the number of leavers to only 5% (that is, 95% x 60 = 57 awards would vest).

At the end of 20X3, awards to 55 employees actually vested.

In accordance with paragraph 26.70 above, the entity should recognise:

- the cost of the original award at grant date (£5 per option) over a three-year vesting period beginning on 1 January 20X1, plus

- the incremental fair value of the re-priced option (£2 per option) at the modification date over a two-year vesting period beginning from the date of modification/re-pricing (1 January 20X2).

The amount recognised as an expense each year would be as follows:

Year	Calculation of cumulative expense		Cumulative expense	Expense for period
	Original award +	Modified award =		
			£	£
31/12/X1	1,000 x 54 x £5 x 1/3 = £90,000		90,000	90,000
31/12/X2	1,000 x 57 x £5 x 2/3 = £190,000	1,000 x 57 x £2 x ½ = £57,000	247,000	157,000
31/12/X3	1,000 x 55 x £5 = £275,000	1,000 x 55 x £2 = £110,000	385,000	138,000

26024

Example 2 – Increase in number of options granted

The facts are the same as in example 1, except that, instead of reducing the option exercise price on 1 January 20X2, the number of options to which each employee was entitled was increased to 1,500. The fair value of each of these additional options was £1.

In accordance with paragraph 26.70 above, the entity should recognise:

- the fair value of the original award at grant date (£5 per option) over a three-year vesting period beginning on 1 January 20X1, plus

- the incremental fair value of the additional option granted – 500 options at £1 at the modification date over a two-year vesting period beginning from the date of modification (1 January 20X2)

The amount recognised as an expense each year would be as follows:

Year	Calculation of cumulative expense		Cumulative expense	Expense for period
	Original award +	Modified award =		
			£	£
31/12/X1	1,000 x 54 x £5 x 1/3 = £90,000		90,000	90,000
31/12/X2	1,000 x 57 x £5 x 2/3 = £190,000	500 x 57 x £1 x ½ = £14,250	204,250	114,250
31/12/X3	1,000 x 55 x £5 = £275,000	500 x 55 x £1 = £27,500	302,500	98,250

Example 3 – Reduction in vesting period

On 1 January 20X1, entity B awarded an employee 100 shares (with no entitlement to dividends during the vesting period), subject only to the employee remaining in service for three years. At the grant date, the fair value of each share was £6.

On 1 December 20X1, entity B decided to reduce the service requirement from three years to two years, thereby reducing the vesting period to two years. It is assumed that the employee remains in service beyond 31 December 20X1.

No dividends are expected to be paid during the vesting period, and the service vesting condition was never factored into the fair value of the award, so changing the service vesting condition from three years to two years has no impact on the fair value of the unvested shares.

In accordance with paragraph 26.12(a) of the standard (see para 26.70 above), where a modification occurs during a vesting period, the incremental fair value granted is included in the measurement of the amounts recognised for services received from the modification date until the date when the modified equity instrument vests. Although the incremental fair value is nil, the effect of the modification should still be accounted for from 1 December 20X1. This is also consistent with paragraph 26.6 of the standard (see para 26.27 above) which requires that, where equity instruments do not vest until the counterparty completes a specified service period, the entity should presume that the services to be rendered by the counterparty will be received during the vesting period.

Share-based payment

Before modification, employee services received as consideration were presumed to be received over a three-year period, and the expense would be recognised on this basis. The presumption changes from three years to two years when the vesting period is modified, and so the modification should be accounted for from the modification date of 1 December 20X1 as follows:

Year	Calculation of cumulative expense	Cumulative expense £	Expense for period £
31/12/X1	Original charge: 11 months to 1 December 20X1: $100 \times £6 \times 1/3 \times 11/12 = £183$ Modification occurs 1 December 20X6. Expense over remaining 13 months to 31 December 20X2: £600 − £183 = £417 Expense for December 20X1: £417/13 = £32 Therefore, total expense for year to 31 December 20X1: £183 + £32 = £215	215	215
31/12/X2	$100 \times £6 = £600$	600	385

Example 4 – Modification of performance condition

On 1 January 20X1, an entity grants 10,000 share options to its sales director, on condition that the sales director remains in the entity's employment for three years and sales revenue increases by 30% over the three-year period. The grant date fair value of each share at 1 January 20X1 is £6.

During 20X1, revenue increased by 8%, and management expects that revenue will increase by 25% over the three-year period; because the revenue condition was not met, no cost of the award was recorded in year 1.

During 20X2, based on current sales, management believes that its previous forecast of achieving an increase in sales revenue of 25% was too optimistic, and it reduces the revenue performance condition to 20%.

By the end of 20X3, revenue over the three-year period increased by 22% and so the share options vest.

The amount recognised as an expense in each period will be as follows:

Year	Calculation of cumulative expense	Cumulative expense £	Expense for period £
31/12/X1	Performance condition not met – no expense recognised	nil	nil
31/12/X2	Management modifies the revenue performance target to 20% and believes it is achievable. It is, therefore, records, an expense of 10,000 x £6 x 2/3 = £40,000. This cost is based on the fair value of the original share option of £6 at the grant date (because the non-performance revenue condition was never factored into the original valuation), so changes in the performance condition have no effect on the fair value.	40,000	40,000
31/12/X3	Performance target met, and so total cost recognised is 10,000 × £6 = £60,000	60,000	20,000

Example 5 – Re-priced options and extension of vesting period

Management granted 100 share options at an exercise price of £10 per share to a senior executive in exchange for services. The grant date was 1 January 20X1 and the options were subject to a two-year vesting period. The grant date fair value of the options was £5,000, and all options were expected to vest at the end of the vesting period.

The options were modified on 1 January 20X2 by reducing the exercise price to £5 per share (the current fair value of the shares) and extending the vesting period by six months to 30 June 20X3. The fair value of the options at 1 January 20X2 was £8,000 prior to the modification and £9,500 after the modification. At the modification date, all options were expected to vest.

In accordance with paragraph 26.70 above, the entity should recognise:

■ the cost of the original award at grant date over the two-year vesting period beginning on 1 January 20X1, plus

■ the incremental fair value of the modification: £1,500 (£9,500 – £ 8,000) over 18 months to 30 June 20X3 beginning from the date of modification (1 January 20X2).

The amount recognised as an expense each year would be as follows:

Year	Calculation of cumulative expense		Cumulative expense £	Expense for period £
	Original award +	Modified award =		
31/12/X1	£5,000 × ½ = £2,500		2,500	2,500
31/12/X2	£5,000 × 1 = £5,000	£1,500 × 12/18 = £1,000	6,000	3,500
31/12/X3		£1,500 × 1 = £1,500	6,500	500

If an employee leaves during the six-month period to 30 June 20X3 (and so fails to meet the revised vesting condition), it is only the modification impact that is reversed; the original grant date fair value expense of £5,000 is unaffected, because the employee satisfied the two-year service condition for the original award.

Modifications that are not beneficial to employees

26.73 An entity might sometimes modify the terms and conditions of a grant of equity instruments in a manner that reduces the arrangement's total fair value or is otherwise not beneficial to employees. The accounting treatment for such modifications is similar to that described above, insofar as the entity should continue to account for the original grant as if the modification had not occurred. [FRS 102 para 26.12(b)].

26.74 For example, if the modification reduces the fair value of the equity instruments granted, this should be ignored. The entity should not recognise reduced expense as a consequence of the modification. This prevents entities from modifying awards simply to reduce the overall income statement charge. Similarly, if the modification is to add a vesting condition or to reduce the likelihood of achieving a vesting condition, this should be ignored for the purpose of estimating the number of awards expected to vest. But, if the modification reduces the number of equity instruments granted, this should be accounted for as a cancellation of that portion of the grant (see para 26.75 below).

Example 1 – Modification that is not beneficial to employees

An entity granted 100 share options to employees at an exercise price of £10 per share. The grant date is 1 January 20X1 and the options are subject to a two-year vesting period. The grant date fair value of each option was £50.

The entity modified the options at 31 December 20X1 by extending the vesting period to 30 June 20X3. At 31 December 20X1, management expected that the number of options outstanding at 31 December 20X2 (that is, the original vesting date), would be 90. The actual number of options outstanding at 31 December 20X2 was 85, of which only 80 vested on 30 June 20X3. The modification did not increase the options' fair value.

The extension of the vesting period should be ignored. Modification of vesting conditions in a manner that is not beneficial to employees should not be taken into account when determining amounts to be recognised.

The amount recognised as an expense in each period will be as follows:

Year	Calculation of cumulative expense	Cumulative expense £	Expense for period £
31/12/X1	90 × £50 × ½	2,250	2,250
31/12/X2	85 × £50	4,250	2,000
31/12/X3	No expense is recognised and no adjustment is made to reflect the fact that only 80 options actually vest, because this occurred after the original vesting period.	-	-

Cancellations and settlements

26.75 Where an entity cancels or settles an equity-settled share-based payment award during the vesting period, it should treat this as an acceleration of vesting; and so it should recognise immediately the amount that otherwise would have been recognised for services received over the remainder of the vesting period. [FRS 102 para 26.13]. In other words, the cancellation or settlement is accounted for as if the awards have vested immediately on the cancellation date.

26.76 This requirement could be interpreted as relating to all awards that are outstanding at the date of cancellation, or relating only to the number of awards that were expected to achieve the performance condition just before the award was cancelled. Our view is that the entity should apply the treatment that is most appropriate to the entity's specific circumstances.

Example 1 – Cancellation and settlement of share options during vesting period

On 1 January 20X1, entity A grants an award of 100 options to each of its 60 employees. The only condition associated with the award is that recipients must remain in the employment of entity A for three years. The grant date fair value of each option is £12.

At the date of the award, management estimated that 10% of employees would leave the entity before the end of three years (that is, 90% x 60 = 54 awards would vest).

Towards the end of 20X2, due to poor trading conditions and a significant fall in the entity's value, management decided to cancel the options at 31 December 20X2. It decided to pay cash compensation to the 57 employees remaining at the end of 20X2 at £4 per share option cancelled; the fair value was £3 per share option at that date.

As stated in paragraph 26.75 above, the entity should account for the cancellation/ settlement as if the awards have vested immediately, as shown below:

Year	Calculation of cumulative expense	Cumulative expense £	Expense for period £
31/12/X1	100 × 54 × £12 × 1/3	21,600	21,600
31/12/X2	100 × 57 × £12 as if the options have vested immediately	68,400	46,800

> Given that the entity has paid compensation amounting to £22,800 (100 x 57 x £4) when the fair value of the option at the date of cancellation amounted to £17,100 (100 x 57 x £3), the question arises as to how the entity should account for this.
>
> In the absence of any specific guidance in the standard, we believe that it would be appropriate to account for £17,100 of the payment as a deduction from equity, and the remaining payment of £5,700, in excess of fair value, should be accounted for in profit or loss. So, the total amount of £74,100 (£68,400 + £5,700) recognised in profit or loss as an expense is represented by a cash payment of £22,800 and a credit to equity of £51,300 (£68,400 – £17,100).

Forfeitures

26.77 A forfeiture occurs where either a service or non-market performance condition is not met during the vesting period, because this affects the number of awards that vest. Failures to meet a market or non-vesting condition are not forfeitures, because such conditions are already taken into account when determining the grant date fair value.

26.78 The accounting for forfeitures is different to that for cancellations (described in para 26.75 onwards above). Where a number of individual awards within a larger portfolio of awards are forfeited, the expense is revised to reflect the best available estimate of the number of equity instruments expected to vest. So, on a cumulative basis, no expense is recognised for goods or services received if the equity instruments do not vest as a result of a service or non-market performance condition (for example, if the employee or counterparty fails to complete a specified service period).

26.79 But the expiry (or lapsing) of a vested award has no accounting implications at the time that the award expires or lapses; if expiry (or lapsing) results from a post-vesting restriction, it will have been incorporated into the grant date fair value.

> **Example – Employee made redundant**
>
> Entity A granted share option awards to a number of its employees, with a three-year service requirement. The individuals were required to remain in service with the entity for three years from the date of grant. After 18 months, one employee is made redundant.
>
> Having been made redundant, the employee is unable to satisfy the three-year service condition, and so this should be treated as a forfeiture rather than a cancellation. The expense recognised to date is reversed. But, if the award was cancelled before the employee was made redundant, there would be an accelerated charge.

Measurement of cash-settled share-based payment transactions

26.80 Cash-settled share-based payment transactions are described at paragraph 26.13 onwards above. As noted in paragraph 26.17 above, the most common examples of cash-settled share-based payment transactions are mandatorily redeemable shares granted by an entity

26.81 An entity should measure the fair value of the liability to settle a cash-settled share-based payment transaction, and the goods or services acquired, at the fair value of the liability. The liability is based on the price (or value) of the entity's equity instruments, so the fair value of the liability should be determined using an option pricing model, taking into account the terms and conditions of the awards. So, the liability would include the intrinsic value (that is, the increase in the share price to date) and the time value (that is, the value of the right to participate in future increases in the share price, if any, that might occur between the valuation date and the settlement date).

26.82 Until the liability is settled, the fair value should be re-measured at each reporting date and at the date of settlement, and changes in fair value should be recognised in profit or loss for the period. [FRS 102 para 26.14]. The measurement reflects the impact of all conditions and all possible outcomes on a weighted-average basis, unlike the measurement for an equity-settled award (see para 26.50 above). This has the effect that, although the liability will ultimately be settled at its intrinsic value, its measurement at reporting dates before settlement is based on its fair value. Although measuring the liability at intrinsic value would be simpler, measuring cash-settled awards at intrinsic value would be inconsistent with the fair value measurement basis applied in the rest of the standard.

26.83 The following example illustrates the application of the above requirements.

> **Example – Cash-settled share-based payment award**
>
> On 1 January 20X1, an entity granted 1,000 share appreciation rights (SARs) to each of its 40 management employees. The SARs provide the employees with the right to receive, at the date the rights are exercised, cash equal to the appreciation in the entity's share price since the grant date. All of the rights vest on 31 December 20X2, and they can be exercised at the end of 20X3 and 20X4. Management estimates that, at grant date, the fair value of each SAR is £11, and that 10% of the employees will leave evenly during the two-year period.
>
> Management estimates the fair value of the SARs at the end of each year in which a liability exists, as shown below. The intrinsic values of the SARs at the date of exercise (equal to the cash paid out) at the end of years 3 and 4 are also shown below:
>
> | Year | Fair value £ | Intrinsic value £ |
> |------|----------|----------------|
> | 31 Dec 20X1 | 12 | - |
> | 31 Dec 20X2 | 8 | - |
> | 31 Dec 20X3 | 13 | 10 |
> | 31 Dec 20X4 | 12 | 12 |

10% of employees left before the end of 20X2. On 31 December 20X3, six employees exercise their options, while the remaining 30 employees exercise their options at the end of 20X4. The amount recognised as an expense in each year, and as a liability at each year end, will be as follows:

Year	Calculation of liability	Calculation of cash paid	Liability £	Cash paid £	Expense for period* £
31/12/X1	36 × 1,000 × £12 × ½		216,000		216,000
31/12/X2	36 × 1,000 × 8		288,000		72,000
31/12/X3	30 × 1,000 x 13	6 × 1,000 × 10	390,000	60,000	162,000
31/12/X4		− 30 × 1,000 × 12	−	360,000	(30,000)

* Expense = Ending liability + Cash paid – Opening liability

Treatment of vesting conditions

26.84 The standard does not specifically deal with the impact of vesting conditions for determining the fair value of cash-settled share-based payment transactions. Where a vesting condition relates to employee service, we believe that the liability should be estimated on the basis of the current best estimate of the number of awards that will vest (that is, similar to an equity-settled transaction), as indicated in the above example. Similarly, non-market performance conditions should be taken into account in determining the liability until vesting, based on the current best estimate of those conditions. So, like equity-settled transactions, the impact of such non-market performance conditions and service conditions should not be factored into the valuation of the cash-settled award.

26.85 As regards satisfaction of market conditions and non-vesting conditions, the probability of achieving the condition should be factored into the fair value of the award. So, no cost will be recognised if a market condition or a non-vesting condition is not satisfied at the reporting date; this is because a liability for a cash-settled transaction must ultimately reflect the amount of cash that will be paid.

26.86 Any later modification to the terms or conditions of a cash-settled share-based payment should be reflected in the re-measurement of the liability at each reporting date. [FRS 102 para 26.14]. So the accounting requirements that apply to the modification of an equity-settled share-based payment are not applicable to cash-settled share-based payments.

Measurement of share-based payment transactions with cash alternatives

26.87 It is common for share-based payment transactions (particularly with employees) to provide either the entity or the counterparty with a choice of settling the transaction in cash (or other assets) or by transferring equity instruments. For share-based payments in which either the entity or the counterparty has the choice of settlement, the entity should account for this arrangement as a cash-settled share-based payment transaction, unless either of the conditions below applies:

■ The entity has a past practice of settling by issuing equity instruments.

■ There is no commercial substance to the option because the cash settlement is not related to the fair value of the equity instrument, and the cash settlement is likely to be lower in value.

[FRS 102 para 26.15].

26.88   Where either of the above conditions is met, the entity should account for the transaction as an equity-settled share-based payment transaction in accordance with paragraph 26.50 above. [FRS 102 para 26.15].

26.89   The first condition above implies that the cash settlement option held by the counterparty has little substance, because the entity's past practice of settling the transaction in shares means that the counterparty has no realistic expectation that the transaction will be settled in cash. Similarly, if the fair value of the cash alternative is less than the fair value of the equity instrument issued (as stated in the second condition), the cash alternative held by the counterparty is effectively worthless.

26.90   It should be noted that, where the counterparty has a choice of settlement, the entity is considered to have issued a compound financial instrument consisting of a debt component (to the extent that the counterparty has the right to demand cash) and an equity component (to the extent that the counterparty has a right to demand settlement in equity instruments by giving up its right to cash). But there is no requirement for an entity to determine the fair value of the debt and equity components separately in order to account for the transaction. This is also consistent with the scope exemption for share-based payment transactions contained in section 22 of the standard that deals with compound financial instruments. [FRS 102 para 22.2(d)]. In other words, the credit entry for share-based payment transactions with cash alternatives will be recognised either as an increase in equity or as a liability, but not both.

> **Example 1 – Share-based payment with employee settlement option**
>
> An entity established a bonus plan on 1 January 20X5. The employees can choose a cash payment equal to the value of 100 shares at 31 December 20X5 or to receive 100 shares on the same date. At the grant date, the fair value of the right to cash is C5,000 and the fair value of the right to shares is C5,000. The entity has not issued shares to any employees in the past.
>
> This is treated as a cash-settled award at the grant date, because the entity does not have an established past practice of settling awards with employees in shares, and also because the value of the cash bonus is equivalent to the value of the shares. If any

employees choose to receive shares when the award vests, the accounting treatment would be to recognise a credit in equity for the grant date fair value of these awards, as if they had always been treated as equity-settled. This cash liability recognised for these awards would be reversed, and any difference would be recognised in profit or loss.

Example 2 – Share-based payment with entity settlement option

An entity has granted (to senior management of its subsidiary entity) the right to either 10,000 phantom shares (that is, the right to receive a cash payment equal to the value of 10,000 shares) or 15,000 shares in the entity. The entity can choose the settlement method. It has never made an award of this nature and it is free to select either settlement method (that is, there is no restriction on its ability to issue shares). In this situation, the commercial substance is that the entity would most likely choose to settle in cash, because this is more cost-effective than purchasing 15,000 shares. So this award is treated as a cash-settled award. But, on settlement, if the entity chooses to settle in shares, the credit would be transferred to equity.

Settlement method contingent on an event outside the control of the entity or employee

26.91 There might be occasions where the conditions of a share-based payment award provide the employee with either cash or equity, but the choice of which option occurs is outside the control of both the employee and the entity. Section 26 of FRS 102 does not address this, but we believe that there are two acceptable approaches to account for an award where the manner of settlement (that is, cash or equity) is contingent on an event that is outside the entity's and counterparty's control.

26.92 One approach is to account for the award as two mutually exclusive awards, of which one is equity-settled and the other is cash-settled:

- The cash-settled alternative is a liability. Although this is affected by the probability of being paid, it always has a fair value which is recognised over the vesting period. If the award is ultimately settled in equity, the fair value of the liability falls to nil.

- The equity-settled alternative is only recognised if it is considered probable. If the award is ultimately settled in cash, the equity alternative would have become improbable, and so no cumulative expense would be recognised for this. The fair value of the liability will have increased to the cash amount ultimately paid.

26.93 The alternative approach is to look to the principles of section 21 of the standard in determining whether or not an uncertain future event gives rise to a liability. Under this approach, only a contingent liability exists when the contingency that triggers cash settlement is not probable. The award should be treated as equity-settled, unless cash settlement becomes probable. The classification is an accounting estimate, and any change in classification is treated as a change in estimate; so the cumulative expense (and related credit to equity or liability) should be the same as if the new classification had always been applied.

26.94 Illustrative examples under both alternatives are provided in our Manual of Accounting – IFRS for the UK.

Measurement of share-based transactions for unidentifiable goods or services

26.95 As noted in paragraph 26.5 above, the standard applies to share-based payment transactions where it is difficult to identify goods or services that have been (or will be) received, under government-mandated plans. [FRS 102 para 26.17]. For example, some jurisdictions operate government-mandated plans which enable investors (including employees) to acquire equity instruments without providing any goods or services.

26.96 In the absence of specifically identifiable goods or services, other circumstances could indicate that goods or services have been (or will be) received in a government-mandated share-based payment plan. In particular, if the identifiable consideration received (if any) appears to be less than the fair value of the equity instruments granted, there is an indication that other consideration (such as past or future employee services) has been (or will be) received.

26.97 In such situations, the standard requires the entity to calculate any difference between the fair value of the share-based payment and the fair value of any identifiable goods or services received (or to be received) at the grant date. If the fair value of the share-based payment is higher than the fair value of the goods or services, this difference should be recognised as a share-based payment. [FRS 102 para 26.17].

Group plans

26.98 In a group plan, a share-based payment is often granted by the parent, or another entity in the group that administers the group scheme (for example the employee share trust), to employees of one or more subsidiaries in the group, where the award is settled in, or based on, the price (or value) of the equity instruments of the parent (or of another group entity). In that situation, where the parent presents consolidated financial statements using either FRS 102 or full IFRS, the cost of the awards recognised in the consolidated financial statements will be measured in accordance with the provisions of those standards.

26.99 Subsidiaries that receive services from their employees as consideration for share-based payments granted by another entity in the group should recognise a cost, even though they are not legally a party to the transaction. However, as an alternative to recognising and measuring this share-based payment in accordance with the full requirements of section 26, such subsidiaries are permitted to recognise and measure the expense in their individual financial statements, on the basis of a reasonable allocation of the group expense. [FRS 102 para 26.16].

26.100   The financial statements of the subsidiary (or other group entity) receiving the goods or services in a group share-based payment transaction should recognise the corresponding credit entry in equity (treating it as an equity settled share-based payment), if that entity has no obligation to settle the transaction [FRS 102 para 16.1(a)(ii)].

26.101   Therefore, there are two scenarios in which the entity receiving the goods or services would be expected to account for the awards as equity-settled. These are where:

- the awards granted are settled with the entity's own equity instruments; or
- the entity has no obligation to settle the share-based payment transaction.

In all other situations, the entity receiving the goods or services would be expected to account for the awards as cash-settled.

26.102   An entity settling a share-based payment transaction when another group entity receives the goods or services will need to record either the issue of its equity instruments or a cash-settled liability. The resulting debit entry would be to recognise an increase in the investment in the subsidiary as a capital contribution. This is because it would be inappropriate to recognise an asset or expense given that no goods or services are received by this entity. The principles of section 26 would indicate that these accounting entries are recognised by the entity settling the share-based payment, over the vesting period.

26.103   The following example illustrates the principles discussed above.

> **Example – Parent entity grants share awards to subsidiary employees**
>
> A parent entity grants its shares directly to employees of subsidiaries A and B. The awards will vest immediately, and the parent will issue new shares directly to the employees. The parent will not charge subsidiaries A and B for the transaction. But subsidiary A has 60% and subsidiary B has 40% of the group's workforce, based on the relative number of employees participating in the scheme.
>
> In the consolidated financial statements, the transaction is treated as an equity-settled share-based payment, because the group has received services in consideration for the group's equity instruments. An expense is recognised in the group income statement for the grant date fair value of the share-based payment over the vesting period, and a credit is recognised in equity.
>
> In the subsidiaries' accounts, each subsidiary bears its proportion of the grant date fair value of the award over the vesting period, with a credit to equity as the subsidiary will not settle the award. The shares vest immediately, so an expense is recognised in the subsidiaries' income statement in full, based on the grant date fair value.

In the parent's separate financial statements, there is no share-based payment charge because no employees are providing services to the parent. So the parent would record a debit, recognising an increase in the investment in the subsidiaries as a capital contribution from the parent and a credit to equity.

If, in the above situation, subsidiaries are required to make a payment to the parent (or any other entity settling the award) , the payment should be charged directly to equity, on the basis that it represents a return of the capital contribution recorded as the credit to equity (as stated above). Any additional payment in excess of the capital contribution, which the subsidiary effectively spends on employee remuneration, should be treated as a distribution. Further guidance on the accounting for recharges is provided in paragraph 26.116 below.

Additional practical implications

Transactions with employees and transactions with shareholders (for example, 'sweet' equity)

26.104 Transactions with employees in their capacity as holders of equity instruments are outside the scope of section 26 of FRS 102. For example, if an entity makes a bonus issue of shares to all of its shareholders, and these include some of the entity's employees, this will not represent a share-based payment transaction to be dealt with in accordance with section 26. But there could be a situation where an employee invests in an entity which is working towards a stock market listing or a trade sale. In these cases, there could be a venture capital entity or similar investor involved in the transaction, and the employee will subscribe for the shares at the same amount as the other investors. The issue is whether the employee is acting as a shareholder or as an employee. Often, the interested parties (including directors, management and other shareholders) have acquired shares for a 'fair' value, which might not equate to grant date fair value for the purposes of section 26 and would typically be tax driven. It is important to note that a fair value determined for tax purposes often reflects factors which it would not be appropriate to allow for under section 26 (that is, lack of marketability), and so it might be lower than the section 26 grant date fair value.

26.105 It could be that there are no conditions or incentives attached to the acquired shares, and so the employee is purely acting as a shareholder. But, in the majority of situations, there are likely to be service conditions or leaver provisions such that the arrangement would be accounted for as a share-based payment transaction under section 26 of the standard. The shares in question are often referred to as 'sweet' or 'sweat' equity, depending on whether they are offered at an advantageous price or in return for services rather than cash.

26.106 There are a number of issues that need to be considered before reaching a conclusion that transactions with employees are not within section 26's scope, including:

■ Whether the instrument that the employees are entitled to is an equity instrument or linked to an equity instrument, as defined by the standard. If the instrument is an equity instrument or linked to an equity instrument, and the value to employees varies depending on the extent to which the employee provides services, the transaction would be within section 26's scope as a share-based payment.

■ Whether the rights and interests of employee shareholders differ from those of other investor shareholders (for example, venture capitalists or private equity investors). Employees might have the right to additional shares, with other investor shareholders giving up their rights – a ratchet mechanism. This ratchet usually depends on the performance of the business, and so employees receive more shares if the business does well. This would qualify as a performance condition, because services from employees contribute towards the entity meeting the performance targets; and so the arrangement is within section 26's scope.

■ Whether holders have different rights following an exit event. Through the articles, employees might be given different rights (cash or shares) if an investor exits through an initial public offering (IPO) rather than a trade sale. This provides evidence of a performance condition (that is, achieving different rights to cash or shares, depending on the exit event that occurs) which could bring the arrangement within section 26's scope.

■ Leaver conditions (the articles or terms and conditions might define good leavers and bad leavers). In this situation, the employees could lose their right to shares by leaving the entity, because the shares are either repurchased or cancelled. Hence, employees might only earn their right to the shares if they stay with the entity or, for example, in the event of an IPO. This would also be considered a service condition, and so the arrangement is in section 26's scope.

■ Whether additional services are being provided. As noted above, employees will often lose their right to shares if they leave the entity. There might be a service requirement (for example, to stay in employment for a number of years or until a change in control). But this might not always be the case, and some employees might have the right to shares, regardless of whether they stay or leave. This does not automatically take the arrangement out of the scope of section 26, because the entity would still need to determine whether additional services are being provided by the shareholders in their capacity as employees.

■ Whether a trust is involved in the transaction. The existence of an employee benefit trust (to buy back and warehouse shares for the benefit of other employees) could well imply that shares are being issued as an incentive, and so the arrangement is in section 26's scope.

The above list is not exhaustive, but it highlights some of the areas that should be considered in order to determine if the transaction is within section 26's scope.

Example – Purchase of shares at fair value, with service condition

A director is offered the opportunity to buy 100,000 shares in entity A at C1 each, the same price paid by the venture capital investor that holds 40% of entity A's shares. If the CEO resigns within two years, he must give the shares back to the entity in return for a payment of the lower of his subscription price and the fair value of the shares.

This transaction is in section 26's scope, because the director accepts a service condition when purchasing the shares. The service condition must be satisfied before he is fully entitled to the risks and rewards of the shares (that is, there is a vesting period of two years).

The director might be paying the section 26 grant date fair value for the shares on grant date (C1); in which case, provided the award was equity-settled, this would result in no charge under section 26. Often, however, the interested parties (including directors, management and other shareholders) have acquired shares for a 'fair' value, which might not equate to grant date fair value for the purposes of section 26 and would typically be tax driven. It is important to note that a fair value determined for tax purposes often reflects factors which it would not be appropriate to allow for under section 26. Either way, since the arrangement is within the scope of section 26, consideration should be given to disclosures prescribed by section 26 (see further para 26.121 below).

Leaver provisions

26.107   Some share-based payment arrangements include good and bad leaver provisions. A good leaver is often defined as an individual who leaves the entity due to injury, disability, death, redundancy or on reaching normal retirement age. A bad leaver is usually defined as any other leaver. The following example considers the accounting implications in relation to typical leaver provisions.

Example – Exit event with good and bad leavers

Entity A's directors have been given an incentive in the form of share options that will vest when an exit event occurs (the entity is unlisted). Each director has paid an up-front exercise price of £10 per share and will become unconditionally entitled to shares in the entity if he or she is still in service when an exit event occurs.

'Exit event' is defined in the plan's terms and conditions as a trade sale, a listing or other change in control. An exit event is expected to occur in the form of a trade sale in three years' time.

The terms and conditions also set out provisions for good and bad leavers. For every share option held, a 'bad leaver' will receive cash equal to the lower of the amount paid (£10) and the market value of the share (market value will be determined by independent valuation consultants). A 'good leaver' will receive cash equal to the higher of the amount paid and the market value in respect of each share option held.

Any director can choose to leave the entity at any time, triggering a contractual 'bad leaver' cash payment that the entity cannot avoid, so entity A has a liability in respect of all directors as part of the share-based payment transaction (that is, for the total number of share options granted). The liability will be measured at the lower of £10 per share and the market value of the share. The payments by the directors are, in effect, advance payments of an exercise price due when the awards vest.

In addition to the bad leaver liability, the arrangement in respect of good leavers, and directors who are still in service at the time of the trade sale, falls within the scope of section 26.

The fair value of share options (which will be incremental to the amount that has already been provided in case each individual becomes a bad leaver) awarded to any director expected to be a good leaver before the exit event occurs will be treated as a cash-settled share-based payment (see para 26.47 onwards above in relation to non-market vesting conditions).

The fair value of share options that are expected to vest as a result of the trade sale will be treated as an equity-settled share-based payment (this will be incremental to the amount that has already been provided in case each individual becomes a bad leaver, and will not include amounts in respect of any individual who is expected to become a good leaver before the exit event). Note that, if the share options do vest as a result of the trade sale, the bad and good leaver liability in respect of each individual for whom the award vests will be transferred into equity.

'Drag along' and 'tag along' clauses

26.108 Some arrangements include 'drag along' and 'tag along' clauses. For example, if an existing majority shareholder chooses to sell his investment in an entity, a 'drag along' clause in an arrangement's terms and conditions might state that the shareholder can force employee shareholders or share option holders to sell their holdings at the same price/date. Or, where an entity is sold, a 'tag along' clause might allow employees to force an acquirer to purchase their holdings at the same price/date.

Awards conditional on IPO or change in control

26.109 Section 26 does not deal explicitly with awards that are conditional on an initial public offering (IPO). As noted above, an expense in respect of an award of, say, options is recognised immediately if the award vests immediately, or over the vesting period if one exists. [FRS 102 paras 26.5, 26.6]. In the case of an award that vests when an IPO (or similar exit event) occurs, but only to employees that are still employed by the entity at that time, it is reasonable to conclude that the vesting period will commence no later than the grant date and end on the date of the IPO. But this raises two questions:

- What will the grant date be?
- How can the date of a future IPO be estimated reliably?

26.110 As regards grant date, the facts of individual awards will vary. Sometimes, an award will be subject to approval at the time of the IPO, in which case the grant date would correspond to the date of the IPO. On other occasions, shareholder approval will have been obtained when the award is made (or at some other time in advance of the IPO). Section 26 does not address situations where the grant date falls after the employees have begun to provide services. In our view, the entity should estimate the grant date fair value at each reporting period until the grant date is established, and then revise it once the grant date has been established.

26.111   Where an award is conditional on an IPO occurring, but employee service up to the IPO date is not required (or perhaps service is only required for part of the period), the IPO condition becomes a non-vesting condition. Non-vesting conditions are considered in paragraph 26.43 above.

26.112   The more difficult question concerns how the date of a future IPO can be estimated reliably. The accounting for a situation where the length of the vesting period varies, depending on when a performance condition is satisfied, is not addressed by section 26 of FRS 102. But one potential approach would be to make an estimate on the basis of the most likely outcome. This is illustrated in the following example.

Example – Estimating listing date

The directors of an entity with a June year end are contemplating a listing of the entity's shares. An award of unvested shares is made to employees on 31 March 20X5, but the shares vest only in the event of an IPO. The entity will not pay dividends before an IPO. Employees leaving the entity before the IPO occurs will lose their entitlement to the shares.

When the award is made, the directors estimate that a stock market listing will be achieved in three years' time. However, during the remainder of 20X5 and the first half of 20X6, the entity performs well and, following discussions with the entity's bankers, the directors decide to seek a listing by the end of 20X6. Due to unforeseen circumstances, this target is not achieved, but the shares are finally listed on 31 August 20X7.

Assuming that the directors have the authority to make the award of shares to the employees, the grant date will be 31 March 20X5, and the fair value of the award will be measured on that date. If the award is subject to shareholder approval at the date of the IPO, fair value will be estimated (for example, by reference to the fair value of the options at each balance sheet date) and revised at grant date when the shareholder approval is obtained.

When the award is made, the directors estimate that the listing might be achieved in three years' time. So an expense in respect of employee services is recognised over this period. By 30 June 20X6, the directors have revised their estimate of the date of listing to the end of 20X6, so the recognition of the expense is accelerated. By 30 June 20X7, the listing has not yet occurred, but the process has commenced, and the directors estimate that it will be achieved within two months. The expense for the year ending 30 June 20X7 will therefore be based on this estimate. So, for the three financial years ending 30 June 20X7, the estimated vesting period for the award of shares for the purposes of recognising an expense in accordance with IFRS 2 will be as follows:

Year	Vesting period
30 June 20X5	Three years ending 31 March 20X8
30 June 20X6	One year and nine months ending 31 December 20X6
30 June 20X7	Two years and five months ending 31 August 20X7

The estimated length of the vesting period is not factored into the grant date fair value of the award. This is because the condition to provide employee services until the date of the IPO is a non-market vesting condition. A single best estimate of the grant date fair value is calculated, given the interaction of the various components of the fair value calculation. In accordance with the guidance in paragraph 26.47 above, the estimate of awards expected to vest should be revised at each reporting date, as a result of the change in service period.

Where awards vest only on an exit event such as an IPO, and an exit event is not deemed to be probable, no expense is recognised. It might be determined that some of the awards will vest in another way, based on the terms of the arrangement.

Employee benefit trusts

26.113 Employee benefit trusts are often created by a sponsoring entity to facilitate employee shareholding, and they are often used as a vehicle for distributing shares to employees under remuneration plans. The structures of employee benefit trusts vary, but typically they are arrangements whereby a trust is set up by a sponsoring entity to acquire shares in that entity for the benefit of its employees, who generally acquire them at a later stage through share option plans, profit-sharing arrangements or other share incentive plans. Section 26 of FRS 102 does not address how to account for employee benefit trusts. Instead, section 9 of the standard addresses the accounting for 'special purpose entities', including employee benefit trusts (see chapter 9 for further guidance).

Save As You Earn plans

26.114 Sharesave plans are plans through which employees are given the opportunity to subscribe for shares, often at a discount to the market price. This might be paid for from a reduction of payroll over a period rather than a lump sum. Save As You Earn (SAYE) plans are typically HMRC-approved plans through which employees are given the opportunity to subscribe for shares at a discount of up to 20% of the market price. Typically, the plans have a term of three, five or seven years. In the case of three- or five-year arrangements, employees must make regular savings throughout the term. In the case of a seven-year term, savings made under a five-year agreement are left to increase in value for a further two years. The amount that can be invested is up to £250 per month across all plans to which an employee belongs. If an employee ceases saving, they receive a reimbursement of all amounts saved to date, plus interest, but they must withdraw from the plan.

26.115 Employee share purchase plans fall within the scope of section 26. So they should be treated like any other equity-settled share-based payment transaction. But, unlike many other arrangements, some employee share purchase plans impose a condition on their members that requires regular saving. If an employee ceases saving, they forfeit their right to subscribe for shares. As discussed in paragraph 26.43 above, a requirement to save is a non-vesting condition (which is included in the fair value calculation); so a failure to save should be treated as a cancellation.

> **Example – Save As You Earn (SAYE) plan cancellation**
>
> An entity enters into an SAYE plan with its employees. The terms of the plan are that:
>
> - Employees will contribute £250 per month to an employee share trust.
>
> - The employee is required to contribute to the SAYE plan for five years, after which the employee can either receive their cash back plus accrued interest or use this cash to acquire shares at a 20% discount to the market price on the grant date.
>
> - An employee who ceases saving receives a reimbursement of all amounts saved to date, plus interest, but must withdraw from the plan and forfeit their right to acquire shares.
>
> The entity should account for the employee's failure to save as a cancellation. The requirement to save does not meet the definition of a service or performance condition, and so a failure to save cannot be interpreted as the failure to fulfil a service or performance condition.
>
> This results in the acceleration of any unvested portion of the award on the date that the employee stops saving and receives their cash.
>
> The probability of employees ceasing to save (and hence losing the equity option) will need to be taken into account when calculating the grant date fair value.

Funding arrangements between the parent and its subsidiary

26.116 As noted above, a parent entity sometimes makes a recharge to the subsidiary in respect of share options granted to the subsidiary's employees. Section 26 of FRS 102 does not address how to account for such intra-group payment arrangements for share-based payment transactions. Taking into account the principles for recognising share-based payment transactions, shareholder funding transactions and the fact that a recharge would otherwise result in a 'double debit' to profit or loss, a sensible approach would be to treat the recharge as an offset against the capital contribution. This would be recognised in the individual financial statements of the subsidiary entity and of the parent entity. We believe that this is particularly appropriate where there is a clear link between the recharge and the share-based payment (for example, where the recharge is based on the intrinsic value or market value of the shares when they vest). If the amount of the inter-company charge exceeded the capital contribution, that excess should be treated as a distribution from the subsidiary to its parent; and this is consistent with the principle of shareholder distributions. We consider this to be an appropriate treatment for such a recharge.

26.117 The return of the capital contribution and any excess distribution payment are separate transactions from the credit to equity arising from the equity-settled share-based payment. So it is necessary to provide separate disclosure of the gross amounts.

26.118 If the recharge in excess of the section 26 charge is treated as a distribution, a question arises whether the distribution would be unlawful if a subsidiary does not have sufficient distributable profits. Tech 02/10, 'Guidance on the determination of realised profits and losses in the context of distributions under the Companies Act 2006', issued by the ICAEW in November 2010, clarifies, *"... it will not be unlawful for the subsidiary to make the reimbursement payment, even in the absence of distributable profits, provided that the payment is not a distribution as a matter of law"*. [Tech 02/10 para 7.54].

26.119 If there is no clear link between the recharge and the share-based payment, we believe that the payment between the subsidiary and its parent should be treated in a manner consistent with management recharges. This would result in an expense recognised in the income statement for the amount recharged. Note that this would result in a 'double debit' to the income statement; this is because the subsidiary would have already recorded the services received under section 26 of the standard.

26.120 Where there is a clear link between the recharge and the share-based payment, the full amount of the recharge would be recorded within equity. It would *not* be acceptable for the subsidiary to split the recharge into two components:

- one equal to the share-based payment expense which is treated as a return of a capital contribution and recorded in equity; and

- the excess of the recharge over the amount above as an additional recharge expense in the income statement.

This would have the effect of creating the same result as if the subsidiary had applied cash-settled accounting.

Disclosures

26.121 Section 26 of FRS 102 requires disclosure for share-based payment arrangements that existed during the period. These requirements are considered under the following headings.

Nature and extent of share-based payment arrangements

26.122 The following disclosure is required:

- A description of each type of share-based payment arrangement that existed at any time during the period, including the general terms and conditions of each arrangement, such as:

  - Vesting requirements.

  - The maximum term of options granted.

  - The method of settlement (for example, whether in cash or equity).

- An entity with substantially similar types of share-based payment arrangements could aggregate this information.

[FRS 102 para 26.18(a)].

- The number and weighted average exercise prices of share options for each of the following groups of options:

  - Outstanding at the beginning of the period.

  - Granted during the period.

  - Forfeited during the period.

  - Exercised during the period.

  - Expired during the period.

  - Outstanding at the end of the period.

  - Exercisable at the end of the period.

[FRS 102 para 26.18(b)].

Determination of fair values

26.123 In the case of equity-settled share-based payment arrangements, disclosure is required of information about how an entity measured the fair value of goods or services received or the value of the equity instruments granted; if a valuation methodology was used, the entity should disclose the method and its reason for choosing it. [FRS 102 para 26.19].

26.124 In the case of cash-settled share-based payment arrangements, disclosure is required of information about how the liability was measured. [FRS 102 para 26.20].

Information about modifications

26.125 If a share-based arrangement has been modified during the period, an entity should provide an explanation of those modifications in the disclosures. [FRS 102 para 26.21].

Group plans

26.126 Entities participating in group share-based payment plans, that recognise and measure the share-based payment expense on the basis of a reasonable allocation of the expense recognised for the group, should disclose that fact and the basis for the allocation (see para 26.99 above). [FRS 102 para 26.22].

Impact on profit or loss

26.127 An entity should disclose the following information about the effect of share-based payment transactions on the entity's profit or loss for the period and on its financial position:

- The total expense recognised in profit or loss for the period.

- The total carrying amount at the end of the period for liabilities arising from share-based payment transactions.

[FRS 102 para 26.23].

Reduced disclosures for qualifying entities

26.128 Chapter 1 of this publication explains the criteria required to qualify for reduced disclosures. For entities that do qualify, paragraph 1.12(e) of FRS 102 provides exemptions from some of the section 26 disclosure requirements, if the equivalent disclosures are given in the group consolidated financial statements. But these exemptions are only available if the share-based payment is being settled in the equity instruments of another group entity. The disclosure exemption applies to the following section 26 disclosures:

- FRS 102 paragraph 26.18(b) (the number and weighted average exercise prices of share options for each of the following groups of options – see para 26.122 above),

- FRS 102 paragraph 26.19 - 26.21 (determination of fair values and information about modifications – see paras 26.123 to 26.125 above), and

- FRS 102 paragraph 26.23 (impact on profit or loss – see para 26.127 above).

Related party disclosures

26.129 Section 33 of FRS 102 contains a requirement to disclose compensation payable to key management personnel, which includes share-based payments. [FRS 102 para 33.6]. This requirement is discussed further in chapter 33.

Directors' emoluments disclosure

26.130 Section 26 of FRS 102 does not deal with the disclosure of directors' emoluments. Disclosure requirements for long-term incentive awards and other share-based payment transactions involving directors are contained in sections 412 and 420 of the Companies Act 2006 and in the Listing Rules. Details of these requirements are covered in chapter 5 of the Manual of Accounting – Narrative Reporting.

Cash flow statements

26.131 Section 7 of FRS 102 requires an entity to report cash flows from operating activities. Employee share-based payment transactions that are equity-settled should be adjusted for in reporting the cash flows from operating activities, because this represents a non-cash item that is operating in nature. [FRS 102 para 7.18]. Cash flow statements are covered in detail in chapter 7.

Materiality

26.132 Section 3 of FRS 102 confirms that disclosure requirements set out in the standard do not need to be applied where the effect of applying them is immaterial. [FRS 102 para 3.16A]. Both the quantitative and qualitative impact of an entity's share-based payment transactions should be assessed in order to determine the impact of applying section 26. It will also be necessary to consider whether the impact of share-based payment transactions is likely to become material in the future. If the impact of applying section 26 is determined to be either quantitatively or qualitatively material, this section of the standard should be applied in full.

Impact on distributable reserves

26.133 Section 26 of FRS 102 is not concerned with how to determine distributable profits. Such matters are dealt with in law. This is instead considered in Tech 02/10 issued by the ICAEW in November 2010. For more details, see our Manual of Accounting – IFRS for the UK, which addresses the impact of share-based payment transactions on distributable reserves.

Transitional issues

26.134 FRS 102 Section 26 must be applied to all share-based payment transactions that are granted on or after an entity's transition date and also to cash settled share based payment transactions that have yet to be settled at the transition date.

26.135 There are some choices available to entities for share-based payment transactions granted (or settled) before transition:

	Equity settled	Cash settled
Entities transitioning from UK GAAP or IFRS	Entities that previously applied FRS20/IFRS2 may continue to apply these standards to equity settled share-based payment transactions granted before the date of transition or they may choose to apply FRS 102 Section 26 at the date of transition.	Cash-settled awards that have been settled prior to transition will not need to be recognised on transition to FRS102.

FRS 102 applies to cash-settled awards that are not yet settled at transition date. |
| Entities **not** transitioning from UK GAAP or IFRS | These entities may choose to ignore equity settled share-based payment transactions granted prior to the transition date or alternatively apply FRS 102 Section 26. | |

[FRS 102 para 35.10(b)].

26.136 The move from old UK GAAP to new GAAP should not cause any significant problems; this because FRS 20 is identical to IFRS 2, on which section 26 of FRS 102 is based. However, entities need to note the matters set out in the following paragraphs when they apply the provisions of this chapter to share-based payments.

26.137 As noted in paragraph 26.32 above, section 26 requires the fair value of an equity-settled award with employees to be calculated at the date of grant. So, if an entity has used an 'intrinsic value' approach under FRS 20 (where it was deemed that the fair value of the equity instrument could not be estimated reliably), the fair value should now be determined under section 26 using the guidance in paragraph 26.30 onwards above. However, for grants made before the transition date where the entity chooses to continue to apply IFRS 2 or FRS 20, the valuation technique under old GAAP would still be used (see para 26.135 above).

26.138 Section 26 of FRS 102 simplifies the recognition of share-based payment transactions for group schemes, by allowing a group entity receiving goods or services to recognise a cost on the basis of a reasonable allocation of the expense recognised by the consolidated group.

Chapter 27

Impairment of assets

Impairment of assets

Objective and scope

27.1 The principle of FRS 102 is that an entity's assets should be carried at no more than their recoverable amount. Recoverable amount is the higher of an asset's (or cash-generating unit's) fair value less costs to sell and its value in use. Where the carrying value of an asset is above its recoverable amount, the asset is impaired, and an impairment loss is required to be recognised.

■ Section 27 of FRS 102 applies in accounting for the impairment of all assets, unless specifically excluded from the scope of section 27. Assets excluded are:

    ■ assets arising from construction contracts (see section 23);

    ■ deferred tax assets (see section 29);

    ■ assets arising from employee benefits (see section 28);

    ■ financial assets within the scope of section 11 or 12;

    ■ investment property measured at fair value (see section 16); and

    ■ biological assets related to agricultural activity measured at fair value less estimated costs to sell (see section 34).

[FRS 102 para 27.1].

27.2 Section 27 does not apply in accounting for the impairment of deferred acquisition costs and intangible assets arising from a contract within the scope of FRS 103. [FRS 102 para 27.1A].

Impairment of inventories

Selling price less costs to complete and sell

27.3 An entity should assess at each reporting date whether there is any indication that inventory is impaired. This assessment should be carried out by comparing the carrying value of each inventory item (or group of similar items) with its selling price less costs to complete and sell. If the selling price less costs to complete and sell is lower than the carrying value, the inventory is impaired and must be written down to its selling price less costs to complete and sell. This reduction is immediately recognised in profit or loss. [FRS 102 para 27.2].

Impairment of assets

27.4 The term 'reporting date' includes not only the year end date, but also interim (half-year or quarterly) reporting dates. So, an entity might be required to complete an impairment test more than once a year. Chapter 13 provides further details and examples on impairment of inventories.

27.5 If an entity cannot determine the selling price less costs to complete and sell by inventory item, even after making every reasonable effort to do so, it could group the inventory relating to the same product line, having similar purposes or end uses, produced and marketed in the same geographical area for the purpose of assessing impairment. [FRS 102 para 27.3].

Reversal of impairment

27.6 The standard requires an entity to make a new assessment of selling price less costs to complete and sell at each reporting date. If there are any indicators that suggest that the circumstances that caused an impairment loss to be recognised in a previous period no longer exist or have changed, the amount of reversal that can be recognised is restricted to increasing the carrying value of the relevant inventory to the carrying value that would have been recognised if the original impairment had not occurred (that is, the new carrying value is the lower of the cost and the revised selling price less costs to complete and sell). [FRS 102 para 27.4].

Impairment of assets other than inventories

General principles

27.7 An asset cannot be carried in the balance sheet at more than its recoverable amount. *"If, and only if, the recoverable amount of an asset is less than its carrying amount, the entity shall reduce the carrying amount of the asset to its recoverable amount. That reduction is an impairment loss".* [FRS 102 para 27.5].

27.8 If an impairment loss has arisen, it should be recognised in profit or loss immediately, unless the asset is carried at a revalued amount according to another section of FRS 102 (for example, according to the revaluation model in chapter 17). For assets that are carried at revalued amounts, an impairment loss is treated as a revaluation decrease until the amount in revaluation reserve relating to the asset is reduced to zero. Any excess is charged to the profit and loss account. [FRS 102 para 27.6].

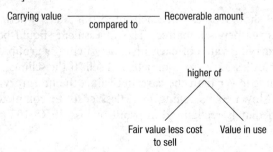

Indicators of impairment

27.9 An entity should assess at each reporting date whether there is any indication that an asset might be impaired. If any indication exists, the entity should estimate the asset's recoverable amount. If there is no indication of impairment, the recoverable amount is not required to be estimated. [FRS 102 para 27.7]. The term 'reporting date' includes not only the year end date, but also interim (half-year or quarterly) reporting dates. So, an entity might be required to complete an impairment test more than once a year.

27.10 The starting point for determining the recoverable amount in impairment testing is at the level of individual assets, unless the asset does not generate cash inflows that are largely independent of other assets or groups of assets. Where there are no such independent cash flows, the recoverable amount is determined for the cash-generating unit (CGU) to which the asset belongs. A CGU is the smallest identifiable group of assets that generates cash inflows that are largely independent of the cash inflows from other assets or groups of assets. [FRS 102 para 27.8]. A CGU can be a single asset.

Decision tree

27.11 The flow chart below gives guidance on determining the level at which to perform an impairment test, whether it is at the individual asset or CGU level.

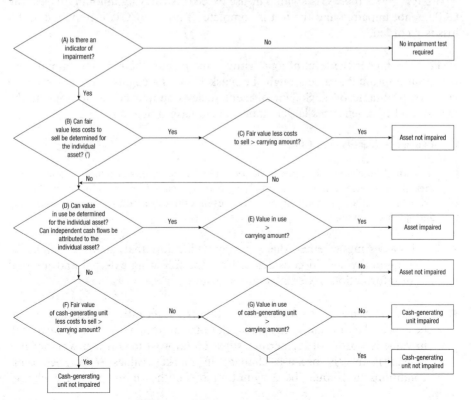

Notes to decision tree:

1. Box B – can the fair value less costs to sell be determined for the individual asset? This will usually be the case. If yes, go to box C and estimate the fair value less costs to sell for the asset. If no, go to Box D.

2. Box C – does the fair value less costs to sell of the asset exceed its carrying amount? If yes, the asset is not impaired and the test is complete. If no, go to Box D.

3. Box D – can value in use be determined for the individual asset (that is, does the asset generate independent cash flows)? If yes, go to box E and determine the asset's value in use. If no, go to Box F and determine the fair value less costs to sell of the CGU to which the asset belongs.

4. Box E – does the asset's value in use exceed its carrying amount? If yes, the asset is not impaired and the test is complete. If no, the asset is impaired and a loss must be recorded.

5. Box F – does the fair value less costs to sell of the CGU to which the asset belongs exceed its carrying amount? If yes, the CGU is not impaired and the test is complete. If no, then go to Box G and calculate the CGU's value in use.

6. Box G – does the CGU's value in use exceed its carrying amount? If yes, the CGU is not impaired and the test is complete. If no, the CGU is impaired and a loss is recorded.

27.12   The higher the level of aggregation, the greater the risk that impairment losses on unprofitable assets might be masked by unrecognised increases in the value of profitable ones. So, impairment reviews should be carried out at the lowest level that generates largely independent cash flows.

> **Example – Identifying a CGU**
>
> Individual hotels usually generate income that is largely independent of others, and their performance is monitored closely by management on an individual basis. So it is probable that they form individual CGUs, even if there are central sales and marketing and finance functions.

27.13   In assessing whether there is any indication that an asset might be impaired, an entity should consider at least the following external and internal sources of information. External sources include:

■   A decline in the asset's market value that is significantly greater than would be expected as a result of the passage of time or normal use. A significant fall in value is worthy of further investigation (at least to consider whether it is relevant); this is because changes in market values reflect economic conditions and could be a symptom of another more pervasive change (for example, technological change or a change in demand for the asset's output).

- Significant adverse changes that have taken place or are expected in the near future in the technological, market, economic or legal environment in which the entity operates or in its markets.

- Increases in interest rates or other market rates of return that could materially affect the discount rate used in calculating the asset's recoverable amount.

- The carrying amount of the entity's net assets exceeds the entity's estimated fair value (or market capitalisation, if it is listed) – for example, in relation to the potential sale of part or all of the entity.

Internal sources of information include:

- Obsolescence or physical damage affecting the asset.

- Significant adverse changes that have taken place or are expected in the near future in the extent to which, or in the way that, an asset is used or expected to be used. This includes the asset becoming idle, plans to discontinue or restructure the operation to which the asset belongs, or the asset's disposal. It also includes reassessing the asset's useful life from indefinite to finite.

- Deterioration in the expected level of the asset's performance.

- Management's own forecasts of future net cash inflows or operating profits might show a significant decline from previous budgets and forecasts.

[FRS 102 para 27.9].

Consider the following examples:

Example 1 – Reduced selling price of recently acquired asset

Entity A bought (and capitalised) a computer system off the shelf for £2 million. Shortly afterwards, the manufacturer dropped the selling price to £1.5 million.

A change in the market value of an asset is an indicator of impairment.

Example 2 – Impairment indicator – global competitor starting business in an existing entity's territory

Entity S is the biggest local supermarket chain in country X, a developing country.

Recently, the global chain, M, has decided to set up operations in the country. Entity M is well known world-wide, and intends to establish its shops close to those of entity S and to offer a wider range of products and international brands to entity S's customers. But, management of entity S expects to retain most of its customer base.

In this example, entity M s market entry is an impairment indicator. Management should perform impairment tests, estimating the recoverable amount of its assets, based on the best available information.

Example 3 – Impairment indicator – change of asset's use

Entity C uses asset M to manufacture product A. There has been a significant reduction in demand for product A as a result of a change in consumer taste. Management has not assessed asset M for impairment because it can, subject to minimal reconfiguration, be used in the manufacture of its new product, T.

Entity C should review asset M for impairment. The change in use is itself an indicator of impairment. Entity C's management will need to assess the impact of both the change in consumer tastes and the asset's proposed change of use on the asset's recoverable amount.

Example 4 – Impairment indicator – government price controls

Entity A is a water and sewage entity with a country-wide water and sewage network. Although entity A is a listed entity, the government is the controlling shareholder.

Management has asked the government to allow a 3% increase in prices in order to cover recent cost increases. This is a regulated business, and any price rise must be authorised by the government. The government has only authorised a 0.5% price increase.

The fact that the government has not approved the requested price increase is an indication that the entity's assets used in the water and sewage network might be impaired. The assets should be tested for impairment, based on the approved business plans and using the information available regarding prices and the assets' current condition.

Example 5 – Impairment indicator – introduction of a superior competitor product

Entity Q produces printers for home computers and has for some time been the market leader. Its chief competitor, entity R, has recently developed a new product that is widely acknowledged as being superior to that of entity Q, because it has the ability to also photocopy documents, send and receive facsimile and colour-print photographs.

Entity Q's management has not performed an impairment review on its plant, on the grounds that annual production and sales are ahead of budget.

Entity Q should review its plant and equipment for impairment. The change in the market for its product can have a significant impact on the equipment's value based on the economic benefit to be obtained from its continued use.

The existence of a conflicting indicator (sales ahead of budget) is not sufficient to negate the need for an impairment review. Management will be required to assess the impact of this new competing product on demand for its existing product and on expected future cash flows.

27.14 Increases in market rates of interest are identified as an indicator for entities to consider. But increases in short-term interest rates would not necessarily trigger an impairment review. Changes in interest rates need to be considered in the context of the level of headroom indicated by previous impairment tests as well as the asset being tested; a long-life asset is tested using discount rates that reflect long-term interest rates. A marginal increase in short-term interest rates is unlikely to lead to an impairment charge where there was significant headroom in the previous test.

27.15 The indicators above and in the standard are examples only, and do not constitute a comprehensive list. Other indicators might present themselves. If there are any, an impairment review should be carried out. This includes reviewing the remaining useful life, the depreciation (amortisation) method or the residual value for the asset, and adjusting it according to the relevant section of FRS 102 applicable to the asset (for example, section 17 for property, plant and equipment, or section 18 for intangible assets other than goodwill), even if no impairment loss is recognised for the asset. [FRS 102 para 27.10].

Consider the following examples:

Example 1 – Test impairment at the individual asset level where possible

An item of PPE (machine B) is one of the assets used within a CGU. Machine B has become redundant and is being abandoned by management. The recoverable amount of machine B's CGU (which is profitable) exceeds its carrying amount.

Impairment should be identified at the individual asset level, where possible. Management should recognise an impairment loss for machine B, as its carrying amount is above recoverable amount.

The recoverable amount should be calculated for the CGU to which the asset belongs only where the recoverable amount for the individual asset cannot be identified. Machine B is being abandoned and, as a result, will no longer be one of the assets used within the CGU. So, machine B is tested for impairment on its own ifi ts recoverable amount can be estimated (which should be straightforward if the asset is being abandoned).

Example 2 – Impairment due to future closure

Entity B is proposing to close a manufacturing unit; this is an indicator of impairment. The closure will take place in two years' time during which, for operational purposes, the unit (a separate CGU) will continue to manufacture, buying in raw materials and making sales as normal. Entity B is considering impairment issues. It has fixed assets at the unit whose useful lives are now two years rather than ten years, which they would have been if the unit was not being closed. The carrying value of the fixed assets is £100, and the 'normal' depreciation charge is £10 per year. Based on the current year impairment review, there is an impairment attributable to the fixed assets of £30, and the residual (that is, realisable) value of the fixed assets in two years' time is £40.

The plant has been reviewed for impairment, and an impairment charge of £30 needs to be recorded in the current year. This gives a remaining net book value of £70; in order to establish the depreciation charge to be recorded, it is necessary to subtract the residual value. This gives a remaining value of £30 to be depreciated over the remaining useful economic life of two years.

Companies Act requirements

27.16 The Companies Act's rules on impairments are set out in SI 2008/410, 'The Large and Medium-sized Companies and Groups (Accounts and Reports) Regulations 2008', and are framed in terms of 'permanent diminutions in value' and 'temporary diminutions in value'. There has often been difficulty in determining what is permanent and what is temporary. The Companies Act requires a company to make provision if any fixed asset (including a fixed asset investment) has diminished in value and this reduction is expected to be permanent. In such a situation, the company must reduce the amount at which it recognises the asset in its financial statements by the amount of this diminution in value. This requirement applies whether or not the asset has a limited useful economic life. [SI 2008/410 1 Sch 19, 20].

27.17 FRS 102 does not specifically use the term 'permanent diminution' or contrast this with a temporary diminution. Where an impairment is identified according to the methodology of the standard, the asset should be written down.

27.18 FRS 102 also introduces the concept of the cash-generating unit (CGU), which contrasts with the Act's requirements that *". . . in determining the aggregate of any item the amount of each individual asset or liability that falls to be taken into account shall be determined separately"*. Whilst the Act, as a result, appears to require each asset or liability to be looked at separately, the standard requires assets and liabilities to be grouped together in some circumstances for the purpose of testing assets for impairment.

27.19 But the standard makes it clear that CGUs are the smallest identifiable group of assets that generate cash inflows that are largely independent of the cash inflows from other assets or groups of assets. So it aims to ensure that the smallest possible grouping of cash-earning assets and liabilities that is independent of the rest of the entity's income is chosen. This aims to come as close to the Act's requirements as is, in practice, possible, whilst at the same time being practical by recognising that assets that are inter-dependent can only be tested as one unit. Nonetheless, the standard emphasises that the value in use of a fixed asset should be estimated individually where reasonably practicable. No individual asset can be written down below the higher of its value in use, fair value less costs to sell, and zero.

Measuring recoverable amount

27.20 'Recoverable amount' is defined as the higher of an asset's (or cash-generating unit's) fair value less costs to sell and value in use. [FRS 102 para 27.11].

27.21 Both fair value less costs to sell and value in use can be difficult to determine in practice. It might be possible to determine fair value less costs to sell, even if an asset is not traded in an active market. Estimating value in use is a matter of judgement, not fact, requiring estimates of cash flows many years into the future and determining appropriate discount rates to bring them back to their present values. The objective is to make the estimates as realistic as possible.

27.22 It is not always necessary to calculate both measures when performing an impairment review. If an asset's fair value less costs to sell or its value in use exceeds its carrying amount, there is no need to estimate the other amount; this is because the asset is not impaired. [FRS 102 para 27.12].

> **Example – Value in use less than fair value less costs to sell**
>
> Entity E is involved in the generation and distribution of electricity. Management is reviewing all of its assets for impairment as a result of a fall in the market price of electricity. One of the entity's power stations is two years old, has a carrying value of £2.5m and a value in use of £2.2m, taking into account the revised electricity price. The market for these assets is an active one, because investors are keen to enter the market to pursue the opportunities arising from market deregulation. A similar asset was recently sold to a US-based global power utility for £2.6m (management considers that the recent fall in the market price of electricity has not impacted asset prices). The estimated incremental costs that would be directly attributable to the disposal are £50,000.
>
> Management has no intention of selling the power station and is proposing to recognise an impairment charge based on its value in use.
>
> This is not correct: management should not recognise an impairment charge, because the recoverable amount (that is, the higher of value in use and fair value less costs to sell) exceeds the carrying amount. Management could recover the asset's carrying amount if it chose to sell it rather than use it in its operations; as a result, no impairment would be recorded in this situation.

27.23 If value in use is found to be lower than the asset's carrying amount, the asset should not automatically be written down to value in use. Before a write-down is booked, the asset's fair value less costs to sell also needs to be estimated in order to determine recoverable amount (being the higher of fair value less costs to sell and value in use).

27.24 If there is no reason to believe that an asset's value in use is materially greater than its fair value less costs to sell, the asset's fair value less costs to sell can be used as its recoverable amount. This is generally the case for an asset that is held for disposal. [FRS 102 para 27.13].

Fair value less costs to sell

27.25 'Fair value less costs to sell' is defined as *"the amount obtainable from the sale of an asset or cash-generating unit in an arm's length transaction between knowledgeable, willing parties, less the costs of disposal".* [FRS 102 para 27.14,

Glossary of terms]. FRS 102 provides a hierarchy of sources for fair value less costs to sell.

27.26 The best indicator of fair value less costs to sell is the price in a binding arm's length sale agreement adjusted for the costs of disposal or a market price in an active market. [FRS 102 para 27.14].

27.27 An 'active market' is defined as:

> *"a market in which all the following conditions exist:*
>
> *(a) the items traded in the market are homogeneous;*
>
> *(b) willing buyers and sellers can normally be found at any time; and*
>
> *(c) prices are available to the public."*

[FRS 102 Glossary of terms].

27.28 There are very few assets tested for impairment under FRS 102 that are traded in an active market (as defined by the standard). If there is neither a binding sale agreement nor an active market, fair value can be estimated as the amount that the entity could obtain from the asset's disposal in an arm's length transaction, based on data from recent market transactions. In determining this amount, an entity should consider evidence from recent transactions for similar assets in the same industry. [FRS 102 para 27.14].

27.29 Any restrictions imposed on the asset should also be considered. Costs to sell should include the cost of obtaining relaxation of a restriction so that the asset can be sold. Similarly, if a restriction applies to any potential buyer of an asset, the asset's fair value might be lower than that of an asset whose use is not restricted. [FRS 102 para 27.14A].

27.30 Where there is an asset for which there is no active market (such as goodwill attaching to a business), fair value less costs to sell can still be derived using estimation techniques such as a discounted cash flow analysis. The discounted cash flow techniques used should incorporate assumptions that market participants would use in estimating the asset's fair value.

27.31 Management will have to determine the inputs into the discounted cash flow analysis, including establishing a discount rate to use for the discounted cash flow. When determining fair value using cash flows, post-tax cash flows should be discounted using a post-tax discount rate (using market participant assumptions).

> **Example – Establishing the discount rate**
>
> Entity C has a capital structure of 25% equity and 75% debt. Its post-tax weighted average cost of capital is 8%. Most of entity C's competitors have a capital structure of 40% equity and 60% debt, and a weighted average cost of capital (WACC) of 10%. Entity C's management proposes to use its own cost of capital as a starting point for determining an appropriate discount rate to use in its impairment reviews.

But entity C's management should not use its own cost of capital as a starting point for determining an appropriate discount rate. The potential willing purchaser, who must be considered in determining fair value, is likely to have a cost of capital in line with the majority of the industry participants. Entity C's management should use the normal industry capital structure of 40% equity and 60% debt, and a WACC of 10%, in determining fair value.

27.32 In practice, a first assessment of the valuation is performed using cash flows from management. There must be, where appropriate, market evidence to support the key assumptions underpinning the cash flow analysis; for example, growth rates could be considered by benchmarking to industry/analyst reports. If some of the assumptions used are not those that a market participant would use, those cash flows must be adjusted to take into account the assumptions that are supported by market evidence.

27.33 It is important that, when comparing carrying amount with recoverable amount, entities ensure that the carrying amount of the CGU being tested for impairment is calculated consistently with the cash flows included in the fair value less costs to sell calculation. For example, if the cash flows include working capital and tax, the carrying amount of the CGU should also include the working capital and tax balances.

27.34 If comparable transactions in similar assets or businesses are available, they should be used as market evidence. Consideration should be given to the comparability of the acquired asset/business to the asset/CGU being tested; for example, adjustments for factors such as size, growth expectations, profitability and risk will need to be considered. This evidence might arise in the implied multiple of earnings before interest, taxes, depreciation and amortisation (EBITDA) or revenue that was paid in a comparable transaction which, when applied to the current model (and adjusted for points of difference), provides support for the valuation. For example, if there are a number of recent transactions in comparable entities where the price paid is six times EBITDA, and management has produced a valuation that is ten times EBITDA, the external data would appear not to support the assumptions made in the valuation. Care is needed in selecting comparable entities; risk profile and size might well be more important than geography. Care is also needed to avoid selection bias: if one transaction in ten provides some support for the EBITDA multiple, but the same transaction is regarded in the financial press as an over-payment and an isolated example, it should not be used.

Value in use

27.35 The definition of 'value in use' is *"the present value of the future cash flows expected to be derived from an asset"* or cash generating unit. [FRS 102 para 27.15].

27.36 In the following, where value in use can only be determined at a cash-generating unit level, the requirements to calculate cash flows at an asset level can be read as applying to that for a cash-generating unit.

27.37 Calculating value in use involves the following steps:

- estimating the future cash flows expected to be derived from the asset's continuing use, including those from its ultimate disposal; and

- applying the appropriate discount rate to those future cash flows.

[FRS 102 para 27.15].

27.38 The following factors should be reflected when calculating an asset's value in use:

- estimated future cash flows expected to be derived from the asset;

- estimating the potential variation in the amount and timing of the future cash flows;

- taking account of the time value of money (discounting), using current market risk-free interest rates;

- estimating the price for bearing the asset's inherent uncertainty (for example, whether the asset will perform as intended); and

- taking account of other factors, such as illiquidity, which would be reflected by the market in pricing future cash flows expected to be derived from the asset.

[FRS 102 para 27.16].

Cash flows

27.39 Cash flows should include:

- cash inflows expected from the continuing use of the asset;

- cash outflows expected to be necessarily incurred to generate the cash inflows from the asset's continuing use (including cash outflows to prepare the asset for use) and that are directly attributed, or allocated on a reasonable and consistent basis, to the asset; and

- net cash flows expected to be received (or paid) for the asset's disposal at the end of its useful life in an arm's length transaction between knowledgeable, willing parties.

The period covered by the cash flow forecast should relate to the useful life of the asset being reviewed for impairment. Recent financial forecasts or budgets can be used to estimate the cash flows. If the useful life of the asset concerned extends beyond the period covered by budgets or forecasts, it might be necessary to extrapolate the cash flow projections. When extrapolating cash flow projections, a steady or declining growth rate can be used for subsequent years, unless an increasing rate can be justified. [FRS 102 para 27.17].

27.40 Estimates of future cash flows should be based on the asset's current condition. Cash flows should exclude:

- Cash flows relating to financing activities (this is because liabilities are excluded from the asset's carrying amount, and the cost of capital is taken into account by discounting the cash flows).

- Income tax receipts or payments (this is because FRS 102 requires value in use to be calculated on the basis of discounting pre-tax cash flows at a pre-tax discount rate).

- Cash flows expected to arise from future restructuring which is not yet committed or those arising from improving or enhancing the asset's performance.

[FRS 102 paras 27.18, 27.19].

27.41 Future expenditure (including improvement-type capital expenditure) and the related benefits should also be excluded from the calculation of value in use to the extent that the expenditure will improve or enhance the asset's performance.

27.42 However, capital expenditure which is necessary to maintain the asset or CGU at its current standard of performance should be included in the calculation of value in use. Similarly, the expected future cost of replacement or restoration expenditure for the component is treated as if it were part of the day-to-day servicing of the larger asset and is included in the cash flows used to assess the recoverable amount of the larger asset; this is because such costs maintain, but do not enhance, the current performance of the CGU.

> **Example – Treatment of costs that maintain the current standard of performance**
>
> The carrying value of a furnace is being reviewed for impairment. The furnace has a useful life of 20 years and requires relining every five years. The lining is treated as a separate asset component under FRS 102. So, the cost of the lining is depreciated over five years, and the remainder of the furnace is depreciated over 20 years.
>
> For calculating the furnace's value in use, the net cash flows forecast for the remainder of the furnace's 20-year useful life would include the costs relating to relining the furnace every five years, because that expenditure is necessary to maintain the current standard of performance.

27.43 In practice, the dividing line between maintenance-type and improvement-type capital expenditure is rarely clear-cut, since businesses are not static; and so judgement must be applied.

Discount rate

27.44 Investment decisions take account of the time value of money and the risks associated with expected future cash flows. These are also reflected in the measurement of an asset's value in use. Projected future cash flows are discounted at a pre-tax rate that reflects both current market assessments of the time value of money and the risks specific to the asset for which the future cash flow estimates have not been adjusted. [FRS 102 para 27.20]. This means that (unless fair value less costs to sell is higher) an asset is regarded as impaired if it is not expected to earn a current market-related rate of return on its carrying value.

27.45 The standard requires that future cash flows should be discounted at a pre-tax discount rate. This is not the same as discounting cash flows as a post-tax discount rate. This is illustrated in the examples below.

> **Example – Deriving a pre-tax rate from a post-tax rate in a simple scenario**
>
> The post-tax market rate of return required from an asset is 14%. Profits are taxed at 30%; there is a tax allowance of 100% of the cost of the asset. All cash flows arise at the end of year 1.
>
> For an asset costing £100, the required post-tax cash flows during year 1 are £114. Pre-tax cash flows of £120 must be earned in order to give the required post-tax return of £114. Pre-tax cash flows of £120 result in a tax charge of £6 – comprising tax on profit before depreciation of £36 (30% of £120) less tax relief on the cost of the asset of £30 (30% of £100). So, the required pre-tax rate is 20%.
>
> The value in use of £100 of an asset with the above cash flows can be derived, either by discounting the post-tax cash flows of £114 at the post-tax rate of 14%, or by discounting the pre-tax cash flows of £120 at the derived pre-tax rate of 20%. The same answer is obtained from both methods, because the cost of the asset is fully deductible for tax purposes as a result of the 100% capital allowances.

27.46 In many cases, where accounting and taxable profits are similar, a reasonable approximation to the pre-tax rate would be to gross up the post-tax rate (often based on an entity's WACC, adjusted to specific risks) by the rate of tax on corporate profits. However, in more complex cases, this might not produce the right answer, as illustrated by the following, more complex example.

> **Example – Calculating a pre-tax discount rate**
>
> Entity A has calculated a WACC of 8% based on market assumptions. Management is aware that this is a post-tax rate and, therefore, wants to determine a pre-tax discount rate by grossing up the 8% by the statutory tax rate in entity A's country, which is 35%. The result is 12.3% (8%/0.65).
>
> The 12.3% is only the correct pre-tax discount rate if the specific amount and timing of the future tax cash flows are reflected by this rate. So, a grossed-up discount rate works only if there is no deferred tax.
>
> As soon as there is deferred tax, an iterative calculation needs to be done that considers the fact that a carrying amount after impairment would trigger new deferred taxes, and this would again change the carrying amount.

The required pre-tax rate is the rate of return that will, after tax has been deducted, give the required post-tax rate of return. The following calculation illustrates how the pre-tax rate could correctly be derived from the post-tax rate.

A CGU is being tested for impairment at the end of 20X0. The CGU comprises a specific asset, which was purchased two years ago for £2,400. The asset has a ten-year useful life for accounting purposes. Tax relief on the asset is available on a straight line basis over the asset's first three years of the life. The tax rate is 35%.

Hence, the carrying value for tax purposes, at the end of 20X0, is £800 (£2,400 × 1/3 years), and the carrying value for accounting purposes is £1,920 (£2,400 × 8/10 years). Applying the tax rate of 35% to the difference gives a deferred tax liability with a carrying value of £392: (£1,920 — £800) × 35%.

Pre-tax profits from the asset are expected to be £125 at the end of 20X1, increasing by £5 for each of the following seven years. The appropriateness of such an increasing rate has been considered and determined reasonable. The results for the seven years in question are as follows:

Currency (£)	20X1	20X2	20X3	20X4	20X5	20X6	20X7	20X8
Pre-tax profit	125	130	135	140	145	150	155	160
Add back depreciation	240	240	240	240	240	240	240	240
Pre-tax cash flow	**365**	**370**	**375**	**380**	**385**	**390**	**395**	**400**
Tax on profit (@ 35%)	(44)	(46)	(47)	(49)	(51)	(53)	(54)	(56)
Post-tax cash flow	**321**	**325**	**328**	**331**	**334**	**338**	**341**	**344**

The post-tax discount rate, determined from the entity's WACC, is 8%.

There are two potential misapplications of the requirements of the standard that are commonly seen. Neither of these gives the correct value in use per the requirements of the standard.

Misapplication 1: Discount post-tax cash flow at post-tax discount rate of 8%. This gives a value in use of £1,904.

Misapplication 2: Discount pre-tax cash flow at post-tax discount rate grossed up for the tax rate. This rate would be 8%/(1 — 0.35) = 12.3%. This gives a value in use of £1,866.

These misapplications fail to achieve the correct result, either by not accounting for varying period-on-period cash flows or by ignoring deferred tax. The correct value in use (VIU) can be achieved by taking the value in use from Misapplication 1 and adjusting for the discounted cash outflows related to deferred tax. This is a complex iterative calculation, because the discounted cash outflows in question relate to the pre-tax value in use – hence, the result of the calculation feeds back into the calculation itself. The calculation is best solved with the aid of a computer, but the following summarises the final calculation for the example above, once the iteration has been completed:

Currency (£)	20X0	20X1	20X2	20X3	20X4	20X5	20X6	20X7	20X8
Pre-tax VIU (*a*)	1,729	1,513	1,296	1,080	864	648	432	216	0
Tax base (*β*)	800								
a – *β*	929	1,513	1,296	1,080	864	648	432	216	0
Change in *a* – *β*		584	(216)	(216)	(216)	(216)	(216)	(216)	(216)
@ 35% (tax)		204	(76)	(76)	(76)	(76)	(76)	(76)	(76)
Discounted (8%)	(175)								
Post-tax VIU	1,904								
Pre-tax VIU	**1,729**								

The 'post-tax VIU' number is as calculated in 'Misapplication 1' above. The iterative process will complete when a set of figures for the first line have been derived which, when discounted at 8%, produce the same number as in the bottom 'pre-tax VIU' line.

Having derived the correct pre-tax VIU, and having the correct pre-tax cash flows, it is possible to 'back-solve' to obtain the pre-tax discount rate that discounts the latter to the former. In this case, the figure is 15.4%.

Assets held for service potential

27.47 FRS 102 is written from the perspective of commercial enterprises where fixed assets are employed to generate cash flows for the business. Where fixed assets are not held for the purpose of generating cash flows (such as some assets held by non-profit-making organisations), the value to such organisations of fixed assets acquired for the purpose of carrying out their activities cannot meaningfully be measured in terms of cash flow, because the benefits are expected to be derived from the asset's use and/or through sale. The value in use for assets held for their service potential is the present value of the asset's remaining service potential, including the net amount expected to be received from its disposal. In some cases, this might be the same as the costs avoided by possessing the asset. As a result, the depreciated replacement cost method is a suitable measurement model, unless an alternative measure is more appropriate. [FRS 102 para 27.20A].

27.48 Assets held for their service potential are usually encountered in non-profit-making entities, such as charities. In practice, an impairment of an asset employed in a non-cash-generating activity is likely to arise only where the asset suffers impairment in a physical sense (for example, where the asset is physically damaged or where the quality of service that it provides has deteriorated). As long as such assets continue to provide the anticipated benefits to the organisation, the consumption of such benefits will be reflected in regular depreciation charges.

Recognising and measuring an impairment loss for a cash-generating unit

27.49 If the recoverable amount of an asset or CGU is less than its carrying amount, the entity recognises an impairment loss. The impairment loss should be allocated to write down the asset's or CGU's carrying amount in the following order:

- Reducing any goodwill allocated to the asset or CGU.

- Against other assets in the CGU on a *pro rata* basis, based on the carrying amount of each asset in the CGU.

[FRS 102 para 27.21].

> **Example – Allocation of impairment to goodwill and then a brand**
>
> Entity A is testing its CGU, which contains goodwill and two brands, X and Y. The CGU needs to be impaired, because the recoverable amount is lower than the carrying amount. Entity A believes this is mainly due to the poor performance of brand Y and wants to allocate the impairment charge to this brand.
>
> If a CGU is considered to be impaired, the goodwill allocated to that CGU is written off first. Entity A must first impair the goodwill before any charge is allocated to the remaining assets in the CGU. However, if the brand was a separate CGU (that is, its fair value can be determined), the allocation of impairment to goodwill and CGU is more complex, and the brand would need to be tested separately.

27.50 But, within this allocation framework, each asset should be reduced only to the highest of:

- its fair value less costs to sell (if this can be determined);

- its value in use (if this can be determined); and

- zero.

[FRS 102 para 27.22].

27.51 In some come circumstances, if the impairment loss cannot be fully allocated (for example, if the assets do not have sufficient value to absorb the impairment loss in its entirety), the impairment loss should be allocated to other assets of the CGU on a pro rata basis of the carrying amounts of those other assets. [FRS 102 para 27.23].

27.52 Where an entity has an asset that is included in a CGU because it does not generate cash flows independently, its recoverable amount would generally be determined at the CGU level to which the asset belongs.

> **Example – Building considered separately for impairment testing**
>
> A CGU includes a head office building, and that asset has a readily determinable market value. The head office building will be considered separately from the CGU for the purpose of impairment testing if its market value (less costs to sell) is clearly higher than its carrying amount. In this case, it will be possible to compare the recoverable amount with the carrying amount for the individual asset, because the fair value less costs to sell is determinable. If the head office building had a market value that was less than the carrying amount, the CGU to which the asset belongs would need to be tested for impairment, because the head office does not generate cash flows independently and so does not have a stand-alone value in use.

Impairment of assets

27.53   The requirement to firstly reduce goodwill and then reduce other assets (on a pro-rata basis) might in some situations seemingly lead to an odd result. For example, when multiple CGUs support a single goodwill amount (that is, 'umbrella' goodwill where it has not been allocated to individual CGUs). It is possible that there is no obvious trigger for impairment in each of the CGUs, but there is an impairment trigger when assessing goodwill at the aggregated level.

27.54   The allocation of impairment between goodwill and multiple supporting CGUs is not straightforward and paragraphs 27.21 and 27.22 of FRS 102 should be considered. It is important to assess the supporting CGUs before dealing with any umbrella goodwill.

> **Example – Allocation of impairment losses to CGUs**
>
> Management has allocated goodwill to a group of CGUs (A, B and C) on an aggregated or 'umbrella' basis. None of the three CGUs have impairment triggers but, when considering the aggregated CGUs plus goodwill, there are indicators of impairment. Management has carried out an impairment test and estimated that the recoverable amount for the group of CGUs is £750. Below are further details of the group of CGUs:
>
> | Assets | Carrying amount £ | Fair value less costs to sell £ | Value in use £ |
> |---|---|---|---|
> | Goodwill (supported by CGUs A, B and C) | 300 | - | - |
> | – CGU A | 500 | 550 | 500 |
> | – CGU B | 90 | 40 | 50 |
> | – CGU C | 250 | 50 | 150 |
> | Total for group of CGUs | 1,140 | 640 | 700 |
> | Total recoverable amount for CGU | 750 | | |
> | Impairment to allocate | 390 | | |

An impairment of £390 has been identified and needs to be allocated between goodwill and each of the CGUs. Following the principles in FRS 102 paragraphs 27.21 and 27.22 each of the individual CGUs is written down to the recoverable amount (that is, the carrying amount of the assets within each CGU are reduced to the higher of fair value less costs to sell, value in use and zero) followed by any additional impairment of the umbrella goodwill by assessing the group of CGUs that support it. So, in practice, the recoverable amount of each asset must also be considered before allocating the impairment loss first to goodwill and then to the CGUs:

Assets	Carrying amount	Recoverable amount	Allocation of impairment	Revised carrying amount based on allocation
Goodwill	300	-	-250(b)	50
- CGU A	500	550	(a)	500
- CGU B	90	50	-40 (a)	50
- CGU C	250	150	-100 (a)	150
	1,140		-390	750

(a) Having identified that CGU B and CGU C are both impaired on an individual CGU basis these are first written down before assessing the 'umbrella' goodwill. Note that no impairment is required for CGU A, because the recoverable amount is greater than the original carrying value.

The remaining balance of the impairment loss of £250 is allocated to goodwill. Goodwill cannot be fully written down, because that would result in an impairment loss greater than that identified when assessing consolidated goodwill. The revised goodwill of £50 refers to consolidated goodwill supported by multiple CGUs.

Note that it would be incorrect to initially impair the umbrella goodwill (that is, write down by £300) because this would result in excess impairment charge overall as a result of needing to impair CGUs B and C by £140 to their recoverable amounts.

Additional requirements for impairment of goodwill

27.55   Goodwill does not generate cash flows independently from other assets or groups of assets, and so the fair value of goodwill as an individual asset cannot be determined directly. But goodwill often contributes to the cash flows of individual or multiple CGUs. As a result, the fair value of goodwill can be derived by measuring the fair value of the CGUs to which goodwill is attributable. [FRS 102 para 27.24].

27.56   Goodwill acquired in a business combination represents future economic benefits arising from assets that are not capable of being individually identified and separately recognised. Such assets might, for example, be a skilled workforce or a non-contractual customer relationship. As a result, goodwill acquired in a business combination is allocated, from the acquisition date, to each of the acquirer's CGUs or groups of CGUs that are expected to benefit from the synergies of the business combination, whether or not the acquiree's other assets or liabilities are assigned to those units. [FRS 102 para 27.25].

27.57   Where goodwill relating to any non-controlling interest is not recognised, it causes a complication when a non-wholly owned CGU to which goodwill has been allocated is reviewed for impairment. The complication is that the carrying amount of the assets and liabilities (other than goodwill) of the CGU includes the non-controlling interest's share of those assets and liabilities, together with the goodwill attributable to the parent's interest. The carrying amount does not include the non-controlling interest in goodwill; but the recoverable amount of the CGU takes no account of the fact that goodwill on the non-controlling interest's share has been omitted from the carrying amount. In order to compare 'like with like', the calculation needs to be adjusted. This is done as follows:

■ First, the carrying amount of the CGU is notionally adjusted to include goodwill attributable to the non-controlling interest. This is done by grossing up the carrying amount of goodwill allocated to the CGU to include the goodwill attributable to the non-controlling interest.

■ Then, the notional carrying amount of the CGU is compared with the recoverable amount of the CGU, to determine whether the CGU is impaired.

[FRS 102 para 27.26].

> **Example – Calculation of impairment where there is a non-controlling interest in the CGU**
>
> Entity A acquires an 80% interest in entity B for £240m on 1 January 20X6. The identifiable net assets and contingent liabilities (after fair valuing) of entity B are £200m on that date. Entity A recognises goodwill only to the extent of its own 80% interest in entity B. So, entity A recognises in its financial statements:
>
> ■ The fair value of net assets and contingent liabilities £200m.
>
> ■ Goodwill of £80m (calculated as £240m – (£200 × 80%)).
>
> ■ Non-controlling interest of £40m (£200m × 20%).
>
> Entity B is a CGU. Goodwill has been allocated to entity B, so it must be tested annually for impairment, and more frequently whenever there is an indication of impairment. It must also be tested before the end of the accounting period in which the acquisition took place.
>
> At the end of 20X6, entity A assesses the recoverable amount of the CGU (that is, entity B) as £100m. Entity A uses straight-line depreciation and a ten-year useful life for entity B's depreciable assets, and anticipates no residual value. (It is assumed, for simplicity, that the depreciable assets are £200m.) It is assumed that goodwill is amortised over a five-year period.
>
> Part of the recoverable amount of £100m is attributable to the non-controlling interest s share of goodwill that has not been recognised. According to the standard, the carrying amount of entity B should first be notionally increased, for the purpose of the impairment test, by the goodwill attributable to the non-controlling interest. That notionally increased carrying amount is then compared with the recoverable amount of £100m. This is shown in the following table:

	Carrying value of CGU	
	£m	£m
Goodwill (attributable to parent's interest) (80 × 4/5)		64
Unrecognised non-controlling interest in goodwill*		16
Gross carrying amount of identifiable net assets	200	
Accumulated depreciation	20	
Carrying amount of identifiable net assets		180
Notionally adjusted carrying amount		260
Recoverable amount		100
Impairment loss (notional)		160

* The goodwill attributable to entity A's interest of 80% was £80m at the acquisition date. So, the goodwill attributable to the non-controlling interest's 20% interest is one quarter of that, namely £16m (20 × 4/5).

The impairment loss then needs to be allocated. This is first attributed to goodwill (of which only £64m is in entity B's balance sheet, because the £16m is attributable to the non-controlling interests) and then allocated to the net assets:

	Carrying value of CGU	Allocation of impairment	After impairment
	£m	£m	£m	£m
Goodwill (attributable to parent's interest)		64	(64)	–
Gross carrying amount of identifiable net assets	200			
Accumulated depreciation	20			
Carrying amount of identifiable net assets		180	(80)	100
				100
Carrying amount[1]		244		
Recoverable amount		100		
Impairment loss (total booked)		(144)	(144)	

[1] Excludes notional amount of non-controlling interest's goodwill.

The balance of the impairment loss of £80m is recognised in full, because it relates to net assets (including both parent and non-controlling interest's share) that are also recognised in full in the financial statements. This remaining impairment loss is allocated pro rata to the identifiable assets (excluding goodwill) on the basis of their carrying amounts. The total impairment loss recognised in entity A's consolidated financial statements is therefore £64m + £80m = £144m.

27.58　If it is not possible to allocate goodwill to a CGU (or a group of CGUs) on a non-arbitrary basis, goodwill can be tested for impairment by determining the recoverable amount of either:

- the acquired entity as a whole (if goodwill relates to a non-integrated acquired entity); or

- the entire group of entities, excluding non-integrated entities (if goodwill relates to an integrated entity).

The term 'integrated' refers to the acquired business that has been restructured or dissolved into the reporting entity or other subsidiaries. When applying this paragraph, the entity will need to separate goodwill into goodwill relating to integrated entities and goodwill relating to entities that have not been integrated. In addition, the entity should follow requirements for CGUs when calculating the recoverable amount and allocating impairment losses and any reversals. [FRS 102 para 27.27].

> **Example – Integrated goodwill**
>
> Entity A is a conglomerate in the mining industry with three divisions. Division X relates to gold mines, division Y relates to diamond mines, and division Z relates to copper mines.
>
> Entity A acquired entity B for £100m on 1 January 20X0. Entity B owns diamond mines, and the identifiable net assets and contingent liabilities (after fair valuing) of entity B are £80m on that date. Entity A recognises goodwill of £20m (£100m – £80m).
>
> During 20X0 the business of entity B is integrated into division Y. For the purposes of impairment testing, goodwill arising from the acquisition of B will be included in the impairment testing of all of the goodwill associated with division Y. Divisions X and Z are excluded from this impairment test.

Reversal of an impairment loss

27.59　An impairment loss that is recognised for all assets, including goodwill, should be reversed in a later period if the reasons for the impairment loss no longer exist. [FRS 102 para 27.28].

27.60　FRS 102 requires an entity to assess, at each reporting date, whether there is any indication that an impairment loss recognised in a previous period either no longer exists or has decreased. Indicators that impairment losses might have reversed are mainly the opposite of those that gave rise to the impairment loss in the first place. If there are indicators, the entity should establish whether all or part of the prior impairment loss should be reversed. The process to establish this will depend on whether the prior impairment loss was based on:

- the recoverable amount for an individual asset; or

- the recoverable amount of the CGU to which the asset belongs.

[FRS 102 para 27.29].

Reversal where recoverable amount was estimated for an individual impaired asset

27.61   The following requirements exist where the impairment loss was based on the recoverable amount for an individual asset:

- The entity is required to estimate the recoverable amount of the asset at the current reporting date.

- If the estimated recoverable amount of the CGU exceeds its carrying amount, the carrying amount of the CGU should be increased to the recoverable amount. This increase is a reversal of an impairment loss and is recognised in profit or loss, unless the CGU is carried at a revalued amount in accordance with another chapter of the standard (for example, section 17 for plant, property and equipment). Any reversal of an impairment loss of a revalued asset should be treated as a revaluation increase in accordance with the relevant chapter of the standard.

- The amount of any reversal that can be recognised is restricted to increasing the carrying value of the relevant assets to the carrying value that would have been recognised if the original impairment had not occurred (that is, after taking account of depreciation or amortisation that would have been charged if no impairment had occurred).

- Once the reversal of an impairment loss is recognised, the depreciation or amortisation amount is based on the asset's revised carrying amount, less any residual value, on a systematic basis over its remaining useful life.

[FRS 102 para 27.30].

Reversal when recoverable amount was estimated for a cash-generating unit

27.62   The following requirements exist where the impairment loss was based on the recoverable amount of the CGU to which the asset, including goodwill, belongs:

- The entity is required to estimate the recoverable amount of that CGU at the current reporting date.

- If the estimated recoverable amount of the asset exceeds its carrying amount, the carrying amount of the asset should be increased to the recoverable amount. This increase is a reversal of an impairment loss and is recognised in profit or loss, unless the CGU is carried at a revalued amount in accordance with another chapter of the standard (for example, section 17 for plant, property and equipment). Any reversal of an impairment loss of a revalued asset should be treated as a revaluation increase in accordance with the relevant chapter of the standard. The reversal amount is allocated to the assets of the CGU, pro rata with the carrying amounts of those assets and goodwill, in the following order:

  - the assets (other than goodwill) in the CGU on a *pro rata* basis based on the carrying amount of each asset in the CGU; and

- any goodwill allocated to the CGU.

■ The amount of any reversal that can be recognised is restricted to the lower of:

- the recoverable amount; and

- the carrying value that would have been recognised if the original impairment had not occurred (that is, after taking account of depreciation or amortisation that would have been charged if no impairment had occurred).

■ Any excess in the reversal amount that cannot be allocated due to the restriction (see previous bullet point) should be allocated, on a pro rata basis, to other assets of the CGU.

■ Once the reversal of an impairment loss is recognised, the depreciation or amortisation amount is based on the asset's revised carrying amount, less any residual value, on a systematic basis over its remaining useful life.

[FRS 102 para 27.31].

Example – Reversal of impairment loss

Entity A operates trains in country X. Entity B operates bus services in the same country. To diversify its business, entity A acquired entity B for £200m on 31 December 20X0. The identifiable net assets and contingent liabilities (after fair valuing) of entity B are £150m on that date. Entity A recognises goodwill of £50m (£200m – £150m).

In June 20X1 the government announced that it would award a major bus contract to a competitor of entity A. This would have a significant adverse impact on entity B's business. Entity A's 20X1 consolidated financial statements disclosed that the goodwill of £50m relating to entity B was impaired, and an impairment loss of £50m was recognised.

During October 20X2 the competitor who had been awarded the major bus contract decided to abort the sector, because it had breached environmental laws. The government decided to award the major contract to entity B. This was a significant boost for entity B's business. Entity A's consolidated financial statements for the year ended 20X2 disclosed that previous impairment losses had been reversed, resulting in an increase in the carrying value of entity B (that is, £50m less 21 months (January 20X1 to September 20X2) of amortisation was added back to goodwill).

27.63 The requirement in FRS 102 to reverse previous impairments in some circumstances is consistent with company law, which states in SI 2008/410 that, where a company has made provision for a diminution in value, but the factors that gave rise to it no longer apply to any extent, the company must write back the provision to that extent. [SI 2008/410 1 Sch 19, 20].

Disclosures

27.64 For each class of assets, an entity should disclose the following:

- The amount of impairment losses recognised in profit or loss for the period, and the line item or items in the statement of comprehensive income (or income statement) in which the losses are included.

- The amount of reversals of impairment losses recognised in profit or loss for the period, and the line item or items in the statement of comprehensive income (or income statement) in which the reversals are included.

- A description of the events and circumstances that led to the recognition or reversal of the impairment loss.

[FRS 102 paras 27.32, 27.33A].

27.65 Examples of classes of asset are:

- inventories;

- property, plant and equipment (including investment property accounted for by the cost method);

- goodwill;

- intangible assets other than goodwill;

- investments in associates; and

- investments in joint ventures.

[FRS 102 para 27.33].

Companies Act disclosures

27.66 The formats in Schedule 1 to SI 2008/410 prescribe the headings under which depreciation of (and other amounts written off) tangible and intangible fixed assets are to be included in the profit and loss account. Under Format 1, where expenses are classified by function, an impairment loss would generally be charged under the same format heading as depreciation of (or other amounts written off) the relevant assets. Under Format 2, where expenses are classified by type, there is a separate heading 'depreciation and amounts written off tangible and intangible fixed assets'.

27.67 SI 2008/410 requires that provisions for diminution in value are made in respect of any fixed asset that has diminished in value if the reduction in its value is expected to be permanent (whether its useful economic life is limited or not). In addition, any such provisions made that are not shown in the profit and loss account must be disclosed (either separately or in aggregate) in a note to the financial statements. [SI 2008/410 1 Sch 19, 20]. Specific disclosure requirements are also given in SI 2008/410. The amounts to be disclosed are:

- The cumulative amount of provisions for depreciation or diminution in value of assets included under that item at the beginning of the financial year and at the balance sheet date.

- The amount of any such provisions made in respect of the financial year.

- The amount of any adjustments made in respect of any such provisions during that year in consequence of the disposal of any assets.

- The amount of any other adjustments made in respect of any such provisions during that year.

[SI 2008/410 1 Sch (51)(3)].

Transition issues

27.68 No special exemptions on impairment of assets are available to first-time adopters under section 35 of FRS 102. So, a first-time adopter must prepare its first financial statements as though the requirements of section 27 of FRS 102 had always applied.

27.69 However, entities transitioning from old UK GAAP (FRS 12) to FRS 102 are unlikely to face any significant issues on transition. This is because there are no differences in substance between the requirements of old UK GAAP and those in section 27 of FRS 102.

27.70 This means that amounts reported under old UK GAAP will be carried forward without any modifications in the opening balance sheet as of the date of transition. However, inevitably there are some differences in disclosure between the two.

Chapter 28

Employee benefits

Chapter 28

Employee benefits

Introduction and scope

28.1 Section 28 of FRS 102 deals with the accounting for employee benefits. Employee benefits include all forms of compensation given by an entity to employees (including directors and management) in exchange for services rendered to the entity.

28.2 Section 28 of the standard divides employee benefits into four categories, as stated below. Each category has different characteristics and, therefore, different requirements:

■ Short-term employee benefits (other than termination benefits), such as wages and salaries, holiday pay, sick leave and bonuses. To fall into this category, benefits must be expected to be settled within 12 months after the end of the reporting period in which the employees render the related service.

■ Post-employment benefits (other than termination benefits and short-term benefits), such as pensions and post-retirement medical insurance that are payable after completion of employment.

■ Other long-term employee benefits, such as long-term incentive plans (LTIPs), long-service awards and bonuses payable more than 12 months after the end of the period in which the employees render the related service. This category includes all employee benefits other than short term, termination or post-employment benefits.

■ Termination benefits provided in exchange for the termination of an employee's employment as a result of either:

■ an entity's decision to terminate an employee's employment before the normal retirement date, or

■ an employee's decision to accept voluntary redundancy in exchange for those benefits.

[FRS 102 para 28.1].

28.3 Employee benefits include benefits provided to employees and their dependants and can be settled by payments (or the provision of goods or services) made directly to the employees, their spouses, children or other dependants, or to others (such as insurance companies). Also, an employee can provide services to an entity on a full-time, part-time, permanent, casual or temporary basis. For the purpose of section 28 of the standard, employees include directors and other management personnel.

28.4 Employee benefits also include share-based payment transactions. However, share-based payment transactions are outside the scope of section 28; instead section 26 deals with them separately. [FRS 102 para 28.1].

General recognition principle

28.5 The general recognition principle stated in the paragraph below applies to all forms of employee benefits that fall within the scope of section 28 of FRS 102, although the manner in which the benefits are measured depends on their characteristics.

28.6 Employees become entitled to benefits as a result of service rendered to the entity during the reporting period. An entity recognises the cost of such employee benefits:

■   As a liability, after deducting amounts that have been paid either directly to the employees or as a contribution to an employee benefit fund.

■   As an expense, unless another section of this FRS requires the cost to be recognised as part of the cost of an asset such as inventories or property, plant and equipment.

[FRS 102 para 28.3].

28.7 Where the amount paid exceeds the liability arising from service before the reporting date (as noted above), the excess should be recognised as an asset to the extent that the prepayment will lead to a reduction in future payments or a cash refund. [FRS 102 para 28.3(a)].

28.8 In some cases an entity may have set up an employee benefit fund as an intermediate payment arrangement. Contributions to an employee benefit fund that is an intermediate payment arrangement are accounted for in accordance with section 9 of FRS 102 (paras 9.33 to 9.38). As a result if the employer is a sponsoring entity the assets and liabilities of the intermediary will be accounted for by the sponsoring entity as an extension of its own business. So in cases like this, the payment to the employee benefit fund does not extinguish the liability of the employer. [FRS 102 para 28.3(a)].

Short-term employee benefits

28.9 Short-term employee benefits are employee benefits (other than termination benefits) that are expected to be settled wholly within 12 months after the end of the annual reporting period in which the employees render the related service. [FRS 102 para 28.1(a)]. They include:

- Wages, salaries and social security contributions.

- Short-term compensated absences (such as paid annual leave and paid sick leave).

- Profit sharing and bonuses.

- Non-monetary benefits (such as medical care, housing, cars and free or subsidised goods or services) for current employees.

[FRS 102 para 28.4].

Recognition and measurement

28.10 Accounting for short-term benefits is generally straightforward. They are recognised in accordance with the general recognition principle (noted in para 28.5 above). This means that the entity recognises an expense (unless costs are capitalised) for services rendered during the period and a liability for the accrued expense. The benefits are measured on an undiscounted basis because of their short-term nature. [FRS 102 para 28.5]. But there are further requirements in respect of short-term compensated absences and profit sharing and bonus plans.

Short-term compensated absences

28.11 Compensated absences are periods during which an employee does not provide services to the employer, but employee benefits continue to accrue. These include absences for annual holiday, sickness, maternity or paternity leave, jury service and military service. These can be either accumulating or non-accumulating compensated absences.

Accumulating compensated absences

28.12 Accumulating compensated absences are defined as those *"that are carried forward and can be used in future periods if the current period's entitlement is not used in full"*. [FRS 102 Glossary of terms]. A typical example is carry forward of unused holidays not taken during the current year. Although the standard makes no distinction for short-term employee benefits, accumulating compensated absences can generally be differentiated into vesting and non-vesting. This is important because the standard requires entities to recognise the *"expected cost of accumulating compensated absences"*. If the benefits are vesting, employees who leave are entitled to a cash payment in respect of an unused entitlement. Non-vesting benefits, on the other hand, are lost if an employee leaves without using them.

28.13 Accumulating compensated absences are typically earned by employees as they provide services. So, in applying the general recognition rule set out in para 28.5 above, an entity should recognise the *"expected cost of accumulating compensated absences"* when the employees render service that increases their entitlement to future compensated absences. The liability is recognised as services are rendered, so no distinction is made between vesting and non-vesting entitlements. But, in measuring non-vesting entitlements, the entity should take into account the possibility of the employees leaving before using their entitlements.

28.14 Accordingly, an entity should measure the expected cost of accumulating compensated absences at the undiscounted additional amount that the entity *"expects to pay"* as a result of the unused entitlement that has accumulated at the end of the reporting period. An entity should present this amount as falling due within one year at the reporting date. [FRS 102 para 28.6].

Non-accumulating compensated absences

28.15 Non-accumulating compensated absences, on the other hand, are those where there is no entitlement to carry forward unused days (that is, any unused entitlement not taken during the current period lapses without payment). They are not generally related to services. Of the examples listed above, sick leave, maternity leave and jury service are usually non-accumulating compensated absences.

28.16 An entity should recognise the cost of other (non-accumulating) compensated absences when the absences occur. The entity should measure the cost of non-accumulating compensated absences at the undiscounted amount of salaries and wages paid or payable for the period of absence. [FRS 102 para 28.7].

28.17 The flow chart below summarises the principles for compensated absences discussed above:

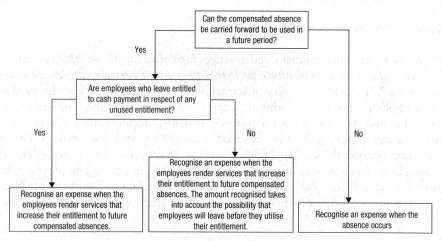

Example 1 – Holiday pay that lapses if employee leaves

Employees of entity A are entitled to 20 days of paid leave each year. The entitlement accrues evenly throughout the year, and unused leave can be carried forward to future periods. There is no cash payment in respect of an unused entitlement if an employee leaves the entity.

At 31 December 20X1, entity A has 100 employees, and the average unused holiday entitlement per employee is two days. Historically, 10% of employees who leave have never taken their unused holiday entitlement, and management expects this trend to continue.

At the reporting date (31 December), entity A should recognise a liability for the expected cost of accumulated absences. In doing so, it should take into account the possibility that employees will leave before they utilise their entitlement. Given that 10% of employees leave without taking their unused holiday, the number of days of accumulated entitlement that the entity expects to have to pay in the future is 180 days (that is, 90% of 200 days).

If entity A were to change its terms and conditions of employment, such that a cash payment was made in respect of unused holiday entitlement when an employee left the entity, the amount provided would be 200 days. This is because it would be irrelevant that 10% of employees never take all of their holiday entitlement, as they would receive a cash payment of equivalent value on leaving the entity.

Example 2 – Unused holiday carried forward for one year only

The facts are as in example 1, except that unused holiday entitlements can be carried forward for one year only. Each year, the current year entitlement is used before any balance is brought forward from the previous year.

At 31 December 20X1, all 100 employees have two days of unused holiday entitlement. Management expects that 75% of employees will take 22 days of holiday in 20X4 (that is, including two days each brought forward from 20X1), 15% will take 20 days (that is, they will lose their two days carried forward), and the remaining 10% will take 18 days (that is, they will lose their two days carried forward from 20X1 and be eligible to carry forward two days from 20X2's entitlement at 31 December 20X2).

How much should be recognised as a liability at 31 December 20X1?

As noted in paragraph 28.14 above, the expected cost (that is, liability) of the accumulated compensated absences is calculated at the level of individual employees, and is based on the additional amount that an entity expects to pay as a result of the unused entitlement that has accumulated at the end of the reporting period. On this basis, the liability would be based on only the 75% of employees who are expected to use their brought-forward entitlement. So, the liability recognised at 31 December 20X1 would be 150 days (that is, two days for each of 75 employees).

Example 3 – Non-accumulating sick leave

Entity B has 100 employees, each of whom is entitled to six working days of paid sick leave for each year. Unused sick leave cannot be carried forward to the next calendar year. Employees are also not entitled to a cash payment for unused entitlement of sick leave on leaving the entity's service.

An entity should not recognise an expense in respect of non-accumulating sick leave until the time of the absence, because employee service does not increase the amount of the benefit. Accordingly, entity B should not recognise a provision for unused sick leave. The use of sick leave is determined by an unpredictable future event (that is, the illness of the employee) and not through the employee's choice. A high or low level of sickness in employees in one year does not cause a lower or higher level of sickness in the following year.

28.18 The previous examples considered the situation where an entity's holiday year corresponds with its financial year. This is not always the case, as illustrated below.

Example – Financial year different to holiday year

Entity A has a March year end but its holiday year runs to the end of September. Employees of entity A are entitled to 20 days of paid annual leave, all of which must be taken by the end of September or it will be lost. On the basis of past experience, management estimates that staff will take only 95% of their holiday entitlement. Staff do not work at weekends or on national holidays, and this means that there are 253 working days per year.

The total annual salary cost for the year ended 31 March 20X4 is £800,000. A pay rise of 4% was awarded with effect from 1 April 20X4, so the total annual salary cost for the year ending 31 March 20X5 will be £832,000.

By 31 March 20X4, staff have earned half of their total annual holiday entitlement (that is, ten days) but have taken only four days. Hence, the amount of holiday earned but not yet taken at 31 March 20X4 is six days. Although this entitlement would be lost if not taken by the end of September, management believe that most will be taken in line with its overall estimates for the year (that is, cumulatively 95%). Four days have been taken so far, so a provision should be made in respect of the remaining five and a half days expected to be taken (95% × 10 days less four days taken).

The amount provided should be based on the pay rate at which management expects the leave to be taken. The annual salary cost with effect from 1 April 20X4 is £832,000, so the amount provided should be £18,087 (that is, 5½/253 × £832,000).

Profit sharing and bonus plans

28.19 In applying the general recognition criteria (discussed in para 28.6 above) to the expected cost of profit sharing and bonus plans, an entity should recognise the expected cost only when:

- it has a present legal or constructive obligation to make such payments as a result of past events (this means that the entity has no realistic alternative but to make the payments); and

- a reliable estimate of the obligation can be made.

[FRS 102 para 28.8].

28.20 The above requirements follow closely the general recognition criteria for provisions discussed in chapter 21. This means that a legal obligation to pay bonuses need not always be present. An entity's past practice of paying regular bonuses could create a constructive obligation that is sufficient for cost recognition. A reliable estimate can normally be made from the terms of the profit sharing and bonus plans, which often contain a formula for determining the amount payable.

Example 1 – One-off compensation payment associated with future operations

To remain competitive, an entity intends to alter the terms and conditions of employment at one factory so that overtime will be paid in future at 1.5 times the normal rate, rather than twice the normal rate as in the past. The entity intends to compensate employees with a one-off payment and has put this offer to the union. The employees are also aware of this impending change. No agreement has been reached with the union at the year end. But, if the offer is not accepted, the entity is likely to switch overtime work to other factories.

Provision should not be made for the planned expenditure to operate in a particular way in the future, because the entity can avoid that expenditure by changing its method of operation. Therefore, the proposed one-off compensation payment that is associated with the future operations (and that could be avoided by switching overtime production to other factories) should not be provided for, in advance, at the year end. But, if agreement for the payment had been reached with the unions by the year end and the payment no longer depended on future events (that is, the structure and recipients of the payment had been identified), a liability should be recognised for the payment at the year end.

Example 2 – Performance bonus based on sales target

A car dealer has a practice of paying a performance bonus to its sales staff.

Past evidence indicates that sales staff who meet their sales targets received a bonus of 10% of their current salary package at the year end. Sales staff who were not in service throughout the whole year received a bonus in proportion to their service period. The bonuses are paid, in the first quarter of the following year, to the sales staff who are still employed by the entity at the year end.

At the year end, seven of the sales staff met their sales targets. Two of the seven began their employment halfway through the year, and one of them left the entity at the year end.

The car dealer should recognise a liability at the expected cost of the bonuses to be paid in the subsequent year, for the following reasons:

- the dealer created a valid expectation among the sales staff that they would receive bonuses if they met their sales targets and were still in the entity's service (that is, there is a constructive obligation); and

- the amount of the payment can be estimated reliably. There are four sales staff who will receive a bonus of 10% of their current salary packages, and two who will receive 5% because their employment commenced halfway through the year. No provision should be recognised for the employee who resigned at the year end, because he left the entity before the year end and will therefore not receive a payment.

Employee benefits

28.21 An annual bonus is often payable after the end of the reporting period and only to those employees who remain in employment at the reporting date (as illustrated in example 2 above). But the terms might sometimes specify that employees are required to remain in service until the date on which the bonus is payable. In that situation, the possibility of employees leaving before receiving their bonuses should be reflected in the measurement of the expected amount payable at the end of the reporting period. It would not be appropriate to defer recognition until the employees complete the entitlement period as illustrated below.

> **Example – Bonus payable to employees three months after the year-end**
>
> An entity has a December year end. It pays a bonus in respect of each year to employees who have provided services during the year and remain on the payroll at 31 March. The bonus pool is determined as 5% of entity profits, and each employee's entitlement is determined as at 31 December. There is no re-allocation of the bonus entitlement of employees who leave before 31 March. On average, 1% of employees leave the entity each month. The financial statements for the year ended 31 December 20X3 showed a profit (for the purpose of the bonus plan) of £100,000 and they were signed on 28 February 20X4.
>
> In the period from 1 January to 31 March, it is expected that an average of 3% of the employees who worked during the previous year will leave the entity. The bonus pool for the year ended 31 December 20X3 was £5,000, so the expected amount payable on 31 March 20X4 would be £4,850 (97% of £5,000). The actual experience (in the period up to the date on which the financial statements were signed) should be taken into account when it is a confirmation of expectations at the balance sheet date. If 3% of employees actually left during January and February 20X4, but it is still expected that a further 1% will leave during March through the normal course of business, the total amount recognised as an expense would be £4,800 (96% of £5,000).

28.22 In the example above, employees are required to provide services until 31 March. The standard does not give any guidance, apart from the general recognition criteria, as to what the liability at year end should be. As a policy choice, the entity could, for example, either recognise the full liability over the shorter 12-month performance period or recognise the expense over the longer 15-month vesting period ending on 31 March. If the entity follows the latter policy, a liability of £3,840 (that is, £4,800 × 12/15) should be recognised at 31 December 20X3. Whichever approach is followed, an entity should apply it consistently year on year.

Disclosures

28.23 The standard has no specific disclosure requirements for short-term employee benefits. [FRS 102 para 28.39]. Section 33 of the standard requires disclosure of key management personnel compensation in total, so any short-term employee benefits payable to key management personnel should be included in the aggregate compensation amount.

Post-employment benefits

28.24 Post-employment benefits are defined as *"employee benefits (other than termination and short-term employee benefits) that are payable after the completion of employment"*; and post-employment benefit plans could be *"formal or informal arrangements under which an entity provides post-employment benefits for one or more employees"*. [FRS 102 Glossary of terms]. They include, for example:

■ retirements benefits, such as pensions; and

■ other post-employment benefits, such as post-employment life insurance and post-employment medical care.

[FRS 102 para 28.9].

28.25 Section 28 applies to all post-employment benefit plans, whether or not they involve the establishment of a separate entity to receive contributions and to pay benefits. Plan arrangements can be imposed by law rather than the action of the entity; or they can arise from the actions of the entity, even in the absence of a formal documented plan.

Types of post-employment benefit plan

28.26 Post-employment benefit plans are classified as defined contribution or defined benefit plans. Classification depends on the principal terms and conditions of the plan and determines the accounting treatment. In addition, section 28 of the standard provides guidance as to how its requirements should be applied to insured benefits, and multi-employer and state plans.

Defined contribution plans

28.27 Defined contribution plans are defined as *"post-employment benefit plans under which an entity pays fixed contributions into a separate entity (a fund) and has no legal or constructive obligation to pay further contributions or to make direct benefit payments to employees if the fund does not hold sufficient assets to pay all employee benefits relating to employee service in the current and prior periods"*. [FRS 102 para 28.10(a)]. Defined contribution plans are sometimes referred to as money purchase plans.

28.28 The amount of the post-employment benefits received by the employee is determined by the amount of contributions paid by an entity (and perhaps also by the employee) to a post-employment benefit plan or to an insurer, and the investment performance achieved on those contributions. [FRS 102 para 28.10(a)]. The rate of contribution to be paid by the employer is normally based on a formula specified in the plan's rules. This formula might consider such factors as age, length of employee service, employer's profits, and compensation level. So, the employer's liability is limited to the contributions that it has agreed to pay. The employee takes both the actuarial risk (that benefits will be less than expected) and the investment risk – if the investments have performed well, the individual will obtain a higher pension than if the investments have performed badly.

Defined benefit plans

28.29   Defined benefit plans are defined as *"post-employment benefit plans other than defined contribution plans"*. [FRS 102 Glossary of terms]. They are pension plans where the rules specify the benefits to be paid and they are financed accordingly. These benefits typically are a function of an employee's years of service and of the compensation level in the years approaching retirement.

28.30   Under defined benefit plans, the employer's obligation is not limited to the amount that it agrees to contribute to the plan. Rather, the employer is obliged (legally or constructively) to provide the agreed benefits to current and former employees. So, the employer bears actuarial risk (namely, that benefits will cost more or less than expected) and investment risk (namely, that returns on assets set aside to fund the benefits will differ from expectations). If actuarial or investment experience is worse than expected, the entity's obligation might be increased; or it might be decreased if actuarial or investment experience is better than expected. [FRS 102 para 28.10(b)]. This is what distinguishes a defined benefit plan from a defined contribution plan: under a defined contribution plan, such risks are borne by the employee.

Funded and unfunded plans

28.31   Defined benefit plans can be funded or unfunded. Funded plans are those where the contributions are paid to a separate entity. In the UK, plan assets are usually placed under the control of trustees, who administer the plan in accordance with the provisions of trust law and the terms of the trust deed governing the particular plan. Most funded plans in the UK that are established under trusts enjoy considerable tax benefits through HMRC recognition as exempt approved plans. The trustees' primary purpose is to safeguard and invest assets so that there will be enough to pay the employer's obligation to the employees. Although the trust is, in form, a separate entity, the trust assets and liabilities belong, in substance, to the employer (that is, as long as the plan continues, the employer is responsible for the payment of the defined benefits). So, the employer must make up any shortfall in the accumulated assets that are insufficient to meet the promised benefits. On the other hand, any surplus can be recognised by the employing entity as an asset but only if it can be recovered either through a refund from the plan or through reduced future contributions (see para 28.58 below).

28.32   Unfunded post-employment benefit plans are plans where no assets are set aside in advance to provide for future liabilities; instead, pension liabilities are met out of the employer's own resources as they fall due.

Multi-employer and state plans

28.33 Some employers participate in industry-wide pension plans, which provide centralised pension arrangements for identifiable groups of unrelated employers. Multi-employer plans are defined contribution plans (other than state plans) or defined benefit plans (other than state plans) that *"(a) pool the assets contributed by various entities that are not under common control, and (b) use those assets to provide benefits to employees of more than one entity, on the basis that contribution and benefit levels are determined without regard to the identity of the entity that employs the employees concerned"*. [FRS 102 Glossary of terms].

28.34 State plans, on the other hand, are *"established by legislation to cover all entities (or all entities in a particular category, for example a specific industry) and are operated by national or local government or by another body (for example, an autonomous agency created specifically for this purpose) which is not subject to control or influence by the reporting entity"*. [FRS 102 Glossary of terms].

28.35 Based on the terms of the plan, which would include any constructive obligation that goes beyond its formal terms, multi-employer plans and state plans are classified as defined contribution plans or defined benefit plans, and they are accounted for accordingly. If sufficient information is not available to use defined benefit accounting for a multi-employer or a state plan that is a defined benefit plan, then an entity accounts for the plan in accordance with paragraphs 28.13 and 28.13A of FRS 102 (that is, as if it was a defined contribution plan; see also paras 28.48 and 49 below). The entity must also provide the disclosures required by paragraphs 28.40 and 28.40A of FRS 102. [FRS 102 para 28.11].

28.36 An agreement with the multi-employer scheme that determines how a deficit will be funded is likely to be disclosed in accordance with paragraphs 28.40 and 28.40A of FRS 102. The information disclosed would include the existence of any contractual agreement, the period over which payments to fund the deficit will be made, and any available information about the expected amount of the payments.

28.37 Where such an agreement exists, an entity participating in a multi-employer defined benefit plan, which is accounted for as a defined contribution plan, should recognise a liability for the contributions payable that arises from the agreement, to the extent that the contributions relate to the deficit. Any resulting expense should be recognised in profit or loss in accordance with paragraphs 28.13 and 13A of FRS 102. [FRS 102 para 28.11A].

28.38 If such a liability is recognised, the company is required to disclose how the liability has been determined. [FRS 102 para 28.40A(c)].

28.39 The requirements of the Pensions Act 2004 (see further para 28.130 below) mean that, where a defined benefit scheme has insufficient assets to cover its liabilities, the trustees must establish a recovery plan setting out how the statutory funding objective (SFO) is to be met and over what period. In detailing the steps to be taken in order to meet the SFO, the recovery plan will specify the contributions sought from each participating company. Although this deals with cash payments rather than each company's share of assets and liabilities, it is through adjustments to normal levels of contribution that the surplus or deficit (being determined as the net sum of the scheme's assets and liabilities) is often recovered or settled. So, it is sometimes possible that a contribution schedule, as set out in the scheme's recovery plan, provides sufficient information to enable defined benefit accounting. In essence, it might therefore be possible to determine how the scheme surplus or deficit (and, hence, the relevant share of scheme assets and liabilities) should be allocated; and therefore defined benefit accounting could be appropriate.

28.40 Also, if the scheme's trust deed and rules specify what would happen on sale of a participating employer (for example, share of fund), these principles could be applied to allocate scheme assets and liabilities. The documentation might set out a rational manner in which to allocate the assets and liabilities.

28.41 As discussed above, an entity accounts for a multi-employer defined benefit plan using defined contribution accounting only if sufficient information is not available. Section 28 of FRS 102 does not address subsequent accounting if sufficient information becomes available in later periods. We consider that there are two alternative approaches that an entity could apply in such a situation. An entity could:

(a) charge or credit the income statement immediately for an amount equal to the deficit or surplus as a past service cost; or

(b) treat the availability of sufficient information as an accounting policy change and adjust opening retained earnings.

28.42 Although both alternatives are acceptable, we believe that there is a stronger argument for alternative (b). Alternative (a) draws support from paragraph 28.21: *"If a defined benefit plan has been introduced or changed in the current period, the entity shall … recognise the increase as an expense … in the current period".* This alternative views the change as analogous to the introduction of a defined benefit plan. However, alternative (b) reflects the view that no new benefits have been introduced, but that the accounting methodology applied has been revised for the existing beneficiaries.

Group plans

28.43 Group pension plans could be considered to be a type of multi-employer plan, except that the participating entities are under common control. Contributions from a number of employers (that is, the members of the group) are pooled, and pension arrangements are administered centrally. As a result of common control the standard expects sufficient information to be available for at least the plan as a whole. The plan as a whole is measured in accordance with section 28 of the standard, on the basis of assumptions that apply to the plan as a whole.

28.44 The accounting guidance in section 28 of FRS 102 for group plans results in at least one entity applying defined benefit accounting for the scheme. If there is a contractual agreement or stated policy for recharging the net defined benefit cost of a defined benefit plan as a whole (measured in accordance with section 28) to the individual group entities, each entity in its individual financial statements recognises the net defined benefit cost of the defined benefit plan so charged. If there is no policy or agreement, the net defined benefit cost of the defined benefit plan are recognised in the individual financial statements of the group entity which is legally responsible for the plan. The other group entities recognise in their individual financial statements a cost equal to their contribution payable in the period. [FRS 102 para 28.38].

This is in contrast to multi-employer plan accounting, where defined benefit accounting is required by all participating entities unless there is insufficient information to use defined benefit accounting.

Example 1 – Stated policy for allocation

Entity A has several trading subsidiaries of similar size. All of the subsidiaries, as well as entity A itself, participate in the 'entity A group defined benefit plan'. The plan rules do not specify how any surplus or deficit should be allocated amongst participating employers. But management has defined a policy for allocating the net defined benefit cost to the individual group entities on the basis of pensionable payroll. Hence, the net defined benefit cost is recognised on this basis in each of the participating entities' individual financial statements. The standard does not give guidance on how any net defined benefit liability would be accounted for; but it would be was appropriate to recognise it on the same basis as the net defined benefit cost (in this case, pensionable payroll).

Example 2 – No contract or stated policy for allocation

Entity B has several subsidiaries. The subsidiaries all trade and are of a similar size. All of the subsidiaries, as well as entity B itself, participate in the 'entity B group defined benefit plan'. The plan rules do not specify how any surplus or deficit should be allocated among participating employers. Also, there is no contractual agreement or stated policy for allocating the net defined benefit cost to the individual group entities. Accordingly, the net defined benefit cost for the plan as a whole should be recognised in the separate or individual financial statements of the entity that is legally responsible for the plan. The other participating entities will recognise a cost equal to their contribution for the period.

The identity of the entity that is legally responsible will often be clear from a plan's trust deed and rules. But, in the absence of such clarity, management might consider the following factors:

- Which entity's management is responsible for making decisions concerning the plan and negotiating with its trustees (such as agreeing contribution rates)?

- How are responsibilities described in the contribution schedule agreed with the plan trustees? Are contributions the responsibility of one entity, with all other participants making payments to that entity rather than to the plan?

- Does one entity guarantee the contributions made by the other group entities?

Employee benefits

Insured benefits

28.45 An entity might enter into an insurance contract and pay insurance premiums to fund a post-employment benefit plan. It should treat such a plan as a defined contribution plan, unless it has a legal or constructive obligation to either:

- pay the employee benefits directly when they become due; or

- pay further amounts if the insurer does not pay all future employee benefits relating to employee service in the current and prior periods.

[FRS 102 para 28.12].

In either of these situations, an obligation exists, so the plan will be treated as a defined benefit plan.

28.46 But, if the insurance company bears all of the actuarial and investment risk and has sole responsibility for paying the benefits, the plan will be treated as a defined contribution plan. In this situation, the insurance premium costs are, in substance, costs of settling the pension obligation. On the other hand, if the employer (either directly, indirectly through the plan, through a mechanism for setting future premiums, or through a relationship with the insurer) retains a legal or constructive obligation, payment of the premiums do not settle the pension obligation. Instead, the plan would be treated as defined benefit, and the insurance policy would be treated as a plan asset or reimbursement right.

Defined contribution plans

28.47 Accounting for defined contribution plans is straightforward; this is because the reporting entity's obligation for each period is determined by the amounts to be contributed for that period. Consequently, no actuarial assumptions are required to measure the obligation or the expense, and there is no possibility of any actuarial gain or loss. Except for contributions outstanding or prepaid, an employer has no assets or liabilities in respect of a defined contribution plan.

Recognition and measurement

28.48 The standard requires that an entity recognises the contribution payable for a period:

- as a liability, after deducting any amount already paid. If contribution payments exceed the contribution due for service before the reporting date, an entity should recognise that excess as an asset to the extent that the prepayment will lead to a reduction in future payments or a cash refund.

■ as an expense, unless another section of FRS 102 requires the cost to be recognised as part of the cost of an asset such as inventories or property, plant and equipment.

[FRS 102 para 28.13].

28.49 FRS 102 requires that, in a specified situation, contributions have to be measured at the present value of the amounts payable, using a discount rate by reference to market yields at the reporting date of high-quality corporate bonds; this is the same discount rate used for the discounting of defined benefit obligations. The situation arises where the contribution is not expected to be settled wholly within 12 months after the end of the reporting period in which the employees render the related service. The entity would present any discount unwinding as finance costs in profit or loss in the period when the unwinding arises. [FRS 102 para 28.13A].

Presentation and disclosures

28.50 Assets and liabilities relating to defined contribution plans are normally of a short-term nature and should therefore be classified in the statement of financial position as 'falling due within one year'.

28.51 An entity should disclose the amount recognised in profit or loss as an expense for defined contribution plans. [FRS 102 para 28.40].

28.52 If an entity treats a defined benefit multi-employer plan as a defined contribution plan, because sufficient information is not available to use defined benefit accounting (see para 28.35 above), it should disclose the following information:

■ The fact that it is a defined benefit plan.

■ The reason why it is being accounted for as a defined contribution plan.

■ Any available information about the plan's surplus or deficit, and the implications, if any, for the entity.

■ A description of the extent to which the company can be liable to the plan for other entities' obligations under the terms and conditions of the multi-employer plan.

■ If a liability has been recognised in accordance with paragraph 28.11A of section 28, disclosure is required on how the liability has been determined (see also para 28.38 above).

[FRS 102 para 28.40A].

28.53 Pension plans are related parties; and so contributions paid into defined contribution plans are transactions with related parties and should be disclosed in accordance with the requirements and guidance in section 33 of the standard.

Defined benefit plans

28.54 Accounting for defined benefit plans is complex; this is because actuarial assumptions and valuation methods are required to measure the obligation and the expense. The entity's obligations under the defined benefit plan are measured on a discounted basis, because they might be settled many years after the employees render the related service. The assumptions used will invariably differ from actual outcomes (resulting in increases or decreases in the entity's obligations), and so the possibility of actuarial gains or losses also arises.

Recognition

28.55 In applying the general recognition principle (in para 28.6 above) to defined benefit plans, an entity should recognise:

- A liability for its obligations (that is, its defined benefit obligation) under defined benefit plans net of plan assets (that is, its net defined benefit liability).
- The net change in that liability during the period as the cost of its defined benefit plans during the period.

[FRS 102 para 28.14].

28.56 The defined benefit obligation is defined as the *"present value, without deducting any plan assets, of expected future payments required to settle the obligation resulting from employee service in the current and prior periods"*. [FRS 102 Glossary of terms].

Measurement of the net defined benefit liability and limits on a plan surplus

28.57 FRS 102 requires that an entity should measure a net defined benefit liability for its obligations under defined benefit plans at the net total of the following amounts:

- the present value of its obligations under defined benefit plans (that is, its defined benefit obligation) at the reporting date; minus
- the fair value at the reporting date of plan assets (if any) out of which the obligations are to be settled.

[FRS 102 para 28.15, Glossary of terms].

28.58 As stated above, a net defined benefit liability should be recognised and measured as a net amount at each reporting date. The plan assets are measured at fair value. The defined benefit obligation is measured on an actuarial basis discounted to present value. But, where this net balance is negative (that is, an asset), that asset would generally also be recognised on the balance sheet. This means that entities recognise on their balance sheet the full overfunded (in the event of plan surplus) or underfunded (in the event of plan deficit) status of their defined benefit pension plan. But there is a recoverability test to be applied with regard to a surplus situation: a plan surplus should be recognised only where the entity is able to recover the surplus through reduced contributions in the future or through refunds from the plan. [FRS 102 para 28.22]. Section 28 does not require that the entity has reached a written agreement with the trustees by the balance sheet date (for example, on reduced future contributions or an agreed refund) to be able to recognise the surplus. To recognise the surplus it would be sufficient if an entity can show that it is able to realise economic benefits. An economic benefit, in the form of a refund or a reduction in future contributions, is available if the entity can realise it at some point during the life of the plan or when the plan liabilities are settled, even if this is not until some distant time in the future, such as when the last benefit is paid to the last pensioner in the scheme.

> **Example – Defined benefit plans**
>
> A defined benefit plan provides an annual pension of 1/60 of final salary for each year of service. The pension is payable from the age of 65. At 31 December 20X1, the actuarial value of the defined benefit obligation amounted to £500,000, and the fair value of the plan assets out of which the obligations are to be settled amounted to £400,000.
>
> In this situation, the plan is underfunded, and the entity would recognise a net pension obligation of £100,000.
>
> If, instead, the fair value of the plan assets were £550,000, the entity would recognise a pension asset of £50,000, but only where it is able to recover the asset through reduced contributions in the future or through refunds from the plan.

28.59 The defined benefit obligation is determined using a number of steps as follows:

- Determine the amount of the benefit that employees have earned in return for services in the current and prior period, including benefits that have not yet vested.

- Make estimates (actuarial assumptions) about demographic variables and financial variables that will influence the cost of the benefit.

- Discount the benefit to present values using actuarial methods.

Attribution of benefits to periods of service

28.60 An estimation of the present value of the defined benefit obligation at the end of the reporting period requires an entity to determine how much of the benefit is attributable to current and prior periods. Such attribution is based on the plan's benefit formula. [FRS 102 para 28.16]. The benefits are payable at or after retirement, so the attribution of benefits to periods of service is discounted. Benefits attributed to the current period are often referred to as current service costs. Benefits attributable to current and prior periods determine the present value of the obligation at the end of the current period. In fact, the present value of the defined benefit obligation at the end of any reporting period is the present value of the benefit attributable during that period multiplied by the number of years of service, up to the end of the reporting period.

> **Example 1 – Lump-sum benefit**
>
> A plan provides a lump-sum benefit of £1,000, payable immediately on retirement, for each year of service.
>
> A benefit of £1,000 is attributed to each year of service. The amount is payable immediately on retirement, so the cost recognised as an expense in each period is the present value of £1,000. Thus, because of the discounting, the benefit is less than the amount that would be determined if the employee left at the balance sheet date. The present value of the defined benefit obligation at the end of the reporting period is the present value of £1,000 at the end of that period multiplied by the number of years of service, up to the end of that reporting period.

> **Example 2 – Annual final salary pension**
>
> A plan provides an annual pension of 1/60 of final salary for each year of service. The pension is payable from the age of 65.
>
> Benefits equal to the present value, at the expected retirement date, of an annual pension of 1/60 of the estimated final salary, payable from the expected retirement date until the expected date of death, are attributed to each year of service. Pension payments begin at the age of 65, so the cost recognised in each period is the present value of that benefit. The present value of the defined benefit obligation is the present value of that benefit multiplied by the number of years of service, up to the end of the reporting period.

28.61 Employee service gives rise to an obligation under a defined benefit plan, even if the benefits are conditional on future employment (in other words, they are not vested). Vested benefits are defined as *"benefits, the rights to which, under the condition of the retirement benefit plan, are not conditional on continued employment"*. [FRS 102 Glossary of terms]. Employee service before the vesting date gives rise to a constructive obligation because, at each successive balance sheet date, the amount of future service that an employee will have to render before becoming entitled to the benefit is reduced. But, when attributing benefits to periods of service, the probability that some employees might not satisfy vesting conditions (which includes performance hurdles) before becoming entitled to benefits is taken into account in the measurement of the defined benefit obligation, but does not determine whether (for accounting purposes) an obligation exists. [FRS 102 para 28.26].

28.62 For example, if the benefits described in example 1 above did not vest until an employee had completed ten years of service, the measurement of the defined benefit obligation in each of the first ten years would reflect the probability that some employees might not complete ten years of service. Similarly, although some post-employment benefits (such as post-employment medical benefits) become payable only if a specified event occurs when an employee is no longer employed (such as an illness), an obligation is created when the employee renders service that will provide entitlement to the benefit if the specified event occurs. The probability that the specified event will occur affects the measurement of the obligation, but does not determine whether the obligation exists.

28.63 A plan's benefit formula might set a point beyond which no further benefit can be earned. In that situation, no benefits are attributed to later years of service, as illustrated in examples 1 and 2 below.

> **Example 1 – Benefits are not earned after a specified period of service**
>
> A plan pays a lump-sum benefit of £1,000 that vests and is paid after ten years of service. The plan provides no further benefit for subsequent service.
>
> A benefit of £100 (£1,000 divided by ten) is attributed to each of the first ten years of service. The present value of the defined benefit obligation is the present value of £100, multiplied by the number of years of service, up to the end of the reporting period. The present value of the obligation reflects the probability that the employee might not complete ten years of service. No benefit is attributed to later years.
>
> **Example 2 – Benefits are only earned before the age of 55**
>
> Employees are entitled to a benefit of 3% of final salary for each year of service before the age of 55.
>
> The benefit of 3% of estimated final salary is attributed to each year up to the age of 55. This is the date when further service by the employee will lead to no material amount of further benefits under the plan. No benefit is attributed to service after that age.

28.64 On the other hand, the plan benefit formula might provide for greater benefits being earned in the later years than the earlier years. In that situation, the attribution of benefits to current and prior periods should reflect that fact. This is required through the words *"including the effects of benefit formulas that give employees greater benefits for later years of service"*. [FRS 102 para 28.16]. We believe that this means that entitlement to benefits at the higher level is attributable to an employee's service throughout the period and not simply to periods over which the greater benefits are earned under the formula, as illustrated in examples 1 and 2 below.

> **Example 1 – Benefit increases after 20 years of service**
>
> A plan provides an annual pension of 1/60 of final salary for each year of service, but this increases to 1/40 of final salary if an employee leaves after more than 20 years' service.
>
> For those employees expected to remain with the employer for at least 20 years, benefit equal to the present value, at the expected retirement date, of an annual pension of 1/40 of the estimated final salary, payable from the expected retirement date until the expected date of death, is attributed to each year of service.

For all other employees, benefit equal to the present value, at the expected retirement date, of an annual pension of 1/60 of the estimated final salary, payable from the expected retirement date until the expected date of death, is attributed to each year of service.

In all cases, the measurement of the defined benefit obligation will reflect the probability that an employee might leave or die before the normal retirement date.

Example 2 – Material increase in benefits in later years

Entity A operates a pension plan that pays a pension of £100 for each of the first three years of service, £500 for each of the years of service from years 4 to 6, and £2,400 for each of the years of service from years 7 to 9. An employee will, therefore, be entitled to a pension of £9,000 (£100 × 3 + £500 × 3 + £2,400 x 3) after nine years of service. Further service after nine years does not give rise to any additional pension.

Company A's employees' services in later years will lead to a materially higher level of benefit than in earlier years. Entity A should, therefore, attribute benefit of £1,000 (£9,000/9 years, ignoring discounting) to each year of service, rather than following the attribution formula in the plan for those employees expected to provide at least 9 years of service.

Actuarial assumptions

28.65   A defined benefit plan specifies benefits in terms of the uncertain future variables; as a result, many assumptions are necessary to estimate the present value of the defined benefit obligations. These are generally referred to as actuarial assumptions, and they comprise both demographic and financial assumptions. [FRS 102 para 28.16].

28.66   Demographic assumptions concern the future characteristics of current and future employees (and their dependants) who are eligible for benefits, and they deal with matters such as:

- Mortality, both during and after employment.
- Rates of employee turnover, disability and early retirement.
- Age, sex and marital status of membership.
- The proportion of plan members with dependants who will be eligible for benefits.
- Claim rates under medical plans.

28.67   Financial assumptions deal with matters such as:

- The discount rate (see para 28.69 below).
- Future salary and benefit levels.
- The expected rate of return on plan assets.

- Price inflation.

- Future medical costs, including (where material) the cost of administering claims and benefit payments.

28.68 Section 28 of the standard requires that actuarial assumptions be unbiased, mutually compatible and represent the employer's best estimate of the variables necessary to determine the future cash flows that will arise under the plan. [FRS 102 para 28.16]. For assumptions to be unbiased, they must be neither imprudent nor excessively conservative. [FRS 102 para 28.16]. For assumptions to be mutually compatible, they must reflect the economic relationships between factors such as inflation, rates of salary increase, returns on plan assets and discount rates. Section 28 of the standard also requires key actuarial assumptions to be disclosed (see para 28.109 below). The assumptions are ultimately the responsibility of the directors, and are generally determined with advice from an actuary (although this is not required).

Discounting

28.69 Given the long timescales, defined benefit obligations are discounted. The discount rate should reflect the time value of money, but not investment risk or actuarial risk, since other actuarial assumptions deal with these items. Furthermore, the discount rate should not reflect the entity-specific credit risk borne by the entity's creditors; nor should it reflect the risk that future experience might differ from actuarial assumptions. The discount rate should reflect simply the estimated timing of benefit payments. For this purpose, the discount rate should be determined by reference to market yields at the reporting date on high-quality corporate bonds of equivalent currency and term to the benefit obligations. [FRS 102 para 28.17].

28.70 The phrase 'high-quality' is not further defined or explained in the standard. In general, high-quality bonds are taken to mean bonds that have been granted at least an AA grade by credit rating agencies. In countries where there is no deep market in such high-quality corporate bonds, the market yields (at the reporting date) on government bonds of equivalent currency and term should be used. [FRS 102 para 28.17].

Actuarial valuation methods

28.71 The third step in the process of measuring the defined benefit obligation is to discount the estimated benefit to present value using an actuarial method. A number of actuarial methods exist in practice, but historically the one that has been most commonly used is the projected unit credit method (sometimes known as the 'accrued benefit method pro-rated on service' or the' benefits/years of service method'). Even though this method can be complex by making use of various actuarial assumptions (see para 28.65 above), the standard requires companies to use it. [FRS 102 para 28.18]. The projected unit credit method is an accrued benefits valuation method under which the accrued benefits are the

Employee benefits

benefits for service up to a given point in time, whether those benefits have vested or not. So, the method uses both the vested and non-vested periods of service. Where benefits are based on future salaries, an estimation of future salary increases is also reflected in the measurement of the obligation. In essence, the method views each period of service as giving rise to an additional unit of benefit entitlement, with each unit being measured separately to build up the total obligation. This is illustrated in the examples below.

Example – The projected unit credit method

An entity operates a defined benefit plan that pays a lump sum on termination of service of 1% of final salary for each year of service. An employee joins the entity at the beginning of year 1 on a salary of £50,000. Salaries are assumed to increase at 7% per annum and the discount rate is 8%. It is expected that the employee will retire after five years of service.

The following table shows how the defined benefit obligation builds up for this employee over the five years of service. It is assumed that there are no changes in actuarial assumptions, and the possibility that the employee might leave the entity before retiring is ignored.

Year	1 £	2 £	3 £	4 £	5 £
Estimated salary (7% growth)	50,000	53,500	57,245	61,252	65,540
Benefit attributable to:					
– current year (1% of final salary)	655	655	655	655	655
– prior years	655	1,310	1,965	2,620	
Cumulative benefit payable	655	1,310	1,965	2,620	3,275
Opening obligation	0	481	1,040	1,686	2,426
Interest (8% on opening obligation)	0	39	84	134	194
Current service cost (discounted at 8%)	481	520	562	606	655
Closing obligation	481	1,040	1,686	2,426	3,275

At the end of year 5, the employee's final salary is £65,540 (£50,000 × (1.07)4). The cumulative benefit earned at the end of five years is 1% of the final salary times five years of service (£655 × 5 = £3,275). The current year benefit earned in each of the five years is one-fifth of this (£655).

The current service cost is the present value of the benefit attributed to the current year. So, in year 3, for example, the current service cost is £655/(1.08)2 = £562.

The closing obligation at the end of year 3 = present value of benefit attributable to the period £562 x number of years of service up to year 3 = £562 × 3 = £1,686.

Frequency of valuations

28.72 The standard does not require an entity to engage a qualified actuary to perform the comprehensive actuarial valuation needed to measure the defined benefit obligation. For practical reasons, an entity might choose to engage a qualified actuary for this purpose. There is also no requirement to perform a comprehensive actuarial valuation on an annual basis. The standard goes on to state that, if the principal actuarial assumptions have not changed significantly, the defined benefit obligation can be measured by adjusting the prior period measurement for changes in employee demographics, such as the number of employees and salary levels. [FRS 102 para 28.20].

28.73 In practice, some aspects of the valuation will need to be updated at each reporting date. For instance, the discount rate should always be the current rate of return on high-grade corporate bonds at the reporting date. Assumptions that are not directly affected by changes in the market conditions need not be updated annually. Similarly, changes to the plan (such as benefit improvements) will need to be factored in. Individual circumstances will dictate whether a full valuation is required subsequent to the previous valuation, or whether an update is sufficient. For instance, if the previous valuation was undertaken some time ago and many changes have occurred since then, an update might not be sufficient to provide a reliable measure of the defined benefit obligation.

Defined benefit plan assets

28.74 Plan assets comprise:

■ Assets held by a long-term employee benefit fund.

■ Qualifying insurance policies.

[FRS 102 Glossary of terms].

28.75 An 'asset held by a long-term employee benefit fund' is defined as an:

"asset (other than non-transferable financial instruments issued by the reporting entity) that:

(a) is held by an entity (a fund) that is legally separate from the reporting entity and exists solely to pay or fund employee benefits; and

(b) is available to be used only to pay or fund employee benefits, is not available to the reporting entity's own creditors (even in bankruptcy), and cannot be returned to the reporting entity, unless either:

(i) the remaining assets of the fund are sufficient to meet all the related employee benefit obligations of the plan or the reporting entity; or

(ii) the assets are returned to the reporting entity to reimburse it for employee benefits already paid."

[FRS 102 Glossary of terms].

28.76 This definition is generally met in funded pension plans that are constituted in the UK, where the assets are usually under the control of the trustee, who administers the plan in accordance with the provisions of the pension trust deed and applicable pension legislation. So, such assets are not generally available to the reporting entity's own creditors (even in bankruptcy), and can only be returned to the reporting entity under strict legal conditions.

28.77 Qualifying insurance policies are defined in FRS 102 as a policy issued by an insurer that is not a related party of the reporting entity, *"if the proceeds of the policy:*

(a) *can be used only to pay or fund employee benefits under a defined benefit plan; and*

(b) *are not available to the reporting entity's own creditors (even in bankruptcy) and cannot be paid to the reporting entity, unless either:*

    (i) *the proceeds represent surplus assets that are not needed for the policy to meet all the related employee benefit obligations; or*

    (ii) *the proceeds are returned to the reporting entity to reimburse it for employee benefits already paid."*

[FRS 102 Glossary of terms].

The definition notes that a qualifying insurance policy does not necessarily have to be an insurance contract.

Measurement of plan assets

28.78 Plan assets should be measured at their fair value at the reporting date. Fair value is defined in the standard's Glossary of terms, and reflects the amount for which an asset could be exchanged in an arm's length transaction between knowledgeable and willing parties. Paragraphs 11.27 to 11.32 of FRS 102 (see chapter 11) provide guidance on determining fair values of plan assets. [FRS 102 para 28.15(b)].

28.79 If the plan asset is an insurance policy that exactly matches the amount and timing of some or all of the benefits payable under the plan, then the fair value of the insurance policy asset is deemed to be the present value of the related obligation. [FRS 102 para 28.15(b)]. We believe that any difference from the amounts paid to acquire a qualifying insurance policy should be recognised (as an actuarial gain or loss) in other comprehensive income. In many cases, the consideration paid could be higher than the defined benefit obligation on the company's books if the third party uses more prudent actuarial assumptions.

28.80 If the present value of the defined benefit obligation at the reporting date is less than the fair value of plan assets at that date, the plan has a surplus. An entity should recognise a plan surplus as a defined benefit plan asset *"only to the extent that it is able to recover the surplus either through reduced contributions in the future or through refunds from the plan"*. [FRS 102 para 28.22].

Reimbursements

28.81 An entity might sometimes look to another party, such as an insurance company, to settle all or part of a defined benefit obligation under a non-qualifying insurance policy. Qualifying insurance policies are plan assets (discussed in para 28.74). Where it is virtually certain that another party will reimburse some or all of the expenditure required to settle a defined benefit obligation (even though this does not represent a qualifying insurance policy or a plan asset), this right to reimbursement should be recognised as a separate asset. [FRS 102 para 28.28].

28.82 In many respects, the above requirement might be considered academic; this is because a right to reimbursement that is virtually certain will satisfy the definition of an asset. It is still important to identify reimbursement rights, because they are not presented in the same way as other assets. Reimbursement rights are recognised as separate assets, rather than as a deduction, in determining the net defined benefit liability. [FRS 102 para 28.28].

28.83 Apart from recognition as a separate asset, the reimbursement right should be treated in the same way as plan assets in all other respects. [FRS 102 para 28.28]. This means it is measured at fair value using the guidance in section 11 paragraphs 11.27 to 11.32. The exception to this would be if the reimbursement right is an insurance policy that exactly matches the amount and timing of some or all of the benefits payable under the defined benefit plan. In such a case, similar to qualifying insurance policies, the fair value would be deemed to be the present value of the related obligation. Any difference from the amounts paid to acquire this reimbursement right would be recognised as an actuarial gain or loss in other comprehensive income (see above para 28.79).

> **Example – Reimbursement rights**
>
> Entity A operates a defined benefit pension plan for its senior management. It has decided to cover its pension obligation with an insurance policy taken out with a leading insurance entity. The policy requires the insurer to reimburse entity A in full for all benefit payments (exact match in timing and amounts); but it also permits entity A to cancel the arrangements, in which case the insurer repays a pre-determined amount to the entity.
>
> The existence of the contractual right to terminate the policy (and receive the proceeds for any purposes) means that entity A can apply the proceeds of the policy in its business, regardless of the benefit obligation. The use of the proceeds is not restricted to paying employee benefits. So, this policy is not a qualifying insurance policy, but it does represent a reimbursement right (as described above). Hence, entity A recognises the reimbursement as a separate asset.
>
> Entity A measures the reimbursement right at the same amount as the related obligation, given that there is an exact match of amount and timing of the payments.

Recognition of the costs of a defined benefit plan

28.84   The plan assets and liabilities are remeasured at each period end, and the standard gives guidance on how to recognise the change in the surplus or deficit. Section 28 of FRS 102 gives detailed guidance on how the costs of a defined benefit plan should be recognised. This will generally be either in profit or loss or in other comprehensive income, depending on the type of the cost (see para 28.79). In some instances, costs could also be capitalised (see para 28.80). But some elements of the net change in the net defined benefit liability should not be recognised in profit or loss or other comprehensive income; these are:

- Benefits paid to employees during the period.
- Contributions made to the plan during the period.

28.85   The net change in the net defined benefit liability is recognised as the cost of a defined benefit plan. The individual components of this net change are recognised as follows:

- The change in the net defined benefit liability arising from employee service rendered during the reporting period in profit or loss.
- Net interest on the net defined benefit obligation during the reporting period in profit or loss.
- Costs of plan introductions, benefit changes, curtailments and settlements in profit or loss.
- Remeasurement of the net defined benefit liability in other comprehensive income.

[FRS 102 para 28.23].

28.86   The net change in the net defined benefit liability during the period (that is recognised as the cost of the defined benefit plan) can be recognised as part of the cost of an asset (such as inventories or property, plant and equipment) if another section of the standard requires it. [FRS 102 para 28.23].

28.87   In some cases the terms of a defined benefit plan may require employees or third parties to contribute to the costs of the plan. The standard requires that contributions by employees reduce the costs of the benefits to the entity. [FRS 102 para 28.23].

28.88   The standard does give any guidance on how such a reduction of the benefit costs to the entity should be classified. For example, the reduction could lower the service costs or alternatively could be included in the actuarial calculations as a negative benefit.

Current service cost

28.89 The change in the net defined benefit liability arising from employee service rendered during the reporting period is often referred to as current service cost. The current service cost is the actuarial present value of the benefits attributed by the pension benefit formula to employee service during the period. That is, the actuary estimates the additional cost that the employer is expected to pay as a result of the employees' current year's service and discounts the cost of those future benefits back to its present value (see example in para 28.71 above). Consequently, it is supposed to reflect the true economic cost relating to each period based on current market conditions. This cost is determined independently of the funding of the plan. So, in principle, for a given set of employees and benefit formula, the current service cost should be the same, irrespective of whether the plan is in surplus, in deficit or unfunded.

28.90 Current service cost is not necessarily a stable percentage of pensionable pay year-on-year. For example, current service cost will vary if the discount rate changes. It will also increase year-on-year as a proportion of pay if the average age of the workforce is increasing, as is likely where a plan is closed to new entrants.

Interest cost

28.91 The defined benefit obligation is discounted, so the interest cost represents the unwinding of the discount on the plan liabilities; this is because benefits are one period closer to settlement. Interest includes also interest income on plan assets. Interest income on plan assets and interest costs on the defined benefit obligation form 'net interest'. The net interest on the net defined benefit liability should be calculated by multiplying the net defined benefit liability by the discount rate (see para 28.69 above for determining the discount rate), both determined at the start of the annual accounting period. [FRS 102 para 28.24]. But changes in the net defined benefit obligation during the period, such as

- transfers into the plan that increase the liability during the year;
- benefits paid to pensioners and transfers out of the plan that reduce the liability during the year; or
- changes in the plan assets as a result of contributions and benefit payments

should be taken into account.

28.92 So, the net interest that is calculated on the net defined benefit liability comprises interest costs on the defined benefit obligation as well as interest income on the plan assets. This excludes the effect of interest on any surplus that is not recoverable and, therefore, not recognised. There will almost always be a difference between actual return on plan assets and the interest income calculated as detailed above. Such difference represents an actuarial gain or loss and is included in the remeasurement of the net defined benefit liability. [FRS 102 para 28.24B].

Remeasurement of the net defined benefit liability

28.93   Remeasurements of the net defined benefit liability are not recognised in profit or loss but in other comprehensive income. A remeasurement comprises the return on plan assets (excluding the amounts that are included in net interest in profit or loss) as well as other actuarial gains and losses. [FRS 102 para 28.25].

28.94   With regard to return on plan assets, pension plan assets out of which pension benefits are paid generally consist of equities, bonds, real estate and qualifying insurance policies. The actual return on these assets comprises interest, dividends and other income, together with realised and unrealised changes in the fair market value of the plan assets. This return on the plan assets (coupled with the contributions that the employer makes to the plan) increases plan assets. Benefits paid to retired employees reduce plan assets. Entities compute the actual return on plan assets from the movements in the fair value of the plan assets during the period (adjusted for contributions paid in and benefits paid out during the year), as illustrated in the following equation:

Actual return on plan assets =

(Closing FV – Opening FV) – (Contributions – Benefits paid)

FV = Fair value of plan assets

28.95   The difference between interest income on plan assets (calculated as part of the net interest calculation) and the actual return on plan assets achieved in the period is part of the remeasurement of the net defined benefit liability and is included in other comprehensive income. The return on reimbursement rights is treated in the same way. [FRS 102 para 28.28].

28.96   The following example illustrates the above principles:

> **Example – Return on plan assets**
>
> Entity A has opening plan assets of £10,000, contributes cash of £4,900 and pays out benefits of £1,900 (net cash contributed £3,000) during the year. The discount is 7.5%.

	£
Return on £10,000 held for 12 months at 7.5%	750
Return on £3,000 held for six months at 3.68% (equivalent to 7.5% annually, compounded every six months)	110
Interest income on plan assets	860

The actual return on plan assets is calculated as follows:

		£
Fair value of plan assets at the end of the reporting period		15,000
Fair value of plan assets at the beginning of the reporting period		10,000
Increase in fair value of plan assets		5,000
Deduct: Contributions to plan during the period	4,900	
Less benefits paid during the period	1,900	
		(3,000)
Actual return on plan assets		2,000

The difference between the actual return on plan assets (£2,000) and interest income on plan assets (£860) is a remeasurement, which is recognised in other comprehensive income (£1,140).

Actuarial gains and losses

28.97 Actuarial gains and losses arise when the values of plan assets and liabilities are remeasured at the balance sheet date. They result from unexpected increases or decreases in the fair value of the plan assets or the present value of the plan liabilities. Examples include the following:

- Experience gains and losses arising where actual events during the year differ from the actuarial assumptions in the previous valuation (for example, unexpectedly high or low rates of employee turnover, early retirement or mortality, or of increases in salaries, benefits or medical costs).

- The effects of changes in actuarial assumptions from one period to the next (for example, to reflect increased life expectancies).

- The effects of changes in the discount rate, which will alter the net present value of the net defined benefit obligation.

- The difference between the expected and actual return on plan assets (as discussed in para 28.93 above).

Example – Events causing actuarial gains and losses

- Actual or estimated mortality rates, or the proportion of employees taking early retirement, will alter the period for which an entity will be required to make benefit payments. For example, accelerating technological change might cause a manufacturer to reduce its workforce gradually by offering early retirement to a number of employees.

- Estimated salaries or benefits will alter the amount of each benefit payment. For example, a software developer might decide to increase its salaries by more than the rate of inflation to retain its skilled work force.

- Estimated employee turnover might alter the number of employees that are expected to transfer their benefits to another pension plan. For example, an unexpected change in tax legislation that makes personal pensions more attractive might lead to a greater number of employees leaving defined benefit plans and making their own pension arrangements.

28.98 An entity is required to recognise all actuarial gains and losses in the period in which they occur. Actuarial gains and losses fall under remeasurements, so an entity recognises them in other comprehensive income and as part of the statement of comprehensive income. [FRS 102 paras 28.23, 28.25].

28.99 Remeasurements that an entity recognised in other comprehensive income are never reclassified into profit or loss in a later period. [FRS 102 para 28.25A].

Plan introductions and changes

28.100 An entity might introduce a new plan, or change its defined benefit plan, in the current period, to provide benefits to employees for years of service before the date of introduction or change. For instance, the entity might amend its existing plan to provide a bonus for early retirement, reduce the pensionable age, provide pension benefits for spouses not previously provided, or extend its pension plan to all employees. Such benefit changes might produce both an increase in the cost of future service relating to active members (reflected in a higher annual current service cost) and an increased liability for past service relating to current and ex-employees. The standard states that the net defined benefit liability should be increased to recognise this additional liability. The cost (that is, the capitalised present value) of benefit changes that relates to past service (whether vested or not) should be charged to profit and loss in the period in which the entity amends the existing plan or introduces a new plan that has a retrospective effect. Such costs are often called 'past service costs'. Some changes in the benefits could result in a decrease in the defined benefit obligation, and result in income (or negative past service costs) for the current reporting period. [FRS 102 para 28.21].

28.101 The recognition of past service costs is illustrated in the following example:

Example – Recognition of past service cost

An entity operates a pension plan that provides a pension of 1% of final salary for each year of service, subject to a minimum of five years' service. On 1 January 20X1 the entity improves the pension to 1.25% of final salary for each year of service, including prior years. As a consequence, the present value of the defined benefit obligation increased by £500,000, as shown below:

	£
Employees with more than five years' service at 1 January 20X1	300,000
Employees with less than five years' service at 1 January 20X1	200,000
(average of three years of service, so two years until vesting)	
Increase in defined benefit obligation	500,000

The entity has changed the present value of the defined benefit obligation as a result of an amendment to the plan. Therefore, a past service cost of £500,000 should be recognised in the income statement immediately. The increase in the defined benefit obligation of £200,000 relating to employees who have not yet vested will include an assumption about how many of them will leave before they complete the five-year vesting condition and thus forfeit their benefit.

Settlements and curtailments

28.102 Settlements and curtailments are events that materially change the liabilities relating to a plan and that are not covered by the normal actuarial assumptions.

28.103 A settlement occurs when the relevant part of the employer's liability under the defined benefit plan is completely discharged. Settlements could occur, for example, when a defined benefit plan is closed and the assets and liabilities are transferred into a defined contribution plan.

28.104 A curtailment occurs when an entity makes a material reduction in the number of employees covered by a defined benefit plan or amends the plan's terms so that a material element of future service by current employees will no longer qualify for benefits, or will qualify only for reduced benefits. A curtailment could arise from an isolated event (such as a factory closure, discontinuance of an operation or the termination or suspension of a plan) or as a result of a reduction in future benefits (for example, following an amendment to the plan rules).

28.105 When a defined benefit plan has been settled or curtailed in the current period, the defined benefit obligation should be decreased or eliminated, and any resulting gain or loss should be recognised in profit or loss in the current period. [FRS 102 para 28.21A].

Illustrative example

28.106 The example below illustrates the accounting for a defined benefit plan discussed above.

Example – Accounting for a defined benefit plan

The following information relates to a defined benefit plan operated by an entity for its employees:

	£
Fair value of plan assets at 1 Jan 20X1	9,200
Present value of plan liabilities at 1 Jan 20X1	11,600
Current service cost	860
Net interest cost	240
Contributions paid by the entity to the fund during the year	350
Benefits paid during the year	400
Fair value of plan assets at 31 Dec 20X1	11,000
Present value of plan liabilities at 31 Dec 20X1	(13,700)

At 1 January 20X1, the entity amended the plan to provide additional benefits to some of its key management. The present value of the past service cost attributable to periods before 1 January 20X1 amounted to £200, of which £50 vests immediately in the current year and £150 is expected to vest over the next three years.

During the year, the entity transferred the accrued benefits of some employees into a defined contribution plan. The accrued benefits at 1 Jan 20X1 relating to these employees amounted to £350, that was settled by transfer of assets from the plan amounting to £400.

The accounting entries that would be made in the financial statements during the year ended 31 December 20X1 are shown below. The memorandum columns on the right maintain the balances in the plan assets and liabilities. The difference between the fair value of the plan assets and the present value of the defined benefit obligation is the net pension asset or liability that is shown in the balance sheet. The pension expense and the actuarial gain or loss recognised in other comprehensive income will be shown in the statement of comprehensive income.

| | Financial statements | | | | Memorandum | |
	Pension expense Dr (Cr) £	Cash Dr (Cr) £	OCI Dr (Cr) £	Net pension asset (liabilities) Dr (Cr) £	Plan liabilities Dr (Cr) £	Plan assets Dr (Cr) £
Balance at 1 Jan 20X1				(2,400)	(11,600)	9,200
Service cost	860				(860)	
Past service cost*	200				(200)	
Net interest cost	240				(1,160)	920
Contribution in year		(350)				350
Benefits paid in year					400	(400)
Liabilities extinguished on settlement	(350)				350	
Assets distributed on settlement	400					(400)
Loss on settlement	50					
Actuarial (gain)/loss (balance)			(700)		(630)	1,330
	1,350	(350)	(700)	(300)		
Balance at 31 Dec 20X1				(2,700)	(13,700)	11,000

*Past service costs includes both vested and non-vested benefits (as discussed in para 28.100 above).

Presentation and disclosure

Presentation

28.107 The standard refers to 'The Large and Medium-sized Companies and Groups (Accounts and Reports) Regulations 2008' (the 'Regulation') for presentation. In particular, paragraph 4.2 of FRS 102 refers to Schedule 1 to the Regulations. Schedule 1 (for non-banking and non-insurance companies) requires that provisions for 'Pensions and similar obligations' are separately disclosed. Schedules 2 and 3 (for banking and insurance companies) require the same: 'Provisions for pensions and similar obligations' are disclosed separately. Paragraph 4.2 of the standard requires generally that an entity classifies a liability as due within one year when the entity does not have an unconditional right to defer settlement of the liability for at least 12 months after the reporting date. But there is no specific requirement to separate portions of assets and liabilities arising from post-employment benefits accordingly. In practice, the net defined benefit obligation or surplus asset would generally be presented in one position outside creditors or debtors that are due within 12 months. But, if a distinction can reliably be made, split classification would be appropriate.

28.108 Where an entity operates more than one plan, some plans might be in surplus and some might be in deficit. In this case, aggregate amounts of net defined benefit assets and net defined benefit liabilities (which include any unfunded benefits) would generally be shown separately (that is, not offset with each other) in the statement of financial position. Section 28 of FRS 102 does not deal with offsetting. But paragraph 38A of section 11 specifies criteria for offsetting of assets and liability balances. Applying similar principles, obligations of one plan can only be offset against a surplus in another plan if the entity:

- currently has a legally enforceable right to use a surplus in one plan to settle obligations in another; and

- the entity intends to settle the obligations on a net basis or to realise the surplus in one plan and settle its obligations under the other plan simultaneously.

Disclosures

28.109   An entity should disclose the following information about defined benefit plans (except for any defined multi-employer benefit plans that are accounted for as a defined contribution plan (see para 28.35 above), for which the disclosures detailed in para 28.52 above apply instead); if an entity has more than one defined benefit plan, these disclosures could be made in aggregate, separately for each plan, or in such groupings as are considered to be the most useful:

(a)   A general description of the type of plan, including funding policy.

(b)   The date of the most recent comprehensive actuarial valuation and, if it was not as of the reporting date, a description of the adjustments that were made to measure the defined benefit obligation at the reporting date.

(c)   A reconciliation of opening and closing balances of the defined benefit obligation, the fair value of plan assets and any reimbursement right recognised as an asset.

(d)   Each of the reconciliations of the opening and closing balances should show separately (if applicable):

- the change in the defined benefit liability arising from employee services rendered during the period in profit or loss;

- interest income or expense;

- remeasurement of the defined benefit liability, showing separately actuarial gains and losses and the return on plan assets less amounts included in interest; and

- plan introductions, changes, curtailments and settlements.

(e)   The total cost relating to defined benefit plans for the period, disclosing separately the amounts:

- recognised in profit or loss as an expense, and

- included in the cost of an asset.

(f)   For each major class of plan assets (which includes, but is not limited to, equity instruments, debt instruments, property, and all other assets), the percentage or amount that each major class constitutes of the fair value of the total plan assets at the reporting date.

(g)   The amounts included in the fair value of plan assets for:

- each class of the entity's own financial instruments, and

- any property occupied by, or other assets used by, the entity.

(h)   The return on plan assets.

(i)   The principal actuarial assumptions used, including (if applicable):

- the discount rates;

- the expected rates of salary increases;

- medical cost trend rates; and

- any other material actuarial assumptions used.

The reconciliations between the opening and closing balances for defined benefit obligations, fair value of plan assets and reimbursement rights recognised as an asset noted above need not be presented for prior periods.

[FRS 102 para 28.41].

28.110   If an entity participates in a defined benefit plan that shares risks between entities under common control (see para 28.43 above), it discloses the following information:

- the contractual agreement or stated policy for charging the cost of a defined benefit plan or the fact that there is no policy;

- the policy for determining the contribution to be paid by the entity;

- if the entity accounts for an allocation of the net defined benefit cost, all the information required as outlined in paragraph 28.109 above; and

- if the entity accounts for the contributions payable for the period, the information about the plan as a whole for items (a), (b), (f) and (g) in paragraph 28.109 above.

This information can be disclosed by cross-reference to disclosures in another group entity's financial statements if:

- that group entity's financial statements separately identify and disclose the information required about the plan; and

- that group entity's financial statements are available to users of the financial statements on the same terms as the financial statements of the entity and at the same time as, or earlier than, the financial statements of the entity.

[FRS 102 para 28.41A].

28.111   With regard to the disclosure requirement in item (e) in paragraph 28.109 above, only the total cost relating to defined benefit plans for the period recognised as an expense need be disclosed as noted above, and not the individual components of the pension cost. In any event, the individual components of the pension cost would be disclosed in the reconciliation between opening and closing balances of the defined benefit obligation that requires separate disclosure of all other changes.

Other long-term employee benefits

28.112   Other long-term employee benefits include for example the following if they are due to be settled 12 months or more after the end of the annual reporting period in which the employees render service:

- Long-term paid absences, such as long-service or sabbatical leave.

- Long-term disability benefits.

- Profit sharing and bonuses.

- Deferred remuneration.

[FRS 102 para 28.29].

28.113   Long-term benefits mentioned above share many of the characteristics of short term benefits (discussed in para 28.9 above). So, one might expect that the same accounting principles would apply, with appropriate adjustment for increased uncertainty and the time value of money. But the standard requires other long-term employee benefits to be accounted for in the same way as defined benefit pension benefits. This means that the cost of the long-term employee benefits should be attributable to the period in which the services that give rise to the obligation are rendered.

28.114   An entity should recognise a liability for other long-term employee benefits measured at the net total of the following amounts:

- the present value of the benefit obligation at the reporting date (calculated using the methodology for selecting a discount rate in para 28.17 of FRS 102), minus

- the fair value at the reporting date of plan assets (if any) out of which the obligations are to be settled directly.

[FRS 102 para 28.30].

28.115   The change in the liability during the period representing the cost of the long-term employee benefit should be recognised in profit or loss (unless the standard elsewhere requires or permits their inclusion in the cost of an asset). [FRS 102 para 28.30].

28.116   The requirement to account for other long-term employee benefits is similar to accounting for defined benefit plans, except that actuarial gains and losses are recognised immediately in profit or loss. This means that the entity should use the projected unit credit method to measure the obligation arising. The mechanics of the projected unit credit method are illustrated in the example in paragraph 28.71 above.

> **Example – Lump-sum disability payments**
>
> Entity A pays, in accordance with a trade union agreement, a lump sum of £10,000 to an employee who becomes disabled as a result of an accident. This payment is the same, regardless of the length of service.
>
> Entity B pays, in accordance with its trade union agreement, a lump sum of £10,000 to an employee who becomes disabled as a result of an accident within the first five years of employment, and £20,000 if the employee becomes disabled after five years of employment.
>
> The future cash outflow of entity A does not depend on past employee service. The obligating event is the occurrence of an accident that causes the disability of an employee. Entity A has no present obligation to make the payment until an accident occurs. No accruals should be made by entity A until such an event.
>
> The level of benefits of entity B's employees depends on the length of employee service. An obligation arises when service is rendered. Entity B's obligation should be measured using the projected unit credit method. It should reflect the probability that payments will be required and the length of service (that is, amount) for which payments are expected to be made.

Disclosures

28.117   For each category of other long-term benefits that an entity provides to its employees, it should disclose the following information:

- The nature of the benefit.
- The amount of the obligation.
- The extent of funding at the reporting date.

[FRS 102 para 28.42].

Termination benefits

28.118   Termination benefits are defined as employee benefits provided in exchange for the termination of an employee's employment as a result of either *"(a) an entity's decision to terminate an employee's employment before the normal retirement date or (b) an employee's decision to accept voluntary redundancy in exchange for those benefits"*. [FRS 102 Glossary of terms].

28.119   Regarding the scope of what might be viewed as termination benefits, *"an entity may be committed, by legislation, by contractual or other agreements with employees or their representatives or by a constructive obligation based on business practice, custom or a desire to act equitably, to make payments (or provide other* *benefits) to employees when it terminates their employment. Such payments are termination benefits".* [FRS 102 para 28.31].

28.120   Termination benefits differ from other post-employment benefits because they arise from termination of employment and not from employee service. The amount of the benefit payable is a one-off payment made at termination and is not linked to periods of service. The following examples illustrate the distinction.

> **Example 1 – Statutory payments to employees leaving after five years' service**
>
> Entity A operates in country C. Local labour laws require that payments are made to employees leaving the entity for any reason after five years' service. The amounts payable are determined by reference to final salary and length of service. Benefits will, therefore, be payable to the workforce, but these will not be termination benefits as defined above. This is because the benefits are earned during an employee's working life, and the entity is obliged to pay them regardless of the reason for the employee's departure; so only the timing of the payment is uncertain. Hence, these benefits are treated as post-employment benefits and accounted for as specified at paragraph 28.29 above.

> **Example 2 – Voluntary redundancy payments**
>
> Entity B also operates in country C and is subject to the same labour laws. But, in connection with a voluntary redundancy programme, entity B has agreed to make additional payments to employees who accept the offer of voluntary redundancy. These additional payments will represent termination benefits as defined above, because the entity had no obligation to make the payments until it made the decision to instigate the voluntary redundancy programme.

Recognition

28.121   Termination benefits do not provide an entity with future economic benefits, so an entity should recognise them as an expense in profit or loss immediately. [FRS 102 para 28.32]. An entity might also have to account for a curtailment of retirement benefits or other employee benefit (see para 28.104 above). [FRS 102 para 28.33].

28.122   With regard to timing of recognition, an entity should recognise a liability when it is demonstrably committed; such commitment could be legal, contractual or constructive, to either:

- terminate the employment of an employee or group of employees before the normal retirement date; or

- provide termination benefits as a result of an offer made in order to encourage voluntary redundancy.

[FRS 102 para 28.34].

28.123 FRS 102 confirms that an *"entity is demonstrably committed to a termination only when the entity has a detailed formal plan for the termination and is without realistic possibility of withdrawal from the plan"*. [FRS 102 para 28.35].

28.124 A *"detailed formal plan"* is not further defined in the standard; in line with general practice, our view would be that a detailed formal plan normally specifies:

- The location, function and approximate number of employees whose services are to be terminated.

- The termination benefits for each job classification or function.

- The timescale for implementation of the plan. Implementation should begin as soon as possible, and the period of time to complete implementation should be such that material changes to the plan are unlikely.

Also, the plan should be communicated to those affected by it (or their representative, union or regulatory body) in order for a demonstrable commitment to exist.

28.125 The above principles for recognition of termination benefits are consistent with those of section 21 of FRS 102. A pre-requisite for making a provision under section 21 of FRS 102 is that a reliable estimate of the amount of the obligation can be made. [FRS 102 para 21.4]. Where this is not possible (and such circumstances are expected to be extremely rare), the obligation is treated as a contingent liability. [FRS 102 para 21.12]. Although the standard is silent on this matter, there is a reference to the disclosure that might be necessary where there is uncertainty about the number of employees who will accept an offer of termination benefits. [FRS 102 para 28.44]. This could be read to imply that the 'normal' principles of section 21 will apply and a provision for termination benefits should be made only where a reliable estimate can be made.

> **Example – Redundancies following restructuring**
>
> The board of an entity has announced two major restructuring plans and, in both cases, has communicated details of the redundancy package to the staff affected:
>
> - Sale of half of the entity's global manufacturing business over a three-year period, starting immediately. This will involve the immediate redundancy of 15% of the machine workers in each factory and 10% of the middle management at each location.
>
> - Re-organisation of the head office over a one-year period, commencing in two years' time; 20% of the head office staff will lose their jobs during the restructuring.
>
> As regards the sale of the manufacturing business, a provision should be recognised for the estimated costs of the disposal and redundancy. The sites and details of the redundancy and other costs have been identified. The scale and complexity of the disposal requires that it be completed over an extended period. Disposal activities will

begin immediately. Three years is the time necessary to complete the disposal and should not prevent the provision from being recognised.

In contrast, the entity should not recognise a provision for the head office's re-organisation. The re-organisation is not due to start for two years. External parties are unlikely to have a valid expectation that management is committed to the restructuring, because the timeframe allows significant opportunities for management to change the details of the plan or even to decide not to continue with it. Also, the degree of identification of the staff to lose their jobs is not sufficient to support recognising a redundancy provision. Details of the departments within head office that will be affected should be identified, together with the approximate numbers of staff from each department.

Measurement

28.126   An entity should measure termination benefits at the best estimate of the expenditure that would be required to settle the obligation at the reporting date. This is consistent with the guidance in section 21 of FRS 102. In the case of an offer made to encourage voluntary redundancy, the measurement of termination benefits should be based on the number of employees expected to accept the offer. [FRS 102 para 28.36].

28.127   Where termination benefits are due more than 12 months after the end of the reporting period, they should be measured at their discounted present value using the methodology for selecting a discount rate specified in paragraph 28.17 of FRS 102. [FRS 102 para 28.37].

Example – Voluntary redundancy payment with a time limit

Entity A restructures its operations in a particular location. It agrees with trade unions during December 20X3 a plan to reduce staff numbers in that location by 100 by February 20X4. Also, in December 20X3, management communicated an offer of £5,000 for voluntary redundancy to be accepted by the end of January 20X4. The offer for any remaining employees can be withdrawn at any time. If sufficient staff do not accept the offer, management will terminate the employment of additional staff to reach the target of 100. Employees terminated involuntarily are entitled to a termination payment of £4,000 each.

At 31 December 20X3, 60 employees have accepted the voluntary termination offer, amounting to a liability of £300,000 (60 employees x £5,000). A further £160,000 (40 employees x £4,000) is recognised as an additional liability because management is demonstrably committed to the plan to terminate 100 staff. A contingent liability of £40,000 for the additional amount that would be payable if the maximum number of employees accepted the termination voluntarily should also be disclosed.

The voluntary termination benefits of £300,000 are based on the number of employees that accepted the offer. The termination benefits of £160,000 are as a result of the company's decision to terminate the remaining 40 employees, and are recorded on communication of the termination plan.

Disclosures

28.128 For each category of termination benefits that an entity provides to its employees, it should disclose the following information:

- The nature of the benefit.

- The accounting policy.

- The amount of the obligation.

- The extent of funding at the reporting date.

[FRS 102 para 28.43].

28.129 When there is uncertainty about the number of employees who will accept an offer of termination benefits, a contingent liability exists (as discussed in para 28.125 above). Section 21 of FRS 102 requires an entity to disclose information about its contingent liabilities unless the possibility of an outflow in settlement is remote. [FRS 102 para 28.44].

Pensions Act 2004 implications

28.130 The Pensions Act 2004, published in November 2004, is a significant piece of legislation and was followed by a web of supporting regulations, codes of practice and other guidance, much of which came into force from April 2005.

28.131 From an accounting perspective, the most significant provisions of the Pensions Act 2004 are in the following areas:

- The launch of the Pension Protection Fund.

- Increased powers for the new Pension Regulator.

- Revised rules for employers ceasing to participate in a pension plan, including section 75 of the Pensions Act 1995 (as amended by the Pensions Act 2004).

28.132 We refer the reader to the section entitled 'Pensions Act 2004 implications' in chapter 11 of our Manual of Accounting – IFRS for the UK, which deals with this topic in more detail.

Transitional issues for UK entities

28.133 No special exemptions on employee benefits are available to first-time adopters under section 35 of FRS 102. So, a UK entity transitioning from FRS 17 ('old UK GAAP') to this standard must prepare its first financial statements as though the requirements of section 28 of the standard had always applied. The main issues that arise on transition are noted below.

28.134 FRS 102 provides specific guidance on dealing with short-term employee benefits (such as holiday pay) for which there is no old UK GAAP equivalent guidance. So, obligations for any unused entitlement for short-term compensated absences at the date of transition to this standard (that might not have been recognised under old UK GAAP) will now need to be recognised as an obligation, with a corresponding adjustment to opening retained earnings at the date of transition.

28.135 The calculation of the net defined benefit liability is similar under old UK GAAP and under this standard, except for any unrecognised past service costs under old UK GAAP. Under old UK GAAP, past service costs relating to benefit improvements were recognised in the profit and loss account on a straight-line basis over the period in which the increases in benefit vested. Where the benefits vested immediately, the past service cost were recognised immediately. Under FRS 102, past service costs are recognised immediately when the plan is amended, whether vested or not. This means that, on the date of transition to this standard, the net defined benefit liability should be amended for any unrecognised past service costs, with a corresponding adjustment to retained earnings.

28.136 For funded or partially funded benefit plans the measurement of pension expenses will differ from old UK GAAP. The change to FRS 102 will result in increased benefit expenses for most entities. FRS 102 requires the annual expense to include net interest expense or income, calculated by applying the discount rate to the net defined benefit asset or liability. This is in contrast to old UK GAAP, which required a finance charge and an expected return on plan assets to be calculated separately with different rates generally being used in practice. The uniform interest rate to be applied to the net defined benefit liability (asset) is a high-quality corporate bond rate where there is a deep market in such bonds and a government bond rate in other markets.

28.137 FRS 102 provides specific guidance on dealing with other long-term employee benefits and termination benefits for which there is no old UK GAAP equivalent. Under old UK GAAP, different accounting practices developed. In practice, FRS 12 was often used to deal with employee benefits other than retirement benefits. Any difference in treatment would have to be brought in line with the requirements of this standard, with a corresponding adjustment to opening retained earnings at the date of transition.

28.138 The accounting under FRS 102 (for both defined benefit multi-employer and for group plans) might differ from that under old UK GAAP, as follows:

- Multi-employer plans – under old UK GAAP, if an entity could not identify its share of plan assets and liabilities in a multi-employer defined benefit plan on a consistent and reasonable basis, it used defined contribution accounting. Under FRS 102, an entity has to recognise a liability where there is an agreement to fund a deficit relating to past service in a multi-employer plan, even though the plan is otherwise accounted for as a defined contribution plan. Under old UK GAAP, there was no clear guidance in this situation.

■ Group plans – under old UK GAAP, if the entities in a group could not identify their share of the defined benefit plan, each entity in the group would apply defined contribution accounting in their individual accounts (with defined benefit accounting applied in the consolidated financial statements). Under FRS 102, in addition to defined benefit accounting for consolidated purposes, at least one entity has to apply defined benefit accounting in its individual financial statements, depending on the policy for recharging pension costs within the group.

28.139 Regarding restrictions on the amount recognised as a defined benefit surplus, old UK GAAP has a harsher test for recognising surpluses compared to FRS 102. Under old UK GAAP there must be either an ability to reduce future contributions or a refund that has been agreed by the pension scheme trustees on the balance sheet date. To recognise a surplus under FRS 102 it is not necessary to have an agreement with the trustee in place on the balance sheet date.

28.140 Further differences might arise on transition, depending on the individual facts and circumstances of each plan and benefit provided. Examples include the lack of guidance under old UK GAAP on reimbursement rights, possible earlier recognition of gains due to curtailment and settlements under FRS 102 compared to old UK GAAP, and differences in the presentation and disclosure requirements between FRS 17 and FRS 102 which are less detailed. We refer the reader to our publication on 'Similarities & Differences — A comparison of old UK GAAP, new UK GAAP (FRS 102) and IFRS' for more detail.

Reduced disclosures for subsidiaries and ultimate parents

28.141 There are no disclosure exemptions for qualifying entities with respect to employee benefits. The disclosures required by section 28 of FRS 102 also need to be applied in full by qualifying entities (see section 1 of the standard).

Companies Act 2006 requirements

Companies Act disclosures

28.142 The Companies Act 2006 contains no specific accounting requirements regarding employee benefits. But there are extensive disclosure requirements for salaries, bonuses, pensions and other benefits payable to directors. Details of these requirements are covered in chapter 5 of the Manual of Accounting – Narrative Reporting.

28.143 Section 411(5) of the Companies Act 2006 requires the following to be disclosed in respect of all persons employed by a company during the financial year:

Employee benefits

- Wages and salaries paid or payable in respect of that year to those persons.

- Social security costs incurred by the company on their behalf.

- Other pension costs so incurred.

Further discussion on the Companies Act disclosure requirements regarding employee costs can be found in chapter 8.

28.144 Also, a UK company that has securities carrying voting rights admitted to trading on a regulated market at the end of its financial year is required to disclose, in its directors' report, details of any agreement with employees (including directors) of the company providing for compensation for loss of office on the takeover of the company. [SI 2008/410 7 Sch 13(2)(k)]. See further chapter 2 of the Manual of Accounting – Narrative Reporting.

Distributable reserves impact

28.145 Areas where the application of the standard could have an impact on distributable profits include the accounting for a company's participation in a group defined benefit plan. For defined contribution plans, the cost charged to the income statement, which is equal to the contributions payable in the period, is a realised loss. Similarly, where multi-employer plans are treated as defined contribution, the income statement charge is a realised loss.

28.146 The Companies Act defines a company's distributable profits not in terms of its assets and liabilities, but as its accumulated, realised profits less its accumulated, realised losses. [CA06 Sec 830(2)(3)]. It is the cumulative gain or loss credited or debited to reserves in respect of a pension plan (whether through the income statement or other comprehensive income), rather than the existence of a surplus or deficit, that affects realised profits. The impact on reserves is not usually the same as the pension surplus or deficit due to net contributions paid into the scheme and any asset or liability introduced as the result of a business combination.

28.147 It is necessary to determine whether an adjustment to reserves is required to arrive at the amount of distributable profits. Firstly it is necessary to identify the cumulative net gain or loss taken to reserves in respect of the pension surplus or deficit, and secondly to establish the extent to which the gain or loss is realised.

- No adjustment is required if a net cumulative debit or loss has been taken to reserves: this represents a realised loss as it results from the creation of, or increase in a provision for a liability or a loss resulting in an overall reduction in net assets.

- A cumulative net credit or gain in reserves is a realised profit only to the extent that it is represented by an asset to be recovered by agreed refunds in the form of qualifying consideration (as defined in Tech 02/10, issued by the ICAEW in November 2010). Any further cumulative net credit (in excess of agreed refunds) is not qualifying consideration so is treated as unrealised, although it will become realised in subsequent periods to the extent that it offsets subsequent net debits to reserves that are treated as realised losses.

28.148   Appendix 4 to Tech 02/10 includes a worked example for a company with a surplus at the year end.

28.149   Where a company operates more than one defined benefit plan, it should assess the impact of a surplus or deficit on its distributable profits separately for each plan. In other words, plans should not be aggregated or offset to reach a single net realised profit or loss, unless two plans are to merge and the trustees have irrevocably agreed to the offset of the surplus and deficit.

28.150   The deferred tax impact of pension accounting generally relates to the pension asset or liability and not the cumulative net debit or credit in reserves. A cumulative debit in respect of a deferred tax liability is a realised loss, and a cumulative credit in respect of a deferred tax asset is an unrealised profit. But, where there is an unrealised cumulative net credit in respect of a pension asset, a deferred tax debit is offset against that unrealised profit. Similarly, where there is a realised cumulative net debit in respect of a pension liability, a deferred tax credit is offset against that realised loss.

Chapter 29

Income tax

Income tax

Chapter 29

Income tax

Introduction

29.1 Tax in the financial statements consists of current tax and deferred tax.

29.2 The amount of tax payable in respect of a particular period often bears little relation to the amount of total comprehensive income reported in the financial statements of the same period. This is because income and expenses are included in tax assessments in different periods from those in which they are recognised in financial statements. For example, some items of income or expenditure in the financial statements might be taxable or tax deductible in a period other than the one in which they were recognised (these are known as 'timing differences').

29.3 So, it is generally accepted that the tax accounting charge or credit should include the tax effects of timing differences resulting from the difference between fiscal and accounting rules. The recognition of these amounts gives rise to deferred tax either payable or receivable in future periods, in addition to the current tax based on based on the tax charge for the current year. This ensures that the total tax charge or credit is recognised in the financial statements in the same period as the income or costs to which it relates.

29.4 The scope of section 29 of FRS 102 is primarily related to income tax, but the section also addresses value added tax (VAT) and other similar recoverable sales taxes. Income tax includes all domestic and foreign taxes that are based on taxable profit and withholding taxes that are payable by a subsidiary associate or joint venture on distributions to the reporting entity. [FRS 102 para 29.1]. VAT should not be included in turnover (see chapter 23). Recoverable VAT should not be included in expenses. Where VAT is irrecoverable, it should be included in the cost of the item to which it relates, where practical and material. For example, the cost of a fixed asset includes irrecoverable VAT (see chapter 17). [FRS 102 para 29.20].

Current tax

29.5 Current tax is based on the taxable and deductible amounts that are included in the tax return for the current year. A number of issues arise in respect of accounting for current tax, and these are discussed in the following sections.

Recognition of current tax liabilities and assets

29.6 Management recognises unpaid current tax expense for the current and prior periods as a liability in the balance sheet. [FRS 102 para 29.3].The amount payable in respect of the current tax expense is based on the taxable and deductible amounts that will be reported on the tax return for the current year, which often involves a degree of judgement.

29.7 The actual tax subsequently paid might differ from the tax liability recognised because a tax rule has been applied or interpreted incorrectly or there is a dispute with the tax authorities. Except where the adjustment is caused by a material error, it is treated as a change in accounting estimate and included in current tax expense of the period when the adjustment arises. Typically, such amounts are disclosed as relating to the prior year. For material adjustments, FRS 102 requires disclosure of the nature of the change in estimate and the effect of the change on the tax accounting for the current period (see chapter 10 for further guidance on changes in estimates).

29.8 If the amount paid for current and prior periods exceeds the amount due for those periods, the excess is recognised as an asset. [FRS 102 para 29.3].

29.9 An entity might incur a tax loss for the current period that can be carried back to set against the profits of an earlier accounting period. [FRS 102 para 29.4]. Because the entity would recover tax paid in a previous period, management should recognise the benefit of the tax loss as an asset in the period in which the tax loss occurs, where such recovery is probable and reliably measurable. If the entity cannot carry back the tax loss, it might be able to carry it forward to set against income in a future period. For recognition of a deferred tax asset for carry-forward of unused tax losses, see paragraph 29.81 below.

Recognition of current tax income or expense

29.10 Current tax is recognised in the same component of total comprehensive income (that is, continuing or discontinuing operations, and profit or loss or other comprehensive income) or equity as the related transaction or event is recognised (or was recognised for tax relating to prior year items). [FRS 102 para 29.22].

29.11 Where an entity pays tax on all its income, including elements recognised outside profit or loss either in other comprehensive income or directly in equity, it can be difficult to determine the amount of current tax attributable to these elements. In such circumstances, the attributable tax should be calculated on a reasonable pro rata basis that is appropriate in the circumstances.

Example – Allocation of tax on exchange loss

A parent entity made a trading profit of C1,500,000 during the year. The parent has a foreign currency loan receivable from a foreign subsidiary on which a tax deductible exchange loss of C500,000 arose. The loan is regarded by the parent as part of its net investment in the foreign subsidiary; so the exchange loss is reported in the parent's profit or loss. The tax rate for the year is 24%. Therefore the parent's tax charge for the year is C240,000 (profit before tax of C1,000,000 @ 24%).

On consolidation, the exchange loss of C500,000 is recognised in other comprehensive income. The total tax charge of C240,000 to be allocated between profit or loss and other comprehensive income is as follows:

	C'000
Tax on trading profit (C1.5m @ 24%)	360
Tax relief on exchange loss (C500,000 @ 24%)	(120)
Total tax charge	240

Profit or loss would bear a tax charge of C360,000, with C120,000 of tax relief being recognised in other comprehensive income in the consolidated financial statements. (The subsidiary's results have been ignored to keep the example simple.)

Dividends and withholding taxes

29.12 In some tax jurisdictions, dividend income might be non-taxable. In jurisdictions where tax is payable on the dividend income, a credit system might apply whereby a tax credit is given to the dividend recipient to acknowledge that the income out of which the dividend has been paid has already been charged to tax in the dividend-paying entity. Alternatively, withholding taxes might be deducted at source and paid to the tax authorities on behalf of the recipient by the dividend-paying entity.

29.13 There is a fundamental difference between the accounting treatment for dividends and other similar income subject to tax credits and for those subject to withholding tax. Tax credits are notional and reduce the tax payable on the dividend income by the recipient entity and not the paying entity. Withholding tax is a real tax suffered by the recipient entity but paid to the tax authorities by the paying entity on the recipient's behalf. Section 29 of the standard requires that outgoing dividends and similar amounts payable are recognised at an amount that:

- Includes any withholding taxes.

- Excludes any other taxes, such as attributable tax credits.

[FRS 102 para 29.18].

29.14 This is logical, because the tax credit is not part of the cost of the dividend, but it benefits the recipient. Section 29 of the standard also requires that dividends and similar income receivable are recognised at an amount that:

■   Includes any withholding taxes.

■   Excludes any other taxes, such as attributable tax credits.

[FRS 102 para 29.19].

29.15 Where the income is reported gross of the withholding tax, the standard requires the withholding tax suffered to be shown as part of the tax charge. [FRS 102 para 29.19].

> **Example 1 – Withholding taxes**
>
> Entity B declares a dividend of £100,000, to be paid to its parent, entity A. The distribution is subject to withholding tax of 15% deductible at source. No tax credits are available, and the income is a non-taxable item.
>
> Entity B will pay £85,000 to entity A and £15,000 to the tax authorities. It will record the gross amount of £100,000 as a distribution in equity.
>
> Entity A will record dividend income of £100,000 in profit or loss, and a tax charge of £15,000 within current tax.

> **Example 2 – Tax credits**
>
> Entity D declares a dividend of £150,000 to be paid to its parent, entity C. When assessing its taxable profit, entity C will receive a tax credit of £37,500 on the dividend, because entity D pays tax at 20% on its profits (£150,000 x 100/80 – £150,000). Entity C pays tax at 25% on its profits.
>
> Entity D will pay the full dividend of £150,000 to entity C and record this amount in equity.
>
> Entity C will record the full dividend of £150,000 in profit or loss. For tax purposes, its dividend income will be £187,500, and tax of £46,875 would ordinarily be payable on the dividend (£187,500 x 25%). But entity C can offset £37,500 against this tax payable, because this is the amount of the tax credit on the dividend received. So, entity C pays tax of £9,375 on the dividend and records the additional £9,375 tax charge in current tax.

Measurement of current tax

29.16 Current tax liabilities and assets are measured at the amounts expected to be paid or recovered using the tax rates and laws that have been enacted or substantively enacted by the balance sheet date. [FRS 102 para 29.5]. The subsequent receipt of information about rates of taxation is a non-adjusting post balance sheet event (see further chapter 32).

29.17 Tax rates are regarded as substantively enacted when the remaining stages of the enactment process historically have not affected the outcome and are unlikely to do so. A UK tax rate is taken as 'substantially enacted' if it is included in either:

■   a Bill that has been passed by the House of Commons and is awaiting only passage through the House of Lords and Royal Assent; or

■   a resolution having statutory effect that has been passed under the Provisional Collection of Taxes Act 1968.

[FRS 102 Glossary].

29.18 Where an entity prepares financial statements for a period that includes a change in tax rates, under UK tax legislation, the entity calculates a pro-rated tax rate for the one year, which applies to all profits for that accounting period.

> **Example – Change of tax rate during accounting period**
>
> An entity has an accounting period ending on 30 October 20X3. The rates of corporation tax for the fiscal years ending 31 March 20X3 and 31 March 20X4 are 24% and 23% respectively. The effective rate of tax to be disclosed in the financial statements for the current tax is calculated as follows:
>
> | | | |
> |---|---|---|
> | Period 1 November 20X2 to 31 March 20X3 | 5/12 @ 24% | 10.00% |
> | Period 1 April 20X3 to 30 October 20X3 | 7/12 @ 23% | 13.42% |
> | Effective rate of corporation tax | | 23.42% |

Uncertain tax positions

29.19 An entity's tax position might be uncertain (for example, where the tax treatment of an item of expense or structured transaction could be challenged by the tax authorities). Uncertainties in income taxes are not addressed specifically in FRS 102. Section 21 of the standard excludes income taxes from its scope and is not used to measure uncertain open tax positions. Uncertain tax positions can reasonably be measured using either an expected value (weighted average probability) approach or a single best estimate of the most likely outcome. The measurement approach is an accounting policy choice.

29.20 It is also necessary to determine the 'unit of account' – that is, whether uncertainties are considered individually or as a group (either together with related uncertainties, or in relation to each taxing authority) – when applying the measurement approach. The determination of the 'unit of account' is an accounting policy choice.

29.21 Where management considers uncertain tax positions individually, it should first consider whether each position taken in the tax return is probable of being sustained on examination by the taxing authority. It should recognise a liability for each item that is not probable of being sustained. The liability is measured using either an expected value (weighted average probability) approach or a single best estimate of the most likely outcome.

29.22   Where management considers uncertain tax positions in related groups or for each taxing authority, the key issue is the measurement of the tax liability, because it is usually probable that an entity will pay tax. Management should calculate the total amount of current tax that it expects to pay, taking into account all the tax uncertainties, using either an expected value (weighted average probability) approach or a single best estimate of the most likely outcome.

29.23   Where an entity has not paid taxes related to an uncertain tax position, it will evaluate the uncertainty surrounding the potential liability. Likewise, where an entity has made payments that are considered to exceed the amount payable under the relevant tax legislation, it will evaluate the recovery of a tax asset. Consistent accounting policies should be applied to uncertain tax assets and uncertain tax liabilities.

29.24   Once an uncertain tax position is determined, management needs to decide whether a change in the tax estimate is justified. We expect that a change in recognition and measurement is justified where circumstances change or where new facts clarify the probability of estimates previously made. Such changes might be further judicial developments related to a specific case or to a similar case, substantive communications from the tax authorities, or a change in status of a tax year (for example, moving from open to closed in a particular jurisdiction). Changes in estimate would be accounted for in accordance with paragraph 29.7 above.

Interest and penalties on uncertain tax positions

29.25   An entity might incur interest or penalties in relation to taxation (for example, where uncertain tax positions have been successfully challenged by the tax authorities).

29.26   There is a strong argument that interest and penalties differ from income tax liabilities, because they are not measured and settled by the tax authorities on the basis of taxable profits. This suggests that interest and penalties should be recognised, measured and presented as provisions under section 21 of FRS 102, and classified as finance or other operating expense, respectively, in the income statement. This is because:

■   such obligations are not based on taxable profits, and so they fall outside section 29's scope; and

■   the economic substance of reducing or delaying a tax payment is no different from other financing arrangements. Interest on tax obligations that increases with time and is, in substance, a financing cost of the liability is interest expense; other penalties represent operating costs.

29.27 But there is no clear guidance in FRS 102 and in some cases, interest and penalties might be accounted for as if they are within section 29's scope, either because they are rolled up into a lump sum settlement and cannot be separated from the taxes, or as a matter of accounting policy. Any associated charge is normally included within the tax line in the income statement; and the liability is included within the income tax liability on the balance sheet.

29.28 Where material amounts are involved, the accounting policy used to recognise, measure and classify interest and tax-related penalties or damages should be disclosed clearly in the financial statements and applied consistently.

Discounting

29.29 Current tax assets and liabilities should not be discounted. [FRS 102 para 29.17].

Deferred tax

Introduction

29.30 Most transactions and events recorded in the financial statements have a tax consequence, whether for the current period or for the future. The future tax consequences of transactions and events that have occurred by the balance sheet date cannot be avoided; whatever happens in the future, the entity will have to pay less or more tax than it would have done if those transactions and events had not happened. So, it is necessary to recognise the tax effects of the transactions and events in the same period in which they are recognised themselves and not in the period in which they form part of taxable profit. This matching of transactions and events with their tax effects gives rise not only to current tax, but also to deferred tax balances that meet the definitions of, and recognition criteria for, assets and liabilities.

29.31 The calculation of deferred tax in FRS 102 follows a method known as the 'timing differences plus' approach, where deferred tax is provided on timing differences and on the initial recognition of a business combination.

29.32 The differences between accounting and taxable profits can be analysed into two categories: permanent differences; and timing differences. Permanent differences arise because specified types of income appearing in the financial statements are not taxable, whilst some types of expenditure are not tax deductible. Timing differences, on the other hand, arise from items that are either taxable or tax deductible, but in periods different from those in which they are dealt with in the financial statements. As a result, such items are included in the measurement of both accounting and taxable profits, but in different periods. These differences are said to 'originate' in one period, and are capable of 'reversal' in one or more subsequent periods.

29.33   Permanent differences are items of income and expense that are included in total comprehensive income but not included in tax assessments, or vice versa. They arise because some types of income and expenditure are non-taxable or disallowable, or because some tax charges or allowances are greater or smaller than the corresponding income or expenses. No deferred tax is recognised on permanent differences, except on those arising on the initial recognition of a business combination. [FRS 102 para 29.10]. Such differences cause the effective tax rate to be different from the statutory rate.

29.34   Regardless of how timing differences impact future tax assessments, the tax charge for the period impacted by such differences will be lower or higher than it would have been if based on reportable profit or loss in the absence of such differences. These known increases or decreases in future tax liabilities (that is, the entity's obligation to pay less or more tax in the future) are recognised in the balance sheet as deferred tax assets and liabilities.

29.35   So, the objective is to recognise the expected tax effects of timing differences either as liabilities for taxes payable in the future or as assets recoverable in the future. Under this method, deferred tax on the timing differences originating in the period are provided using the tax rates and laws that have been enacted or substantively enacted by the reporting date expected to apply when the asset is recovered or the liability is settled (see para 29.61). [FRS 102 para 29.12].

Timing differences

29.36   Timing differences are defined as *"differences between taxable profits and total comprehensive income as stated in the financial statements that arise from the inclusion of income and expenses in tax assessments in periods different from those in which they are recognised in financial statements"*. [FRS 102 para 29.6]. Timing differences originate in one period and are capable of reversal in one or more subsequent periods.

29.37   It follows from the above definition that there are only two situations under which timing differences can arise, as illustrated below:

■   An item of income or expense is included in total comprehensive income of the period, but recognised in taxable profit in later periods. For example, income receivable might be accrued in the financial statements in one year, but be taxed in the subsequent year when received. Similarly, provisions might be made for restructuring costs in the financial statements in one period, but qualify for tax deduction in a subsequent period when the expenditure is incurred.

■   An item of income or expenditure is included in taxable profit of the period, but recognised in total comprehensive income in later years. For example, development expenditure might be tax deductible in the year in which it is incurred, but capitalised and amortised over a period for financial reporting purposes. Similarly, income received in advance might be taxed in the period of receipt, but treated as earned in the financial statements in a later period.

Accounting for some specific timing differences

Accelerated capital allowances

29.38 In the UK, tax relief in respect of capital expenditure on plant and machinery is given by means of capital allowances that are a form of standardised tax depreciation. Since capital allowances are deducted from accounting profit to arrive at taxable profit, the amount of depreciation charged in the financial statements is always disallowed in the tax computation. Although depreciation for taxation and accounting purposes will normally be the same over the life of the asset, they will differ from year to year, thus giving rise to timing differences. In many cases, the capital allowances depreciate the asset at a faster rate for tax purposes than the rate of depreciation charged in the financial statements. For this reason, the timing differences created are often referred to as 'accelerated capital allowances'. The following example illustrates the creation of the timing differences:

Example – Origination and reversal of timing differences

An entity purchases a machine in 20X1 for £100,000. The asset is expected to be sold at the end of its useful life of five years for £10,000. Depreciation is charged on a straight-line basis for accounting purposes and amounts to £18,000 ((£100,000 – £10,000)/5) per annum. For the purpose of this example, the rate of capital allowances is assumed to be 25% per annum on a reducing balance basis.

The timing difference will arise as follows:

	20X1 £'000	20X2 £'000	20X3 £'000	20X4 £'000	20X5 £'000
Per financial statements					
Carrying value of asset	100	82	64	46	28
Depreciation charge	18	18	18	18	18
Book written down value	82	64	46	28	10
Per tax computation					
Carrying value of asset	100	75	56	42	32
Capital allowance	25	19	14	10	8
Tax written down value	75	56	42	32	24
Timing difference					
Capital allowance allowed	25	19	14	10	8
Depreciation charged	18	18	18	18	18
Originating (reversing)	7	1	(4)	(8)	(10)
Cumulative	7	8	4	(4)	(14)

29.39 Deferred tax should be provided on all tax-deductible assets where timing differences arise, even if the assets are not depreciated. However, if and when the conditions for retaining the tax allowances have been met, the deferred tax should not be recognised. For example, if tax allowances are received in advance of depreciation but, on disposal of the asset, no further amounts of tax are payable (even if the proceeds received exceed the asset's tax written down value), no deferred tax liability would be recognised, because the profit on disposal is a permanent difference. [FRS 102 para 29.8].

Provisions

29.40 Provisions (such as those made for refurbishment, or for plant closures following a reorganisation) may give rise to timing differences, because tax relief is obtained when the expenditure is actually incurred and not when it is recognised in the financial statements. It follows that such provisions will give rise to a deferred tax asset, because taxable profits are higher than total comprehensive income in the year in which the provisions are made. The tax asset will be recovered in the year in which the actual expenditure is incurred.

Deferred expenditure

29.41 Deferred expenditure, on the other hand, usually gives rise to deferred tax liabilities. In this situation, tax relief is typically obtained on the full amount of the expenditure in the year in which it is incurred; only a proportion of the expenditure is recognised in the financial statements of the same period, and the balance is carried forward as an asset to be charged to income over a period of time. The difference between accounting and tax treatment gives rise to a deferred tax liability to reflect the fact that the entity has obtained full tax benefit on expenditure of which only a proportion has passed through total comprehensive income in the year.

Leases

29.42 Many entities enter into leases and hire purchase contracts, under which they obtain the right to use or purchase assets. Assets acquired under leases and hire purchase contracts give rise to timing differences between the amounts recorded in total comprehensive income and the amounts recorded in the tax computations.

29.43 Where the asset is purchased under a hire purchase agreement, the hirer will normally account for the acquisition of the fixed asset in question and will be able to claim the capital allowances. So, no particular deferred tax problems arise.

29.44 Similarly, no deferred tax problems normally arise in accounting for an operating lease. This is because the amount that is charged to rentals in total comprehensive income, for financial reporting purposes, is likely to be the same as the amount charged in arriving at the taxable profit. An exception to this will arise where there are accrued rentals that could give rise to a potential short-term timing difference.

29.45   A timing difference will arise in circumstances where the lessee enters into a finance lease that is accounted for under section 20 of FRS 102 and where the tax legislation provides that capital allowances are claimed by the lessor, rather than the lessee. The asset is capitalised and depreciated over the lease term or the useful economic life of the asset. The liability is recognised and reduced by the rents payable, less an allocation for the finance charge.

29.46   If the finance lessee does not qualify for capital allowances, but is able to obtain a tax deduction for the whole of each rental payment, a timing difference arises if tax relief is given on the rentals paid, as a result of the differing treatment for accounting and tax purposes. Some taxation authorities might accept the section 20 accounting treatment for tax purposes, in which case there are no deferred tax consequences. But, in principle, a timing difference arises, and this is illustrated in the following example.

> **Example – Finance lease where lessee does not receive capital allowances**
>
> An entity leases a fixed asset under a finance lease over a five-year period. The annual lease payments amount to £12,000 per annum. The asset is recorded at the present value of the minimum lease payments of £48,000 and is depreciated at £9,600 per annum.
>
> The timing difference arising is calculated as follows:
>
> | | Year 1 | Year 2 | Year 3 | Year 4 | Year 5 |
> |---|---|---|---|---|---|
> | | £ | £ | £ | £ | £ |
> | Rentals | 12,000 | 12,000 | 12,000 | 12,000 | 12,000 |
> | Finance cost @ 7.93% | (3,806) | (3,158) | (2,455) | (1,699) | (882) |
> | Capital repayment | 8,194 | 8,842 | 9,545 | 10,301 | 11,118 |
> | **Timing difference** | | | | | |
> | Tax computations: rentals | 12,000 | 12,000 | 12,000 | 12,000 | 12,000 |
> | Profit and loss account: | | | | | |
> | Finance cost | 3,806 | 3,158 | 2,455 | 1,699 | 882 |
> | Depreciation | 9,600 | 9,600 | 9,600 | 9,600 | 9,600 |
> | | 13,406 | 12,758 | 12,055 | 11,299 | 10,482 |
> | Timing difference | (1,406) | (758) | (55) | 701 | 1,518 |
> | Net book value of fixed asset | 38,400 | 28,800 | 19,200 | 9,600 | – |
> | Outstanding obligation (capital) | 39,806 | 30,964 | 21,419 | 11,118 | – |
> | Cumulative timing difference | (1,406) | (2,164) | (2,219) | (1,518) | – |

So, finance leases capitalised under section 20 of FRS 102 tend to produce an originating negative timing difference (in other words, a deferred tax asset), because greater finance charges are allocated to earlier years to reflect the reducing capital amount owed under the lease.

Pensions

29.47   In the UK, tax relief on employers' pension contributions (or payment of unfunded benefits) is often given in the period in which they are paid, rather than when the costs are recognised in the financial statements. For large one-off contributions the tax relief might be spread over a number of periods. On the other hand, pension costs and other post-retirement benefits are recognised in the financial statements at the time when service is provided by the employee. Where the total of the pension costs differs from the actual contributions (or unfunded benefits) paid, the resulting asset or liability recognised in the balance sheet is a timing difference for deferred tax purposes. This is the case whether the defined benefit scheme is in a net deficit or a net surplus position.

29.48   Complications can arise due to actuarial gains and losses. Actuarial losses often give rise to defined benefit liabilities. Normally, contributions are increased in future years to address the deficit, resulting in related tax deductions. So, actuarial losses will give rise to timing differences. As a result it is necessary to build up a deferred tax asset as the pension deficits arises and to reverse this asset as deficits are recovered. The probability of future taxable profits should be considered when determining the extent of the deferred tax assets to recognise (see further para 29.81 below).

29.49   Similarly actuarial gains are recorded in the entity's financial statements in the year in which they arise. Normally, as a result of a surplus, contributions are reduced in future years, and so the pension asset will be recovered because the pension cost accrued each year will exceed the contributions that will be paid. These gains are not taxed in the years in which they arise but, in a sense, they are taxed in future years because as future contributions to the scheme are reduced, fewer tax deductions will be received. So, actuarial gains will give rise to timing differences. As a result, it is necessary to build up a deferred tax liability as surpluses arise and to reverse this liability as such surpluses are recovered.

29.50   Further complications can arise on the allocation of the current and deferred tax charge or credit between profit or loss and other comprehensive income. For instance where an entity reduces its defined benefit liability through the payment of a large contribution to the scheme and receives tax relief on that payment, it might not be clear whether the liability arose through profit or loss or other comprehensive income and therefore where the current tax relief should be recognised. Entities should ensure that the charge or credit is allocated on a reasonable pro rata basis (see further paragraph 29.10 above).

Share-based payment transactions

Equity-settled transactions

29.51   Section 26 of FRS 102 requires entities to recognise the cost of equity-settled share-based awards on the basis of the fair value of the award at the date of grant, spread over the vesting period (see further chapter 26). But generally the amount of any deduction available for tax purposes in the case of equity-settled transactions does not correspond to the amount charged to the profit and loss account in accordance with section 26 of the standard.

29.52 Under current UK tax law, a tax deduction in connection with an employee share option scheme is generally available at the date of exercise, measured on the basis of the share option's intrinsic value at that date (that is, the difference between the share's market price at the date of exercise and the option's exercise price).

29.53 To the extent that the tax deduction for the award is more or less than the ultimate total accounting charge, this is a permanent difference and not a timing difference. Deferred tax is not recognised on permanent differences. [FRS 102 para 29.10].

29.54 However, there is a timing difference for the cumulative accounting charge that will be tax deductible in the future on exercise of the award. This timing difference results in a deferred tax asset, which will be recognised if there are sufficient future taxable profits (see para 29.81 onwards below).

29.55 If the accounting charge is revised as a result of a change in the number of options expected to vest (see further chapter 26 on share-based payment accounting), there will be a corresponding adjustment to the deferred tax asset, because the future tax deduction will also change. Similarly, if it appears that the share options will not be exercised because they are out of the money, it is likely that any deferred tax asset recognised should be written off.

29.56 FRS 102 provides no guidance regarding how such the difference between the share based payment charge and the related tax deduction should be reflected over the accounting periods impacted, so entities must adopt an approach as a policy choice to be applied consistently. There are two principle approaches for calculating and reflecting the permanent and timing differences resulting from share based payments. One alternative is based on comparing the cumulative share-based payment charge to the intrinsic value of the related awards at each balance sheet date. The second alternative is based on comparing the cumulative charge to a pro rata amount of the intrinsic value at each balance sheet date over the life of the option.

> **Example – Deferred tax on an equity-settled share-based award**
>
> On 1 January 20X3, 100,000 options are issued with a fair value of £360,000. The vesting period is 3 years and all the share options are expected to be exercised. All of the share options are exercised in year 4. The tax rate is 30%. The intrinsic value of the share options (being market value of the underlying shares less exercise price) at the end of years 1, 2, 3 and at the date of exercise in year 4 is £330,000, £300,000, £380,000 and £400,000, respectively.

The total share-based payment charge recognised in each year of the three year period is £120,000 (£360,000/3). Tax deductions are not received until the share options are exercised and so a timing difference arises.

Acceptable accounting policies for determining timing differences resulting from share-based payments are to base calculation of the timing difference on:

(a) the cumulative share-based payment charge — which is the fair value at date of grant (that is, £360,000/3 = £120,000 for year 1), capped, if necessary, at the total intrinsic value (£330,000 for year 1); or

(b) on pro rata share of the intrinsic value (that is, £330,000/3 = £110,000 for year 1), capped if necessary at the cumulative share-based payment charge so that any permanent difference is not recognised.

Approach (a) can be described as a first-in first-out basis for allocating the future tax deductions to the cumulative share-based payment charge. Approach (b) can be described as a weighted average allocation basis. These approaches are illustrated below.

(a) Deferred tax based on cumulative share-based payment charge

At the end of year 1, the cumulative share-based payment charge is £120,000, which is less than the expected tax deduction of £330,000, and hence fully available. It is considered acceptable for the timing difference for deferred tax purposes to be based on the cumulative share-based payment charge, up to the options' total intrinsic value. Therefore, at the end of year 1, the deferred tax asset is £36,000 (30% × £120,000).

At the end of year 2, the cumulative share-based payment charge is £240,000, which is less than the expected tax deduction of £300,000. Therefore, at the end of year 2, the deferred tax asset is £72,000 (30% × £240,000).

At the end of year 3, the cumulative share-based payment charge is £360,000, which is less than the expected tax deduction of £380,000. Therefore, at the end of year 3, the deferred tax asset is £108,000 (30% × £360,000). The cumulative position at the end of year 3 is shown in the table below.

		Profit and loss account Dr (Cr)		Balance sheet Dr (Cr)	
		Current tax	Deferred tax	Current tax	Deferred tax
Year	Expense				
	£	£	£	£	£
1	120,000		(36,000)		36,000
2	120,000		(36,000)		72,000
3	120,000		(36,000)		108,000
Cumulative position at the end of year 3	360,000		(108,000)		

(b) Deferred tax based on a pro rata share of intrinsic value at balance sheet date

Under this policy, the cumulative timing difference (that is, the tax deductions relating to the cumulative share-based payment charge) is based upon a pro rata share of the options' total intrinsic value at the balance sheet date, capped at the cumulative share-based payment charge. Therefore, at the end of year 1, the timing difference is £110,000 (£330,000 × $^1/_3$) and the related deferred tax asset is £33,000 (£110,000 × 30%).

At the end of year 2, the deferred tax asset is £60,000 (£300,000 × $^2/_3$ × 30%).

At the end of year 3, the deferred tax asset is £108,000 (£360,000 × 30%). A deferred tax asset is not recognised in respect of the excess of the option's intrinsic value (£380,000) over the cumulative share-based payment charge (£360,000). The cumulative position at the end of year 3 is shown in the table below.

		Profit and loss account Dr (Cr)		Balance sheet Dr (Cr)	
		Current tax	Deferred tax	Current tax	Deferred tax
Year	Expense				
	£	£	£	£	£
1	120,000		(33,000)		33,000
2	120,000		(27,000)		60,000
3	120,000		(48,000)		108,000
Cumulative position at end of year 3	360,000		(108,000)		

29.57   Where the timing difference is capped, such as in year 1 in the second example above, the shortfall is a permanent difference and no deferred tax should be recognised on this amount (as noted in para 29.53).

29.58   If the share options' intrinsic value is negative (that is, the options are out of the money) and is not expected to recover, then accordingly, an entity will not expect the options to be exercised nor the related a tax deduction received. In this situation, a deferred tax asset would not be recognised.

Cash-settled transactions

29.59   Cash-settled share-based payment transactions (such as share appreciation rights issued to employees) give rise to a liability and not a credit to equity. The fair value of the liability is remeasured at each reporting date until the liability is settled. A timing difference arises on the cumulative difference between the share-based payment charge in total comprehensive income and the related deduction for tax purposes where that will be received in the future, resulting in a deferred tax asset (if there are sufficient future taxable profits).

Revaluation of assets

29.60   In accordance with sections 11, 16 and 17 of FRS 102, entities can revalue some assets. In some circumstances, such as certain financial instruments, the gains and losses are subject to current tax when they are recognised, and no timing difference (and hence no deferred tax) arises on the revaluation. But a question arises regarding how to account in circumstances where the gains and losses are not taxed until realised at a later date. In this case, revaluation of the asset creates a timing difference, because the gain or loss is recognised in total comprehensive income in the current period, but it will be recognised in taxable profits in a latter period (either when the asset is sold and a gain is realised, or as the asset is used, generating taxable income). So a deferred tax asset or liability should be recognised.

Example – revaluation of non-monetary asset

On 1 January 20X1, an asset is purchased for £100,000. Its original useful economic life is five years, and it is expected to have nil residual value. Depreciation, charged on a straight-line basis, amounts to £20,000 per annum. On 1 January 20X2, the asset is revalued to £120,000; a gain of £40,000. Its useful economic life is four remaining years, so revised depreciation of £30,000 is charged per annum.

For the purposes of this example, the rate of capital allowances is 25% per annum on a reducing balance basis and the tax written down value of the asset is not adjusted for the revaluation.

The timing difference will arise as follows:

	20X1 £	20X2 £	20X3 £	20X4 £	20X5 £
Per financial statements					
Carrying value b/f	–	80,000	90,000	60,000	30,000
Addition	100,000	–	–	–	–
Revaluation	–	40,000	–	–	–
Depreciation	(20,000)	(30,000)	(30,000)	(30,000)	(30,000)
Carrying value c/f	80,000	90,000	60,000	30,000	–
Per tax computation					
Pool b/f	-	75,000	56,250	42,188	31,641
Addition	100,000	–	–	–	–
Capital allowances	(25,000)	(18,750)	(14,063)	(10,547)	(7,910)
Pool c/f	75,000	56,250	42,188	31,641	23,730
Timing differences					
Capital allowances allowed	25,000	18,750	14,063	10,547	7,910
Revaluation	–	40,000	–	–	–
Depreciation charged	(20,000)	(30,000)	(30,000)	(30,000)	(30,000)
Originating (reversing)	5,000	28,750	(15,938)	(19,453)	(22,090)
Cumulative timing differences	5,000	33,750	17,813	(1,641)	(23,730)

Measurement issues

Tax rates

29.61   Deferred tax should be measured using the tax rates and laws that have been enacted or substantively enacted at the balance sheet date that are expected to apply to the reversal of the timing differences (subject to the two exceptions discussed below). [FRS 102 para 29.12]. The meaning of 'substantively enacted' is considered in paragraph 29.17 above.

29.62   Timing differences might reverse over many years and, since the rate of tax will not normally be known in advance of those years, entities are required to use rates that have been enacted or substantially enacted at the balance sheet date as a proxy for the future rates.

29.63   The tax rate applicable to an entity could change as a result of changes in relevant legislation. The impact of such changes in tax rate will vary, depending on the nature and timing of the legislative changes made. Any impact of the changes will be recognised in accounting periods ending on or after the date of substantive enactment (and might be disclosable prior to that date). In many cases, changes in tax rates will be prospective, and so there will be no impact on current tax assets and liabilities that have arisen before the effective date of the change. However, deferred tax balances are likely to be affected.

29.64   In some jurisdictions, different tax rates might apply to different levels of taxable income. For instance, the first five million of profit might be taxed at 20%, and any further profits might be taxed at 30%. In order to measure deferred tax assets and liabilities, an average enacted or substantially enacted tax rate for the periods over which the timing difference is expected to reverse would need to be calculated. [FRS 102 para 29.13]. This would require the entity to estimate future taxable profits.

29.65   Other complications might arise if different tax rates apply to trading income and capital gains. Section 29 of the standard requires deferred tax assets and liabilities to be measured using the rate that is expected to apply to the reversal of the timing difference.

29.66   It might be difficult to determine the rate at which a timing difference will reverse if some element of the difference will reverse in trading income and some in capital gains. The standard provides no further guidance on how to measure deferred tax in this scenario. The entity will have to determine an accounting policy to use either the income or capital rate or a mix of both. The mix of both rates is commonly known as the 'dual manner of recovery' and is the method specified in IFRS. Further guidance on this method can be found in the IFRS manual of accounting chapter 13. That said, FRS 102 does not mandate this approach.

29.67   Recognising these difficulties (as noted above), section 29 of the standard contains two exceptions to this measurement principle. Where a non-depreciable asset, such as land, is measured using the revaluation model under section 17, any deferred tax should be measured at a rate applicable to the sale of the asset. [FRS 102 para 29.15].

29.68 Similarly, deferred tax arising on investment properties measured at fair value under section 16 of the standard (except those with limited useful lives where the entity will consume significantly all of the economic benefits through on-going rental) should also be measured at a rate applicable to the sale of the asset. [FRS 102 para 29.16].

Tax consequences of dividends

29.69 Measurement can be complicated where distributed and undistributed income are taxed at different rates. In some jurisdictions, corporate taxes are payable at a higher or lower rate if part or all of the net profit or retained earnings are distributed as dividends. For example, undistributed profits might be taxed at 45% and distributed profits at 30%. In such situations, deferred tax is measured using the tax rates on undistributed profits (that is, 45%). [FRS 102 para 29.14].

29.70 In other jurisdictions, income taxes might be refundable or payable if part or all of the profit or retained earnings is paid out as dividends to the entity's shareholders. So, deferred tax is measured using the tax rates on undistributed profits. The tax consequences of dividends are recognised when the dividend is subsequently declared and recognised as a liability.

29.71 The tax consequences of a transaction (for example, the tax credit at 15% shown above) is required to be recognised in the same component of total comprehensive income or equity as the underlying transactions or events. [FRS 102 para 29.22]. The question arises whether the tax impact of dividends should be recognised within profit or loss or in equity. If the underlying transaction is viewed as a distribution to shareholders, this suggests that the tax should be recorded in equity. But viewing the underlying transactions as the income and expense that gave rise to the dividend suggests that the tax should be recorded in profit or loss.

29.72 We believe that the incremental tax effect of the dividend payment should generally be recognised in profit or loss; this is because the tax is more clearly linked to the past events than to distributions to owners.

29.73 But we believe that an alternative is acceptable when the amounts payable are, in effect, a withholding tax for the benefit of the shareholders. The recipients of the dividend would typically be entitled to a tax credit at least equal to the tax paid by the entity. In this case, the subjects of the taxation are the shareholders and not the entity, so the tax is charged directly to equity as part of the dividends.

Discounting

29.74 Despite deferred tax balances generally reversing over a number of years, entities should not discount deferred tax assets or liabilities. [FRS 102 para 29.17].

Uncertain tax positions

29.75 We feel that the uncertain tax positions relating to deferred tax should be recognised in the same manner as current tax. For guidance on uncertain tax positions relating to current tax, see paragraph 29.19 above.

29.76 Where the income or expense has been included in the tax assessment before the financial statements, an entity would assess the uncertainty in calculating its current tax position. The deferred tax recognised should only be to the extent that the uncertain current tax has been recognised.

29.77 Where the income or expense has been included in the financial statements before the tax assessment, an entity should estimate the future deductible or taxable amount in the same manner as for current taxes and recognise the deferred tax up to this amount.

29.78 If the full extent of the timing difference is not recognised, the difference is a permanent difference and will be recognised in profit or loss when it originates.

Change in tax status

29.79 The tax status of an entity can change because of, say, public listing of its equity instruments, restructuring of its equity or a change in tax jurisdictions of its shareholders. The change could affect current tax assets and liabilities as well as deferred tax assets and liabilities. The entity could be taxed at a different rate in the future, or it might lose or gain various tax incentives that affect the tax bases of its assets and liabilities.

29.80 An entity should re-assess its current and deferred tax balances based on the new tax status. Any impact of the changes will be recognised in the accounting period in which the change has occurred.

Deferred tax assets

General

29.81 Deferred tax assets usually result from timing differences, such as differences arising on provisions made for refurbishment or differences arising on pensions and retirement benefits where tax deductions are obtained only when the expenditure is actually incurred, rather than when the expense is recognised in the financial statements. Also, unrelieved tax losses and unused tax credits give rise to deferred tax assets. [FRS 102 Glossary].

29.82   Deferred tax assets should be recognised only to the extent it is probable that they will be recovered against the reversal of deferred tax liabilities or other future taxable profits. [FRS 102 para 29.7].

29.83   Where recovery of a deferred tax asset is dependent on future taxable profits, an entity would have to do more than simply *'not make losses'* in future: it must have *'enough taxable profits to recover the deferred tax assets',* having regard to any limitations on their availability or life. Further, prudence would suggest that more evidence of the likelihood of future profits is needed for recognition of a deferred tax asset. The standard notes that the very existence of unrelieved tax losses is strong evidence that there might not be 'other future taxable profits' against which the losses will be relieved.

Future taxable profits

29.84   The standard gives little guidance on how an entity should assess the likelihood of future profits for determining the deferred tax asset to be recognised. But it stands to reason that entities should project their future taxable profits and consider other persuasive and reliable evidence to support recoverability of the asset. As noted above, the existence of deferred tax losses is considered to be strong evidence that other future taxable profits might not be forthcoming.

29.85   Our view is that, when an entity is projecting future taxable benefits, new originating timing differences should not be taken into account in determining the future taxable profits available for the recovery of deferred tax assets at the balance sheet date. This is because the new originating timing differences will themselves reverse, so there is no overall impact on taxable profits.

29.86   Issues can arise where brought-forward tax losses need to be utilised within a specified time period or else they are lost. Where future deductible temporary differences arise within that time period, but reverse afterwards, it is necessary to ensure that these deductible temporary differences carried forward can also be recovered later against future taxable profits before recognising a deferred tax asset for the brought-forward tax losses.

> **Example – Interaction of losses and deductible timing differences**
>
> An entity has unused losses of £300,000 and is assessing whether it can recognise a deferred tax asset. The losses expire in five years' time. In year 1, the entity is forecasting an accounting loss of £100,000, but this is after charging £400,000 for a loss on a loan. The tax deduction for the loan can be carried forward for up to 10 years, and the entity intends to claim this after year 5 (that is, in years 6 to 10).
>
> Accounting profits in years 2 to 5 are forecast to be nil, and in years 6 to 10 to be £600,000 in total.

	Years 1 to 5 £'000	Years 6 to 10 £'000	Total £'000
Accounting result before loan loss	300	600	900
Loan loss	(400)	–	(400)
Accounting result	(100)	600	500
Taxable profit before loan loss deduction	300	600	900
Loan loss deduction	–	(400)	(400)
Loss carry-forwards utilised	(300)	–	(300)
Taxable profit	–	200	200

Overall, sufficient taxable profits are expected over the next 10 years (£900,000) to recover both the loss carry-forwards (£300,000) and the loan loss deduction (£400,000). So, a deferred tax asset in respect of the loss carry-forwards is recognised in the current year (subject, of course, to confidence of the recoverability of the asset in the future).

If there were no taxable profits in years 6 to 10, the loan loss deduction would not be recoverable in that period, but would instead reduce the taxable profits in years 1 to 5 to nil. So the loss carried forward would not be recoverable and no deferred tax asset would be recognised.

Tax planning opportunities

29.87 We believe that an entity can include the effects of tax planning opportunities in its assessment of the future taxable profits. At first sight, this might seem at odds with the general principle that no account should be taken of future events. But, putting in place a tax scheme that might reduce future expenses or create additional income is, in substance, no different from procuring orders that will result in future sales. Both actions will create future taxable profits necessary for the recovery of the deferred tax asset.

29.88 A tax planning opportunity is an action that the entity would not normally take, but would do so to prevent, say, an unused tax loss from expiring. Such actions could include:

■ Accelerating taxable amounts or deferring claims for writing down allowances to recover losses (perhaps before they expire).

■ Changing the character of taxable or deductible amounts from trading gains or losses to capital gains or losses, or vice versa.

■ Switching from tax-free to taxable investments.

29.89 Tax planning strategies should only be considered in determining the extent to which an existing deferred tax asset will be realised. They cannot be used to create a new deferred tax asset or to avoid recognition of, or reduce, a deferred tax liability.

29.90 The feasibility of the strategy is assessed based on the individual facts and circumstances of each case. Whatever tax planning opportunities are considered, management must be capable of undertaking them and must have the ability to implement them.

Re-assessment of recoverability

29.91 The carrying amount of a deferred tax asset should be reviewed at each balance sheet date. This means that an entity would need to assess whether a net deferred tax asset recognised in the balance sheet is still recoverable and has not been impaired. For example, an entity might have recognised a deferred tax asset in respect of tax losses in a previous period, based on information then available. A year later, circumstances might have changed so that it is no longer probable that the entity will earn sufficient future taxable profits to absorb all the tax benefit. In that situation, the asset has suffered an impairment and should be written down.

29.92 Similarly, where an entity has been unable to recognise a deferred tax asset because of the unavailability of sufficient taxable profit, it should review the situation at each subsequent balance sheet date to ascertain whether some or all of the unrecognised balance should now be recognised.

29.93 The re-assessment of recoverability of the deferred tax assets is a change in estimate that should be reflected in the current year (see para 29.118).

Tax treatment in consolidated financial statements

29.94 The treatment of taxation in the consolidated financial statements involves considerations that are different from those that apply to individual financial statements. In a group, the tax positions of the individual group entities are unlikely to be similar. Some group entities might be profitable, whilst others might be loss making, leading to different tax considerations. Some might operate in the same tax jurisdiction, whilst others might operate in different tax jurisdictions. Given that consolidated financial statements are prepared as if the parent entity and its subsidiary undertakings were a single entity, it follows that the group's tax position needs to be viewed as a whole.

29.95 The total tax liability of a group is determined by aggregating the actual tax liability assessed under local tax laws and borne by individual group entities. Consolidation adjustments could have tax consequences. Consolidation adjustments can give rise to timing differences if, for group purposes, income and expenses are included in total comprehensive income in a different period from when they are included in the individual tax assessments of group entities. Similarly, consolidation adjustments can give rise to permanent differences. So the provisions of section 29 of FRS 102 apply equally to consolidated financial statements.

> **Example — Tax effects of a consolidation adjustment**
>
> A subsidiary sells goods costing £50,000 to its parent entity for £60,000, and these goods are still held in inventory at the balance sheet date. A consolidation adjustment is required to eliminate the profit of £10,000 from the consolidated profit and loss account. The subsidiary records a current tax charge of £3,000 (£10,000 @ 30%).
>
> At a group level, the current tax charge provided by the subsidiary is eliminated on consolidation, through the recognition of a deferred tax credit in profit or loss and a deferred tax asset. The consolidation adjustment results in a timing difference on consolidation, because the profit on the sale of the stock to the parent is recognised in the subsidiary's tax return in a different period from when it is recognised in total comprehensive income of the group. So a deferred tax asset is recognised.
>
> The tax asset should be recognised and subsequently released at the tax rate of the selling entity when it was included in the tax return. No adjustments should be made for changes in the tax rate.

Business combinations

Fair value adjustments

29.96   As noted previously, deferred tax balances generally result from income or expense that is recognised in total comprehensive income in one period but, under tax laws, is included in taxable income in a different period. But deferred tax balances also arise from business combinations, even where differences between book and tax bases arising will never impact taxable profit.

29.97   In a business combination (as defined in the Glossary of terms in FRS 102), the identifiable assets and liabilities of the acquired business are recognised in the consolidated financial statements at their fair values as at the date of acquisition (subject to limited exceptions). The fair values of these individual assets and liabilities often differ from the amounts that will be deducted or assessed for tax in the future in respect of the assets and liabilities, which often will be the original book values appearing in the acquired entity's own financial statements.

29.98   Deferred tax should be recognised for differences between the amounts recognised on acquisition for accounting purposes and the amounts deductible or chargeable for tax purposes in respect of the assets and liabilities acquired; and an adjustment is made to the goodwill for the deferred tax recognised. [FRS 102 para 29.11].

Goodwill

29.99   In some jurisdictions outside the UK (and where goodwill arises in the UK on the acquisition of trade and assets), tax relief is available on goodwill, which is amortised for tax purposes over a pre-determined life or in accordance with any amortisation for accounting purposes. Where the goodwill is amortised over the same period for accounting purposes, there is no timing difference. But, where a different period is used for tax purposes, deferred tax will arise. For example, it is common in the UK for entities to make an election to claim annual deductions at 4%, so that deductions are received over a 25-year period; but, for accounting purposes, the period over which amortisation is recognised does not exceed five years, unless a longer period can be justified (see further chapter 19).

Investments in subsidiaries, associates, branches and joint ventures

29.100   Subsidiaries, associates, branches and joint ventures incur income and expenses which are included in the consolidated financial statements of the group and impact the group's net assets. But the amounts will not impact the parent's financial statements until the entity is sold. This generates a timing difference in the group financial statements between the recognition of the income and expenses and the allowance for tax.

29.101   The parent should recognise deferred tax on the timing difference, except where:

■   the parent is able to control the reversal of the timing difference; and

■   it is probable that the timing difference will not reverse in the foreseeable future.

[FRS 102 para 29.9].

Foreign exchange differences

29.102   Gains or losses arising on the translation of the financial statements of overseas subsidiaries associates and joint ventures are not taxable, and so they are permanent differences. But gains or losses arising on the translation of an entity's own overseas assets and liabilities could give rise to timing differences, depending on whether or not the gains or losses have a tax effect.

Presentation and disclosures

General

29.103   It is generally accepted that tax effects (regardless of how they have been calculated) should be shown in the financial statements separately from the items or transactions to which they relate. There is an overriding principle that an entity should disclose sufficient information for the users of the financial statements to understand and appraise the tax consequences (both current and deferred) of transactions and events in the period. [FRS 102 para 29.25]. Both section 29 of the standard and UK company law (SI 2008/410) contain disclosure requirements for taxation (discussed below). The disclosure requirements apply to the financial statements of individual entities as well as to consolidated financial statements.

Accounting policies

29.104 There is no specific requirement in section 29 of FRS 102 to disclose accounting policies in respect of current and deferred tax. But section 8 of the standard and SI 2008/410 require disclosure of significant accounting policies that are relevant to an understanding of the entity's financial statements. In respect of deferred tax, the policy note should state the measurement basis on which deferred tax has been recognised and any other accounting policy choices.

Balance sheet

29.105 Section 29 of FRS 102 does not contain any specific requirements for the presentation of current tax assets or liabilities in the balance sheet, presumably because the requirements of SI 2008/410 are sufficient. The section does contain requirements for the presentation of deferred tax balances.

29.106 Deferred tax assets should be presented within the balance sheet heading 'Debtors', and deferred tax liabilities should be presented within the heading 'Provisions for liabilities'. [FRS 102 para 29.23].

29.107 Company law does not state how current tax assets and deferred tax assets should be presented. But section 29 of the standard requires entities to present deferred tax assets within 'Debtors', so we would expect current tax assets to be included under the same balance sheet heading but separately disclosed in the notes.

29.108 The requirements of SI 2008/410 that relate to the presentation of taxation liabilities are as follows:

- Liabilities for taxation must be included in the balance sheet heading 'Other creditors including taxation and social security', and the liability for taxation and social security is shown separately from 'other creditors'. [SI 2008/410 1 Sch Balance sheet formats note 9]. 'Other creditors including taxation and social security', like other categories of creditors, must be split between amounts that will fall due within one year and amounts that will fall due after more than one year. [SI 2008/410 1 Sch Balance sheet formats note 13]. No corporation tax balances payable in over one year should arise, because all entities are due to pay UK corporation tax within nine months of the financial year end.

- The provision for deferred taxation should be included under the balance sheet heading 'Provisions for liabilities' as part of the provision for 'Taxation, including deferred taxation', and stated separately from any other provision for other taxation. [SI 2008/410 1 Sch 60, Balance sheet formats 1 and 2].

Offsetting

29.109   Current tax assets and liabilities and deferred tax assets and liabilities are separately measured and recognised. Current tax assets and liabilities should only be offset for presentation purposes if the entity:

- has a legally enforceable right to offset the recognised amounts; and

- intends either to settle on a net basis, or to realise the asset and settle the liability simultaneously.

[FRS 102 para 29.24].

29.110   Deferred tax assets and liabilities should only be offset for presentation purposes if:

- the entity has a legally enforceable right to offset current tax assets against current tax liabilities; and

- the deferred tax assets and liabilities relate to income taxes levied by the same taxation authority on either the same taxable entity or different taxable entities which intend either to settle current tax liabilities and assets on a net basis, or to realise the assets and settle the liabilities simultaneously, in each future period in which significant amounts of deferred tax liabilities or assets are expected to be settled or recovered.

[FRS 102 para 29.24A].

29.111   The 'legal right of offset' criterion is met only where income taxes are levied by the same tax authority that accepts or requires settlement on a net basis.

29.112   In consolidated financial statements, current tax assets of one group entity could be offset against a current tax liability of another entity if they relate to income taxes levied by the same authority, where there is a legally enforceable right to offset the recognised amounts and the entities intend to make settlement on a net basis or to recover the asset and settle the liability simultaneously.

Performance statements and equity

29.113   All changes in current tax assets and liabilities and deferred tax assets and liabilities should be recognised as tax expense or income, except where they arise from the initial recognition of an asset or liability at fair value in a business combination. [FRS 102 para 29.21].

29.114   For the implications of deferred tax assets and liabilities arising from the initial recognition of assets and liabilities at fair value in business combinations, see paragraph 29.96 above.

29.115 An entity accounts for the tax consequences of transactions and other events in the same way that it accounts for the transactions and other events themselves. In other words, where tax expense or income has arisen from transactions or events recognised in total comprehensive income (that is, continuing or discontinuing operations, and profit or loss or other comprehensive income) or equity, the tax expense or income is presented in the same statement. [FRS 102 para 29.22].

29.116 UK company law requires the tax in the profit and loss account to be disclosed separately (as applicable) for each of 'tax on profit or loss on ordinary activities', 'tax on extraordinary profit or loss' and 'other taxes not shown under the above items'. These are separate headings included in each of the four profit and loss account formats. [SI 2008/410]. SI 2008/410 does not indicate the type of information to be included under 'other taxes not shown under the above items', and no such 'other taxes' are presently collected in the UK, so this heading in the format appears to be superfluous for the time being.

29.117 The carrying amount of deferred tax assets and liabilities can change without a change in the timing difference. Such changes might arise as a result of:

■ a change in tax rates or laws; or

■ a re-assessment of the recoverability of deferred tax assets.

29.118 The resulting change in deferred tax should be recognised in the same way as above, and the tax expense or income should follow the presentation of the underlying transaction or event.

Disclosures in the notes

29.119 A considerable amount of information about current and deferred tax is required to be disclosed in the notes. The disclosure requirements set out below are grouped under appropriate headings for ease of reference.

Analysis of tax expense

29.120 The major components of the tax expense or income should be identified and disclosed separately. Such components might include:

■ Current tax expense or income.

■ Any adjustments recognised in the period for current tax of prior periods.

■ The amount of deferred tax expense or income relating to the origination and reversal of timing differences.

■ The amount of deferred tax expense or income relating to changes in tax rates or the imposition of new taxes.

■ Adjustments to deferred tax expense or income arising from a change in the tax status of the entity or its shareholders.

- The amount of tax expense income relating to changes in accounting policies and material errors (see chapter 10).

[FRS 102 para 29.26].

29.121 UK company law also requires the taxation charge to the profit and loss account to be analysed, distinguishing between:

- UK corporation tax, both before and after double tax relief;

- UK income tax; and

- overseas tax (that is, tax imposed outside the UK).

[SI 2008/410 1 Sch 67(2)].

29.122 The total current and deferred tax relating to items that are charged or credited to other comprehensive income or equity should be disclosed. [FRS 102 para 29.27(a)].

29.123 An entity that conforms to the above requirement would also meet the UK company law requirements to present the amounts credited or debited to the revaluation and fair value reserves. [SI 2008/410 1 Sch 35(6), 41(2)].

Reconciliation of tax expense

29.124 A reconciliation is required between (i) tax expense included in profit or loss and (ii) the product of the profit or loss on ordinary activities multiplied by the applicable rate of tax for the period. [FRS 102 para 29.27(b)]. This relationship can be affected by factors including: significant tax-free income and disallowable expenses; utilisation of tax losses; different tax rates in the locations of foreign-based operations; adjustments related to prior years; unrecognised deferred tax assets; and tax rate changes occurring during the period. An explanation of these matters enables users of the financial statements to understand the relationship between tax expense and accounting profit, as well as the significant factors that could affect that relationship in the future.

29.125 The starting point for preparing the reconciliation is to determine an applicable tax rate. In the context of a single economic entity (that is, the group), it is important to use an applicable tax rate that provides the most meaningful information to users of the financial statements. The most relevant rate is often the rate applicable in the reporting entity's country. This rate could be used even if some of the group's operations are conducted in other countries. In that situation, the impact of different tax rates applied to profits earned in other countries would appear as a reconciling item.

29.126 Alternatively, the rate used could be a weighted average of the rates applicable in the individual jurisdictions in which the entity operates.

29.127 In either case, changes from the prior period in the applicable rate of tax should be disclosed (FRS 102 para 29.27(d)), as well as the basis on which the rate has been determined.

Analysis of deferred tax assets and liabilities

29.128 Deferred tax assets and liabilities (of the current and previous periods) should be analysed by each type of timing difference and the amount of unused tax losses and tax credits. [FRS 102 para 29.27(e)]. The significant types of timing difference that generally need to be disclosed separately will include the following: accelerated capital allowances; revaluation of assets; short-term timing differences; and tax losses and tax credits carried forward.

29.129 If relevant, entities should also disclose the expiry dates of the timing differences, unused tax losses and unused tax credits. [FRS 102 para 29.27(f)].

29.130 Disclosure should also be provided of the net amount of deferred tax assets and liabilities that are expected to reverse within one year of the balance sheet date, together with a brief explanation for the expected reversal. [FRS 102 para 29.27(c)]. Disclosure is on a net basis, which takes account of both the reversal of existing timing differences and the origination of new ones. This is considered to provide information that is relevant to an understanding of an entity's future cash flows, even though it means forecasting future new timing differences. [FRS 102 Advice to the FRC para 91].

29.131 Deferred tax liabilities are presented within provisions, so company law disclosure requirements for provisions should also be adhered to. Where there has been a transfer to or from a provision (other than the utilisation of the provision for the purpose for which it was set up), the following information should be disclosed:

■ The aggregate amount of the provision at the beginning and end of the financial year.

■ Any amounts transferred to or from the provision during the financial year.

■ The source and the application of any amounts so transferred.

[SI 2008/410 1 Sch 59(1),(2)].

Post balance sheet changes in tax rates

29.132 Section 29 of FRS 102 requires the use of tax rates and laws that have been substantively enacted by the balance sheet date (rather than by the date when the financial statements are authorised for issue); this means that information received after the year end about changes in tax rates and laws is not an adjusting post balance sheet event. But changes in tax rates or laws enacted or announced after the balance sheet date that have a significant effect on current and deferred tax assets and liabilities should be disclosed under section 32 of the standard.

Estimation uncertainty

29.133   Section 8 of FRS 102 requires entities to disclose information about key sources of estimation uncertainty for assets and liabilities at the balance sheet date. Areas within taxation that could require disclosure in respect of estimation uncertainty are:

■   Status of negotiations with tax authorities.

■   Assessing the probabilities that sufficient future taxable profits will be available to enable deferred tax assets resulting from timing differences and tax losses to be recognised.

■   Other assumptions about the recoverability of deferred tax assets.

[SI 2008/410 1 Sch 59(1),(2)].

Tax consequences of dividends

29.134   As discussed in paragraph 29.69 above, tax rates in some jurisdictions vary between distributed and undistributed profits. In such situations, an entity should explain the potential income tax consequences that would result from payment of dividends. [FRS 102 para 29.27(g)]. Where dividends have been proposed or declared before the financial statements were authorised for issue (but are not recognised as a liability in the financial statements), we would expect that the tax consequence of the approval of the dividends would be quantifiable, and so it would be disclosed.

Group relief

29.135   Under UK tax legislation, some profits and losses can be offset between entities in the same group by way of group relief. A loss-making subsidiary might be able to surrender its loss for that accounting period to another group entity that made a profit during the same accounting period, thereby reducing the group's tax charge. A number of accounting issues might arise on the presentation of group relief, depending on whether a payment has been made to the surrendering entity and whether any payment represents the tax saving or not. For further guidance, see chapter 13 in the Manual of Accounting – IFRS for the UK.

Transitional issues

29.136   No special exemptions on current and deferred tax are available to first-time adopters under section 35 of FRS 102. So, a first-time adopter must prepare its first financial statements as though the requirements of section 29 of the standard had always applied.

29.137   The accounting for current tax is similar to old UK GAAP, but the new standard specifically precludes discounting of current tax. [FRS 102 para 29.17].

29.138 FRS 102 uses a 'timing differences plus' approach for deferred tax. This is similar to the old UK GAAP 'timing differences' approach, but with some key differences. The main difference is that, under FRS 102, deferred tax is recognised on the revaluation of non-monetary assets, including fair value adjustments in a business combination. Under old UK GAAP, deferred tax was only recognised on the revaluation of non-monetary assets when there was a binding sale agreement and any gains or losses on the sale had been recognised.

29.139 FRS 102 does not allow entities to discount deferred tax assets or liabilities, whereas old UK GAAP (FRS 19) permitted this as an accounting policy choice.

29.140 The new standard also requires the recognition of deferred taxes for timing differences arising from the unremitted earnings of subsidiaries, associates and joint ventures, except where the entity can control the reversal of the timing difference and it will not reverse in the foreseeable future. Under old UK GAAP, deferred tax was only recognised when the dividends from the subsidiary, associate or joint venture were accrued or there was a binding agreement to distribute them.

29.141 Any adjustments to deferred tax arising as a result of adopting FRS 102 for the first time are recognised directly in retained earnings (or, if appropriate, another category of equity) at the date of transition to the FRS. [FRS 102 para 35.8].

29.142 So, deferred tax recognised on transition to FRS 102 in respect of fair valued assets in a business combination where the election to not retrospectively restate business combinations has been applied, would be included in opening retained earnings; goodwill is not adjusted (see chapters 19 and 35). Where the election has not been applied and the business combination is restated, any associated deferred tax would adjust goodwill.

29.143 Deferred tax recognised for the first time on revalued property would be included in the same reserve as the revaluation gains or losses. Similarly, where a first-time adopter has elected to use a previous revaluation (or fair value) as the deemed cost of the asset, deferred tax should be recognised and recorded in the related revaluation reserve (see chapter 17).

29.144 FRS 102 requires the tax expense to be recognised in the same component of comprehensive income (that is, continuing or discontinued operations, and profit or loss or other comprehensive income) or equity as the transaction or other event that resulted in the tax expense. This is slightly different from old UK GAAP, where no tax expense was recognised directly in equity.

Chapter 30

Foreign currency translation

Chapter 30

Foreign currency translation

Introduction

30.1 Entities conduct businesses that are not confined within national boundaries. This can be done in a number of ways. First, entities might buy goods and services from overseas suppliers, and sell goods and services to overseas customers. Secondly, they might conduct international business through overseas subsidiaries, branches and associates.

30.2 In the first situation, transactions are often expressed in foreign currencies. The results of these transactions are translated into the entity's functional currency for financial reporting purposes. In the second situation, it is common for the foreign operation to maintain its accounting records in the local currency. It is not possible to directly combine amounts expressed in different currencies, so management must translate the foreign operation's results and financial position into the currency in which the reporting entity presents its consolidated financial statements.

30.3 So, accounting for foreign currencies involves the translation of financial data denominated in one currency into another currency. The translation process does not change the essential characteristics of the assets and liabilities measured; it merely restates assets and liabilities, initially expressed in a foreign currency unit, to a common currency unit by applying a rate of exchange — a translation rate.

30.4 Different translation rates are used, depending on the circumstances. These are:

- the historical rate (that is, the exchange rate at the date when the transaction or revaluation occurred);
- the closing rate (that is, the exchange rate at the balance sheet date); or
- the average exchange rate during the year.

The average rate is generally only applied to income and expenditure items. The rates used for balance sheet items (historical or closing) depend on whether the assets and liabilities are monetary or non-monetary. These methods are addressed later in this chapter.

30.5 Exchange differences that arise on foreign currency transactions are treated differently from those that arise on foreign currency translation.

Objectives

30.6 Section 30 of FRS 102 prescribes how to:

- include foreign currency transactions and foreign operations in an entity's financial statements;

- specify which exchange rates to use and how to report the effects of changes in exchange rates in the financial statements; and

- translate the financial statements into a presentation currency.

Scope

30.7 Section 30 of the standard sets out the requirements for foreign currency translation. It also applies to any entity that comes within its scope by engaging in foreign currency operations. The standard is applied in:

- Accounting for transactions and balances in foreign currencies.

- Translating the results and financial position of foreign operations that are included in an entity's financial statements by consolidation, or equity accounting.

- Translating an entity's results and financial position into a presentation currency.

30.8 Accounting for financial instruments denominated in a foreign currency is outside the scope of section 30 (and is included, instead, in sections 11 and 12 of FRS 102). The standard also does not apply to hedge accounting for foreign currency items, including the hedging of a net investment in a foreign operation (see chapter 12).

The functional currency approach

Introduction

30.9 Section 30 of FRS 102 requires each individual entity to determine its functional currency and to measure its results and financial position in that currency. So, each individual entity included in a consolidation has its own functional currency; there is no such thing as a group functional currency.

30.10 The requirement to identify each entity's functional currency is a key feature of section 30 of the standard. The functional currency serves as the basis for determining whether the entity is engaging in foreign currency transactions. Additionally, identifying the functional currency has a direct impact on the treatment of exchange gains and losses arising from the translation process and, thereby, the reported results.

Determining functional currency

30.11 An entity's functional currency is a matter of fact. In some cases, the facts will clearly identify the functional currency; in other cases, they will not, and judgement will be required. Section 30 provides guidance on how to determine an entity's functional currency.

30.12 An entity's functional currency is the currency of the primary economic environment in which it operates. [FRS 102 para 30.2]. It should, therefore, be determined at the entity level. The primary economic environment in which an entity operates is normally the economic environment in which it primarily generates and expends cash. [FRS 102 para 30.3]. The functional currency is normally the currency of the country in which the entity is located. It could, however, be a different currency.

30.13 Section 30 of the standard requires entities to consider primary and secondary indicators when determining the functional currency. Primary indicators are closely linked to the primary economic environment in which the entity operates and are given more weight. Secondary indicators provide supporting evidence to determine an entity's functional currency. Both of these indicators, and the factors needing consideration, are shown in the table below.

30.14 FRS 102 gives greater emphasis to the primary indicators because, as stated above, these indicators are closely linked to the primary economic environment in which the entity operates. The currency of the economy in which the entity operates generally determines the pricing of transactions; this is considered to be more influential than the currency in which the transactions are denominated and settled. The reason for this is that transactions can be denominated and settled in any currency management chooses, but the pricing of the transaction is normally done by reference to the economy of the country whose competitive forces and regulations affect the transaction, so the currency of that economy becomes the functional currency by definition. In other words, the currency of the country whose economy drives the business and (determines the gains and losses to be recognised in the financial statements) most faithfully reflects the economic effects of the underlying transactions, events and conditions.

30.15 The standard's intention that the primary and secondary indicators should be looked at as a hierarchy is intended to avoid practical difficulties in determining an entity's functional currency. For example, if all the primary indicators, which should be considered together, identify a particular currency as the functional currency, there is no need to consider the secondary indicators. Secondary indicators serve to provide additional supporting evidence in determining an entity's functional currency.

Primary indicators of functional currency

Indicators	Factors to be considered by the entity in determining the functional currency
Sales and cash inflows	(a) The currency that *mainly influences* sales prices for its goods and services. This will often be the currency in which sales prices for goods and services are denominated and settled. [FRS 102 para 30.3(a)(i)]. In other words, where an active local sales market exists for the entity's products that are also priced in the local currency, and revenues are collected primarily in that local currency, the local currency is the functional currency.
	(b) The currency of the country whose competitive forces and regulations *mainly determine* the sales prices of its goods and services. [FRS 102 para 30.3(a)(ii)]. Where sales prices of the entity's products are determined by local competition and local government regulations, rather than worldwide competition or by international prices, the local currency is the functional currency. For example, aircraft manufacturers often price aircraft in US dollars or in euros, but the legal and regulatory environment of the country in which the manufacturer is located might inhibit the entity's ability to pass hard currency costs (that is, dollars or euros) to its customers. Therefore, while the business is influenced by the hard currency, its ability to generate revenue is determined by the local environment, which could indicate that the local currency is the functional currency.
Expenses and cash outflows	The currency that *mainly influences* labour, material and other costs of providing goods and services. This is often the currency in which such costs are denominated and settled. [FRS 102 para 30.3(b)]. For example, where labour, material and other operating costs are primarily sourced and incurred locally, the local currency is likely to be the functional currency, even though there also might be imports from other countries.

[FRS 102 para 30.3].

Secondary indicators of functional currency

Indicators	Factors to be considered by the entity in determining the functional currency
Financing activities	The currency in which funds from financing activities (for example, issuing debt and equity instruments) are generated. [FRS 102 para 30.4(a)]. For example, where financing is raised in and serviced by funds primarily generated by the entity's local operation, this could indicate that the local currency is the functional currency, in the absence of other indicators to the contrary.
Retention of operating income	The currency in which receipts from operating activities are usually retained. [FRS 102 para 30.4(b)]. This is the currency in which the entity maintains its excess working capital balance, which would generally be the local currency.

[FRS 102 para 30.4].

30.16 The above primary and secondary indicators for determining the functional currency must be considered by all entities.

If the entity is a foreign operation (that is, a subsidiary, branch, associate or joint venture of a reporting entity), the activities of which are based or conducted in a country or currency other than those of the reporting entity, FRS 102 specifies four additional factors that should be considered in determining the functional currency of the foreign operation and whether it is the same as that of the reporting entity. Even though branches are not separate legal entities, it is still necessary to determine their functional currency.

These additional factors are shown in the table below. They set out the conditions that point to whether the foreign operation's functional currency is the same as, or different from, the reporting entity.

Additional indicators for foreign operations

Indicators	Conditions pointing to functional currency being *different from* that of the reporting entity	Conditions pointing to functional currency being the *same as* that of the reporting entity
Degree of autonomy	Activities are carried out with a significant degree of autonomy. An example is when the operation accumulates cash and other monetary items, incurs expenses, generates income and arranges borrowings, all substantially in its local currency.	No significant degree of autonomy – activities are carried out as an extension of the reporting entity. An example is when the foreign operation only sells goods imported from the reporting entity and remits the proceeds to it. It follows that such an entity must have the same currency as the reporting entity. This is because it would be contradictory for an integral foreign operation that carries on business as if it were an extension of the reporting entity's operations to operate in a primary economic environment that is different from its parent.
Frequency of transactions with reporting entity	Few inter-company transactions with the reporting entity.	Frequent and extensive inter-company transactions with the reporting entity.
Cash flow impact on reporting entity	Mainly in local currency and do not affect reporting entity's cash flows.	Directly impact the reporting entity's cash flows and are readily available for remittance to the reporting entity.
Financing	Primarily in the local currency and serviced by funds generated by the entity's operation.	Significant financing from, or reliance on, the reporting entity to service existing and normally expected debt obligations.

[FRS 102 para 30.5].

30.17   The relative importance of the various indicators will vary from entity to entity. For example, the primary and secondary indicators apply to many entities that provide goods and services, but they might not be directly relevant in some other situations (for example, treasury entities, structured or special purpose entities, ultimate holding entities and intermediate holding entities). In those situations, management might need to consider the additional indicators (stated in para 30.13 above) when determining the functional currency.

30.18   In assessing the indicators' relative importance, management might find it useful to consider the following aspects of each indicator:

■   The significance of that indicator to the entity's operation. For example, the existence of sterling-denominated debt in a foreign entity of a UK parent might not be significant if the foreign entity is primarily self-financing through retained earnings.

■   How clearly the indicator identifies a particular currency as the functional currency. For example, if the same entity purchases raw materials both from the UK and locally, the 'expenses' indicator might be inconclusive. By contrast, if the majority of sales occur in the host country at prices determined by local conditions, the 'sales' indicator might be regarded as the key determinant in concluding that the local currency is the functional currency.

30.19   After considering all the factors, the functional currency might still not be obvious. The operation could be diverse, with cash flows, financing and transactions occurring in more than a single currency. In these situations, judgement is required in determining the functional currency that most faithfully represents the economic effects of the underlying transactions, events and conditions. In exercising that judgement, management should give priority to the primary indicators before considering the secondary indicators and the additional factors set out above.

30.20   When considering the 'autonomy' indicator in paragraph 30.5 of FRS 102 (see para 30.14 above), a non-autonomous subsidiary or branch typically derives its functional currency from its parent. Many intermediate holding companies fall into this category. Associates and joint ventures are likely to be autonomous from an individual investor, given the lack of control in the relationship and the fact that the additional indicators in paragraph 30.5 of the standard are not likely to be relevant.

Foreign currency transactions

Introduction

30.21   Foreign currency transactions are transactions denominated in a currency other than the entity's functional currency. Foreign currency transactions might produce receivables or payables, that are fixed in terms of the amount of foreign currency that will be received or paid. For example, an entity might buy or sell goods or services in a foreign currency; borrow or lend money in a foreign currency; acquire or dispose of assets; or incur and settle liabilities in a foreign currency. [FRS 102 para 30.6].

Initial recognition

30.22 A foreign currency transaction is recorded, on initial recognition in the functional currency, by applying to the foreign currency amount the spot exchange rate between the functional currency and the foreign currency at the date of the transaction. [FRS 102 para 30.7]. This process is known as 'translation', whereby financial data denominated in one currency is expressed in terms of another currency. The date of transaction is the date on which the transaction first qualifies for recognition in accordance with FRS 102. For practical reasons, a rate that is approximate to the actual rate at the date of the transaction is often used (for example, the average rate for the week or month). [FRS 102 para 30.8].

Determining the average rate

30.23 Management can use an average rate for a period for recording foreign currency transactions instead of the actual rate prevailing at the date of each transaction, provided that there is no significant change in rates during that period. [FRS 102 para 30.8]. An average rate is unlikely to be used by entities undertaking few transactions in a foreign currency. It is also unlikely to be used for translating large, one-off transactions. The flexibility allowed in section 30 of the standard is likely to be most beneficial to entities that enter into a large number of transactions in different currencies, or that maintain multi-currency ledgers. However, no guidance is provided in the standard as to how such a rate is determined.

30.24 Determining an average rate, and its use in practice, depends on a number of factors, such as: the frequency and value of transactions undertaken; the period over which the rate will apply; the extent of any seasonal trade variation and the desirability of using a weighting procedure; the acceptable level of materiality; and the nature of the entity's accounting systems. There are a large number of methods by which an average rate can be calculated. These range from simple monthly or quarterly averages to more sophisticated methods, using appropriate weighting that reflects changes both in exchange rates and in the volume of business. The choice of the period to be used for calculating the average rate will depend on the extent to which daily exchange rates fluctuate in the period selected. If exchange rates are relatively stable over a period of one month, for example, the average exchange rate for that month can be used as an approximation to the daily rate. If, however, there is volatility of exchange rates, it might be appropriate to calculate an average rate for a shorter period, such as a week. Whatever period is chosen, materiality is likely to be an important consideration.

Subsequent measurement

30.25 A foreign currency transaction could give rise to assets and liabilities that are denominated in a foreign currency. The procedure for translating such assets and liabilities into the entity's functional currency at each balance sheet date will depend on whether they are monetary or non-monetary.

Translation of monetary items

30.26 Monetary items are units of currency held, and assets and liabilities to be received or paid in a fixed or determinable number of units of currency. The essential feature of a monetary item is a right to receive (or an obligation to deliver) a fixed or determinable number of units of currency. Examples are:

■ Financial assets, such as cash, bank balances and receivables.

■ Financial liabilities, such as debt.

■ Provisions that are settled in cash.

■ Pensions and other employee benefits to be paid in cash, deferred taxes and cash dividends that are recognised as a liability.

■ Derivative financial instruments, such as forward exchange contracts, foreign currency swaps and options. These are also monetary items, because they are settled at a future date (although they are outside the scope of section 30 of FRS 102 – see para 30.8 above).

30.27 Section 30 of the standard requires entities to translate foreign currency monetary items outstanding at the balance sheet date using the closing rate. [FRS 102 para 30.9(a)]. The closing rate is the spot exchange rate at the balance sheet date. The treatment of the exchange differences that arise on translating a monetary item at the balance sheet date is considered in paragraph 30.34 onwards below. A rate of exchange that is fixed under the terms of the relevant contract cannot be used to translate monetary assets and liabilities. Translating a monetary item at the contracted rate under the terms of a relevant contract is a form of hedge accounting that is not permitted under section 12 of FRS 102.

Translation of non-monetary items

30.28 Non-monetary items are all items other than monetary items. In other words, the right to receive (or an obligation to deliver) a fixed or determinable number of units of currency is absent in a non-monetary item. Typical examples are:

■ Intangible assets.

■ Goodwill.

■ Property, plant and equipment.

- Inventories.

- Amounts pre-paid for goods and services (pre-paid rent).

- Equity investments.

- Provisions that are to be settled by the delivery of a non-monetary asset.

30.29 Advances paid and received (including pre-payments) can be difficult to classify as monetary or non-monetary. An example of a non-monetary item is an advance payment for goods that, in the absence of a default by the counterparty, must be settled by the counterparty delivering the goods. However, if an advance is refundable in circumstances other than a default by either party, this might indicate that it is a monetary item, because the item is receivable in units of currency.

30.30 Translation of non-monetary items depends on whether they are recognised at historical cost or at fair value. For example, property, plant and equipment might be measured in terms of historical cost or revalued amounts in accordance with section 17 of FRS 102.

30.31 Non-monetary items that are measured in terms of historical cost in a foreign currency are translated using the exchange rate at the date of the transaction. [FRS 102 para 30.9(b)]. This means that such assets are recorded at historical cost, and no retranslation of the asset is required at subsequent balance sheet dates. But, if the asset is impaired, the recoverable amount is translated at the exchange rate applicable at the date when that value is determined (for example, the closing rate at the balance sheet date). Comparing the previously recorded historical cost with the recoverable amount might or might not result in recognising an impairment loss in the functional currency.

30.32 For example, an entity's functional currency is sterling. A foreign currency asset costing FC925,000 is recorded at the date of purchase at £500,000, when £1 = FC1.85. At a subsequent balance sheet date, the asset's recoverable amount in foreign currency is FC787,500, when £1 = FC1.5. Although there is impairment loss in foreign currency, no impairment loss is recognised, because the recoverable amount at the balance sheet date of £525,000 is higher than the carrying value.

30.33 Non-monetary assets that are measured at fair value in a foreign currency are translated using the exchange rates at the date when the fair value was determined. [FRS 102 para 30.9(c)]. For example, a UK entity has a euro-denominated investment property located in France that is carried at fair value, where gains and losses from changes in fair value are recognised in profit or loss for the period in which they arise, in accordance with section 16 of the standard. The fair values, measured initially in euros due to the property's appreciation in value, are translated to sterling at the exchange rate applicable at the relevant measurement dates. The resulting change in fair value in sterling includes foreign exchange differences arising on the retranslation of the opening euro carrying value. This exchange difference is recognised as part of the change in fair value in profit or loss for the period.

Recognition of exchange differences

Monetary items

30.34 Exchange differences arising on the settlement of monetary items, or on translating monetary items at rates different from those at which they were translated on initial recognition during the period or in previous financial statements, are recognised in profit or loss in the period in which they arise, except as described in paragraph 30.40 below. [FRS 102 para 30.10].

30.35 Where monetary items arise from a foreign currency transaction, and there is a change in exchange rate between the transaction date and the date of settlement, an exchange difference results. Where a transaction is settled within the same accounting period at an exchange rate that differs from the rate used when the transaction was initially recorded, the exchange difference is recognised in the income statement of the period in which the settlement takes place. It is appropriate to recognise such exchange differences as part of the profit or loss for that year, because the exchange difference will have been reflected in the cash flow at the time of the settlement.

> **Example – Treatment of a foreign currency denominated purchase of plant**
>
> In March 20X5, a UK entity purchases plant for use in the UK from an overseas entity for FC1,980,000. At the date when the entity purchases the plant, the exchange rate is £1 = FC1.65. The purchase price is to be settled in three months, although delivery is made immediately. The UK entity records both the plant and the monetary liability at £1,200,000 (FC1,980,000/1.65). The entity will not need to translate the plant again. At the settlement date of the liability, the exchange rate is £1 = FC1.75. So, the actual amount that the UK entity will pay is £1,131,429. The entity should include the gain on exchange of £68,751 (that is, £1,200,000 – £1,131,429) in arriving at its profit or loss.

30.36 Where a monetary item arising from a foreign currency transaction remains outstanding at the balance sheet date, an exchange difference arises as a consequence of recording the foreign currency transaction at the rate applicable at the date of the transaction (or when it was translated at a previous balance sheet date) and the subsequent retranslation of the monetary item to the exchange rate at the balance sheet date. Such exchange differences are reported as part of the profit or loss for the year.

Non-monetary items

30.37 Where a gain or loss on a non-monetary item is recognised directly in other comprehensive income, any exchange component of that gain or loss is recognised directly in other comprehensive income. [FRS 102 para 30.11]. An example is where a property denominated in a foreign currency is revalued. Any exchange difference arising when the property is translated at the exchange rate applicable at the valuation date is reported directly in other comprehensive income, along with other changes in value.

Example – Translation of a revalued foreign asset

A UK entity with a sterling functional currency has a property located in the US, which it acquired at a cost of US$1.8m when the exchange rate was £1 = US$1.6. The property was revalued to US$2.16m at the balance sheet date. The exchange rate at the balance sheet date was £1 = US$1.8.

Ignoring depreciation, the amount that would be reported directly to equity is:

	£
Value at balance sheet date = US$2,160,000 @ 1.8 =	1,200,000
Value at acquisition date = US$1,800,000 @1.6 =	1,125,000
Revaluation surplus recognised in other comprehensive income	75,000

The revaluation surplus can be analysed as follows:

	£
Change in fair value = US$360,000 @ 1.8 =	200,000
Exchange component of change = US$1,800,000 @ 1.8 — US$1,800,000 @ 1.6	(125,000)
Revaluation surplus recognised in other comprehensive income	75,000

30.38 On the other hand, where a gain or loss on a non-monetary item is recognised in profit or loss, any exchange component of that gain or loss is also recognised in profit or loss. [FRS 102 para 30.11].

Example – Translation of an impaired foreign asset

A UK entity with a sterling functional currency has a property located in the US, which it acquired at a cost of US$1.8m when the exchange rate was £1 = US$1.6. The property is carried at cost. At the balance sheet date, the recoverable amount of the property (as a result of an impairment review) amounted to US$1.62m. The exchange rate at the balance sheet date was £1 = US$1.8.

Ignoring depreciation, the impairment loss that would be reported in the income statement:

	£
Carrying value at balance sheet date – US$1,620,000 @ 1.8 =	900,000
Historical cost – US$1,800,000 @ 1.6 =	1,125,000
Impairment loss recognised in profit or loss	(225,000)
The impairment loss can be analysed as follows:	
Change in value due to impairment = US$180,000 @ 1.8 =	(100,000)
Exchange component of change = US$1,800,000 @ 1.8 — US$1,800,000 @ 1.6	(125,000)
Impairment loss recognised in profit or loss	(225,000)

Net investment in a foreign operation

30.39 A 'net investment in a foreign operation' is *"the amount of the reporting entity's interest in the net assets of that operation"*. [FRS 102 Glossary of terms]. A monetary item that is receivable from or payable to a foreign operation, such as long-term loans and receivables and long-term payables, could be regarded as an extension of, or reduction, in the reporting entity's net investment in that foreign operation (see further para 30.41 below). In those situations, it might not be appropriate to include the resulting exchange differences arising on the retranslation of such monetary items in consolidated profit or loss, because exchange differences arising on equivalent financing with equity capital would be taken to other comprehensive income on consolidation.

30.40 Section 30 of FRS 102 recognises the above situation and requires exchange differences arising on a monetary item that forms part of a reporting entity's net investment in a foreign operation (that is, a subsidiary, branch, associate or joint venture) to be treated as follows:

- In the separate financial statements of the reporting entity (or the individual financial statements of the foreign operation, as appropriate), such exchange differences are recognised in the income statement.

- In the financial statements that include the foreign operation and the reporting entity (for example, consolidated financial statements where the foreign operation is a subsidiary), such exchange differences are recognised in other comprehensive income and they accumulate in equity. They are not recognised in the profit or loss on disposal of the net investment (see further para 30.36 below).

[FRS 102 para 30.13].

30.41 The inclusion of long-term loans and receivables as part of the net investment in the foreign operation is only permitted where settlement is neither planned nor likely to occur in the foreseeable future. [FRS 102 para 30.12]. In other words, the parent must regard them as 'permanent as equity'. For example, a loan to a foreign entity that is repayable on demand might seem to be a short-term item, rather than part of capital; but, if there is demonstrably no intent or expectation to demand repayment (for example, the short-term loan is allowed to be continuously rolled over, whether or not the subsidiary is able to repay it), the loan has the same economic effect as a capital contribution. On the other hand, a long-term loan with a specified maturity (say 10 to 15 years) does not automatically qualify to be treated as being part of the net investment simply because it is of a long duration, unless management has expressed its intention to renew the note at maturity. The burden is on management to document its intention to renew by auditable evidence, such as board minutes. Otherwise, in the absence of management's intention to renew, the note's maturity date implies that its settlement is planned in the foreseeable future.

30.42 For consolidated accounts purposes, a large number of entities treat cross-border long-term loans to other group entities as 'permanent as equity', in order to avoid recognising foreign exchange movements on these loans in the consolidated profit and loss account. For accounts purposes, if a long-term loan to a foreign operation is neither planned nor likely to be settled in the foreseeable future, it can be treated as forming part of the reporting entity's net investment in the foreign operation ('permanent as equity'). [FRS 102 para 30.12]. Paragraph 30.13 of the standard allows exchange differences on such loans to be taken to other comprehensive income on consolidation. As noted above, it is our view that 'permanent as equity' treatment is only available where management has expressed its intention to renew the long-term note at maturity. Given that paragraph 30.12 of the standard refers to *"an item for which settlement is neither planned nor likely to occur in the foreseeable future"*, the documentation given by management should be specific to the loan that is being treated as 'permanent as equity'. Representations that acknowledge that the loan will be repaid as part of a wider refinancing, whereby the overall funding levels will be maintained for the foreseeable future, do not meet the requirements of section 30 of FRS 102.

30.43 The Finance Act 2012 incorporates a new controlled foreign companies (CFC) regime which had previously been announced as part of the Government's corporate tax reform package. A big change under the new rules is the introduction of a partial (or, in some cases, full) exemption for interest income arising in an offshore finance company. Under the rules, the offshore lender can exempt the interest income on the long-term loan from tax, whilst the offshore borrower can typically claim a tax deduction for the finance expense, thus making it tax efficient to fund overseas foreign operations in this way. That said, it appears that some tax authorities are increasingly scrutinising the tax deduction for the interest expense, particularly where management has documented its intention to renew the note at maturity to achieve 'permanent as equity' treatment on consolidation to avoid taking foreign exchange movements to the consolidated income statement. Where overseas foreign operations are funded by loans, if the desired accounting treatment is to treat the loan as 'permanent as equity' on consolidation, evidence is required from management of its intention to renew or roll over the loan (see para 30.41 above).

30.44 Some might argue that inter-company accounts of a trading nature should qualify for the same treatment as above because, although individual transactions are settled, the account's aggregate balance never drops below a specified minimum. In other words, as a minimum amount is permanently deferred, an appropriate amount of the resulting exchange difference should also be deferred in equity. This treatment is not permitted; the standard prohibits its application to trade receivables and payables. [FRS 102 para 30.12]. The rationale is that, as each individual transaction included in the overall inter-company balance is settled and replaced by a new transaction, settlement is always contemplated; and so exchange gains and losses arising on such active accounts (as described above) would not qualify for deferral treatment.

Hedging a net investment

30.45 On consolidation, management might decide to hedge against the effects of changes in exchange rates in the entity's net investment in a foreign operation. This could be done by taking out a foreign currency borrowing or a forward contract to hedge the net investment (see chapter 12).

Change in functional currency

30.46 Once the functional currency of an entity is determined, it should be used consistently, unless significant changes in economic facts, events and conditions indicate that the functional currency has changed. [FRS 102 para 30.15]. For example, a branch that carried out its operations as an extension of the reporting entity's business might become independent as a result of changed circumstances.

30. 47 A change in functional currency should be accounted for prospectively from the date of change. [FRS 102 para 30.14]. In other words, management should translate all items (including balance sheet, income statement and statement of comprehensive income items) into the new functional currency, using the exchange rate at the date of change. [FRS 102 para 30.16]. Because the change was brought about by changed circumstances, it does not represent a change in accounting policy, and so a retrospective adjustment under section 10 of the standard is not relevant. All items are translated using the exchange rate at the date of change, so the resulting translated amounts for non-monetary items are treated as their historical cost. There is no specific guidance in section 30 of FRS 102 on what should be done with equity items, but it would be consistent that these are also translated using the exchange rate at the date of the change of functional currency. This means that no additional exchange differences arise on the date of the change.

30.48 It might not be practicable to determine the date of change at a precise point during the year. It is also likely that the change might have occurred gradually during the year. If so, it might be acceptable to account for the change as of the beginning or end of the accounting period in which the change occurs, whichever more closely approximates to the date of change.

> **Example – Change in functional currency**
>
> A UK entity has a branch in France, with sterling as its functional currency. A significant change in trading operations and circumstances occurred during the first quarter of the financial year ended 30 June 20X6. This meant that sterling no longer faithfully represented the underlying transactions, events and conditions of the foreign branch. The UK management decided that the euro should be the functional currency of its foreign operation, and that all transactions undertaken from the beginning of the financial year ended 30 June 20X6 should be recorded in euros.
>
> The foreign branch's financial statements at 30 June 20X5, previously prepared in sterling, are translated to euros at the rate of exchange applicable at the date of change — in this situation, 1 July 20X5, the first day of the current financial year. All items in

the balance sheet are translated at the rate of exchange applicable at 30 June 20X5, which approximates to the date of change. Retrospective application is not permitted, because the change in functional currency is accounted for prospectively.

30.49 Entities should also consider presentation currency (see further para 30.50 below) where there is a change in functional currency. It might be that the presentation currency does not change. For example, a stand-alone UK entity previously presented its financial statements in its sterling functional currency, and its functional currency changes to US dollar. The entity is based in the UK and has UK shareholders. It does not wish to change its presentation currency, and so continues to present its financial statements in sterling. Alternatively, the entity is part of a group, and the presentation currency of the group does not change following the change in functional currency of a foreign operation. In such a case, the numbers in the entity's own financial statements for the period up to the change in functional currency do not change in presentational currency terms. From the point that the functional currency changes, new foreign exchange differences will arise in the entity's own financial statements when items expressed in the new functional currency are translated into the presentation currency.

Use of a presentation currency other than the functional currency

Translation to the presentation currency

30.50 An entity can present its financial statements in any currency. Selecting a presentation currency that is different from the functional currency requires a translation from the functional currency into the presentation currency. For example, where a group contains individual entities with different functional currencies, the results and financial position of each entity are expressed in a common currency, so that consolidated financial statements can be presented. Section 30 of FRS 102 has prescribed a translation methodology for translating from the functional currency to a different presentation currency. This translation methodology (described in the next paragraph) seeks to ensure that the financial and operational relationships between underlying amounts established in the entity's primary economic environment and measured in its functional currency are preserved when translated into a different measurement currency. [FRS 102 para 30.17]. A different translation methodology (described in chapter 31) applies to an entity whose functional currency is the currency of a hyper-inflationary economy. [FRS 102 para 30.21].

30.51 The translation methodology referred to above requires the results and financial position of an entity, whose functional currency is not the currency of a hyper-inflationary economy, to be translated into a different presentation currency using the following procedures:

■   Assets and liabilities for each balance sheet presented (including comparatives) are translated at the closing rate at the date of that balance sheet.

Use of a constant rate of exchange for all items on the balance sheet maintains the same relationship in the retranslated financial statements as existed in the foreign operation's financial statements. So, for example, fixed assets are the same proportion of long-term liabilities.

■ Income and expenses for each statement of comprehensive income (that is, including comparatives) are translated at exchange rates at the dates of the transactions. For practical reasons, a rate that approximates to the exchange rates at the dates of the transactions (for example, an average rate for the period) is often used to translate income and expense items. However, if exchange rates fluctuate significantly, the use of the average rate for a period is inappropriate (see para 30.57 below).

The use of a closing rate is more likely to preserve the financial results and relationships that existed prior to translation, but the use of an actual or average rate reflects more fairly the profits or losses and cash flows as they accrue to the group throughout the period.

■ All resulting exchange differences are recognised in other comprehensive income. They accumulate in equity, but there is no requirement to report them in a separate reserve (see further below).

[FRS 102 paras 30.18; 30.19].

30.52 The exchange differences referred to in the last bullet point above comprise:

■ Differences arising from translating the income and expenses in total comprehensive income at exchange rates at the dates of the transactions or at average rates, and assets and liabilities at the closing rate.

■ Differences arising on the opening net assets' retranslation at a closing rate that differs from the previous closing rate.

[FRS 102 para 30.20].

30.53 The above exchange differences are not recognised in the income statement. This would distort the results from trading operations shown in the functional currency financial statements. Such differences, which primarily result from a translation process, are unrelated to the foreign operation's trading performance or financial operations; in particular, they do not represent or measure changes in actual or prospective cash flows. So, it is inappropriate to regard them as profits or losses, and they are recognised in other comprehensive income.

30.54 FRS 102 does not require translation differences to be presented as a separate component of equity. There is no requirement to track previous translation differences by foreign operation, because there is no requirement for them to be recycled through the income statement on disposal. Entities may of course choose to separately identify and disclose foreign currency translation adjustments.

Non-performance statement items

30.55 FRS 102 is silent on how to translate items that are recognised directly in equity (that is, items that have not been recognised through the performance statements). These will generally be recognised as a result of a transaction with a shareholder, such as share capital, share premium or treasury shares. Management has a choice of using either the historical rate or the closing rate for these items. The chosen policy should be applied consistently.

30.56 Any exchange differences arising on retranslating equity items at closing rate are recognised directly in equity and not in other comprehensive income. The policy choice has no impact on the amount of total equity.

Determining the average rate for translating the income statement

30.57 FRS 102 permits a foreign operation's income statement to be translated at an average rate for the period. Section 30 of the standard does not prescribe any definitive method of calculating the average rate, probably because the appropriate method might justifiably vary between individual entities. For further information, see paragraphs 30.23 and 30.24 above.

Change in presentation currency

30.58 Entities are allowed a free choice of the currency in which they present their financial statements. [FRS 102 para 30.17]. The question, therefore, arises how a change in presentation currency should be treated. An entity might choose to change its presentation currency when there is a change in its functional currency, although this is not required (see para 30.49 above). The choice of presentation currency represents an accounting policy, and any change should be applied fully retrospectively in accordance with section 10 of the standard, unless impracticable. This means that the change should be treated as if the new presentation currency had always been the entity's presentation currency, with comparative amounts being restated into the new presentation currency. Since using a presentation currency is purely applying a translation method, and does not affect the underlying functional currency of the entity or any entities within a group, it is straightforward to apply a change in presentation currency to assets, liabilities and income and other performance statement items. All assets and liabilities are translated from their functional currency into the new presentation currency at the beginning of the comparative period, using the opening exchange rate and retranslated at the closing rate. Income statement and other performance statement items are translated at an actual rate or at an average rate approximating to the actual rate.

30.59 However, for non-performance statement items, such as share capital and share premium, management has a choice of translating these equity items from an entity's functional currency into its presentation currency at either the closing rate or the historical rate (see para 30.55 above).

Consolidated financial statements

Translation of a foreign operation

30.60 Translating foreign currency financial statements into the presentation currency is necessary so that the foreign operation's financial statements can be included in the reporting entity's financial statements by consolidation or the equity method. The method of translation is described in paragraph 30.51 above. This translation method is illustrated by the example below. Once the foreign operation's financial statements have been translated into the reporting entity's presentation currency, its incorporation into the reporting entity's consolidated financial statement follows normal consolidation procedures. [FRS 102 para 30.22].

> ### Example – Translation of a foreign subsidiary
>
> Entity A, a UK entity, whose accounting period ended on 30 September 20X5, has a wholly owned US subsidiary, S corporation, which was acquired for US$500,000 on 30 September 20X4. The fair value of the net assets at the date of acquisition was US$400,000, giving rise to goodwill of US$100,000. The exchange rate at 30 September 20X4 and 20X5 was £1 = US$2.0 and £1 = US$1.5 respectively. The weighted average rate for the year ended 30 September 20X5 was £1 = US$1.65. During the year, S corporation paid a dividend of US$14,000 when the rate of exchange was £1 = US$1.75.
>
> The foreign currency movements in this example have been exaggerated. In reality, if exchange rates were this volatile, an entity would not be permitted to use average rates for translating the income statement. [FRS 102 para 30.19].
>
> The summarised income statement of S corporation for the year ended 30 September 20X4, and the summarised balance sheets at 30 September 20X3 and 20X4 in dollars and sterling equivalents, are as follows:
>
> **S corporation: Income statement for the year ended 30 September 20X5**
>
> | | $'000 | Exchange rate | £'000 |
> |---|---|---|---|
> | Operating profit | 135 | 1.65 | 81.8 |
> | Interest paid | (15) | 1.65 | (9.0) |
> | Profit before taxation | 120 | | 72.8 |
> | Taxation | (30) | 1.65 | (18.2) |
> | Profit after taxation | 90 | | 54.6 |

Foreign currency translation

Balance sheets of S corporation

	20X5 $'000	20X4 $'000	20X5 $'000	20X4 $'000
Closing exchange rate £1 =			$1.50	$2.00
Property, plant and equipment				
Cost (20X5 additions: $30)	255	225	170.0	112.5
Depreciation (20X5 charge: $53)	98	45	65.3	22.5
Net book value	157	180	104.7	90.0
Current assets:				
Inventories	174	126	116.0	63.0
Debtors	210	145	140.0	72.5
Cash at bank	240	210	160.0	105.0
	624	481	416.0	240.5
Current liabilities:				
Trade creditors	125	113	83.3	57.5
Taxation	30	18	20.0	9.0
	155	131	103.3	65.5
Net current assets	469	350	312.7	175.0
Loan stock	150	130	100.0	65.0
Net assets	476	400	317.4	200.0
Share capital	200	200	100.0	100.0
Retained profits	276	200	217.4	100.0
	476	400	317.4	200.0

Analysis of retained profits

	$'000	£'000
Pre-acquisition profit brought forward	200	100.0
Profit for the year	90	54.6
Dividends paid in the year *	(14)	(8.0)
Exchange difference	-	70.8
Retained profits	276	217.4

* Dividend paid during the year is translated at the actual rate $1 = $1.75

Analysis of exchange difference:

Arising on retranslation of opening net assets (excluding goodwill – see below)

at opening rate — $400,000 @ $2 = £1	200.0
at closing rate — $400,000 @ $1.5 = £1	266.7
Exchange gain on net assets	66.7
Exchange gain arising from translating retained profits from average to closing rate – $90,000 @1.5 – £54.6	5.4
	(1.3)

Exchange loss arising from translating dividend from actual to closing rate –
$14,000 @1.5 – £8.0

Total exchange difference arising on translation of S corporation	70.8

Exchange difference on goodwill of US$100,000 treated as a currency asset
(see para 30.63 below)

at opening rate — US$100,000 @ $2 = £1	50.0
at closing rate — US$100,000 @ $1.5 = £1	66.7
Exchange gain on goodwill included in consolidation	16.7
Total exchange difference included in consolidated balance sheet that accumulates in equity (see below)	87.5

It is assumed that parent entity A's functional currency is the pound sterling. It has received a dividend from S corporation during the year. The summarised balance sheets of entity A at 30 September 20X4 and 20X5 are as follows:

Entity A — Balance sheets

	20X5 £'000	20X4 £'000
Investments in S corporation ($500,000 @ $2 = £1)	250	250
Cash	208	200
Net assets	458	450
Share capital	450	450
Retained profits (dividend received: $14,000 @ $1.75 = £1 *)	8	-
	458	450

* actual rate on the date when the dividend was received

The summarised consolidated income statement for the year ended 30 September 20X5, and the consolidated balance sheet as at date prepared under the closing rate/net investment method, are as follows:

Consolidated income statement for the year ended 30 September 20X5

	£'000
Operating profit of S corporation	81.8
Operating profit of entity A	8.0
	89.8
Elimination of inter-company dividend *	(8.0)
Net operating profit	81.8
Interest paid	(9.0)
Profit before taxation	72.8
Taxation	(18.2)
Profit after taxation	54.6
Other comprehensive income	87.5

Foreign currency translation

Consolidated balance sheet as at 30 September 20X5

	£'000
Goodwill	66.7
Property, plant and equipment	104.7
	171.4
Current assets:	
Inventories	116.0
Debtors	140.0
Cash (S corporation: £160; entity A: £208)	368.0
	624.0
Current liabilities:	
Trade creditors	83.3
Taxation	20.0
	103.3
Net current assets	520.7
Loan stock	100.0
Net assets	592.1
Capital and reserves	
Share capital	450.0
Retained profit including translation adjustments	142.1
	592.1

Different reporting dates

30.61 Where a foreign subsidiary's financial statements are drawn up to a date that is different from that of the parent, the foreign subsidiary often prepares additional financial statements, as of the same date as the parent, for inclusion in the parent's financial statements. Therefore, the foreign subsidiary's financial statements are translated at the exchange rate at the parent's balance sheet date. Where additional financial statements are not prepared, section 9 of FRS 102 allows the use of a different reporting date that is not more than three months before the reporting entity's balance sheet date. The foreign subsidiary's financial statements are translated at the exchange rate applicable at the foreign operation's balance sheet date. However, if significant transactions or events occur between the date of the subsidiary's financial statements and the date of the parent's financial statements, adjustments are made. This might include changes to the exchange rate.

Non-controlling interest

30.62 Exchange differences arising on the retranslation of a foreign subsidiary's financial statements are recognised in other comprehensive income, and they accumulate in equity. Where the foreign subsidiary is not wholly owned, the accumulated exchange differences that are attributable to the non-controlling interest are allocated to, and reported as part of, the non-controlling interest in the consolidated balance sheet. [FRS 102 para 30.20].

Goodwill and fair value adjustments arising on an acquisition

30.63 Goodwill arising in a business combination is measured as the excess of the consideration transferred for the combination over the acquirer's interest in the net fair value of the acquiree's identifiable assets and liabilities and any non-controlling interest.

30.64 Goodwill and fair value adjustments to the acquired entity's assets and liabilities are treated as assets and liabilities of the foreign operation. They are expressed in the foreign operation's functional currency and are translated at the closing rate (in accordance with paras 30.50 and 30.51 above). [FRS 102 para 30.23].

Intra-group trading transactions

30.65 Where normal trading transactions take place between group entities located in different countries, the transactions give rise to monetary assets (liabilities) that might either have been settled during the year or remain unsettled at the balance sheet date. The transactions will be recorded in the functional currency of one of the entities in question, so exchange differences will arise. These are reported in the entity's income statement in the same way as gains or losses on transactions arising with third parties (as explained in para 30.52 above). Where the monetary asset or liability is settled during the year, the exchange gain or loss will have affected group cash flows. It is, therefore, included in consolidated results for the year. The exchange difference arising simply reflects the risk of doing business with a foreign party, even though that party happens to be a group member. Where the transaction remains unsettled at the balance sheet date, and the monetary asset (liability) in one group entity is eliminated against the corresponding liability (asset) in another group entity, the exchange difference reported in the group entity's own income statement continues to be recognised in consolidated profit or loss. This is because the monetary item represents a commitment to convert one currency into another and exposes the reporting entity to gain or loss through currency fluctuations. [FRS 102 para 30.22].

Disposal or partial disposal of a foreign operation

30.66 The cumulative amount of exchange differences recognised in other comprehensive income is not carried forward as a separate component of equity (as discussed in para 30.51 above). These amounts cannot be recognised in the profit or loss on the disposal of the related foreign operation (consistent with old UK GAAP SSAP 20 and different to FRS 23, which required the recognition of such exchange differences in profit or loss on disposal of a net investment in a foreign operation). [FRS 102 para 30.13].

Disclosure

30.67 In respect of exchange differences, the following are required to be disclosed:

- The amount of exchange differences recognised in profit or loss, except for those arising on financial instruments measured at 'fair value through profit or loss' in accordance with sections 11 and 12 of FRS 102.

- The amount of exchange differences arising during the period and classified in equity at the end of the period.

[FRS 102 para 30.25].

30.68 The disclosures required above are on an aggregate net basis.

The total amount of exchange differences recognised in profit or loss includes exchange differences recognised on subsequent settlement and retranslation to closing rate on balances arising on foreign currency transactions. However, the standard is silent as to where in profit or loss they should be included. A cue can be taken from IFRS (particularly IAS 12), which states that exchange differences arising on foreign deferred tax assets and liabilities can be included as part of the deferred tax expense (income) if that presentation is considered to be the most useful to financial statement users. Therefore:

- Foreign exchange differences arising from trading transactions can be included in the results of operating activities.

- Foreign exchange differences arising from financing can be included as a component of finance cost/income.

30.69 A reporting entity is permitted to present its financial statements in a currency that is different from its functional currency and, in this situation, the following should be disclosed:

- The fact that the presentation currency is different from the functional currency.

- The disclosure of the functional currency.

- The reasons for using a different presentation currency.

[FRS 102 para 30.26].

30.70 Where there is a change in the functional currency of either the reporting entity or a significant foreign operation, that fact and the reason for the change in functional currency are required to be disclosed. [FRS 102 para 30.27]. A change in functional currency could be due to a number of reasons, so it is not possible to say what disclosure might be required in a particular case. However, it will certainly require a more substantial disclosure than, for example, 'this currency was chosen because it gives the most appropriate presentation'.

Other matters

Tax effects of all exchange differences

30.71 Gains and losses on foreign currency transactions, and exchange differences arising on translating the results and financial position of an entity (including a foreign operation) into a different currency, might have tax effects. Section 29 of FRS 102 applies to these tax effects (see chapter 29).

Cash flow statements

30.72 Cash flows arising from transactions in foreign currency and cash flows of a foreign subsidiary are translated at the exchange rates between the functional currency and the foreign currency at the dates of the cash flows. Section 7 of FRS 102 applies to foreign currency cash flows (see chapter 7).

Transition requirements

30.73 On transition to FRS 102, an entity adopts the requirements of the standard retrospectively. That is, with specified exceptions, the opening balance sheet should be presented in accordance with the standard. [FRS 102 para 35.7]. Therefore, any changes from the previously applied accounting policies are accounted for retrospectively in accordance with FRS 102.

30.74 For foreign currency translation, there are no transitional exemptions which should not cause any hardship as FRS 102 does not require translation differences to be taken to a separate component of equity and, unlike FRS 23/IFRS, amounts are not recycled to the income statement on disposal of a foreign operation. Therefore, where entities have previously disclosed a separate cumulative translation reserve, this can be released directly to retained earnings on adoption of FRS 102.

Entities previously applying IAS 21 or FRS 23

30.75 For entities previously applying IAS 21 (or FRS 23), there are unlikely to be transitional issues for foreign currency transactions, due to the similarities between the standards.

Entities previously applying SSAP 20

30.76 Transitional issues might arise on the application of hedge accounting for foreign investments. SSAP 20 contained specific guidance for individual financial statements, allowing foreign investments to be retranslated where foreign currency borrowings had been taken out to finance the purchase of the foreign investment. FRS 102 contains no similar guidance. Section 12 of the standard only permits the foreign exchange risk in a net investment in a foreign operation to be hedged; a 'net investment in a foreign operation' is defined as *"the amount of* *the reporting entity's interest in the net assets of that operation"*. [FRS 102 Glossary of terms]. Because the net assets of the foreign operation are reported only in the reporting entity's consolidated financial statements, the foreign exchange risk, for which hedge accounting can be applied under section 12 of the standard, only exists on consolidation. For stand-alone entities that include branches that are foreign operations, hedge accounting can be applied to the foreign exchange risk in the net assets of the branch. Hedge accounting is covered by section 12 of FRS 102 (see chapter 12).

30.77 For foreign currency transactions, one of the main transition issues that entities previously applying SSAP 20 are likely to encounter concerns hedging transactions. SSAP 20 allowed transactions to be translated at a rate specified in a matching or related forward contract. The item translated could be, for example, a sale and debtor, a fixed asset or the purchase of an item of inventory. [SSAP 20 para 46]. FRS 102 requires all transactions to be translated at the rate of exchange applicable at the date of the transaction. In addition, monetary items, and non-monetary items that are carried at fair value, are retranslated at closing rates or rates applicable when the fair values were determined. [FRS 102 para 30.9]. Translating an item at the contracted rate under the terms of a relevant contract is a form of hedge accounting that is not permitted under FRS 102. FRS 102 details strict criteria that must be fulfilled before hedge accounting can be applied, and it specifies the appropriate accounting treatment for the hedged item and hedging instrument where hedge accounting is permitted.

30.78 FRS 102 states that an entity should determine its functional currency and measure its results and financial position in that currency. 'Functional currency' is defined as *"the currency of the primary economic environment in which the entity operates"*. [FRS 102 Glossary of terms]. The standard goes on to give guidance as to the factors that will determine an entity's functional currency. [FRS 102 para 30.3]. Under SSAP 20, an entity was required to prepare its financial statements in its local currency, and to translate the results of foreign operations that had been prepared in their local currencies. The definition of 'local currency' was *"the currency of the primary economic environment in which an entity operates and generates net cash flows"*. [SSAP 20 para 39]. In principle, therefore, the move from SSAP 20 to FRS 102 should not cause difficulties in this respect, because the definitions are close. However, where an entity is a foreign operation and is not autonomous from (or acts as a conduit/extension of) its parent, such as some intermediate holding companies, the functional currency should be reconsidered.

30.79 As noted above, UK entities applying SSAP 20 were required to present their financial statements in their local currency. Although FRS 102 requires entities to measure their results and position in their functional currencies, they might choose to present their financial statements in a different currency. Broadly, the method of translation is that assets and liabilities for all balance sheets should be translated at the closing rate existing at the date of each balance sheet presented, and income and expense items for all periods presented should be translated at transaction rates (or average rates as an approximation). Exchange differences resulting from retranslation should be taken to equity. First-time adopters might, therefore, choose to present their financial statements in a currency other than their local (or functional) currency. This would generally only be the case where more useful information would result.

30.80 There is one additional disclosure in FRS 102 for which UK entities that have applied SSAP 20 will have to ensure that they have the systems in place to collect the information. FRS 102 requires the total amount of exchange differences included in profit or loss for the period to be disclosed. SSAP 20, on the other hand, required disclosure only of the exchange differences included in the profit and loss account that had arisen on foreign currency borrowings less deposits.

Chapter 31

Hyper-inflation

Chapter 31

Hyper-inflation

Scope

31.1 Conventional financial reporting can be distorted by inflation. This is especially the case where financial statements are prepared in an economy that is impacted by a very high level of inflation ('hyper-inflation'). Adjustments to stabilise the unit of measurement (that is, to measure items in units of constant purchasing power) can make the financial statements more relevant and reliable. Section 31 of FRS 102 applies to an entity whose functional currency is the currency of a hyper-inflationary economy; and it requires that the entity's financial statements are adjusted for the effects of hyper-inflation.

Characteristics of hyper-inflation

31.2 Section 31 does not provide a definition of hyper-inflation, nor does it provide an absolute rate at which an economy is deemed to be hyper-inflationary. Instead, the standard sets out the following indicators that management should consider when judging whether an economy is hyper-inflationary:

- The general population prefers to accumulate its wealth in non-monetary assets or in a relatively stable foreign currency. Amounts of local currency are invested immediately to maintain purchasing power.

- The general population regards monetary amounts not in terms of the local currency, but in terms of a relatively stable foreign currency. Prices (for example, rent, wages and capital goods) might be quoted in that foreign currency.

- Sales and purchases on credit take place at prices that compensate for the expected loss of purchasing power during the credit period, even if the period is short.

- Interest rates, wages and prices are linked to a price index.

- The cumulative inflation rate over three years is approaching, or exceeds, 100%.

[FRS 102 para 31.2].

31.3 A cumulative three-year inflation rate exceeding 100% might be a strong indicator of hyper-inflation, but the qualitative factors should also be considered. The factors have to be carefully weighed because it is not desirable to move in and out of hyper-inflationary reporting within a short time period.

31.4 Other characteristics that are not mentioned in the section, but that can be useful in determining the presence of hyper-inflation, include:

■   Severe exchange controls to protect the local currency.

■   Frequent central bank intervention in the currency.

Applying section 31

31.5 The key principle of section 31 is that all amounts (including comparatives) in the financial statements of an entity whose functional currency is the currency of a hyper-inflationary economy should be stated in terms of the measuring unit current at the end of the reporting period. [FRS 102 para 31.3]. This is achieved in a number of steps, which are discussed in the following paragraphs and can be summarised as follows:

■   Select a general price index (see para 31.6 below).

■   Segregate monetary and non-monetary items (see para 31.8 below).

■   Restate non-monetary items (excluding shareholders' equity) (see para 31.15 below).

■   Restate shareholders' equity (see para 31.19 below).

■   Restate comprehensive income (see para 31.21 below).

■   Restate the cash flow statement (see para 31.23 below).

■   Calculate the gain or loss on net monetary position (see para 31.25 below).

Selection of a general price index

31.6 Section 31 requires the use of a general price index to reflect changes in general purchasing power. [FRS 102 para 31.4]. The most reliable indicator of changes in general price levels is normally the consumer price index. In most cases, the consumer price index is closest to the concept of the general price index required by section 31 because it is at the end of the supply chain and reflects the impact of prices on the general population's consumption basket.

31.7 The general price index selected is used to restate historical amounts to units of current purchasing power. Conversion factors are calculated on the basis of the change in the levels of the index over a period. An example is given below.

Example – Conversion factors

An entity purchased an item of property, plant and equipment in December 20X0 at a price of C200m. The general price indices and conversion factors as at 31 December 20X0 and 20X2 are given below.

	General price index	**Conversion factor**
31 December 20X0	54.224	4.114 (223.100 ÷ 54.224)
31 December 20X2	223.100	1.000 (223.100 ÷ 223.100)

The restated fixed asset cost at 31 December 20X2 is C823m (that is, C200m × 4.114), current at 31 December 20X2.

Segregation of monetary and non-monetary items

31.8 As noted above, the key principle of section 31 is that all amounts in the financial statements of an entity whose functional currency is the currency of a hyper-inflationary economy should be stated in terms of the measuring unit current at the end of the reporting period. So, an entity should restate all amounts in the statement of financial position that are not expressed in terms of the measuring unit current at the reporting date. [FRS 102 para 31.5].

31.9 Monetary items do not need to be restated, because they represent money held, to be received or to be paid, so are already expressed in terms of the measuring unit current at the reporting date. [FRS 102 para 31.6]. Accordingly, balance sheet items should be analysed into monetary and non-monetary items in order to segregate the latter for the purpose of restatement.

31.10 Most balance sheet items are obviously monetary or non-monetary. In less straightforward cases, determining whether a component is monetary depends on its underlying characteristics. For example, a provision for doubtful receivables is considered monetary because receivables are monetary; and a provision for inventory obsolescence is non-monetary because inventory is non-monetary.

31.11 Examples of monetary items are:

Monetary assets	**Monetary liabilities**
Cash and amounts due from banks	Trade payables
Marketable debt securities	Accrued expenses and other payables
Trade receivables	Current income taxes payable
Notes receivable and other receivables	Borrowings and notes payable

31.12 Examples of non-monetary items are:

Non-monetary assets	Non-monetary liabilities
Prepaid expenses	Advances received on sales
Advances paid on purchases	Deferred income
Inventories	
Equity securities	
Investments in associates	
Property, plant and equipment	
Intangible assets	

Advances paid or received are considered non-monetary if they are linked to specific purchases or sales; otherwise, they should be considered monetary.

31.13 Provisions for liabilities and charges could be monetary or non-monetary. Their classification depends on the nature of the liability. For example, if warranty obligations are limited to a refund of a defined original amount, the provision is monetary. But, if the entity's obligation is specified as a repair or exchange of the item under warranty, the provision is non-monetary.

31.14 Monetary assets and liabilities linked by agreement to changes in prices, such as index linked bonds and loans, are adjusted in accordance with the agreement in order to determine the amount outstanding at the end of the reporting period. These items are carried at this adjusted amount. [FRS 102 para 31.7].

Restatement of non-monetary items (excluding shareholders' equity)

31.15 Having identified its non-monetary assets and liabilities, an entity should restate them in terms of the measuring unit current at the end of the reporting period. An exception to this is non-monetary assets and liabilities that are carried at amounts current at the end of the reporting period, such as net realisable value or fair value; and so those assets and liabilities are not restated. [FRS 102 para 31.8(a)]. The treatment of shareholders' equity and retained earnings is discussed separately at paragraph 31.19 onwards below.

31.16 Most non-monetary items are carried at cost (or cost less depreciation); and so they are expressed at amounts current at the date of acquisition. The restated cost, or cost less depreciation, of each item is determined by applying, to its historical cost and accumulated depreciation, the change in the general price index (identified in para 31.6 above) from the date of acquisition to the end of the reporting period. [FRS 102 para 31.8(b)].

31.17 Some non-monetary items might be carried at amounts current at dates other than that of acquisition or the reporting date (for example, property, plant and equipment that has been revalued at some earlier date, under the alternative revaluation model allowed by section 17 of FRS 102). In such cases, the carrying amounts need to be updated so that they are expressed in terms of the measuring unit current at the end of the reporting period. In order to do this, the revalued carrying amounts are restated from the date of the revaluation.

31.18   The recoverable amount of an asset might be less than its restated amount. So, application of the normal impairment requirement would result in a write-down of the carrying amount in the restated financial statements, even if no impairment of the asset was required in the historical cost financial statements [FRS 102 para 31.8(c)].

Restatement of shareholders' equity

31.19   At the beginning of the first period when section 31 of FRS 102 is applied, the components of shareholders' equity, excluding retained earnings, should be restated by applying the general price index (identified in para 31.6 above) from the dates on which the items were contributed, or otherwise arose, to the end of the reporting period. The amount of restated retained earnings is the balancing figure derived from all the other amounts in the restated statement of financial position. [FRS 102 para 31.9].

31.20   At the end of the first period and in subsequent periods, all components of shareholders' equity are restated by applying a general price index from the beginning of the period (or the date of contribution, if later). The movements for the period are disclosed in the statement of changes in equity (see chapter 6). [FRS 102 para 31.10]. In addition, dividends paid during the period should be restated from the date at which the shareholders' right to receive payment is established.

Restatement of comprehensive income

31.21   The principle described above (that is, all amounts in the financial statements of an entity whose functional currency is the currency of a hyper-inflationary economy should be stated in terms of the measuring unit current at the end of the reporting period) also applies to the statement of comprehensive income. All items in the statement of comprehensive income, including the income statement if presented separately, should be restated by applying the change in the general price index (identified in para 31.6 above) from the dates when the items of income and expense were originally recorded to the end of the reporting period. [FRS 102 para 31.11].

31.22   It is often not practical to restate individual items, so average indices can be used as approximations, provided items of income and expense arise evenly throughout the period and general inflation is approximately even throughout the period. [FRS 102 para 31.11]. In periods of unstable inflation or where there have been seasonal fluctuations influencing comprehensive income, quarterly or monthly indices would be more appropriate. Significant one-off transactions should be dealt with in isolation.

Restatement of statement of cash flows

31.23 Similar to the statement of comprehensive income, all items in the statement of cash flows should be stated in terms of the measuring unit current at the reporting date. [FRS 102 para 31.12]. So, all items in the statement of cash flows are restated by applying the same approach as that adopted for items in the statement of comprehensive income (see para 31.21 onwards above).

31.24 The preparation of a statement of cash flows under section 31 of the standard presents some challenges. All activity should be presented in terms of current purchasing power, but readers of the financial statements must also be able to follow cash flows between the restated statements of financial position and comprehensive income. So, it is useful to disclose the amount of the monetary gain or loss in the year, to enable users of the financial statements to reconcile cash flows to the movements in balance sheet items.

Gain or loss on net monetary position

31.25 One of the main objectives of section 31 of FRS 102 is to account for the financial gain or loss that arises from holding monetary assets or liabilities during a reporting period (the monetary gain or loss). In a period of inflation, an entity holding an excess of monetary assets over monetary liabilities loses purchasing power, and an entity with an excess of monetary liabilities over monetary assets gains purchasing power. So an entity should include in profit or loss any gain or loss arising on its net monetary position. [FRS 102 para 31.13].

31.26 Section 31 does not set out how the monetary gain or loss is calculated. There are two possible methodologies:

■ All monetary assets and liabilities (net monetary position) held during the year are represented in the financial statements, either by non-monetary assets and liabilities recorded in the statement of financial position or by transactions recorded in comprehensive income or directly in equity. The monetary gain or loss can be calculated as the difference resulting from the restatements described in this chapter of non-monetary items, shareholders' equity, items in the statement of comprehensive income and the adjustment of index-linked items to year end purchasing power and comparing the restated values to the historical cost amounts.

■ It is also possible to calculate the gain or loss on the entity's daily net monetary position. But the costs of such a calculation might well be onerous. An approximation of the monetary gain or loss can be made by applying the change in a general price index to the weighted average for the period of the difference between monetary assets and monetary liabilities. This could be done as a test of the reasonableness of the monetary gain or loss derived by restating non-monetary assets and liabilities.

31.27 Whichever method is adopted, an entity should offset the adjustment to assets and liabilities linked to changes in prices described in paragraph 31.14 above against the gain or loss on net monetary position. [FRS 102 para 31.13].

Calculation and proof

31.28 Calculation and proof of the monetary gain or loss that arises on the carrying amounts of monetary assets and liabilities is an important element of applying section 31 of the standard. Restatement in accordance with section 31 requires the application of certain procedures and judgement. So it is necessary to verify that the results are reasonable; the proof might well reveal restatement errors. The monetary gain or loss can be estimated by applying the change in a general price index to the weighted average difference between monetary assets and monetary liabilities. The weighted average of the opening monetary position, and of the monetary position at year end, can be used for the purpose of this calculation. But it is possible for a large difference to arise between the monetary gain or loss in the comprehensive income and income statement, on the one hand, and the estimate as calculated by the proof, on the other, if the monetary position has not been relatively constant throughout the year.

31.29 If the monetary position is changing significantly, a more accurate proof of the monetary gain or loss can be obtained by using the quarterly or monthly weighted average monetary position.

31.30 A simple example with a constant monetary position is set out below. It would be appropriate to use the weighted average of the opening and closing monetary position in this example.

> **Example – Proof – statement of source and application of net monetary assets and liabilities method**
>
> A statement of source and application of net monetary assets or liabilities is often prepared as an alternative proof of the net monetary gain or loss. The items that cause changes in the monetary assets or liabilities are analysed, and the net balance of the monetary assets or liabilities is initially determined as if there were no changes before being adjusted for current year movements. Restatements are performed, and the comparison with the actual net balance and movements of monetary assets or liabilities enables the monetary gain or loss to be approximated.

Conversion factor 1.649 for the year	Opening position currency units	Inflation adjustment	Closing position currency units at end of reporting period
	C	C	C
Statement of financial position:			
– cash	10,000	–	10,000
– share capital	10,000	6,490	16,490
– retained earnings	–	(6,490)	(6,490)
Comprehensive income and income statement:			
– monetary loss		(6,490)	(6,490)

Monetary loss proof:

Average monetary position for the year (C10,000 + C10,000)/2	C10,000
Change in inflation factor (1.649 – 1.000)	0.649
Monetary loss estimated for the year	C6,490

31.31 The procedures needed to prepare a statement of source and application of net monetary assets and liabilities are as follows:

Historical column

1   Calculate the net monetary position at the beginning of the period under restatement.

2   Identify all items that caused changes in the monetary position during the period. These should be the actual or uninflated changes in the monetary position. These items can be obtained from the historical cost statements of comprehensive income and cash flow.

3   Arrive at the monetary position at the end of the period by adding or subtracting the changes as identified. Check that the monetary position as calculated is equal to the actual monetary position at the end of the period.

Restated column

4   Calculate the net monetary position at the beginning of the period (as in step 1 above), but restate it for inflation for the entire period. The inflation adjustment restates the opening monetary position as if there was no monetary gain or loss (that is, by adjusting the opening monetary position as if the opening monetary assets and liabilities were not eroded as a result of inflation).

5   Inflate the changes in the monetary position (as in step 2 above). Adjusting the changes in monetary position for inflation restates the monetary changes as if the monetary assets and liabilities obtained or disposed of during the period were not eroded as a result of inflation. These items could be obtained from the inflation-adjusted statements of comprehensive income and cash flow.

6   Determine the net monetary position restated at the period end as if inflation had not affected the monetary assets and liabilities. Note that the real monetary position does not change as a result of the inflation adjustment.

Proof

7   Compare the actual net monetary position at the end of the period included in the 'historical' column with the restated net monetary position at the end of the period in the 'restated' column. The difference between the actual position and the restated monetary position is the estimate of the monetary gain or loss. This estimate should be compared to the actual gain or loss in the statement of comprehensive income.

A simple example is set out below. In this example, the inflation factor was 1.650 and there were two types of transaction that occurred evenly throughout the period.

Example – Calculation of monetary gain or loss

	Opening position	Closing position	Inflation adjustments	Closing position at period end purchasing power
Statement of financial position				
– cash	100	100	–	100
– trade receivables	–	200	–	200
	100	300		300
– trade payables	–	100	–	100
– share capital	100	100	65	165
– current profit	–	100	(65)	35
	100	300		300
Comprehensive income and income statement				
– credit sales		200	60	260
– cost of sales		(100)	(30)	(130)
– monetary loss*		–	(95)	(95)
– profit		100	(65)	35

*Monetary loss is calculated as follows:

Monetary loss from sales	60
Monetary gain from cost of sales	(30)
Restatement of share capital	65
	95

31009

Monetary loss proof – statement of source and application of net monetary assets and liabilities

	Historical	Restated
	C	C
Net monetary asset at the beginning of the period	100	165
Add movement in receivables	200	260
Deduct movement in payables	(100)	(130)
	200	295

The monetary loss is C95 (C200 — C295)

31.32 The proof of the monetary gain or loss might be more challenging if adjustments to those monetary items that are linked to the inflation index are offset against the monetary gain or loss (as described in para 31.27 above).

Group reporting

31.33 A foreign subsidiary operating in a hyper-inflationary economy might be required, for group purposes, to report to its overseas parent in a stable currency, usually the group's presentation currency. Section 30 of FRS 102 requires the foreign subsidiary to restate its local currency financial statements in accordance with section 31 before translation into the group's presentation currency. This would include restating goodwill and any fair value adjustments to the carrying amounts of assets and liabilities arising on acquisition.

Example – Restatement of goodwill

Goodwill is a non-monetary item. The carrying value of goodwill should be restated by applying the change in the general price index from the beginning of the period (or the date of acquisition, if later) to the end of the reporting period.

There is no explicit guidance on how to treat the credit to the goodwill uplift, as it is outside the local financial statements of the subsidiary. We consider that it is acceptable to recognise the credit in equity instead of comprehensive income (monetary gain or loss). This can be based on the argument that, if the goodwill was pushed down to the subsidiary's financial statements, the credit would go to equity. The non-monetary gain or loss would be offset by the uplift of goodwill and the corresponding equity item. It would also be supportable because it does not contribute to any changes in the monetary position of the subsidiary.

Economies that cease to be hyper-inflationary

31.34 Judgement should be applied to determine when an economy ceases to be hyper-inflationary. A number of qualitative and quantitative indicators should be considered (for example, stabilisation of price levels and increased preference to keep wealth in the local currency rather than stable foreign currency or non-monetary assets). Although there is a clear indication where the quantitative measure of cumulative three-year inflation falls below 100%, other qualitative factors might indicate that the price stabilisation is only temporary, and so the country is not out of hyper-inflation (that is, overall economic trends and developments should be taken into account). It is not beneficial for an entity's financial reporting to go into and out of hyper-inflation within a short period of time.

31.35   An entity should cease applying section 31 at the end of the reporting period that immediately precedes the period in which hyper-inflation ceases. The amounts in the financial statements as at that date should be considered as the carrying amounts for the subsequent financial statements (that is, those restated amounts should be the cost bases of the non-monetary items in later financial statements). [FRS 102 para 31.14].

31.36   If, for example, a country moves out of hyper-inflation at 31 October 20X2, an entity's last financial statements for the year ended 31 December 20X1 would be used to derive cost bases for non-monetary items at the end of any reporting period on or after 1 November 20X2. The effects of hyper-inflation for the period of 10 months from 1 January 20X2 to 31 October 20X2 are ignored. But the inflation in the last period before moving out of hyper-inflation should be less significant, because the decrease in inflation reflects one of the reasons for an economy ceasing to be hyper-inflationary.

31.37   An entity might have presented interim reports before the country moves out of hyper-inflation. These interim reports should not be subsequently amended to exclude the hyper-inflationary restatement. An entity should consider the closing date of the last interim report as the 'end of the previous reporting period' for the purpose of deriving the cost bases for non-monetary items at the end of later reporting periods in post-hyper-inflationary periods.

Disclosures

31.38   An entity should disclose the following:

- The fact that the financial statements and other prior period data have been restated for changes in the general purchasing power of the functional currency.

- The identity and level of the price index at the reporting date and changes during the current and previous reporting periods.

- The amount of gain or loss on monetary items.

[FRS 102 para 31.15].

Transitional issues

31.39   Old UK GAAP included two sources of guidance on accounting for the effects of hyper-inflation. Entities that adopted the 'new' financial instruments standards (equivalent to IFRS) were required to apply FRS 24, which was substantially the same as section 31 of FRS 102. So, no significant change is expected for these entities.

31.40 Entities using the 'old' financial instruments guidance in SSAP 20 and FRS 4 would follow the guidance in UITF 9. UITF 9 permitted a choice of methods: the first was to restate financial statements for the impact of price changes; and the second was to adopt a stable currency for reporting. Section 31 of FRS 102 allows only the first of these approaches, and so entities applying the second approach under UITF 9 might find that there are some changes on adoption of FRS 102.

Chapter 32

Events after the end of the reporting period

Chapter 32

Events after the end of the reporting period

Scope

32.1   This chapter considers the requirements of section 32 of FRS 102, which sets out principles for recognising, measuring and disclosing events after the end of the reporting period.

32.2   Events after the end of the reporting period are all those events, favourable and unfavourable, that occur between the end of the reporting period and the date when the financial statements are authorised for issue. This is the case even when the events occur between the public announcement of profit or loss (or other selected financial information) and the date when the financial statements are authorised for issue. [FRS 102 paras 32.2-32.3].

32.3   Section 32 of the standard distinguishes between those events that require changes in the amounts to be included in the financial statements ('adjusting events') and those events that require only disclosure ('non-adjusting events') in the notes to the financial statements. The classification of an event as 'adjusting' or 'non-adjusting' depends on whether the additional information it presents relates to conditions already existing at the reporting date (that is, the balance sheet date) or to conditions that arose after the reporting date. [FRS 102 para 32.2(a), (b)].

Adjusting events after the end of the reporting period

32.4   An adjusting event after the end of the reporting period ('adjusting event') is one that provides evidence of conditions that existed at the end of the reporting period. [FRS 102 para 32.2(a)]. FRS 102 requires an entity to adjust the amounts recognised in the financial statements, including related disclosures, to reflect adjusting events. [FRS 102 para 32.4].

32.5   Examples of adjusting events are given in FRS 102 and include:

- The settlement of a court case after the balance sheet date (that is, the 'reporting date') that confirms that the entity had a present obligation at that date. The entity adjusts any existing provision for the obligation or creates a new provision. Provisions in relation to court cases are considered in chapter 21. Favourable settlements in court cases are considered in paragraph 32.16.

- The receipt of information after the balance sheet date that indicates that an asset was impaired as at that date or that the amount of a previously recognised impairment loss needs to be adjusted; for example, the bankruptcy of a customer that occurs after the balance sheet date or the sale of inventories after the balance sheet date that gives evidence about their net realisable value at that date.

- The determination after the balance sheet date of the consideration for assets sold or purchased before that date.

- The determination after the balance sheet date of profit-sharing or bonus arrangements, if the entity had an obligation to make such payments as a result of events that occurred before that date.

- The discovery of fraud or errors that show that the financial statements are incorrect.

[FRS 102 para 32.5].

Assets sold before the year end

32.6 Whether the sale of an item of property, plant and equipment is recognised in the financial statements will depend on whether the sale is conditional or unconditional at the balance sheet date. For example, where a property is being sold, the sale completion might be *conditional* on the grant of planning permission. In such a case, where that permission is granted after the balance sheet date, the sale is not recognised at that date. This is because there is no existing condition at the balance sheet date for which the grant of planning permission provides additional evidence.

32.7 On the other hand, where the property is *sold unconditionally* before the balance sheet date, and only the amount of the consideration depends on whether planning permission is obtained, the sale is recognised. In such a situation, the potential for planning permission would be taken into account in determining the fair value of the receivable at the balance sheet date in accordance with section 12 of the standard. Any adjustment to the receivable's value resulting from the granting or refusal of planning permission after the balance sheet date is a non-adjusting event.

Information that indicates impairment or provides evidence of net realisable value

32.8 An entity should consider recording an impairment loss if it becomes aware after the balance sheet date of conditions that existed at that date. Whilst a restructuring and discontinuance of operations by sale or closure occurring after the balance sheet date are not in themselves adjusting events, they might have been prompted by a downturn in profitability. This might mean that the carrying amounts of the entity's assets at the balance sheet date are not fully supported by the amounts to be recovered through the use or sale of those assets.

Example 1 – Impairment of trade receivables

A customer's insolvency after the year end normally provides evidence that, at the balance sheet date, receivables due from that customer were impaired, because the customer was unable to pay. This type of event is typically treated as an adjusting event, because it is unusual (although not impossible) for a customer's business to fail only as a result of events occurring after the balance sheet date and before approval of the financial statements.

Example 2 – Destruction of an asset

Destruction or expropriation of an asset after the balance sheet date represents a new impairment indicator arising after that date that is a non-adjusting event. The event is not indicative of a condition existing at the balance sheet date. But management should disclose the nature of such an event and an estimate of its financial effect (see para 32.17).

32.9 Market deterioration is not defined by a specific event, but occurs gradually over time. Where such a decline occurs after the balance sheet date, it is not an adjusting event. Provided the budgets on which any impairment review was based (1) were in existence at the balance sheet date, (2) represented management's best estimate of the future outlook at that time, and (3) were based on reasonable and supportable assumptions (in view of market conditions), no impairment loss would be recorded as a result of the post-balance sheet date decline.

32.10 Impairments of current assets that become evident as a result of events after the end of the reporting period are usually fairly straightforward to identify and quantify; this is because they are generally the direct result of a debtor's insolvency or the sale of inventory. Where either a current or a fixed asset is sold at a loss or revalued downwards after the balance sheet date, this could provide additional evidence of a diminution in value that existed at the balance sheet date and would indicate that an impairment review should be carried out in accordance with section 27 of FRS 102 (see chapter 27).

Example 1 – Impairment of inventory

An entity supplies parts to a car manufacturer in respect of a particular model of car. At the balance sheet date the entity has a high level of inventory of parts due to low order levels. After the balance sheet date, the car manufacturer announces that the specific model will no longer be produced. There is no alternative market for the inventory. Does the subsequent event trigger a write-down of inventory to net realisable value?

Estimates of net realisable value are based on the most reliable evidence available when the estimates are made. These estimates consider fluctuations of price or cost directly relating to events occurring after the end of the period to the extent that such events confirm conditions existing at the end of the period.

The inventory should be written down to net realisable value. The high inventory levels indicated slow demand from the manufacturer. The announcement after the balance sheet date confirmed the over-supply at year end.

If, on the other hand, the level of inventory was appropriate for the order levels being achieved up to the balance sheet date, the post-balance sheet car manufacturer's announcement is a non-adjusting event and the inventory is not written down.

Example 2 – Impairment of properties

After the balance sheet date and the approval of the financial statements, a company in trading difficulties obtained an external valuation of its properties for the purpose of providing additional security to its bankers. In view of its trading difficulties, the company is also considering selling some properties to generate cash. The amount shown by the valuation is materially lower than the historical cost carrying amount attributed to the properties in the balance sheet. How should this be reflected in the financial statements?

In absence of any particular events after the balance sheet date that would have caused a decline in the properties' value, we consider that the external valuation is an indicator of impairment that had occurred before the balance sheet date. An impairment review should be carried out in accordance with section 27 of FRS 102. A provision to write down each property would be made at the balance sheet date if the carrying value at that date is more than the recoverable amount of the properties (see chapter 27).

Fraud, error and other irregularities

32.11 Internal fraud, error and other irregularities that occur before the balance sheet date, but that are only identified after that date, are adjusting events. This type of adjusting event sometimes gives rise to uncertainties about the entity's ability to continue its operations. Often, the consequences of failures in internal controls extend back to earlier years, necessitating not only adjustments to the current year figures, but also a prior year adjustment (see chapter 10).

Going concern

32.12 When preparing financial statements, management is required to assess the entity's ability to continue as a going concern. [FRS 102 para 3.8]. Where management either intends to liquidate the entity or cease trading, or has no realistic alternative but to do so, it should not prepare the entity's financial statements on a going concern basis. Section 32 of the standard makes it clear that, where management determines *after the balance sheet date* that the entity is not a going concern, the financial statements are not prepared on a going concern basis. [FRS 102 para 32.7A].

32.13 It might be that management believed at the balance sheet date that the entity was a going concern, but deterioration in operating results and financial position after that date brings that assessment into question. [FRS 102 para 32.7B]. If management determines that the entity is not a going concern, it prepares the financial statements on a break up basis, disclosing the basis of accounting and the reason why the entity is not regarded as a going concern. If management determines that the entity is a going concern, it prepares the financial statements on a going concern basis, but discloses the material uncertainties that cast doubt on the entity's ability to continue as a going concern. [FRS 102 para 3.9].

Non-adjusting events

32.14 Adjustments to amounts recognised in the financial statements are not made for non-adjusting events after the end of the reporting period. [FRS 102 para 32.6]. A non-adjusting event is an event that arises after the balance sheet date concerning conditions that did not exist at that time. [FRS 102 para 32.2(b)]. Examples of non-adjusting events are given in paragraphs 32.15, 32.16 and 32.18.

Decline in market value of investments

32.15 A decline in the market value of investments after the balance sheet date is a non-adjusting event. The amounts included in the financial statements (and related notes) in respect of such investments are not adjusted; this is because the decline normally relates to circumstances that have arisen after the balance sheet date. Disclosure of the decline in the market value of the investments might be required under paragraph 32.10 of the standard (see para 32.18). [FRS 102 para 32.7(a)].

Favourable judgement in a court case

32.16 A favourable judgement or settlement in a court case might be obtained after the balance sheet date in respect of loss or damage incurred before that date. In this situation, under section 21 of the standard, an asset is not recognised because an inflow of economic benefits is not virtually certain at the balance sheet date; the amount receivable is a contingent asset that is disclosed if, at the balance sheet date, its receipt is considered probable. Only when the final judgement is obtained should the asset be recognised. Where a judgement is obtained before the balance sheet date but a receivable is not recognised because it could not be measured reliably, agreement of the amount of damages to be received might be an adjusting event. [FRS 102 para 32.7(b)].

Disclosure of non-adjusting events

32.17 For each category of non-adjusting event, the entity discloses the nature of the event and an estimate of its financial effect. Where it is not possible to make an estimate of the event's financial effect, that fact must be disclosed. [FRS 102 para 32.10].

32.18 The standard lists the following as examples of non-adjusting events after the end of the reporting period that would generally result in disclosure:

- A major business combination or disposal of a major subsidiary.

- Announcing a plan to discontinue an operation.

- Major purchases of assets, disposals or plans to dispose of assets, or expropriation of major assets by government.

- The destruction of a major production plant by fire.

- Announcing, or commencing the implementation of, a major restructuring.

- Issues or repurchases of an entity's debt or equity instruments.

- Abnormally large changes in asset prices or foreign exchange rates.

- Changes in tax rates or tax laws enacted or announced that have a significant effect on current and deferred tax assets and liabilities.

- Entering into significant commitments or contingent liabilities (for example, by issuing significant guarantees).

- Commencing major litigation arising solely out of events that occurred after the balance sheet date.

[FRS 102 para 32.11].

Acquisitions and disposals

32.19 Significant acquisitions and disposals that are made after the balance sheet date are examples of non-adjusting events that should be disclosed in financial statements.

32.20 Section 4 of FRS 102 requires specific disclosures in respect of assets held for disposal. If, at the balance sheet date, an entity has a binding sale agreement for a major disposal of assets, or a disposal group (see chapter 4), it discloses the following information:

- A description of the asset(s) or disposal group.

- A description of the facts and circumstances of the sale or plan.

- The carrying amount of the assets or, for a disposal group, the carrying amounts of the underlying assets and liabilities.

[FRS 102 para 4.14].

Major restructuring

32.21 As noted in paragraph 32.8, a restructuring might be undertaken after the balance sheet date in response to a decline in financial performance that occurred before that date. Any related impairment loss is recognised in the financial statements; and, in that sense, the restructuring is an event that provides evidence of conditions existing at the balance sheet date and is an adjusting event. But, under section 21 of the standard, a provision is not made for future restructuring costs until a legal or constructive obligation to restructure arises. Where an entity commences a restructuring after the balance sheet date but before the approval of the financial statements, disclosure of the restructuring is required.

Changes in foreign exchange rates or asset prices

32.22 Changes in currency exchange rates or in asset prices occurring after the balance sheet date do not normally reflect the conditions at that date, because the recoverable amount at the balance sheet date was defined by the market (that is, by knowledgeable and willing participants).

> **Example – Movement in foreign exchange rates**
>
> An adverse movement on the foreign exchange rate after year end has resulted in exchange differences arising on the retranslation of the bank overdraft that exceed the profit for the period under review. How should this be reflected in the financial statements?
>
> Exchange rate changes are included in the list of non-adjusting events set out in paragraph 32.11 of FRS 102. Although the bank overdraft existed at the balance sheet date, the conditions that gave rise to the loss did not. The exchange rate fluctuation occurred after the balance sheet date. So, no adjustment is made in the financial statements for the effect of the exchange rate fluctuations. But the exchange rate fluctuations and a quantification of their financial effect should be disclosed in the notes to financial statements.

Changes in tax rates

32.23 Proposed or expected changes in tax laws and rates are not reflected in the financial statements, unless they have been enacted or substantively enacted by the balance sheet date (see chapter 29). [FRS 102 para 29.12]. But section 32 of the standard requires disclosure of changes in the tax laws and rates enacted or announced after the balance sheet date that have a significant effect on current or deferred tax.

> **Example – Announcement of change in tax rates**
>
> An entity has deferred tax assets recognised in the balance sheet at 31 December 20X1 in respect of unused tax losses that can be used to reduce taxable income in future years. The income tax rate used to calculate the deferred tax asset was 40%, which was the current rate of tax applicable at the balance sheet date. In January 20X2, legislation announced in December 20X1 was passed such that, on 17 January 20X2, the income tax rate was reduced to 33% with immediate effect.
>
> The change in the income tax rate was announced before, but enacted after, the balance sheet date; so it is a non-adjusting event. Management should not adjust the amounts recognised in its financial statements because of this event.

> If the effect of the new tax rate on the deferred tax asset will be material, management should disclose details of the change in income tax rate (and its related effects on the entity) in the notes to the financial statements. Where applicable, the disclosure should consider the impact on the different performance statements (see para 32.24).

32.24 It is necessary to consider whether the accounting impact of a change in tax rates will be reflected in profit or loss, in other comprehensive income or in the statement of changes in equity. Section 29 of FRS 102 requires tax expense to be recognised in the same component of total comprehensive income (that is, continuing operations, discontinued operations, or other comprehensive income) or equity as the transaction or other event that resulted in the tax expense. This applies to changes in deferred tax resulting from a change in tax rates. So, where the impact is likely to be material for the purpose of disclosing the non-adjusting event, entities will need to consider how the transactions that gave rise to deferred tax were accounted for and trace the impact of the change in tax rate to the same place. Backwards tracing of adjustments to deferred tax is considered further in chapter 29.

Dividends payable and receivable

32.25 Dividends on equity instruments can be considered under the following categories:

- Dividends declared and paid in a reporting period. These dividends are recognised in that reporting period.

- Interim dividends announced by the directors but unpaid at the balance sheet date. These dividends are not a liability at the balance sheet date because the directors retain the discretion to cancel interim dividends until they are paid (see para 32.28).

- Final dividends proposed by the directors but not declared (see para 32.26). These are not recognised as a liability until they are declared.

- Final dividends declared before, but paid after, the balance sheet date. These are recognised as a liability at the balance sheet date.

- Final dividends declared after the balance sheet date (see para 32.26). Dividends declared after the balance sheet date are not recognised as a liability at the balance sheet date.

[FRS 102 para 32.8].

32.26 Final dividends proposed by directors are not a liability of the company until they are declared; dividends are declared by the company in general meeting or by the members passing a written resolution. Final dividends should be recognised as a liability in the period in which they are declared (that is, when they are no longer at the entity's discretion). They remain as liabilities until they are paid or waived by the shareholders. In practice, final dividends are usually proposed by the directors after the balance sheet date for declaration by the company at the annual general meeting at a date even further removed from the balance sheet date. If directors propose a final dividend before the balance sheet date, its declaration would not happen until the next general meeting. Even where an entity has a history of paying dividends, this does not give rise to a liability at the balance sheet date.

32.27 The accounting treatment reflects the legal status of dividends under the Companies Act 2006. The legal position is set out in ICAEW Tech Release 02/10, 'Guidance on the determination of realised profits and losses in the context of distributions under the Companies Act 2006'. In particular, paragraph 2.10 of Tech 02/10 states that:

> *"A distribution is made when it becomes a legally binding liability of the company, regardless of the date on which it is to be settled. In the case of a final dividend, this will be when it is declared by the company in general meeting or, for private companies, by the members passing a written resolution. In the case of an interim dividend authorised under common articles of association (eg 1985 Act Table A), normally no legally binding liability is established prior to payment being made of the dividend ..."*

32.28 The standard articles of association (Table A) stipulate that, subject to the provisions of the Companies Act 2006, directors are permitted to declare and pay interim dividends without shareholders' authorisation at a general meeting. As stated in paragraph 2.10 of Tech 02/10, an interim dividend declared by directors only becomes a liability when it is paid. This is because their resolution is not irrevocable. The directors have discretion over whether the interim dividend is paid (that is, the directors are able to reverse their resolution to pay an interim dividend at any time up to the date of payment).

32.29 Under their common law duties, directors have to be able to revoke their resolution because they must test for sufficient distributable profits at both the date of declaration and the date of payment. The distributable profits might be sufficient at the first date but, if by the latter date they have been eroded by subsequent losses, the dividend must not be paid. [Tech 02/10 paras 2.1 to 2.3]. For example, if an interim dividend is declared by the directors on 4 May and is payable on 4 July, but profits available for distribution are insufficient at the date of payment (4 July), the dividend will not be paid and will not be recognised as a liability at either date. However, where the dividend is a final dividend, declared by the company in general meeting on 4 May and payable on 4 July, but profits available for distribution are insufficient at the date of payment, the dividend will not be paid; but it will remain as a liability of the company until sufficient profits are available for distribution to allow it to be paid, or until it is waived by the shareholders.

32.30 In the same way that dividends declared after the balance sheet date are not recognised by the paying company at that date because they do not meet the definition of a liability, the recipient of such dividends does not recognise them as an asset and, consequently, as income at the balance sheet date. Dividends receivable are recognised when the shareholder's right to receive payment is established. [FRS 102 para 23.29(c)]. This principle is consistent with paragraph 9.7 of Tech 02/10 which states:

> "A dividend will be accrued as receivable by a parent company only when the subsidiary has a legally binding obligation to make the distribution."

Where a parent company depends on dividends from its subsidiaries to create distributable profits to support its own dividends to shareholders, it will be vital that the subsidiaries' dividends are declared before the balance sheet date.

32.31 Disclosure of dividends is considered in chapter 6.

Date of authorisation of the financial statements for issue

32.32 FRS 102 requires an entity to disclose the date on which the financial statements were authorised for issue and who gave that authorisation. [FRS 102 para 32.9]. The disclosure of the date of authorisation informs users that the financial statements do not reflect events after that date. If the board authorises the financial statements for issue, section 32 of the standard requires the financial statements to disclose that the board (or similar body for unincorporated entities) gave the authorisation. The standard also requires that, if the entity's owners or other parties have the power to amend the financial statements after issue, that fact should be disclosed. [FRS 102 para 32.9].

32.33 The Companies Act 2006 permits a company's directors to prepare revised annual financial statements where it appears to them that its previously approved financial statements did not comply with the Act. The Secretary of State, or a person authorised by the Secretary of State (such as the FRRP), can apply to the court for an order that revised financial statements should be prepared. [CA06 Sec 454]. Companies seldom prepare revised financial statements voluntarily; corrections are usually dealt with in the current period financial statements through prior period adjustments (see chapter 10). SI 2008/373, 'The Companies (Revision of Defective Accounts and Reports) Regulations 2008' sets out the detailed rules applying to the preparation of revised financial statements. These regulations require the revised financial statements to be prepared as if they were prepared and approved by the directors as at the date of approval of the original financial statements; this basis of preparation must be stated in the revised financial statements. As a result, events that take place between the date of approval of the original financial statements and the date of approval of the revised financial statements are not reflected in the measurement or disclosure of items in the revised financial statements.

Transitional issues

32.34 No special exemptions in respect of events after the end of the reporting period are available to first-time adopters under section 35 of FRS 102. So, a first-time adopter must prepare its first financial statements as though the requirements of section 32 of FRS 102 had always applied.

32.35 Entities transitioning from old UK GAAP (FRS 21), 'Events after the balance sheet date,' to FRS 102 are unlikely to face any significant issues on transition. This is because there are no differences in substance between the requirements of old UK GAAP and those in section 32 of FRS 102.

32.36 An entity should not retrospectively change the accounting that it followed for accounting estimates under its previous financial reporting framework. [FRS 102 para 35.9(c)]. It might be that, between the date when the previous 'old UK GAAP' financial statements were approved and the date of signing the first FRS 102 financial statements, events occur that provide further evidence of conditions that existed at the previous balance sheet date or at the date of transition. No adjustments are made to the comparative financial statements in respect of such events; the comparative financial statements are presented on the basis of the information available when they were approved, and the adjustments are dealt with in the current period. Only if the previous estimates were incorrect as a result of an error in calculation (as opposed to a judgement which was later shown to be incorrect) is a retrospective adjustment made to the comparative information (see chapter 10).

Chapter 33

Related party disclosures

Chapter 33

Related party disclosures

Introduction

33.1 Related party transactions can take a variety of forms. Many of them include transactions in the normal course of business (for example, purchases or sales of goods at market values). But others include significant one-off transactions at a fair value on an arm's length basis or at book value or some other amount that differs from market prices. Section 33 of FRS 102 aims to ensure that financial statements contain the disclosures necessary to draw attention to the possibility that the reported financial position and results might have been affected by the existence of related parties and by transactions and outstanding balances with them. [FRS 102 para 33.1].

Scope

33.2 Section 33 of FRS 102 sets out how related party relationships, transactions and balances should be identified and what disclosures should be made. But transactions entered into between two or more members of a group do not need to be disclosed, provided that any subsidiary that is a party to the transaction is wholly owned by such a member. [FRS 102 para 33.1A]. Although the wording of this exemption is somewhat ambiguous, we believe that 'wholly owned by such a member' encompasses situations where 100% ownership is achieved indirectly. This is illustrated in the following examples.

> **Example 1 – 100% ownership achieved indirectly**
>
> Entity A has two wholly owned subsidiaries, entities B and C. Entity B owns 60% of entity D, while entity C owns 40% of entity D.

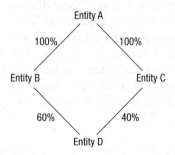

> FRS 102 does not require disclosure of transactions between entities A and B, A and C or B and C, given that entities B and C are wholly owned within entity A's group.

Indirectly (that is, through entities B and C), entity D is also 100% owned within entity A's group. So, the disclosure exemption in paragraph 33.1A of FRS 102 can be applied to transactions entered into between entity D and entities A, B and C.

Example 2 – 100% ownership achieved indirectly as part of a wider group

Entity E owns 100% of entity F. Entity F owns 80% of entity G, and the remaining 20% of entity G is held by entity E.

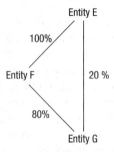

Entity E's financial statements

As explained in example 1 above, FRS 102 does not require disclosure of transactions between entities E and F, E and G or F and G, given that entities F and G are wholly owned within entity E's group.

Entity F's financial statements

In its financial statements, entity F could apply the exemption in paragraph 33.1A of FRS 102 in relation to transactions entered into with entity G. Entity G is 100% owned, indirectly, within entity E's group. We believe that the term 'group' in this situation can be taken to mean the wider E group (as opposed to only entity F's reporting group).

The exemption also applies to transactions between entities F and E, given that entity F is a wholly owned member within entity E's group.

33.3　While FRS 102 does not specify that balances between two or more wholly owned members of a group are exempt from disclosure, transactions are exempt; so we believe that, by implication, balances are also exempt. The exemption also covers parent entities, provided the subsidiaries with which they have transacted are wholly owned. But specified information regarding balances with group members needs to be provided, because the Companies Act's balance sheet formats require the disclosure of amounts owed by and to group undertakings. The disclosure of control of the reporting entity is also required (see para 33.46 below).

33.4　FRS 102 requires transactions between a reporting entity and its related parties to be disclosed in the reporting entity's financial statements. Where an entity is preparing its separate financial statements, it will be the reporting entity. But, where a parent entity is preparing consolidated financial statements, the reporting entity will be the group headed by the parent entity. It follows that transactions and balances between group entities that are eliminated on consolidation are not transactions and balances with the 'group reporting entity', and so those items are not disclosed in the consolidated financial statements.

Related parties

33.5   A related party can be a person, an entity or an unincorporated business. The standard's definition is in two parts. The first part of the definition identifies criteria that result in a *person,* or a close member of that person's family, being a related party of the reporting entity (see para 33.6 onwards). The second part of the definition identifies conditions that result in an *entity* being related to the reporting entity (see para 33.17 onwards).

Relationships with persons

33.6   A person, or a close member of that person's family (see further para 33.14 onwards), is a related party of the reporting entity if that person:

- has control or joint control over the reporting entity;

- has significant influence over the reporting entity; or

- is a member of the key management personnel of the reporting entity or of a parent of the reporting entity.

[FRS 102 para 33.2(a)].

33.7   The criteria for persons involve the application of the terms 'control', 'joint control' and 'significant influence'. Such terms are familiar, because they are used elsewhere in FRS 102 in relation to consolidated financial statements (see chapter 9), joint ventures (see chapter 15) and associates (see chapter 14). Further guidance on how to determine whether an entity is subject to control, joint control or significant influence is included in the chapters referenced above. But, in the context of section 33 of FRS 102, an entity could be subject to the control, joint control or significant influence of a person as well as of another entity.

Key management personnel

33.8   A member of the key management personnel of an entity or of a parent of the reporting entity, as well as a close member of that person's family, is a related party of the entity. The term 'key management personnel' is defined in FRS 102 as *"those persons having authority and responsibility for planning, directing and controlling the activities of the entity, directly or indirectly, including any director (whether executive or otherwise) of that entity"*. [FRS 102 para 33.6; Glossary of terms].

33.9   The definition clearly includes directors, and the term 'or otherwise' is intended to cover non-executive directors and supervisory boards, as well as those who have responsibility for the management and direction of a significant part of the business without holding the title 'director'.

33.10 In the UK, directors can be of three kinds: de jure directors (that is, executive or non-executive directors who have been validly appointed); de facto directors (that is, directors who act as directors without having been appointed validly or at all); and shadow directors. A shadow director is defined as a person in accordance with whose directions or instructions the directors of a company are accustomed to act. [CA06 Sec 251].

33.11 Apart from directors, the term 'key management personnel' includes people who are not appointed directors, but whose activities encompass duties normally carried out by directors. For example, where management commentary refers to managers by name, entities should consider whether this indicates that they are key managers.

33.12 As a reporting entity can be a group as well as a separate entity, key management personnel must also be considered in relation to directing or controlling the group's resources. Whilst the term 'key management personnel' in the group context could include a divisional director or the director of a subsidiary, such a person would need to direct or control a major part of the group's activities and resources in order to be key management personnel of the group. The following examples illustrate situations where the persons included in the key management personnel disclosures might include persons who are not directors of the entity.

Example 1 – Divisional managers

An entity has two equal-sized operating divisions. Each of the operating divisions is headed by a 'divisional manager'. Neither divisional manager is a director of the entity, but each is responsible for an operating division and reports to the board of directors on its performance.

Although the divisional managers are not directors of the entity, they fall within the definition of 'key management personnel' in FRS 102, because they have authority and responsibility for planning, directing and controlling approximately half of the entity's activities.

Example 2 – Members of a management committee

A financial services entity has a board of directors that makes high-level decisions about the markets in which the entity operates. It delegates decisions about the products that should be offered within those markets, and the customers to whom those products should be marketed, to a management committee.

The management committee has authority for planning, directing and controlling the entity's activities, and so its members, together with the board of directors, are key management personnel.

Example 3 – Directors of subsidiaries as key management personnel of a group

A parent entity has three subsidiaries, and its main activity is to coordinate its subsidiaries' operations.

A director of a subsidiary is not automatically presumed to be a related party of the group. A subsidiary's director is a related party of the group if he is a member of the group's key management personnel (that is, he has authority for planning, directing and controlling a major part of the group's activities). Because this group has three subsidiaries, the significance of each subsidiary for the group would need to be considered.

33.13 The term 'key management personnel' also includes people who have responsibilities for the administration or direction of reporting entities, such as trusts, which are not incorporated.

Close family members

33.14 Close family members of a person are defined in FRS 102 as those family members who could be expected to influence, or be influenced by, that person in their dealings with the entity, including:

■ The person's children and spouse or domestic partner.

■ Children of the person's spouse or domestic partner.

■ Dependants of the person or the person's spouse or domestic partner.

[FRS 102 Glossary of terms].

33.15 The term 'domestic partner' would encompass any person, whether of a different sex or the same sex, who lives with the member of key management personnel as a partner in an enduring family relationship. In relation to children, it is worth noting that step-children are included in the definition and that the examples do not restrict the definition to infant children (or step-children). Dependants include foster children and, where they are dependent on the person or the person's partner, could also include elderly and infirm parents, brothers, sisters, mothers-in-law or fathers-in-law, ex-partners receiving alimony, and even more distant relatives such as cousins.

33.16 The examples in the standard are not complete, because the wider definition of a close family member makes it clear that anyone who is a member of the family (whether blood-related or not) is potentially a close family member for the purposes of the standard. They will be close family members if they could be expected to influence, or be influenced by, the person in their dealings with the entity.

Relationships with other entities

33.17 FRS 102 identifies certain parties that are always treated as related parties. The following entities are related to each other:

- Members of the same group (which means that parents, subsidiaries and fellow subsidiaries are all related to each other).

- One entity is an associate or joint venture (including the associate or joint venture's subsidiaries) of the other entity or a member the other entity's group (see para 33.22 onwards).

- Two joint ventures of the same third party.

- A joint venture of a third party and an associate of that same third party (see para 33.22 onwards).

- Where a person (or close member of that person's family):

  - controls or jointly controls an entity;

  - has significant influence over the entity; or

  - is a member of that entity's (or the entity's parent's) key management personnel;

  that entity is a related party of another entity controlled or jointly controlled by the same person (or close member of that person's family) (see para 33.24 onwards).

- An entity and a post-employment benefit plan (such as a pension scheme) for the benefit of that entity's employees, or employees of any other entity related to the entity. If the reporting entity is itself such a plan, the sponsoring employers are also related parties of the plan.

[FRS 102 paras 33.2(b), 33.4A].

Parties that are not necessarily related

33.18 The following are not related parties of an entity:

- Two entities simply because they have a director or other member of key management personnel in common, or because a member of key management personnel of one entity has significant influence over the other entity.

- Two venturers simply because they share joint control over a joint venture.

- Any of the following simply by virtue of their normal dealings with an entity (even though they could affect the freedom of action of an entity or participate in its decision-making process):

  - Providers of finance.

- Trade unions.

- Public utilities.

- Government departments or agencies.

■ A customer, supplier, franchisor, distributor or general agent with whom an entity transacts a significant volume of business, simply by virtue of the resulting economic dependence.

[FRS 102 para 33.4].

Substance of the relationship

33.19 There is an important principle that, in considering each possible related party relationship, attention is directed to the substance of the relationship and not merely the legal form. [FRS 102 para 33.3].

33.20 For example, as set out above, FRS 102 states that two entities are not related parties simply because they have a director or other member of key management personnel in common. But the words 'simply by virtue' indicate that, even where two entities simply have a director in common, there is still a need to consider the possibility that the two entities might be related.

33.21 So, the standard places more emphasis on what actually happens in practice (that is, substance) than on the legal form of an arrangement. For example, if the director prevents one or both of the entities from pursuing its separate interests, the existence of the common director could mean that the director has control or significant influence over one or both of the entities; and, as such, the parties could be related.

Examples

Group situations – subsidiaries, joint ventures and associates

33.22 Where entity A has a subsidiary (entity B) and significant influence or joint control over another entity (entity C), entities A, B and C are related parties of one another. [FRS 102 para 33.2(b)(ii)]. Entities A and B would also be related parties of any subsidiary held by entity C. [FRS 102 para 33.4A]. This situation is illustrated in the following examples.

Example 1 – Control, significant influence or joint control from the same source

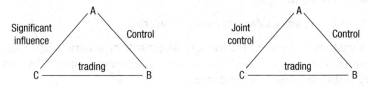

In each of the above scenarios:

- Entities A and B are related parties because they are members of the same group. [FRS 102 para 33.2(b)(i)].

- Entities A and C are related parties because C is A's associate or joint venture. [FRS 102 para 33.2(b)(ii)].

- Entities B and C are related parties because C is an associate or joint venture of a member of B's group. [FRS 102 para 33.2(b)(ii)].

Example 2 – Entity with joint control and significant influence

Entity H has joint control over entity J and significant influence over entity K:

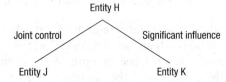

Entity H has a joint venture (entity J) and an associate (entity K). So, both entities J and K are entity H's related parties. [FRS 102 para 33.2(b)(ii)].

For the purposes of entity J's financial statements, entities H and K are entity J's related parties. [FRS 102 para 33.2(b)(ii), (iv)].

Similarly, for the purposes of entity K's financial statements, entities H and J are entity K's related parties. [FRS 102 para 33.2(b)(ii), (iv)].

Note that, if entity H had joint control, as opposed to significant influence, over entity K, similar principles would apply, and each entity within the structure shown would be related. [FRS 102 para 33.2(b)(ii), (iii)].

33.23   The standard is clear that a reporting entity's associates and joint ventures are its related parties. But the question arises whether a reporting entity is related to the related parties of its associate or joint venture. This is considered in the examples below.

Example 1 – Transactions with the related parties of an associate or joint venture

Entity A owns 30% of entity B's share capital and has the ability to exercise significant influence over it.

Entity B holds the following investments:

- 70% of the share capital of its subsidiary, entity C; and

- 30% of the share capital of entity D, with the ability to exercise significant influence.

The structure is illustrated as follows:

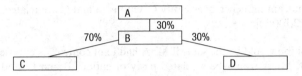

Entity C is a related party of entity A because entity C is the subsidiary of entity A's associate, entity B. [FRS 102 para 33.4A]. Entity C is also a related party of entity B because they are members of the same group. [FRS 102 para 33.2(b)(i)].

Entity D is a related party of entity B because entity D is entity B's associate. [FRS 102 para 33.2(b)(ii)]. But entity D is not a related party of entity A because entity A has no ability to exercise control or significant influence over entity D.

Example 2 – Transactions between different investors in a joint venture

Entity D is a related party of each of entities A, B and C because it is a joint venture of those entities. [FRS 102 para 33.2(b)(ii)]. Entity A sells goods to entity B, and entity C provides services to entity B:

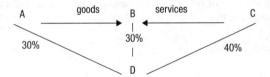

Entities A, B and C are related parties of entity D, but not necessarily related parties of each other. So, unless there is some other relationship between entities A, B and C (other than the fact that they are all investors in entity D) that would make them related parties, the transactions between entities A and B and between entities C and B would not be disclosable in any of the financial statements of entity A, B, C or D. (For example, if entities A, B and C were all fellow subsidiaries of another entity, they would be related parties of each other, but for a reason other than their investment in entity D.) [FRS 102 paras 33.2(b), 33.4(b)].

Entities in which related party persons have an interest

33.24   The following examples concern persons with control, joint control and/or significant influence over more than one entity.

Related party disclosures

Example 1 – Investor controls one entity and has significant influence over another

Mr A owns 70% of entity B and 30% of entity C:

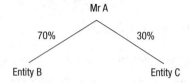

Mr A controls entity B and so is a related party of that entity. [FRS 102 para 33.2(a)(i)]. Mr A has significant influence over entity C and so is a related party of that entity. [FRS 102 para 33.2(a)(ii)]. Because Mr A has control over entity B and significant influence over entity C, entities B and C are related parties. [FRS 102 para 33.2(b)(vii)].

The position would be the same if Mr A had joint control, as opposed to control, over entity B. Mr A would be a related party of entities B and C, and entities B and C would be related parties of one another.

Example 2 – Investor has significant influence over two entities

Mr X owns 40% of entity Y and 25% of entity Z:

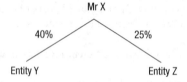

Mr X has significant influence over entities Y and Z, and so is a related party of both entities. [FRS 102 para 33.2(a)(ii)]. Entities Y and Z are not related to each other. Investees are not related simply because they are subject to significant influence from the same investor.

Key management personnel

33.25 The following examples concern key management personnel and their close family members.

Example 1 – Key management personnel

Mr A owns all of entity X's share capital. He is also a member of entity Y's key management personnel. Entity Y owns all of entity Z's share capital:

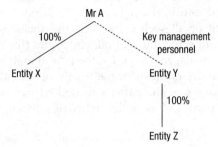

Entity Y is a related party of entity X because Mr A is a member of entity Y's key management personnel and he also controls entity X. [FRS 102 para 33.2(b)(vii)]. Entity Z is also a related party of entity X, given that Mr A is a member of the key management personnel of its parent (that is, entity Y). [FRS 102 para 33.2(b)(vii)].

Viewed from the perspective of entity Y, entities X and Z are related parties, given that Mr A (who is a member of entity Y's key management personnel) controls entity X, and entity Y itself controls entity Z. [FRS 102 paras 33.2(b)(vi), 33.2(b)(i)]. In addition, entity X is a related party of entity Z because Mr A controls entity X and he is also a member of entity Z's parent's key management personnel. [FRS 102 para 33.2(b)(vi)].

Example 2 – Close family members

Mr L controls entity M, and his spouse is Mrs L. Mrs L has significant influence over entity N:

In view of Mr L's control of entity M and Mrs L's significant influence over entity N, the two entities are related parties.

For the purposes of entity M's financial statements, a close family member of the person who controls entity M has significant influence over entity N. [FRS 102 paras 33.2(a)(i), 33.2(b)(vii)].

Similarly, for the purposes of entity N's financial statements, a close family member of a person who has significant influence over entity N controls entity M. [FRS 102 para 33.2(b)(vi)].

Post-employment benefit plans

33.26   Pension funds and similar post-employment arrangements for the benefit of employees of the entity, or of any entity that is a related party of the entity, are related parties of the entity. [FRS 102 para 33.2(b)(v)]. As well as applying to funds for the benefit of all such employees, this includes pension funds whose membership is open to some, but not all, employees (for instance, those open to directors and senior managers only). On the other hand, industry-wide and state pension schemes that are not just for the benefit of the entity's employees, or for the benefit of employees of the entity's related parties, would generally not be regarded as related parties of an entity under this definition.

33.27   In contrast, a pension fund that is operated for the benefit of employees in a group is a related party of each entity within the group whose employees participate in the fund. This is because the entities and the fund are subject to control and influence from the same source.

33.28   The fact that pension funds are related parties is not intended to call into question the independence of the trustees of the scheme. Transactions between the reporting entity and the pension fund might be in the interest of members, but they still need to be reported in the reporting entity's financial statements.

33.29   'Post-employment plans' is a broad term and is interpreted widely to include, for example, funds maintained by employers to pay pensions to employees disabled at work.

33.30   It should be noted that it is not just pension funds for the benefit of employees in group entities that are related parties of the reporting entity. Instead, pension funds and similar post-employment arrangements for the benefit of employees of any entity that is a related party of the entity are related parties of the entity.

33.31   If the reporting entity itself is a post-employment benefit plan, the sponsoring employers are also related to the reporting entity. [FRS 102 para 33.2(b)(v)].

Related party transactions

Definition of related party transactions

33.32   A 'related party transaction' is defined in FRS 102 as *"a transfer of resources, services or obligations between a reporting entity and a related party, regardless of whether a price is charged"*. [FRS 102 para 33.8].

33.33   FRS 102 gives the following examples of common related party transactions:

■   Transactions between an entity and its principal owners.

- Transactions between one entity and another controlled by the same person or entity.

- Transactions in which a controlling person or entity incurs expenses that the reporting entity would otherwise have borne.

[FRS 102 para 33.8].

33.34 The standard goes on to provide a list of transactions that must be disclosed by a reporting entity if they are with a related party:

- Purchases or sales of goods (finished or unfinished).

- Purchases or sales of property and other assets.

- Rendering or receiving of services.

- Leases.

- Transfers of research and development.

- Transfers under licence agreements.

- Transfers under finance arrangements (including loans and equity contributions in cash or in kind).

- Provision of guarantees or collateral.

- Settlement of liabilities on behalf of the entity or by the entity on behalf of another party.

- Participation by a parent or subsidiary in a defined benefit plan that shares risks between group entities (see chapter 28).

[FRS 102 para 33.12].

33.35 The above lists are not exhaustive, and it is our view that a number of other transactions, such as agency arrangements, should also be disclosed.

33.36 A common form of corporate reorganisation is for the business of a subsidiary to be transferred to the parent, but the subsidiary continues to invoice customers as agent for its parent. In such circumstances, it is important that the fact and details of the agency arrangement are disclosed in the financial statements of the individual entities involved (note that the transactions would be eliminated on consolidation, so disclosure in the consolidated financial statements would not be required), so that customers and others are aware of the role played by the subsidiary.

33.37 The definition of a related party transaction envisages that some related party transactions might not be entered into an entity's accounting records or might not involve the passing of any consideration. Examples of such transactions are:

- Management services provided by one entity to another free of charge.

- Goods manufactured under a patent owned by a fellow subsidiary which makes no charge.

- Guarantees given by directors.

- Rent-free accommodation or the loan of vehicles or other assets at no charge.

Materiality

33.38 As with other standards, the disclosure of related party transactions is required only if the transactions are material. The glossary to FRS 102 provides a definition of material: *"Omissions or misstatements of items are material if they could, individually or collectively, influence the economic decisions that users make on the basis of the financial statements. Materiality depends on the size and nature of the omission or misstatement judged in the surrounding circumstances. The size or nature of the item, or a combination of both, could be the determining factor"*.

33.39 In respect of disclosures, FRS 102 states: *"An entity need not provide a specific disclosure required by this FRS if the information is not material"*. [FRS 102 para 3.16A].

33.40 FRS 102 does not deal with a situation that arises with related party transactions, particularly where such transactions involve a person; the issue is that, even though the amount of a transaction might be immaterial to the entity, it might not be immaterial to the person; and so the question is whether materiality should be judged from the person's or the entity's perspective.

33.41 In a straightforward situation, it might be clear that a transaction is immaterial to both the person and the entity, but situations are seldom that straightforward. For example, a director buying a chocolate bar in the staff canteen is not of interest to users of financial statements, but the director or his close family buying a six-bedroom house from the entity at a price other than fair value certainly would be. If the director bought the house from the entity at its fair value, the situation (interpreted by reference only to the above definition of materiality) would require further consideration.

33.42 In recent times, there has been a considerable growth in shareholder interest in the rewards paid to persons, particularly directors. There has been much criticism of the payment of large rewards when entities have not been performing well. The interest and concern have focused both on the cost to the entity and on the benefit derived by the person. This implies that materiality should be judged from both the entity's and the person's perspective.

33.43 So, in the examples given above, not only the significance to the entity, but also the transaction's significance to the director would need to be considered in order to form a judgement as to whether the transaction involving the purchase of the house was material. The transaction could be small to the entity, but a major investment for the director. In our view, the intention of FRS 102 is that transactions of the type and size shown in the example in paragraph 33.41 above (that is, the purchase of a house, whether at market value or not) would be regarded as material to the director and, therefore, disclosable.

33.44 Although it is clear that the purchase of a house is material, from the director's point of view, and the purchase of a chocolate bar is not, there will in practice be transactions between these two extremes whose materiality is borderline. It is not possible to be definitive about how materiality should be established, because much will depend on the facts of each case. But a transaction at arm's length and on normal commercial terms would contribute to its being regarded as immaterial. Equally, a transaction that is on terms advantageous to the director would contribute to its being regarded as material and, therefore, disclosable.

33.45 In addition, if a director enters into several small transactions in a financial year, the transactions will need to be aggregated in order to determine whether they are material from the director's point of view. If these transactions are material when aggregated, they will need to be disclosed in accordance with the standard.

Disclosure requirements

Summary

33.46 FRS 102 requires the following information about related parties to be disclosed in an entity's financial statements:

- Relationships between a parent and its subsidiaries, irrespective of whether there have been transactions between them.

- The name of its parent and, if different, the name of the ultimate controlling party (see para 33.48 onwards below).

- Key management personnel compensation (see para 33.68 onwards below).

- Details of transactions between the entity and any related parties (see para 33.88 onwards below).

- Details of balances due to, or from, related parties at the balance sheet date, including information on bad and doubtful debts (see para 33.88 onwards below).

[FRS 102 paras 33.5, 33.6, 33.9].

33.47 There is no requirement in FRS 102 to disclose information about related party transactions in any specific note. But it is likely to be more helpful to users to present the information in one comprehensive note, instead of including different aspects of related party disclosures in several notes to the financial statements. Where information is also required by other standards, cross-references can be used to avoid duplicated information.

Related party disclosures

Disclosure of control

Parent and ultimate controlling party

33.48   An entity must disclose the name of its parent and, if different, the name of the ultimate controlling party. If neither the parent nor the ultimate controlling party produces consolidated financial statements available for public use, the name of the next most senior parent that does so must also be disclosed. [FRS 102 para 33.5].

33.49   The standard notes that related party relationships need to be disclosed where control exists, irrespective of whether there have been transactions between the parties.

33.50   Disclosure of the ultimate controlling party is in addition to the requirements of Schedule 4 to SI 2008/410, 'The Large and Medium-sized Companies and Groups (Accounts and Reports) Regulations 2008'. SI 2008/410 requires disclosure of the following information in respect of both the largest and the smallest group of undertakings for which group accounts are drawn up and of which the company is a member:

- The name of the parent undertaking.

- Where the parent undertaking is incorporated outside the United Kingdom, the country in which it is incorporated.

- Where the parent is unincorporated, the address of its principal place of business.

- If copies of the group accounts are available to the public, the addresses from which copies of those accounts can be obtained.

33.51   The Act also requires a company to disclose the name of the company (if any) that is regarded by the directors as being the company's ultimate parent company. If the ultimate parent company is incorporated outside the United Kingdom, the company must also disclose the country in which the ultimate parent is incorporated. In this context, the ultimate parent company is a corporate entity, as opposed to the ultimate controlling party which is required to be disclosed by paragraph 33.5 of FRS 102, which could be a person, partnership or other entity.

> **Example – Disclosure where the ultimate controlling party is not an entity**
>
> XYZ Limited directly owns 100% of the shares of entity C, and the ultimate controlling party of entity C is Mr A. XYZ Limited does not publish financial statements available for public use.
>
> Entity K is the immediate parent of XYZ Limited. Entity L is the immediate parent of entity K. Both entities K and L produce consolidated financial statements filed with the local stock exchange.

The following diagram shows the structure of the group:

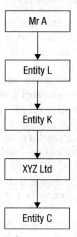

Which controlling parties need to be disclosed by entity C?

Entity C must disclose the name of XYZ Limited as the direct parent and Mr A as the ultimate controlling party, irrespective of whether there were transactions between them during the year. [FRS 102 para 33.5].

Entity K is also disclosed as the next most senior parent that produces consolidated financial statements available for public use. The next most senior parent is the first parent in the group above the immediate parent that produces consolidated financial statements available for public use. [FRS 102 para 33.5]. Further, entity C should disclose that K is the parent of the smallest group which prepares consolidated accounts that include entity C.

In addition to the above, entity L must be disclosed as the ultimate parent entity of entity C, and as the parent of the largest group to prepare consolidated financial statements containing entity C. [SI 2008/410].

33.52 Although the term 'parent' relates to an entity, the term 'ultimate controlling party' could relate to a person, partnership or other entity. Alternatively, it could be a group of persons or entities acting together (see para 33.55 onwards below) if the persons or entities, although each with small shareholdings, actively co-operate to control the entity.

33.53 Where the ultimate parent entity is itself controlled by, say, a person or a trust, the ultimate controlling party would be that person or trust.

33.54 Where control is shared in the form of a joint venture, the question arises whether the venturers should be disclosed as a controlling party under FRS 102. This is considered in the following example.

Example – Controlling parties and joint control

An entity is owned 50% by one entity and 50% by another. It is a joint venture under the definition in FRS 102. Should the two venturers be treated as the controlling party, thus requiring them to be disclosed as such under FRS 102?

FRS 102 does not deal with entities or persons working together to exercise joint control. Two venturers are not necessarily related parties simply because they share joint control over a joint venture. [FRS 102 para 33.4(b)].

But, if the venturers were acting together, and despite the lack of explicit reference to this situation in FRS 102, disclosure would be required, because of the general requirement in paragraph 33.5 of FRS 102 for disclosure of the ultimate controlling party. Paragraph 33.5 of the standard does not specifically limit disclosure to situations where the controlling party is a single person or entity.

In practice, such a situation is unusual and might indicate that one of the parties was in fact acting as a nominee for the other in order to disguise the fact that the other party actually had control. In considering each possible related party relationship, attention should be directed to the substance of the relationship and not merely its legal form. [FRS 102 para 33.3]. If one of the parties was in fact a nominee of the other, only that other party would be disclosed as the controlling party. Notably, this might also call into question whether the reporting entity itself had been appropriately classified as a joint venture. It would be expected that consistent conclusions be reached in relation to the control structure when considering the treatment of the reporting entity in the financial statements of investors and the disclosure requirements of section 33.

Joint control and significant influence exercised by groups of persons

33.55 As noted in paragraph 33.52 above, the term 'ultimate controlling party' could relate to a group of persons acting together if the persons actively co-operated to control the entity.

33.56 The key consideration, particularly given the lack of guidance in the standard in this area, is substance. As noted in paragraph 33.19 above, *"in considering each possible related party relationship, an entity shall assess the substance of the relationship and not merely the legal form"*. [FRS 102 para 33.3]. So, each arrangement should be assessed to determine the substance of relationships.

33.57 The Companies Act 2006 deals with similar arrangements in the context of interests in shares. Each party to an agreement is deemed to be interested in all the shares held by the other parties to the agreement. [CA06 Sec 825(1)]. 'Agreement' includes undertakings, expectations or understandings operative under any arrangement. Existence of such an agreement in relation to a UK company would be strong evidence that the parties are, in substance, acting as one, and that, if they held sufficient voting rights to give them control or significant influence, they should be treated as a related party of the entity under FRS 102.

33.58 The principle that a contractual arrangement between persons might result in them controlling the reporting entity could also be extended to situations where parties are contractually obliged to act together and, by doing so, in substance have joint control or significant influence over the reporting entity. In such a situation, we consider that the parties would be related parties of the reporting entity under the 'related party' definition in paragraph 33.2(a)(i) and (ii) and paragraph 33.3 of FRS 102.

33.59   When considering whether or not a small group of shareholders is operating together such that joint control or significant influence exists, the specific circumstances need to be carefully examined. For example, the shares in an entity might be held by two (or more) brothers, or by two or more parties in a normal joint venture. In the absence of a contractual arrangement, the fact that they co-operate or vote the same way would not, in itself, make them related parties. They would just be shareholders working in the normal way for their collective benefit. But a related party relationship will exist where there is a contractual arrangement that requires the parties to act together.

33.60   Where investors in a joint venture act as intermediaries for an ultimate controlling party, disclosure of that party is required, as shown in the following example.

> **Example – Ultimate control is exercised through a joint venture**
>
> Mr A owns shares that entitle him to 100% of the voting rights in entities B and C.
>
> Entities B and C jointly control entity P, which controls entity S.
>
> The following diagram shows the structure of the group:
>
>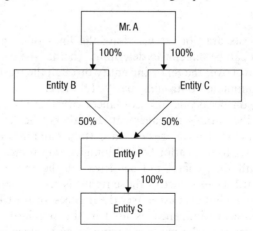
>
> Entity S's management should disclose Mr A as the ultimate controlling party of entity S, irrespective of whether there were transactions between them during the year. [FRS 102 para 33.5].
>
> Mr A controls entities B and C, which jointly control entities P and S. Entities B and C form a group which will vote according to Mr A's instruction.

Control by trusts

33.61 Where the controlling party is a trust, it will be necessary to consider whether the trust itself is controlled by a person or persons who will need to be disclosed as the ultimate controlling party (see para 33.53 above).

33.62 The definition of control comprises two elements:

- the power to govern the financial and operating policies of an entity; and

- the ability to benefit from its activities.

So, the question of establishing whether control exists is particularly difficult in relation to trusts. Trusteeship could be viewed as an example of where the two aspects of control are divided between two parties: the trustee has the power to deploy the trust assets; and the beneficiary benefits from their deployment. In what might be called a pure trust, neither the trustee nor the beneficiary controls the trust. Not all vehicles created in the legal form of a trust will fall into the category of a pure trust, and the rights and duties of the trustees and beneficiaries might be divided differently where the trust is not a pure trust. In a pure trust, however, it is possible to argue that there is no controlling party of the trust, because neither the trustee nor the beneficiary has both elements of control. The question of whether or not control exists over a trust is one that will need particular care and scrutiny of the facts of each individual case.

33.63 In view of the above argument, where a 'pure trust' holds shares in the reporting entity, it would follow that, other than disclosure of the trust as the controlling party, there would be no further requirement to disclose an ultimate controlling party.

33.64 Many trusts are not set up along the lines of a 'pure trust'. In these circumstances, it can be difficult to determine whether the trustees or any outside parties have control over the reporting entity through the trust for the purposes of establishing its ultimate controlling party. In the case of some trusts, trustees might be acting on occasions in accordance with the wishes of the settlor, the beneficiaries or the entity's management. In others, the settlor might have the power to appoint or remove trustees in certain circumstances, or the trustees might need to refer to the settlor before doing certain things. If these matters do not interfere with the general independence of the trustees, it might not be necessary to regard the existence of those rights as giving the settlor (or any other party, as the case might be) control over the trustees, or the trust, in the sense that control (as opposed to influence) is used in the standard. Alternatively, there might be no evidence of the trustees having given independent consideration to matters relevant to the reporting entity in the light of independent advice. These circumstances could point to trustees allowing outside parties (such as settlors or beneficiaries), who are in a position to do so, to exercise unrestricted control. If they do exercise control, such parties would need to be disclosed as the ultimate controlling party of the reporting entity.

33.65 It would seem from the above that the following reasoning can be applied to ascertaining the party, if any, to be disclosed as the controlling party of a trust for the purposes of FRS 102. That is, the controlling party is likely to be the party that both:

■ has the ability to direct the trust or to limit its powers (by pre-determination or otherwise), so as to ensure the implementation of its wishes concerning the trust's financial and operating policies; and

■ derives the principal economic benefit, whether or not that party is a named beneficiary under the trust.

Partnerships

33.66 Where a partnership controls over 50% of the shares with voting rights in a reporting entity, the question arises as to who controls the reporting entity. The partnership holds the majority of the voting rights in the reporting entity and would control it. One particular partner might be the reporting entity's controlling party, particularly where this partner has control over the management of the partnership and where it has a substantial partnership interest as well. But this partner might itself have a parent undertaking or ultimate controlling party, which it discloses in its financial statements. This would mean that the reporting entity would have to disclose that party as its ultimate controlling party.

33.67 In the UK, such a situation commonly occurs where a general partner acts as manager of a limited partnership.

Key management personnel compensation

33.68 The identification of key management personnel is dealt with at paragraph 33.8 onwards above. This section considers the disclosure requirements for key management personnel compensation.

33.69 Total key management personnel compensation is required to be disclosed. [FRS 102 para 33.7]. However, note that qualifying entities, which choose to take advantage of the reduced disclosure framework, are exempt from the disclosure requirements of paragraph 33.7 [FRS 102 para 1.12 (e)]. (See chapter 1).

33.70 FRS 102 explains that compensation includes all employee benefits as defined in section 28, including in the form of share-based payments. (See chapters 28 and 26 for further detail.) It includes all forms of compensation paid, payable or provided (for example, through benefits in kind) by the entity, or on its behalf, in return for services rendered to the entity. Also included is any such compensation paid on behalf of the entity's parent in respect of the entity. These requirements are illustrated in the following example. Further guidance on disclosure of key management personnel compensation in a group situation is given at paragraph 33.79 onwards below.

33.71 For some types of short-term employee benefits, it is not clear what the cost of the benefit is, as illustrated in the example below.

> **Example – Benefits in kind**
>
> Mr A is a member of key management personnel of an entity. As part of his employment package, he has the benefit of staying in a residential property owned by the entity. The entity bought the residential property 30 years ago at a low price. The property is carried at cost and is still being depreciated. The value of the property has increased significantly. The market rental of a similar property is also significantly higher than the depreciation charge on this property.
>
> At what value should the benefits given to Mr A be included in total compensation?
>
> In our view, the amount of the depreciation expense is not representative of the amount of compensation to Mr A. Depreciation does not meet the definition of employee benefits compensation.
>
> Additional disclosure is required where it is necessary for users to understand the potential effect of the relationship on the financial statements. [FRS 102 para 33.9]. In this situation, it might be appropriate to disclose details (such as the market rental of a similar property) in narrative information below the key management personnel compensation disclosure, if the information is necessary for an understanding of the potential effect of the relationship on the financial statements.

33.72 Another benefit in kind frequently granted as key management personnel compensation is the use of a company car. Such cars might be leased or owned by the entity. If an entity owns the vehicle, there will be no cash cost to the business on an ongoing basis. Consistent with the example above, we do not consider it appropriate to include the depreciation charge on the car in the amount of compensation. It would be appropriate to show an estimation of the benefit to the employee in some narrative disclosure. This might, for example, be calculated with reference to the amount that the employee would have to pay to lease a similar vehicle. Care should be exercised if management is considering disclosure of the taxable benefit in the narrative as being the benefit to the employee: in many jurisdictions, the taxable benefit might not be equal to the actual value of the benefit that the employee is receiving. Alternatively, if the car is leased by the business, there will be a cash cost to the business. We consider that this cash cost should be included in the numerical information.

33.73 For other types of key management personnel compensation (for example, post-employment benefits and share-based payment), the requirements are less clear. We consider that, for these categories, the principle underlying the standard is to disclose the cost of remunerating an entity's key management personnel for their services during the period covered by the financial statements. This would include the cost to the entity itself and any costs borne by other entities on its behalf (see para 33.77 below).

33.74 For defined contribution post-employment benefit schemes, we consider it most appropriate that the disclosure includes the cost of the aggregate contributions payable in the period by the entity to schemes for members of key management personnel.

33.75 For defined benefit schemes, we consider it most appropriate that the disclosure includes the total cost of the defined benefit scheme (including recognised actuarial gains and losses) calculated in accordance with section 28 of FRS 102 in respect of key management personnel. Where a defined benefit pension scheme is not operated solely for key management personnel (for example, an entity-wide scheme in which members of key management personnel participate), it might not be practicable to calculate the total recognised cost in respect of key management personnel. Under these circumstances, we consider that an acceptable alternative is to include the current service cost attributable to key management personnel (calculated in line with section 28 of the standard). There is also an argument for including the value of the change in benefits accrued in the scheme that could be transferred into another pension scheme, net of management's contributions (that is, a net change in 'transfer value'), where this information is available.

33.76 We consider it most appropriate that the amount included for compensation in the form of share-based payment is the expense in respect of the share-based payments, attributable to key management personnel, recognised by the entity in the period in accordance with section 26 of FRS 102. This is in addition to any disclosures that might be required under paragraph 33.9 of FRS 102 (details of transactions and outstanding balances – see para 33.88 below). It is also in addition to the details required by section 26 of the standard to be disclosed in respect of total awards in the notes to the financial statements, such as numbers of options granted and exercised in the period and options held at the beginning and end of the period. [FRS 102 para 26.18].

33.77 As noted in paragraph 33.73 above, key management personnel compensation includes compensation provided, on the entity's behalf, for services rendered to the entity. This will apply, for instance, where share-based payment awards are made by an entity's owners.

33.78 FRS 102's requirements are unlikely to be met by disclosure of directors' remuneration in compliance with the Companies Act 2006, either for a quoted company that prepares a directors' remuneration report or for an unquoted company that does not. The key reasons for this are:

- Where both the consolidated and the parent's separate financial statements are being prepared in accordance with FRS 102, disclosure is required in respect of the group's key management personnel for their services to the group and in respect of the parent's key management personnel for their services to the parent company. The Companies Act disclosures are of the parent company's directors' remuneration for services to the parent company and its subsidiaries, regardless of whether consolidated financial statements are prepared.

- The FRS 102 disclosure in respect of key management personnel might include persons who are not the company's directors, particularly where the 'entity' is a group preparing consolidated financial statements.

- The FRS 102 disclosures differ from those required by the Act.

Group situations

33.79 For entities that are not 'qualifying entities' or which choose not to take advantage of the reduced disclosure framework (see chapter 1) problems commonly arise with the disclosure of key management personnel compensation in a group context. Consider the following examples where a director of a parent entity is also a director of one of its subsidiaries. In each situation, it is assumed that the director is compensated by the parent entity in connection with services to the parent entity. It is also assumed that all the relevant information concerning compensation is available to the reporting entity.

Example 1 – Subsidiary bears cost for services received

The subsidiary pays the director directly in respect of services as a director of the subsidiary, as well as the parent entity compensating the director for services to the parent.

In this situation, the parent entity will need to disclose, within key management personnel compensation in its separate financial statements, the amount paid to the director in respect of services to the parent entity (which is the same as the amount paid by the parent entity). The subsidiary will need to disclose, within key management personnel compensation, the amount paid to the director by the subsidiary (that is, the amount earned by the director in respect of services to the subsidiary).

Example 2 – Subsidiary bears cost indirectly via a management charge

The parent entity pays the director directly for services as a director to both the subsidiary and the parent, and recharges the subsidiary for the services as a director of the subsidiary.

The amount that needs to be disclosed, within key management personnel compensation, in the parent's separate financial statements is the same as in example 1. The notes to the subsidiary's financial statements must disclose, within key management personnel compensation, the amount receivable by the director for services to the subsidiary (that is, the amount recharged by the parent in respect of the director's services).

Example 3 – Subsidiary bears no cost for services received

The parent entity pays the director directly for services as a director to both the subsidiary and the parent, but no recharge is made to the subsidiary.

Again, the amount that needs to be disclosed, within key management personnel compensation, in the parent's separate financial statements is the same as in example 1. But the notes to the financial statements of the subsidiary must include details of the compensation paid by the parent entity in respect of the director's services to the subsidiary. An explanation that the charge for director's compensation has been borne by the parent might be useful, although it is not required. In order to give this disclosure, it will be necessary to apportion the director's compensation between the parent and the subsidiary for disclosure purposes. Management of the entities might apportion it in any way they consider appropriate, although the method of apportionment should usually be consistent over time.

Example 4 – No significant services are received by subsidiary

In some cases, the parent entity might pay the director directly, but the director's role is to represent the parent's interests in the management of the subsidiary.

The director is a member of the subsidiary's key management personnel. So it will be necessary to consider the services for which the director is being compensated in order to allocate the compensation between that relating to services to the subsidiary and that relating to services to the parent. The substance of such an arrangement might be that, through a presence at board meetings of the subsidiary, the director is primarily performing services to the parent (that is, representing the parent's interests) and not to the subsidiary. Thus, it could be argued that much of the compensation paid by the parent should be included in the disclosure in the parent's separate financial statements. It should be noted that the director will have fiduciary duties to the subsidiary, so that some compensation might need to be allocated to the subsidiary, even if there is no recharge made between the entities. The amount disclosed in the subsidiary's financial statements should reflect the compensation paid to the director relating to services rendered to the subsidiary.

33.80 Practical difficulties might arise in connection with disclosure of compensation in a subsidiary's financial statements where a member of the subsidiary's key management personnel is also:

■ a member of key management personnel or an employee of the parent and is paid by the parent; or

■ a member of key management personnel of another subsidiary and is paid by that other subsidiary.

33.81 In such cases, it is often difficult to ascertain the compensation of the director that is paid to (or receivable in respect of services to) the subsidiary in question. This difficulty might be increased if there is no charge made to the subsidiary by the payer of the compensation. It might also sometimes be aggravated by a desire, on the part of either the parent or the subsidiary, to limit the amount of disclosure in the subsidiary's financial statements (for instance, if the parent-appointed director is more highly rewarded than other members of key management personnel).

33.82   Where there are difficulties in obtaining information, one or more of the steps described below might be taken.

33.83   If the subsidiary is a party to the key manager's service agreement, and that agreement stipulates what is paid in respect of services to the subsidiary, those elements of the total compensation should be disclosed in the subsidiary's financial statements.

33.84   If the subsidiary is not a party to the service agreement (possibly because the agreement is with the parent or a fellow subsidiary), the subsidiary or its management should *make reasonable efforts* to obtain the information (for instance, by asking the parent or fellow subsidiary for details of the terms of the service agreement, or by obtaining a detailed breakdown of any management charge).

33.85   If the information needed is not obtainable by any of the above means, it is necessary to make an apportionment. This is relatively simple where the person performs services for only two or maybe three entities. It is less simple if the person is, for example, a director (and, hence, a member of key management personnel) of a large number of different subsidiaries. We suggest that, where apportionment is relatively straightforward, it could be the best way of determining the compensation to be disclosed in each entity. It should be noted that, while an apportionment should be as accurate as possible, it need only be 'reasonable'. Hence, situations where it is not possible should be rare.

33.86   If, in rare circumstances, the necessary information is not available to an entity's management and a reasonable apportionment is not practicable, we consider that the financial statements would not give a true and fair view if no disclosure were made of the facts. So, in these circumstances, some narrative information is required to ensure that the financial statements give a true and fair view.

33.87   We suggest that appropriate notes for two situations that could arise, where no information is available, would be as follows:

> **Example 1 – Subsidiary cannot separately identify the cost of key management personnel compensation**
>
> A recharge is made to the subsidiary by the parent entity or fellow subsidiary, but the management charge includes other costs and the compensation cannot be separately identified.
>
> *"The above details of key management personnel compensation do not include Mr X's compensation, which is paid by the parent (fellow subsidiary) and recharged to the entity as part of a management charge. This management charge, which in 20XX amounted to C95,000, also includes a recharge of*

administration costs borne by the parent (fellow subsidiary) on behalf of the entity and it is not possible to identify separately the amount of Mr X's compensation."

If Mr X was also a member of the parent's key management personnel, it would be appropriate to state that his total compensation is disclosed in the parent's consolidated financial statements.

It is envisaged that this situation would be rare, because a full breakdown of management charges should normally be possible.

Example 2 – No reasonable allocation of costs is practicable

The director is also a director of, and carries on work for, a number of other subsidiaries. The director is actively involved in the management of each subsidiary and is paid by the parent, which makes no recharge to the subsidiaries.

"Mr X's compensation is paid by the parent, which makes no recharge to the entity. Mr X is a director of the parent and a number of fellow subsidiaries, and it is not possible to make a reasonable apportionment of his compensation in respect of each of the subsidiaries. Accordingly, the above details include no compensation in respect of Mr X. His total compensation is included in the aggregate of key management personnel compensation disclosed in the consolidated financial statements of the parent."

It is suggested that, where a similar situation applies but the compensation is paid by a fellow subsidiary, there should normally be a recharge. This is because the situation where a subsidiary pays compensation to other group directors normally only arises where the subsidiary is a group services entity, and such an entity would usually recharge for these services. In this type of situation, the note would not be needed, because the appropriate amount to be disclosed should be ascertainable.

Disclosure of transactions and balances

Information to be disclosed

33.88 FRS 102 states that, if there have been transactions between related parties, an entity should disclose the nature of the related party relationship, together with information about the transactions, outstanding balances and commitments. The information should be such as is necessary for an understanding of the potential effect of the relationship on the financial statements. The disclosures are additional to the disclosures referred to above in respect of key management personnel compensation. The information to be disclosed should, as a minimum, include the following:

- The amount of the transactions.

- The amount of outstanding balances and:

  - the terms and conditions and whether the balances are secured, together with the type of consideration to be given in settlement; and

- details of any guarantees given or received.

- Provisions for uncollectible receivables and the amount of expense recognised in the period in respect of bad and doubtful debts.

[FRS 102 para 33.9].

33.89 Other than for parent/subsidiary relationships (see para 33.48 onwards above), FRS 102 does not specifically require disclosure of the related parties' names. But this disclosure might be necessary, depending on the circumstances, in order to disclose the nature of the related party relationship and to provide an understanding of the potential effect of the relationship on the financial statements.

33.90 The standard states that the elements of disclosure set out in paragraph 33.88 above represent a minimum. Other relevant facts should be disclosed where this is necessary to enable users to understand the effect of related party transactions or balances. For example, disclosure of the amount of a transaction involving a sale of assets to a related party might be insufficient if the amount is materially different from that obtainable on normal commercial terms; in that case, a statement giving an indication that such sales or purchases or other transfers have taken place at amounts materially different from that obtainable on normal commercial terms might be necessary for an understanding of the financial statements.

33.91 Where a related party transaction is carried out at market value, judgement will be needed to determine the information necessary for an understanding of the potential effect of the relationship on the financial statements.

33.92 Disclosure that transactions were carried out on an arm's length basis between related parties should not be made unless such arm's length terms can be substantiated. [FRS 102 para 33.13]. The term 'arm's length basis' is generally taken to mean that transactions have been undertaken on terms that could have been obtained in a transaction with an external party, in which each side bargained knowledgeably and freely, unaffected by any relationship between them.

33.93 The requirement to disclose balances between related parties arises independently of the requirement to disclose details of specific transactions undertaken during the year. For example, a balance might arise from a prior year transaction. If (after what might be an unusually long credit period) a balance due from a related party is written off, that information could be significant for users.

Categories of disclosure

33.94 The disclosures referred to in paragraphs 33.88 to 33.90 above should be made separately in respect of each of the following:

- Entities with control, joint control or significant influence over the entity.

- Entities over which the entity has control, joint control or significant influence.

- Key management personnel of the entity or its parent (in the aggregate).

- Other related parties.

[FRS 102 para 33.10].

33.95 As noted above, paragraph 33.10 of the standard requires disclosures to be made separately for key management personnel of the entity and its parent. The disclosures for key management personnel should therefore include transactions with key management personnel of the entity and *any* parent of the entity (that is, not only the entity's immediate parent).

33.96 Generally, related party transactions and balances will be disclosed in the notes, although major balances might need to be disclosed on the face of the balance sheet if that is necessary for a proper understanding of the financial position. For example, a major intra-group loan might be disclosed on the face of the balance sheet if it is the major source of finance for an entity and the entity is dependent on such support for it to be able to continue its operations.

Aggregation — general

33.97 The disclosure of related party transactions could be very extensive and, in order to avoid excessive detail, the standard permits aggregation of transactions and balances in certain circumstances. Aggregation is allowed for items of a similar nature, except where separate disclosure is necessary for an understanding of the effects of related party transactions on the financial statements. [FRS 102 para 33.14].

33.98 Items of a similar nature should not be aggregated if:

- Separate disclosure of an item is required by law.

- Aggregation would obscure the importance of significant transactions. Material transactions should not be hidden or concealed by aggregation with other transactions. For example, the sale of a major item of property, plant and equipment to a related party should not be included in the aggregated disclosures for normal sales of trading inventory to that party, but should instead be separately disclosed.

33.99 An example of aggregation is where purchases or sales of similar items, such as trading inventory, are aggregated and described as such. But sales cannot be aggregated with purchases because they are not 'items of a similar nature', and so the netting of such transactions is not permitted.

33.100 Where permitted, aggregation can be by type of related party, provided that disclosure is given for each of the categories listed in paragraph 33.94 above.

Within each of these categories, the entity can aggregate similar transactions with the entities in that category. Where such aggregation is made, disclosure of the individual names of the related parties in that category is not necessarily required. The extent of detail to be disclosed will depend on materiality.

> **Example – Aggregation by counterparty**
>
> An entity has six associates and makes sales of goods to those associates. Half of those sales are to two of the associates. If the amount of the sales is not material to the entity as a whole, the sales to associates can be aggregated because they are similar in nature. But it might be necessary to identify the two associates to which half of the sales are made and to disclose the extent of the sales to those associates. If, on the other hand, the sales to associates are a material proportion of the entity's sales as a whole, it might be necessary to disclose separately the details of the transactions with the two associates to which half of the sales are made and the amounts of the sales transactions and accounts receivable balances for each of those associates. If the sales to the remaining four associates are not material to the entity as a whole, disclosure for those can continue to be aggregated.

Aggregation — transactions with key management personnel

33.101 Special considerations arise in connection with transactions with key management personnel and particularly with directors. Except for the disclosures in respect of compensation for services to the entity, FRS 102 would not generally permit the aggregation of other transactions with directors. This is because such transactions are not usually of a similar nature, but rather tend to be one-off transactions, such as the purchase or sale of an asset. For example, separate disclosure is needed where a director of an entity buys a property from the entity. But aggregation could be an acceptable approach in cases such as the following:

- A situation sometimes arises where all directors have material transactions with the entity. For example, where the entity is an association or co-operative serving all its members, the members could put all or most of their sales or purchases through the entity. Some of the members are elected directors for certain periods and they enter into similar transactions as all other members and on the same terms. Here, it would be acceptable to aggregate the transactions for disclosure purposes. But this approach cannot be used to conceal unusual transactions.

- In other circumstances, some or all directors might enter into transactions with the entity that are or might be material, but less material than the transactions described in the previous bullet point. An example would be insurance policies taken out by directors of insurance entities on normal or staff terms. Here again, it seems reasonable to aggregate the transactions for disclosure purposes. But this approach would not apply to unusual contracts or heavily discounted policies.

33.102 In contrast to these two cases, consider the following example. Some directors of a house-building entity might, over a period of a few years, buy houses from that entity for their own or family use. But, given the nature of house purchases, they are likely to be less frequent than is the case with the insurance policy example. Moreover, they would be more clearly material to the directors. Hence, in this example we do not believe that aggregation is appropriate, even where house-building is the entity's normal business and the transactions are on normal commercial terms.

Comparatives

33.103 Section 33 of FRS 102 is silent on comparatives. The rule in section 3 of the standard is that, except where the standard provides otherwise (which section 33 does not), comparative information must be given for all amounts reported in the financial statements. Comparative information should be included for narrative and descriptive information where it is relevant to an understanding of the current period's financial statements. [FRS 102 para 3.14]. In the case of related party disclosure, comparative information is likely to be relevant for all narrative and descriptive information.

33.104 The comparative information should disclose transactions with parties that were related at the time the transaction took place, but need not include information about transactions with parties that were unrelated at that time. It could be that the persons or entities that were related parties in the previous period are not the same as those that are related parties in the current period. For example, a person might have been promoted into a key management position in the current year, having previously been a non-management member of staff. Such a person is a related party since the date of his appointment to key management, but not before that date. Any transactions with the person in the previous period are not related party transactions and are not disclosable as related party comparative information. Similarly, it could be that an entity was a related party in the previous period but, as a result of a change in ownership, it is no longer related to the reporting entity. Transactions with such an entity were related party transactions at the time they took place, and should therefore be included in the comparative information. See further paragraph 33.105 onwards below.

Practical application

Subsidiaries acquired and disposed of in the year

33.105 In practice, questions arise as to what transactions are disclosable in consolidated and separate financial statements where a group has acquired or disposed of a subsidiary during the year. It is considered that disclosure should be made on the following basis.

Consolidated financial statements

- Where a group has acquired a subsidiary, transactions between the members of the acquiring group and the acquired subsidiary before the date of acquisition are not disclosable in the consolidated financial statements. This is because an acquired subsidiary is deemed to be a related party of the group only for the period during which the related party relationship exists. Post-acquisition transactions would also not be disclosable in the consolidated financial statements because they are eliminated on consolidation.

- Where a group has disposed of a subsidiary during the year, post-disposal transactions between the members of the group and the subsidiary disposed of are not disclosable in the consolidated financial statements, because the related party relationship ceases on disposal. Pre-disposal transactions are eliminated on consolidation, so no disclosure is required.

Parent's separate financial statements

- Where an entity acquires a subsidiary that is not wholly owned by the group (and so intra-group transactions are not exempt from disclosure under paragraph 33.1A of FRS 102), only transactions between the parent and the subsidiary after the date of acquisition are disclosable in the entity's separate financial statements. This is because it is this period during which the related party relationship exists.

- Where an entity disposes of a subsidiary (that was not wholly owned), only transactions between the parent and the subsidiary up to the date of disposal are disclosable in the entity's separate financial statements. Again, this is because it is this period during which the related party relationship exists.

Subsidiary's financial statements

- Where an entity is acquired in the period (but less than 100% is acquired, so intra-group transactions are not exempt from disclosure under paragraph 33.1A of the standard), only transactions after the date of acquisition are disclosable in its financial statements, because this is the period during which the related party relationship exists.

- Where a subsidiary (that was not wholly owned) is disposed of during the period, only transactions up to the date of disposal are disclosable in its financial statements, because this is the period during which the related party relationship exists.

33.106 If an entity acquired and then disposed of an associate (or joint venture) during one financial period, the treatment in the entity financial statements of the parent and the associate (or joint venture) would be similar to that discussed in the example above. Transactions occurring during the period when the parties were related would be disclosable as related party transactions by both entities. In this scenario, transactions between the parent and the associate (or joint venture) during the period the parties were related would also be disclosable in any consolidated financial statements prepared by the parent. This is because the transactions between the related parties would not eliminate on consolidation.

Pension funds

33.107 Post-employment benefit plans, such as pension funds, are related parties of an entity if they are for the benefit of employees of the entity or of any entity that is a related party of the entity (see para 33.26 onwards above). Transactions with post-employment plans will be disclosable as related party transactions in the entity's financial statements. These will include contributions paid to the plan; although, in practice, the amount of contributions for defined benefit schemes is likely to be disclosed under the requirements of section 28 as part of the reconciliation of movements in the net liability or asset recognised in the balance sheet. Other related party disclosures might include details of pension fund expenses charged to, or recharged by, the entity and more complex transactions (such as the sale and leaseback of property).

33.108 FRS 102 also specifies that participation by a parent or subsidiary in a defined benefit plan that shares risks between group entities is a transaction between related parties. Paragraph 28.41A of FRS 102 contains specific disclosure requirements in this situation. These are dealt with in chapter 28.

Government-related entities

33.109 FRS 102 includes an exemption from the disclosure requirements of paragraph 33.9 of the standard (see para 33.88 above) in relation to related party transactions, and outstanding balances and commitments, with:

■ a state (a national, regional or local government) that has control, joint control or significant influence over the reporting entity; and

■ another entity that is a related party because the same state has control, joint control or significant influence over both the reporting entity and the other entity.

[FRS 102 para 33.11].

33.110 The following is an example of a situation where the exemption might be applied.

Example — Government holding significant influence

Government G has significant influence over entity I. Entity I has significant influence over entity J and controls entity K.

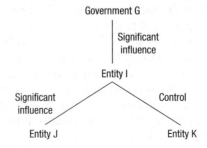

Entities I and K could take the exemption from disclosure for government-related entities, because government G has significant influence over entities I and K (because entity I controls entity K). But the exemption does not extend to any transactions with entity J because, even though government G has significant influence over entity I, entity I's significant influence over entity J is not sufficient to assert that government G also has significant influence over entity J. So, transactions between entities J and I and between entities J and K are subject to the full disclosure requirements of FRS 102. [FRS 102 para 33.2(b)(ii)].

33.111   If a reporting entity applies the exemption described in paragraph 33.109 above, it must still disclose the parent-subsidiary relationship as required by paragraph 33.5 of FRS 102 (see para 33.48 above).

Non-disclosure and the position of the auditor

33.112   Where there is a material misstatement in the financial statements that relates to the non-disclosure of information (such as the ultimate controlling party), the auditor is guided by the requirements of ISA (UK&I) 705. Where such circumstances arise, the auditor should:

■ discuss the non-disclosure with those charged with governance;

■ describe, in the 'basis for modification' paragraph, the nature of the omitted information; and

■ unless prohibited by law or regulation, include the omitted disclosures, provided it is practicable to do so and the auditor has obtained sufficient appropriate audit evidence about the omitted information.

[ISA (UK&I) 705 para 19].

33.113   This means that qualified audit opinions will generally contain omitted disclosures (including, for example, details of the ultimate controlling party).

33.114   The ISA's application guidance describes circumstances where it would not be practicable to disclose the omitted information, as follows:

- the disclosures have not been prepared by management or are not readily available to the auditor; or

- the auditor judges the disclosures to be unduly voluminous in relation to the auditor's report.

[ISA (UK&I) 705 para A19].

Transition to FRS 102

Scope

33.115 FRS 8 provided certain reliefs from disclosure that are not carried forward to FRS 102.

33.116 FRS 8 did not require disclosure of key management compensation; but, under FRS 102, disclosure of the total of key management compensation is required unless the entity is a 'qualifying entity', which chooses to take the exemptions from disclosure set out in the reduced disclosure framework (see para 33.69 above).

33.117 Paragraph 3(b) of FRS 8 provided an exemption from disclosure of contributions to a pension fund; but there is no such exemption in FRS 102.

33.118 The exemption in FRS 8 from disclosing transactions with other wholly owned subsidiaries is retained in FRS 102, although the wording of the exemption is slightly amended to align it with the Companies Act (see para 33.2 above). Unlike FRS 8, there is no requirement to state that this exemption has been taken. [FRS 8 para 3].

33.119 FRS 8 did not include an exemption from disclosing transactions with governments, but an exemption is included in FRS 102. [FRS 102 para 33.11].

33.120 Related party disclosures were not required by FRS 8 if disclosure would conflict with the reporting entity's duties of confidentiality arising by operation of law (but not from contractual provisions relating to confidentiality). So, banks that were legally required to observe a strict duty of confidentiality about their customers' affairs did not have to disclose details concerning related parties that would be in conflict with that duty. [FRS 8 para 16]. There is no such exemption in FRS 102.

33.121 FRS 8 stated that, in consolidated financial statements, any transactions or balances that were eliminated did not need to be disclosed. This explicit exemption is not included in FRS 102, but disclosure of such transactions and balances is not required (for the reasons set out in para 33.3 above).

Other minor differences

33.122 There are also some minor differences between FRS 8 and FRS 102, although we would expect these to have little practical effect for UK GAAP reporters.

33.123 There is a minor change in the definition of a related party, in that paragraph 33.2(b)(v) of the standard refers to 'post-employment benefit plans' rather than 'retirement benefit schemes'; this is because the scope of section 28 of FRS 102 is broader than that of FRS 17.

33.124 FRS 102 requires that relationships between a parent and its subsidiaries are disclosed irrespective of whether there have been transactions between them. An entity discloses the name of its parent and (if different) the ultimate controlling party. FRS 8 required disclosure of the controlling party and ultimate controlling party, but did not otherwise require disclosure of relationships between group companies. [FRS 8 para 5]. Under FRS 102, if neither the entity's parent nor the ultimate controlling party produces consolidated financial statements available for public use, the name of the next most senior parent that does so is disclosed. Although not all of the FRS 102 requirements as regards parents and subsidiaries were contained within FRS 8, the disclosure requirements of UK company law cover most of the same ground.

33.125 Although the disclosure requirements of FRS 102 and FRS 8 are expressed slightly differently, they will normally result in similar disclosures. For example:

- FRS 8 required disclosure of the name of the related party, but FRS 102 does not. However, both standards require disclosure of the nature of the related party relationship, and this will often mean that the related party is named. In addition, both FRS 102 and FRS 8 permit aggregation of disclosures by type of related party so that related parties are not always named individually.

- FRS 102 requires disclosure of *"outstanding balances, including commitments"*. Although FRS 8 made no reference to the disclosure of commitments, it required disclosure of *"any elements of the transactions necessary for an understanding of the financial statements"* and, in our view, this requirement would necessitate the disclosure of commitments.

- FRS 102 requires disclosure of the terms and conditions, including any secured balances or guarantees given. Again, although these disclosures were not specifically required in FRS 8, the requirement to disclose *"any elements of the transactions necessary for an understanding of the financial statements"* would likely mean that such information was already disclosed by UK GAAP reporters.

33.126 As noted above, both FRS 102 and FRS 8 allow aggregation by type of related party. Unlike FRS 8, FRS 102 sets out specific categories for which aggregated disclosure of related party transactions is required (see para 33.94 above). [FRS 102 para 33.10].

33.127 Both FRS 8 and FRS 102 provide examples of the types of related party transaction that require disclosure. [FRS 8 para 19; FRS 102 para 33.12]. These lists of examples are largely the same but there are some differences. FRS 8 did not include the following FRS 102 examples:

- Settlement of liabilities on behalf of the entity, or by the entity on behalf of that related party.

- Participation by a parent or subsidiary in a defined benefit plan that shares risks between group entities. However, FRS 8 did exempt from disclosure contributions to a pension plan.

33.128 FRS 8 included agency arrangements and management contracts as examples of types of transaction that should be disclosed. Although not specifically mentioned as examples in FRS 102, we believe they should also be disclosed under FRS 102.

Chapter 34

Specialised activities

34.1 – Agriculture

34.1 – Agriculture

Introduction

34.1.1 Section 34 of FRS 102 prescribes the accounting treatment, measurement and disclosures required for agricultural activity and its related agricultural produce. Depending on the accounting policy choice made for each class of biological asset and its related agricultural produce, an entity will follow either the fair value or cost model.

Definitions and scope

34.1.2 'Agricultural activity' is defined as *"the management by an entity of the biological transformation of biological assets for sale, into agricultural produce or into additional biological assets".* [FRS 102 Glossary of terms]. Examples of agricultural activity include:

- Raising livestock, fish or poultry.

- Stud farms (for example, breeding horses or cattle).

- Forestry.

- Cultivating vineyards, orchards or plantations.

- Floriculture.

34.1.3 There are several key terms used in the standard, namely 'biological asset', 'agricultural produce' and 'management'.

Biological assets

34.1.4 A 'biological asset' is defined as a *"living animal or plant".* [FRS 102 Glossary of terms]. This is a broad definition and, in the context of agriculture, biological assets include (amongst others) the following:

- Sheep, pigs, beef cattle, dairy cattle, poultry and fish.

- Trees in a plantation forest.

- Plants for harvest (such as wheat, maize and vegetables).

- Cultivating vineyards, orchards or plantations.

- Trees, plants and bushes from which agricultural produce is harvested (such as fruit trees, tea bushes, vines, tobacco plants and sugar cane).

34.1.5 It is evident that the above items represent living plants or animals. However, a more complex question concerns other living organisms, such as cultures, cells, bacteria and viruses used in the pharmaceutical and biotechnology industries. Generally, such organisms would not be regarded as animals or plants under either the common or the scientific usage of those words. However, the Collins English Dictionary defines a plant as *"any living organism that typically synthesises its food from inorganic substances, lacks specialised sense organs, and has no powers of locomotion"*. Arguably, such a definition could encompass cultures etc.

34.1.6 However, as noted above, agricultural activity is the management by an entity of the biological transformation of biological assets for sale, into agricultural produce, or into additional biological assets. The development of organisms for research purposes does not qualify as agricultural activity, because the organisms are not being developed for sale or for transformation into agricultural produce or additional biological assets; as such, we consider that cultures, cells, bacteria, viruses and similar organisms used in the pharmaceutical and biotechnology industries are not biological assets within the scope of section 34 of FRS 102.

Agricultural produce

34.1.7 'Agricultural produce' is defined as *"the harvested product of the entity's biological assets"*. [FRS 102 Glossary of terms]. The following table gives examples of biological assets, together with examples of the agricultural produce or additional biological assets that they yield:

Biological assets	Additional biological assets	Agricultural produce
Dairy cattle	Calves	Milk/Carcass/Hides
Beef cattle	Calves	Carcass/Hides
Fruit trees	Saplings	Fruit
Wheat	–	Wheat
Sheep	Lambs	Carcass/Wool
Trees	Saplings/Seeds	Felled trees/Rubber latex
Vines	Saplings/Seeds	Harvested grapes

Management and transformation of biological assets

34.1.8 Biological transformation is a natural change in a biological asset. It includes growth of living animals or plants, reduction in output due to age or disease, and the production of new biological assets through a managed reproductive programme. The following are examples of biological transformation in the context of cattle:

■ Calves are born (procreation).

- Calves grow into mature cattle (growth).

- Dairy cattle yield milk (production).

- Beef cattle are reared for meat (production).

34.1.9 All of these changes are observable, measurable and have a direct relationship to future economic benefits. Hence, biological transformation has an effect on the value of biological assets. This is relevant for the measurement of biological assets, as discussed in paragraph 34.1.14 onwards below.

34.1.10 Having identified biological transformation, it is necessary to determine whether it is managed before it can be considered to represent agricultural activity. Management of biological transformation normally takes the form of activity to enhance, or at least stabilise, the conditions necessary for the process to take place. For example, management of cattle (discussed above) would involve providing shelter and food as well as maintaining their health. The following are examples of management of biological transformation:

- Raising fish in captivity on a fish farm for subsequent slaughter or sale.

- A managed breeding programme carried out to produce animals for sale.

This management distinguishes agricultural activity from other activities. For example, harvesting from unmanaged sources (such as ocean fishing) is not agricultural activity.

Scope

34.1.11 Section 34 of FRS 102 applies to the following where they relate to agricultural activity:

- biological assets, and

- agricultural produce at the point of harvest.

34.1.12 Section 34 of the standard does not apply to the following:

- Land related to agricultural activity. Land owned by the entity and used for agricultural activity is dealt with by section 17 of the standard (see chapter 17). Land owned by a third party and rented to the entity for the purposes of agricultural activity is likely to be the third party's investment property and is dealt with by section 16 of the standard (see chapter 16).

- Intangible assets related to agricultural activity; these are dealt with by section 18 of the standard (see chapter 18).

- Leased biological assets held by a lessee under an operating lease; these are accounted for under section 20 of the standard (see chapter 20).

- Agricultural produce after the point of harvest. It is likely that such produce will be inventory in the scope of section 13 of the standard (see chapter 13).

However, while the produce is still growing or is still attached to the biological asset, its value forms part of the value of the biological asset.

Recognition

34.1.13 The recognition criteria for biological assets and agricultural produce are the same as for any other type of asset. Biological assets and agricultural produce should be recognised when:

- the entity controls the asset as a result of past events;

- it is probable that future economic benefits associated with the asset will flow to the entity; and

- the fair value or cost of the asset can be measured reliably.

[FRS 102 para 34.3].

Measurement

34.1.14 An entity has an accounting policy choice as to whether it applies the cost or fair value model. This accounting policy is made for each class of biological asset and its related agricultural produce. The fair value and cost models are covered, respectively, in paragraphs 34.1.16 and 34.1.31 onwards below.

34.1.15 Where an entity selects the fair value model for a class of biological asset and its related produce, it should not subsequently change its accounting policy to the cost model. [FRS 102 para 34.3B]. See paragraph 34.1.26 below for situations where it is not possible to establish fair values reliably.

Measurement – fair value model

34.1.16 Biological assets should be measured, both at initial recognition and at each subsequent reporting date, at fair value less costs to sell, and changes in fair value less costs to sell should be recognised in profit or loss. [FRS 102 para 34.4]. Agricultural produce should be measured at fair value less costs to sell at the point of harvest. This amount will then represent cost for the purposes of section 13 of the standard.

34.1.17 Costs to sell are the incremental costs incurred in selling the asset and include commissions to brokers and dealers, levies by regulatory agencies and commodity exchanges, and transfer taxes and duties.

34.1.18 'Fair value' is defined as *"the amount for which an asset could be exchanged or a liability settled, between knowledgeable, willing parties in an arm's length transaction"*. [FRS 102 Glossary of terms]. It represents a market price for the asset, based on current expectations. Section 34 of the standard includes a hierarchy of valuation measures. The hierarchy can be summarised as follows:

- Price for the asset in an active market.

- Recent transaction price for the asset if there is no active market.

- Market prices for similar assets, adjusted for the points of differences.

- Sector benchmarks.

- Present value of the future cash flows expected to be generated from the asset.

34.1.19 Many biological assets have relevant market-determined prices or values available, because biological produce in general are basic commodities that are traded actively. For example, there are usually market prices for calves and piglets, because there is an active market for these. Where there is an active market for a biological asset or agricultural produce, the quoted price in that market is the appropriate basis for determining the fair value of that asset. [FRS 102 para 34.6]. An active market is a market where all of the following conditions exist:

- The items traded within the market are homogeneous.

- Willing buyers and sellers can normally be found at any time.

- Prices are available to the public.

34.1.20 If an entity has access to different markets, it should refer to the most relevant one when measuring fair value. For example, if an entity has access to two active markets, it should refer to the price prevailing in the market that it expects to use. [FRS 102 para 34.6].

34.1.21 The nature of consumable biological assets and agricultural produce is such that an active market will normally exist. Some bearer biological assets, on the other hand, might seldom be sold, so other techniques for measuring fair value might be necessary. If an active market does not exist, one or more of the following methods should be used to estimate fair value, if such data are available:

- the most recent market transaction price, provided that there has not been a significant change in economic circumstances between the date of that transaction and the end of the reporting period;

- market prices for similar assets, with adjustment to reflect differences; and

- sector benchmarks, such as the value of an orchard expressed per export tray, bushel, or hectare, and the value of cattle expressed per kilogram of meat.

[FRS 102 para 34.6(b)].

34.1.22 Sometimes, the information sources listed in paragraph 34.1.21 above might suggest different conclusions as to the fair value of a biological asset or agricultural produce. In such circumstances, management will need to exercise judgement to determine the most reliable estimate of fair value within a relatively narrow range of reasonable estimates.

34.1.23 Where market-based prices or values are not available for a biological asset in its present location and condition, fair value should be estimated on the basis of the present value of expected net cash flows from the asset, discounted at a current market-based rate. [FRS 102 para 34.6].

34.1.24 The cash flow model should include all directly attributable cash inflows and outflows, and only those cash flows. The inflows will be the price in the market of the harvested crop for each crop over the asset's life. The outflows will be those incurred in raising or growing the asset and getting it to market (for example, direct labour, feed, fertiliser and transport to market). The 'market' is where the asset will be sold. For some assets, this will be an actual market; for others, it might be the 'factory gate'.

34.1.25 Consistent with the objective of estimating fair value, the cash flows should be based as far as possible on market data. For example, while there is a market for fully grown salmon, there is no market for partly grown salmon. The fair value of a partly grown salmon is measured by projecting the cash flows from the sale of the salmon fully grown, less the cash outflows needed to grow the salmon to its marketable weight and discounting them to a present-day value.

34.1.26 Where fair value cannot be reliably established, biological assets should be measured using the cost model [FRS 102 para 34.6A], but only until fair values can once again be determined. The cost model is considered in paragraph 34.1.31 onwards below.

Disclosures – fair value model

34.1.27 An entity should provide a description of each group of its biological assets. [FRS 102 para 34.7]. The groupings could take many forms, but an entity is encouraged to distinguish between consumable and bearer biological assets, or between mature and immature biological assets, as appropriate.

34.1.28 An entity should disclose the methods and significant assumptions applied in determining the fair value of each group of biological asset. [FRS 102 para 34.7; SI 2008/410 1 Sch 58(2)].

34.1.29 The opening and closing carrying amounts of biological assets should be reconciled for each group of biological assets. This reconciliation should show, as a minimum:

- Gains or losses arising from changes in fair value less costs to sell.
- Increases due to purchases.
- Decreases resulting from harvest.
- Increases resulting from business combinations.

■   Other changes.

The reconciliation does not need to be presented for prior periods.

[FRS 102 para 34.7].

34.1.30   Where an entity applies cost rather than fair value, it should disclose the reasons why fair value could not be reliably measured. If the fair value of a biological asset subsequently becomes reliably measureable during the current period, the entity should explain why the fair value has become reliably measureable, and it should disclose the effect of the change. [FRS 102 para 34.7A].

Measurement – cost model

34.1.31   Where an entity applies the cost model, biological assets should be measured at cost less accumulated depreciation and impairment losses (if any). [FRS 102 para 34.8]. For this purpose, cost, accumulated depreciation and any accumulated impairment losses should be determined in accordance with sections 17 and 27 of the standard, as appropriate. These sections are considered further in chapters 17 and 27 respectively.

34.1.32   Agricultural produce harvested from an entity's biological assets is measured at the point of harvest, at either:

■   the lower of cost and estimated selling price less costs to complete and sell; or

■   its fair value less costs to sell. Any gain or loss arising on initial recognition of agricultural produce at fair value less costs to sell is included in profit or loss for the period in which it arises.

This cost then becomes the cost when applying section 13 (or another applicable section) of the standard.

[FRS 102 para 34.9].

Disclosures – cost model

34.1.33   For each biological asset measured in accordance with the cost model, an entity should disclose:

■   a description of each class of biological asset;

■   the depreciation method used; and

■   the useful lives or the depreciation rates used.

[FRS 102 para 34.10].

34.1.34 In addition, the opening and closing carrying amounts of biological assets should be reconciled for each group of biological assets. This reconciliation should show, as a minimum:

- Increases resulting from purchases.

- Decreases attributable to sales.

- Decreases resulting from harvest.

- Increases resulting from business combinations.

- Impairment losses recognised or reversed in profit or loss in accordance with section 27 of the standard.

- Other changes.

This reconciliation does not need to be presented for prior periods.

[FRS 102 para 34.10].

34.1.35 An entity should disclose the methods and significant assumptions applied in determining the fair value of each group of agricultural produce at the point of harvest of each class of agricultural produce. [FRS 102 para 34.10A].

Transitional issues

34.1.36 No special exemptions are available to first-time adopters under section 35 of FRS 102. So, a first-time adopter must prepare its financial statements as though the requirements of section 34 of the standard had always applied.

34.1.37 Under previous UK GAAP, there was no specific guidance on accounting for biological assets, and as such, entities might have followed guidance on fixed assets and applied a cost model. If the entity previously applied a cost or fair value model and maintains that basis, it is unlikely that there would be measurement differences. On the other hand, if an entity changes basis from fair value to cost, or from cost to fair value, the change is applied retrospectively, and adjustments are recognised in reserves.

34.2 – Extractive activities

34.2 – Extractive activities

Scope

34.2.1   This part of the chapter deals with the accounting for the exploration for and/or evaluation of mineral resources (extractive activities) and should be read in combination with IFRS 6, 'Exploration for and evaluation of mineral resources'. [FRS 102 para 34.11].

34.2.2   When applying the requirements of IFRS 6, references made to other IFRS standards within that standard should be taken to be references to the relevant section or paragraph within FRS 102. [FRS 102 para 34.11A].

34.2.3   As there is no equivalent section in FRS 102 the reference in IFRS 6 to IFRS 8 'operating segments' is replaced by a reference to the definitions of cash generating unit and operating segment in the glossary. [FRS 102 para 34.11B]. This in effect prevents the relevant cash generating units from being larger than an operating segment in the same way that FRS 6 does.

Transitional issues

34.2.4   When adopting FRS 102 for the first-time and where it is not practical to apply a particular requirement of paragraph 18 of IFRS 6 to the previous comparative amounts an entity should disclose that fact in the note that explains the transition. [FRS 102 para 34.11C].

34.2.5   Under previous GAAP, entities that accounted for exploration and development costs for oil and gas properties in the development or production phases in cost centres that included all properties in a large geographical area, can elect on transition to FRS 102 to measure those oil and gas assets on the following basis:

(a)   Exploration and evaluation assets at the amount established under the entity's previous GAAP.

(b)   Assets in the development or production phases at the amount determined for the cost centre under the entity's previous GAAP. The entity should allocate this amount to the cost centre's underlying assets pro rata using reserve volumes or reserve values that existed at the date of transition.

34.2.6   The entity then needs to test the exploration and evaluation assets and assets in the development and production phases for impairment in accordance with section 34, '*Specialised activities*' or section 27, '*Impairment of assets*', and if necessary, reduce the amounts determined above. [FRS 102 para 35.10(j)].

34.3 – Service concession arrangements

34.3 – Service concession arrangements

Introduction

34.3.1   In a service concession arrangement, a government or other public sector body ('the grantor') contracts with a private sector entity ('the operator') to develop or upgrade, operate and maintain infrastructure assets such as roads, bridges, tunnels, airports, energy distribution networks, prisons and hospitals for an agreed period of time ('the concession period'). [FRS 102 para 34.12]. The operator receives payment over the concession period either from the grantor or from users of the infrastructure assets, or from both.

34.3.2   A common feature of all service concession arrangements is the public service nature of the obligation undertaken by the operator. All of the activities described in the previous paragraph (such as provision of a transport infrastructure or hospital) might be considered essential for a nation such that they are provided or guaranteed by the public sector. Even where they are provided by the private sector, they are usually subject to regulation going beyond that applying to most businesses.

34.3.3   Accounting for service concession arrangements is considered in section 34 of FRS 102. Guidance is provided in respect of the accounting by both operators (see para 34.3.11 onwards below) and grantors (see para 34.3.29 onwards below).

Scope

34.3.4   Section 34 of FRS 102 applies to public-to-private service concession arrangements, as described in paragraph 34.3.1 above. Arrangements are accounted for as service concession arrangements when:

- "
■   *the grantor controls or regulates what services the operator must provide using the infrastructure assets, to whom, and at what price; and*

- ■   *the grantor controls, through ownership, beneficial entitlement or otherwise, any significant residual interest in the assets at the end of the term of the arrangement.*"

[FRS 102 para 34.12A].

34.3.5   Control of services might be exercised by contract as well as through other forms of regulation. For this purpose, the grantor and any related parties, such as regulators acting in the public interest, should be considered together. Control might also include the grantor specifying who is permitted to access the infrastructure (for example, through rights to nominate tenants for rented property).

34.3.6 Control of prices applies to amounts that the grantor is required to pay to the operator, as well as amounts that the operator can charge to members of the public. Where the grantor has complete control over the price charged by the operator, the condition is clearly met. But it is not necessary for the grantor to have complete control of the price. It is sufficient for the price to be regulated by the grantor in some way, which could include capping or profit-sharing mechanisms. Any restriction that is highly unlikely to apply in practice should be ignored.

34.3.7 Control of the residual interest in the infrastructure assets effectively restricts how the operator might use the infrastructure after the end of the concession period. Such control might arise if the infrastructure is transferred to the grantor (with or without payment), or the grantor can restrict the operator's ability to sell or pledge the infrastructure and give the grantor a continuing right of use throughout the concession period. [FRS 102 para 34.12A]. This control concept is not the same as the 'risks and rewards' approach to accounting for service concession arrangements previously applied under UK GAAP.

34.3.8 Where the infrastructure assets' residual value is not significant (that is, the arrangement is for its entire useful life), it is only necessary to consider whether the grantor controls or regulates what services the operator must provide with the infrastructure, to whom it must provide them, and at what price (that is, the first criterion set out in para 34.3.4 above). [FRS 102 para 34.12A]. If this is the case, it would confirm that the grantor controls the infrastructure throughout its useful economic life, and the arrangement would fall within the scope of section 34 of FRS 102.

34.3.9 In some arrangements, the use of infrastructure is partly controlled by the grantor and partly unregulated. Although such arrangements vary, consider the following examples:

- Infrastructure that is physically separable and capable of being operated independently should be analysed separately if used wholly for unregulated purposes. For example, this might apply to a private wing of a hospital, where the remainder of the hospital is used to treat NHS patients.

- Any purely ancillary activities (such as a hospital shop) should be ignored, because they do not detract from the grantor's control over the infrastructure assets.

In either of the above situations, there might in substance be a lease from the grantor to the operator of the assets that are separable or used for the additional services. If so, this lease should be accounted for in accordance with section 20 of FRS 102.

34.3.10 The contractual terms of service concession arrangements are often complex and might contain groups of contracts and sub-arrangements. Such an arrangement should be treated as a whole where the groups of contracts and sub-arrangements are linked in such a way that the commercial effect cannot be understood without reference to them as a whole. Where this is the case, and the arrangement taken as a whole meets the scope requirements of both sections 34 and 20 of FRS 102, the former should prevail, and the arrangement should be accounted for as a service concession arrangement. [FRS 102 para 34.12C].

Accounting by the operator in a service concession arrangement

34.3.11 The notion of control described in the previous paragraphs has important implications for the accounting for service concession arrangements. Control of any infrastructure assets constructed or acquired by the operator is transferred to the grantor, so these assets should not be recognised as the operator's property, plant and equipment. [FRS 102 para 34.12I]. Instead, the operator has rights to operate the infrastructure assets to provide public services on the grantor's behalf. This applies whether the infrastructure is constructed or acquired by the operator or is provided to the operator by the grantor for the purposes of the concession.

34.3.12 Given that the operator is not permitted to recognise the infrastructure, the asset that it recognises instead reflects the consideration that it receives from the grantor in exchange. The consideration received can take a variety of forms but usually involves:

■ an unconditional contractual right to receive a specified or determinable amount of cash or another financial asset from, or at the direction of, the grantor (including where the grantor guarantees to pay any shortfall between amounts received from users of the infrastructure assets and specified or determinable amounts); and/or

■ a right to charge users directly for use of the infrastructure assets.

34.3.13 Where the operator has an unconditional contractual right to receive cash or another financial asset, this should be recognised as a financial asset. [FRS 102 para 34.13(a)]. By contrast, if the operator has a right to charge users for access to the infrastructure, there is no contractual right to receive cash from any party, even if receipt of cash is highly probable. Instead, the operator has an intangible asset. [FRS 102 para 34.13(b)]. Whatever form the consideration takes, it should be measured at fair value (see paras 34.3.17 and 34.3.21 below).

34.3.14 In some service concession arrangements, the operator might have both a contractual right to receive cash and a right to charge users. For example, where the grantor has given an unconditional guarantee of payment for the construction of an infrastructure asset, the operator has a financial asset; where the operator has to rely on the public using the infrastructure in order to obtain payment, it has an intangible asset. [FRS 102 para 34.13].

34.3.15 In most service concession arrangements, the operator does not receive cash, either from the grantor or users, until construction of the infrastructure assets is completed and services have commenced. From that point on, the operator will receive payments from the grantor or from users of the public service, but it is highly unlikely that any payments will identify the specific transaction or service to which they relate (that is, construction, upgrade, maintenance or operation). Where the operator receives payment from the grantor, it will be necessary to allocate those payments between construction or upgrade of the infrastructure assets and provision of services. The standard does not prescribe a method for this allocation, although it is commonly made on the basis of the relative fair values of the components of the arrangement. There is further discussion in chapter 23 of allocating consideration in a multiple element arrangement.

Operator recognises a financial asset

34.3.16 Where the operator has an unconditional contractual right to receive a specified or determinable amount of cash or another financial asset from, or at the direction of, the grantor, it recognises a financial asset as consideration for constructing or upgrading the infrastructure assets. [FRS 102 para 34.14]. In substance, the operator is paid for constructing or upgrading the grantor's assets, so the transaction is treated as a construction contract in accordance with section 23 of FRS 102. Accordingly, revenue is recognised by reference to the stage of completion of the construction or upgrade services. [FRS 102 para 23.17].

34.3.17 The financial asset that is recognised as consideration for construction or upgrade services is measured initially at fair value, based on the fair value of the construction or upgrade services provided. [FRS 102 para 34.14]. In view of the complexity of many service concession arrangements, and the many elements they might contain, it will seldom be obvious from the contract how much the grantor will pay specifically for construction or upgrade services. Accordingly, it will be necessary to estimate fair value, typically by applying an appropriate profit margin to the construction costs incurred

34.3.18 After initial recognition, the operator accounts for the financial asset in accordance with sections 11 and 12 of FRS 102. [FRS 102 para 34.14]. Typically, the financial asset will represent a basic financial instrument falling within the scope of section 11 of the standard and measured at amortised cost. But this should not be presumed, and the terms of the arrangement need to be considered carefully. Further guidance on financial instruments is provided in chapters 11 and 12.

34.3.19 The following example illustrates the accounting where an operator recognises a financial asset.

Example – operator recognises a financial asset

The terms of a service concession arrangement require an operator to construct a road (completing construction within two years) and maintain and operate the road to a specified standard for eight years (that is, years 3 to 10). At the end of year 10, the arrangement will end.

The arrangement's terms require the grantor to pay the operator C200 per year in years 3 to 10 for making the road available to the public. For the purpose of this illustration, it is assumed that all cash flows take place at the end of the year.

The operator estimates that the costs it will incur to fulfil its obligations, and the margins that it expects to earn on the various activities, will be as follows:

	Year	Cost	Mark-up on cost	Fair value
Construction services	1	500	5%	525
	2	500	5%	525
Operation services per year	3–10	10	20%	12

Given that the operator receives annual payments of C200 during the operation phase, it is necessary to allocate the consideration between the various services by reference to their relative fair values (as explained in para 34.3.15 above). Clearly, the total cash received over the term of the arrangement (C1,600) exceeds the sum of the fair values of the individual components (C1,146). The difference of C454 represents finance income earned by the operator as the financial asset is settled over time.

The operator recognises contract revenue and costs during the construction phase in accordance with section 23 of FRS 102. So, the operator will recognise construction revenue and costs in years 1 and 2 of C525 and C500 respectively, and record a profit of C25 in each of those years. In later years, revenue of C12 and costs of C10 will be recognised in respect of operation services (see para 34.3.25 below).

As explained above, the revenue of C525 in years 1 and 2 will be received in cash from years 3 to 10. The effective interest rate for this series of cash flows can be calculated using a financial calculator or a spreadsheet, and it amounts to 7.75%. This interest rate is used to measure the amortised cost of the financial asset in accordance with section 11 of FRS 102.

The operator's cash flows, income statement and statement of financial position over the term of the arrangement will be as follows:

Cash flows

Year	1	2	3	4	5	6	7	8	9	10
Receipts	–	–	200	200	200	200	200	200	200	200
Contract costs	(500)	(500)	(10)	(10)	(10)	(10)	(10)	(10)	(10)	(10)
Net inflow/ (outflow)	(500)	(500)	190	190	190	190	190	190	190	190

Income statement

Year	1	2	3	4	5	6	7	8	9	10
Revenue	525	525	12	12	12	12	12	12	12	12
Contract costs	(500)	(500)	(10)	(10)	(10)	(10)	(10)	(10)	(10)	(10)
Finance income *	–	41	84	76	68	59	49	38	26	13
Net profit	25	66	86	78	70	61	51	40	28	15

* Amount due from grantor at start of year x 7.75%

Statement of financial position

Year	1	2	3	4	5	6	7	8	9	10
Amount due from grantor	525	1091	987	875	755	626	487	337	175	–
Cash/(debt)	(500)	(1,000)	(810)	(620)	(430)	(240)	(50)	140	330	520
Net assets	25	91	177	255	325	386	437	477	505	520

Operator recognises an intangible asset

34.3.20   Where the operator has a right to charge users directly for use of the infrastructure assets, it recognises an intangible financial asset as consideration for constructing or upgrading the infrastructure assets. [FRS 102 para 34.15]. In substance, the operator is granted a licence as consideration for constructing or upgrading the grantor's assets, so the transaction is treated as a construction contract in accordance with section 23 of FRS 102. Accordingly, revenue is recognised by reference to the stage of completion of the construction or upgrade services (similar to where the operator recognises a financial asset). [FRS 102 para 23.17].

34.3.21   The intangible asset that is recognised as consideration for construction or upgrade services is measured initially at fair value, based on the fair value of the construction or upgrade services provided. [FRS 102 para 34.15]. For the reasons set out in paragraph 34.3.17 above, fair value is typically estimated by applying an appropriate profit margin to the construction costs incurred.

34.3.22   After initial recognition, the operator accounts for the intangible asset in accordance with section 18 of the standard. [FRS 102 para 34.15]. Further guidance on intangible assets other than goodwill is provided in chapter 18.

34.3.23 The following example illustrates the accounting where an operator recognises an intangible asset.

Example – operator recognises an intangible asset

The terms of a service concession arrangement require an operator to construct a road (completing construction within two years) and maintain and operate the road to a specified standard for eight years (that is, years 3 to 10). At the end of year 10, the arrangement will end.

The arrangement's terms allow the operator to collect tolls from drivers using the road. The operator forecasts that vehicle numbers will remain constant over the duration of the arrangement, and that it will receive tolls of C200 in each of years 3 to 10. The operator also estimates that its annual running costs for the road will amount to C10 in each of years 3 to 10.

The operator estimates that the costs it will incur to construct the road, and the margin that it expects to earn, will be as follows:

	Year	Cost	Mark-up on cost	Fair value
Construction services	1	500	5%	525
	2	500	5%	525

In other words, the licence granted by the grantor (and hence the intangible asset recognised by the operator) has a fair value of C1,050. For the purpose of this example, borrowing costs incurred by the operator are ignored (see para 34.3.24 below). The intangible asset is amortised over the period in which it is expected to be available for use by the operator (that is, years 3 to 10).

The operator recognises contract revenue and costs during the construction phase in accordance with section 23 of FRS 102. So, the operator will recognise construction revenue and costs in years 1 and 2 of C525 and C500 respectively, and record a profit of C25 in each of those years. In later years, revenue of C200 will be recognised as tolls are collected, and running costs of C10 will be incurred. In addition, the intangible asset will be amortised.

The operator's cash flows will be the same as in the example in paragraph 34.3.19 above. Its income statement and statement of financial position over the term of the arrangement will be as follows:

Income statement

Year	1	2	3	4	5	6	7	8	9	10
Revenue	525	525	200	200	200	200	200	200	200	200
Contract costs	(500)	(500)	(10)	(10)	(10)	(10)	(10)	(10)	(10)	(10)
Amortisation of intangible asset	–	–	(131)	(131)	(131)	(131)	(131)	(131)	(131)	(133)
Net profit	25	25	59	59	59	59	59	59	59	57

Statement of financial position

Year	1	2	3	4	5	6	7	8	9	10
Intangible asset	525	1050	919	788	657	526	395	264	133	–
Cash/(debt)	(500)	(1,000)	(810)	(620)	(430)	(240)	(50)	140	330	520
Net assets	25	50	109	168	227	286	345	404	463	520

Borrowing costs

34.3.24 Borrowing costs incurred by an operator and directly attributable to a service concession arrangement fall within the scope of section 25 of FRS 102. The accounting treatment depends on whether the operator recognises a financial asset or an intangible asset. Borrowing costs should be recognised as an expense when incurred, unless the operator recognises an intangible asset. In that case, borrowing costs can be capitalised during the construction phase of the arrangement where the operator has adopted a policy of capitalisation in accordance with section 25 of FRS 102. [FRS 102 para 34.16A]. See further chapter 25.

Revenue in respect of operating services

34.3.25 The operator should account for revenue and costs relating to operating services in accordance with section 23 of FRS 102. [FRS 102 para 34.16]. Revenue will be recognised as those services are delivered.

Obligations for infrastructure maintenance

34.3.26 Service concession arrangements usually require the operator to maintain the infrastructure assets during the concession term. In some cases, this maintenance will require renewal, replacement or upgrade of life-expired components. For example, a toll road might need to be resurfaced. If the operator receives additional payment for meeting such obligations, it should treat them as a separate revenue-earning activity in accordance with section 23 of FRS 102. Alternatively, if no additional payment is received, the operator would need to consider the requirements of section 21 of the standard and make provision where it has an obligation under the terms of the arrangement to repair or replace damaged or worn-out assets. See further chapter 21.

34.3.27 If a service concession arrangement requires the operator to enhance or upgrade existing infrastructure during the operation phase, such activity is treated in the same way as construction, and it is accounted for as described in paragraph 34.3.11 onwards above.

Cash or other assets provided to the operator by the grantor

34.3.28 A grantor might sometimes contribute cash or other assets to the operator during (or at the end of) an arrangement's construction phase. A cash payment is treated in the same way as any other payments made in settlement of the financial asset. If a non-cash asset is provided and is necessary for the operator to meet its obligations under the arrangement, it remains the grantor's property, and no further accounting entries are required. But, if the operator is given assets that it can keep or deal with as it wishes, these will be the operator's assets that it should recognise at fair value. In substance, they represent a component of the grantor's consideration for the services provided under the arrangement.

Accounting by the grantor in a service concession arrangement

34.3.29 Infrastructure assets constructed or acquired by an operator in a service concession arrangement are controlled by the grantor (as explained in para 34.3.11 above). Hence, such assets should be recognised by the grantor as its assets. [FRS 102 para 34.12E]. The assets should be recognised as property, plant and equipment or as intangible assets, as appropriate, and accounted for in accordance with section 17 or 18 of FRS 102. [FRS 102 para 34.12H].

34.3.30 Where the grantor has an unconditional obligation to pay cash or another financial asset to the operator, it recognises a liability that is accounted for as a finance lease liability in accordance with section 20 of FRS 102. [FRS 102 paras 34.12F, 34.12G]. Amounts payable to the operator in respect of the operation or maintenance of the infrastructure assets are not included in the lease liability, or the initial recognition of the assets, but are recognised as expenses when incurred.

34.3.31 FRS 102 does not provide explicit guidance on the accounting by the grantor where it grants an operator a right to charge users directly for use of the infrastructure assets (that is, the operator recognises an intangible asset as described in para 34.3.20 above). But it does state that, if (as a result of applying section 20 of FRS 102) the grantor does not recognise a liability to make payments to the operator, it should not recognise the infrastructure assets (in other words, the assets described in paragraph 34.3.29 above cannot be recognised if there is no corresponding liability to pay for them). [FRS 102 para 34.12F].

34.3.32 In its advice to the FRC, the Accounting Council noted that the International Public Sector Accounting Standards Board has issued a standard (IPSAS 32) that includes two models for accounting by the grantor, depending on the terms of its arrangement with the operator. In addition to the finance lease model (described in para 34.3.30 above), IPSAS 32 includes a 'grant of right to the operator model' that applies to 'user pays' arrangements (that is, where the grantor grants the operator a right to charge users directly for use of the infrastructure assets). In this case, a grantor reporting in accordance with IPSAS 32 treats the credit arising on recognition of the infrastructure assets as deferred income, which it recognises as revenue in accordance with the economic substance of the service concession arrangement. The Accounting Council did not include this model in FRS 102 because, in its view, it results in the recognition as liabilities of amounts that might not meet the definition of a liability. Nevertheless, it has advised that further research should be carried out on the most appropriate accounting for 'user pays' service concession arrangements.

34.3.33 A grantor might sometimes contribute cash or other assets to the operator during (or at the end of) an arrangement's construction phase. A cash payment is held as a pre-payment when made, and it is then debited to the grantor's liability when initially recognised and measured. If a non-cash asset is provided and is necessary for the operator to meet its obligations under the arrangement, it remains the grantor's property, and no further accounting entries are required. But, if the operator is given assets that it can keep or deal with as it wishes, these will be the operator's assets, so the grantor should de-recognise them and treat them in the same way as a cash contribution. In substance, they represent a component of the grantor's consideration for the services provided under the arrangement.

Transitional issues

Accounting by operators

34.3.34 A first-time adopter is not required to apply paragraphs 34.12E — 34.16A of FRS 102 to service concession arrangements that were entered into before the date of transition to the standard. [FRS 102 para 35.10(i)]. Such arrangements should continue to be accounted for using the same accounting policies being applied at the date of transition.

Accounting for grantors

34.3.35 The Accounting Council considered whether the transitional provisions referred in paragraph 34.3.34 above should be available for grantors. It noted that, for some grantors, the proposals would result in recognising assets and liabilities for infrastructure assets that are not presently recognised. However, it considered that this provides more relevant information to users, and so it advised the FRC that special transitional provisions should not be available for grantors. As a result, grantors will not be permitted to apply, by analogy, the transitional exemptions available to operators (described above). Hence, grantors should give full retrospective effect to paragraphs 34.12E — 34.12H of FRS 102.

34.4 – Financial institutions: Disclosures

34.4 – Financial institutions: Disclosures

Scope

34.4.1 Section 34 of FRS 102 contains disclosure requirements about financial instruments and related risks. The disclosures apply only to financial institutions, which is defined to capture entities that have significant exposures to financial instruments. The disclosures are similar to those of IFRS 7, but the number of disclosures and level of detail required are significantly less in some areas. Detailed guidance on IFRS 7 can be found in chapter 6.9, 'Financial instruments: Presentation and disclosure', of the Manual of Accounting — IFRS for the UK. Financial institutions must provide these disclosures in addition to the disclosure requirements in sections 11 and 12 of FRS 102. [FRS 102 para 34.17].

34.4.2 The disclosure requirements apply to financial institutions (with the exception of retirement benefit plans) in both the individual financial statements and the consolidated financial statements of a group containing the financial institution. In the case of consolidated accounts, the disclosures apply regardless of the principal activity of the group. However, the disclosures are only required if they are material to the group and, if they are material, are only for entities in the group that are financial institutions.

34.4.3 A 'financial institution' is defined as:

- A bank which:

  - has permission under Part IV of the Financial Services and Markets Act 2000 to accept deposits and:

    - which is a credit institution; or

    - whose Part IV permission includes a requirement that it complies with the rules in the General Prudential sourcebook and the Prudential sourcebook for Bank, Building Societies and Investment Firms relating to banks, but which is not a building society, a friendly society or a credit union;

  - an EEA bank which is a full credit institution;

- a building society which is defined in section 119(1) of the Building Societies Act 1986 as a building society incorporated (or deemed to be incorporated) under that Act;

- a credit union, being a body corporate registered under the Industrial and Provident Societies Act 1965 as a credit union in accordance with the Credit Unions Act 1979, which is an authorised person;

- a custodian bank, broker-dealer or stockbroker;

- an incorporated friendly society incorporated under the Friendly Societies Act 1992 or a registered friendly society registered under section 7(1)(a) of the Friendly Societies Act 1974 or any enactment which it replaced, including any registered branches;

- an entity that undertakes the business of effecting or carrying out insurance contracts, including general and life assurance entities;

- an investment trust, Irish Investment Company, venture capital trust, mutual fund, exchange traded fund, unit trust, open-ended investment company (OEIC);

- a retirement benefit plan; or

- any other entity whose principal activity is to generate wealth or manage risk through financial instruments.

[FRS 102 Glossary of terms].

34.4.4 The final part of the definition above is intended to cover entities which have similar business activities to those listed above. It is not intended to include a parent entity whose sole activity is to hold investments in other group entities. It will, however, cover many group treasury companies who use financial instruments to manage cash, liquidity and financial risk for the group.

34.4.5 The definition of a financial institution includes retirement benefit plans, but the disclosures for financial institutions do not apply to retirement benefit plans (either in separate financial statements or for a group containing a retirement benefit plan). Instead, the disclosure requirements of section 34 of FRS 102 concerning retirement benefit plans apply.

Objectives

34.4.6 The objective of section 34 of FRS 102 is to provide information to users of financial statements about an entity's exposure to risks and how the entity manages those risks. To do this, the standard requires an entity to provide disclosures in its financial statements that enable users to evaluate:

- the significance of financial instruments for the entity's financial position and performance; and

- the nature and extent of credit, liquidity and market risks arising from financial instruments to which the entity is exposed (quantitative disclosure), and how the entity manages those risks (qualitative disclosures).

[FRS 102 paras 34.19, 34.23].

34.4.7 The first bullet point above covers disclosures about the figures in the balance sheet and the income statement. In addition, it requires various disclosures by 'class' of financial instruments (see para 34.4.9 below).

34.4.8 The second bullet point covers disclosure of qualitative and quantitative information about an entity's exposure to risks arising from financial instruments. Section 34 of the standard expands the qualitative disclosure to include information on the process that an entity uses to manage and measure risk. Some minimum disclosures are also required. Entities are required to communicate how they perceive, manage and measure risk.

34.4.9 The standard requires some disclosures to be given by class of financial instrument, including the following:

- The reconciliation of an allowance account (see para 34.4.15 below).

- Specific disclosures relating to credit risk (see para 34.4.21 below).

34.4.10 The standard itself does not provide a prescriptive list of classes of financial instrument. Therefore, management should determine the appropriate classes for disclosure, based on the nature of the entity's business and the financial instruments to which it has exposure. Classes are potentially determined at a lower level than the measurement categories in sections 11 and 12 of FRS 102, and need to be reconciled back to the balance sheet. The level of detail for a class should be determined on an entity-specific basis and could be defined for each individual disclosure in a different way. In determining classes of financial instrument, an entity should, at a minimum:

- Distinguish between instruments measured at amortised cost, at cost less impairment and at fair value.

- Treat as a separate class or classes those financial instruments outside section 11's scope which are accounted for in accordance with section 12 of the standard.

34.4.11 For entities applying the recognition and measurement provisions of IAS 39/IFRS 9 (see para 12.2(b) of FRS 102), a 'class' of financial instrument is not the same as a 'category' of financial instrument; classes are potentially determined at a lower level (as discussed above).

34.4.12 For example, in the case of banks, 'loans and receivables' comprises more than one class, unless the loans have similar characteristics. In this situation, it might be appropriate to group financial instruments into classes based on the following factors:

- types of customer (for example, commercial loans and loans to individuals); or

- types of loan (for example, mortgages, credit cards, unsecured loans and overdrafts).

However, in some cases, 'loans to customers' can be one class if all the loans have similar characteristics (for example, a savings bank providing only one type of loan to individuals).

34.4.13 Fair value assets could be split into equity and other investment classes. The equity investments could be further subdivided into those that are listed and those that are unlisted.

34.4.14 Section 34 of FRS 102 requires both qualitative and quantitative disclosure about risks associated with financial instruments. In the context of financial instruments, risk arises from the uncertainty in cash flows, which in turn affects both the future cash flows and fair values of financial assets and liabilities. The following are the types of financial risk that are related to financial instruments:

- Market risk – the risk that the fair value or cash flows of a financial instrument will fluctuate, because of changes in market prices. Market risk embodies not only the potential for loss, but also the potential for gain. It comprises three types of risk, as follows:

    - Interest rate risk – the risk that the fair value or future cash flows of a financial instrument will fluctuate because of changes in market interest rates.

    - Currency risk – the risk that the fair value or future cash flows of a financial instrument will fluctuate because of changes in foreign exchange rates.

    - Other price risk – the risk that the fair value or future cash flows of a financial instrument will fluctuate because of changes in market prices (other than those arising from interest rate risk or currency risk), whether those changes are caused by factors specific to the individual financial instrument or its issuer, or factors affecting all similar financial instruments traded in the market.

- Credit risk – the risk that the counterparty to a financial instrument will cause a financial loss for the entity by failing to discharge an obligation.

- Liquidity risk – the risk that an entity will encounter difficulty in meeting obligations associated with financial liabilities.

Allowance amount for credit losses

34.4.15 Where financial assets are impaired by credit losses and the entity records the impairment in a separate account (for example, an allowance account used to record individual impairments or a similar account used to record a collective impairment of assets) rather than directly reducing the asset's carrying amount, it should disclose a reconciliation of changes in that account during the period for each class of financial assets. [FRS 102 para 34.21].

Fair value

34.4.16 For financial instruments held at fair value on the statement of financial position (and only such instruments), financial institutions are required to disclose an analysis of the fair value using the hierarchy in paragraph 11.27 of the standard. [FRS 102 para 34.22].

34.4.17 The hierarchy in paragraph 11.27 has three levels which are used to estimate the fair value of a financial instrument, referred to as (a), (b) and (c). Therefore, the fair value disclosures for financial instruments held at fair value should be given for the following three levels. The standard states that:

(a) The best evidence of fair value is a quoted price for an identical asset in an active market. This is usually the current bid price.

(b) When quoted prices are unavailable, the price of a recent transaction for an identical asset provides evidence of fair value as long as there has not been a significant change in economic circumstances or a significant lapse of time since the transaction took place. If the entity can demonstrate that the last transaction price is not a good estimate of fair value (eg because it reflects the amount that an entity would receive or pay in a forced transaction, involuntary liquidation or distress sale), that price is adjusted.

(c) If the market for the asset is not active and recent transactions of an identical asset on their own are not a good estimate of fair value, an entity estimates the fair value by using a valuation technique. The objective of using a valuation technique is to estimate what the transaction price would have been on the measurement date in an arm's length exchange motivated by normal business considerations.

The hierarchy in paragraph 11.27 refers specifically to investments in ordinary or preference shares, but it is stated that, where other sections of the standard refer to the hierarchy, it should be read to include the types of assets covered by those sections. [FRS 102 para 11.27].

34.4.18 Because section 34 of the standard requires the disclosure of a fair value hierarchy for *financial instruments*, this will include both financial assets and financial liabilities held at fair value.

Qualitative disclosures

34.4.19 For each type of risk arising from financial instruments, an entity should disclose:

■ The exposures to risk and how they arise. This information about risk exposures might describe exposures, both gross and net of risk transfer and other risk-mitigating transactions.

■ Its objectives, policies and processes for managing the risk and the methods used to measure the risk. This might include, but is not limited to:

■ The structure and organisation of the entity's risk management functions, including a discussion of independence and accountability.

- ■ The scope and nature of the entity's risk reporting or measurement systems.

- ■ The entity's policies for hedging or mitigating risk, including its policies and procedures for taking collateral.

- ■ The entity's processes for monitoring the continuing effectiveness of such hedges or mitigating devices.

- ■ The entity's policies and procedures for avoiding excessive concentrations of risk.

■ Any changes in the above for the period.

Entities should disclose the reasons for the change. Such changes might result from changes in exposure to risk or from changes in the way those exposures are managed.

[FRS 102 para 34.24].

Quantitative disclosures

34.4.20   For credit, liquidity and market risks arising from financial instruments, an entity should disclose:

■ Summary quantitative data about its exposure to that risk at the reporting date.

■ The items described in paragraphs 34.4.21 to 34.4.50 below, to the extent that they are not provided in the previous bullet point. These are section 34's minimum disclosure requirements.

Credit risk

34.4.21   The standard requires an entity to disclose information about its exposure to credit risk by class of financial instrument. Financial instruments in the same class share economic characteristics with respect to the risk being disclosed (in this case, credit risk). For example, an entity might determine that residential mortgages, unsecured consumer loans and commercial loans each have different economic characteristics. The information that an entity should disclose, by class of financial instrument, is as follows:

■ The amount that best represents its maximum exposure to credit risk at the reporting date, without taking account of any collateral held or other credit enhancements. This is typically the gross carrying amount of the related asset, net of any impairment losses recognised in accordance with section 11 of FRS 102; examples of the maximum exposure to credit risk for various instruments are given below. This disclosure is not required for financial instruments whose carrying amount best represents the maximum exposure to credit risk.

■ A description of collateral held as security and of other credit enhancements. A description is required of the financial effect of collateral held as security and of other credit enhancements (for example, a quantification of the extent to which collateral and other credit enhancements mitigate credit risk) in respect of the amount that best represents the maximum exposure to credit.

■ The amount by which any related credit derivatives or similar instruments mitigate that maximum exposure to credit risk.

■ Information about the credit quality of financial assets that are neither past due nor impaired.

[FRS 102 para 34.25].

34.4.22 The above disclosures do not apply to equity investments such as non-convertible preference shares and non-puttable ordinary or preference shares. This is because, for these shares, the issuer has no obligation to pay cash or transfer other assets. Therefore, such equity investments are subject to price risk, and not credit risk.

34.4.23 Activities that give rise to credit risk, and the related maximum exposure to credit risk, include (but are not limited to):

■ Granting loans and receivables to customers and placing deposits with other entities. In these cases, the maximum exposure to credit risk is the carrying amount of the related financial assets.

■ Entering into derivative contracts (for example, foreign exchange contracts, interest rate swaps and credit derivatives). Where the derivative contract has a positive fair value (that is, it is an asset) and is measured at fair value, the maximum exposure to credit risk will equal the carrying amount.

■ Granting financial guarantees. In this case, the maximum exposure to credit risk is the maximum amount that the entity could have to pay if the guarantee is called on, which might be significantly greater than the amount recognised as a liability.

■ Making a loan commitment that is irrevocable over its life, or is revocable only in response to a material adverse change. If the issuer cannot settle the loan commitment net in cash or another financial instrument, the maximum credit exposure is the full amount of the commitment not yet drawn. This is because it is uncertain whether the amount of any undrawn portion might be drawn on in the future and, if it is drawn, whether the borrower will be able to repay it. This might be significantly greater than the amount recognised as a liability.

Collateral and other credit enhancements

34.4.24 In respect of the second bullet point in paragraph 34.21 above, an entity's description about collateral held as security and other credit enhancements might include:

- The policies and processes for valuing and managing collateral and other credit enhancements obtained.

- A description of the main types of collateral and other credit enhancements (examples of the latter being guarantees, credit derivatives and other netting agreements).

- The main types of counterparties to collateral and other credit enhancements and their creditworthiness.

- Information about risk concentrations within the collateral or other credit enhancements.

34.4.25 Where an entity obtains financial or non-financial assets during the period by taking possession of collateral that it holds as security or calling on other credit enhancements, and such assets meet the recognition criteria in other sections, an entity should disclose, for such assets held at the reporting date:

- the nature and carrying amount of the assets; and

- where the assets are not readily convertible into cash, its policies for disposing of such assets or for using them in its operations.

[FRS 102 para 34.27].

Credit quality of financial assets that are neither past due nor impaired

34.4.26 In respect of the fourth bullet point in paragraph 34.21 above, information about credit quality of financial assets that are neither past due nor impaired might include:

- An analysis of credit exposures using an external or internal credit rating system.
  - Where an entity manages its credit exposures using an external credit rating system, an entity might disclose information about:
    - The carrying amounts of credit exposures for each external credit rating.
    - The rating agencies used.
    - The amount of an entity's rated and unrated credit exposures.
    - The relationship between internal and external ratings.

- Where an entity manages its credit exposures using an internal credit rating system, an entity might disclose information about:

    - The internal credit ratings process.

    - The amounts of credit exposures for each internal credit rating.

    - The relationship between internal and external ratings.

- The nature of the counterparty.

- Historical information about counterparty default rates.

- Any other information used to assess credit quality.

Financial assets that are either past due or impaired

34.4.27 In addition to the above disclosures, the required disclosures about credit risk also cover financial assets that are either past due or impaired.

34.4.28 A financial asset is past due where the counterparty has failed to make a payment when contractually due. As an example, an entity enters into a lending agreement that requires interest to be paid every month. On the first day of the next month, if interest has not been paid, the whole loan is past due, not just the interest. Past due does not mean that a counterparty will never pay, but it can trigger various actions such as renegotiation, enforcement of covenants, or legal proceedings. An entity should disclose by class of financial asset:

- An analysis of the age of financial assets that are past due as at the reporting date but not impaired. The purpose of this disclosure is to provide users of the financial statements with information about those financial assets that are more likely to become impaired, and to help users to estimate the level of future impairment losses. Thus, the entire balance which relates to the amount past due should be disclosed, rather than only the amount that is past due, as this is the amount of the impaired financial assets that would be disclosed if impairment crystallises.

    Other associated balances due from the same debtor are not included if the debtor has not yet failed to make a payment on these balances when contractually due.

    In preparing such an age analysis of financial assets, an entity uses its judgement to determine an appropriate number of time bands. For example, an entity might determine that the following time bands are appropriate:

    - Not more than three months.

    - More than three months but not more than six months.

    - More than six months but not more than one year.

    - More than one year.

- An analysis of financial assets that are individually determined to be impaired as at the reporting date, including the factors that the entity considered in determining that they are impaired. These disclosures are given not only in the year of impairment, but also in each subsequent reporting period during which the financial asset remains impaired. Such an analysis might include:

  - The carrying amount, before deducting any impairment loss.

  - The amount of any related impairment loss.

Example – Assessment of receivables individually determined to be impaired

Entity M has £300m of receivables, which it has analysed as follows:

- £120m have been assessed individually for impairment and are considered to be impaired.

- £40m represent a group of receivables, each with a small balance, that are individually determined to be impaired, but the amount of the impairment is calculated on the whole £40m amount.

- £140m represent a portfolio of receivables for which there is observable data indicating a measurable decrease in the estimated future cash flows, although the decrease cannot be identified with individual balances. A collective impairment provision has been recognised.

Of these, only the first two amounts have been individually assessed for impairment and so would require disclosure under section 34 of FRS 102. Disclosure would not be required in respect of the third amount, because the receivables have been assessed on a collective basis rather than individually.

Liquidity risk

34.4.29 At a minimum, an entity should disclosure the following with regard to liquidity risk:

- A maturity analysis for non-derivative financial liabilities (including issued financial guarantee contracts) that shows the remaining contractual maturities.

- A maturity analysis for derivative financial liabilities. The maturity analysis should include the remaining contractual maturities for the derivative financial liabilities.

- A description of how it manages the liquidity risk inherent in the above.

[FRS 102 paras 34.24, 34.28].

34.4.30 This information can be summarised in one or several maturity analysis tables. It should be clear whether the financial liabilities are derivatives or non-derivatives.

34.4.31 In preparing the contractual maturity analyses described above, an entity uses its judgement to determine an appropriate number of time bands. For example, an entity might determine that the following time bands are appropriate:

- Not later than one month.

- Later than one month but not later than three months.

- Later than three months but not later than one year.

- Later than one year but not later than five years.

34.4.32 Where the counterparty has a choice of when an amount is paid, the liability is included on the basis of the earliest date on which the entity can be required to pay. For example, financial liabilities that an entity can be required to repay on demand (for example, demand deposits) are included in the earliest time band.

34.4.33 Where an entity is committed to make amounts available in instalments, each instalment is allocated to the earliest period in which the entity can be required to pay that instalment.

34.4.34 Where an entity has issued a financial guarantee contract, the maximum amount of the guarantee is allocated to the earliest period in which the guarantee could be called.

34.4.35 The maximum amount of an undrawn loan commitment should also be included in the maturity analysis, and it is allocated to the earliest period in which the commitment could be called. Once a loan is drawn down, it will be included in the maturity analysis as a non-derivative financial liability.

34.4.36 The amounts disclosed in the maturity analyses on a contractual basis are the contractual undiscounted cash flows (including principal and interest payments). For example:

- Gross finance lease obligations (before deducting finance charges).

- Prices specified in forward agreements to purchase financial assets for cash.

- Net amounts for pay-floating receive-fixed interest rate swaps for which net cash flows are exchanged.

- Contractual amounts to be exchanged in a derivative financial instrument (for example, a currency swap) for which gross cash flows are exchanged.

- Gross amounts that can be drawn under loan commitments.

34.4.37 The undiscounted cash flows described above differ from the amounts included in the balance sheet, which are based on discounted cash flows. There is no specific requirement to reconcile the amounts disclosed in the maturity analysis to the amounts included in the balance sheet.

34.4.38 Where the amount payable is not fixed, the amount disclosed in the maturity analyses is determined by reference to the conditions existing at the end of the reporting period. For example, where the amount payable varies with changes in an index, the amount disclosed might be based on the level of the index at the end of the period. For floating rate financial liabilities and foreign currency denominated instruments, the use of forward interest rates and forward foreign exchange rates might be conceptually preferable, but the use of a spot rate at the end of the period is also acceptable. Whichever approach is adopted (that is, current/spot rate or forward rate at the reporting date), it should be applied consistently.

Market risk

34.4.39 Unless an entity complies with paragraph 34.4.45 below, it should disclose:

- A sensitivity analysis for each type of market risk to which the entity is exposed at the reporting date, showing how profit or loss and equity would have been affected by changes in the relevant risk variable that were reasonably possible at that date. The sensitivity analysis should show the effect of changes over the period until the entity next presents these disclosures, which usually is its next annual report. Note that the standard requires this disclosure based on reasonably possible changes and not on a 'worst case scenario' or 'stress test'. Risk variables that are relevant to disclosing market risk include (but are not limited to):

  - The yield curve of market interest rates. It might be necessary to consider both parallel and non-parallel shifts in the yield curve.

  - Foreign exchange rates.

  - Prices of equity instruments.

  - Market prices of commodities.

- The methods and assumptions used in preparing the sensitivity analysis.

- Changes from the previous period in the methods and assumptions used and the reasons for such changes.

[FRS 102 para 34.29].

34.4.40 In providing the sensitivity analysis for each type of market risk, an entity should decide how it aggregates information, to display the overall picture without combining information with different characteristics about exposures to risks from significantly different economic environments. For example, an entity that trades financial instruments might disclose this information separately for financial instruments held for trading and those not held for trading. Similarly, an entity would not aggregate its exposure to market risks from areas of hyperinflation with its exposure to the same market risks from areas of very low inflation. Conversely, if an entity has exposure to only one type of market risk in only one economic environment, it would not show disaggregated information.

34.4.41 An entity might disclose a sensitivity analysis for interest rate risk for each currency in which the entity has material exposures to interest rate risk. Similarly, a sensitivity analysis is disclosed for each currency to which an entity has significant exposure.

34.4.42 If an entity presents its financial statements in a currency other than its functional currency, it should provide the foreign currency risk disclosures with reference to its functional currency rather than its presentation currency. The entity's exposure to currencies other than the functional currency will affect its future performance, and details of these exposures are provided in the financial statements.

34.4.43 Because the factors affecting market risk vary, depending on the specific circumstances of each entity, the appropriate range to be considered in providing a sensitivity analysis of market risk varies for each entity and for each type of market risk. However, entities are not required to disclose the effect for each change within a range of reasonably possible changes of the relevant risk variable; disclosure of the effects of the changes at the limits of the reasonably possible range would be sufficient.

34.4.44 An entity is not required to determine what the profit or loss for the period would have been if relevant risk variables had been different. Instead, it should disclose the effect on profit or loss and equity at the balance sheet date, assuming that a reasonably possible change in the relevant risk variable had occurred at the balance sheet date and had been applied to the risk exposures in existence at that date. For example, if an entity has a floating rate liability at the end of the year, it would disclose the effect on profit or loss (that is, interest expense) for the current year if interest rates had varied by reasonably possible amounts and the floating rate liability had been outstanding for the entire year.

34.4.45 If an entity prepares a sensitivity analysis, such as value-at-risk (VaR), that reflects interdependencies between risk variables (for example, interest rates and exchange rates) and uses it to manage financial risks, it could use that sensitivity analysis in place of the analysis described above. However, a precondition for disclosing sensitivity in such a format (VaR) is that the entity uses VaR in managing its financial risks. It cannot choose just to apply VaR for disclosure purposes but continue to manage each risk variable separately. In addition, it is likely that outstanding inter-entity foreign currency receivables and payables at the year end are not considered in the VaR model. If this is the case, the entity will need to prepare additional sensitivity disclosures for these amounts. The entity should also disclose details of the methods and assumptions used. [FRS 102 para 34.30].

Capital

34.4.46   An entity is required to disclose information that will enable users of its financial statements to evaluate the entity's objectives, policies and processes for managing capital. [FRS 102 para 34.31].

34.4.47   To satisfy the above requirement, a financial institution discloses the following, on the basis of information provided internally to key management personnel:

- Qualitative information about its objectives, policies and processes for managing capital, including:

    - a description of what it manages as capital;

    - where an entity is subject to externally imposed capital requirements, the nature of those requirements, and how those requirements are incorporated into the management of capital; and

    - how it is meeting its objectives for managing capital.

- Summary quantitative data about what it manages as capital.

- Any changes in the above from the previous period.

- Whether, during the period, it complied with any externally imposed capital requirements to which it is subject and, if not, the consequences of such non-compliance.

[FRS 102 para 34.31(a)–(e)].

34.4.48   'Capital' is not defined in FRS 102. As noted above, an entity is required to describe what it manages as capital on the basis of information provided internally to key management personnel. Whilst capital would often equate to equity for the purposes of this disclosure, it might also include some financial liabilities or exclude some components of equity. For example, some entities regard forms of subordinated debt as part of capital, while others exclude a hedge reserve. In practice, some entities also include interest-bearing debt as part of capital.

34.4.49   A financial institution might manage capital in a number of ways, and it might be subject to a number of different capital requirements. For example, a group might include both banking and insurance activities, or a non-financial services group might have a financial services subsidiary. In such circumstances, where aggregate capital disclosures would not provide useful information or would distort a user's understanding of an entity's capital resources, the entity should disclose separate information for each capital requirement to which it is subject. [FRS 102 para 34.32].

Reporting cash flows on a net basis

34.4.50   A financial institution that presents a statement of cash flows (see chapter 7) might report cash flows arising from each of the following activities on a net basis:

- cash receipts and payments for the acceptance and repayment of deposits with a fixed maturity date;

- the placement of deposits with, and withdrawal of deposits from, other financial institutions; and

- cash advances and loans made to customers and the repayment of those advances and loans.

This does not impose a requirement to produce a cash flow statement (see chapter 7).

[FRS 102 para 34.33].

Transition requirements

34.4.51   On transition the standard requires the disclosure of comparative information, for the previous period, for all monetary amounts presented in the financial statements, as well as specified narrative and descriptive information. [FRS 102 para 35.6]. Therefore, in order to present a complete set of financial statements, financial institutions are required to disclosure comparative amounts for all the disclosures included in section 34 of the standard.

34.5 – Public benefit entities

34.5 – Public benefit entities

Introduction

34.5.1 Traditionally, UK accounting standards have not dealt specifically with the non-commercial transactions of public benefit entities (PBEs). Instead guidance has generally been provided by the Statements of Recommended Practice (SORPs) for the individual sectors (housing, education and charities). In some cases, the SORPs took different approaches to apparently similar financial reporting issues, such as the accounting for government grants. In an attempt to improve consistency, in 2007 the Accounting Standards Board (ASB) published its Statement of Principles for Public Benefit Entities, which led to a few changes to the SORPs.

34.5.2 In 2011 the ASB published Financial Reporting Exposure Draft (FRED) 45 setting out proposals for a Financial Reporting Standard for Public Benefit Entities (FRSPBE) to accompany the proposed FRS 102. In response to the consultation, the ASB decided to incorporate into FRS 102 the specific requirements for public benefit entities. The three existing SORPs relating to public benefit entities are being updated to reflect FRS 102.

34.5.3 Most of the public benefit entity requirements are located in section 34 of FRS 102 and are identified by a 'PBE' prefix to the paragraph number. There are a few requirements which can be found elsewhere in the standard, such as accounting for heritage assets and funding commitments, which are not specifically identified as relating to PBEs but are relevant nonetheless.

What is a public benefit entity (PBE)?

34.5.4 A 'public benefit entity' is defined as one "*whose primary objective is to provide goods or services for the general public, community or social benefit and where any equity is provided with a view to supporting the entity's primary objectives rather than with a view to providing a financial return to equity providers, shareholders or members*". [FRS 102 Glossary of terms].

34.5.5 The following types of entity will normally fall within this definition:

- charities (including charitable companies);

- registered social landlords (also known as housing associations);

- further education colleges (including academies);

- higher education institutions (for example, universities); and

- other bodies that meet the definition, which might include clubs, associations, societies and trade unions.

34.5.6 FRS 102 notes that 'public benefit entity' does not necessarily mean that the purpose of the entity is for the benefit of the whole public. Many PBEs exist for the direct benefit of a particular group of people, although it is possible that society as a whole also benefits indirectly. The key factor is that the entity's primary purpose is not to provide economic benefit to its investors. For example, entities such as mutual insurance companies, mutual co-operative entities – and clubs which provide dividends or other economic benefits directly and proportionately to their owners, members or participants – are not PBEs. [FRS 102 Glossary of terms, footnote 28].

34.5.7 Some PBEs undertake activities intended to make a surplus in order to fund their primary activities. An entity should consider the primary purpose of its (or its group's) activities when assessing whether it meets the definition of a PBE. [FRS 102 Glossary of terms, footnote 28].

34.5.8 PBEs might receive contributions in the form of equity even though the PBE does not have a primary profit motive. However, because of the fundamental nature of PBEs, any such contributions are made by the equity holders of the entity primarily to enable the provision of goods or services to beneficiaries rather than with a view to a financial return for themselves. This is different from the position of lenders; loans do not fall into the category of equity. [FRS 102 Glossary of terms, footnote 28].

What is a public benefit entity group?

34.5.9 A public benefit entity group is defined as "*a public benefit entity parent and all of its wholly-owned subsidiaries*". [FRS 102 Glossary of terms]. It is important to note that this definition is different from the general, more well-known, definition of a group in the standard because it limits the group members to the parent and its 'wholly-owned' subsidiaries.

34.5.10 The inclusion of the 'PBE group' definition, together with allowing PBE group members to apply some specific elements of the PBE accounting requirements (as described below), is a useful feature of FRS 102. For example, where a charity has a wholly owned trading subsidiary company, that company can make use of some of the PBE accounting requirements, even though it is not a PBE in its own right. So, if the parent charity gives the subsidiary a concessionary loan, both the parent and the subsidiary can take advantage of the simplified accounting for PBE concessionary loans in their individual financial statements.

Which entities apply the PBE elements?

34.5.11 FRS 102 restricts the use of the PBE elements to specific types of entity; this is because, in some cases, the PBE requirements diverge from those for similar commercial transactions found elsewhere in the standard.

34.5.12 As noted above, the standard identifies the elements through a 'PBE' prefix to the paragraph number, and the majority of these paragraphs are located in section 34. Paragraphs with this 'PBE' prefix are applied only by public benefit entities and, where specifically directed, by members of a public benefit entity group (as defined above). These paragraphs cannot be applied (directly or by analogy) by other entities. [FRS 102 para 1.2].

34.5.13 The standard is not clear on whether PBEs must apply the PBE elements to their relevant transactions. For example, if a PBE is the acquirer in a business combination that meets the definition of the gift of a business in section 34 of FRS 102, can it nevertheless choose to apply acquisition accounting in accordance with section 19 of the standard? In practice, this could be academic for those PBEs that must apply a SORP, because it is likely that the SORPs will require the use of the PBE paragraphs in the standard.

34.5.14 Where a PBE applies one or more of the PBE elements it must also include in its accounts an unreserved statement that it is a public benefit entity. [FRS 102 para PBE3.3A]. Where a non-PBE member of a PBE group is entitled to apply a PBE element and does so, it is not required to make this unreserved statement; but, in our view, it should instead state in its accounts that it is a member of the PBE group.

PBE-specific elements in FRS 102

34.5.15 FRS 102 contains requirements on the following transactions:

- Property held for the provision of social benefits. [FRS 102 para 16.3A].
- Incoming Resources from Non-Exchange Transactions. [FRS 102 paras PBE34.64-PBE34.74].
- Public Benefit Entity Combinations. [FRS 102 paras PBE34.75-PBE34.86].
- Public Benefit Entity Concessionary Loans. [FRS 102 paras PBE34.87-PBE34.97].

34.5.16 In addition, FRS 102 contains requirements on accounting for heritage assets and funding commitments which, although not PBE paragraphs, are more likely to be relevant to PBEs than to other types of entity. These are discussed in chapters 34.6 and 34.7.

Property held for the provision of social benefits

34.5.17 Where an entity holds property primarily for the provision of social benefits, such as property held for social housing purposes, the property is not classified as an investment property. [FRS 102 para 16.3A]. This is directly relevant to registered social landlords, but might also be relevant to some charities.

34.5.18   For example registered social landlords that charge social housing rent on their dwellings (that is, less than a market rent for the properties) are assumed to be holding the properties for social housing purposes rather than seeking to maximise the return on the properties. So, the standard confirms that, despite the assets being cash-generating, they are not held to generate profits for the PBE and it is inappropriate to classify them as investment properties . The assets should instead be accounted for as property, plant and equipment in accordance with section 17 of the standard.

34.5.19   Where a PBE does not hold a property primarily for social purposes but for income generation and/or capital appreciation, it must account for it as an investment property. [FRS 102 para 16.2].

Incoming resources from non-exchange transactions

Definition

34.5.20   The FRS defines a 'non-exchange transaction' as one *"whereby an entity receives value from another entity without directly giving approximately equal value in exchange or gives value to another entity without directly receiving approximately equal value in exchange"*. [FRS 102 para PBE34.65].

34.5.21   Such transactions can include donations of cash, goods, and services and legacies — such as leaving a specific amount of money or a percentage of an estate in a will to a PBE. [FRS 102 para PBE34.66].

34.5.22   Government grants received and receivable are excluded from the scope of non-exchange transactions because the requirements in section 24 of the standard take precedence. [FRS 102 para PBE34.64].

Scope

34.5.23   PBEs and entities within a public benefit entity group apply the accounting requirements of paragraphs PBE34.67 — PBE34.74 and Appendix B to section 34 of the standard to incoming resources from non-exchange transactions. [FRS 102 para PBE34.65]. These accounting requirements are described below.

Recognition

34.5.24   The receipt of resources will usually result in a PBE recognising an asset (such as cash) and corresponding income for the fair value of resources when those resources become received or receivable. However, in some cases this might differ where:

- the PBE receives the resources in the form of services (see further below); or

- there are performance-related conditions attached to the resources, which have yet to be fulfilled.

[FRS 102 para PBE34B.1].

34.5.25 The standard establishes principles for recognising receipts of resources from non-exchange transactions as follows:

Feature of the non-exchange transaction	Recognition treatment
(a) The transaction **does not** impose performance-related conditions on the recipient.	Recognise in income when resources are received or receivable.
(b) The transaction **does** impose performance-related conditions on the recipient.	Recognise in income only when the performance-related conditions are met.
(c) Incoming resources are received in advance and before the revenue recognition criteria are satisfied	Recognise a liability.

[FRS 102 para PBE34.67].

34.5.26 As described in the table above, where no performance conditions are imposed, an entity recognises the income when the resources are received or receivable. The point at which resources are receivable is, in our view, the point at which the entity recognises an asset for the future inflow of the resources. This occurs when it is probable that the future economic benefits will flow to the entity and the asset has a cost or value that can be measured reliably. [FRS 102 para 2.37].

34.5.27 The standard requires an entity to recognise a liability where resources are received in advance of the recognition criteria in (a) or (b) in the table being met. This would most likely be presented as deferred income in the balance sheet.

Performance-related conditions

34.5.28 It can be seen from the above principles that where the PBE receives incoming resources that impose conditions on it, it needs to examine the conditions to determine whether they are performance-related.

34.5.29 A 'performance-related condition' is a *"condition that requires the performance of a particular level of service or units of output to be delivered, with payment of, or entitlement to, the resources conditional on that performance"*. [FRS 102 Glossary of terms].

34.5.30 In some cases, the PBE might receive resources with performance-related conditions attached which require it to use the resources to provide a specified level of service in order to be entitled to retain the resources. A PBE does not recognise income from those resources until these performance-related conditions have been met. [FRS 102 para PBE34B.13].

34.5.31 However, in other cases, the requirements might be stated so broadly that in practice they do not impose any performance-related condition on the PBE. In these cases the PBE recognises income when the resources are received or receivable. [FRS 102 para PBE34B.14].

34.5.32 Where a condition is not performance-related, it may represent a restriction. A 'restriction' is a "*requirement that limits or directs the purposes for which a resource may be used that does not meet the definition of a performance-related condition*". [FRS 102 Glossary of terms]. The existence of a restriction does not prohibit a PBE from recognising a resource in income when it is receivable. [FRS 102 para PBE34.68]. For example, an individual might donate money to a PBE to fund the construction of a property for use by the PBE in its services. The donation does not specify the services for which the PBE must use the property, nor the level of services to be provided, nor the recipients. The donation does however require that if the PBE ever sells the property, the original donation amount must be returned to the donor, so this is a restriction. The obligation to repay the donation does not arise unless and until the PBE sells the property. So, the PBE can recognise the donation in income once the property has been constructed.

Can the resource be measured reliably?

34.5.33 When applying the recognition requirements above, a PBE also considers whether the resource can be measured reliably and whether the benefits of recognising the resource outweigh the costs. [FRS 102 para PBE34.69]. Where a PBE meets the criteria for recognising the resources, it only recognises resources when it can measure the fair value of those resources reliably. [FRS 102 para PBE34B.2]. A PBE considers the concepts of materiality and balance between benefit and cost when deciding which resources received to recognise in its financial statements. [FRS 102 para PBE34B.3].

34.5.34 If it is not practicable for a PBE to estimate the value of the resource with sufficient reliability, the PBE should recognise income in the financial period when the resource is sold. [FRS 102 para PBE34.70]. This might commonly occur with high-volume, low-value second-hand goods donated to charity shops for resale. [FRS 102 para PBE34B.4]. In such cases, the PBE recognises the resource at an amount equal to the consideration received or receivable.

Timing of recognition – legacies

34.5.35 A PBE recognises donations arising from legacies when it is probable that the PBE will receive the legacy and it can measure its value reliably. These criteria will normally be met following probate, once the executor of the estate has established that there are sufficient assets in the estate, after settling liabilities, to pay the legacy. [FRS 102 para PBE34B.5].

34.5.36 The standard notes that agreement of the estate's accounts, or notification that payment will be made, might give rise to evidence that the executor has determined that a payment can be made. Where a PBE receives notification after the year-end, but it is clear that the executor has agreed before the year-end that the legacy can be paid, the PBE accrues the legacy in its financial statements. [FRS 102 para PBE34B.6].

34.5.37 Where a PBE receives numerous immaterial legacies, where individual identification would be burdensome, it could take a portfolio approach by grouping similar legacies. [FRS 102 para PBE34B.7].

Resources received in the form of services – quantification and recognition

34.5.38 Donated services which can reasonably be quantified include:

■ donated facilities, such as office accommodation;

■ services that would otherwise have been purchased (such as legal or financial advice); and

■ services usually provided by an individual or an entity as part of their trade or profession for a fee.

[FRS 102 para PBE34B.10].

34.5.39 Also, it is expected that contributions made by volunteers cannot reasonably be quantified, and so these services should not be recognised in the financial statements. [FRS 102 para PBE34B.11]. While there is an argument that volunteer services could be quantified by reference to a metric such as the minimum wage, this does not take into account an organisation's requirements for volunteers, and it might not reflect the skills, experience or role of the volunteer. [FRS 102 Advice to FRC para 157].

34.5.40 Where a PBE can reasonably quantify donations of services, it recognises these in the financial statements when the services are received (for example an audit service provided for free to a charity). [FRS 102 para PBE34B.8].

34.5.41 The PBE will usually recognise the corresponding income when the services are provided to it. Where it consumes the services immediately, it will usually recognise this as a corresponding expense. [FRS 102 paras PBE34.72; PBE34B.9]. The PBE recognises an asset, instead of an expense, only when those services are used for the production of an asset and the services received will be capitalised as part of the cost of that asset. [FRS 102 para PBE34.72]. For example, the PBE might use a service in the erecting a building (an asset). In such a case, the PBE would recognise the associated donated service (for plumbing and electrical services) as a part of the cost of that asset. [FRS 102 para PBE34B.9].

Non-compliance with performance conditions

34.5.42 If a PBE recognises a resource in income, and subsequently fails to meet a restriction or performance-related condition such that repayment becomes probable, it recognises a liability for the amount repayable. [FRS 102 para PBE34.71]. In the example from paragraph 34.5.32 above, if at a later time, the PBE considers that it might sell the property, it will need to assess if and when to recognise an obligation in accordance with section 21 of the standard.

Measurement

34.5.43 A PBE measures incoming resources from non-exchange transactions as follows:

a) Donated services and facilities, which would otherwise have been purchased, are measured at the value to the PBE.

b) All other incoming resources from non-exchange transactions are measured at the fair value of the resources received or receivable.

[FRS 102 para PBE34.73].

34.5.44 The requirement in (a) above applies only to donated services and facilities that a PBE would otherwise have purchased. The value to the PBE is the estimated value to the PBE of the service or facility received, which is the price that the PBE estimates it would have to pay in the open market for a service or facility of equivalent utility to the PBE. [FRS 102 para PBE34B.15]. Where the service received is to a higher standard, and so of a higher value, than the PBE would have purchased itself, in our view it should measure the resource and expense based on the standard of service it would actually have purchased. The PBE might also consider disclosing that it has actually received services of a higher standard and the 'excess' value.

34.5.45 A PBE measures other resources received or receivable, that are not services or facilities, at their fair value. These fair values are usually the price that the PBE would have to pay on the open market for an equivalent resource [FRS 102 para PBE34B.16].

34.5.46 Where there is no direct evidence of an open market value for an equivalent item, a PBE could derive a value from sources such as:

a) the cost of the item to the donor; or

b) in the case of goods that are expected to be sold, the estimated resale value (which might reflect the amount actually realised) after deducting the cost to sell the goods.

[FRS 102 para PBE34B.17].

34.5.47 A PBE recognises donated services as income and an equivalent amount as an expense in income and expenditure, unless it can capitalise the expense as part of the cost of an asset. [FRS 102 para PBE34B.18].

Disclosure

34.5.48   A PBE must disclose:

- the nature and amounts of resources receivable from non-exchange transactions that are recognised in the financial statements;

- any unfulfilled conditions or other contingencies that are attached to resources from non-exchange transactions that have not been recognised in income; and

- an indication of other forms of resources from non-exchange transactions from which the entity has benefited (such as unrecognised volunteer services).

[FRS 102 paras PBE34.74; PBE34B.12].

Public benefit entity combinations

34.5.49   A 'business combination' is the "*bringing together of separate entities or businesses into one reporting entity*" [FRS 102 Glossary of terms]. Where a PBE is involved in a business combination which involves an entity (or parts of an entity) combining with another entity, it considers the nature and substance of the business combination and applies the relevant accounting requirements, as set out in the following table:

Type of Business Combination	Required Accounting
In-substance gift of a business for nil or nominal consideration	Recognition of assets/liabilities at fair value with corresponding gain/loss (FRS 102 paras PBE34.76 – PBE34.79)
Combination meets the definition and criteria of a merger	Merger accounting at book value (FRS 102 paras PBE34.80 – PBE34.85)
Acquisitions	Acquisition accounting at fair value (FRS 102 section 19)

[FRS 102 paras PBE34.75; PBE34.76].

Combinations that are in substance a gift

34.5.50   Such a combination is defined as "*a combination carried out at nil or nominal consideration that is not a fair value exchange but in substance the gift of one entity to another*". [FRS 102 Glossary of terms]. For example, a charity might gift a charity shop subsidiary to another charity with similar objectives.

Accounting treatment and disclosure

34.5.51   For a PBE business combination that is, in substance, a gift, the PBE accounts for it as an acquisition in accordance with section 19 of the standard, except for the following elements of the transaction [FRS 102 para PBE34.77]:

■   the recipient PBE recognises any excess of the fair value of the assets received over the fair value of the liabilities assumed as a gain in income and expenditure. The gain represents the gift of the value of one entity to another and is recognised as income by the recipient PBE [FRS 102 para PBE34.78]; and

■   where the fair value of the liabilities assumed exceeds the fair value of the assets received, the recipient PBE recognises this excess as a loss in income and expenditure. The FRS notes that this loss represents the net obligations assumed, for which the receiving PBE has not received a financial reward and therefore recognises the loss as an expense [FRS 102 para PBE34.79].

Combinations which meet the definition and criteria of a merger

34.5.52   A 'merger' is a business combination "*that results in the creation of a new reporting entity formed from the combining parties, in which the controlling parties of the combining entities come together in a partnership for the mutual sharing of risks and benefits of the newly formed entity and in which no party to the combination in substance obtains control over any other, or is otherwise seen to be dominant*". [FRS 102 Glossary of terms].

34.5.53   In order for a business combination to meet the definition of a merger, all of the following criteria must be met:

(a)   No party to the combination is portrayed as either acquirer or acquiree, either by its own board or management or by that of another party to the combination.

(b)   There is no significant change to the classes of beneficiaries of the combining entities or the purpose of the benefits provided as a result of the combination.

(c)   All parties to the combination, as represented by the members of the board, participate in establishing the management structure of the combined entity and in selecting the management personnel, and such decisions are made on the basis of a consensus between the parties to the combination rather than purely by exercise of voting rights.

[FRS 102 Glossary of terms].

Accounting treatment

34.5.54   The PBE does not adjust the carrying value of the assets and liabilities of the combining entities to fair value, although it does make adjustments to achieve uniformity of accounting policies across the combining entities. [FRS 102 para PBE34.82].

34.5.55 The newly formed entity brings the assets, liabilities, equity, income, expenditure and cash flows of all the combining entities into its financial statements from the beginning of the financial period in which the merger occurs. [FRS 102 para PBE34.83].

34.5.56 The newly formed entity reports comparative amounts that include the results for all the combining entities for the previous accounting period and their statements of financial position for the previous reporting date. The resulting comparative figures are described as 'combined' figures in the accounts. [FRS 102 para PBE34.84].

34.5.57 All costs incurred by the entities in connection with the merger are to be charged as expenses in the periods when they are incurred. [FRS 102 para PBE34.85].

Disclosure

34.5.58 For each merger in the reporting period, the newly formed entity discloses the following in its financial statements:

- names and descriptions of the combining entities or businesses;

- date of the merger;

- an analysis of the principal components of the current period's total comprehensive income, to indicate:

  - the post-merger amounts relating to the newly formed merged entity; and

  - the pre-merger amounts relating to each party.

- an analysis of the previous period's total comprehensive income between each party to the merger;

- the aggregate carrying value of the net assets of each party to the merger at the date of the merger; and

- the nature and amount of any significant adjustments required to align accounting policies and an explanation of any further adjustments made to net assets as a result of the merger.

[FRS 102 para PBE34.86].

Transition to FRS 102

34.5.59 A PBE adopting FRS 102 for the first time could elect not to apply the above requirements to PBE combinations that occurred prior to the PBE's date of transition to the FRS. However, if a PBE entity does restate any such previous entity combination to comply with the above requirements, it must also restate all later entity combinations [FRS 102 para 35.10(q)].

Public benefit entity concessionary loans

Introduction and scope

34.5.60 Public benefit entities often provide loans to third parties at lower rates of interest than the other parties could obtain from commercial lenders. Such loans are usually provided as a form of financial assistance, for example to other PBEs, or from a PBE to its trading subsidiary.

34.5.61 In general, loans given or received normally fall within the scope of sections 11 or 12 of FRS 102 which deal with basic financial instruments and other issues relating to financial instruments. Under those sections, if an entity provides a loan at less than a market rate of interest, it will need to measure the loan at amortised cost, using an effective rate of interest that reflects a market rate rather than the actual rate on the loan. This will result in the entity initially recognising the loan receivable at an amount which is less than the loan principal amount and, consequently, recognising the difference between the two amounts as a 'day one loss' charged to expenses.

34.5.62 To recognise the common use by PBEs of such loans, FRS 102 contains requirements for accounting for 'public benefit entity concessionary loans' which permit an alternative accounting treatment to that required by sections 11 and 12 of the standard. These requirements also apply to public benefit entity concessionary loans given or received by a member of a PBE group.

Definition

34.5.63 A 'public benefit entity concessionary loan' is defined as:

"A loan made or received between a public benefit entity or an entity within a public benefit entity group and another party:

(a) at below the prevailing market rate of interest;

(b) that is not repayable on demand; and

(c) is for the purposes of furthering the objectives of the public benefit entity or public benefit entity parent."

[FRS 102 para PBE34.88;Glossary of terms].

All three elements of this definition need to be met in order for the loan to fall within the scope of the accounting policy choice below. If at least one element is not met, the PBE must account for the loan in accordance with the requirements of section 11 or 12 as appropriate.

Accounting policy choice

34.5.64   Where the public benefit entity concessionary loan definition is met, the standard permits a choice of accounting policy.

34.5.65   A PBE (or PBE group member) making or receiving a public benefit entity concessionary loan must apply either:

■   the recognition, measurement and disclosure requirements of section 11 (or, if appropriate, section 12) of FRS 102; or

■   the accounting treatment set out in paragraphs PBE34.90 to PBE34.97 of the standard, which are described below.

[FRS 102 para PBE34.89].

34.5.66   FRS 102 requires the entity to apply its choice of accounting policy consistently to all PBE concessionary loans that it makes and receives. [FRS 102 para PBE34.90]. So this prohibits, for example, an entity from recognising concessionary loans that it receives under section 11 of the standard (and recognising a 'day one gain' for the present value of the interest subsidy obtained), while recognising concessionary loans that it provides under section 34 of the standard (and recognising the loss — for the interest subsidy provided — over the life of the loan).

Required accounting (paras PBE34.90 — PBE34.97 of FRS 102)

34.5.67   Where the PBE chooses not to apply section 11 (or section 12) of FRS 102 to the accounting for its concessionary loans, it instead applies the following accounting requirements.

Recognition and measurement

Loans provided by the entity

34.5.68   The entity measures the concessionary loan in the statement of financial position initially at the amount of loan principal paid to the other party. [FRS 102 para PBE34.90]. Subsequently, the entity adjusts the carrying amount of the concessionary loan in each accounting period to reflect any interest receivable. [FRS 102 para PBE34.91].

34.5.69   The effect of the above requirements is to permit the entity to measure the loan at its stated principal amount and, subsequently, to accrue interest receivable using the interest rate set out in the loan contract, rather than the effective interest rate that is required by the accounting requirements of sections 11 and 12 of FRS 102. So a 'day one loss' is not recognised and, instead, the loss is automatically spread over the life of the loan.

34.5.70 Where the entity determines that part, or all, of the loan is not recoverable, it must recognise an impairment loss in expenses. [FRS 102 para PBE34.92].

Loans received by the entity

34.5.71 The entity measures the concessionary loan in the statement of financial position initially at the amount of loan principal received from the other party. [FRS 102 para PBE34.90]. Subsequently, the entity adjusts the carrying amount of the concessionary loan in each accounting period to reflect any interest payable. [FRS 102 para PBE34.91].

34.5.72 The effect of the above requirements is to permit the entity to measure the loan at its stated principal amount and, subsequently, to accrue interest payable using the interest rate set out in the loan contract, rather than the effective interest rate that is required by the accounting requirements of sections 11 and 12 of FRS 102. So a 'day one gain' is not recognised and, instead, the gain is automatically spread over the life of the loan.

Presentation

34.5.73 Entities that choose to apply Section 11 or 12 to their concessionary loans must apply the presentation and disclosure requirements of those sections. [FRS 102 para PBE 34.89(a)]. Entities that follow PBE accounting must apply the requirements below.

34.5.74 Entities must present concessionary loans made and received as separate line items on the face of the statement of financial position, or alternatively as separate line items in the notes to the accounts. [FRS 102 para PBE34.93]. This presentation must show separately the amounts due within one year and the amounts due after more than one year. [FRS 102 para PBE34.94].

Disclosure

34.5.75 In its summary of significant accounting policies, the entity must disclose the measurement basis that it has used for its concessionary loans, together with any other accounting policies which are relevant to understanding these transactions. [FRS 102 para PBE34.95].

34.5.76 The entity must also disclose:

- the terms and conditions of its concessionary loan arrangements (such as the interest rate(s), any security for the loans provided to or by the entity, and the repayment terms of the loans); and

- the value of concessionary loans which the entity has made commitments to provide to other parties but which have not been taken up by the other parties at the year end.

[FRS 102 para PBE34.96].

34.5.77 In providing the disclosures, the entity must disclose information for concessionary loans provided separately from that for concessionary loans received. But, where the entity has provided multiple concessionary loans, it can aggregate these disclosures – and similarly for multiple concessionary loans received, provided that the aggregation does not obscure the significant information. [FRS 102 para PBE34.97].

34.6 – Heritage assets

34.6 – Heritage assets

Scope

34.6.1   Heritage assets are defined as *"tangible and intangible assets with historic, artistic, scientific, technological, geophysical, or environmental qualities that are held and maintained principally for their contribution to knowledge and culture"*. [FRS 102 Glossary of terms]. This definition matches that previously set out in FRS 30, except that it now also includes intangible assets (which were outside the scope of FRS 30).

34.6.2   A commercial entity might hold works of art and similar objects. These are generally not heritage assets because they are not usually held by the entity principally for their contribution to knowledge and culture. The entity should instead treat such assets as property, plant and equipment and account for them in accordance with section 17 of the standard. [FRS 102 para 34.50].

34.6.3   Where an asset falls within the definition of a heritage asset, but the entity uses it in an operational capacity (for example an education establishment uses buildings for teaching that are historic assets), the entity should treat such an asset as operational and account for it under section 17 as property, plant and equipment. This is because FRS 102 takes the view that an operational perspective is likely to be most relevant for most users of financial statements, and this view drives the accounting treatment. However, entities with such operational heritage assets might also wish to consider providing the heritage asset disclosures, in addition to those required for property plant and equipment (as described below). [FRS 102 para 34.50].

Recognition and measurement

34.6.4   Entities are required to recognise and measure heritage assets in accordance with section 17 of the standard, using the cost model or revaluation model, but subject also to the requirements set out below. [FRS 102 para 34.51].

34.6.5   However, where an entity has intangible heritage assets, in our view it should instead recognise and measure them in accordance with section 18 of the standard, subject to the requirements below.

34.6.6   FRS 102 notes that, where a heritage asset has previously been capitalised or has recently been purchased, the entity will have information on the cost or value of the asset. Where the entity does not have such information and cannot obtain it at a cost which is commensurate with the benefits to users of the financial statements, it should not recognise the asset in its statement of financial position.

34.6.7   FRS 30 encouraged entities to recognise heritage assets using valuations employing any method that an entity considered to be appropriate or relevant. In practice, this often meant that entities recognised heritage assets at a value provided by internal valuers or at an insurance valuation. FRS 102, however, requires entities to apply either the cost or revaluation model in section 17 (or for intangible assets, in our view, section 18), and this does not permit the use of 'any valuation approach'. So, this leaves the following possibilities for entities that, under FRS 30, measured their tangible heritage assets using valuation methods that do not comply with the revaluation model in section 17:

■   value these heritage assets using a basis that complies with the revaluation model;

■   restate these heritage assets to their cost (where available); or

■   de-recognise these heritage assets.

34.6.8   Entities adopting the standard for the first time are permitted to measure an item of property, plant and equipment at the date of transition at cost, by using the existing GAAP valuation as the deemed cost. [FRS 102 para 35.10(d)]. Although this transitional provision does not explicitly include tangible heritage assets, in our view it is reasonable to apply this approach for such assets.

34.6.9   At each reporting date, an entity is required to apply section 27 of the standard to determine whether a heritage asset is impaired and, if so, how to recognise and measure the impairment loss. A heritage asset might be impaired, for example, where it has suffered physical deterioration or breakage, or doubts arise as to its authenticity. [FRS 102 para 34.54].

34.6.10   Where an entity has unrecognised heritage assets, it must provide disclosures in accordance with the requirements described below. [FRS 102 para 34.53].

Presentation

34.6.11   An entity presents heritage assets in the statement of financial position separately from other assets. [FRS 102 para 34.52].

Example – Presentation of heritage assets

	2012 £'000	2011 £'000
Non-current assets		
Property, plant and equipment	1,000	1,500
Heritage assets	100	100
Non-current available for sale financial assets	11,000	10,000
	12,100	11,600

Disclosure

34.6.12 An entity provides the disclosures below for all heritage assets (that is, recognised and unrecognised) that it holds:

(a)   An indication of the nature and scale of heritage assets held by the entity.

(b)   The policy for the acquisition, preservation, management and disposal of heritage assets (including a description of the records maintained by the entity of its collection of heritage assets and information on the extent to which access to the assets is permitted).

(c)   The accounting policies adopted for heritage assets, including details of the measurement bases used.

(d)   For heritage assets that have not been recognised in the statement of financial position, the notes to the financial statements shall:

    (i)   explain the reasons why;

    (ii)   describe the significance and nature of those assets; and

    (iii)   disclose information that is helpful in assessing the value of those heritage assets.

(e)   Where heritage assets are recognised in the statement of financial position, the following disclosure is required:

    (i)   the carrying amount of heritage assets at the beginning of the reporting period and the reporting date, including an analysis between classes or groups of heritage assets recognised at cost and those recognised at valuation; and

    (ii)   where assets are recognised at valuation, sufficient information to assist in understanding the valuation being recognised (date of valuation, method used, whether carried out by external valuer and, if so, their qualification and any significant limitations on the valuation).

(f)   A summary of transactions relating to heritage assets for the reporting period and each of the previous four reporting periods, disclosing:

    (i)   the cost of acquisitions of heritage assets;

    (ii)   the value of heritage assets acquired by donations;

    (iii)   the carrying amount of heritage assets disposed of in the period and proceeds received; and

    (iv)   any impairment recognised in the period.

The summary should show separately those transactions included in the statement of financial position and those that are not.

(g)   In exceptional circumstances where it is impracticable to obtain a valuation of heritage assets acquired by donation the reason should be stated.

[FRS 102 para 34.55].

34.6.13   An entity can provide aggregated disclosures for groups or classes of heritage assets, provided that, in doing so, the entity does not obscure significant information. [FRS 102 para 34.55].

34.6.14   An entity need not provide the disclosures in (f) above for any accounting period earlier than the previous comparable period, where it is impracticable for the entity to do so (for example, if the information is not available). In such cases, the entity discloses that it is impracticable to do so. [FRS 102 para 34.56].

34.7 – Funding commitments

34.7 – Funding commitments

Introduction

34.7.1 The accounting requirements for funding commitments were initially introduced into FRS 102 for the purpose of public benefit entities (and, in particular, charities) which often make commitments to provide funding to other parties for a period of several years. The Accounting Council considered, however, that the principles were equally applicable to other entities, and so decided not to make these requirements specific to PBEs. In practice, the requirements are likely to be most relevant to PBEs.

34.7.2 Entities often make commitments to provide cash or other resources to other entities. In such situations, the entity making the commitment needs to determine whether it should recognise the commitment as a liability. The definition of a liability requires there to be a present obligation, and not merely an expectation of a future outflow. [FRS 102 para 34A.1]

Accounting requirements

34.7.3 Where an entity makes a commitment to provide resources to other entities, it applies the requirements described below, except for commitments to make a loan, to which it applies either section 11, or section 12 of the standard, as applicable [FRS 102 para 34.57].

34.7.4 Where an entity applies the requirements below, it considers the substance of the commitment, and in doing so takes into account the requirements of sections 2 and 21 of the standard. [FRS 102 para 34.58].

Recognition

34.7.5 An entity recognises a liability and, usually, a corresponding expense, when it makes a commitment to provide resources to another party, if (and only if):

(a) the definition and recognition criteria for a liability are satisfied (that is, there is an expected outflow of future economic benefits from the entity);

(b) the obligation (which might be a constructive obligation) is such that the entity cannot realistically withdraw from it (such as a written commitment to a specific party and a past pattern of the entity meeting similar commitments); and

(c)   the entitlement of the other party to the resources does not depend on the satisfaction of performance-related conditions.

[FRS 102 para 34.59].

34.7.6   For example, where a charity communicates to another party that it:

- will provide funding to that party for a three-year period for use on a specified purpose;

- will require the other party to provide it with evidence each year to demonstrate that the funds have been applied for the specified purpose; and

- will not release a subsequent year's funding until it is satisfied that the funding has been so applied;

the charity does not recognise the full commitment initially because it depends on the satisfaction of performance conditions by the recipient (that is, applying the resources to the specified purpose and providing evidence to satisfy the entity of this).

34.7.7   In contrast, if the charity does not specify any purpose, leaving the other party to use the funding at its discretion, and does not require evidence of how it has been spent before releasing the grant in the subsequent years, the charity will normally need to recognise the full multi-year commitment as a liability.

34.7.8   Where an entity makes a general statement that it intends to provide resources to specified classes of potential beneficiaries in accordance with its objectives, this does not in itself give rise to a liability, because the entity can amend or withdraw its policy, and potential beneficiaries are not able to insist on the entity fulfilling its statement. [FRS 102 para 34A.2].

34.7.9   Similarly, an entity might make a promise to another party to provide it with cash, but the promise is conditional on the entity obtaining future income to fund the commitment. This in itself does not give rise to a liability: there is not a probable transfer of economic benefit because the entity does not have to meet its promise. [FRS 102 para 34A.2].

34.7.10   An entity only recognises a liability for a commitment that gives the recipient a valid expectation that payment will be made and from which the entity realistically cannot withdraw. One of the implications of this is that a liability only exists where the entity has communicated the commitment to the recipient. [FRS 102 para 34A.3].

Commitments with performance-related conditions

34.7.11   Where an entity makes a commitment that imposes conditions on the other party, it needs to examine these to determine whether they are performance-related conditions.

34.7.12 A 'performance-related condition' is a *"condition that requires the performance of a particular level of service or units of output to be delivered, with payment of, or entitlement to, the resources conditional on that performance"*. [FRS 102 Glossary of terms].

34.7.13 An entity does not recognise a commitment if it is subject to performance-related conditions. In such a case, the entity is required to fulfil its commitment only where the performance-related conditions are met by the other party and no liability exists for it until that occurs. [FRS 102 para 34A.4]. So, an entity recognises commitments with performance-related conditions only when those conditions are met. [FRS 102 para 34.60].

34.7.14 An entity might make a commitment that contains conditions that are not performance-related conditions. For example, a requirement for the other party to provide the entity with an annual financial report might serve mainly as an administrative tool, because failure by the other party to comply would not release the entity from its commitment. This can be contrasted with a requirement for the other party to submit to the entity a detailed report for its review and consideration of how the funds will be utilised, in order to secure payment by the entity. [FRS 102 para 34A.5]. But if the entity pays out the funds without first conducting the review, or it performs only a superficial review, then the requirement to submit the report might not, in substance, be a performance condition.

34.7.15 Where a condition is not performance-related, it might represent a restriction. A 'restriction' is a *"requirement that limits or directs the purposes for which a resource may be used that does not meet the definition of a performance-related condition"*. [FRS 102 Glossary of terms]. A mere restriction on the specific purpose for which funds are to be used does not in itself constitute a performance-related condition. [FRS 102 para 34A.5].

Measurement

34.7.16 An entity measures the liability at the present value of the resources committed. [FRS 102 para 34.61].

Disclosure

34.7.17 Where an entity has made a commitment (whether recognised or unrecognised), it includes the following disclosures:

(a) the commitment made;

(b) the time-frame of that commitment;

(c) any performance-related conditions attached to the commitment; and

(d) details of how it will fund the commitment.

[FRS 102 para 34.62].

347003

34.7.18 The entity could provide these disclosures in aggregate, provided that the aggregation does not obscure significant information. However, the entity must make separate disclosures for recognised and unrecognised commitments. [FRS 102 para 34.63].

34.7.19 For funding commitments that are not recognised by the entity, it is important that the entity makes full and informative disclosures of the existence of the commitments and of the anticipated sources of funding for the commitments. [FRS 102 para 34A.6].

34.8 – Insurance

34.8 – Insurance

Introduction

34.8.1   FRS 103 (to which FRS 102 cross-refers) will deal with the accounting for insurance contracts (including reinsurance contracts) and financial instruments with a discretionary participation feature that a company issues and for reinsurance contracts that a company holds. FRS 103 will not address accounting by policyholders for direct insurance contracts held; and reimbursements by way of insurance claims within the scope of section 21 of FRS 102 are discussed in chapter 21.

34.8.2   An exposure draft of FRS 103 was published in July 2013. But FRS 103 has not yet been issued and so the proposed requirements in the exposure draft are subject to change and are not covered in this chapter. It is expected that FRS 103 will incorporate the requirements of IFRS 4, 'Insurance Contracts', and the liability measurement requirements that were previously set out in FRS 27, 'Life Assurance'. Until such time as FRS 103 is finalised, FRS 27 remains in force. The requirements of FRS 27 are not covered in this chapter as, in practice, it not expected that UK life insurers will seek to apply FRS 102 prior to the issuance of FRS 103.

34.8.3   Not all contracts issued by insurance companies meet the definition of an insurance contract or a financial instrument with a discretionary participation feature; and such contracts (which are commonly referred to as 'investment contracts') will be subject to provisions elsewhere within FRS 102 (for example, in respect of financial instruments).

34.8.4   The general provisions that relate to the format and content of insurance company financial statements are detailed in Schedule 3 to SI 2008/410, 'The Large and Medium-sized Companies and Groups (Accounts and Reports) Regulations 2008' (referred to here as 'Schedule 3'). Schedule 6 to SI 2008/410 (referred to here as 'Schedule 6') deals with the format of consolidated financial statements; and Part 3 of that Schedule contains modifications specific to insurance groups. Not all companies that issue insurance contracts (as defined in FRS 102) are insurance companies. Companies that are not insurance companies are not subject to Schedule 3's requirements.

34.8.5   The Association of British Insurers (ABI) has historically maintained a Statement of Recommended Practice (SORP) on Accounting for Insurance Business which has been followed by UK insurance companies and groups reporting under UK GAAP. It is expected that FRS 103 will include material originally from the ABI SORP as an appendix, providing application guidance and that, going forward, no separate insurance SORP will be maintained.

34.8.6   Where a company is within the scope of a SORP, early adoption of FRS 102 is not permitted if this would conflict with the requirements of a current SORP. [FRS 102 para 1.14]. If the current SORP is not withdrawn or updated, early adoption of FRS 102, prior to the issuance of FRS 103, by insurance companies within the scope of the SORP would only be permissible if the requirements of FRS 102 do not conflict with the SORP. Once FRS 103 is issued, it is proposed that insurers will be free to early adopt FRS 102 and FRS 103 irrespective of any inconsistency with the current SORP. Except as set out in paragraph 34.8.23, this chapter does not consider the recommendations of the current SORP; this is because that SORP was not drafted in contemplation of FRS 102 and FRS 103, and it is not expected that the SORP will apply to entities reporting under FRS 102 and FRS 103.

34.8.7   In practice, it is expected that many UK insurance companies and groups will continue to report under old UK GAAP at least until FRS 103 is published. Early adoption of FRS 102 by insurance companies might not be permissible until the current SORP is either updated or withdrawn (for the reasons set out in para 34.8.6). In addition, it appears unlikely that an insurance company would wish to apply FRS 102 until the requirements of FRS 103 are known with certainty; this is because FRS 102 does not itself prescribe a framework for accounting for insurance contracts, and any accounting policies developed by insurance companies under FRS 102 would be subject to change on application of FRS 103.

34.8.8   Section 1 of this chapter covers the requirements of FRS 102 applicable to insurance contracts and financial instruments with a discretionary participation feature. As FRS 103 has not yet been issued, this section covers only the very limited requirements set out in FRS 102. The provisions of Section 1 of this chapter are not applicable to investment contracts issued by insurance companies which do not transfer significant insurance risk and which do not contain a discretionary participation feature.

34.8.9   Section 2 of this chapter deals with requirements and guidance applicable to insurance companies and groups preparing accounts in accordance with Schedule 3 and Schedule 6. This section will not be relevant to issuers of insurance contracts or financial instruments with a discretionary participation feature (as defined in FRS 102) which are not insurance companies or insurance groups. This section does not consider requirements that are specific to friendly societies.

Section 1 – Insurance contracts and financial instruments with a discretionary participation feature

Definitions

34.8.10   An insurance contract is defined as *"a contract under which one party (the insurer) accepts significant insurance risk from another party (the policyholder) by agreeing to compensate the policyholder if a specified uncertain* *future event (the insured event) adversely affects the policyholder".* [FRS 102 Glossary of terms].

34.8.11 The definition of an insurance contract is identical to that contained in IFRS 4. But the glossary to IFRS 4 further defines certain terms used in this definition (for example, 'insurance risk') which are not defined in FRS 102. In addition, Appendix B to IFRS 4 contains further guidance on the application of this definition (such as determining whether an insurance risk is significant). The content of Appendix B to IFRS 4 has not been replicated in FRS 102, but it might be relevant to consider its content when applying the FRS 102 definition. The Manual of Accounting IFRS for the UK considers this guidance in more detail.

34.8.12 A reinsurance contract is defined as *"an insurance contract issued by one insurer (the reinsurer) to compensate another insurer (the cedant) for losses on one or more contracts issued by the cedant".* [FRS 102 Glossary of terms]. References within this chapter to insurance contracts include reinsurance contracts.

34.8.13 A discretionary participation feature is defined as:

"a contractual right to receive, as a supplement to guaranteed benefits, additional benefits:

- *that are likely to be a significant portion of the total contractual benefits;*

- *whose amount or timing is contractually at the discretion of the issuer; and*

- *that are contractually based on:*

  - *the performance of a specified pool of contracts or a specified type of contract;*

  - *realised and/or unrealised investment returns on a specified pool of assets held by the issuer; or*

  - *the profit or loss of the company, fund or other entity that issues the contract."*

[FRS 102 Glossary of terms].

34.8.14 In the UK, with-profits contracts are likely to be the most common form of financial instrument containing a discretionary participation feature.

Scope

34.8.15 Paragraph 1.6 of FRS 102 requires that FRS 103 is applied to insurance contracts (including reinsurance contracts) and financial instruments with a discretionary participation feature that a company issues and to reinsurance contracts that a company holds.

34.8.16 FRS 103 will be a new UK Financial Reporting Standard dealing with insurance contracts and financial instruments with a discretionary participation feature. FRS 103 has not been issued yet. References in FRS 102 to FRS 103 will not have effect until FRS 103 has been issued. As a result, until FRS 103 is issued, FRS 102 does not set out a specific accounting framework for insurance contracts or financial instruments with a discretionary participation feature.

34.8.17 Except for section 18's disclosure requirements in respect of intangible assets, deferred acquisition costs and intangible assets arising from contracts within the scope of FRS 103 are excluded from the scope of section 18 of FRS 102 dealing with intangible assets other than goodwill and section 27 of FRS 102 dealing with impairment of assets. [FRS 102 paras 18.1A, 27.1A].

34.8.18 Section 21 of FRS 102 dealing with provisions and contingencies does not apply to contracts within the scope of FRS 103. [FRS 102 para 21.1B].

34.8.19 In general, financial guarantee contracts are within the scope of FRS 102. But some financial guarantee contracts might also be insurance contracts; and will be within the scope of FRS 103 where an entity has elected under FRS 103 to continue the application of insurance accounting. [FRS 102 para 21.1A].

34.8.20 Insurance contracts and financial instruments with a discretionary participation feature that a company issues and reinsurance contracts that a company holds are excluded from the scope of sections 11 and 12 of FRS 102 dealing with financial instruments and section 22 of FRS 102 dealing with liabilities and equity. [FRS 102 paras 11.7(f)(g), 12.3(d)(j), 22.2(e)(f)].

Section 2 — Insurance company specific company law requirements

34.8.21 Schedule 3 prescribes the format of an insurance company's balance sheet and profit and loss account; sets out requirements regarding the recognition and measurement of items in an insurance company's financial statements; and sets out disclosure requirements applicable to insurance companies.

34.8.22 Some Schedule 3 provisions distinguish between 'general business' (being business which consists of effecting or carrying out contracts of general insurance as defined for regulatory purposes) and 'long-term business' (being business which consists of effecting or carrying out contracts of long-term insurance as defined for regulatory purposes). [SI 2008/410 3 Sch 91]. The Schedule 3 provisions relating to long-term business apply to any significant amounts of accident or sickness general insurance contracts which are transacted exclusively or principally according to the technical principles of long-term business. [SI 2008/410 3 Sch 7].

34.8.23 The ABI SORP has historically provided guidance on the application of some Schedule 3 requirements. In particular, it has served to limit some of the options that would otherwise be permissible under Schedule 3 in areas such as:

- Recommending that underwriting results should be determined on an annual basis and so the fund basis or deferred annual basis permitted by Schedule 3 should not be used (see paras 34.8.90–34.8.92). [SORP 83].

- Recommending that the balance sheet and long-term business technical account headings in respect of bonuses and rebates (see paras 34.8.46 and 34.8.60) should not be used. [SORP 178].

- Recommending that investment return should only be allocated between elements of the profit and loss account (see para 34.8.65) on one of two prescribed bases. [SORP 292].

34.8.24   As set out in paragraph 34.8.5, it is expected that FRS 103 will include material originally from the ABI SORP as an appendix, providing application guidance.

34.8.25   Where the requirements of Schedule 3 are the same as those set out within Schedule 1 to SI 2008/410 (referred to here as 'Schedule 1') as applicable to the generality of companies, these are not considered in this chapter and are addressed elsewhere in this book. The table at paragraph 34.8.125 highlights areas where the disclosure requirements of Schedule 3 replicate those in Schedule 1.

Format of the financial statements

34.8.26   The profit and loss account and balance sheet of insurance companies are required to follow the format prescribed by Schedule 3. [SI 2008/410 Reg 6(1)].

34.8.27   Although Schedule 3 prescribes that items should be set out in the order and under the headings and sub-headings given in the format, it does permit items to be disclosed in greater detail than so required. In addition, the profit and loss account and balance sheet might include items not specifically covered by the headings listed in the prescribed format. [SI 2008/410 3 Sch 1, 2].

34.8.28   Where the format requires both a gross amount and reinsurers' share of an amount to be shown, a sub-total should also be given. [SI 2008/410 3 Sch 9(1)].

Modifications to the format of financial statements for insurance groups

34.8.29   An insurance group is defined as a group where the parent company is an insurance company or where:

- the parent company's principal subsidiary undertakings are wholly or mainly insurance companies; and

- the parent company does not itself carry on any material business apart from the acquisition, management and disposal of interests in subsidiary undertakings.

[CA06 Sec 1165(5)].

34.8.30 The profit and loss account and balance sheet of insurance groups are required to follow the format prescribed by Schedule 3, with the modification that the items in both the balance sheet and the profit and loss account dealing with participating interests are split between associated undertakings and other participating interests. [SI 2008/410 6 Sch 20, 37].

34.8.31 Insurance groups' consolidated financial statements have to comply, as far as practicable, with the provisions of Schedule 3 as if the undertakings included in the consolidation were a single company. [SI 2008/410 6 Sch 1(1), 32].

The balance sheet

34.8.32 An insurance group is defined as a group where the parent company is an insurance company or where:

- Their individual amounts are not material for the purpose of giving a true and fair view. [SI 2008/410 3 Sch 3(1)(a)].

- The combination facilitates the assessment of the state of affairs of the company for the financial year in question. Where this applies, the detailed breakdown of the combined items should be given in the notes to the financial statements. [SI 2008/410 3 Sch 3(1)(b), 3(2)].

34.8.33 The format of the insurance company balance sheet is set out below:

Assets

A   Called-up share capital not paid
B   Intangible assets
     1   Development costs
     2   Concessions, patents, licences, trademarks and similar rights and assets.
     3   Goodwill
     4   Payments on account
C   Investments
    I   Land and buildings
    II   II Investments in group undertakings and participating interests
     1   Shares in group undertakings
     2   Debt securities issued by, and loans to, group undertakings
     3   Participating interests
     4   Debt securities issued by, and loans to, undertakings in which the company has a participating interest
    III   Other financial investments
     1   Shares and other variable-yield securities and units in unit trusts
     2   Debt securities and other fixed-income securities
     3   Participation in investment pools
     4   Loans secured by mortgages
     5   Other loans

            6   Deposits with credit institutions
            7   Other
      IV   Deposits with ceding undertakings
D   Assets held to cover linked liabilities
Da   Reinsurers' share of technical provisions
            1   Provision for unearned premiums
            2   Long-term business provision
            3   Claims outstanding
            4   Provisions for bonuses and rebates
            5   Other technical provisions
            6   Technical provisions for unit-linked liabilities
E   Debtors
      I   Debtors arising out of direct insurance operations
            1   Policyholders
            2   Intermediaries
      II   Debtors arising out of reinsurance operations
      III Other debtors
      IV   Called-up share capital not paid
F   Other assets
      I   Tangible assets
            1   Plant and machinery
            2   Fixtures, fittings, tools and equipment
            3   Payments on account (other than deposits paid on land and
                 buildings) and assets (other than buildings) in course of
                 construction
      II   Stocks
            1   Raw materials and consumables
            2   Work in progress
            3   Finished goods and goods for resale
            4   Payments on account
      III Cash at bank and in hand
      IV   Own shares
      V   Other
G   Prepayments and accrued income
      I   Accrued interest and rent
      II   Deferred acquisition costs
      III Other prepayments and accrued income

Assets

A   Called-up share capital not paid
B   Intangible assets
            1   Development costs
            2   Concessions, patents, licences, trademarks and similar rights and
                 assets
            3   Goodwill
            4   Payments on account
C   Investments

I   Land and buildings

II   II Investments in group undertakings and participating interests
1. Shares in group undertakings
2. Debt securities issued by, and loans to, group undertakings
3. Participating interests
4. Debt securities issued by, and loans to, undertakings in which the company has a participating interest

III   Other financial investments
1. Shares and other variable-yield securities and units in unit trusts
2. Debt securities and other fixed-income securities
3. Participation in investment pools
4. Loans secured by mortgages
5. Other loans
6. Deposits with credit institutions
7. Other

IV   Deposits with ceding undertakings

D   Assets held to cover linked liabilities

Da   Reinsurers' share of technical provisions
1. Provision for unearned premiums
2. Long-term business provision
3. Claims outstanding
4. Provisions for bonuses and rebates
5. Other technical provisions
6. Technical provisions for unit-linked liabilities

E   Debtors

I   Debtors arising out of direct insurance operations
1. Policyholders
2. Intermediaries

II   Debtors arising out of reinsurance operations

III   Other debtors

IV   Called-up share capital not paid

F   Other assets

I   Tangible assets
1. Plant and machinery
2. Fixtures, fittings, tools and equipment
3. Payments on account (other than deposits paid on land and buildings) and assets (other than buildings) in course of construction

II   Stocks
1. Raw materials and consumables
2. Work in progress
3. Finished goods and goods for resale
4. Payments on account

III   Cash at bank and in hand

IV   Own shares

V   Other

G   Prepayments and accrued income

I   Accrued interest and rent

    II   Deferred acquisition costs
    III   Other prepayments and accrued income

Liabilities

A   Capital and reserves
    I   Called-up share capital or equivalent funds
    II   Share premium account
    III Revaluation reserve
    IV Reserves
        1   Capital redemption reserve
        2   Reserve for own shares
        3   Reserves provided for by the articles of association
        4   Other reserves
        5
    V   Profit and loss account
B   Subordinated liabilities
Ba Fund for future appropriations
C   Technical provisions
        1   Provision for unearned premiums
           (a) gross amount
           (b) reinsurance amount
        2   Long-term business provision
           (a) gross amount
           (b) reinsurance amount
        3   Claims outstanding
           (a) gross amount
           (b) reinsurance amount
        4   Provision for bonuses and rebates
           (a) gross amount
           (b) reinsurance amount
        5   Equalisation provision
        6   Other technical provisions
           (a) gross amount
           (b) reinsurance amount
D   Technical provisions for linked liabilities
           (a) gross amount
           (b) reinsurance amount
E   Provisions for other risks
        1   Provisions for pensions and similar obligations
        2   Provisions for taxation
        3   Other provisions
F   Deposits received from reinsurers
G   Creditors
    I   Creditors arising out of direct insurance operations
    II   Creditors arising out of reinsurance operations
    III Debenture loans
    IV Amounts owed to credit institutions

V   Other creditors including taxation and social security

H   Accruals and deferred income

34.8.34   Paragraphs 34.8.35 — 34.8.51 discuss some practical aspects of the application of the balance sheet format above, including requirements specified in Schedule 3 as notes to the balance sheet format .

Debt securities and other fixed-income securities

34.8.35   Any debt securities or other fixed-income securities that represent investments in group undertakings or participating interests are shown under asset item C.II.2 or C.II.4 and not within item C.III.2. [SI 2008/410 3 Sch Balance sheet format note 5].

Deposits with credit institutions

34.8.36   This item comprises sums the withdrawal of which is subject to a time restriction. Amounts which can be withdrawn on demand should be shown within 'cash at bank and in hand'. [SI 2008/410 3 Sch Balance sheet format note 8].

Deposits with ceding undertakings

34.8.37   This amount comprises any amounts owed by undertakings from which reinsurance has been accepted corresponding to guarantees which represent amounts either withheld by the ceding undertaking or deposited back with them or with a third party. Such amounts should not be combined with, or offset against, other amounts owed by or to the ceding undertaking. [SI 2008/410 3 Sch Balance sheet format note 10].

Assets held to cover linked liabilities

34.8.38   This item comprises investments made pursuant to long-term policies under which the benefits payable to the policyholder are wholly or partly determined by reference to the value of, or income from, property of any description or by reference to fluctuations in, or an index of, the value of any property. [SI 2008/410 3 Sch Balance sheet format note 11].

Reinsurers' share of technical provisions

34.8.39   Schedule 3 permits the reinsurers' share of technical provisions to be presented either on the asset side of the balance sheet or as a deduction from the gross amounts of the relevant technical provisions. [SI 2008/410 3 Sch Balance sheet format note 12]. But FRS 102 prohibits the offsetting of assets and liabilities; and so the reinsurers' share of technical provisions should be presented as assets. [FRS 102 para 2.52].

Group debtors

34.8.40 Amounts owed by group undertakings and undertakings in which the company has a participating interest should be shown separately as sub items of asset items E.I, II and III. [SI 2008/410 3 Sch Balance sheet format note 13].

Deferred acquisition costs

34.8.41 The cost of acquiring insurance policies which are incurred during a financial year, but which relate to a subsequent financial year, are deferred as an explicit asset in the balance sheet, except where such costs are either explicitly or implicitly recognised in the computation of the long-term business provision or allowed for via a deduction from the provision for unearned premiums. Deferred acquisition costs arising in general business should be distinguished from those arising in long-term business. [SI 2008/410 3 Sch Balance sheet format note 17].

Long-term business unrealised profits

34.8.42 The balance sheet of an insurance company which carries on long-term business should show separately as an additional item the aggregate of any amounts included in capital and reserves which are not realised profits under section 843 of the Companies Act 2006. [SI 2008/410 3 Sch 11(1)]. This disclosure is not required in respect of an insurance group's consolidated balance sheet. [SI 2008/410 6 Sch 40(2)].

Subordinated liabilities

34.8.43 This item comprises all liabilities in respect of which there is a contractual obligation that, in the event of a winding up or of a bankruptcy, they are to be repaid only after the claims of all other creditors have been met. [SI 2008/410 3 Sch Balance sheet format note 18].

Fund for future appropriations

34.8.44 This item comprises all funds the allocation of which (either to policyholders or to shareholders) has not been determined by the end of the financial year. [SI 2008/410 3 Sch Balance sheet format note 19]. Such amounts most commonly arise in the with-profits funds of long-term insurance companies.

Claims outstanding

34.8.45 This item represents the total estimated ultimate cost of settling all claims arising from events which have occurred up to the end of the financial year (including, in the case of general business, claims incurred but not reported) less amounts already paid in respect of such claims. [SI 2008/410 3 Sch Balance sheet format note 22].

Provisions for bonuses and rebates

34.8.46 This item comprises amounts intended for policyholders or beneficiaries by way of bonuses and rebates which have not yet been credited to them and which are not included in the fund for future appropriations or the long-term business provision. [SI 2008/410 3 Sch Balance sheet format note 23].

Unexpired risks provision

34.8.47 Any unexpired risks provision (see para 34.8.85) should be included within 'Other technical provisions' and, if it is significant, be disclosed separately, either in the balance sheet or in the notes to the financial statements. [SI 2008/410 3 Sch Balance sheet format note 25].

Technical provision for linked liabilities

34.8.48 This item comprises provisions to cover liabilities relating to investment in the context of long-term policies under which the benefits payable to the policyholder are wholly or partly determined by reference to the value of, or income from, property of any description or by reference to fluctuations in, or an index of, the value of any property. Any additional technical provisions constituted to cover death risks, operating expenses or other risks are included in the long-term business provision. [SI 2008/410 3 Sch Balance sheet format note 26].

Deposits received from reinsurers

34.8.49 This item comprises any amounts deposited by or withheld from reinsurers under reinsurance contracts ceded, including any amounts owed by virtue of the deposit of securities which have transferred to the company's ownership. Such amounts should not be combined with other amounts owed to or by the reinsurer. [SI 2008/410 3 Sch Balance sheet format note 27].

Group creditors

34.8.50 Amounts owed to group undertakings and undertakings in which the company has a participating interest should be shown separately as sub-items. [SI 2008/410 3 Sch Balance sheet format note 28].

Investment contracts

34.8.51 Schedule 3 does not contain specific requirements regarding the presentation of amounts relating to investment contracts in the balance sheet where such contracts are accounted for as financial instruments under FRS 102. We consider that the following presentations would be appropriate:

■ Financial liabilities in respect of linked investment contracts – include within 'Technical provisions for linked liabilities'.

- Financial liabilities in respect of non-linked investment contracts either – include within 'Other technical provisions' or 'Other creditors, including tax and social security'. Or a case could be made for creating a new line for non-linked financial liabilities in respect of such investment contracts on the grounds that such liabilities are not 'specifically covered' in any of the prescribed headings. [SI 2008/410 3 Sch 2(2)].

- Any costs incurred in acquiring an investment contract that qualify for deferral as an asset under the provisions of FRS 102 – include within 'Deferred acquisition costs'.

- Initial fee income which is deferred and recognised in line with the performance of the related contract – include within 'Accruals and deferred income'.

- Amounts recoverable under contracts that, although legally in the form of reinsurance, are accounted for as financial assets – show within 'Other financial investments' or 'Assets held to cover linked liabilities'.

The profit and loss account

34.8.52 Items (other than those within the headings showing the derivation of net earned premiums, net claims incurred or changes in other technical provisions) to which lower case letters in parentheses have been assigned in the profit and loss account format could be combined in the insurance company's financial statements where either of the following circumstances apply:

- The individual amounts are not material for the purpose of giving a true and fair view. [SI 2008/410 3 Sch 3(1)(a)].

- The combination facilitates the assessment of the profit or loss of the company for the financial year in question. Where this applies, however, the detailed breakdown of the combined items should be given in the notes to the financial statements. [SI 2008/410 3 Sch 3(1)(b), 3(2)].

34.8.53 Where an item designated by an Arabic number is required to be sub-analysed, a sub-total should be given (for example, a sub-total of 'Earned premiums, net of reinsurance' is required). [SI 2008/410 3 Sch 9(1)].

34.8.54 The profit and loss account is divided into three sections: a technical account for long-term business; a technical account for general business; and a non-technical account. All contracts that are long-term business for regulatory purposes should be included in the Technical account – Long-term business. All contracts that are general business for regulatory purposes should be included in the Technical account – General business. [SI 2008/410 3 Sch 10]. This requirement is based on the regulatory definition, so it applies to all contracts regulated as insurance, including those investment contracts that will not be within the scope of FRS 103.

34.8.55   The format of the insurance company profit and loss account is set out below:

I Technical account—General business

1   Earned premiums, net of reinsurance
    (a)   gross premiums written
    (b)   outward reinsurance premiums
    (c)   change in the gross provision for unearned premiums
    (d)   change in the provision for unearned premiums, reinsurers' share
2   Allocated investment return transferred from the non-technical account (item III.6)
2a   Investment income
    (a)   income from participating interests, with a separate indication of that derived from group undertakings
    (b)   income from other investments, with a separate indication of that derived from group undertakings
        (aa) income from land and buildings
        (bb) income from other investments
    (c)   value re-adjustments on investments
    (d)   gains on the realisation of investments
3   Other technical income, net of reinsurance
4   Claims incurred, net of reinsurance
    (a)   claims paid
        (aa) gross amount
        (bb) reinsurers' share
    (b)   change in the provision for claims
        (aa) gross amount
        (bb) reinsurers' share
5   Changes in other technical provisions, net of reinsurance, not shown under other headings
6   Bonuses and rebates, net of reinsurance
7   Net operating expenses
    (a)   acquisition costs
    (b)   change in deferred acquisition costs
    (c)   administrative expenses
    (d)   reinsurance commissions and profit participation
8   Other technical charges, net of reinsurance
8a   Investment expenses and charges
    (a)   investment management expenses, including interest
    (b)   value adjustments on investments
    (c)   losses on the realisation of investments
9   Change in the equalisation provision
10   Sub-total (balance on the technical account for general business) (item III.1)

II Technical account—Long-term business

1 Earned premiums, net of reinsurance
   (a) gross premiums written
   (b) outward reinsurance premiums
   (c) change in the provision for unearned premiums, net of reinsurance
2 Investment income
   (a) income from participating interests, with a separate indication of that derived from group undertakings
   (b) income from other investments, with a separate indication of that derived from group undertakings
      (aa) income from land and buildings
      (bb) income from other investments
   (c) value re-adjustments on investments
   (d) gains on the realisation of investments
3 Unrealised gains on investments
4 Other technical income, net of reinsurance
5 Claims incurred, net of reinsurance
   (a) claims paid
      (aa) gross amount
      (bb) reinsurers' share
   (b) change in the provision for claims
      (aa) gross amount
      (bb) reinsurers' share
6 Change in other technical provisions, net of reinsurance, not shown under other headings
   (a) Long-term business provision, net of reinsurance
      (aa) gross amount
      (bb) reinsurers' share
   (b) other technical provisions, net of reinsurance
7 Bonuses and rebates, net of reinsurance
8 Net operating expenses
   (a) acquisition costs
   (b) change in deferred acquisition costs
   (c) administrative expenses
   (d) reinsurance commissions and profit participation
9 Investment expenses and charges
   (a) investment management expenses, including interest
   (b) value adjustments on investments
   (c) losses on the realisation of investments
10 Unrealised losses on investments
11 Other technical charges, net of reinsurance
11a Tax attributable to the long-term business
12 Allocated investment return transferred to the non-technical account (item III.4)
12a Transfers to or from the fund for future appropriations
13 Sub-total (balance on the technical account—long-term business) (item III.2)

III Non-technical account

1   Balance on the general business technical account (item I.10)
2   Balance on the long-term business technical account (item II.13)
2a Tax credit attributable to balance on the long-term business technical account
3   Investment income
    (a) income from participating interests, with a separate indication of that derived from group undertakings
    (b) income from other investments, with a separate indication of that derived from group undertakings
        (aa) income from land and buildings
        (bb) income from other investments
    (c) value re-adjustments on investments
    (d) gains on the realisation of investments
3a Unrealised gains on investments
4   Allocated investment return transferred from the long-term business technical account (item II.12)
5   Investment expenses and charges
    (a) investment management expenses, including interest
    (b) value adjustments on investments
    (c) losses on the realisation of investments
5a Unrealised losses on investments
6   Allocated investment return transferred to the general business technical account (item I.2)
7   Other income
8   Other charges, including value adjustments
8a Profit or loss on ordinary activities before tax
9   Tax on profit or loss on ordinary activities
10 Profit or loss on ordinary activities after tax
11 Extraordinary income
12 Extraordinary charges
13 Extraordinary profit or loss
14 Tax on extraordinary profit or loss
15 Other taxes not shown under the preceding items
16 Profit or loss for the financial year

34.8.56 Paragraphs 34.8.57 — 34.8.66 discuss some practical aspects of the application of the profit and loss account format above, including requirements specified in Schedule 3 as notes to the profit and loss account format.

Gross premiums written

34.8.57 This item comprises all amounts due during the financial year in respect of insurance contracts entered into, regardless of the fact that such amounts might relate (in whole or in part) to a later financial year. The amount is stated after deductions of cancellations and portfolio withdrawals. Taxes or duties levied with premiums (for example, Insurance Premium Tax) should not be included. [SI 2008/410 3 Sch Profit and loss account format note 1].

Outwards reinsurance premiums

34.8.58 This item comprises all premiums paid or payable in respect of outwards reinsurance contracts entered into. Portfolio entries payable on the conclusion or amendment of outward reinsurance contracts should be added; and portfolio withdrawals receivable should be deducted. [SI 2008/410 3 Sch Profit and loss account format note 2].

Claims incurred

34.8.59 This item comprises all payments made in respect of the financial year, together with movements in the provision for outstanding claims. These amounts should include annuities, surrenders, entries and withdrawals of loss provisions to and from ceding insurance undertakings and reinsurers, and external and internal claims management costs and charges for claims incurred but not reported. The liability is presented net of sums recoverable on the basis of subrogation and salvage. [SI 2008/410 3 Sch Profit and loss account format note 4].

Bonuses and rebates

34.8.60 Bonuses comprise all amounts chargeable for the financial year which are paid or payable to policyholders and other insured parties or provided for their benefit, including amounts used to increase technical provisions or applied to the reduction of future premiums, to the extent that such amounts represent an allocation of surplus or profit arising on business as a whole or a section of business, after deduction of amounts provided in previous years which are no longer required. Rebates comprise such amounts to the extent that they represent a partial refund of premiums resulting from the experience of individual contracts. [SI 2008/410 3 Sch Profit and loss account format note 5].

Acquisition costs

34.8.61 These comprise the costs arising from the conclusion of insurance contracts and include direct costs (such as acquisition commissions) and indirect costs (such as advertising and the administrative expenses connected with the processing of proposals and the issuing of policies). Policy renewal commissions for long-term business should be included under administrative expenses in the long-term business account. [SI 2008/410 3 Sch Profit and loss account format note 6].

Administrative expenses

34.8.62 These costs include costs arising from premium collection, portfolio administration and inwards and outwards reinsurance, together with policy renewal commissions. This item includes staff costs and depreciation provisions in respect of office furniture and equipment, insofar as these do not need to be shown under acquisition costs, claims expenses or investment charges. [SI 2008/410 3 Sch Profit and loss account format note 7].

Investment return

34.8.63 Investment income, expenses and charges arising in the long-term fund, and any unrealised gains or losses recognised in the profit and loss account in respect of investments attributed to the long-term fund, are initially recorded in the long-term business technical account. [SI 2008/410 3 Sch Profit and loss account format notes 8, 9].

34.8.64 Investment income, expenses and charges not arising in the long-term fund can initially be disclosed in the non-technical account or attributed between the appropriate technical and non-technical accounts. Any unrealised gains or losses recognised in the profit and loss account in respect of investments not attributed to the long-term fund are initially recorded in the non-technical account [SI 2008/410 3 Sch Profit and loss account format notes 8, 9].

34.8.65 Investment return can be transferred from one part of the profit and loss account to another. [SI 2008/410 3 Sch Profit and loss account format note 10].

Investment contracts

34.8.66 Schedule 3 does not contain specific requirements regarding the presentation of amounts relating to investment contracts in the profit and loss account where such contracts are accounted for as financial instruments under FRS 102. We consider that the following presentations would be appropriate:

- Fee income – include under the technical heading 'Other technical income, net of reinsurance'.

- Where the financial liability is classified in the balance sheet as either 'Technical provisions for linked liabilities' or 'Other technical provisions' – present movements in that liability (not arising from deposits or withdrawals) within changes in other technical provisions.

- Where the financial liability in respect of a non-linked investment contract is classified in the balance sheet as either 'Other creditors, including tax and social security' or as a new line item – present movements in that liability (not arising from deposits or withdrawals) within other technical income/ expenses or as a new line item.

Recognition and measurement

34.8.67 Schedule 3 sets out requirements regarding the recognition and measurement of many of the items set out in the prescribed format. In some cases, the valuation bases prescribed by Schedule 3 are consistent with the requirements of FRS 102 and do not serve to limit any of the options available under the relevant sections of that standard; these items are not discussed further in this chapter. Discussed further below are the significant areas where Schedule 3's requirements might, in practice, impact recognition or measurement.

Investments and investment return

34.8.68   Under Schedule 3, assets of insurance companies shown as investments should be measured at current value, except for those investments where the option to measure at fair value (see para 34.8.71) or amortised cost (see para 34.8.73) has been applied. [SI 2008/410 3 Sch 21(1), 22].

34.8.69   For assets other than land and buildings, current value represents market value (reduced for realisation costs where the investments are to be sold within the short term). Except where the equity method of accounting is applied, the current value of assets for which no market exists should be determined on a basis which has prudent regard to the likely realisable value. [SI 2008/410 3 Sch 25].

34.8.70   For land and buildings, current value represents market value at the date of most recent valuation (which should be carried out at least every five years) reduced by subsequent diminishments in value. Where it is impossible to determine the market value, the value arrived at (on the basis of the principle of purchase price or production cost) is deemed to be current value. [SI 2008/410 3 Sch 26].

34.8.71   Schedule 3 also permits certain financial instruments and investment property to be valued at fair value. For financial instruments, fair value is defined by reference to market value (or a reasonable approximation thereof). For investment property, fair value is defined by reference to EU-endorsed IFRS. [SI 2008/410 3 Sch 30, 31, 33(3)].

34.8.72   In practice, valuations meeting the Schedule 3 definition of fair value will, in many cases, also be capable of representing current value. So, where valuation at either current value or fair value is permitted, the distinction between the two bases might not necessarily impact the actual carrying value. But valuation at current value might not always represent fair value. For example, the current value of land and buildings (determined in accordance with para 34.8.70) might not equate to fair value where the value has increased since the date at which the valuation to determine current value was performed.

34.8.73   Investments which are debt securities and other fixed income securities can be shown at amortised cost. [SI 2008/410 3 Sch 24].

34.8.74   Unrealised gains and losses on investments are permitted, but not required, to be included within the profit and loss account. [SI 2008/410 3 Sch Profit and loss account format note 9].

Investments — Land and buildings

34.8.75 Land and buildings are required to be valued either at current value or, in the case of investment property, fair value. [SI 2008/410 3 Sch 21(1), 22(1)].

34.8.76 To comply with the requirements of Schedule 3, the fair value model (as set out in section 16 of FRS 102) will generally need to be applied to investment property. Under FRS 102, the cost-depreciation-impairment model in section 17 is applied to investment property where fair value cannot be measured reliably without undue cost or effort on an ongoing basis. [FRS 102 para 16.1]. But, under Schedule 3, the use of a cost-based method for valuing investment property would only be permissible where it is impossible to determine market value.

34.8.77 Land and buildings other than investment property (for example, owner-occupied property) will generally need to be accounted for under the revaluation model in section 17 of FRS 102. The alternative cost-depreciation-impairment model will only be appropriate where it is impossible to determine market value.

Investments — Interests in subsidiary undertakings, associated undertakings and joint ventures

34.8.78 Investments in subsidiary undertakings, associated undertakings and joint ventures are required to be valued either at current value or, where permitted under EU-endorsed IFRS, fair value. [SI 2008/410 3 Sch 21(1), 22(1), 30].

34.8.79 The use of the cost model set out in sections 9, 14 and 15 of FRS 102 will not be consistent with this requirement and so should not be used.

Assets held to cover linked liabilities

34.8.80 All investments included as assets held to cover linked liabilities should be held at current value or fair value. [SI 2008/410 3 Sch 21(1), 22(2)]. Unrealised gains and losses on such investments should be included within the profit and loss account. [SI 2008/410 3 Sch Profit and loss account format note 9]. To ensure compliance with this requirement, any valuation bases permitted under FRS 102 that involve a cost-based valuation, or the inclusion of unrealised gains and losses in other comprehensive income, should not be applied to such assets.

Deferred acquisition costs – general business

34.8.81 The amount of deferred acquisition costs in respect of general business should be established on a basis compatible with that used for unearned premiums (see para 34.8.83). [SI 2008/410 3 Sch 13, Balance sheet format note 17].

Technical provisions

34.8.82   The amount of technical provisions should at all times be sufficient to cover any liabilities arising out of insurance contracts, as far as can be reasonably foreseen. [SI 2008/410 3 Sch 49].

Provision for unearned premiums

34.8.83   This comprises the amount representing that part of gross premiums written which is estimated to be earned in following financial years. In respect of long-term business, such amounts could be included in the long-term business provision; and there is a similar choice regarding the presentation of movements in this amount in the long-term business technical account. [SI 2008/410 3 Sch Balance sheet format note 20, Profit and loss account format note 3].

34.8.84   The provision for unearned premiums should, in principle, be computed separately for each insurance contract (except that statistical methods can be used where they are likely to give approximately the same results as individual calculations). Where the pattern of risk varies over the life of a contract, this should be taken into account in the calculation methods. [SI 2008/410 3 Sch 50].

Provision for unexpired risks

34.8.85   The provision for unexpired risks represents the amount set aside in respect of risks to be borne by the company after the end of the financial year, in order to provide for all claims and expenses in connection with insurance contracts in force in excess of the related unearned premiums and any premiums receivable on those contracts. The provision should be computed on the basis of claims and administrative expenses likely to arise after the end of the financial year from contracts concluded before that date, insofar as their estimated value exceeds the provision for unearned premiums and any premiums receivable under those contracts. [SI 2008/410 3 Sch 91, 51].

General business – claims outstanding

34.8.86   A provision should, in principle, be computed separately for each claim on the basis of the costs still expected to arise (except that statistical methods can be used if they result in an adequate provision, having regard to the nature of the risk). The provision should allow for claims incurred but not reported ('IBNR'), having regard to experience as to the number and magnitude of claims reported after previous balance sheet dates. The provision should include all direct and indirect claims settlement costs. [SI 2008/410 3 Sch 53(1)-(3)].

34.8.87   Salvage and subrogation recoveries should be estimated on a prudent basis and either deducted from claims outstanding or shown as assets. [SI 2008/410 3 Sch 53(4)].

34.8.88   Where benefits resulting from a claim are paid in the form of an annuity, the amounts set aside for that purpose should be calculated by recognised actuarial methods. [SI 2008/410 3 Sch 53(6)].

34.8.89   Implicit discounting of outstanding claims is not permitted. For claims other than those paid in the form of an annuity, explicit discounting to take account of investment income is only permitted where all the following conditions are met:

- The expected average interval between the date for the settlement of claims being discounted and the accounting date is at least four years.

- The discounting is performed on a recognised prudential basis.

- When calculating the total cost of settling claims, account is taken of all factors that could cause increases in that cost.

- The company has adequate data to construct a reliable model of the rate of claims settlements.

- The rate of interest used does not exceed a prudently estimated rate to be earned on assets appropriate to back the outstanding claims provisions. The rate should not exceed a rate justified by the performance of such assets over either the preceding five years or the preceding year.

[SI 2008/410 3 Sch 53(6)(7), 54(1)].

Use of non-annual basis of accounting

34.8.90   Where, because of the nature of the class or type of insurance business in question, information about premiums receivable or claims payable is insufficient when the accounts are drawn up for reliable estimates to be made, Schedule 3 permits the use of either the fund basis of accounting or the deferred annual basis of accounting. [SI 2008/410 3 Sch 57].

34.8.91   Under the fund basis of accounting, the excess of premiums written over claims and expenses paid (or, where appropriate to the type of risk insured, a given percentage of premium) is included in the technical provision for claims outstanding (increased, as necessary, to make them sufficient to meet present and future obligations). This provision is replaced with one calculated in accordance with paragraph 34.8.86 as soon as sufficient information is available (and no later than the end of the third year following the financial year in which the contract commenced). [SI 2008/410 3 Sch 58].

34.8.92   Under the deferred annual basis of accounting, the figures shown in the technical account (or a part thereof) relate to a year which wholly or partly precedes the financial year (but by no more than 12 months). The amount of technical provisions should, if necessary, be increased to make them sufficient to meet present and future obligations. [SI 2008/410 3 Sch 59].

Equalisation provision

34.8.93 This item includes those equalisation provisions maintained in respect of general business in accordance with the FSA Handbook, together with any other amounts which are required to be set aside to equalise fluctuations in loss ratios by the European Directive dealing with credit and suretyship insurance (Council Directive 87/343/EEC). [SI 2008/410 3 Sch 56, Balance sheet format note 24].

Long-term business

34.8.94 The long-term business provision item represents the actuarially estimated value of the company's liabilities (excluding technical provisions for linked liabilities). The long-term business provision includes bonuses already declared, and is stated after deducting the actuarial value of future premiums. This item also comprises claims incurred but not reported, plus the estimated costs of settling such claims. As set out in paragraph 34.8.83, this item can also include the provision for unearned premiums. The long-term business provision should, in principle, be computed separately for each long-term contract (except that statistical methods can be used where they are likely to give approximately the same results as individual calculations). The computation should be made annually by a Fellow of the Institute or Faculty of Actuaries on the basis of recognised actuarial methods, with due regard to the actuarial principles laid down in the Consolidated Life Directive (2002/83/EC). [SI 2008/410 3 Sch 52, Balance sheet format note 21].

34.8.95 The amount of the provision for claims for long-term business should equal the sums due to beneficiaries plus the cost of settling claims. [SI 2008/410 3 Sch 55].

Disclosure

Basis of preparation

34.8.96 The accounts of insurance companies should contain a statement that they have been prepared in accordance with the provisions of SI 2008/410 relating to insurance companies ; and the same applies to insurance groups. [SI 2008/410 Reg 6(3), 9(4)].

Owner-occupied land and buildings

34.8.97 The amount of any land and buildings occupied by the insurance company for its own activities should be disclosed. [SI 2008/410 3 Sch Balance sheet format note 4].

Other loans

34.8.98 The amount of loans to policyholders for which the policy is the main security should be disclosed. Where the amount of other loans not secured by policies is material, an appropriate breakdown should be given. [SI 2008/410 3 Sch Balance sheet format note 7].

Other financial investments – other

34.8.99   Where the amount of 'other financial investments – other' is significant, it should be disclosed in the notes to the accounts. [SI 2008/410 3 Sch Balance sheet format note 9].

Other assets — other

34.8.100   Where the amount of 'other assets – other' is material, it should be disclosed in the notes to the accounts. [SI 2008/410 3 Sch Balance sheet format note 15].

Deferred acquisition costs

34.8.101   The accounts should detail how deferred acquisition costs have been treated. Disclosure should be given of the amount of any deferred acquisition costs which have been included as a deduction from the provision for unearned premiums or explicitly recognised in the computation of the long-term business provision or the technical provision for linked liabilities. [SI 2008/410 3 Sch Balance sheet format note 17].

Equalisation reserves

34.8.102   If an insurance company constitutes reserves to equalise fluctuations in loss ratios in future years or to provide for special risks, and these reserves are not required to be shown as equalisation provisions, this fact should be disclosed. [SI 2008/410 3 Sch Balance sheet format note 24].

Basis of calculation of long-term business provision

34.8.103   A summary of the principal assumptions in making the long-term business provision should be given. [SI 2008/410 3 Sch 52(2)].

Value of long-term fund

34.8.104   An insurance company conducting long-term business should disclose the total value of assets representing the long-term fund. [SI 2008/410 3 Sch 11(2)]. This disclosure is not required in an insurance group's consolidated financial statements. [SI 2008/410 6 Sch 40(2)].

Managed funds

34.8.105   The notes to the accounts should detail the amounts included within each balance sheet item in respect of any assets and liabilities that fall to be recognised on the balance sheet in respect of managed funds. For this purpose, managed funds are funds of a group pension fund:

- the management of which constitutes long-term insurance business;

- which the insurance company administers in its own name but on behalf of others; and

- to which it has legal title.

[SI 2008/410 3 Sch 12].

Attribution or allocation of investment return

34.8.106 Where investment income, expenses or charges not arising in the long-term fund are attributed between technical and non-technical accounts, the basis for attribution should be disclosed. [SI 2008/410 3 Sch Profit and loss account format note 8]. The bases on which any transfers of investment return between technical and non-technical accounts are made should be disclosed. [SI 2008/410 3 Sch Profit and loss account format note 10].

Material run-off deviation

34.8.107 Disclosure should be made of any material surplus or deficiency in claims provisions established at the previous year-end, broken down by category and amount. [SI 2008/410 3 Sch Profit and loss account format note 4].

Bonuses and rebates

34.8.108 Where material, the amount charged for bonuses and that charged for rebates should be disclosed separately. [SI 2008/410 3 Sch Profit and loss account format note 5].

Items shown at current cost or current value

34.8.109 Where items are valued at either current value or current cost under paragraph 22 or 23 of Schedule 3, the items affected and the basis of valuation adopted should be disclosed. [SI 2008/410 3 Sch 28(2)].

34.8.110 The purchase price of investments valued at current value should be disclosed. [SI 2008/410 3 Sch 28(3)].

34.8.111 For intangible assets (other than goodwill), tangible assets, own shares or stocks valued at current cost or current value, one of the following should be disclosed:

- The comparable amounts determined according to the historical cost accounting rules (without any provision for depreciation or diminution in value).

- The differences between the amounts determined according to the historical cost accounting rules and the corresponding amounts actually shown in the balance sheet.

[SI 2008/410 3 Sch 28(4)].

Valuation of fixed interest securities at amortised cost

34.8.112 Where debt securities or other fixed interest securities are valued at amortised cost, the following disclosures should be made:

- the aggregate totals of the purchase price and current value; and

- the net excess/deficit of the amounts payable at maturity over the amortised cost.

[SI 2008/410 3 Sch 24 (4)(5)(6)].

Use of non-annual basis of accounting

34.8.113 Where a non-annual basis of accounting is adopted, this should be disclosed, together with the reasons for adopting it. Where the fund basis of accounting is used, the length of time that elapses before a year is closed should be disclosed. Where a deferred annual basis of accounting is adopted, the period of deferral and the magnitude of transactions concerned should be disclosed. [SI 2008/410 3 Sch 57(2), 58(5), 59(3)].

Salvage and subrogation recoveries

34.8.114 Any material salvage and subrogation recoveries which have been deducted from general business outstanding claims should be disclosed. [SI 2008/410 3 Sch 53(4)].

Discounting of general business outstanding claims

34.8.115 Where general business outstanding claims are discounted, the following should be disclosed:

- The total amount of provisions before discounting.

- The categories of claim which are discounted.

- For each category of claims: the methods used; the rate of claims settlement; the rate of interest; and the criteria adopted for estimating the period that will elapse before settlement.

[SI 2008/410 3 Sch 54(2)].

Particulars of business

34.8.116 In respect of general business, the following should be disclosed:

- Gross premiums written.

- Gross premiums earned.

- Gross claims incurred.

- Gross operating expenses.

- Reinsurance balance.

[SI 2008/410 3 Sch 85(1)].

34.8.117 Where reinsurance acceptances amount to more than 10% of gross written premiums, the amounts set out in paragraph 34.8.116 should be broken down between direct insurance and reinsurance acceptances. [SI 2008/410 3 Sch 85(2)].

34.8.118 An analysis of the amounts set out in paragraph 34.8.116 by class of business is required to be made in respect of direct insurance business where the amount of gross premiums written for a particular class exceeds 10 million euros (and, in any event, for the three largest classes). The classes of business are:

- Accident and health.

- Motor (third-party liability).

- Motor (other classes).

- Marine, aviation and transport.

- Fire and other damage to property.

- Third-party liability.

- Credit and suretyship.

- Legal expenses.

- Assistance.

- Miscellaneous.

[SI 2008/410 3 Sch 85(3)(4)].

34.8.119 In respect of long-term business, the following should be disclosed:

- Gross premiums written, sub-analysed between direct business and reinsurance business.

- A sub-analysis of gross premiums written by way of direct business between:

  - Individual premiums and premiums under group contracts.

  - Periodic premiums and single premiums.

- ■ Premiums from non-participating contracts, premiums from participating contracts, and premiums from contracts where the investment risk is borne by policyholders.

■ The reinsurance balance.

[SI 2008/410 3 Sch 86(1)(2)].

34.8.120 Disclosure of the sub-analyses referred to in paragraph 34.8.119 is not required if it does not exceed 10% of the gross premiums written or (as the case might be) of the gross premiums written by way of direct insurance. [SI 2008/410 3 Sch 86(3)].

34.8.121 An insurance company should, separately for general and long-term business, analyse total gross premiums between premiums resulting from contracts concluded:

■ In the EU member State of the insurance company's head office.

■ In other EU member States.

■ In other countries.

34.8.122 The disclosure in paragraph 34.8.121 is not required of any amounts not exceeding 5% of total gross premiums. [SI 2008/410 3 Sch 87(1)].

34.8.123 The disclosures regarding particulars of business set out at paragraphs 34.8.116 – 34.8.122 are not required in the consolidated accounts of insurance groups. [SI 2008/410 3 Sch 40(6)].

Commissions

34.8.124 The total amount of commissions for direct insurance business accounted for in the financial year (including acquisition, renewal, collection and portfolio management commissions) should be disclosed. [SI 2008/410 3 Sch 88]. Disclosure is not required in the consolidated accounts of insurance groups. [SI 2008/410 6 Sch 40(6)].

Areas where Schedule 3's disclosure requirements replicate Schedule 1

34.8.125 The table below highlights areas where the disclosure requirements applicable to insurance companies in Schedule 3 replicate those applicable to the generality of companies as set out in Schedule 1. The Schedule 1 disclosure requirements are discussed in more detail in the relevant chapters of this book.

Topic	Schedule 3 reference	Schedule 1 reference
Corresponding amounts	5(2)	7(2)
Debenture loans	Balance sheet format note 29	Balance sheet format note 7
Departure from accounting principles	15	10(2)
Revaluation reserve	29(6)	35(6)
Fair value reserve	35(2)	41(2)
Depreciation and diminution in value	38(4)	19(3)

Note: under Schedule 1, this requirement applies to 'fixed assets' which are not separately presented in the Schedule 3 format. In Schedule 3, this requirement applies to intangible assets, investments, tangible assets and own shares valued under the historical cost accounting rules.

Topic	Schedule 3 reference	Schedule 1 reference
Development costs	41(2)	21(2)
Goodwill	42(4)	22(4)
Excess of money owed over value received as an asset item	43(2)(b)	25(2)(b)
Determination of cost	45(3), 46(3)	27(3), 28(3)
Disclosure of accounting policies	61, 62	44, 45
Sums denominated in foreign currencies	63	70
Reserves and dividends	64	43
Share capital and debentures	65–68	47–50

Note: Schedule 3 does not replicate the requirement of paragraph 47(1)(b) of Schedule 1 to give disclosures regarding treasury shares.

Topic	Schedule 3 reference	Schedule 1 reference
Assets	69–71	51–53

Note: under Schedule 1, these requirements relate to fixed assets. The disclosure requirements of paragraph 69(1) of Schedule 3 apply to intangible assets, land and buildings and investments in group undertakings and participating interests. The disclosures required by paragraphs 69(3) and 70 of Schedule 3 are not limited to fixed assets.

Topic	Schedule 3 reference	Schedule 1 reference
Investments	72	54(1)
Information about fair value of assets and liabilities	73–75	55–57

348029

Note: Schedule 3 additionally requires disclosure of the items affected, the basis of valuation and the purchase price. [SI 2008/410 3 Sch 73(2), (3)].

Information where investment property and living animals and plants included at fair value	76	58
Reserves and provisions	77	59
Provision for taxation	78	60
Details of indebtedness	79–80	61–62
Guarantees and other financial commitments	81	63

Note: under Schedule 3, the disclosure regarding contingent liabilities and other financial commitments does not extend to those arising from insurance contracts. Schedule 3 additionally requires insurance companies to separately analyse commitments undertaken on behalf of any parent undertaking or fellow subsidiary and commitments undertaken on behalf of any subsidiary. [SI 2008/410 3 Sch 81(6)].

Miscellaneous matters	82, 89	64, 69
Separate statement of certain items of income and expenditure	83	66
Particulars of tax	84	67
Related party transactions	90	72

Chapter 35

Transition to FRS 102

Chapter 35

Transition to FRS 102

Scope

35.1 For first-time adopters, the underlying principle is retrospective application of FRS 102's requirements in the opening balance sheet and all periods presented in the first financial statements prepared under the standard. This is consistent with what might be expected for a change in accounting policies under section 10 of FRS 102. But section 35 of FRS 102 replaces section 10 in the context of first-time adoption, and it contains some mandatory exceptions and optional exemptions from the general requirement of retrospective application.

> *"An entity that presents its first annual financial statements that conform to this FRS, regardless of whether its previous accounting framework was EU-adopted IFRS or another set of accounting standards."* [FRS 102 Glossary of terms].

35.3 Section 35 of FRS 102 applies to first-time adopters moving from IFRS, national accounting standards (for instance, 'old UK GAAP'), or another framework such as the local income tax basis. [FRS 102 para 35.1]. In most cases, entities transitioning in the UK to FRS 102 will be moving from old UK GAAP; and, in some cases, they will be moving from IFRS.

35.4 This chapter summarises the requirements in section 35 of FRS 102 for first-time adopters of the standard. Practical issues arising on first-time adoption are dealt with in sections on 'Transitional issues' in each of the other chapters in this book.

Repeated first-time application

35.5 A question arises as to whether section 35 can be applied by an entity more than once. For example, an entity might have previously transitioned to FRS 102 (applying section 35) and then changed to IFRS on being acquired by a group reporting under IFRS. If the entity later leaves the group and wishes to revert back to FRS 102, the question is how it accounts for the transition (that is, on 'repeated first-time application').

35.6 An entity that has applied FRS 102 in a previous reporting period, but whose most recent previous annual financial statements did not contain an explicit and unreserved statement of compliance with the FRS, has a choice of applying (i) section 35 or (ii) FRS 102 retrospectively in accordance with section 10, as if the entity had never stopped applying the FRS. [FRS 102 para 35.2].

First annual financial statements

35.7 Section 35 of the standard applies to an entity's first financial statements that conform to FRS 102. These are the first financial statements (excluding interims) in which the entity makes an explicit and unreserved statement of compliance with the FRS. [FRS 102 paras 35.3, 35.4].

35.8 Financial statements prepared under FRS 102 are an entity's first such financial statements if, for example, the entity:

■ did not present financial statements for previous periods;

■ presented its most recent previous financial statements under previous UK and Republic of Ireland requirements, and so they are not consistent with FRS 102 in all respects; or

■ presented its most recent previous financial statements under IFRS.

[FRS 102 para 35.4].

35.9 Generally, section 35 does not apply where an entity has, in its most recent previous financial statements, presented an explicit and unreserved statement of compliance with FRS 102, even if those financial statements were accompanied by an audit report that was qualified. In other words, those previous financial statements are still FRS 102 financial statements.

Date of transition

35.10 An entity should disclose, in a complete set of financial statements, comparative information in respect of the preceding period for all amounts presented in the financial statements, as well as specified comparative narrative and descriptive information. [FRS 102 para 3.14]. Comparative information can be given for more than one prior period. For the purpose of first-time adoption, an entity's date of transition to FRS 102 is the beginning of the earliest period for which the entity presents full comparative information in accordance with the standard in its first financial statements that comply with the FRS. [FRS 102 para 35.6].

35.11 For entities adopting FRS 102 when it is mandatory (that is, for accounting periods beginning on or after 1 January 2015), and assuming that one year's comparatives are given, the relevant dates of transition are shown below:

Year end	First FRS 102 financial statements required for year ending	Date of transition
31 December	31 December 2015	1 January 2014
31 March	31 March 2016	1 April 2014
30 June	30 June 2016	1 July 2014
30 September	30 September 2016	1 October 2014

Initial recognition and measurement

35.12 Apart from some specified exceptions and exemptions, the general principle applied to an entity's opening balance sheet at its date of transition (that is, the beginning of the earliest period presented) is that items should be recognised and measured in accordance with FRS 102. So, entities apply the following rules:

■ Recognise all assets and liabilities whose recognition is required by the standard.

■ Do not recognise items as assets or liabilities if the standard does not permit such recognition.

■ Reclassify items that it recognised under its previous financial reporting framework as one type of asset, liability or component of equity, but that are a different type of asset, liability or component of equity under the standard.

■ Apply the standard in measuring all recognised assets and liabilities.

[FRS 102 para 35.7].

35.13 Although section 35 of FRS 102 sets out the accounting requirements for the opening balance sheet, as a starting point for the adoption of the new standard, it does not require the opening balance sheet (that is, the balance sheet at the date of transition) to be presented. [FRS 102 para 35.7].

35.14 The accounting policies that an entity uses in its opening balance sheet under FRS 102 might differ from those that it used for the same date under its previous financial reporting framework. The resulting adjustments arise from transactions, other events or conditions before the date of transition. So, section 35 of FRS 102 requires these adjustments to be recognised directly in retained earnings (or, if appropriate, another category of equity) at the date of transition to the standard. [FRS 102 para 35.8].

35.15 Examples of adjustments that could be made to a category of equity other than retained earnings include:

■ The result of remeasuring derivative financial instruments classified as hedges under paragraph 12.23 of FRS 102.

■ The difference between cost of property, plant and equipment and fair value where a deemed cost is used or where a revaluation policy is adopted on transition to FRS 102.

■ Deferred tax recognised for the first time on revalued property, included in the same reserve as the revaluation gains.

35.16 The requirement to recognise adjustments on transition to FRS 102 in retained earnings (or another category of equity) applies also in the case of previous business combinations; no adjustment is made to the carrying value of goodwill. [FRS 102 para 35.10(a)].

Exceptions to retrospective application

35.17 The general requirement of FRS 102 is full retrospective application. Section 35 of FRS 102 has two categories of exceptions to full retrospective application: mandatory exceptions (see immediately below); and optional exemptions (see para 35.30 below).

35.18 The mandatory exceptions derive from the IFRS for SMEs, and they were included on the following grounds: the IASB believed either that retrospective application could not be performed with sufficient reliability, or that there would be potential for abuse because retrospective application would require judgements about past conditions after the outcome of a particular transaction was already known. So, the exceptions to retrospective application listed in paragraph 35.9 of FRS 102 are mandatory for all first-time adopters.

35.19 Paragraph 35.9 of FRS 102 states that, on first-time adoption of the standard, an entity should not retrospectively change the accounting that it followed under its previous financial reporting framework for any of the following transactions:

Mandatory exceptions from full retrospective application	Scope – exception applies to	Dealt with from
Derecognition of financial assets and liabilities	Financial assets and liabilities derecognised before the date of transition.	Para 35.20
Hedge accounting	Hedging relationships that no longer exist at the date of transition.	Para 35.22
Estimates	All estimates.	Para 35.25
Discontinued operations	All discontinued operations previously accounted for.	Para 35.28
Non-controlling interests	All equity in a subsidiary not attributable, directly or indirectly, to a parent.	Para 35.29

Derecognition of financial assets and liabilities

35.20 There is a mandatory exception from full retrospective application of FRS 102 in respect of the derecognition of financial assets and liabilities. Financial assets and liabilities derecognised under an entity's previous accounting framework before the date of transition are not recognised on adoption of FRS 102.

35.21 Also, for financial assets and liabilities that would have been derecognised under FRS 102 in a transaction that took place before the date of transition, but were not derecognised under an entity's previous accounting framework, an entity can choose:

■ to derecognise them on adoption of the standard; or

■ to continue to recognise them until disposed of or settled.

[FRS 102 para 35.9(a)].

Hedge accounting

35.22 There is a mandatory exception in section 35 of FRS 102 related to hedge accounting. An entity should not change its hedge accounting before the date of transition to FRS 102 for hedging relationships that no longer exist at the date of transition. [FRS 102 para 35.9(b)].

35.23 For hedging relationships that exist at the date of transition, an entity should follow the hedge accounting requirements of section 12 of FRS 102, including the requirements for discontinuing hedge accounting for hedging relationships that do not meet the conditions of section 12 of the standard.

35.24 Further guidance on the practical implications of hedge accounting on transition to FRS 102 is given in chapter 12.

Accounting estimates

35.25 Another mandatory exception from full retrospective application of FRS 102 is in the area of estimates. An entity should not retrospectively change the accounting that it followed for estimates under its previous financial reporting framework. [FRS 102 para 35.9(c)].

35.26 This means that management's estimates at the date of transition to FRS 102 should be consistent with estimates made for the same date in accordance with previous GAAP (after adjustments to reflect any difference in accounting policies). In other words, hindsight cannot be used to improve the estimates. If more information comes to light about estimates made under previous GAAP, it should be treated as non-adjusting and accounted for in the current period. This applies unless there is clear evidence that those estimates were wrong.

35.27 Some estimates might not have been required by a first-time adopter's previous GAAP, but are required by FRS 102 (for instance, fair valuing some financial instruments). The standard does not include any specific guidance for first-time adopters, but the general approach should be to base the initial estimates of fair values for the opening balance sheet on conditions that existed at the date of transition.

Discontinued operations

35.28 FRS 102 requires separate disclosure to be given in the statement of comprehensive income (or income statement, if presented) in respect of discontinued operations. This is covered in chapter 5. The definition of a discontinued operation in FRS 102 is similar to that in IFRS, but differs from that in old UK GAAP (FRS 3). On first-time adoption of FRS 102, an entity should not retrospectively change the accounting that it followed under its previous financial reporting framework for discontinued operations. [FRS 102 para 35.9(d)]. So, no reclassification or remeasurement is recognised for discontinued operations previously accounted for using the previous financial reporting framework.

Non-controlling interests

35.29 Section 35 of FRS 102 requires that, on first-time adoption of the standard, an entity should not retrospectively change the accounting that it followed under its previous financial reporting framework for measuring non-controlling interests. The requirements of paragraph 5.6 of FRS 102 for:

(i)   allocating profit or loss and total comprehensive income between non-controlling interest and the parent's owners;

(ii)   accounting for changes in the parent's ownership interest in a subsidiary that do not result in a loss of control; and

(iii) accounting for a loss of control over a subsidiary,

are applied prospectively from the date of transition to the FRS (or, if business combinations are restated, from that earlier date – see para 35.31 below). [FRS 102 para 35.9(e)].

Exemptions from full retrospective application

35.30 Paragraph 35.10 of FRS 102 lists a number of exemptions that a first-time adopter can use in preparing its financial statements. Any, all or none of these exemptions could be taken. They are summarised below:

Optional exemptions from full retrospective application	Scope – where exemption taken, it applies to	Dealt with from
Business combinations, including group reconstructions	All business combinations before the date of transition; or, if an entity chooses to apply FRS 102 to a combination before that date, the exemption applies to all combinations prior to that one.	Para 35.31
Share-based payment transactions	Equity share-based payment transactions granted (or liability share-based payment transactions settled) before the date of transition. But a first-time adopter previously applying FRS 20 or IFRS 2 can apply those standards (as applicable) or section 26 of FRS 102 for equity share-based payment transactions at the date of transition.	Para 35.47
Fair value as deemed cost	Any tangible fixed asset, investment property and a limited number of intangible assets.	Para 35.37
Revaluation as deemed cost	Any tangible fixed asset, investment property and a limited number of intangible assets.	Para 35.38
Individual and separate financial statements	Any investments in subsidiaries, jointly controlled entities and associates in individual and separate financial statements.	Para 35.56
Compound financial instruments	Compound financial instruments where the liability component has been settled by the date of transition.	Para 35.44
Service concession arrangements	Accounting by operators for service concession arrangements entered into before the date of transition.	Para 35.48
Extractive activities	Measurement of oil and gas assets at the date of transition.	Para 35.50
Arrangements containing a lease	Arrangements existing at the date of transition.	Para 35.45
Decommissioning liabilities included in the cost of property, plant and equipment	Decommissioning liabilities included in the cost of property, plant and equipment.	Para 35.41
Dormant companies	All dormant companies.	Para 35.58
Deferred development costs at deemed cost	Development costs deferred under old UK GAAP.	Para 35.42

Borrowing costs	All borrowing costs relating to qualifying assets.	Para 35.40
Lease incentives	Lease incentives for leases that commenced before the date of transition.	Para 35.46
Public benefit entity combinations	All public benefit entity combinations before the date of transition; or, if an entity chooses to apply FRS 102 to a combination before that date, the exemption applies to all combinations prior to that one.	Para 35.36
Assets and liabilities of subsidiaries, associates and joint ventures	All assets and liabilities of individual subsidiaries, jointly controlled entities and associates whose transition date is different from the parent/group.	Para 35.52
Designation of previously recognised financial instruments	Specified debt instruments.	Para 35.43

Business combinations, including group reconstructions

35.31 A first-time adopter can elect not to apply section 19 of FRS 102 to business combinations effected before the date of transition to the standard. But, if a first-time adopter restates any business combination to comply with section 19 of the standard, it has to restate all later business combinations. If a first-time adopter does not apply section 19 of the standard retrospectively, it still has to recognise and measure its assets and liabilities relating to past business combinations in accordance with FRS 102 (subject to the exceptions and exemptions in section 35) at the date of transition, except that:

■   intangible assets subsumed within goodwill are not separately recognised; and

■   no adjustment is made to the carrying value of goodwill.

[FRS 102 para 35.10(a)].

35.32 The effect of this exemption is that, although business combinations before the transition date do not have to be restated in full, the assets and liabilities relating to those combinations have to be recognised and measured in accordance with FRS 102 (subject to the exceptions and exemptions in section 35). It means that, even if an entity uses the business combination exemption, it might have to restate deferred tax arising on business combinations before the date of transition to FRS 102 (for example, on fixed assets revalued to fair value on acquisition), because there is no specific exemption for this.

35.33 Any adjustments made in recognising and measuring the assets and liabilities relating to past business combinations are made against opening retained earnings on transition to FRS 102 (as noted in para 35.16 above), because goodwill cannot be adjusted. This means that, where a company has acquired an unincorporated business in a trade and asset deal, adjustments (for example, for deferred tax liabilities) will impact distributable profits.

35.34 If an entity previously determined that goodwill had an indefinite useful life, it will need to reassess this on transition. FRS 102 does not permit goodwill to have an indefinite useful life. So, on transition to FRS 102, entities that previously did not amortise goodwill will need to determine its remaining useful life, and subsequently amortise the goodwill over that period. [FRS 102 Advice to FRC para 161].

35.35 Further guidance on the exemption for business combinations, and on transitional issues relating to goodwill, is given in chapter 19.

35.36 There are also separate transitional provisions for public benefit entity combinations. A first-time adopter can elect not to apply the paragraphs in section 34 of FRS 102 relating to public benefit entity combinations (see chapter 34) to combinations that were effected before the date of transition to the FRS. But if, on first-time adoption, a public benefit entity restates any entity combination to comply with section 34 of the standard, it should restate all later entity combinations. [FRS 102 para 35.10(q)].

Valuations as deemed cost

35.37 There are two 'valuation as deemed cost' exemptions: fair value as deemed cost; and revaluation as deemed cost. The first of these is that a first-time adopter can elect to measure an:

- item of property, plant and equipment;
- investment property; or
- intangible asset which meets the recognition criteria and the criteria for revaluation in section 18 of FRS 102,

on the date of transition to the FRS at its fair value and use that fair value as its deemed cost at that date. [FRS 102 para 35.10(c)].

35.38 Alternatively, a first-time adopter can elect to use a previous GAAP revaluation of the above items at, or before, the date of transition to FRS 102 as the deemed cost at the revaluation date. [FRS 102 para 35.10(d)].

35.39 Guidance on applying the deemed cost exemptions is given in chapters 16 (investment property), 17 (property, plant and equipment) and 18 (intangible assets).

Borrowing costs

35.40 An entity electing to adopt an accounting policy of capitalising borrowing costs as part of the cost of a qualifying asset can elect to treat the date of transition to FRS 102 as the date on which capitalisation commences. [FRS 102 para 35.10(o)]. See chapter 25.

Decommissioning liabilities included in the cost of property, plant and equipment

35.41 Under paragraph 17.10(c) of FRS 102, the cost of an item of property, plant and equipment includes the initial estimate of the costs of dismantling the item and restoring the site on which it is located. A first-time adopter can elect to measure this component of the property, plant and equipment's cost at the date of transition to the FRS, rather than on the date(s) when the obligation initially arose. [FRS 102 para 35.10(l)].

Deferred development costs as a deemed cost

35.42 A first-time adopter can elect to measure the carrying amount at the date of transition to FRS 102 for development costs deferred in accordance with SSAP 13 as its deemed cost at that date. [FRS 102 para 35.10(n)]. See chapter 18.

Designation of previously recognised debt instruments

35.43 A first-time adopter is permitted to designate, at the date of transition to FRS 102, any financial asset or liability at fair value through profit or loss, provided the asset or liability meets the criteria in paragraph 11.14(b) of FRS 102 at that date. [FRS 102 para 35.10(s)]. This applies to specified debt instruments. Normally, these can only be designated at fair value through profit or loss on initial recognition. The exemption permits this designation if the instrument already existed on transition to FRS 102.

Compound financial instruments

35.44 Paragraph 22.13 of FRS 102 requires an entity to split a compound financial instrument into its liability and equity components at the date of issue. A first-time adopter need not separate those two components if the liability component is not outstanding at the date of transition to the standard. [FRS 102 para 35.10(g)]. But, since the principles of section 22 of FRS 102 are the same as FRS 25, it is unlikely that there will be classification differences on transition.

Leases

35.45 A first-time adopter can elect to determine whether an arrangement existing at the date of transition to FRS 102 contains a lease (as in para 20.3A of FRS 102) on the basis of facts and circumstances existing at that date, rather than when the arrangement was entered into. [FRS 102 para 35.10(k)]. See further chapter 20.

35.46 Also, a first-time adopter is not required to apply the standard's requirements to spread benefits from lease incentives over the lease term on a straight-line basis or another systematic basis, provided the term of the lease commenced before the date of transition to FRS 102. The first-time adopter continues to recognise any residual benefit or cost associated with these lease incentives on the same basis as that applied at the date of transition to the standard. [FRS 102 para 35.10(p)]. See chapter 20.

Share-based payment transactions

35.47 A first-time adopter is not required to apply section 26 of FRS 102 to equity instruments that were granted before the date of transition to the standard, or to liabilities arising from share-based payment transactions that were settled before the date of transition to the standard. But a first-time adopter previously applying FRS 20 or IFRS 2 should, in relation to equity instruments that were granted before the date of transition to FRS 102, apply either FRS 20 or IFRS 2 (as applicable) or section 26 of FRS 102 at the date of transition. [FRS 102 para 35.10(b)]. For further guidance on transition, see chapter 26.

Service concession arrangements

35.48 A first-time adopter that is an operator in a service concession arrangement is not required to apply paragraphs 34.12E to 34.16A of FRS 102 to arrangements that were entered into before the date of transition to the standard. Such service concession arrangements continue to be accounted for using the same accounting policies being applied at the date of transition. [FRS 102 para 35.10(i)]. For further guidance, see the section on service concession arrangements in chapter 34.

35.49 For grantors, the requirements in FRS 102 might mean recognising assets and liabilities for infrastructure assets that were not presently recognised. The Accounting Council considers that this provides more relevant information to users; so grantors are not permitted to apply the transitional exemptions that are available to operators by analogy. [FRS 102 Advice to the FRC para 104].

Extractive activities

35.50 A first-time adopter that under a previous GAAP accounted for exploration and development costs for oil and gas properties in the development or production phases, in cost centres that included all properties in a large geographical area, can elect to measure oil and gas assets at the date of transition to FRS 102 on the following basis:

- Exploration and evaluation assets at the amount determined under the entity's previous GAAP.

- Assets in the development or production phases at the amount determined for the cost centre under the entity's previous GAAP. The entity should allocate this amount to the cost centre's underlying assets pro rata, using reserve volumes or reserve values as of that date.

[FRS 102 para 35.10(j)].

35.51 Section 35 of FRS 102 contains requirements on testing the above assets for impairment on transition. For further guidance, see the section on extractive activities in chapter 34.

Assets and liabilities of subsidiaries, associates and joint ventures

35.52 If a subsidiary becomes a first-time adopter later than its parent, the subsidiary should (in its financial statements) measure its assets and liabilities at either:

■ the carrying amounts that would be included in the parent's consolidated financial statements, based on the parent's date of transition to FRS 102, if no adjustments were made for consolidation procedures and for the effects of the business combination in which the parent acquired the subsidiary; or

■ the carrying amounts required by FRS 102, based on the subsidiary's date of transition to the standard. These carrying amounts could differ from those described in the first bullet where:

(a) the exemptions in FRS 102 result in measurements that depend on the date of transition to the standard; or

(b) the accounting policies used in the subsidiary's financial statements differ from those in the consolidated financial statements. For example, for property, plant and equipment, the subsidiary might use as its accounting policy the cost model in section 17 of the standard, whereas the group might use the revaluation model.

[FRS 102 para 35.10(r)].

35.53 A similar election is available to an associate or joint venture that becomes a first-time adopter later than an entity that has significant influence or joint control over it. [FRS 102 para 35.10(r)].

35.54 If an entity becomes a first-time adopter later than its subsidiary (or associate or joint venture), the entity should, in its consolidated financial statements, measure the assets and liabilities of the subsidiary (or associate or joint venture) at the same carrying amounts as in the financial statements of the subsidiary (or associate or joint venture), after adjusting for consolidation (and equity accounting) adjustments and for the effects of the business combination in which the entity acquired the subsidiary (or transaction in which it acquired the associate or joint venture). Similarly, if a parent becomes a first-time adopter for its separate financial statements earlier or later than for its consolidated financial statements, it should measure its assets and liabilities at the same amounts in both financial statements, except for consolidation adjustments. [FRS 102 para 35.10(r)].

35.55 Further guidance on the above exemption is available in chapter 9.

Investments in subsidiaries, jointly controlled entities and associates

35.56 Where an entity prepares individual or separate financial statements, it should account for its investments in subsidiaries, associates and jointly controlled entities either at cost less impairment or at fair value. [FRS 102 paras 9.26, 14.4 and 15.9]. If a first-time adopter measures such an investment at cost, it measures that investment at one of the following amounts in its individual or separate opening balance sheet:

- cost determined in accordance with section 9, 14 or 15 of FRS 102; or

- deemed cost, which is the carrying amount at the date of transition, as determined under the entity's previous GAAP.

[FRS 102 para 35.10(f)].

35.57 Further guidance on the above exemption is available in chapter 9.

Dormant companies

35.58 A company within the Companies Act definition of a dormant company can elect to retain its accounting policies for reported assets, liabilities and equity at the date of transition to FRS 102 until there is any change to those balances or the company undertakes any new transactions. [FRS 102 para 35.10(m)]. This means that, for as long as the company remains dormant, it can retain its previous accounting policies. For the definition a dormant company, see chapter 3 of the Manual of Accounting – Other statutory requirements.

Applying the first-time adoption rules

35.59 If it is impracticable for an entity to restate the opening balance sheet at the date of transition for one or more of the adjustments required by section 35 of FRS 102, the entity makes the adjustments in the earliest period for which it is practicable to do so. FRS 102 says *"Applying a requirement is impracticable when the entity cannot apply it after making every reasonable effort to do so"*. [FRS 102 Glossary of terms]. The entity should identify the data presented for prior periods that are not comparable with data for the period in which it prepares its first financial statements under FRS 102. [FRS 102 para 35.11].

35.60 Also, if it is impracticable for an entity to provide any disclosures required by FRS 102 for any period before the period in which it prepares its first financial statements under FRS 102, the omission should be disclosed. [FRS 102 para 35.11].

35.61 The standard makes it clear that, where the exemptions in section 35 of FRS 102 have been applied at the date of transition on first-time adoption of the standard, they can continue to be used in subsequent financial statements until the related assets and liabilities are derecognised. [FRS 102 para 35.11A].

35.62   But the standard goes on to say that, where there is subsequently a significant change in the circumstances or conditions associated with transactions, events or arrangements that existed at the date of transition, to which an exemption in section 35 of FRS 102 has been applied, an entity should reassess the appropriateness of applying that exemption in preparing subsequent financial statements in order to maintain fair presentation in accordance with section 3 of FRS 102. [FRS 102 para 35.11B].

Disclosures

35.63   An entity should explain how the transition from its previous financial reporting framework to FRS 102 affected its reported financial position and financial performance. To do this, an entity's first financial statements prepared using FRS 102 should include:

- A description of the nature of each change in accounting policy.

- Reconciliations of its equity determined in accordance with its previous financial reporting framework to its equity determined in accordance with FRS 102, for both of the following dates:

  - the date of transition to FRS 102; and

  - the end of the latest period presented in the entity's most recent annual financial statements determined in accordance with its previous financial reporting framework.

- A reconciliation of the profit or loss determined in accordance with its previous financial reporting framework for the latest period in the entity's most recent annual financial statements to its profit or loss determined in accordance with FRS 102 for the same period.

[FRS 102 paras 35.12, 35.13].

35.64   An entity that is preparing its first FRS 102 financial statements for the year to 31 December 2015, with one year of comparative information, will disclose reconciliations for equity (that is, net assets) at 1 January 2014 and 31 December 2014, and profit for the year to 31 December 2014.

35.65   FRS 102 does not specify the format of the reconciliations of equity and profit or loss. The FRC's Staff published a draft guidance note on FRED 48 setting out two alternatives reconciliations. This notes that entities will need to determine the most suitable format for their reconciliations, taking into account the nature and amount of their own adjustments. These illustrative reconciliations below are based on those in the draft guidance note.

Example – Illustrative formats for transition reconciliation disclosures

Suggested format 1

Reconciliation of equity

	Note	As previously stated £	Effect of transition £	FRS 102 (as restated) £	As previously stated £	Effect of transition £	FRS 102 (as restated) £
		At 1 Jan 20X4			At 31 Dec 20X4		
Fixed assets		5,868	–	5,868	5,416	–	5,416
Current assets	(i)	2,475	15	2,490	2,520	17	2,537
Creditors: amounts falling due within one year	(i) (iii)	(2,355)	(16)	(2,371)	(1,824)	(20)	(1,844)
Net current assets		120	(1)	119	696	(3)	693
Total assets less current liabilities		5,988	(1)	5,987	6,112	(3)	6,109
Creditors: amounts falling due after more than one year	(i)	(2,900)	(6)	(2,906)	(2,840)	(3)	(2,843)
Provisions for liabilities		(410)	–	(410)	(465)	–	(465)
Net assets		2,678	(7)	2,671	2,807	(6)	2,801
Capital and reserves		2,678	(7)	2,671	2,807	(6)	2,801

Transition to FRS 102

Reconciliation of profit or loss for the year

	Note	As previously stated £	Effect of transition £	FRS 102 (as restated) £
		Year ended 31 Dec 20X4		
Turnover		832	–	832
Cost of sales	(ii)	(520)	(3)	(523)
Gross profit		312	(3)	309
Administrative expenses	(i), (ii), (iii)	(65)	4	(61)
Other operating income		42	–	42
Operating profit		289	1	290
Interest receivable and similar income		5	–	5
Interest payable and similar charges		(130)	–	(130)
Taxation		(35)	–	(35)
Profit on ordinary activities after taxation and for the financial year		129	1	130

Suggested format 2

Reconciliation of equity

	Note	At 1 Jan 20X4 £	At 31 Dec 20X4 £
Capital and reserves (as previously stated)		2,678	2,807
Recognition of derivative financial instruments	(i)	(2)	1
Re-measurement of stock using spot exchange rate	(ii)	–	(1)
Short-term compensated absences	(iii)	(5)	(6)
Capital and reserves (as restated)		2,671	2,801

Reconciliation of profit or loss for the year

	Note	Year ended 31 Dec 20X4 £
Profit for the year (as previously stated)		129
Recognition of derivative financial instruments	(i)	3
Re-measurement of stock using spot exchange rate	(ii)	(1)
Short-term compensated absences	(iii)	(1)
Profit for the year (as restated)		130

Notes to the reconciliations

The following notes are applicable to both formats set out above.

Financial instruments

(i)   [Name] was not within the scope of FRS 26 'Financial instruments: Recognition and measurement'and had not previously applied it voluntarily. As a result [Name] was not required to recognise derivative financial instruments on the balance sheet. Instead the effects of the derivative financial instruments were recognised in profit or loss when the instruments were settled. Derivative financial instruments are classified as 'other financial instruments' in FRS 102 and are recognised as a financial asset or a financial liability, at fair value, when an entity becomes party to the contractual provisions of the instrument. Consequently financial assets of £15,000 and financial liabilities of £17,000 have been recognised in the opening balance sheet at 1 January 20X4.

(ii)   The derivative financial instruments are foreign exchange forward contracts. In applying SSAP 20 'Foreign currency translation', [Name] previously chose to translate purchases in foreign currencies at the rate of exchange specified in a matching forward contract. This is not permitted by FRS 102, which requires purchases to be translated using the spot exchange rate on the date of the transaction. FRS 102 does not provide an exemption from measuring stock bought in a foreign currency and paid for before the transition date in accordance with its required accounting policies, but the difference is not material and accordingly no adjustment has been made. Items purchased since the transition date have been re-measured based on spot exchange rate. Consequently stock at 31 December 20X4 has been reduced by £1,000 and costs of £2,000 have been recognised in administrative expenses rather than cost of sales.

Short-term compensated absences

(iii)   Prior to applying FRS 102, [Name] did not make provision for holiday pay (that is, holiday earned but not taken prior to the year-end). FRS 102 requires the cost of short-term compensated absences to be recognised when employees render the service that increases their entitlement. Consequently an additional accrual of £5,000 at 1 January 20X4 has been made to reflect this.

35.66   If an entity becomes aware of errors made under its previous financial reporting framework, the reconciliations required by paragraph 35.13 of FRS 102 should, to the extent practicable, distinguish the correction of those errors from changes in accounting policies. [FRS 102 para 35.14].

35.67   If an entity did not present financial statements for previous periods, it should disclose that fact in its first financial statements that conform to FRS 102. [FRS 102 para 35.15].

Index

Locators are:
   paragraph numbers: 11.149, for Chapter 11, paragraph 149

Entries are in word-by-word alphabetical order, where a group of letters followed by a space is filed before the same group of letters followed by a letter, eg 'capital structure and treasury policy' will appear before 'capitalisation'. In determining alphabetical arrangement, initial articles, conjunctions and small prepositions are ignored.

Index

definition, 34.1.4–34.1.6
management and transformation, 34.1.7–34.1.10
definitions
  agricultural activity, 34.1.2–34.1.3
  agricultural produce, 34.1.7
  biological assets, 34.1.4–34.1.6
disclosures
  cost model, 34.1.33–34.1.35
  fair value model, 34.1.27–34.1.30
'fair value', 34.1.18
introduction, 34.1.1
measurement
  cost model, 34.1.31–34.1.32
  fair value model, 34.1.16–34.1.26
  generally, 34.1.14–34.1.15
recognition, 34.1.13
scope, 34.1.11–34.1.12
transitional issues, 34.1.36–34.1.37

Allocation of cost
business combinations, and
  identifiable assets and liabilities, 19.73–19.
  introduction, 19.70–19.72
inventories, and
  joint products, 13.19–13.20
  production overheads, 13.17–13.18

Amortisation
intangible assets, and
  change of method, 18.120
  depreciable amount, 18.114–18.117
  estimates of useful lives, 18.103–18.113
  generally, 18.98–18.102
  methods, 18.118–18.120
  residual lives, 18.114–18.117

Ancillary services to occupants
investment property, and, 16.15–16.16

Assets
financial position, and, 2.10

Associates
accounting for investments
See also **Investment in associates**
  cost model, 14.63–14.66
  definition, 14.2–14.25
  disclosure, 14.74–14.82
  equity method of accounting, 14.28–14.62
  fair value model, 14.67–14.70
  measurement, 14.26–14.70
  presentation, 14.71–14.73
  scope, 14.1
  transitional issues, 14.83–14.87
accounting policies, 14.50
date of financial statements, 14.48–14.49
definition
  generally, 14.2–14.3
  'participating interest', 14.5–14.8
  'significant influence', 14.3–14.25
investment property, and, 16.17–16.18
net liability position at transaction date, in, 14.87
'participating interest', 14.5–14.8
potential voting rights
  equity method of accounting, 14.34–14.35
  significant influence, 14.17–14.19
'significant influence'
  demonstrating in practice, 14.20–14.24
  generally, 14.3–14.4
  loss of, 14.25
  'participating interest', 14.5–14.8
  potential voting rights, 14.17–14.19
  voting power, 14.9–14.16
transactions with, 14.44–14.47
voting power
  generally, 14.9–14.16

potential rights, 14.17–14.19

Auditors' remuneration
notes to financial statements, and, 8.37

Balance sheet
See also **Statement of financial position**
alternative positions, 4.12
disclosure exemptions, and, 1.23
generally, 4.1
insurance companies
  assets held to cover linked liabilities, 34.8.38
  bonus provisions, 34.8.46
  claims outstanding, 34.8.45
  debt securities, 34.8.35
  deferred acquisition costs, 34.8.41
  deposits received from reinsurers, 34.8.49
  deposits with ceded undertakings, 34.8.37
  deposits with credit institutions, 34.8.36
  fixed-income securities, 34.8.35
  format, 34.8.33
  fund for future appropriations, 34.8.44
  group creditors, 34.8.50
  group debtors, 34.8.40
  introduction, 34.8.32
  investment contracts, 34.8.51
  linked liabilities, 34.8.48
  long-term business unrealised profits, 34.8.42
  practical aspects, 34.8.34–34.8.51
  rebate provisions, 34.8.46
  reinsurers' share of technical provisions, 34.8.39
  subordinated liabilities, 34.8.43
  unexpired risks, 34.8.47

Bank loans
statement of financial position, and, 4.28

Beneficial contracts
business combinations, and, 19.93–19.98

Best estimate
provisions, and, 21.41–21.43

'Bill and hold' sales
revenue, and, 23.82–23.83

Bills of exchange payable
statement of financial position, and, 4.28

Biological assets
agricultural produce at point of harvest
  generally, 13.28
  introduction, 13.4
disclosure exemptions, and, 1.23
impairment, and, 27.1
revenue, and, 23.3

Bonus issue of shares
financial liabilities and equity, and, 22.86–22.88

Bonus schemes
employee benefits, and
  generally, 28.112
  short-term benefits, 28.19–28.22
selection of approach within new regime, and, 1.53

Borrowing costs
capitalisation
  directly attributable costs, 25.12–25.15
  eligible costs, 25.12–25.15
  introduction, 25.9
  period, 25.16–25.20
  'qualifying asset', 25.9
  'ready for its intended use or sale', 25.11
  'substantial period of time', 25.10
definition, 25.2–25.5
disclosure, 25.21–25.24
exchange differences, 25.6–25.7
introduction, 25.1
inventories, and, 13.20.1
presentation, 25.21–25.24
recognition, 25.8

Index

Index

Index

Index

major inspections or overhauls, 17.16–17.18
replacement parts, 17.14–17.15
servicing equipment, 17.13
spare parts, 17.13
renewals accounting, 17.144–17.145
replacement parts, 17.14–17.15
residual values, 17.143
revaluation
bases, 17.59–17.64
fair value, 17.59–17.64
frequency, 17.50–17.54
gains, 17.65–17.67
introduction, 17.43
losses, 17.68
model, 17.45–17.49
valuers, 17.55–17.58
scope, 17.1–17.7
servicing equipment, 17.13
spare parts, 17.13
tangible assets, as, 17.4
transitional issues
component depreciation, 17.142
deemed cost, 17.137–17.141
introduction, 17.135–17.136
renewals accounting, 17.144–17.145
residual values, 17.143
unknown price or cost, 17.25–17.26

Equity
financial position, and, 2.10
statement of changes
generally, 6.3–6.7
introduction, 6.1–6.2
transitional issues, 6.11–6.12

Equity instruments
business combinations, and, 19.43–19.47
disclosure exemptions, and, 1.22

Equity investments
comparison of FRS 102 with old UK GAAP, and,
1.33

Equity method of accounting
investments in associates, and
accounting policies, 14.50
adjustments to carrying amount, 14.33
date of financial statements, 14.48–14.49
discontinuance of, 14.55–14.60
distributions, 14.33
exemption from, 14.61–14.62
fair value adjustments, 14.36–14.39
impairment, 14.40–14.43
implicit goodwill, 14.36–14.39
introduction, 14.28
investment portfolios, and, 14.61–14.62
losses in excess of investment, 14,.51–14.54
potential voting rights, 14.34–14.35
share accounted for, 14.29–14.32
transactions with associates, 14.44–14.47
investment in joint ventures, and, 15.30

Equity-settled share-based payment transactions
See also Share-based payment transactions
accounting for vesting conditions
generally, 26.44–26.46
market vesting conditions, 26.48
non-market vesting conditions, 26.47
non-vesting vesting conditions, 26.48
service vesting conditions, 26.47
cancellations, 26.75–26.76
definition, 26.11
employees, with, 26.32
example, 26.12
fair value of equity instruments, 26.50–26.52
forfeitures, 26.77–26.79

generally, 26.11–26.12
grant date, 26.35–26.38
income tax, and, 29.51–29.58
market vesting conditions
accounting for, 26.48
generally, 26.42
measurement
accounting for vesting conditions, 26.44–26.49
cancellations, 26.75–26.76
employees, with, 26.32
fair value of equity instruments, 26.50–26.52
forfeitures, 26.77–26.79
general, 26.30–26.31
grant date, 26.35–26.38
market vesting conditions, 26.42
modifications, 26.67–26.
non-market vesting conditions, 26.42
non-vesting conditions, 26.43
parties other than employees, with, 26.33–26.34
performance conditions, 26.41–26.42
service conditions, 26.40
settlements, 26.75–26.76
share appreciation rights, 26.59–26.66
share options, 26.59–26.66
shares, 26.53–26.58
vesting conditions, 26.39–26.49
modifications, 26.67–26.
non-market vesting conditions
accounting for, 26.47
generally, 26.42
non-vesting conditions
accounting for, 26.48
generally, 26.43
overview, 26.1
parties other than employees, with, 26.33–26.34
performance conditions, 26.41–26.42
service conditions
accounting for, 26.47
generally, 26.40
settlements, 26.75–26.76
share appreciation rights, 26.59–26.66
share options, 26.59–26.66
shares, 26.53–26.58
vesting conditions
accounting for, 26.44–26.49
introduction, 26.39
performance conditions, 26.41–26.42
service conditions, 26.40

Equity share capital
financial liabilities and equity, and, 22.54
Equivalence
disclosure reductions, and, 1.41–1.43
Equivalent disclosures
generally, 1.23
Errors
events after end of reporting period, and, 32.11
Estimates of useful lives
depreciation, and, 17.79–17.85
intangible assets, and, 18.103–18.113
Estimation
notes to financial statements, and, 8.16–8.21
provisions, and
expected value method for number of obligations,
21.47
generally, 21.44
most likely outcome for single obligation, 21.45–
21.46
revenue, and, 23.119–23.121
Events after end of reporting period
acquisitions, 32.19–32.20
adjusting events

Index

Index

Index

Index

Index

introduction, 13.13–13.12.1
joint products, 13.19–13.20
other costs, 13.21–13.26
production overheads, 13.17–13.18
service provider's inventories, 13.27
cost formulas, 13.33–13.37.1
cost of conversion.
allocation of production overheads, 13.17–13.18
generally, 13.16
cost of purchase, 13.13–13.15
cost of sales, and, 5.13
derecognition, 13.46–13.48
disclosure
generally, 13.50–13.53
subsidiaries, for, 13.54
excepted inventories, 13.4
impairment, and
generally, 13.38–13.44
reversal, 13.45, 27.6
selling price less costs to complete and sell, 27.3–27.5
introduction, 13.1–13.5
joint products, 13.19–13.20
measurement
generally, 13.10–13.11.1
techniques, 13.29–13.32
non-exchange transactions, and, 13.12.1
other costs, 13.21–13.26
presentation, 13.49
production overheads, 13.17–13.18
public benefit entities, and, 13.12.1
recognition, 13.6–13.9
scope, 13.1–13.5
service providers, of, 13.27
transitional issues, 13.54–13.56
Investment income
individual accounts, and, 5.41–5.45
Investment portfolios
investments in associates, and, 14.61–14.62
Investment property
ancillary services to occupants, 16.15–16.16
associates, and, 16.17–16.18
buildings, 16.10–16.12
comparison of FRS 102 with old UK GAAP, and, 1.33
deferred payment terms, 16.29
definition
ancillary services, 16.15–16.16
interest held under operating lease, 16.19–16.21
introduction, 16.7–16.9
land and building, 16.10–16.12
mixed-use property, 16.22–16.24
occupation by group members, etc, 16,17–16.18
other assets, 16.13–16.14
disclosure
exemptions, 1.23
generally, 16.50–16.54
disposals, 16.49
fair value, 16.32–16.36
group members, and, 16.17–16.18
impairment, and, 27.1
initial recognition
ancillary services, 16.15–16.16
interest held under operating lease, 16.19–16.21
introduction, 16.7–16.9
land and building, 16.10–16.12
measurement, 16.25–16.30
mixed-use property, 16.22–16.24
occupation by group members, etc, 16.17–16.18
other assets, 16.13–16.14
integral parts of land, 16.10

interest held under a operating lease
after initial recognition, 16.40–16.44
at initial recognition, 16.30
generally, 16.19–16.21
introduction, 16.1–16.6
joint ventures, and, 16.17–16.18
land and building, 16.10–16.12
leases, and, 20.8
measurement
after initial recognition, 16.31–16.
at initial recognition, 16.25–16.30
measurement after initial recognition
fair value, 16.32–16.36
interest held under a lease, 16.40–16.44
introduction, 16.31
self-constructed property, 16.37–16.39
measurement at initial recognition
deferred payment terms, 16.29
interest held under a lease, 16.30
introduction, 16.25–16.28
mixed-use property, 16.22–16.24
occupation by group members, etc, 16,17–16.18
other assets, 16.13–16.14
presentation, 16.50–16.54
realised profits, 16.55–16.58
redevelopment of property, 16.12
revenue, and, 23.3
scope, 16.1–16.6
self-constructed property, 16.37–16.39
short-term holdings, 16.11
transfers
disposals, 16.49
generally, 16.45–16.48
transitional issues, 16.59–16.64
Investments
associates, in
cost model, 14.63–14.66
definition, 14.2–14.25
disclosure, 14.74–14.82
equity method of accounting, 14.28–14.62
fair value model, 14.67–14.70
measurement, 14.26–14.70
presentation, 14.71–14.73
scope, 14.1
transitional issues, 14.83–14.87
inventories, and, 13.3
joint ventures, in
accounting, 15.21–15.33
definition, 15.2–15.13
disclosure, 15.42–15.45
forms, 15.14–15.20
introduction, 15.1
investor without joint control, 15.40
jointly controlled assets, 15.24–15.26
jointly controlled entities, 15.27–15.33
jointly controlled operations, 15.21–15.23
presentation, 15.41
scope, 15.1
transactions between venturer and JV, 15.34–15.39
transitional issues, 15.46–15.48
statement of financial position, and
generally, 4.13–4.14
participating interests, 4.15
Investments in associates
accounting policies, 14.50
adjustments to carrying amount, 14.33
'associate'
generally, 14.2–14.3
'participating interest', 14.5–14.8
'significant influence', 14.3–14.25
'associated undertaking', 14.4

Index

Index

changes in foreign exchange rates, 32.22
changes in tax rates, 32.23–32.24
disposals, 32.19–32.20
generally, 32.17–32.18
restructuring, 32.21
disposals, 32.19–32.20
dividends, 32.25–32.31
error, 32.11
evidence of net realisable value, 32.8–32.10
foreign exchange rates, 32.22
fraud, 32.11
going concern, 32.12–32.13
impairment, 32.8–32.10
irregularities, 32.11
judgment in court case, 32.16
non-adjusting events
  decline in market value of investments, 32.15
  disclosure, 32.17–32.24
  generally, 32.14
  introduction, 32.3
  judgment in court case, 32.16
restructuring, 32.21
scope, 32.1–32.3
settlement of court proceedings, 32.5
tax rates, 32.23–32.24
transitional issues, 32.34–32.36
Potential voting rights
investments in associates, and
  equity method of accounting, 14.34–14.35
  significant influence, 14.17–14.19
Preference shares with rights
financial liabilities and equity, and, 22.39–22.40
Prejudicial disclosures
provisions, and, 21.104–21.106
Preparation of financial statements
selection of approach within new regime, and, 1.53
Prepayments
statement of financial position, and
  alternative positions in balance sheet, 4.12
  generally, 4.20
Presentation
borrowing costs, and, 25.21–25.24
debtors, and, 4.18–4.19
employee benefits, and
  defined benefit plans, 28.107–28.108
  defined contribution plans, 28.50–28.53
financial instruments, and, 12.85
financial statements, and
  aggregation, 3.26–3.35
  comparative information, 3.22–3.25
  compliance with FRS 102, 3.4–3.7
  consistency, 3.17–3.21
  contents of complete set, 3.37–3.42
  fair presentation, 3.2–3.3
  frequency of reporting, 3.15–3.16
  going concern, 3.8–3.14
  identification, 3.43–3.48
  introduction, 3.1
  materiality, 3.26–3.35
  offsetting, 3.36
  transitional issues, 3.49–3.51
government grants, and, 24.31–24.32
heritage assets, and, 34.6.11
income tax, and, 29.103
intangible assets, and, 18.125
inventories, and, 13.49
investments in associates, and, 14.71–14.73
investment in joint ventures, and, 15.41
investment property, and, 16.50–16.54
property, plant and equipment, and, 17.115–17.122
profit and loss account, and, 5.3

provisions, and, 21.90
Presentation currency
change, 30.58–30.59
determining the average rate, 30.57
non-performance statement items, 30.55–30.56
translation from functional currency, 30.50–30.54
Price
costs of purchase, and, 13.13
property, plant and equipment, and, 17.20–17.24
Price index
hyper-inflation, and, 31.6–31.7
Principals
revenue, and, 23.21–23.24
Principles
accruals basis, 2.29
expenses, 2.17–2.19
financial position, 2.8–2.11
going concern, 2.32
income, 2.15–2.16
introduction, 2.1–2.4
measurement, 2.22–2.26
objectives of financial statements, 2.5–2.6
offsetting, 2.30–2.31
performance, 2.12–2.19
purpose, 2.3
qualitative characteristics of financial statements, 2.7
recognition, 2.20–2.21
selection of accounting policies, 2.27
Prior period errors
correction of material errors, 10.58–10.59
disclosure, 10.60–10.63
identification, 10.55–10.57
re-issue of financial statements, 10.64
Product development
cost of sales, and, 5.13
Production cost
property, plant and equipment, and, 17.20–17.24
Production overheads
inventories, and, 13.17–13.18
Professional charges
administrative costs, and, 5.15
Profit and loss account
consolidated accounts
  generally, 5.52–5.56
  parent's profit and loss account, 5.57–5.59
financial performance, and, 5.1
generally, 5.5–5.7
individual accounts
  administrative costs, 5.15
  allocation of costs, 5.16
  amounts written off assets, 5.18–5.20
  analysis of costs, 5.17
  classification of expenses by function, 5.11–5.20
  classification of expenses by type, 5.21–5.25
  cost and expenses, 5.13–5.17
  depreciation, 5.18–5.20, 5.23
  discontinued operations, 5.34–5.40
  distribution costs, 5.14
  exceptional items, 5.27–5.33
  extraordinary items, 5.50–5.51
  generally, 5.5–5.7
  individual accounts, 5.8–5.10
  'interest payable and other charges', 5.46–5.48
  investment income, 5.41–5.45
  material items, 5.27–5.33
  operating profit, 5.26
  ordinary activities, 5.49
  'other external charges', 5.24
  'other operating charges', 5.25
  own work capitalised, 5.22
  revenue, 5.12

Index

Index

restricted cash balances, 4.26
set-off on bank balances, 4.22–4.25
consolidated formats, 4.49–4.52
debenture loans, 4.40
debtors, 4.18–4.19
deferred income
alternative positions in balance sheet, 4.12
disclosure, 4.28
generally, 4.43–4.44
disposal groups, 4.62–4.64
dividends, 4.54–4.56
format of individual accounts
Format 1, 4.9–4.10
Format 2, 4.11
introduction, 4.6–4.7
types, 4.8
formats
alternative positions in balance sheet, 4.12
Format 1, 4.9–4.10
Format 2, 4.11
insurance companies, and, 4.2
interests in group undertakings, 4.46–4.48
introduction, 4.1–4.2
investments
generally, 4.13–4.14
participating interests, 4.15
liabilities
accruals, 4.43–4.44
amounts received on account, 4.41
debenture loans, 4.40
deferred income, 4.43–4.44
disclosure, 4.28–4.39
other, 4.45
social security, 4.42
taxation, 4.42
net current assets and liabilities, 4.27
off-balance sheet arrangements, 4.57–4.61
overdrafts, 4.28
own shares, 4.16
payments on account
disclosure, 4.28
generally, 4.17
prepayments
alternative positions in balance sheet, 4.12
generally, 4.20
presentation of debtors, 4.18–4.19
related undertakings, 4.53
reporting date, and, 4.1
reserves and dividends, 4.54–4.56
scope, 4.3–4.5
share capital, 4.54–4.56
social security, 4.42
taxation, 4.42
trade creditors, 4.28
transitional issues, 4.65–4.66
Statements of recommended practice (SORPs)
generally, 1.56
Statements of standard accounting practice (SSAPs)
generally, 1.1–1.2
Subscriptions to publications
revenue, and, 23.98
Subsidiaries
consolidated financial statements, and
acquisition, 7.56–7.58
'control', 9.38–9.84
control of board of directors, 9.68–9.76
definition, 9.34
disposal, 7.56–7.58
excluded from consolidation, 9.101–9.1
generally, 9.36–9.37
passive control, 9.46–9.47

potential voting rights, 9.78–9.81
power to govern under statute or agreement, 9.64–9.67
employee benefits, and, 28.141
funding by parent, and, 26.116–26.120
inventories, and, 13.54
related party disclosures, and, 33.105–33.106
transition to FRS 102
assets and liabilities, 35.52–35.54
investments, 35.56–35.57
Substance over form
characteristics of financial statements, and, 2.7
'Sweet' equity
share-based payment transactions, and, 26.104–26.106
Tag along clauses
share-based payment transactions, and, 26.108
Tangible assets
property, plant and equipment, and, 17.4
Tax liabilities
selection of approach within new regime, and, 1.53
Tax rates
events after end of reporting period, and, 32.23–32.24
Taxation
costs of purchase, and, 13.13
statement of cash flows, and, 7.46–7.50
statement of financial position, and, 4.42
Termination benefits
definition, 28.118
'detailed formal plan', 28.124
disclosure, 28.128–28.129
examples, 28.120
generally, 28.118–28.120
introduction, 28.2
measurement, 28.126–28.127
recognition, 28.121–28.125
scope, 28.119
Timeliness
characteristics of financial statements, and, 2.7
Tools and consumables
inventories, and, 13.3
Total comprehensive income
introduction, 5.1
other comprehensive income, and, 5.60
presentation, 5.3–5.4
statement of changes in equity, 6.3
Trade creditors
statement of financial position, and, 4.28
Trade discounts
costs of purchase, and, 13.13
cost of sales, and, 5.13
revenue, and, 23.17–23.18
Transfer of business around a group
by dividend, 9.239
from subsidiary to parent, 9.232–9.235
from one group member to another, 9.236–9.238
introduction, 9.231
Transfer of economic benefits
provisions, and, 21.24
Transfers
investment property, and
disposals, 16.49
generally, 16.45–16.48
Transition to FRS 102
accounting estimates, 35.25–35.27
applying first-time adoption rules, 35.59–35.62
borrowing costs, 35.40
business combinations, 35.31–35.36
compound financial instruments, 35.44
date of transition, 35.10–35.11
decommissioning liabilities, 35.41

Index